I0819692

SALEHE
I MAKE SHOES

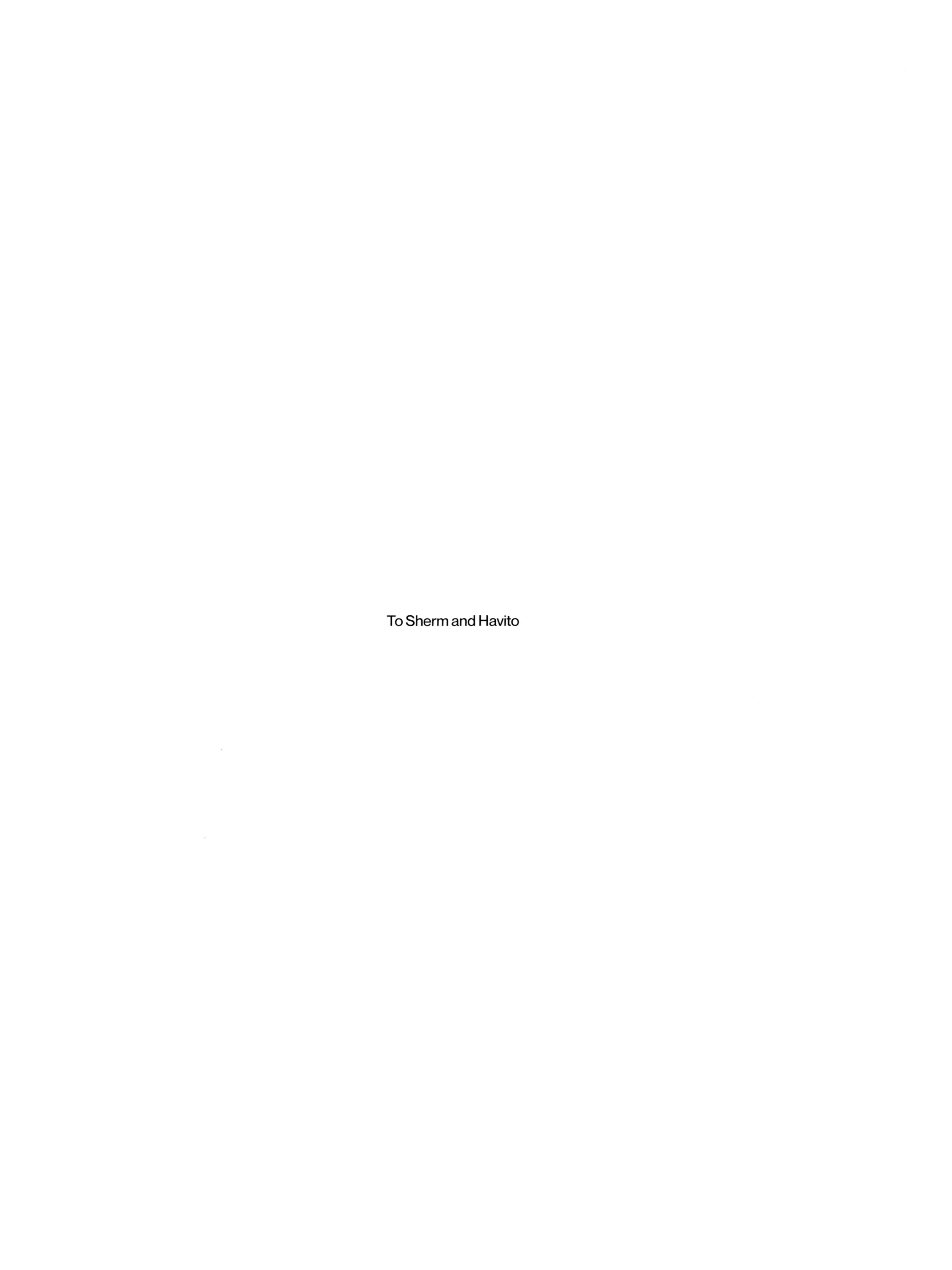

To Sherm and Havito

SALEHE

I MAKE SHOES

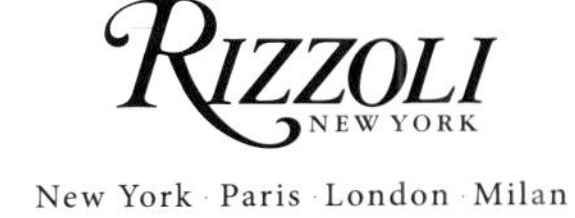

New York · Paris · London · Milan

SALEHE BEMBURY: CARVING OUT HIS OWN LANE

JIAN DELEON

In the pantheon of heralded footwear designers, two names that have fairly large shoes to fill are Tinker Hatfield and the late, great Virgil Abloh. Both defined and redefined innovation in their own ways, but also pushed the boundaries of what a shoe meant to the average person. For Hatfield, his relationship with Michael Jordan forever changed how athletes and shoe companies work together—building product that didn't just match a player's style and taste, but became a very extension of themselves. The codes of the Jordan brand and black-and-cement elephant print fundamentally challenged what signature shoes looked and felt like, and in many ways elevated the humble sneaker from a strictly performance item into a modern object of desire.

Abloh took those ideas and simultaneously interrogated and reinvented them. A bona fide student of the game, he knew and understood the "rules" so well that he expertly bent and broke them to his will. And yet, another thread the two have in common is their shared experience as trained architects. For both, the work of Georges Pompidou and Mies van der Rohe shaped their approach to design. Hatfield's way of working with Michael Jordan was not unlike the relationship a respected architect would have with a high-profile client. They took the idea of designing a communal, permanent space that would have a life long after it was built, and set the stage for a time when shoes would have the same staying power.

Which is precisely what makes Salehe Bembury an iconoclast in his own right. A student of industrial design, he is a rare example of someone who began his career as a footwear designer, but let that discipline shape his evolution as a multi-faceted creative. Like generations of sneaker enthusiasts who build their outfits from the ground up, Bembury's initial focus on footwear influenced how he approached design holistically.

It's not strange that one of his earliest obsessions as an industrial design student at Syracuse University was wood. As a material it continues to be one of his favorites and an enduring source of inspiration, not just because of the organic, naturally occuring motifs that have become synonymous with his codes, but also because of the childhood nostalgia it gives him. And in some ways, his growth as a designer is reflected in the inherent characteristics of the sturdy natural resource. After all, depending on weather conditions, the age of the wood, and other factors, wood is susceptible to evolving over time and can be both as malleable as a young sapling or as permanent as petrified wood, at times given a new sheen thanks to the intake of hardy minerals like quartz or agate.

With that in mind, it's the ideal jumping-off point when thinking about what makes quality footwear. For athletic shoes, that young-wood sponginess and pliability are ideal for sneakers that feel both responsive and resilient. For classic footwear and dressier options, the burnished browns of old redwood and maple trees and the permanence of aged oaks are living testaments to the kinds of things that will stand the test of time.

It was during his time at Syracuse that Bembury learned to embrace a self-aware side of the burgeoning streetwear movement, too. He met designer Bobby Waltzer at a pre-college program at the Rhode Island School of Design, and was instantly drawn to his sense of style, pairing shoes like beat-up Jordan VIs with a vintage Tupac Shakur tee and Orlando Magic basketball shorts, an offbeat, semi-discordant uniform that suited him well. As one of the founders of seminal early-2000s New York streetwear brand PEGLEG, Waltzer and his cohorts championed fluorescent colors and a humorous approach to Americana and streetwear at a time when many brands were self-serious and couldn't be bothered to show models smiling. Meanwhile, these guys were hawking candy-colored G-SHOCK watches at buzzy shops like Opening Ceremony and clearly having a great time doing it. That in-your-face, unapologetic sense of self-authenticity is something that can be clearly felt in the world Bembury has created today.

Take for example, Bembury's first New Balance shoe, a fuzzy orange suede iteration of the 2002R called "Peace Be the Journey," a phrase that's Jamaican in origin but, through the platform of the sneaker, became something else entirely. At face value, a predominantly orange shoe with contrasts of yellow mesh and burnt sienna soles may be polarizing, but the project was one where Bembury really got to dig into his talents as a storyteller.

Bringing in the inspiration from Arizona's Antelope Canyon and enlisting actor and activist Jesse Williams to helm the campaign, the result is a fully realized project of uncompromising vision. In many ways, it was the first big step into Bembury's now-recognizable brand universe. There's the foundational sense of tribalism, the elements of mysticism and appreciation for nature,

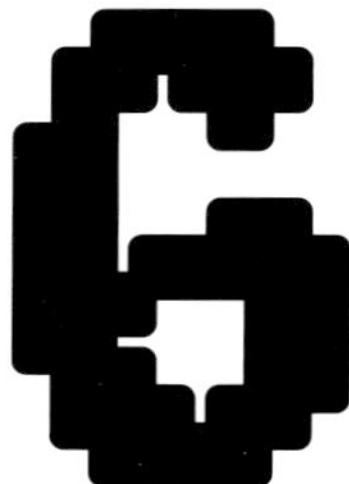

and a clear identity for the community that freely engages with the work. It's not only a well-defined creative statement, but a pretty damn good recruitment vehicle that entices outsiders to want to sit at Bembury's table.

It would be remiss to mention that honing in on the spirit of community wasn't just an important part of Bembury coming into his own as a designer, but also because his penchant for successfully mixing the physical and digital realms is something that was inspired by an online creative collective that similarly paved their own way on the internet. One of Bembury's other inspirations is Phillip Annand and the work he did as part of the Madbury Club. During the blog boom of the early 2000s, the online crew stood out as a group of digital renegades with a knack for amplifying things they were enthusiastic about. Bucking trends in favor of trusting their own taste, their work was a breath of fresh air at a time when so many digital publications and pre-influencers with a WordPress account were busy aggregating the news about the latest release. You didn't go to the Madbury Club for the weather report; you went because they were creating their own forecast.

But before Salehe Bembury could express himself as fully as he could with that first New Balance project, there was also the part of his career where he operated more behind-the-scenes and did the work. Perhaps one of the reasons he's able to play to multiple audiences—mainstream crowds with Crocs, sneaker enthusiasts with New Balance, and high fashion with Canada Goose and Moncler Genius—is because he really understands the needs of all those customers simultaneously.

Keep in mind, one of his first jobs as a designer was for Payless ShoeSource, a company whose humble mission is in its very name. That prepped him well for his next gig at Cole Haan, where the prices were higher but the mass audience had a ton of crossover, and it also gave him an eye for what the wear-to-work and more suit-and-tie-centric crowd of consumers look for. Then to take that experience to a fashion house like Versace gives him a unique purview that not many designers have—the ability to understand the needs of the mainstream but have an astute understanding of the taste level of the niche.

That's a mindset that came in especially handy during his time at Yeezy, where he was allowed a great degree of creative freedom, but was also put in the unenviable position of having to answer that very conundrum: How do you find the balance between mass appeal, elevated execution, and modern cultural relevance?

In due time, that answer came in the form of a shoe mold. At a time when Crocs was fighting for relevance and credibility among a more discerning consumer, Bembury literally found a way to put his fingerprint on a silhouette that would change the trajectory of his own career, and the company's perception on the finicky spectrum of taste. When it came time to think about how he would brand his inaugural project with Crocs, Bembury was hesitant to use his own name—not necessarily to be self-effacing, but because he was coming from a background where the work and the client it was for spoke for itself.

But he realized that many of the designers and artists that inspired him had established signatures that were consistent, subtle, and yet instantly recognizable. Thinking back on his longtime fixation with wood and wood grain, he devised the idea of implementing a fingerprint design onto the shoe. That evolved into a deconstruction of the Croc itself, distilling the silhouette into its fundamental essence before injecting himself into the mold, resulting in the kind of item that really is the best of all worlds. In many ways, the Salehe Bembury Crocs Pollex is the culmination of everything Bembury has worked towards. He imbued one of the most democratic and divisive footwear silhouettes and made it into a status symbol—while still keeping the retail price well within the reach of the average consumer.

And while the fingerprint motif has become an ongoing signature for Bembury, popping up in his capsule collections for Moncler, Canada Goose, and his ever-evolving practice at Spunge, it remains a welcome callback to the radical individualism he first discovered during his time at Syracuse University. So whether he continues to have fun with designs like putting a whistle on the back of a New Balance 574, making progressive new silhouettes for Crocs, or simply paying homage to one of his favorite countries on a T-shirt with WTAPS, one thing is certain: Bembury's fingerprints have that magic touch.

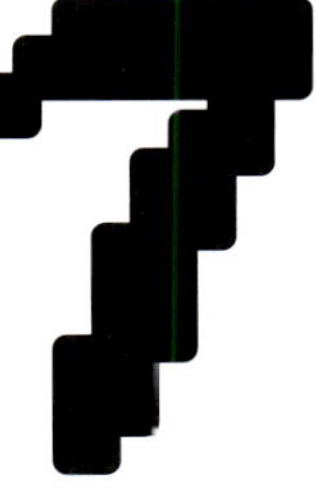

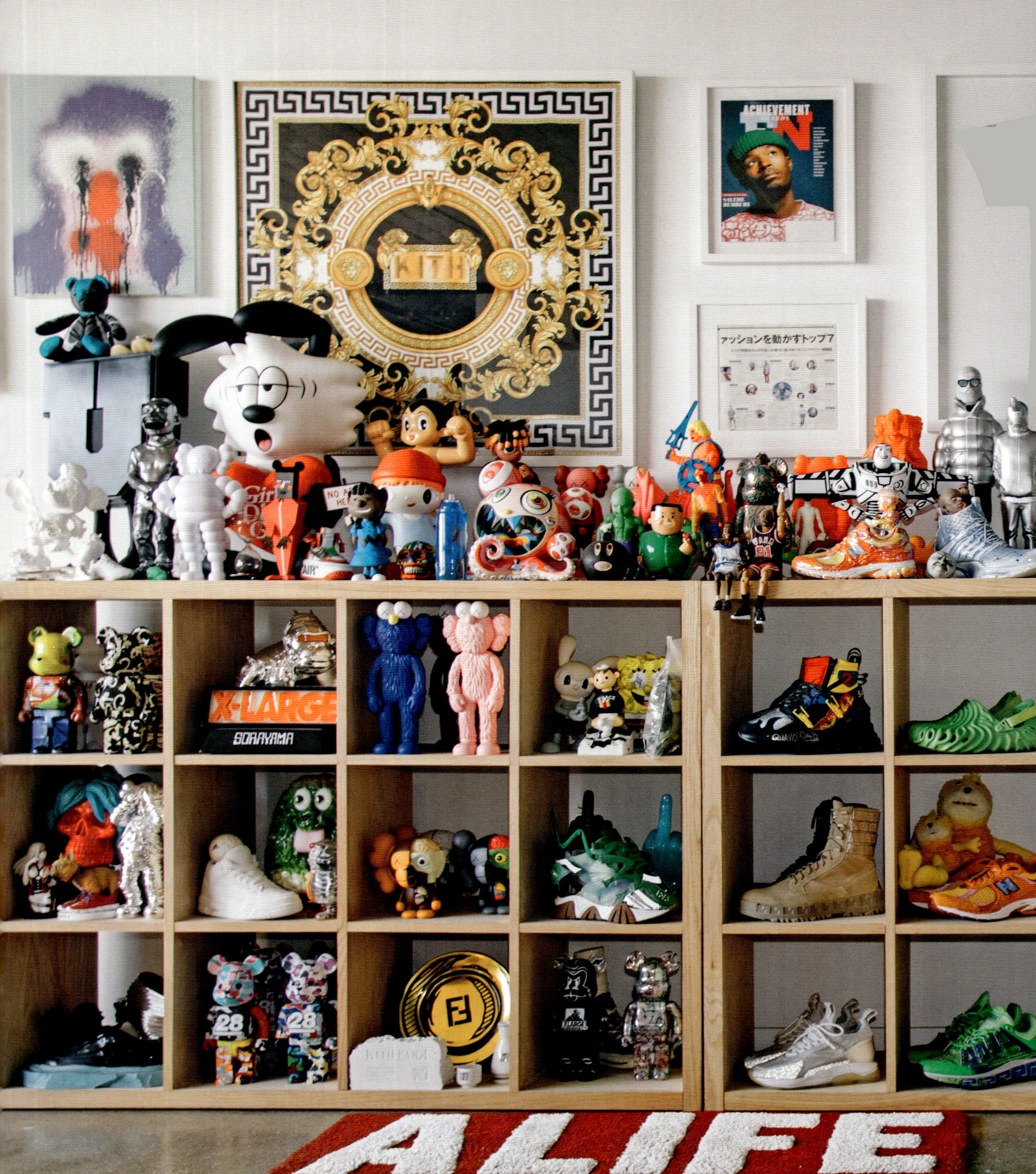
KITH
ACHIEVEMENT
X-LARGE
SORAYAMA
ALIFE

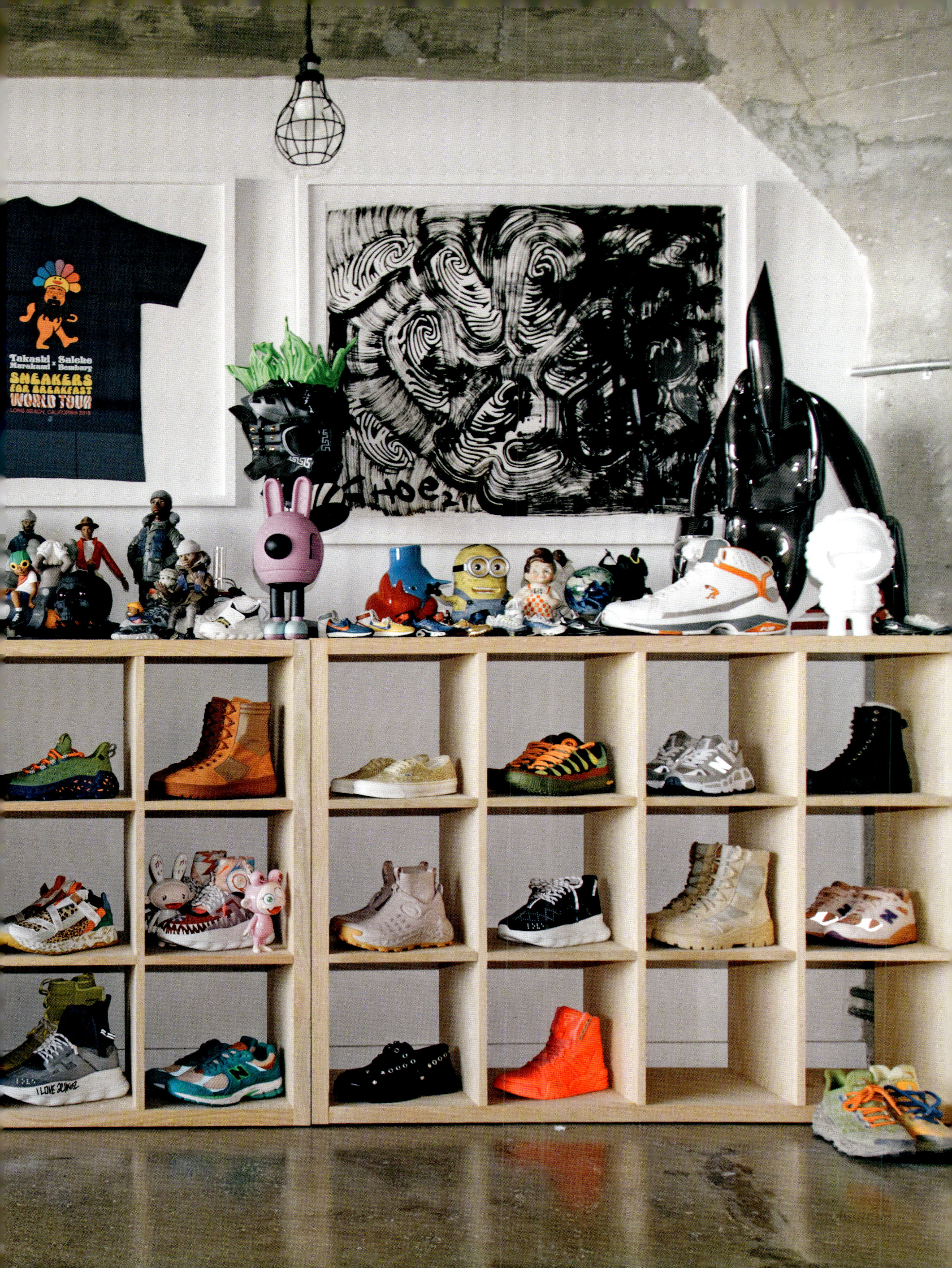

Takashi Murakami x Salehe Bembury
SNEAKERS FOR BREAKFAST
WORLD TOUR

10

COLE HAAN **(2011)**

BE A STUDE

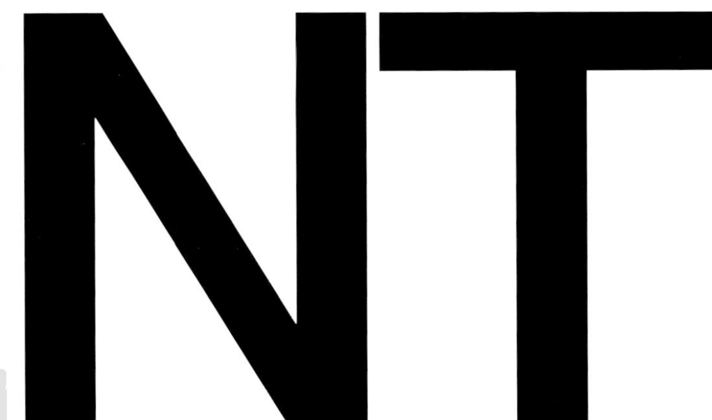

COLE HAAN
BE A STUDENT

By the time I got to Cole Haan, after my beginnings with Payless and freelance work for other brands, I had essentially accomplished the first task I had set myself, which was to grow, move on, and work for a brand I could be more proud of—a brand with more opportunity, a bigger pay check, and better association all round. The most appealing thing for me about Cole Haan was the fact that they were owned by Nike. Since the masterplan back then was to design for Nike, I thought to myself: if I work for this brand that is owned by Nike, then I'm one step closer—theoretically I'm under the Nike company umbrella, if you will—and I had heard through the grapevine that Nike liked to hire internally.

When I got to Cole Haan, I had a very insignificant role that may even have been technically temporary, similar to my position with Payless before that. My first week there, I saw a six-foot two-inch bald Black man with massive beads and some Jordan 1s I'd never seen before in my life; me being the aficionado and connoisseur that I am, I was like, who is this guy? I found out that his name was Jeff Henderson. He had been at Nike, and he was about to start a team at Cole Haan. I went back to my desk, opened up my sketchbook to what I believed to be one of the dopest pages, and slid it to the edge of the desk, hoping he would walk by and see—and that's exactly what happened. He asked me if I wanted to join what was going to be an innovation team, the goal of which would be to utilize the Nike technology we had access to through the brand's ownership, and create completely new and utilitarian professional footwear.

(There are certain characters that some of us are blessed to have in our lives. These characters ultimately give us tools to be able to get through the obstacles that they once encountered, and in many cases those people can be called mentors. I believe that on a subconscious level I had always wanted a mentor. I've always had my parents and they've always given me great guidance; but design is a very niche profession, and industrial design and footwear design are even more specific niches themselves. So I think that on some level I always wanted someone who could relate to me in all of those languages. And that was Jeff Henderson. Jeff recently let me know that he hired me because I was Black; I thought it was all down to that sketchbook, but in actuality he was just trying to hold the door open for me as someone had once held the door open for him. I owe much to Jeff, and he continues to be a participant in my life.)

Our innovation team lived in a back closet of the Cole Haan office. We took a space that no one wanted and outfitted it with different images of design and the city, different trinkets, references, samples, and factory parts, and suddenly it felt like we were living and creating in this kind of Willy Wonka chocolate factory of creative expression. Our team was tasked with extreme and aggressive disruption of the formal footwear space, which, up to that point, was something that had not really been explored. Right around then, Mark McNairy had started doing die-cut EVA Oxfords, which might not have been revolutionary but at the time was genius, because he was a pioneer in breaking convention in that space.

When the innovation team began, Jeff did an amazing job of tasking myself and Jin with both necessary and unnecessary tasks to get our minds working, to get us to ask why, and to get us to challenge the norms that had long existed in the formal fashion space. Sometimes he would give us tasks that actually had to do with projects that were happening in the company; other times, on some OG designer Jedi shit, he was just trying to get us to think, or to challenge us, or to get us to figure out solutions for things that may not have been even necessary for a task at hand, the exploration of which would load us up with tools for tasks of the future.

Jeff was trying to get me to explore my creativity on product that most people would be afraid to scuff. I was getting to cut up, paint, destroy, and explore the new

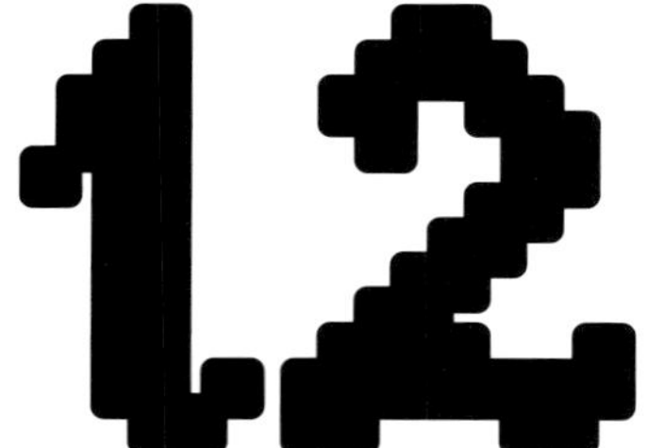

visuals and opportunities that formal footwear could bring the company. On one occasion, in a back hallway of the office on 18th Street and 5th Avenue, I spray-painted a bunch of Cole Haan wingtips and Oxfords for a Nike presentation. John Hoake and the heads of Nike were coming to see the different things we were working on, and Jeff thought it would be good for us to have some aggressive creative explorations on formal footwear. At the time I remember being extremely confused as to what I was doing and why I was doing it; but it was a break from the desk and it allowed me to be creative, which in some corporate spaces is neither encouraged nor explored.

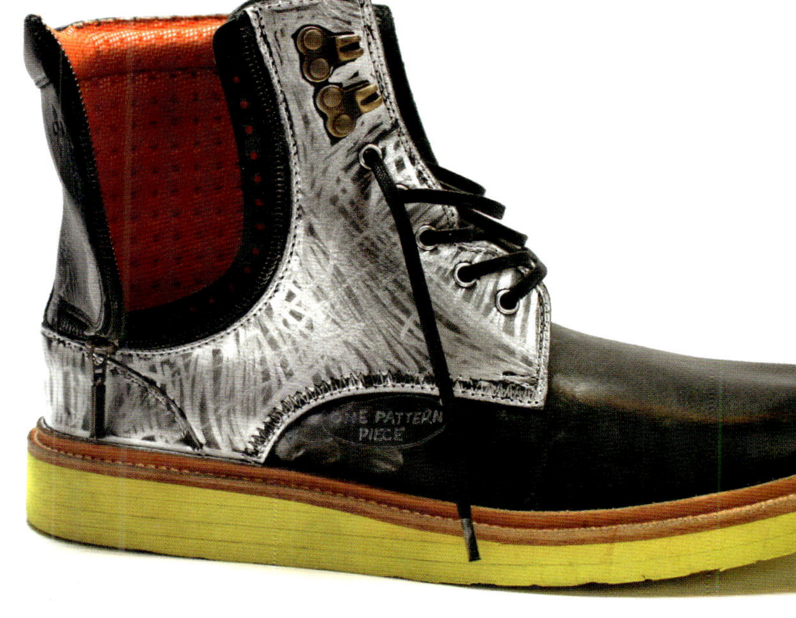

The innovation team moved with an autonomy no other team could move with. If we needed to go anywhere in the office, needed to take anything, borrow anything, cut up or paint anything, it was allowed, because we were this mysterious team that was working our magic in our back room. So it was really an amazing position to hold in the early stages of my career; not only did I get to learn about design, but I also got to learn a lot about how to move within a corporate space, when your job potentially isn't something others in the space are familiar with.

Something that fascinates me looking back at this period is how angry I look in photographs. I wasn't angry at all, but this is what I thought you had to do. I'm mimicking what I believed to be the way a designer–a "cool guy," a fashion participant–was supposed to look. That's what I was seeing in the space at the time: it was about being too cool, taking yourself too seriously. Photos I posed for then remind me of the artificial and fragile disposition I had to take on as a way to fit into a role. I really believe I found my design–and myself–when I realized that the only role I can fill is the one that exists within myself, and that leaning into who I am authentically was the answer to all of this.

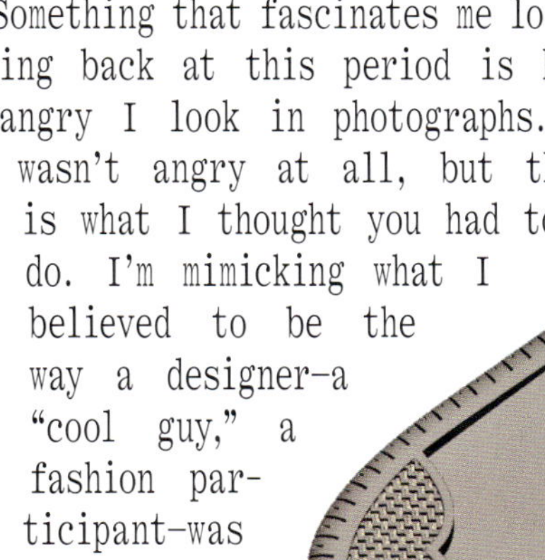

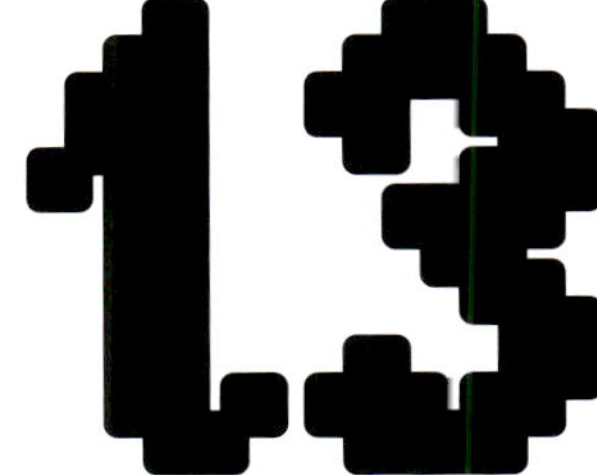

Salehe Bembury's Cole Haan Desk

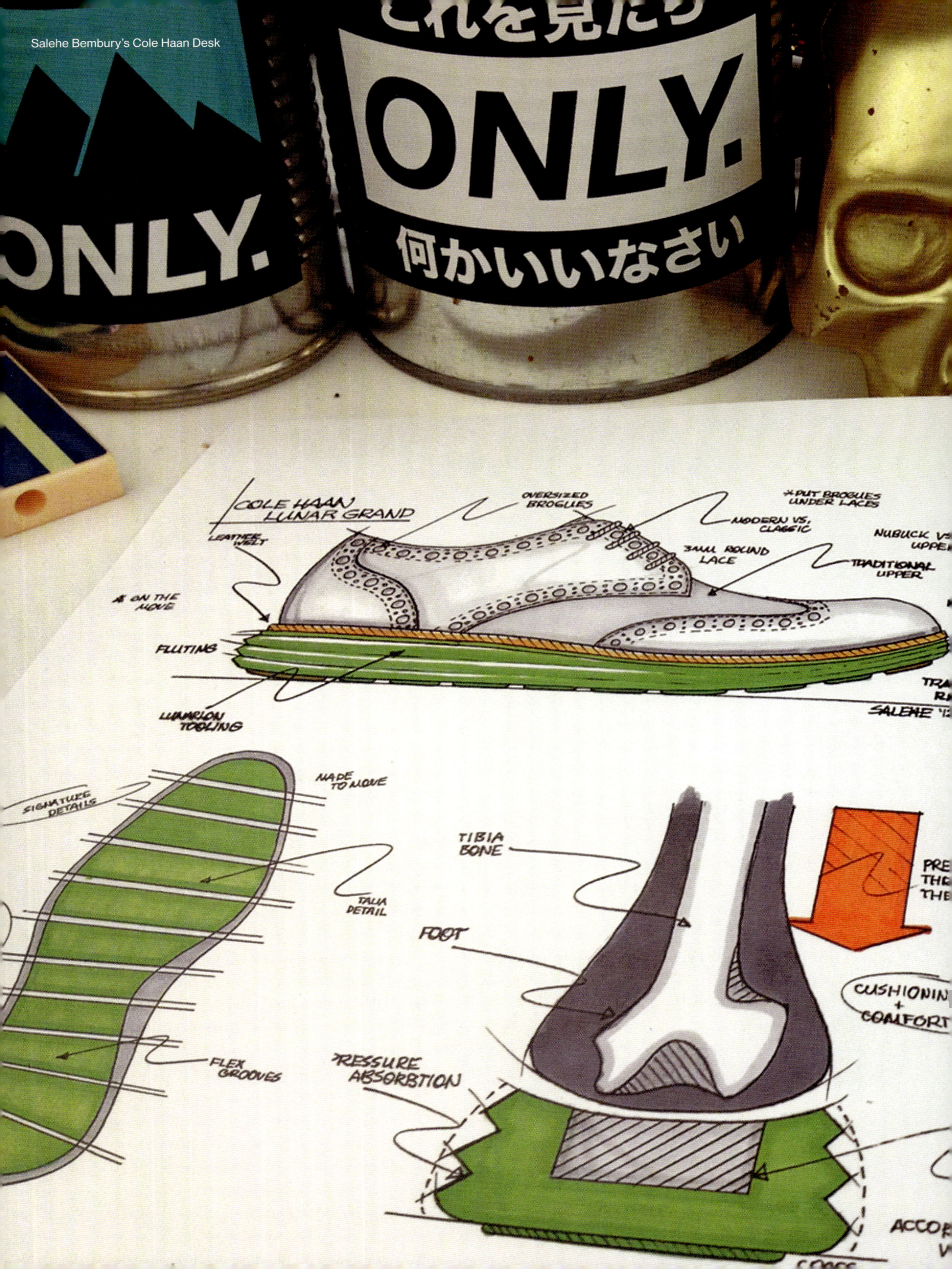

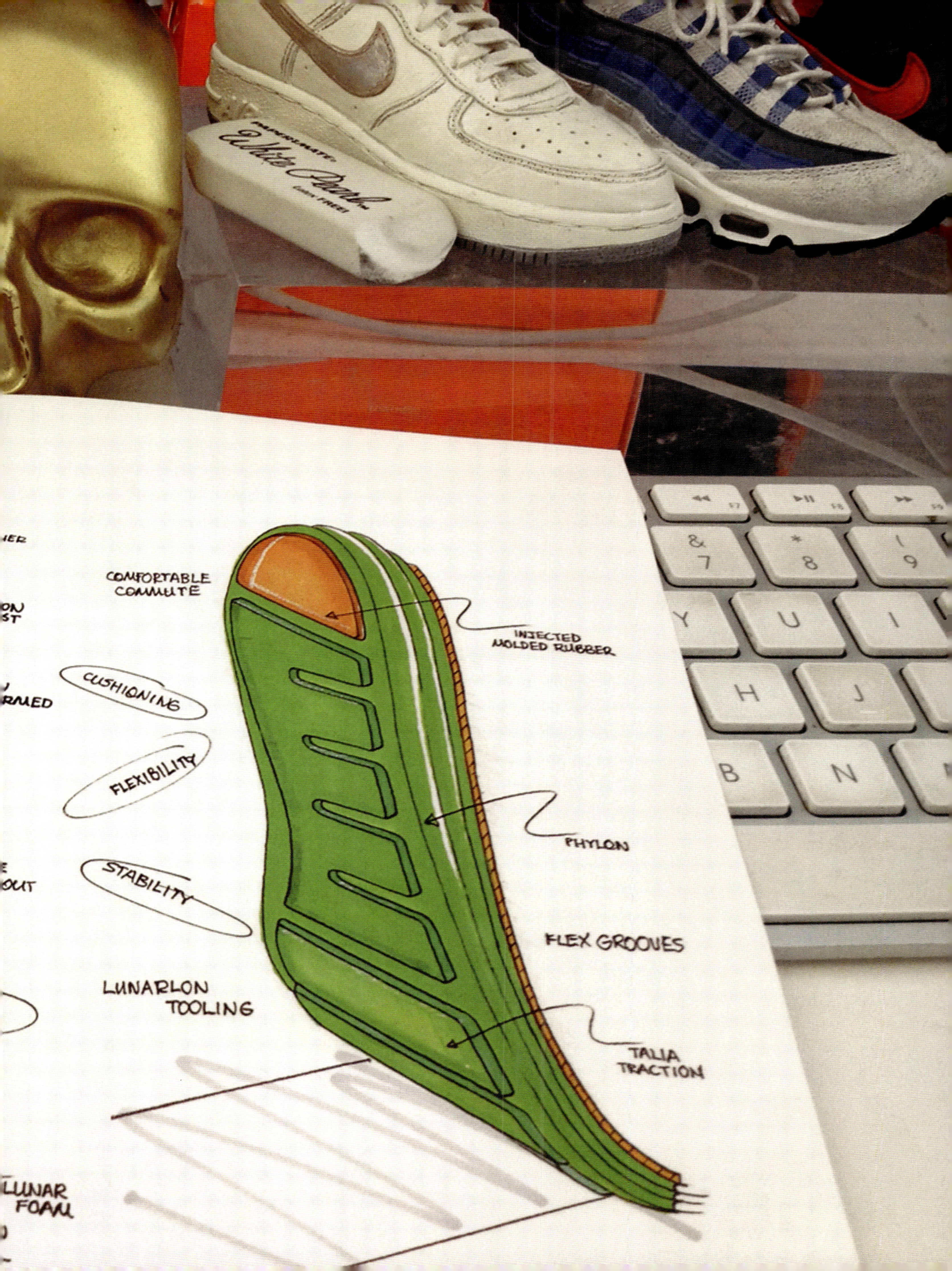
PAPERMATE
White Pearl
COMFORTABLE COMMUTE
INJECTED MOLDED RUBBER
CUSHIONING
FLEXIBILITY
PHYLON
STABILITY
FLEX GROOVES
LUNARLON TOOLING
TALIA TRACTION
LUNAR FOAM

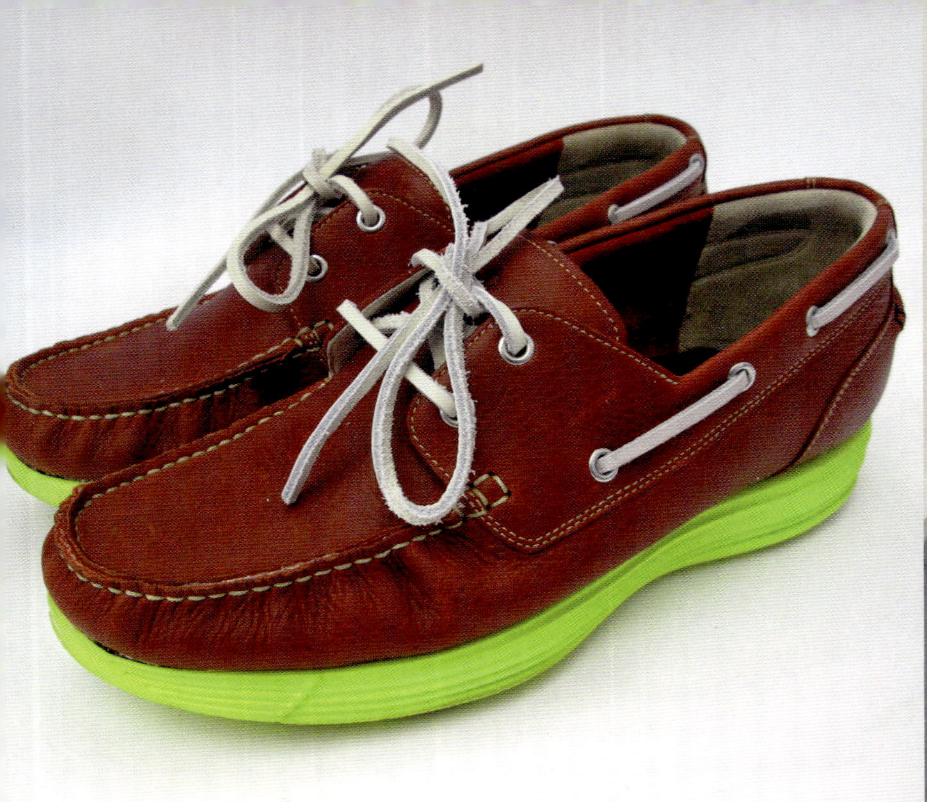

Nike Lunar loafer concept

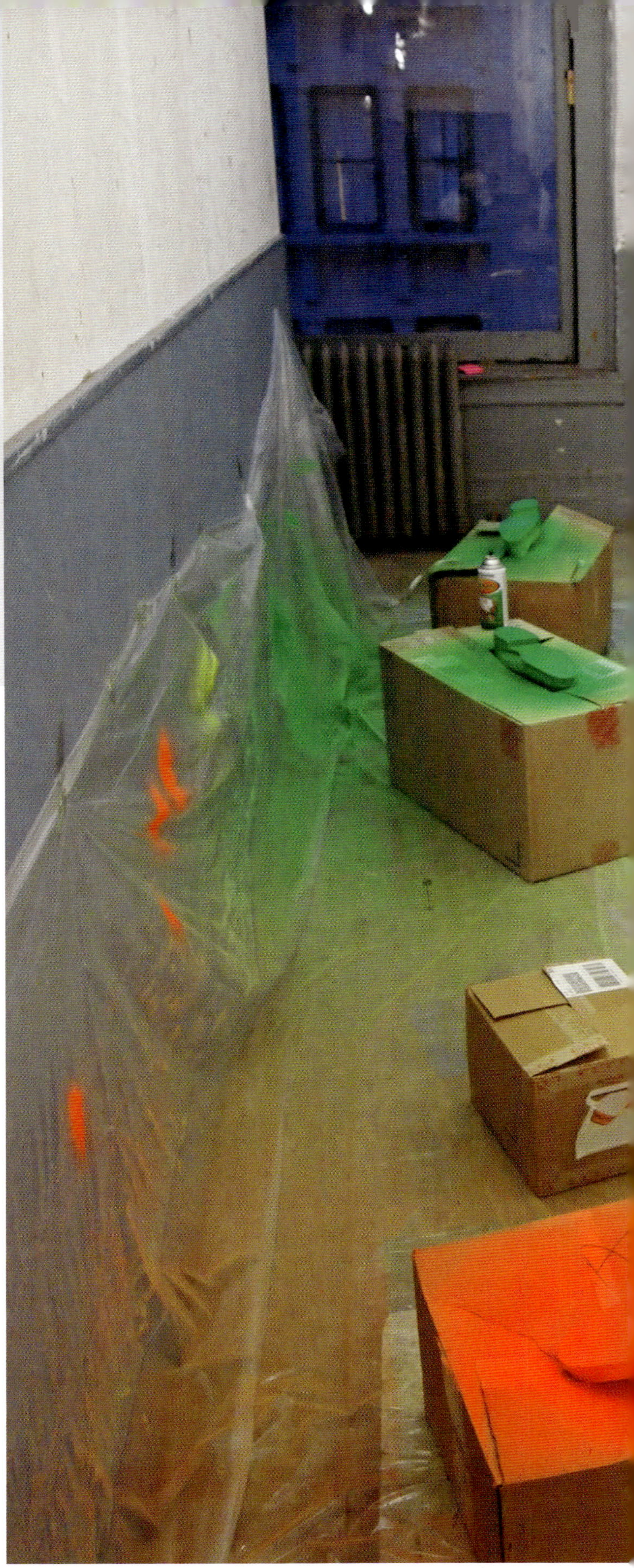

Cole Haan

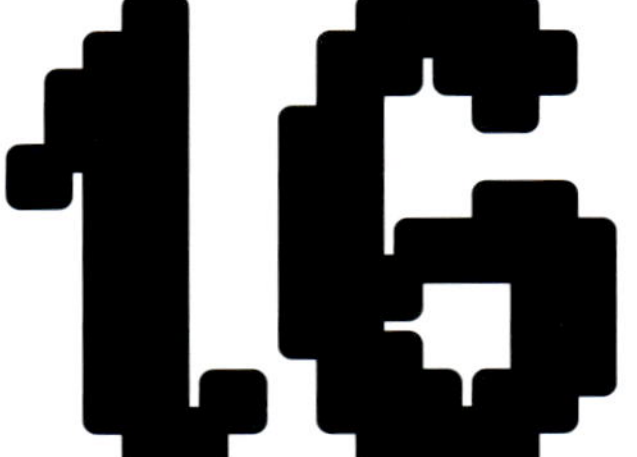

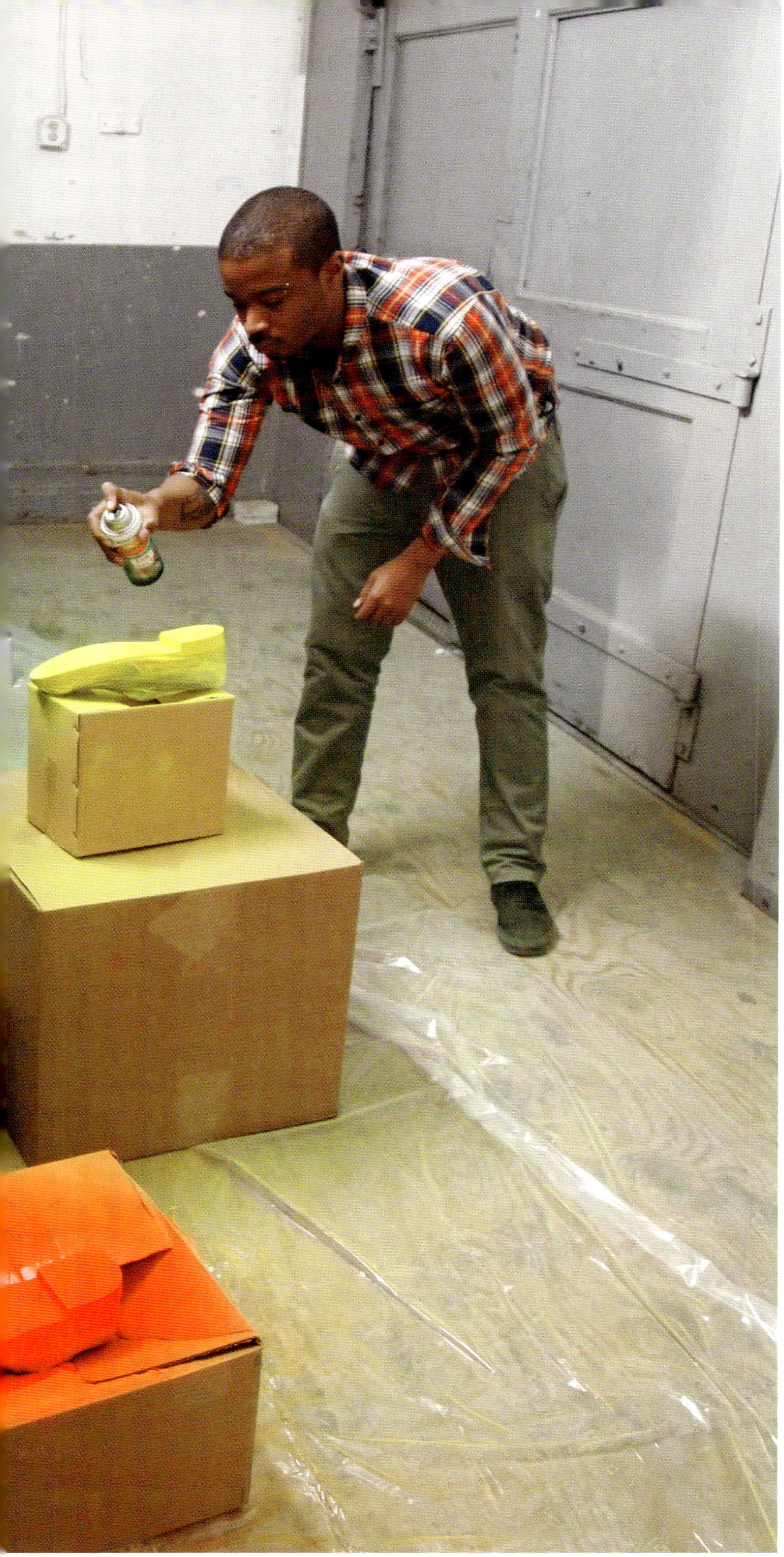

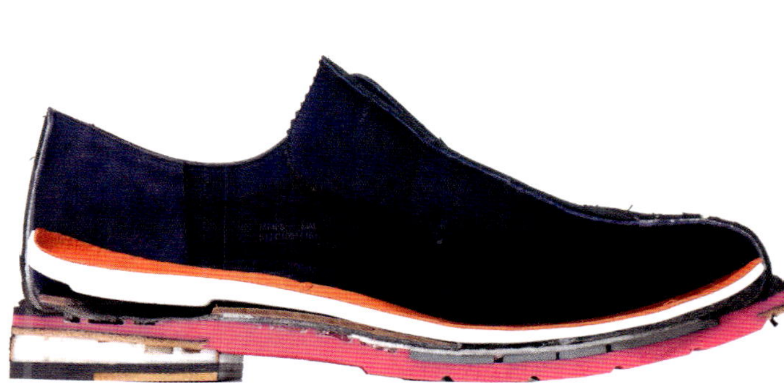

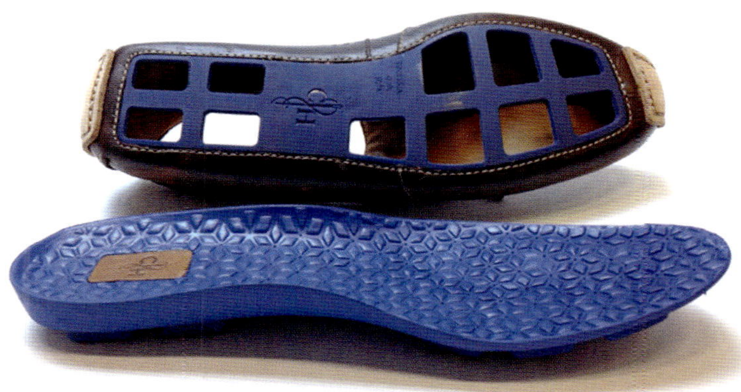

Cole Haan innovation deconstruction

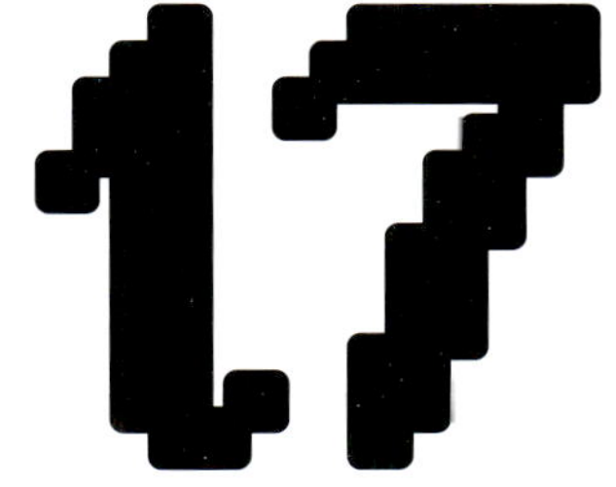

COLE HAAN (2011)

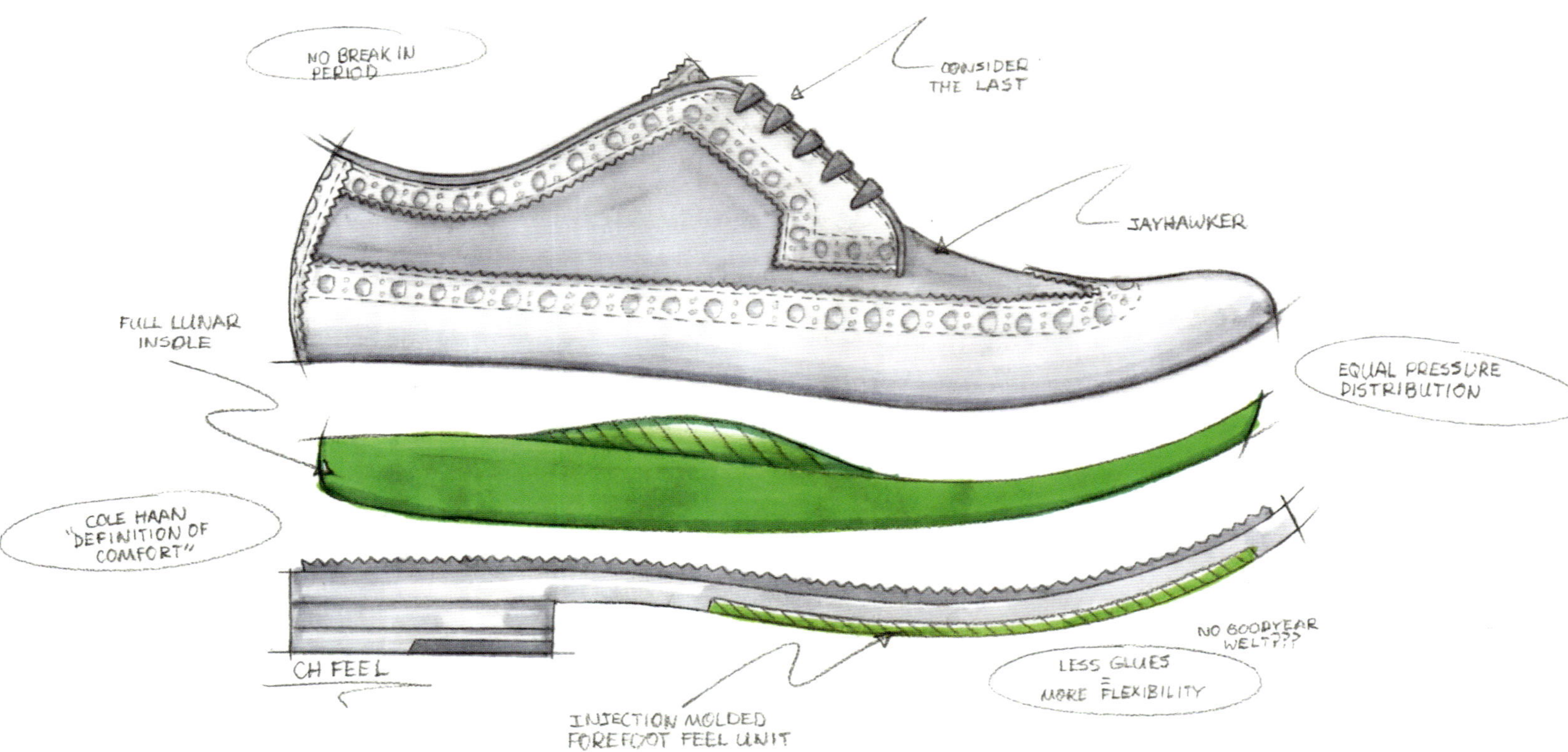

Cole Haan Innovation insole sketch

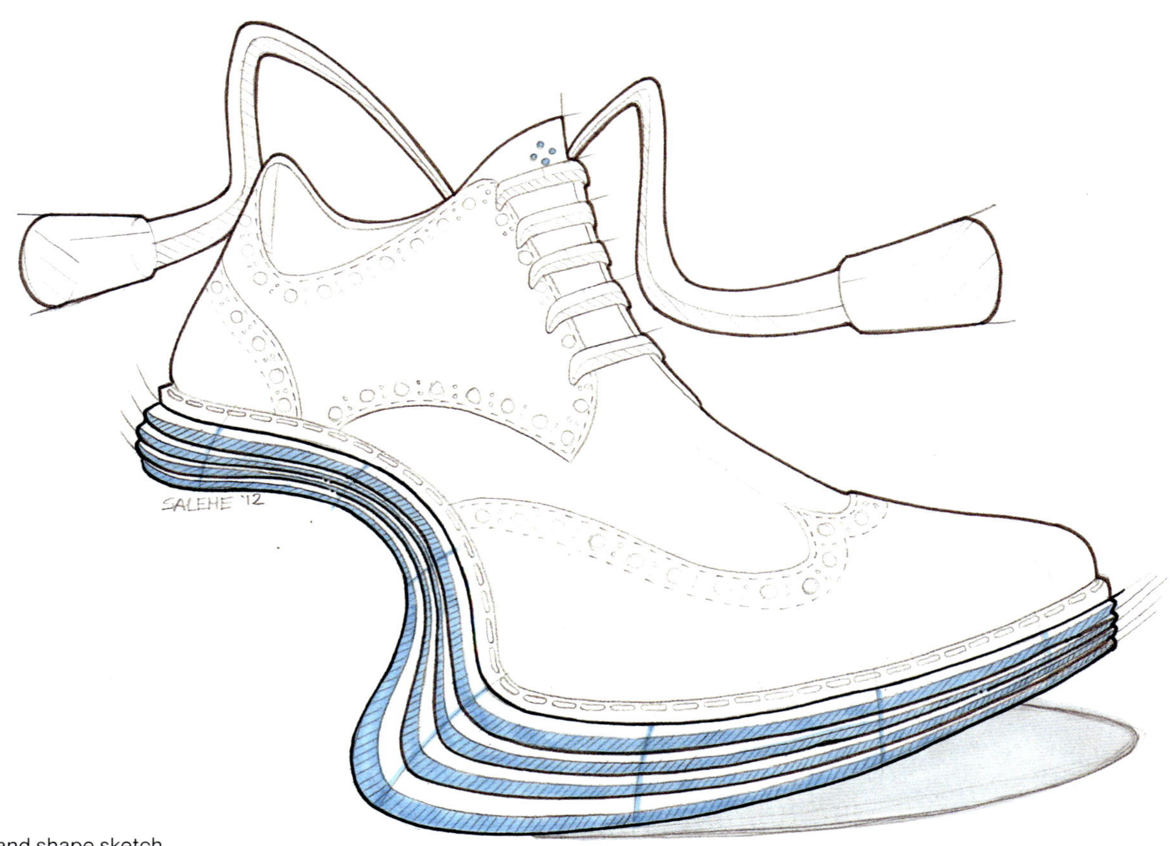

Cole Haan Lunargrand shape sketch

18

(2011)

COLE HAAN

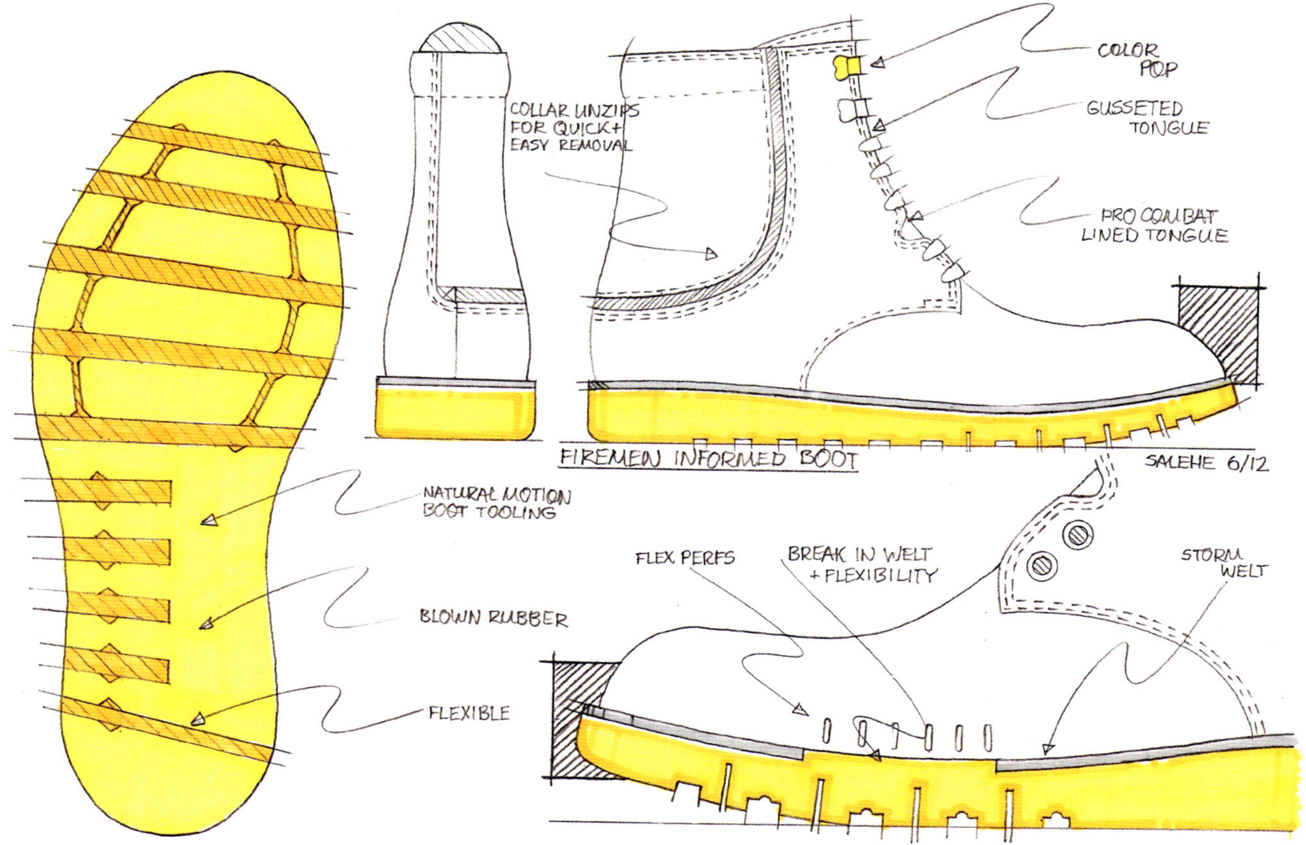

Cole Haan Fireboot exploration sketch

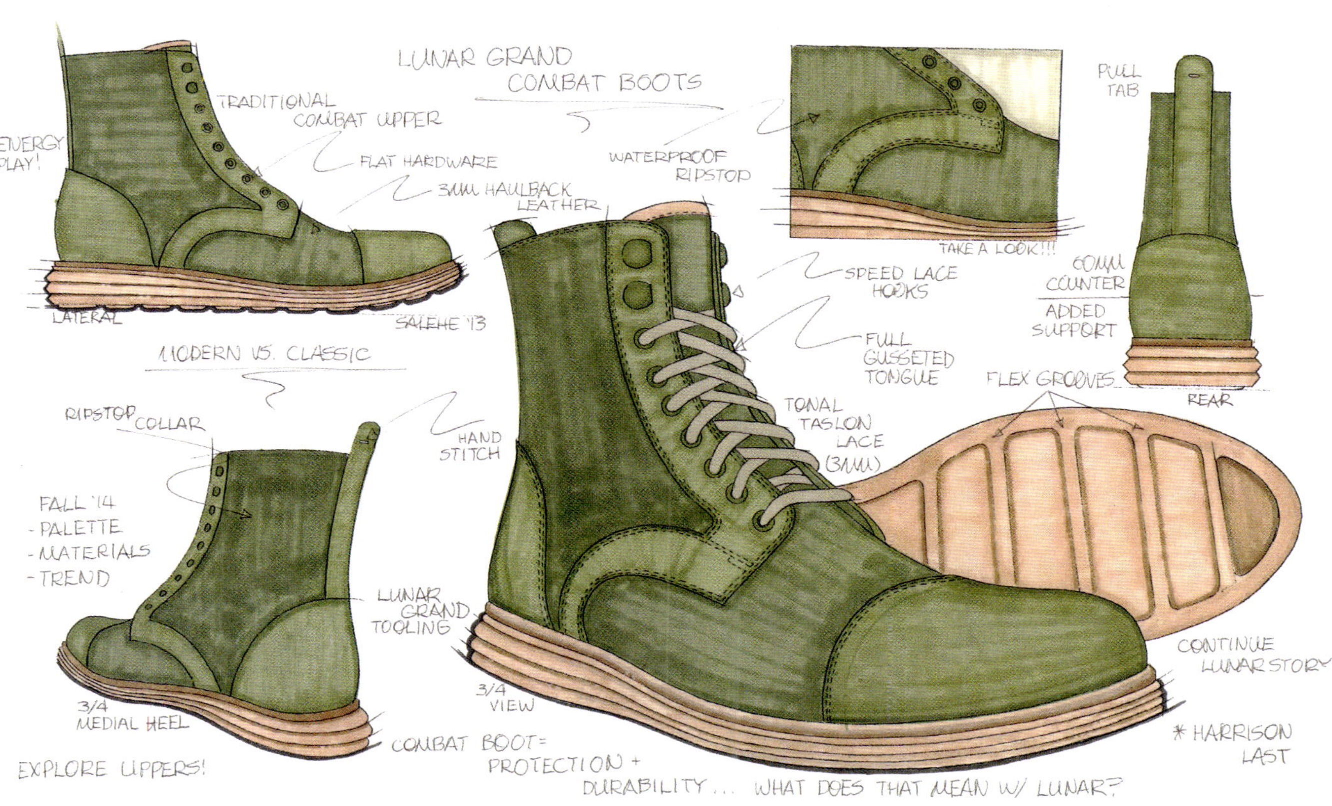

Cole Lunargrand boot rendering

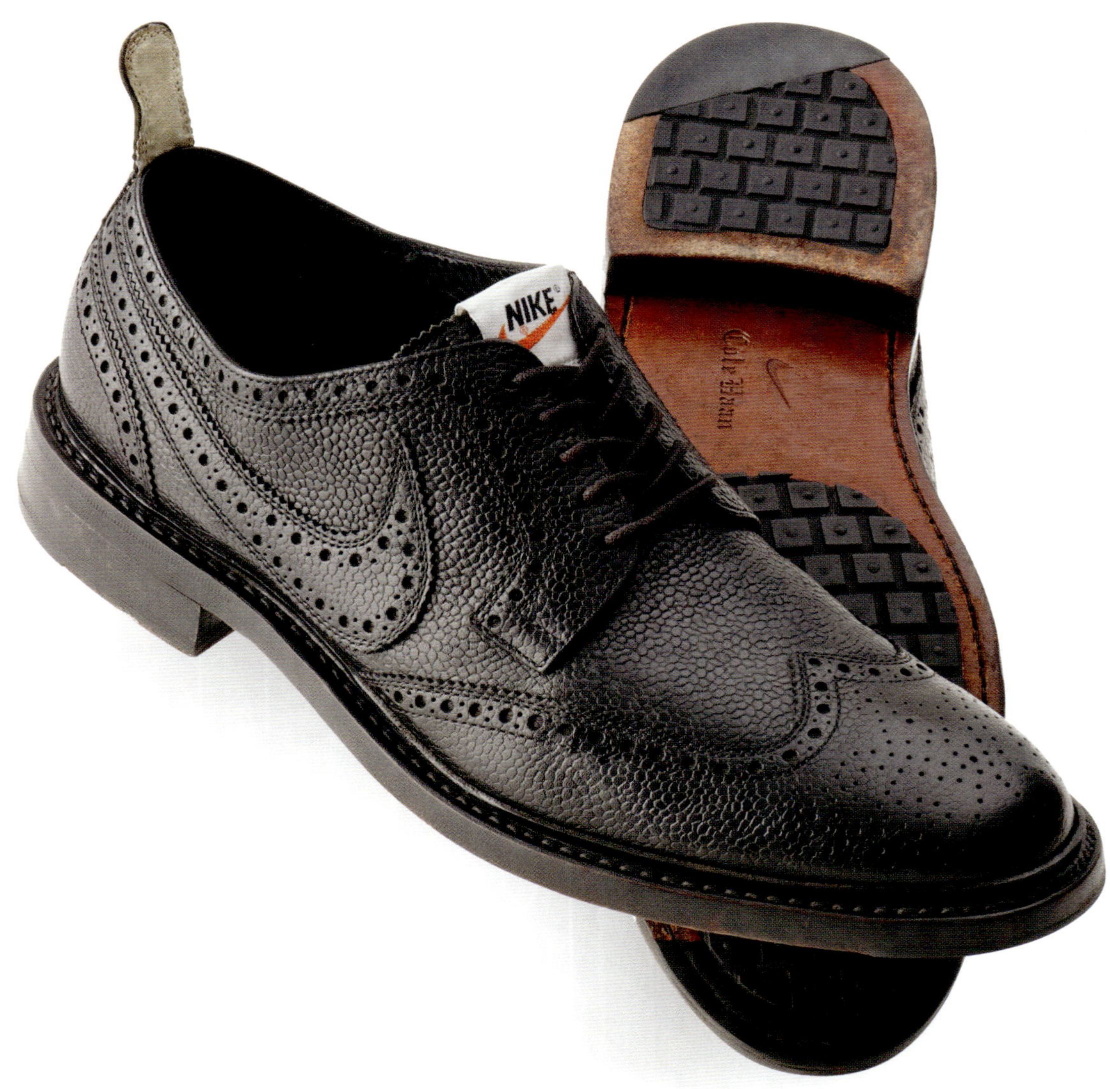

Cole Haan brogue concept

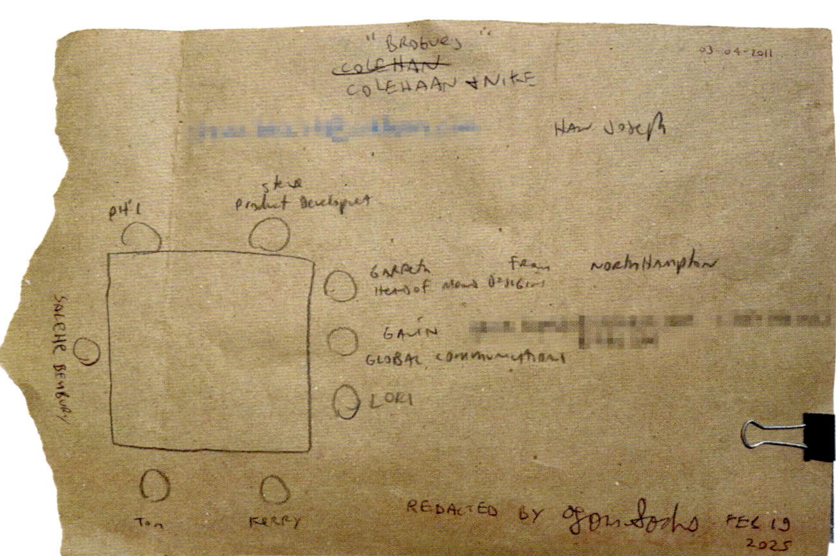

Tom Sachs notes from Cole Haan meeting

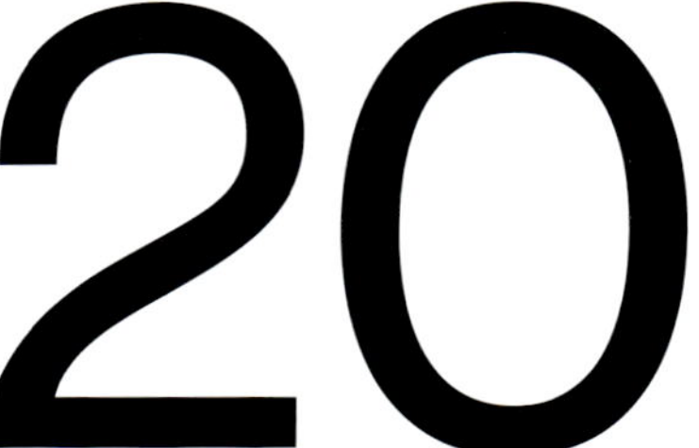

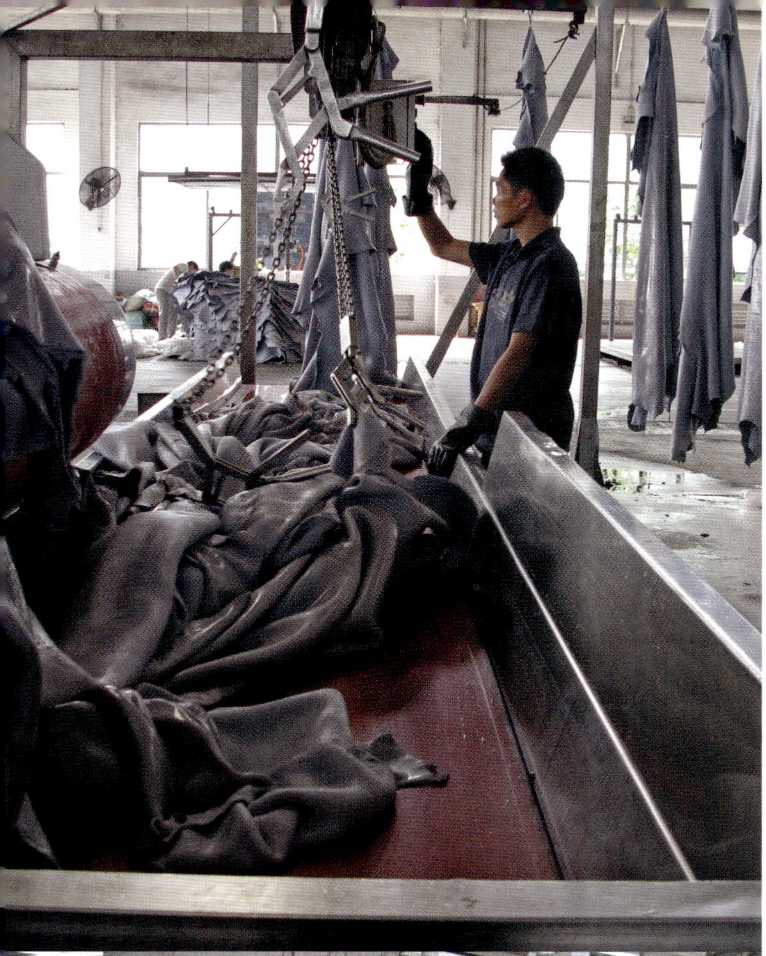

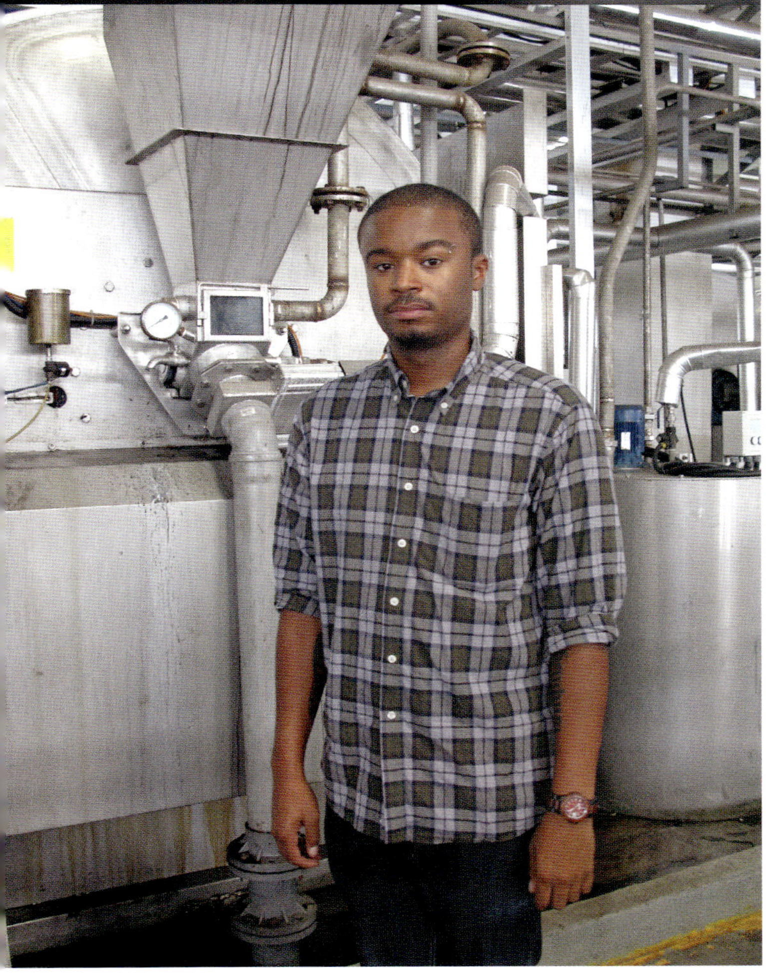

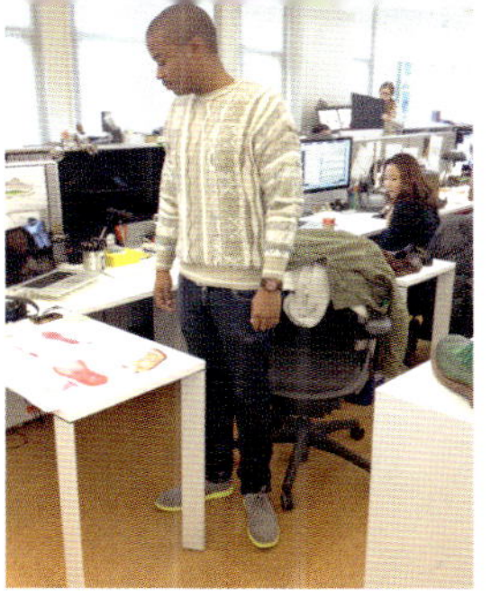

Salehe's Cole Haan desk

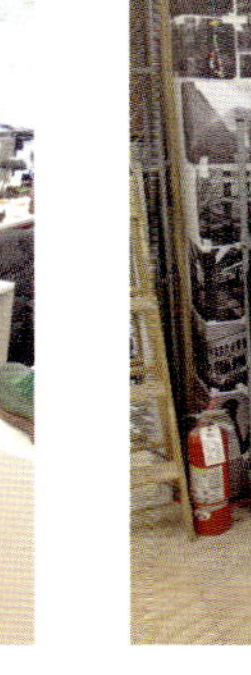

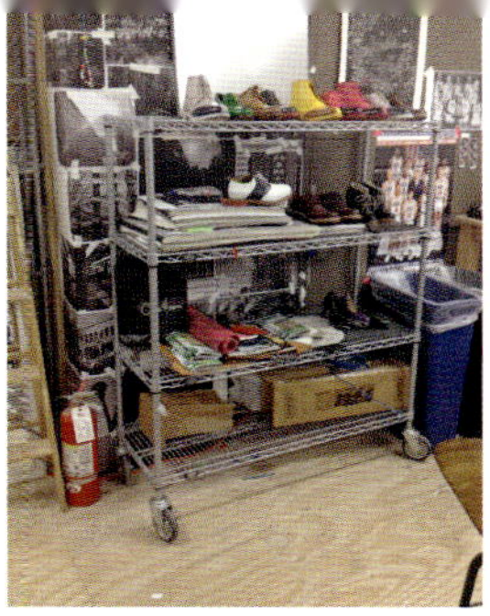

Cole Haan Innovation Room

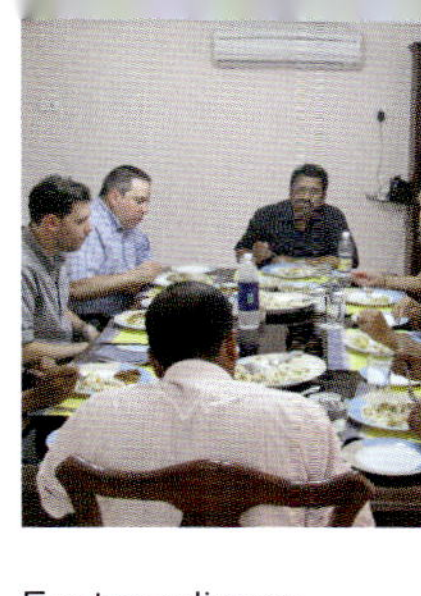

Factory dinner
in Chennai, India

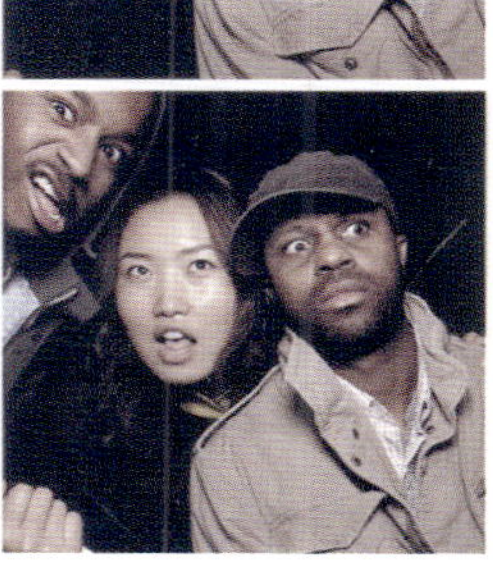

Cole Haan Innovation Team
(Jeff Henderson, Jin Hong)

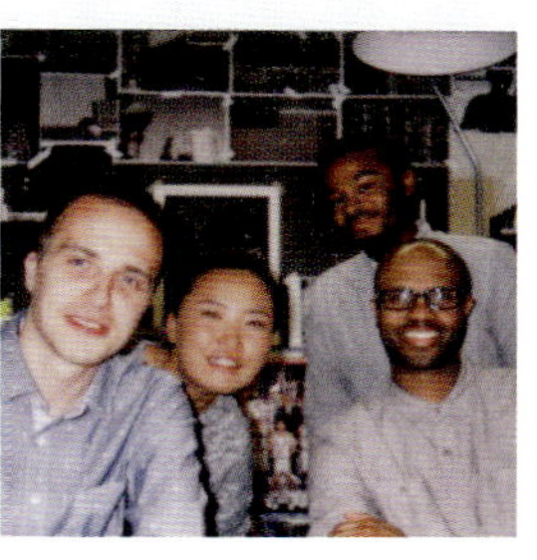

Cole Haan Innovation Team
and some guy from Nike

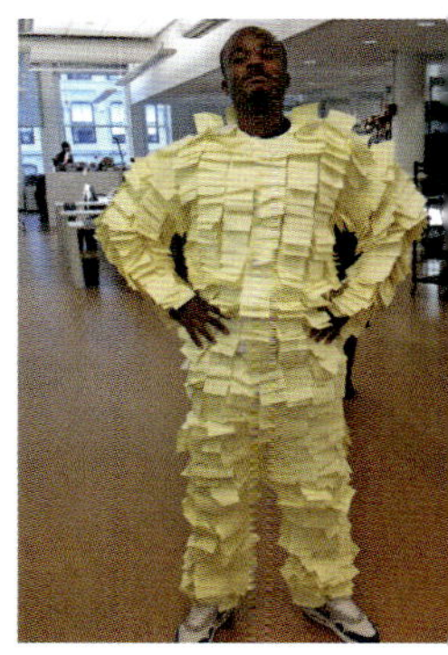

"Post-It Note Man"

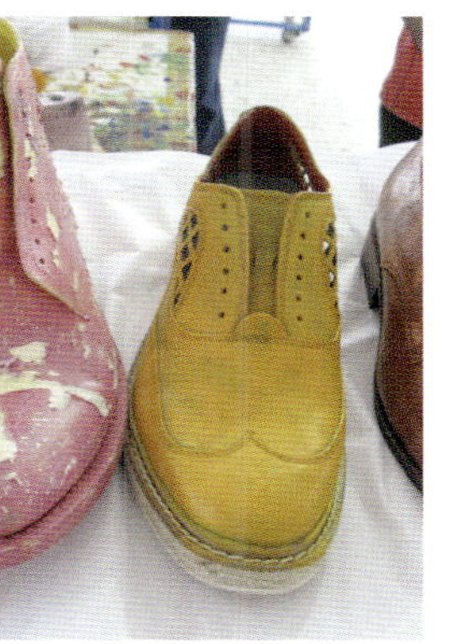

Sample development

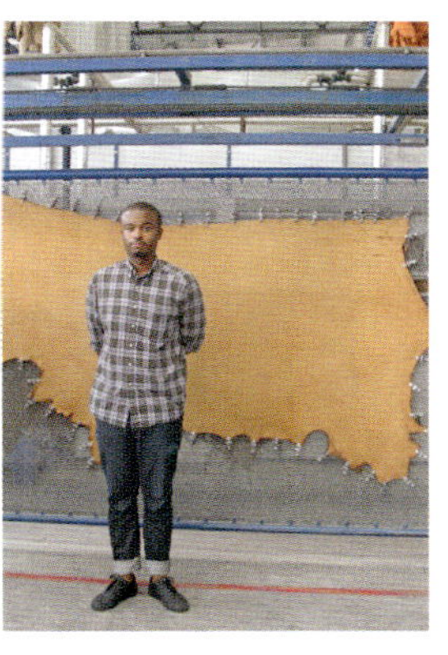

Leather factory -
Chennai, India

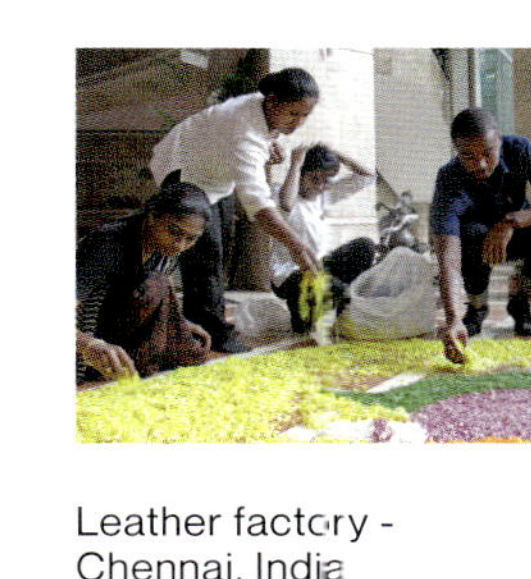

Leather factory -
Chennai, India

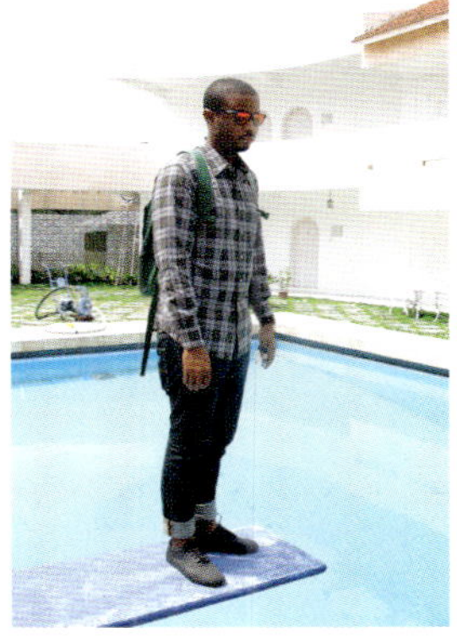

Leather factory housing
facility - Chennai, India

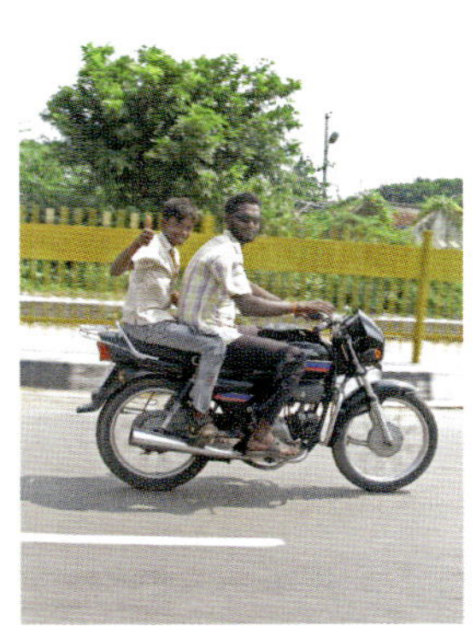

Leather factory commute -
Chennai, India

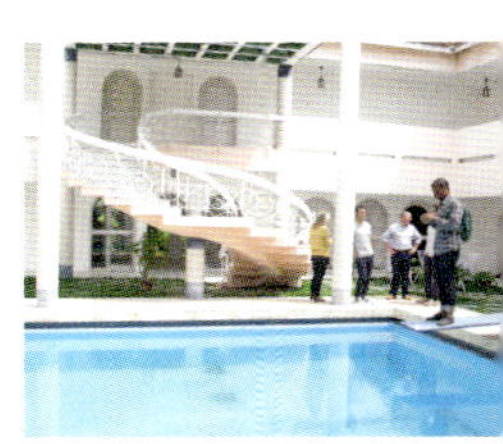

Leather factory housing
facility - Chennai, India

Leather factory - Chennai, India

21

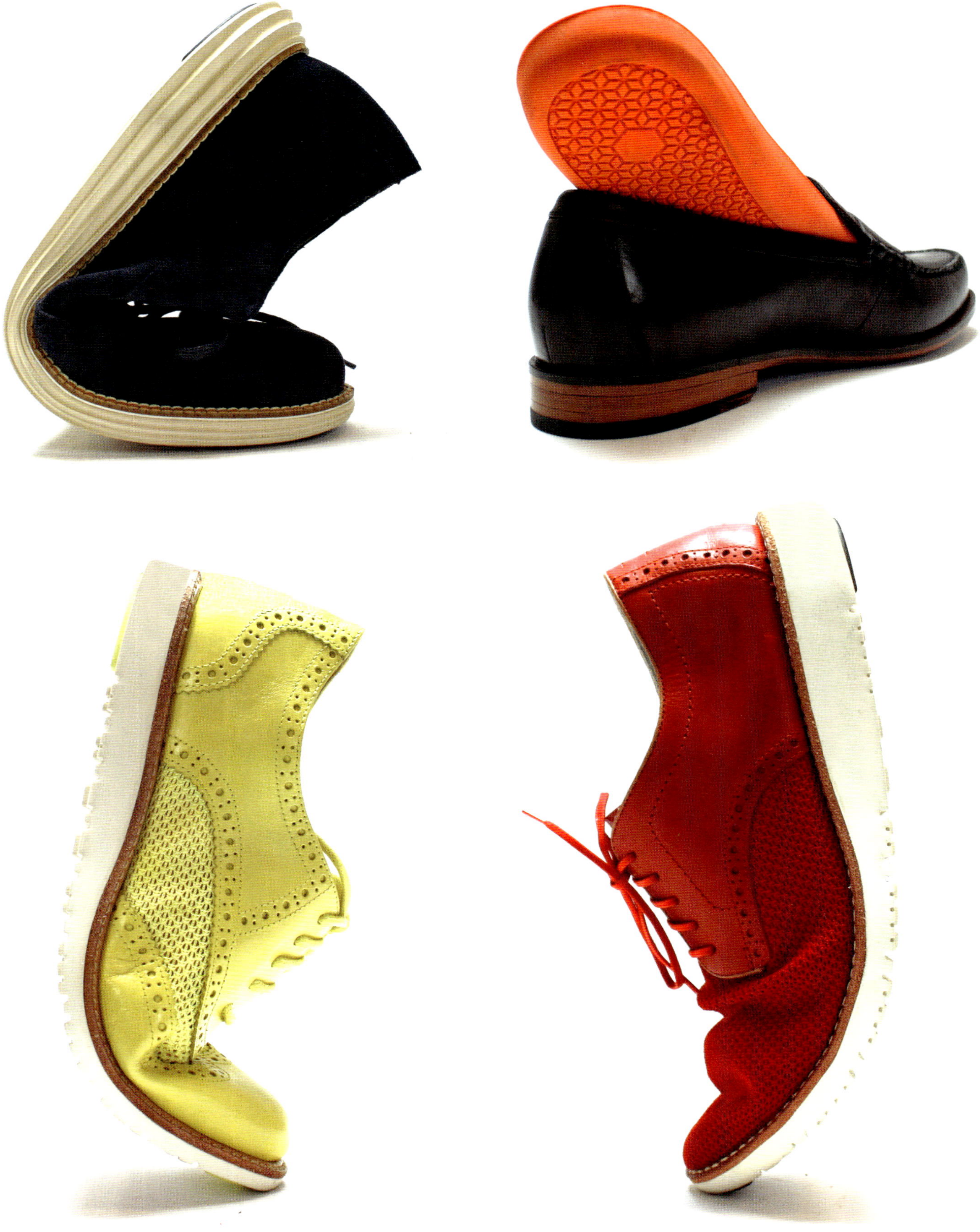

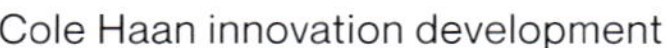

Cole Haan innovation development

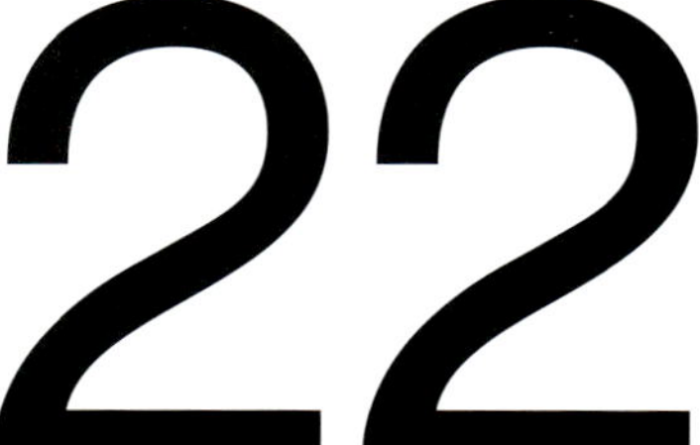

22

(2011)

COLE HAAN

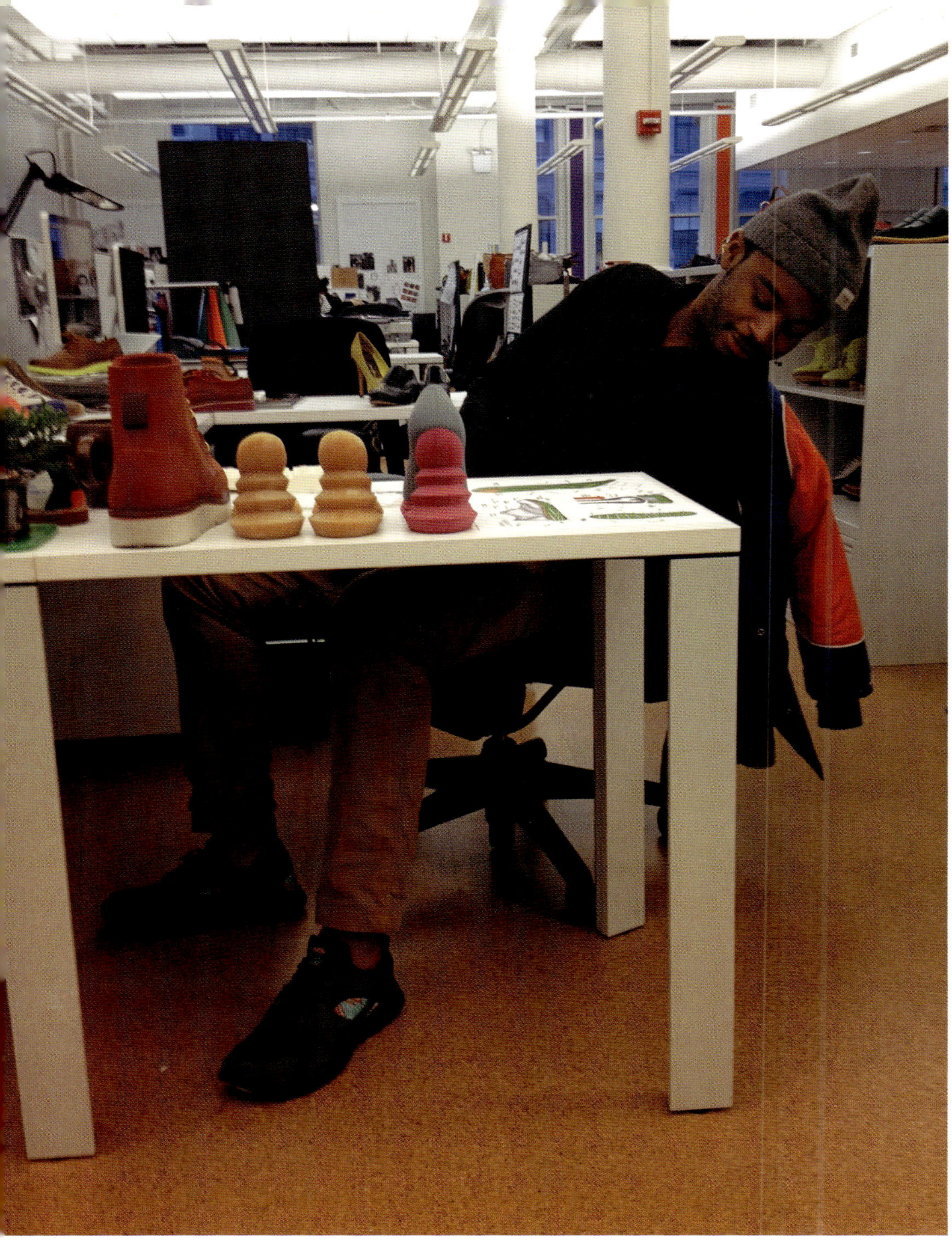

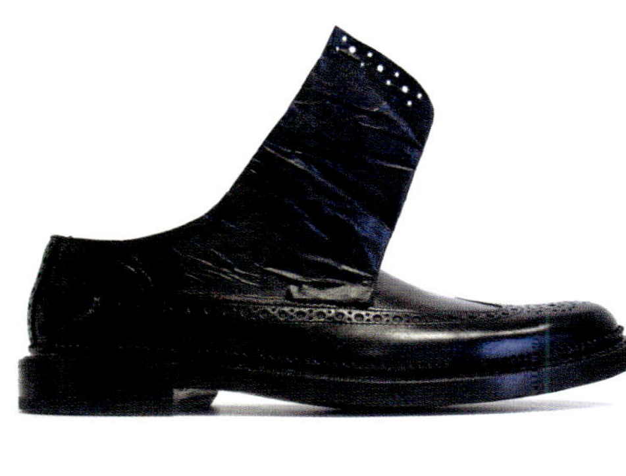

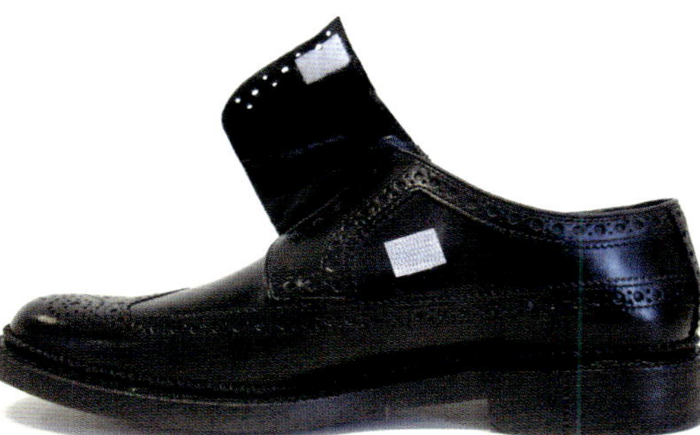

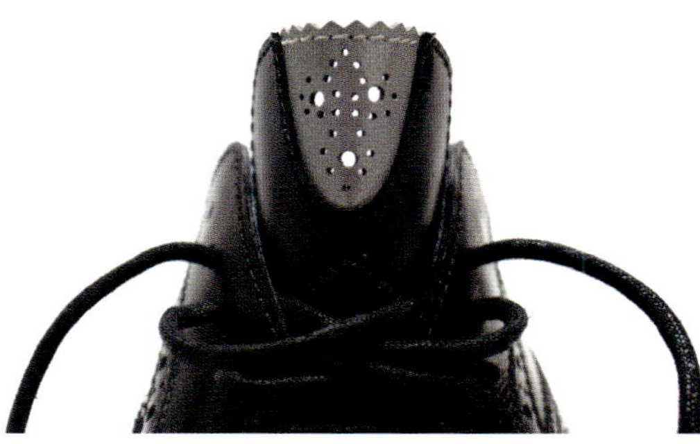

Cole Haan innovation development

Salehe Bembury's Cole Haan desk

23

COLE HAAN (2011)

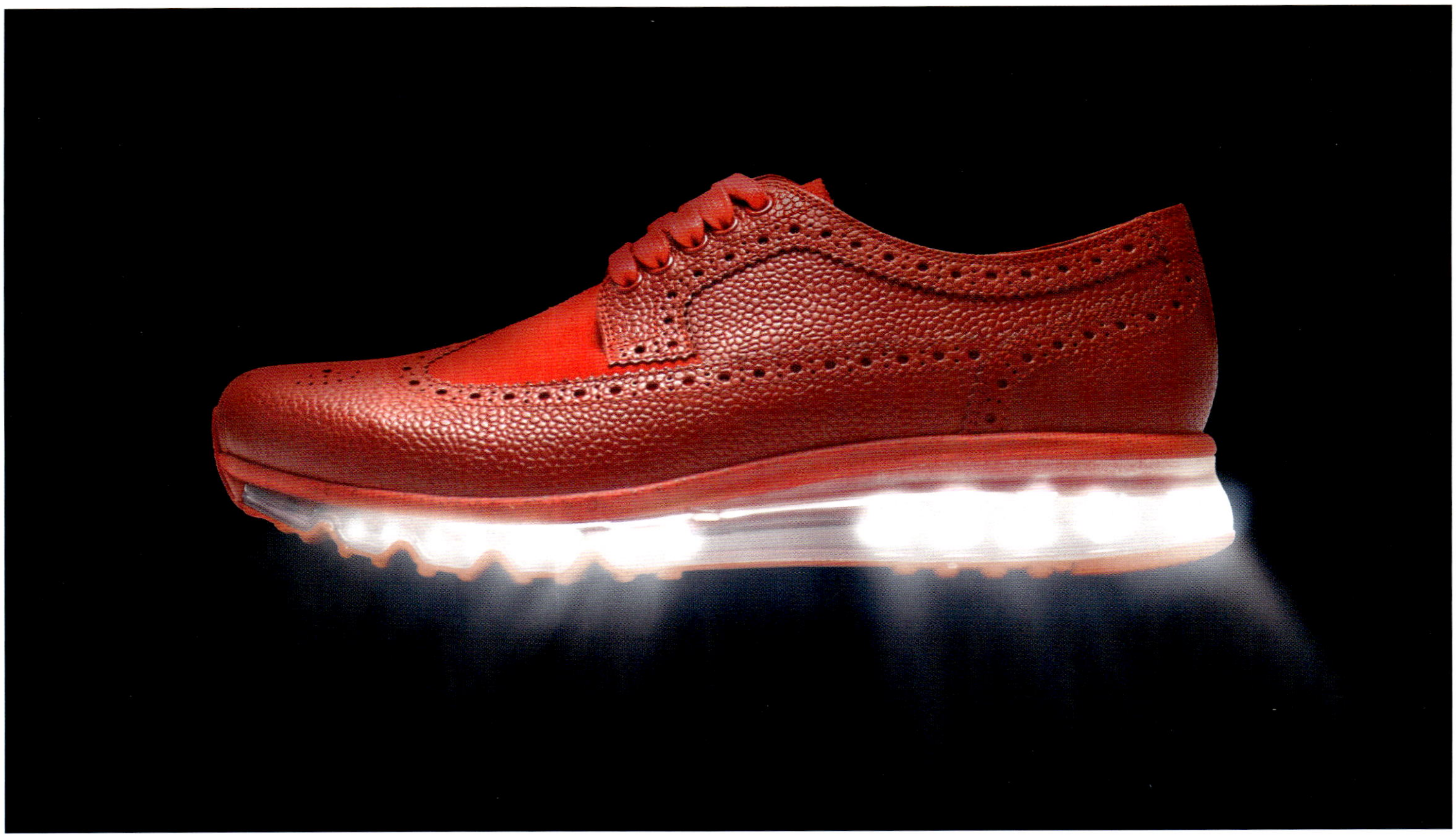

Cole Haan innovation development

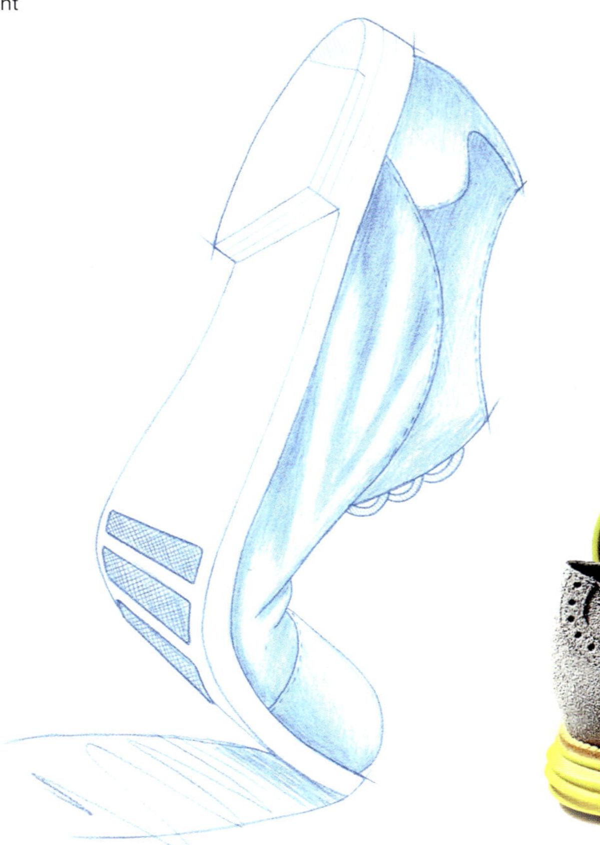

Cole Haan innovation development

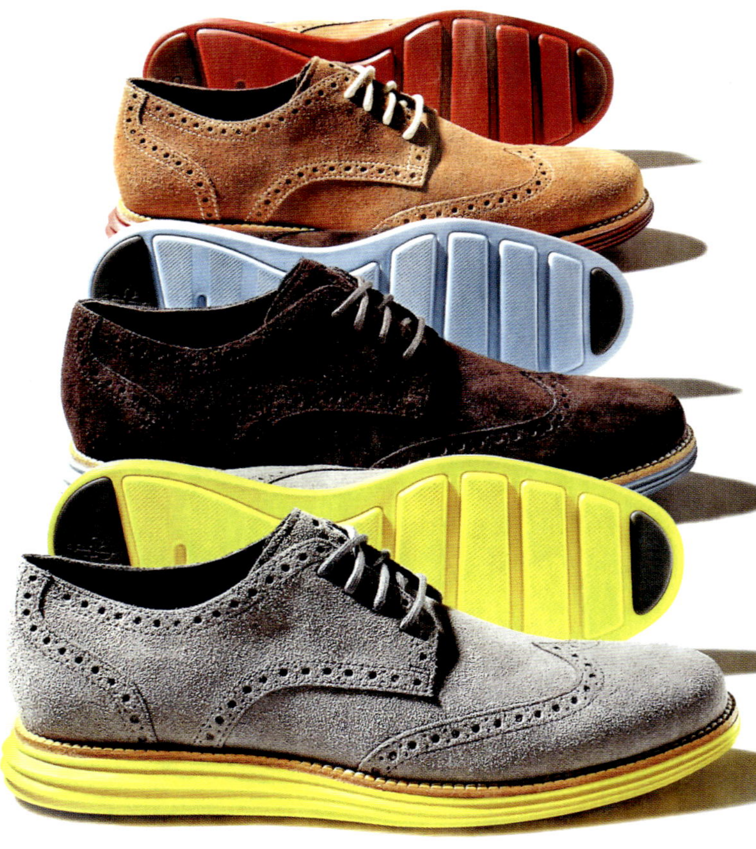

Cole Haan innovation development

24

(2011)

COLE HAAN

(12) **United States Design Patent** (10) **Patent No.: US D759,365 S**
Henderson et al. (45) **Date of Patent: ** Jun. 21, 2016**

(54) **SHOE WELT**

(71) Applicant: **Cole Haan LLC**, New York, NY (US)

(72) Inventors: **Jeff Henderson**, New York, NY (US); **Salehe Bembury**, New York, NY (US); **Steve Beccia**, New York, NY (US); **TJ Papp**, Interlaken, NJ (US)

(73) Assignee: **Cole Haan LLC**, New York, NY (US)

(**) Term: **14 Years**

(21) Appl. No.: **29/460,880**

(22) Filed: **Jul. 16, 2013**

(51) **LOC (10) Cl.** **02-04**

(52) **U.S. Cl.**
USPC **D2/977**

(58) **Field of Classification Search**
USPC .... D2/896, 915, 916, 923, 925, 918, 922, D2/946, 964–966, 969, 970, 976; 36/17 R, 36/17 PW, 18, 19 R, 34 R, 72 B, 72 R, 73, 36/78, 83, 136
CPC A43B 21/00; A43B 21/36; A43B 21/39; A43B 21/52; A43B 9/02; A43B 9/04; A43B 9/06
See application file for complete search history.

(56) **References Cited**

U.S. PATENT DOCUMENTS

4,450,632	A	*	5/1984	Bensley	36/17 PW
D336,766	S	*	6/1993	Sjosward	D2/902
D402,795	S	*	12/1998	Moll et al.	D2/923
D481,860	S	*	11/2003	Robbins	D2/969
D504,011	S	*	4/2005	Robbins et al.	D2/969
D504,560	S	*	5/2005	Robbins et al.	D2/969
D507,864	S	*	8/2005	Robbins et al.	D2/969
D524,016	S	*	7/2006	Robinson et al.	D2/902
D561,452	S	*	2/2008	Belley et al.	D2/969
7,836,609	B2	*	11/2010	Covatch	36/17 R
D641,964	S	*	7/2011	Schwartz et al.	D2/969
2005/0262728	A1	*	12/2005	Robbins	36/16

OTHER PUBLICATIONS

Timberland PRO Men's Pitboss 6" Steel-Toe Boot, announced Oct. 2007, [online], site visited Mar. 16, 2015. Available from Internet, <URL: http://www.amazon.com>.*
Timberland PRO Men's Pitboss 6" Steel-Toe Boot, announced Oct. 2007, [online], site visited Jun. 20, 2015. Available from Internet, <URL: http://www.amazon.com>.*

* cited by examiner

Primary Examiner — Derrick Holland
Assistant Examiner — Janice Lim
(74) *Attorney, Agent, or Firm* — Thompson Coburn LLP

(57) **CLAIM**

The ornamental design for a shoe welt, as shown and described.

DESCRIPTION

FIG. **1** is a perspective view of a shoe welt showing our new design;
FIG. **2** is a top plan view thereof;
FIG. **3** is a lateral side elevational view thereof;
FIG. **4** is a medial side elevational view thereof;
FIG. **5** is a front elevational view thereof; and,
FIG. **6** is a rear elevational view thereof.
The broken line portions of FIGS. **1-6** show unclaimed subject matter only and form no part of the claimed design.

1 Claim, 4 Drawing Sheets

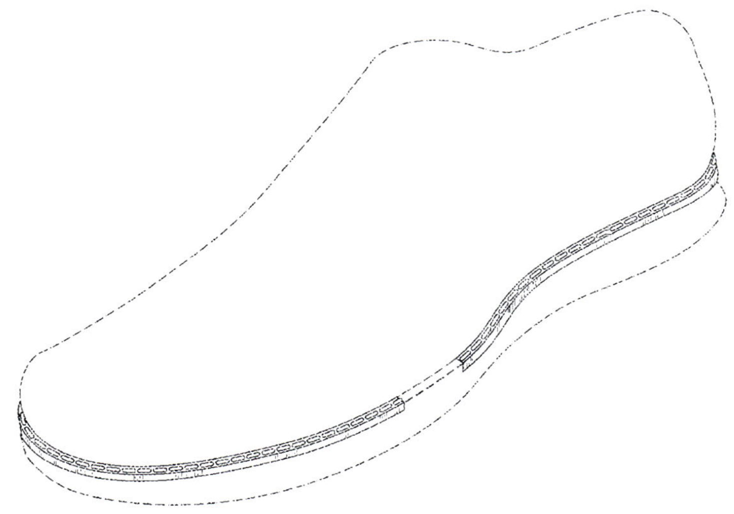

US Patent for Cole Haan medial midsole welt split

25

COLE HAAN **(2011)**

26

GREATS (2014)

G LEA
CAPTA

GUE
IN

GREATS
G LEAGUE CAPTAIN

Up until this point in my career, I felt like I was the subordinate. I was constantly learning, being told what to do; I was the young padawan to Jeff Henderson's Jedi. And that was exactly what I should've been doing at that point in my career. I knew nothing, even though I thought I did, and I really needed someone like Jeff to show me the way—to teach me how to fail, to hold my hand and explain to me the different ways to navigate both my design career and corporate America, or even white corporate America, to take it a step further. And he did an amazing job doing so.

But my next job along the path was Greats. Greats was a small startup started by Jon Buscemi, who at the time was also starting a brand called Buscemi. He was creating a footwear company that would be straight-to-consumer, with an accessible price point, and they were looking for a designer to take them to the top. This position appealed to me because prior to this my career had been very much about working for someone else, listening to what somebody else told me to do; I didn't really feel like I'd had a perspective. This job felt like an opportunity to grow, an opportunity to make decisions, and it felt like a place where I could evolve into being the designer that I wanted to be.

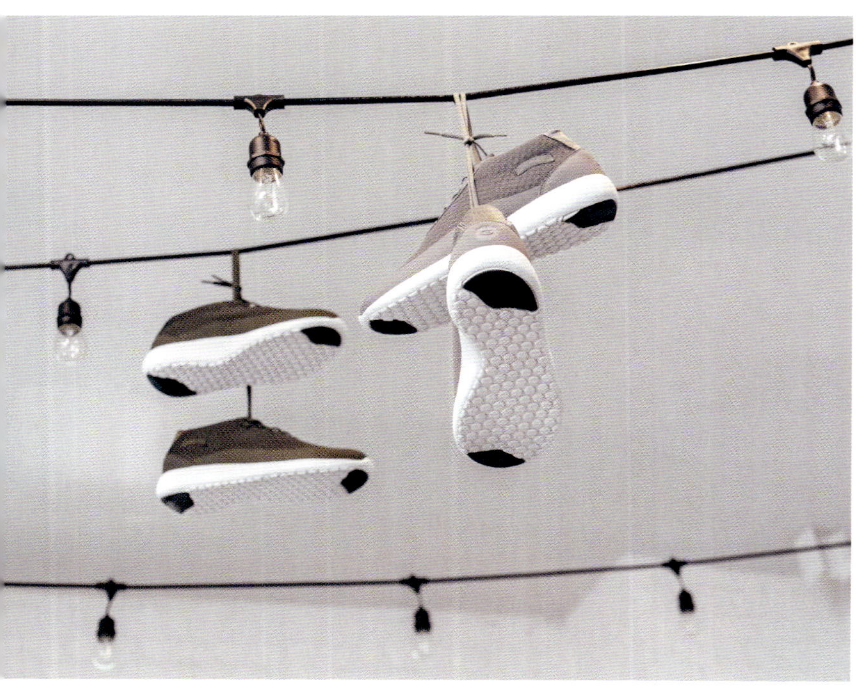

Greats office

Additionally, even though Cole Haan was a Nike-owned company, Greats felt somehow even closer to Nike because I was getting to make sneakers that I wanted to make. Whether it was for Cole Haan, or Payless, or some of the licensed stuff that I'd done before then, none of the work thus far had been about making a traditional sneaker—and Greats was. What made this opportunity even better was that I would be the only footwear designer: not only was I coming into a fresh position filled with many different opportunities, I was also going to be the one making a lot of the design decisions. I felt like I was going to be teaching, and I felt like I was going to be leading. So in the overall journey, this felt like an appropriate next step. It was a step forward, and a natural evolution.

For the first time in my career, I also got the opportunity to participate in marketing. At that stage, I didn't realize I was doing it; it was more that I felt like I was mimicking the designers I'd seen in the past—the Tinkers, the Petries, and the Coopers. Getting to participate in interviews and blogs that were interested in knowing about me and what I did in my off time, having pictures published of my desk and what I was wearing—this was a whole culture that I'd spent many years looking at from a distance from one side of the fence, and I was now slowly climbing over to the other side of the fence. This was one of the first times people cared about me and what the fuck I was doing. I grew up reading *Slam* magazine, or the one time of the year they would have *Kicks* magazine, and I would always become hyper-obsessed with Tinker's desk and what he did in his off time, and all that kind of stuff. So when *Complex* interviewed me for a feature and photographed my office, every single thing on my desk was placed there meticulously: I wanted the consumer to see exactly what I wanted them to see and how I wanted them to see it. This is an early example of how meticulous I am with my execution and my presentation, because I think it really matters. The desk photo probably took an hour to set up, but at that point in my career I had that kind of time, and something as simple as a *Complex* feature was worth spending an hour organizing my desk for. It was something that made my week, if not my month. These were the early stages that felt like a step toward the career that I wanted.

These were also the early stages of Instagram. At the time I didn't personally have an account, but I knew the importance of it. We were tasked with getting more eyes to pay attention to the brand, creating a moment. At the time, it was extremely

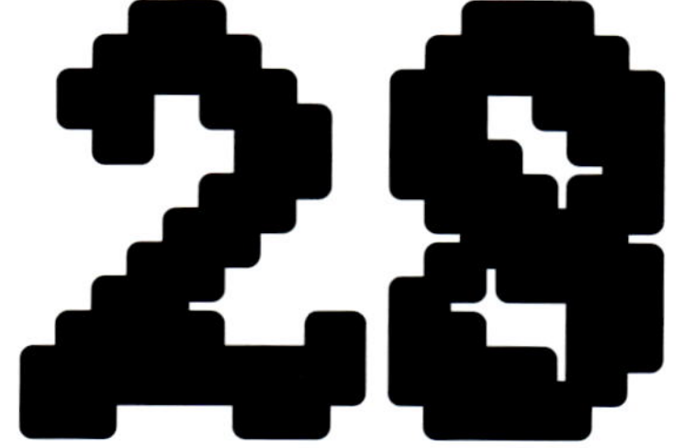

easy to get likes and follows by simply having an "influencer" post a picture of a product–these were the early days of exploring and trying to conquer the algorithm. (I don't think we were even using the word "algorithm" back then, but that's what we were trying to conquer.) I'm friends with Josh Ostrovsky, a.k.a. The Fat Jewish, and at the time he was easily one of the biggest people on Instagram. I thought to myself, if we do a quick shoot with him wearing the shoes, given his influence in social media and on Instagram, we will have a massive reaction, and that will add to the momentum we're trying to create with this brand. So we did, and it was a big success. I didn't consider this to be marketing at the time, because I really was focusing on myself as a designer, and in moments like that I saw myself as an old-school phone operator–I was just putting in the plugs where they needed to be. But in retrospect, this was one hundred percent an attempt at viral marketing.

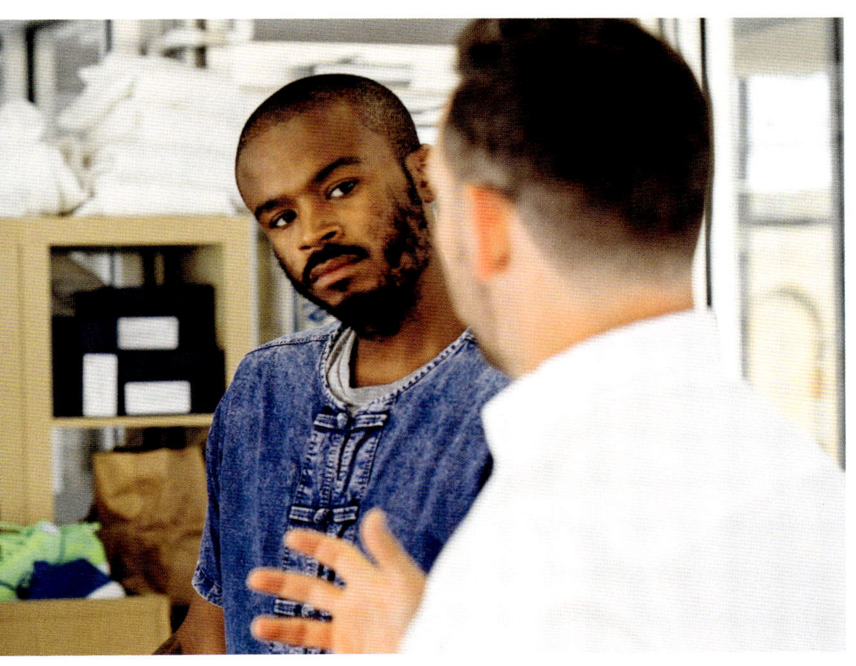

Salehe Bembury in Greats office

This was also the first time in my life I'd worked on a product where I felt comfortable approaching known individuals and asking them if they wanted a pair. This was an idea that existed at Cole Haan, but it didn't feel authentic to me because they weren't sneakers; I felt somewhat of a fraud trying to push dress shoes on people because that's not what was running through my blood. But at Greats, I was working on sneakers that I could put my name on, and that

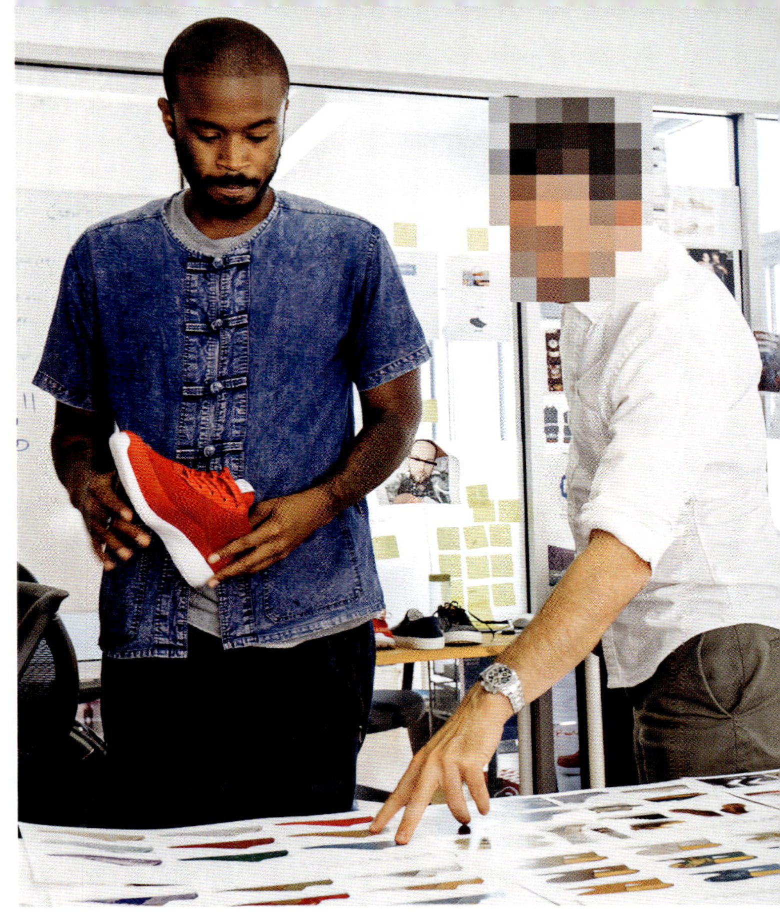

Salehe Bembury in Greats design review

I knew others would potentially enjoy too. One day I was walking around Williamsburg, Brooklyn, during lunch and I ran into Michael Kenneth Williams. I basically said, "Hey, I got these shoes, I think you'd like them," and within an hour he was at the Greats office. He met everybody, we went to the roof, spoke for a little bit, and I gave him some shoes. Unfortunately, he's no longer with us, but my picture with him is representative of how the most seemingly insignificant moments can actually turn out to be tremendously important. All moments are to be respected and honored.

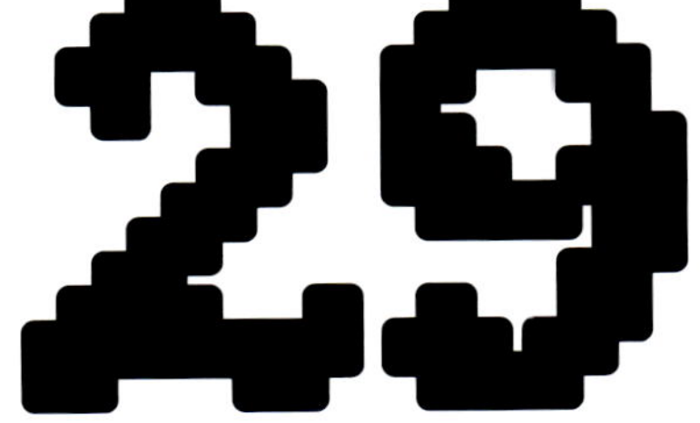

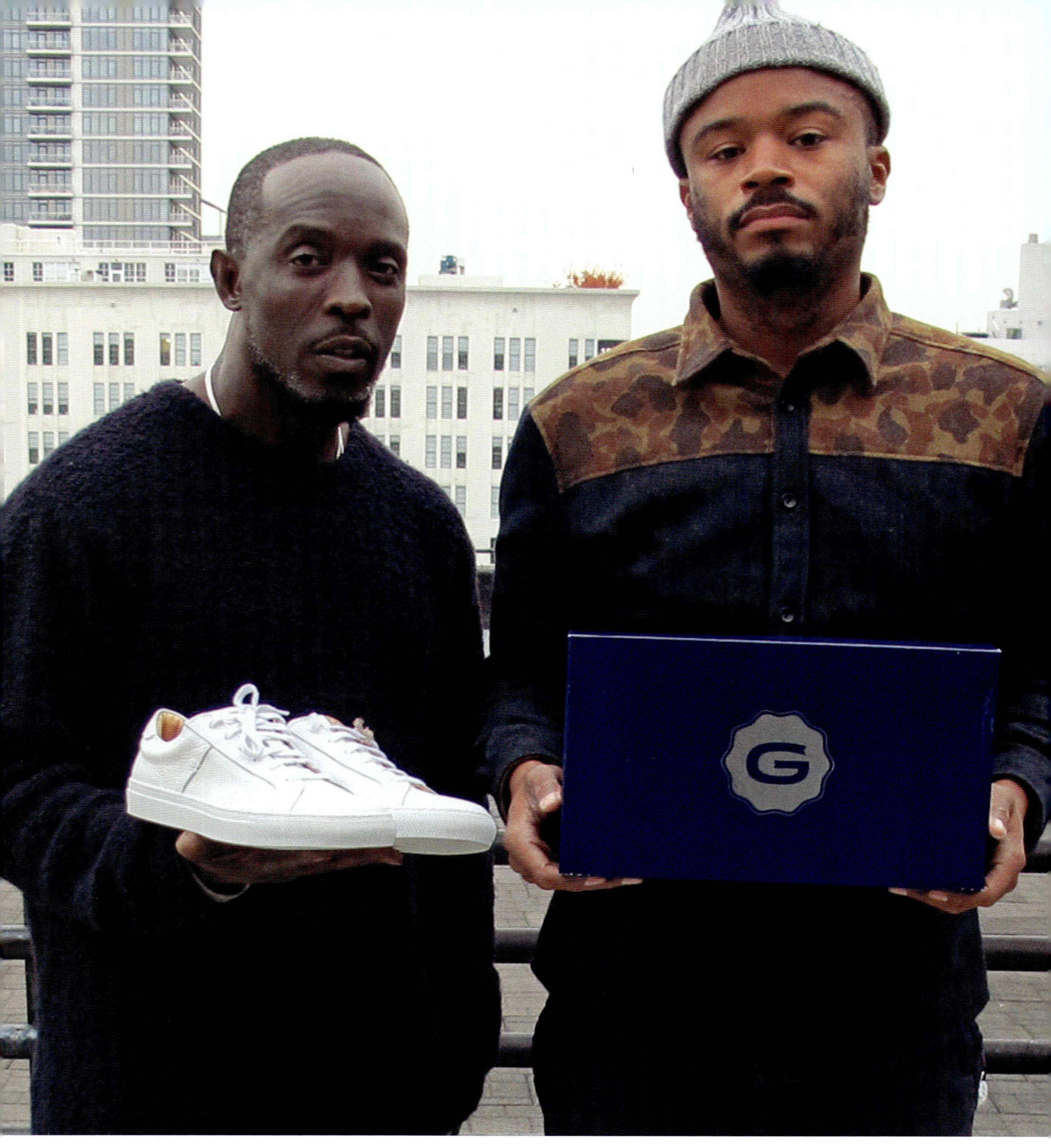

Michael K. Williams and Salehe Bembury

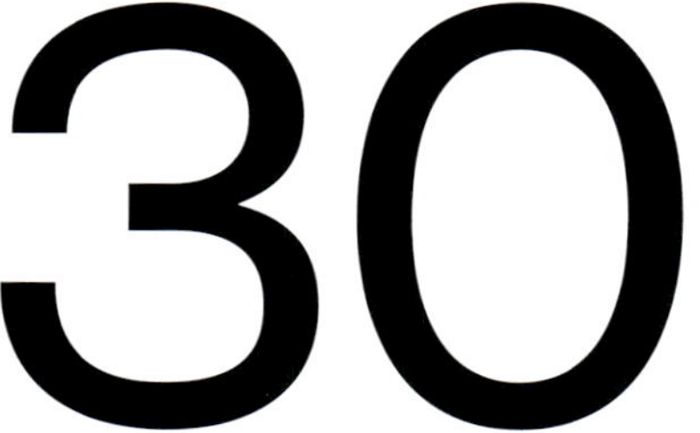

(2014)

GREATS

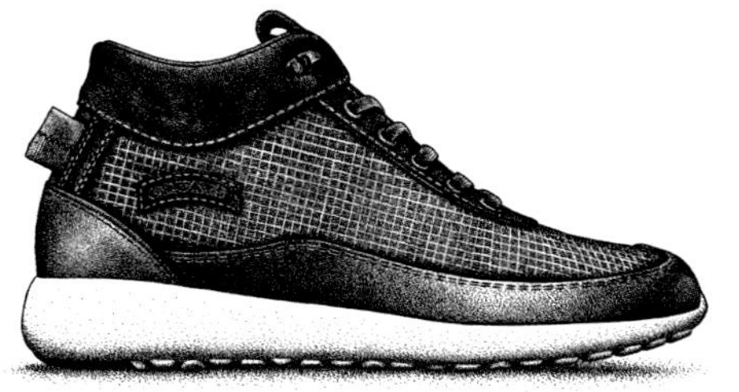
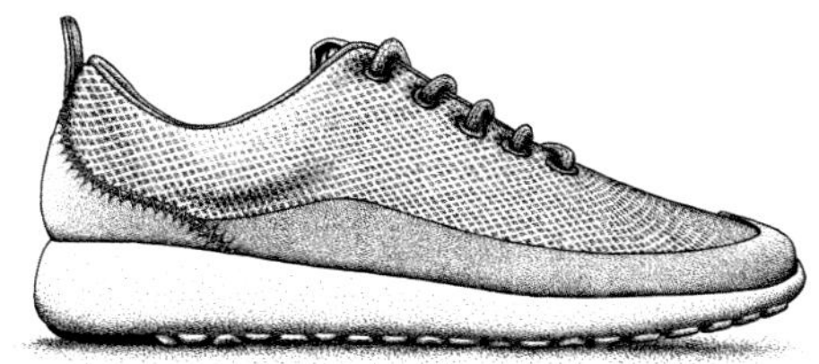
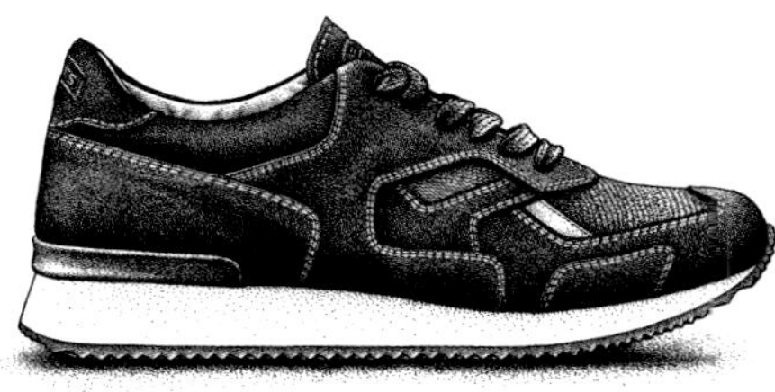
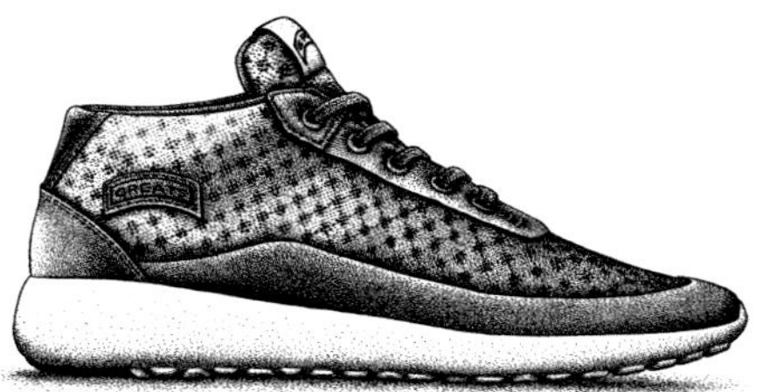
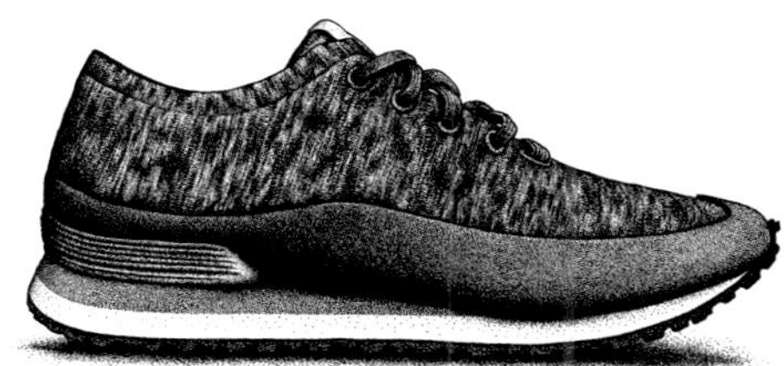
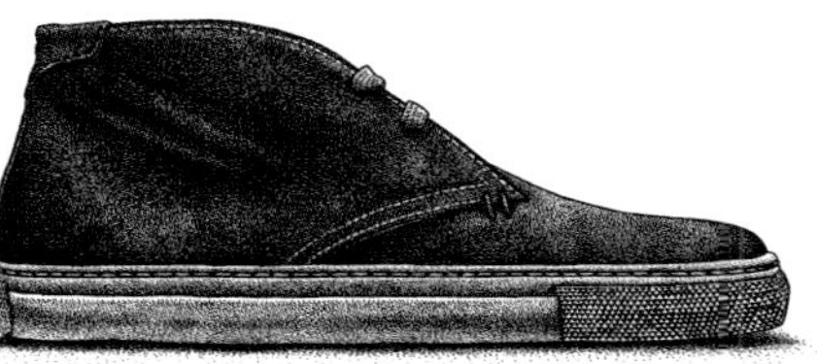
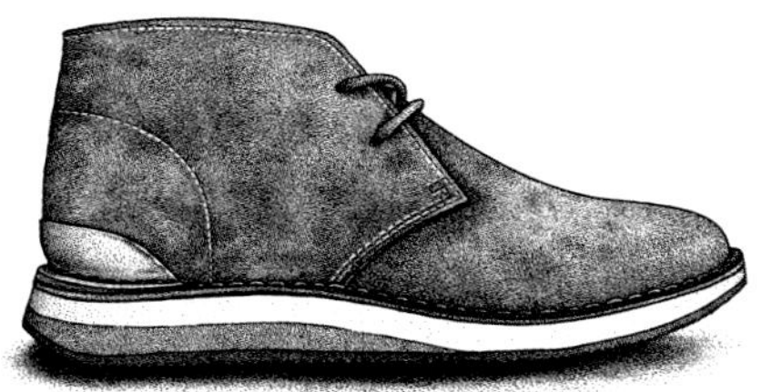
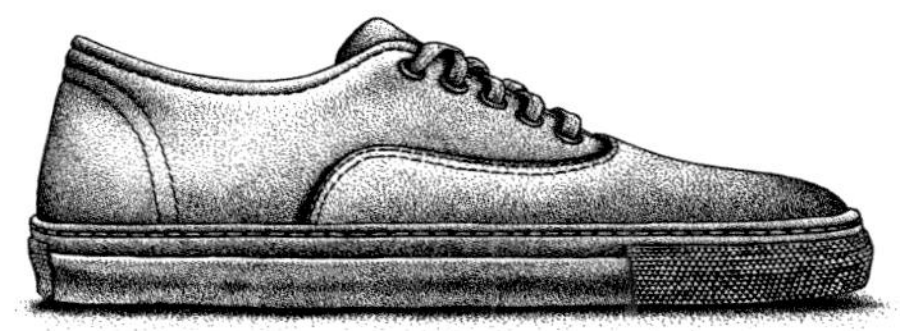
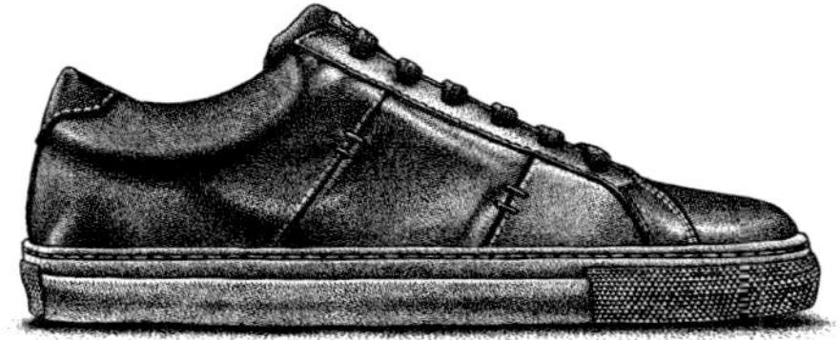
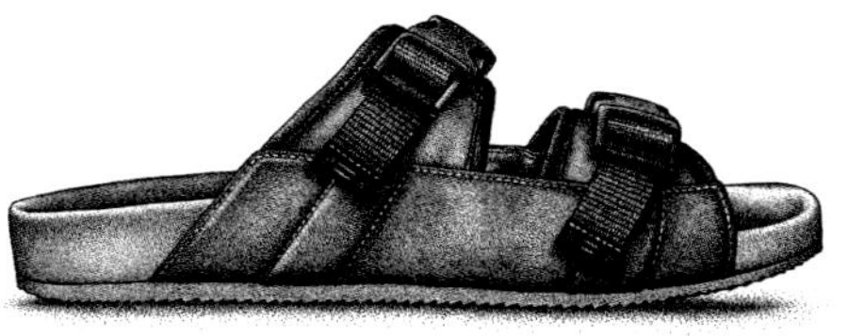
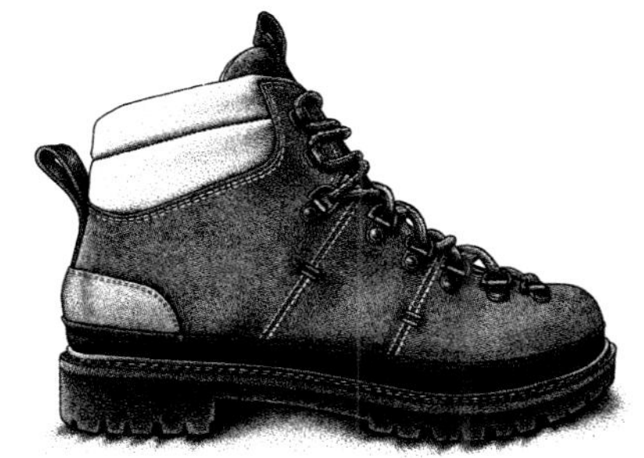
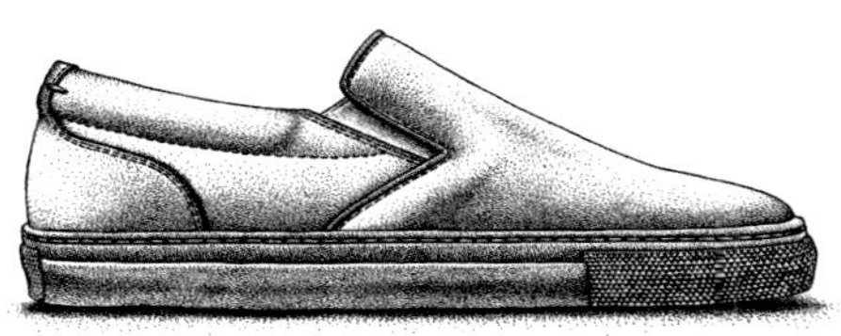
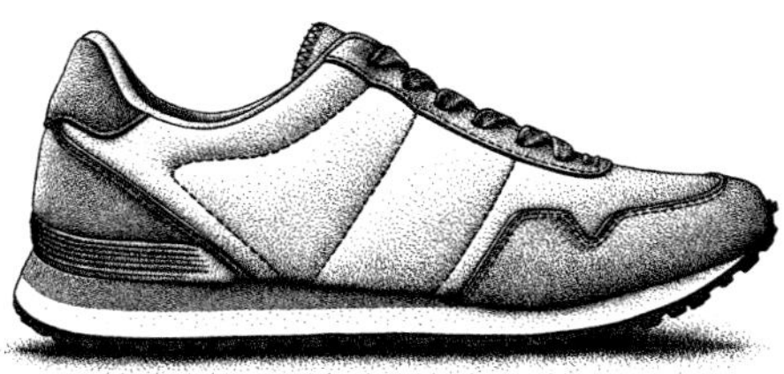
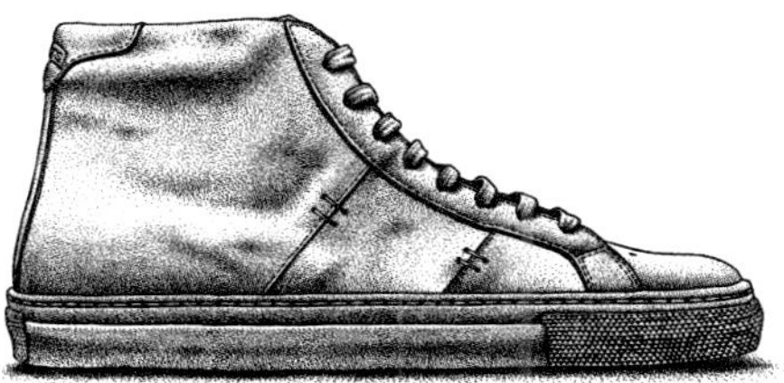
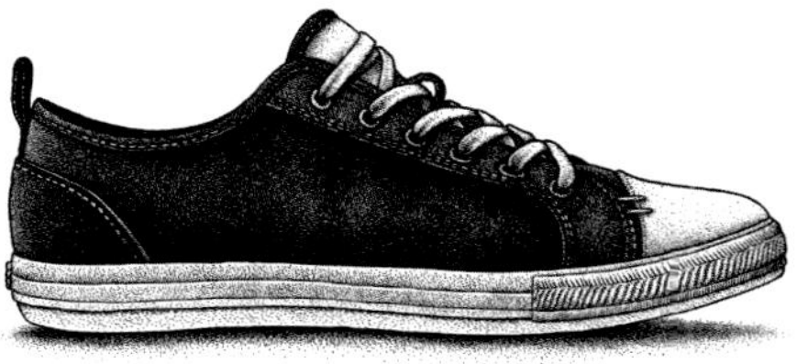

31

GREATS

(2014)

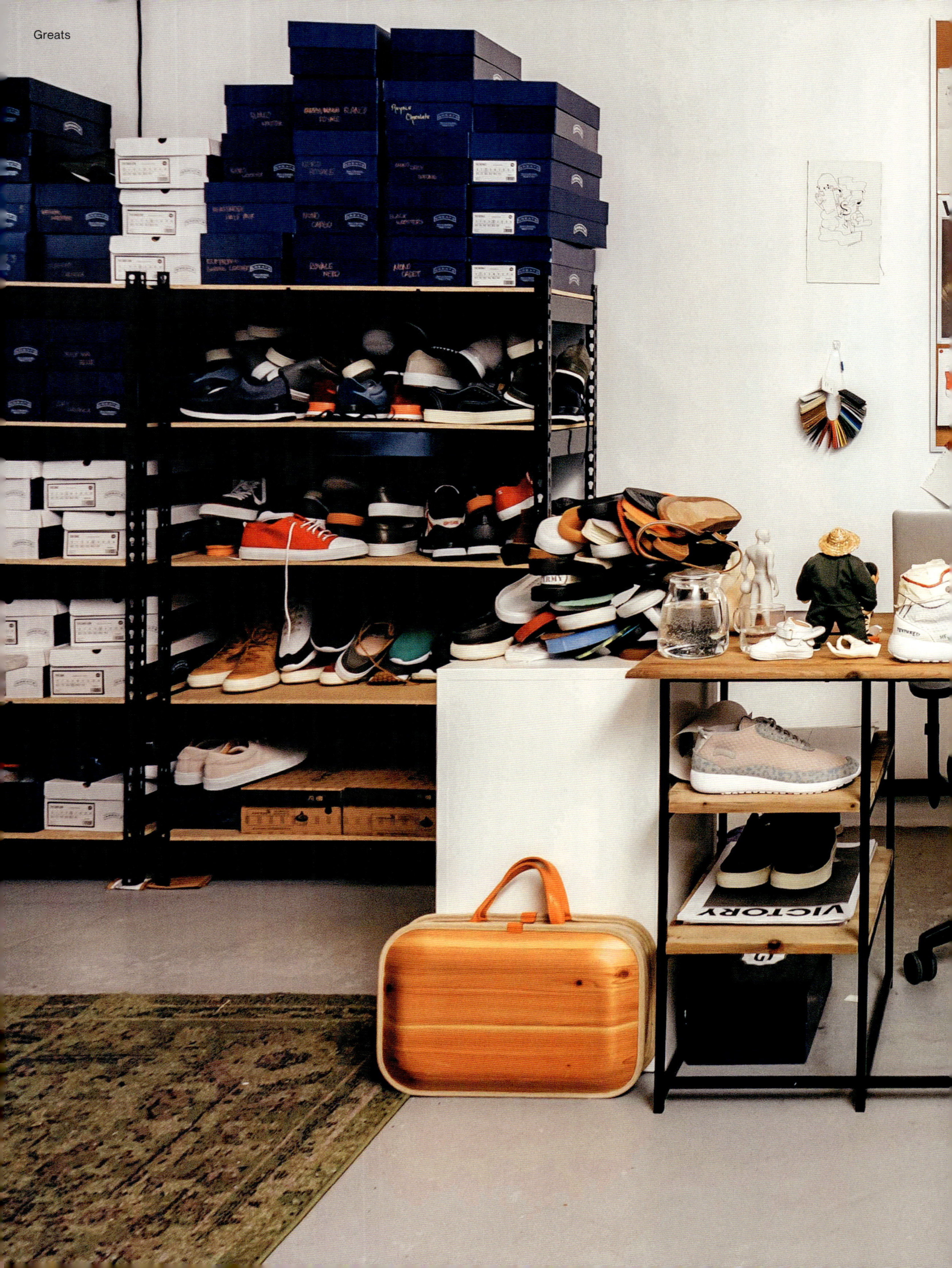
VICTORY

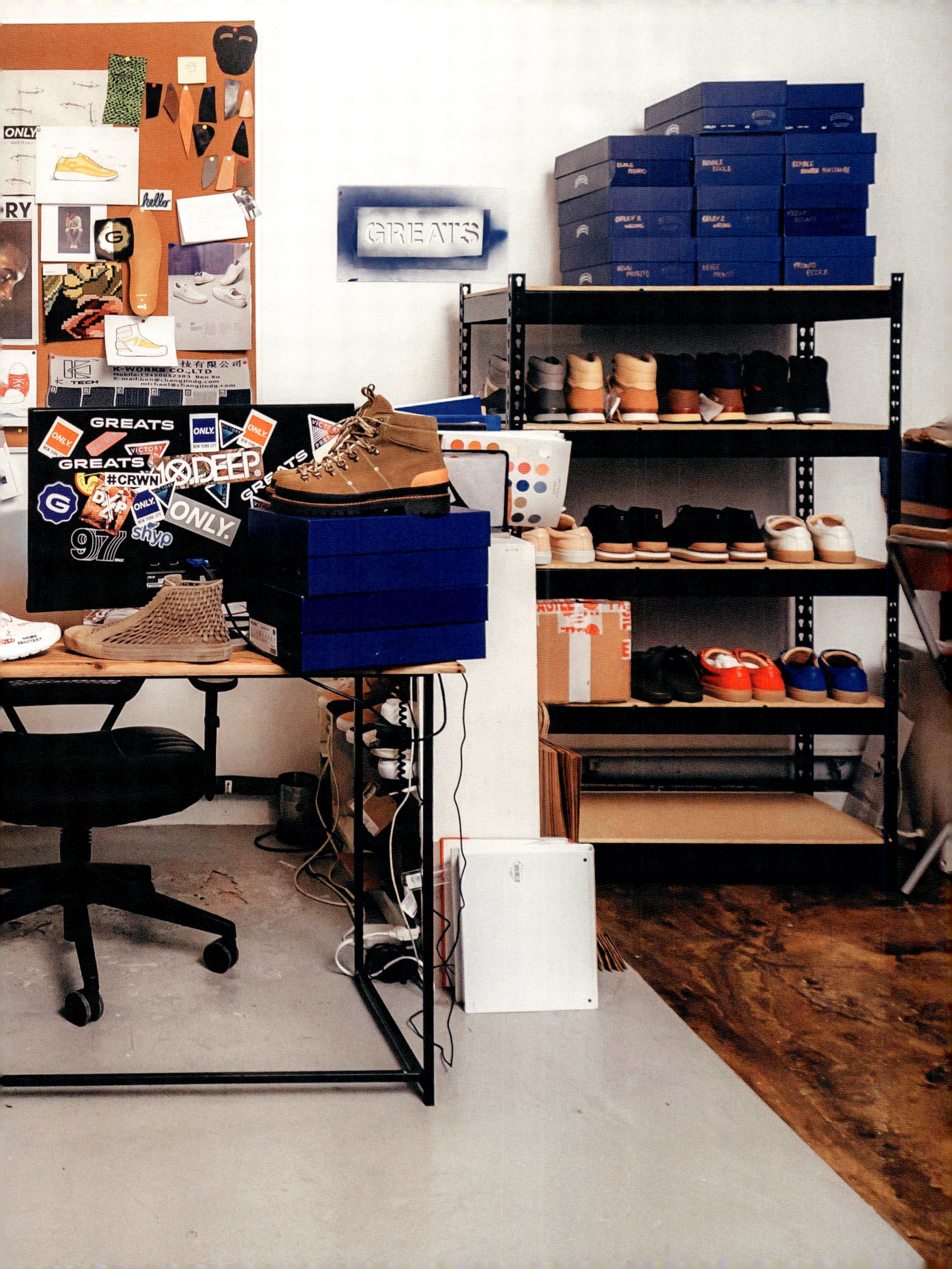
GREATS
GREATS
#CRWN
10DEEP
ONLY.
shyp
K-WORKS CO.,LTD

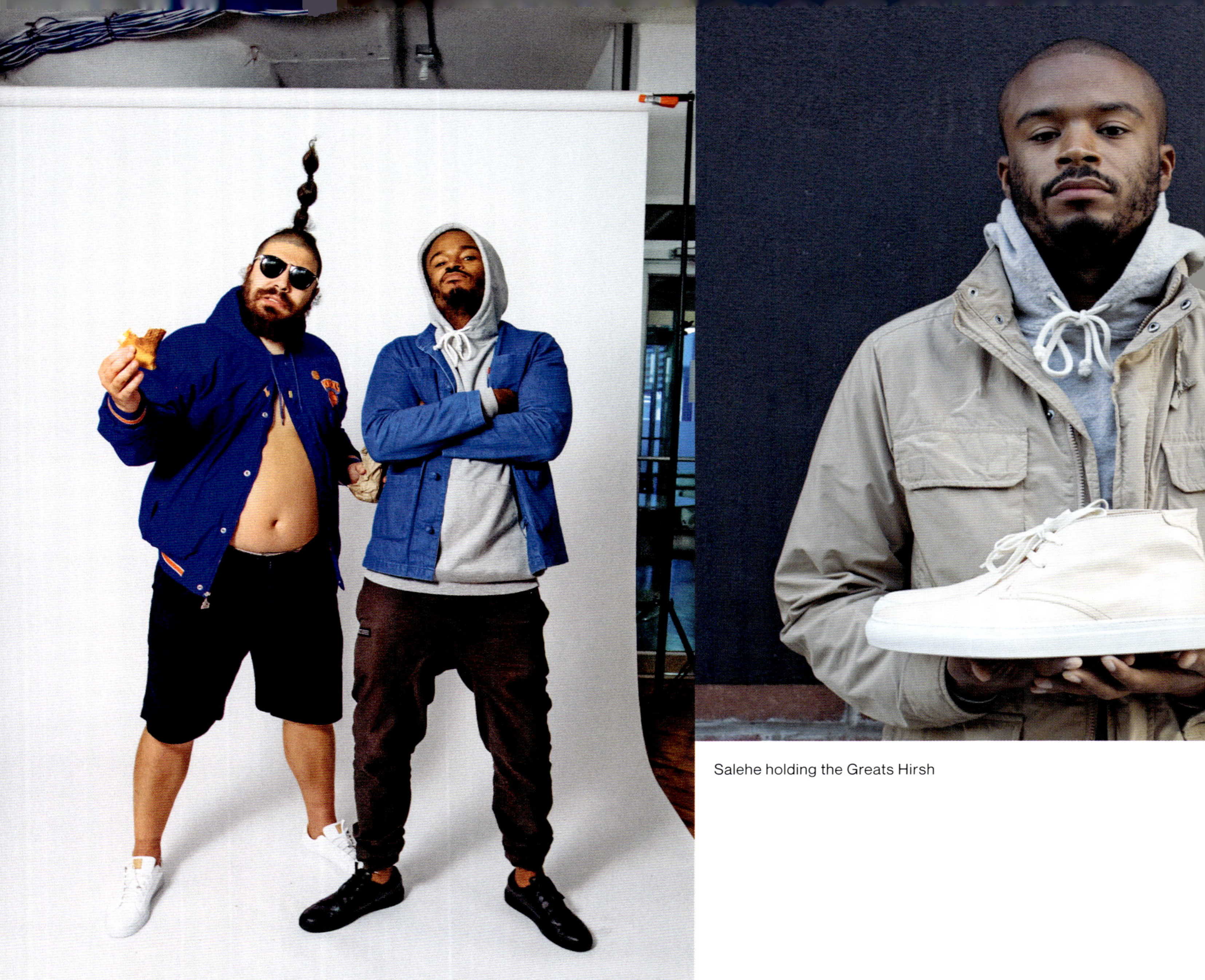

The Fat Jewish for Greats campaign

Salehe holding the Greats Hirsh

34

(2014)

GREATS

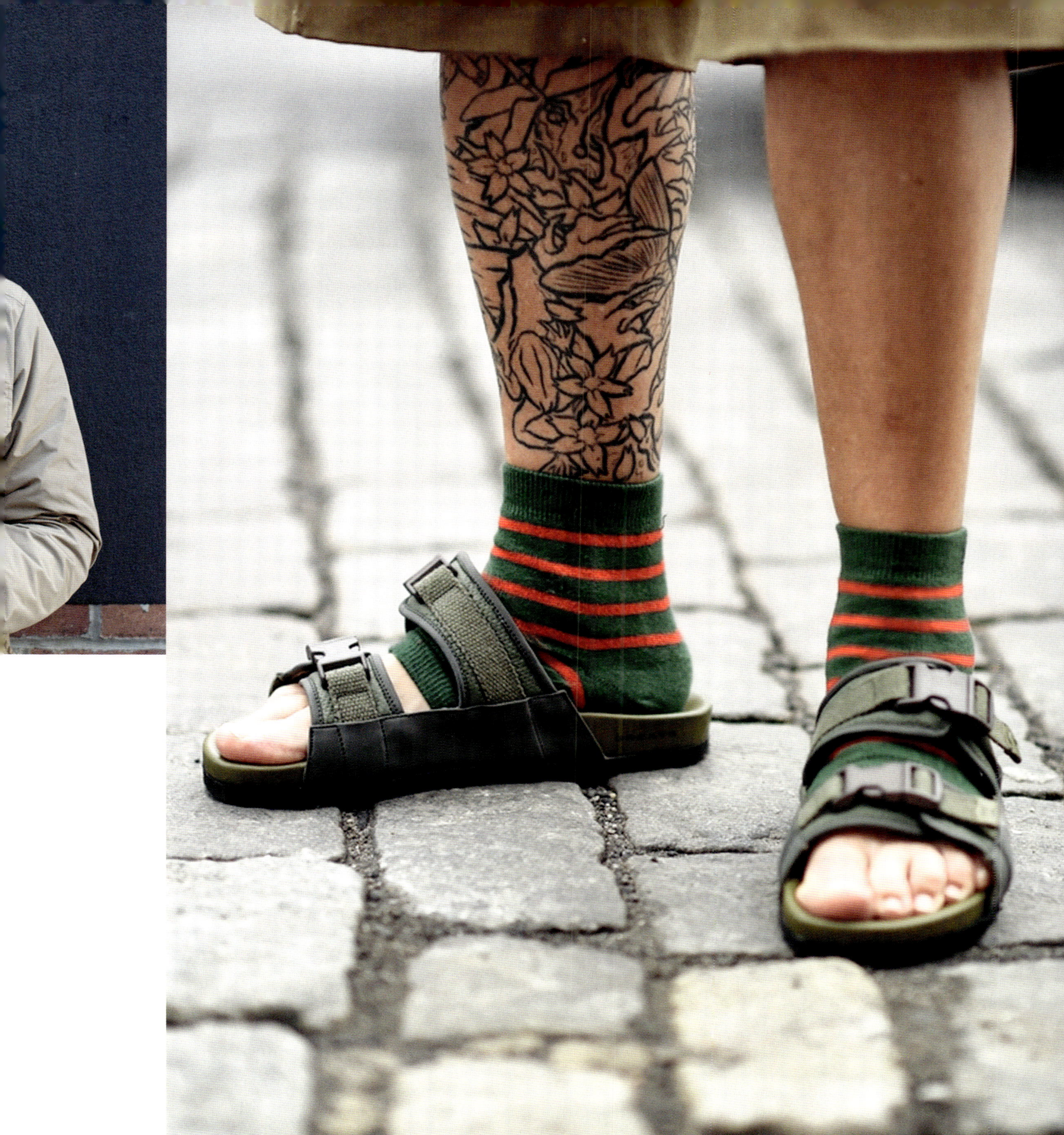

Nick Wooster wearing the Greats Canarsee

35

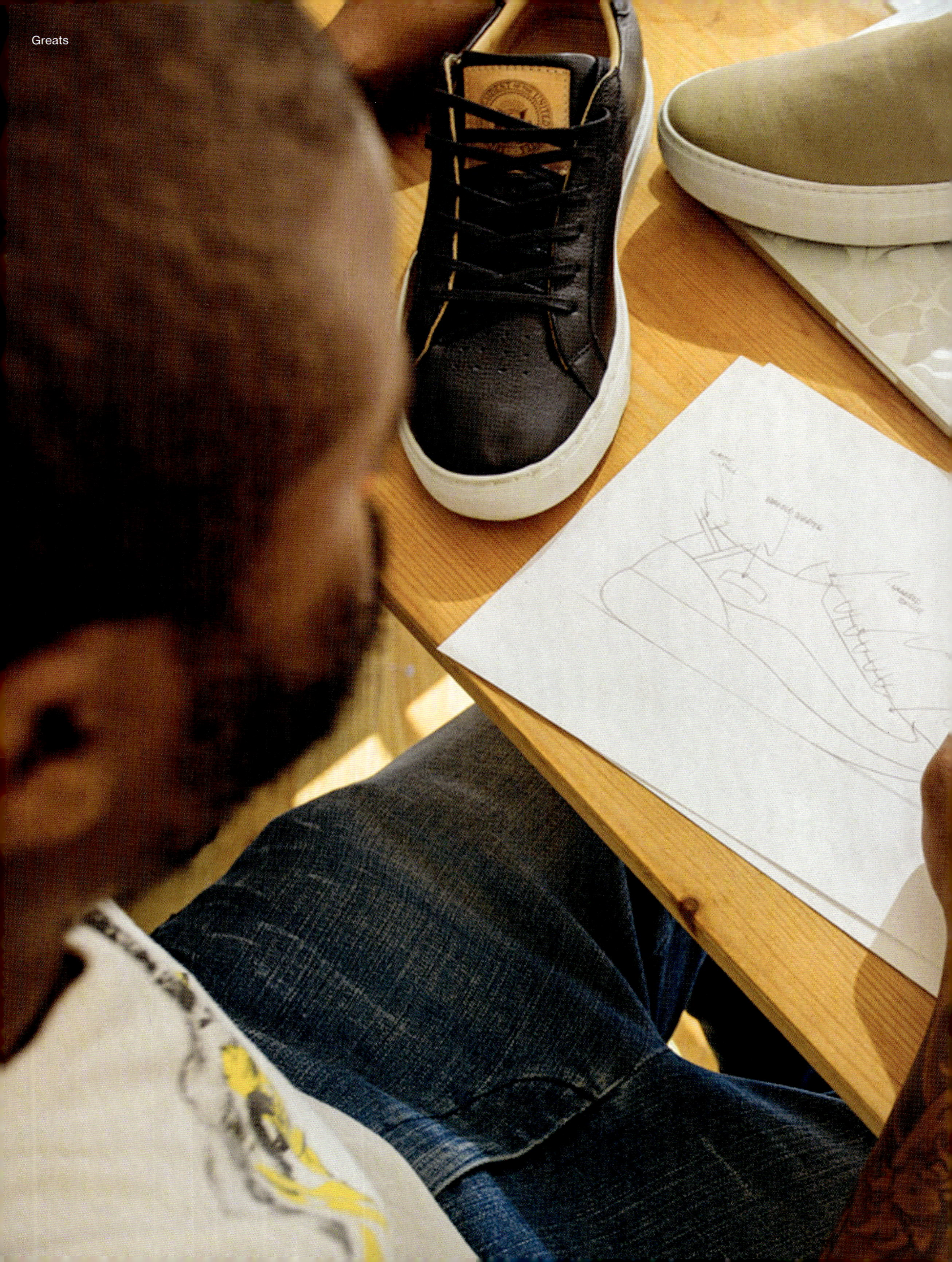

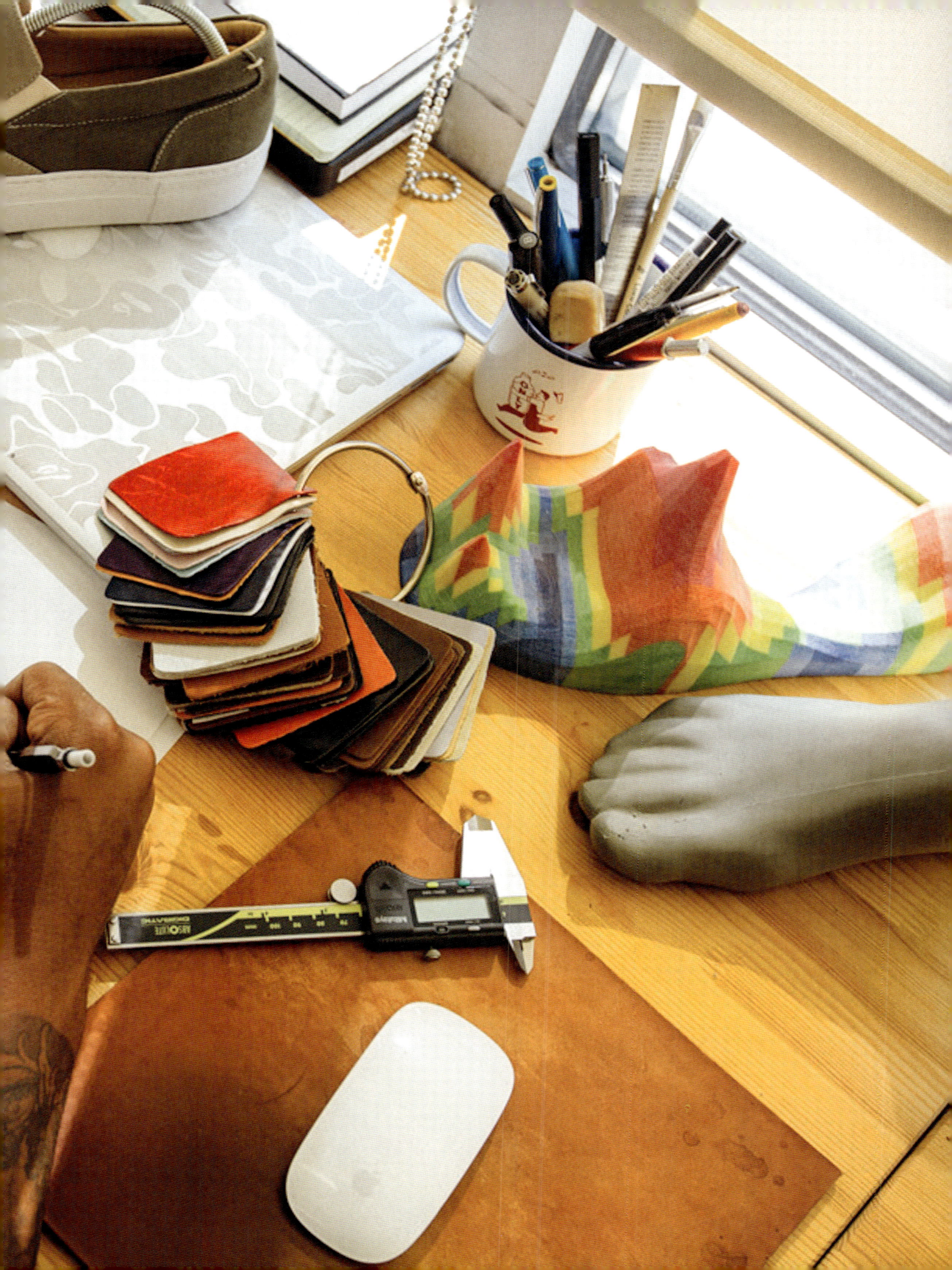

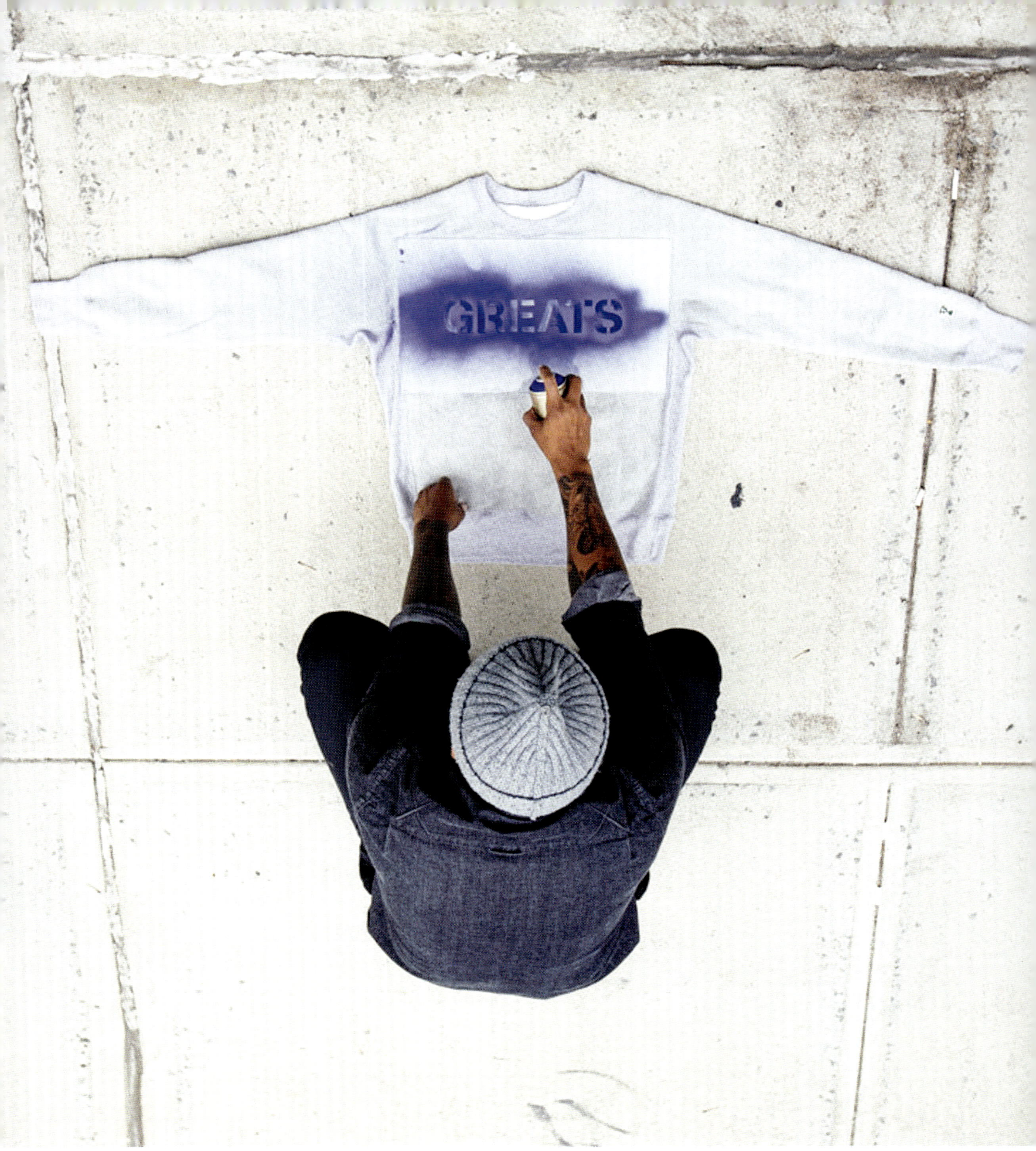

38

(2014)

GREATS

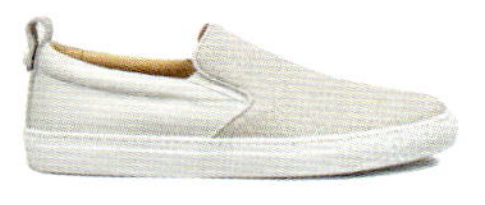
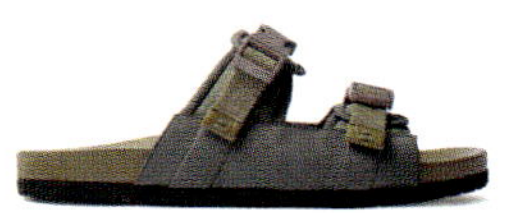
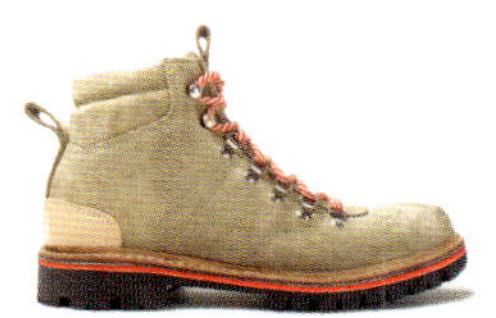
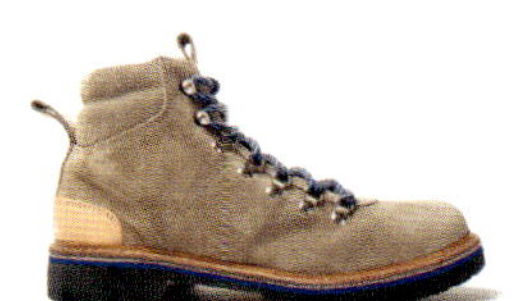
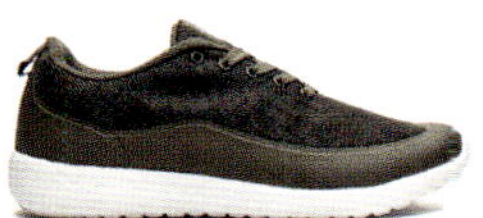
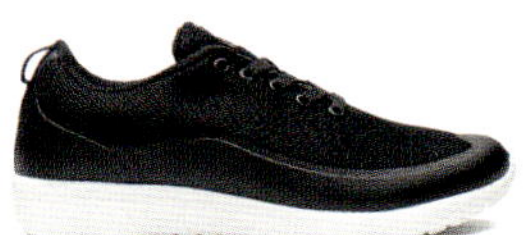
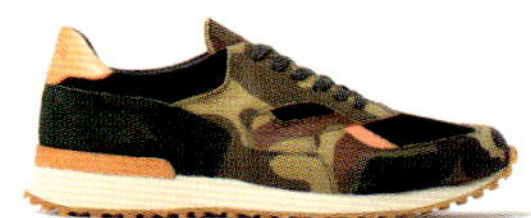
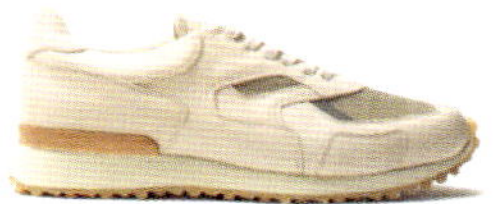
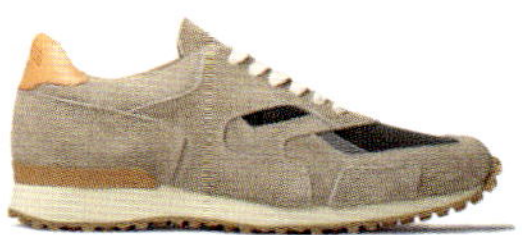
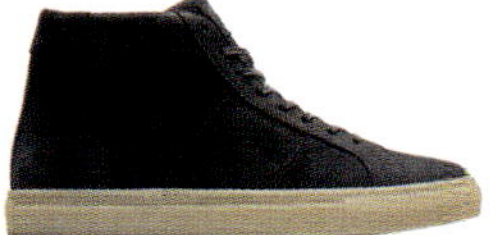
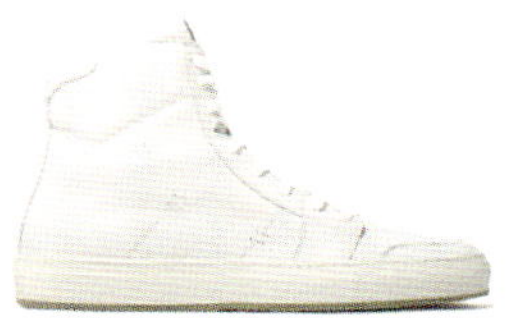
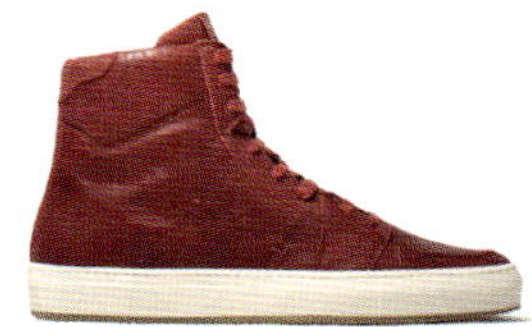
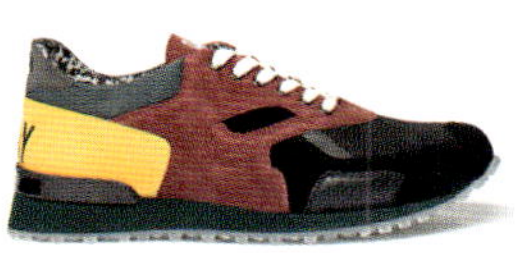
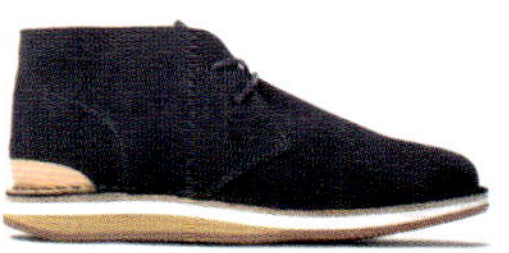
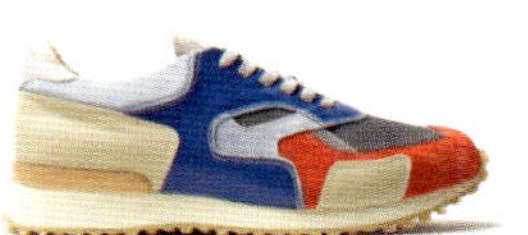

39

GREATS

(2014)

40

YEEZY (2015)

OBSER
RINSE
REPEA

RVE
&
T

YEEZY
OBSERVE RINSE & REPEAT

1

My former boss and mentor Jeff Henderson let me know that he was working with Kanye West. I couldn't believe it. He explained that Kanye was looking for someone to move to Los Angeles and help him with design and footwear creation. This was the craziest and most unexpected opportunity I ever thought I would encounter. I'd been on this Nike hunt and all of a sudden I get Nike x 20. So I'm told to put together a portfolio of work and show Kanye what my creative ability is. I had just done a design charrette for United Nude, an extremely design-forward brand, which meant I had a lot of decent work to show, so I put together a presentation. And then months and months and months passed, and those months felt like years because I was waiting for "the call"–twiddling my thumbs, waiting next to my phone, and sweating.

After close to a year, I get the call. I'm told that I need to come out to LA, not necessarily for the job but to meet with Kanye, sit in on a presentation, and ultimately so that he could get a vibe check of me. I fly to LA and I stay at the Wyndham Hotel in Santa Monica, right next to the ocean, which for a New Yorker was easily the craziest kind of Los Angeles, California welcome I could've encountered. I'm going from trains and streets and sidewalks to the ocean, mountains, and sunsets, things that I saw in the movies that appeared in front of me just because I designed shoes.

The next morning I'm picked up by Jeff, who was there basically to facilitate this introduction and meeting. We get in a car and we drive along the PCH, which again is extremely surreal to me–I'm driving along the ocean, heading to meet Kanye West. What the fuck is my life? We cut a right into a canyon and now we're driving with mountains on either side of us, and all of a sudden we're in Calabasas and I'm on the E! network, I see that Calabasas sign that I've seen on the *Kardashians*. I hear that we're five minutes away and my heart is fucking fluttering. Obviously I have completely overthought the fact that I'm meeting him and so I've thought about what outfit I wear to meet Kanye West. I can't peacock, I can't try to go crazy, so I wore all black and what I thought were exclusive New Balances. We get there, he shows up, I don't have much to say, I'm kind of there to learn and listen. They're having an Adidas meeting about maybe the 350 or the 750, and I'm just sitting there. I have a lot of locked and loaded comments and ideas that I want to say, but I'm waiting to be summoned, waiting to be called on, I didn't want to just blurt them out. At one point during the meeting he turns to me and says, "What do you think about all this?" And then I just go off. I start rattling off a bunch of six-syllable words and he just kind of gives a nod of approval. It wasn't anything dramatic, it was just a very calm nod, and then he kept on with the meeting. I end up going back home. Maybe a week or two passes and then I find out that he's interested in working with me. And now it's time to move to LA.

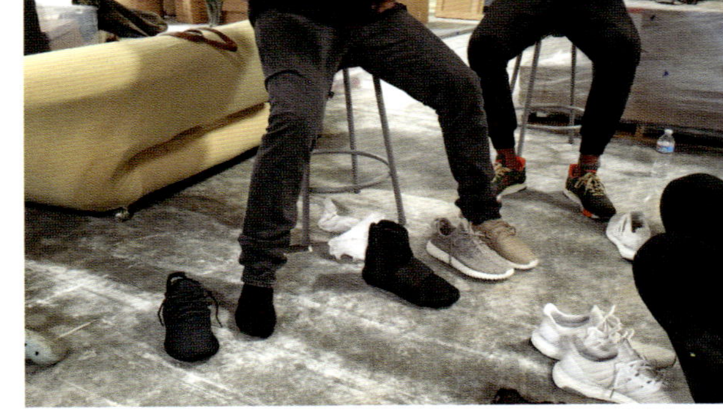

Salehe Bembury meeting Kanye for the 1st time.

2

So now I had the job at Yeezy. It was a unique company structure day-to-day, there was really no paperwork. I ultimately got my paycheck and I knew what my role was, and that was understood between myself, the team, and Kanye. But to simplify it into a corporate title, I was the head of men's footwear, and my counterpart, whose name was Lucette Holland, was the head of women's footwear. It was our job ultimately to bring Kanye's ideas to fruition. We were his pencils. He would come to us with ideas, with inspiration images and references, or "vibes," as he liked to call them, and we would then discuss how to see that idea through the Yeezy lens, or how to juxtapose different ideas and put them in the Yeezy machine, or how to deconstruct an idea and then bring it back to life through the Yeezy execution.

This was the first time I was a part of a company that had a culture. There were things that were unspoken and things that were damn near the law. One of the more subtle things was that there was a dress code: you basically had to dress within the Yeezy color palette. He was not a fan of logos and that rule was aggressively enforced in the office, which I actually thought was cool. It's really no different than working for Nike–if you worked at Nike you had to wear Nike. So it was really about enforcing a company culture, an aesthetic among the internal staff, and ultimately that helps push the goals of the brand.

3

I had a small office within the overall Yeezy office, which was extremely surreal to me. I was still unsure if Kanye was going

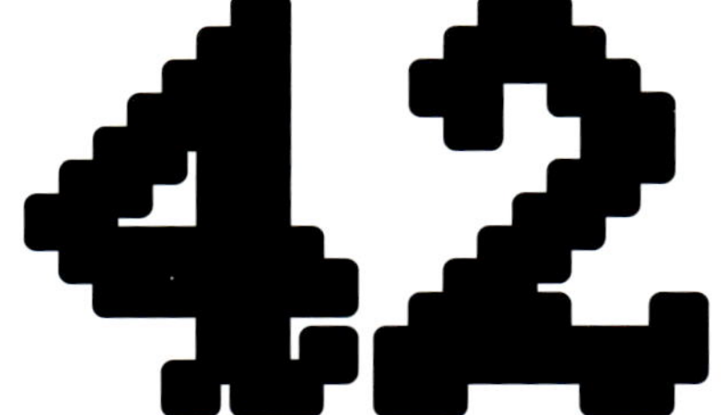

to be in the office every day, or, considering he's a worldwide superstar, if we weren't going to see him that often. It ended up being the former—he was pretty much there every single day that he wasn't touring. I remember the first day he came in, he walked in on his phone—he always walked with a kind of purpose, he was always going somewhere—and went directly to my office. I was pinning up designs and in my head I was thinking, holy fucking shit, Kanye West is my boss and I work here and he's walking towards me right now—again, what is my life? He walked in with his phone on his ear, he was talking, and I started saying, "Oh my god, man, listen, I'm so excited to be here, I have so many ideas, I'm going to kill it for you, thank you so much for this opportunity." I was so grateful I was throwing gratitude bombs at him, constantly. He looked up from his phone and he just said, "Let's change the world," and walked away. And that feeling was so powerfully magical. I genuinely felt like he did want to change the world, and regardless of his success or lack thereof with different projects, he wasn't kidding. It was so crazy how impactful those four words were to me.

4

At the time, there were two entities: Yeezy Adidas and Yeezy. Yeezy Adidas were the products like the 350, the 750, the 950—things with Adidas logos on them. Yeezy were the military boots, the women's heels, the Lucite thigh-high boots, stuff like that. That was produced in Italy and that was the product that I worked on. My time with Yeezy coincided with Seasons 3 and 4. Season 3 was the show that took place at Madison Square Garden. The premier footwear items at that show were the military boot and the Adidas 350 V2. That show featured Young Thug, Ian Connor, Lil Yachty, and other participants of the culture, and they were surrounded by about 500 extras, all wearing vintage items that had been hand-dyed to fit the Yeezy palette. During this period of time I was extremely sleep-deprived and constantly running around trying to solve the problems that come with footwear production, and solve the problems that come with working for a person as famous as Kanye West.

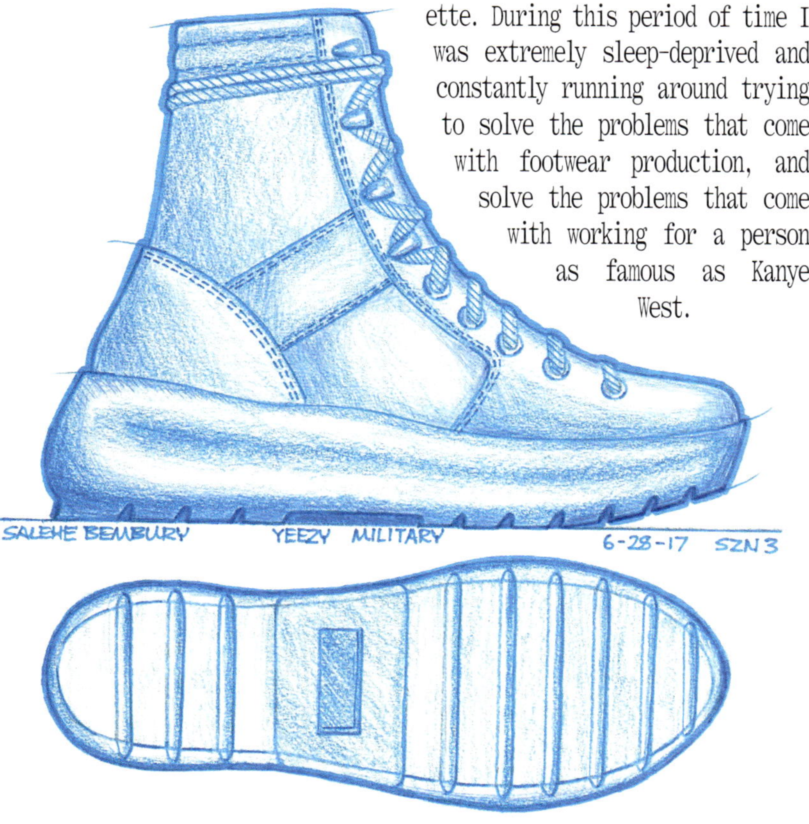

Kanye was a big believer in having direct contact with everyone on his staff. He had my phone number, we would frequently have exchanges about product, life, and the day, and those exchanges would happen at all hours of the day and night. And a lot of times I had to be available for them. I was traveling casually to Italy to develop and produce Yeezy footwear, which was extremely surreal in itself. I felt like an adult, I had a little disposable income, but I didn't look like an adult—I wasn't wearing khakis—and I felt cool, I felt independent, and I felt like there was a lot of opportunity in front of me. And getting to be behind the scenes with someone like Kanye West, who I was a huge fan of—it was a really special time and I'm honored to have been a part of it.

5

There were many different arms to the Yeezy operation: there were internal arms, there were things happening at Adidas, Kanye would work with different designers from around the world. But there were some days where a lot of people working on similar projects would come together to discuss or review samples. On one particular day, everybody was there—the entire Adidas team was there, Don C. was there, Virgil was there—and then Kanye also had two videographers filming everything. So there was this giant circle of extremely talented creative individuals, and then Adidas pulls out the 350 V2. At the time, the 350 had no stripe on it. Kanye puts the shoe on, and as he's looking at it, all of a sudden he sees a random piece of trash on the ground that looked like it was some kind of woven ribbon. He looks at me and he says, "Hey Salehe, can you pin that on the side of the shoe, starting at the middle of the toe, and then going up the side?" So I nervously and quickly take some safety pins and pin this strip of woven ribbon onto the side of the 350, while simultaneously pricking myself. I feel like I'm bleeding, and I'm trying to make sure that none of the pins are pricking the inside of the foot because I know Kanye's going to be putting this shoe on his foot, and if I poke his foot, that would not be good. After about thirty seconds of attaching this ribbon—and I have all of these influential people staring at me and I'm being recorded from two different angles—I finally put it on. Kanye takes the shoe, he puts it on his foot, he observes it, he looks in the mirror, he changes the angle. Then he takes it off his foot, holds it in his hand, smirks a little bit and goes, "New wave." I'll never forget it. I don't think we all clapped, but there was a kind of unified feeling of relief. Those shoes ended up being called the Bowies because David Bowie had just passed away. That story represents how random creative expression and design can sometimes be.

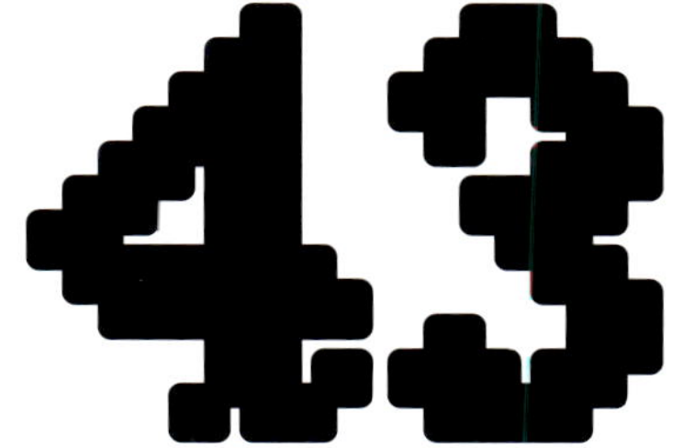

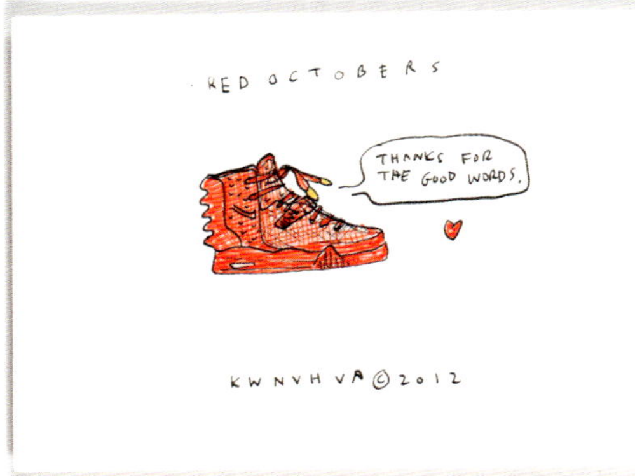

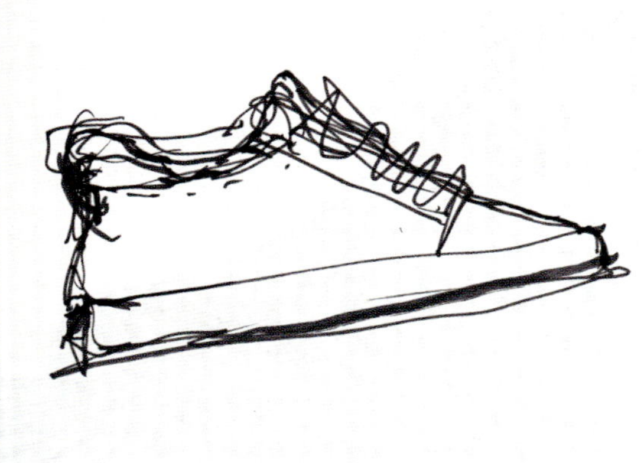

Above: Nathan VanHook sketch
Below: Kanye West sketch

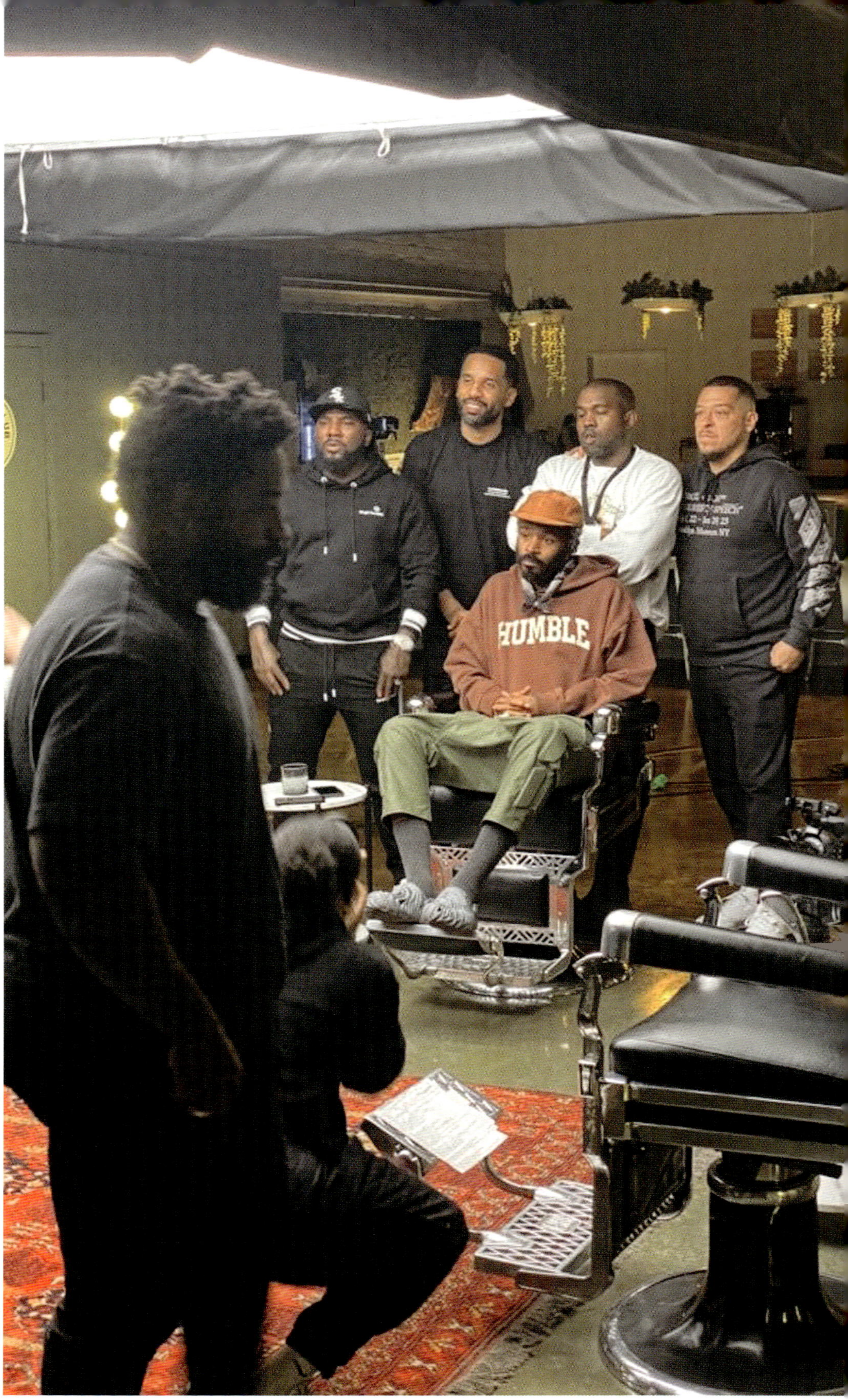

HBO's *The Shop* taping, featuring Salehe Bembury, Ye, Paul Rodriguez, Maverick Carter, and Jeezy

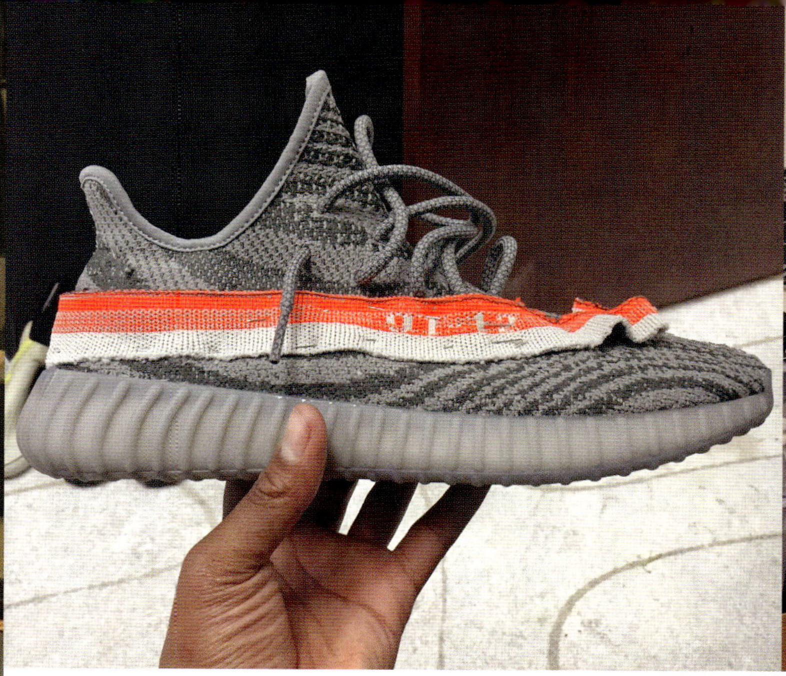

Yeezy 350 V2 "Bowie" 1st prototype

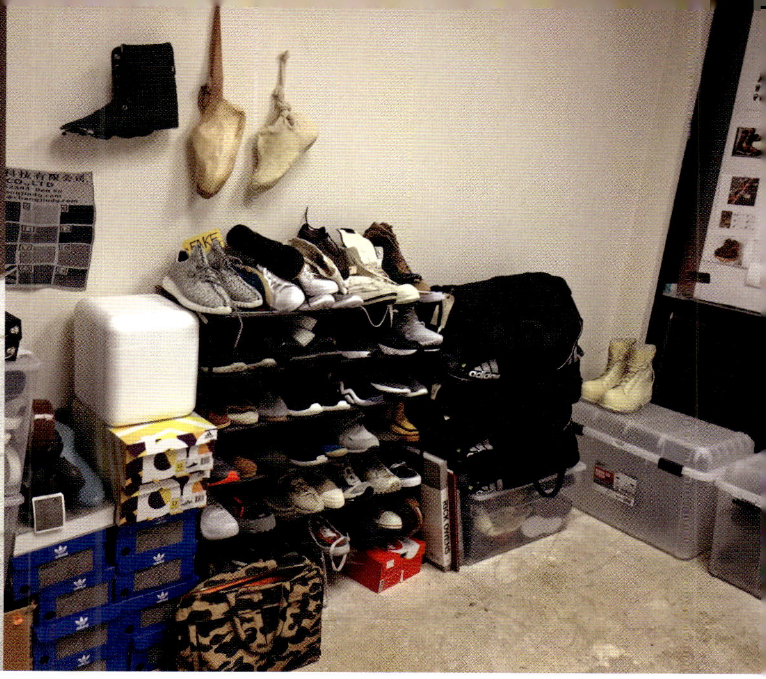

Salehe Bembury Yeezy office

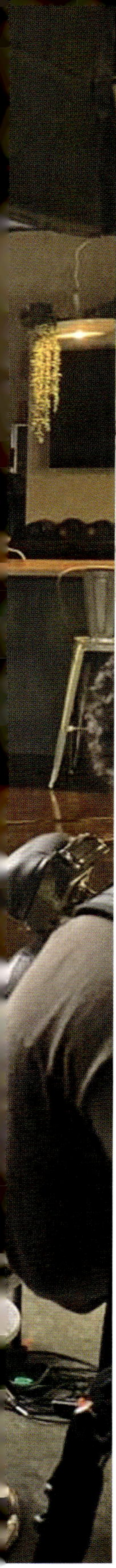

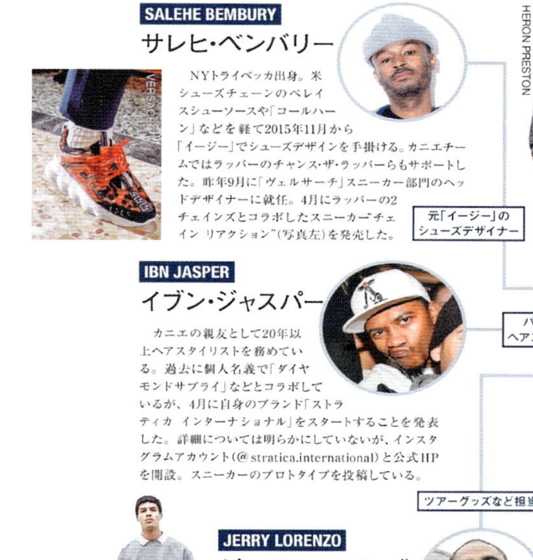

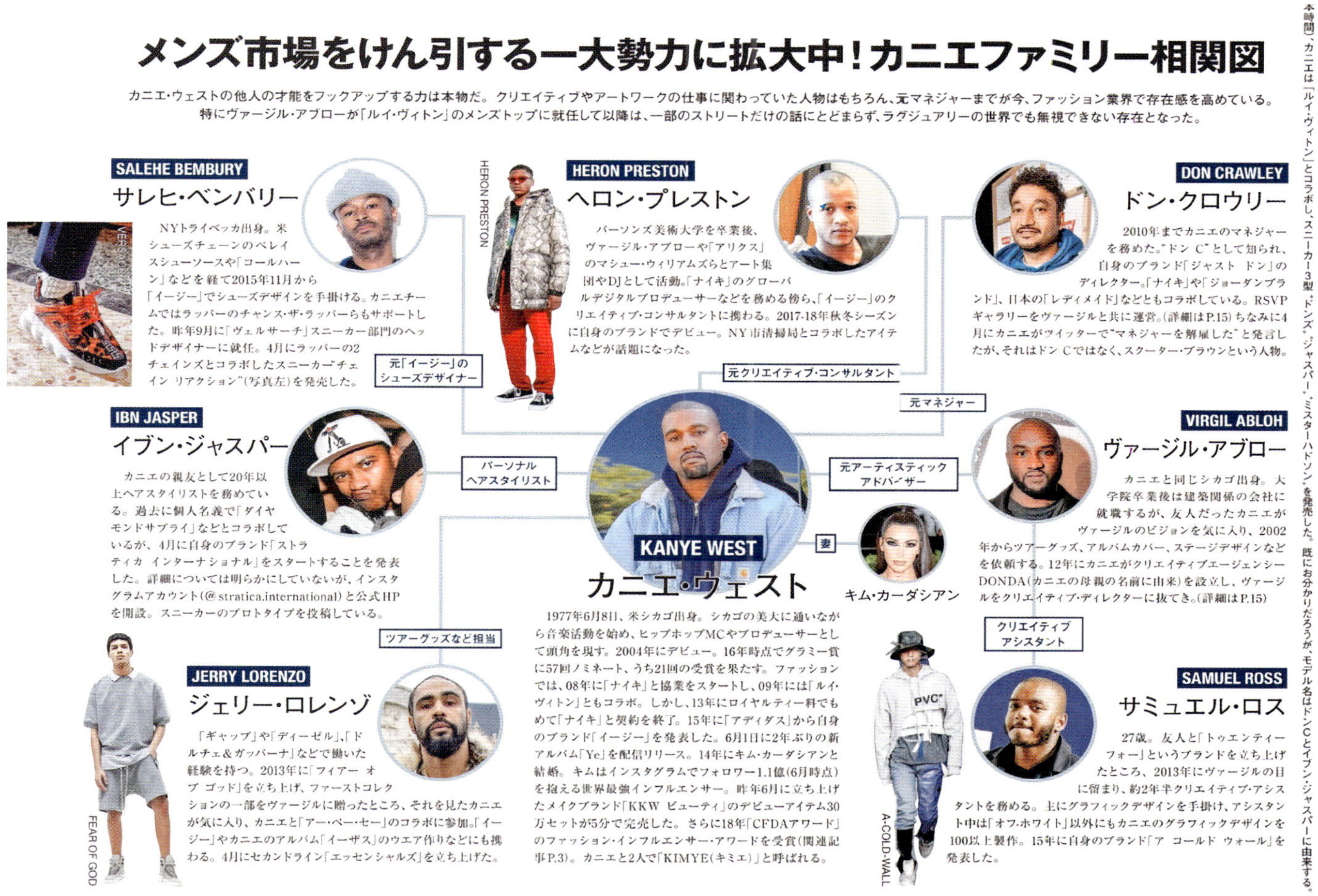

メンズ市場をけん引する一大勢力に拡大中！カニエファミリー相関図

カニエ・ウェストの他人の才能をフックアップする力は本物だ。クリエイティブやアートワークの仕事に関わっていた人物はもちろん、元マネジャーまでが今、ファッション業界で存在感を高めている。特にヴァージル・アブローが「ルイ・ヴィトン」のメンズトップに就任して以降は、一部のストリートだけの話にとどまらず、ラグジュアリーの世界でも無視できない存在となった。

SALEHE BEMBURY

サレヒ・ベンバリー

NYトライベッカ出身。米シューズチェーンのペイレスシューソースや「コールハーン」などを経て2015年11月から「イージー」でシューズデザインを手掛ける。カニエチームではラッパーのチャンス・ザ・ラッパーらもサポートした。昨年9月に「ヴェルサーチ」スニーカー部門のヘッドデザイナーに就任。4月にラッパーの2チェインズとコラボしたスニーカー"チェイン リアクション"(写真左)を発売した。

VERSACE

元「イージー」の シューズデザイナー

HERON PRESTON

ヘロン・プレストン

パーソンズ美術大学を卒業後、ヴァージル・アブローや「アリクス」のマシュー・ウィリアムズらとアート集団やDJとして活動。「ナイキ」のグローバルデジタルプロデューサーなどを務める傍ら、「イージー」のクリエイティブ・コンサルタントに携わる。2017-18年秋冬シーズンに自身のブランドでデビュー。NY市清掃局とコラボしたアイテムなどが話題になった。

HERON PRESTON

元クリエイティブ・コンサルタント

DON CRAWLEY

ドン・クロウリー

2010年までカニエのマネジャーを務めた。"ドン C"として知られ、自身のブランド「ジャスト ドン」のディレクター。「ナイキ」や「ジョーダンブランド」、日本の「レディメイド」などともコラボしている。RSVPギャラリーをヴァージルと共に運営。(詳細はP.15) ちなみに4月にカニエがツイッターで"マネジャーを解雇した"と発言したが、それはドン Cではなく、スクーター・ブラウンという人物。

元マネジャー

IBN JASPER

イブン・ジャスパー

カニエの親友として20年以上ヘアスタイリストを務めている。過去に個人名義で「ダイヤモンドサプライ」などとコラボしているが、4月に自身のブランド「ストラティカ インターナショナル」をスタートすることを発表した。詳細については明らかにしていないが、インスタグラムアカウント(@stratica.international)と公式HPを開設。スニーカーのプロトタイプを投稿している。

パーソナル ヘアスタイリスト

KANYE WEST

カニエ・ウェスト

1977年6月8日、米シカゴ出身。シカゴの美大に通いながら音楽活動を始め、ヒップホップMCやプロデューサーとして頭角を現す。2004年にデビュー。16年時点でグラミー賞に57回ノミネート、うち21回の受賞を果たす。ファッションでは、08年に「ナイキ」と協業をスタートし、09年には「ルイ・ヴィトン」ともコラボ。しかし、13年にロイヤルティー料でもめて「ナイキ」と契約を終了。15年に「アディダス」から自身のブランド「イージー」を発表した。6月1日に2年ぶりの新アルバム「Ye」を配信リリース。14年にキム・カーダシアンと結婚。キムはインスタグラムでフォロワー1.1億(6月時点)を抱える世界最強インフルエンサー。昨年6月に立ち上げたメイクブランド「KKW ビューティ」のデビューアイテム30万セットが5分で完売した。さらに18年「CFDAアワード」のファッション・インフルエンサー・アワードを受賞(関連記事P.3)。カニエと2人で「KIMYE(キミエ)」と呼ばれる。

妻

キム・カーダシアン

元アーティスティック アドバイザー

VIRGIL ABLOH

ヴァージル・アブロー

カニエと同じシカゴ出身。大学院卒業後は建築関係の会社に就職するが、友人だったカニエがヴァージルのビジョンを気に入り、2002年からツアーグッズ、アルバムカバー、ステージデザインなどを依頼する。12年にカニエがクリエイティブエージェンシーDONDA(カニエの母親の名前に由来)を設立し、ヴァージルをクリエイティブ・ディレクターに抜てき。(詳細はP.15)

ツアーグッズなど担当

JERRY LORENZO

ジェリー・ロレンゾ

「ギャップ」や「ディーゼル」、「ドルチェ＆ガッバーナ」などで働いた経験を持つ。2013年に「フィアー オブ ゴッド」を立ち上げ、ファーストコレクションの一部をヴァージルに贈ったところ、それを見たカニエが気に入り、カニエと「アー・ペー・セー」のコラボに参加。「イージー」やカニエのアルバム「イーザス」のウエア作りなどにも携わる。4月にセカンドライン「エッセンシャルズ」を立ち上げた。

FEAR OF GOD

クリエイティブ アシスタント

SAMUEL ROSS

サミュエル・ロス

27歳。友人と「トゥエンティーフォー」というブランドを立ち上げたところ、2013年にヴァージルの目に留まり、約2年半クリエイティブ・アシスタントを務める。主にグラフィックデザインを手掛け、アシスタント中は「オフ-ホワイト」以外にもカニエのグラフィックデザインを100以上製作。15年に自身のブランド「ア コールド ウォール」を発表した。

A-COLD-WALL

本時間)、カニエは「ルイ・ヴィトン」とコラボし、スニーカー3型"ドンズ"、"ジャスパー"、"ミスターハドソン"を発売した。既にお分かりだろうが、モデル名はドンCとイブン・ジャスパーに由来する。

WWD Japan Kanye West family tree

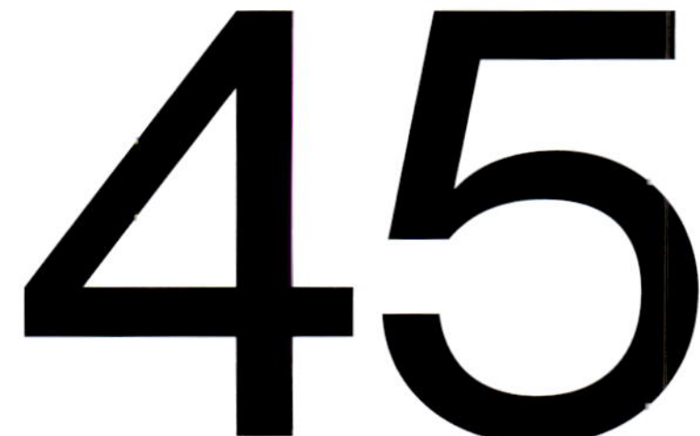

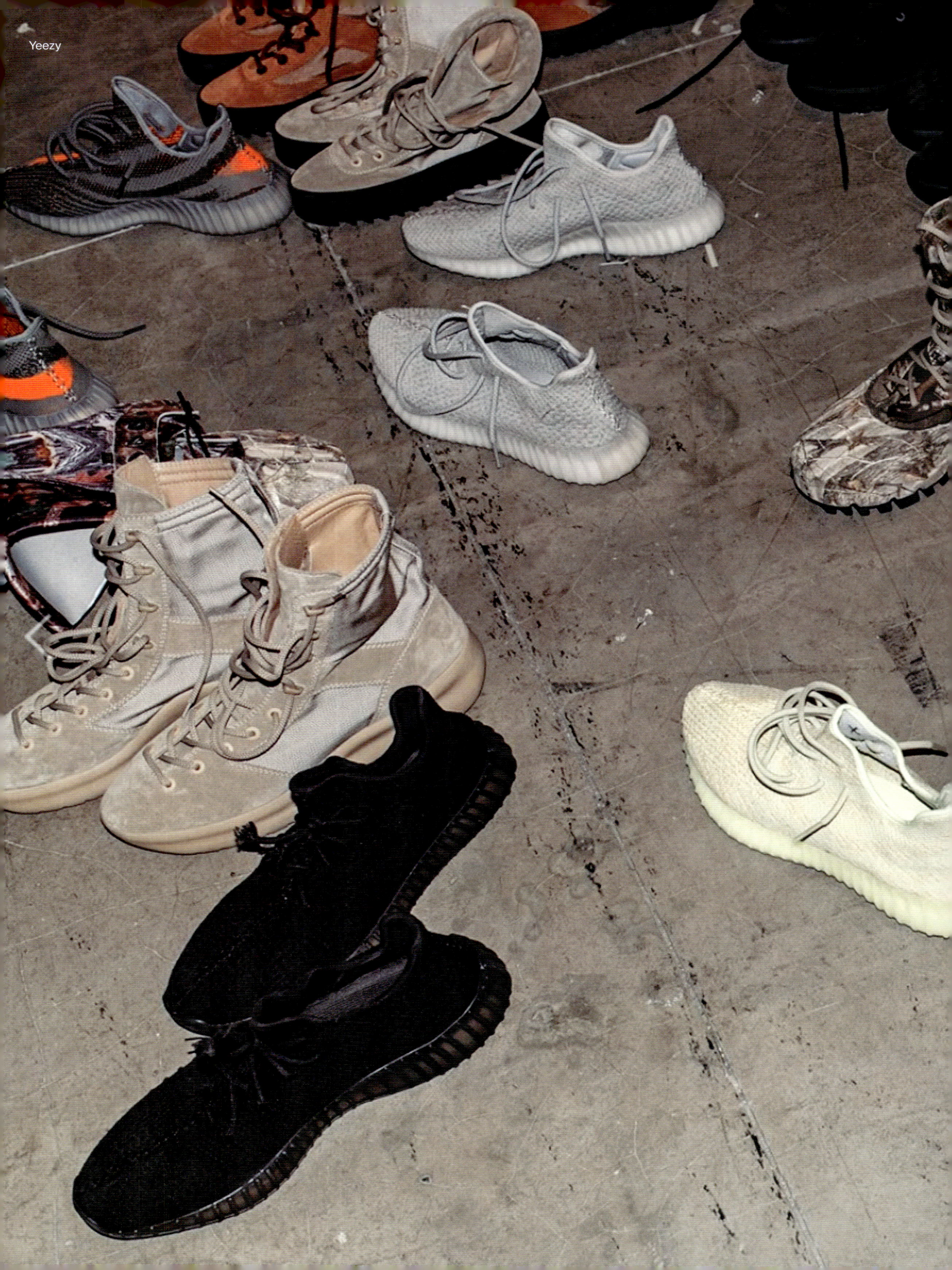

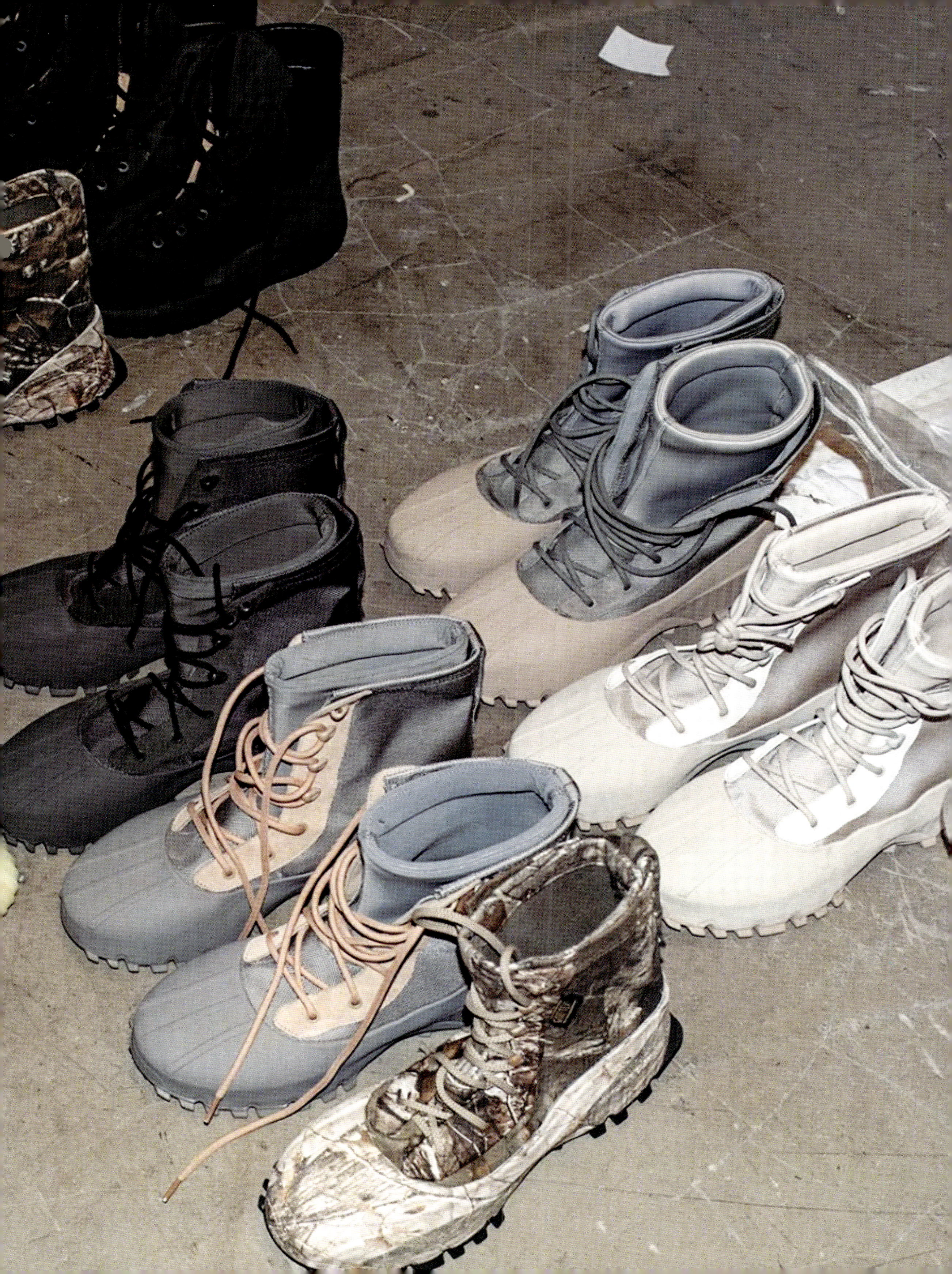

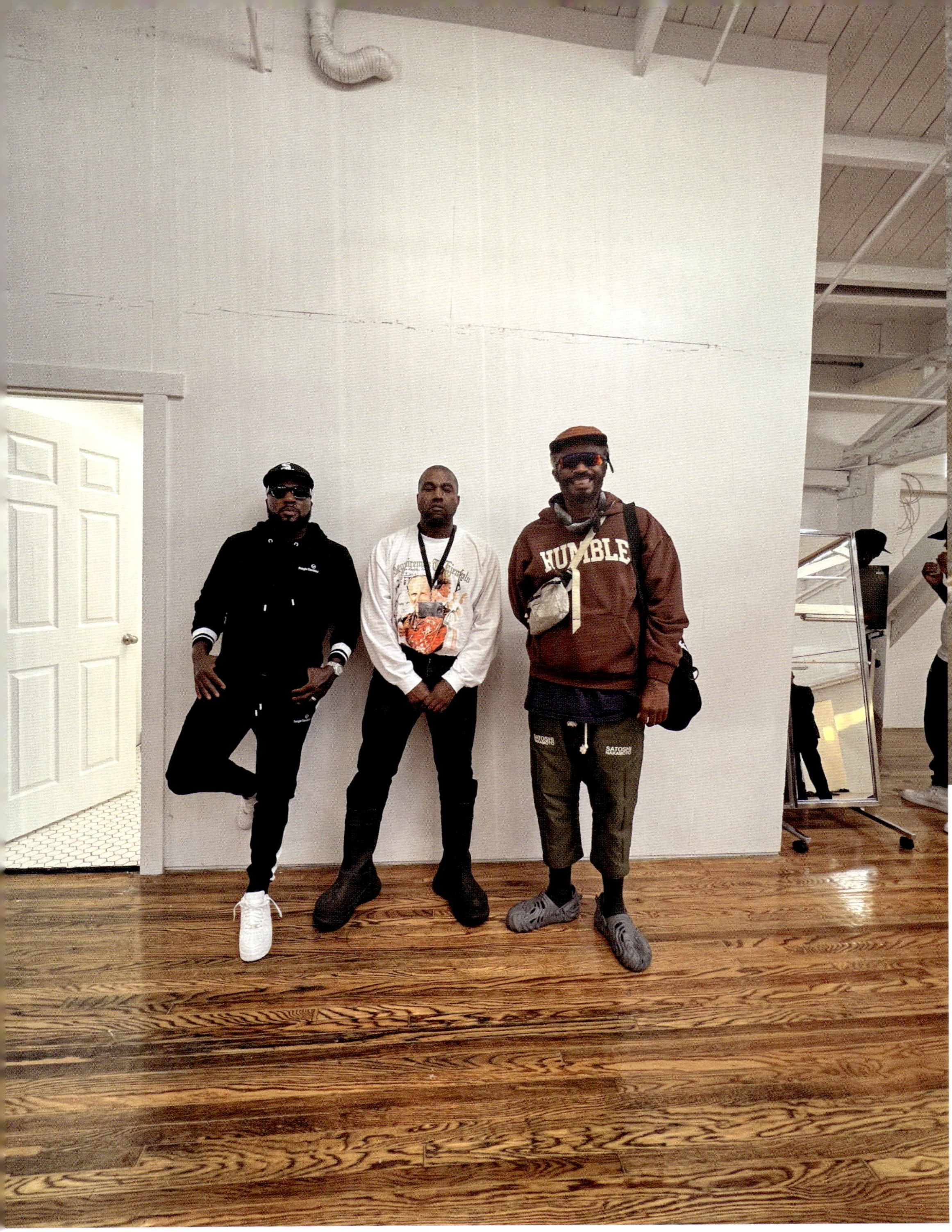

Jeezy, Ye, and Salehe Bembury

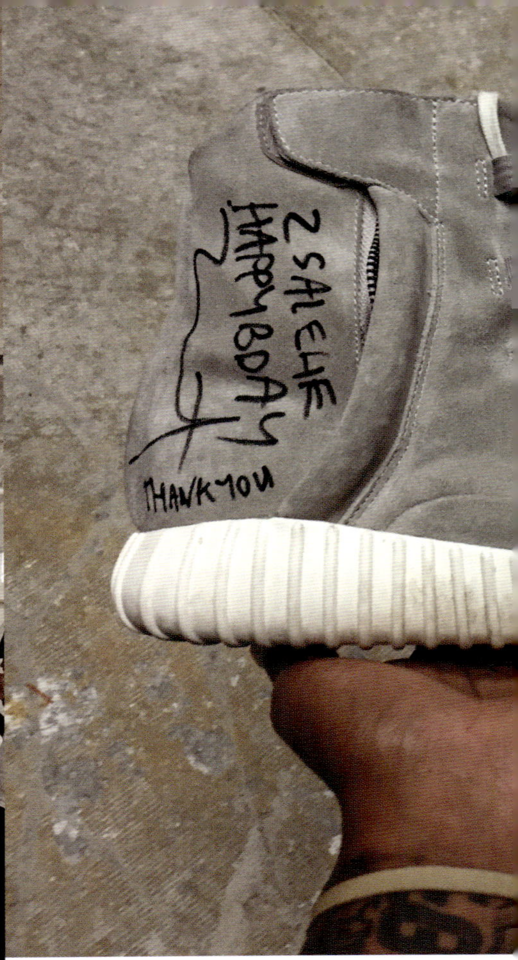

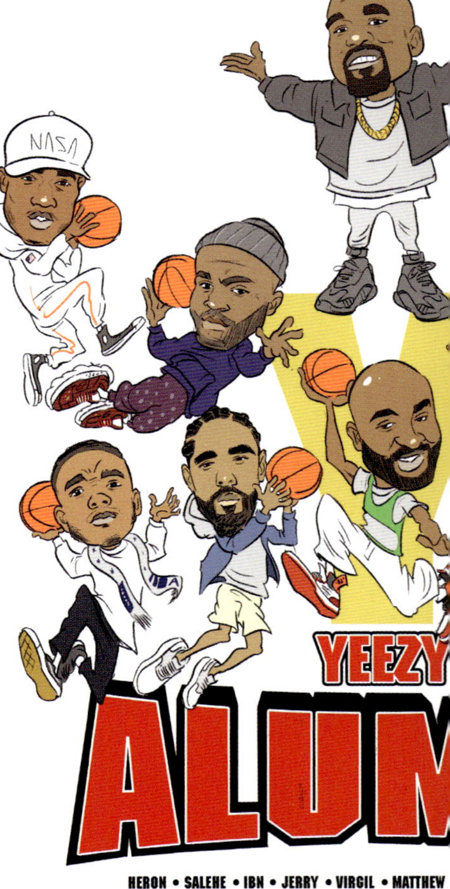

Above: Yeezy 750 signed by Kanye West
Below: Yeezy alumni

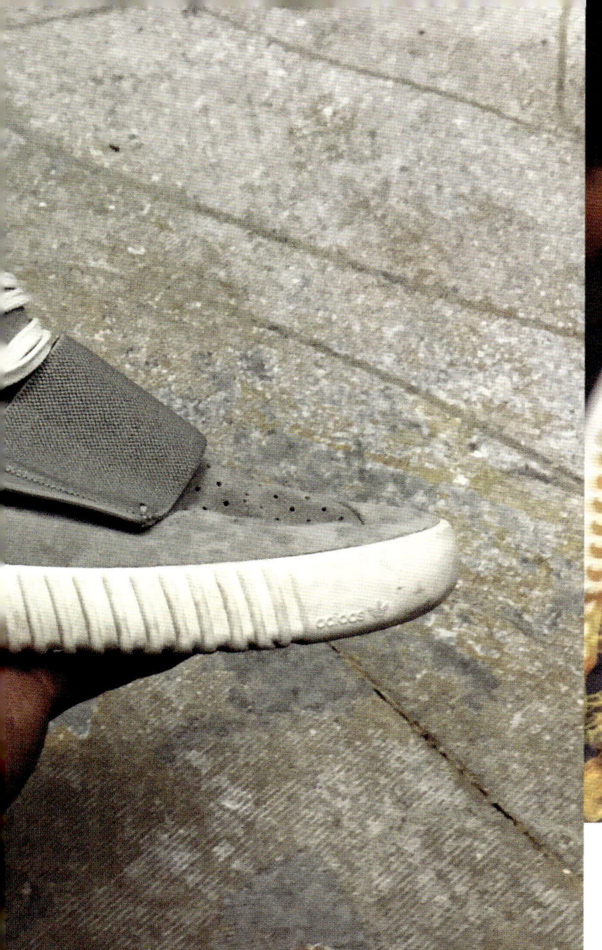

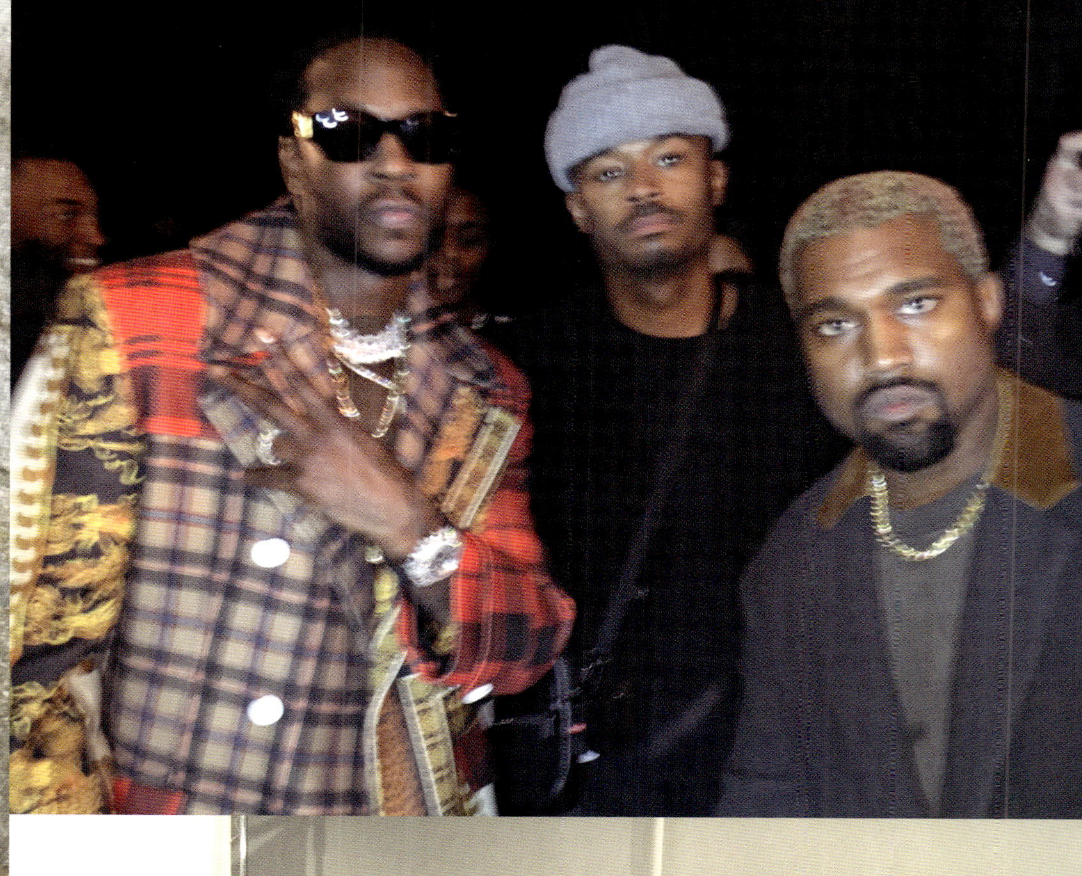

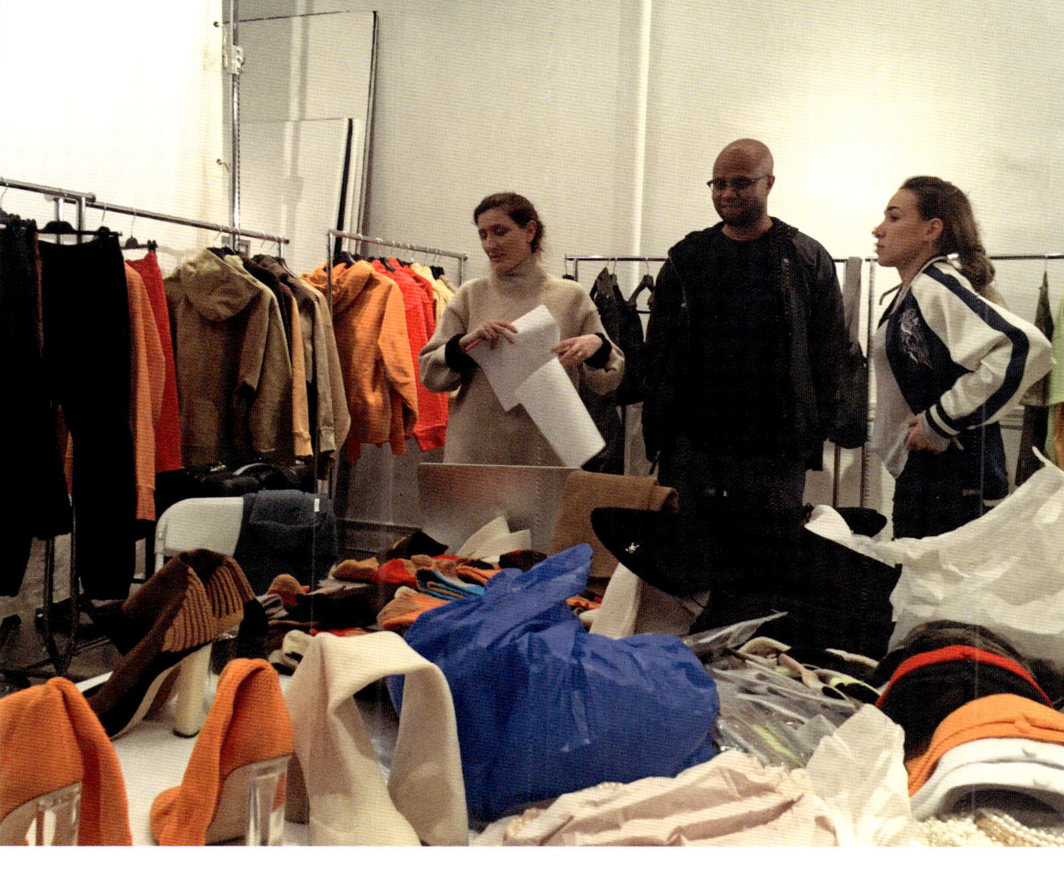

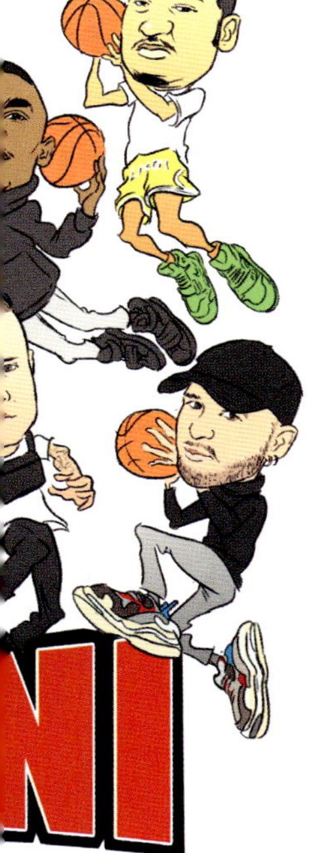

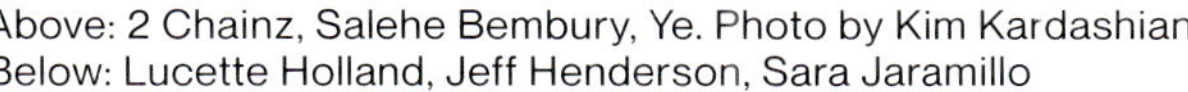

Above: 2 Chainz, Salehe Bembury, Ye. Photo by Kim Kardashian
Below: Lucette Holland, Jeff Henderson, Sara Jaramillo

Yeezy Season 3 Military Boot - Burnt Sienna (2016)

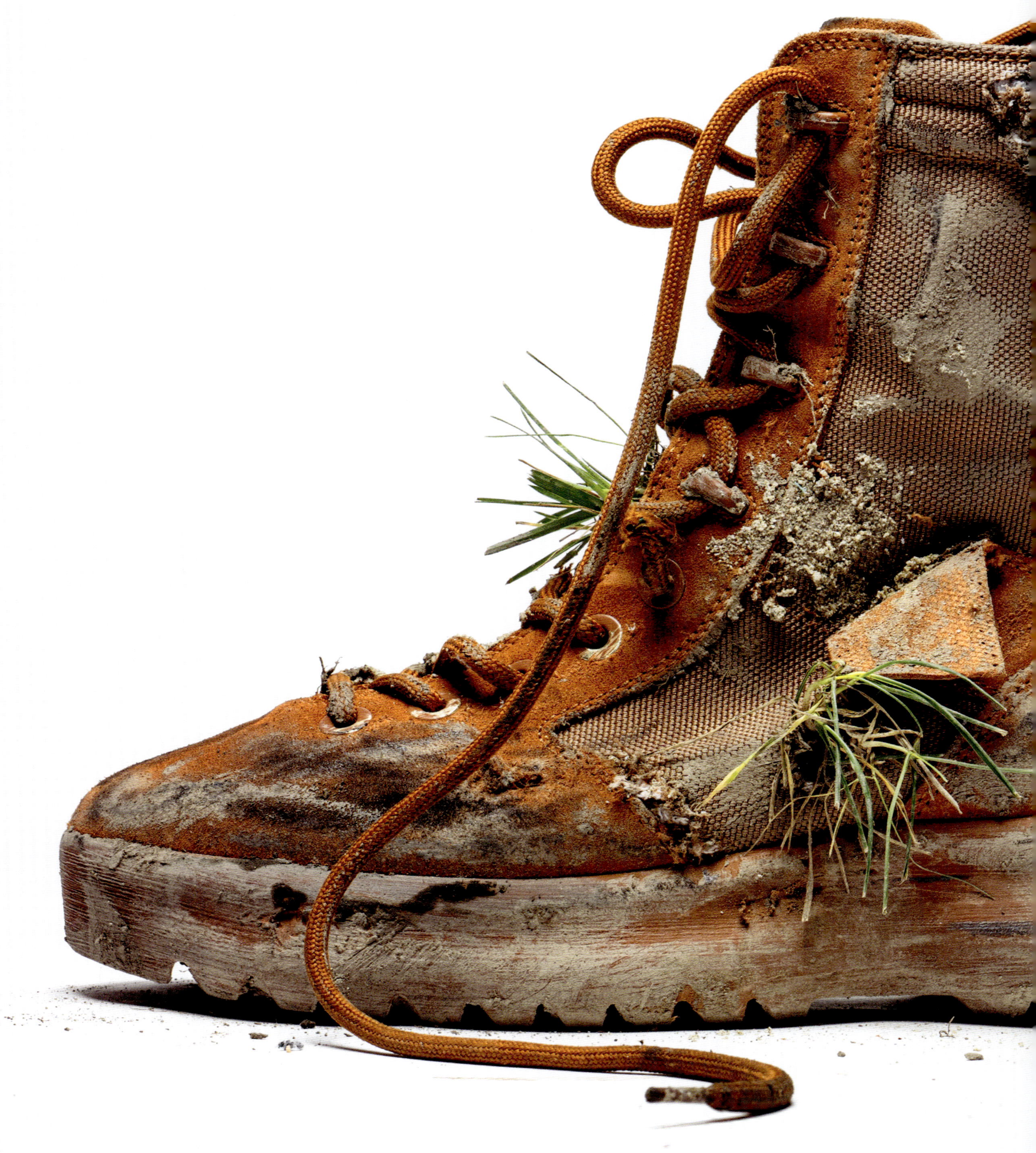

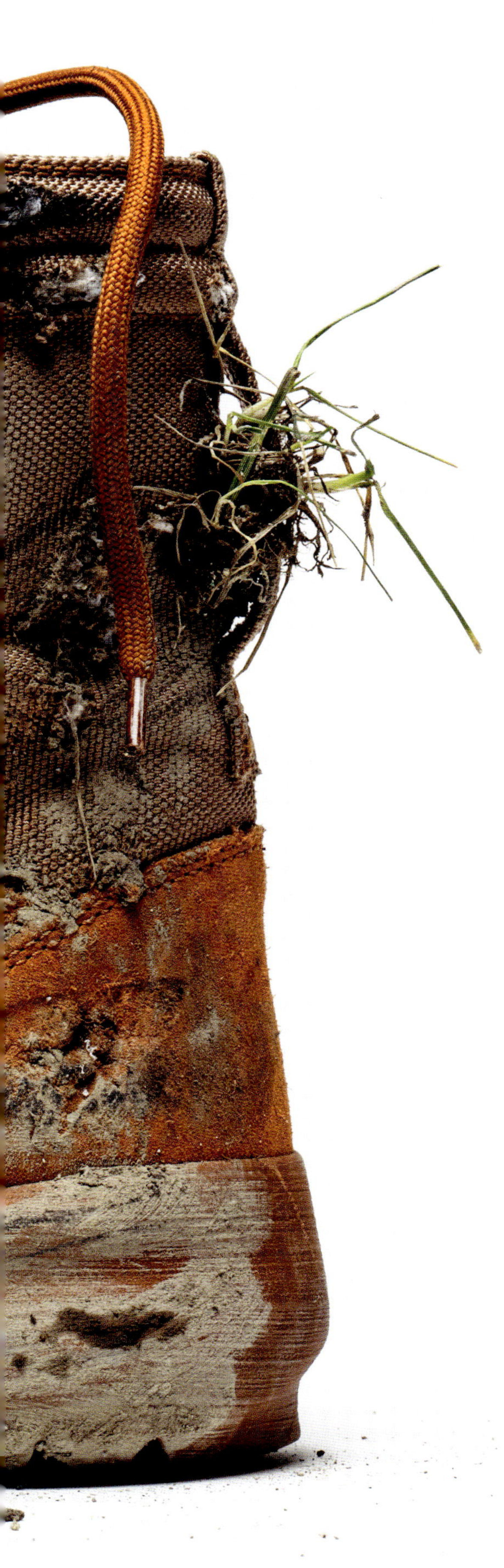

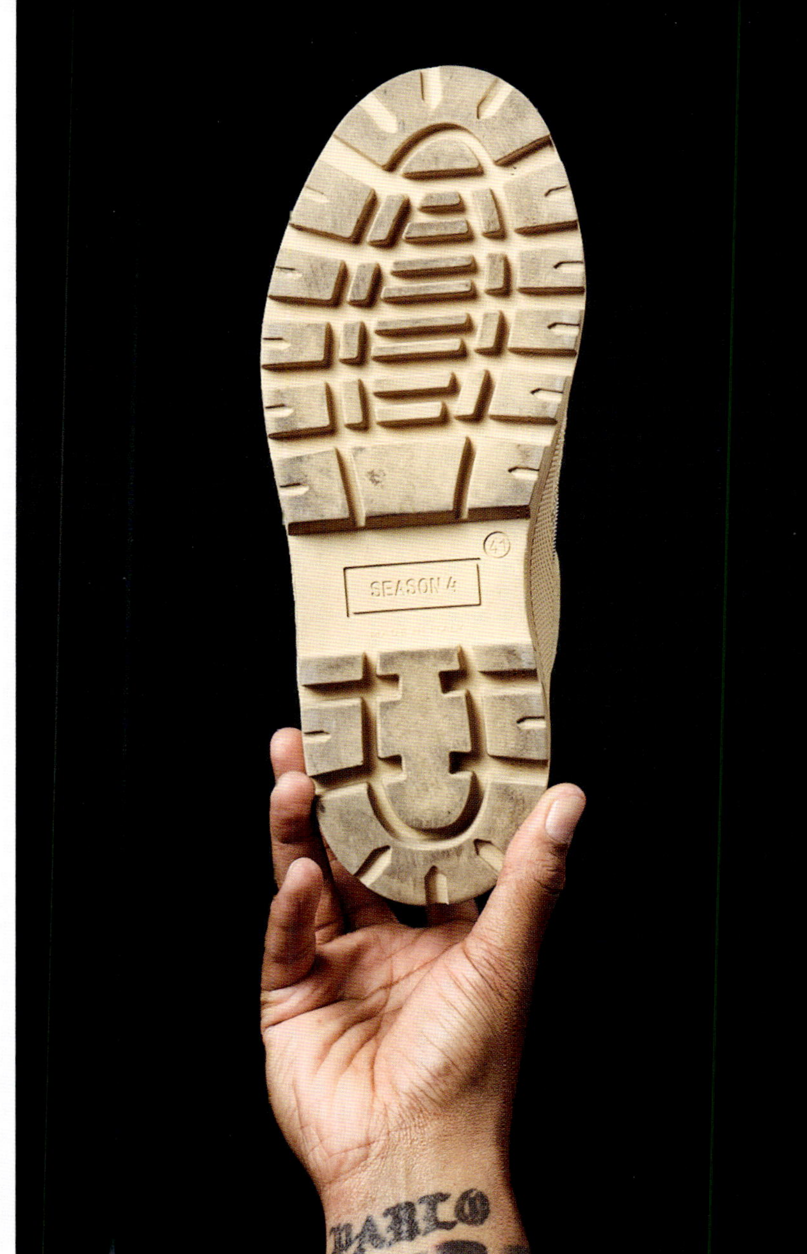

Yeezy Season 4 Combat Boot

51

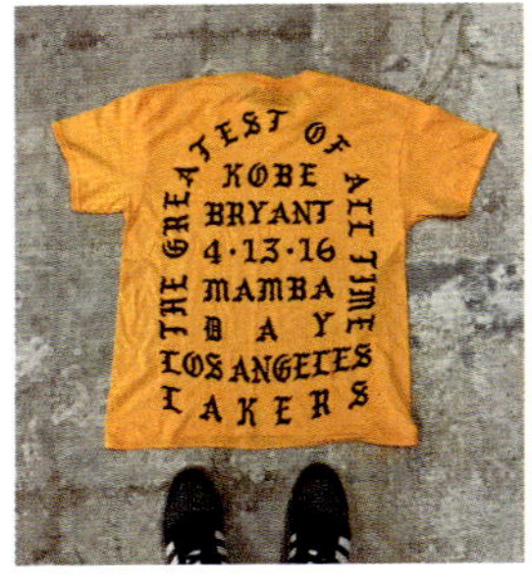

“I Feel Like Kobe” shirt

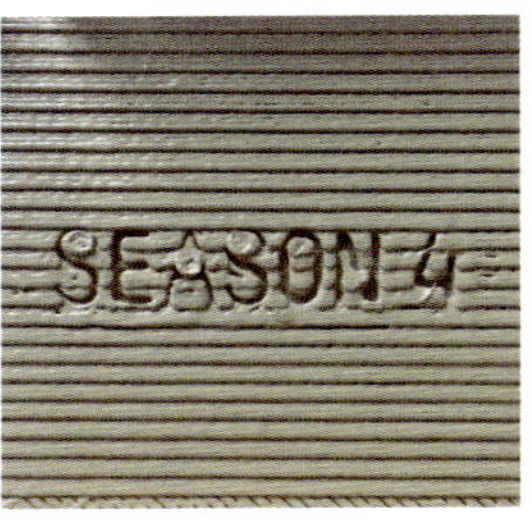

Yeezy Season 4 3D print

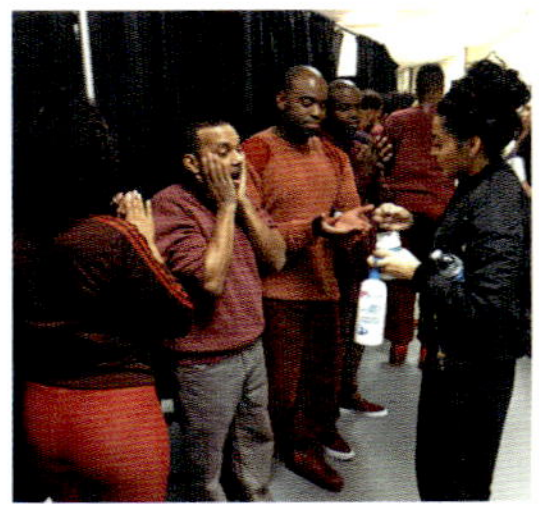
Yeezy Season 3 backstage

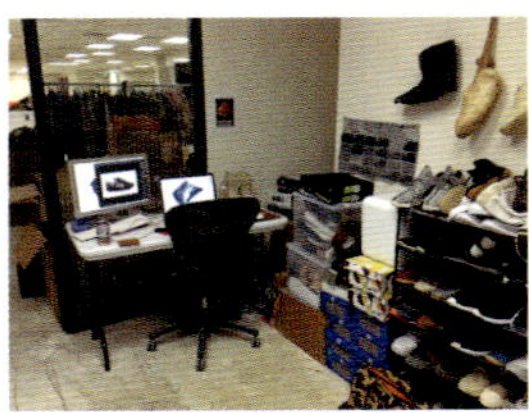
Salehe’s desk

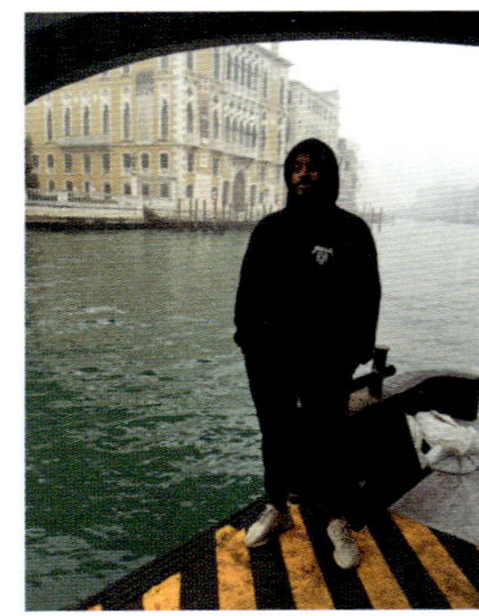
Salehe Bembury in Venice, Italy

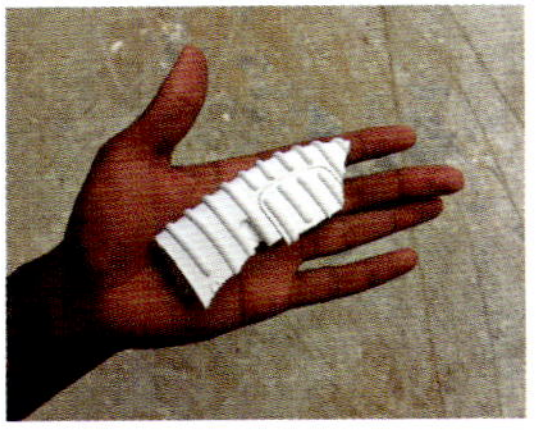
Yeezy 350 outsole part

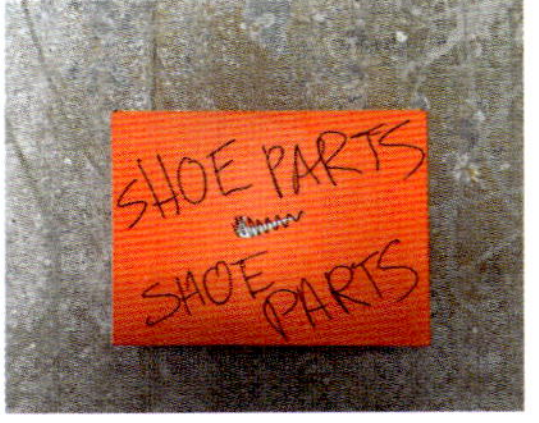

“Shoe Parts” box

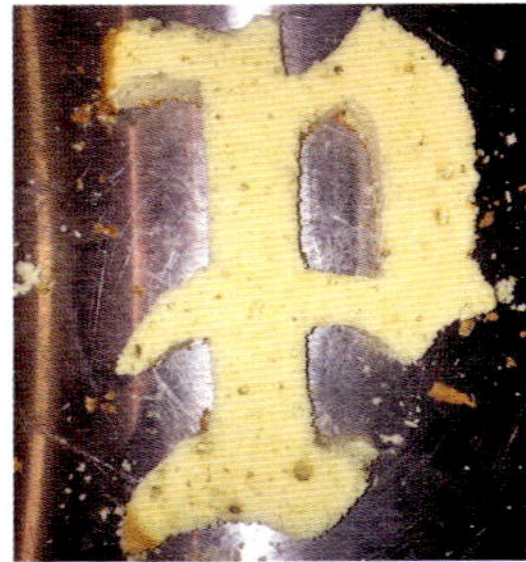
“Pablo” birthday cake

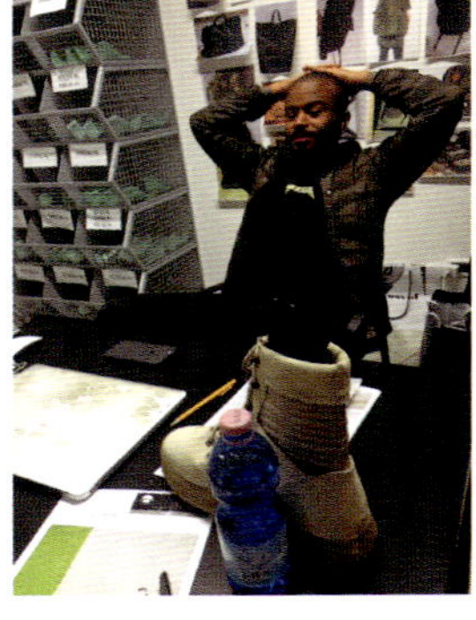
Salehe Bembury on Yeezy factory trip - Italy

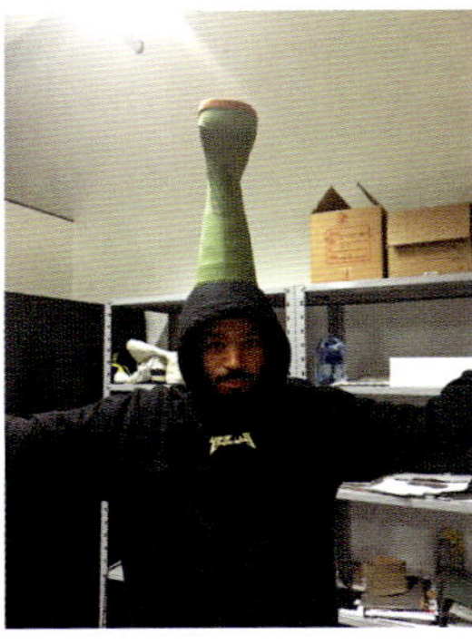
Salehe Bembury on Yeezy factory trip - Italy

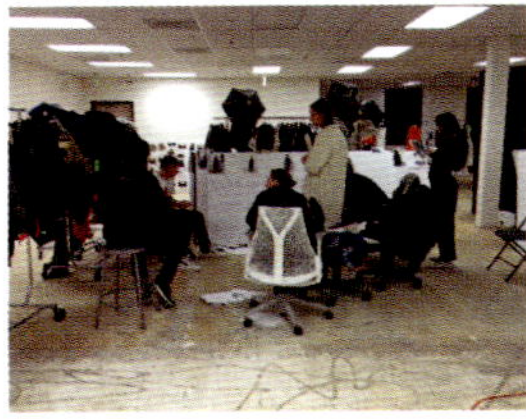
Design meeting

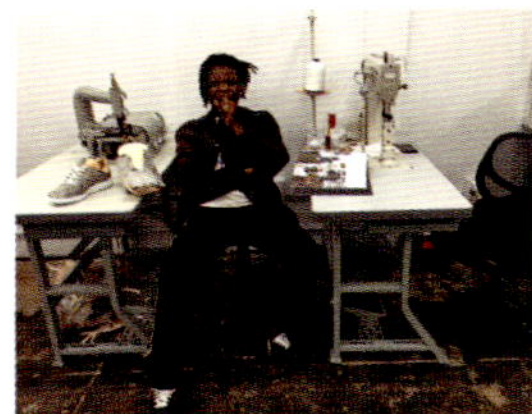
Ian Connor in Yeezy studio

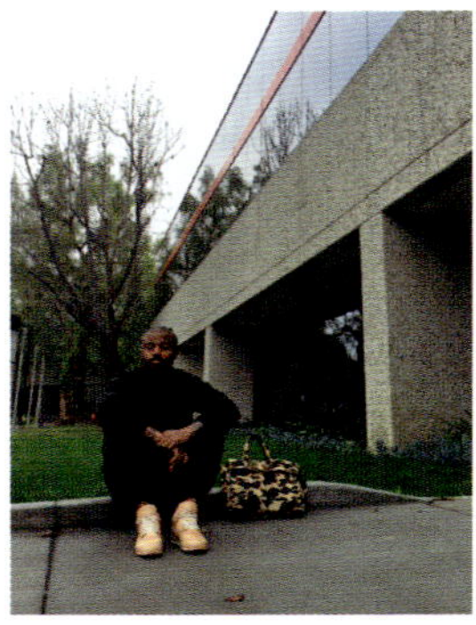
Salehe Bembury outside of Yeezy office

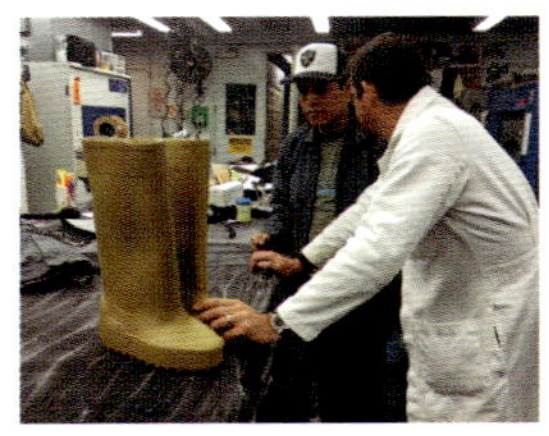
Yeezy Rain Boot development

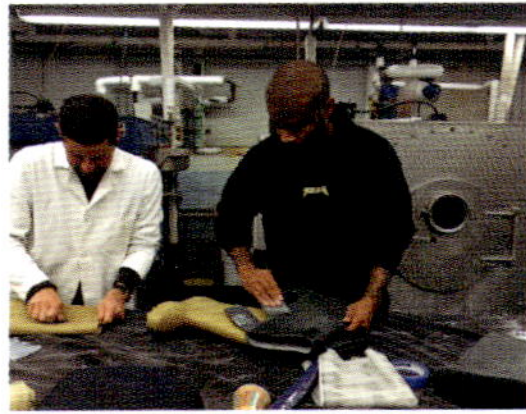
Yeezy Rain Boot development

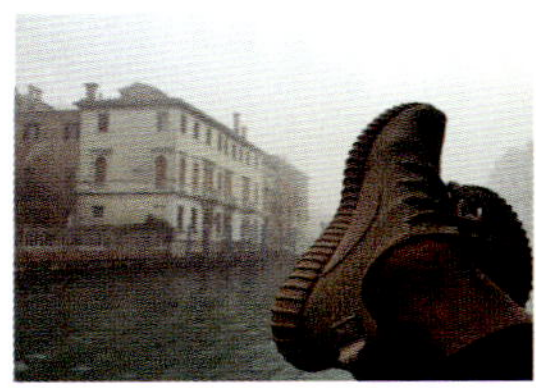
Salehe Bembury in Venice, Italy

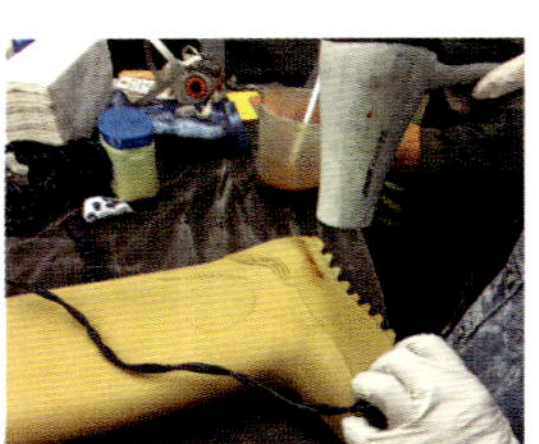
Yeezy Rainboot development

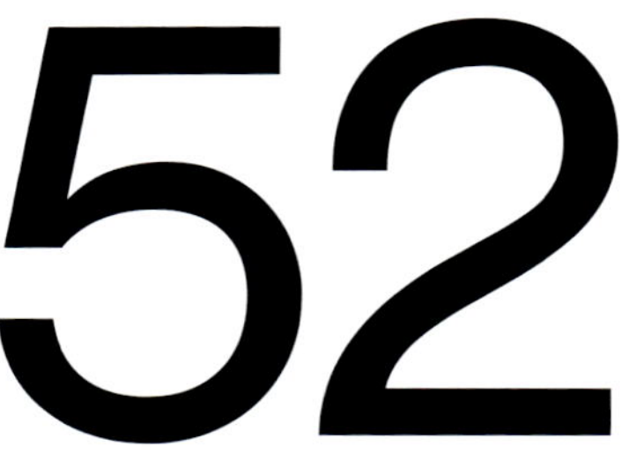

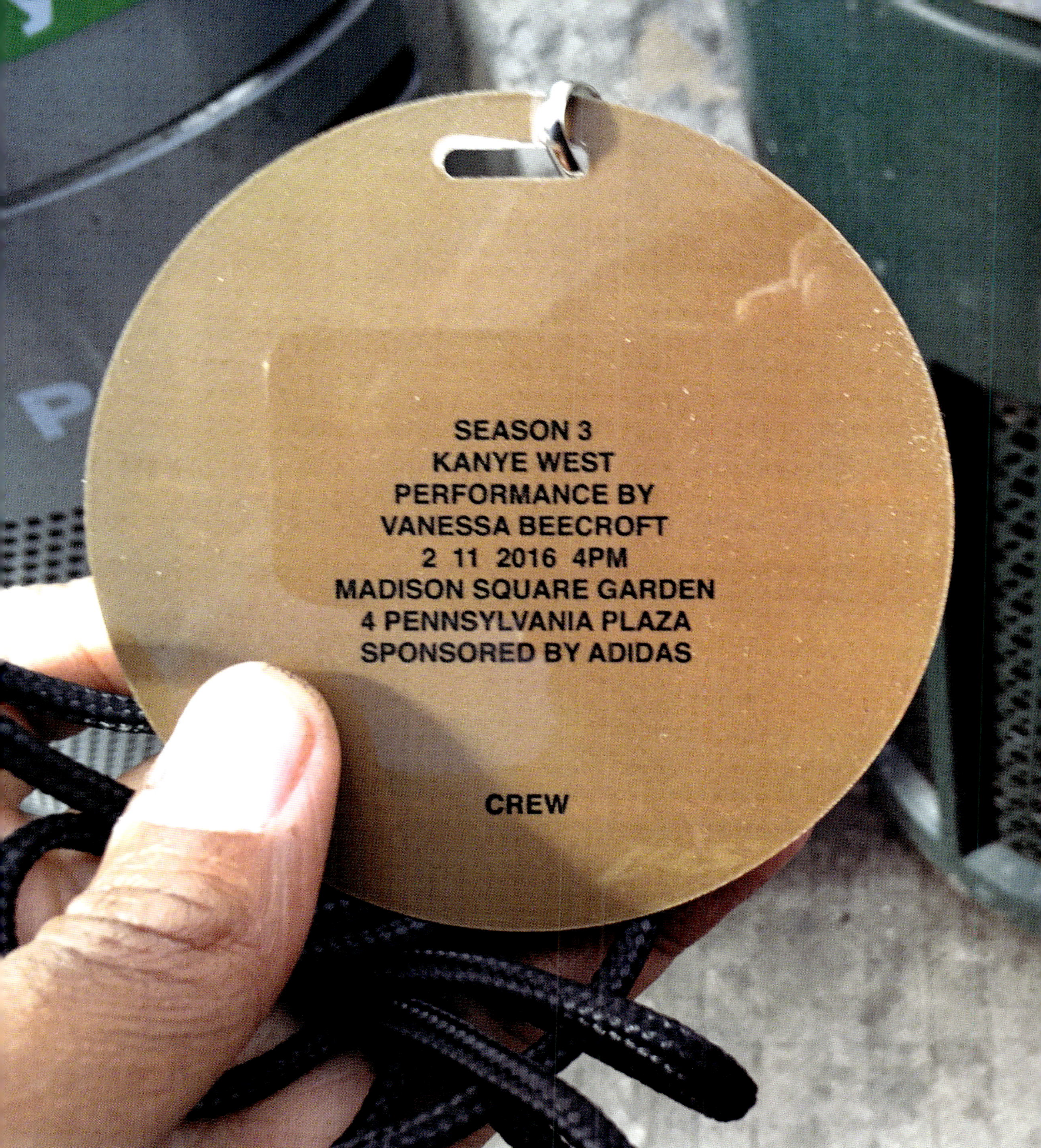

Yeezy Season 3 credentials - Madison Square Garden

53

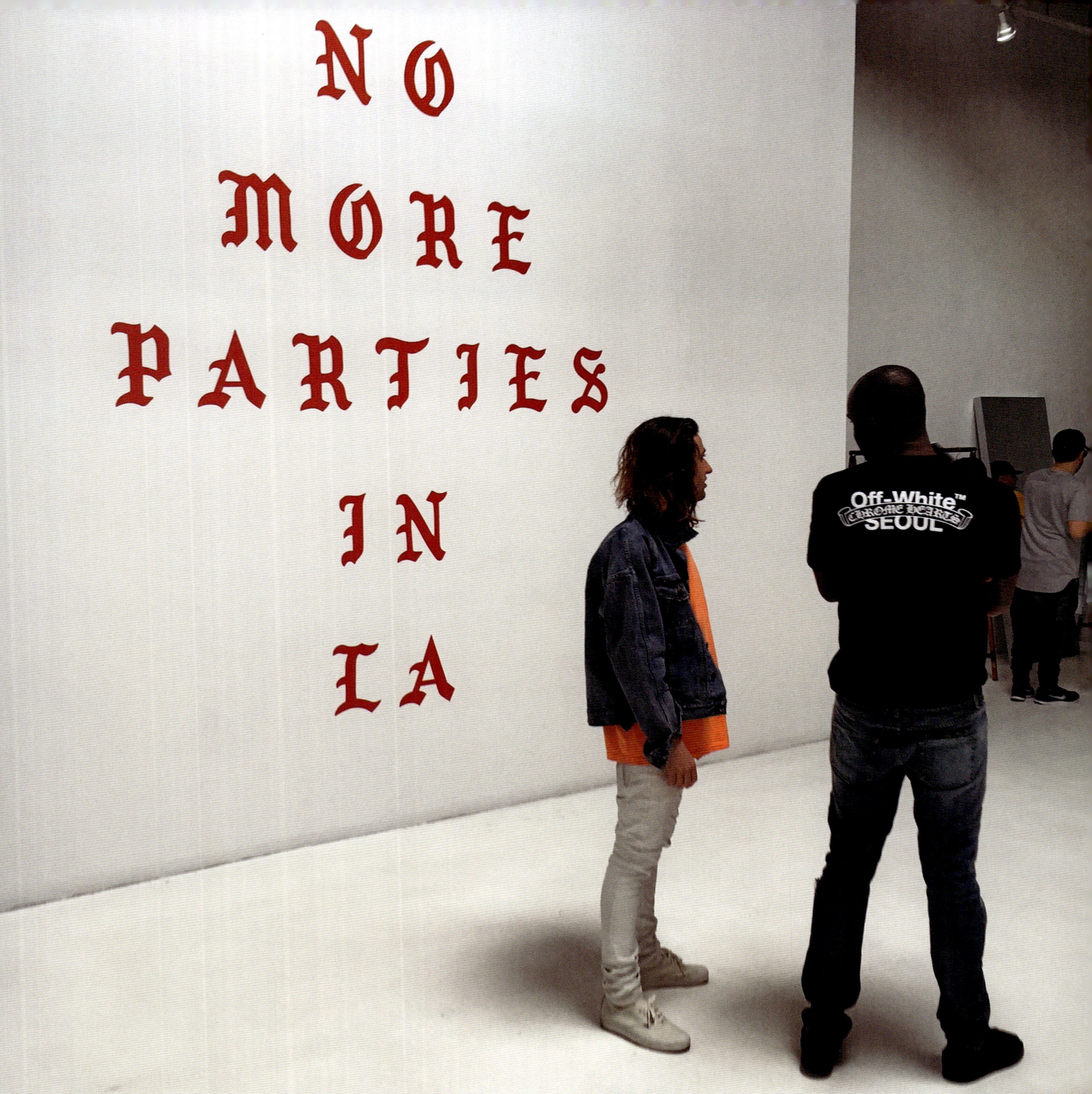

Mark Seekings and Virgil Abloh at “No More Parties in LA” Los Angeles pop-up

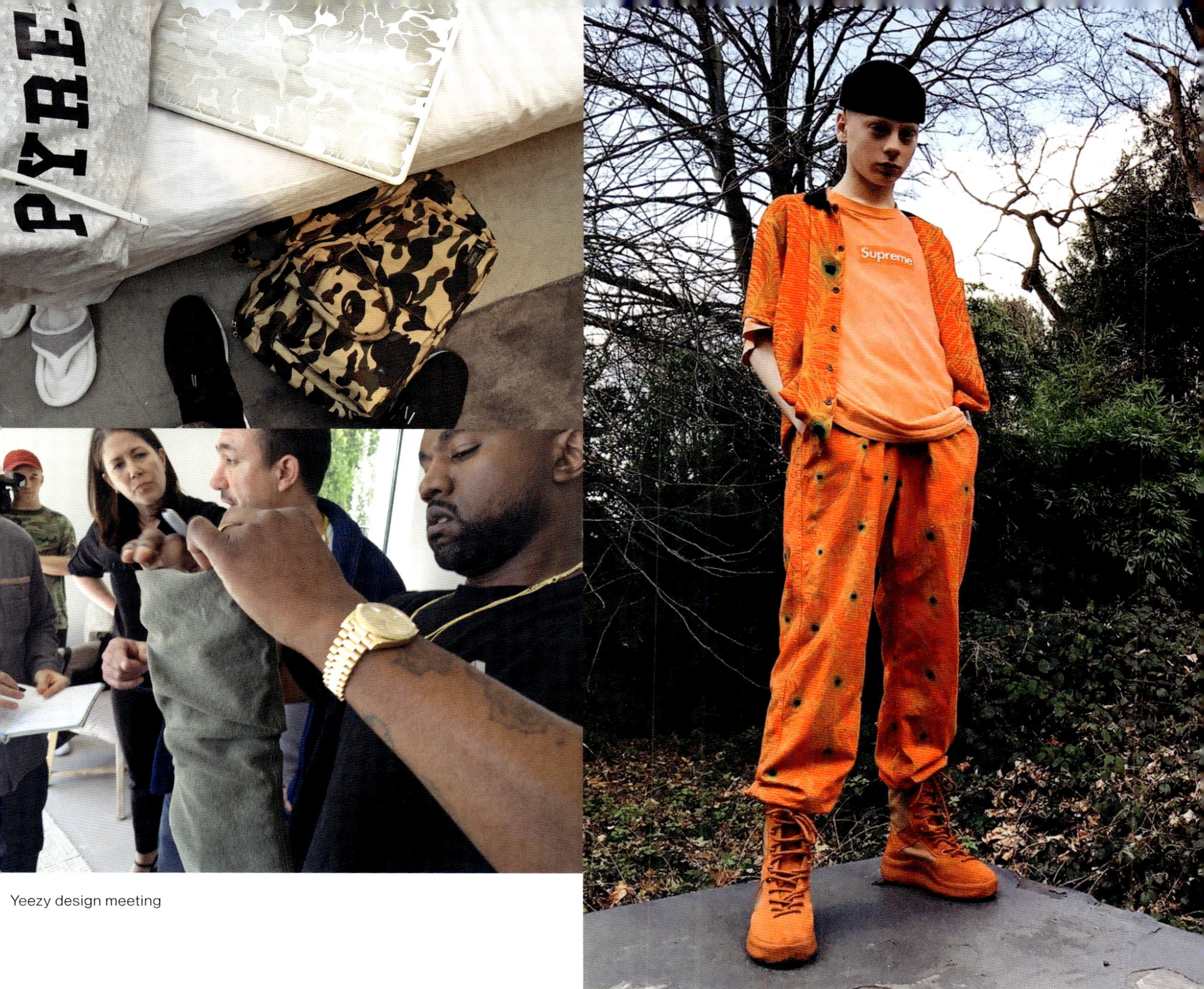

Yeezy design meeting

Gully Guy Leo wearing Yeezy Season 3 Military Boot (2016)

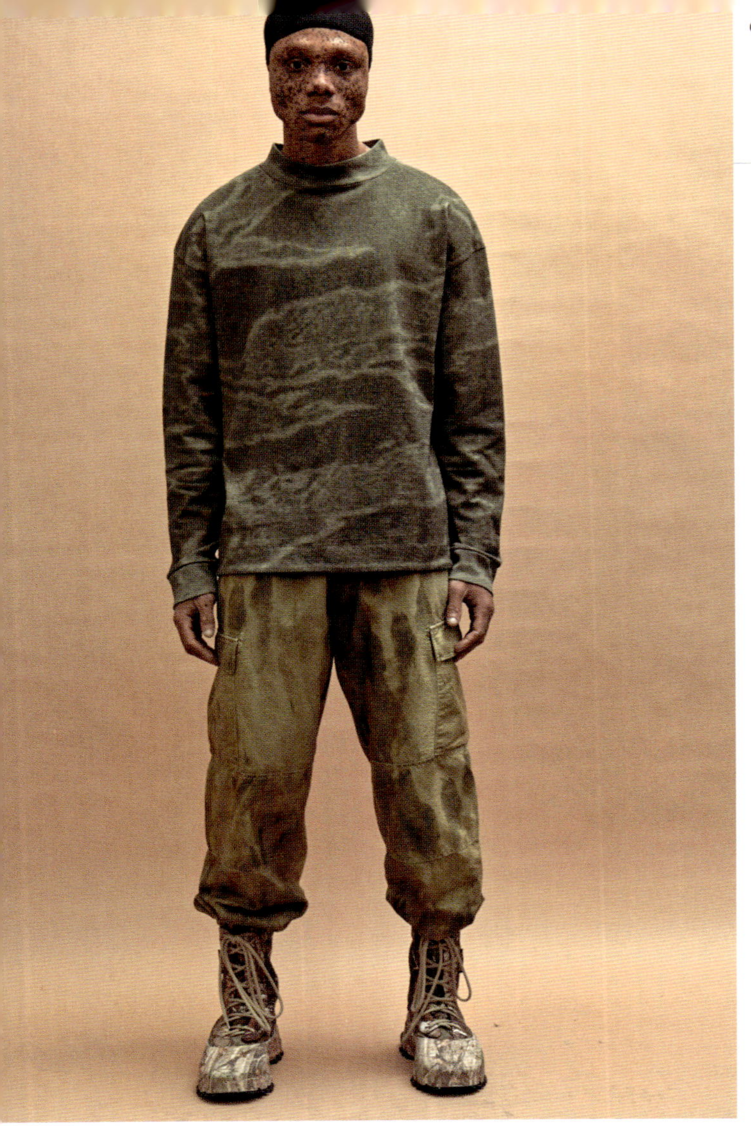

Ralph Souffrant - Yeezy Season 3 lookbook

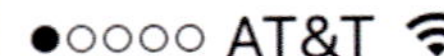

●○○○○ AT&T 5:52 PM

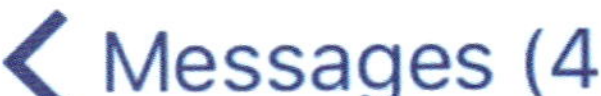

Messages (4) Kanye Detail

Today 5:37 PM

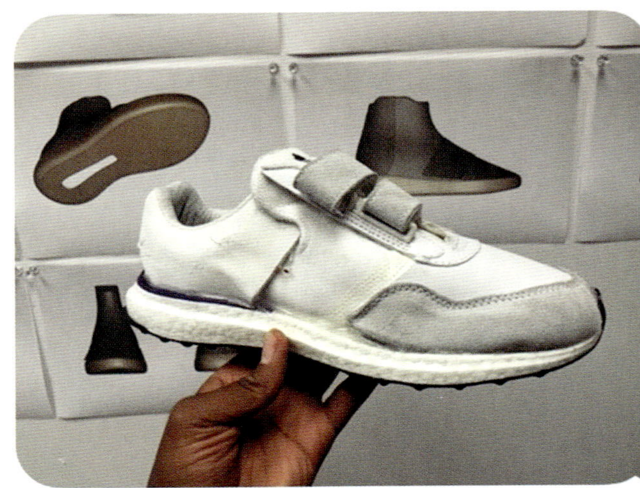

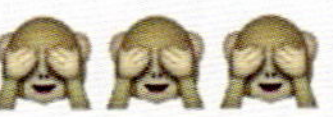

Can't tell if that's a positive or negative response ha

Negative. Who is getting pussy in these?

Ha ok, just cutting up some shoes to try a new balance type vibe you've mentioned

Delivered

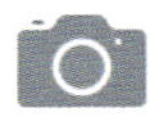

iMessage

Text between Kanye West and Salehe Bembury

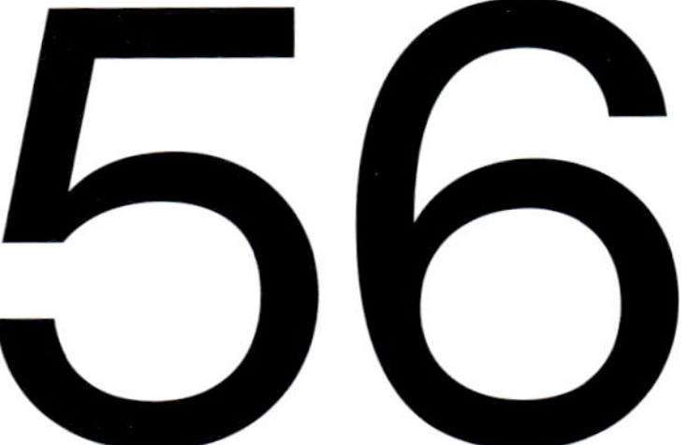

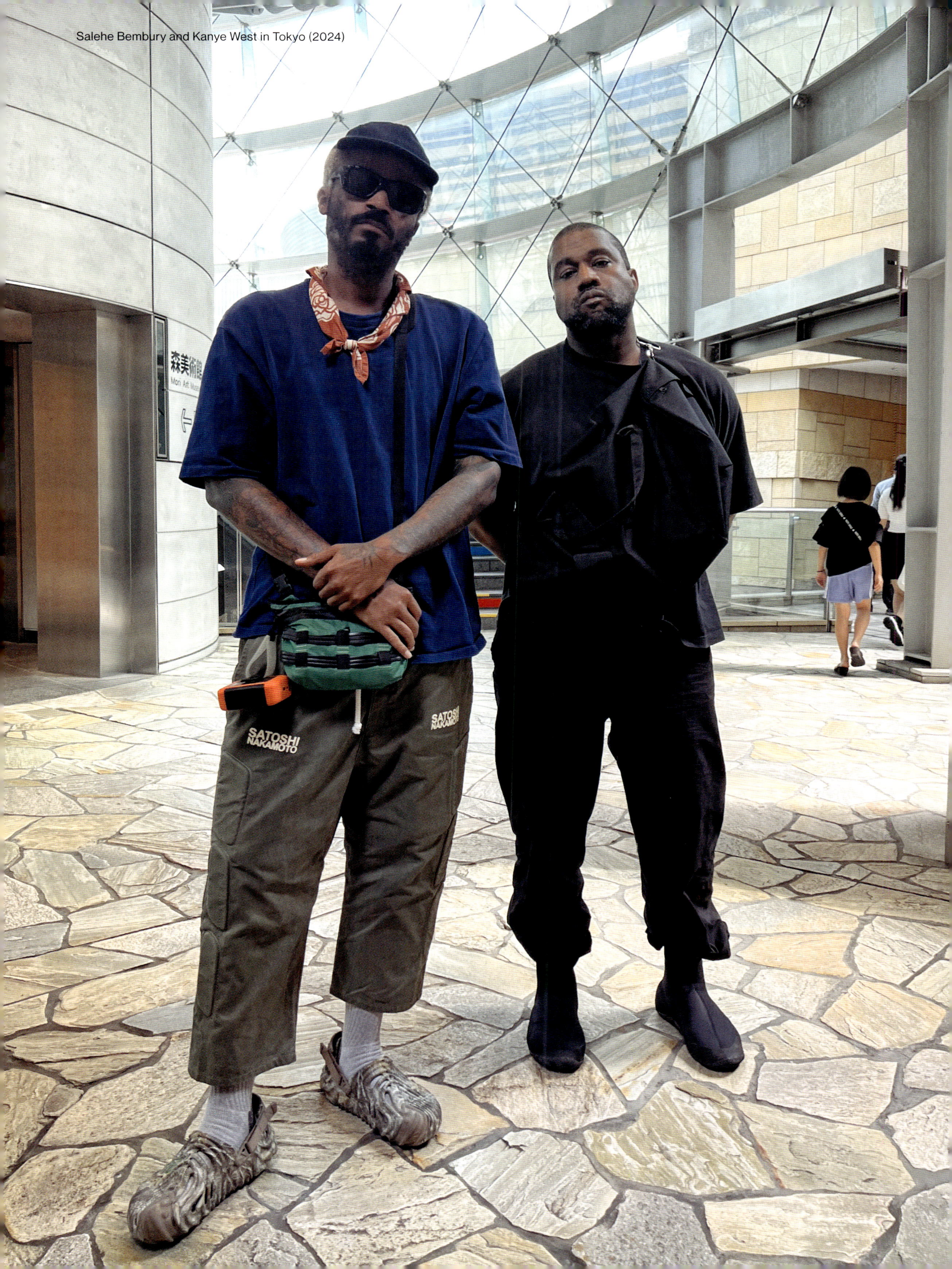

Salehe Bembury and Kanye West in Tokyo (2024)

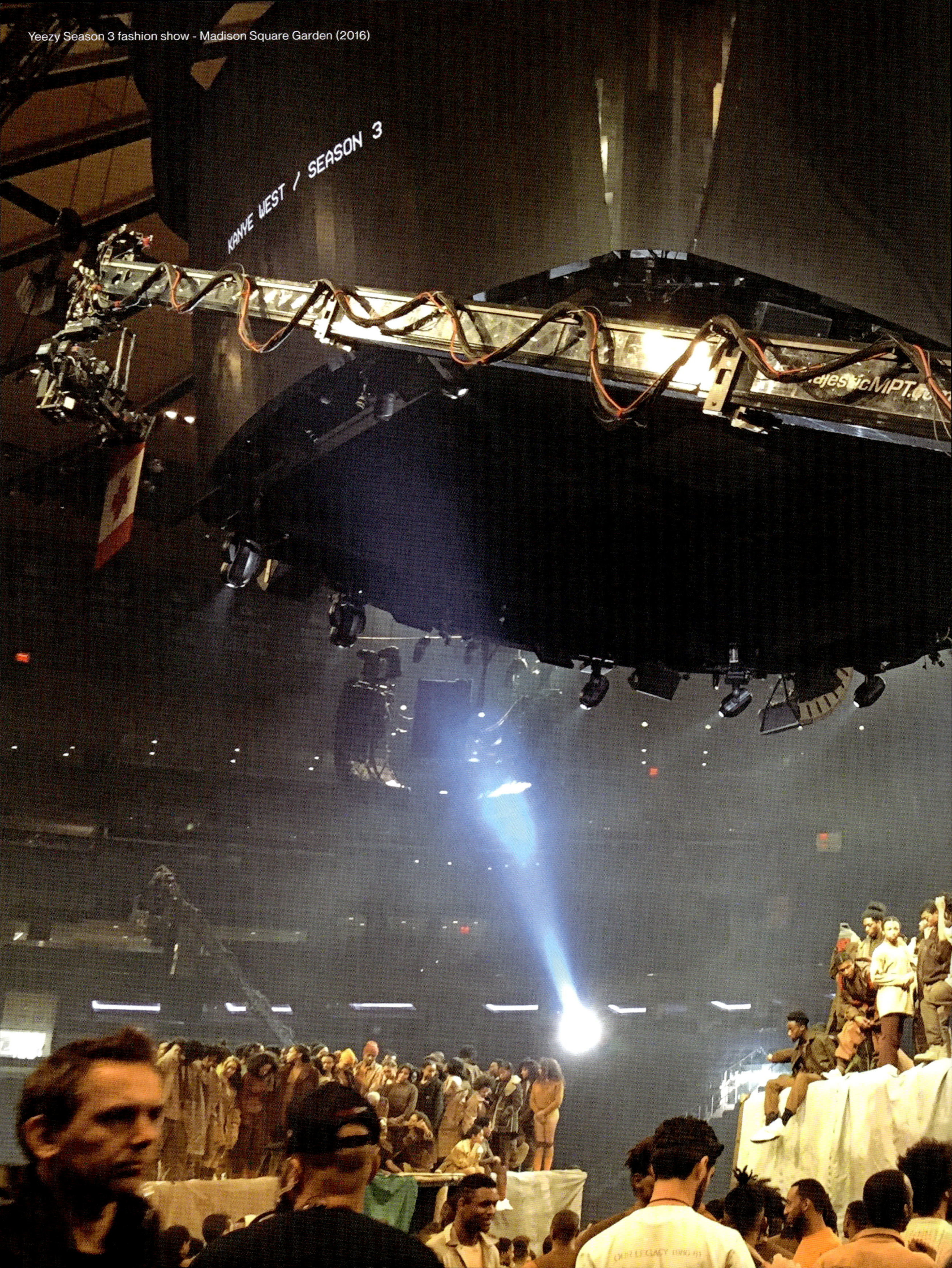

Yeezy Season 3 fashion show - Madison Square Garden (2016)

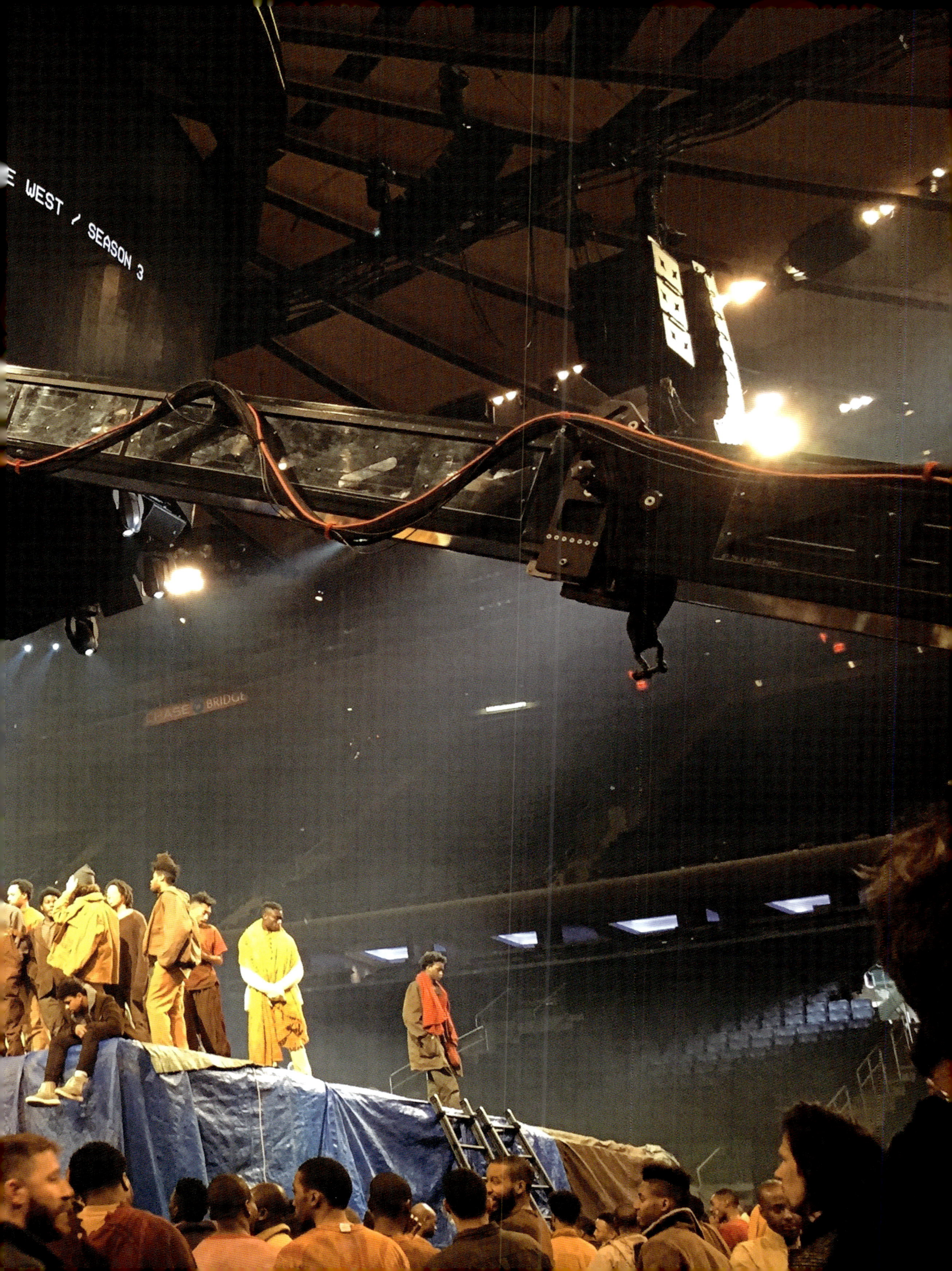
E WEST / SEASON 3
CHASE BRIDGE

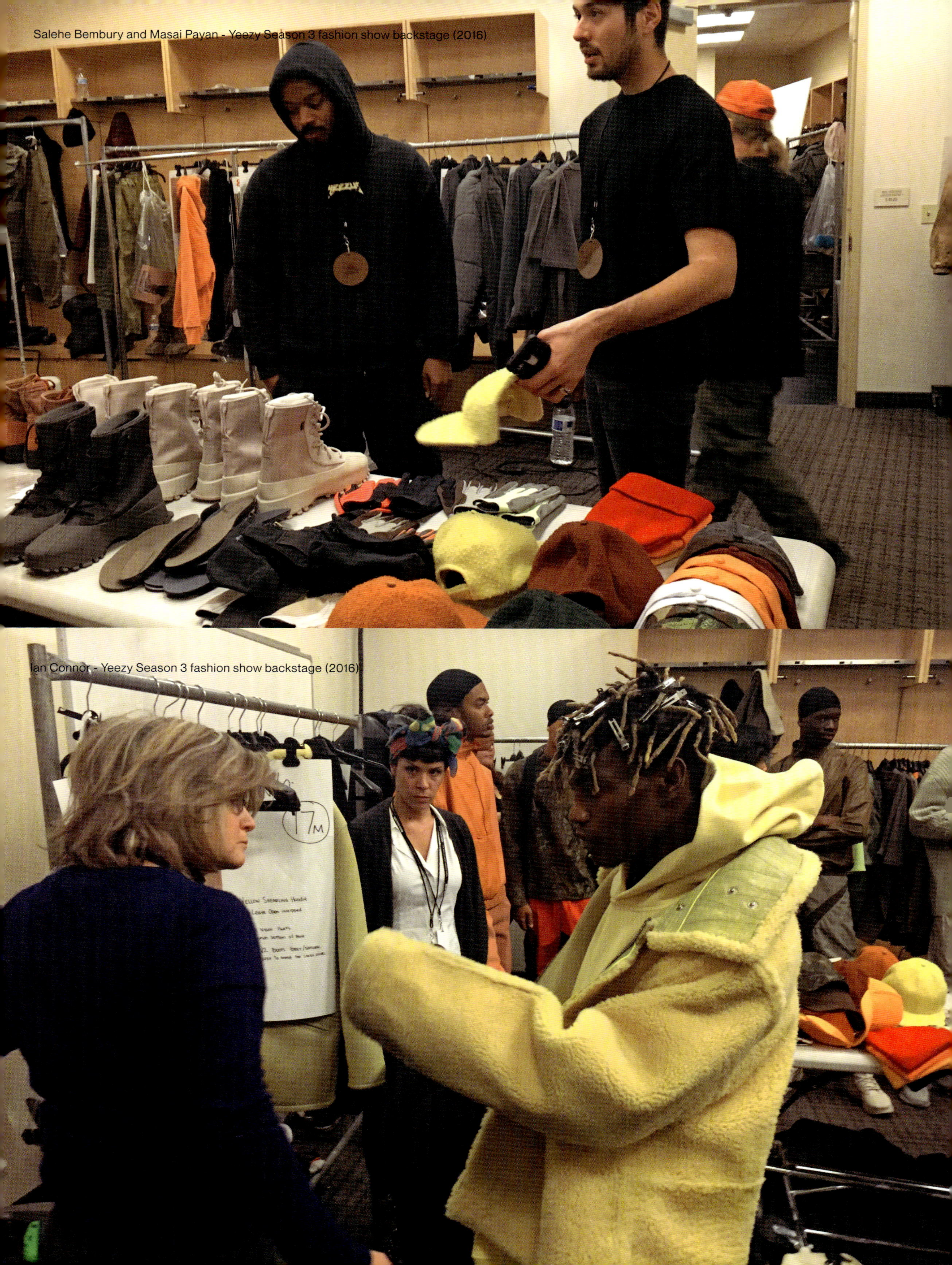

Salehe Bembury and Masai Payan - Yeezy Season 3 fashion show backstage (2016)

Ian Connor - Yeezy Season 3 fashion show backstage (2016)

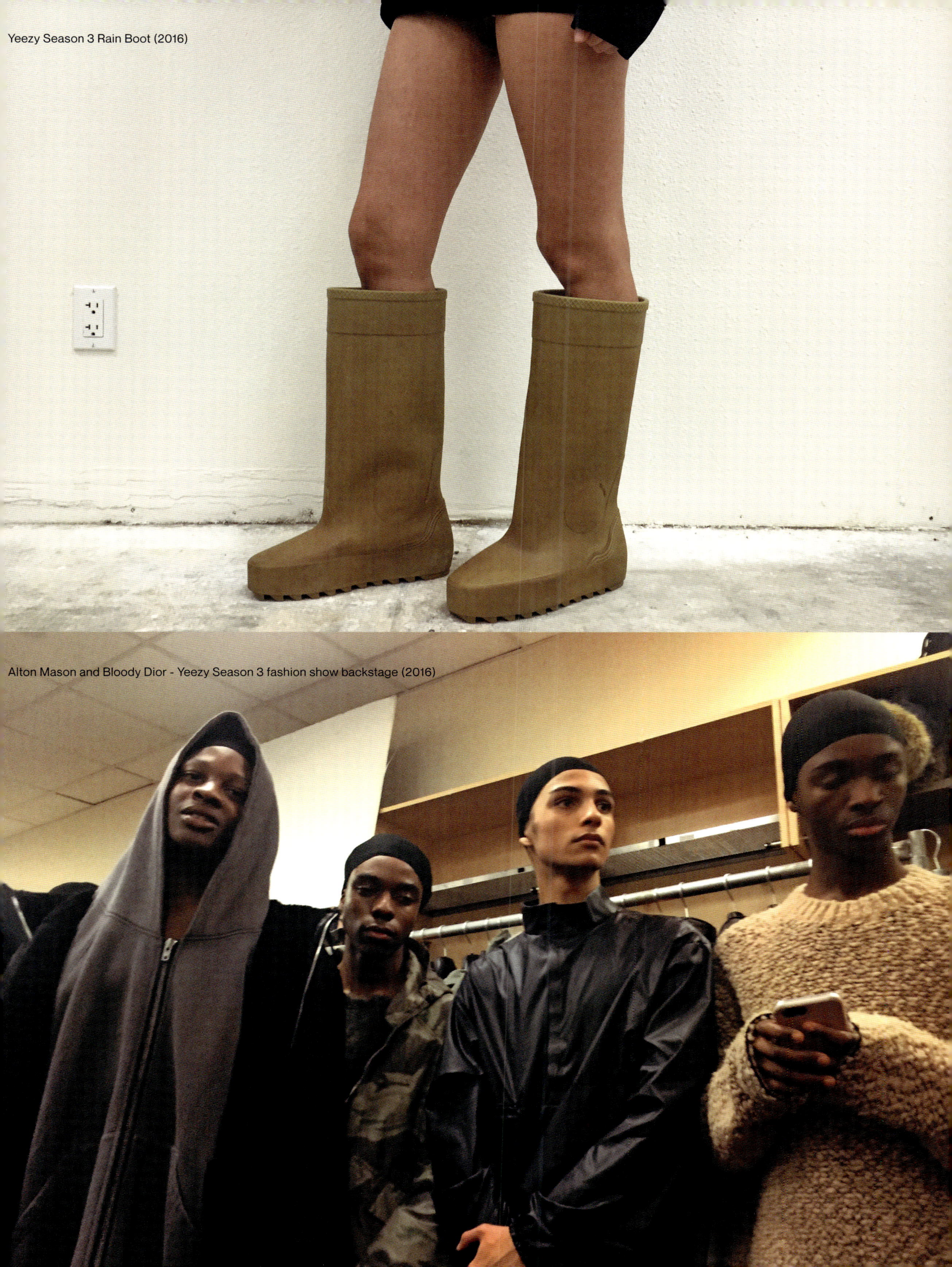

Yeezy Season 3 Rain Boot (2016)

Alton Mason and Bloody Dior - Yeezy Season 3 fashion show backstage (2016)

62

PYER MOSS **(2016)**

MAKE A FRIE

WITH
ND

PYER MOSS
MAKE WITH A FRIEND

1

I bet Kerby Jean-Raymond at a dinner. I didn't know anyone there–Virgil might've been the common denominator. At that time, I wouldn't necessarily say I was "in fashion," but I'm designing shoes, so at some level I'm in fashion. Kerby was in fashion as well. Kerby grew up in New York City. Kerby was Black. Kerby was my age. And so, with all those mirrors existing between us, a friendship grew immediately, and a level of familiarity, nostalgia, and similarity bonded us.

2

He and I were in different stages of our careers at that time. Pyer Moss was off the ground–Rihanna had famously worn a camo leather jacket that he'd made–and he'd had a few fashion shows, whereas I was just starting at Yeezy and exploring that space. So he had a brand while I was still a budding designer, albeit working for probably the most famous person in the world. So we had a lot to talk about.

3

I would visit Kerby at his office in midtown. It wasn't the stereotypical example of a young creative's small warehouse space. This was a proper office, with glass doors, a secretary, a security guard. It made no sense to me, but I was inspired, fascinated, and I really wanted to know more about him and get closer to him. Not only was he similar to me in terms of where he came from and what he did, but he looked like me. And that was very important for me to see.

About a year into the friendship, Kerby told me he was having a fashion show and that he wanted to create footwear that followed the theme of the show. The theme was Wall Street, or something to do with feeling financially stuck. He called me and asked if I could make footwear that would illustrate this idea, and let me know that he had some kind of deal with Doc Martens, so we would use those shoes to produce the concept.

4

Immediately I thought about concrete–but obviously the shoe needed to function, so I knew that concrete wouldn't work for a runway shoe. I needed to use a material that had the visual of stagnation and stiffness, but still had utility and function. So I experimented with silicone on my kitchen counter. I made a one-off sample that was extremely crude, brutalist almost. I sent a picture of it to Kerby and he loved it. That night he bought a ticket for me to come to New York and participate in his fashion show.

5

I got to New York and I spent the next 48 hours pouring silicone onto Doc Martens shoes and a few Nikes, too, in an effort to make 16 show shoes. I remember feeling out of my element, feeling like a fly on the wall, but at the same time being very much involved in the operation. It was extremely educational, and it was amazing exposure. In retrospect it's funny because on paper this project is written as "Salehe Bembury for Pyer Moss," but at the time I didn't see it remotely like that–for me it was simply "Salehe Bembury helping out his boy." I got to use my creative abilities and witness a fashion show for one of the first times in my life. And yes, I did design for Kanye at the time, so being involved with someone who was also involved with Kanye was certainly a benefit to Kerby. But I was just very excited to be there, to be a part of "fashion."

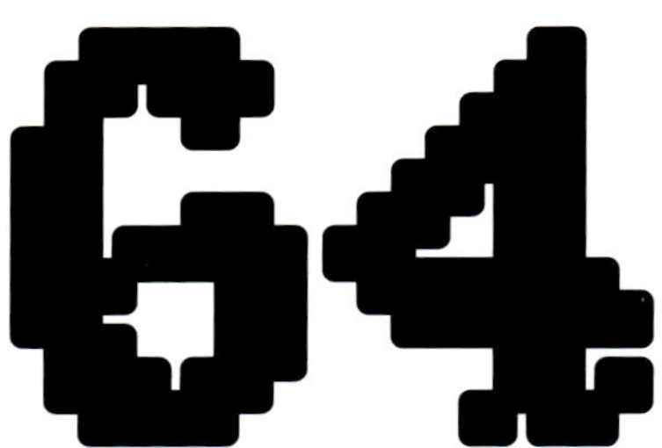

(2016) PYER MOSS

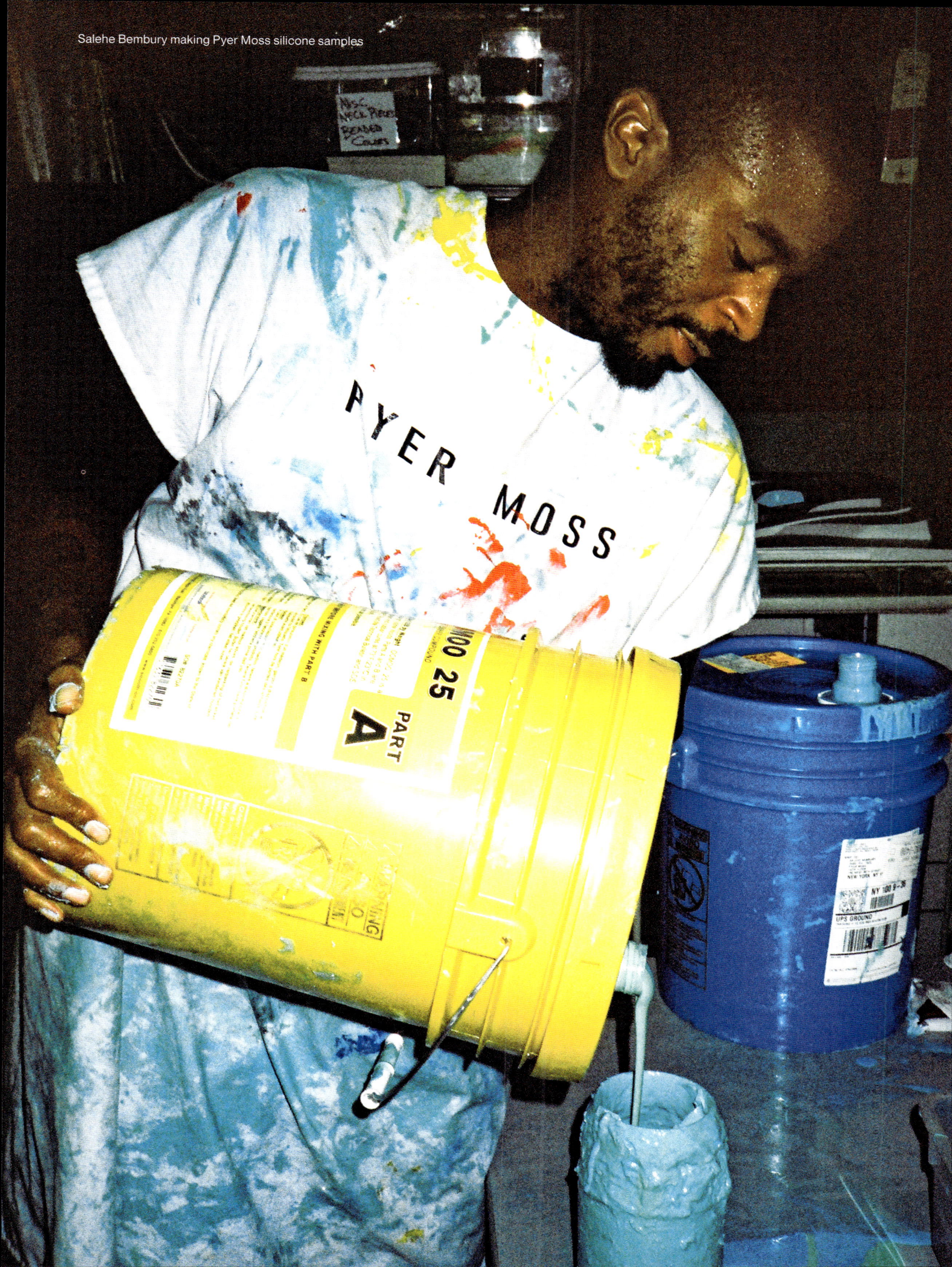

Salehe Bembury making Pyer Moss silicone samples

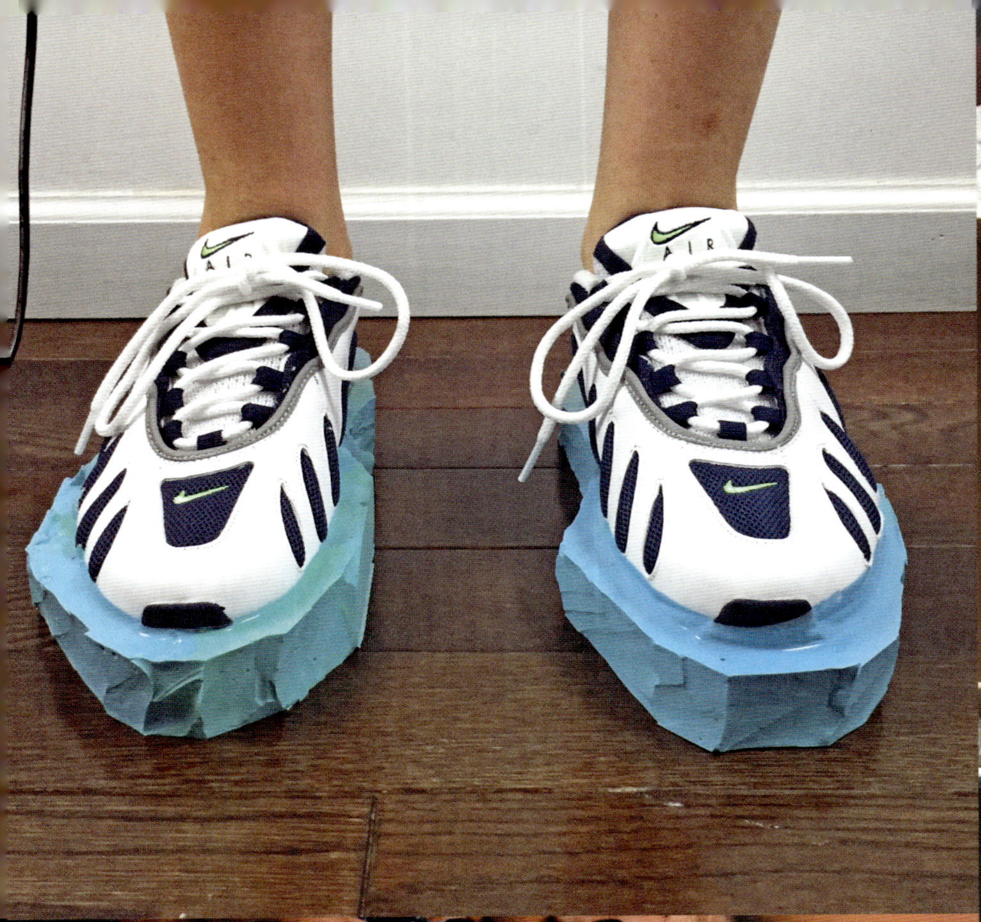

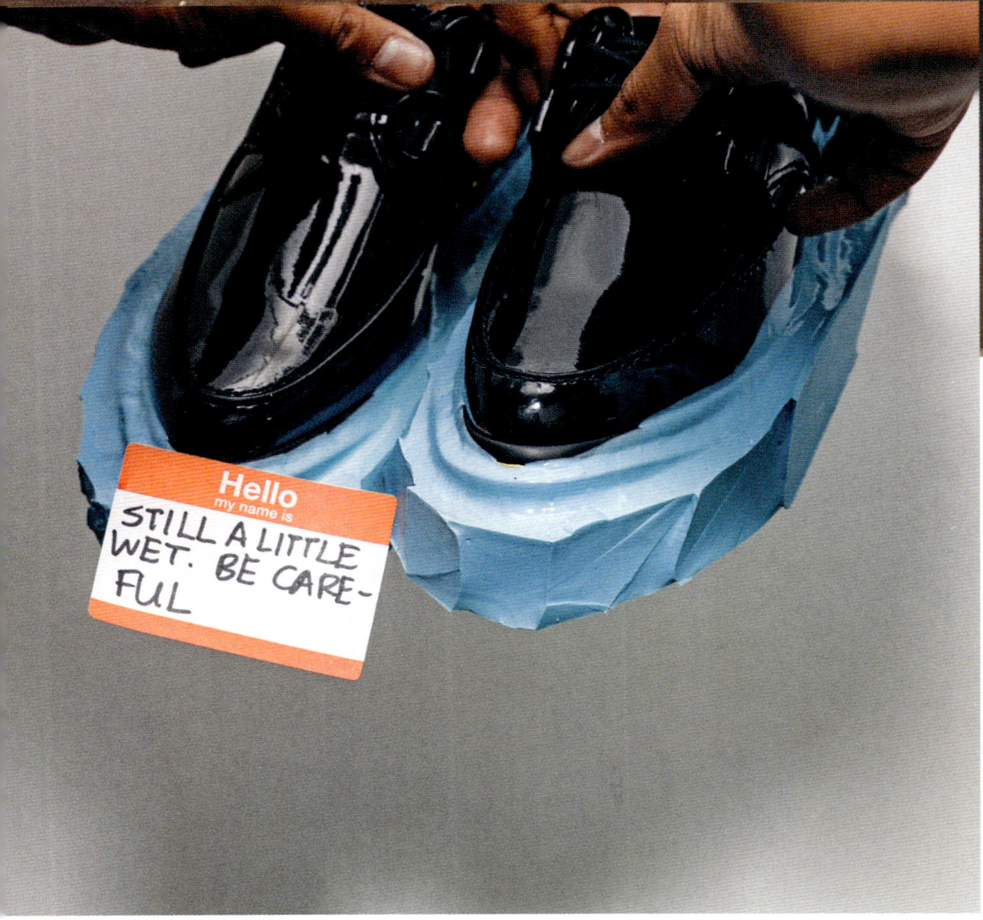

Silicone tests

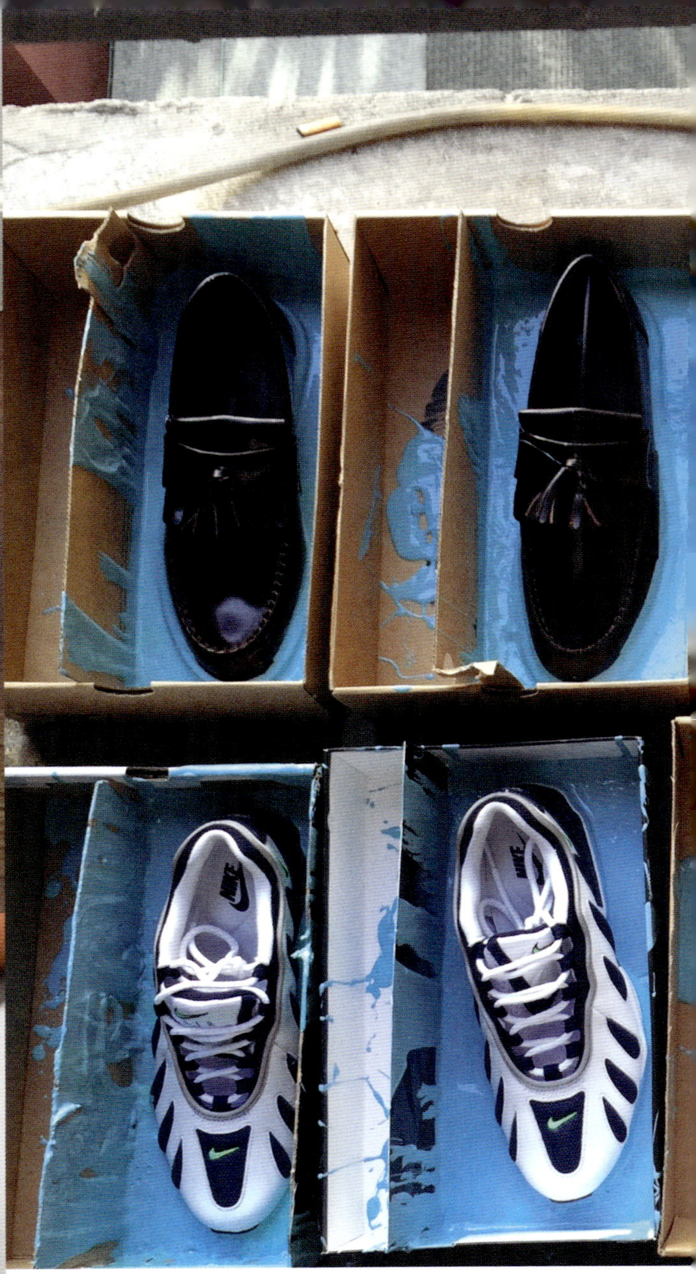

Silicone tests

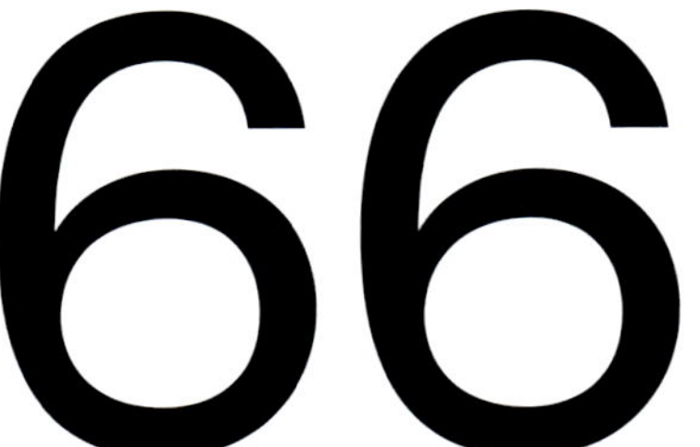

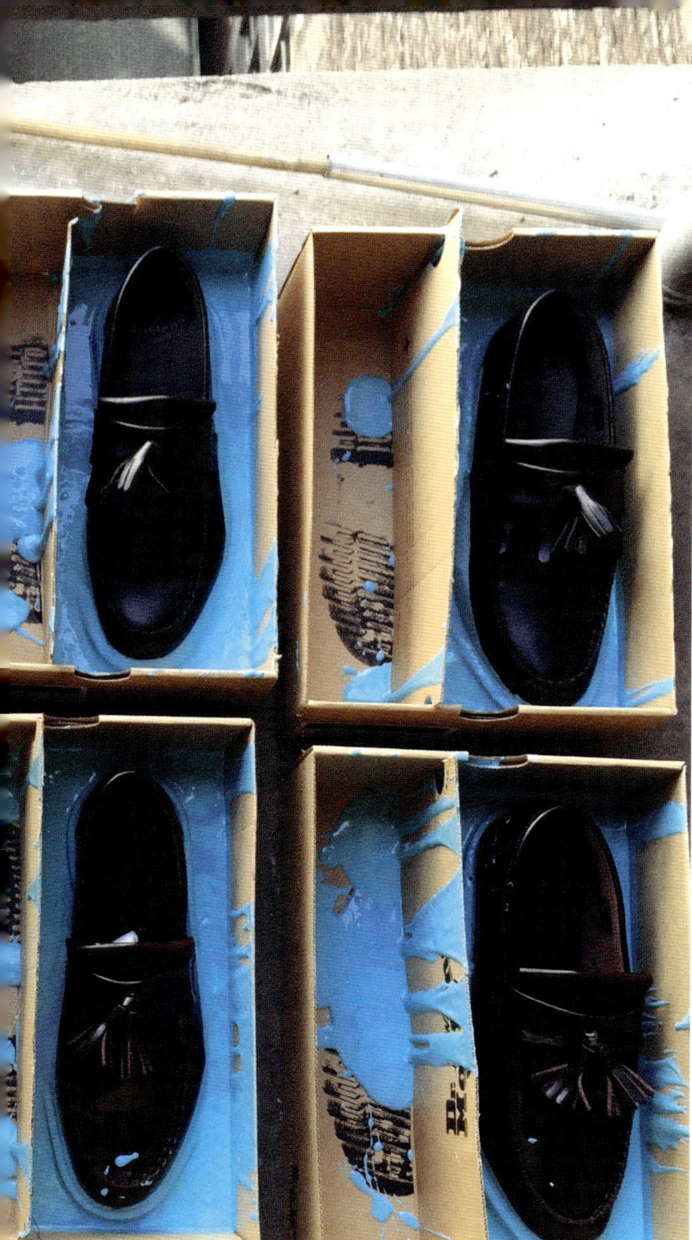

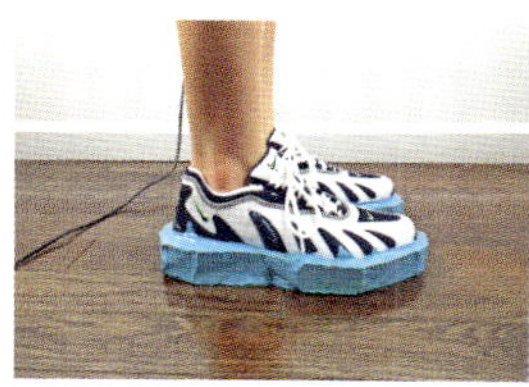

Air Max silicone test

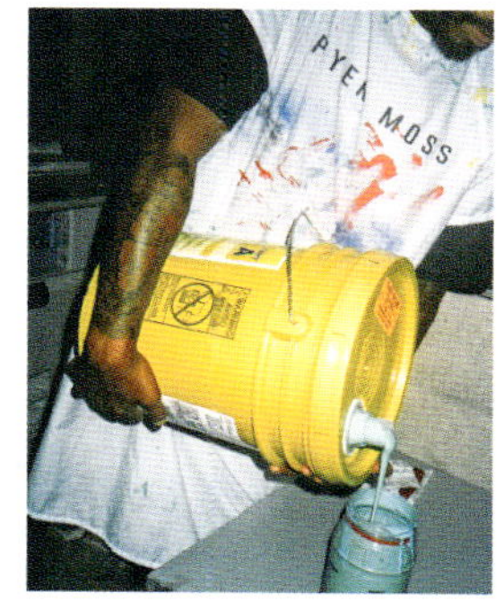

Salehe Bembury pouring silicone

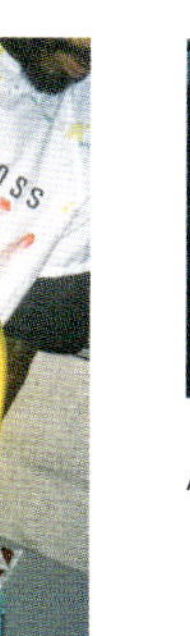

Air Max silicone test

Salehe Bembury pouring silicone

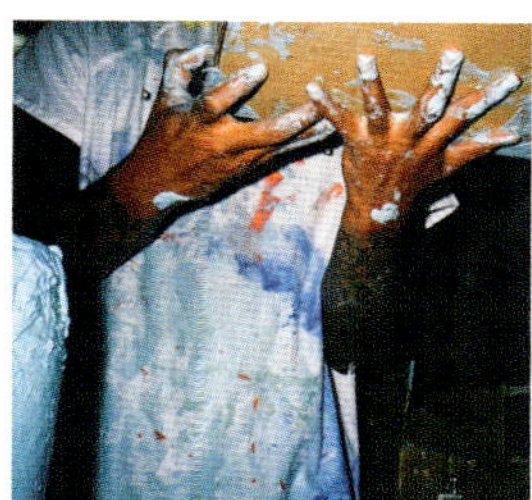

Salehe Bembury pouring silicone

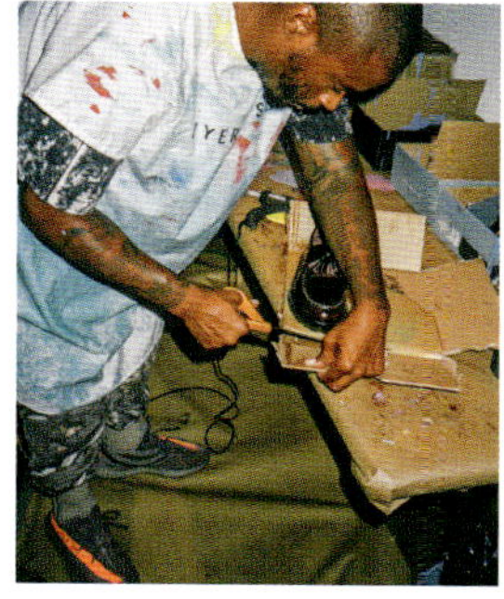

Salehe Bembury pouring silicone

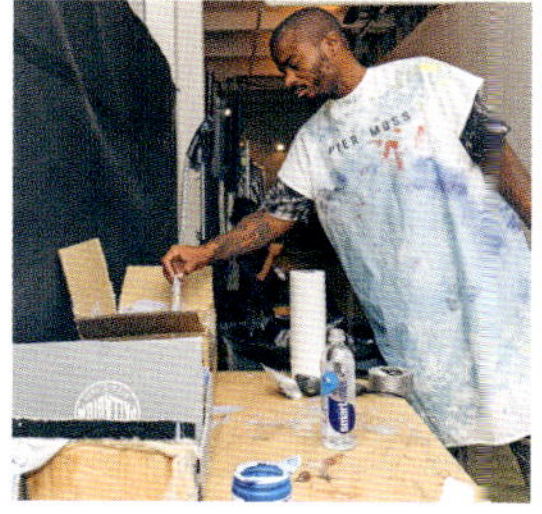

Salehe Bembury cutting cardboard

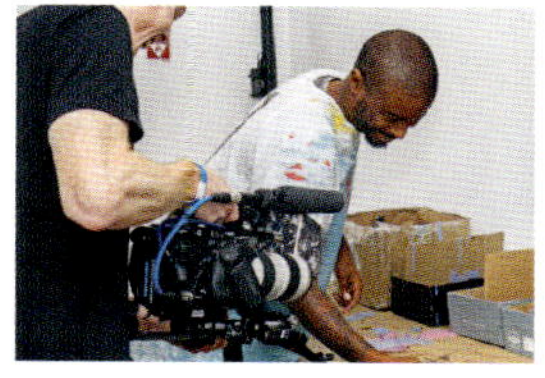

Salehe Bembury pouring silicone

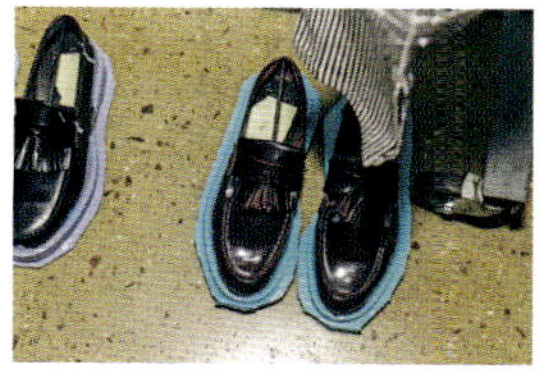

Salehe Bembury for Pyer Moss sample

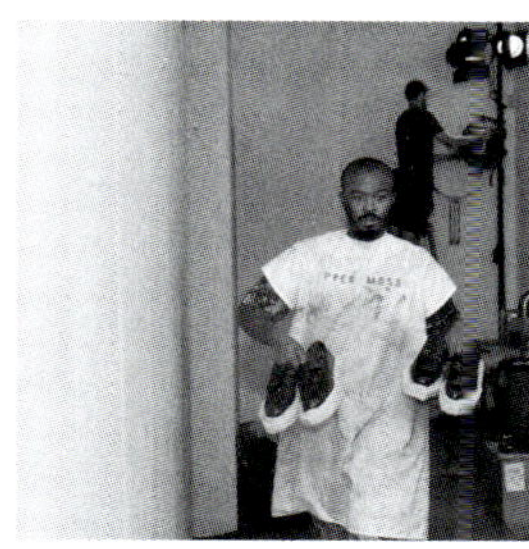

Salehe Bembury holding Pyer Moss samples

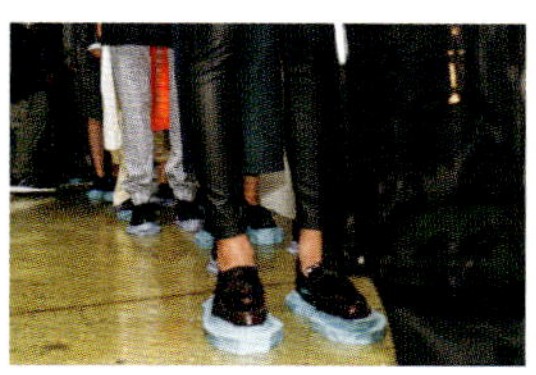

Models wearing Salehe Bembury for Pyer Moss

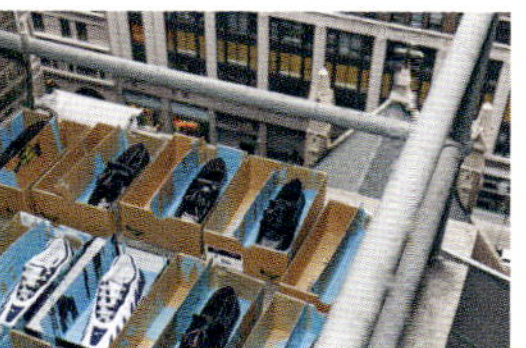

Silicone poured samples

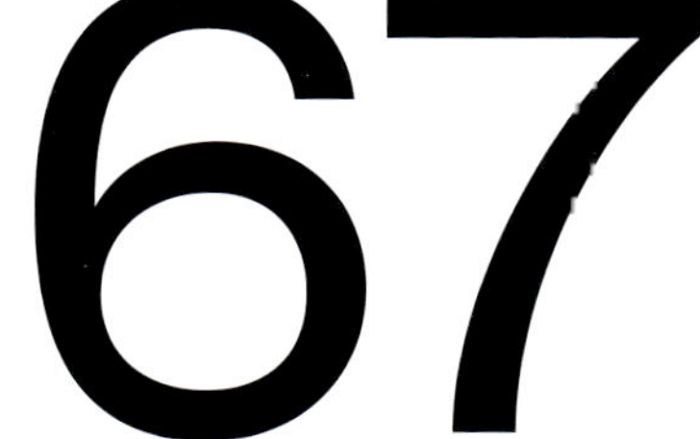

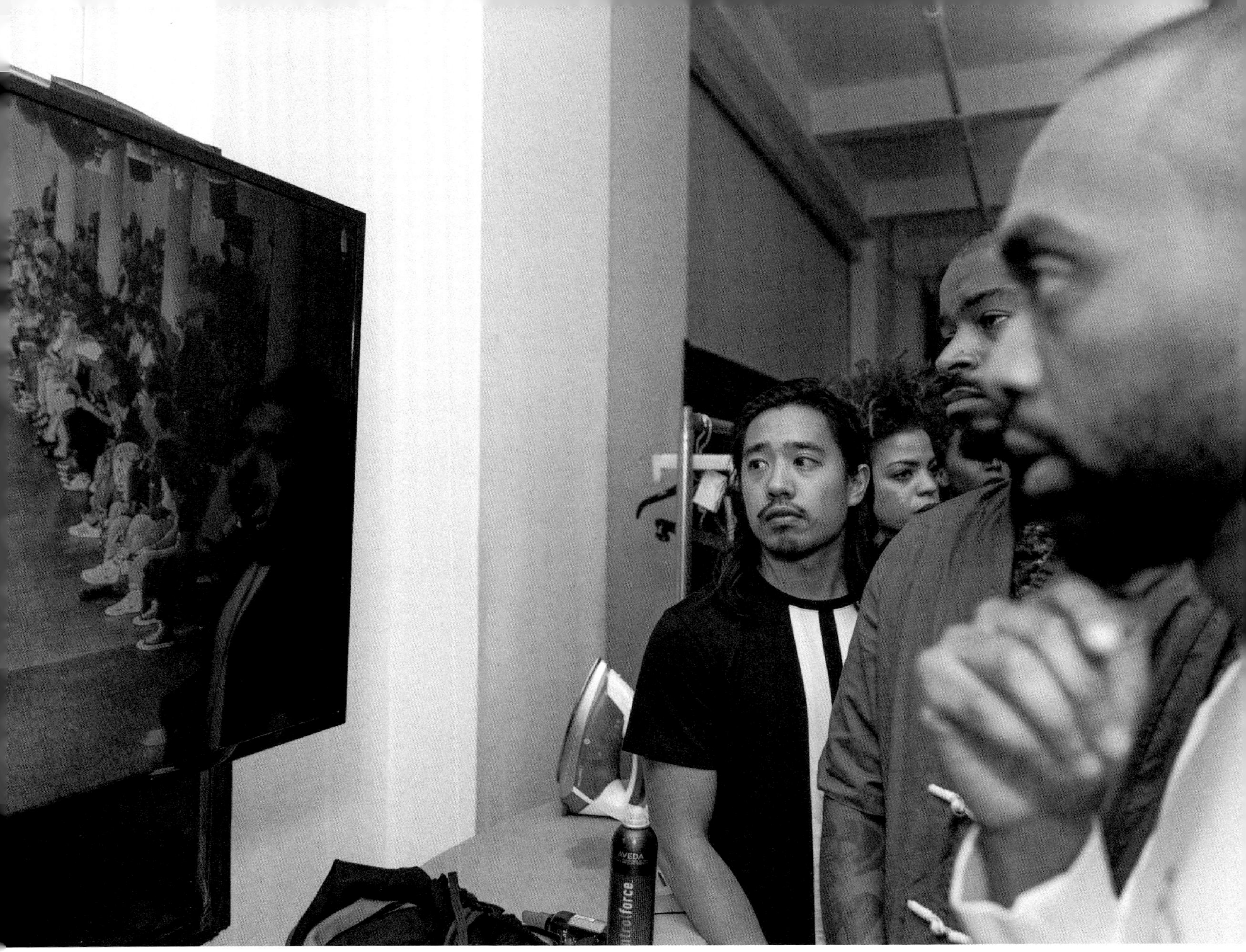

Kerby Jean Raymond and Salehe Bembury watching Pyer Moss show (2016)

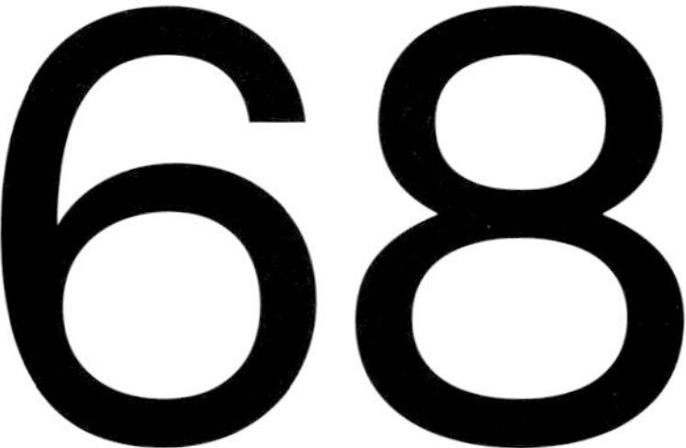

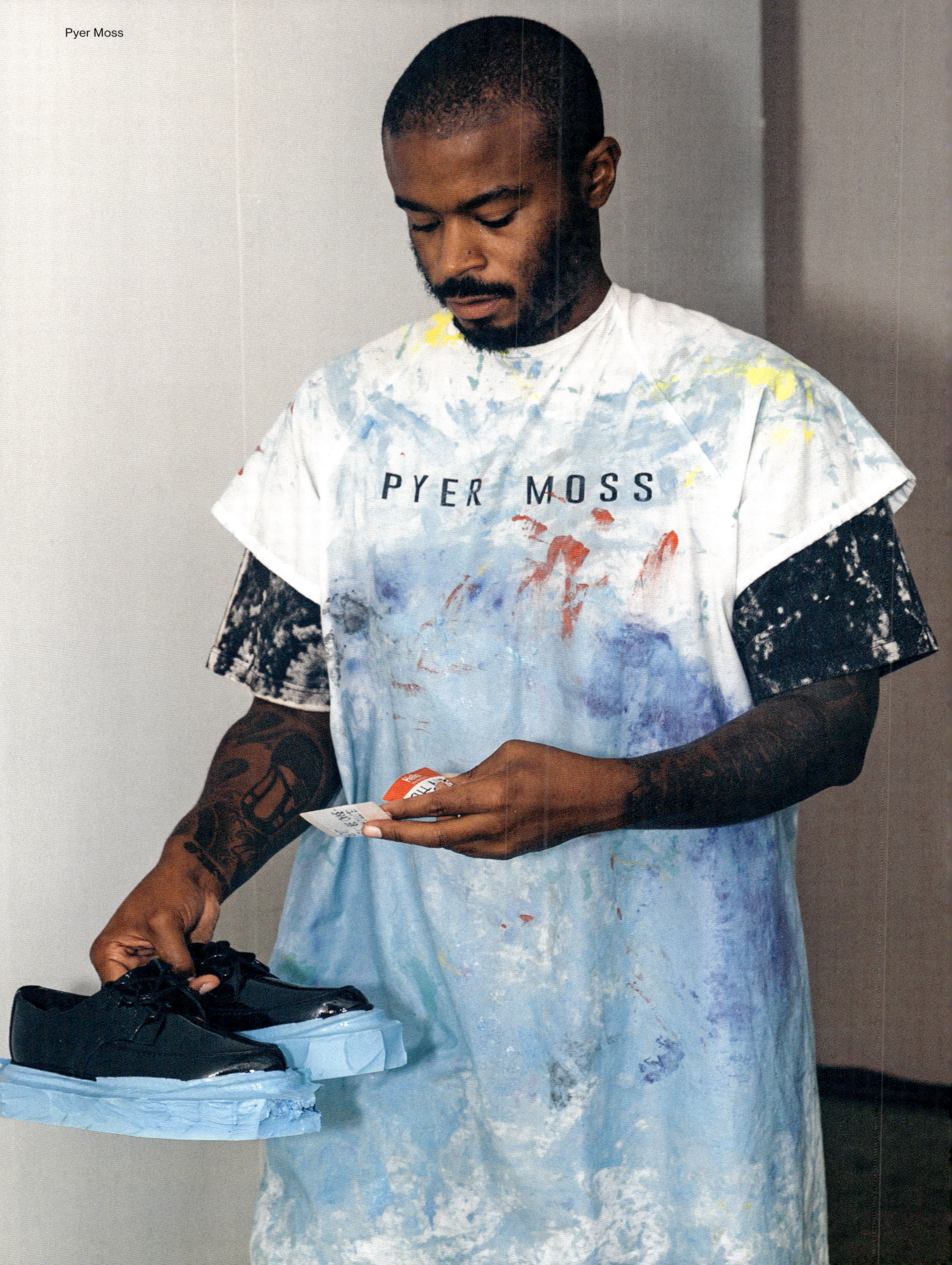
PYER MOSS

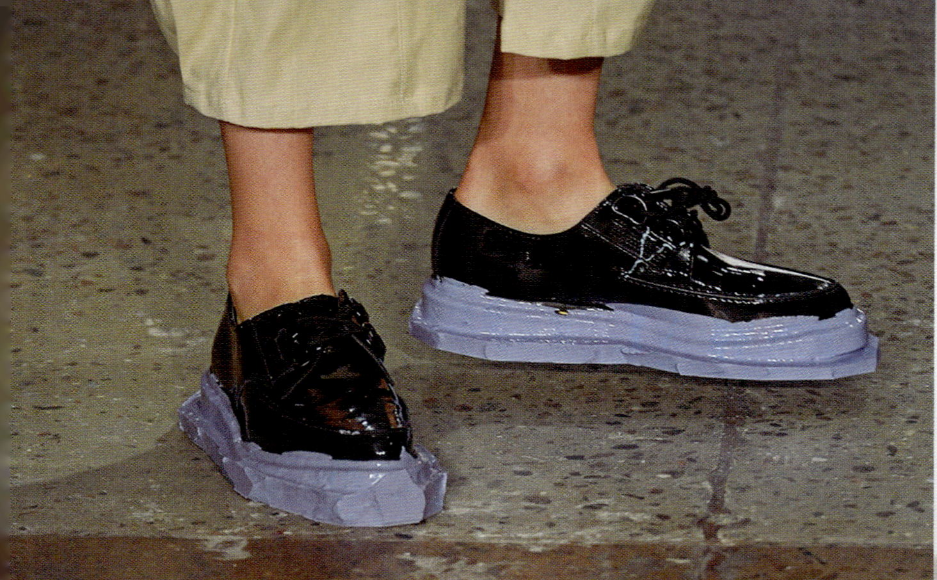

Pyer Moss fashion show (2016)

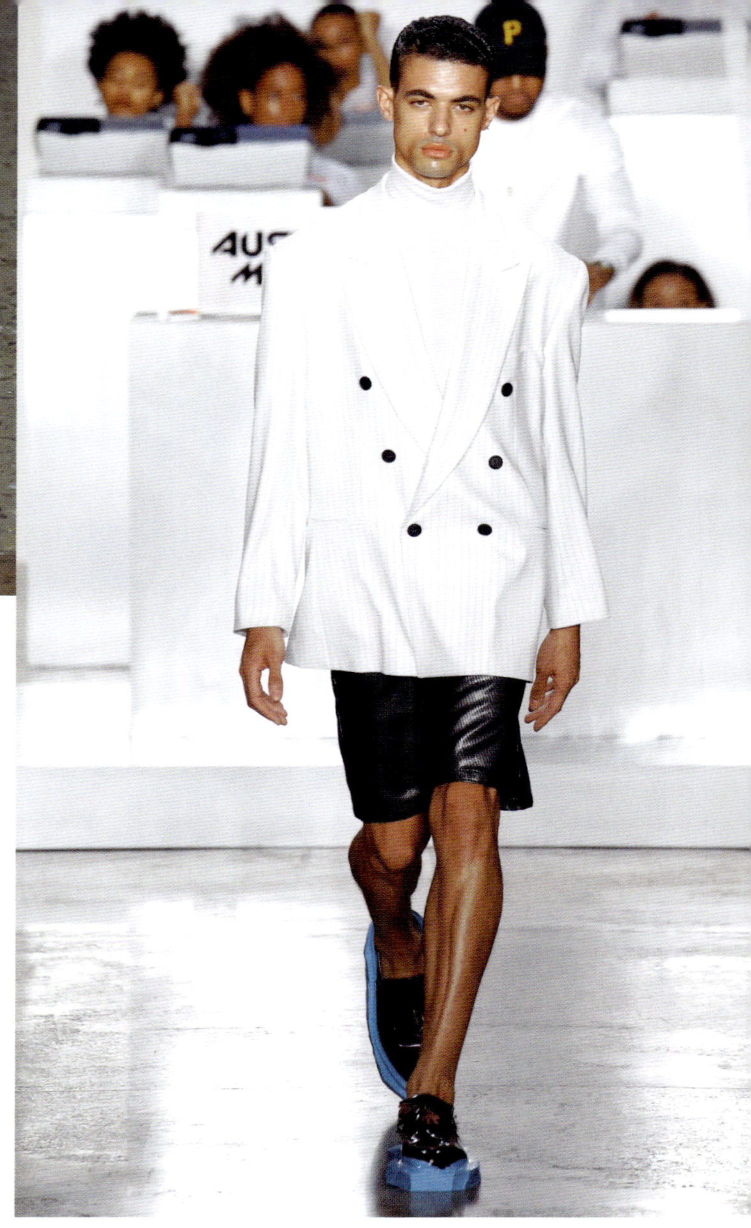

Pyer Moss fashion show (2016)

70

(2016)

PYER MOSS

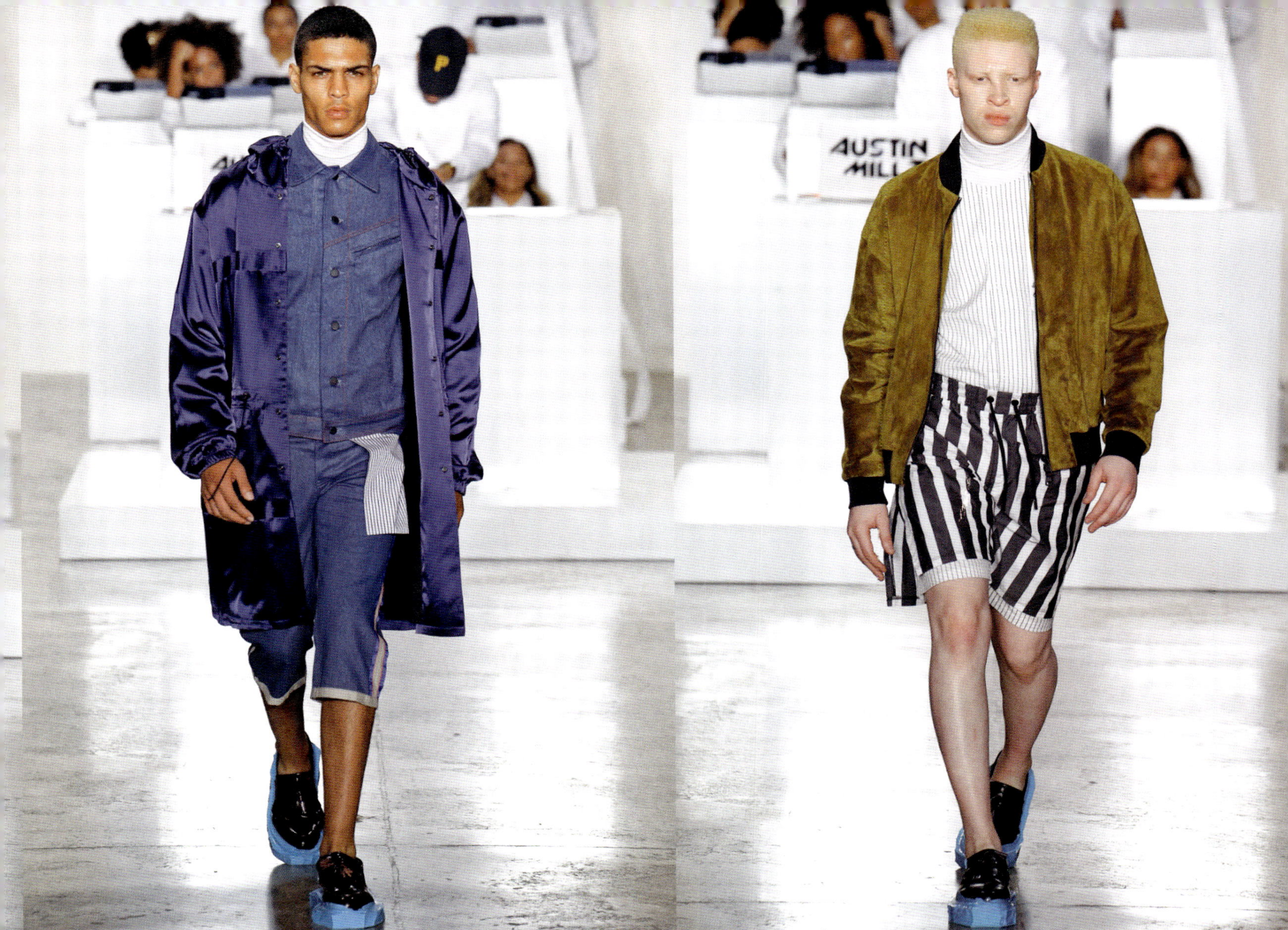

71

PYER MOSS (2016)

From the
King Towers
and
St. Nicholas
projects.

Damnb, Im only 18

Dear My Nigga Salehe,

Firstoff this is not a letter. This is a piece of art. This is an 18 year old project kid talking to a nigga that inspire him. Right now im in my 1 bedroom apartment with my mom, dad, and sister. I got two bottles of ginger ale on the table. Im drinking bothmy nigga. I want you to have this gear some I made some we made. Some I wore but I look at them and the public look at them as something RARE! They be wylin. The Telfar shirt thats for Kanye though. Thats my nigga. People like You, Kerby, and Yé inspire me. Why! Because ya black men with white man jobs. And I know they hate it. My house is small and got like an African scent so the clothes smell like pepper. But lately Im torn between two constant things Nike and Adidas. They both want me because I'm to valuble. I KNOW WHAT THE FUCK THE STREETS WANT! I rap, I model, I play ball, I design, I be onna block, I be in the 25k a month penthouse. Im good at everything I do and know what people in these fields want. So they try to pick my brain all the time for ideas. And they using ALL of THEM. i aint get a ~~single~~ single dime. Don't NIKE know how I live. Don't they know bills be short. Why they aint give me my

Letter from Sheck Wes (2016)

30k they promised me. I just love the brand IG. They send shoes to my house. I'm lost b. Kids dm me like your music is so refreshing. You inspire me. I AINT EVEN do nothing yet. SMH. Ima make it tho. Inshallah. My mom couldn't accept me modeling. She called me gay. I LIKE Bitches tho SMH. So she sent me to AFRICA for 100 days. That was the worst best time of my life. I missed out on 32k and I was mad at that like Im 18 I need that money. But I saw the world for what it really is. I wanna go back. Everything is about the youth. Every body old wants to be young. Everything is for US. Focus on what the kids want. I wish I can keep writing but my Air Max 96's are getting roach infested and got scuffs I got to tend to. Hope we can sit and talk again my g. Never stop innovating.

Sincerely, The most valuble
lil nigga on planet earth.

Sheck Wes 2x

The New Old Dirty Bastard.

Ps. I wear a 10.5
750s are fire
Those boots I wore em in Season 3
They're fire too.

BRANDON ‘JINX’ JENKINS IN CONVERSATION WITH SALEHE BEMBURY

I

JINX: Does making a book freak you out?

SALEHE: There’s a quote that says we die twice. The first time is when you transition and leave this planet. The second time is when that last person says your name for the last time. A book is legacy and a book is forever, so I feel like it means—I don’t want to say I’m not going to die a second time, but it’s going to probably take a whole lot longer for me to die that second time. So that feels really special. And in recent years, I’ve become more familiar with the responsibility I hold in leading by example, sharing my story, keeping the door open, and sharing gems. It’s kind of like a video game: along the way you learn these cheat codes, and the cheat codes may not necessarily work for you or the other person, but it’s still worth knowing—A, B, A, B, up, down, up, down.

JINX: This responsibility that you have... Is it something you gradually grew into? Or did something happen that made you think, “Maybe I’m not just telling Salehe’s journey, it’s bigger than my own personal timeline?”

SALEHE: In the beginning of my career when I started doing interviews, they were super buttoned-up because I was afraid that if I talked about getting fired or a negative work experience, that would negatively affect or prevent a future opportunity. So I never really would share too much in interviews. They’re very surface level, if you look back in my early interviews.

But at this point in my career, talking about getting fired is not going to negatively affect things at all. I’m pretty good. I recently did an interview with Idea Generation where I spoke about those things. I spoke about the feelings of vulnerability, feeling like your value had disappeared, and then what it took me to get back on my feet. I was in New York a few months later and I saw a guy on the street, and he was like, “Oh my god, Salehe, it’s you, I just saw your Idea Generation interview.” And I was like, “Oh wow, cool.” And then he said, “I just found out my job was trying to fire me, but I quit before they could.” He was holding a piece of paper with a paragraph and two signatures on it. He’d just got fired that day and he had the paper in his hand and he just kept looking at me, and then he started crying. I mean, I’m a hugger, but this is New York and he’s some random guy. So I hit him with the far-off pat-pat and then I got out of there. But on that day, I realized the responsibility I hold.

If you think about the intimate relationships you’ve had with YouTube videos, where you watch them in your room over and over and over again, or you watch them even in bed—you take a lot of those moments of wisdom and you apply them to your own life. So it made me realize, despite my extreme fear of public speaking, that for the rare space that I find myself in and the pioneer that I am or am working to be, I have a responsibility.

JINX: And it takes a long time to unlearn shit you learned. There’s this Miles Davis quote, “Sometimes you have to play a long time to be able to play like yourself.”

SALEHE: Well, I like that I got to discover my own version of responsibility. Because there’s the responsibility that’s preached to us by our parents—it’s like the old Black people responsibility, and that has its relevance and value as well—but the things that are preached to us as children, we don’t necessarily take them seriously. When it kind of presented itself to me, it definitely was something that lived within skin color. But it also just lived within being a man and leaving those gems for people who wanted to follow in similar footsteps.

JINX: How does growing up in TriBeCa jump to where you’re at?

SALEHE: It relates, I just probably haven’t spoken much about it. I grew up in TriBeCa, went to middle school in the West Village. I was going to school in a gay neighborhood, which wasn’t necessarily a thing in the early 1990s. Then I went to high school on the Upper West Side, at Calhoun. All throughout this time I had an interest in sneakers, but I didn’t necessarily know sneakers. And then during high school, I discovered all the boutiques—I think my first moment was seeing a picture of Alife in a magazine, and I thought, “This is a fucking regal-ass store that sells shoes.” And then it just turned into this pathway of discovery: Alife, Nom de Guerre, Recon, Nort, Classic Kicks, Dave’s Quality Meat. So I come from that world, and I would go through the circuit of all those stores and just hope that the guys behind the desk would talk to me. I used to camp out, watching *Family Guy* on portable DVD players and taking shits in bodegas. I grew up in that world, so that’s why it really is just beautiful that I have now achieved this position, because I grew up obsessing over it.

JINX: I used to work at Foot Locker in high school. I was in central New Jersey, so there was no version of the New York shit there. It was just proper malls and then your hood boutiques—and no one would even call them boutiques back then, this was just the hood spot. I remember the first time I went to New York City... I went to Supreme, I went to Clientele, I went to Dave’s Quality Meat when it still looked like a butcher’s shop. I was just asking questions—“How come they have different sneakers than us?” And they were like, “What do you mean? This is New York City. This is where all the shit starts.” And I just completely pivoted—“Oh, I’m in this world now.” It was massively influential. But my start was still having an interest in a very mainstream world. Go to the mall, go to Foot Locker, wait for the Jordans, get in line, hope they’re selling one pair at a time, and then shoot off. So our environment does inform things. We might end up at the same place, but our entry point informs how we see shit.

SALEHE: One hundred per cent. And the common ground was NikeTalk. What was so beautiful about that platform was that it was uniting people from the middle of fucking Indiana to wherever you were at to myself in New York. But we all spoke a similar language in sneakers. That was almost like sneaker IG before sneaker IG.

Now people see sneakers as status symbols. I believe that’s a significant reason why people participate in the culture. It’s not about how they look. People will fucking wear anything if it’s cool. The Big Red Boot is an example of that. That just speaks to the importance of marketing and storytelling and getting people to feel like they’re part of a community.

JINX: Much of what you’re talking about relates to our age bracket, too. Even if you had access to it with that physical proximity growing up, the way we approach things—the way we look at things—is fueled by the Internet. And you combine that with growing up in a Black

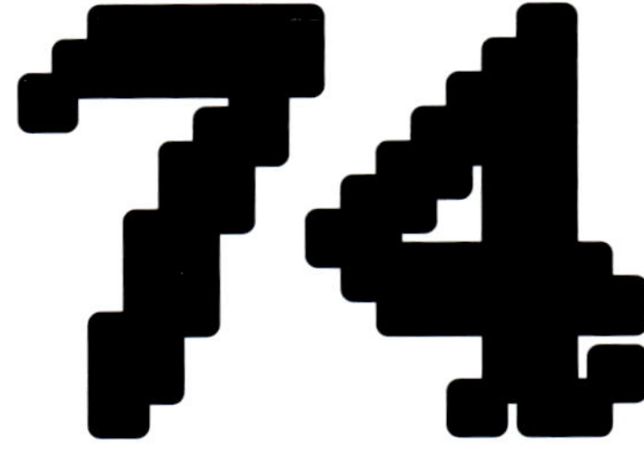

household, where you have another layer of constraint, or rules, or a lane to live in that is very different. Taking risks, for example—did your parents understand risk-taking? Or were they like, "We want you to do this for your own safety, we want good things to happen to you?"

SALEHE: It was kind of both. I grew up in an artist's neighborhood with artist parents, and so they absolutely inspired and cultivated my creative expression. But they were instrumental in helping me decide a major because they didn't want me to be a starving artist. Ironically, I have a bunch of friends who are really successful drawers or painters or artists. But my parents told me to major in industrial design or architecture, because they saw that as a way to take my artistic talent and apply it to something that was potentially more lucrative. So they kind of had both sides. They weren't the traditional minority parents, if you will; not just Black, but minority parents, who might force you to be a doctor. They wanted me to explore my passion, but they also wanted to protect my ability to earn.

JINX: So you chose industrial design. Were you aware that that could lead to the world of sneakers?

SALEHE: My parents did the research. My parents strangely didn't know what industrial design is, but did enough research to know that that's what their kid should do. I knew it was product design, and I also knew that it was a unique route to take because it wasn't fashion. I thought that since it armed you with so many tools and created so much design versatility, shoes were just going to be one of the tools I was going to be able to get off.

JINX: Were you designing before you knew what it was?

SALEHE: I just loved shoes. I would just draw them. I didn't see it as design. It was no different than drawing fucking Rugrats or Mickey Mouse. I would go home and draw Jordan 11s, and it would make me feel great. I don't know if that was design—maybe. Ultimately, design is about evoking an emotional response from its audience. So even at a young age, it was like design was working on me. I just didn't realize what it was.

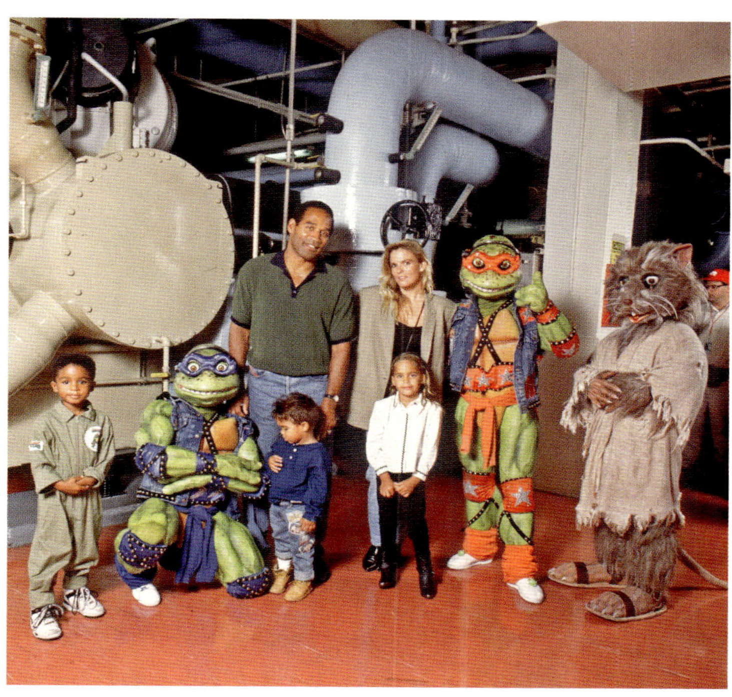

Salehe Bembury with OJ Simpson, Nicole Brown Simpson, and the Ninja Turtles.

JINX: Maybe the emotional response was your own, then, at that point.

SALEHE: Footwear was something that embodied an energy that I didn't see in any other product, just in regard to the organic lines, especially in the 1990s. Now things are more organic and futurist, but in the 1990s, things were very linear and geometric. So to see these alien, organic things that also had function just fascinated me. And similar to the way a pair of Louboutins or high heels makes someone feel sexy, I loved how putting on a pair of shoes throughout the different stages of life affected my psyche.

JINX: Sometimes you have these weird paths that make sense in hindsight. I've always loved sneakers, I've always loved music. But then I realized what I actually liked was a whole different level of design. And this design carried sneakers and carried music. There's a picture of me in fourth grade when we got to bring a prop for whatever reason—they tried something different for the class pictures—and last minute, I panicked and grabbed a Nintendo video game magazine that I really liked. The cover was glossy and it was a special edition, so it had gold foil on the front. It had design in it, but I didn't have the vocabulary for that. I just knew I liked it.

SALEHE: That same unintentional emotional reacting can happen to adults.

JINX: And I'm chasing that in so many ways now. I can draw a line to that moment because I have that photo somewhere in this house. Were there moments for you where, looking back, you're like, "Yeah, it was that commercial, or this poster"?

SALEHE: Yes. I can honestly say that I watched the Nike Freestyle basketball commercial once every two months. I remember seeing that commercial and just being hypnotized. That commercial was such a game changer. Nike was trying to respond to AND1, who was taking the market share for street basketball. So Nike was trying to capture the street basketball market again, and they put out this commercial and they did it. This featured my favorite player for a very long time, Jason Williams, and then Darius Miles and Quentin Richardson. It was a great time in basketball. Wieden+Kennedy did that campaign, that was one that stuck with me forever.

And then whenever a Nike would release, they would have a little advertisement in *Slam* magazine or *Kicks*. It would be a little graphic with the player, and then a phone number. You'd call it, they'd pick up, and it'd be a recording. But being a little kid, and with technology being where it was in 1995, I'd think it was really the player.

There's the Maya Angelou quote: "People may not remember what you said, but they'll always remember how you made them feel." And these things left me with a feeling. So in a lot of my marketing and my creative projects, I try to leave the audience with a feeling. I want to make people smile or laugh or think about when they were a child... For one of my *New Balance* campaigns, the premise was the first episode of Fresh Prince when he was at dinner and he started hitting the crystal glasses. That was a fucking hilarious episode, and it was also such a commentary on culture. There were some people that may not have caught that reference at all, and that's fine because it still was entertaining for them. But for the people that did, it was powerful.

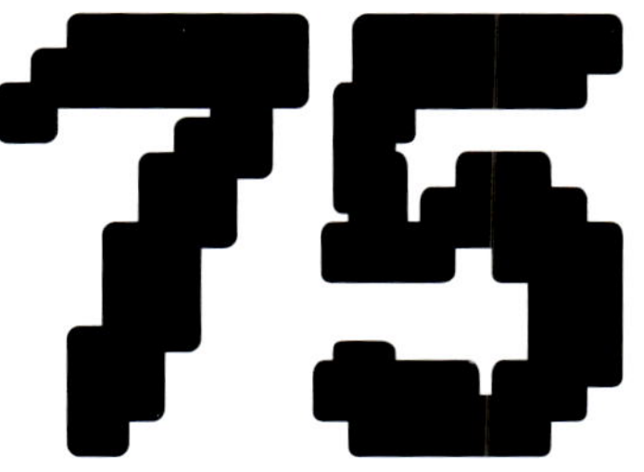

JINX: Was there a non-cultural marketing moment that created a similar feeling?

SALEHE: One of the best Instagram comments that I received, probably ever, was when someone recently said, "This feels like an iPhone release or something." It was in response to my Juniper release. And I was like, "That's exactly what I'm going for." Because with an iPhone or really any Apple product, they just show you the corner and you're like, "Oh, shit..." So I really am just trying to treat these product release moments like Apple. As creatives, all we have is the reveal. As humans, all we have is our first impression. So our product is the reveal. I put a lot of time and thought into that, and it's always calculated, even if it seems as if it's not.

When it comes to the iPhone, from the moment that you see the corner of it and it excites you, and then eventually you see more, and then you see the whole thing, and then you learn the specs, down to the moment of finally purchasing it and peeling off that piece of plastic, and that happening slow—and even that subtle sticky noise it makes as you're pulling it off—that's all part of the product experience, and it's all magical. I'm really trying to influence that and make sure that when I release a product, down to the packaging, people see that it's intentional and that there was thought put into it. You can see that with the Crocs packaging, for instance—that's made out of paper pulp and has a clear top so you can see the shoe, and it feels like this organic womb or vessel. So yeah, I would say Apple inspires me. Obviously shoes sit in a different space, but when it comes to product, it's all the same.

JINX: Why do you think that makes us feel something? For some people, it's the needle drop on a song, or the line to get into a restaurant. But I love products. I love a fucking great commercial.

SALEHE: I think unfortunately we live in a capitalist society where everyone's trying to just get ahead. So a lot of the time people produce what works. They're afraid to take chances because that can also result in loss of money. So the mark of a good designer is one that exercises restraint. It's really hard to find that thin line between new, exciting, and innovative, and then commercial and safe. A lot of people go the safe route. So I think the reason it excites you is because you've never seen it before.

When you see people actually execute from a place of perspective or with insight, then it surprises you. One term that's thrown around a lot these days is "genius." People call me a genius, and I think that's so fucking strange, because ultimately I think that what they're witnessing is passion, extreme passion. And in this era, there are not many passionate people. So when people witness passion, they confuse it with genius.

JINX: That's probably the first thing I observed in you. I remember I was out in LA and somehow we were talking, and straight away you were like, "Yo, come through." And I'm not like that—give me a week's notice, I have a hesitation in me to do things. And then I paid more attention to you having that trait in other things you did and said—I was watching how you were hopping through opportunity and understanding a moment. I thought, "This guy feels really fucking alive." Where does that come from?

SALEHE: I would say New York, for one. I think just New Yorkers have that in them. And then my dad's an entrepreneur. He's a photographer, he owns his photography business. I grew up in a loft, so the loft had really high ceilings, but then the walls only went up halfway so sound really traveled. And I would always hear my dad cold-calling people, just asserting himself and putting himself out there with no shame. And I was just playing Dreamcast, not paying attention. But I think on a subconscious level, I was absorbing. You got to put yourself out there and you got to get after it. So it's partly that.

And the worst thing that can happen a lot of the time is "no." So it's like, who gives a fuck? At this point in my life, I've seen how putting yourself out there and asking—in regard to Versace, for example—changed my entire life.

There's this Steve Jobs clip—I'm going to play this for you:

[I've never found anyone who said no or hung up the phone when I called. I just asked. And when people ask me, I try to be as responsive, pay that debt of gratitude back. Most people never pick up the phone and call. Most people never ask. And that's what separates sometimes the people that do things from the people that just dream about them. You got to act. And you've got to be willing to fail. You've got to be willing to crash and burn, with people on the phone, with starting a company, with whatever. If you're afraid of failing, you won't get very far.]

And that's it.

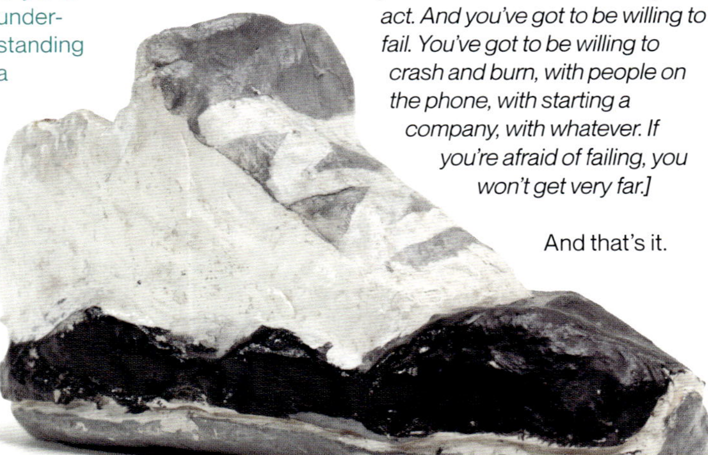

Ceramic Jordan XI made by Salehe circa 1996

That's fucking it. A lot of people think that if they ask for things, they're going to get laughed out of the room, and they're spending all their time overthinking things. But life is short. So it just comes from that, you know what I mean? And if they tell you no, you just keep pushing.

JINX: Do you have a moment early on that's the opposite of that, though, or a moment before it started to feel like it was a positive trait? When the reward to that decision-making wasn't there?

SALEHE: Well, I think it's relatable to being in high school and trying to get a girl to kiss you. Maybe you try the first time and it fails and you're like, "Okay, I need to try it this way." Then it fails again. And then you finally get a girl to kiss you and you're like, "Oh shit, I got to do it like that." So with every step in the game, you just learn new tools. As you continue to ascend or move laterally, you take tools from those experiences and apply them appropriately. That's what I'm doing.

JINX: That is a theme that I feel like I see just in your work—there is a through line. Whether it's your campaigns, your designs, or even what I believe is your maneuvering through the public sphere—you're clearly stacking up ideas, information, insights, responses, and then going forward. And it feels like you're picking up speed because of that.

I remember asking you about your design process, and you said that at that moment you were "focusing on material," and that you'd focus on color one year, and then form the next. There is iteration.

SALEHE: I grew up loving basketball and I remember you'd hear that Dwight Howard was practicing with Olajuwon to work on his hook shot all summer, or even about Kobe strictly working on defense. So it was a similar thing to that: I am a design athlete, if you will, and again I have tools—I just need to make sure they're all sharp.

JINX: Is there an athletic equivalent? If you were to say, "Yo, this is me," just because of that structure?

SALEHE: That's interesting, I've never been asked that question. Maybe someone like Ricky Rubio, who was interesting because it almost seemed like he took the sensibilities of soccer, football, and brought them into basketball.

JINX: You've talked about your idea of professionalism. Is that an inherited idea? Why did you want to break out of that mold?

SALEHE: I don't know if that's a Black household idea, or if it was just what the professional traditions were in 2010. I'd see my dad come home from work and he'd be in hard bottoms and slacks, so that would be this strange visual representation, or really nightmare, of what adulthood was. My only relationship with that style of dress prior to my job at Payless was for church, and it sucked. You would just want to rip that shit off as soon as you got home. I knew working in design was slightly more casual, but it was still an office. It was still a corporate office.

Being a "kid," I felt like I had to immediately transition and put on this mask of adulthood. And that mask consisted of hard bottom shoes, fucking khakis, and a button-down shirt of some type. That's what that was, and it was extremely uncomfortable. And in that time, I met Kanye. When I worked at Payless, I was wearing that outfit, and I believe that's why he didn't reach out to me. That wasn't the reason, but that was my grandiose reason back then—because he saw me in this fucking uniform that wasn't myself.

JINX: Did you resent the mold? It seems like you had an awareness that there was a path.

SALEHE: I look back now and I'm like, "Damn, I don't think any employer ever checked to see if I really went to the college I went to." But then at the same time, I think I really benefited from the path, because college taught me how to play the game and how to finesse and how to deal with obstacles and all those kinds of things. And it did give me some design tools. I don't think many, but some. I'm not sure I knew I was on some kind of path—I more so was just listening to my mom. I grew up in a strict Black household, so I got to go to high school, then I got to go to college. So it was more about just doing what I was supposed to be doing. Maybe I was brainwashed, but I'm very thankful for that brainwashing.

JINX: Speaking about your transitions from Payless to Yeezy and then Versace, there's a moment where you ask yourself—"What is my life?" Do you find yourself asking that often? And do you have an answer?

SALEHE: I just think my surreal experiences are really diverse. I used to say in interviews that I've drank tea with Donatella Versace in her home, and I've smoked blunts with Migos backstage. There's not many people on the planet—well, there's probably a few people on the planet that could say they did that. But I think that's an example of my versatility, the types of people I know, the places and circles I find myself in. What I find more ridiculous is the juxtaposition of ridiculous moment with ridiculous moment. They've been going on for so long, now I'm a little jaded to them. But I'm absolutely a voyeur and I'm extremely observant, and I love to see how the world works behind closed doors.

JINX: Observation seems like a superpower for you. But you have to have both—you have to be able to see something, an approach, an opportunity, and have the willingness to do it. I feel like you can't do what you do without optimism.

SALEHE: I don't know if it's optimism... The moments of unemployment or uncertainty of what is next are extremely scary. I don't think the descriptive word for those moments is optimism. It's more just drive and motivation. And I have the most plentiful fuel, which is passion. For a lot of people, their fuel is money or ego. For me, it's passion. I used to just run home and draw shoes for free. Now I get paid well to draw shoes, you know what I mean? And that still isn't necessarily fueling me doing it. It's still the passion. So that's what I hang my hat on.

JINX: What is the source of that? I have different motivators—sometimes that is inspiration, other times it can be ego or competition. So where does that tank of passion come from?

SALEHE: Luckily, I think if it is something that you loved when you were a kid, it can't disappear. If you loved fire trucks, you still love fire trucks. This is Jeff Staple's, so I can't claim it as mine, but Jeff always said that when it comes to taking on a project, so that you can really have that passion for it, it needs to hit two of the three Fs—and those three Fs are: fun, funds, and 'folio, for portfolio. If it hits two of those, then you're solid. I really follow that. Coupled with a passion for shoes that really stems from a deep and aggressive childhood obsession... Yeah, I fly high.

JINX: When you jump from project to project—say, from Payless to Cole Haan—each time you're iterative, you're adding things on. But what things are you shedding as well?

SALEHE: Well, I thank God that my early jobs were at companies that, in the grand scheme of things, were less significant to my overall career goals, because that allowed me to make mistakes. Maybe just getting too socially close to coworkers, or maybe not hitting deadlines properly, or not representing the company in the best light. Maybe using my company email to try to get product, or whatever it was. You want to make those mistakes at the companies that aren't as important, because if you make them at the big ones, it could severely affect your career. So I'm lucky that my career has really been a set of stairs. At each company, the same way that I took tools, I was able to self-edit and leave better.

JINX: Is there a point in time where you tripped on those stairs?

SALEHE: Absolutely. I was at Cole Haan, and we created the Lunargrand. Cole Haan was Nike-owned, so it was using Lunar technology. I got to be a part of all that because we were this three-person innovation team, with Jeff Henderson as the lead designer on that. At that point, we didn't know that Nike was about to sell Cole Haan. They let us know that they wanted us to create another hybrid shoe that this time used Air technology, and Jeff gave me the project. Whereas the Lunargrand was a group innovation project, this was my project. So I created a wingtip with a full 360 Air Max bottom. During the time, there weren't many company shoes for me to wear, so it really made me excited. I had been trying to orbit the sun that is Nike for my entire life, this was the closest I had gotten. I worked on the shoe for about eight months and then, I think because of the sell, they deaded the project. Any seasoned designer will know how it feels to work on something for almost a year, if not more, and then lose it—it's the worst feeling ever. And considering this was going to be me dipping my toe in the Nike pond, it was devastating.

At the time I had a blog—this was the time of blogs—and there was a little bit of traffic. I asked Jeff, "Yo, is it okay if I just put this on my blog at least, because I've worked on this?" He knew all the history of my feelings for Nike and he said, "Yeah, sure, whatever, not a big deal." So I post the shoe. It

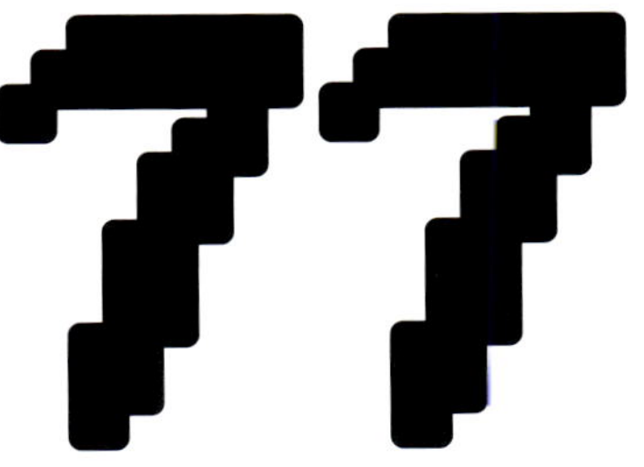

was a blog, so it wasn't like you got responses or comments, but I assume people liked it. But within maybe thirty minutes, Nike lawyers were calling Cole Haan. It was a huge deal. I would argue that there are some people that still harbor feelings from that day today. Based on the information on paper, I didn't do anything wrong, but at the same time, being someone that understands confidentiality, non-disclosure agreements, and all that kind of stuff now, that's an example of exercising a level of green in my early career.

JINX: But they exist out in the world, those Cole Haans with the Air Max sole, because of that?

SALEHE: Throughout my career, regardless of being told that I couldn't, I've found interesting ways to make shoes seen. Because I understand and value that the Internet is forever—our Google search page is forever—and one of the most valuable assets that we have, whether or not we realize it. So I was not willing to accept working on things and not getting the credit for it. That was at a point in my career where I needed my name attached to things. Now I ghost-design shoes. There's shoes for other brands, one of the big five brands, if you will, that are very hyped that I've designed, and the world doesn't know. And that's because I am doing business and I don't really care about the name recognition. But at that point, if I'd chosen some fucking laces on a shoe, I wanted the world to know. I honestly can't confirm, I don't remember, but I believe that shoe's been seen.

JINX: You've spoken about Jeff Henderson training you to disrupt—being able to fuck with product, in a way—and making you do these artistic tasks that maybe open up your mind or break molds again. Is there something you remember from back then that you still use for process today, to either actually make shoes or generate ideas?

SALEHE: Jeff was a Nike OG that worked there for eighteen years, I really viewed him in a certain light—maybe not like a god, but he worked for God. He would give me all these tasks that I thought were going to be things, but they were just missions for me to complete. It was really some Padawan shit, missions for me to complete just to get another tool to understand how to navigate corporate life or corporate obstacles or even just design tasks.

One was to create a boot—Cole Haan had a contract with the New York City Fire Department and we were going to make a Cole Haan boot for the firemen. Jeff told me to go and interview firemen, so I spoke to maybe fifteen around New York. I'd just walk up to firehouses. And even that was important, because now I'm stepping out of my comfort zone with this kind of safety net of just doing my job. It was arming me with a bunch of life tools and design tools. Doing your research is one of the first steps, and then figuring out an insight from that. I get my insight, which I realize for firemen's boots is about protection from fire and hard items and then the ability to be put on quickly—entry and exit, really quickly. I ended up creating a boot where the medial had this asymmetrical zip from the bottom of the shoe to the collar, so you could just zip it up, zip it open. Wasn't the most groundbreaking idea, but that was a project and I was really excited. And then I created an EVA outsole that was supposed to be flexible so they could move faster. Was it a good boot? No. But I was really thinking of all the aspects of what they need. So that was a perfect example of him just—he kind of broke down everything I knew about design and then built me up from a pure place.

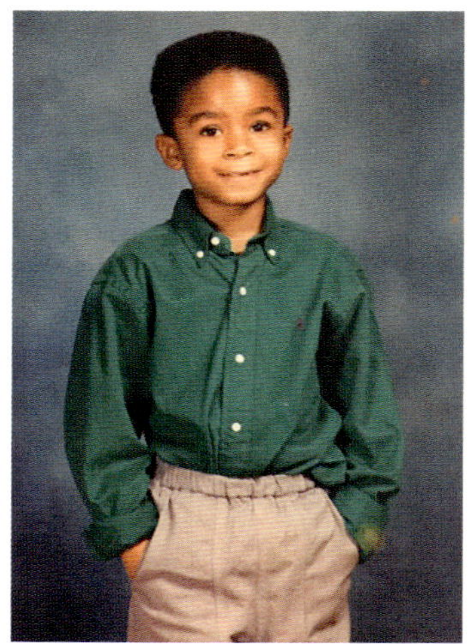

JINX: There's something very pragmatic about being able to go project by project and identify what tools you pulled out of each.

SALEHE: Well, it's funny you say that. People always tell me what my codes are. But the strange thing is, I'm designing from the gut, so I'm like, "Damn, really?" Even a couple years ago, I saw a picture of some New Balances with some Crocs and some ANTAs, and they were cohesive—all the pinks were kind of the same—and I was like, "I did not do that on purpose." I just chose that. I'm designing from such an authentic place. So I was thinking that for this book, I need to think of my process and analyze these moments in my career and create some codes, some tools.

JINX: I think they're there. Obviously, you can tell us, but people on the outside can tell you as well. When you follow someone's work personally—especially an individual creating, rather than Nike at large or another brand—I think the thread is clear. And there's also an iterative way you share information—even your ads, your campaigns, your packaging. I wonder if everyone thinks you're the nature guy? There's so much of that thread in what you do.

SALEHE: Well, that's kind of happened organically I guess, pun intended, because I moved to LA and started hiking. I'm not "wild nature guy," but it works for my brand. I just signed with Puma and am starting to tell basketball stories. I grew up balling my entire life. And it's kind of hilarious, because I'm from New York, I talk shit, but no one from this "Salehe Bembury designer life" that I live now has seen me hoop. So people think I'm ridiculous, but I actually hoop. My skills are court vision and I'm a shooter. I'm a sharp shooter. I don't have hops, but I can shoot.

JINX: That's exciting, because it's going to feel different to people. And I see threads between the Chain Reaction and what you're doing. "Any player can become a star in the right system" is a basketball term. But the way that works in the ecosystem is with the right product. It happened for Crocs: I was not wearing Crocs. They had a certain connotation. Yours were my first pair of Crocs, I'm sure you've heard that several times. Good design, and then on top of that, great marketing—which has to be built on good design, because great marketing without good design is content. But when it all goes together, it's next level, it's that feeling you're talking about, being a kid watching that Freestyle commercial. I don't remember any of those sneakers from that commercial. Doesn't matter.

SALEHE: I do.

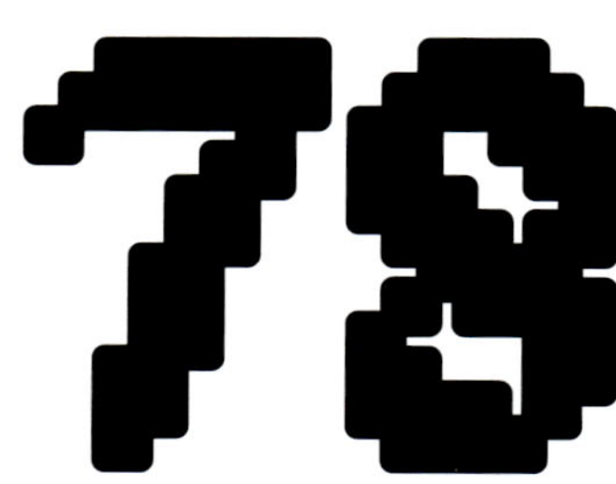

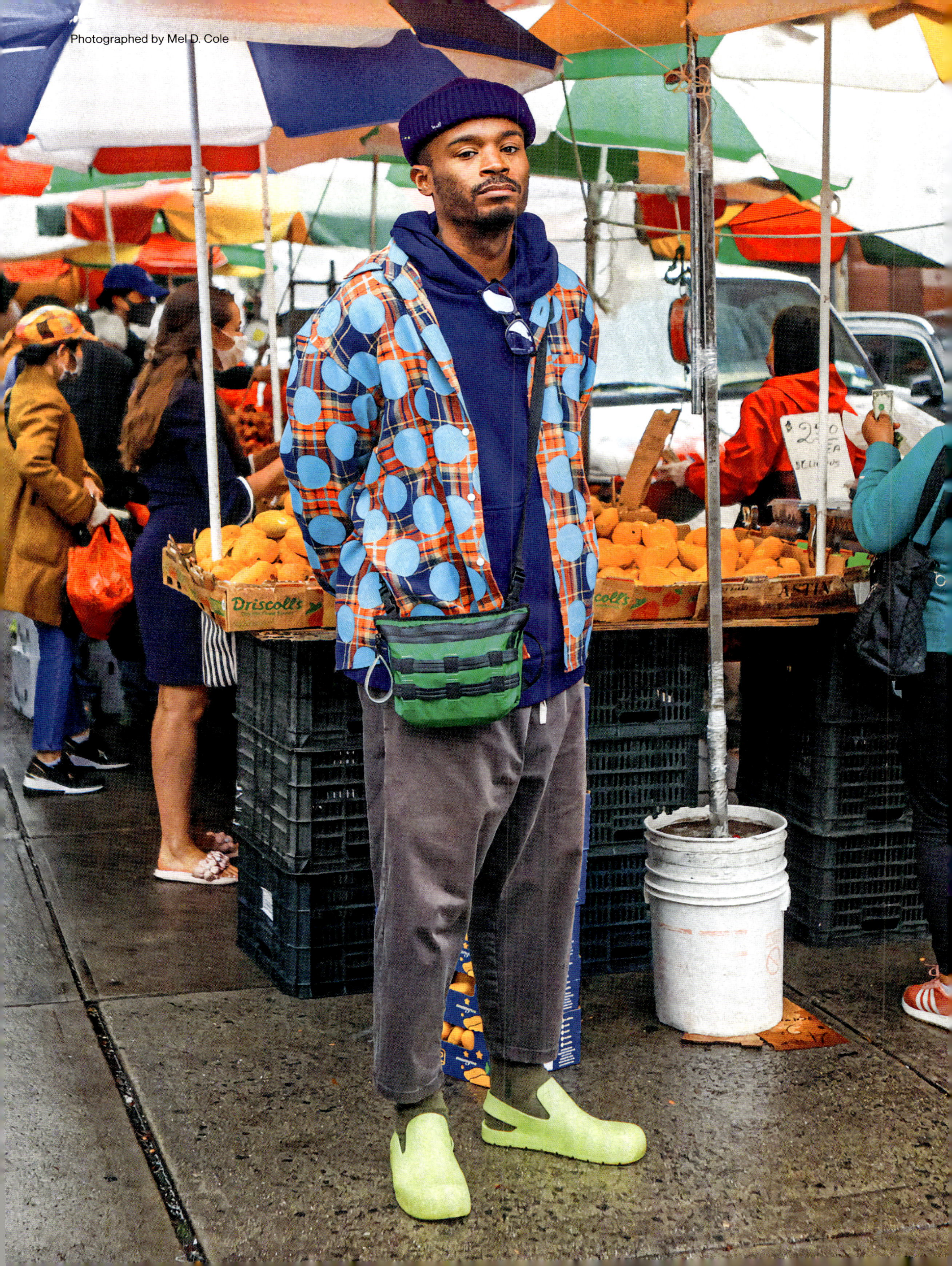

Photographed by Mel D. Cole

80

VERSACE (2017)

SHOOT YOUR

SHOT

VERSACE
SHOOT YOUR SHOT

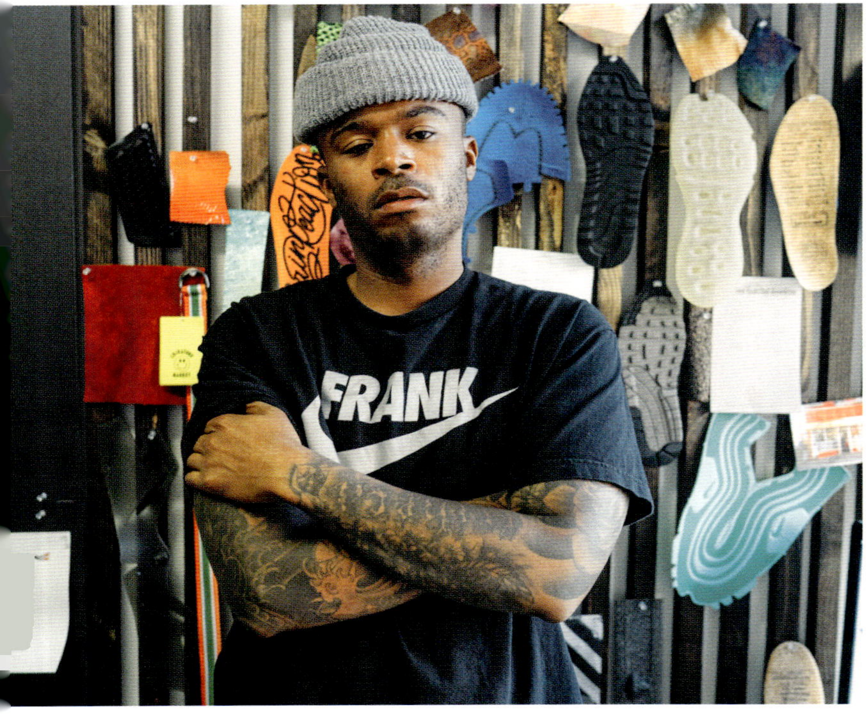

1

When Yeezy ended, I was in Los Angeles without a job. At the time, Yeezy was the top of the mountain. So where do you go when you've been eating at the top of the mountain for the past year?

My funds were dwindling, and I had to start freelancing for brands. I freelanced for the brand Clae. They were a mid-tier skate brand, it was only a few months, but I made ends meet. One shoe I touched made it onto the market. I did some work with Android Homme and Javier Laval–entry-level design work just to make some dollars. Then, at the end of that year, things were getting scary. I only had a couple months' rent left, I didn't really have a job in sight, and I had to ask myself–what do I do?

It's not as if homelessness was around the corner–at least I had my parents to move in with–but it felt like I was failing at adulthood. And I was defeated, because I have wanted to be a footwear designer my entire life, and I had been one for the better part of a decade, and now, having been at the top of the mountain with things feeling very bright, I found myself unemployed. I didn't feel like I had value because it didn't seem like anyone wanted me, and I didn't feel like I had a purpose. In retrospect I would say that we should not think that we are our professions; but mine is my passion and it's something I've been obsessed with and passionate about since way before I saw it as a profession or a means to make money. Footwear was something I would run home to do before I got paid to do it.

2

At the end of that year–defeated, unemployed, on my couch in my underwear essentially–I was on LinkedIn, and in the "people you may know" section I saw a Versace design director named Dean Quinn. I reached out to him and explained that sneakers were a multi-billion-dollar industry. Growing up, we all wore Adidas, New Balance, Nike, and Reebok, and we knew it was really about the logo on the quarter panel of the shoe. And now, because of collaborations that existed about ten years ago–Raf Simons and Adidas, or Nike and Comme Des Garçons, or when Balenciaga started making sneakers that the common sneaker consumer could appreciate–now the billion-dollar consumer was aware of the fact that fashion houses have the ability to participate in the footwear space. I explained that with Versace being a brand with such overt and recognizable brand DNA and heritage, it would be extremely easy to translate that ethos into a footwear program and, more specifically, a sneaker program.

This was not my one shot. This was fishing. I had sent out a lot of other messages. At that time I was also in talks with Zara and was waiting to hear from them. It really wasn't about working in high fashion, or working here or there–it was about a paycheck.

3

Three days later, Donatella Versace emailed me herself and said she loved my ideas and wanted me to come to Milan and tell her more. I was completely stunned by the fact that I got a response, period, let alone by the fact that it was from Donatella. I didn't go to school for fashion, so while I was familiar with the image of this blonde woman from "fashion" that wears black, and I obviously knew Versace as a house, I didn't exactly know who she was. That is not intended disrespectfully; but it's important to understand that I didn't have the education of what she had accomplished and who she was. I really was coming into this situation somewhat ignorantly, which I believe helped me.

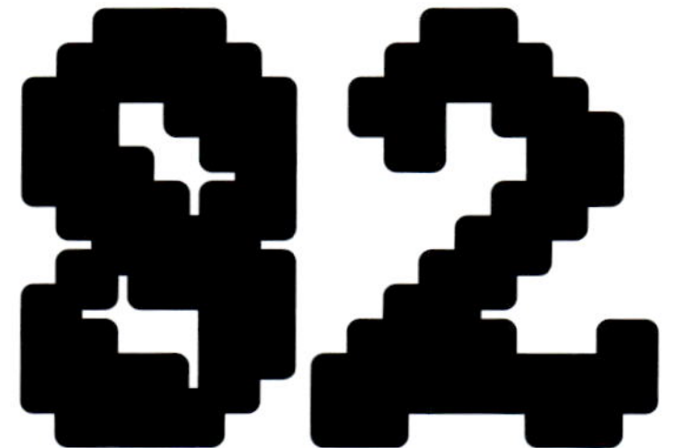

I started to put together a kind of trend presentation of what I thought was cool. Initially I wasn't going to do more than take some screenshots off Hypebeast, because I thought that fashion houses weren't looking to places like that for inspiration. But strangely, in the weeks leading up to my first meeting, I had some extremely influential conversations with a diverse group of people in my life. I was told that I should put sample design work in the presentation, and that I shouldn't assume that they knew I had the ability to design, or design through their lens. I was told that I should visit the Versace store and see how they merchandised, see what they were selling and ask how it was selling—do my research on the brand in that sense. Someone reminded me that there weren't too many people that look like me in the high fashion space, and that an opportunity like this was bigger than me, that I'd be paving a way with this and needed to take it seriously and lead with the right foot. What was going to be a three- or four-page presentation turned into a 40-page one, ultimately breaking down their business, their sneakers, and presenting a lot of information that I was able to regurgitate naturally just because I've been a footwear fanatic for such a long period of time. I was really just opening their eyes to the potential of what their sneaker business could be.

4

I flew to Milan and met with Donatella one-on-one in her office, which was extremely regal. I was surrounded by gold and Greca patterns. She walked in with her giant cup. I showed the presentation to her on my laptop, and as I presented, she loved it so much that she started to bring a couple of other people in. By the end, she let me know that she loved me, she wanted me to work for her, and she wanted to know how it would work. She asked if I wanted to consult, she asked if I wanted to move to Milan, she asked if I wanted to design something for a season—she was extremely flexible. And because she was so flexible, I made an attempt at achieving the most convenient professional situation I could think of, which was having my own design studio in Los Angeles, paid for by Versace, and then flying to Milan once a month for meetings, fashion shows, sample approvals, and all the other things that would come with the gig. She immediately agreed. I went outside and either actually or damn-near cried, because to me, I just saw a paycheck: I saw security and safety and food and a roof.

I've told this story to many, who see my appointment there as this kind of 4th-quarter poetic accomplishment—that I went for it, bet on myself. I can see that perspective. But from my own perspective it truly was a paycheck. A week or two after I got the Versace job, Zara hit me up and offered me a job. If Versace hadn't offered me that position, I would absolutely have accepted the Zara job. It's interesting how easily your life can change with a simple decision.

5

The Versace job began. I had an extremely small studio space in Downtown Los Angeles. It didn't even have its own bathroom. I could reach the other side of it in about eight steps. However, after a decade of working in the corporate office space with coworkers, lunchtimes, rules, having to show up at certain times, and reporting to a boss, I felt like I had reached the promised land. Obviously I still had a boss in Donatella and in Versace as a company, and still had emails to respond to and meetings to take—but on a day-to-day basis, what I did and when did not necessarily matter. I was trusted to execute based on my experience. I really felt like I had made it at that point. I forget what the paycheck was, but it was definitely a good one—I was flying business class to Milan, which was not something I had ever done. My life had really somewhat changed overnight.

In some of the earlier trips to Milan, the city felt like a completely different planet. I remember I had to go to McDonald's just to feel a sense of normalcy or a sense of home. Once a month I would spend seven or eight days in Milan as a nine-to-five employee, and during that time I would get the face time that I did not get to have while in America. I would also visit factories, review materials and suppliers, take meetings, and all that good stuff. Back in

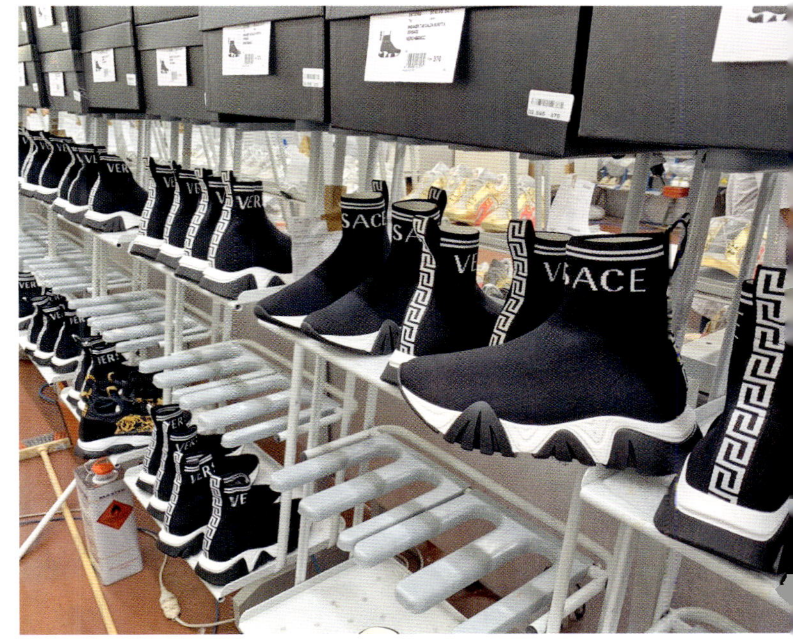

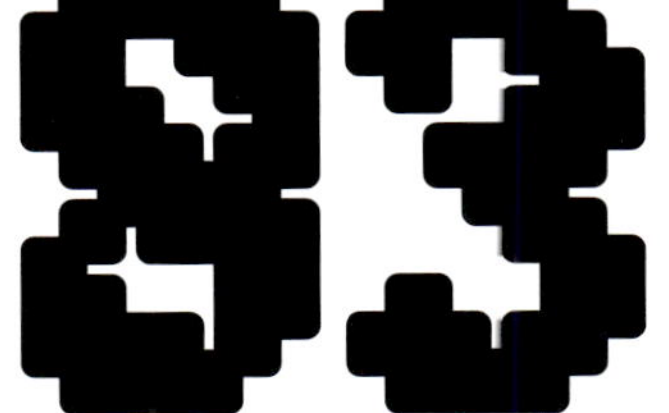

Los Angeles, I would spend my time designing and creating footwear.

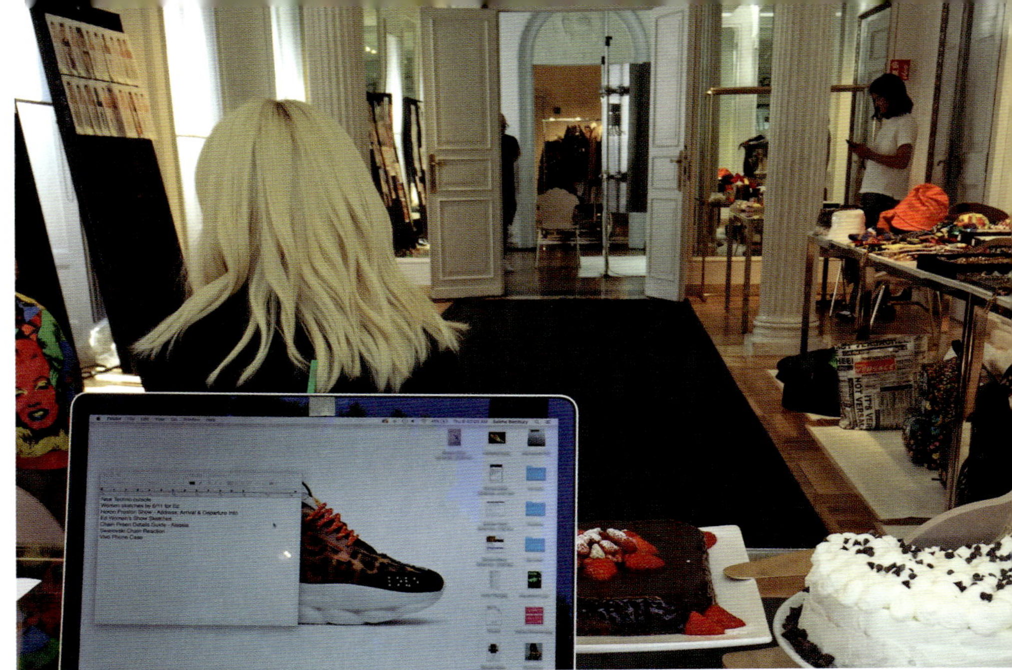

The first task I was given was to create a sneaker that simultaneously took the sneaker industry, the fashion world, and the culture by storm. This was easier said than done. However, given my experience and my lifelong obsession with footwear, I was sure that I was the correct individual to take on the task. I had to maintain a very thin line and careful balance between overt, innovative, and new; and commercial, familiar, and nostalgic. I was looking to have a conversation with many different consumers: the existing Versace consumer, the younger sneaker consumer, and then, to quote Virgil, the "tourist," the person that's just popping up for the day and doesn't know what's going on. So how do you have a conversation with all of them?

The first thing I did was break down the signature details of Versace. The baroque print, the Greca, the medusa, and all the elements by which we as the consumer at whatever level would be able to identify the product and associate it with Versace as a house. After doing that, I began to identify if any of these elements could work functionally. This was me using one of my industrial design tools; we were often taught to think with utility and function. After conducting this exercise, I figured out that the chain–and specifically the Cuban link chain, because of its flat elements–could function as an outsole. I initially started playing with clay, and then I sat down with my good friend NAME, who helped me make a 3D model. That model was what I presented to Donatella the first time I showed her my work as an employee. I gave an entire presentation on the DNA of Versace as I understood it. I had other shoes to present as well, but this was kind of the peacock product–a peacock spreads its feathers, everyone looks–and I simply handed her the outsole.

I've since come to learn that the extreme advantage that 3D printing and design gives us is that instead of having to point to a piece of paper and talk through a design, you can simply hand an object over to someone and say nothing at all. That simplification in design communication makes the translation of an idea a lot easier, especially when you're speaking to someone that may not have the experience or the knowledge about what you're trying to present. In this case, presenting a sneaker to someone who has prioritized high fashion most of her life–the model made it easy. I handed it to her, she understood it immediately, she absorbed it immediately, and she approved it immediately. And that was the birth of the Chain Reaction.

6

After I created the Chain Reaction, I realized that one of the most important things to do with this shoe was to inject it into the culture. You cannot simply create a good shoe and expect it to take off, especially if it's coming from an outlet that the consumer is not used to seeing that kind of product come from. If Coca-Cola all of a sudden started making cars, you probably wouldn't drive them. I explained this to Donatella and she gave me 100 pairs of the shoe to personally seed to a network of people I did not yet have. However, I was familiar with the idea and the success that seeding could have. I put my boots to the ground and hit up every individual that I knew who had any direct or indirect connection with a celebrity. One individual that helped me a lot during that time was Edith Bo, who did an amazing job of putting me in touch with people. And like the Versace job itself, it goes to show the importance of asking for something. I barely knew Edith back then and she was still so kind to me, and I will never forget that–so if you're reading this Edith, thank you very much.

One of the people Edith put me in touch with was 2 Chainz. We had a call while I was in Milan, and I told him I had a shoe that really aligned with his brand. I had him sign an NDA, I showed him the shoe, and just said: "Holy shit, I can't believe it's made of two chains," which was both a joke and extremely literal. We continued to talk and we clicked immediately. He really respected that I was in the position that I was in,

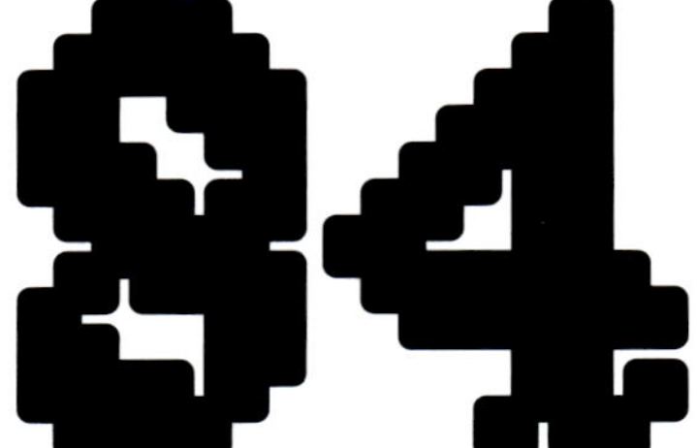

given that there aren't too many people that look like us in my position, and he wanted to learn from me, as I did him.

The first step in both our budding relationship and his new relationship with the brand was attending the fashion show. We invited 2 Chainz to come to Milan so I could bring him to the first Versace show with me. I met him at his hotel, and he was smoking, there was jewelry and clothing everywhere—in my head I was thinking, "This is fucking insane: I work for Versace and I'm in Milan in 2 Chainz's hotel room—again, what is my life?"

Then it was time to head to the show. I had my Chain Reactions on, he was fully fitted by Versace. I started to get nervous because of my phobia of being the center of attention. There was a lot of traffic on the way, and we learned that they were actually holding up the show for us. When we finally got there, photographers started going crazy—they started yelling "Tity Boi," which surprised me just because that was 2 Chainz's original rapper name, and I didn't expect people in Italy to have that kind of hip-hop knowledge. We walked in, and I expressed just so much gratitude to him for being a part of this and coming and helping me make a splash stepping into this new job. I could tell that this was just another day for him, he wasn't fazed in the least. As we walked into the show I was like a deer in the headlights, so nervous, I didn't know what the fuck was going on, and 2 Chainz just looked like he was going to the supermarket.

And then the show happened. The Chain Reaction had an insane response. It went on to be one of the top two or three sneakers in high fashion. Through my personal seeding I got it to a lot of people in the industry that mattered from a fashion perspective. And that really helped move the needle and inject it into the culture.

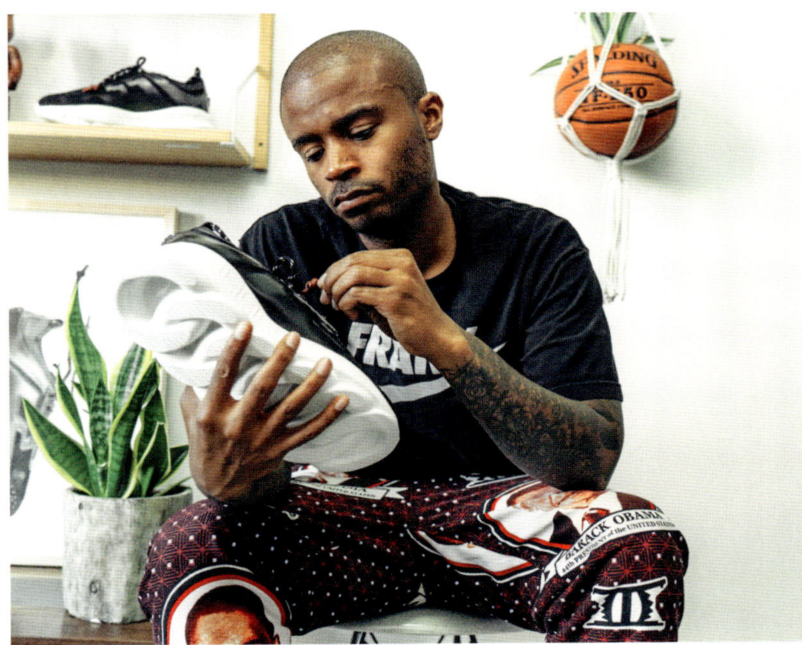

7

Now my goal was to create other footwear silhouettes that successfully filled out a strong sneaker program. We had to create the perfect runner, the perfect boot, the perfect casual slip-on sneaker. And if we were able to do that successfully, the next task would be more about color and material than a silhouette quest, which is what many brands find themselves focusing on.

While doing that I simultaneously had to maintain the momentum—create moments, launch collaborations, and continue to engage this new and young sneaker audience that was starting to peep over the fence at what we were doing. Some of those projects were collaborations with Kith, 2 Chainz, Migos, United Arrows, and Swarovski crystal; and Takashi Murakami's Sneakers for Breakfast project.

On a personal level, this was the first time I'd created a shoe that was garnering the kind of attention it was. At Yeezy, while I had created the military boot and the combat boot, these were Kanye's ideas and I was used as a pencil to bring them to fruition. While I one-hundred-percent take credit for that work, I ultimately was helping Kanye realize his brainchildren. In the case of the Chain Reaction, it was solely my creation—this sneaker that the fashion world is obsessed with, the sneaker community is obsessed with, and for lack of a better term, the influential crowd is obsessed with.

In previous years I had been someone that was always looking at the Paris street snaps for inspiration, and to learn, and now I was seeing my shoe worn by these people at Pitti and at fashion weeks around the world. It was a surreal time for me, but I wasn't stopping to appreciate or think about those things because I was still moving at 1000 miles a minute. I was there for a paycheck. There's a lot of poetry and emotion and thought that can be put into something after the fact—but in the moment it was about go, go, go, what's next.

At that time I was also still alone, essentially doing the work of what would typically be a four- or five-person team by myself. After an extremely

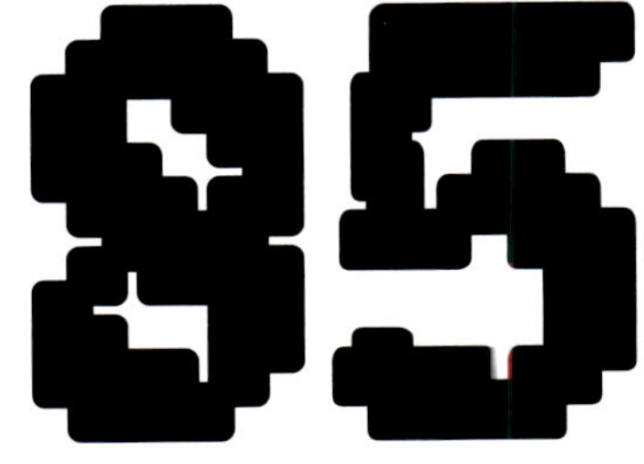

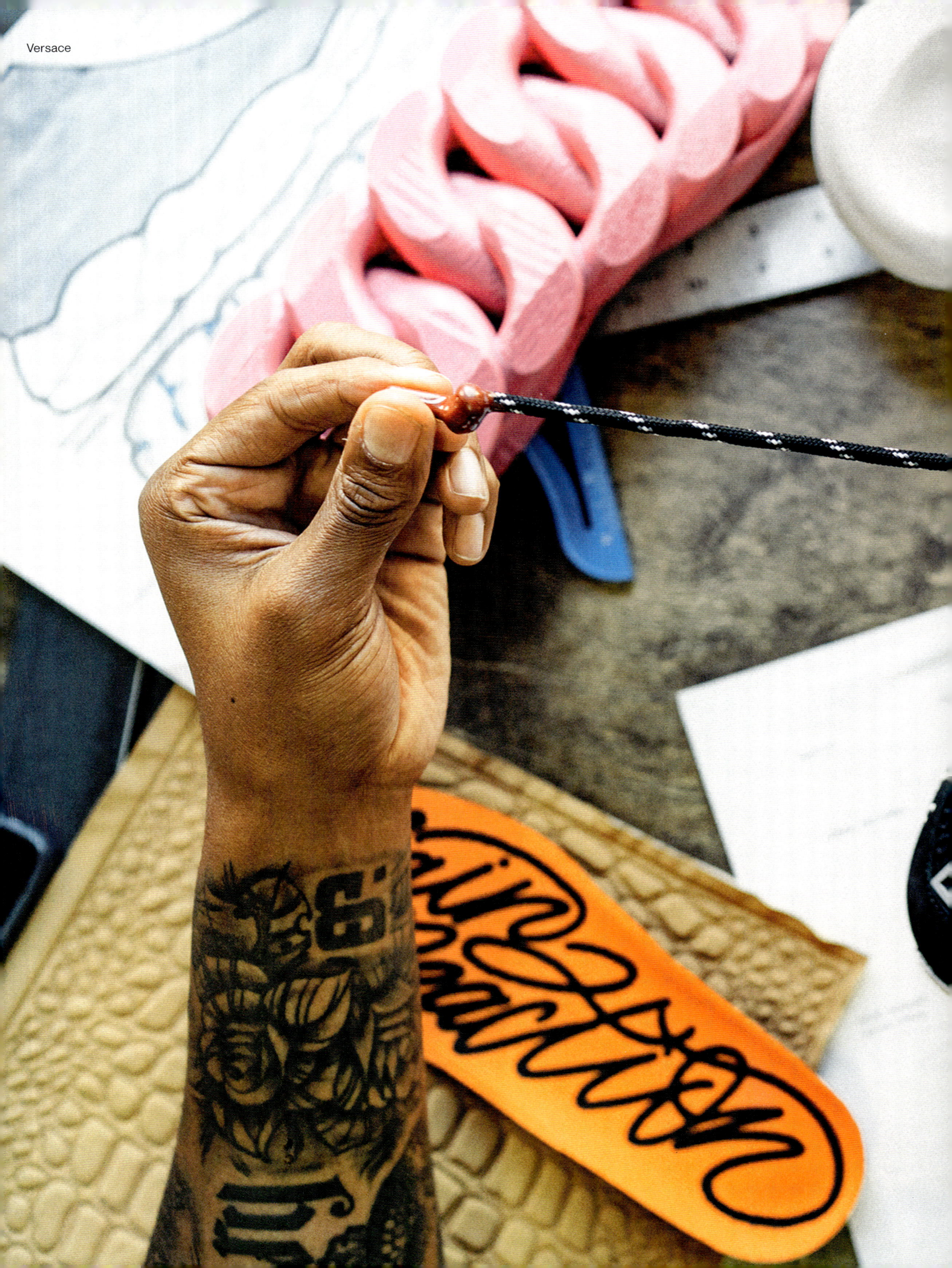

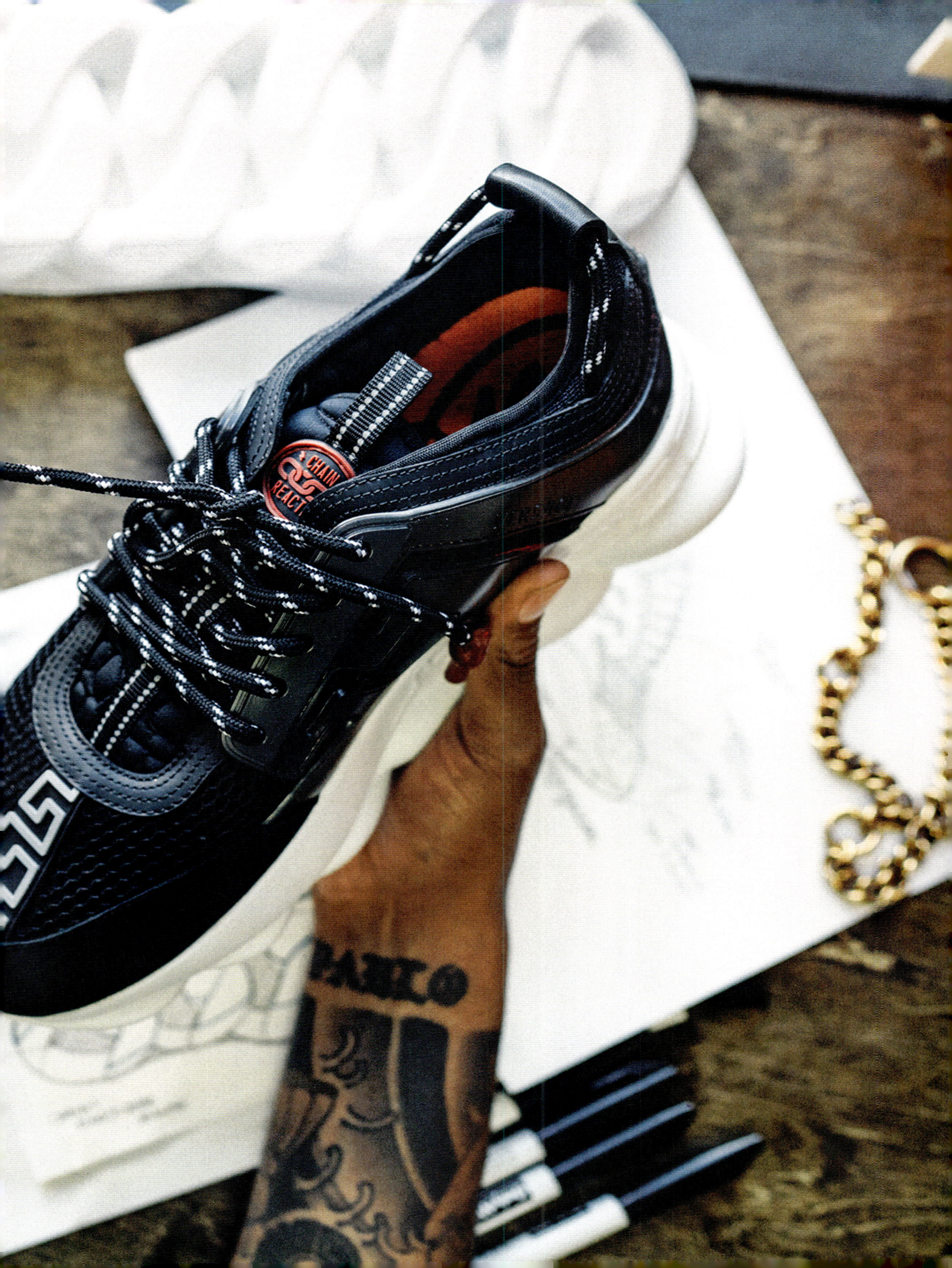
CHAIN
PABLO

successful year of sales that Versace had never seen from sneakers or even footwear before, they appointed me the head of men's footwear. From that point it was my task to create the formal footwear offering as well. I asked if I could hire an assistant designer, because we would be doing the work of about eight people, and I did not have the bandwidth to do all of that.

So I hired Fardin Hazratizadeh, who came from a short stint at New Balance. He was a very green designer, and I essentially had to do to him what Jeff Henderson had done to me. That in itself was rather poetic, because a lot of the things Jeff had told me were going to happen in my career, or warned me about, or armed me for, did happen—and now I found myself with this wide-eyed young designer in my studio looking to me to show him that same path. I wasn't used to being that person, I was used to being the padawan. NAME was extremely talented but his abilities needed some fine tuning and some challenging. I had to grow him, he needed to learn a lot before he could truly contribute to the operation.

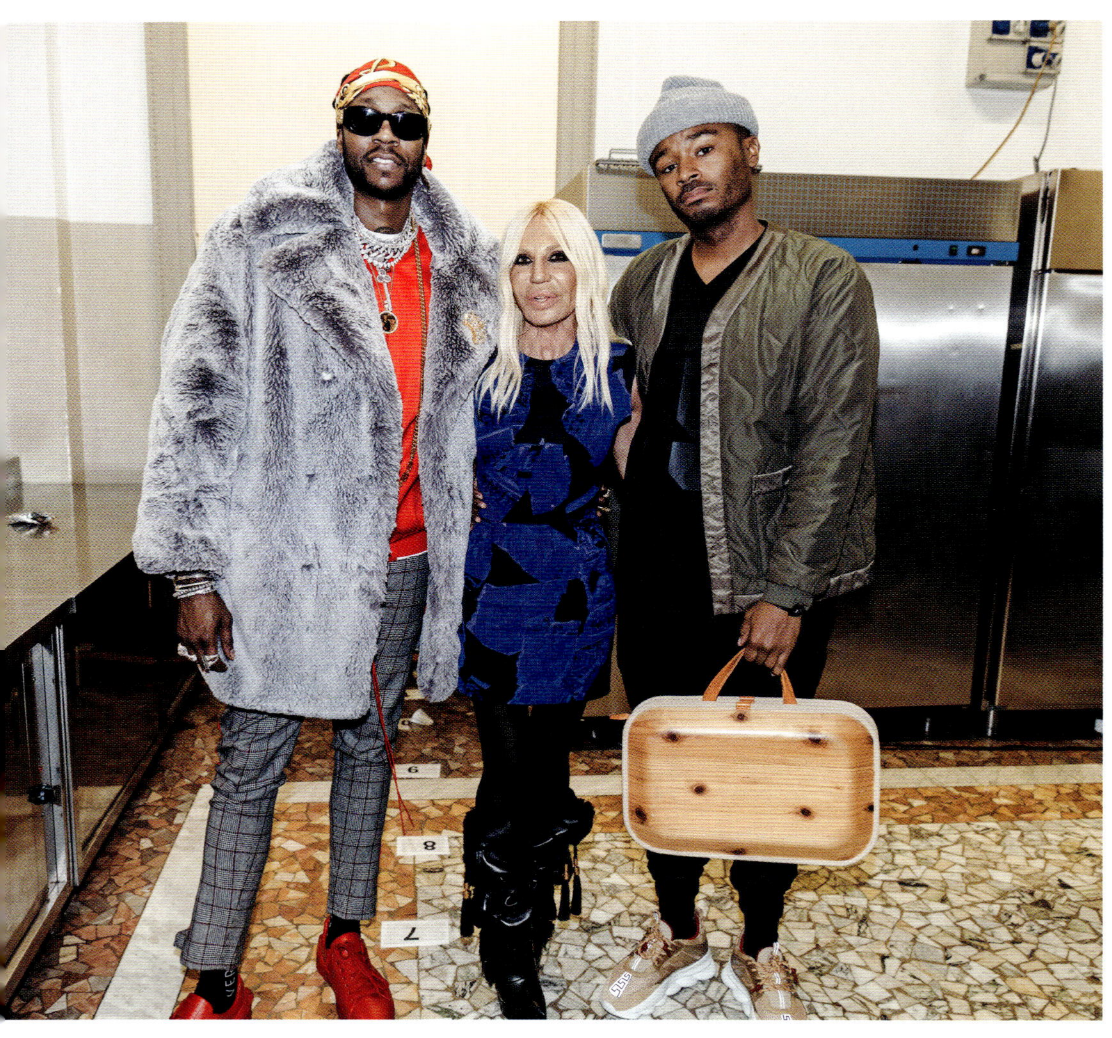

But I had help, and that was extremely important. We had to coexist in an extremely small studio space, which was still better than being in a massive office space with coworkers and having to participate in the rituals of an office environment. So we moved forward and designed all the sneakers and formal footwear for Versace. There continued to be an uprise in sales, and the Chain Reaction was one of the top selling products, if not the top selling product, at Versace for a few seasons, which is unheard of for a fashion house—short of McQueen and their Stan Smith, maybe. It was a lot of success, success, success.

8

At this point, some of my peers, some of my friends, and even my lawyer began telling me that given all the success I've had at Versace, I had the ability to go out and be on my own.

To me this did not seem realistic. I was taught and conditioned that you work for a paycheck, that you're happy with that paycheck, and that you work harder so your paycheck will increase. But I never saw myself as someone that would put my name on something for people to wear it. In previous years, I had received attention for my involvement in projects, and that seemed like a comfortable space that I wanted to see evolve. However, being the brand was something I never saw for myself, and something that was also extremely intimidating.

However, in an effort to keep me creatively motivated, and also I think to let me be somewhat free, Versace allowed me to conduct two collaborations while retaining my position as head of men's footwear. Those collaborations were with Anta, a sportswear brand from China, and New Balance. The sneakers I created for these collaborations did well—the New Balance sold out immediately, and the Anta was an extremely successful collaboration for their brand, which did not do many. And this taught me that I had an audience, that there were people out there that would buy things because my name was on them. Even though that was initially uncomfortable, now I see that that step was an extremely important one for me to take. This was the proof of concept that I could, in fact, move on.

I remember being backstage at one of the Versace fashion shows. Donatella was getting ready, everyone was getting ready, when all of a sudden this crowd of people gathered, and Jonathan Anderson was back. He had been a designer at Versace and had moved on to do great things with JW Anderson as well as with Loewe, and he was back and everyone was so excited. He was there to say hello to Donatella, and they took photos together, and in that moment I daydreamed—how crazy would it be to work at Versace and then leave Versace, become a name in the space, and then return as that name and be greeted as such? It was a next step in this journey that I was never aware of, nor did I think I wanted, but was just cool to witness. Then, a year or two after I left Versace myself, I did come back as a name in the space. I've made some successful collaborations that have sold out and really been at the pinnacle of the sneaker conversation. And now I was coming back, and it felt as if I was about to experience this JW Anderson moment. I went to the show, and afterward I saw Donatella starting to slowly walk out, with a massive crowd of people surrounding her trying to take photos. So I took advantage of the fact that I was a 6'3" male in Italy, and I slowly slid to the front of the group. But Donatella didn't see me, nor did her PR person. I eventually tapped her on the shoulder; she looked at me, a millisecond of confusion before she realized it was me, and then had a massive smile on her face. We had a big hug, it was a great moment. And not one photographer took a photo. Maybe they didn't know who I was, maybe they didn't give a fuck, I don't know. But I had to capture this moment, so I handed my phone to a security guard who basically took one or two photos without even looking—and didn't even include my shoes.

This is just a story that proves you can't really plan how things are going to play out. It's just not in your hands. Either way, regardless of that, it was great to return as a designer in the space. People were happy to see me and happy for me, proud of me, and it was very full circle.

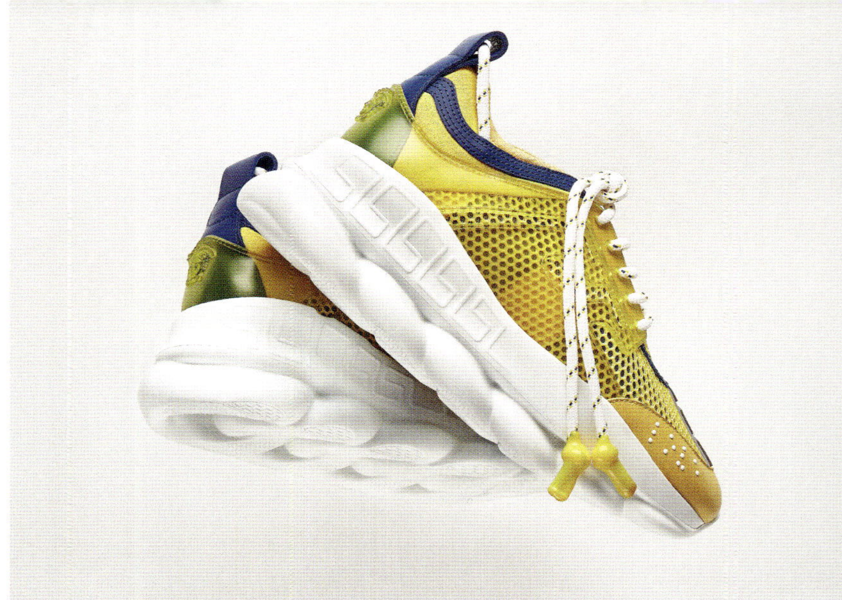

9

I took a job for a paycheck. It happened to be an amazing job. I capitalized, I created a lot of different moments that you would not normally see in high fashion. I was inspired by looking at what Virgil was doing at Louis Vuitton, which was kind of happening simultaneously. And the level of freedom was very similar. This is actually something I learned at Cole Haan: when you report to the top and you have a kind of obscure job where no one knows exactly what it is, you can really do anything you want. So that was the case at Versace: I reported directly to Donatella. I had many obstacles but none of them were real because I reported to Donatella. The fact that I was the only Black person, and one of few straight and few American people there, meant that I was fighting against a lot of anthropological obstacles that may not have existed for me if I'd checked some of the boxes on that list. It's very human for people not to like what's different, for people not to like change or a shift in culture; but overall my experience there was extremely positive. When I arrived at Versace I started garnering attention and press, which is something that was not typically allowed at the brand, but they for whatever reason allowed me to get that attention. A lot of those moments allowed me to step out and become an independent designer. So I have to thank Donatella for giving me the platform to tell my story, and to stand out, and to have the freedom to create beautiful footwear with her.

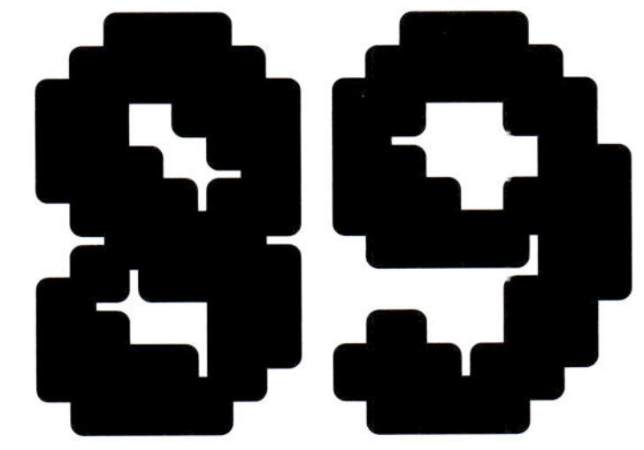

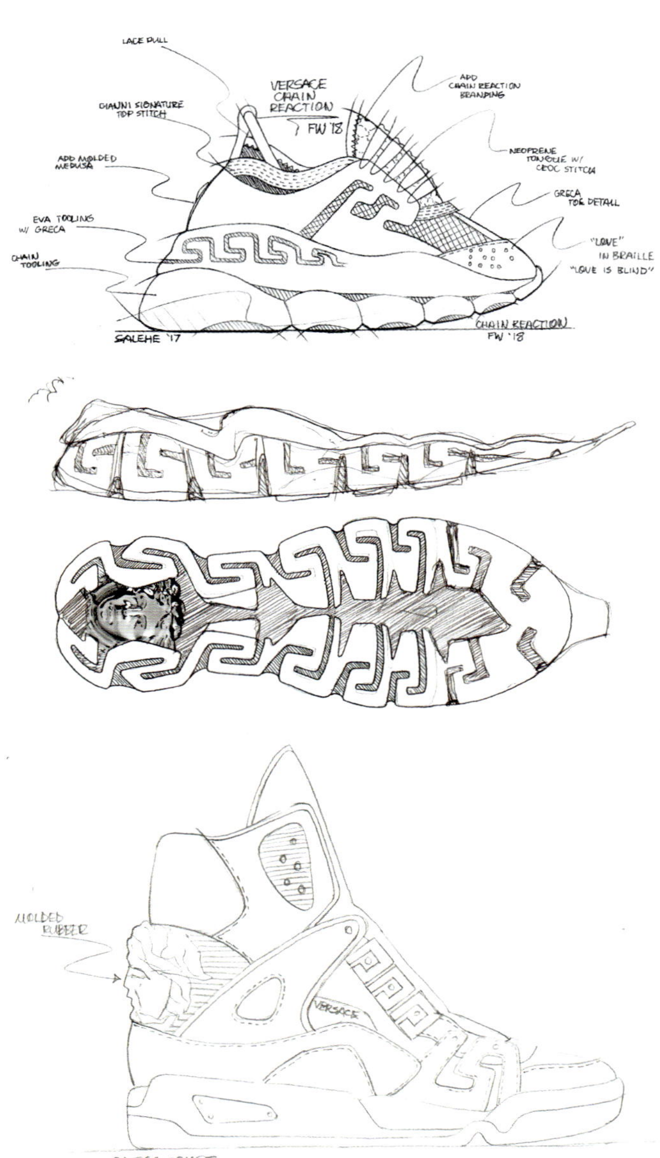

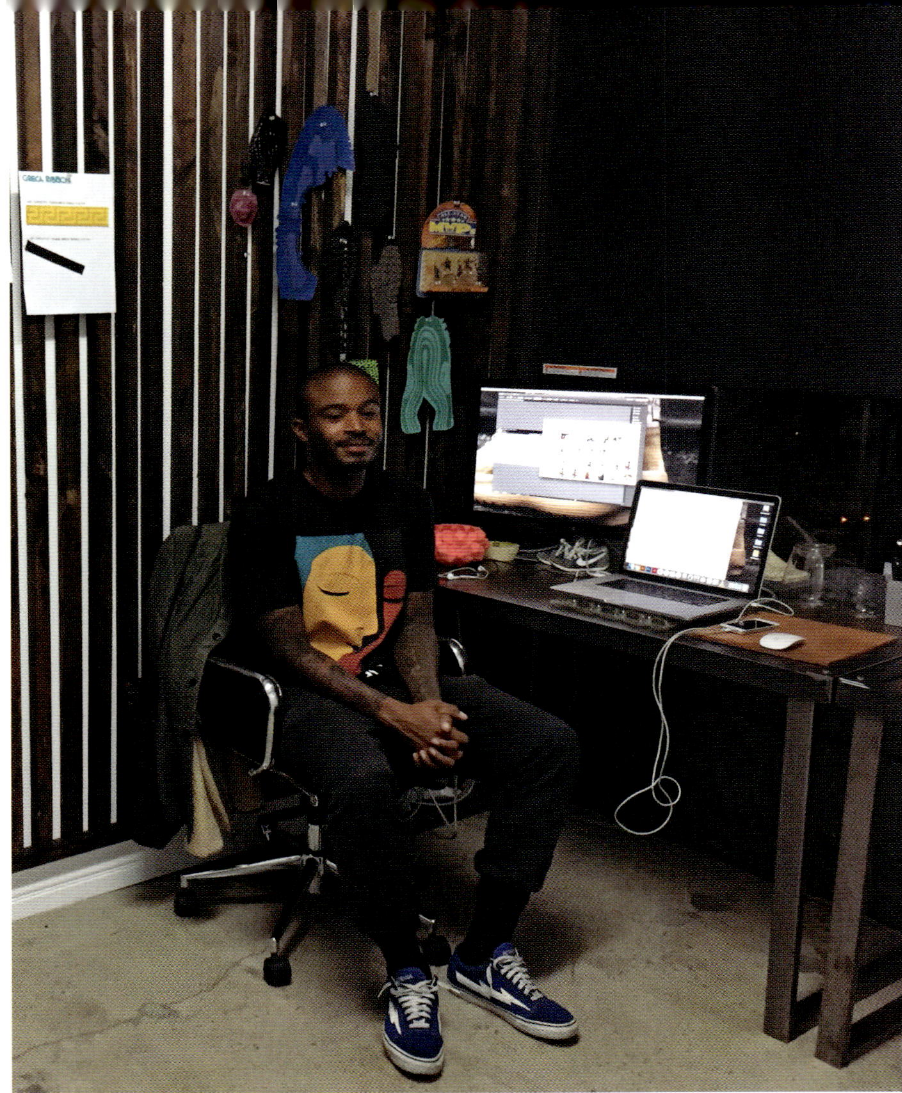

Salehe Bembury in his personal design studio

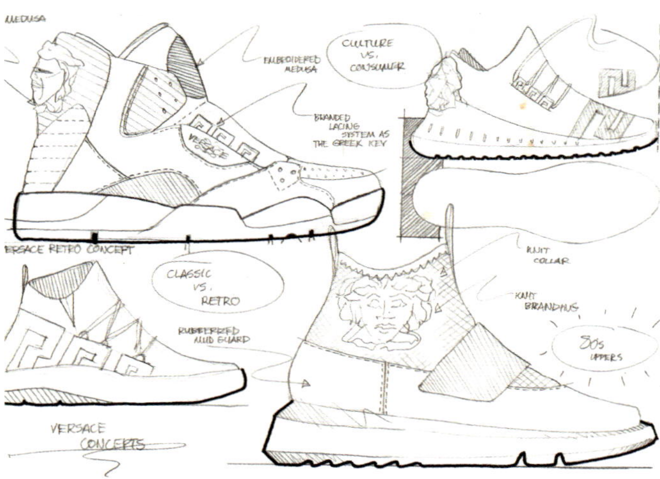

Versace sketches

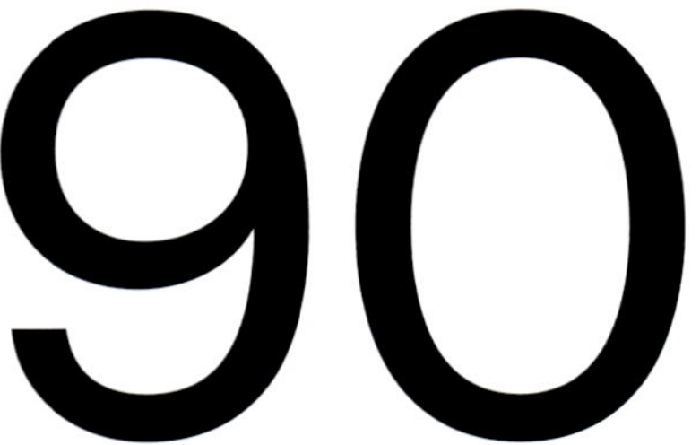

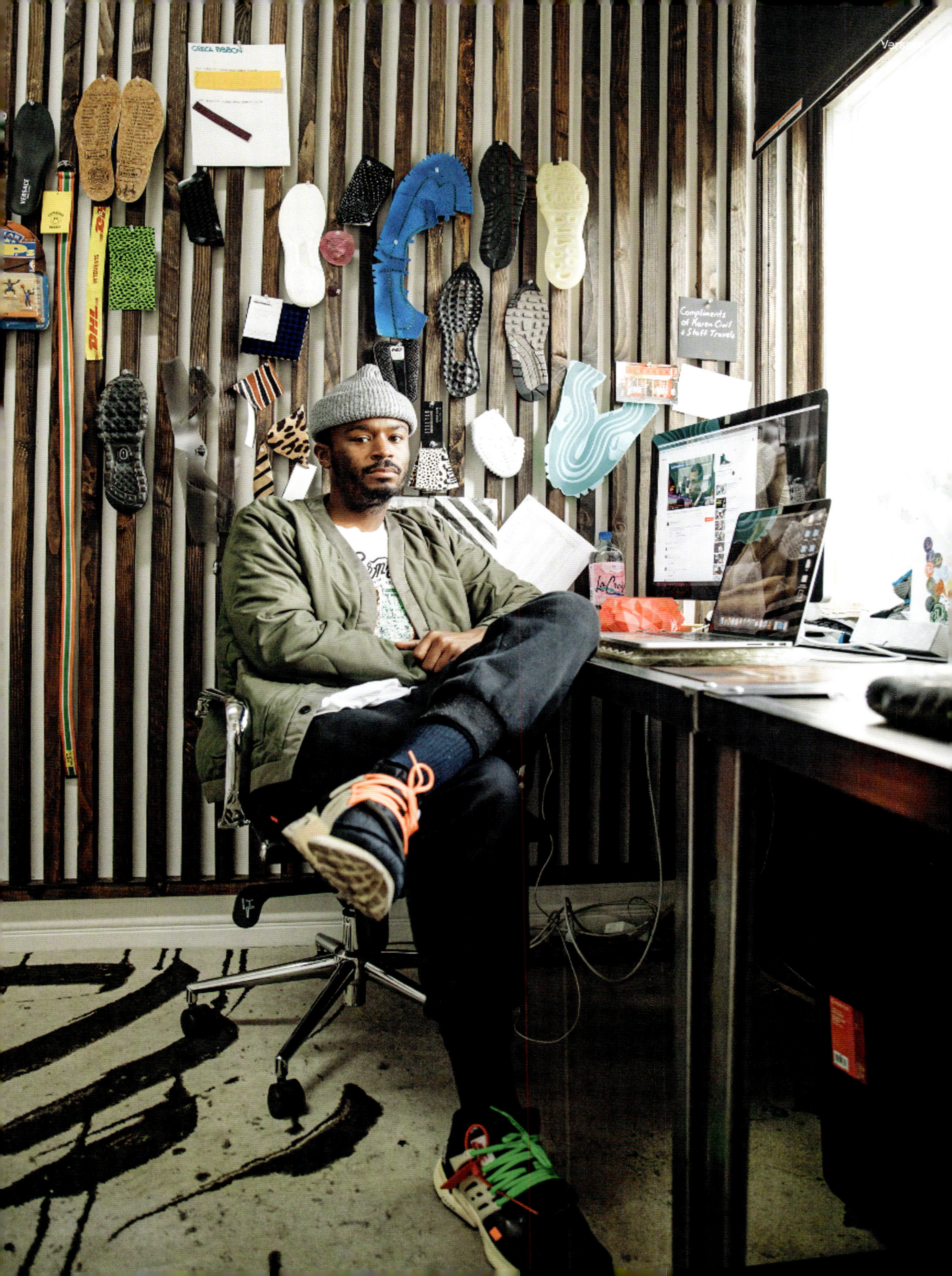
GRECA RIBBON
DHL
Compliments
of Karen Civil
& Staff Travels

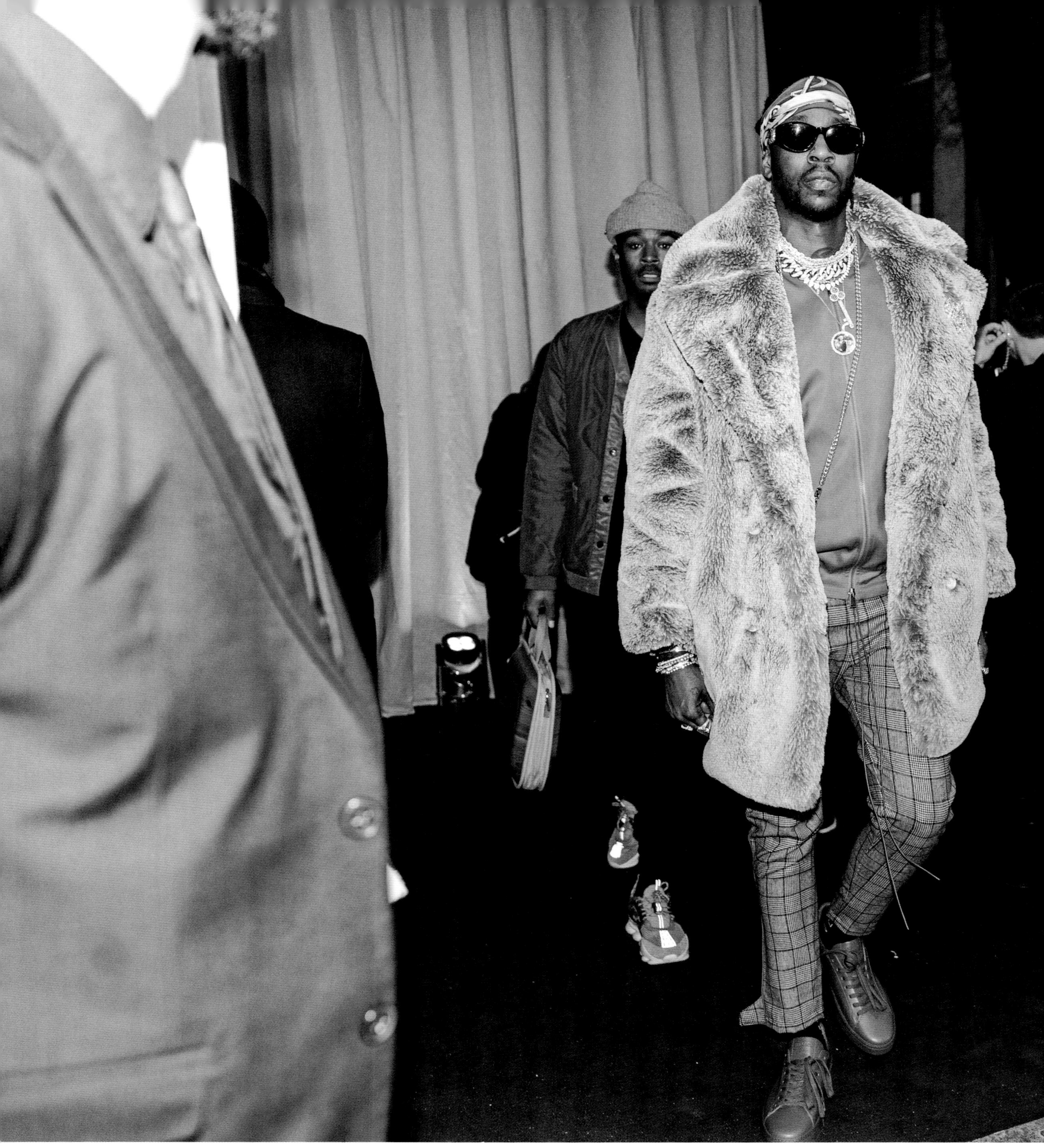

Salehe Bembury and 2 Chainz - Versace FW18 fashion show - Milan, Italy

92

(2017)

VERSACE

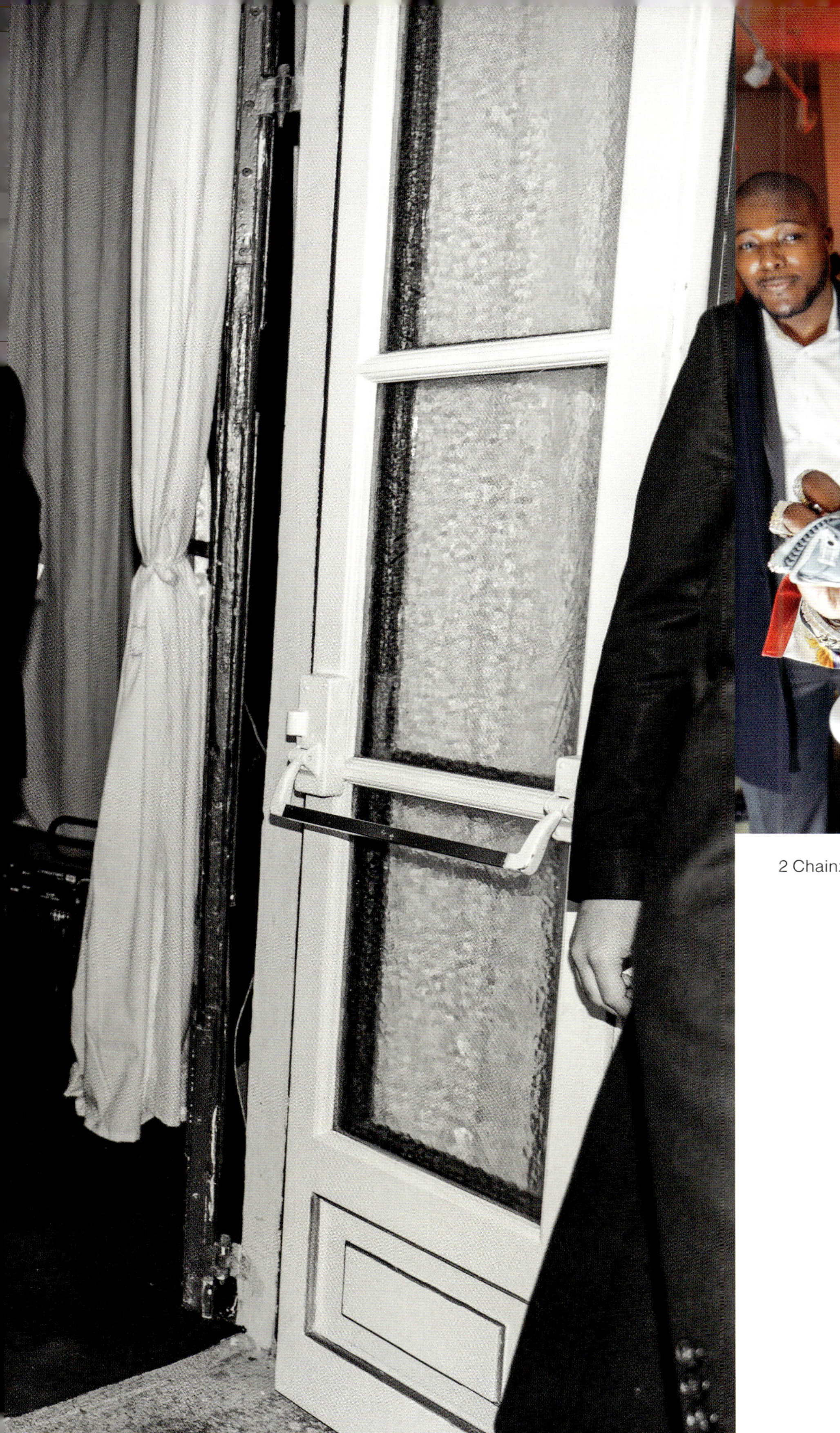

2 Chainz at 2 Chainz x Versace Chain Reaction Atlanta launch

93

VERSACE (2017)

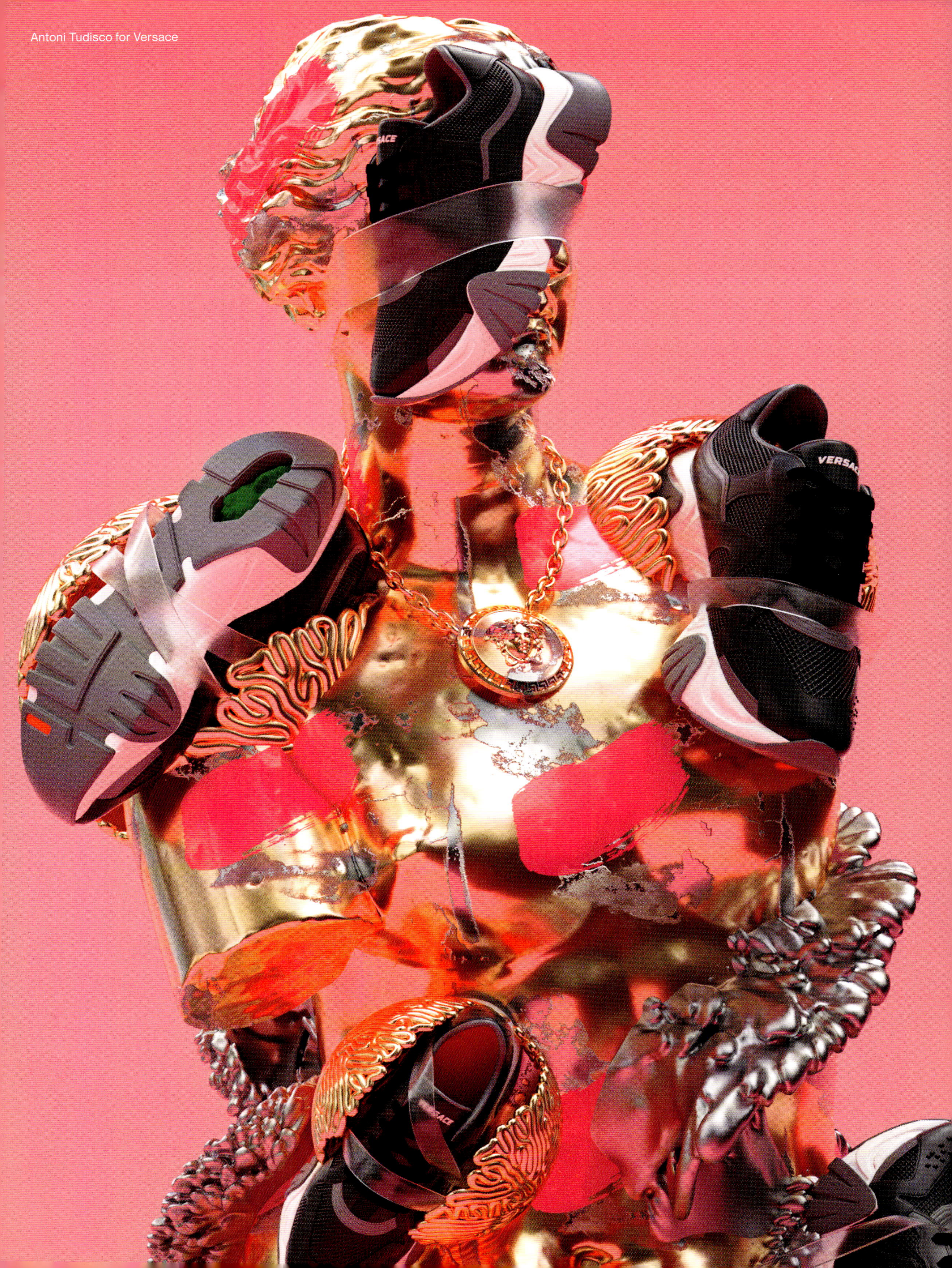
Antoni Tudisco for Versace

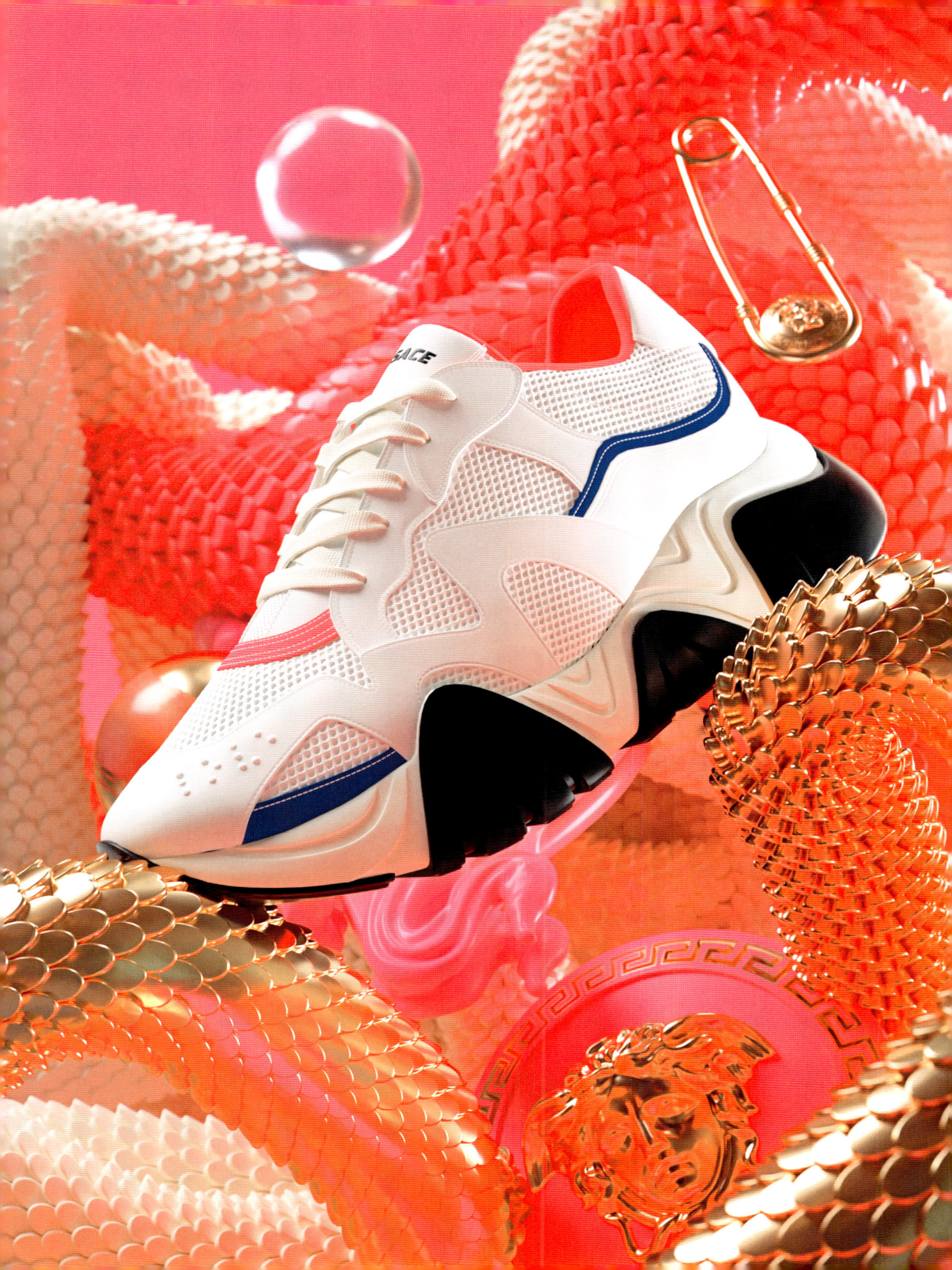

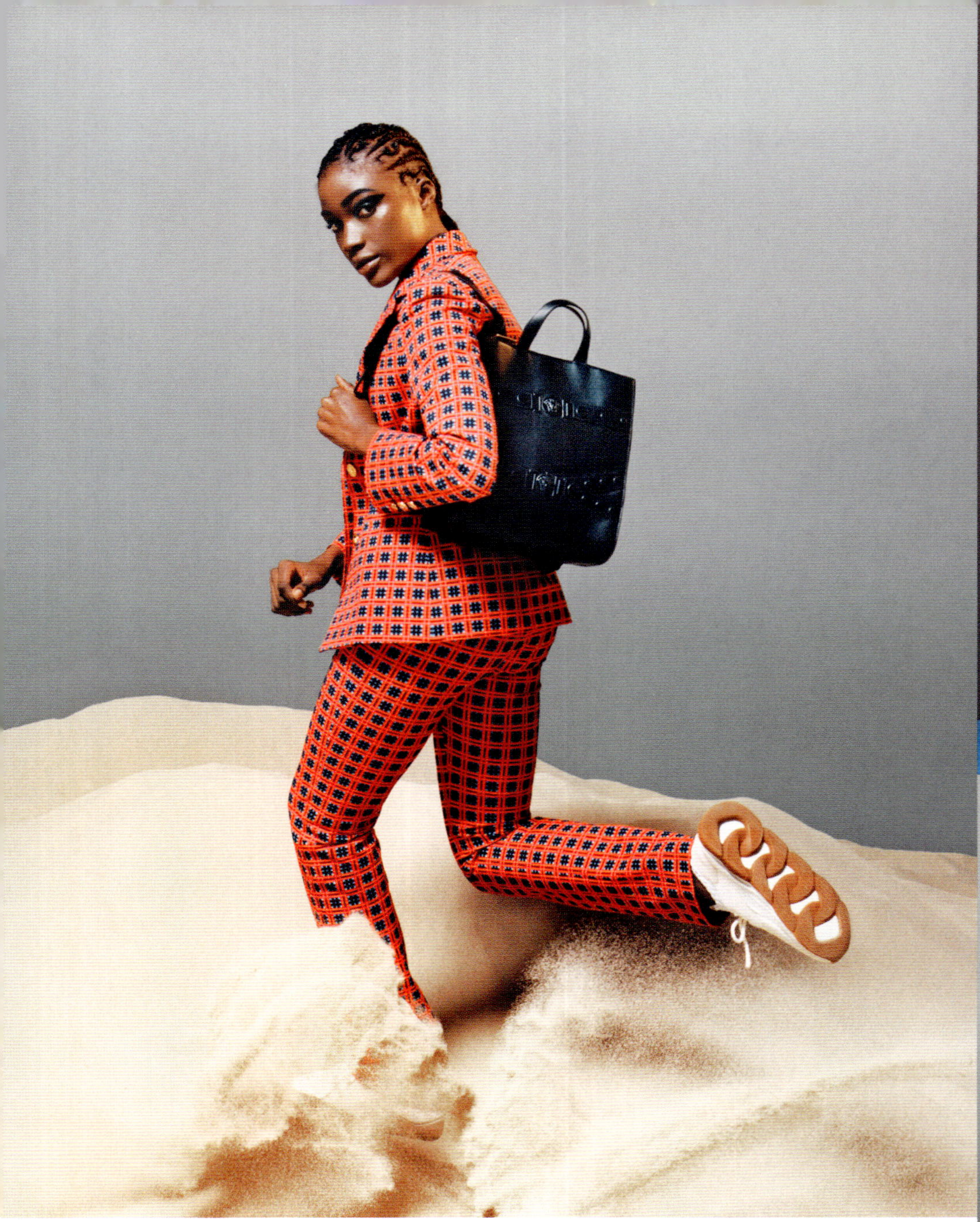

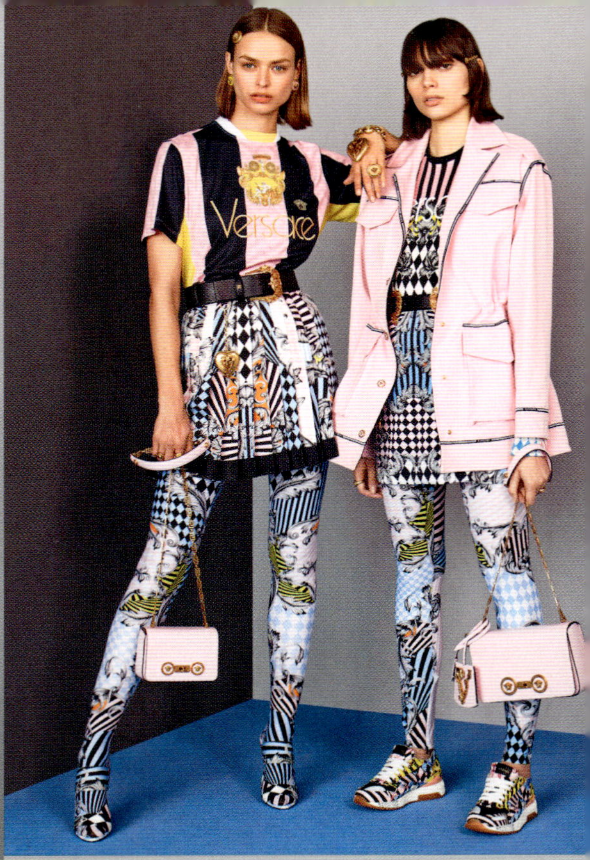

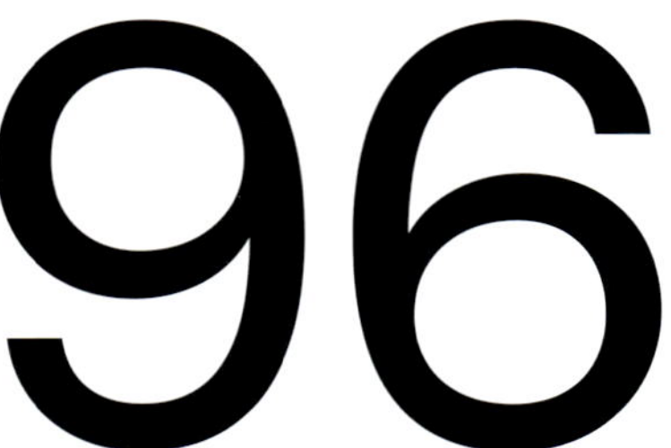

(2017)

VERSACE

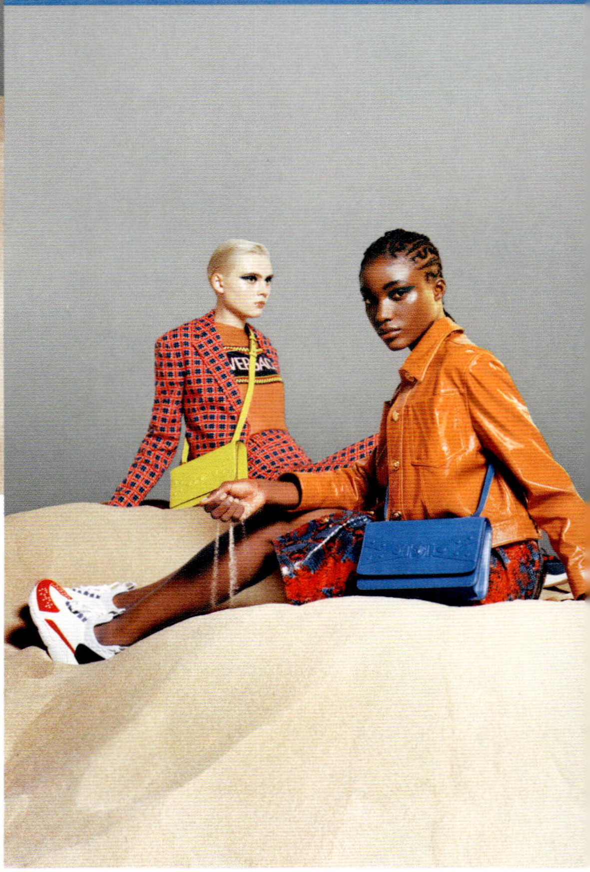

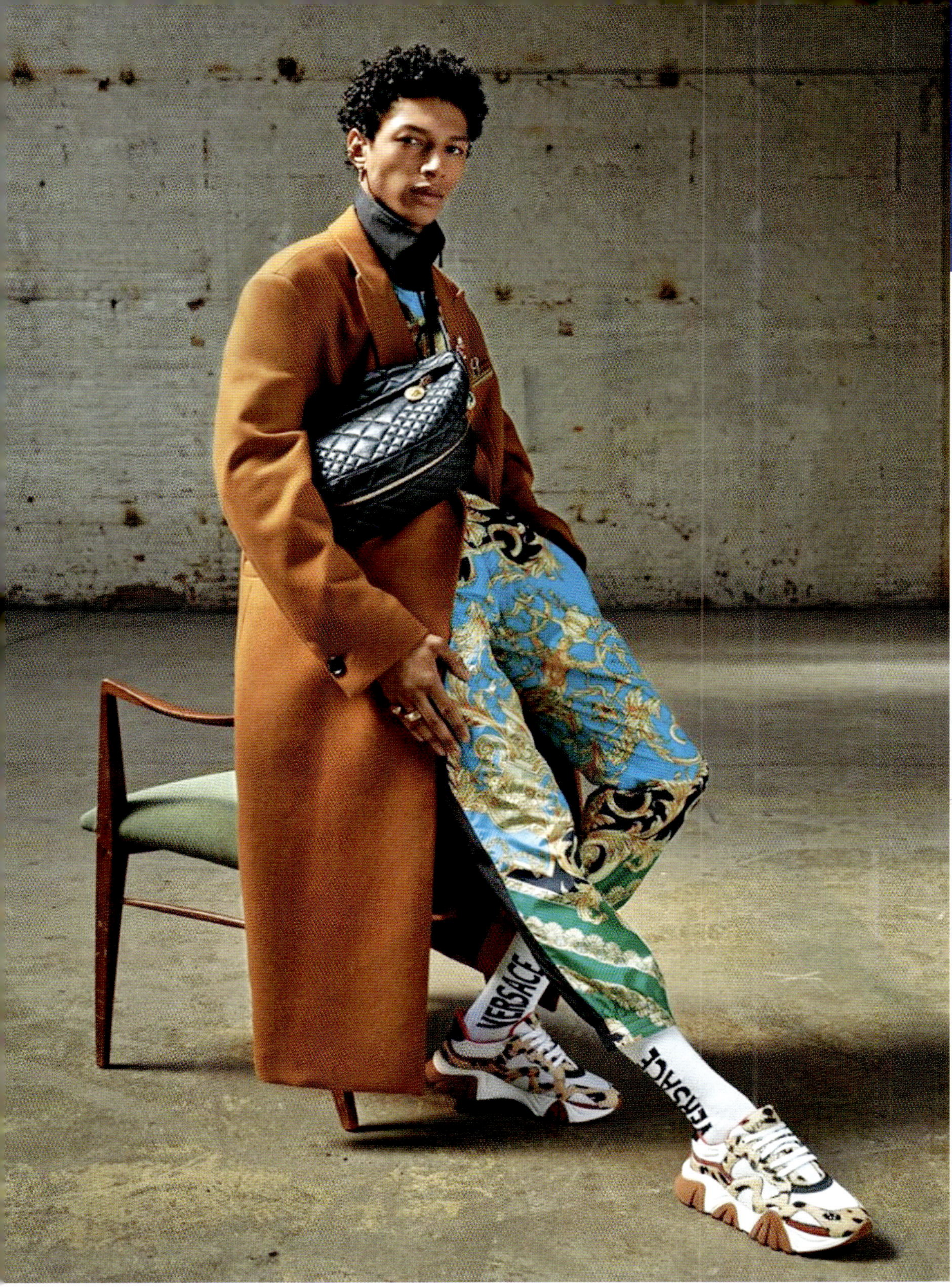

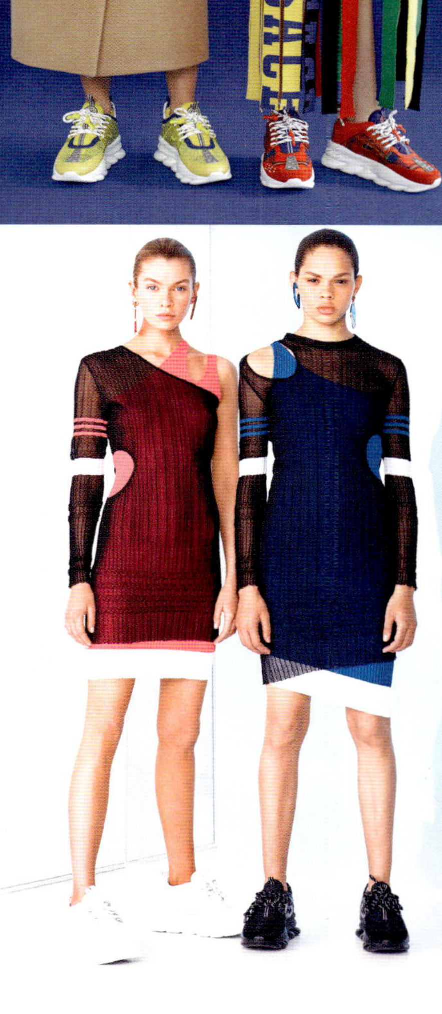

97

VERSACE (2017)

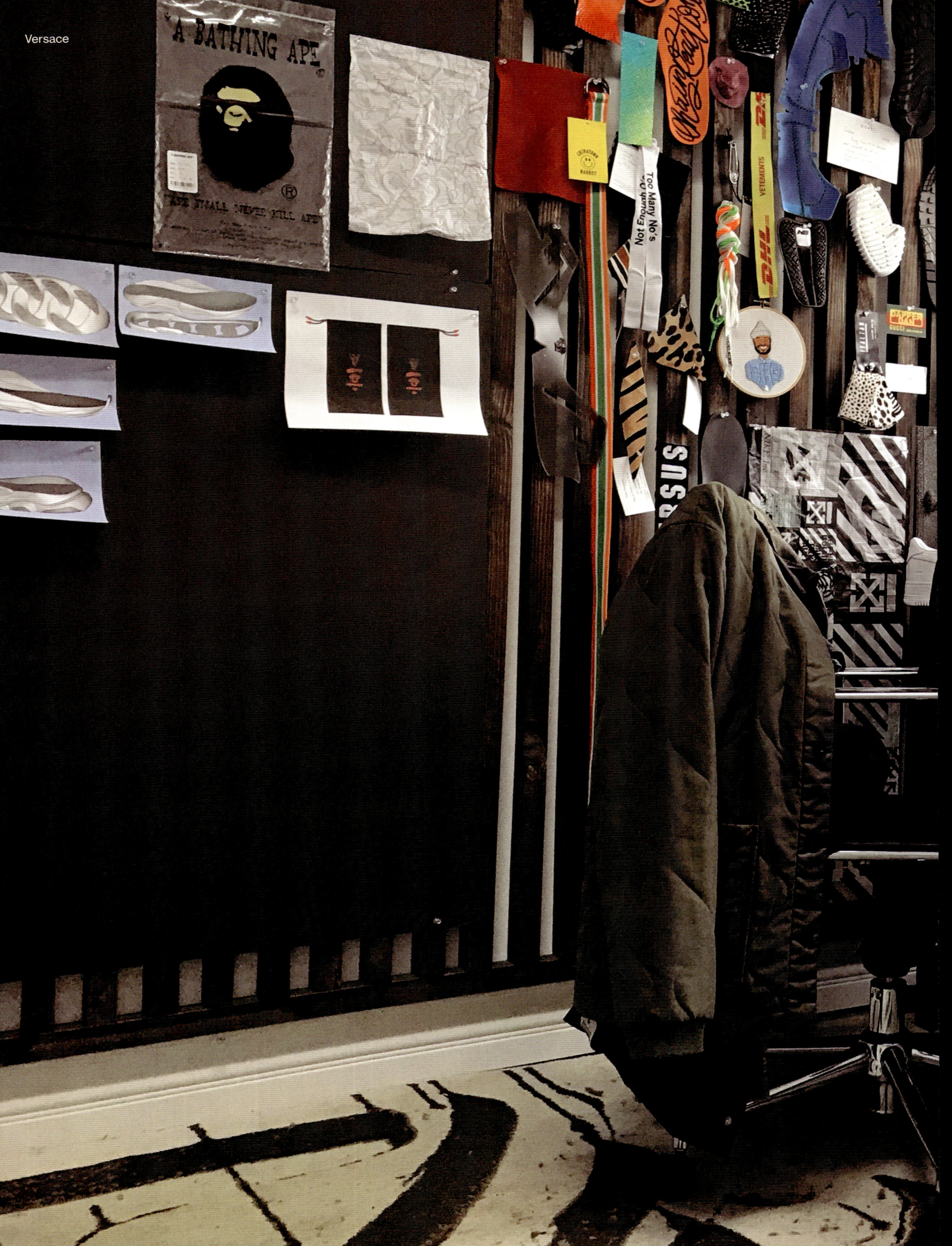
A BATHING APE
APE SHALL NEVER KILL APE
Too Many No's
VETEMENTS
DHL

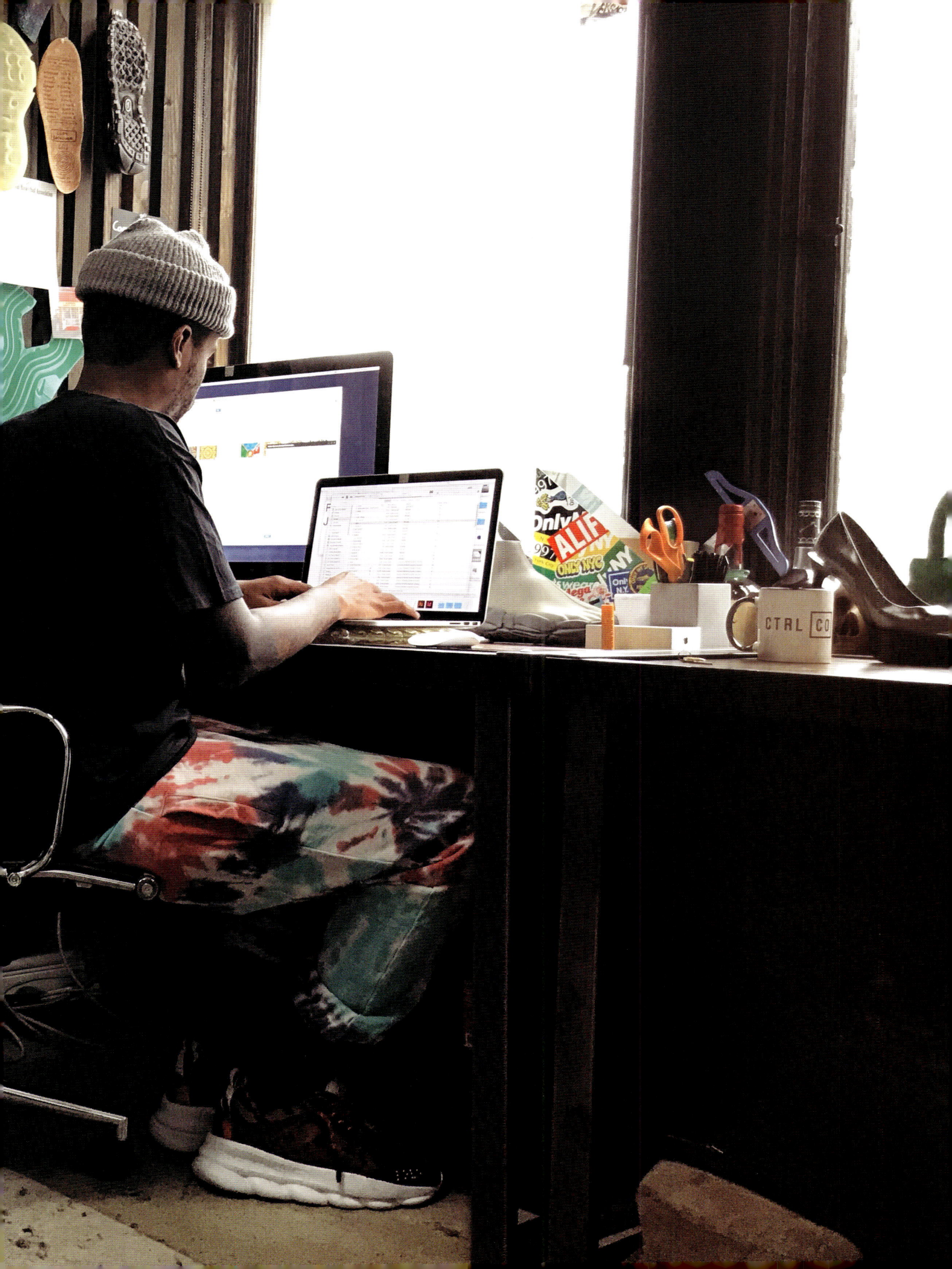
ALIF
ONLY NYC
CTRL CO

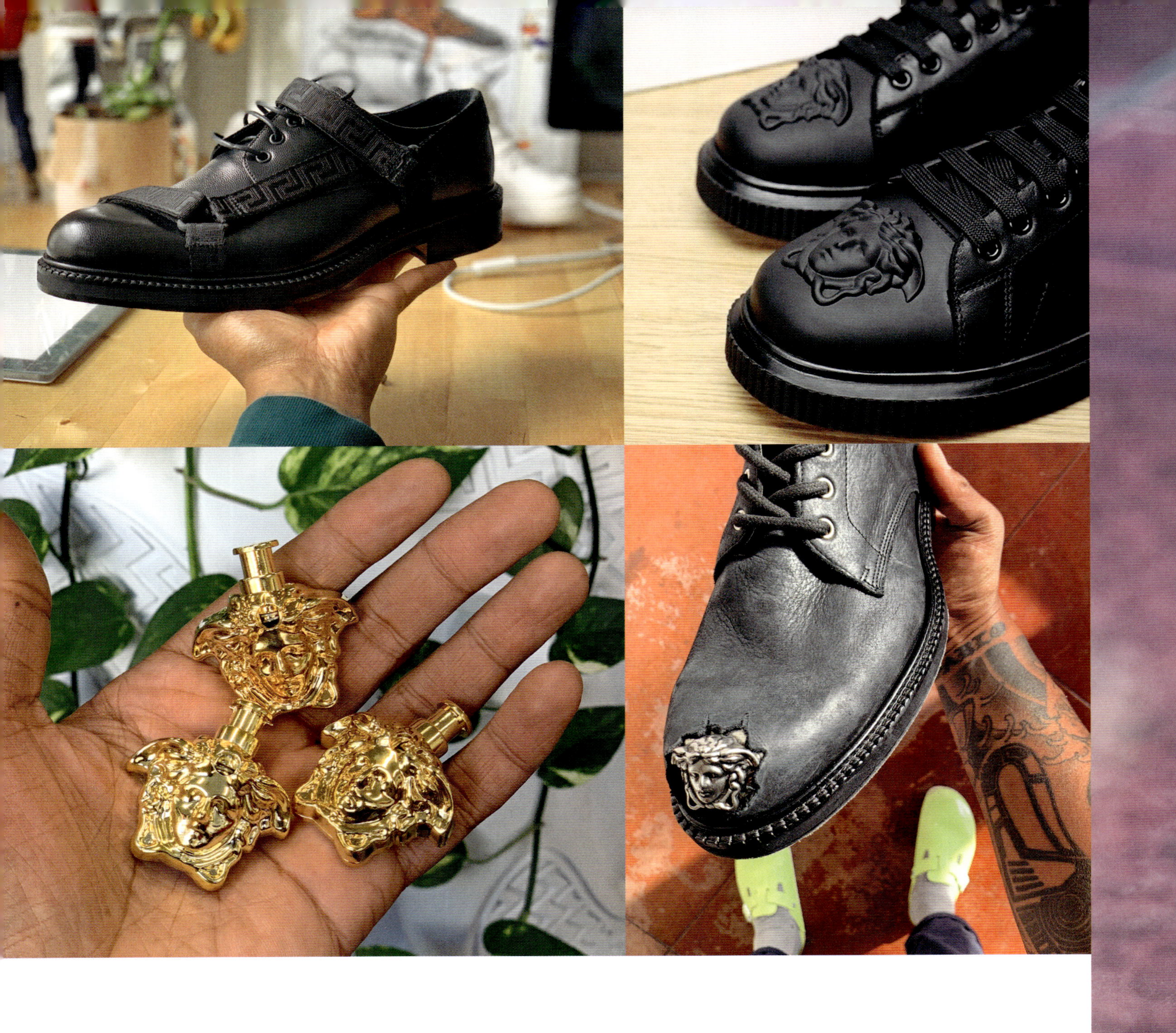

100

(2017)

VERSACE

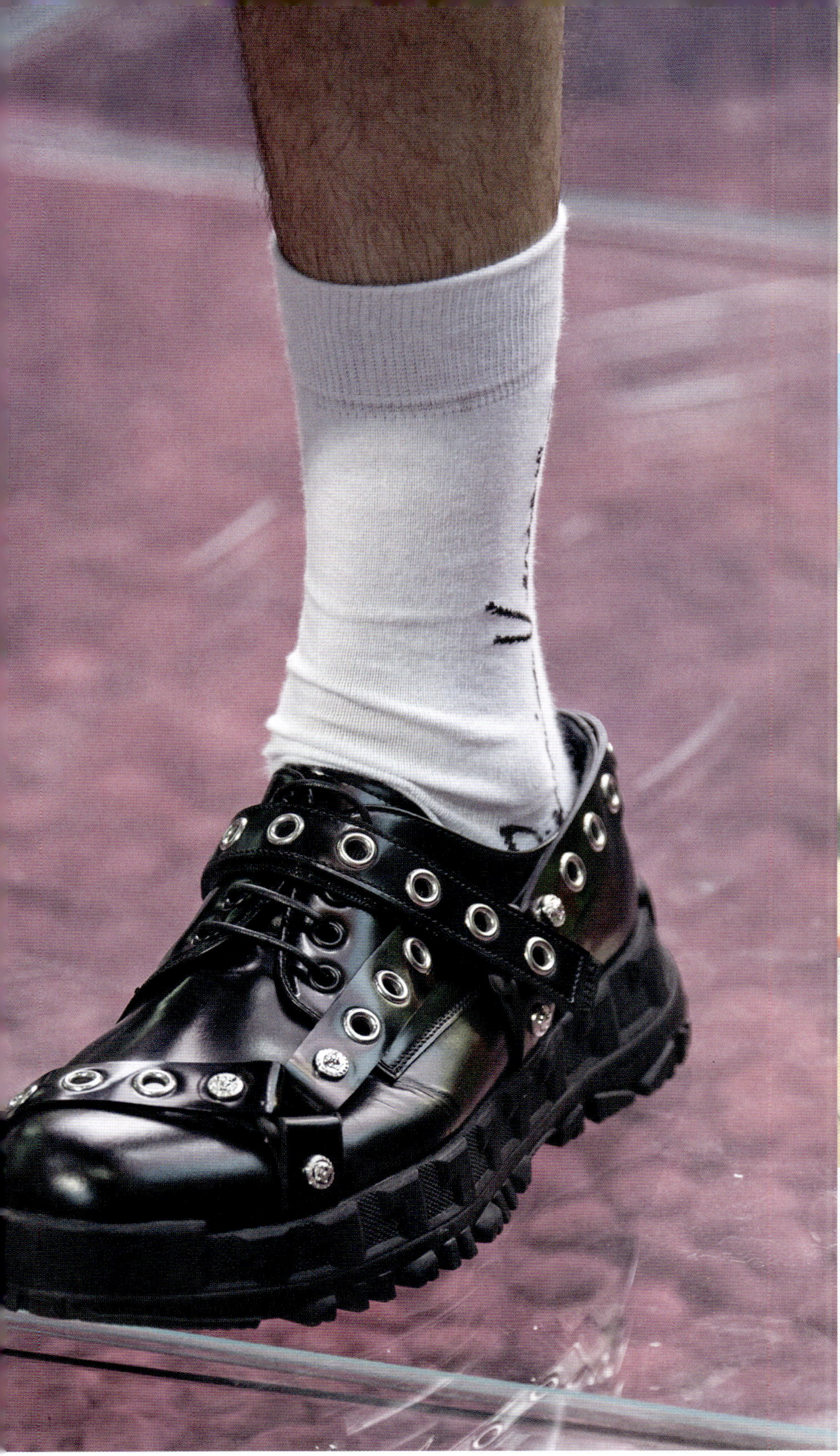

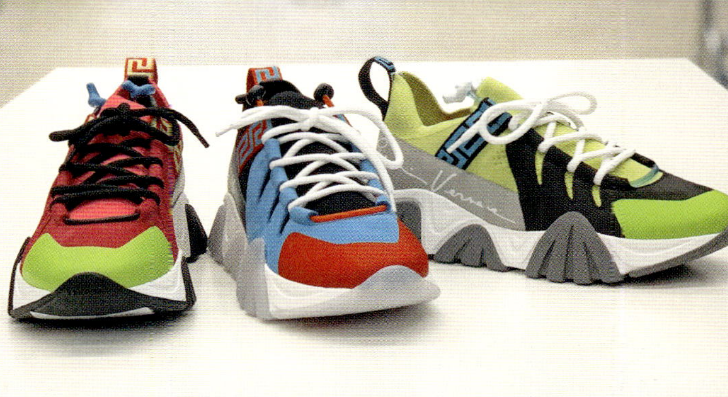

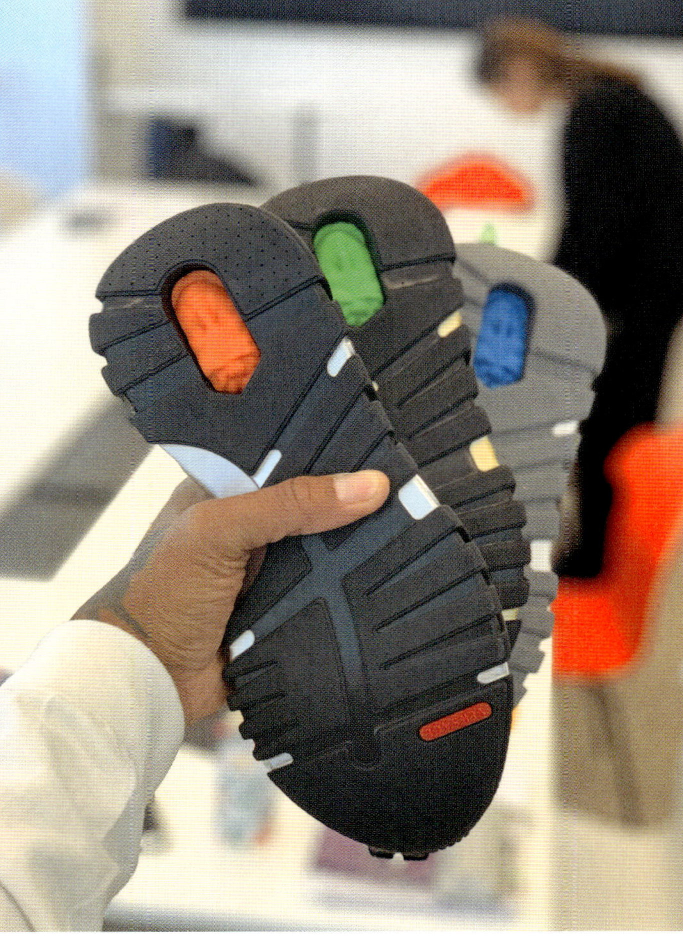

VERSACE

(2017)

101

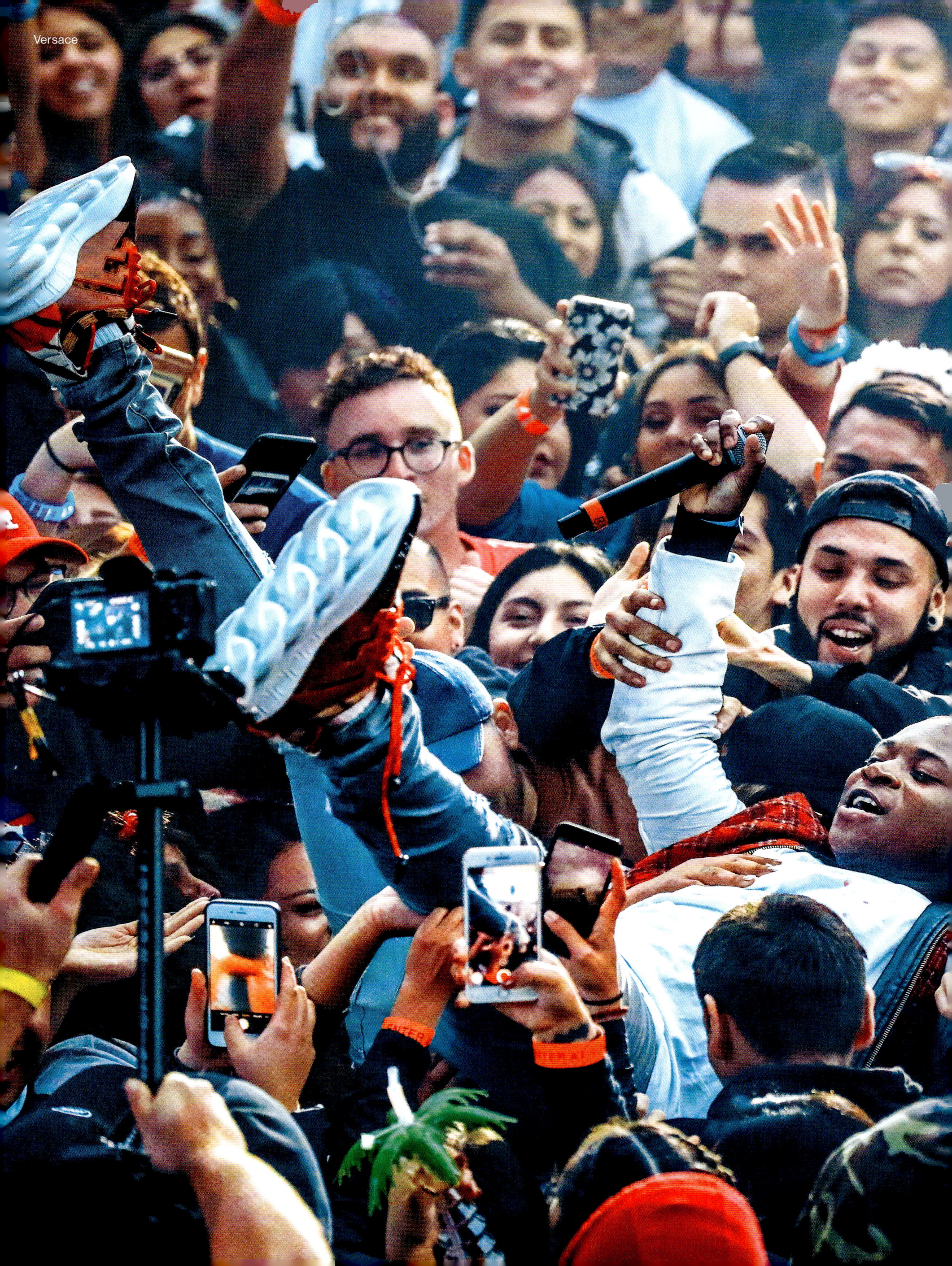

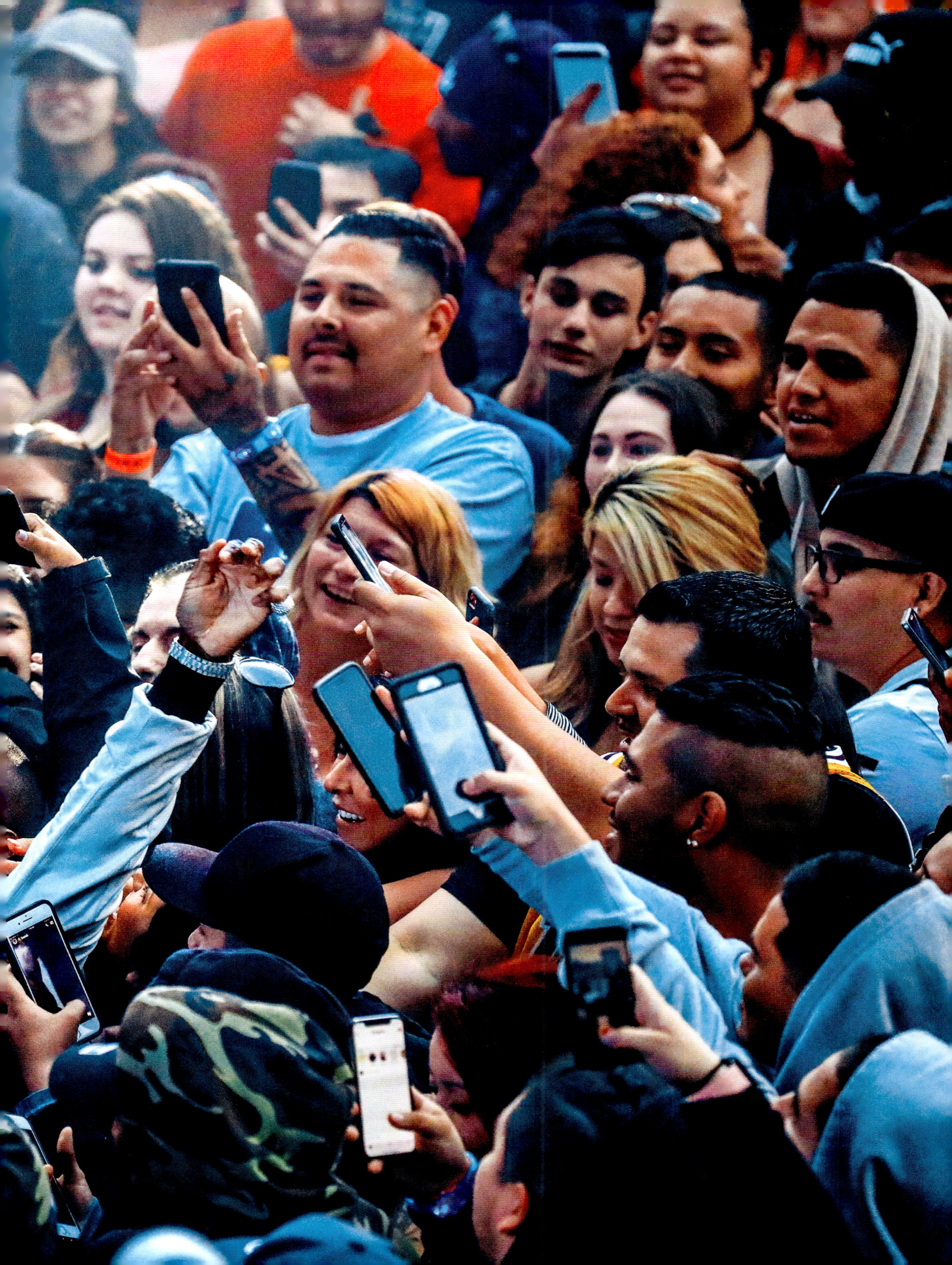

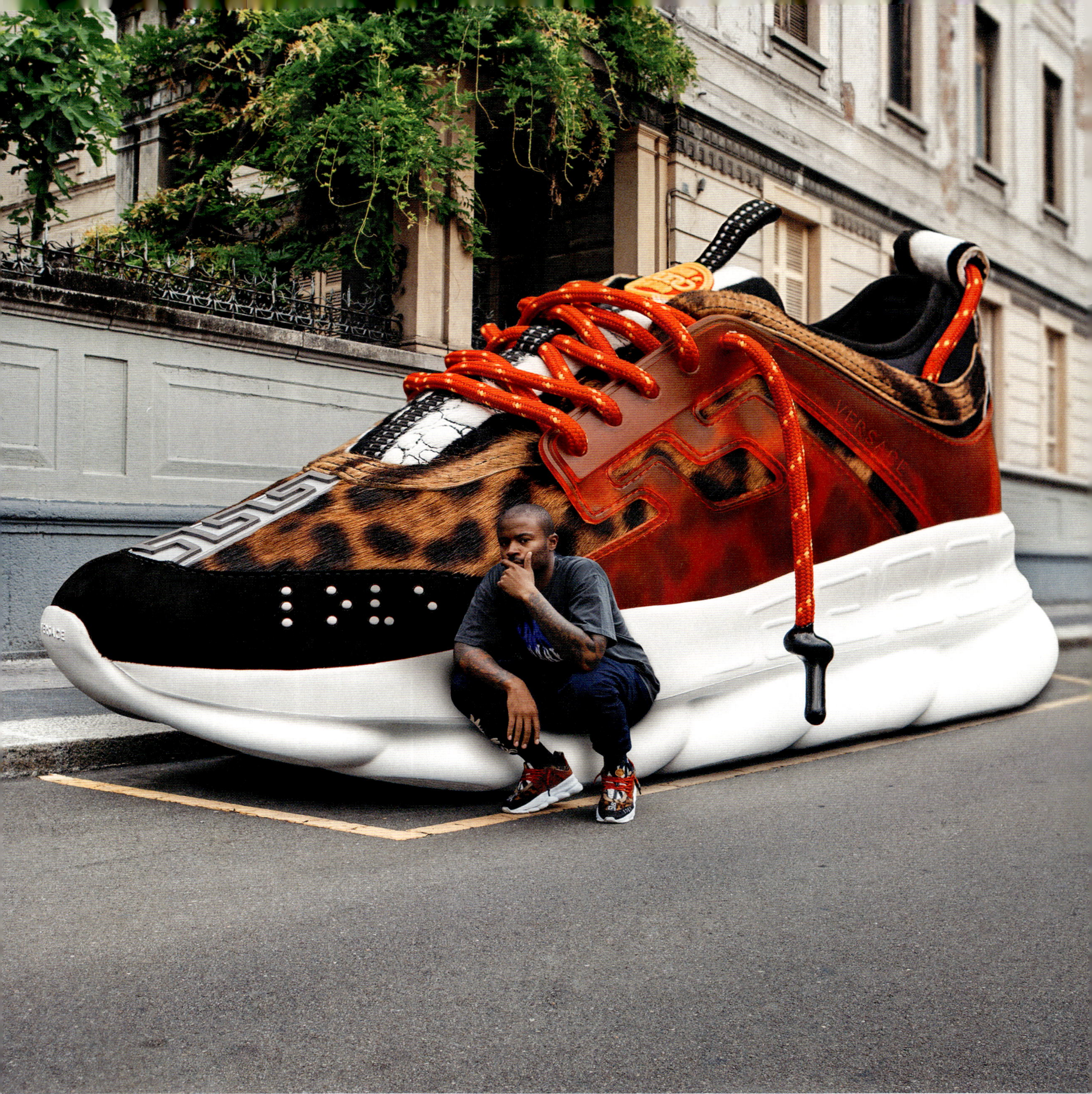

Versace marketing c/o Alessandro Bigi

104

(2017)

VERSACE

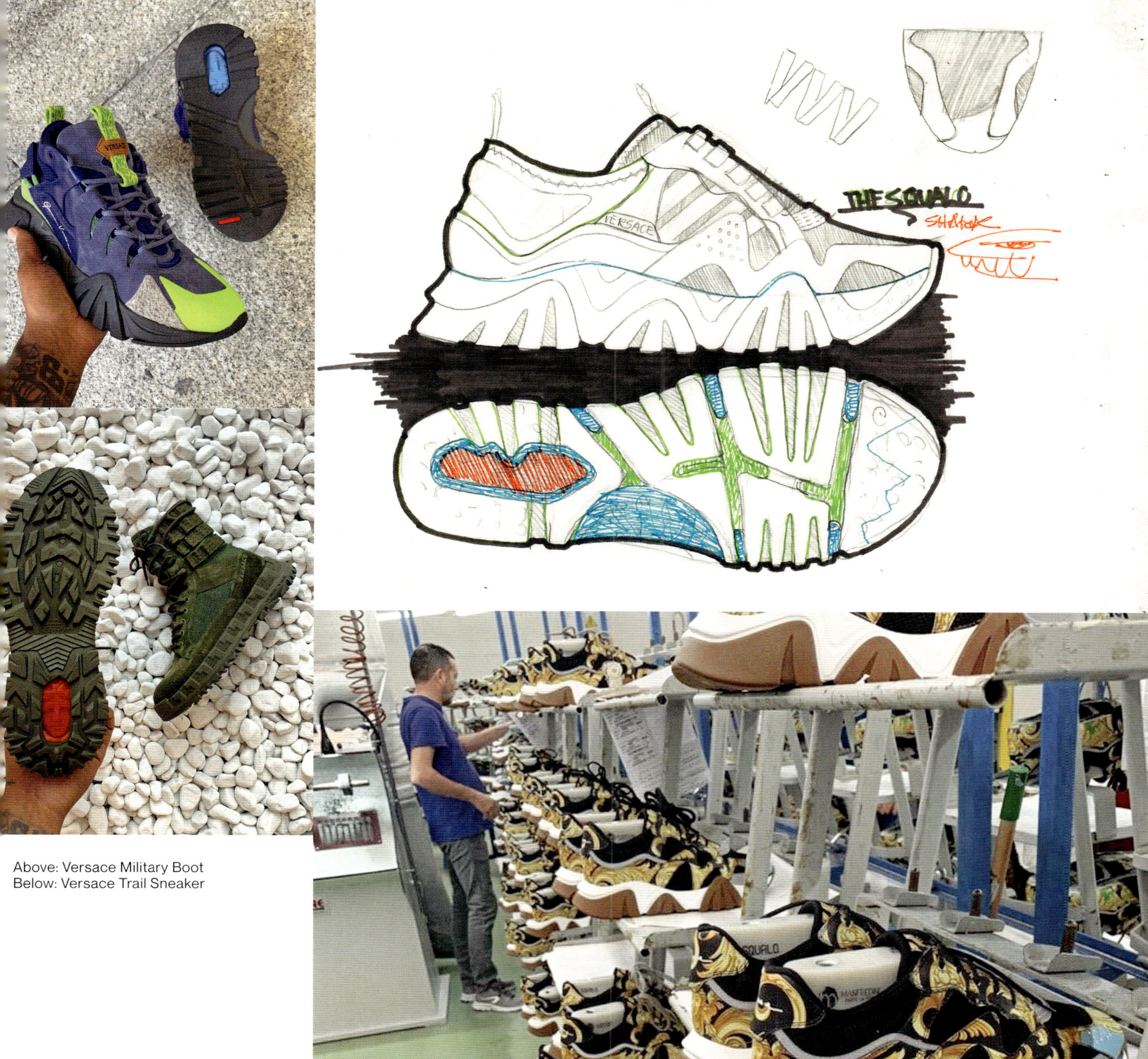

Above: Versace Military Boot
Below: Versace Trail Sneaker

Above: Versace Squalo sketch
Below: Versace Squalo at the factory

105

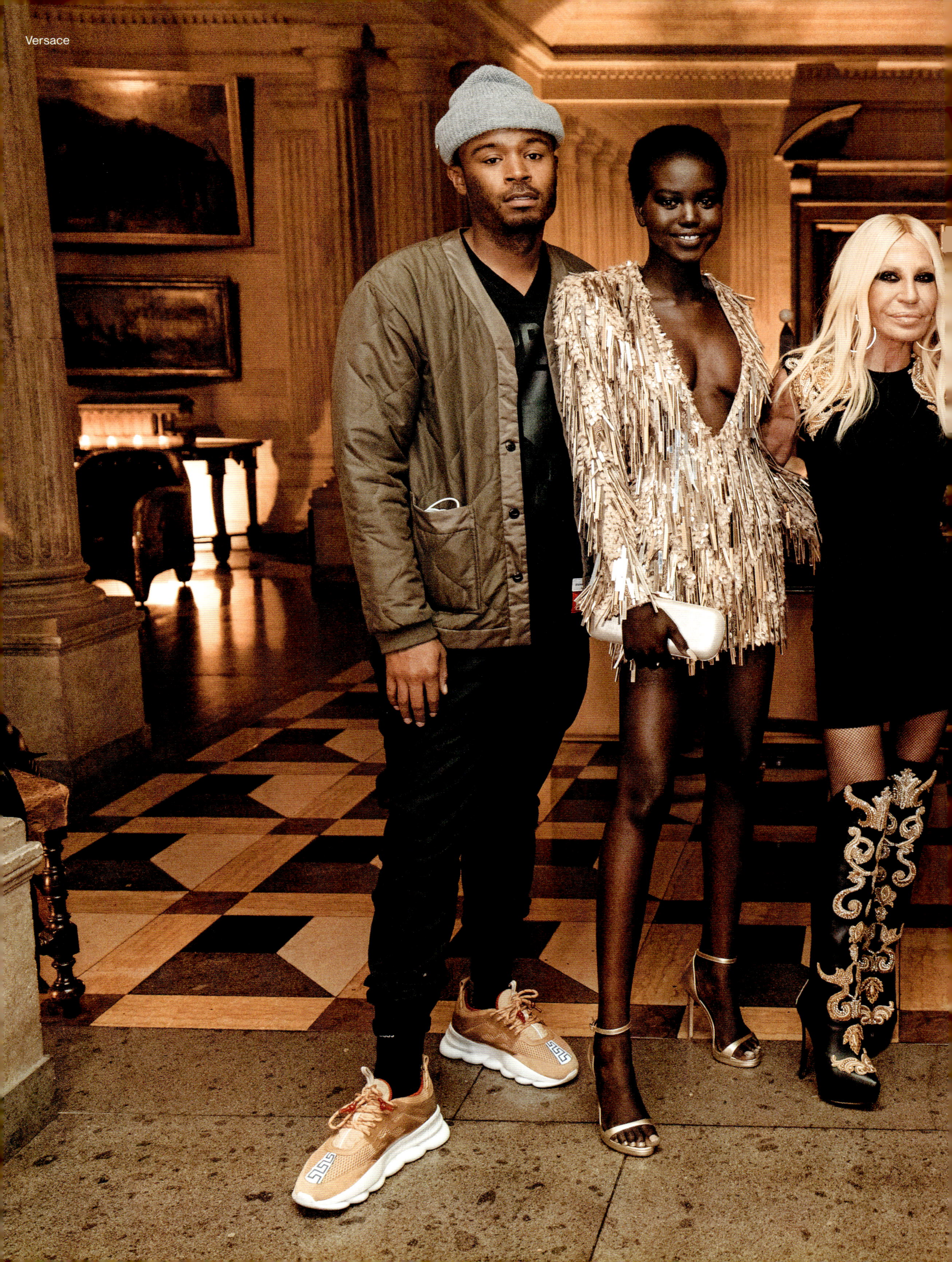

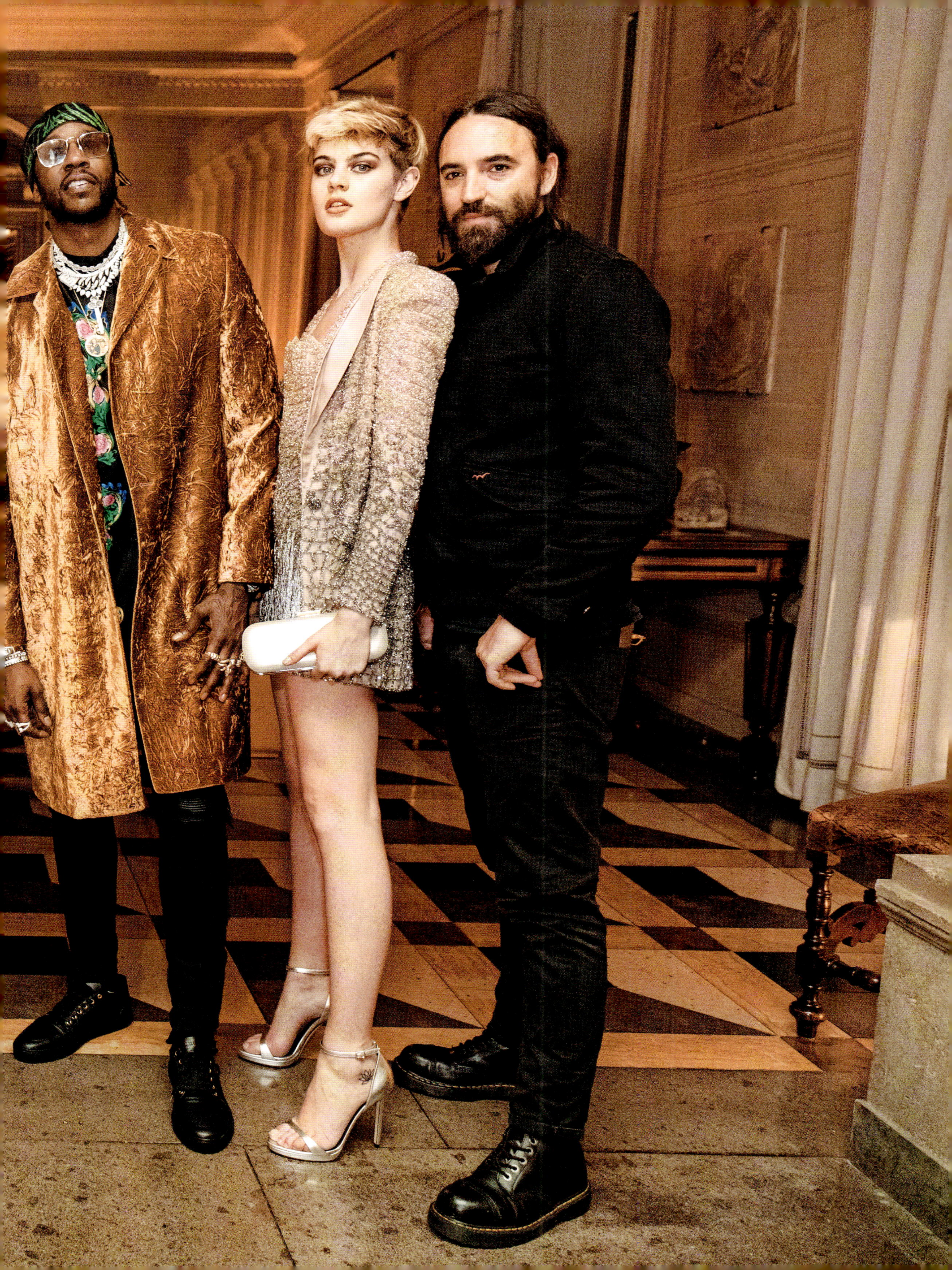

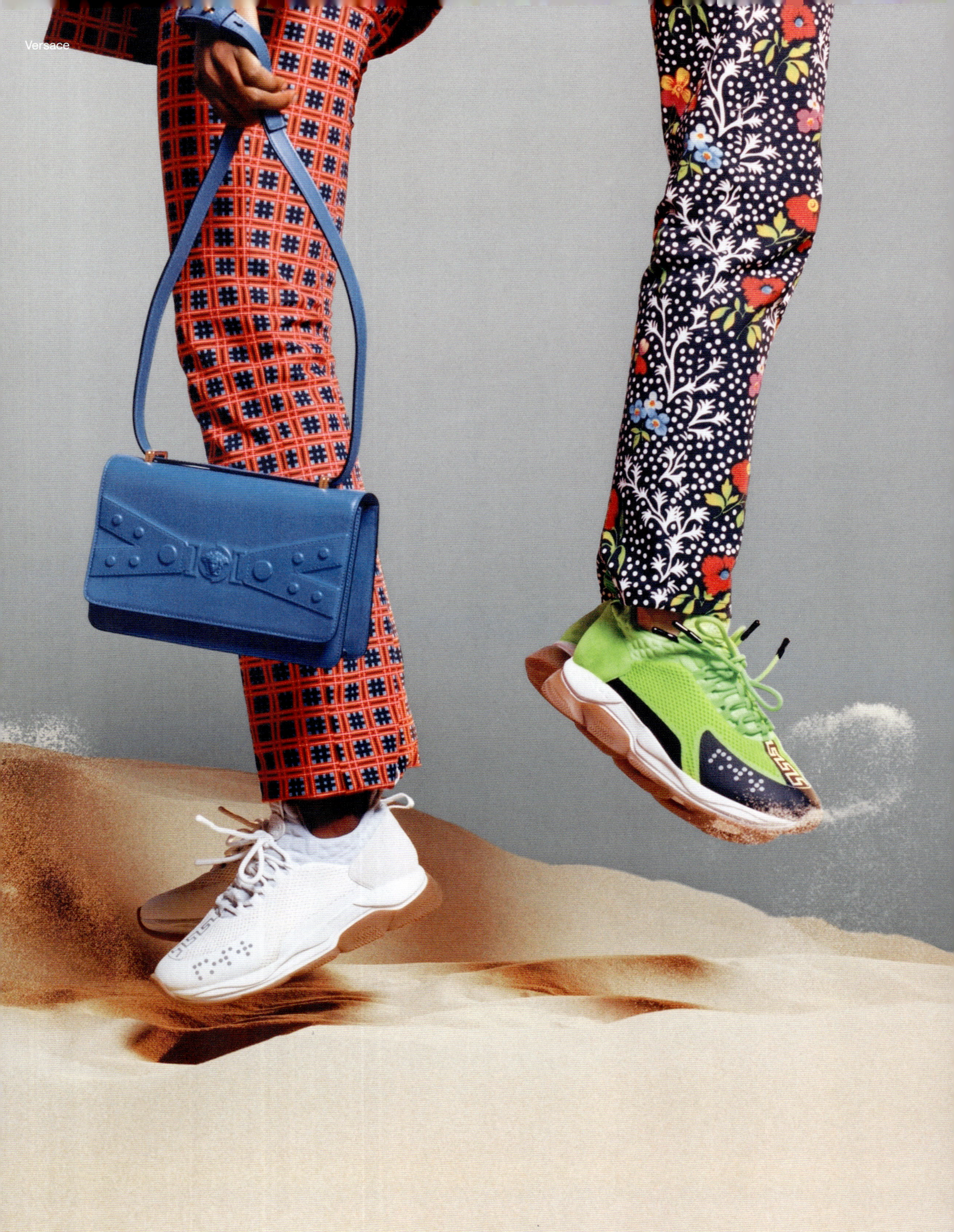

Versace

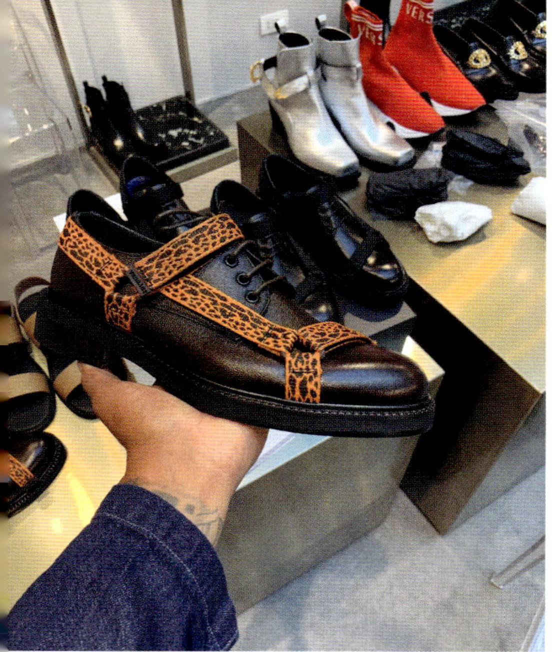

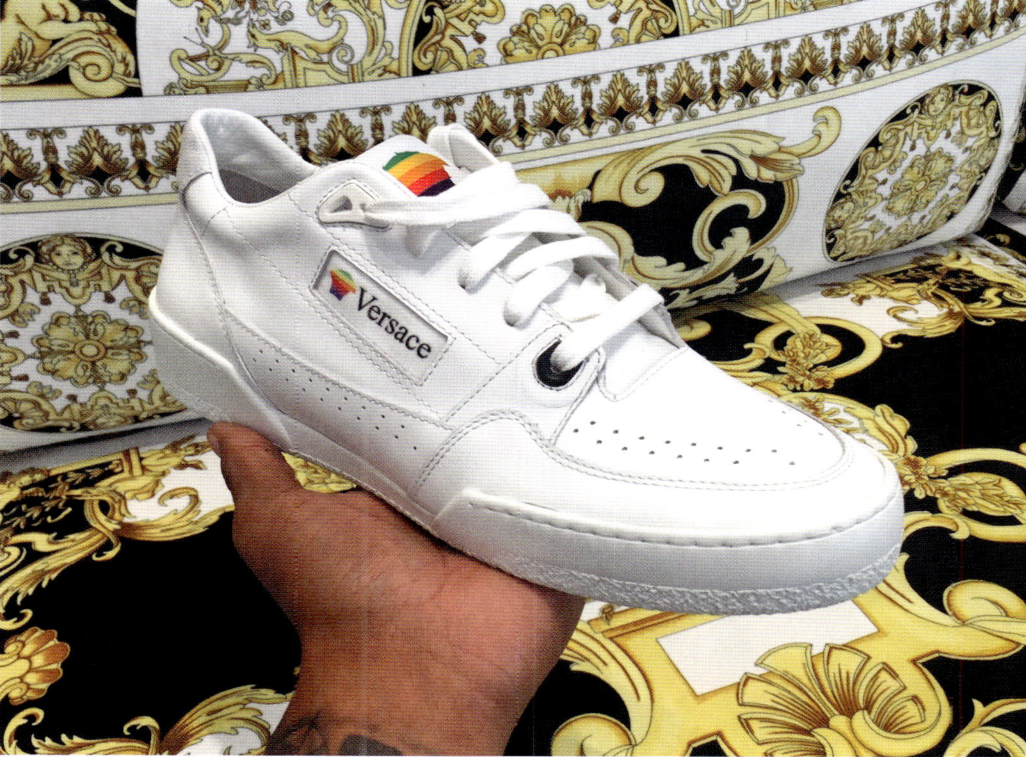

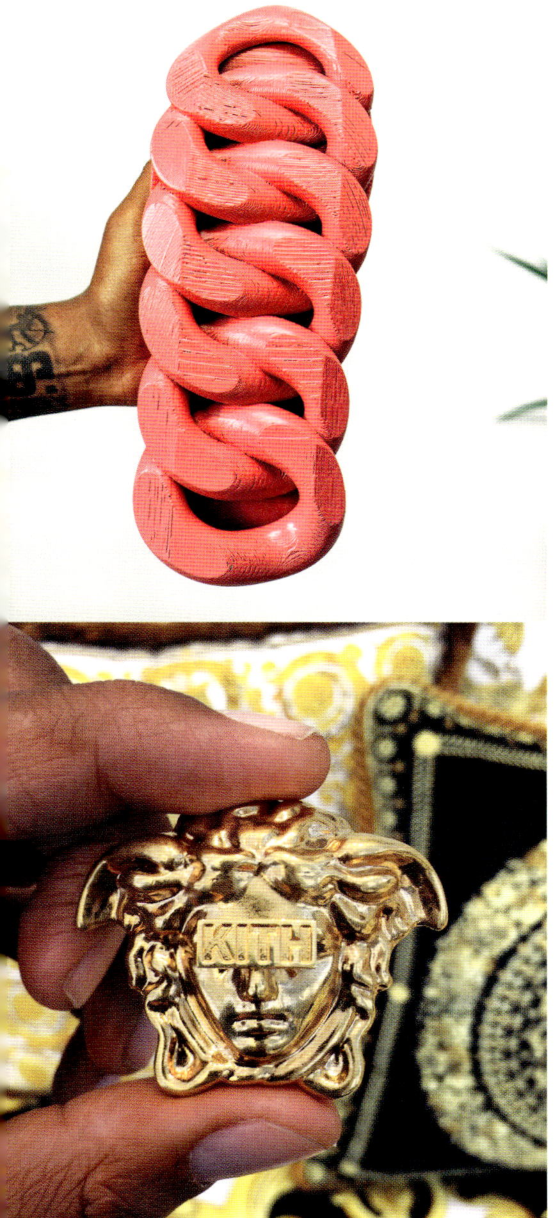

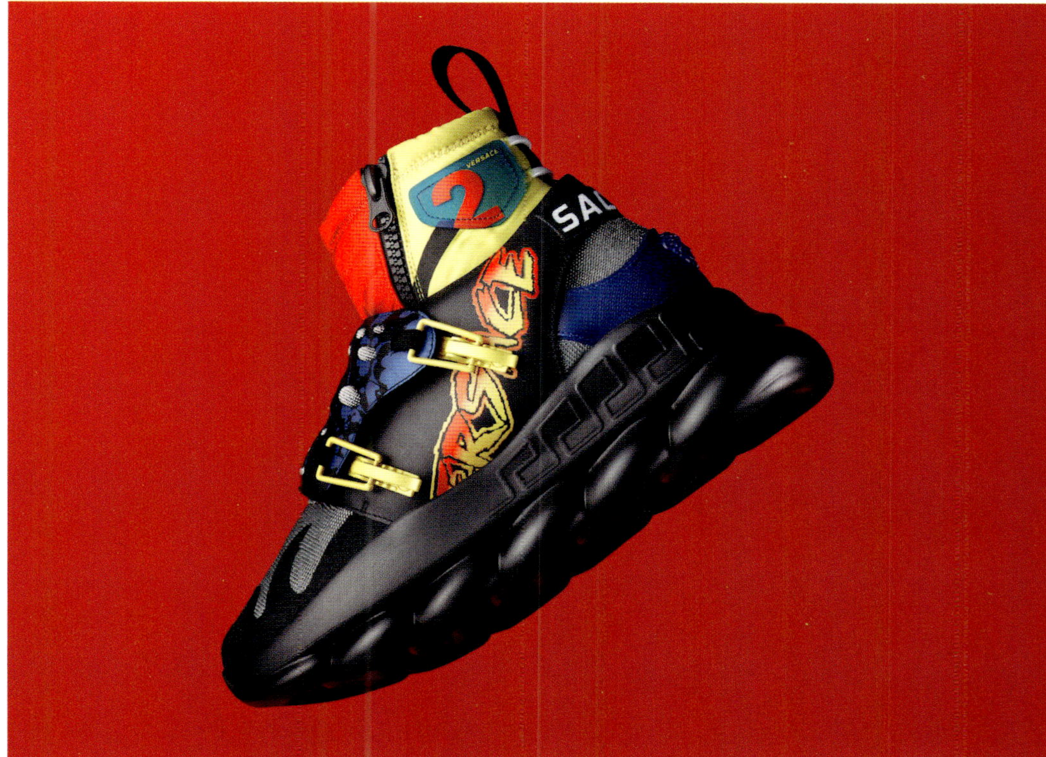

Above: Apple-inspired Versace sample
Below: Versace x Migos Chain Reaction Boot

Above: Versace sample
Middle: Versace Chain Reaction tooling prototype
Below: Versace x Kith lace lock

109

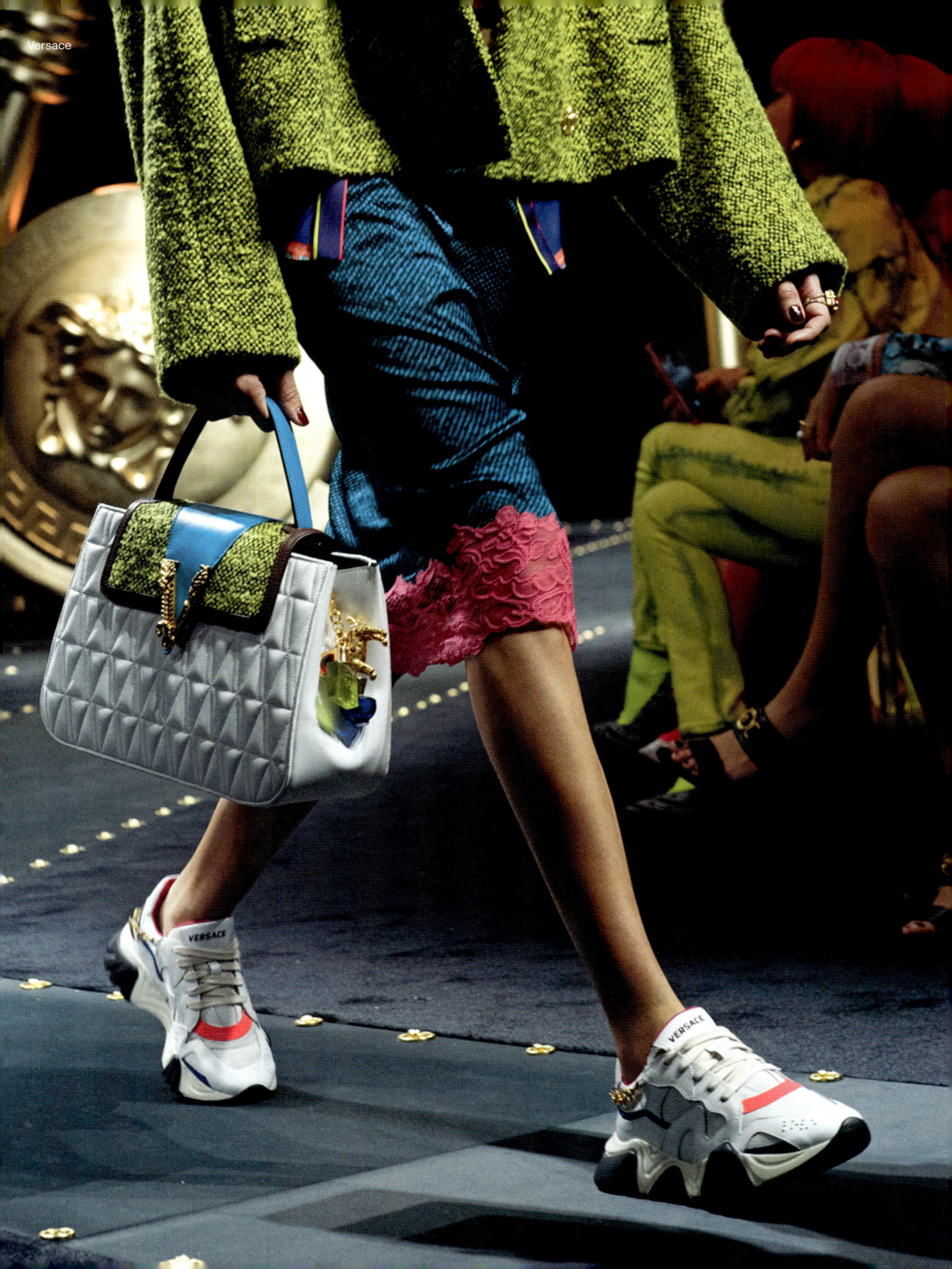
VERSACE
VERSACE

THE GREATEST SNEAKER DESIGNER IN THE WORLD

—DONATELLA VERSACE

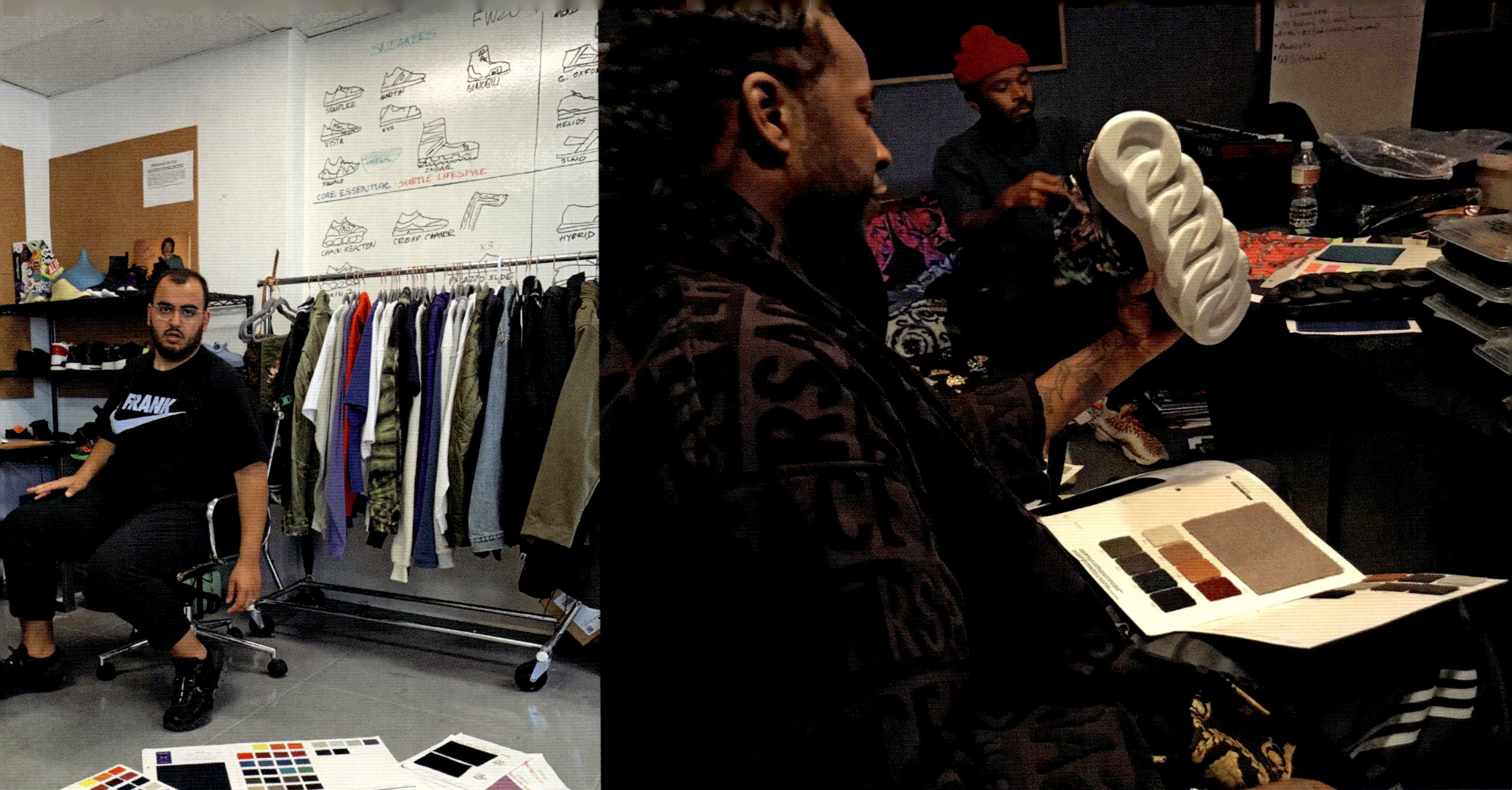

Fardin Hazratizadeh (Salehe's design assistant)

2 Chainz and Salehe designing his Versace collaboration

112

(2017)

VERSACE

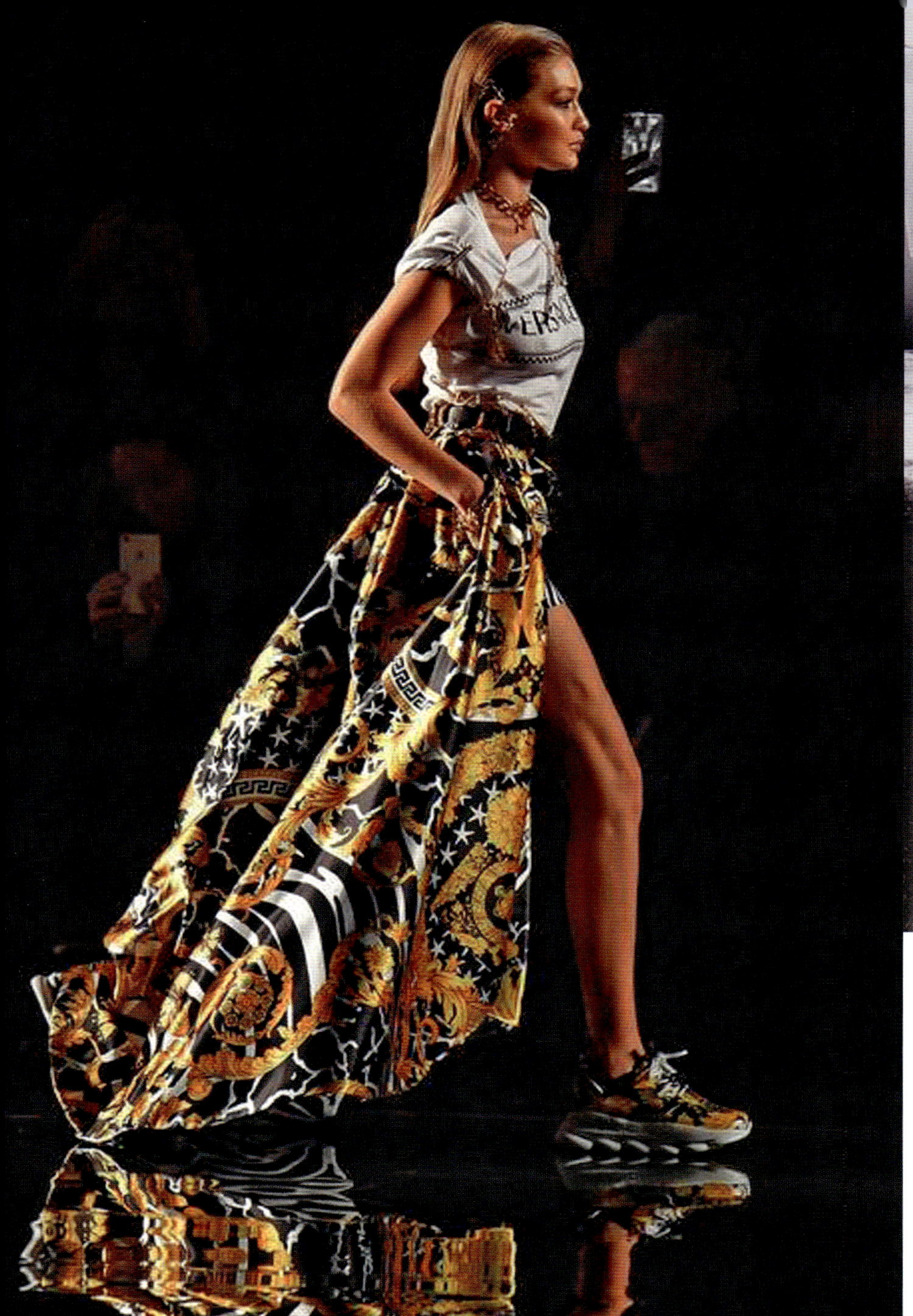

Gigi Hadid on runway

Kendall Jenner, Bella Hadid, and Gigi Hadid

VERSACE (2017)

113

Versace

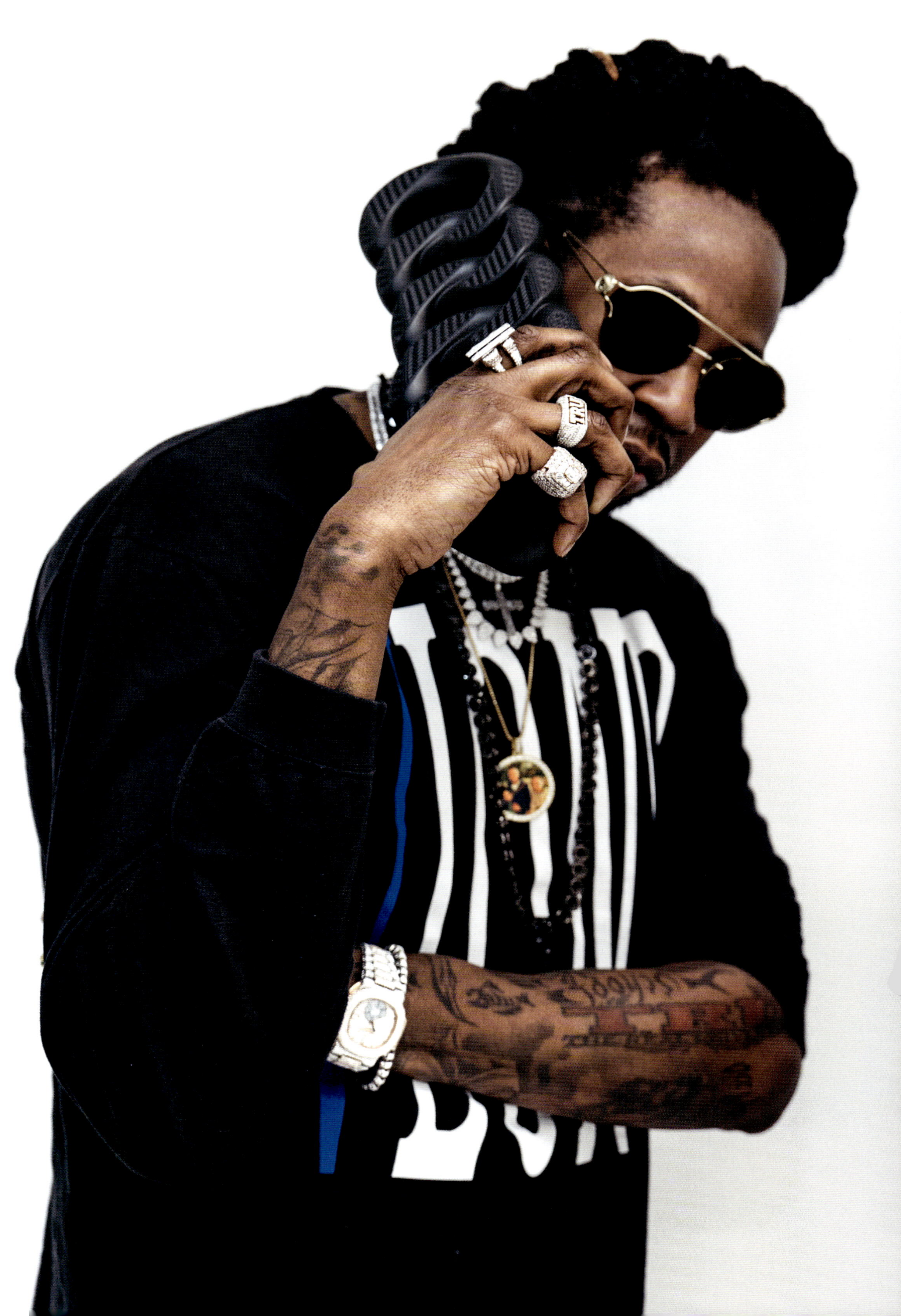

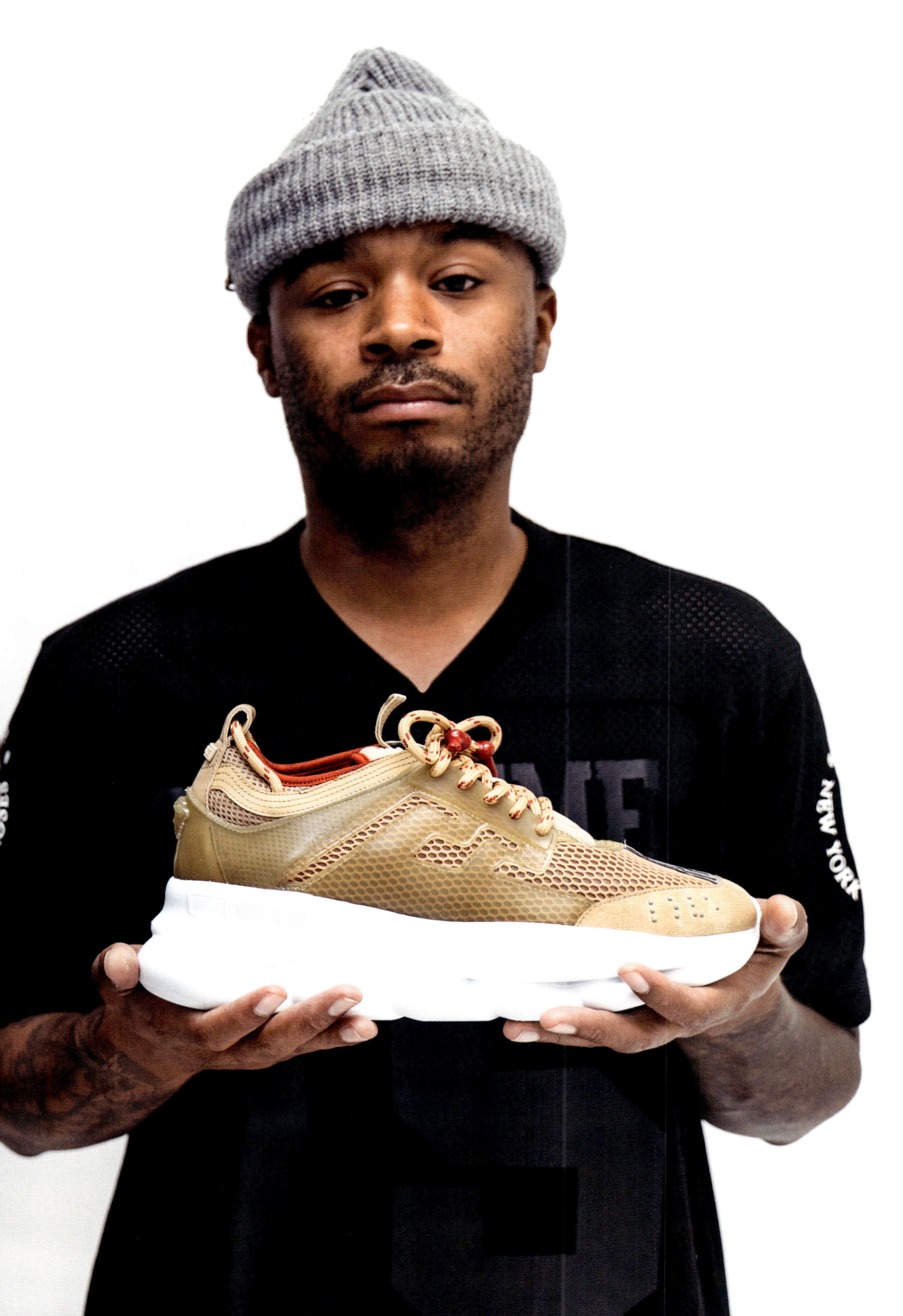
NEW YORK

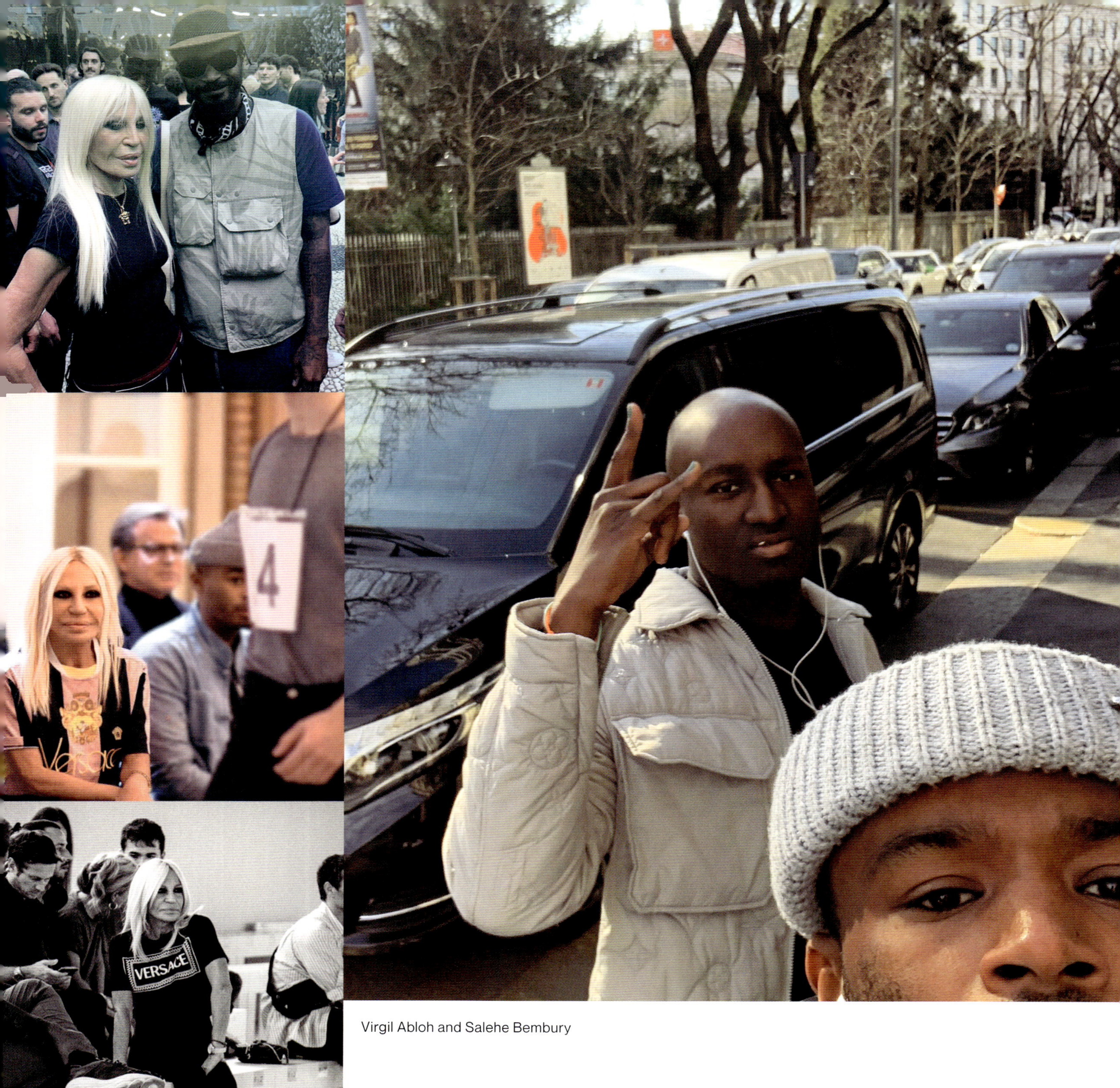

Virgil Abloh and Salehe Bembury

Donatella Versace

116

(2017)

VERSACE

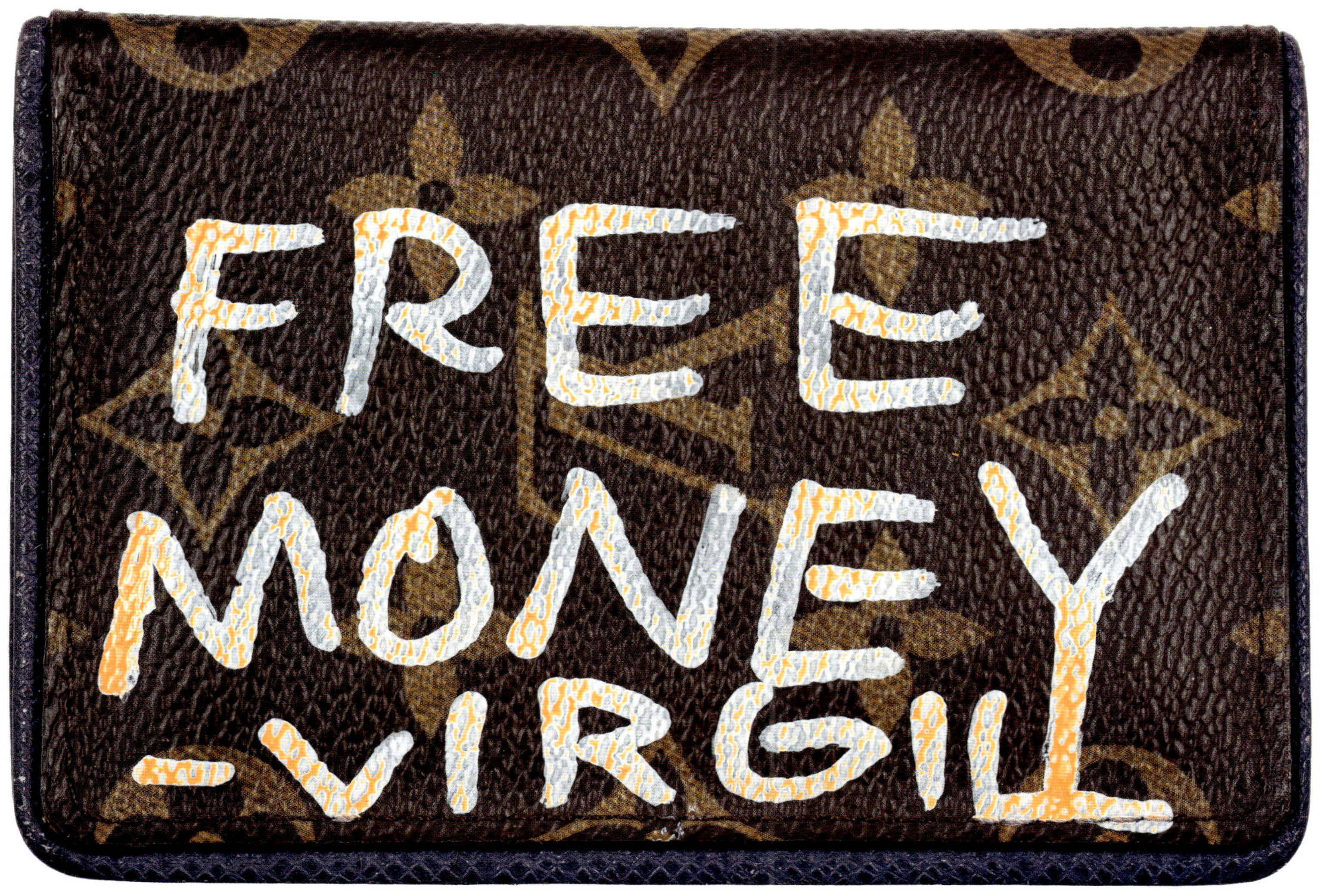
FREE
MONEY
-VIRGIL

(12) **United States Design Patent** (10) **Patent No.: US D882,229 S**
Bembury (45) **Date of Patent: ** Apr. 28, 2020**

(54) **SOLE FOR FOOTWEAR**

(71) Applicant: **Gianni Versace S.p.A.**, Milan (IT)

(72) Inventor: **Salehe Bembury**, New York, NY (US)

(73) Assignee: **GIANNI VERSACE S.p.A.**, Milan (IT)

(**) Term: **15 Years**

(21) Appl. No.: **29/647,665**

(22) Filed: **May 15, 2018**

(30) **Foreign Application Priority Data**

Mar. 23, 2018 (EM) 005017043

(51) **LOC (12) Cl.** **02-04**

(52) **U.S. Cl.**
USPC **D2/956**; D2/947; D2/951; D2/954

(58) **Field of Classification Search**
USPC .... D2/902, 906, 908, 916, 918, 925, D2/946–962, 977; 36/3 B, 22 R, 24.5, 36/25 R, 28, 32 R, 34 R, 59 C, 67 A, 103
CPC A43B 13/00; A43B 13/02; A43B 13/023; A43B 13/026; A43B 13/04; A43B 13/08; A43B 13/10; A43B 13/12; A43B 13/14; A43B 13/141; A43B 13/143; A43B 13/16; A43B 13/18; A43B 13/181; A43B 13/187; A43B 13/189; A43B 13/20; A43B 13/22; A43B 13/223; A43B 13/24; A43B 13/28; A43B 13/30; A43B 13/32; A43B 13/34; A43B 13/36
See application file for complete search history.

(56) **References Cited**

U.S. PATENT DOCUMENTS

D267,366 S * 12/1982 Davis D2/951
4,494,320 A * 1/1985 Davis A43B 13/223 36/103
D282,123 S * 1/1986 Davis D2/959
D475,514 S * 6/2003 Burg D2/956
D677,866 S * 3/2013 Vestuti A43B 13/32 D2/947
D716,535 S * 11/2014 Seo D2/951
D719,331 S * 12/2014 Christensen A43B 13/12 D2/951
D807,621 S * 1/2018 Davis A43B 13/04 D2/946
D807,623 S * 1/2018 Vestuti A43B 13/223 D2/954
D823,583 S * 7/2018 Petrie A43B 1/0045 D2/954
D838,452 S * 1/2019 Christensen A43B 13/223 D2/955
D854,295 S * 7/2019 Nethongkome D2/953
D854,798 S * 7/2019 Nethongkome D2/953
D858,964 S * 9/2019 Vestuti D2/953
(Continued)

Primary Examiner — T Chase Nelson
(74) *Attorney, Agent, or Firm* — Thomas | Horstemeyer, LLP

(57) **CLAIM**

The ornamental design for a sole for footwear, as shown and described.

DESCRIPTION

FIG. **1** is a perspective view of a sole for footwear showing my new design;
FIG. **2** is a front elevational view thereof;
FIG. **3** is a rear elevational view thereof, opposite that of FIG. **2**;
FIG. **4** is a right side elevational view thereof;
FIG. **5** is a left side elevational view thereof, opposite that of FIG. **4**;
FIG. **6** is a top view thereof; and,
FIG. **7** is a bottom view thereof.
The broken lines in FIGS. **2** and **6** illustrate portions of the sole for footwear that form no part of the claimed design.

1 Claim, 5 Drawing Sheets

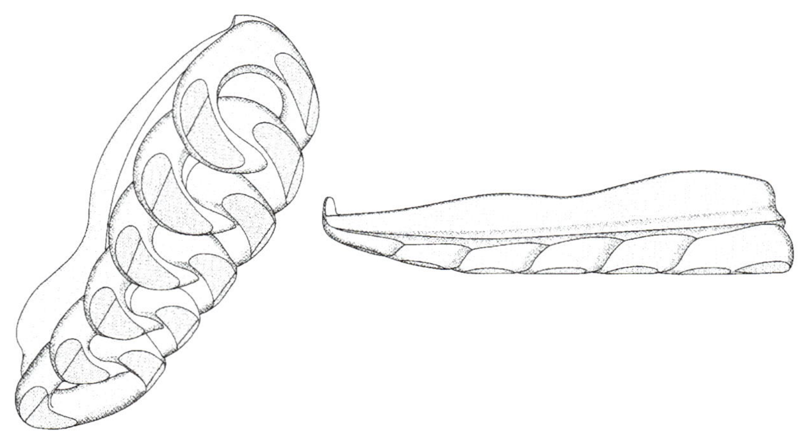

Versace

118 (2017) VERSACE

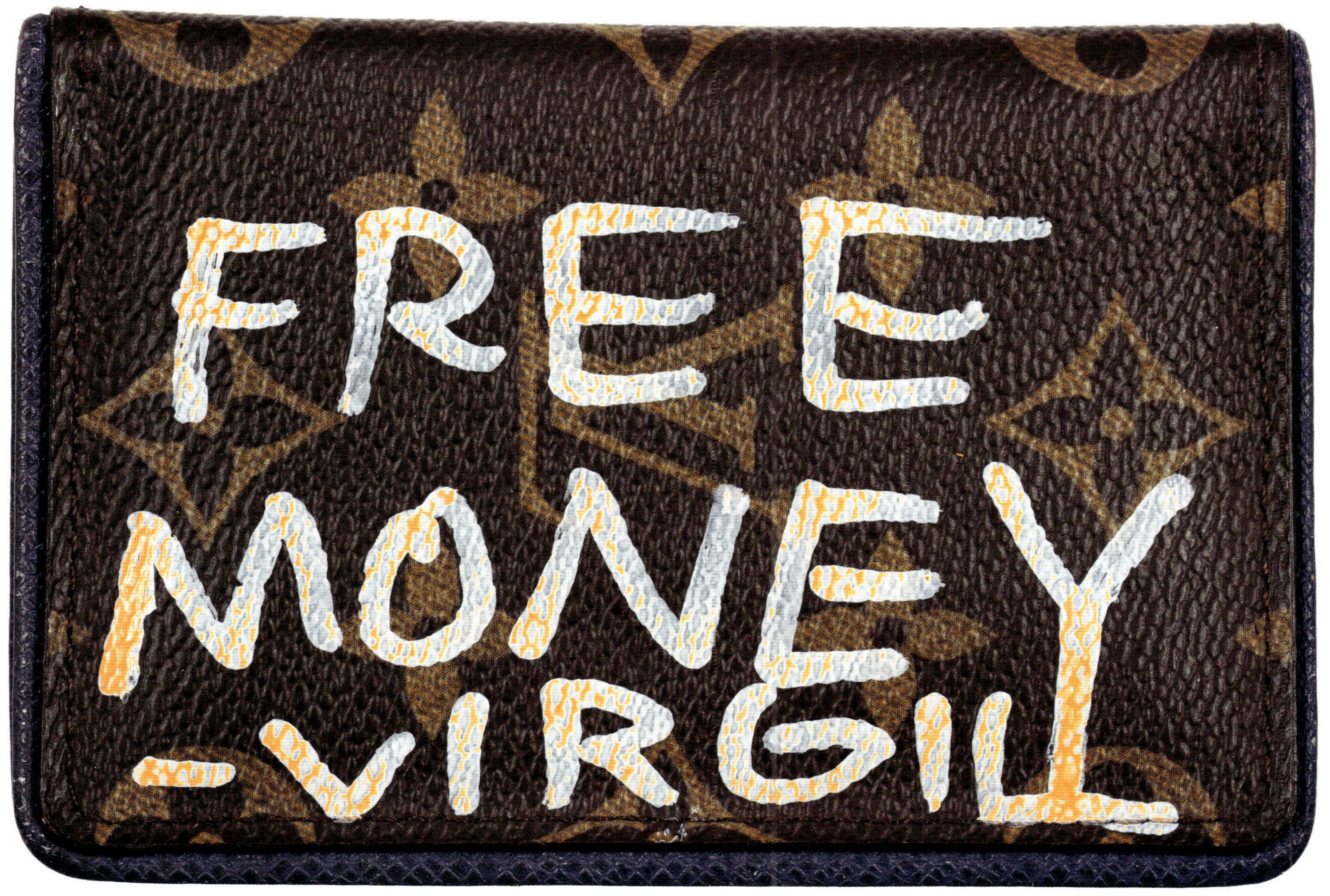
FREE
MONEY
-VIRGIL

(12) **United States Design Patent**
Bembury

(10) **Patent No.:** **US D882,229 S**
(45) **Date of Patent:** ** **Apr. 28, 2020**

(54) **SOLE FOR FOOTWEAR**

(71) Applicant: **Gianni Versace S.p.A.**, Milan (IT)

(72) Inventor: **Salehe Bembury**, New York, NY (US)

(73) Assignee: **GIANNI VERSACE S.p.A.**, Milan (IT)

(**) Term: **15 Years**

(21) Appl. No.: **29/647,665**

(22) Filed: **May 15, 2018**

(30) **Foreign Application Priority Data**

Mar. 23, 2018 (EM) 005017043

(51) **LOC (12) Cl.** **02-04**

(52) **U.S. Cl.**
USPC **D2/956**; D2/947; D2/951; D2/954

(58) **Field of Classification Search**
USPC .... D2/902, 906, 908, 916, 918, 925, D2/946–962, 977; 36/3 B, 22 R, 24.5, 36/25 R, 28, 32 R, 34 R, 59 C, 67 A, 103
CPC A43B 13/00; A43B 13/02; A43B 13/023; A43B 13/026; A43B 13/04; A43B 13/08; A43B 13/10; A43B 13/12; A43B 13/14; A43B 13/141; A43B 13/143; A43B 13/16; A43B 13/18; A43B 13/181; A43B 13/187; A43B 13/189; A43B 13/20; A43B 13/22; A43B 13/223; A43B 13/24; A43B 13/28; A43B 13/30; A43B 13/32; A43B 13/34; A43B 13/36
See application file for complete search history.

(56) **References Cited**

U.S. PATENT DOCUMENTS

D267,366 S * 12/1982 Davis D2/951
4,494,320 A * 1/1985 Davis A43B 13/223 36/103
D282,123 S * 1/1986 Davis D2/959
D475,514 S * 6/2003 Burg D2/956
D677,866 S * 3/2013 Vestuti A43B 13/32 D2/947
D716,535 S * 11/2014 Seo D2/951
D719,331 S * 12/2014 Christensen A43B 13/12 D2/951
D807,621 S * 1/2018 Davis A43B 13/04 D2/946
D807,623 S * 1/2018 Vestuti A43B 13/223 D2/954
D823,583 S * 7/2018 Petrie A43B 1/0045 D2/954
D838,452 S * 1/2019 Christensen A43B 13/223 D2/955
D854,295 S * 7/2019 Nethongkome D2/953
D854,798 S * 7/2019 Nethongkome D2/953
D858,964 S * 9/2019 Vestuti D2/953

(Continued)

Primary Examiner — T Chase Nelson
(74) *Attorney, Agent, or Firm* — Thomas | Horstemeyer, LLP

(57) **CLAIM**

The ornamental design for a sole for footwear, as shown and described.

DESCRIPTION

FIG. **1** is a perspective view of a sole for footwear showing my new design;
FIG. **2** is a front elevational view thereof;
FIG. **3** is a rear elevational view thereof, opposite that of FIG. **2**;
FIG. **4** is a right side elevational view thereof;
FIG. **5** is a left side elevational view thereof, opposite that of FIG. **4**;
FIG. **6** is a top view thereof; and,
FIG. **7** is a bottom view thereof.
The broken lines in FIGS. **2** and **6** illustrate portions of the sole for footwear that form no part of the claimed design.

1 Claim, 5 Drawing Sheets

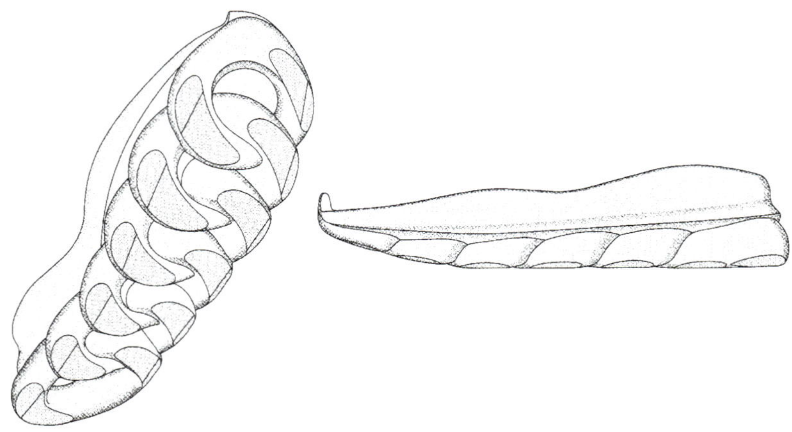

Versace

118

(2017)

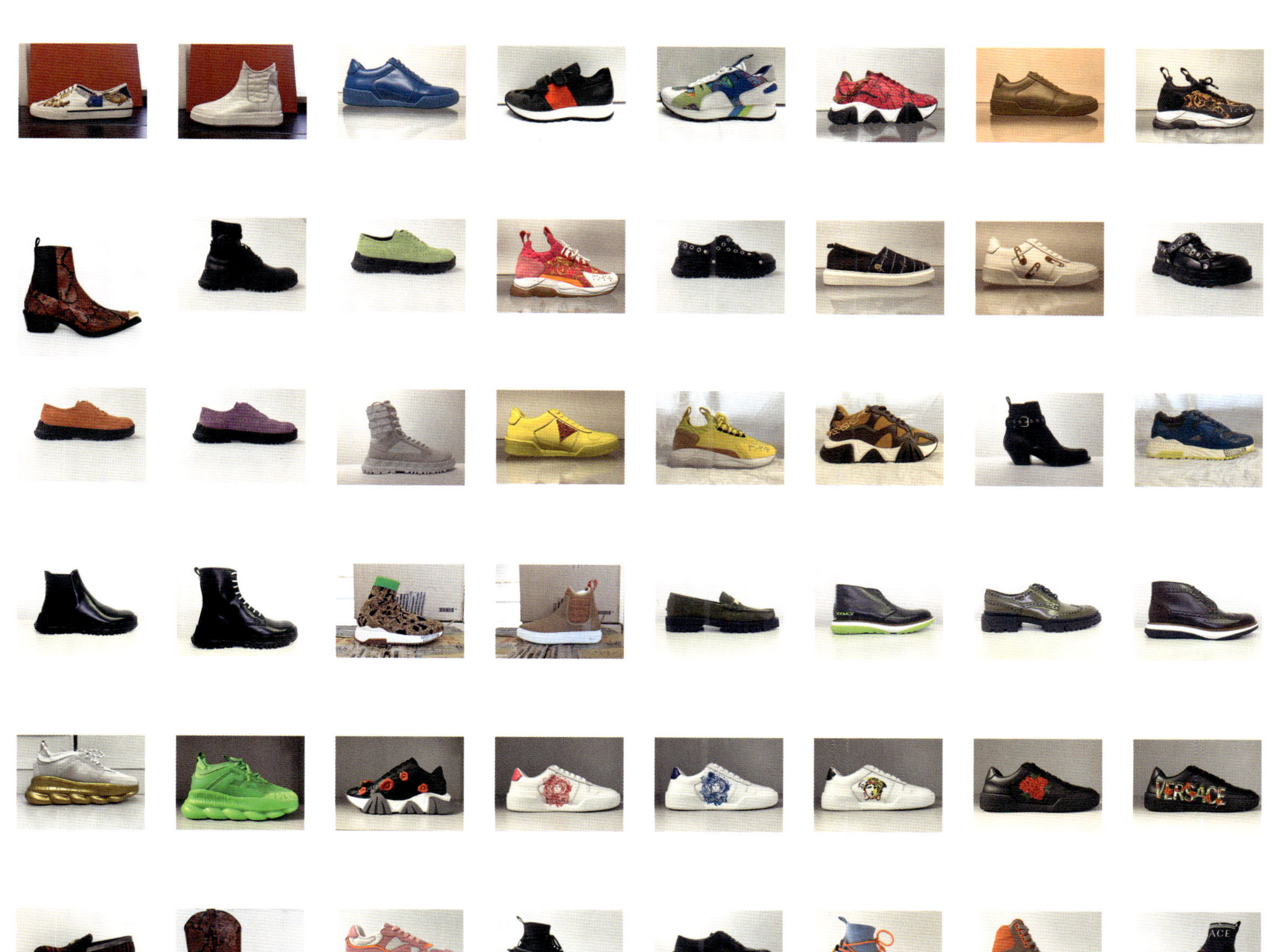

127

VERSACE (2017)

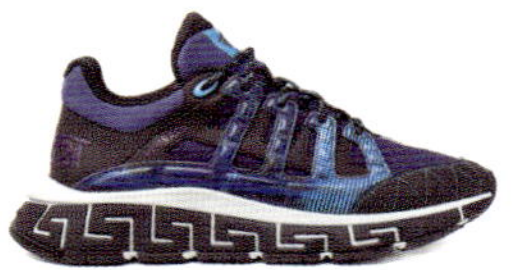
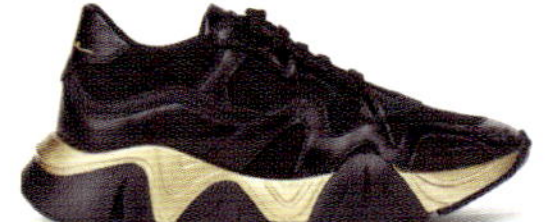
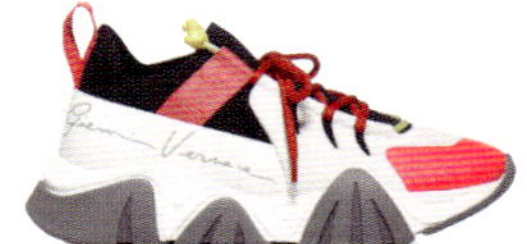
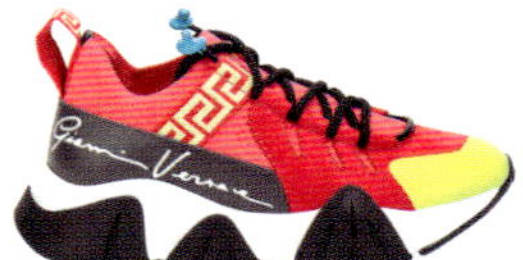
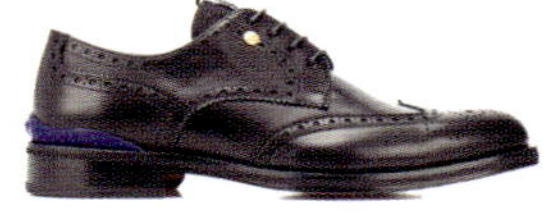
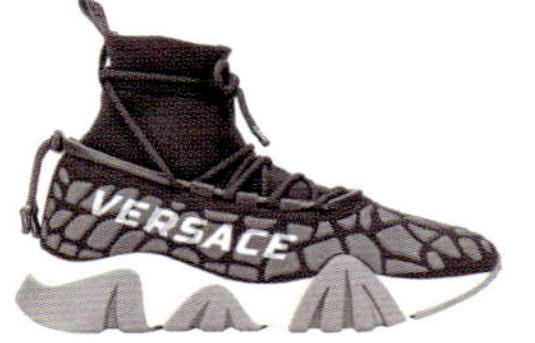
VERSACE
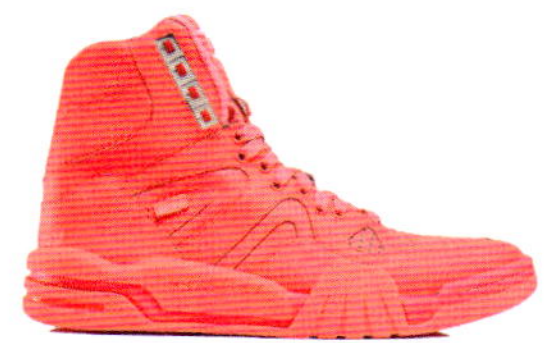
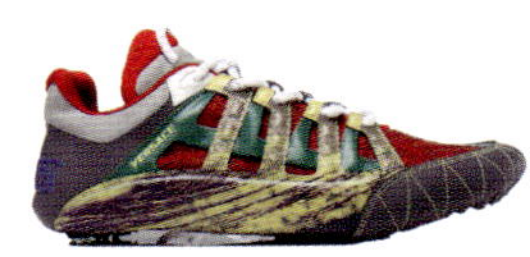
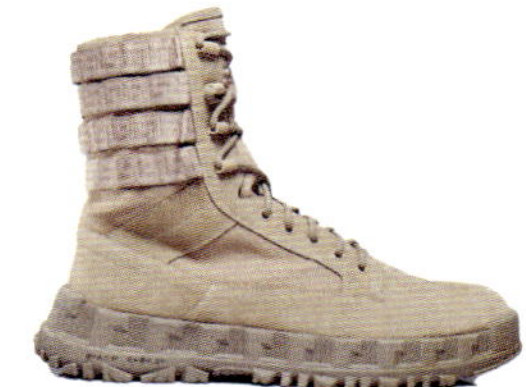
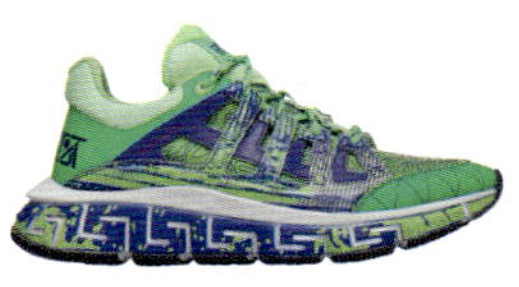
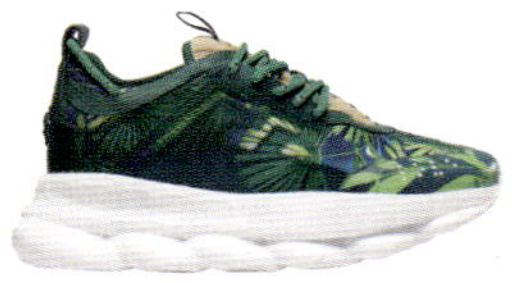
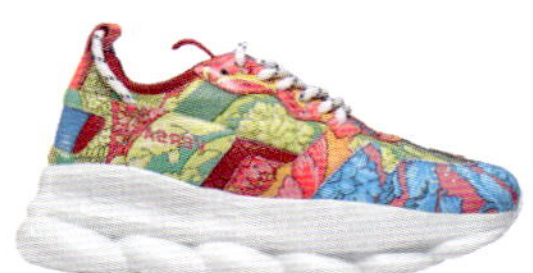
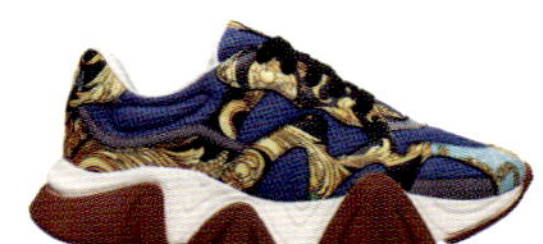
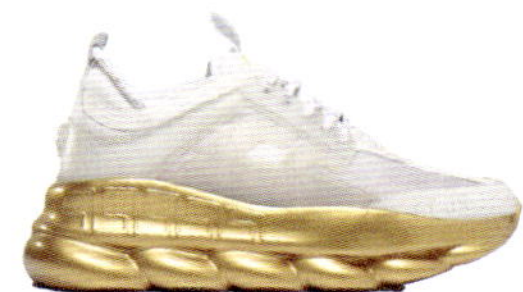
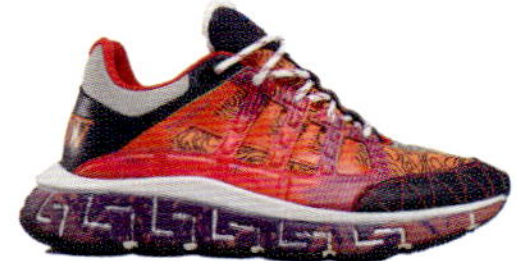
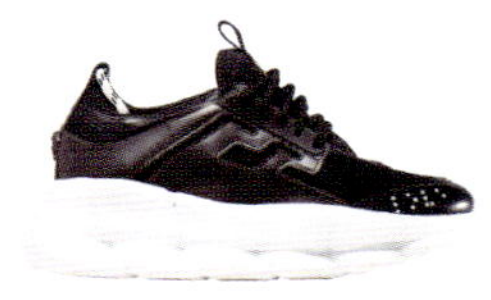
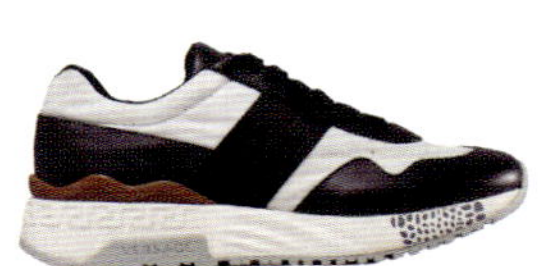
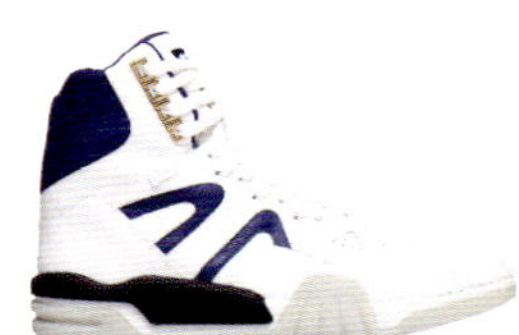
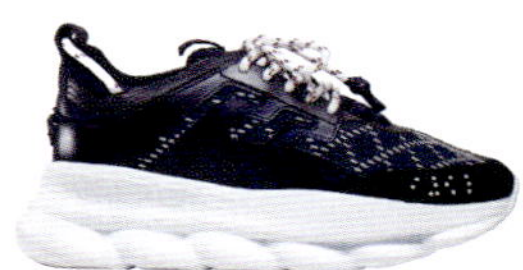
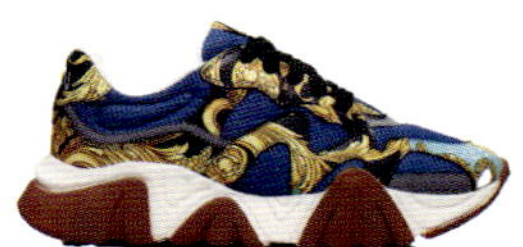
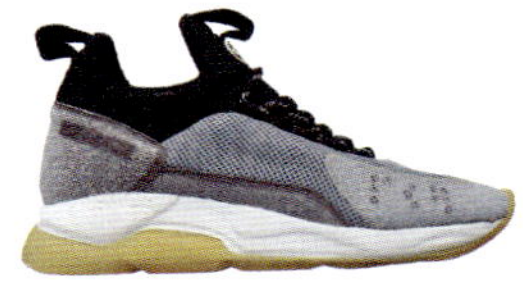
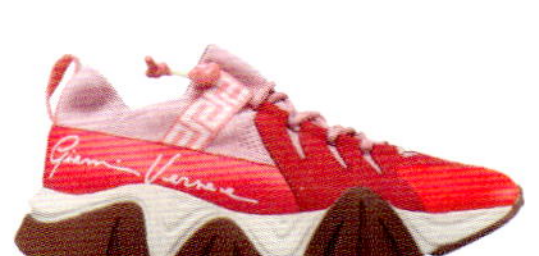
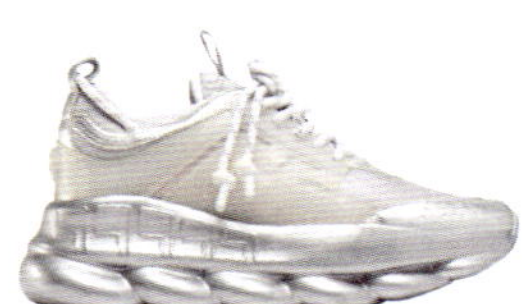
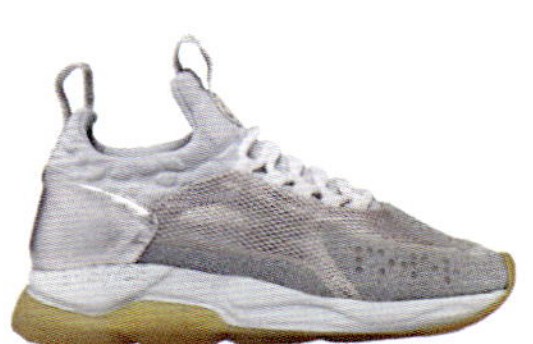
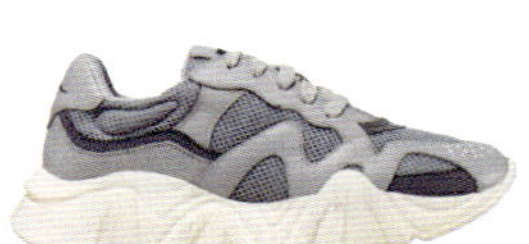

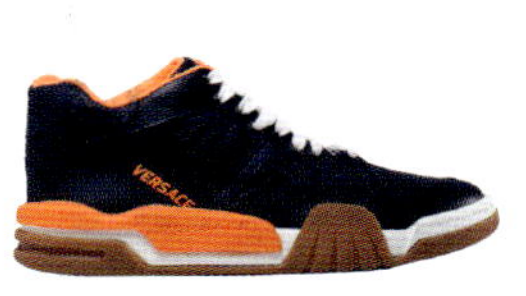
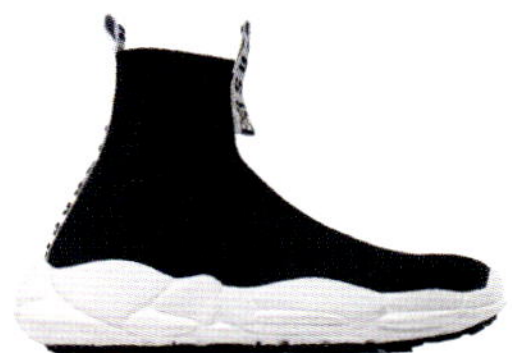
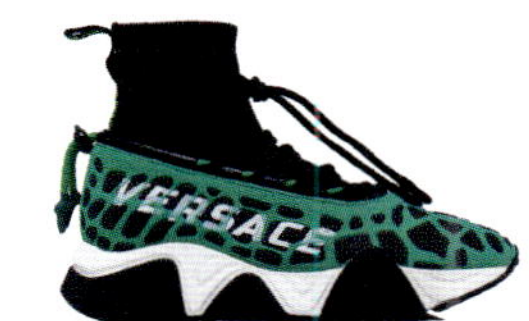
VERSACE
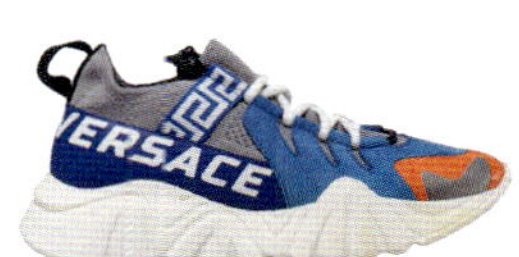
VERSACE
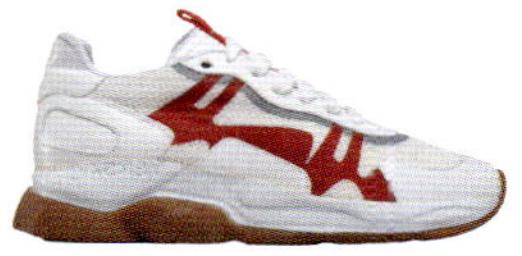
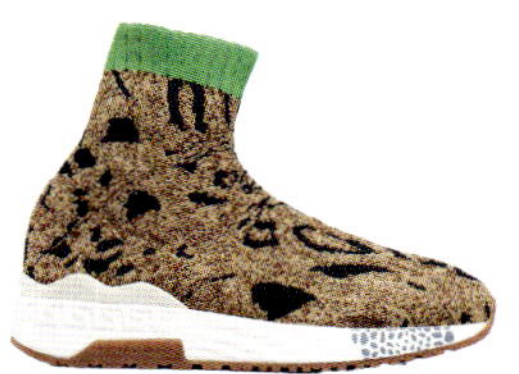
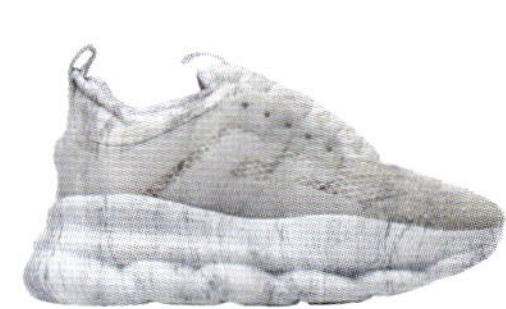
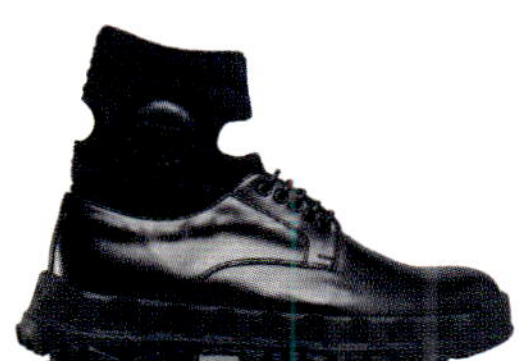
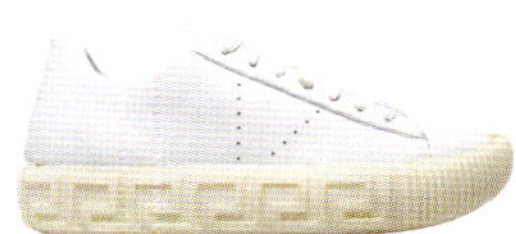
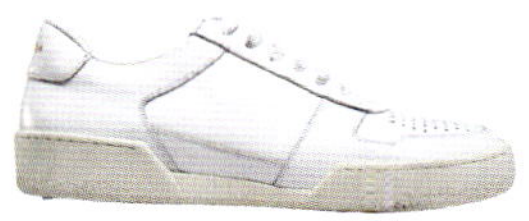
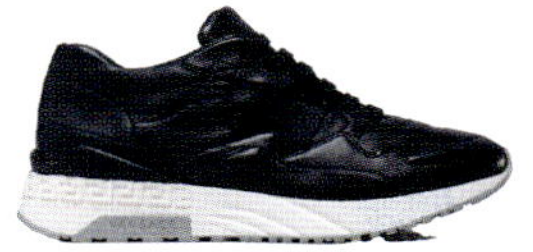
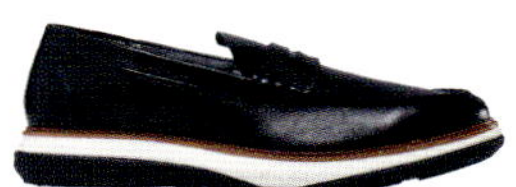
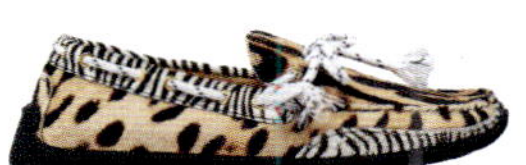
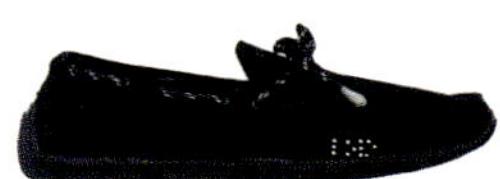
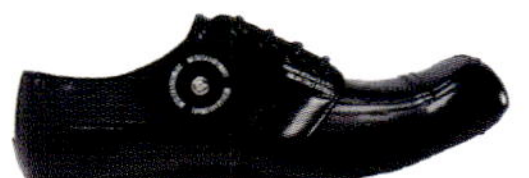
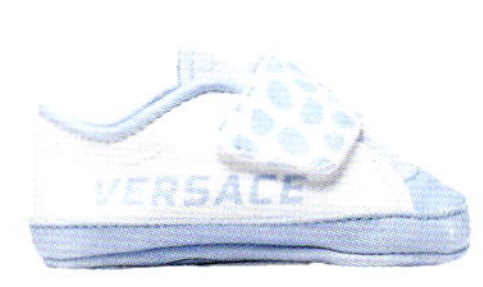
VERSACE
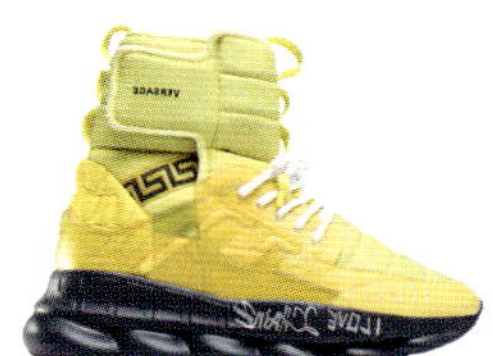
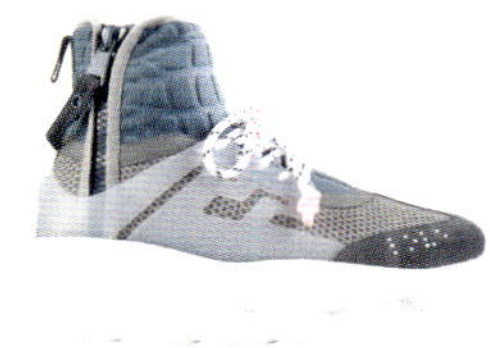
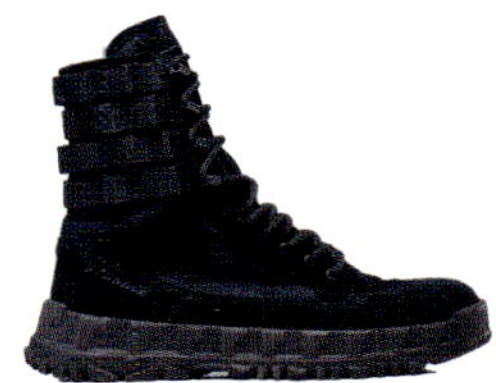
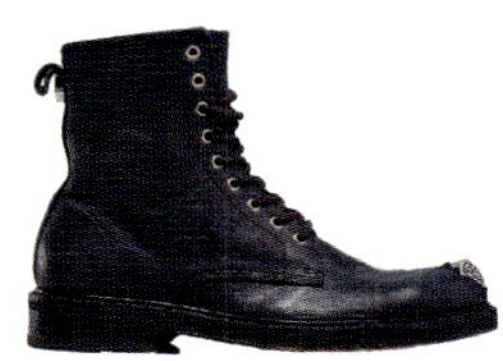
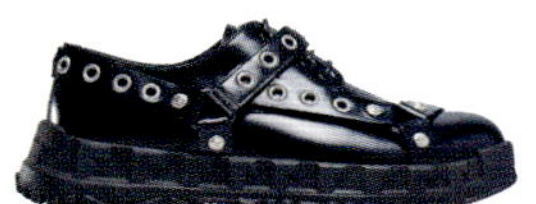

130

SNEAKERS FOR BREAKFAST (2018)

SHOO' YOUR AGAIN

T

SHOT

SNEAKERS FOR BREAKFAST
SHOOT YOUR SHOT AGAIN

A lot of industry relationships happen by chance. I first met Takashi Murakami with Don C. Our design offices were in the same building in Los Angeles, and he let me know that Takashi Murakami was waiting for him at his store, RSVP Gallery, down the block. He asked if I wanted to go with him, so I went and quickly met Takashi.

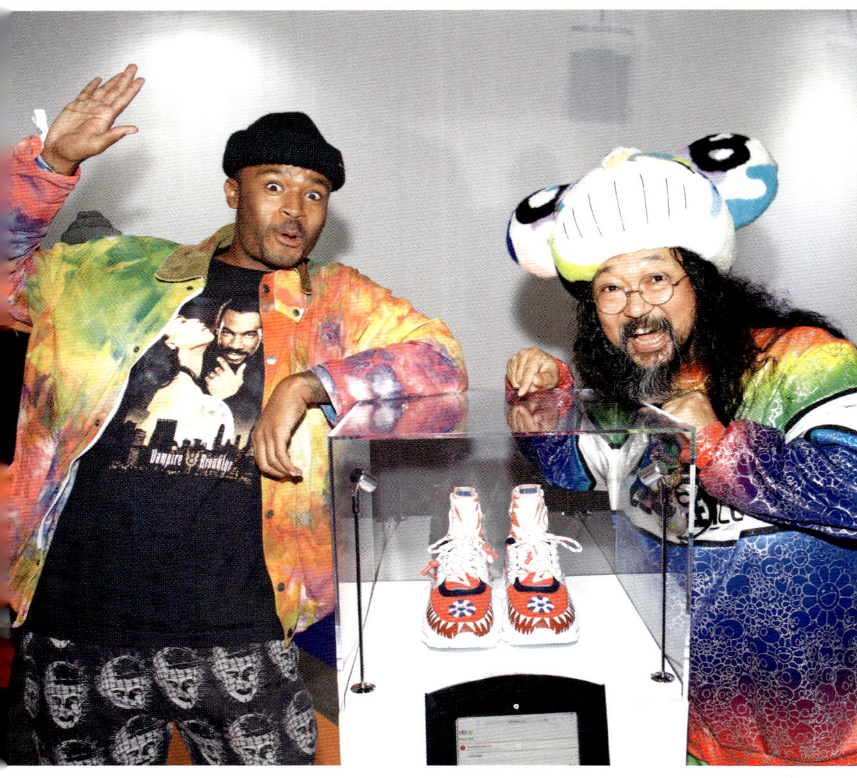

A couple of years later, I was in Paris for Fashion Week. I had been a designer at Versace for about a year. The Chain Reaction was a massive hit, and I was in the mode of trying to create moments–marketing moments, collaborative moments–to bring eyes, attention, and most importantly sales to the newly anointed Versace sneaker business. I saw Takashi again at the Off-White show. He was extremely warm, and he took a look at my shoes. I was wearing the Chain Reaction, which was still a pretty new shoe, so not many people were wearing them at the time. He told me he wanted to meet with me at the Gagosian gallery in a couple of days, which was an unexpected invitation that I immediately accepted.

A few days later I met him at Gagosian. I found him sitting at a low table that felt Japanese in execution, eating lunch. He had no shoes on and was eating with his hands. I've since learned that Takashi's English is amazing, but at the time he was using a translator for the most part when we spoke. We had a very surface-level yet intimate conversation about footwear, sneakers, and the culture, about where things were headed, and about my participation in the space and my experience at Versace. He let me know that he had become recently really interested in the subculture of sneakers as a whole, and that he wanted to create some kind of project in sneakers. He showed me the sneakers that he had–in a corner of the room was a lineup of about 20 pairs of sneakers in his personal collection, of which 3 or 4 were my designs. Not only was I surprised to see that Takashi Murakami had a rotation, but I was double surprised to see that he was a fan of my work.

Throughout the meeting I was thinking to myself, "I'd love if he signed something for me." I was very familiar with his work, I was a fan of his work, and I knew that I had to create a memory of this moment by getting him to sign something just to mark the occasion. We live in an era where people want selfies to create memories with people that they admire, but I love a signature. Just as I was about to muster up the courage to ask him, he whispered something in Japanese to his translator, and all of a sudden my Chain Reactions in red came out and he asked if I could sign his shoes. It was extremely surreal. I signed what was at the time my most popular creation for him, and I was honored and humbled.

After the meeting ended, we went our separate ways, we went back to Fashion Week, and we went to the drawing board. We tried to figure out how we could capitalize on his recent interest in sneakers and what we could do that would attract an audience and cultivate a conversation. I thought that creating art within the footwear space would be an amazing project, and we collaboratively came up with Sneakers for Breakfast, which would be a charity auction of 6 custom sneakers. They were auctioned off at ComplexCon, with different charities assigned to each pair. The participants in the collaboration were all young up-and-coming footwear designers: Mattieu Hagelaars, Daniel Bailey, Helen Kirkum, Suzanne Oude Hengel, David Mawdsley, and myself.

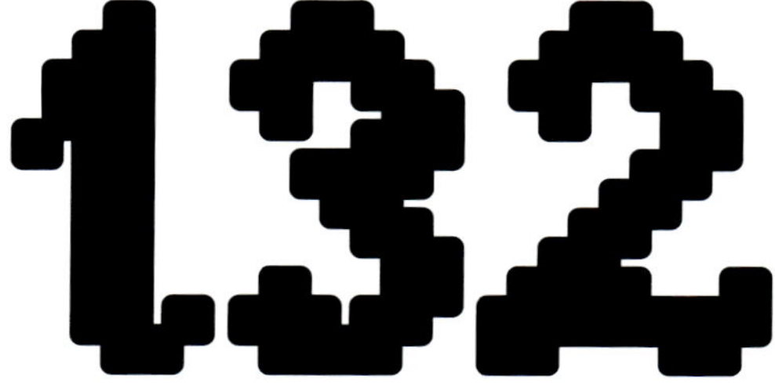

The premise of the project was that we were six different footwear designers from six different backgrounds, from different parts of the world with different resources. The shoe that I was going to make would be a Versace shoe; someone else was going to create something handmade from different shoe parts; another designer was going to create something at a shoe factory with one-off pieces. So there were many different paths being taken, and this was represented in the final outcome of the footwear itself. The sneaker I created was an exaggerated version of my Chain Reaction for Versace. The upper featured a beaded vamp that featured Takashi's iconic flower logo, and then the collar featured more of Takashi's art, which he made available for the project. Marc Ecko ended up being the one to purchase mine, which actually sparked the friendship we have to this day.

This project did an amazing job of pulling in that young hype-hungry consumer that goes to ComplexCon. Normally you don't see high fashion participation in a space like that, and this was an example of the freedom I had to create moments for Versace, which Donatella trusted me to execute. This was also one of the first times that 360 experiential marketing was put into my hands: Takashi asked me how we should do it, how we could make it special and different. One of the things Takashi did was create characters of all of the designers in his artistic vision, which were featured at the booth. He had prints made and gave them to all of the designers, which was a great gift—it's awesome to have a one-of-one Takashi piece that's of myself. Each designer also made a collaborative t-shirt, so now I have a t-shirt that says "Takashi Murakami x Salehe Bembury Sneakers for Breakfast Long Beach California 2018." That to me really marks the moment. It is a significant memory, and even just seeing the year makes me realize how much time has passed, how long I've been friends with Takashi, and how significant that moment was.

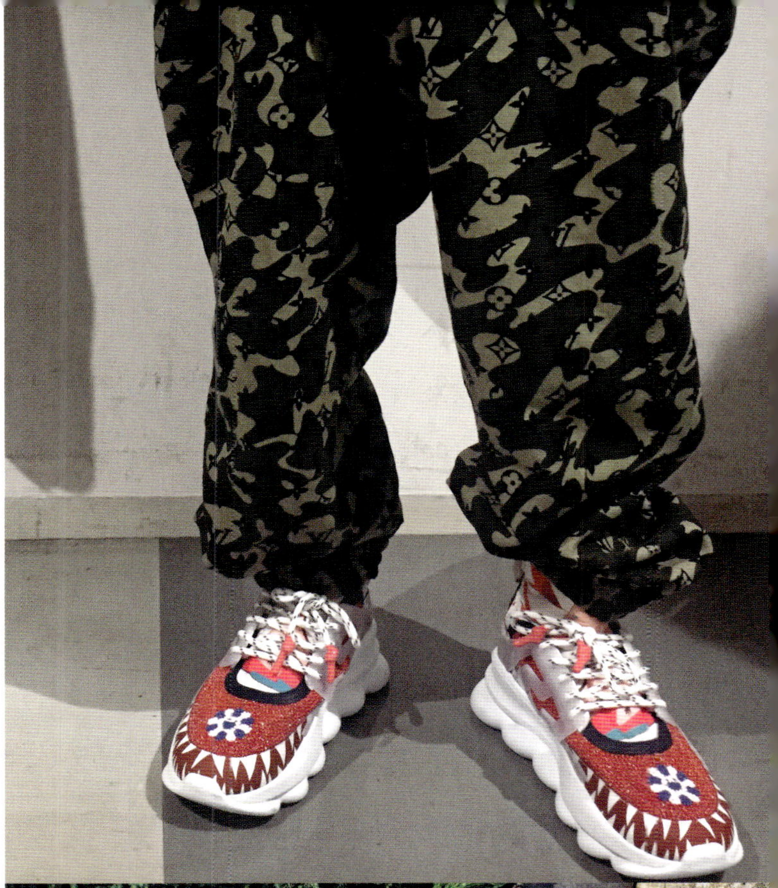

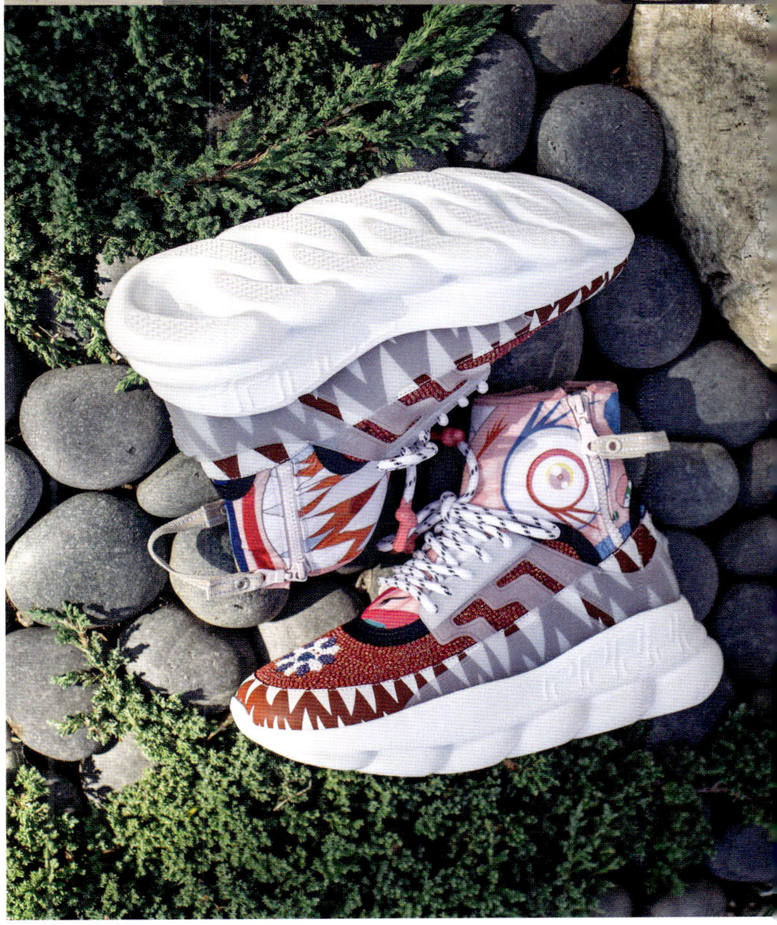

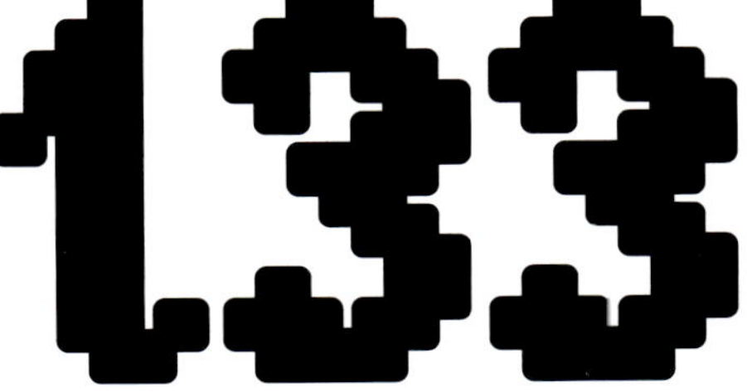

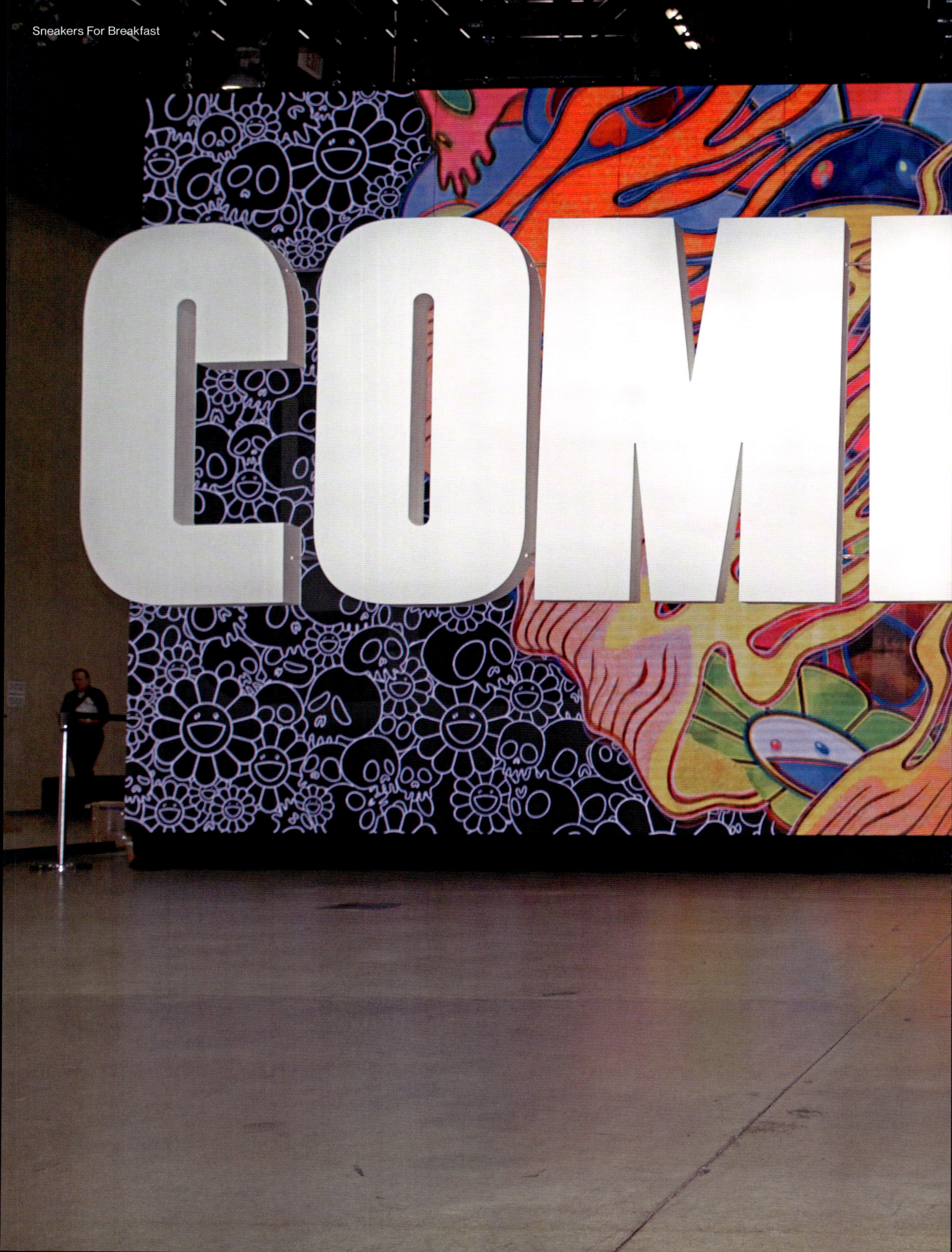

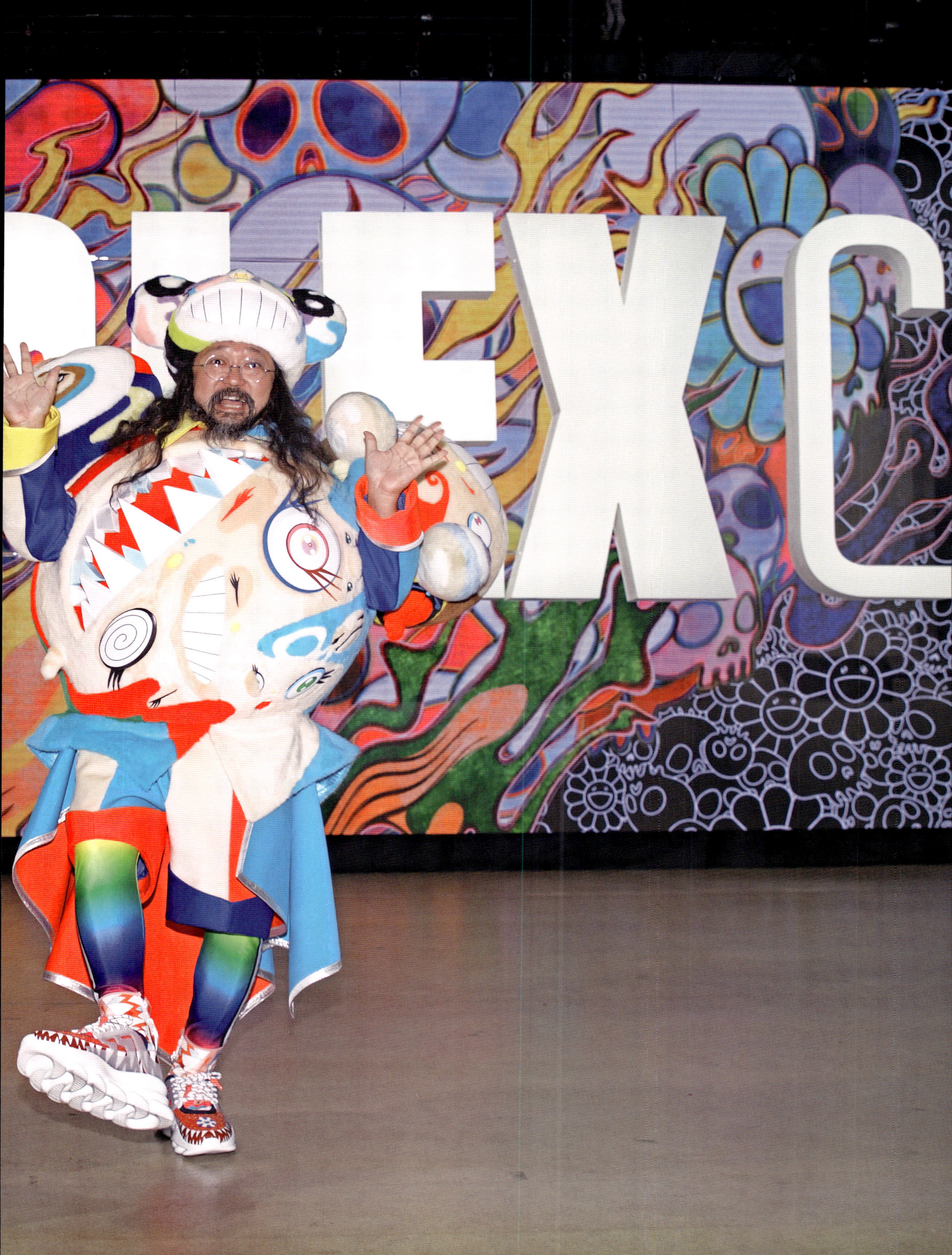

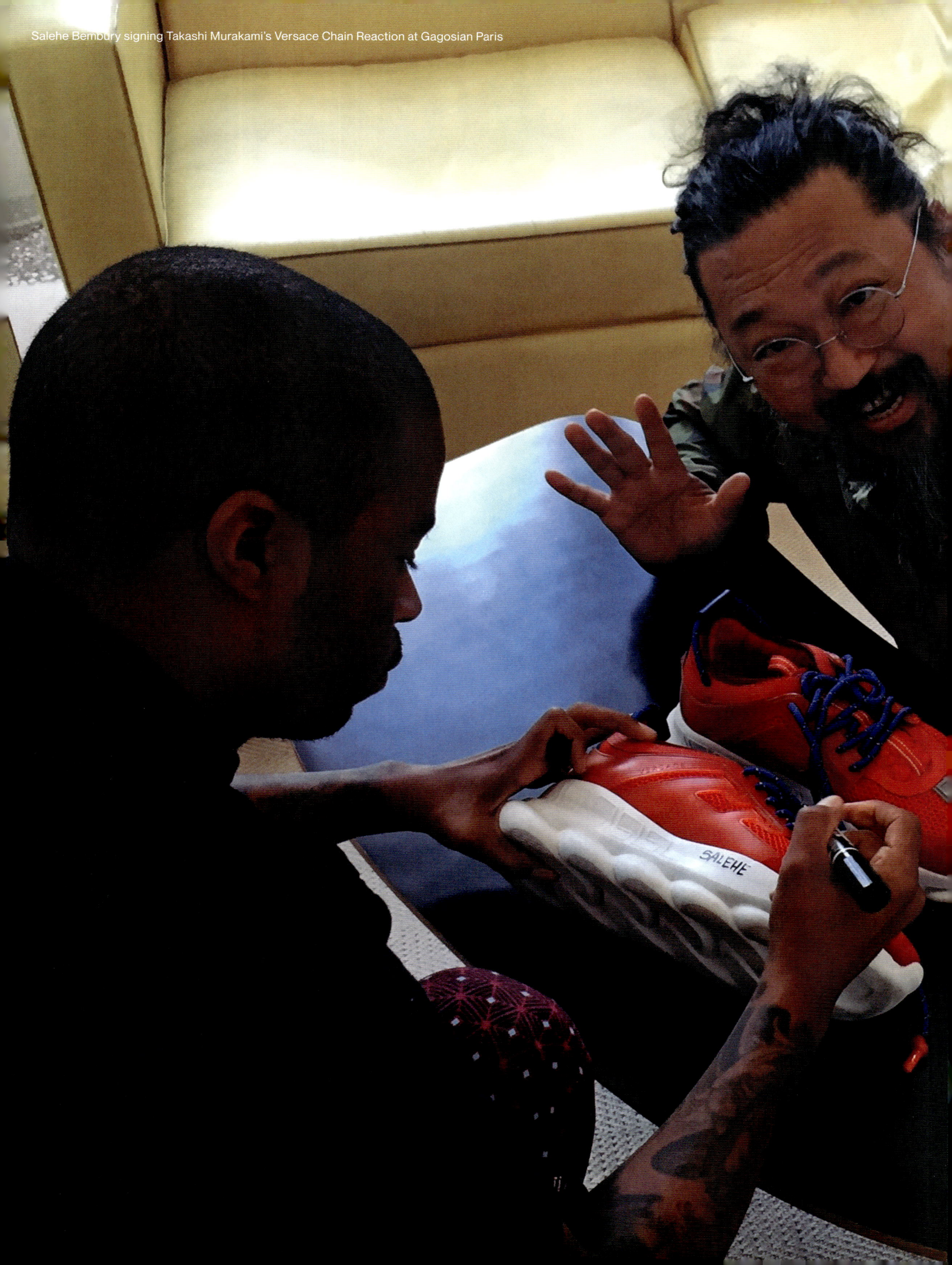

Salehe Bembury signing Takashi Murakami's Versace Chain Reaction at Gagosian Paris

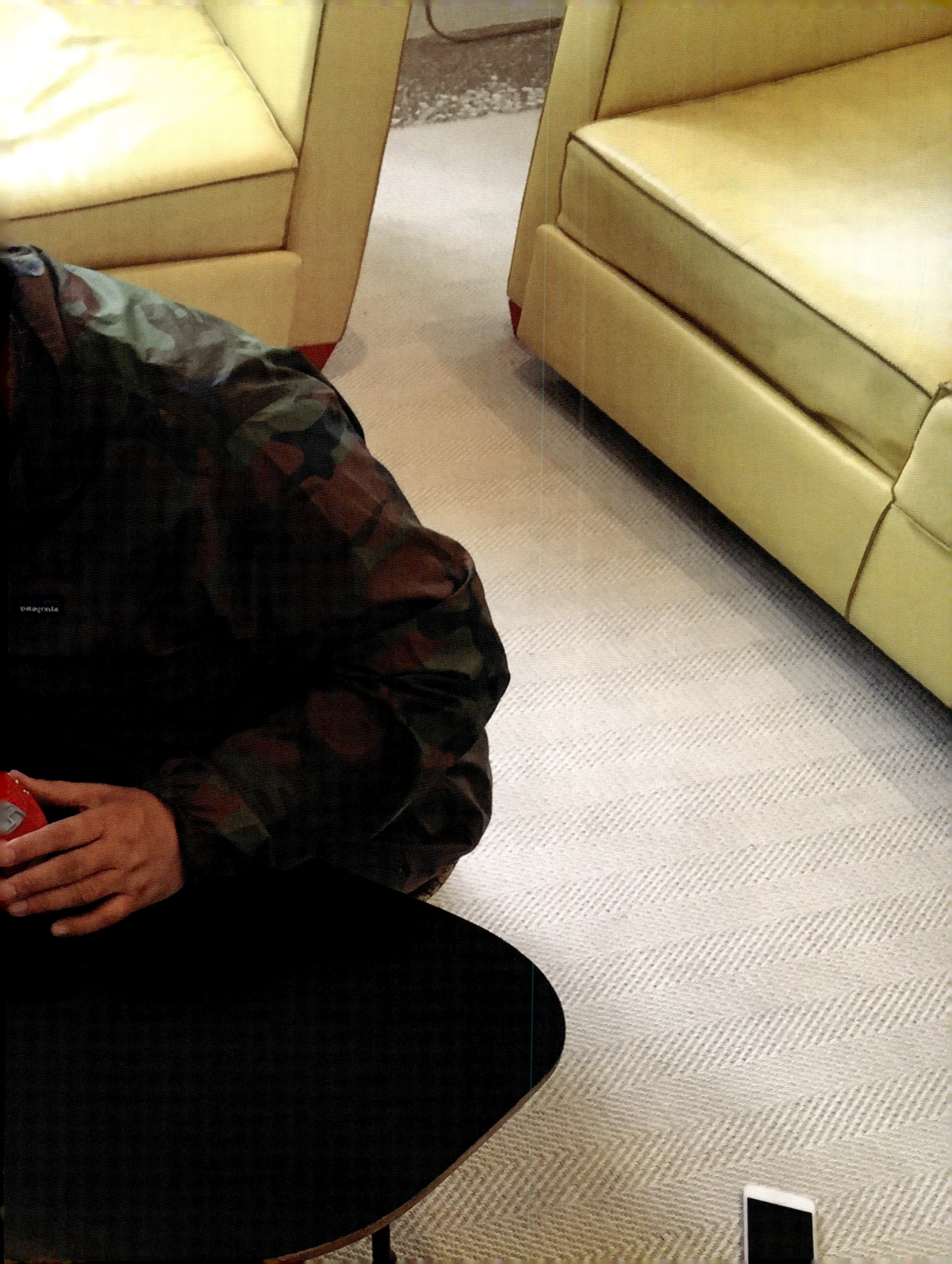

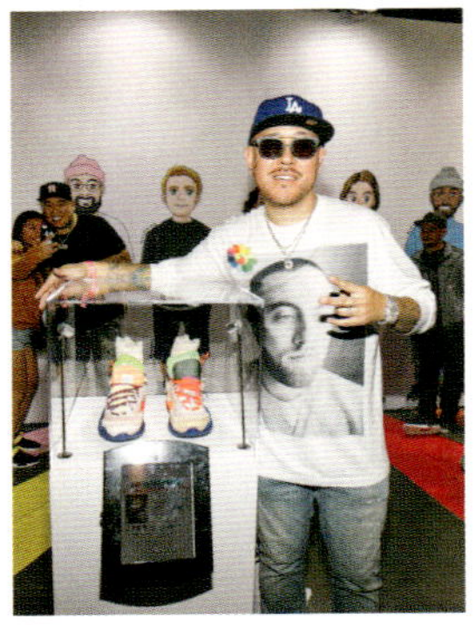

Ben Baller at Sneakers for Breakfast

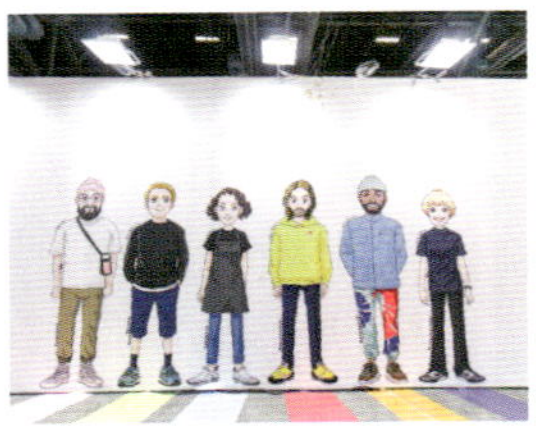

Takashi Murkami Sneakers for Breakfast illustrations

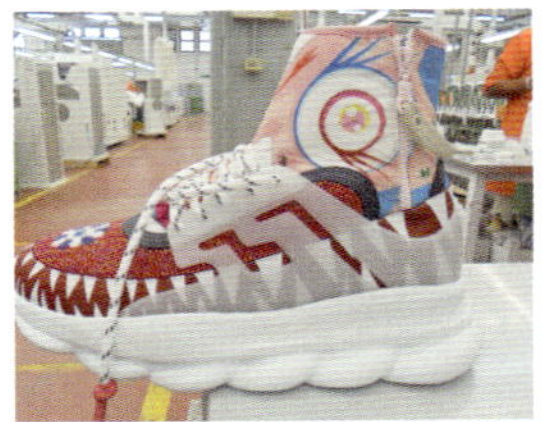

Salehe Bembury x Takashi Murakami Versace Chain Reaction "Sneakers for Breakfast" sample

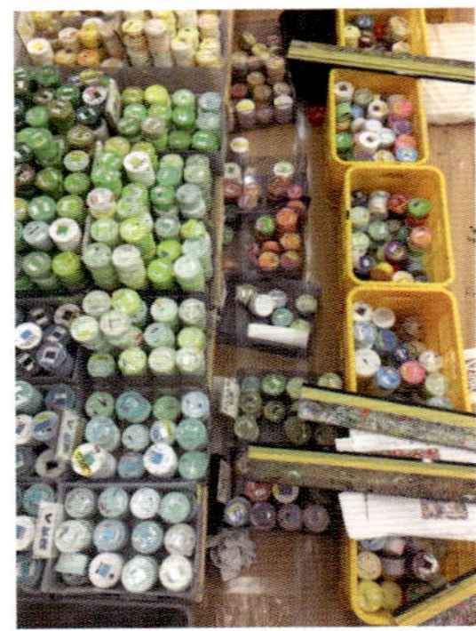

Takashi Murakami studio visit

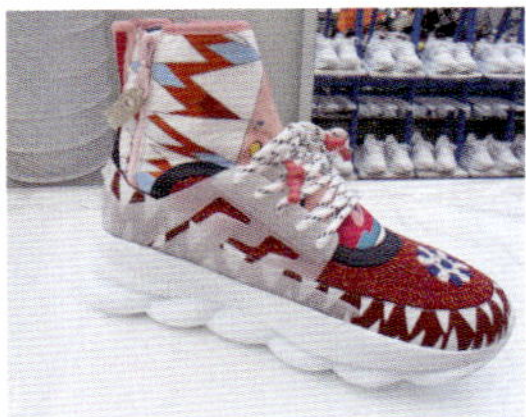

Salehe Bembury x Takashi Murakami Versace Chain Reaction "Sneakers for Breakfast" sample

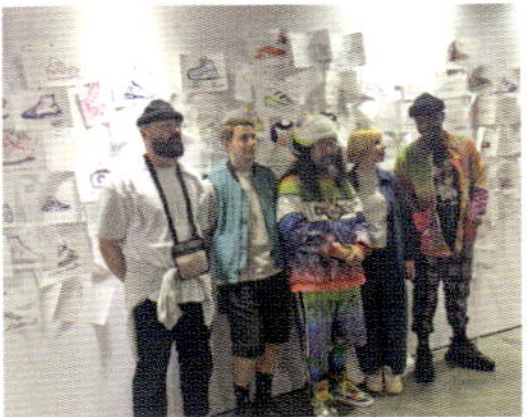

Suzanne Oude Hengel, Takashi Murakami, David Mawdsley, Daniel Bailey, and Salehe Bembury

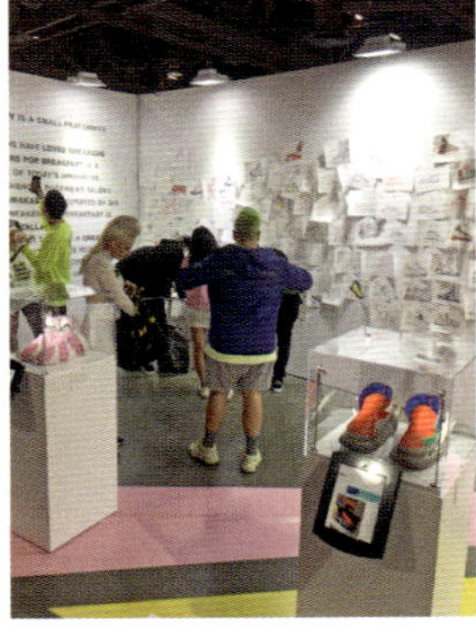

Sneakers for Breakfast sketch wall

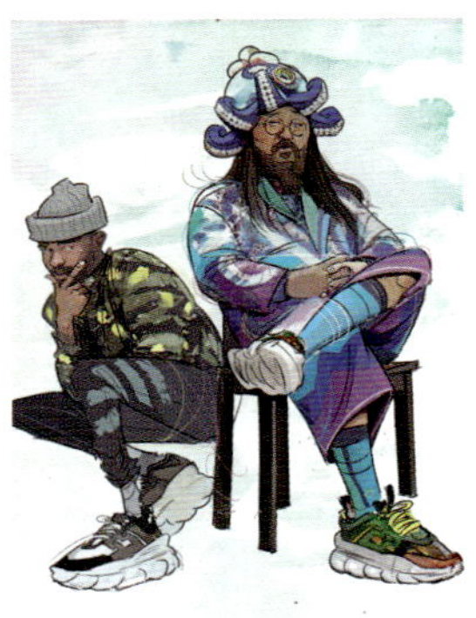

Salehe Bembury and Takashi Murakami fan art

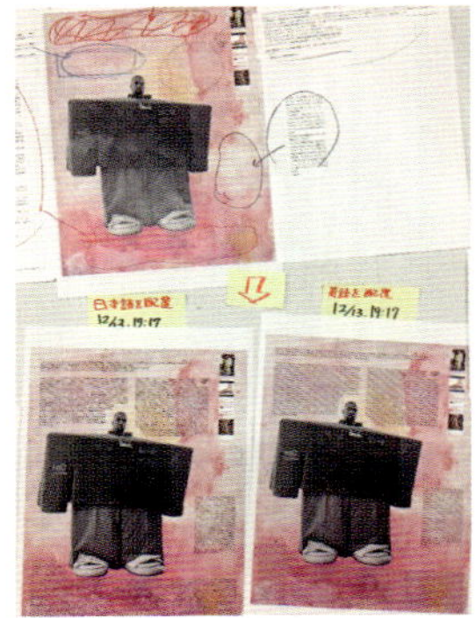

Takashi Murakami studio visit

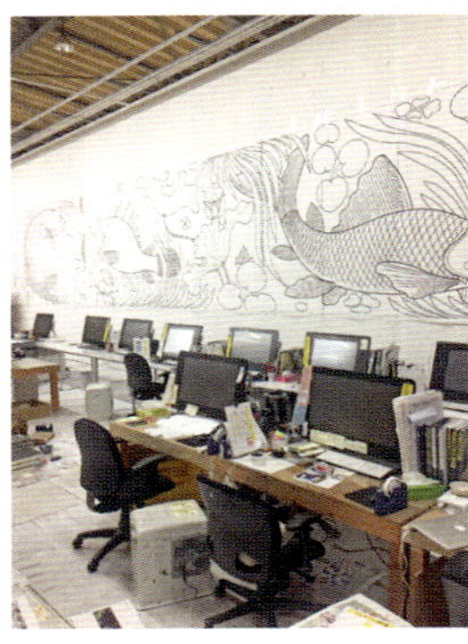

Takashi Murakami studio visit

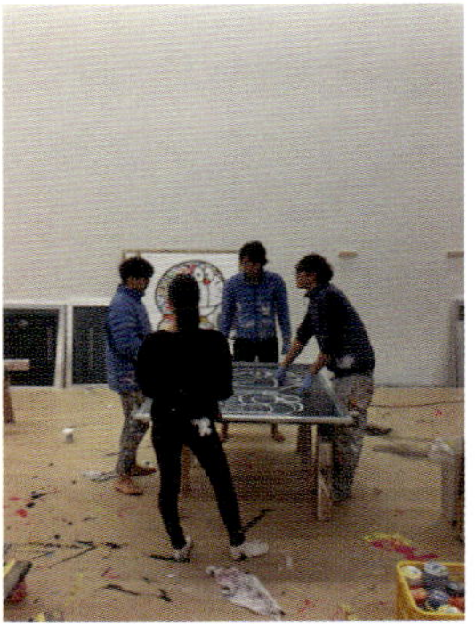

Takashi Murakami studio visit

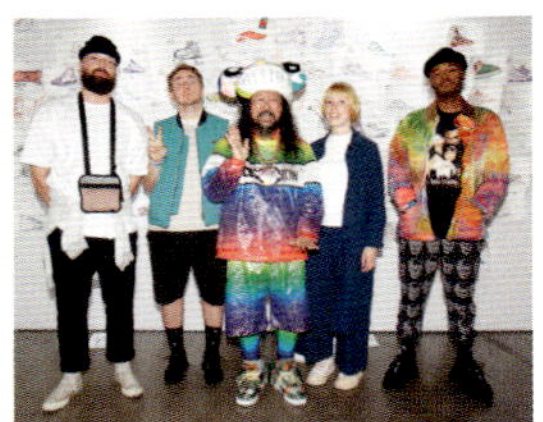

Suzanne Oude Hengel, Takashi Murakami, David Mawdsley, Daniel Bailey, and Salehe Bembury

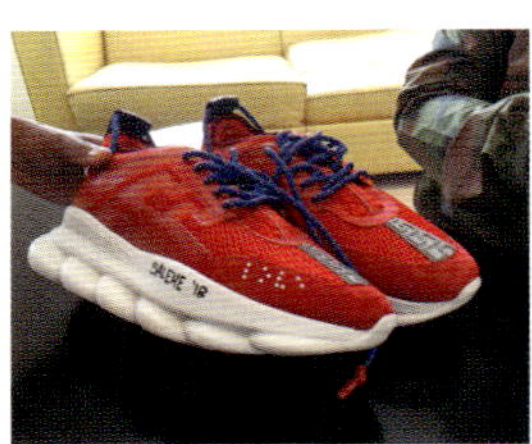

Salehe Bembury's signature on Takashi Murakami's Versace Chain Reaction

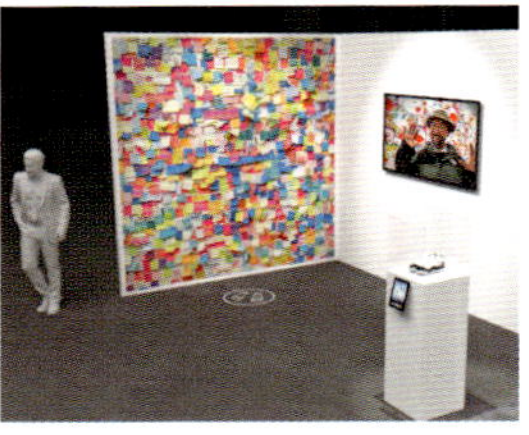

Sneakers for Breakfast exhibition render

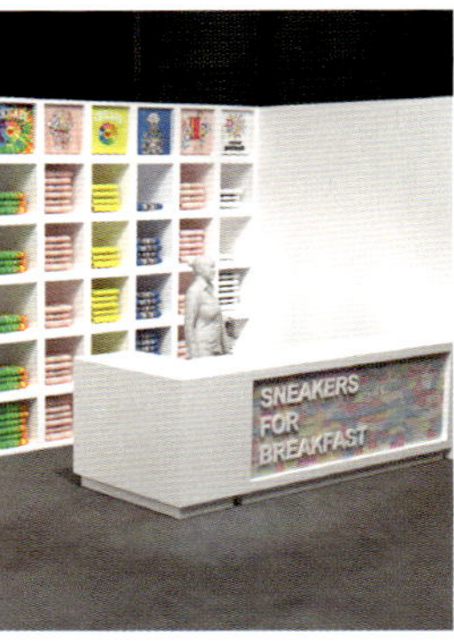

Sneakers for Breakfast exhibition render

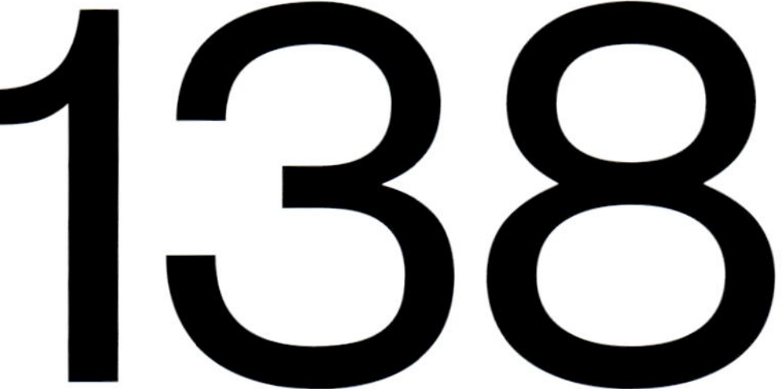

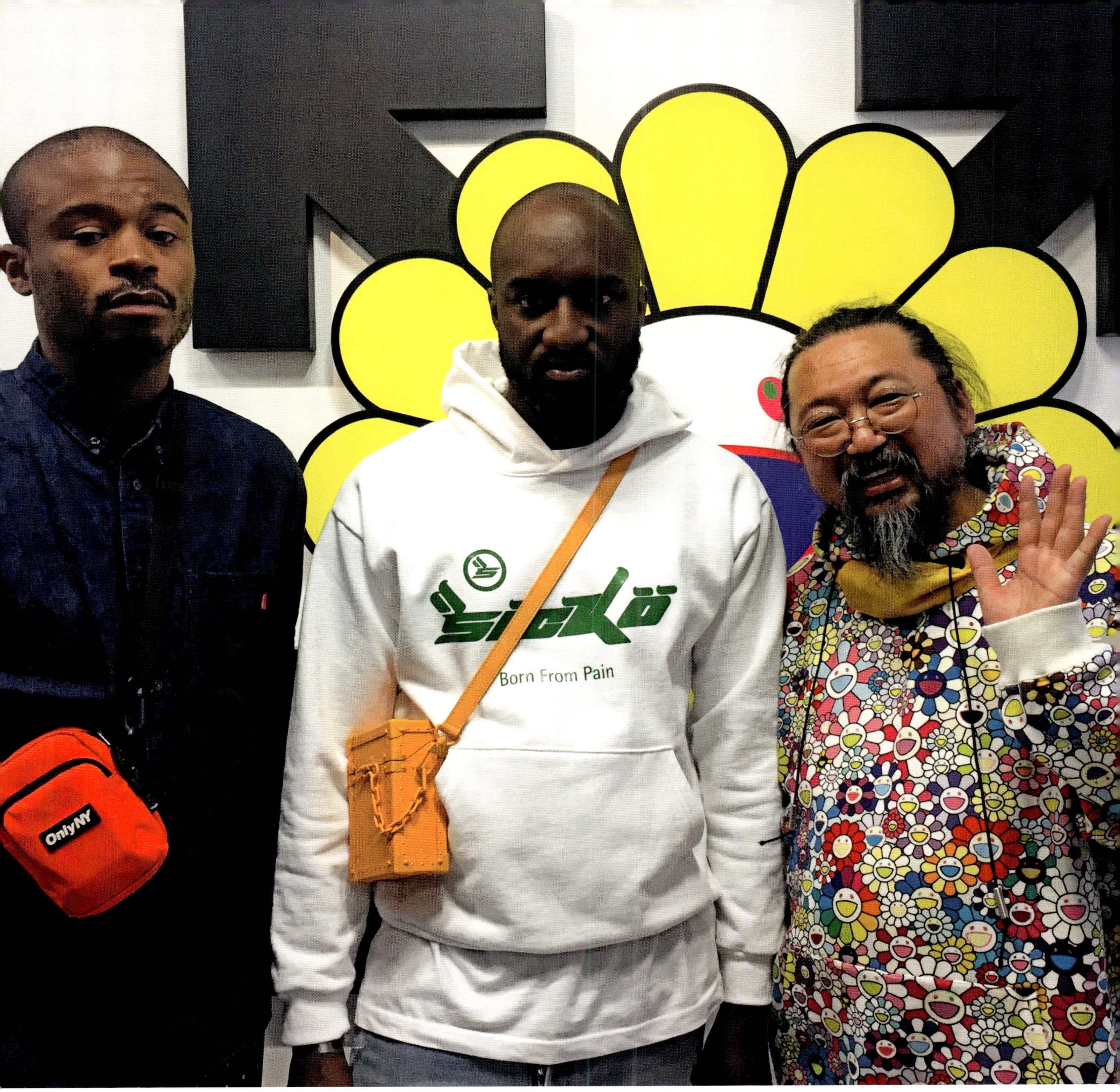

Salehe Bembury, Virgil Abloh, and Takashi Murakami

139

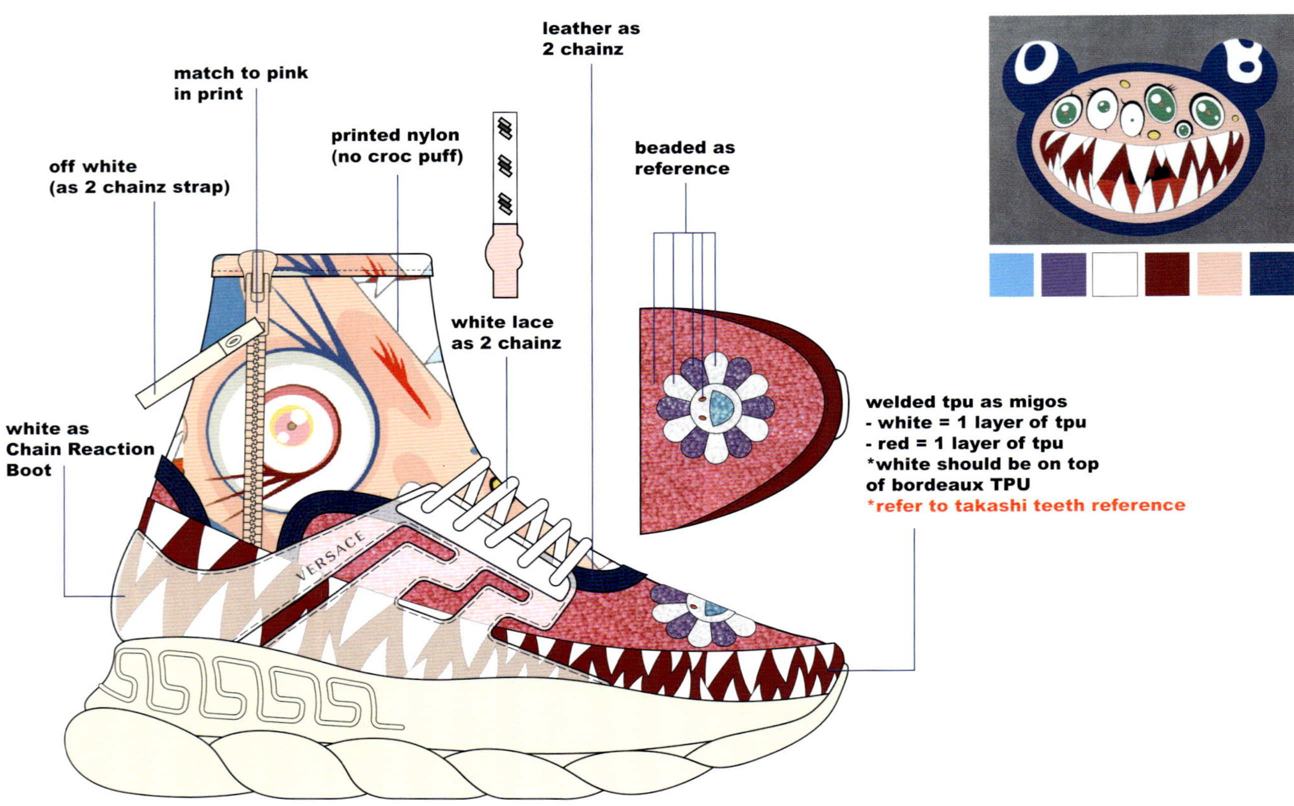

Sneakers for Breakfast

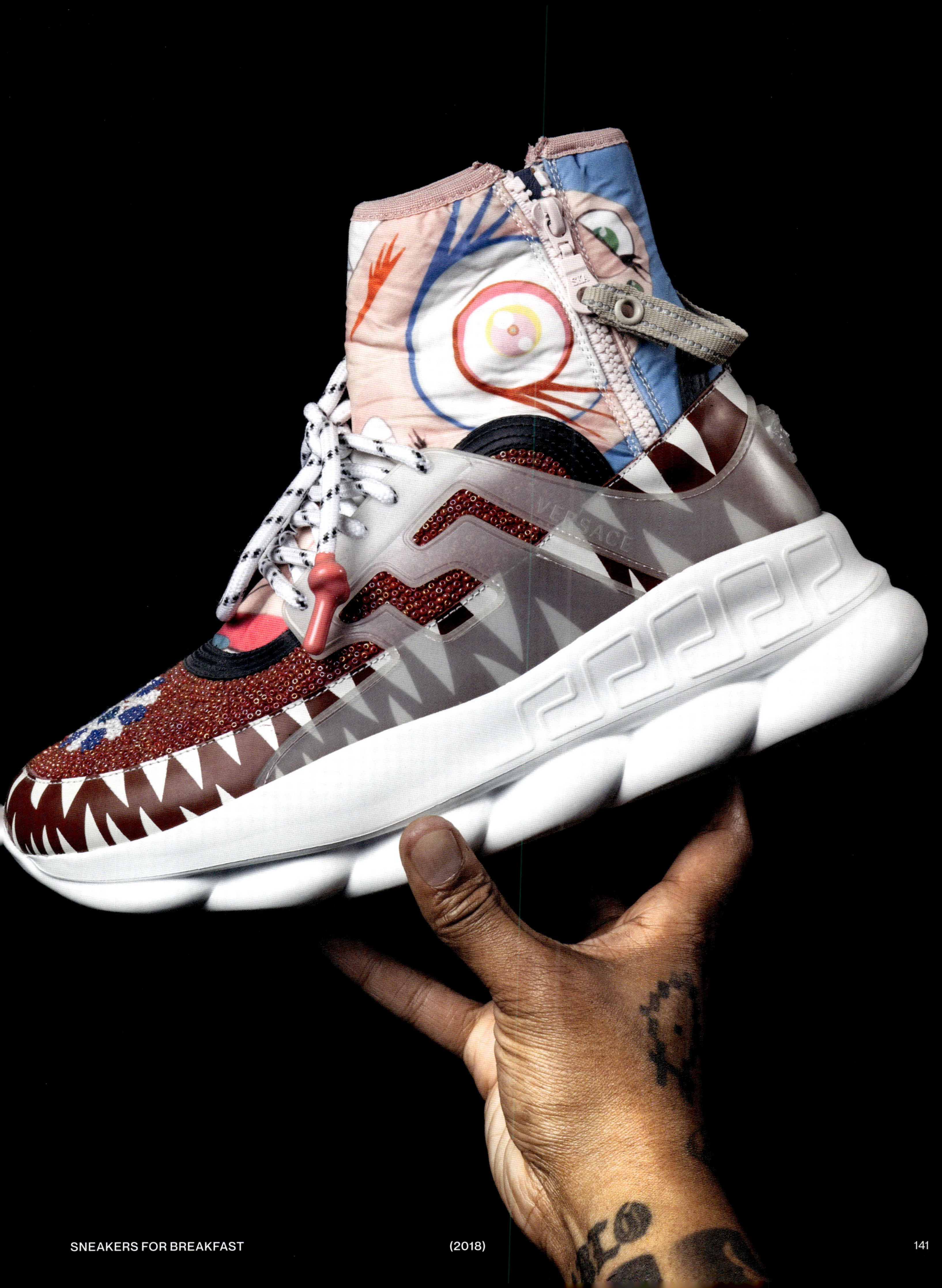
VERSACE

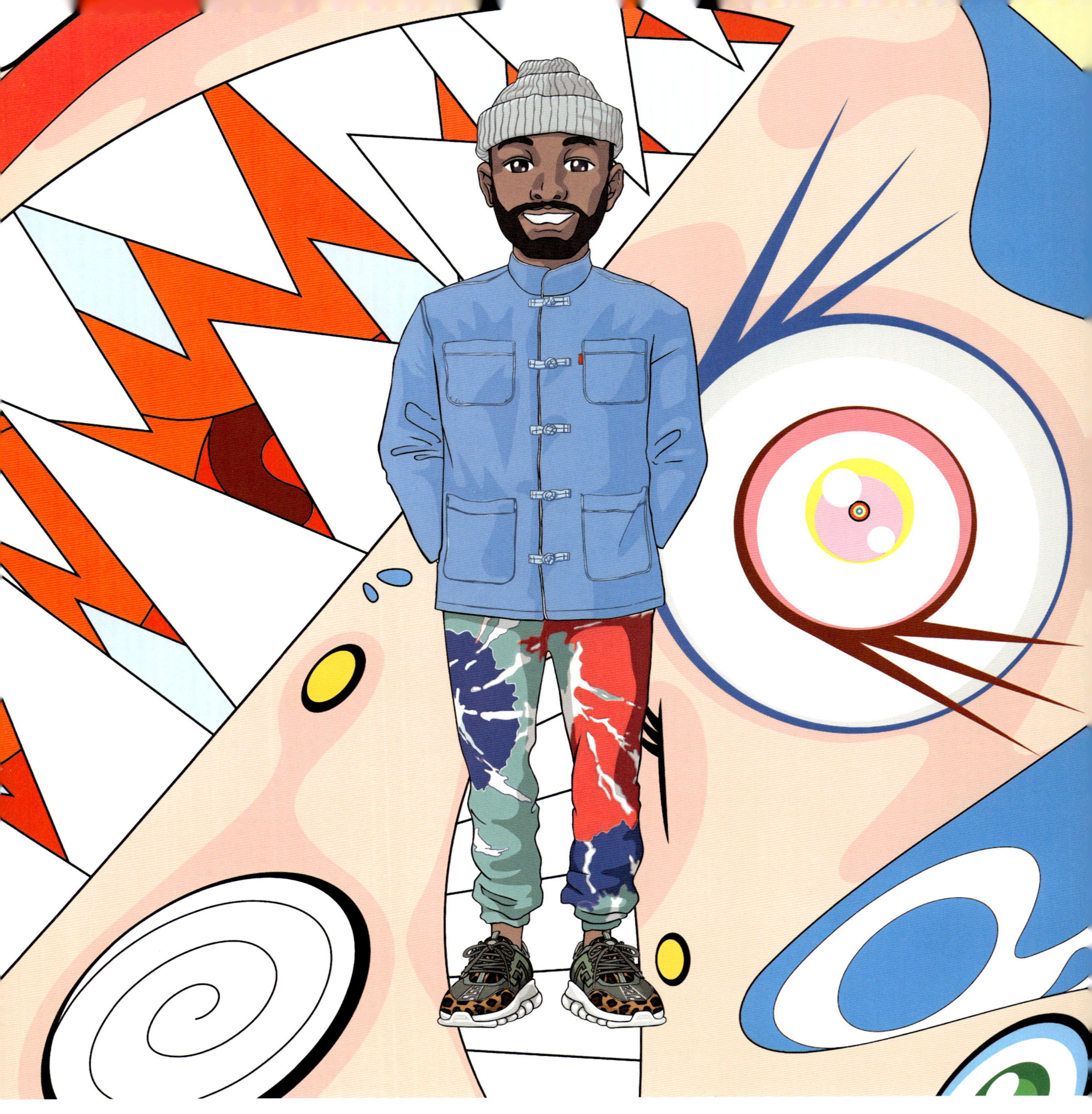

Takashi Murakami work - Salehe Bembury

142

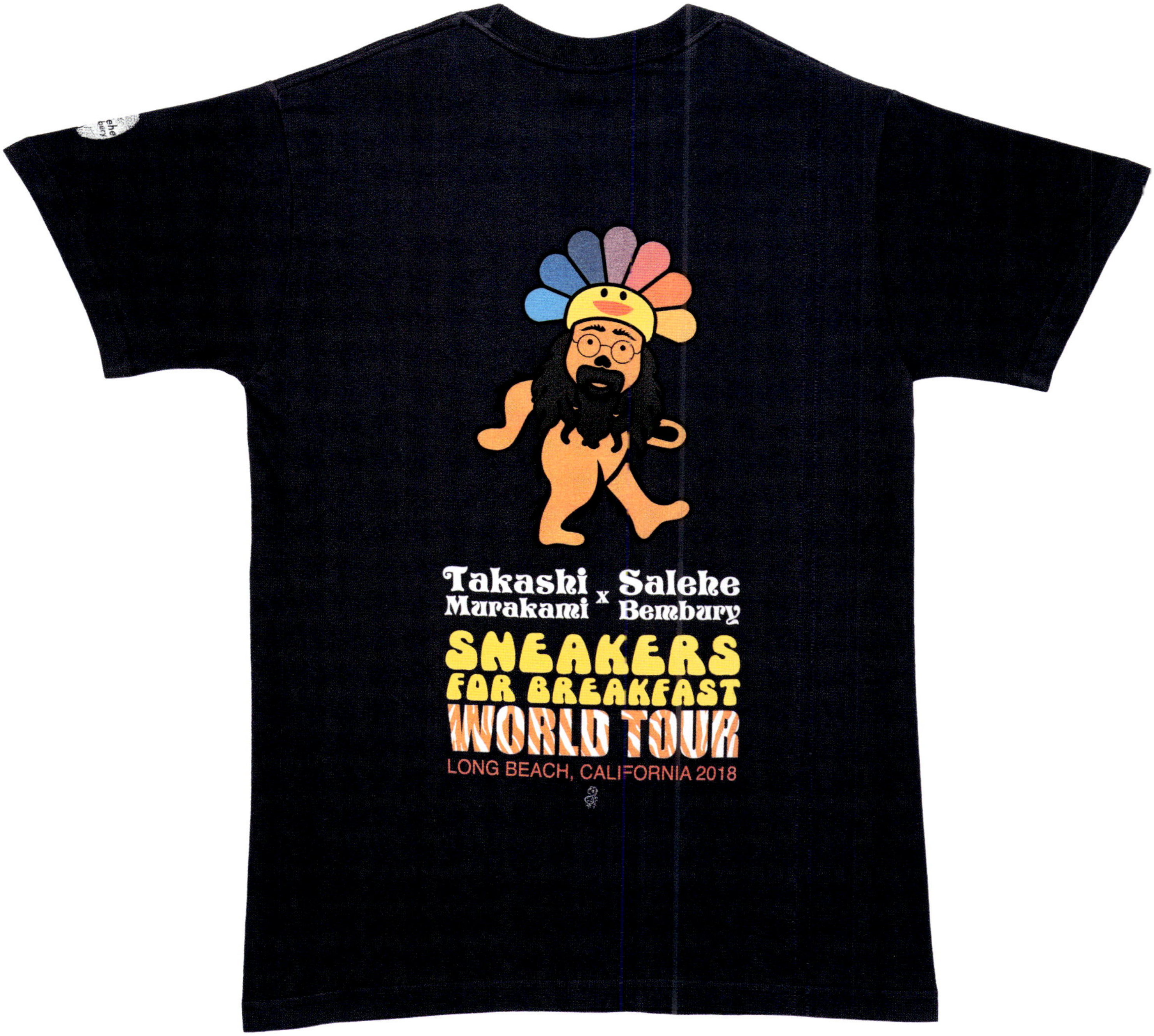

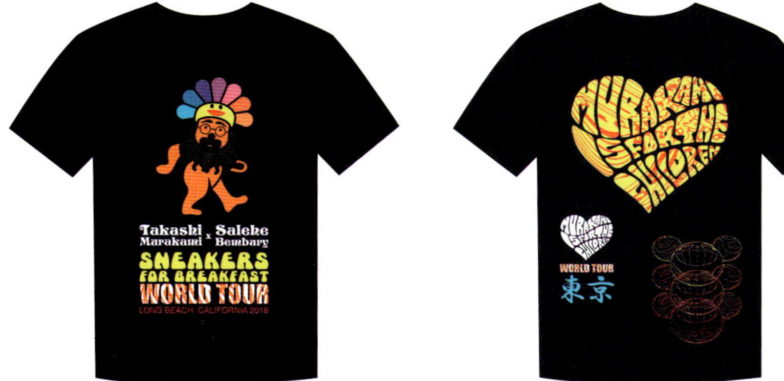

Salehe Bembury x Takashi Murakami Sneakers for Breakfast collaborative shirt design

143

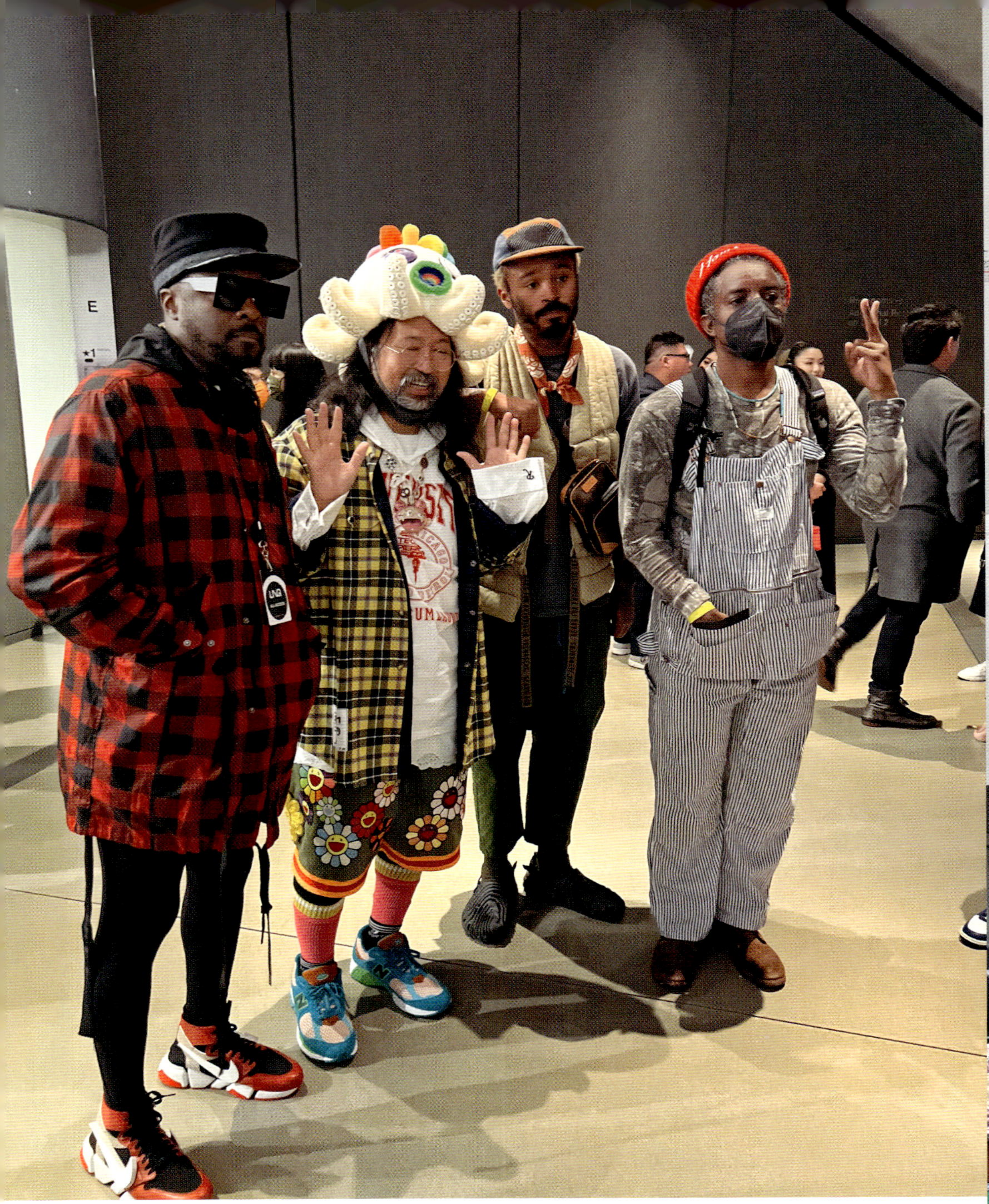

Will.i.am, Takashi Murakami, Salehe Bembury and André Benjamin at Takashi Murakami's Broad Exhibit

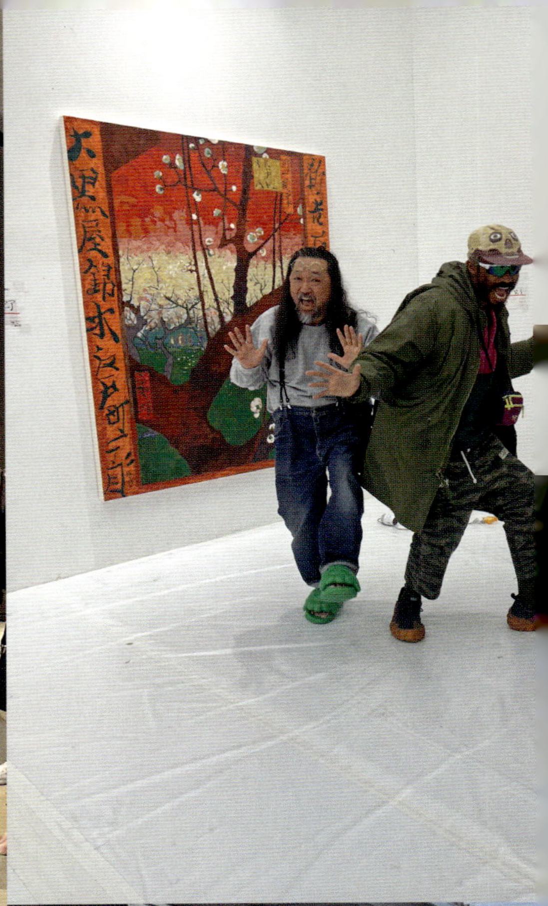

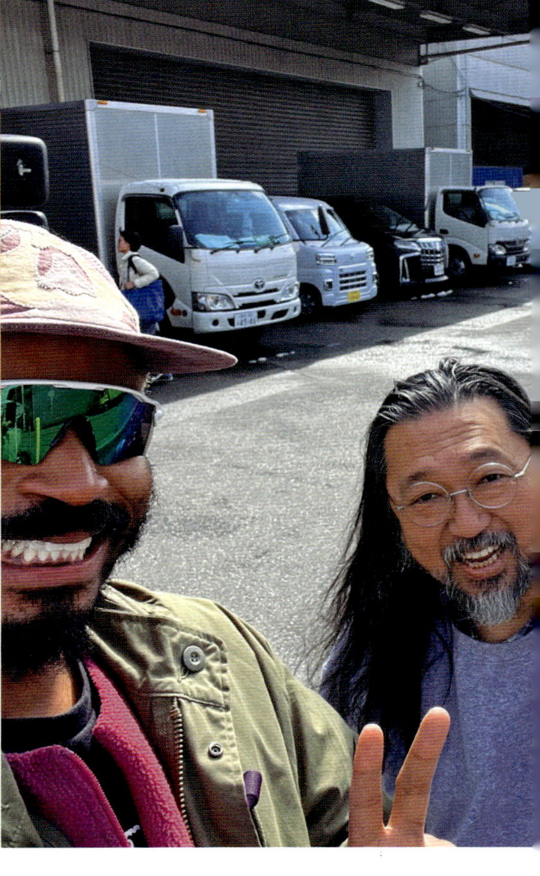

Salehe Bembury at Takashi Murakami's Studio in Japan

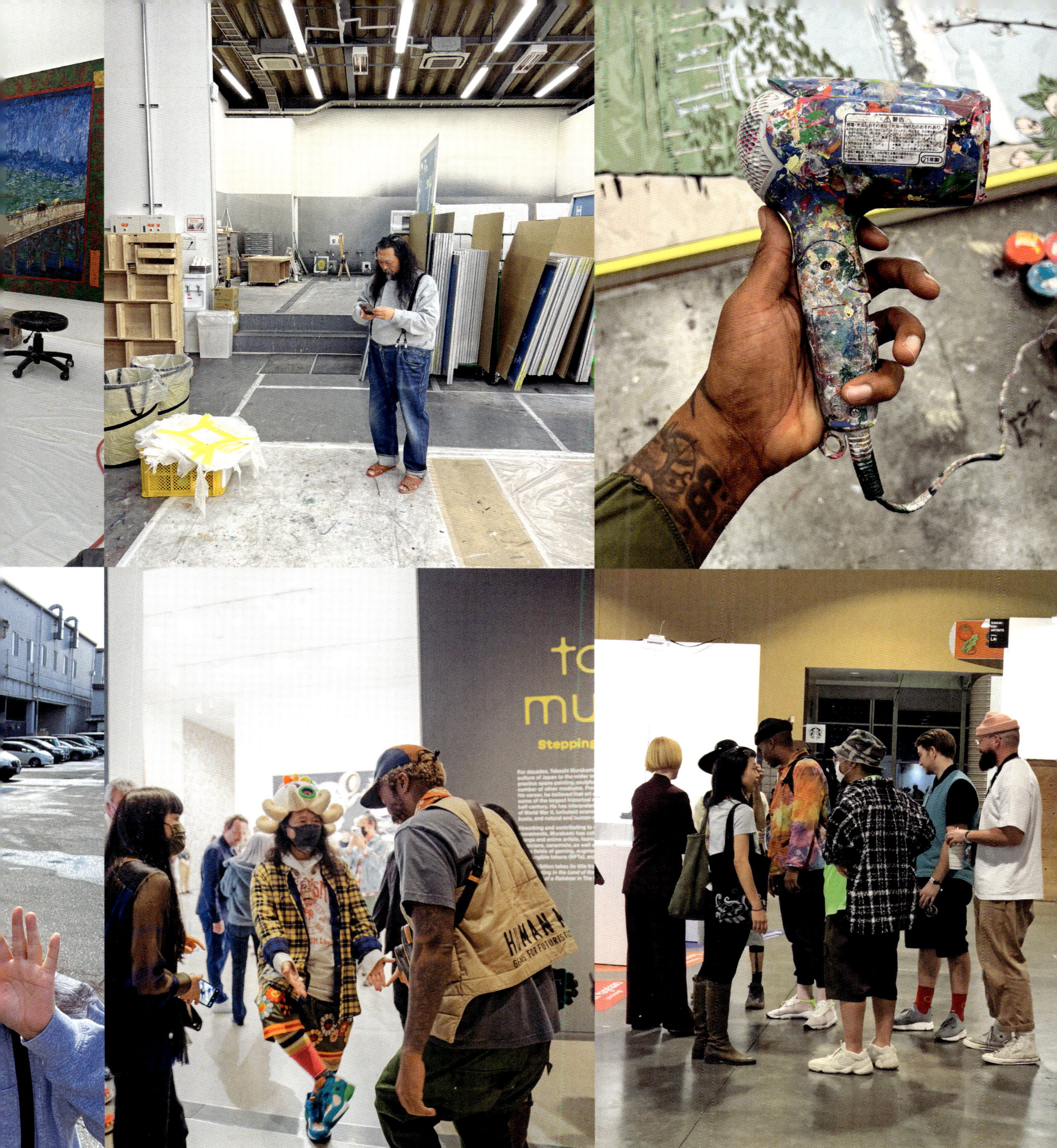

Top Left: Takashi Murakami in his Studio in Japan | Top Right: A canvas blow dryer from Takashi Murakami's Studio in Japan | Bottom Left: Takashi Murkami showing Salehe Bembury his "Water Be The Guide" New Balance sneakers. | Botton Right: Suzanne Oude Hengel, Cherry, Takashi Murakami, David Mawdsley, Daniel Bailey, Yuko Sakata Burtless, and Salehe Bembury setting up

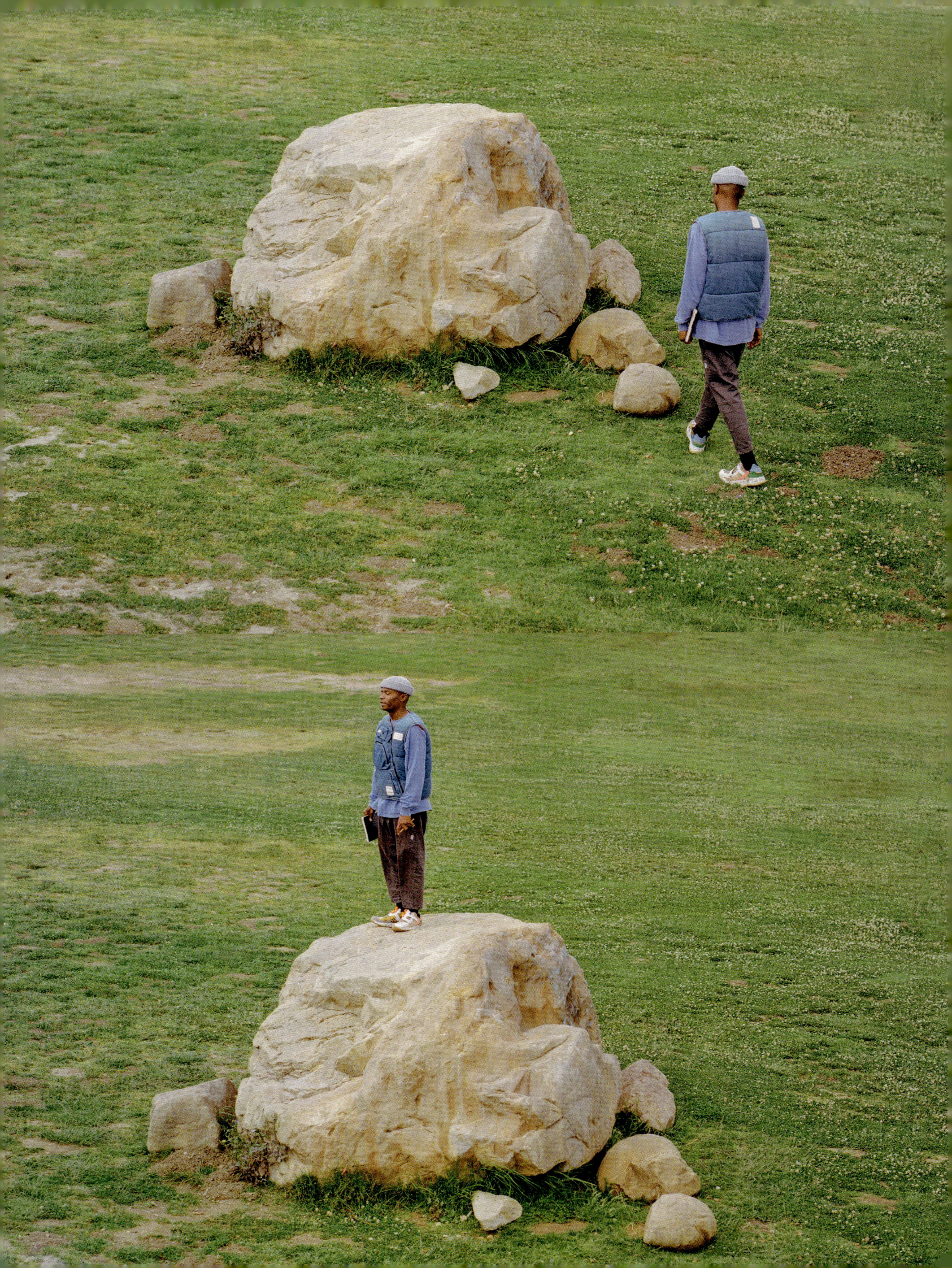

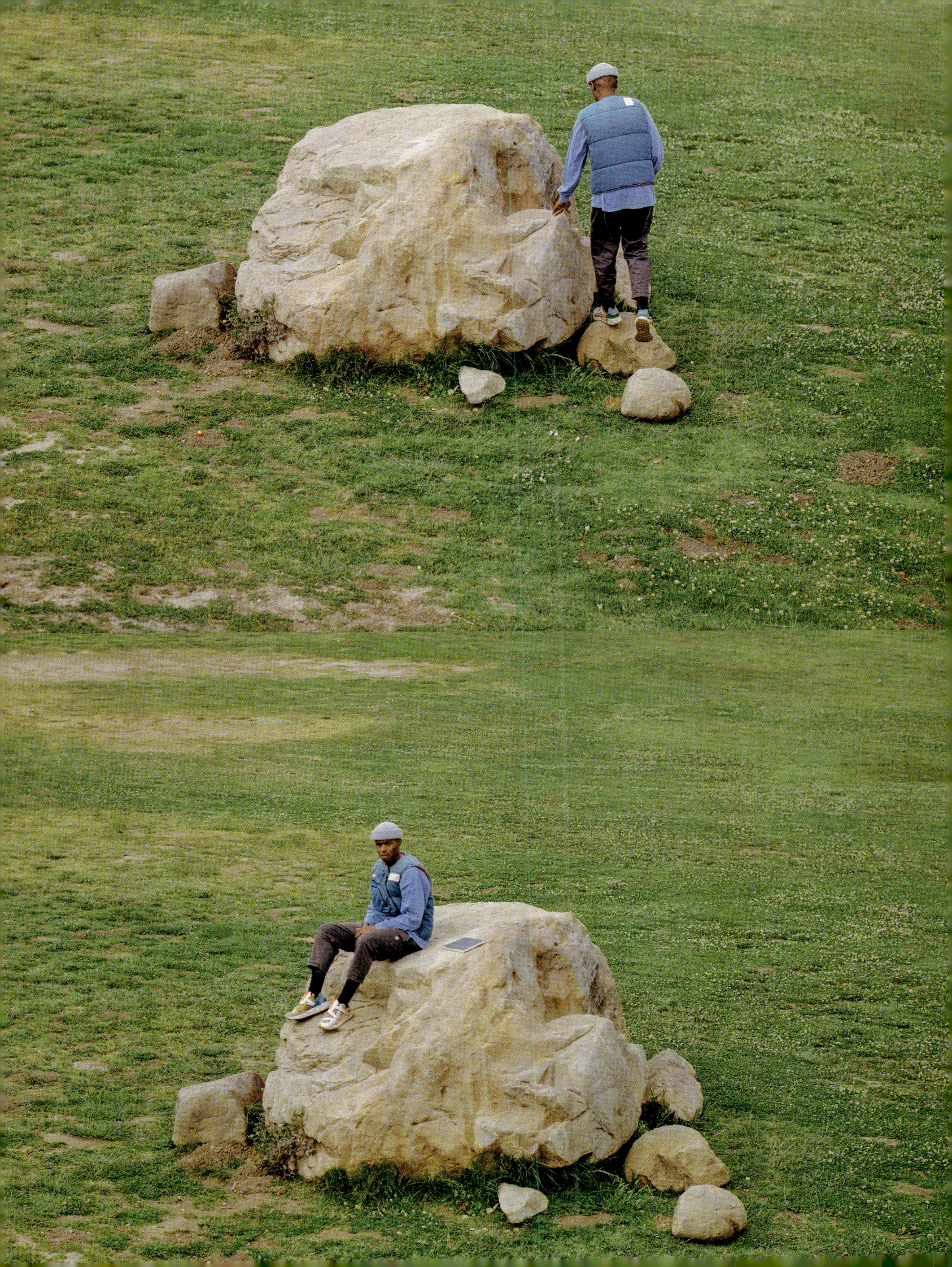

148

ANTA (2020)

FIRST CHEF

TIME

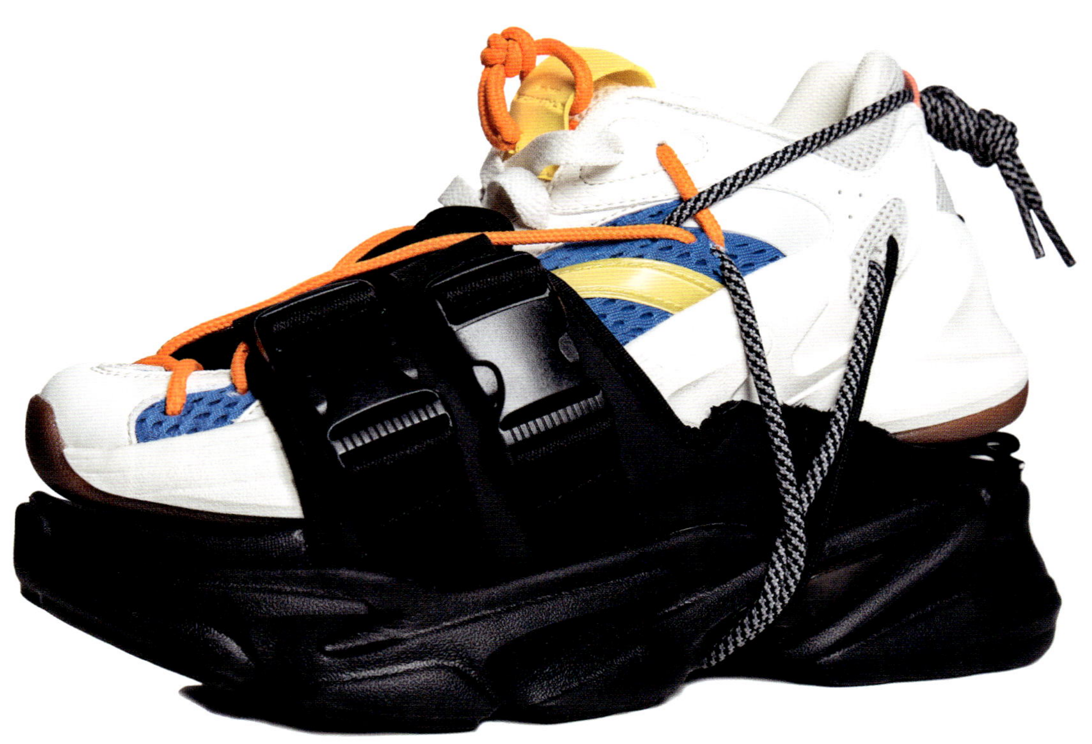

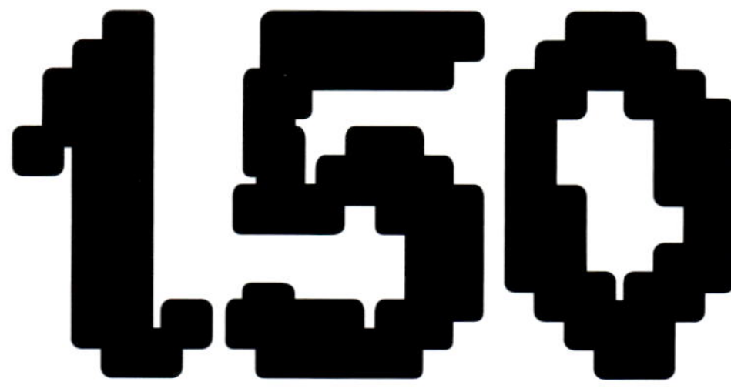

(2020)

ANTA

ANTA
FIRST TIME CHEF

Anta was my first collaboration as an independent designer.

Nike was the goal. At first, I was torn about working with Anta: if I worked with this sportswear brand that not many American people had heard of, and which didn't have much history in the NBA or sportswear–even though they're massive in China–would this positively affect my career, would people want the shoe? I still worked at Versace when I took on the project, which was pivotal, because it allowed me to dip my toes into the waters of entrepreneurship and design independence without fully leaving the security of my full-time job and biweekly paycheck.

As a brand, Anta were comparable to Nike in terms of resources and capabilities. They could develop and produce a shoe with the exact same technology and materials, and in some instances their shoes were made in the same factory as Nike's. They also had large budgets, so I could market my shoes and create events globally the way I wanted to–opportunities I was never given as a full-time employee at a company. Furthermore, they offered me a sum of money that would've taken me years upon years upon years to obtain working at my current job with Versace. This was proof that the independent design world and the opportunities that lived there were going to be way more lucrative than any full-time job I could have at any company.

At the time I had a manager, who was one of the people motivating me to work with Anta. He traveled me to China for some of the first meetings. This was the first time that I was sitting down with the entire team of a company, where they were all focused on me. This was the first time that I was getting a tour of the facilities and grounds, in hopes that I would utilize them for motivation for the collaboration, and the first time I was seeing ideas for budgets and ways to engage the Chinese consumer. I was in completely unfamiliar territory, but at the same time I felt comfortable; I had witnessed a lot of the same things from the other side of the fence, whether as a corporate office participant or as a consumer, so I was familiar with a lot of these initiatives.

I already knew the importance of documentation, because my dad's a photographer, but I started to value and execute on the importance of documentation by bringing a photographer with me to China. We spent a week at the Anta offices in Jinjiang, meeting with the team, and I created what I called "Make and Play"–an exercise which is where we basically took a bunch of Anta sneakers and samples, arts and crafts, bits and pieces, and made about 25 very cool Mr. Potato Head sneakers. From an Anta perspective, this allowed us to have a small brainstorm of ideas with some of the motivated young designers of the company; from my perspective it did the same, but it also was an intentional initiative to create assets for marketing. During this period, Virgil Abloh was holding workshops where people were making t-shirts and customizing sneakers, and that made me realize that engaging the audience more than just engaging their pockets was the wave of the future. So I thought it was really important to use these methods to create storytelling. With all of the assets from this– pictures from the trip, pictures of the work, pictures of designs and CADS–I myself went into InDesign and put together a book. I had it printed and bound, and then pitched it to Anta as a booklet that should come in every friends-and-family shoebox to bring this new audience along with me on the journey of this trip, the creation of the sneaker, and just the overall collaboration.

I was also given the opportunity to execute the packaging for the sneakers, and we were planning out in-store installations–I was being given the reins to execute every aspect of this collaboration and I took the fullest advantage of it. These were things I was involved in at Versace, but not

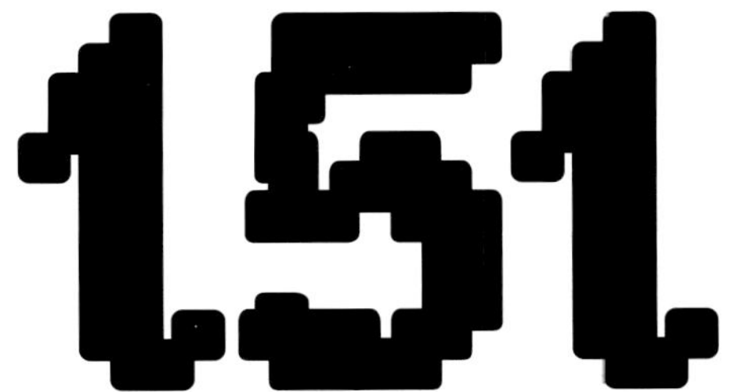

to this extent, and the major difference was that at Anta I didn't need an approval. They were looking to me to make the decisions and to inject my taste and creative ability into their brand. This was just new territory completely. It might have been more intimidating if this had been my sole thing, but I had a job, so this felt like a fun experiment that at the time I thought was probably temporary. I didn't really see myself going into a becoming an independent designer. It felt like a cool test...

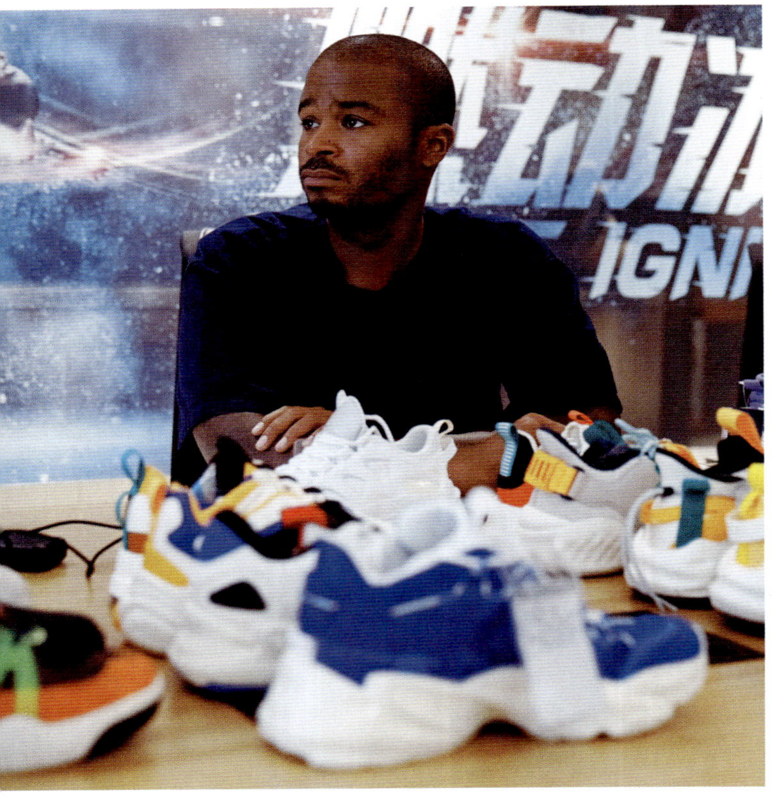

The two sneakers that were created for the collaboration were called the SB01 and the SB02. I was not used to putting my name on anything, and now I was giving shoes my initials. And this collaboration was truly where my outdoor brand identity was born. It was design over everything, but in a very close second was storytelling and purpose. I knew that the footwear that I created couldn't be just some cool shoe. It needed to have a purpose, it needed to have utility, it needed to have a reason. So I dug not so deep into what is and was my day-to-day activity of hiking, and thought: What if I create tools to assist in this in this practice?

From this insight, the SB01 and SB02 were born. The way in which I marketed them was very similar to what I did at Versace. I seeded them and I tried to create a campaign that was clickable, shareable, rewatchable, and likeable. I compiled the list of names, which now I had from my Versace dealings; and I created a beautiful friends-and-family package that was sealed in a utilitarian-looking shipping wrap that you would not normally see on a sneaker. I hand wrote everyone's name on duct tape. It felt extremely industrial, yet intentional. On the other side, I worked with a slow-motion capturing director Steve Giralt. He was the kind of director that made cereal commercials or Chili's commercials–cereal falling into the bowl and milk flowing out in slow motion, or meat sizzling on a grill and seeing the flames pop up in slow motion. I'd always loved those shots and I thought, why not take a shot like that and apply it in footwear? From this, my first sneaker campaign was born. I didn't have much of an audience at the time, so I don't think it was seen by that many, but I think it's some of my best campaign work.

At launch events in China, I got to see the brand identity that I had created through this collaboration explored further. My sneaker was sitting in a massive bird's nest, which was the original inspiration for the collaboration; there were walls of plants, real-life lizards. Having a team of people to deconstruct, analyze, and execute your ideas at the highest level with a budget is something I had never really had to work with before; it was really the truest expression of seeing my ideas play out. In a sense, this collaboration was an opportunity to prove myself. Prove myself to myself, prove myself to the industry, and prove myself to Versace. This was a designer's dream project, because you're being paid a lot of money to do what you love with no rules–pretty much the sky's the limit. So I told myself, I need to impress with my campaign, I need to impress with the product I'm creating from scratch because I have such amazing development resources–the entire operation has to be impressive. I need to prove to myself that I can do this.

The outcome, I would argue, was a huge success. Both shoes performed amazingly, the campaign was received very well, my relationship with Anta remains strong, and I'm honored that they saw potential in me to give me my first collaboration as an employee within a company. To this day I think the SB02 is one of my best-ever designs. I've always said that I wish that it was my first personal design, the first shoe I put out under my own name–I almost wish I had just used the Anta design for that. But hey–I've got millions of ideas.

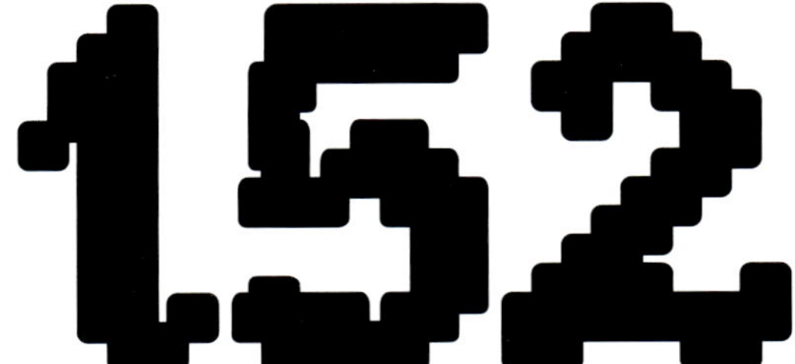

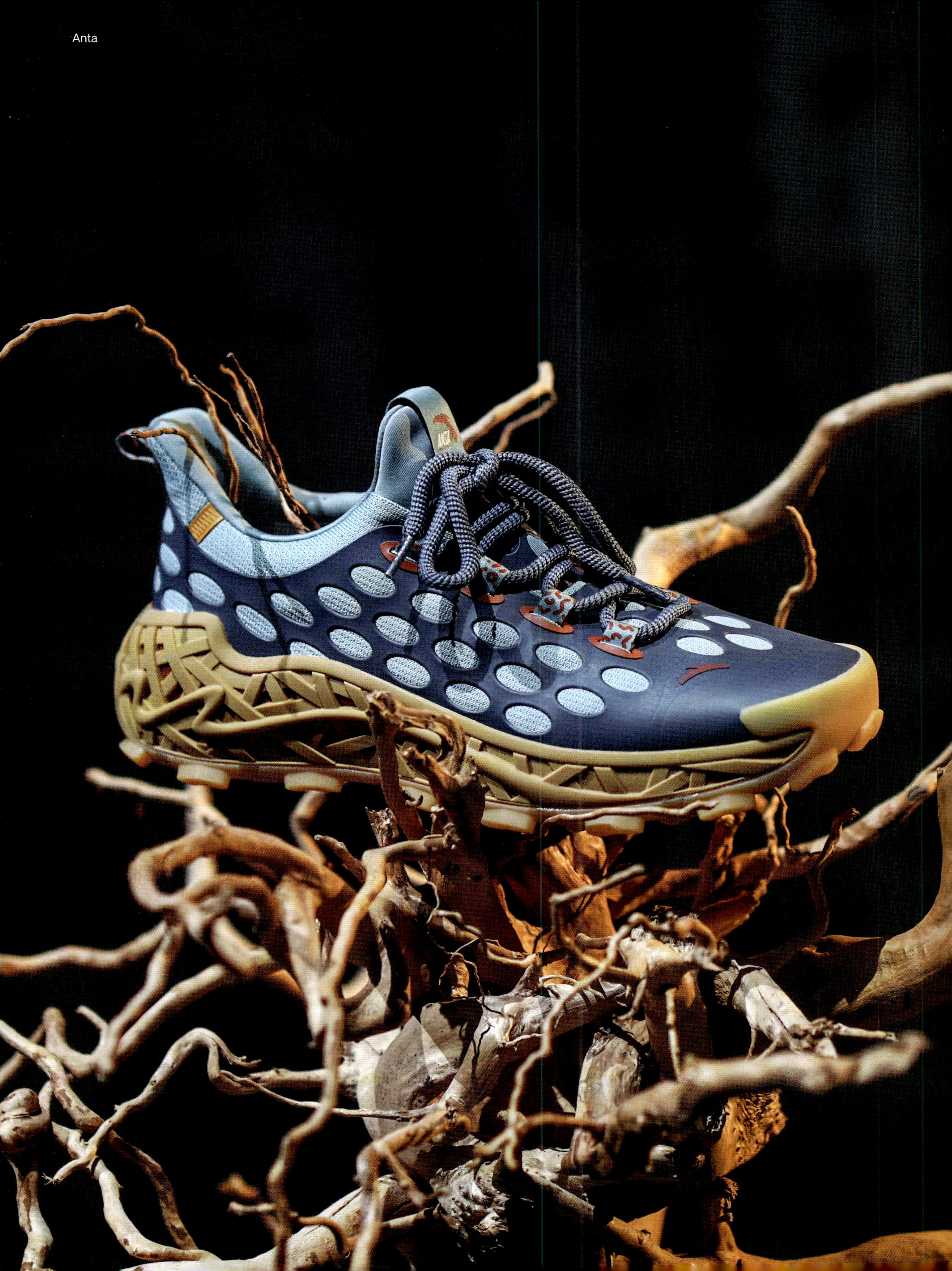
Anta

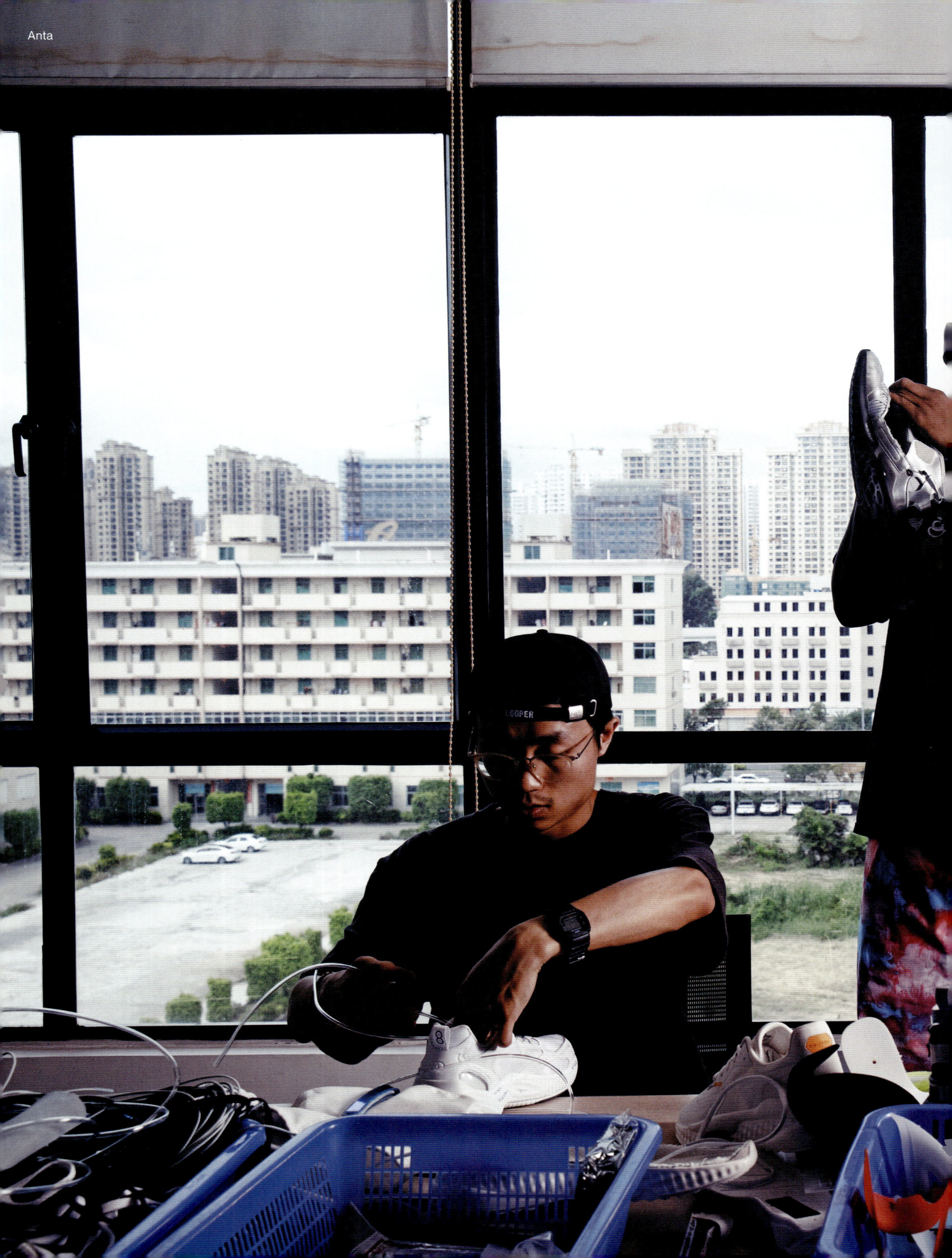

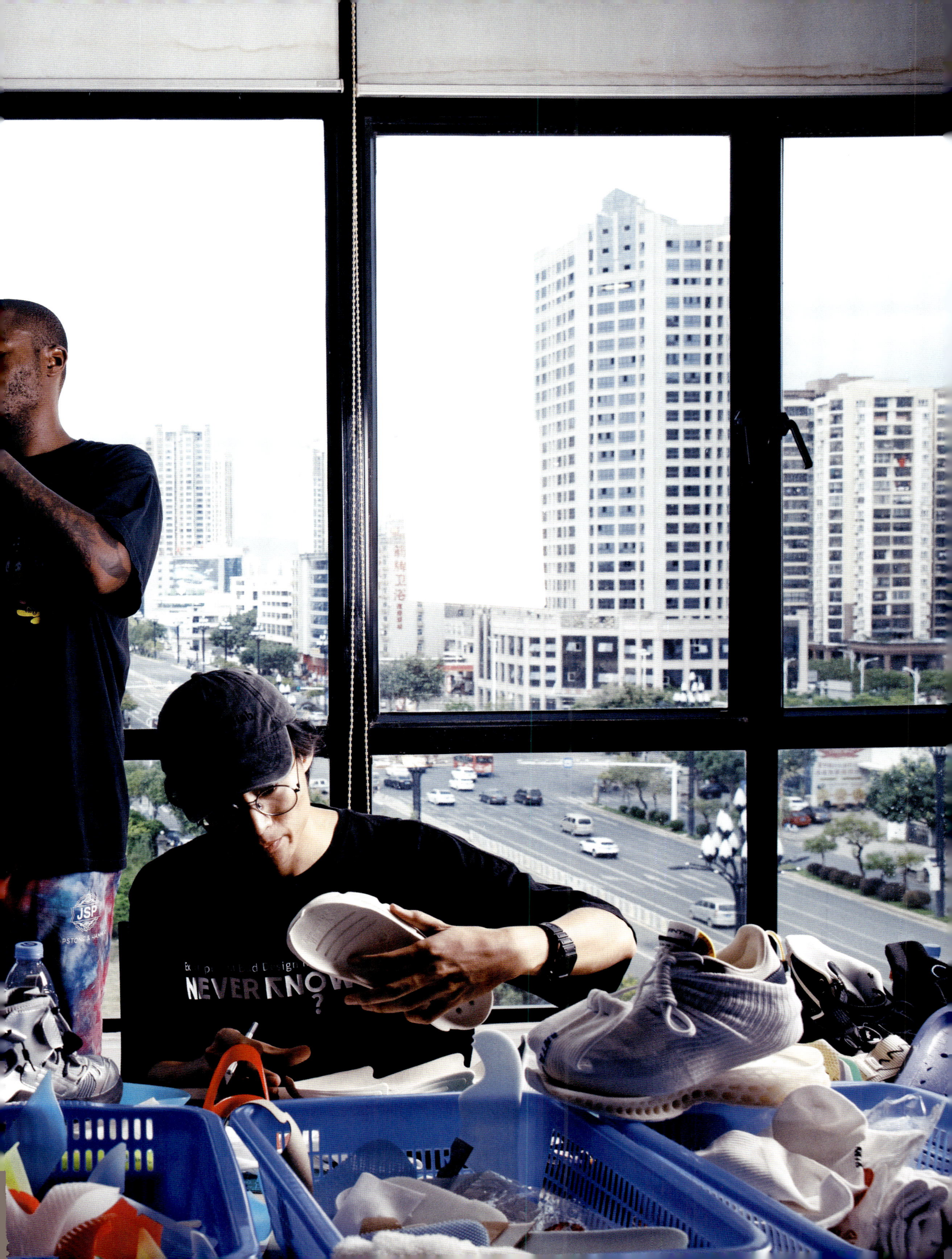
JSP
NEVER KNOW

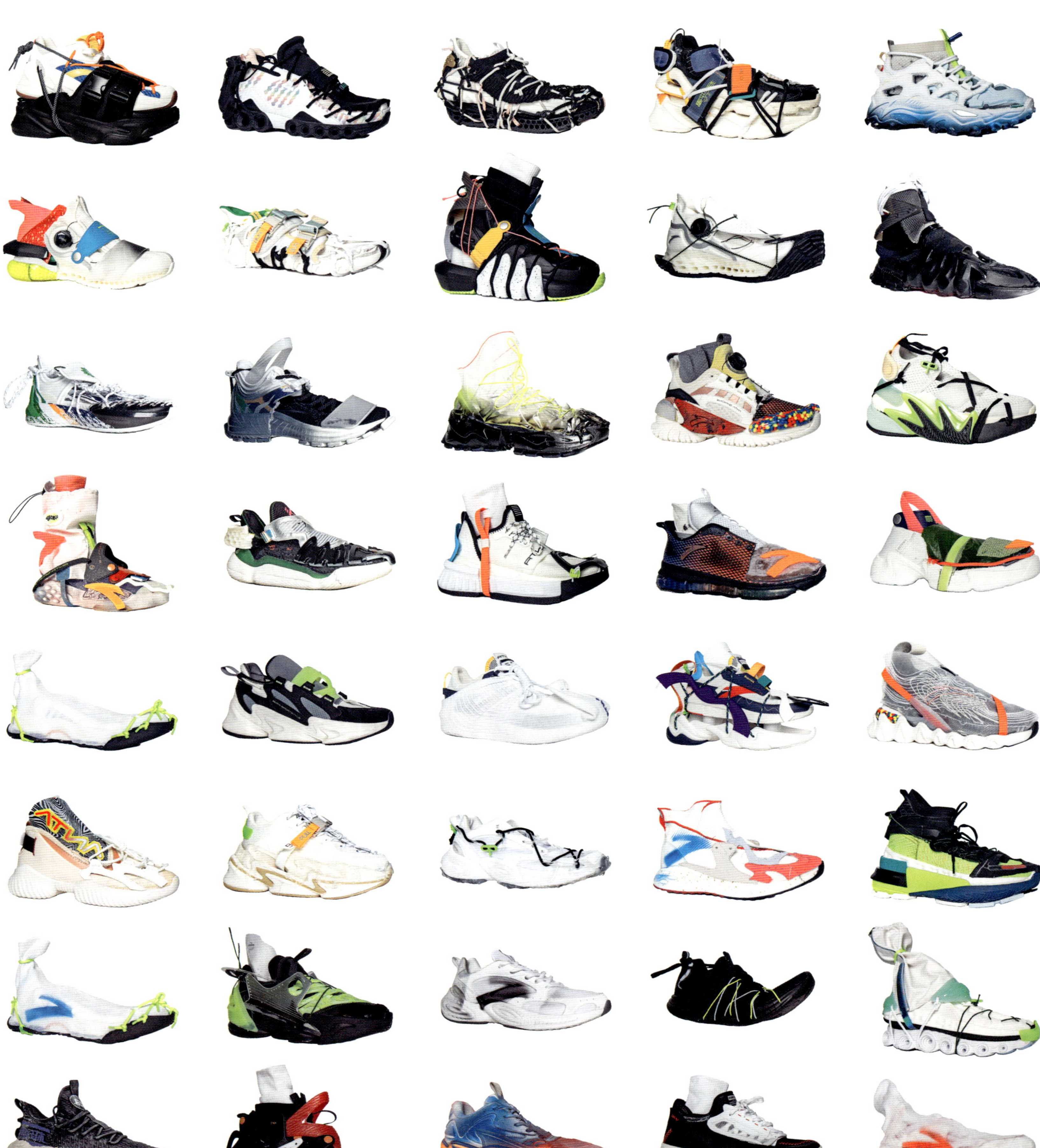

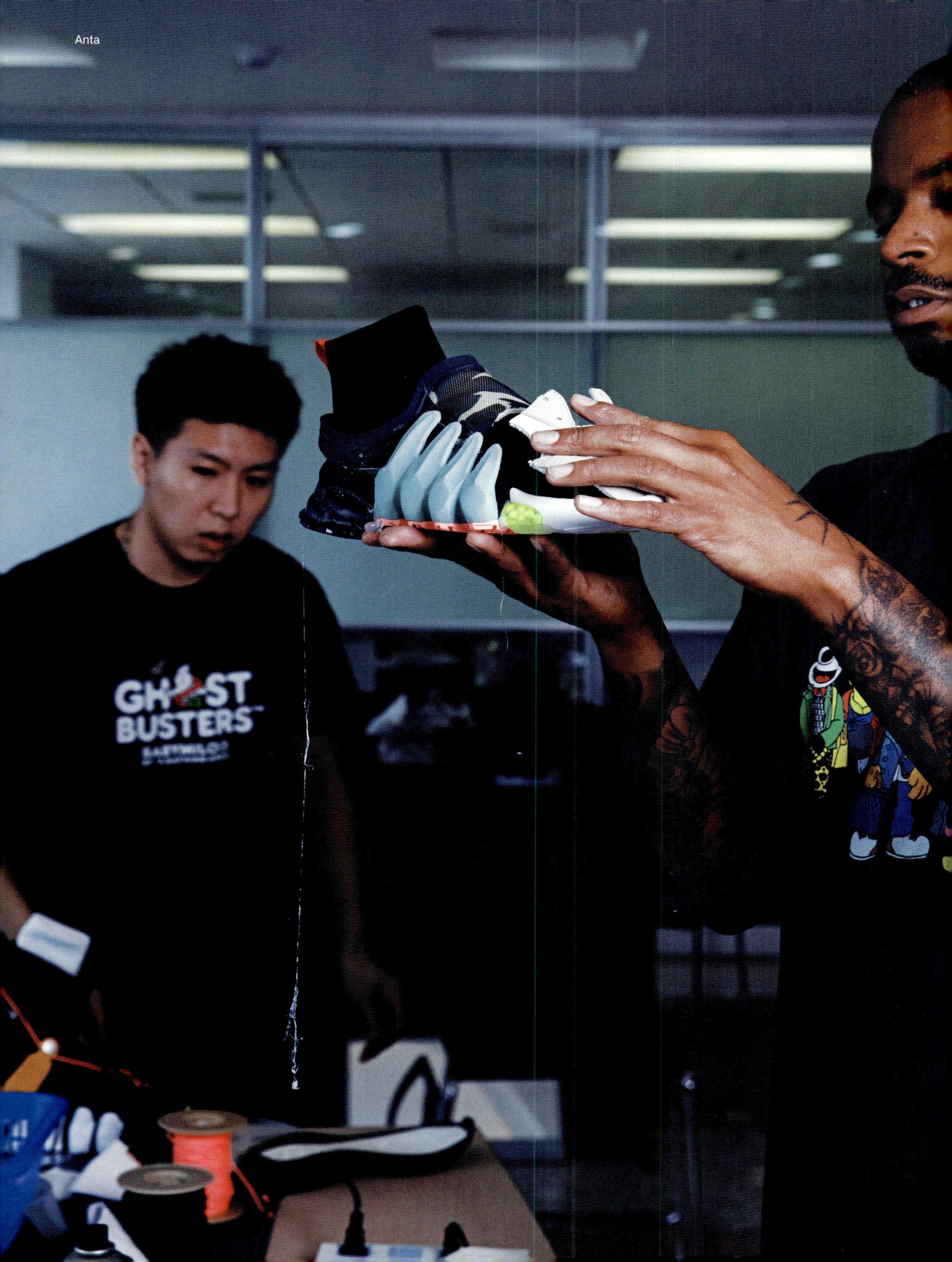
BUSTERS

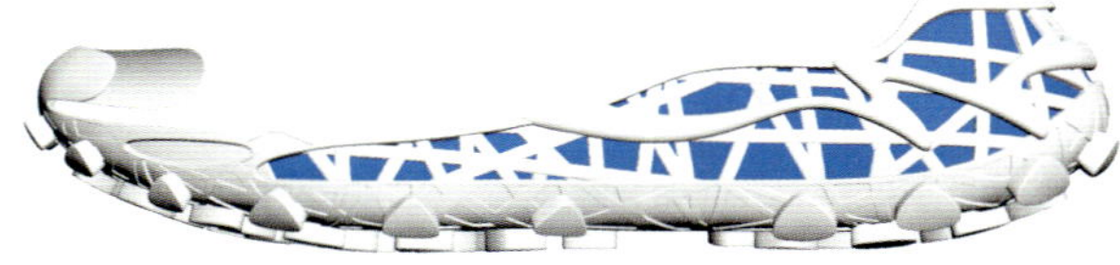

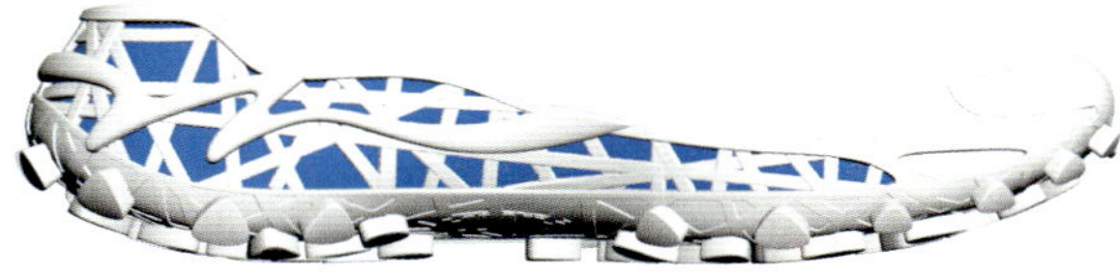

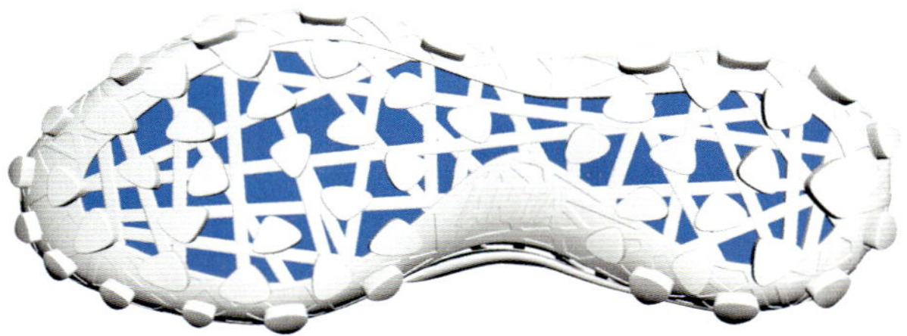

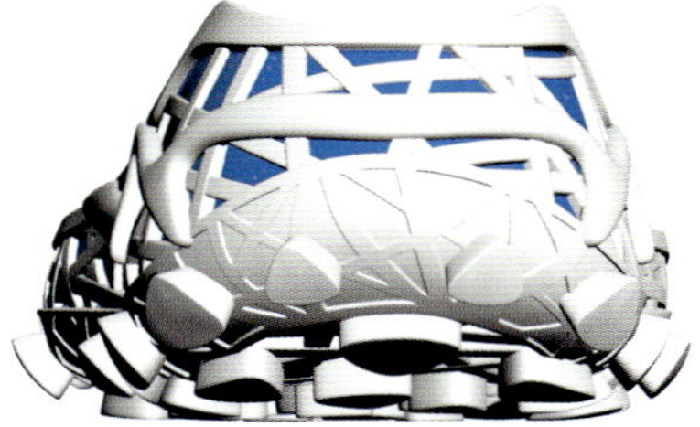

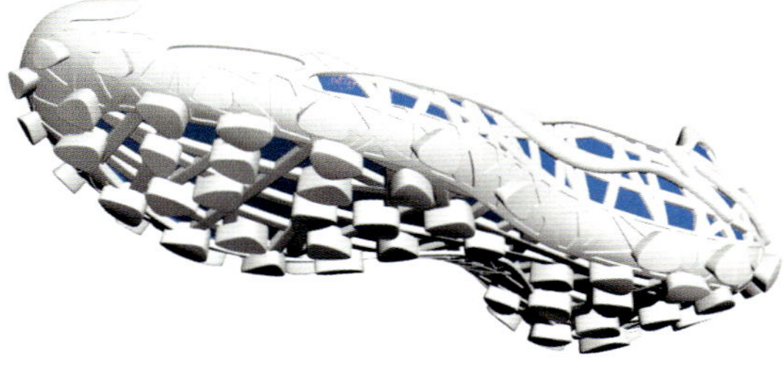

Anta SB-01 development sample

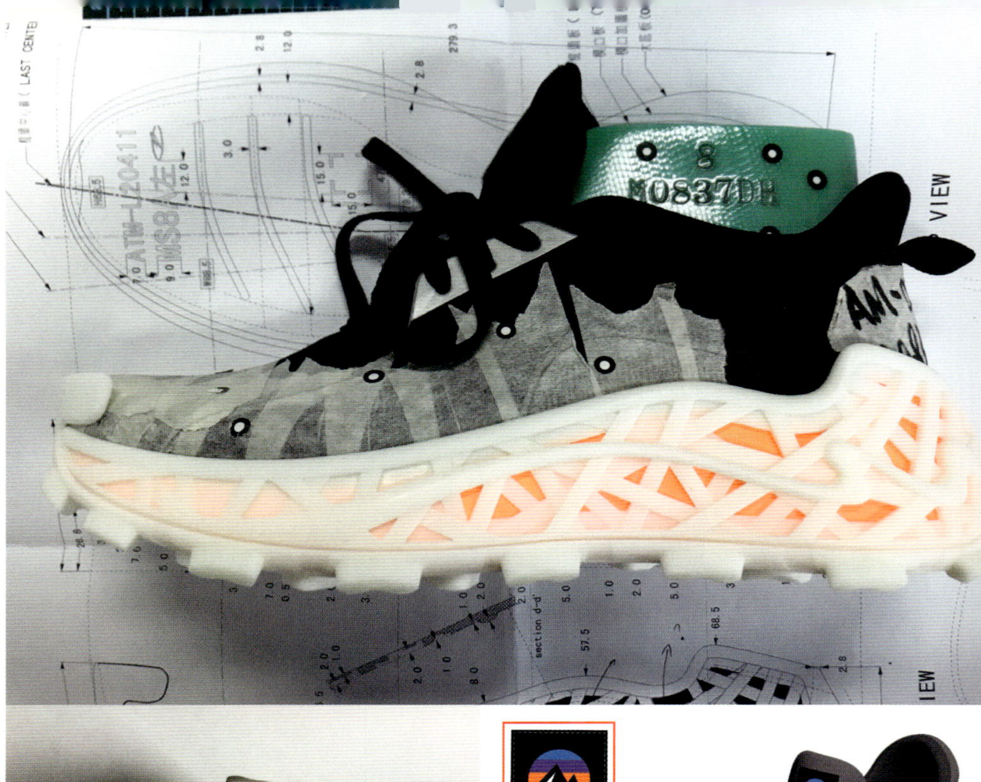

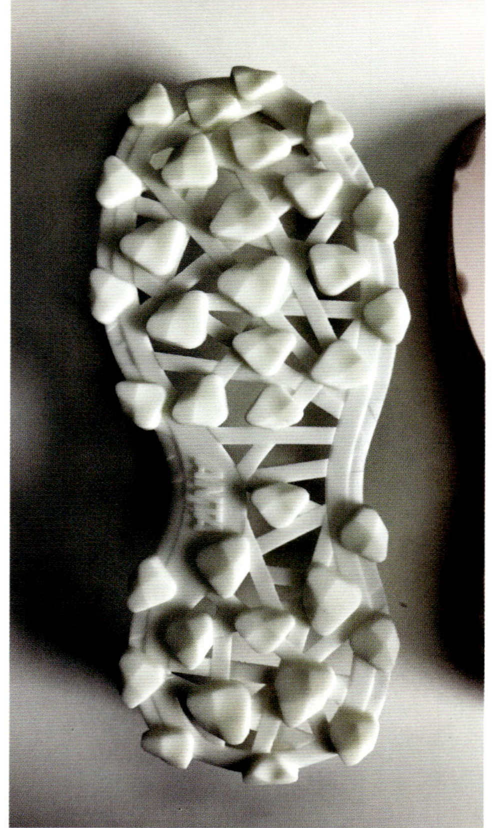

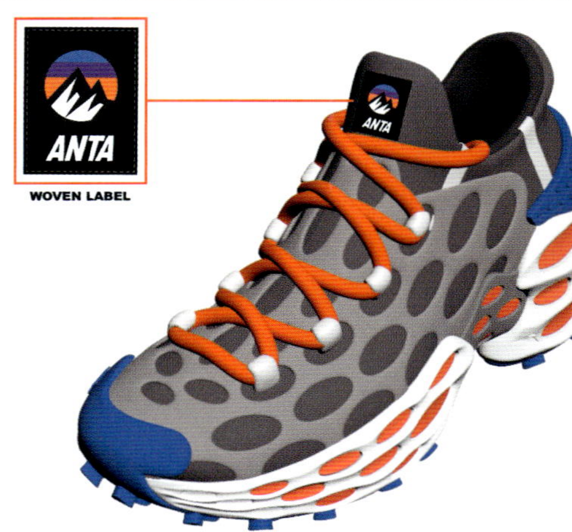

Above: Anta SB 3D design exploration
Bottom left: Anta SB-01 tooling model | Bottom right: Anta SB-01 tooling 3D exploration

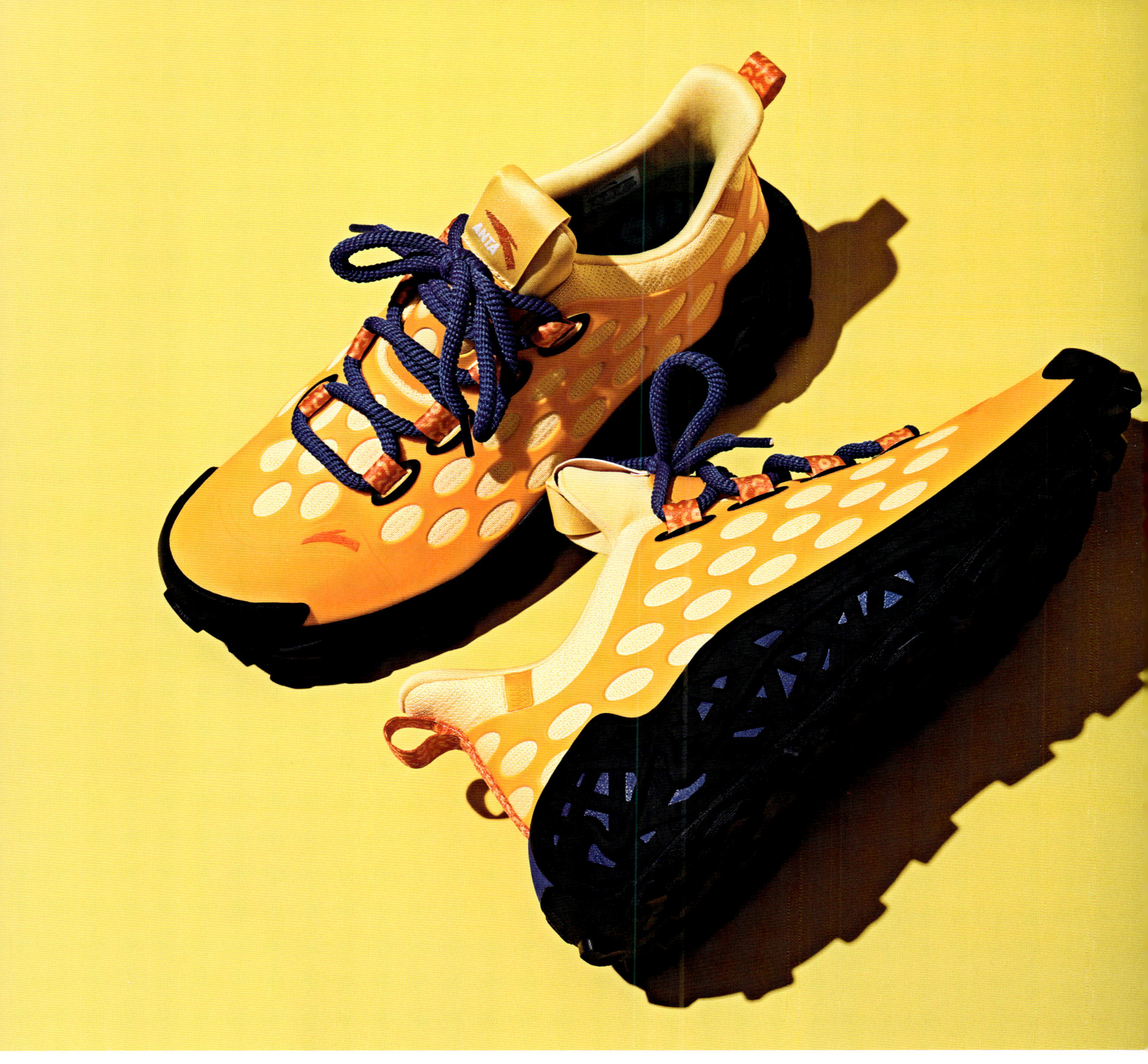

Anta SB-01 sample

ANTA

(2020)

159

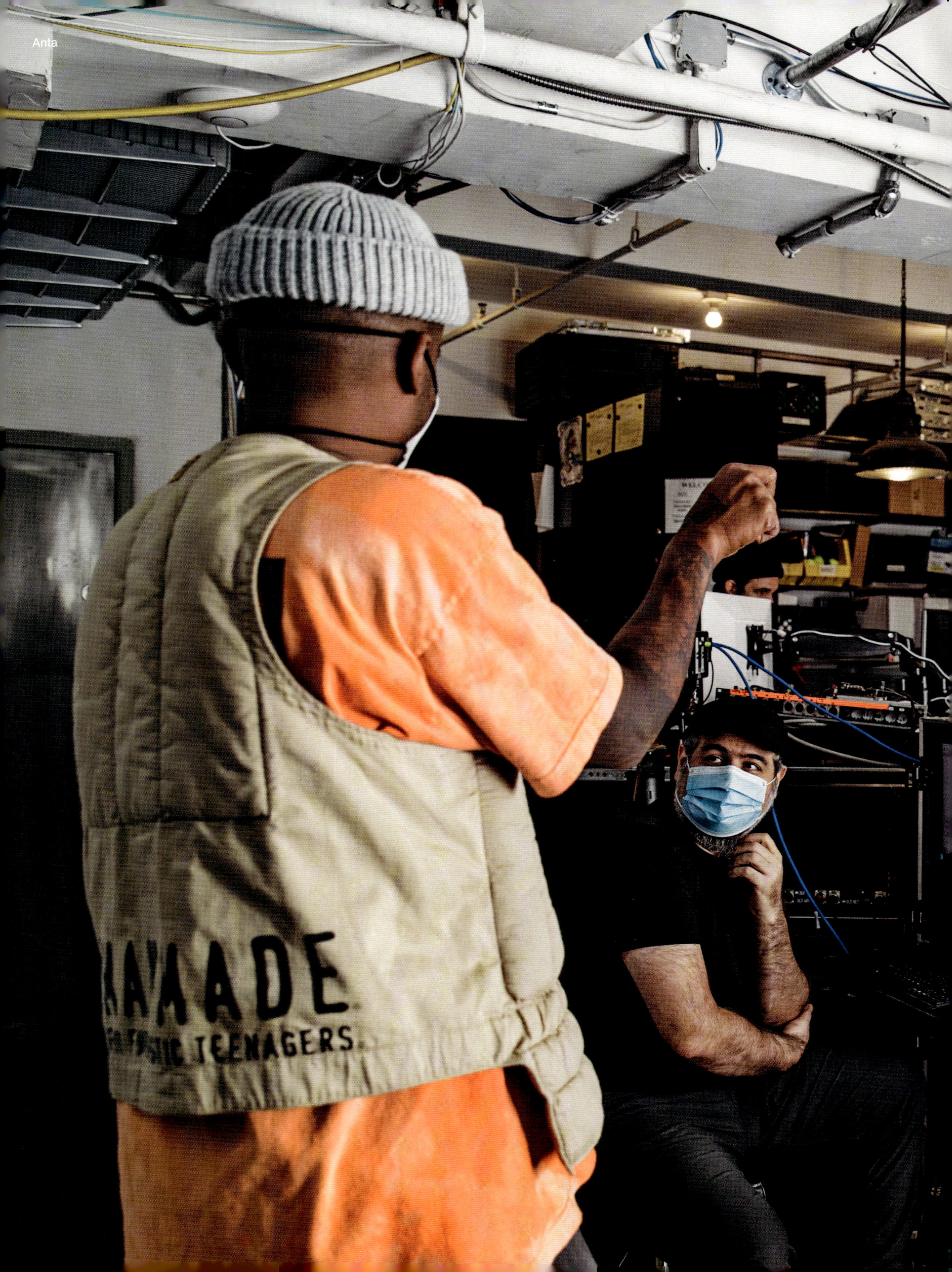

Anta

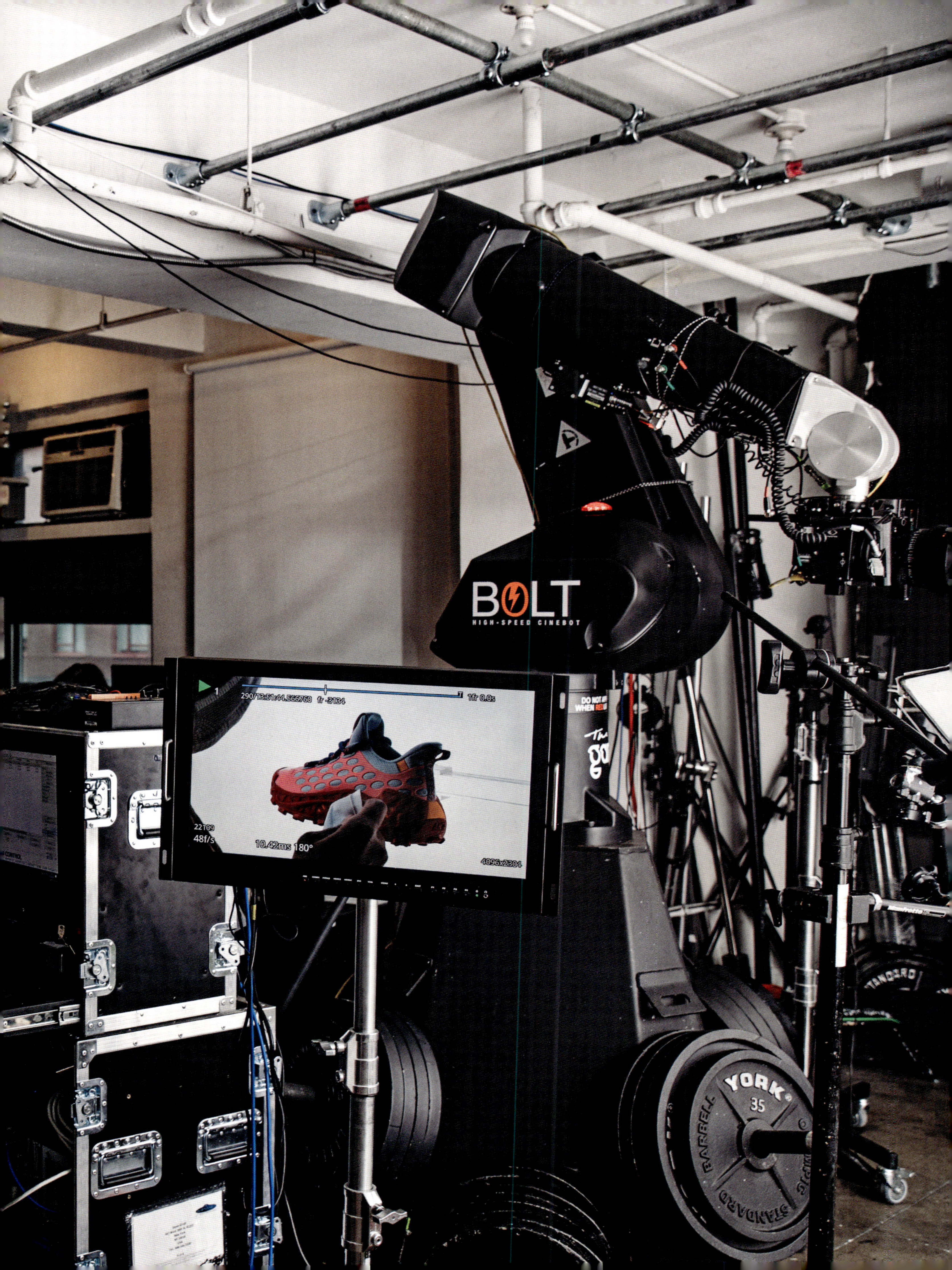
BOLT
HIGH-SPEED CINEBOT
48f/s
10.42ms 180°
4096x2304
YORK
35
BARBELL
STANDARD

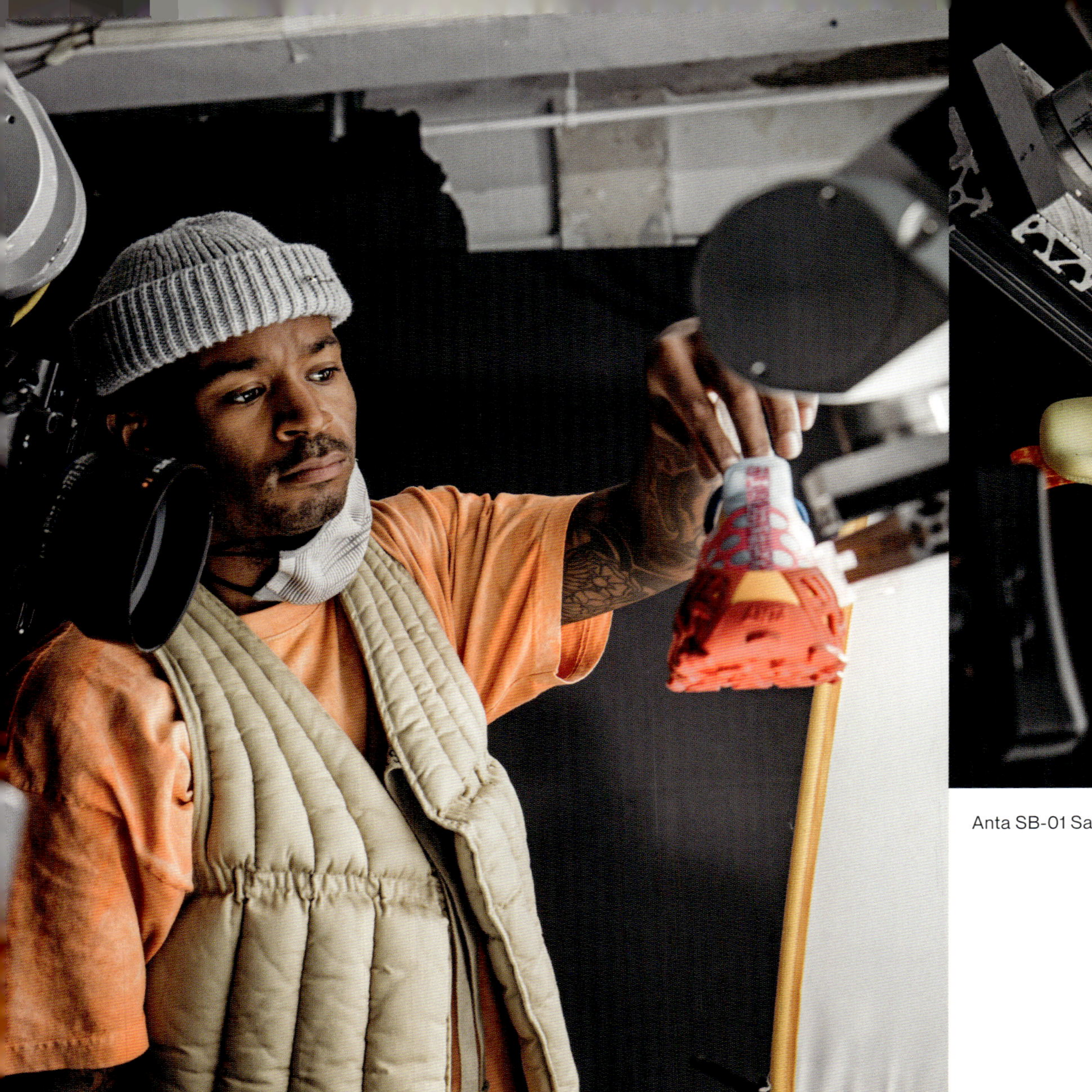

Salehe shooting Anta campaign

Anta SB-01 Salehe Bembury

162

(2020)

ANTA

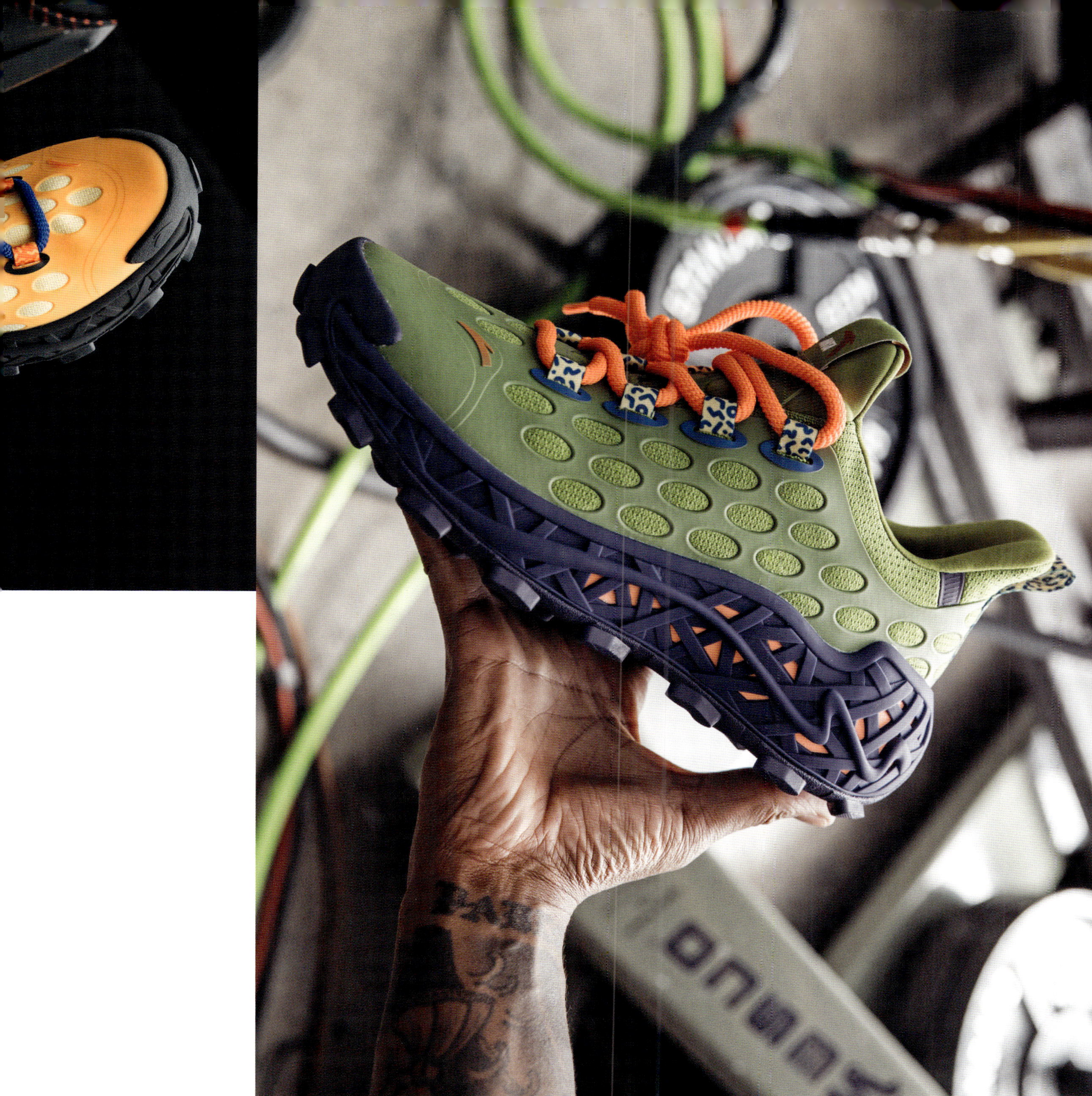

Anta SB-01 Salehe Bembury

Amine wearing Anta SB-01 Salehe Bembury

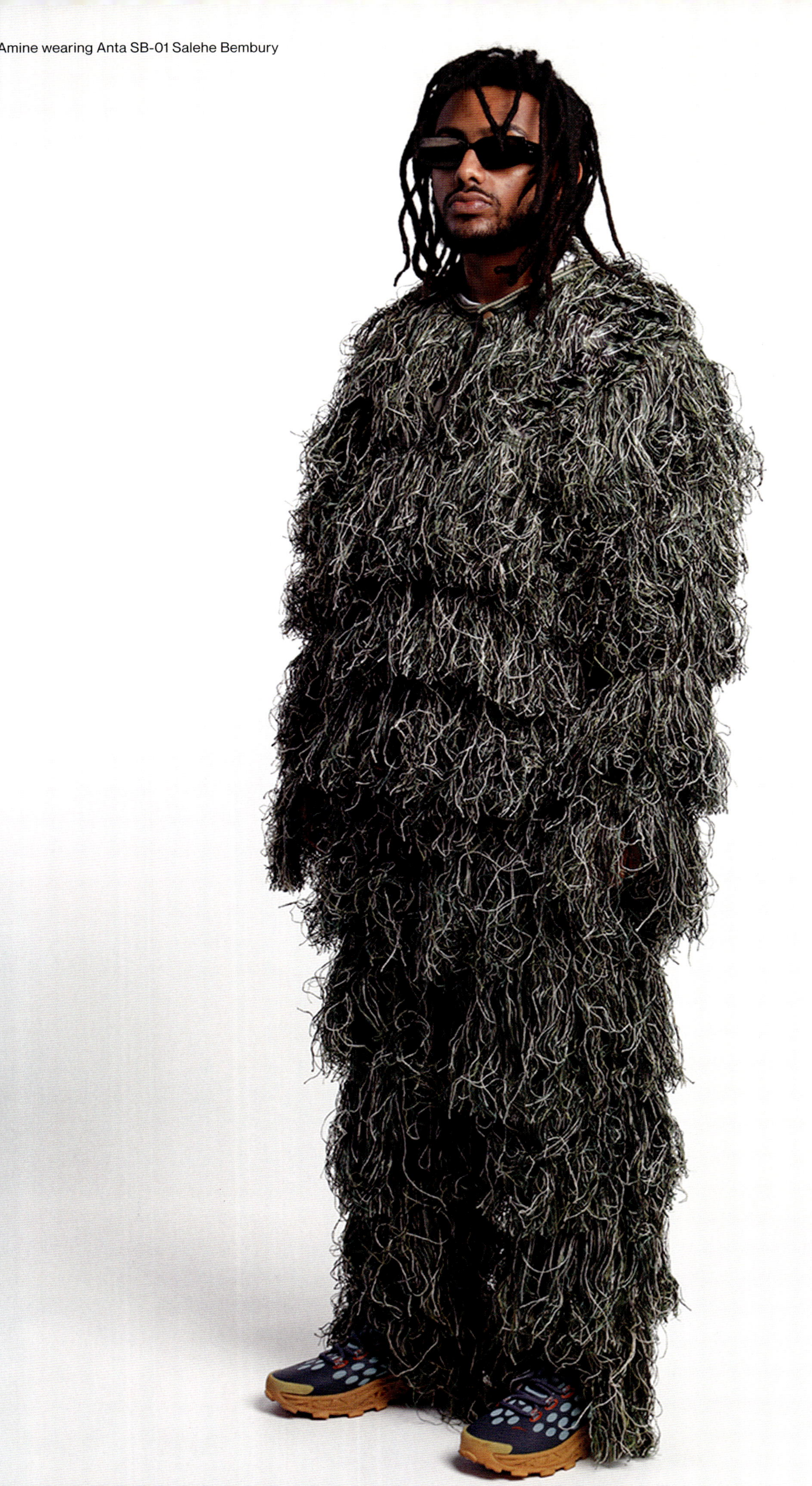

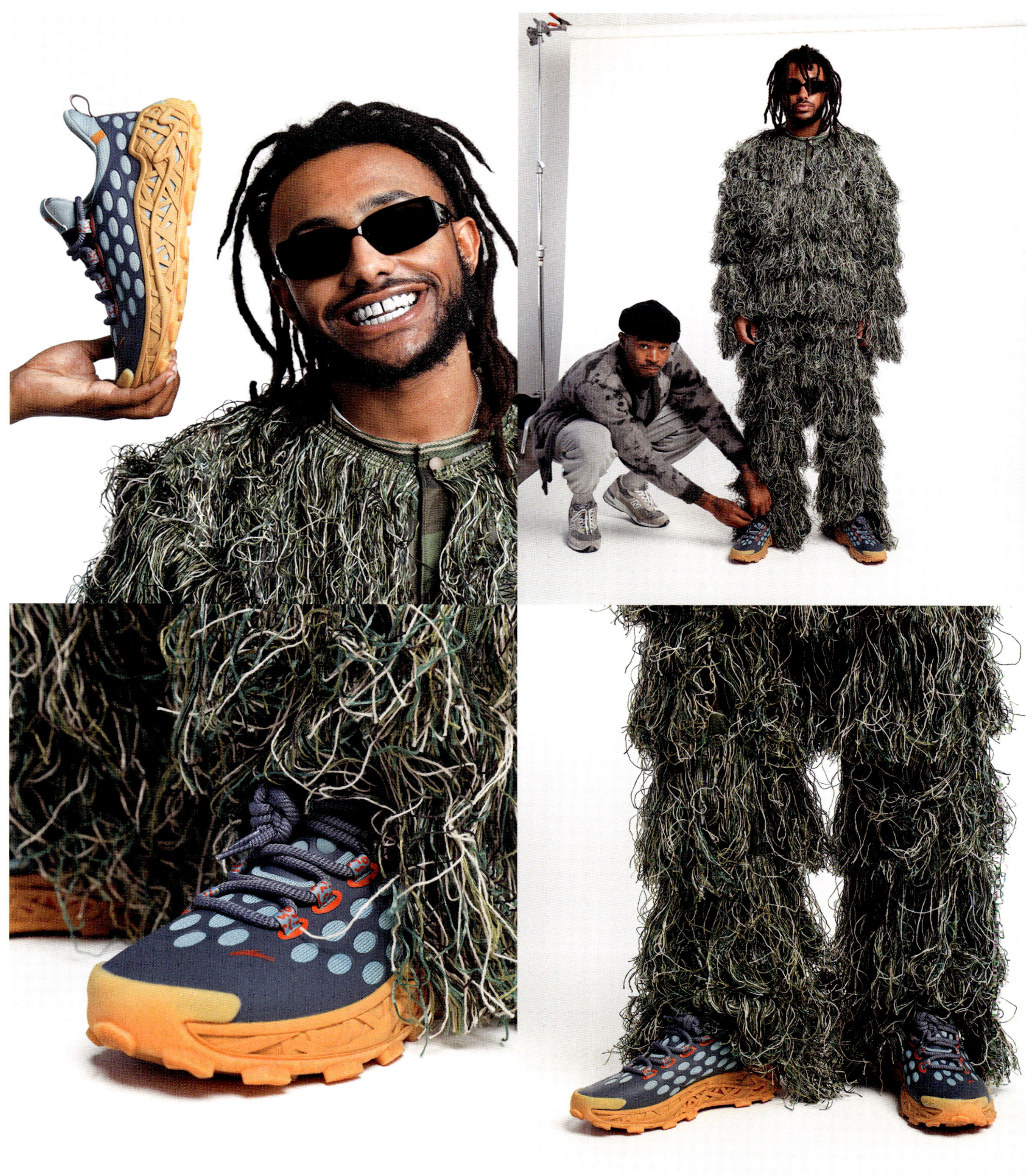

Amine wearing Anta SB-01 Salehe Bembury

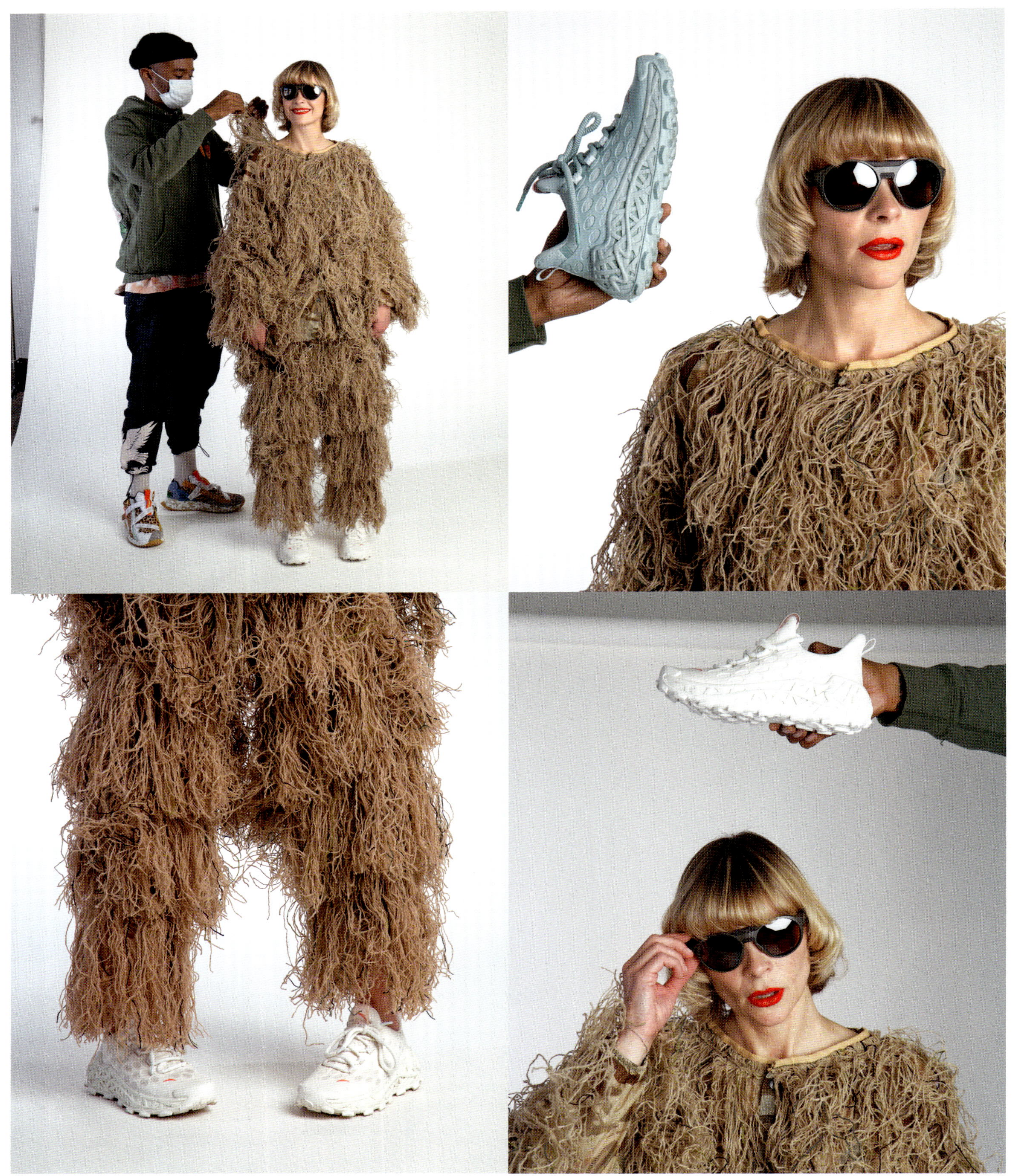

Jaime King wearing Anta SB-01 Salehe Bembury

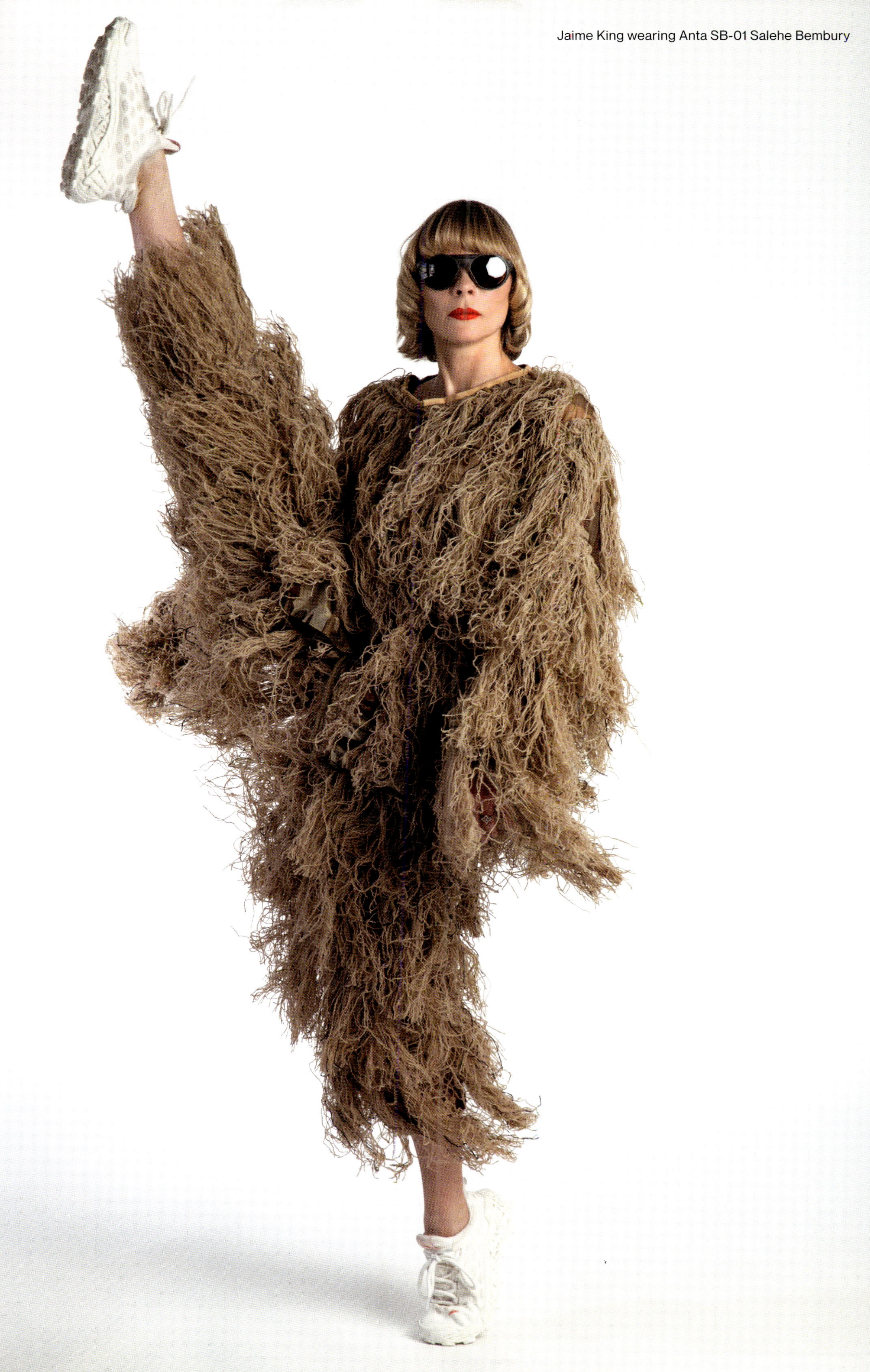

Jaime King wearing Anta SB-01 Salehe Bembury

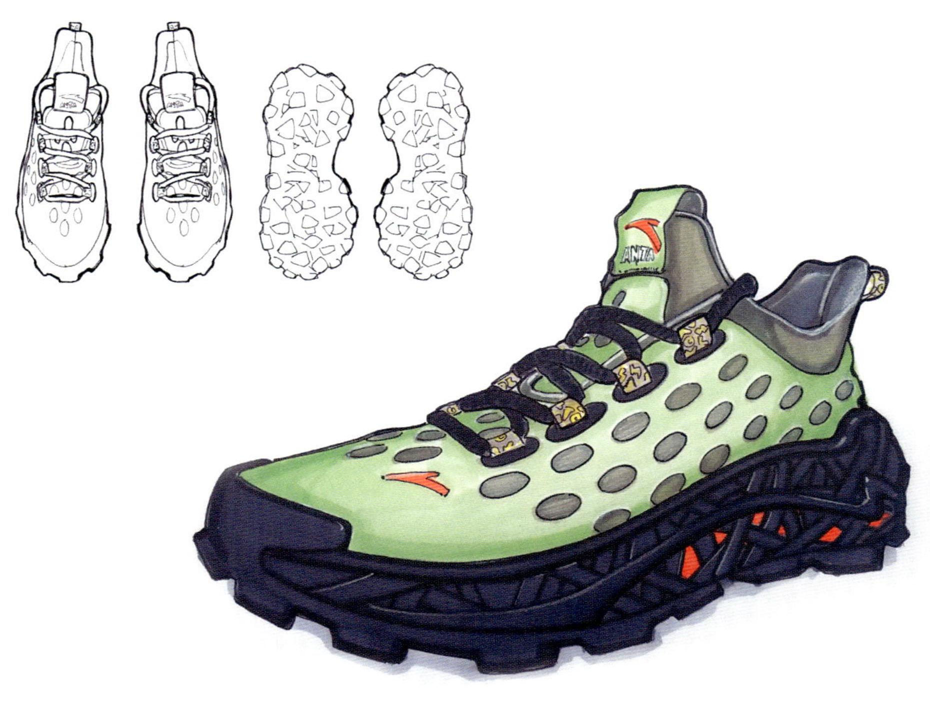

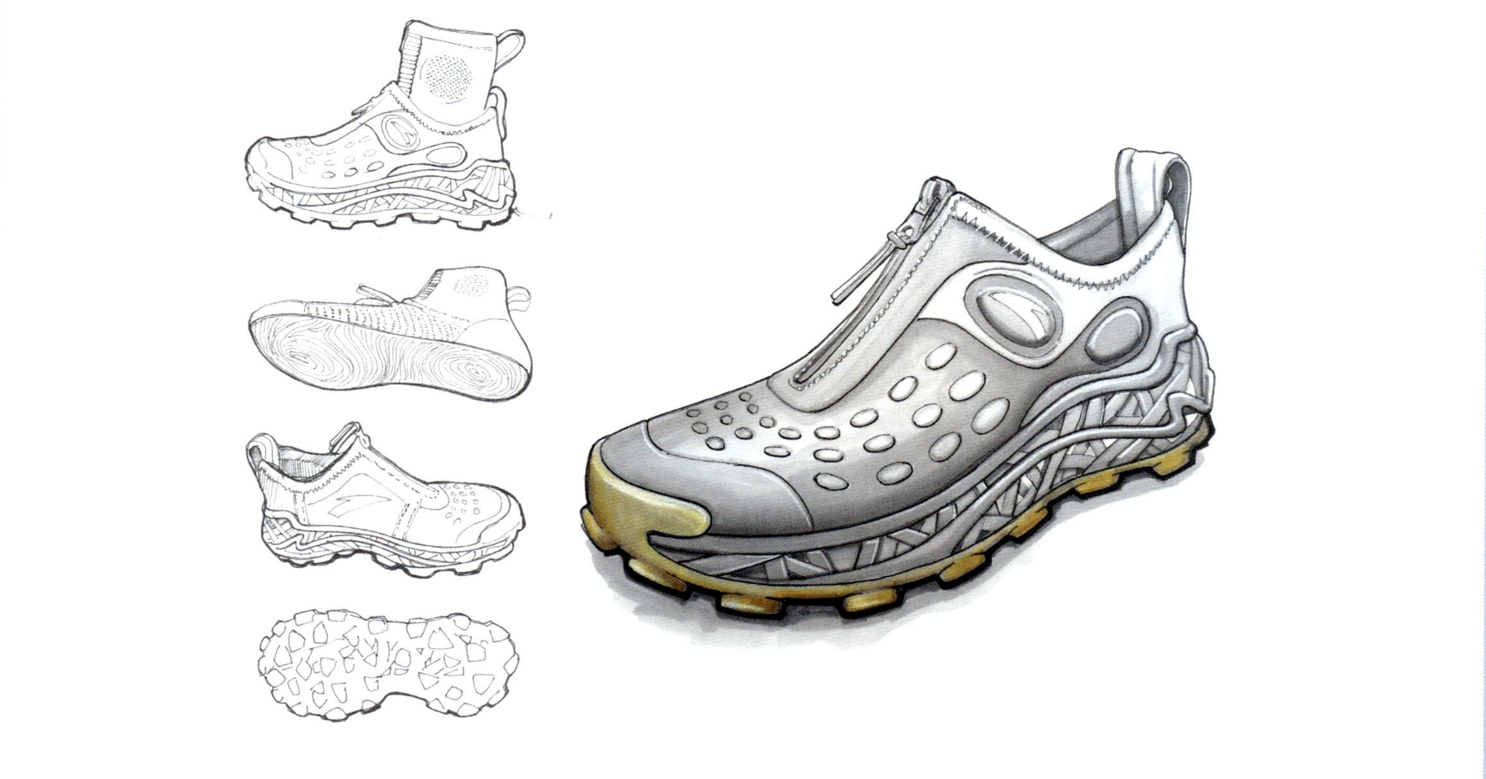

Above: Anta SB-01 Salehe Bembury marker rendering | Below: Anta SB-02 Salehe Bembury marker rendering

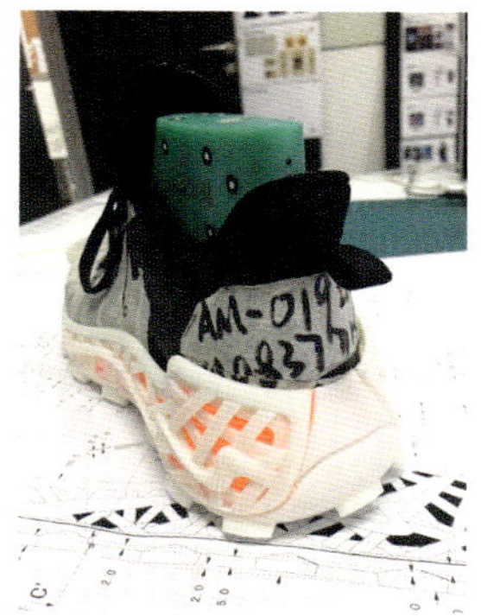

Anta SB-01 development sample

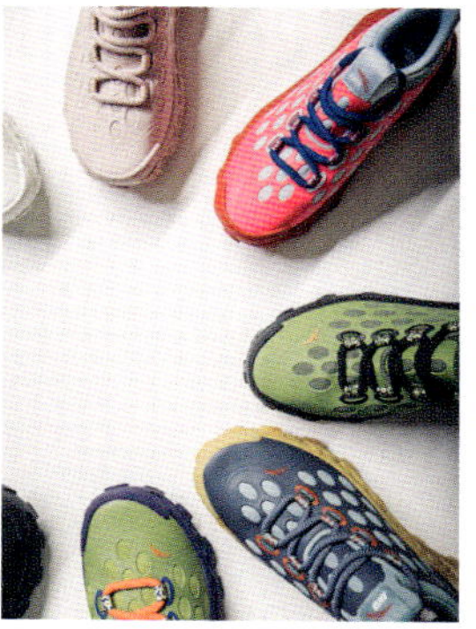

Anta SB-01 Salehe Bembury

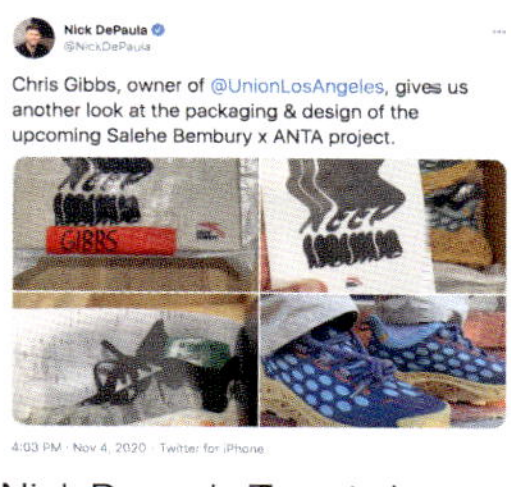

Nick Depaula Tweet about Anta x Salehe Bembury

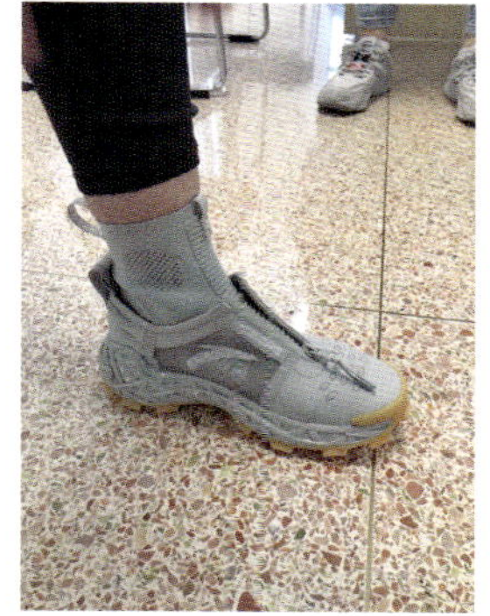

Anta SB-01 Salehe Bembury sample

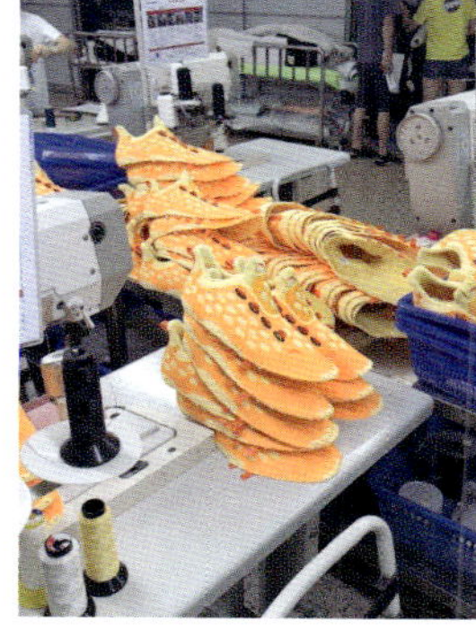

Anta factory

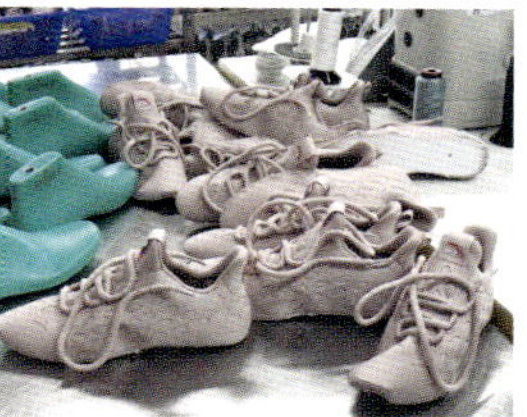

Anta factory

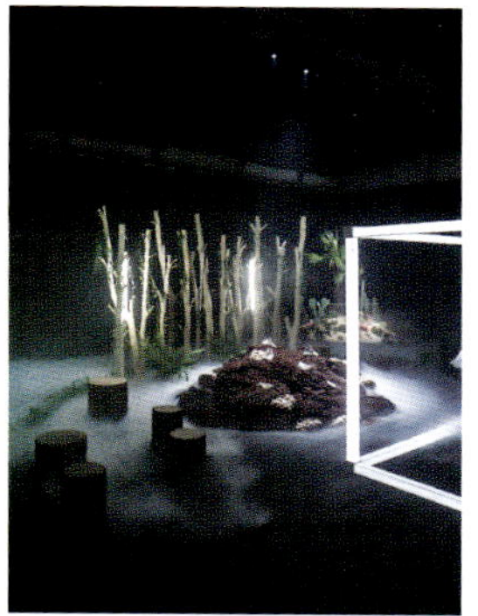

Anta x Salehe Bembury Pop-Up

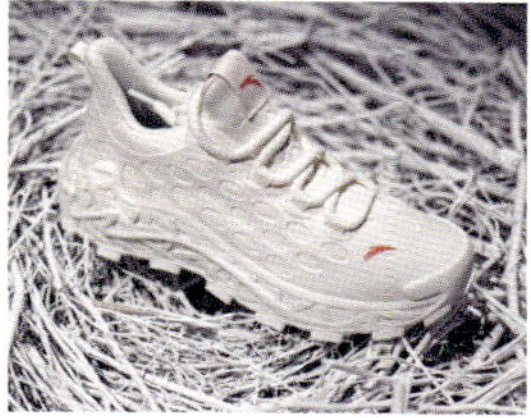

Anta x Salehe Bembury Pop-Up

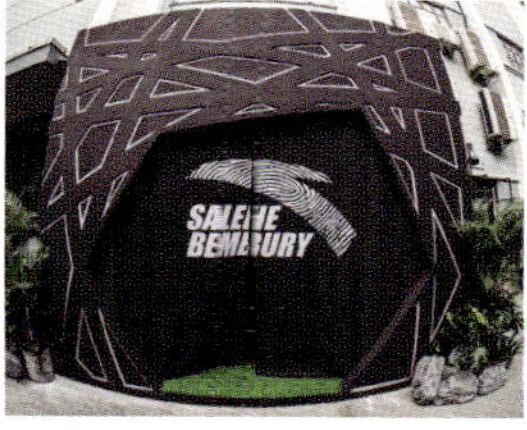

Anta x Salehe Bembury Pop-Up

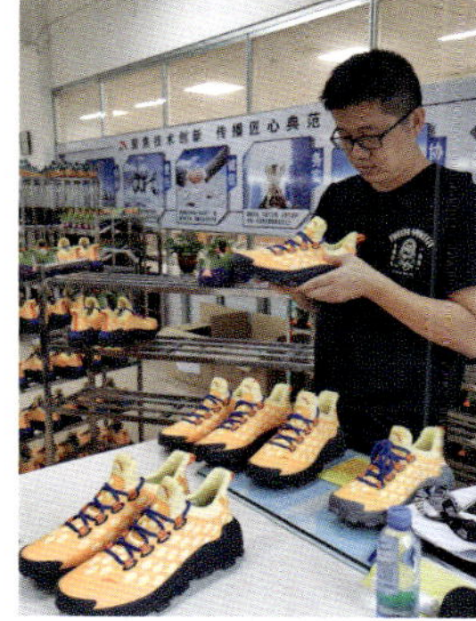

Anta factory

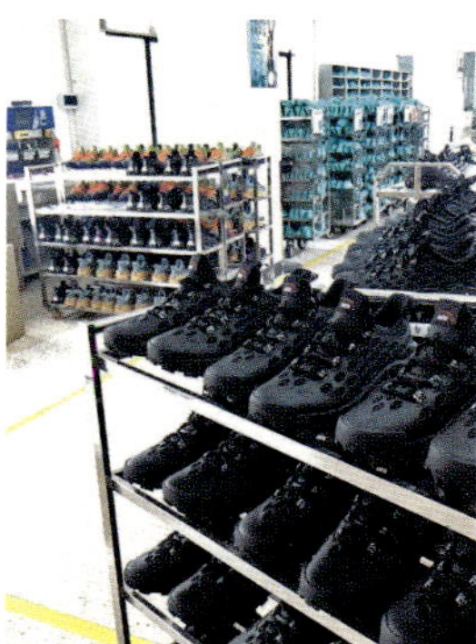

Anta factory

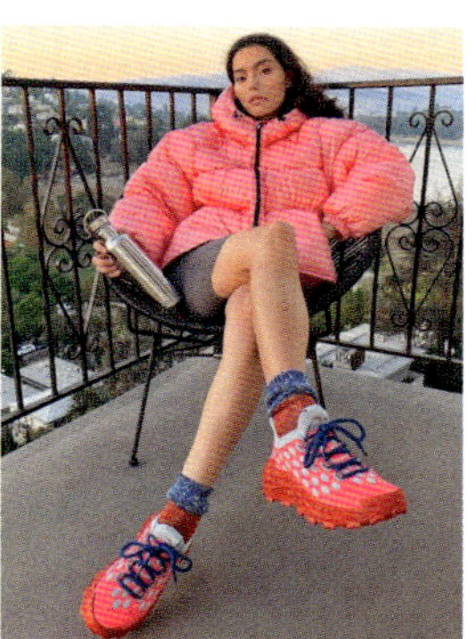

Adrianne Ho wearing Anta SB-01 Salehe Bembury

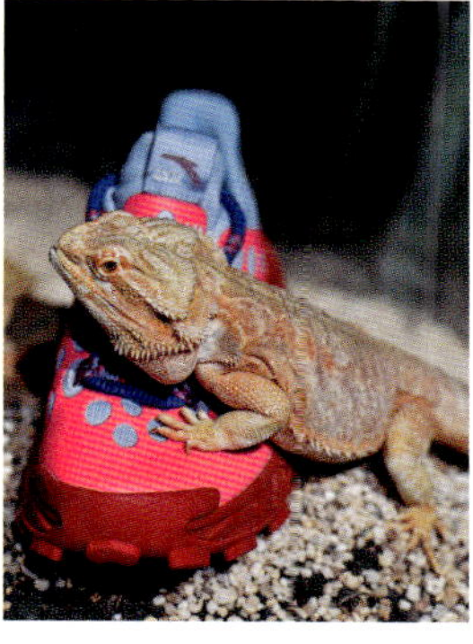

Anta x Salehe Bembury Pop-Up

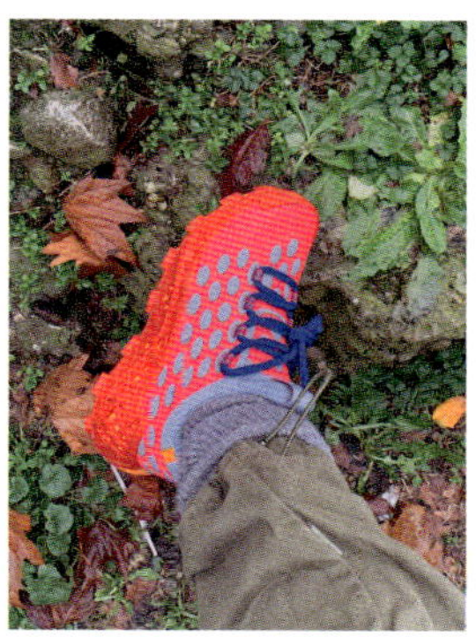

Anta SB-01 Salehe Bembury

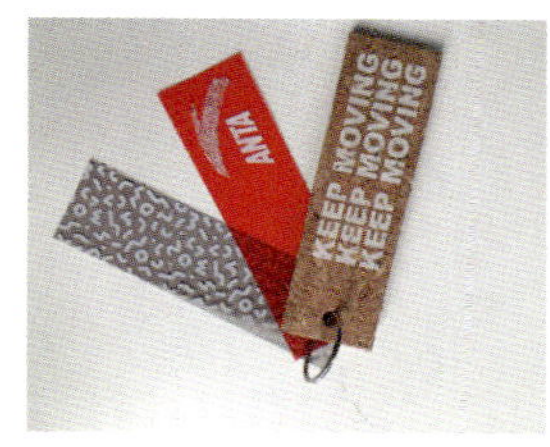

Anta x Salehe Bembury hang tag

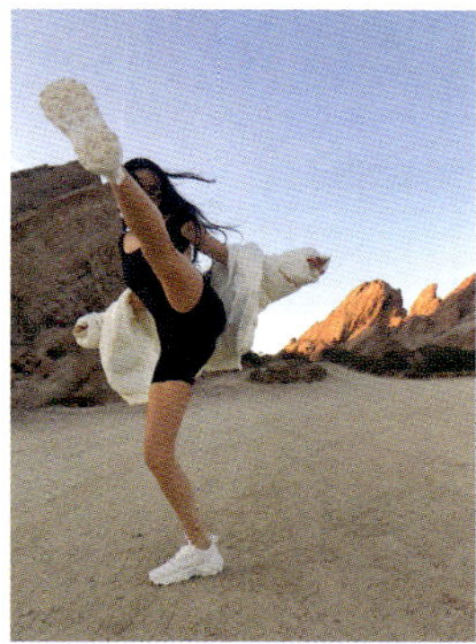

Genelle Seldon wearing Anta SB-01 Salehe Bembury

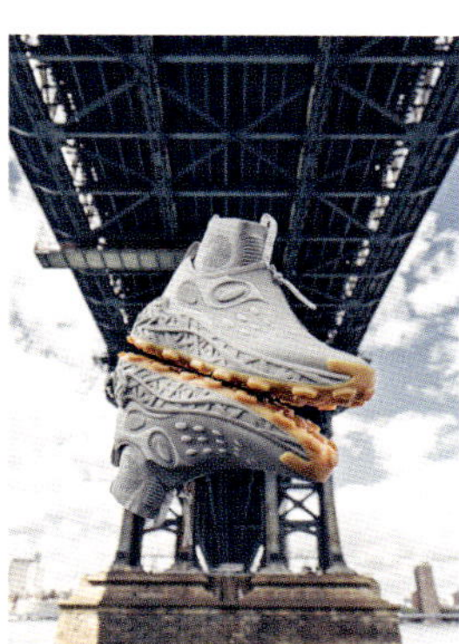

Anta SB-02 Salehe Bembury

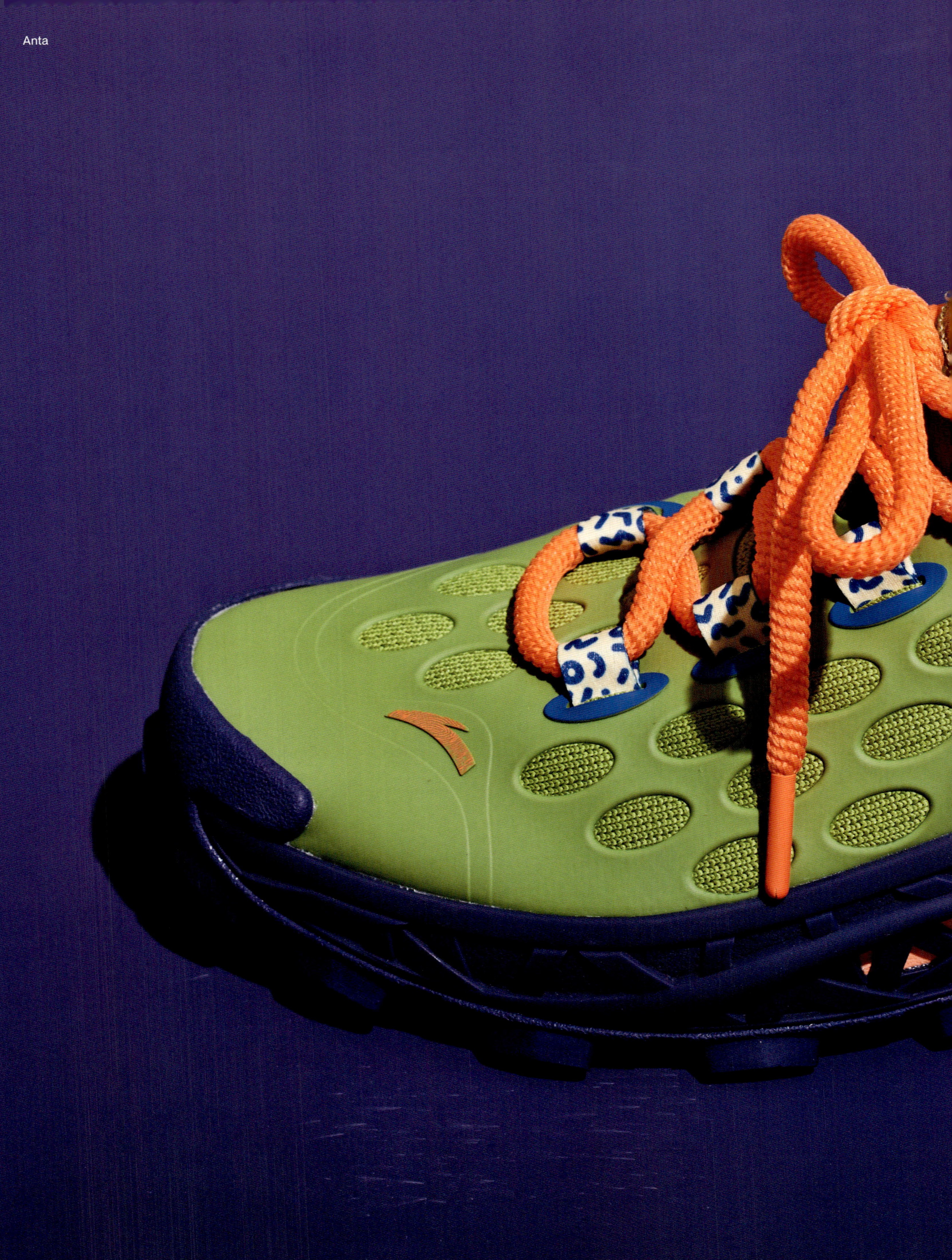

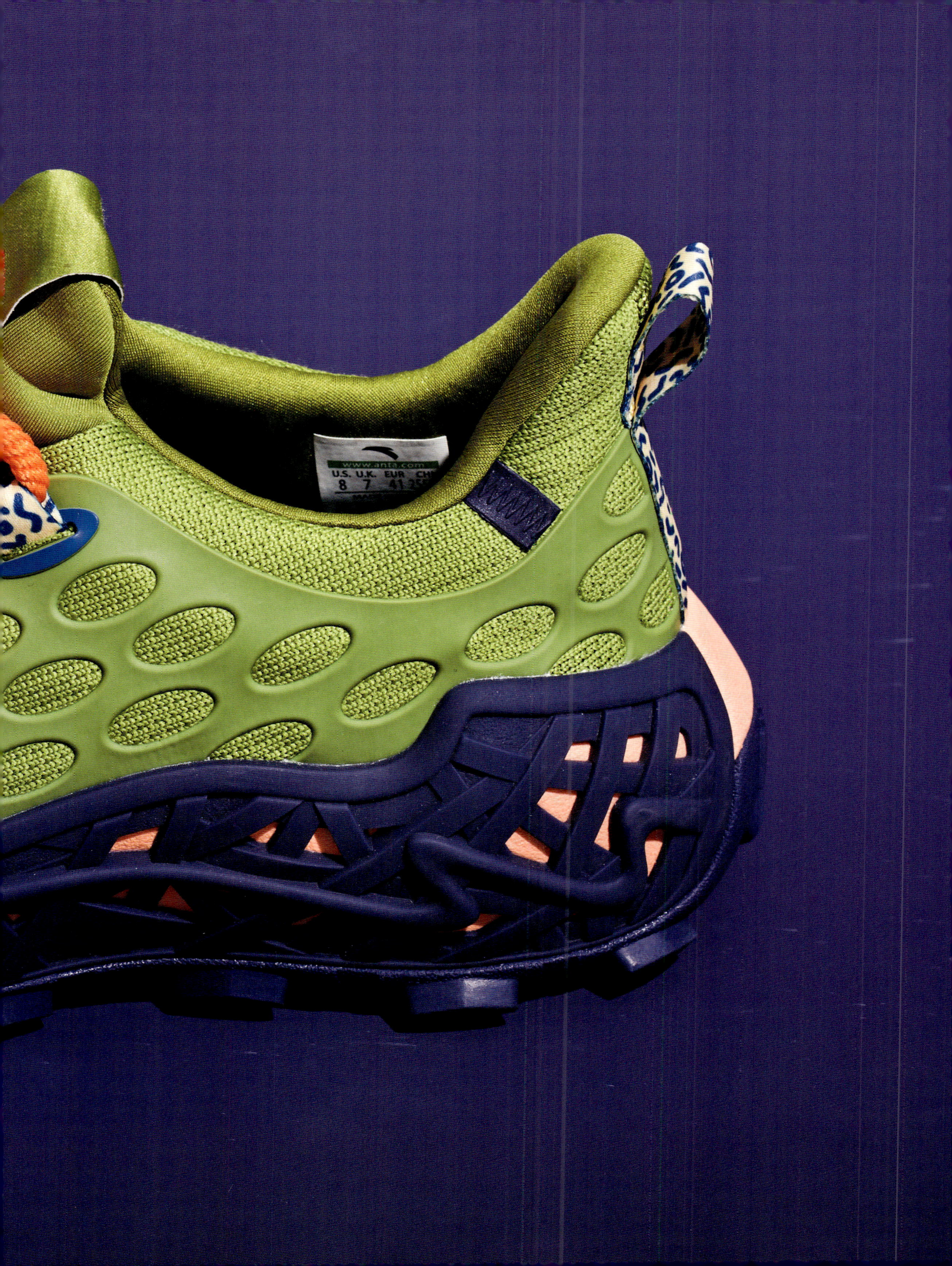
www.anta.com
U.S. U.K. EUR
8 7 41

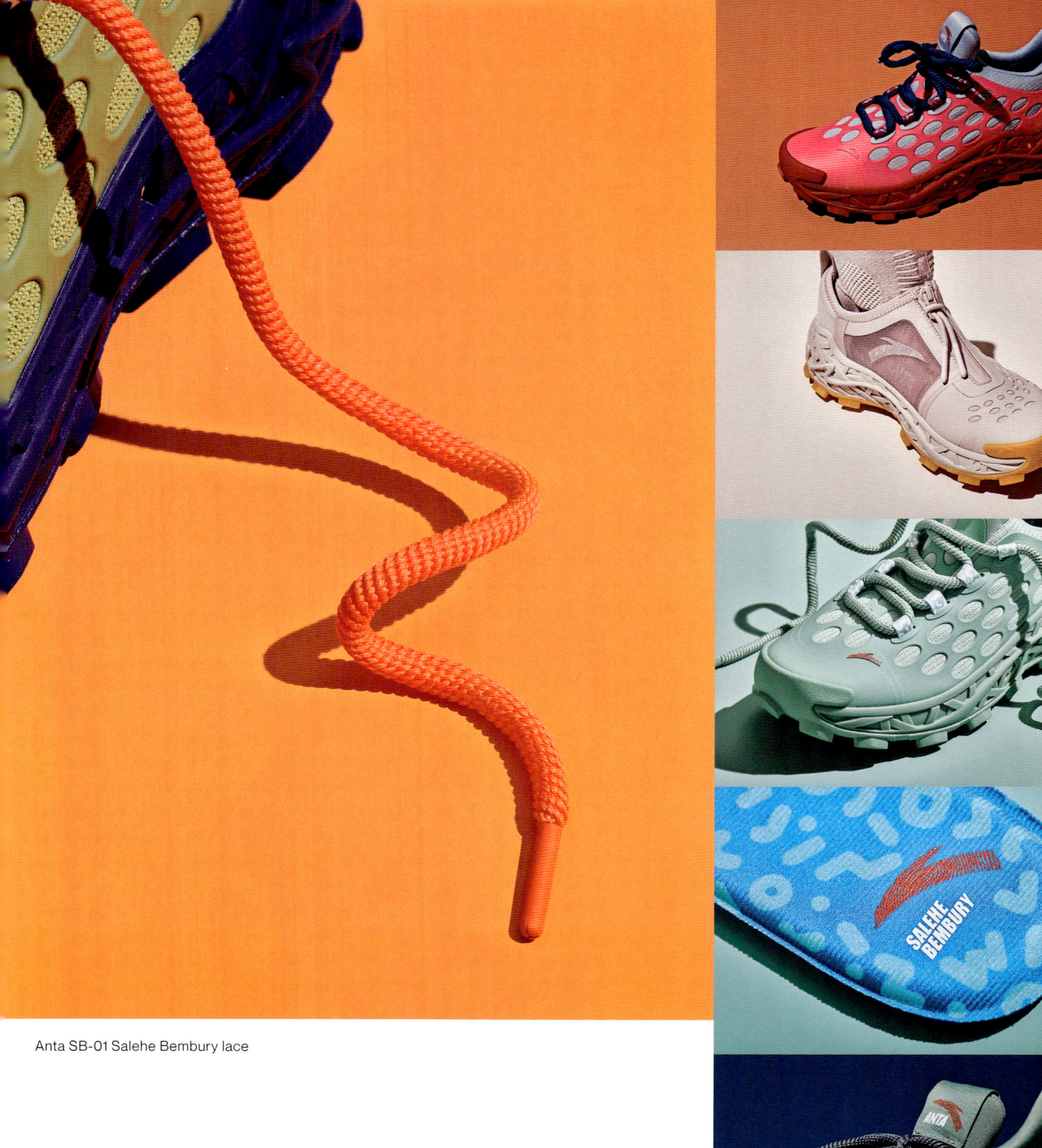

Anta SB-01 Salehe Bembury lace

Anta SB-01 Salehe Bembury

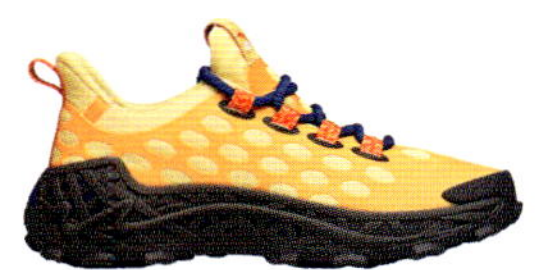
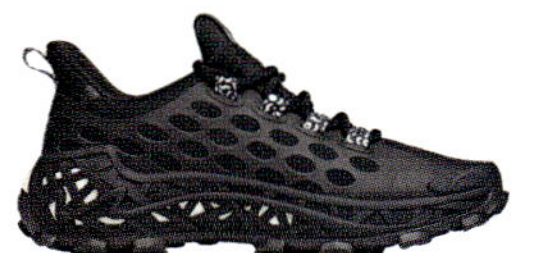
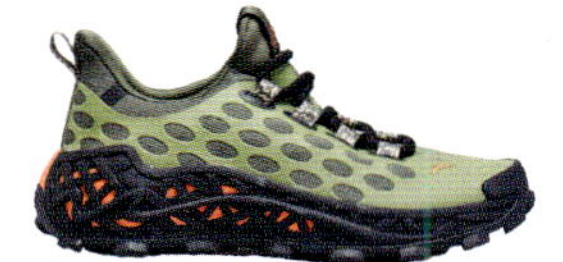
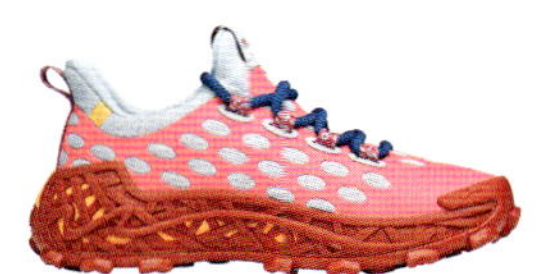
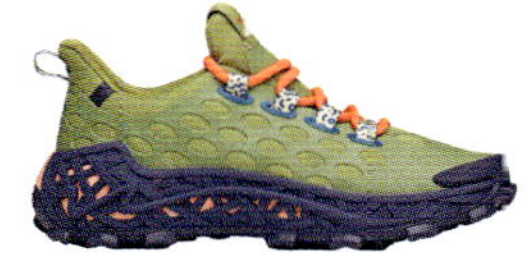
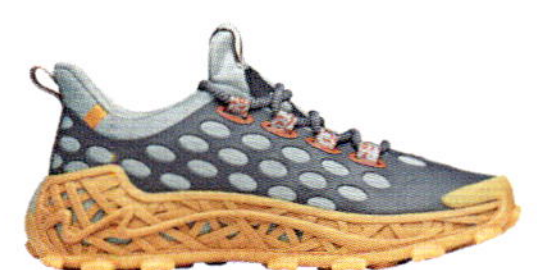
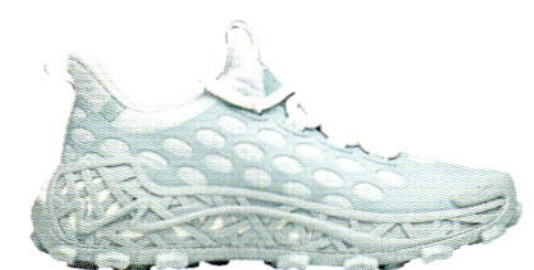

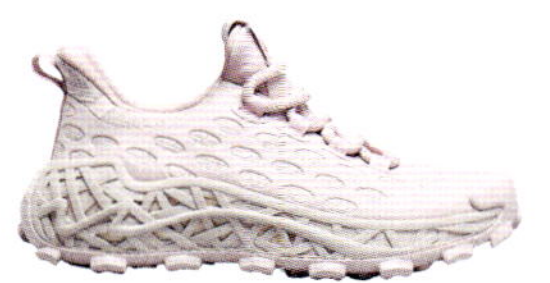
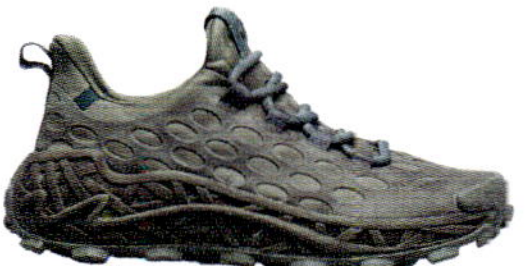
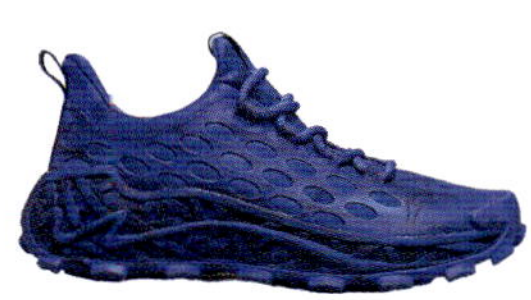
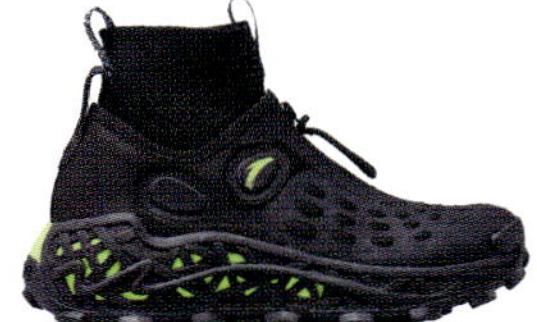
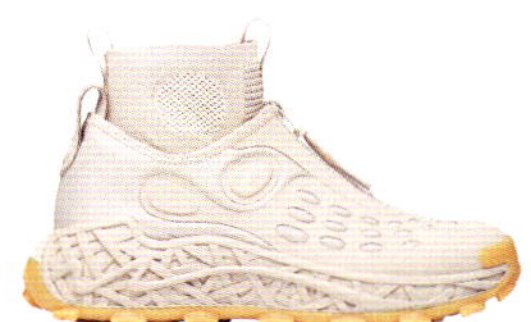
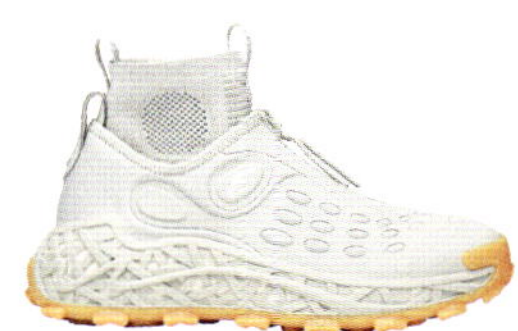
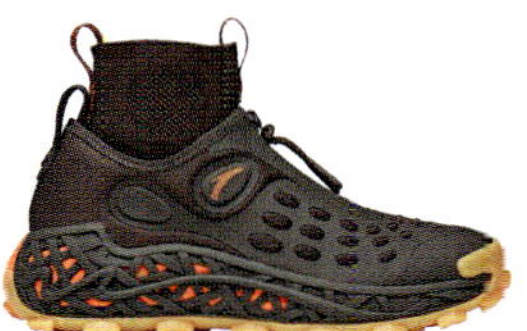

BRANDON 'JINX' JENKINS IN CONVERSATION WITH SALEHE BEMBURY

II

JINX: What was it like working at Yeezy?

SALEHE: It felt extremely surreal. It felt like I was almost home, in the sense that this is the place that I always wanted to be, but I never knew I could get to, and it was just a very hit-the-ground-running role. I wasn't able to stop and absorb the moment, because it was, "Get to work immediately, we're flying to Italy." Kanye was always in contact and I was always playing catch up, because his ideas were being presented at such a fast rate and his expectations were so high that we were always working on something, chasing something. It was a sport. It felt like a sport, like you had to be in shape for it.

JINX: And at this point, you're going from being under the tutelage of someone like Jeff, who's a proper designer, to Kanye—which is not to say he's not a proper designer, but it's a little bit different. In this case, he's a man with taste, he's a man with insight, and he has a high consumption rate, but maybe isn't going to speak in the same way as you and Jeff, who might have a similar education, right?

SALEHE: I would say the number one thing it hindered was potentially the design communication, the creative jargon. You'd have to figure out different bridges and words to have mutual understanding. But then it also offered a completely different and, in some cases, better set of tools, because he was able to think outside of the box. You know, as designers, we often speak a similar language. We put design obstacles or design projects through a similar machine. But for him, he was thinking on a larger scale, and he wasn't maybe considering obstacles or costs or materials. He was just thinking of his dreams. In the moment, I found it frustrating, because it was my job to get these things done. He would come in and say, "Man, I had a vision last night." And I'd be like, "Well, can you draw it?" And it wouldn't necessarily make sense, but then he's gone, and now it's my job within the next two days to make that real. And granted, I have a cellphone and I can ask him questions; but then there was that fear of reaching out and making it known that I didn't understand what he wanted. So it was definitely sometimes tough. But at the same time, that was what my job was, what my expertise was—to translate his ideas that sometimes didn't have full visibility, and make them candid.

JINX: Also, you might not have a shorthand in design language, or even proper professional structure, but maybe you guys have a shorthand in culture, right? Reference points, points of view, things he cares about. "Who's getting pussy in these?" is shorthand.

SALEHE: Strangely, though, reference points and cultures are somewhat like trends. They come and they go. What was cool for his generation? Not that he's that much older than me, but what was cool for his generation wasn't necessarily cool for mine. While working for him, he often spoke about the Jordan 1 toe—they called it the GPT, which meant the "good pussy toe." And the reason they called it that is because when they were growing up in Chicago, all the drug dealers were wearing Jordan 1s and other shoes, maybe Pradas, with sleek toes. So they called it the GPT. So often when designing for him, there was a lot of attention paid to the shape and the sleekness of the toe. For me, being a designer and me being a consumer—well, sure, the vamp and the last of a shoe is important, but I was not obsessing over the toe. So I thought that that was a perfect example of how, within a decade, the interest in the details of a product, or more specifically, a shoe that a group of people see, can change.

JINX: In that process, what did you learn about decision-making? You're coming into this as a person who's ambitious, a person who's constantly leveling up and trying to soak up information and experience around you. You're essentially tasked with more decision-making, but you're still dealing with the decision maker.

SALEHE: It's a tough one, because this was definitely a job where I felt like I had independence. No one's clocking me in or out, I'm traveling to Italy to produce shoes, and I'm a team of one, because I was the men's designer and Lucette Holland was the women's designer. So I really felt like I was in control of my future. But at the same time, I had a boss in Kanye who was very involved in the process and loved to text and call at all hours of the day and night. I knew that this wasn't product that necessarily I could say was mine; I was more so bringing something to fruition that Kanye wanted. At the end of the day he was presenting a design brief, and it was my job to design. So, you know, there are shoes in the Yeezy line that one hundred percent have my name on them. But at the end of the day, every Yeezy ever created is Kanye's brainchild, and I can't ever claim credit for those things.

JINX: Did that give you that itch? You're at the bar with your friends, you see the sneaker walk in, and wanting to say, "Yo, I worked on that"—especially at that age? I've had moments like that in my career, of trying to balance a sense of what I hope is humility with ambition, being confused about what that is.

SALEHE: Well, in the earlier stages of my career, I would exaggerate my involvement in things just to level up. I've said this in past interviews, but I didn't design the Cole Haan Lunargrand. I was on the team, I helped do some colors, maybe, helped with some cad, spec, or proto stuff. But I did not design the Lunargrand. But I also realized that the association with the Lunargrand aligned me with Nike. It made me seem like this really innovative designer. I actually did this colorful Prisma sketch page of the Lunargrand—I got picked up by Hypebeast and my name became synonymous with the shoe, which was fully like a curated operation that now I speak to honestly. But there was a point to that: that got my name on Hypebeast, and that put my name in a couple people's mouths. It wasn't that successful, compared to where things are now, obviously, but that's the smartest thing in the world.

It's this weird double-edged sword, because a lot of the time brands and bigger designers try to prevent their designers from claiming the work or associating with the designs for reasons of confidentiality or NDAs; but a young designer should absolutely do whatever they can to get that association, that digital association, with their work. Because if you work on something and someone can't Google that you worked on something, short of them getting in contact with you and getting your

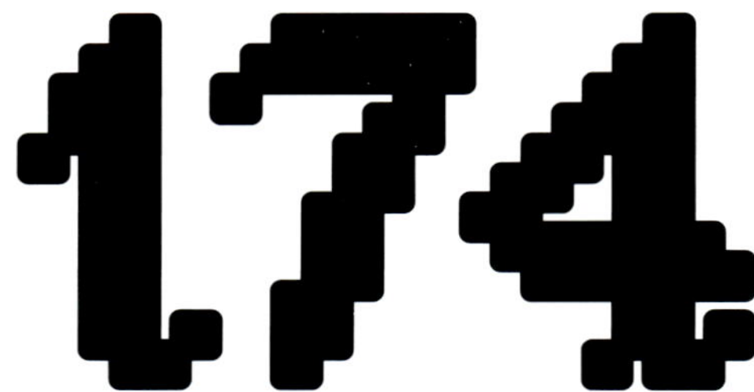

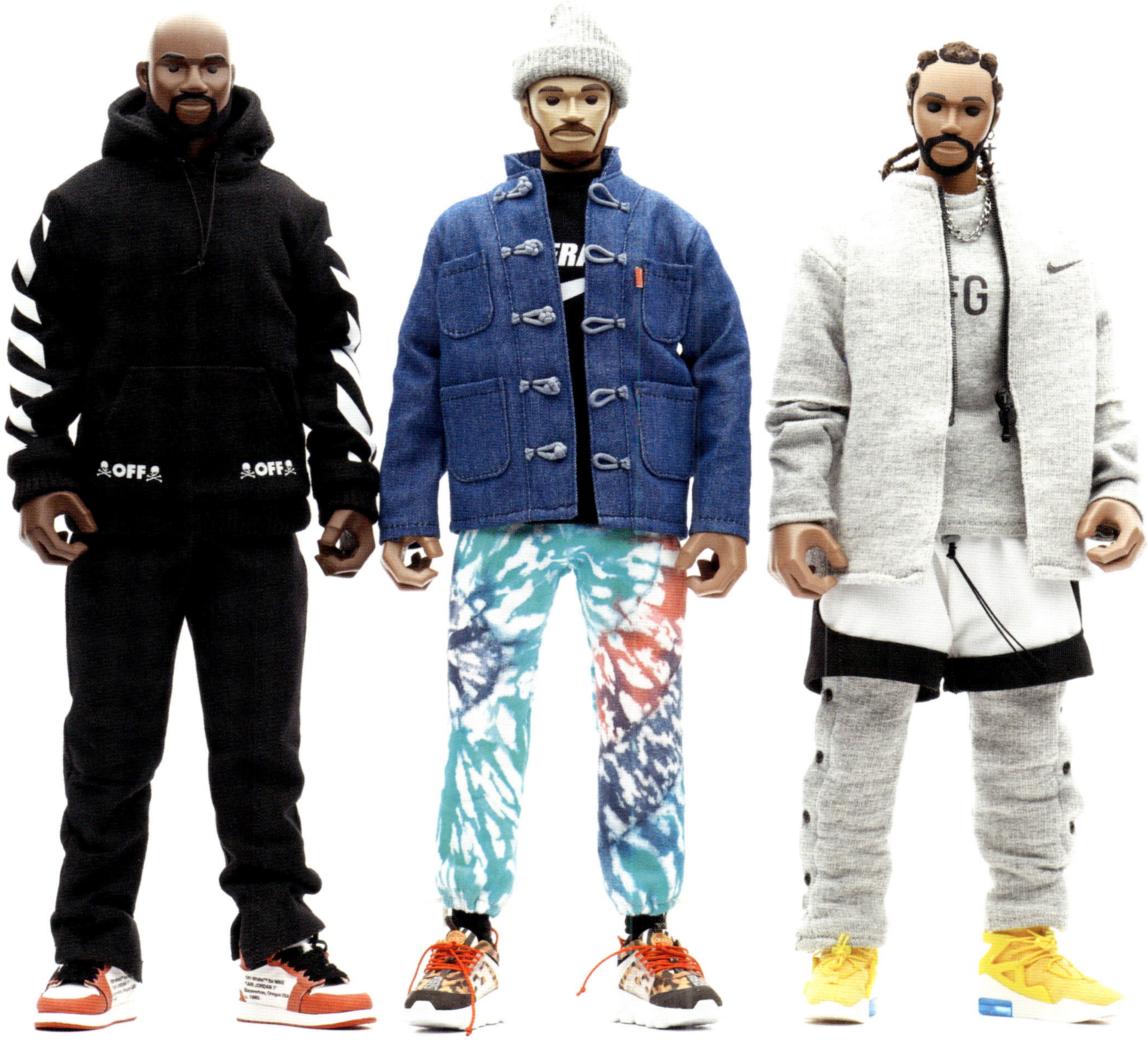

In Conversation with Salehe Bembury

Brandon 'Jinx' Jenkins

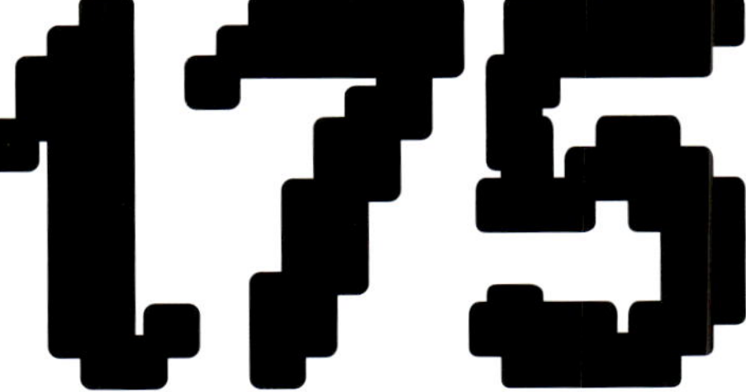

portfolio, it's like it never happened. So in the early stages of my career, I was always on that, even when it came to Yeezy. Like, you couldn't photograph the Yeezy office, but the one thing that you were allowed to photograph was the floor. And that floor became extremely identifiable. When you rip up carpet and it has that kind of glue—those glue marks on that rough floor became identifiable as the Yeezy floor. And I was aware of that—if you were a detail-oriented person, you noticed that. So I was always taking floor pics to kind of let people know I was there. That was a way of showing people I was there without actually telling them I was there.

JINX: It's funny, because the culture has a lot of that, right? Just the way in which we signal, "Hey, I'm doing something"—that in itself is its own code. I remember coming to your office when you did the prototype for the Croc, and you were like, "Hey, you want to take a picture of it?" You had immediately understood the value of that language—of how to show, maybe not tell, or to tell and to not tell at the same time. There was a "show the corner of this thing" about what that was, and I think you can find that in product culture, or just culture, period, today. A lot of people that have earned that DNA.

And how does that chapter change your point of view? Maybe "violent" is not the word, but it could shake your whole shit up, right? "I'm working with fucking Kanye West." There's only one of this guy in the world—it's very specifically Kanye. You're working on this sort of offshoot of Adidas, but it's still Kanye. It's a very exciting time in culture, the number of people that are coming into his universe. And I imagine just a sense of possibility arises out of that, given that your prior stuff had been with Greats, Cole Haan, and Payless.

SALEHE: I would say the culmination of it was witnessing the Season 3 show. That was maybe four or five months into my time there. I grew up in New York City and grew up a Knicks fan, and to see this one individual man take over Madison Square Garden—just to be behind the scenes of that and see all the people that showed up—was to witness something that never even happened before. A fucking fashion show happening in a stadium like that. And to have been a fan of Kanye for the period of time that I had been a fan of him, and the inspiration that he was for me and Black men, and the possibility that he showed. He really promoted that Black

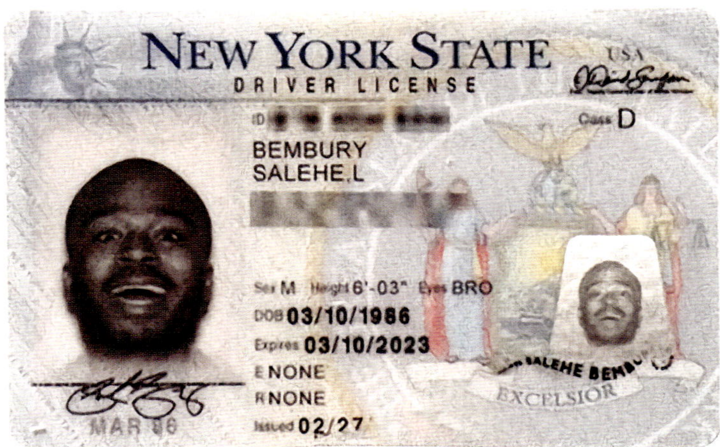

people—and more specifically, Black men—are not a monolith, we exist on a spectrum, and we can be anything. I always kind of had mentioned two people as my inspiration—my inspiration of being confident in self—and that's Phillip Annand and Bobby Waltzer. But it's also Kanye, Pharrell, and Tyler—these individuals that really leaned into just being themselves. So when it came to Kanye and being on the inside, it was just so much inspiration from someone that so leaned into being themselves. In instances of not even knowing how to accomplish certain things that he wanted to, he didn't give a fuck because he was so confident in himself.

JINX: Thinking of the Madison Square Garden show: I went t o a Knicks game a couple months ago, and it's weird to still have that leak-over effect. You're there, they're doing the organ, and suddenly I remember: Yo, bro had an aux cord. Like, an actual stupid cord that he connected to his iPhone. It wasn't even like there was some pre-recorded shit—he literally was like, "Hold on, hold on one second." And that's a song off his phone in Madison Square Garden. He connected his iPhone to Madison Square Garden.

You mentioned having these figures, especially, too; I think the Blackness of it all is such an interesting dynamic. Obviously there are other people in your field that do what you do. But I think when you appear as a Black person, specifically a Black man, it comes with this context—context around whatever people think, whatever you think. There are a couple of figures in our space that have sort of—I'm not going to say they defined new territory, as much as they didn't affirm a thought people already had. And that immediately starts to open doors, the way we feel this connectivity to them because they got a new language to say the things we want to say. Do you feel like you're in that space now? Do you feel a sense of responsibility about that?

SALEHE: Yeah. But again, I think it exists on a spectrum. At the most dramatic end of that spectrum, there have been Black men, like Prince or Michael Jackson, where their entire presentation was showing you that "I am different and I am other." That almost seemed like this asserted effort, you know, to literally be this thing. Whereas with me, I'm really just like the person I am now. I couldn't be more organically just who I am in my heart, and I think that I naturally obtain that association just because I lean into who I am.

And as far as responsibility goes, I think representation is extremely important. From something as obvious and simple as Obama being president, to something less expected like maybe me being a designer in high fashion. I think it's very important for little kids to see—hey, there's someone that looks like me that can do that position. Even going back to what I was saying about my fear of public speaking: in the past five years, I've realized that it's fucking selfish, and I have a responsibility to inspire, and I have to share these cheat codes, and I have to hold the door open. So, yeah, I have a huge responsibility, and it exists on many levels. Something as simple as my audience seeing me on a business-class flight to Paris—while that's some jiggy shit, that's also inspirational as fuck and no different from when I remember seeing Virgil doing that and thinking, "Wow, so this is how you move to the airport." Before that, we only saw executive men doing it in suits. And now, we see like, this is a Black man in a hoodie. This is what I mean about the scale of it. It could be as crazy as seeing Virgil walk down the L.V. runway, waving. That's a moment, and that's crazy. But then on a smaller, yet equally important level, it's like, wow—this is a Black man going to the airport, business class, eating a good meal, getting picked up by a car. What does that look like? And now, wow, this is Virgil in these white European environments, but they're all respecting him, and he belongs, and he gathers all the tools he needs to be there. So those are some of the things that inspired me and gave me the balls to be able to walk into an environment like Versace and feel like I was going to be able to do what I needed to do. Obviously Virgil has no idea he inspired on that—I mean, I'm sure he had an idea of many ways that he inspired, but I don't think he knew that something as simple as just showing the shot of him in the back of the car was inspiration. You know what I mean? That's inspiration. This motherfucker is in Paris getting picked up by a sixty-year-old white man in the newest BMW. And that's how it's supposed to be.

JINX: I remember running into you in the airport, you were on the moving walkway or something, and as you went by you were like, "Yo, what up?" And I was like, Yo, Salehe looks cool as fuck. And that's an exciting thing. That's important. Anytime I see a friend in the airport, you feel like you both know something that someone else doesn't know. But how important is it not just to feel confident, but to feel cool—how important is cool in this space?

SALEHE: "Cool" is this very intangible thing. I also think cool exists on a spectrum, because my cool is so different from, say, a Jerry Lorenzo's cool. A Jerry Lorenzo's cool is very, like, serious—it's a color palette, and it is direct—whereas I believe my cool lives within authenticity and a level of freedom and nostalgia. I think it's just important because people want to look like something they can relate to. I think my cool might be a little bit more relatable—maybe the lifestyle that I live, or the clothes that I wear, make people happy. I don't know how to dissect my cool, really, because I've had people tell me I'm cool, and I've had people tell me I'm a nerd. I think that strangely, being confident in being a nerd is fucking cool. So that's what I think my cool is. I can pantomime the other versions of cool pretty easily, but it's the me shit that I'm most excited about.

JINX: What's an early code from your life—a code that you realize is probably still with you today?

SALEHE: Probably one of the most important ones for designers is just to document. I'm thanking my 24-year-old self, because now I'm at 38 years old, I'm working on a book, and I have a very well-organized hard drive of pretty much everything I've ever worked on. So documentation is a very important one. And then I would also say that corporate movement, corporate finessing, is extremely important, because at every job you have, you're going to have allies and you are going to have obstacles. Those obstacles might exist because they need to exist; they might be ego-driven, they might be age-driven, or gender-driven. You never know. You can be the most talented person in the world, the coolest person in the world, the best-dressed person in the world, have celebrity friends—but if you do not know how to navigate the corporate space, you will be lost. And so, you know, simply understanding how to identify who's your obstacle and how to work with them or not work with them, or how to collect allies and use those things—it's really all a game of chess.

JINX: Do you have a memorable moment of having to navigate obstacles?

SALEHE: I remember with Cole Haan, we were the innovation team. It was Jeff Henderson, who I mentioned millions of times, and then Jen Hong, and we were the innovation team. They gave us this back closet that was really big, but it was still a closet, and we outfitted it with design images and samples. It felt like this little kind of Nike kitchen, right? Jeff came from Nike, so I'm sure it was inspired by that. And because we were part of the innovation team, we could literally go anywhere in the building and do anything—we could go up to the CEO and be like, "I need your shoe for a second." And it'd be like, "Oh, innovation team's up to something," you know, and they'd give it to us. It was cool, because it was kind of like we had this police badge.

With Yeezy, it was like that too. If I went to a 3D place and said I need everything in here, they'd be like, "Whoa, buddy, what are you doing?" I'd be like, "Yeezy." "Oh, okay." And for Yeezy, there was the 1050 boot. It was kind of like the super shredder of the 950, it just had more. For the season three show, we did a tree camo version, and it was a duck boot—the bottom was rubber foam and the upper was this woven material. But the sample came in three days before the show, and for whatever reason it was over-dyed red—and tree camo is obviously like a mixture of the browns. For any designer or any brand, if a sample comes in three days before the show and obviously you can't use it—and given it's coming from Italy or China with shipping time—there's no fixes. But Kanye took that boot and he looked at me, and he said: "Fix it." So for the next two days, I had to drive around the tri-state area, going to Dick's Sporting Goods and whatever outdoor stores I could find. I had to find the correct tree camo that matched what the upper was, and then I had to take that material—which came, I believe, from some duffle bags—and find a tailor that could work on shoes. The tailor took the patterns of the 1050, remade the upper out of the tree camo that I found, and then I remade the boot. The night before the season three show, I'm in my room in the Ace Hotel, hot-glueing the shoe back together. Then the day of that show, it was being worn, and they put it on the Madison Square Garden Jumbotron, and while everyone else was like, "Oh my God, there's a tree camo," I'm like, begging that bitch doesn't fall apart. So for me, that was just an example of being faced with a seemingly impossible obstacle, and then really just taking it upon myself to solve it. And obviously, maybe there was a little bit of fear. There was a motivator. But sometimes you need fear to motivate.

JINX: I feel like that's relevant in your career going forward—how you did everything with New Balance, made sure you're on top of the marketing, made sure that it's still extremely hands on. It's not a note you're sending off and hoping it comes back okay. You're saying, "Wherever I can have my hands involved, I'm going to do that."

SALEHE: Well, I also think, like all great chefs—they put in the time developing the expertise of washing the dishes or cutting the vegetables or whatever. I just want to make sure that I can wear all the hats, I'm able to speak the language, and that I have that experience. So then, when I'm faced with those obstacles, I have the tools to deal with it.

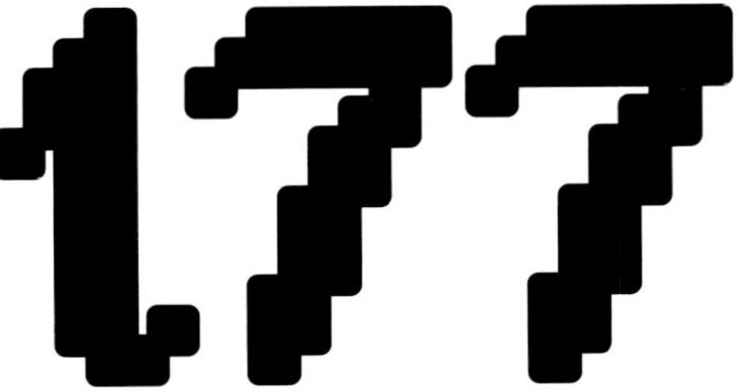

178

NEW BALANCE (2020)

LEGAC
NOSTA

CY VS.
ALGIA

NEW BALANCE
LEGACY VS. NOSTALGIA

1

Joe Grondin reached out to me through my manager and let me know he was interested in me being a collaboration partner of New Balance. This request was confusing to me because at that point in my career and my life I saw myself as a hired gun for a brand. I was very used to a guaranteed paycheck and I for sure was never putting my name on product. The Anta collaboration hadn't played itself out yet so I still was very uncertain, unsure about my ability to be an independent designer.

I met with Joe in a hotel room in Paris. Having heard all the Yeezy tales of meetings with Mark Parker and all this stuff, it felt strangely appropriate to be meeting at a hotel in Paris, because it seemed to fit the fairytale I had in my head of how these things happen. We met, he showed me some things they were working on, some things they had coming up in the future. When we met again in my office in LA, he brought a duffle bag of different things, he brought Nicole Underwood, and basically they showed me what they had in mind. It was really a surprise to me because growing up I saw New Balance more or less as a 990 silhouette that came in different colors. On that day I learned that New Balances come in many different colors, silhouettes, and styles. And not only were there a lot of old-school silhouettes, but they had a lot of ideas for silhouettes for the future. So I was flattered to be approached by one of the iconic sneaker brands of our time, and I was also surprised by what they were capable of from a product standpoint.

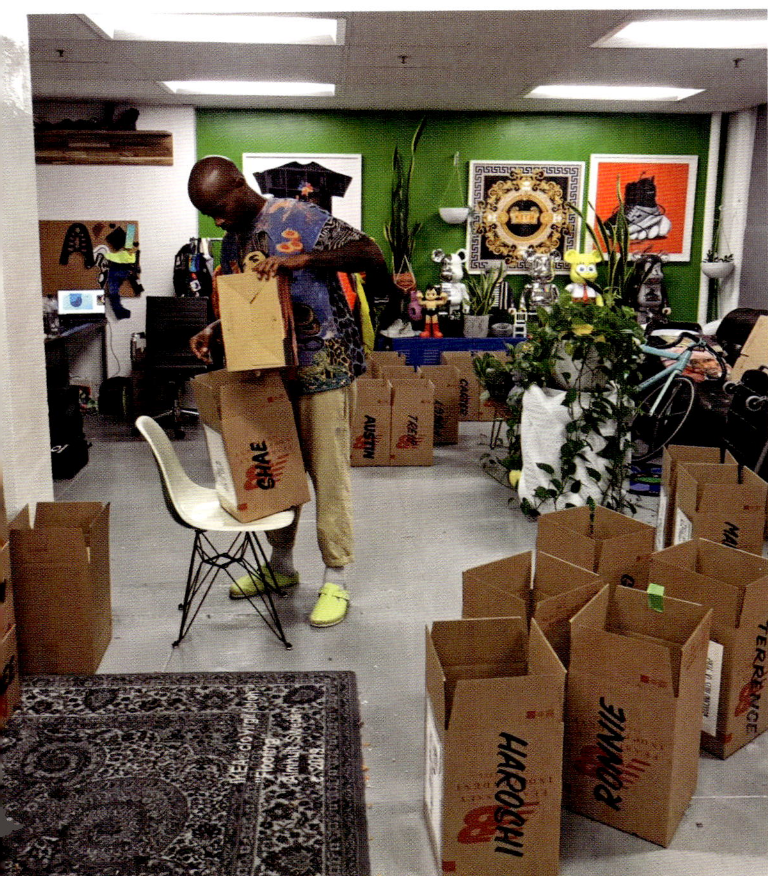

Once we agreed to terms (which at this point in my career was simply me saying yes, there wasn't much negotiation happening—I was just happy to see an agreement for a single collaboration that was worth close to the amount of money I was making yearly), my then-manager and I went to Boston to meet the New Balance team. I had created an entire PDF for presentation, which goes back to my "decks lead to checks" mantra that's gotten popular on the Internet. In this deck I basically mapped out the entire collaboration from product and storytelling to marketing. I mapped out the whole world. And that came from me being a student of the game, from being a lifelong consumer of sneakers and essentially regurgitating what I had been absorbing for all those decades, and from having waited for that moment a long, long time.

Anta was a different kind of opportunity because it was an unknown brand. I saw Anta as a product development opportunity—as in, I could make a Nike shoe at this brand. But New Balance is a very well-known brand within America, so with this brand I realized: I can prove myself to a lot of people, to the culture, the audience, myself as a professional. Prove that I can execute an amazing collaboration that will sell out, that'll be remembered, and that'll be impactful.

2

I gave the New Balance team the context of the lifestyle I was living, being a somewhat outdoors individual. I never want to claim expertise because I was fresh from New York City, or a few years at least. But it was what I spent a lot of my time doing, so I told that story. I thought it would be appropriate to create footwear that aligned with those experi-

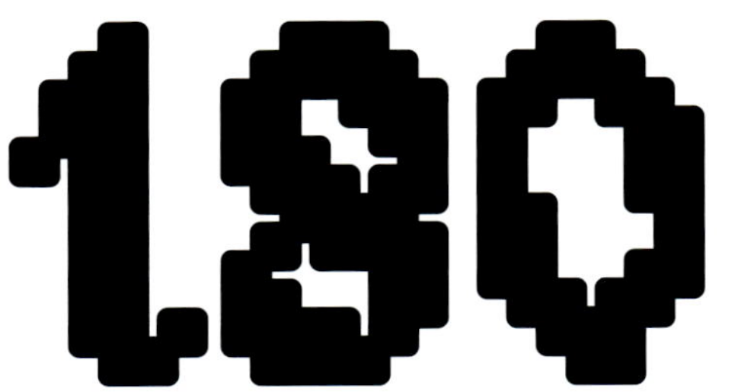

ences, that came from a place of authenticity. The most recent place I had traveled to was Antelope Canyon, and I thought it would be great to have my first show represent that trip. So the tagline for the shoe was "Peace Be the Journey." The shoe itself was an extremely hairy orange suede, which was meant to represent the sand and dirt in Antelope Canyon; the New Balance logo was a light blue shearling to represent the sky; and all the other materials on the shoe fell in line with this narrative. The box is an area of real estate I find many collaborators don't take advantage of—often you'll see a logo or a color, but I saw the box as a blank canvas to further tell the story and communicate value. So I created a box where the panels featured a digitally illustrated section of Antelope Canyon and of those experiences. So now you're figuratively doing some storytelling through product but then you're literally doing storytelling through packaging, and it makes everything a bit more full circle.

I remember hearing that the New Balance team was extremely impressed with my ability to story-tell backwards. I came in with a story and then we worked backwards to the product. They let me know that most collaborators come in with a rendering, or a picture of a shoe, or some reference colors, and then from there they make a shoe. And a lot of the time it's up to the New Balance team to fill some of the voids in the storytelling. In my case, I came in with a story, we worked our way back to the product, it was fully thought through. And this was very representative of how long I had been studying footwear and footwear launches. The shoe released, it sold out immediately, the sneaker audience seemed to be extremely engaged in the story I was telling and the packaging design, really in the entire collaboration. Coupled with my Anta experience, this let me know that I too had an audience resonating with the story and the product that I was putting out there, creating a runway for me to explore entrepreneurship, a further relationship with NB, and new product.

3

When I created this first New Balance, I realized that once we figured out what the storytelling and the product was going to be, the next thing would be seeding. With all of the contacts I'd acquired from Versace, I had an amazing Rolodex of influential figures all over the world to send my work to. And not only that, they were looking forward to the package. I tried to create as much poetry within the package as possible. Being someone that receives a lot of free things, I realized that just receiving something in a brown box—while always amazing and I'm always appre-

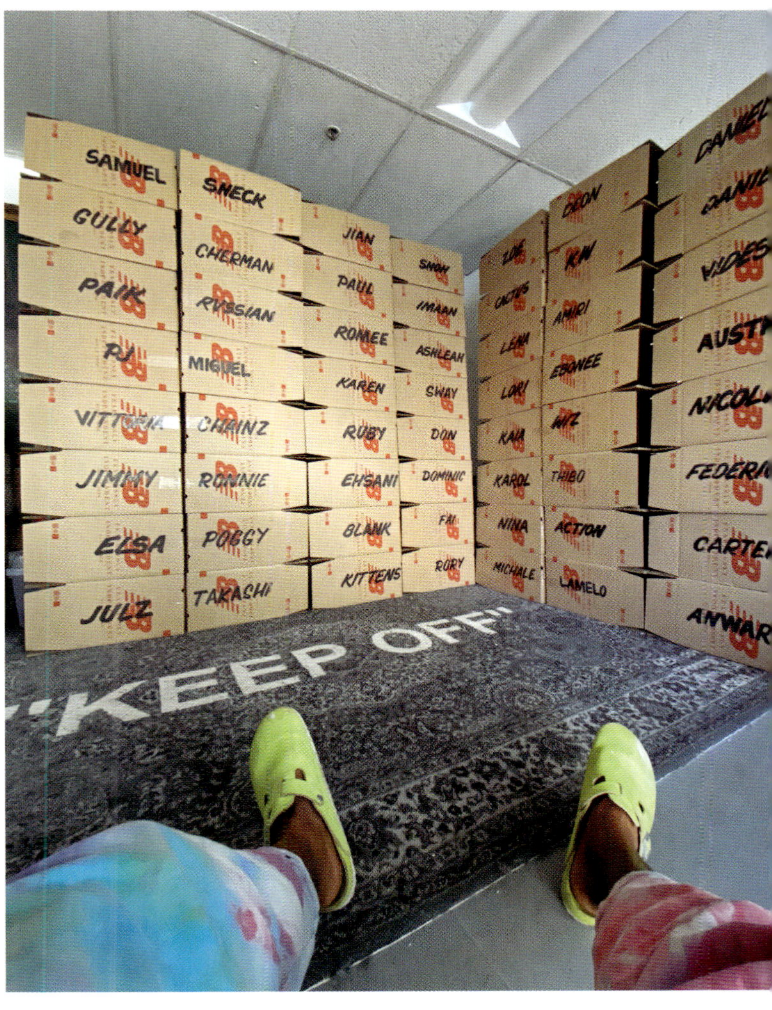

ciative for it—sometimes packaging can make the experience more memorable. So I bought garbage bags of orange moss, which I felt to align with the story of material and color that I had been telling. I personally filled every box I was seeding with orange moss; I then hired a hand-letterer to write everyone's names on the boxes I was shipping; with my own money I had bandanas produced that I put in the boxes; and I reached out to a company called Kleen Kanteen and for their promotional association they gave me 100 free canteens that I was able to customize within the branding and color of the collaboration. This was just me trying to give more accessories that I thought at the time, without any other collection, would further tell my story of the outdoors and ultimately speak to what my brand was. At the time it was unknown, I was virtually unknown to the audience. You only have one opportunity to make a first impression, and this was what that was. I would take about

20 boxes at a time—that was how many would fit inside my Jeep Renegade—and drive to UPS in downtown LA and ship them. They would be received by those influential peoples and those people would post them on their social media, and all of their audiences would now see that shoe. It really created a wave of momentum. I would seed by the truckload to most of the influential people in the space, so it would really create an impact. The shoe sold out immediately, the seeding initiative was very successful, and this set the stage for what was to come.

4

What is the concept of the campaign? Who do I use? What do they wear? What is the tone of the campaign? These are questions I'd never asked myself, these are things I'd never considered. But they're significant because it's first-impression shit. It's the thing that people are going to remember when they wear the product. It's the thing that people are going to associate with the product.

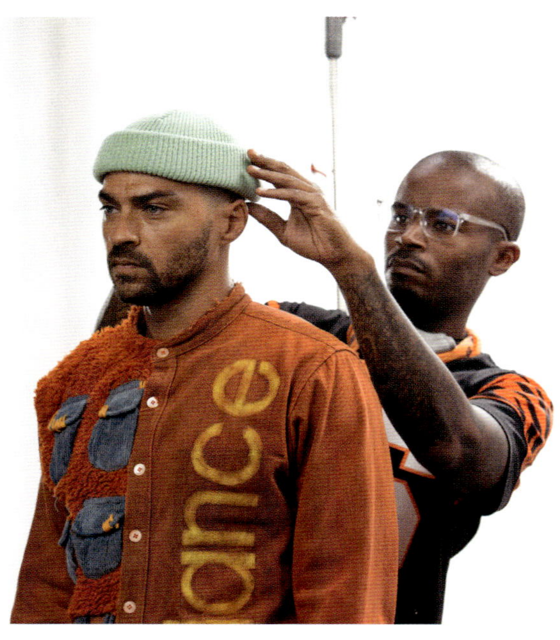

I knew it had to take place in some type of Antelope Canyon setting, though it didn't have to take place there literally. I worked with one of my oldest friends, Nat Prinzi, who owns Betterdays Productions, and so this was already progress. Now I had someone that was familiar with the world of creating campaigns and commercial making, and now I have at least an idea of the environment I want it to take place in.

Coincidentally, around that time someone had hit me up about working together, and this individual owned an inflatables business. He would look up malls with empty lots and rent out those lots for a couple of weeks or a month at a time, and he would put his inflatables in those lots and create kids' fun zones, comparable maybe to a Chuck E. Cheese. He told me that he was a huge fan of mine, and that if I ever needed any kind of inflatable that he'd love to make me one for free. It was the most random offer ever, but I was kind of intrigued by it. He was such a unique individual and had such a unique business, it stuck in my head. And all of a sudden I have a lightbulb and I think to myself: how cool would it be if the climax of this campaign was a New Balance logo inflating out of nowhere? I saw this campaign also as a kind of hello to the industry—it was an introduction to my new career, to myself. "Hello, I'm here."

So next I have to ask myself: what is the person going to wear? Initially, not being familiar with being the designer who's center stage, I start thinking of brands with interesting silhouettes or brands that I like that might add to the depth of the concept. And then I realized: I'm a designer now. Theoretically they should be wearing my stuff. So now the task at hand is to create something myself. Unfortunately, this is also the beginning of Covid, so many of the tailors I would normally work with were not available to help. So I essentially had to create this look all by myself. I wanted it to have a handmade feel to it, to really speak to the outdoorsy aesthetic and the brand I was trying to establish. The items are my old clothes that I bleached and dyed. I hand-painted the New Balance logo on it, I hand-dyed fabric, and everything was really just a DIY attempt at being a fashion designer, which I was freestyling on the run.

Lastly I had to ask myself: who was going to be in this campaign? When it came to casting, which was a word I had never even used before, I wanted to do something that was still utilizing all of the benefits that a model gives you, just with a slightly different perspective so it didn't feel stale or like something you'd seen before. I thought to myself, I need this person to have somewhat of a universal or ambiguous appeal. I didn't want to lean too much into any one direction because I was really trying to cultivate a conversation with a large audience, and I didn't want

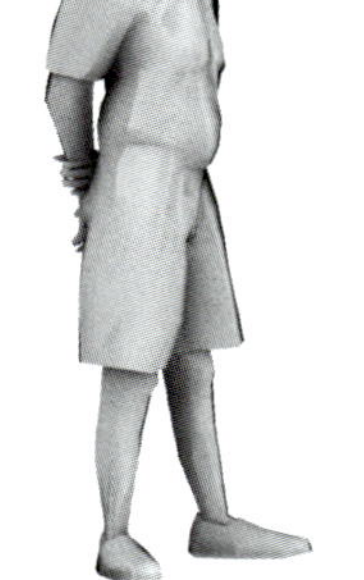

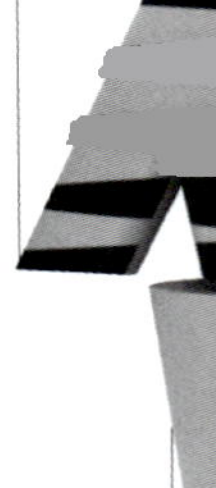

to exclude anyone. I reached out to Jesse Williams. He did not know who I was at the time. Eventually he told me he needed to come to my office to try the look on, and it seemed like when he tried it on, that was a moment of convincing for him. This actual moment of him trying on these orange, tattered clothes that I'm telling him are about to be amazing in this campaign—all of a sudden something clicked, and it felt like he got it. Everything used in the campaign was purchased on Amazon with the exception of the inflatable logo. We imported one or two tons of sand to mimic the Antelope Canyon environment. And a lot of it was freestyled—we didn't really have a shot list, we just did it as we went. Nat Prinzi knocked it out of the park, I will always be indebted to him he's done the majority of my campaigns since. And we created a great campaign that had an amazing response and that was a catalyst in allowing the shoe to sell out immediately.

5

The success of Peace Be The Journey was such that New Balance asked if we could slip in one more colorway. So that was the beginning of Water Be The Guide. This time the environment to be explored was Havasu Falls. We did the exact same exercise: we told a story, we created packaging, we worked with Jesse again, I created another look. This time I also had my friend Austin Mahone make a cameo in the campaign

This time the campaign was inspired by the first episode of The Fresh Prince of Bel-Air. Will, who is from West Philadelphia, born and raised, is sitting down at his first ever formal dinner in Bel-Air, and they are drinking from crystal glasses. At one point Will hits one of the glasses with a knife and it makes an angelic "ding" noise. Being a rhythmic individual, then turns that ding into a beat, and that moment has gone down in culture. I grew up on that show and I love playing with nostalgia as a vehicle for marketing or really just to get someone's attention. I used this as the concept for the campaign.

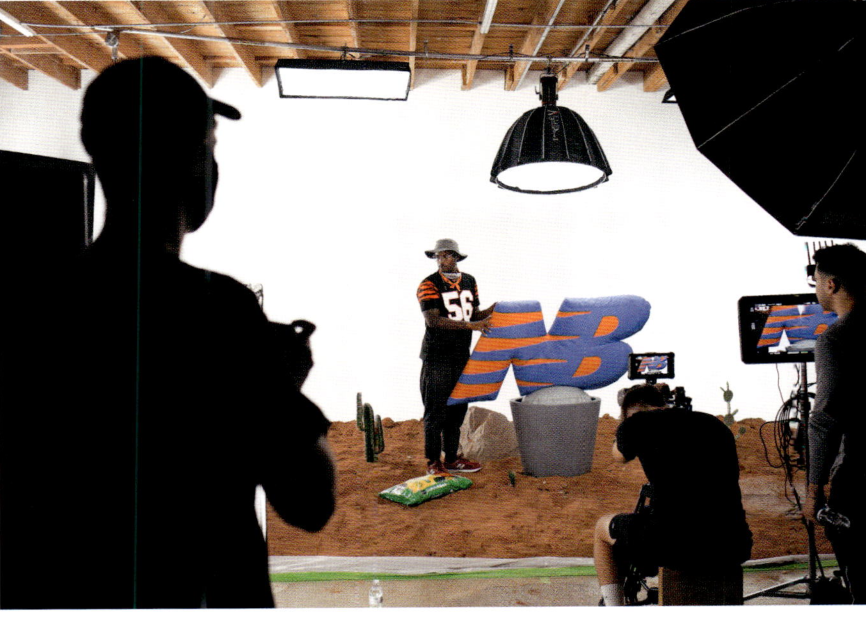

6

Next was the planned Yurt collaboration. (At this point I'm feeling myself.) My last two collaborations have sold out, I feel very comfortable in my ability to create a campaign. I've seen the response of the audience both through sales of product and digital and social media response. It's all positive. And now I'm getting the opportunity to create a sneaker and I'm getting to make apparel. I couldn't be happier and it just seems like the beginning of a really special output.

The first question is, what do I make for the sneaker. I realize that New Balance is a brand that really puts their flagpole deep within their brand identity, in their heritage, and in their signature details. So I knew that whatever I designed could not be completely new—it had to have some of the New Balance DNA in it so that it felt like it was a part of the family.

One aspect of the project that needed to remain was that it had to be a 574. Coincidentally, the 574 is my least favorite New Balance, it always has been. I pleaded with them to change it to a 990 or anything else, but it had to be a 574. So my way of opposing that was essentially to create a shoe that did have the previously established signature details of the 574, but then to add so many things to it that it no longer felt like a 574. The justification for adding all of these things was that within the worlds of hiking and outdoor equipment, you need tools, accessories, zippers, and pulls to get the job done. So I was essentially doing the same exercise with footwear.

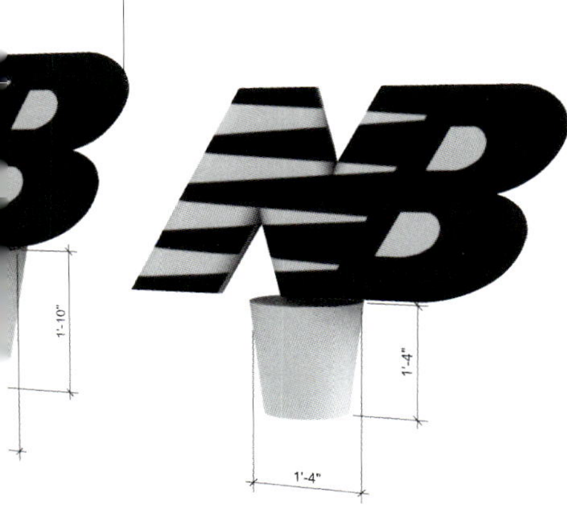

(Side note: All of my time spent with Jeff Henderson prepared me for corporate opposition like this. Jeff was a complete fucking master jedi at dealing with corporate obstacles and debates, and he has passed down those

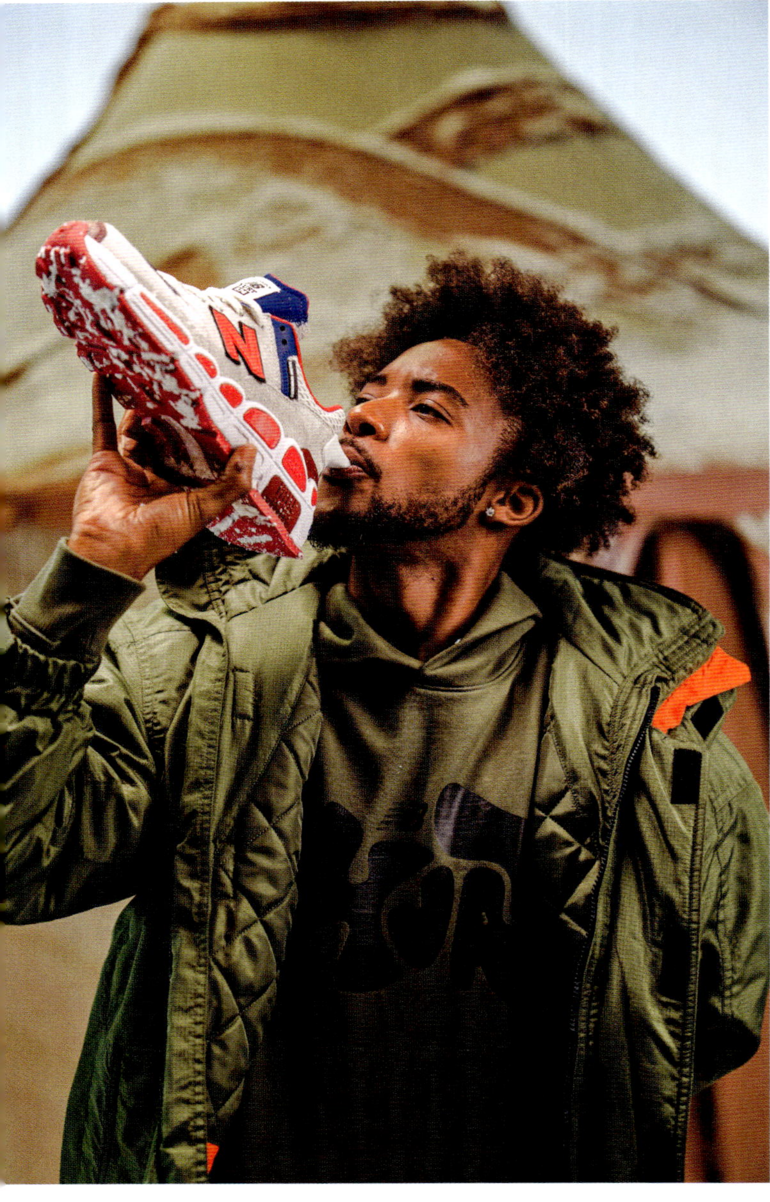

tools to me. I openly welcome professional debate. It is something that I welcome with open arms and it is very much a part of the job, because frequently you will be met with obstacles for reasons of finance, ego, or logistics, and you will have to figure out a way to accept those obstacles or give new points and perspectives to get your way. I'm very fucking good at that, and I'm proud of it.)

The main concept for the Yurt features a safety whistle. I thought about tools that you need in the outdoors, and then I thought about how we could arm a shoe with some or one of these tools? At the same time I was wearing the Samuel Ross A-Cold-Wall Nike Zoom Vomero. Before his collab, that sneaker originally did not feature a 3 x 3" molded plastic part on the back heel. I personally had never seen that material on a sneaker, it was a very strange detail, and more specifically it was real estate on a sneaker that I had really never seen explored. Any time I would wear those sneakers, I would always be asked what that thing did. And when I told the person it did nothing, they seemingly accepted it. To me that was fascinating: if I saw something on a shoe that was weird,and asked what its function was, expecting it to perform, and was told me it did nothing, I would kind of reject it. I guess that reflects that I'm a designer that looks for function and purpose, and maybe so. But it made me think, "Wow, what if this plastic piece had function?" So I started thinking of those different functions that could be obtained, and a very obvious one to me was a whistle. In order to create a whistle, there's no electronics, there's no maintenance—it's simply form manipulation that alters the air to make a noise. So before my meeting, I cut up a pair of 574s—I think they were Junya Watanabes—and I cut a hole in the back, put in a whistle, hot-glued it really well, and then we went to New Balance.

Coming from streetwear and downtown New York, the collection was very representative of that. I wasn't reinventing the wheel, I was staying within a comfort zone of what I was familiar with. All of the cut-and-sew pieces from my first New Balance collection are actually reinterpretations of vintage New Balance pieces. I thought that was extremely important because one of the most valuable things that any brand has is its heritage, so getting the opportunity to work with New Balance was not only something that I needed to honor but a situation where I had to pay respects to the heritage and use those as ingredients for whatever I was creating.
I meet with the team—Brian Sterling, Joe Grondin, Jordan, James, Kevin, Nicole—and I tell them I'd like to continue the narrative of the outdoors that has been so successful in the past. I proceed to tell them a story of camping with friends, going for a long walk before

dusk and stopping to see some deer. You have your camera with you, so you decide to take some pictures of the deer, and you get lost in the photo experience. After a few minutes you look up and your friends are gone. It's about to be dark and you have no idea where you are. And then all of a sudden from a bag beneath the table I pull out the handcrafted 574 with the glued-in whistle, and I blow it. You could tell that they immediately got it–whether they understood it from a perspective of outdoor safety, or from a perspective of just seeing a fun thing on a shoe that we've never seen before, or a tool, or even just a "I didn't see this coming"–and everyone was engaged, everyone was on board. And that was the birth of the Yurt. I then had to design it.

That collection featured the Yurt in 5 colors. It also featured a jacket, a fleece, some T shirts, a hat, and pants. This was my first attempt at making a collection. Elementary in execution–there was nothing that reinvented the wheel–but cohesive, it was representative of what was to come, and I believe that it came from an authentic place. I wasn't trying, I was just executing authentically. And I think the best fuel for creativity is executing from a place of authenticity.

I had now established a campaign style which was very Wes Anderson in execution; they were always on a set, which made the audience feel like the model was in that environment but at the same time you knew he wasn't, which gave it a kind of fun tongue-in-cheekiness. I had an identity, and I was able to explore it.

I called up Jesse Williams – but this time, given that it was 5 colorways of shoes and an apparel collection, this was the first time I was going to use multiple models. So I used Jesse Willams, Kim Johansson, Ron Holden, and Algee Smith. The Yurt campaign video is by far my most viewed video on Youtube, and I believe it is because I told a story.

7

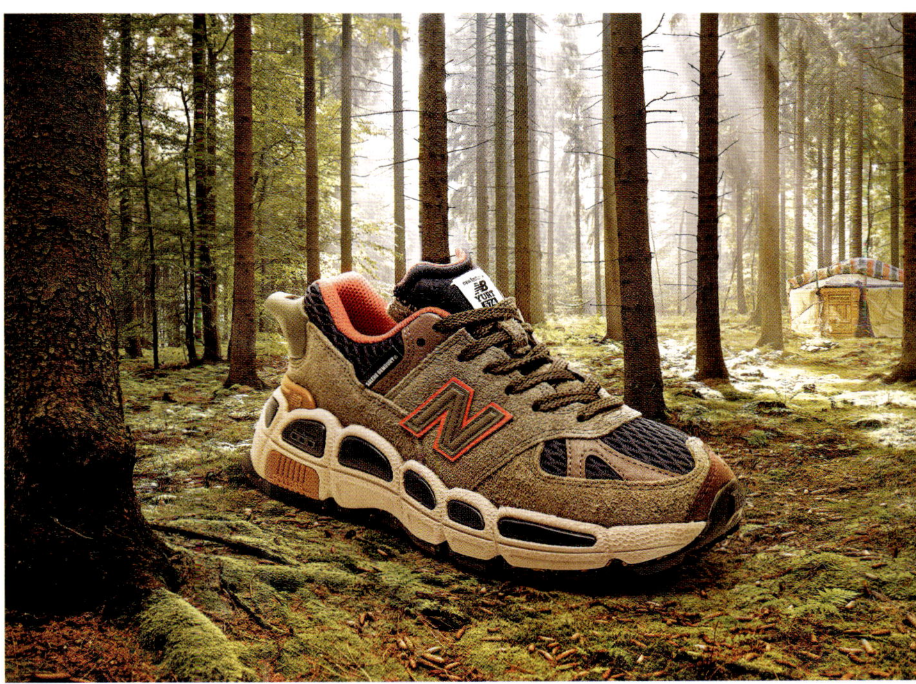

In the early 2000s, the brand Orchard Street collaborated with Nike on a project where they made around 20 Dunks that were yellow and red, and they hung them up around New York City for anyone to find. Today, these Dunks go for around $20,000 because they are so rare, and they created an experience in a time when there was no social media and really no way to confirm or classify if any of the shoes that were dropped were found. Over the years I had always heard tales of this marketing exercise–which at the time I didn't realize was marketing,–and when New Balance gave me the opportunity to do a smaller project during Covid, this was the initiative that came to mind.

New Balance allowed me to create 50 of a sneaker for the sole purpose of hiding them around Los Angeles and creating a scavenger hunt for my local audience. Given that the purpose of this shoe was not for sale, it meant that the shoe could look however I wanted. In instances of trying to sell a shoe, while you want to make it how you'd like, you still do have to consider the consumer and try to make

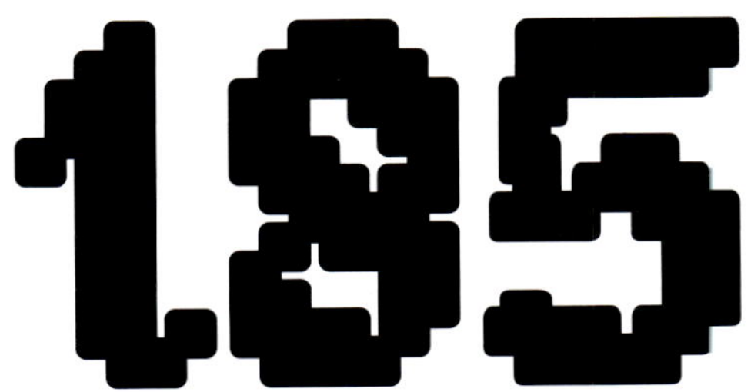

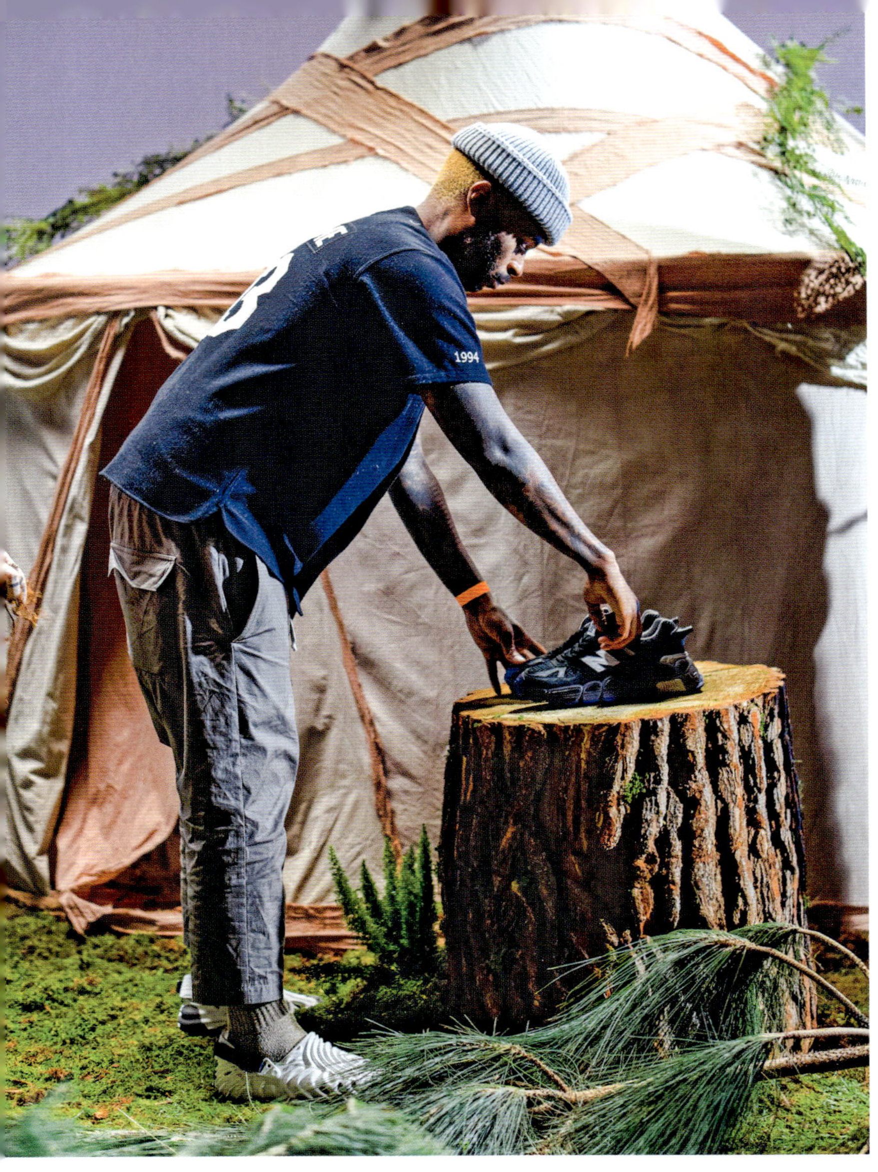

where the audience had to stay in their car, hop out for one second then get back in their car, was not only a fun exercise but was also Covid-safe.

I was driven around Los Angeles by friends and participants in the culture—Josh Vides, Anwar Carrots, Jeff Staple, Ron Holden—and I made an effort to hit all of the neighborhoods so that no one felt left out. I would go to a random, quiet section of that neighborhood, record myself placing the bag of shoes in a tree behind a dumpster in a nondescript place, and then put that video on my story, either showing that exact address or a clue of where I was. Within a minimum of a minute and a maximum of five, someone would show up and grab the shoes, and they would immediately be theirs.

During this period of time I was still brand-building, I was still trying to get peoples' attention. And this exercise left a lot of people with a memory, with an experience. There's a famous Maya Angelou quote—"People may not remember what you said but they'll always remember how you made them feel."

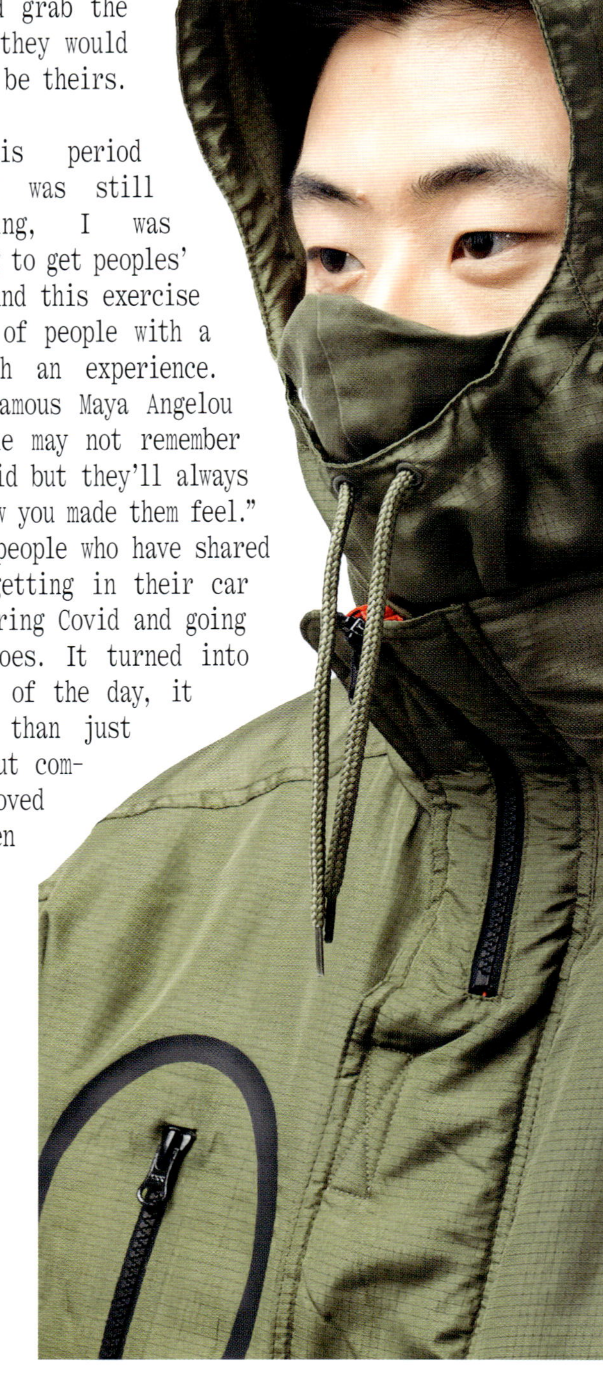

something that will be commercial. Making an all-yellow shoe is not advisable, for example, as yellow is not a color that sells in high demand. So in this case I made the shoe with three different kinds of leopard print, ten different colors, and it really was a shoe for the few and not the many. I created screen-printed garbage bags that were meant to stand as a second layer of packaging. The premise was that I would go to different parts of Los Angeles, let people know in my stories where I was, and within minutes the consumer would come running in their cars or on foot and get the shoes. The scavenger hunt was called Finders Keepers.

What made this exercise unique and rather appropriate for its time is that it was during Covid. There were no social gatherings happening, we were in many cases not legally allowed to be around each other. So executing something

There are a lot of people who have shared their memories of getting in their car at a random time during Covid and going out to look for shoes. It turned into a game. At the end of the day, it became about more than just shoes—it became about community, about loved ones. It didn't even have to be about getting the shoes—there were a lot of people e telling me that they never even got a shoe or saw one, but just the experience of

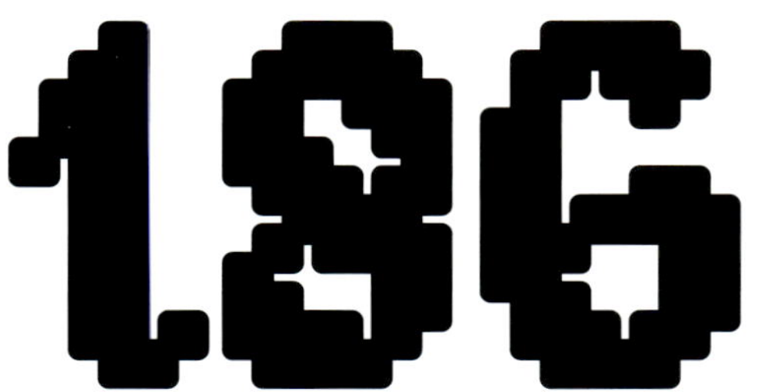

getting in their car and sitting there, waiting and holding their phone and hoping that maybe I'd post, that in itself was fun.

8

New Balance has been my longest partner. They're one of the partners I'm most honored to be collaborating with. They have been established in the industry for decades, and having the opportunity to put my name with their logo not only brings a lot of value to my brand but also allows me to execute at a level that I wouldn't be able to on my own. I also see the partnership as an ability to show my peers and show the industry what I'm capable of with a partner like New Balance. Not many creatives are given the opportunity to work with partners that have the development capabilities of a New Balance, or even the other partners; the roster that New Balance currently has of collaborators also adds to the value not only of New Balance but of myself. I've always told New Balance that there should be a moment when all of the collaborators get an opportunity to stand next to each other. Joe Grondin was able to compose a team of the untapped. Somehow, at a time when it seemed like every potential collaborator was already allied with a brand, Joe had a certain taste level and a certain vision to find collaborators that were untapped. He planted the seed of what the collaborative initiative could look like at New Balance, and a lot of the results seen now stem from him.

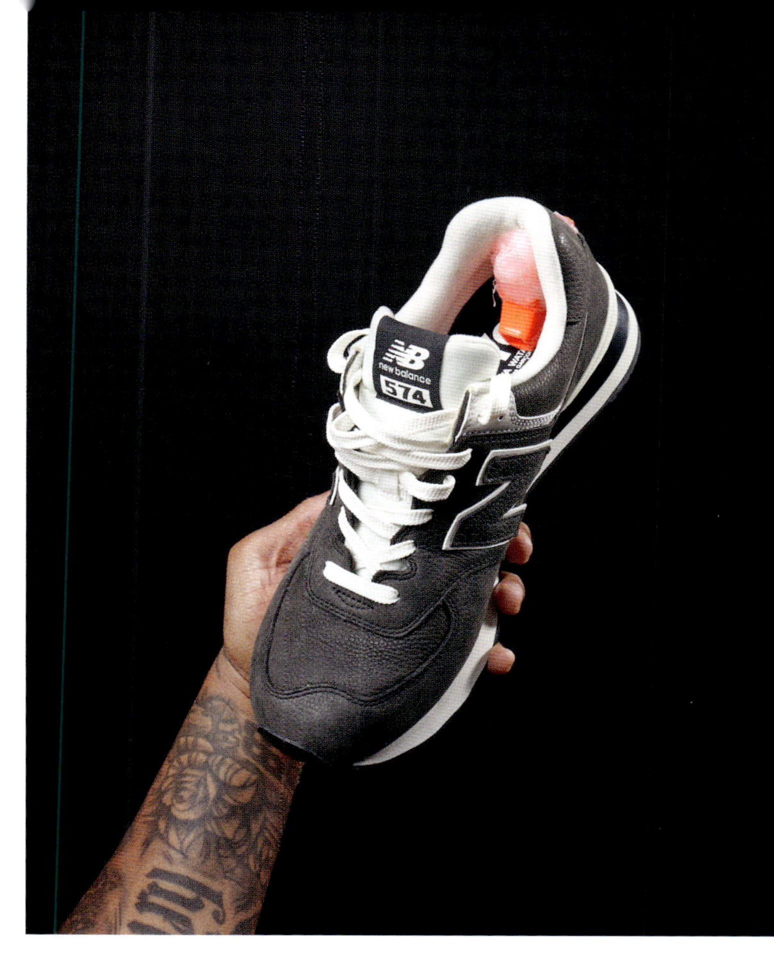

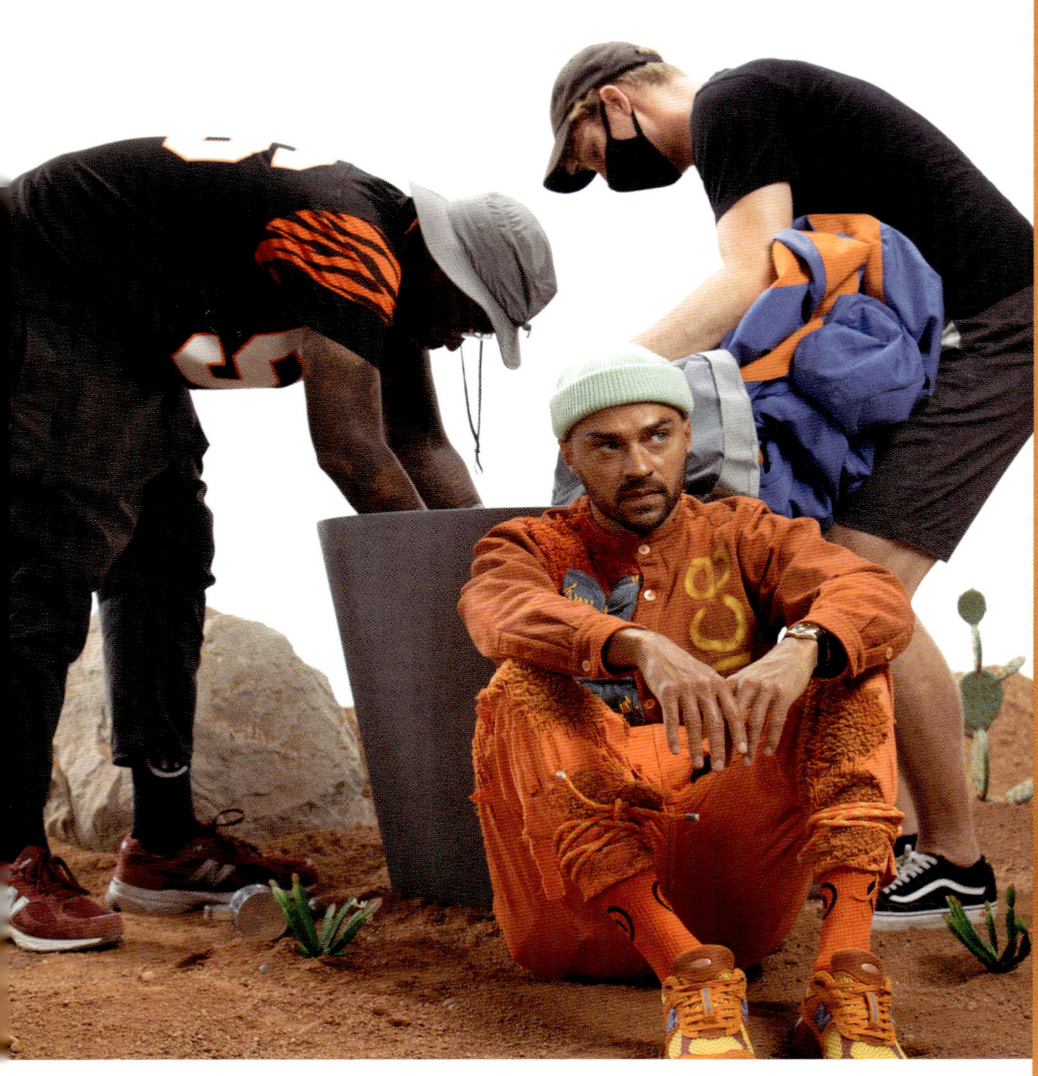

New Balance 2002r Salehe Bembury “Peace Be The Journey” campaign featuring Jesse Williams

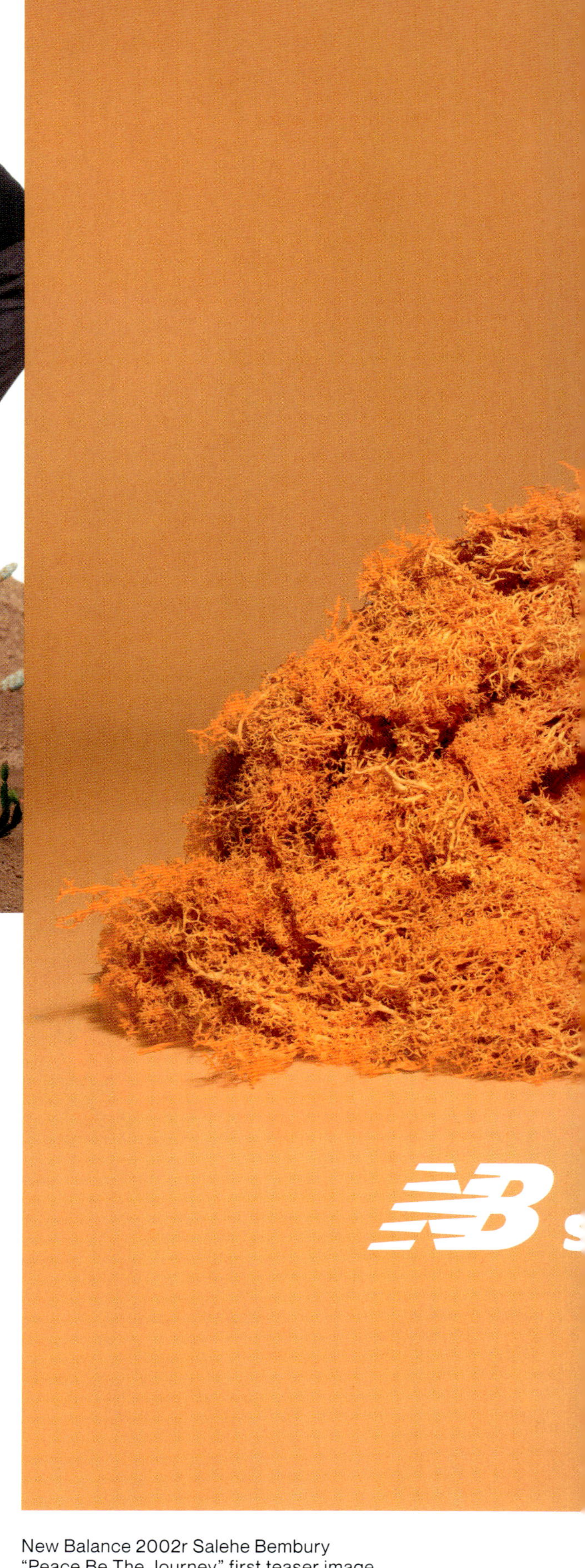

New Balance 2002r Salehe Bembury
“Peace Be The Journey” first teaser image.

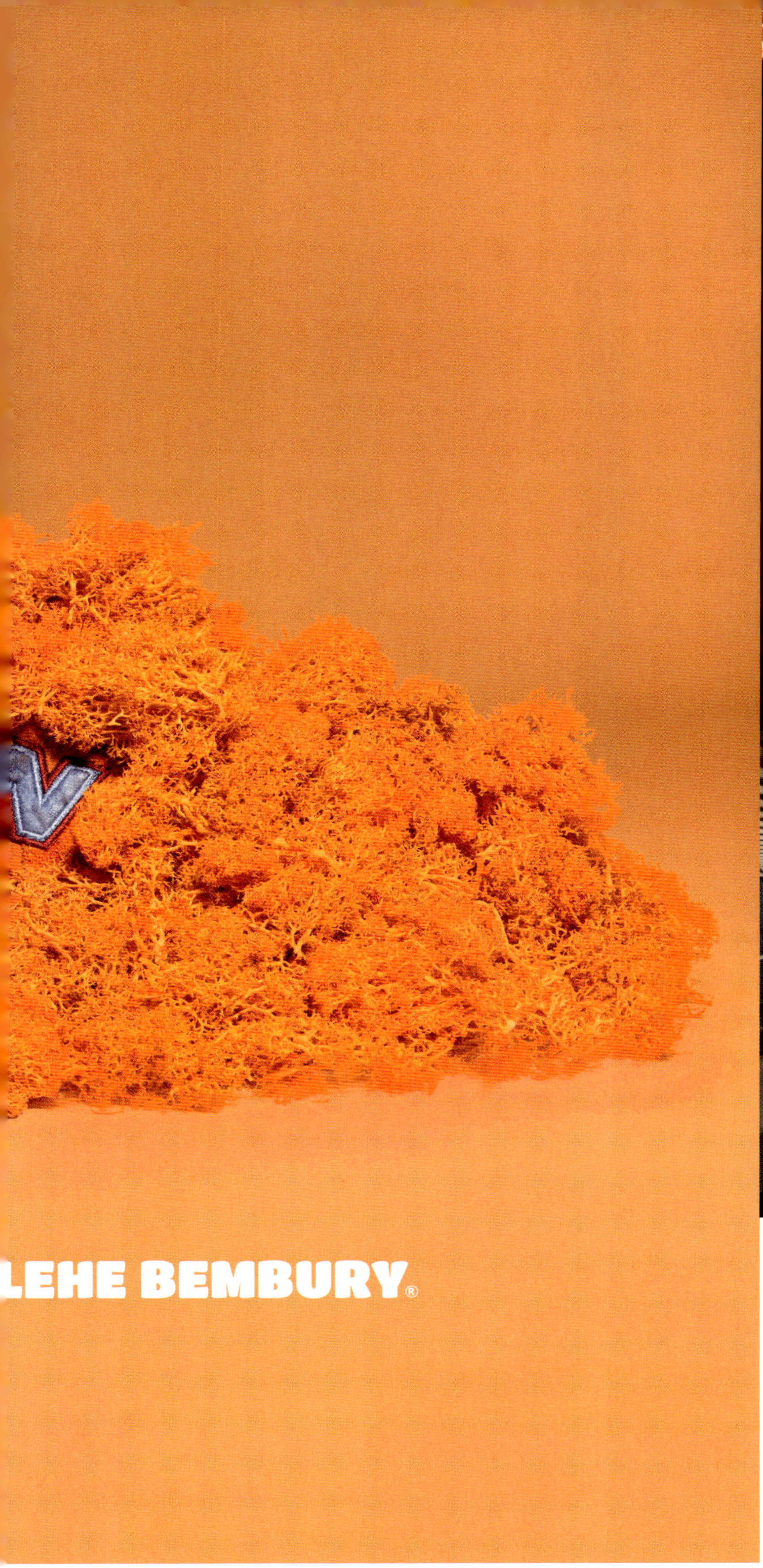

LEHE BEMBURY®

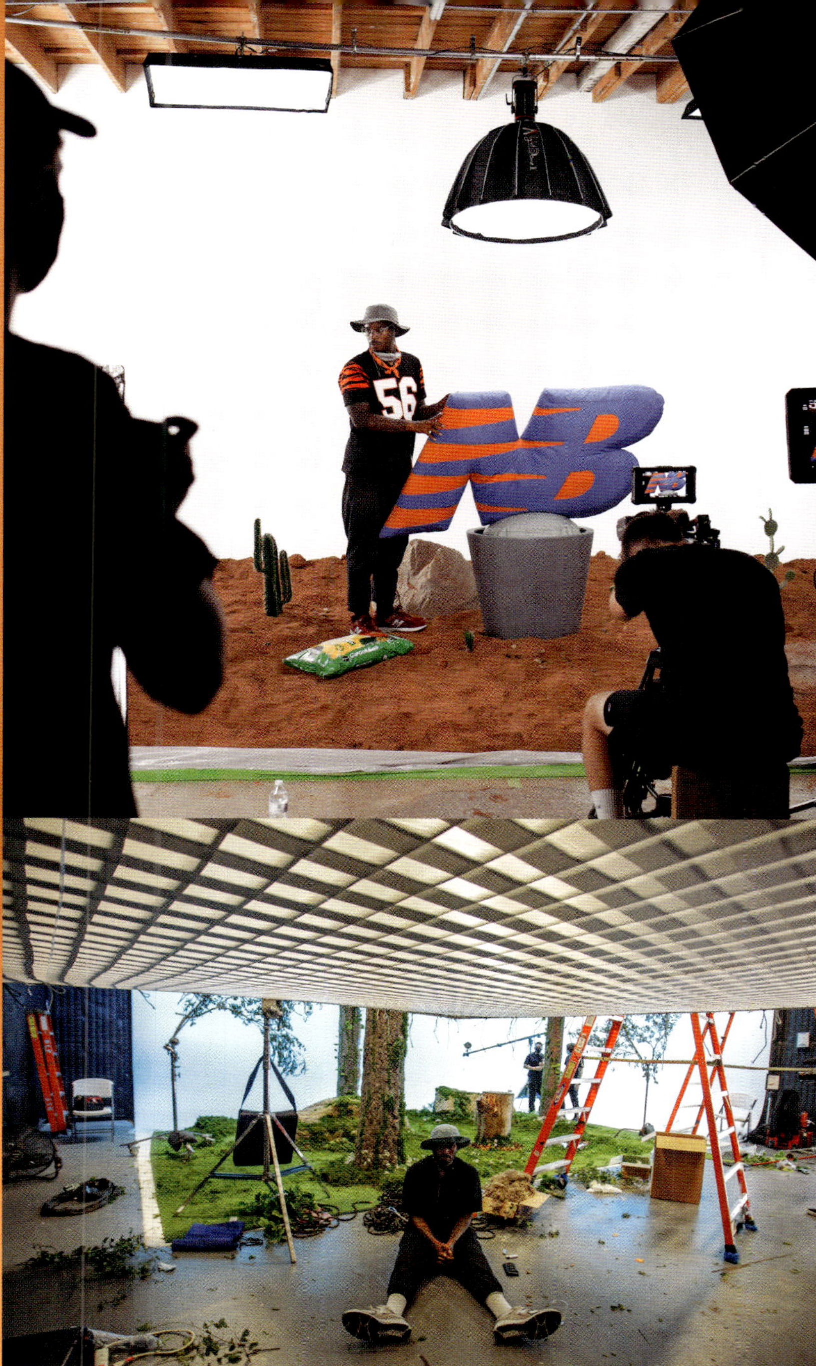

Above: New Balance 2002r Salehe Bembury "Peace Be The Journey" campaign featuring Jesse Williams

Below: New Balance 2002r Salehe Bembury "Water Be The Guide" campaign set

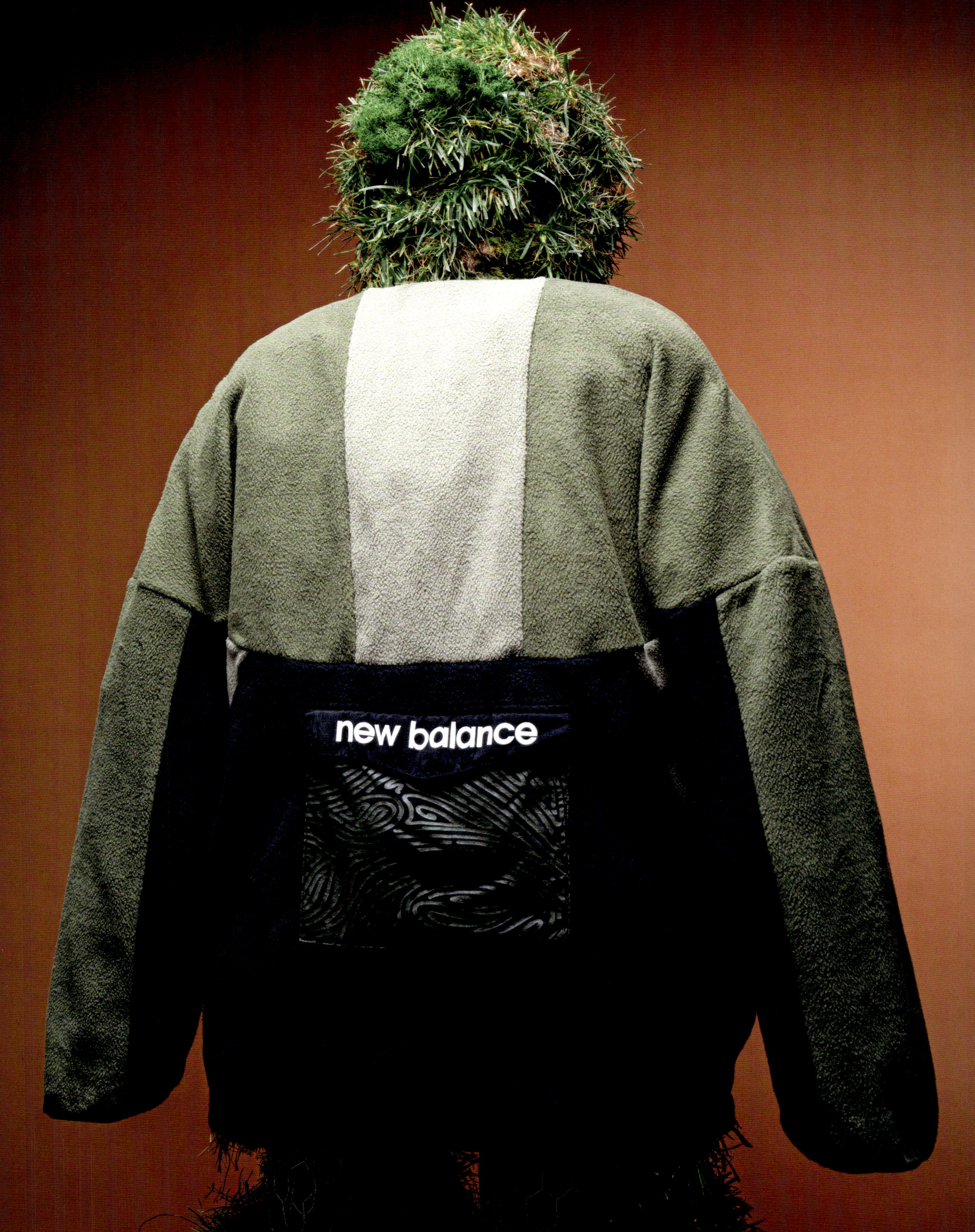
new balance

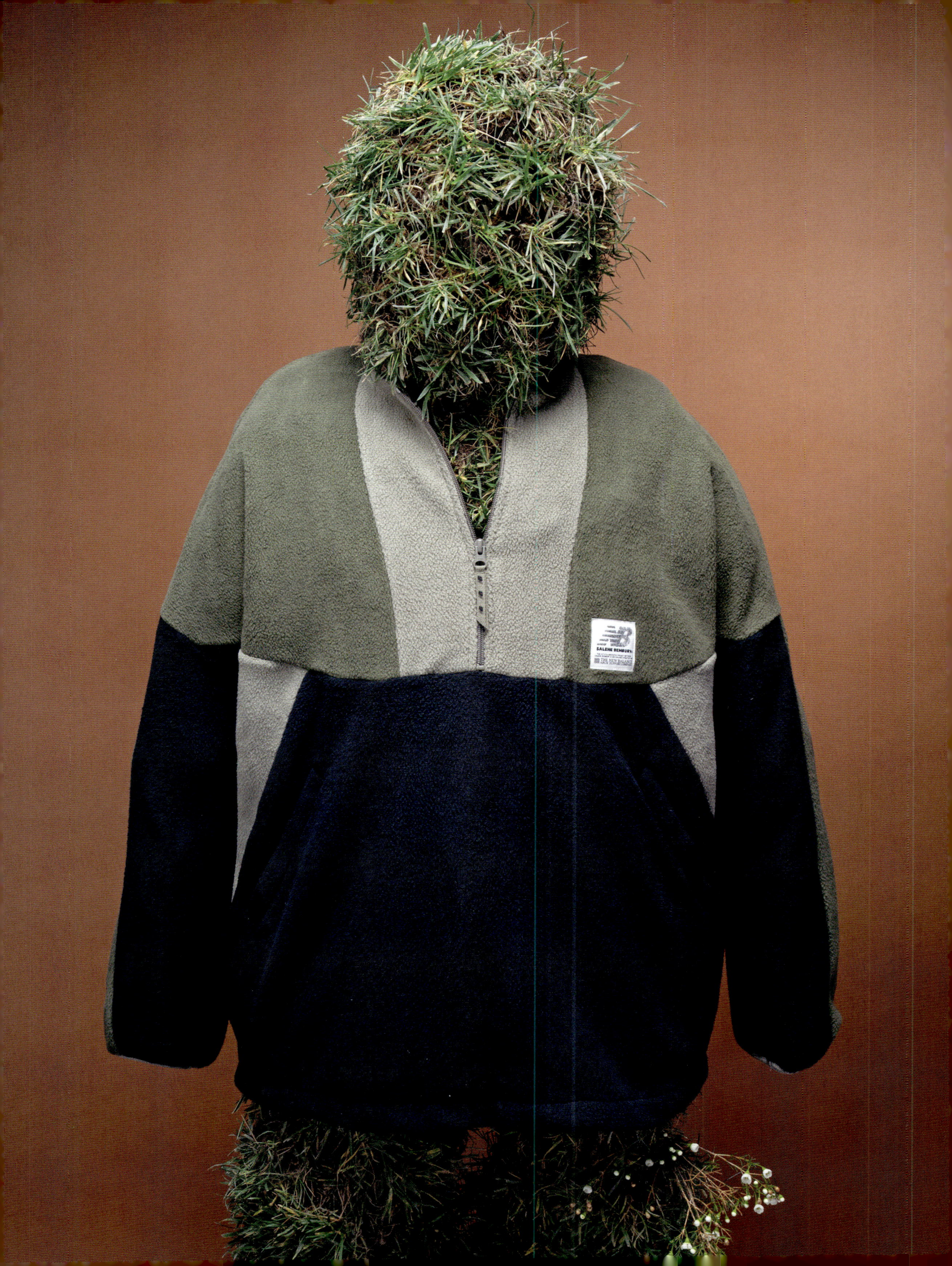
SALEHE BEMBURY

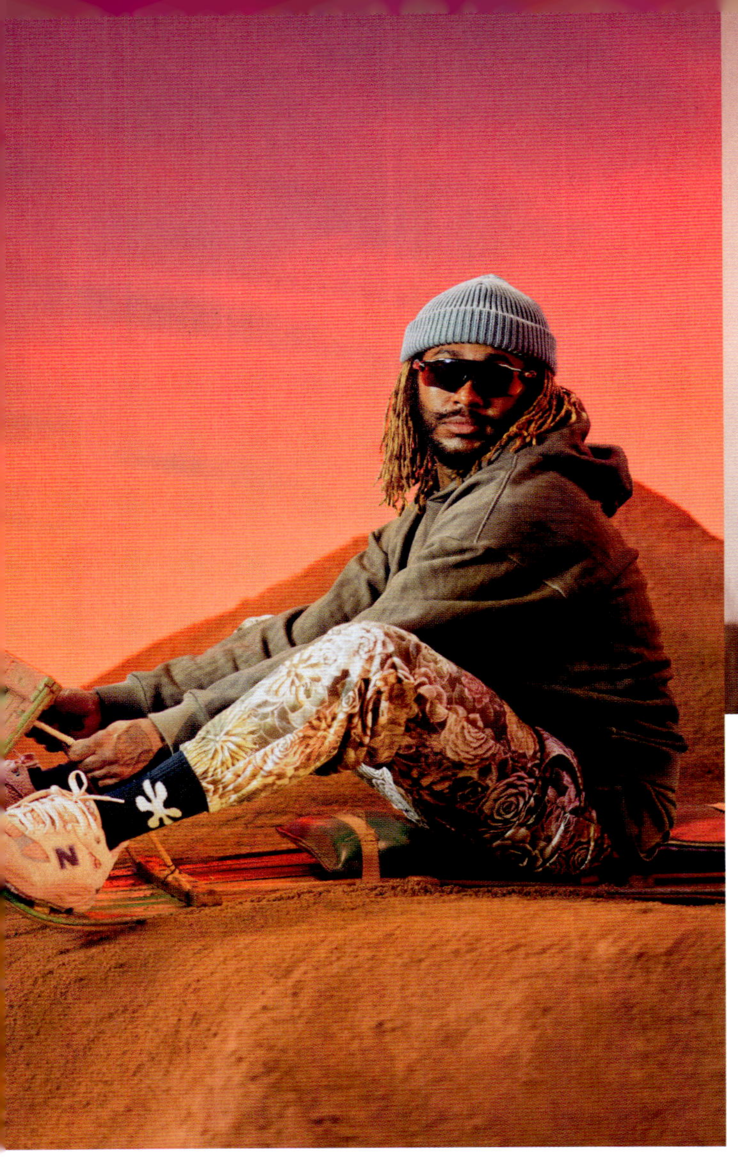

New Balance 990v2 Salehe Bembury "Sand Be The Time" Campaign featuring Thundercat

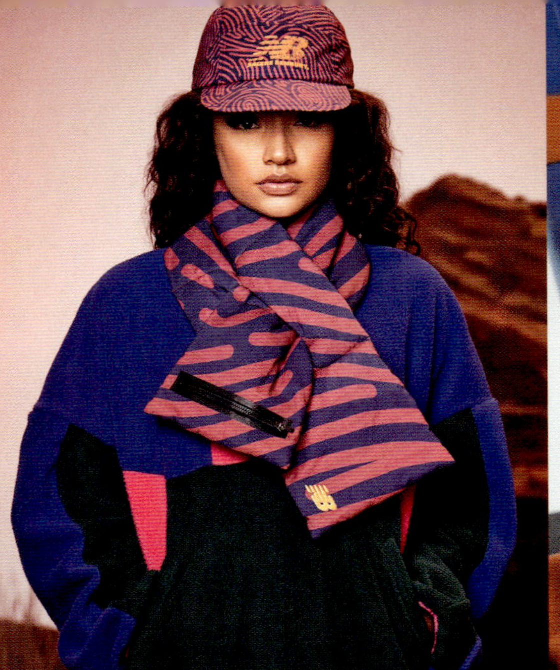

New Balance 574 Yurt Salehe Bembury Campaign featuring Kim Johansson

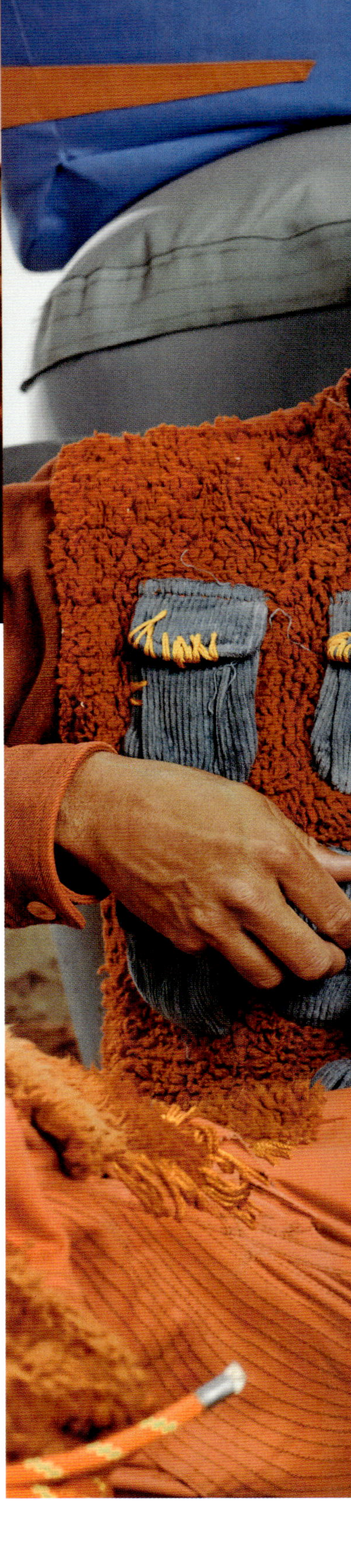

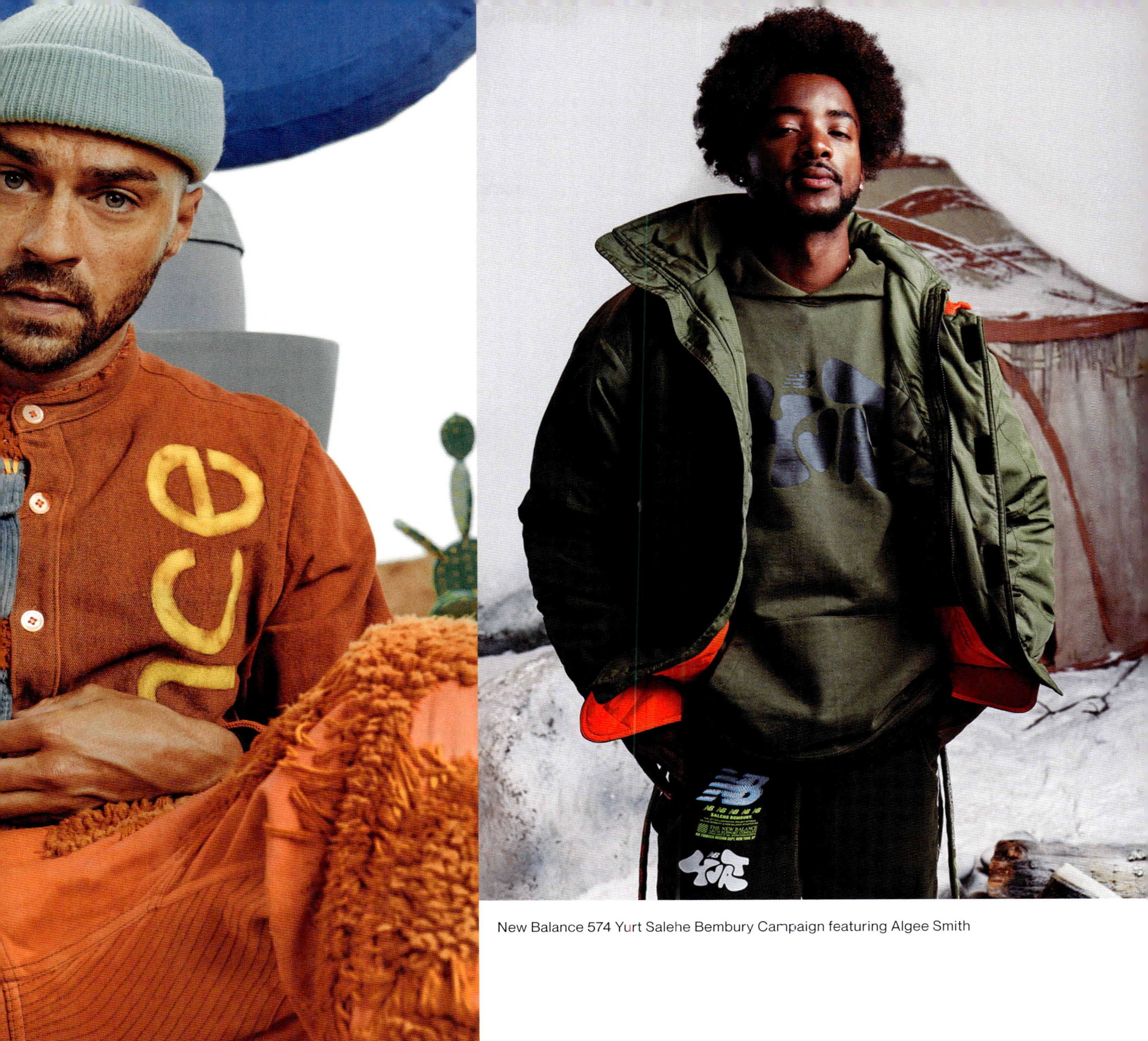

New Balance 574 Yurt Salehe Bembury Campaign featuring Algee Smith

New Balance 2002r Salehe Bembury "Peace Be The Journey" Campaign featuring Jesse Williams

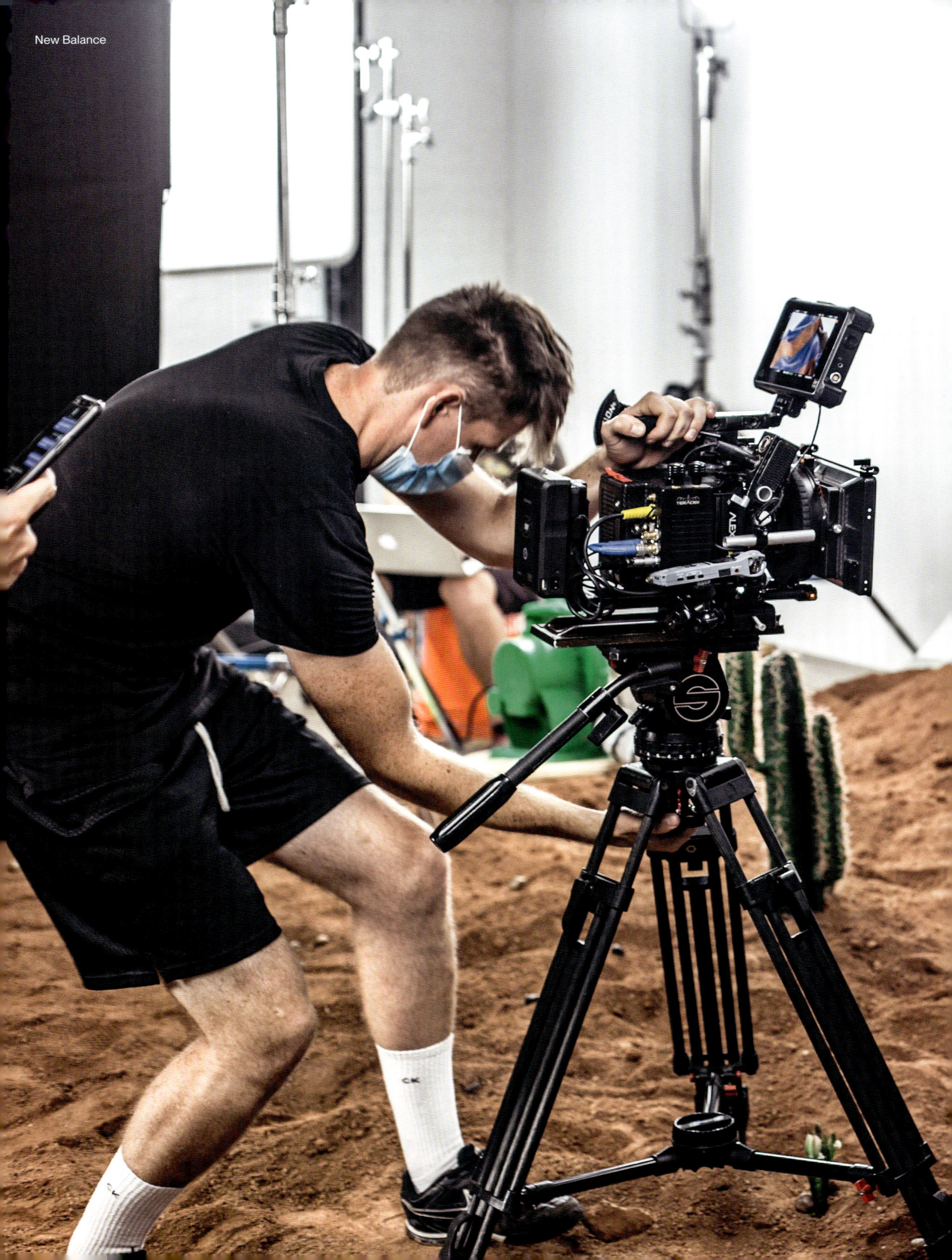

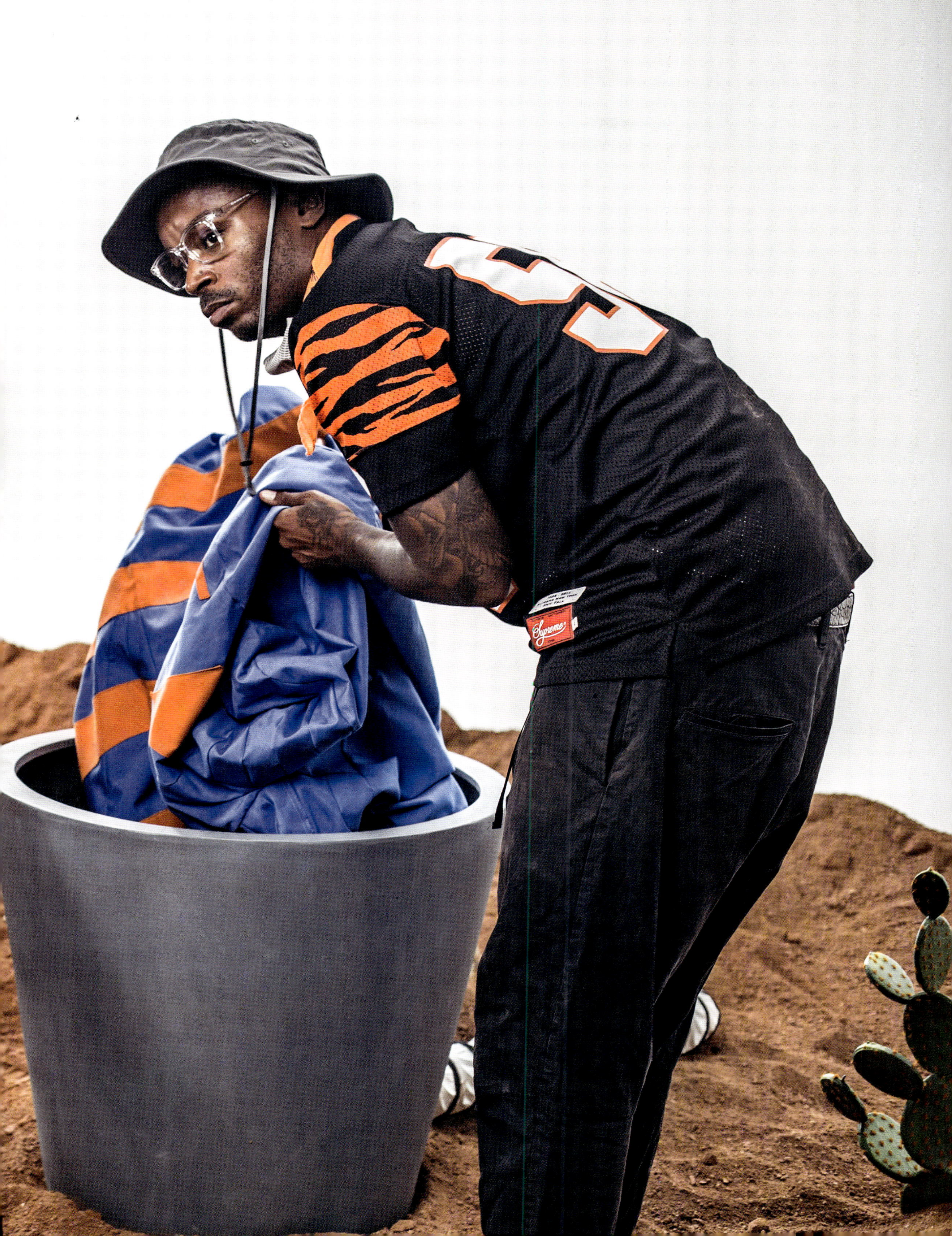

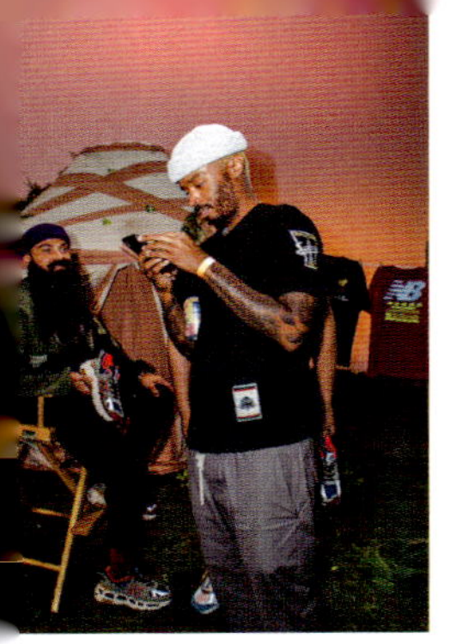

Salehe Bembury and Jesse Williams

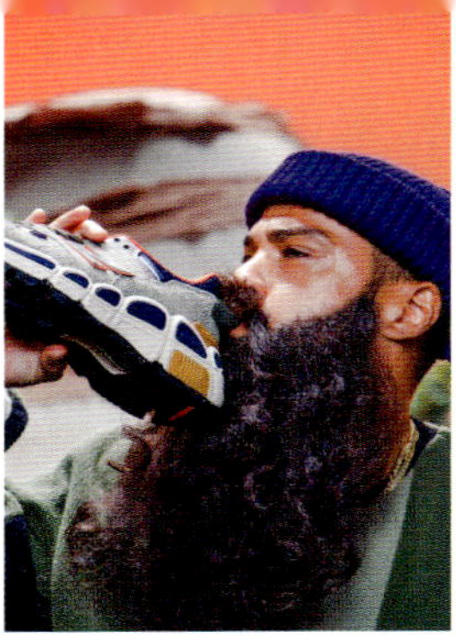

Jesse Williams blowing Yurt whistle

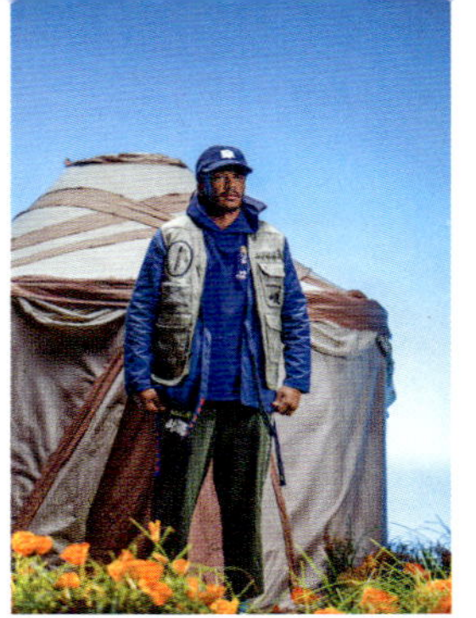

Ron Holden for New Balance Yurt campaign

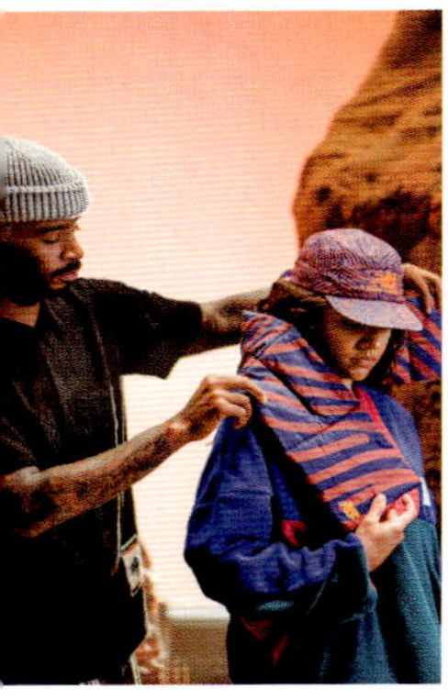

Kim Johansson for New Balance Yurt campaign

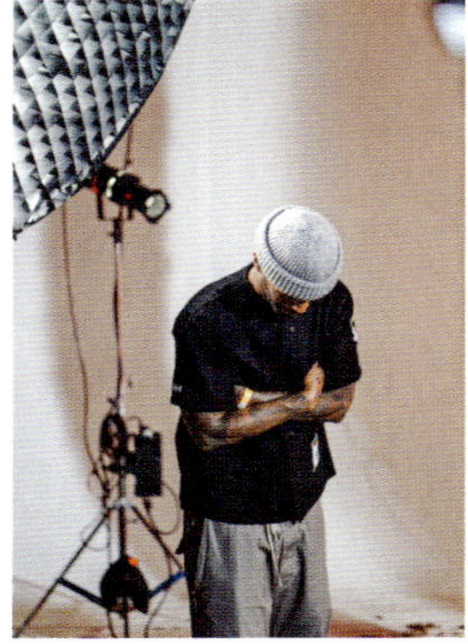

Salehe Bembury on Yurt campaign set

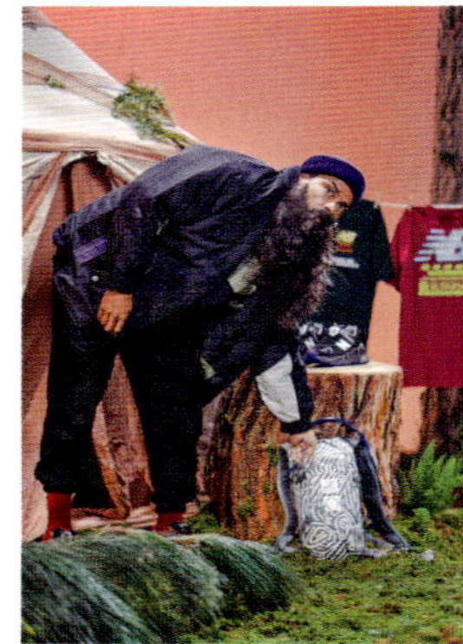

Jesse Williams for New Balance Yurt campaign

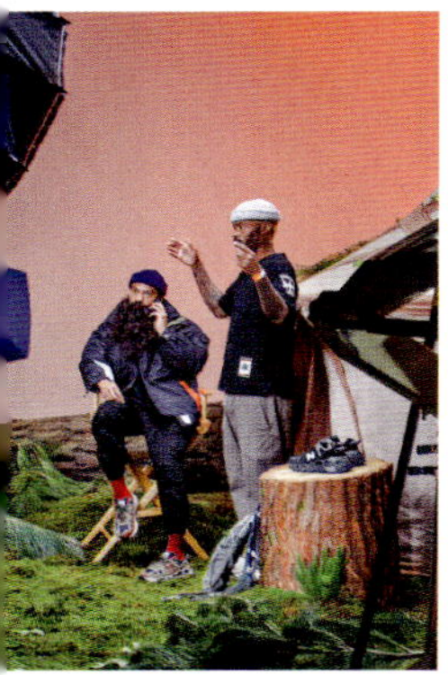

Salehe Bembury and Jesse Williams

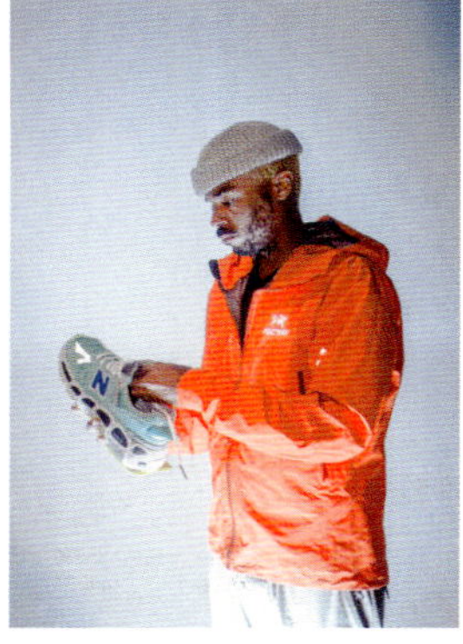

Salehe Bembury on Yurt campaign set

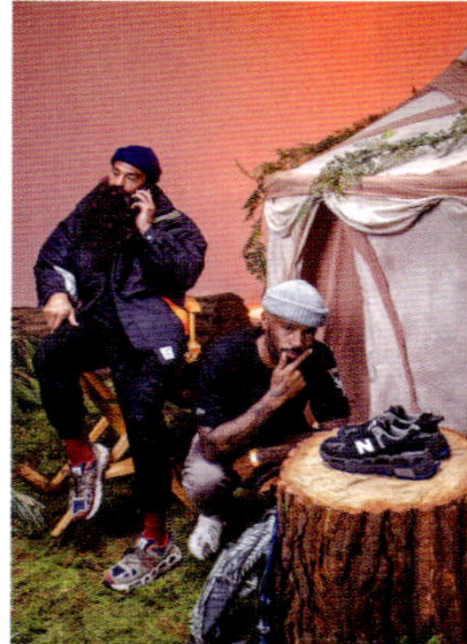

Salehe Bembury and Jesse Williams

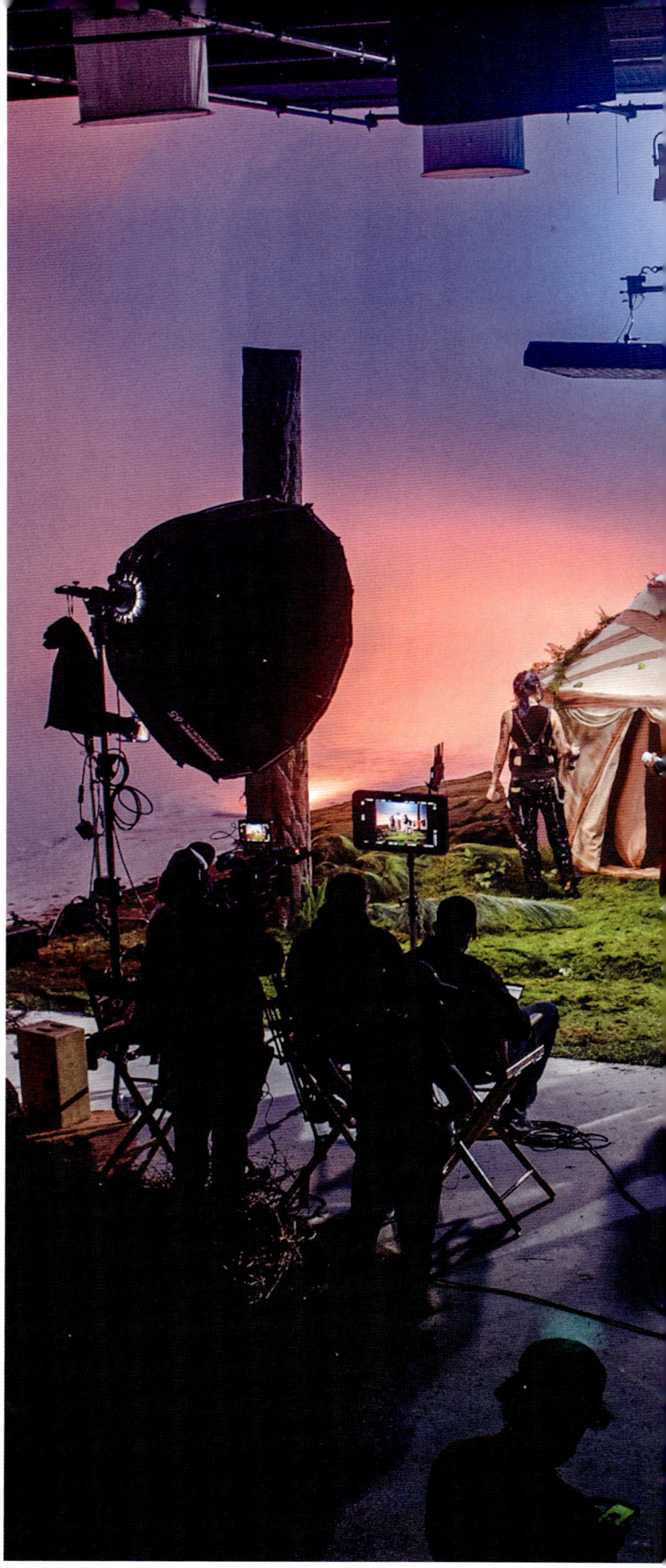

New Balance 574 Yurt Salehe Bembury campaign

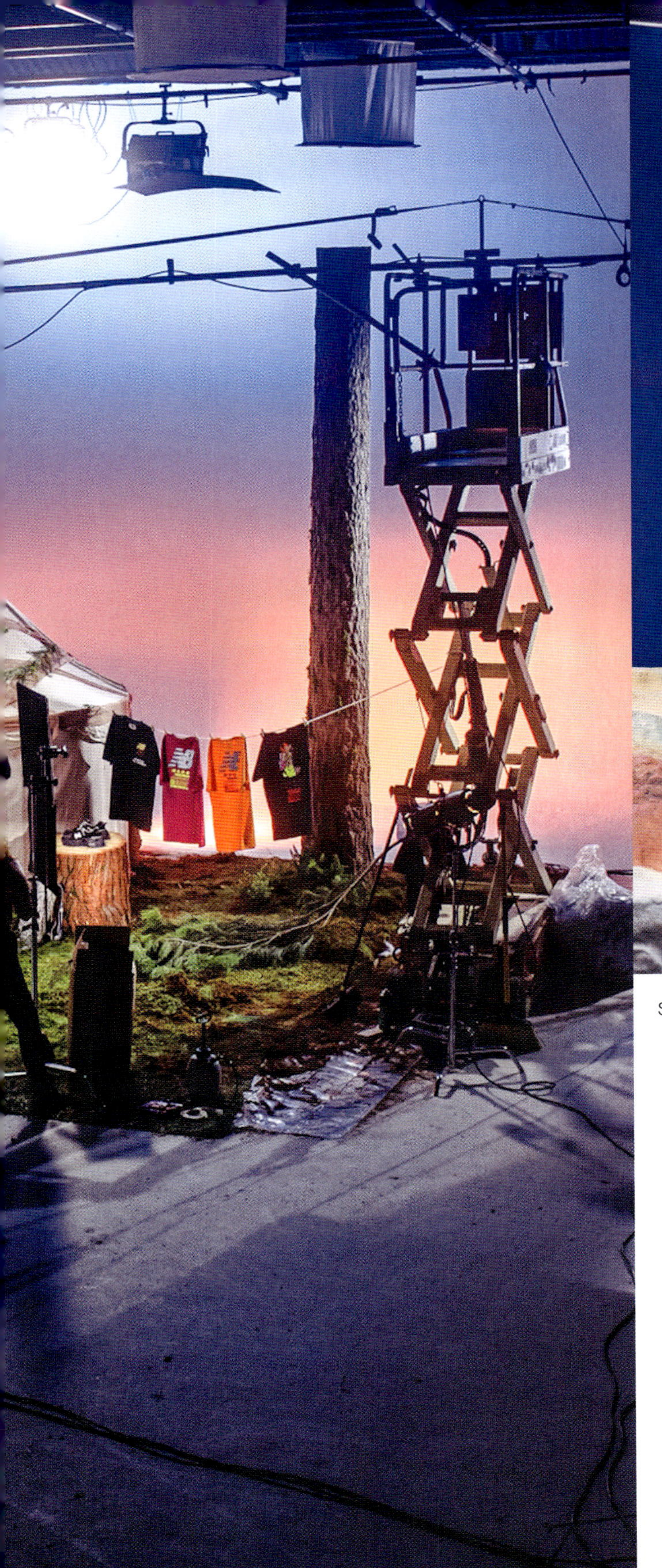

Salehe Bembury and Blake Anderson

197

NEW BALANCE (2020)

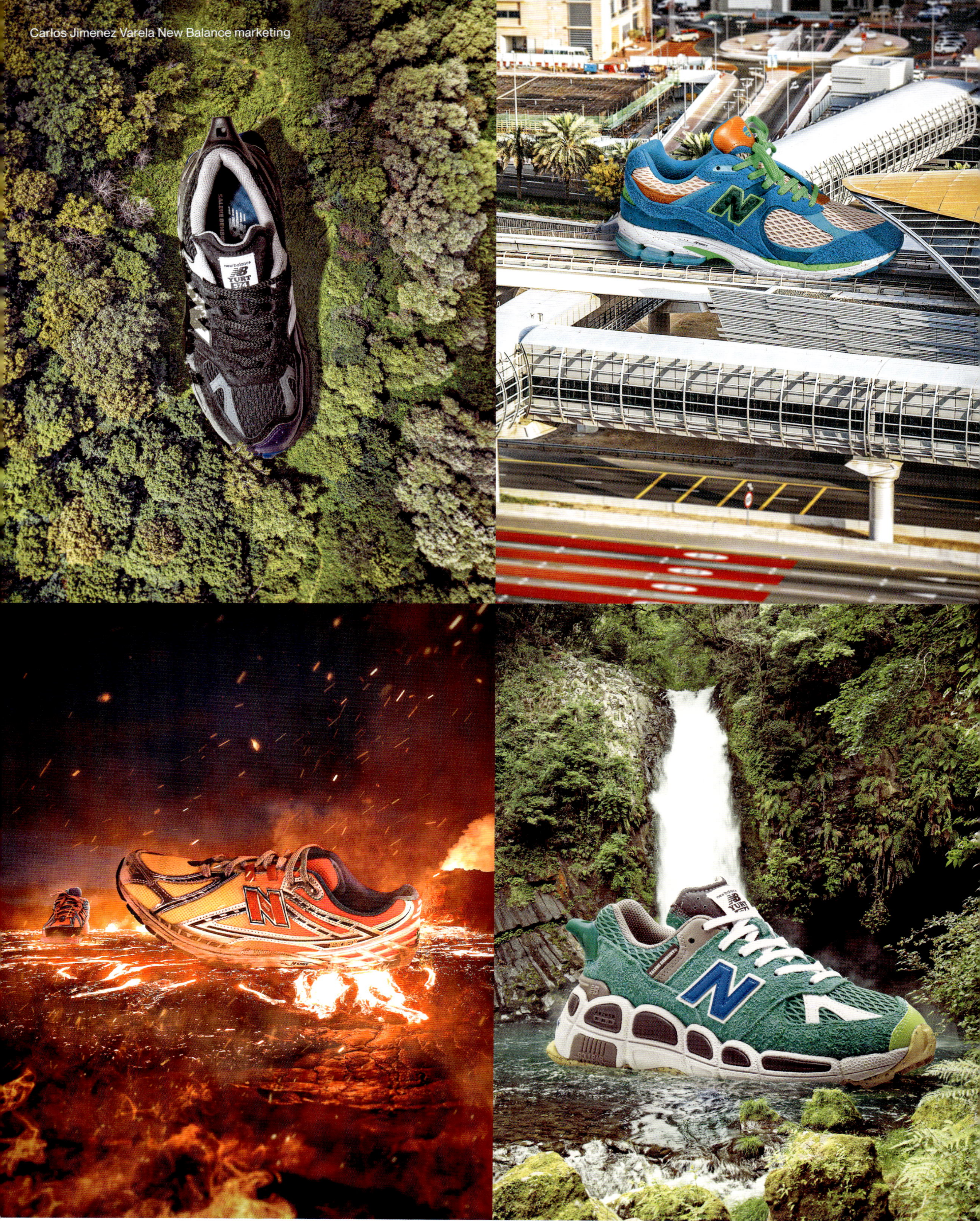
Carlos Jimenez Varela New Balance marketing

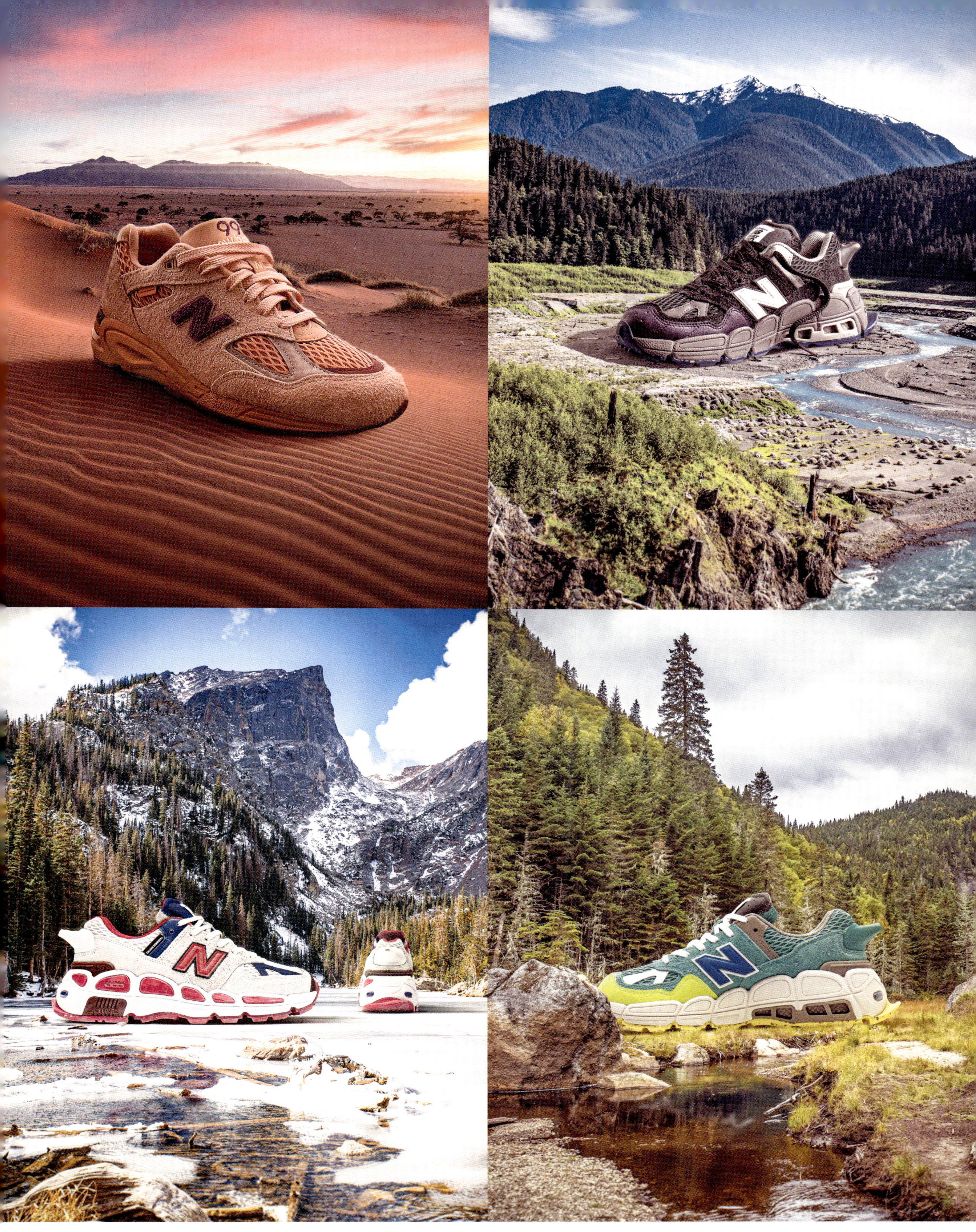

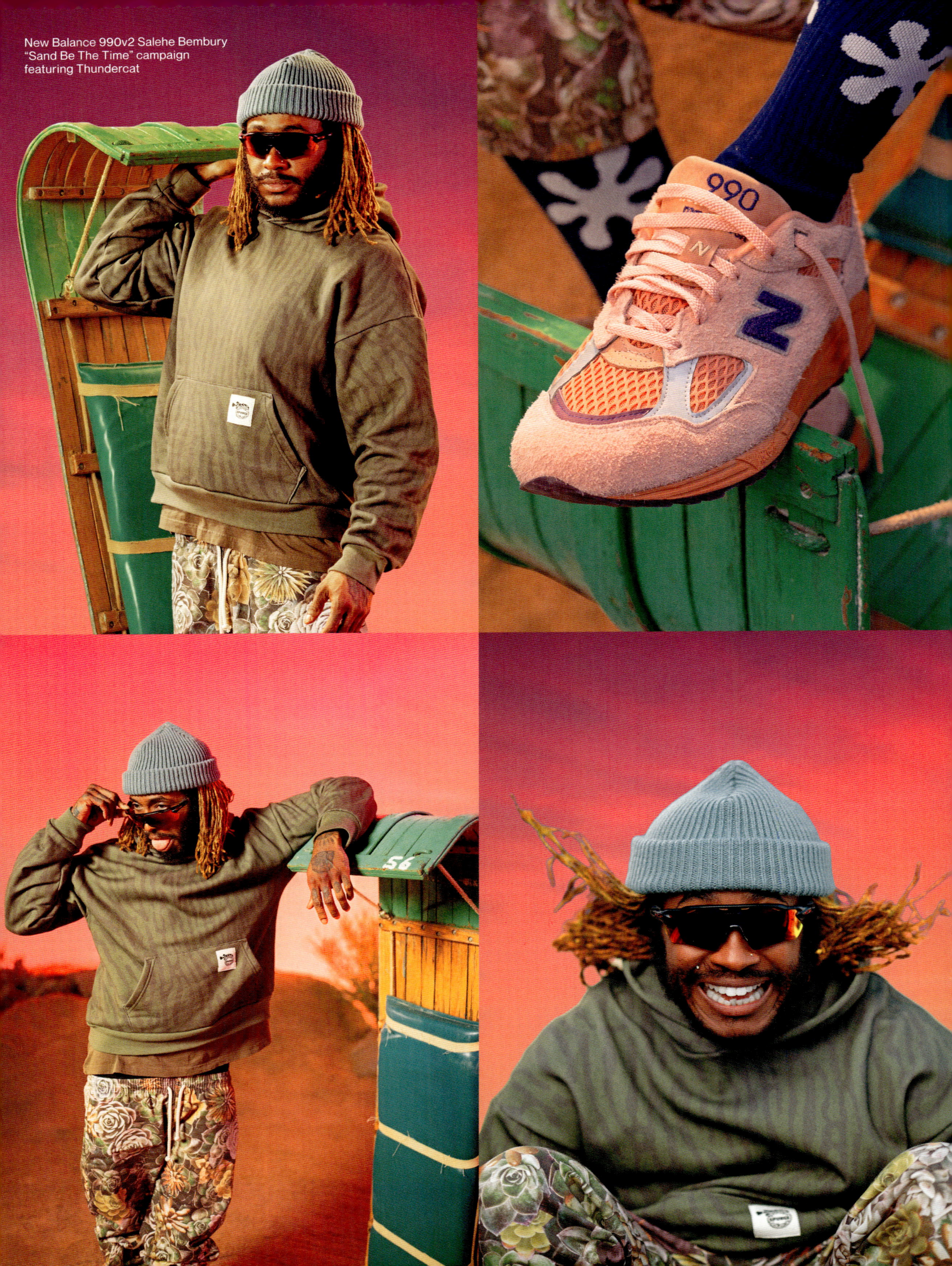

New Balance 990v2 Salehe Bembury
"Sand Be The Time" campaign
featuring Thundercat

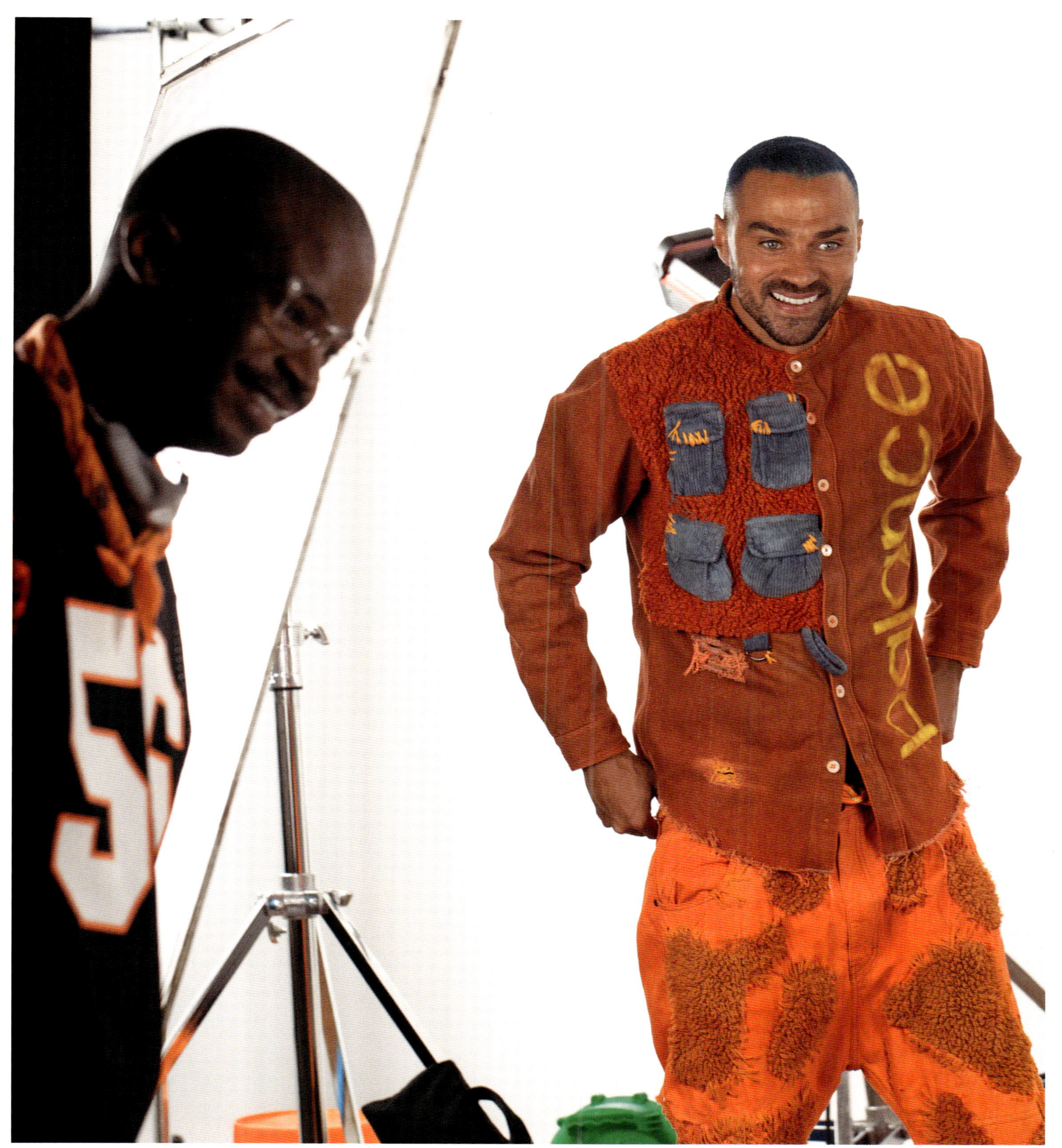
Balance

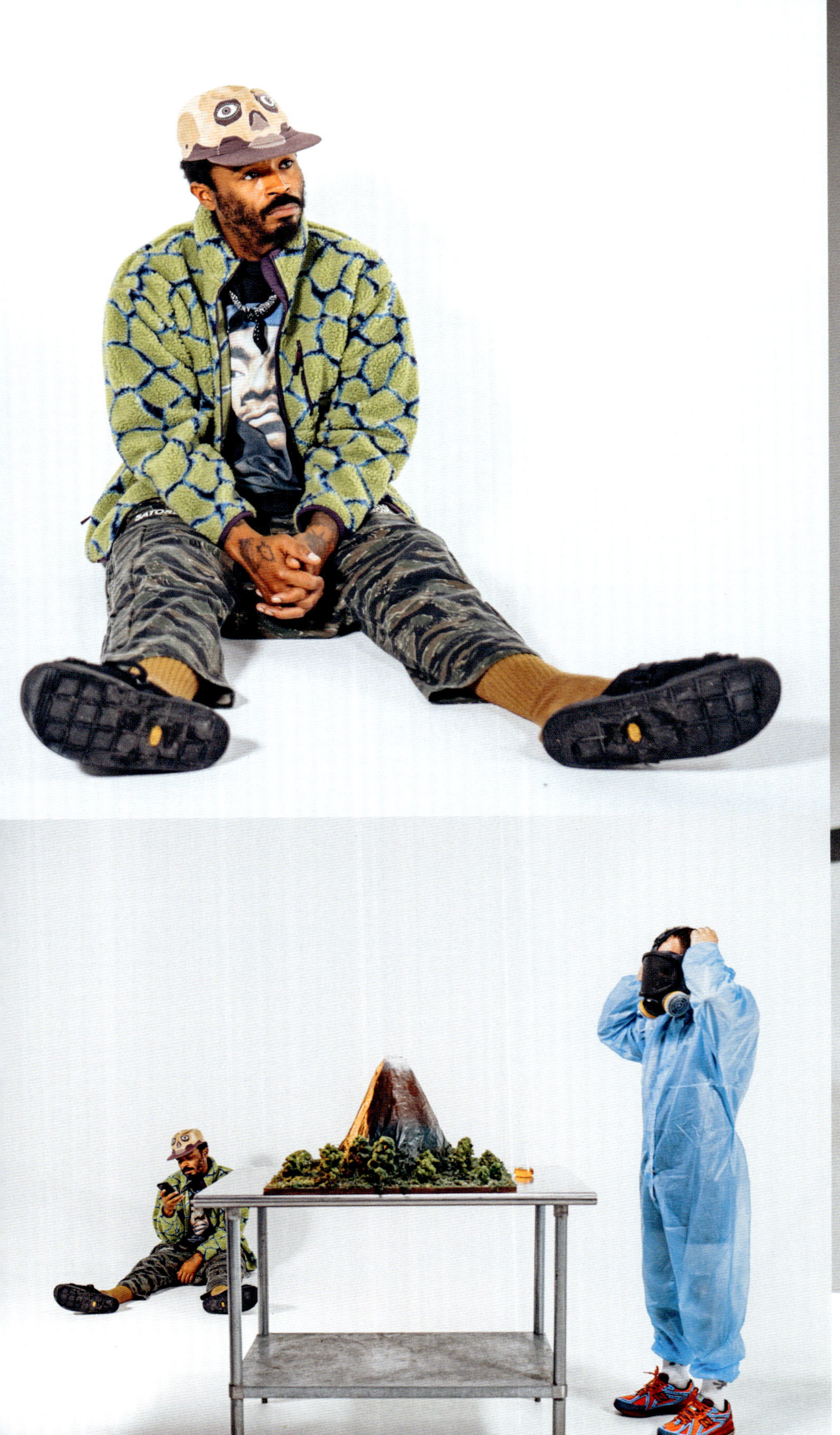

New Balance “Heat Be Hot” campaign set

New Balance “Heat Be Hot” campaign set

202

(2020)

NEW BALANCE

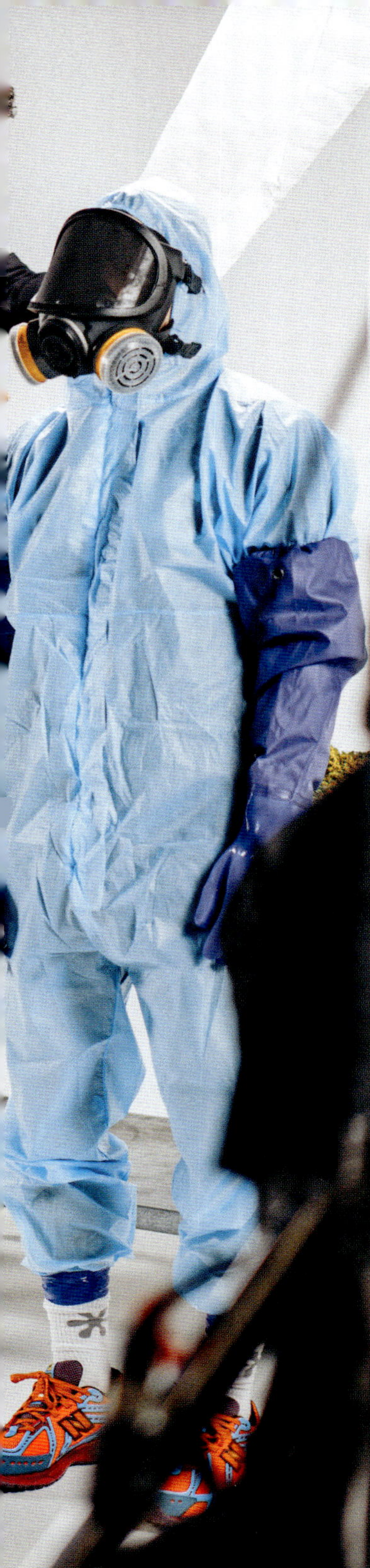

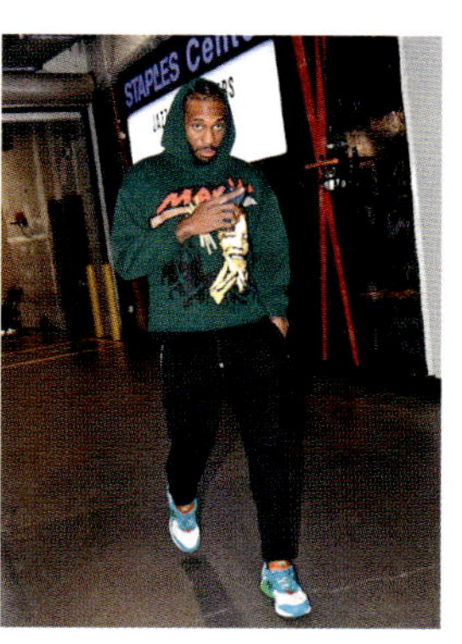

Kawhi Leonard wearing New Balance 2002r Salehe Bembury "Water Be The Guide"

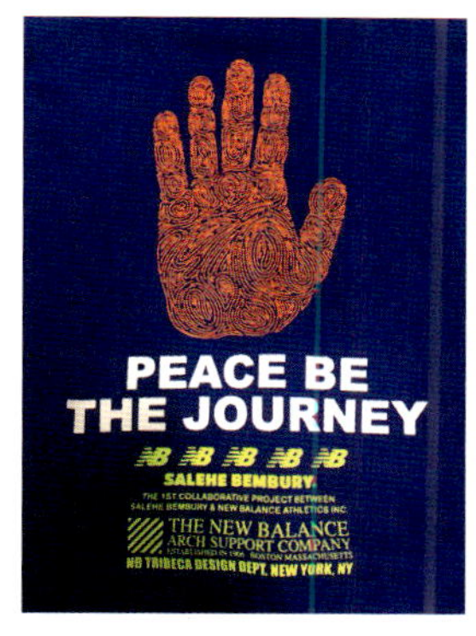

New Balance Yurt Salehe Bembury hoodie

New Balance Yurt Salehe Bembury development

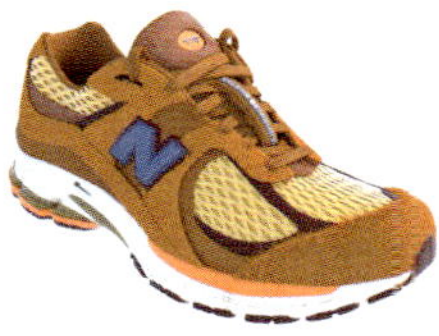

New Balance 2002r Salehe Bembury "Peace Be The Journey" 3D render

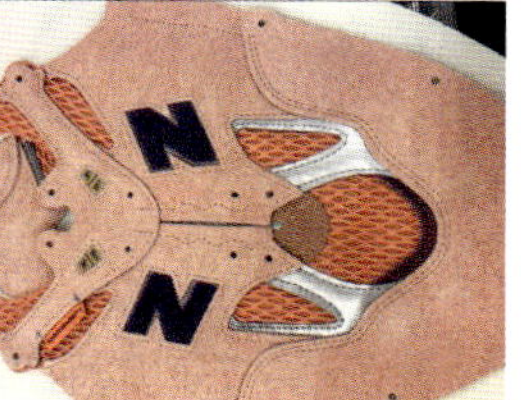

New Balance 990v2 Salehe Bembury "Sand Be The Time" development sample

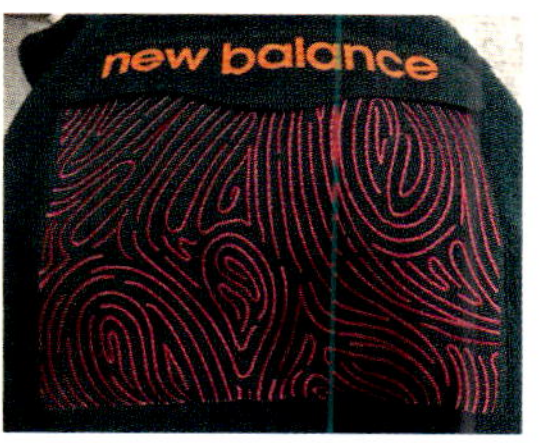

New Balance Yurt Salehe Bembury fleece

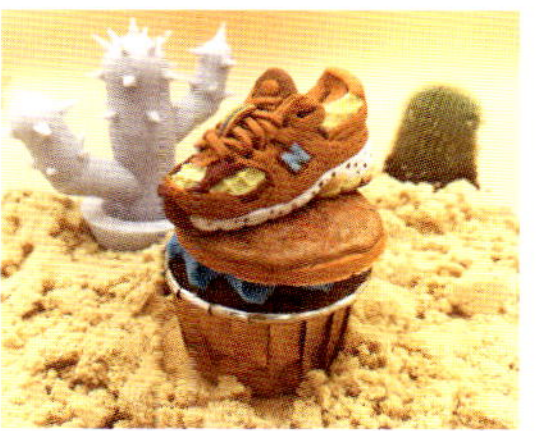

New Balance 2002r Salehe Bembury "Peace Be The Journey" cupcake

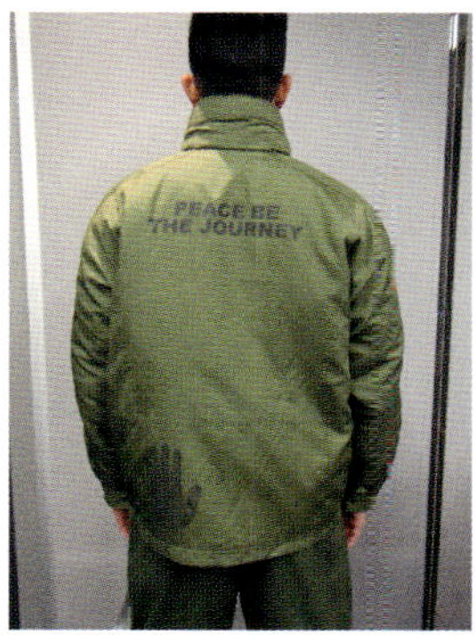

New Balance Yurt Salehe Bembury jacket

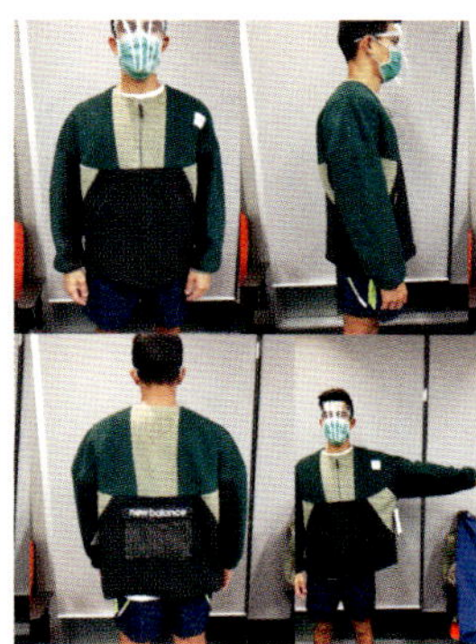

New Balance Yurt Salehe Bembury fleece

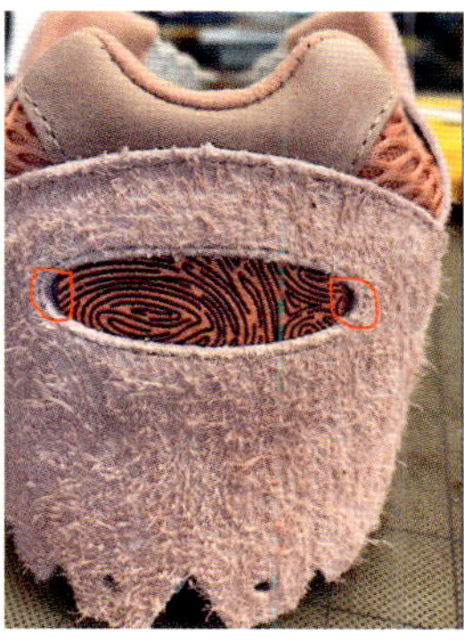

New Balance 990v2 Salehe Bembury "Sand Be The Time" development sample

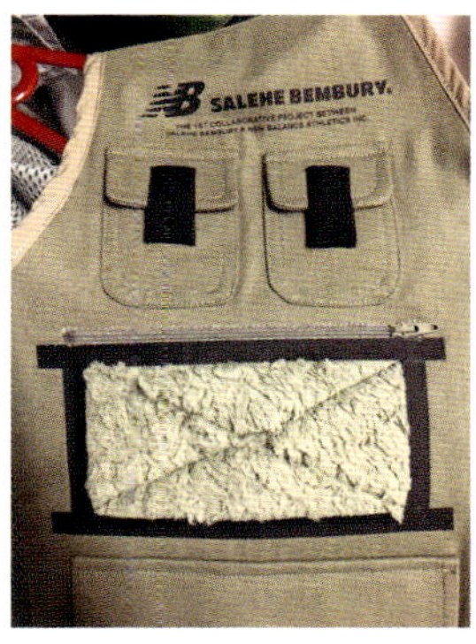

New Balance Yurt Salehe Bembury vest development

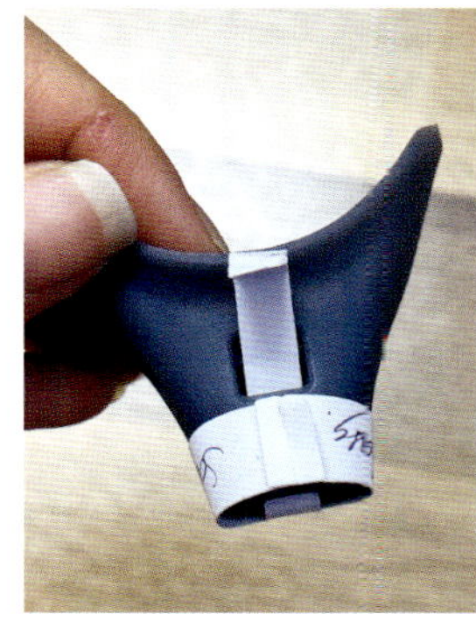

New Balance Yurt Salehe Bembury whistle development

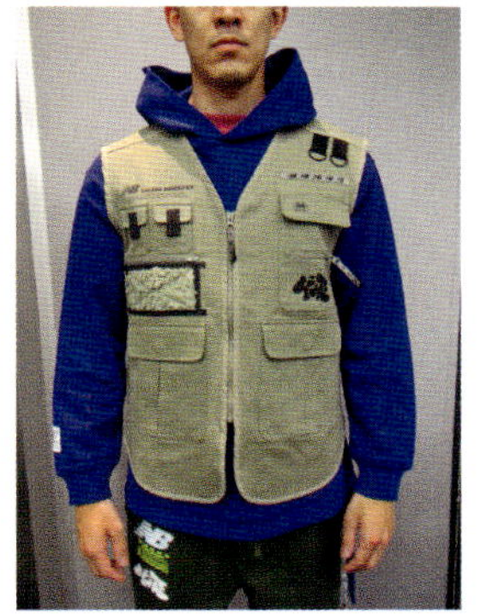

New Balance Yurt Salehe Bembury vest development

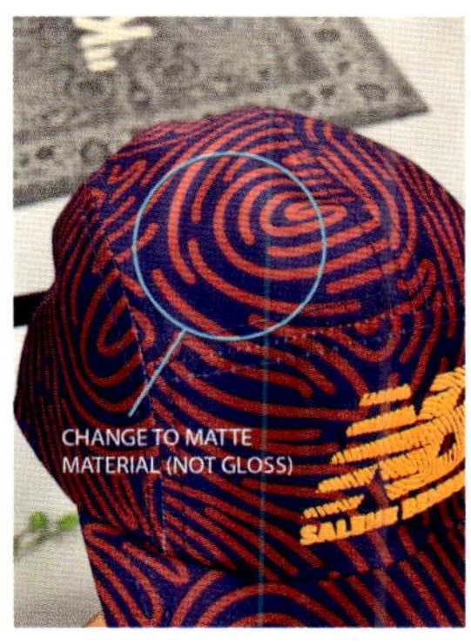

New Balance Yurt Salehe Bembury hat development

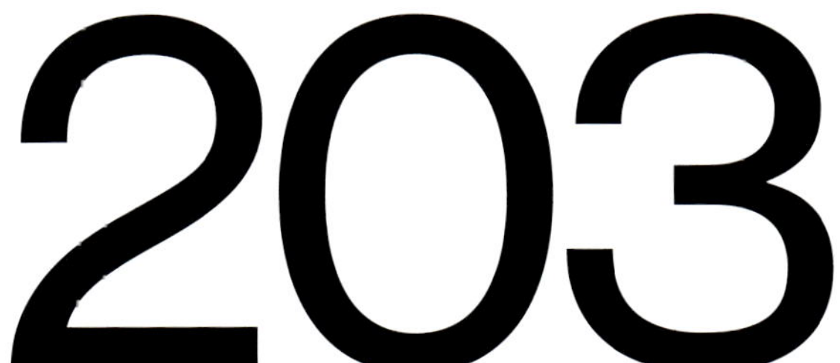

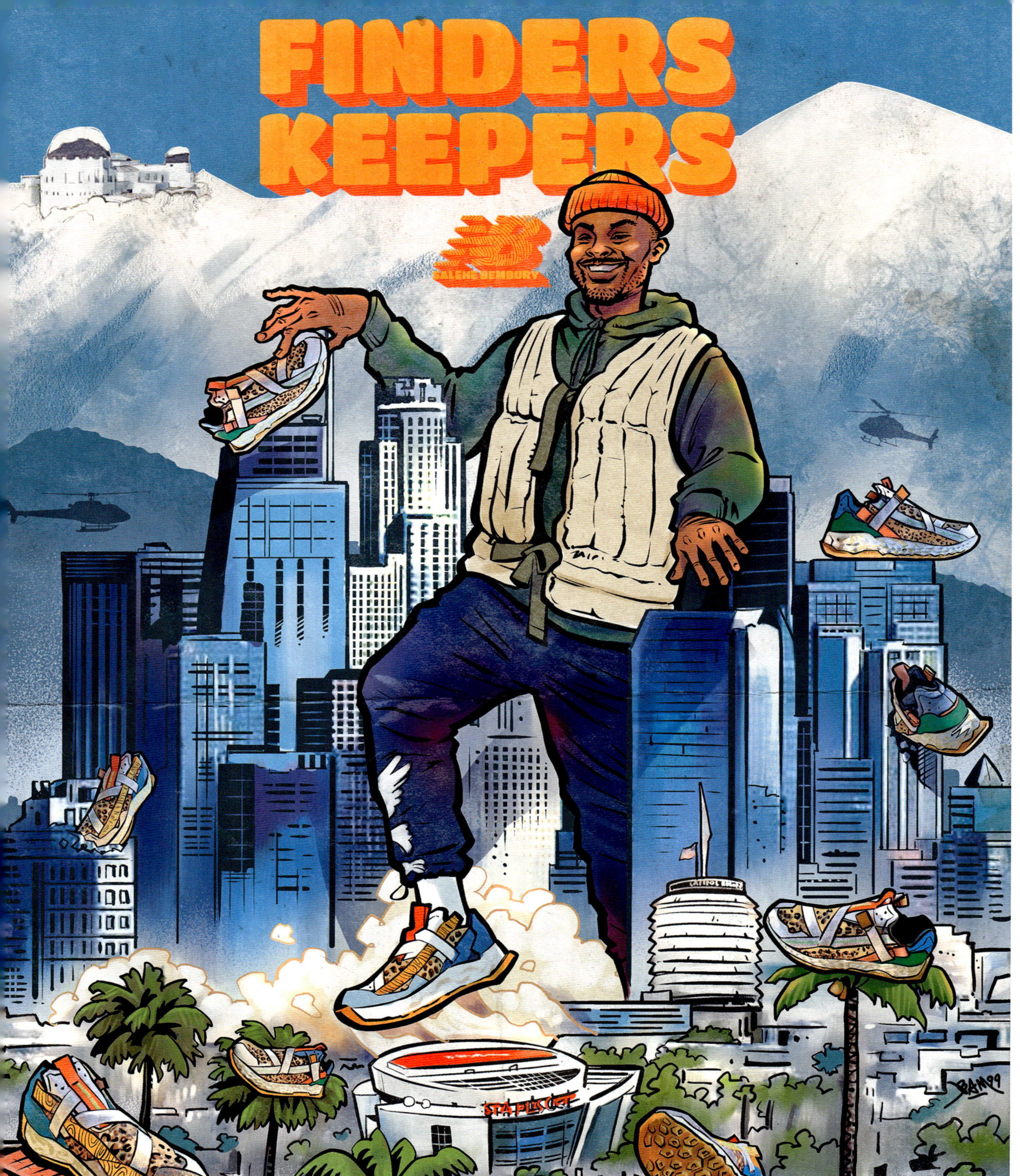

New Balance Finders Keepers ad

204

(2020)

NEW BALANCE

free footwear for folks.

SALEHE BEMBURY

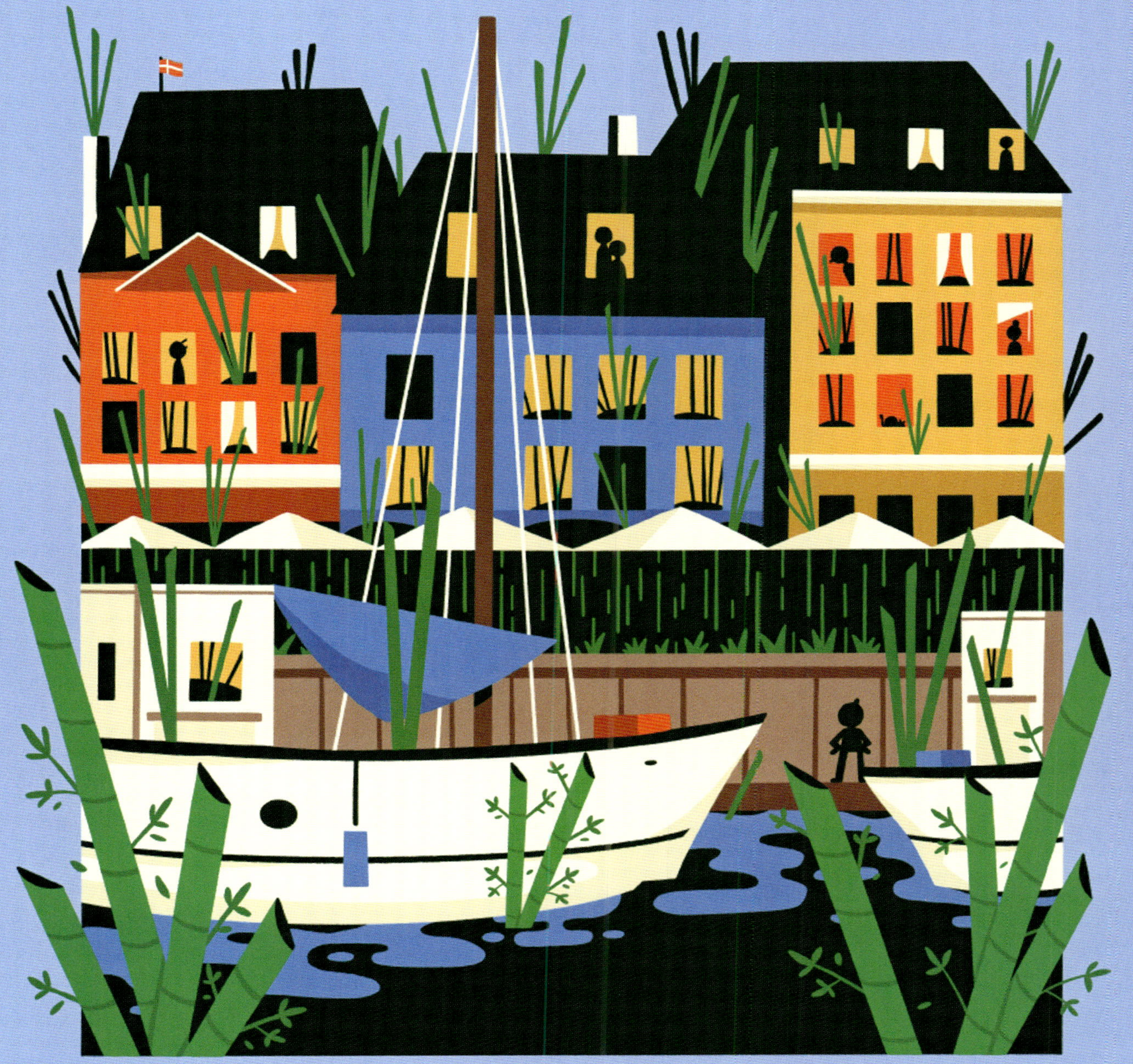

thursday august 8th 12-5pm

etage projects, borgergade 15e
1300 københavn, denmark

New Balance 530 Bamboo Copenhagen Pop-Up ad

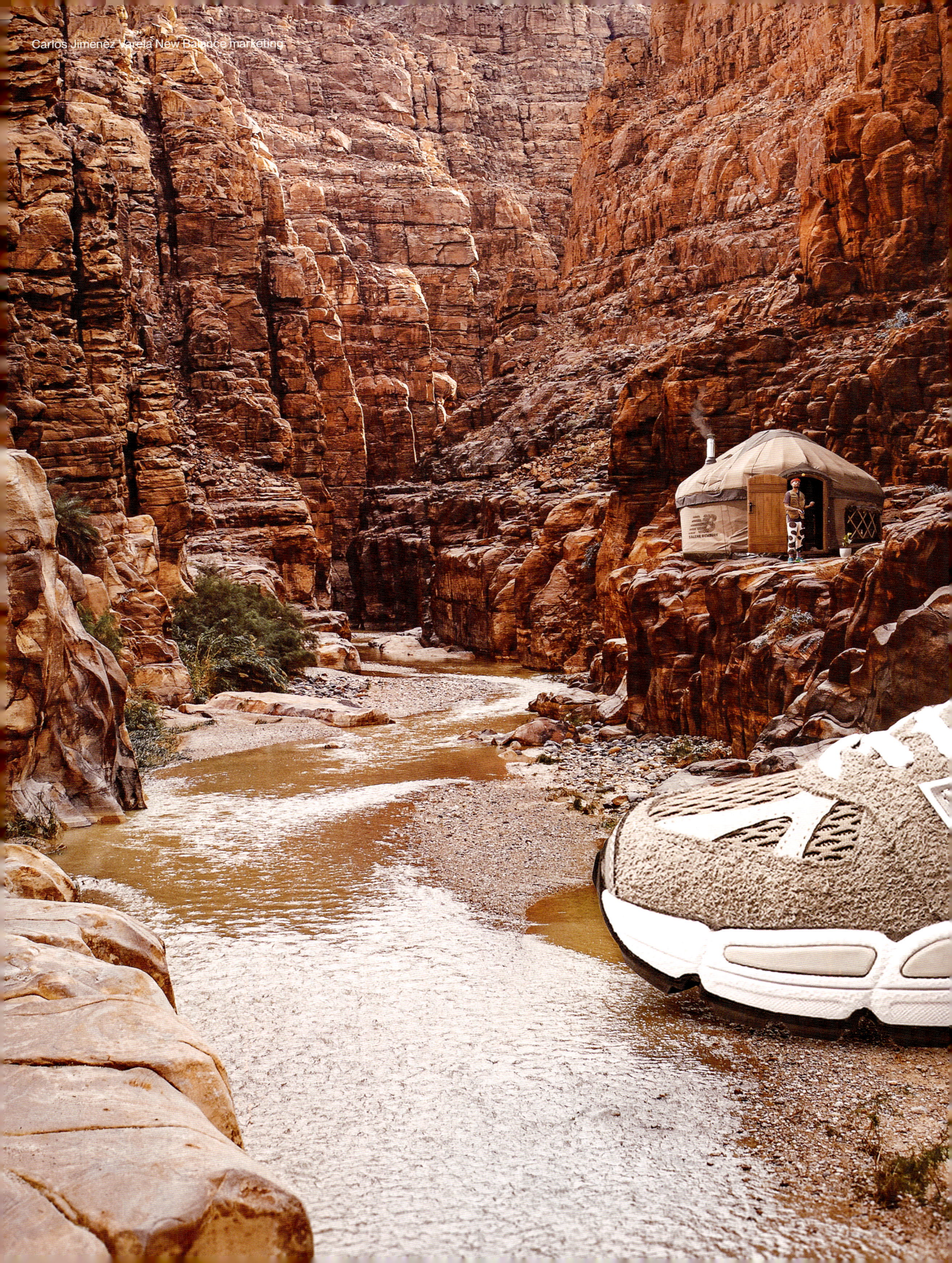

Carlos Jimenez Varela New Balance marketing

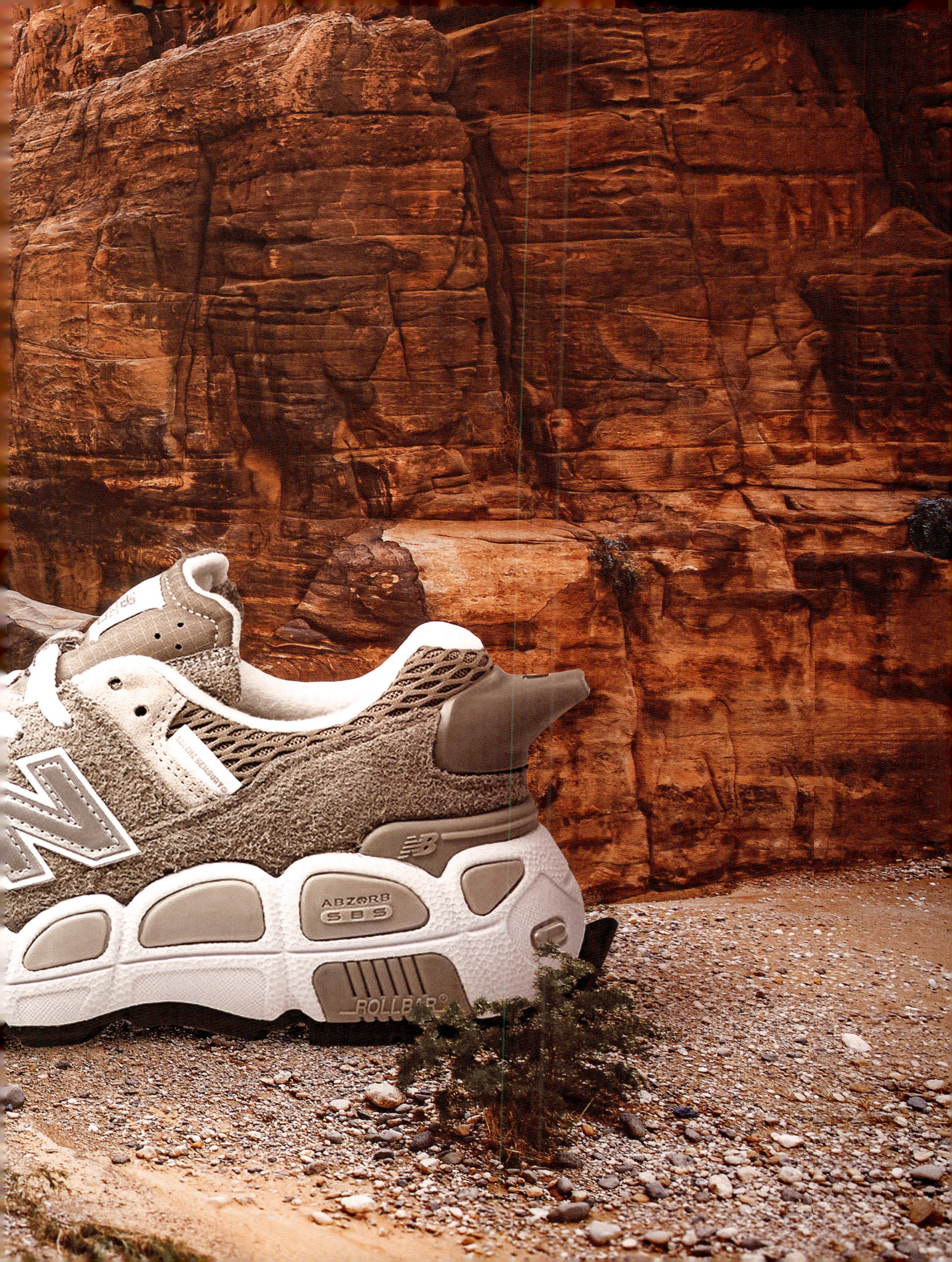
ABZORB
SBS
ROLLBAR

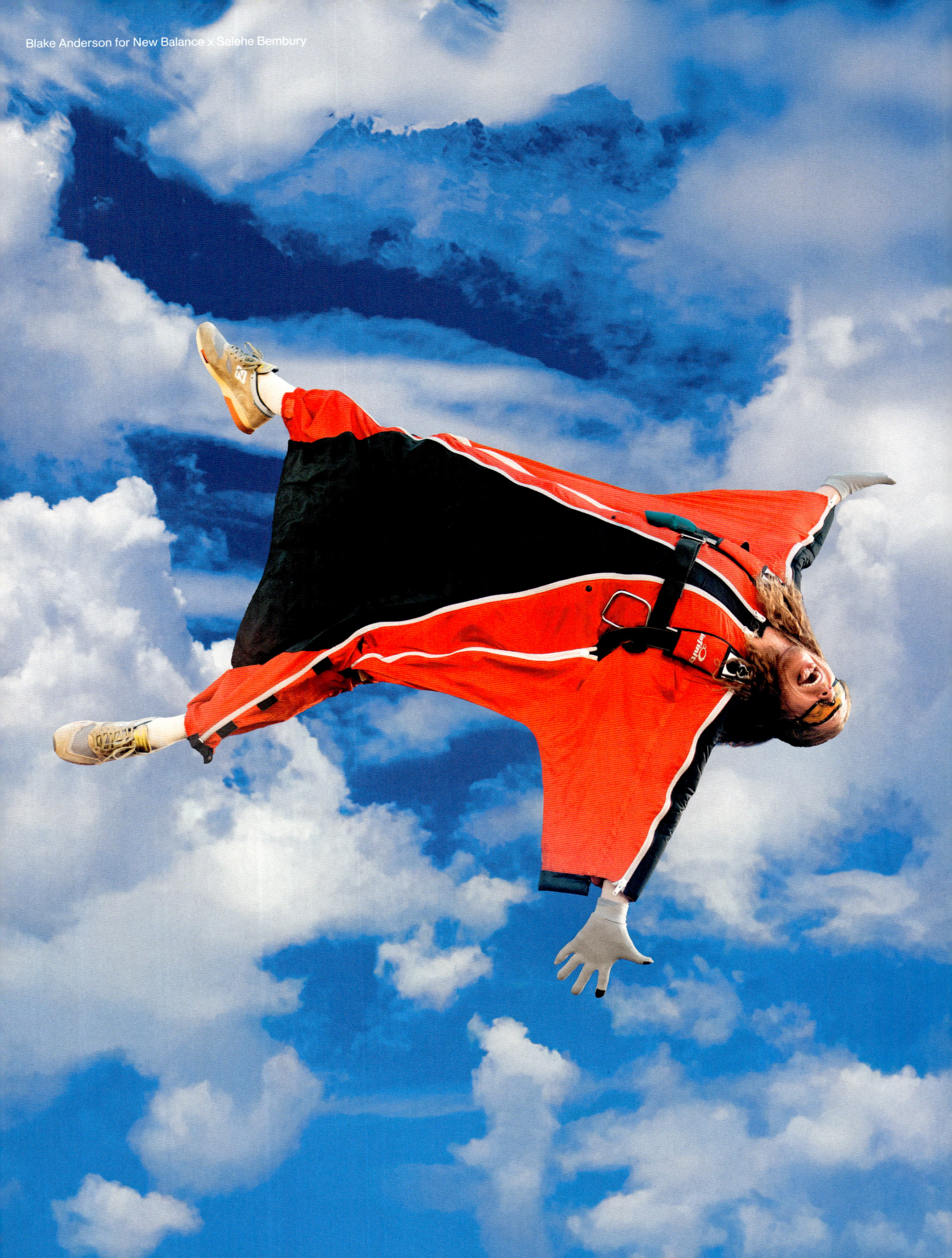
Blake Anderson for New Balance x Salehe Bembury

New Balance Test Run 3.0 "Finders Keepers"

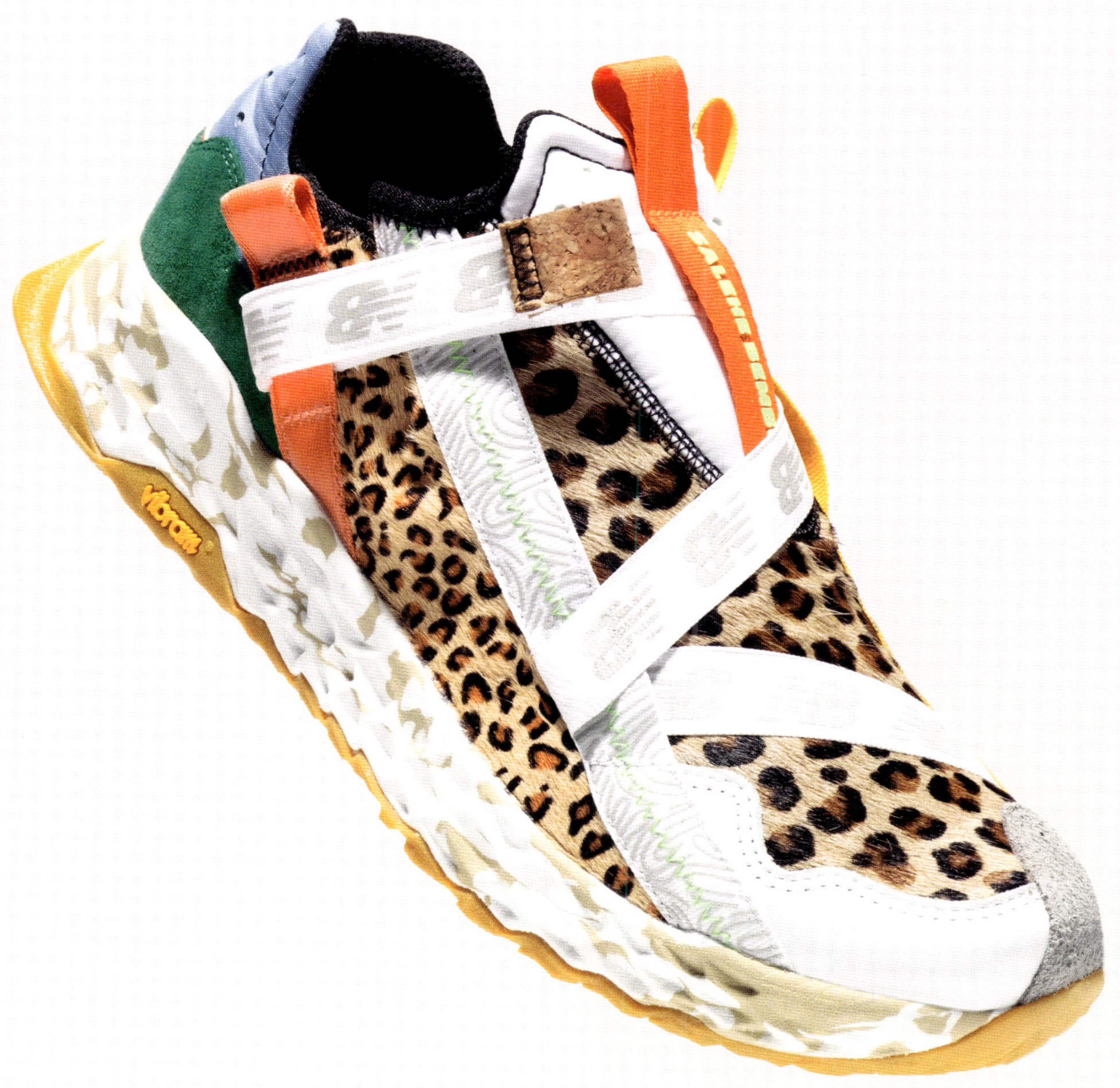

NEW BALANCE

(2020)

209

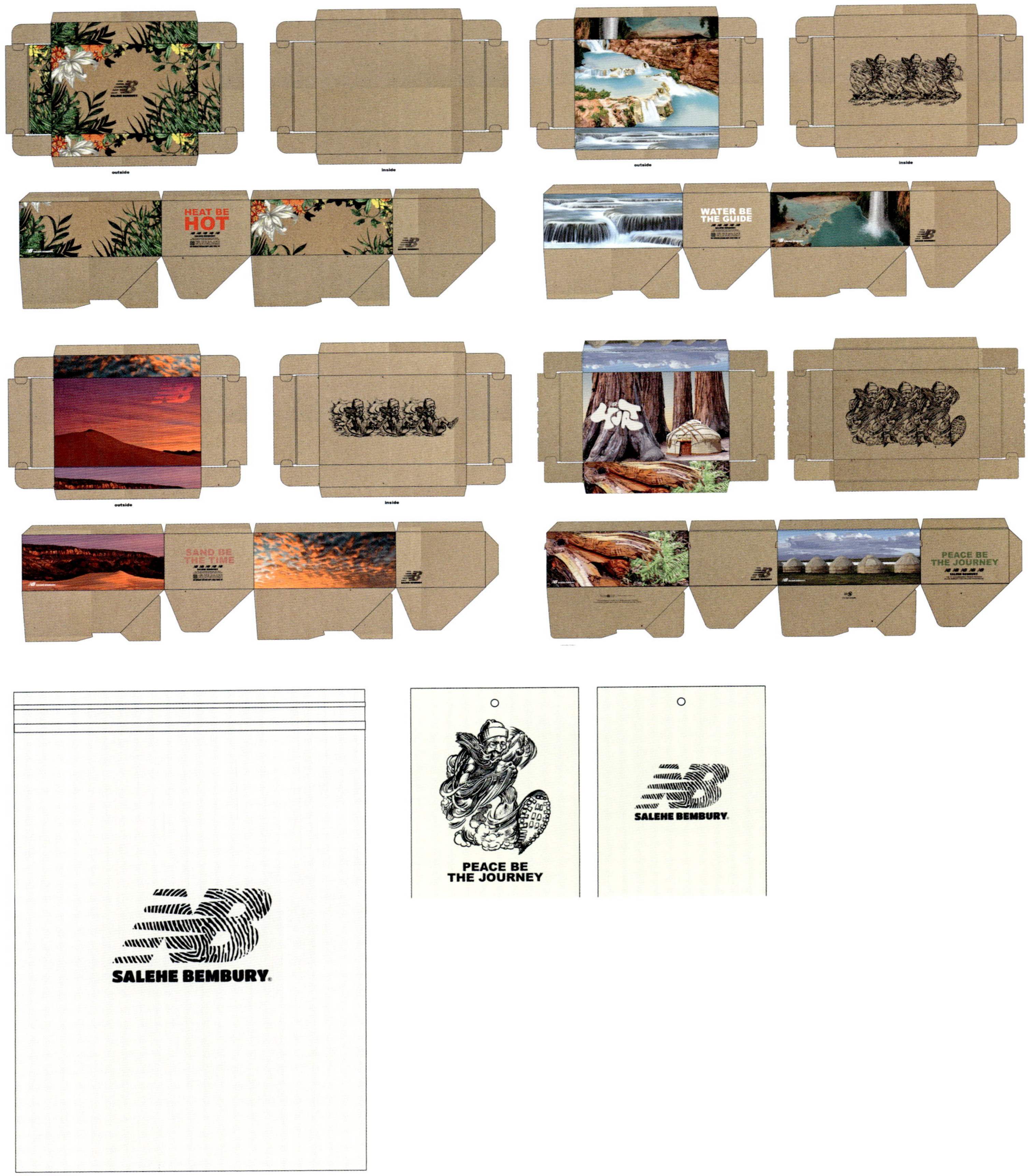

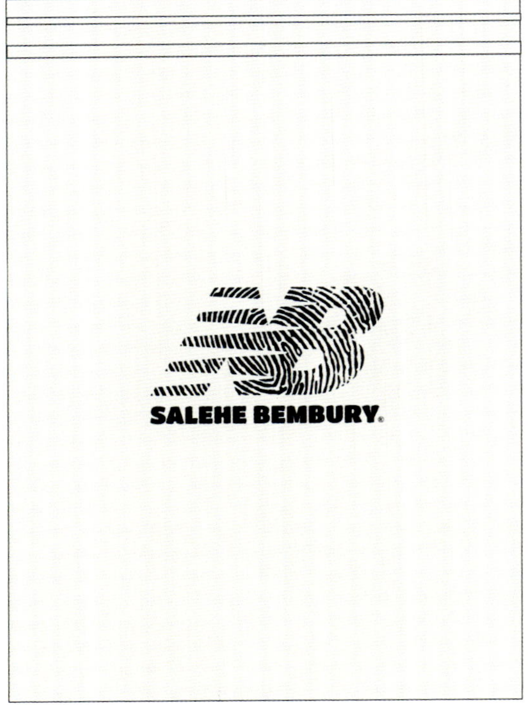

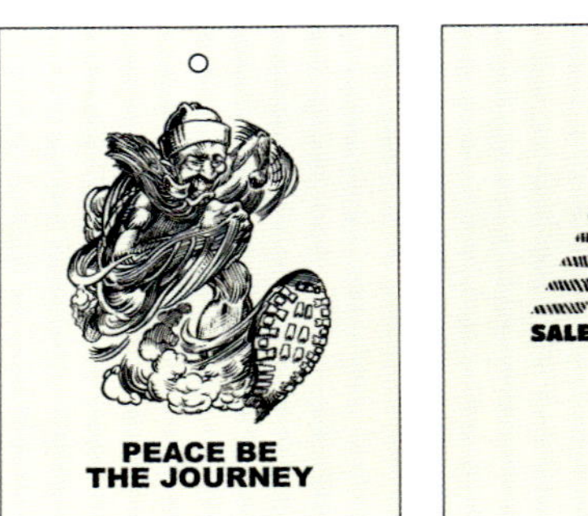

New Balance x Salehe Bembury packaging designs

210

(2020)

NEW BALANCE

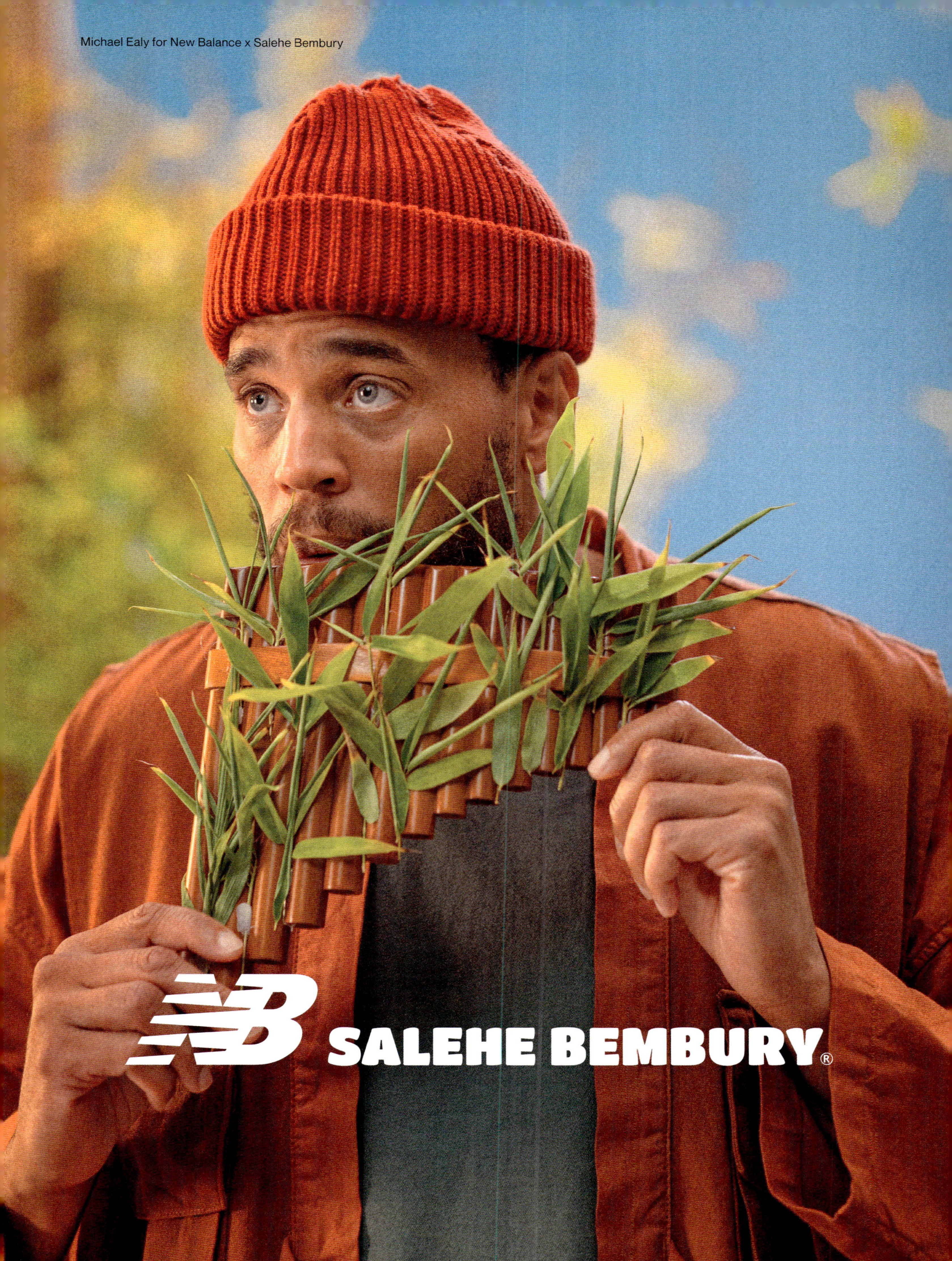
Michael Ealy for New Balance x Salehe Bembury
SALEHE BEMBURY®

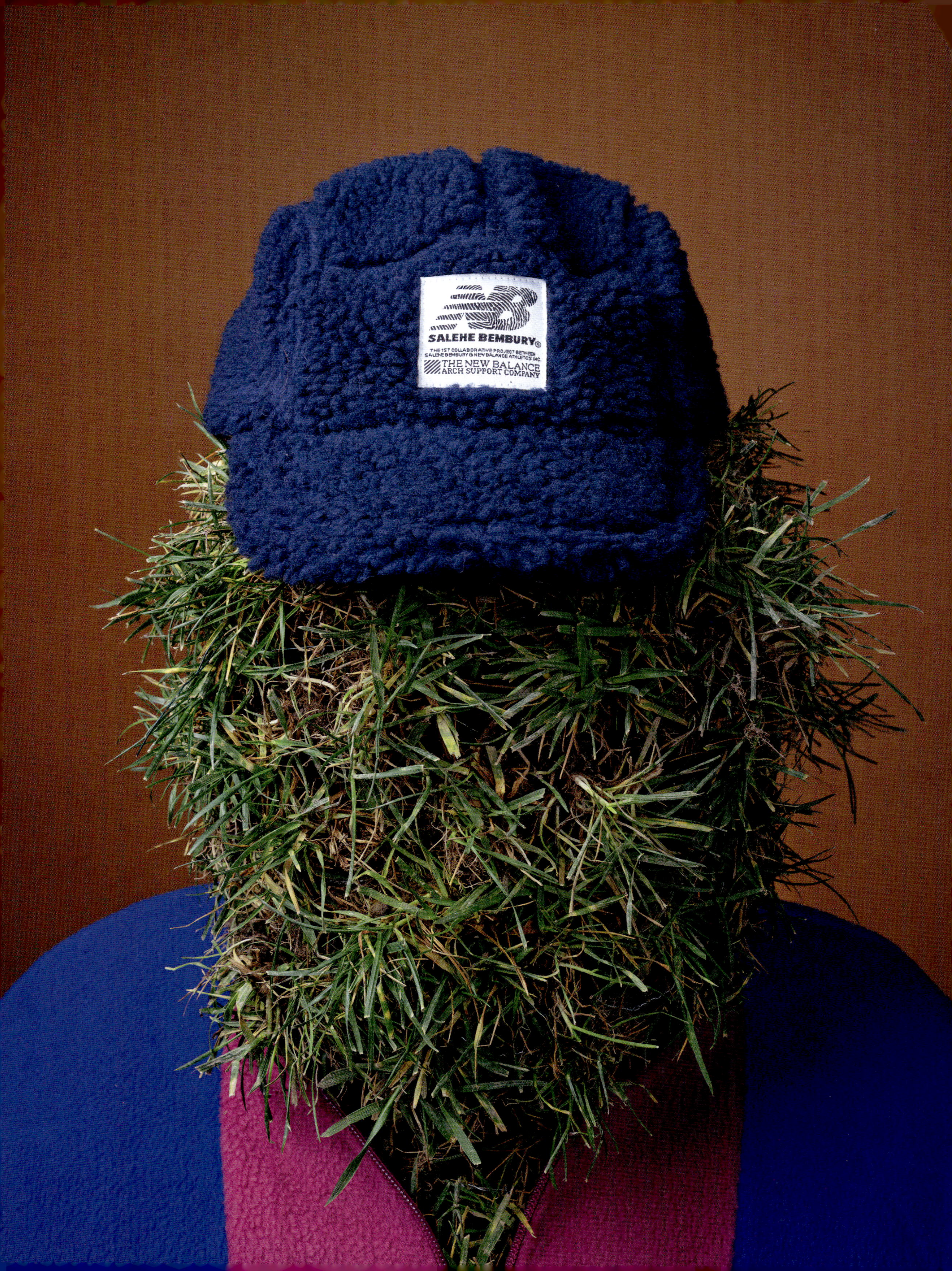
SALEHE BEMBURY®
THE 1ST COLLABORATIVE PROJECT BETWEEN SALEHE BEMBURY & NEW BALANCE ATHLETICS INC.
THE NEW BALANCE
ARCH SUPPORT COMPANY

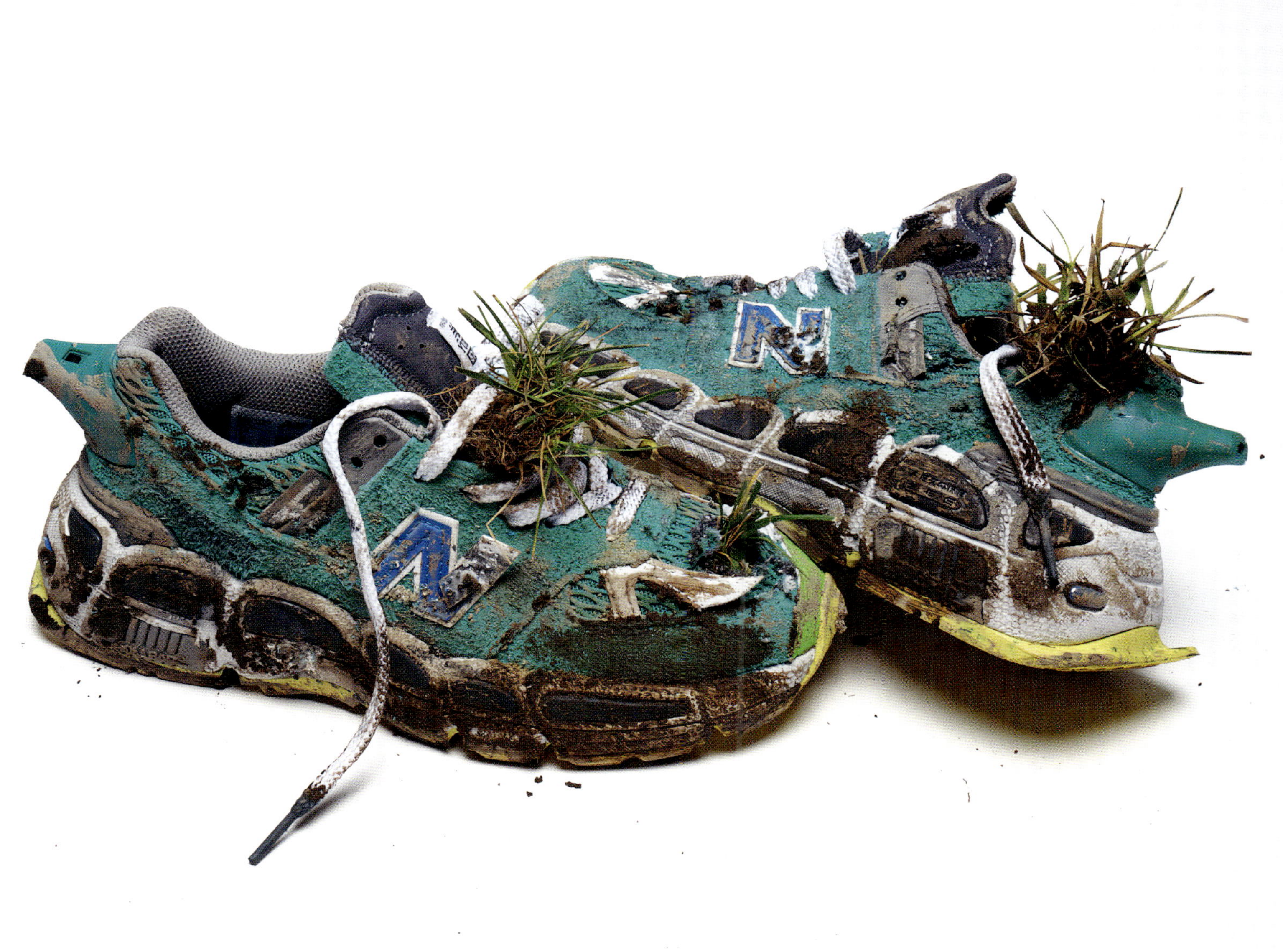

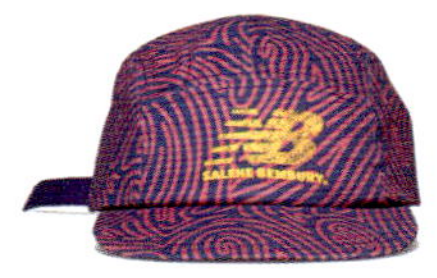
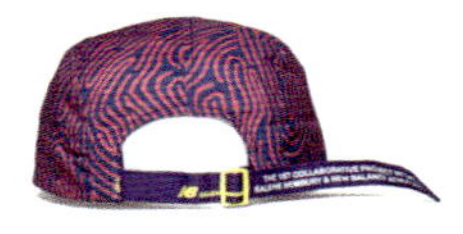
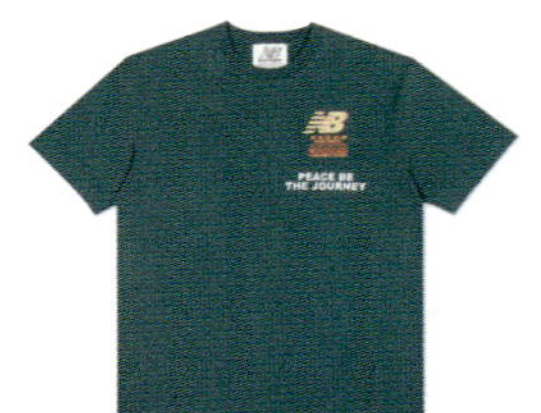
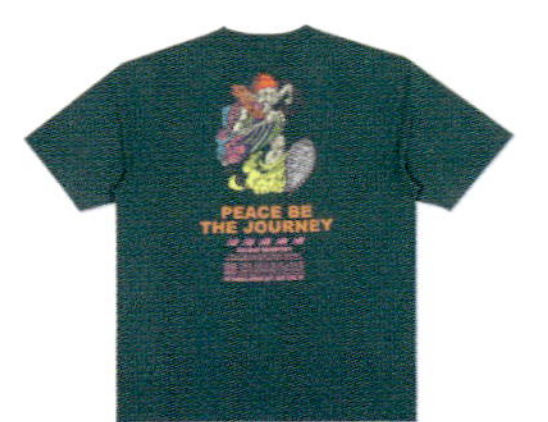
PEACE BE
THE JOURNEY
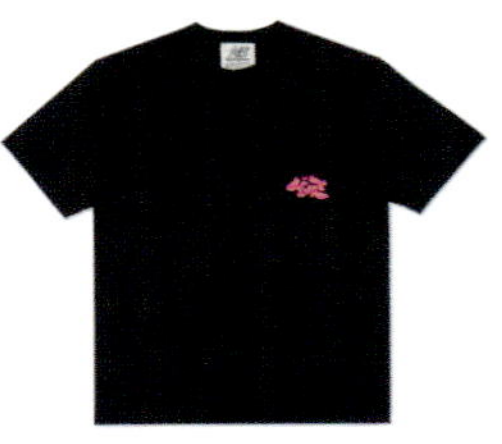
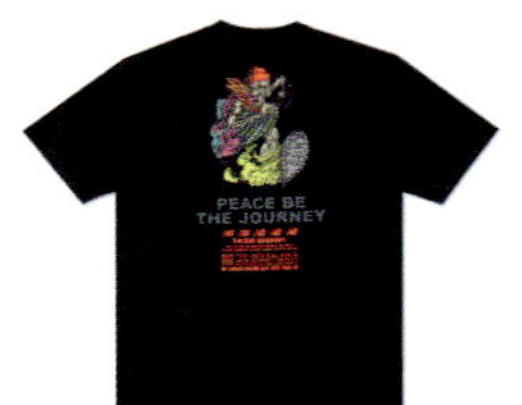
PEACE BE
THE JOURNEY
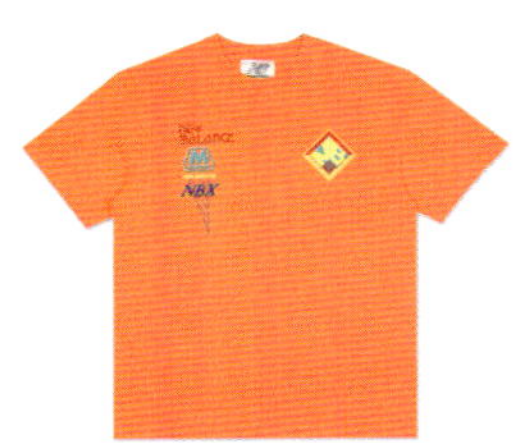
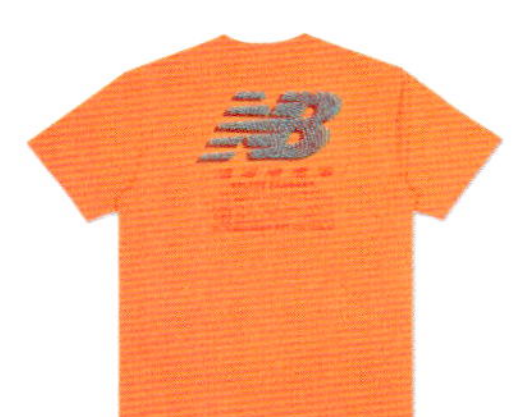
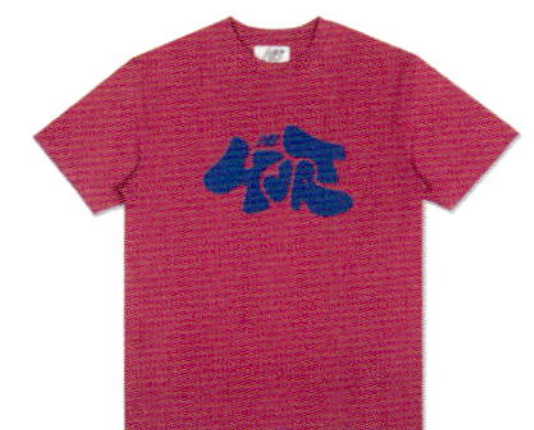
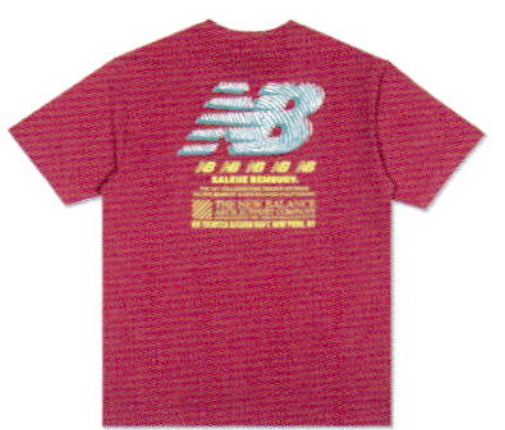
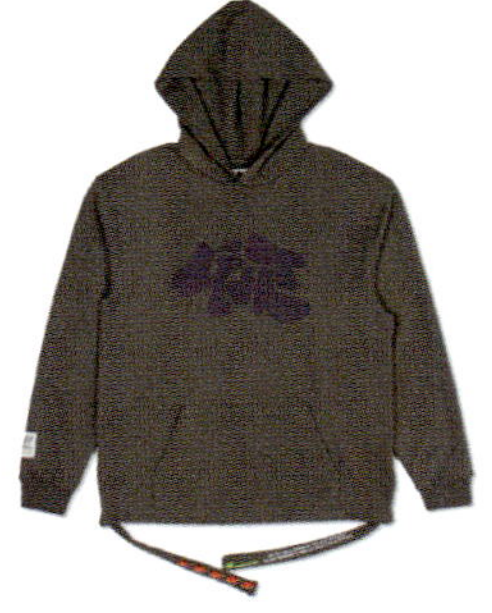
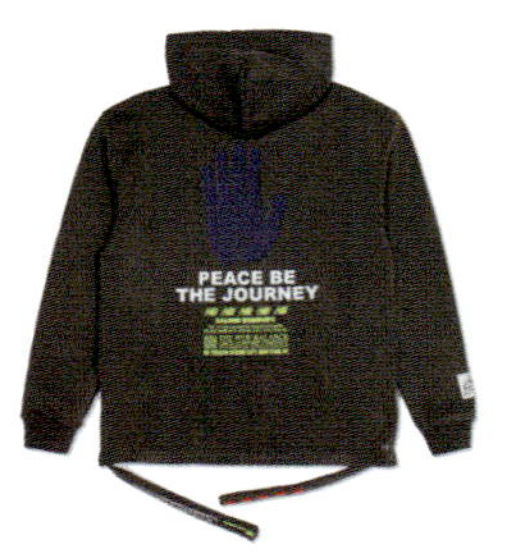
PEACE BE
THE JOURNEY
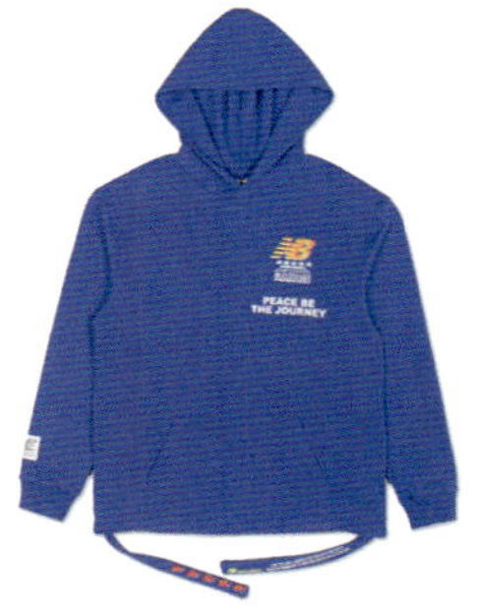
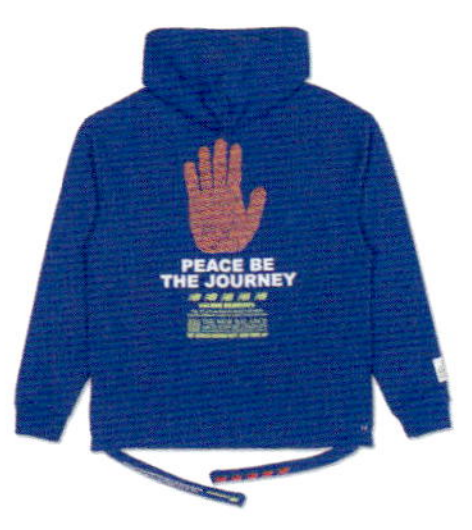
PEACE BE
THE JOURNEY
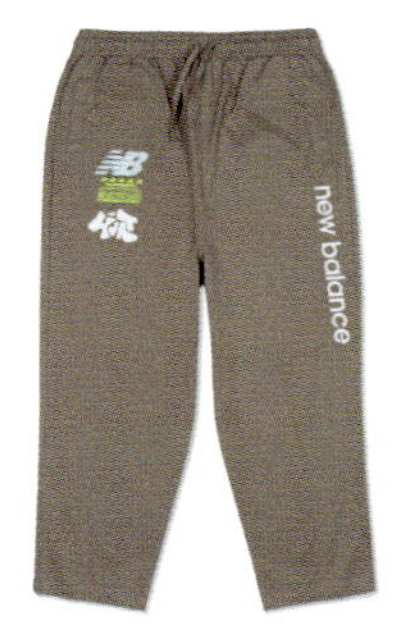
new balance
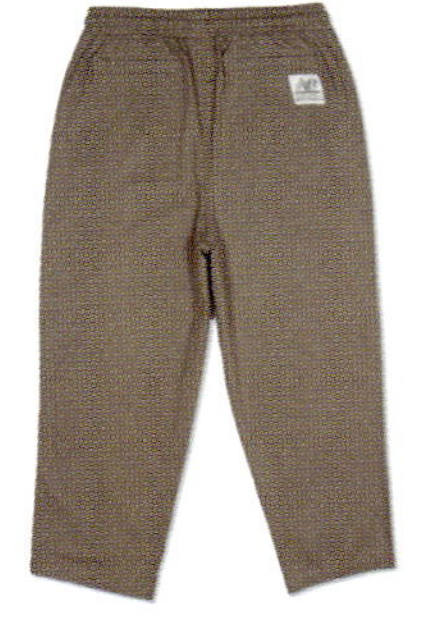
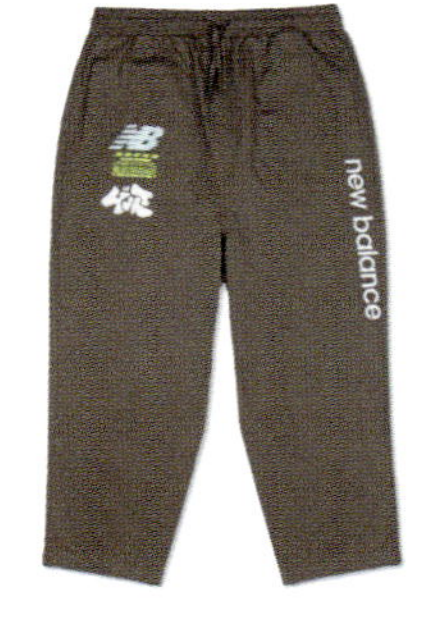
new balance
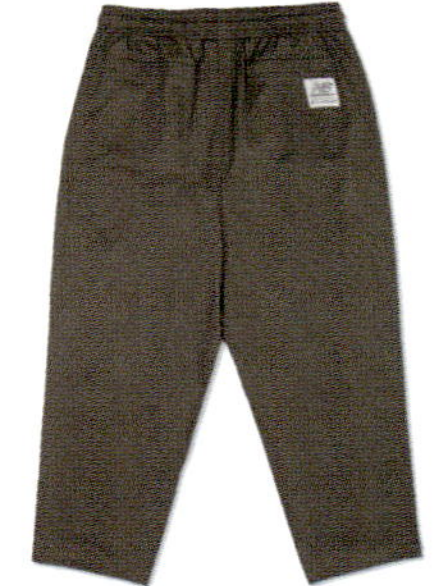
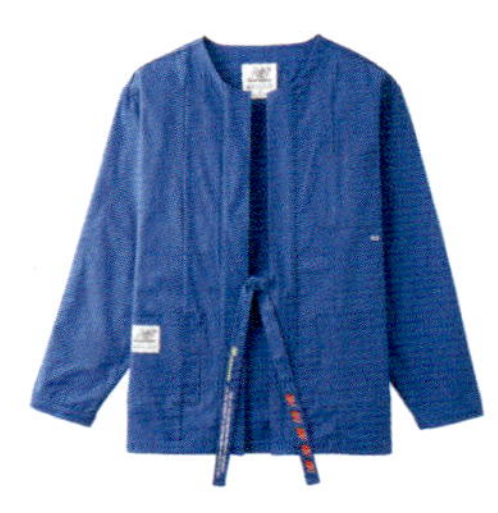
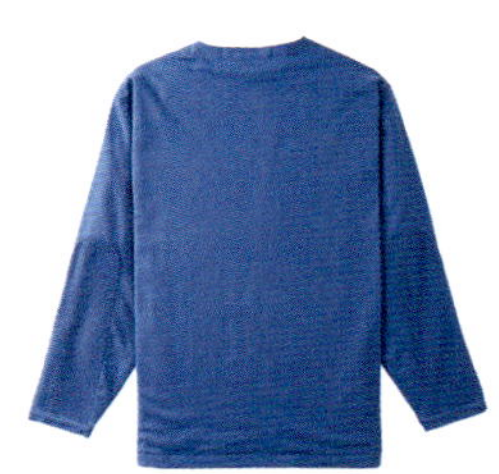
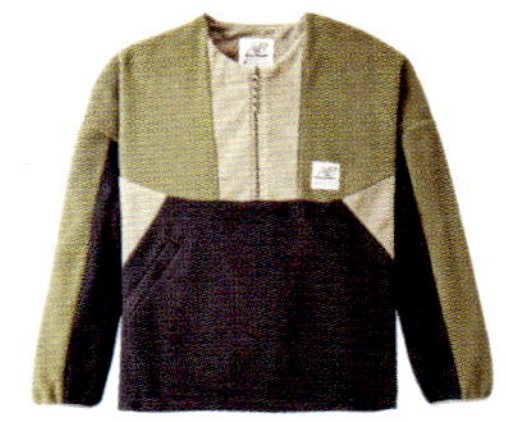
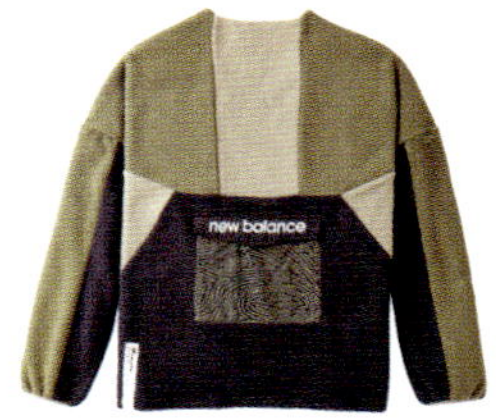
new balance
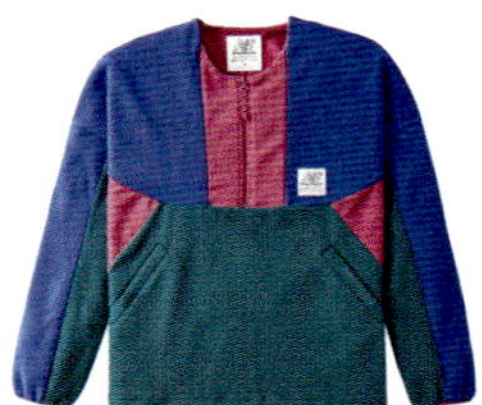
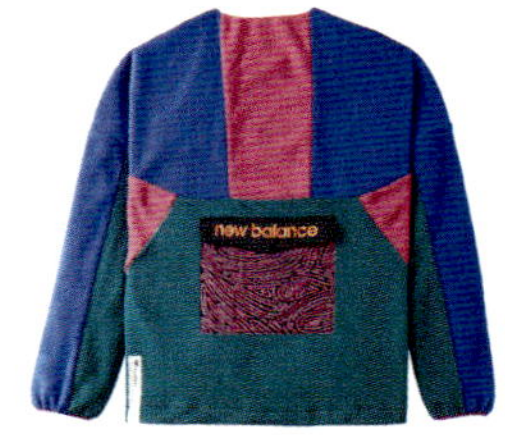
new balance
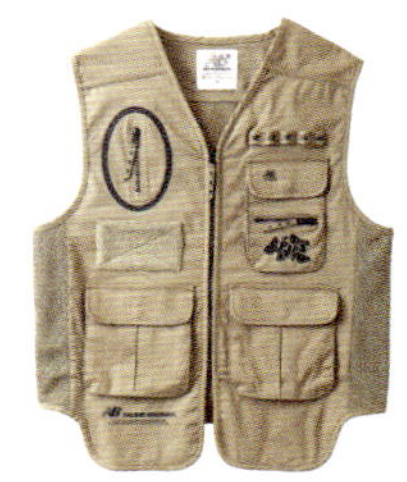
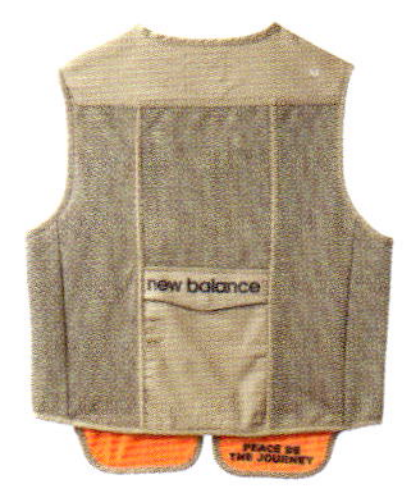
new balance
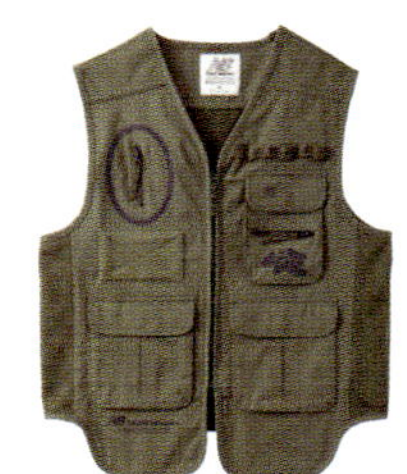
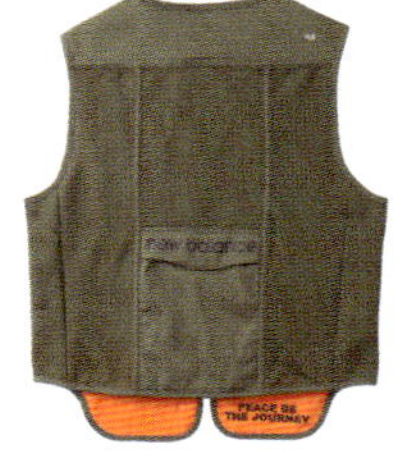
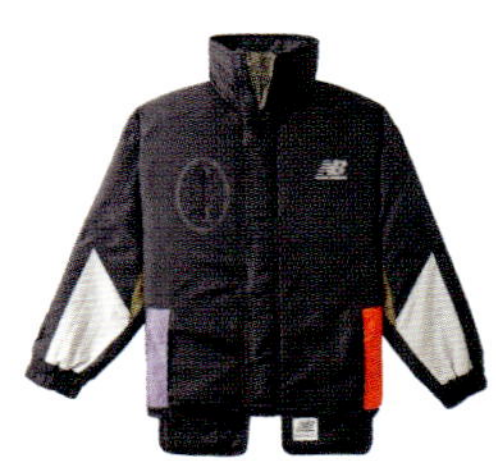
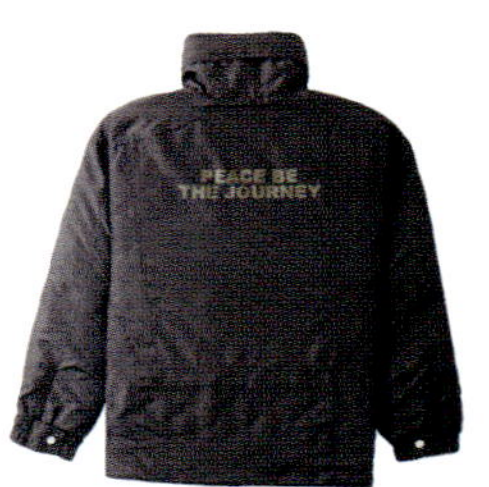
PEACE BE
THE JOURNEY

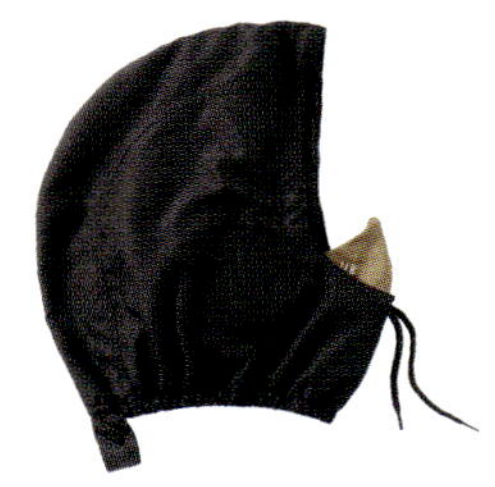
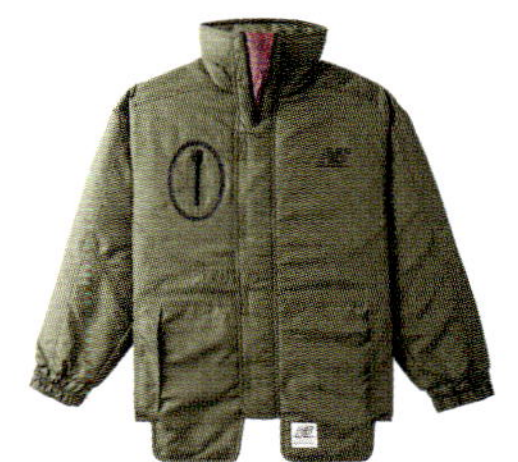
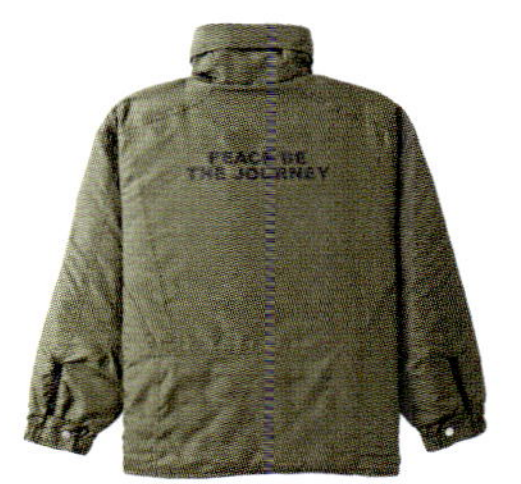
PEACE BE
THE JOURNEY
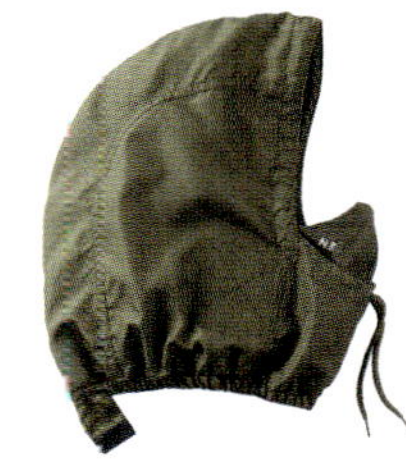
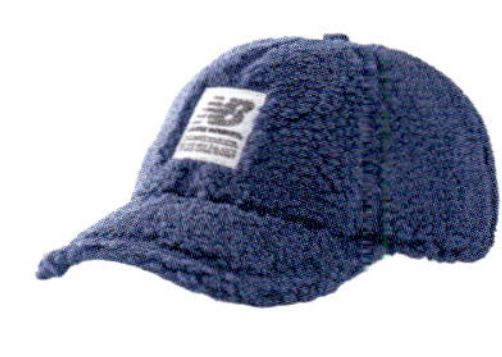
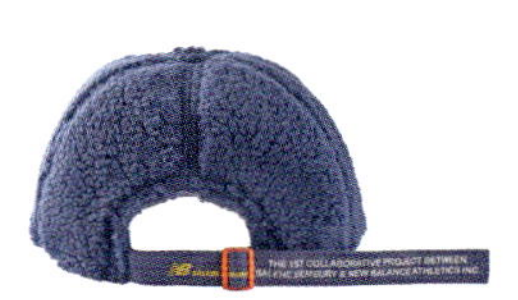
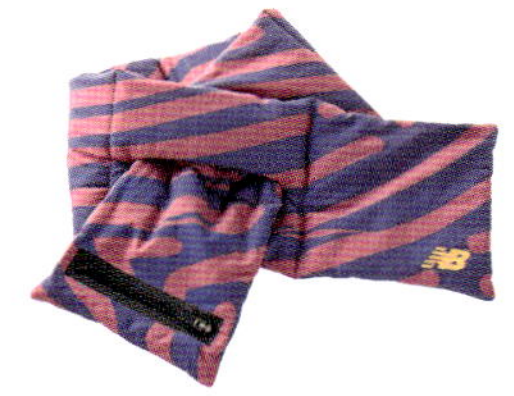
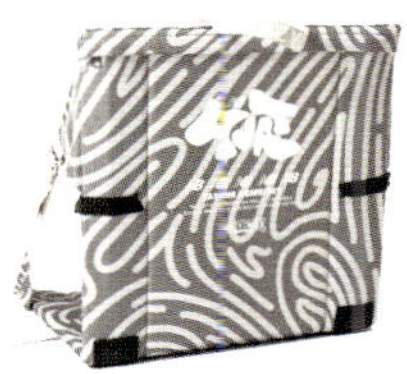
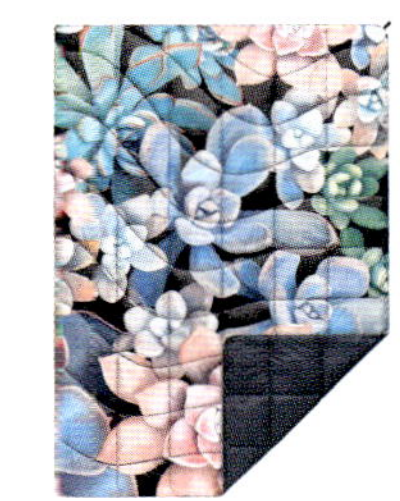
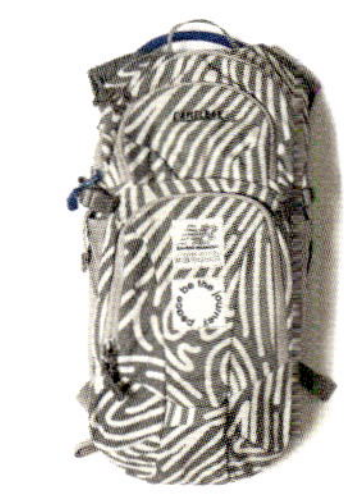
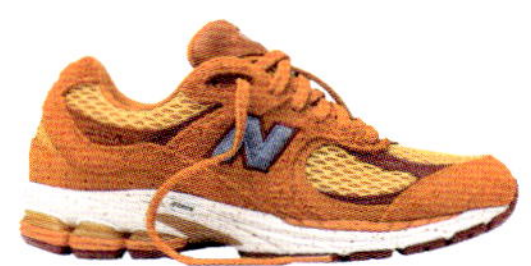
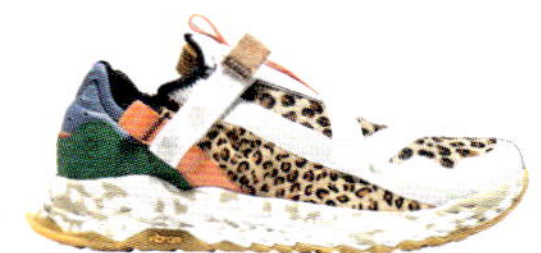
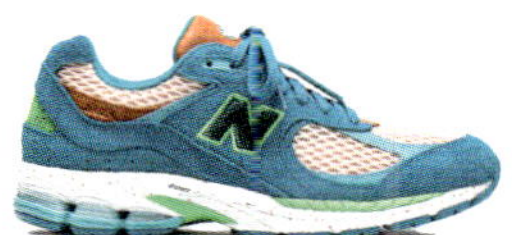
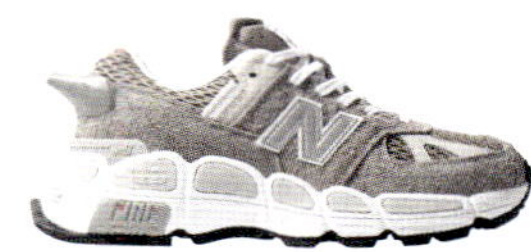
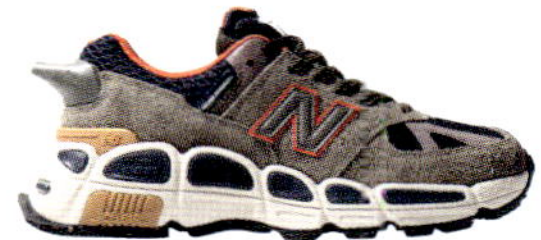
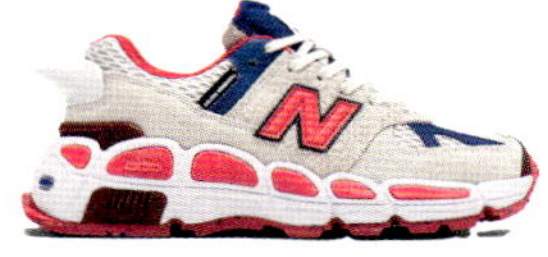
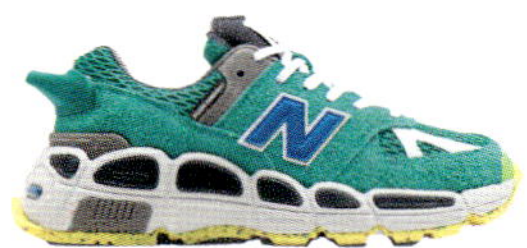
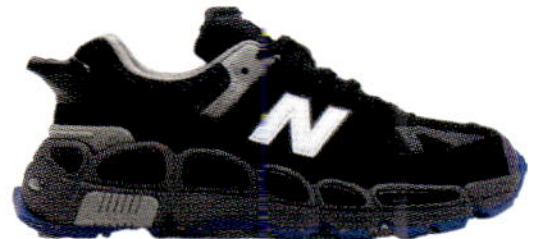
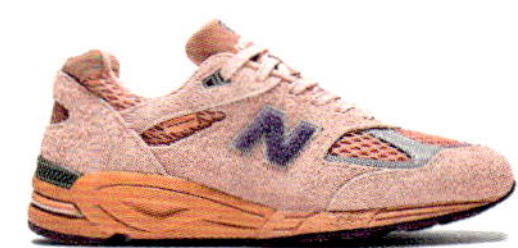
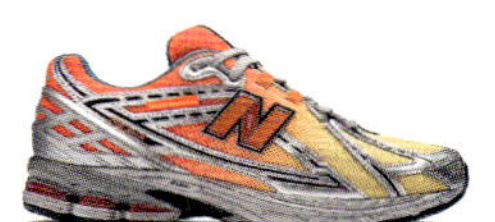
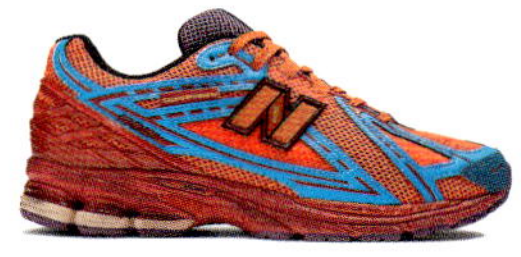
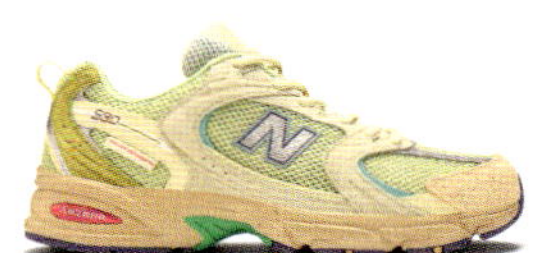
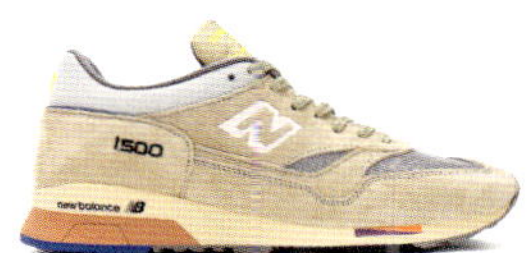
1500
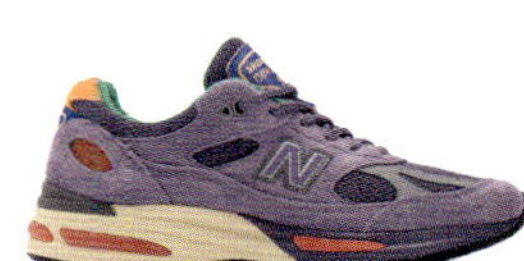
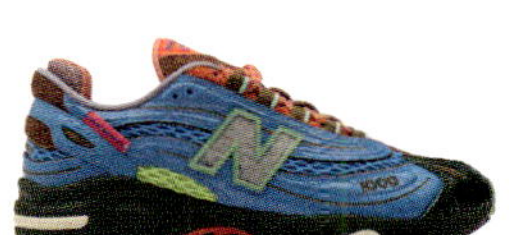
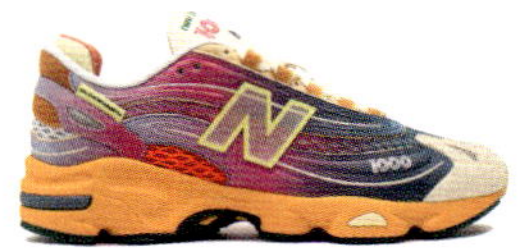
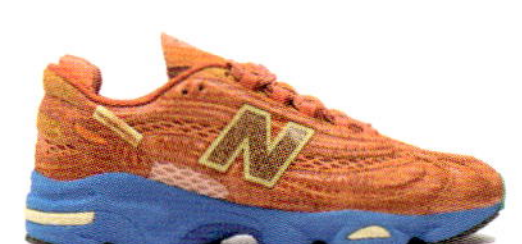
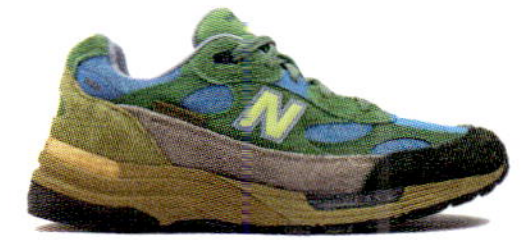
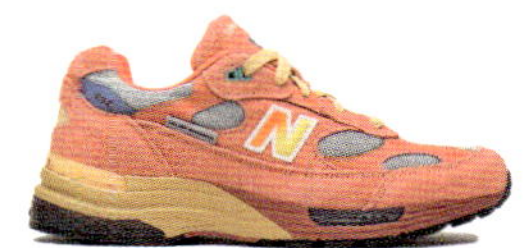

216

CROCS **(2020)**

MAKE AN ICO

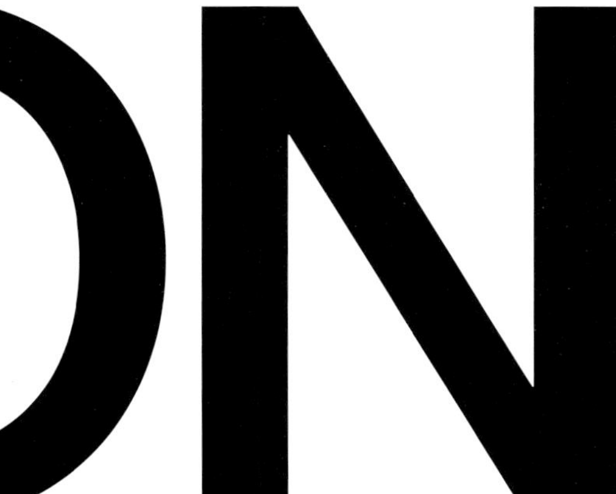

CROCS
MAKE AN ICON

1

1When attacking this design project I thought about how I could do something new but also not scare the existing Crocs consumer. I also saw this as an opportunity to explore my very infant brand identity at the time, which was the fingerprint. I came to the conclusion that all great designers and artists have a consistent brand identity, a consistent visual language, that the consumer or an audience can recognize without ever seeing a logo. Through my love of woodgrain and organic design lines, I stumbled upon the fingerprint, which it seemed that no one owned or was exploring. And now I can confidently say that I own the fingerprint.

That really was the foundation of the design for the Pollex, which at the time didn't have a name. We played around with fingerprint lines, we played around with brain lines, we played around with woodgrain lines, changed contours and dimensions, changed composition, placement. Is the heel closed, is it not? What are the signature details, the heritage details of Crocs that need to be maintained, so that their existing consumer recognizes the shoe as a Croc? So that it doesn't scare them away, but it also excites the new consumer and potentially welcomes the sneaker consumer. So I was really trying to tackle a few different things at once. And after about three weeks of rather intense design, we created the Pollex.

The 3D modeler's name was Michal Kukucka, and he was an important player in the opportunity. I met him when I designed for United Nude, he was the 3D modeler there. He lived in Venice. I spent three weekends at his house, where we would just jam on 3D all day long and I would be communicating to him exactly what I wanted—"shift this, change that, move this, move that, reference this." Ultimately we were digitally playing with clay all day long, and then we'd go to the bar, drink, I'd sleep on his couch, and we'd wake up and do it again the next day. And given that I personally do not execute 3D design, I needed to have someone be my hands—my digital hands. That's what Mikhail was, and he really helped me realize my vision.

When we had the final model, it didn't look like the Pollex you see now, in terms of the holes on the front of the shoe. Initially I had the holes live more on the side of the shoe because I was doing a lot of thinking about what are the least attractive parts of the foot, and not wanting those parts of the foot to be revealed. Some of the first models we printed were strictly of the reveal points in the shoe, for reasons of heat release and breathability—but also because no one wants their pinky toe hanging out of a shoe. We really had to make sure that we show parts of the foot for both utilitarian reasons and aesthetic, but we also had to hide other parts of the foot. I was really treating this like a work of art. But in that moment, I realized that the three signature details of the Croc were the strap, the toe pitch, and the front toe perforations. And while they're not the same as the Croc, we shifted some of those perforations to the front of the toe, to better mimic the understood, classic Croc visual language.

There are some shoes I've made in my career where as soon as I see the 3D model I know that it's a winner. And the Pollex was absolutely one of them.

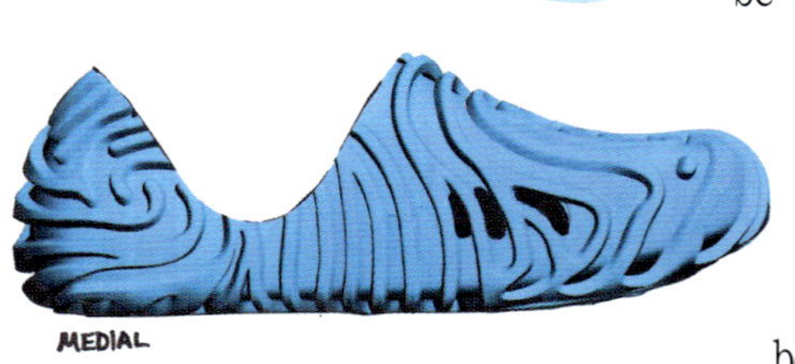

Initial Crocs Pollex sketch

2

So now that we have this shoe, we have the visual language, the next two things to be created are packaging and marketing.

For packaging design I first looked at what Crocs offered for their collaborators. Crocs being a sustainability-first company, often their collaborations would be packaged in a type of bag. This didn't work for me for a few reasons. Within sneaker culture there are some rituals that are unbreakable, and one of them is the shoe-box stacking ritual. And if we're creating this shoe that we want to be both accepted and owned by the sneaker community, I thought it was important to explore some of these rituals within our shoe. So a bag would not suffice. I then knew whatever we did create would need to be a box and would need to have roughly the same dimensions as your average

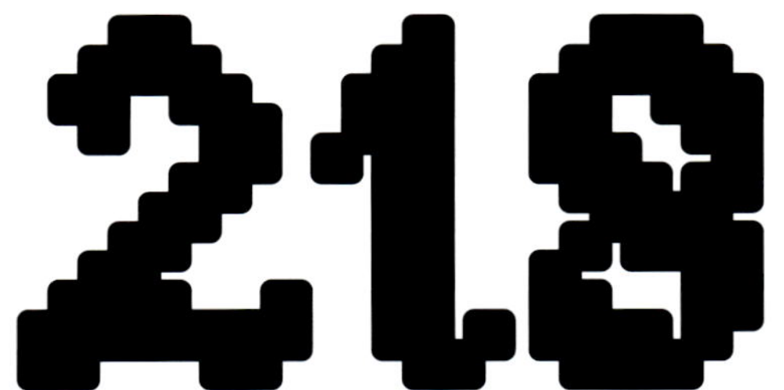

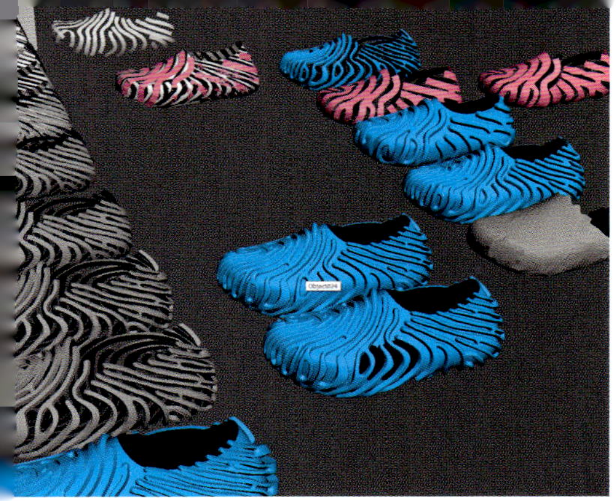

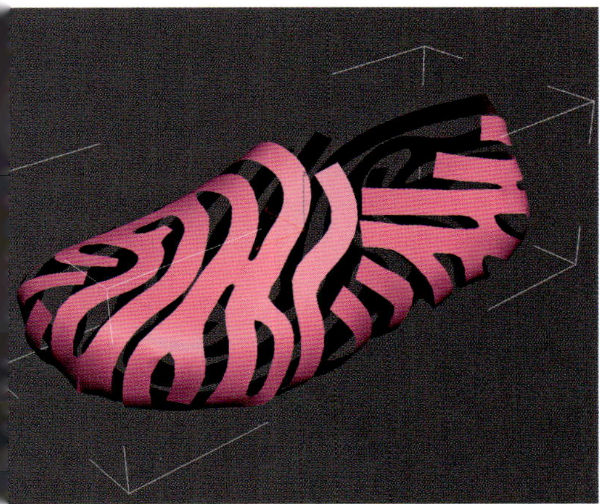

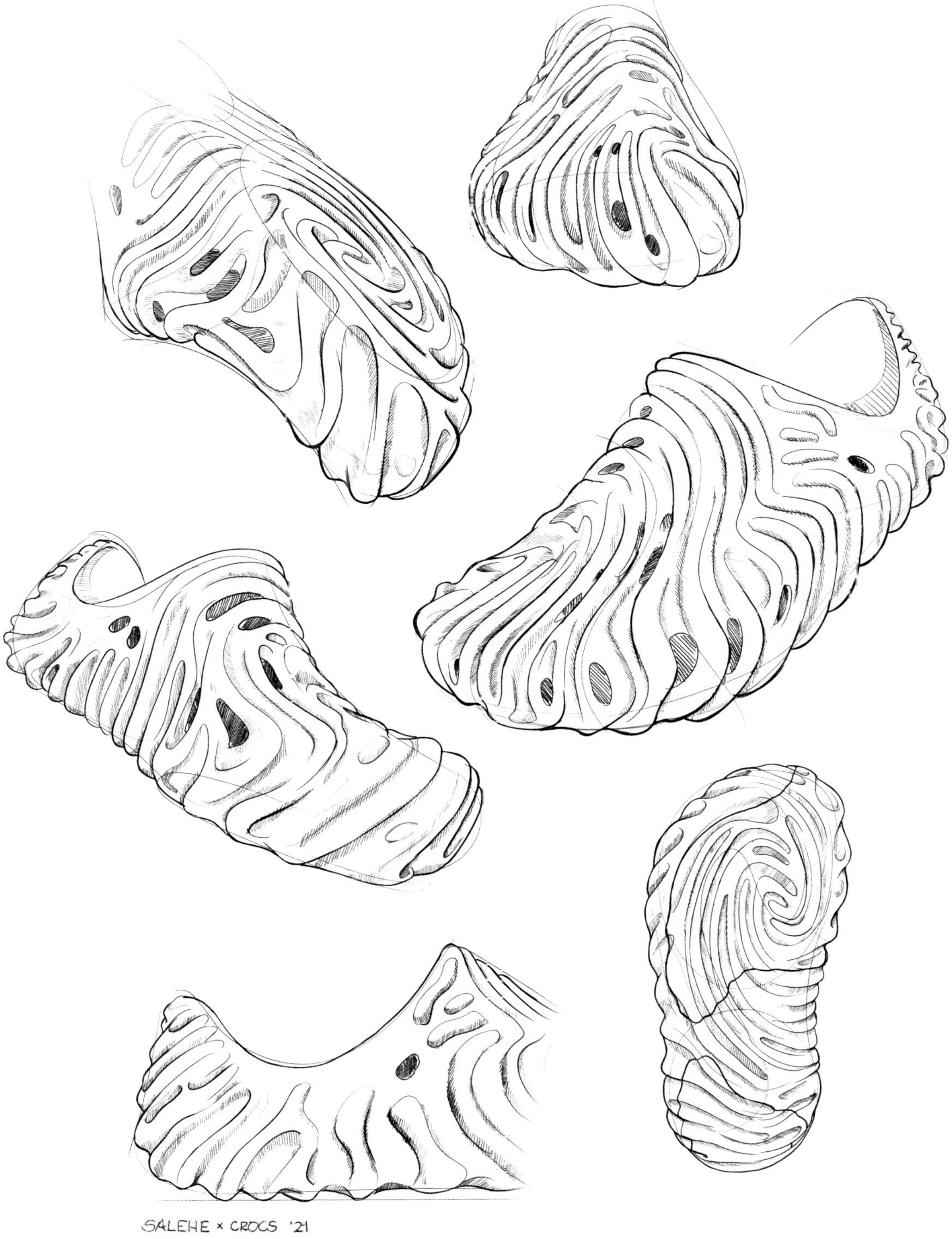

SALEHE × CROCS '21

Crocs Pollex sketch

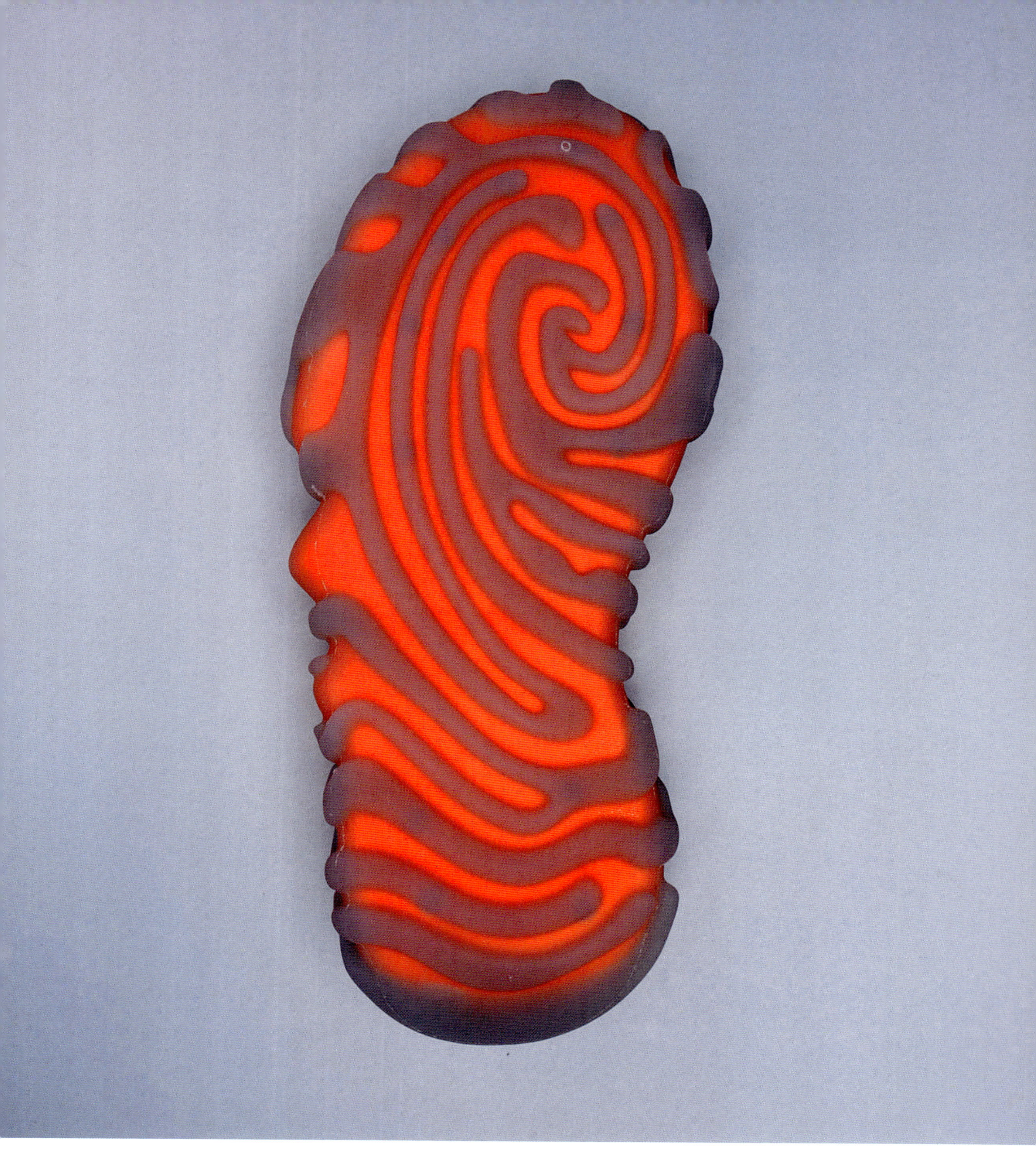

220

(2020)

CROCS

sneaker box, so it could be stacked and participate in that space or real estate in your home. And now visually, too, you immediately couple these Crocs with your sneaker collection.

How could we keep the box sustainable while potentially introducing a new idea, a new shape, or a new presentation of the product? I was looking at egg cartons and I was really fascinated by the capabilities and the structural integrity of paper pulp. So I started sketching, started playing with 3D a little bit, and eventually we created what is considered the launch box of my Crocs collaboration. And that consists of a paper-pulp box with two shoe-shaped cavities that hold the Pollex, covered by a clear cover that features the logos and keeps the shoes visible while the box is closed. This box accomplished a few things: It used what I believe to be a material never seen in sneaker packaging; it allowed the consumer to see the product while the box was closed; it still participated in the box-stacking ritual of sneaker culture, which I deemed very important; and it made the Pollex feel like a specimen, because you could see it through this clear barrier. And given that it was a time when we were introducing a new shape, a new idea, a new brand identity, I thought it was important that the consumer and the audience saw the product even before they saw the product.

3

The Croc became a niche success, and then a slightly larger success, and then it continued to grow into a shoe that I would argue is one of the most important pieces of footwear in the last ten years, which I'm extremely proud of.

Because of that, we then had to create moments and marketing that helped extend the lifespan and increase the momentum of this once-in-a-decade project. One example were pop-ups. The first pop-up we did was in Paris, at Paris Fashion Week. It was in a really small retail space in the Marais. We basically painted the entire thing black with a small logo at the top left. This space was sourced and executed by Michael Dupouy. We also did one in Dubai, we did one in Japan. All of them represented the momentum that this one shoe has created globally. And with different marketing initiatives, campaigns, and seedings, we cultivated a community that is now extremely engaged in myself, my work, and the collaboration.

4

Another marketing exercise that we did was the giant Pollex around the world. Essentially we created a giant Pollex (with Team Epiphany) that was about the size of a car, versions in different colors, and we placed them in urban environments so that passersby could discover the shoe, recognize the shoe, take pictures, document, post, share, discuss, hate it, love it. From being a really invested sneaker consumer my entire life, I understand capitalizing on marketing, nostalgia, making people smile, giving people perspective, and adding utility to one's life. This giant Croc thing was an example of that, and it was extremely successful. It was also extremely surreal to see something I designed sitting in the middle of New York City, on Houston Street—a street that I'd walked by many, many times, and now my shoe is sitting there at roughly ten feet in length. That was a testament to the success of the shoe, a testament to the marketing dollars that were put behind this collaboration, and many of the decisions made have resulted in a lot of success.

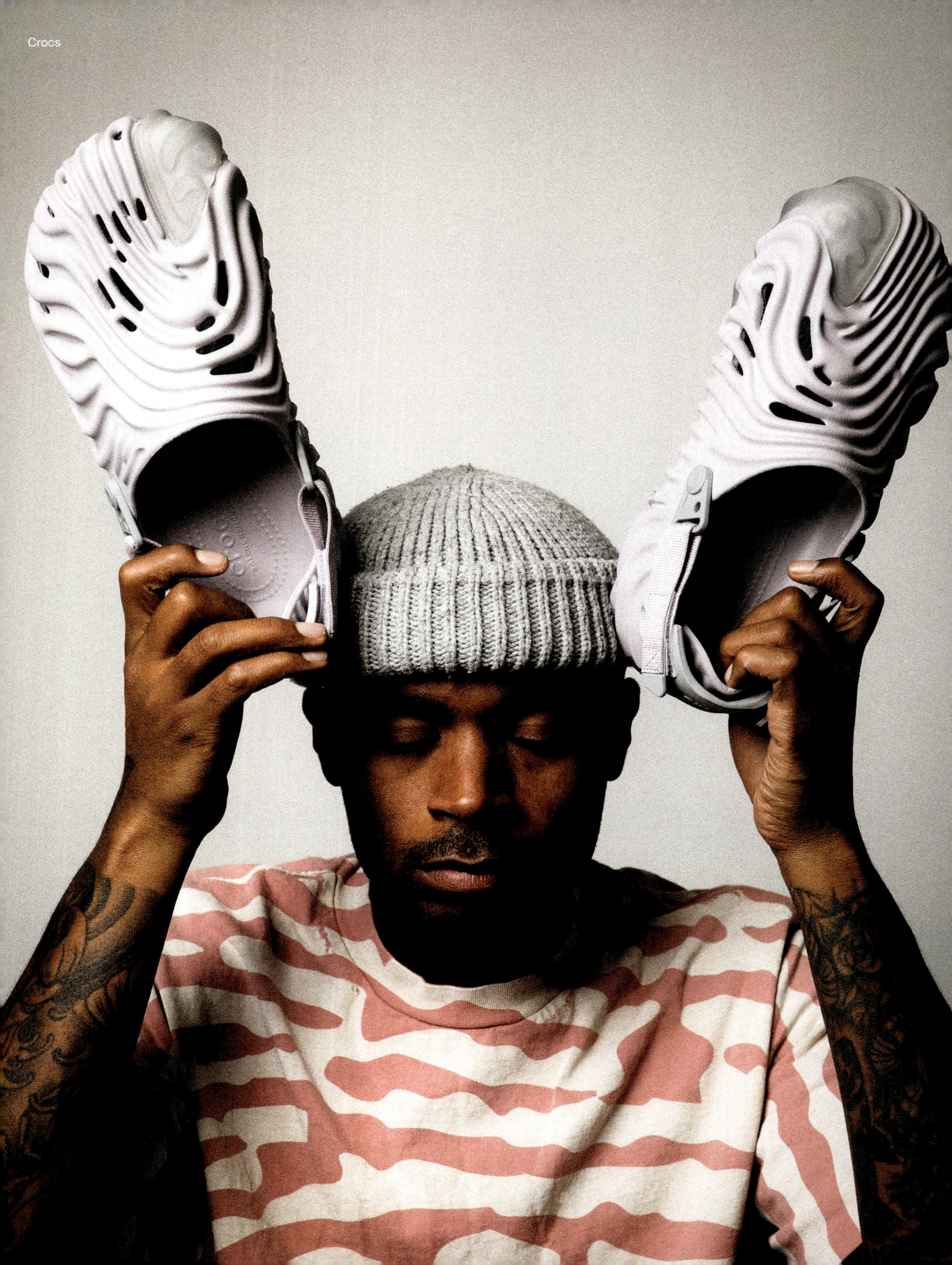

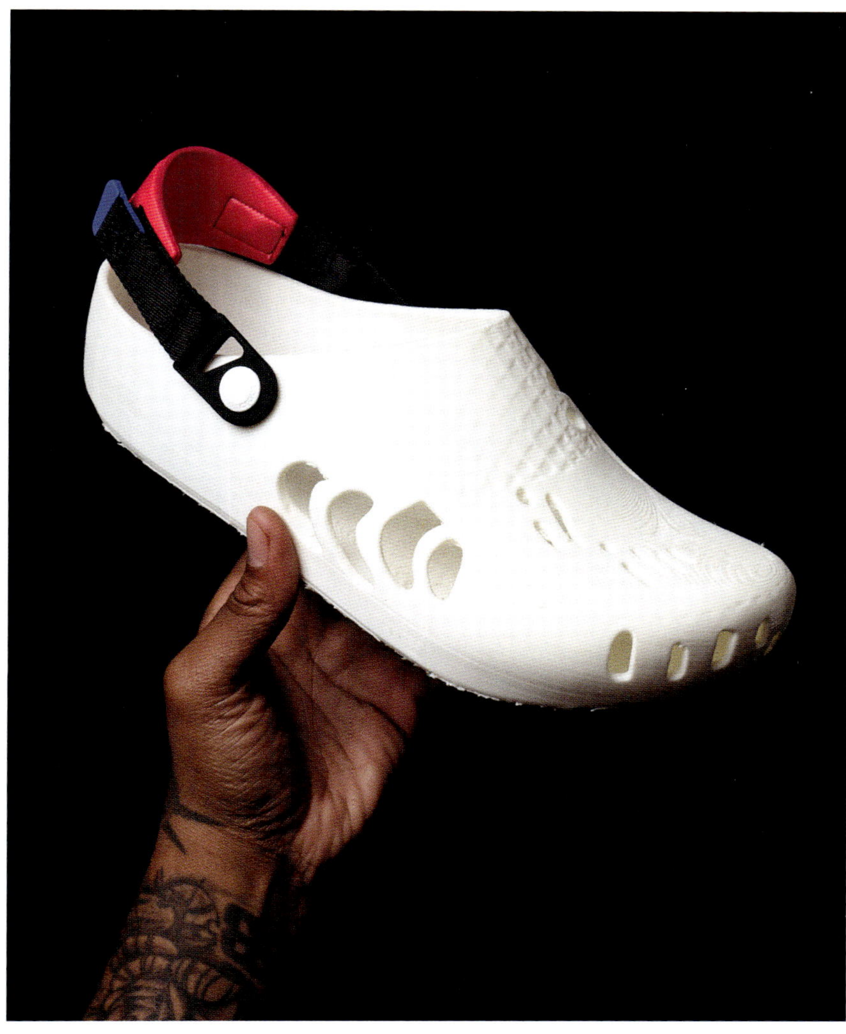

First Crocs Pollex 3D prototype

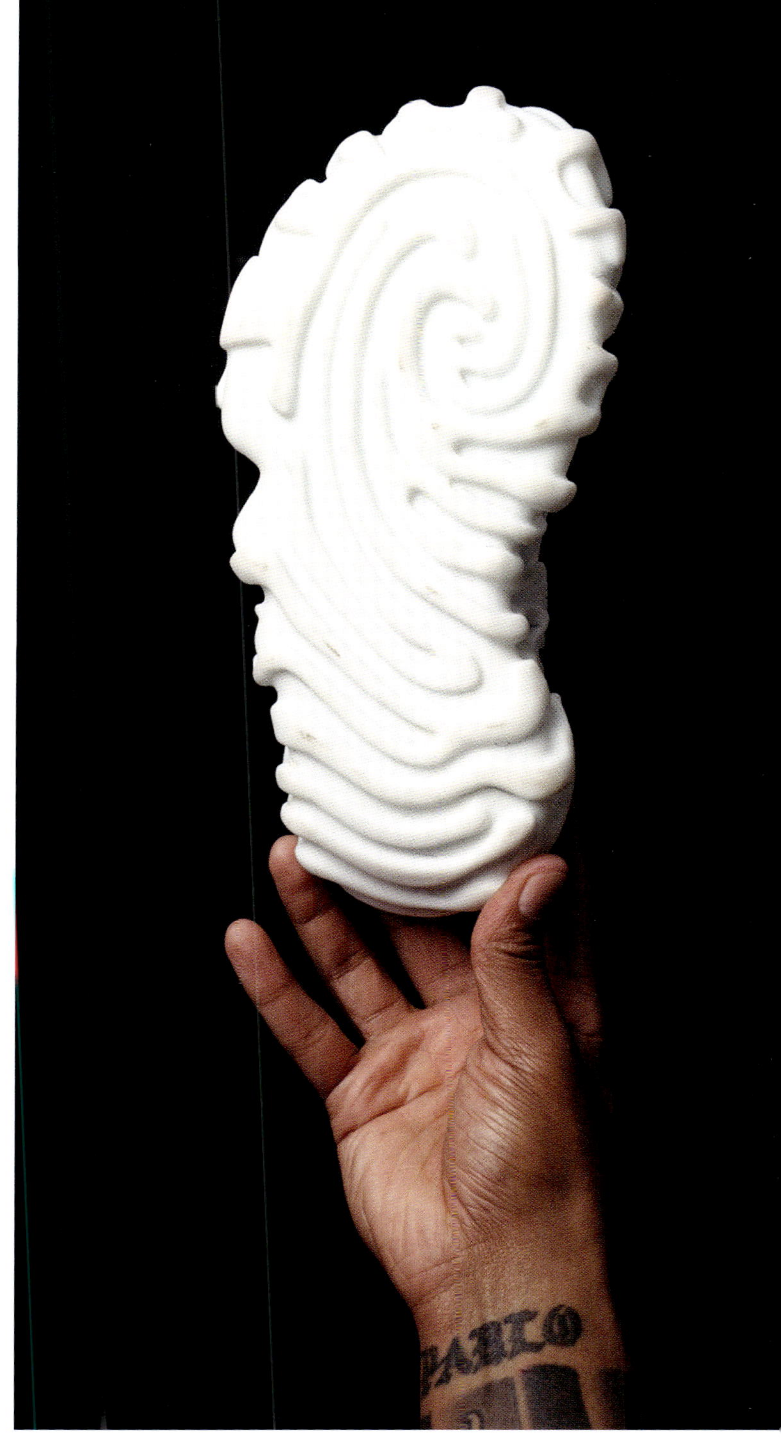

Crocs

223

Crocs Pollex by Salehe Bembury Miami activation by Team Epiphany

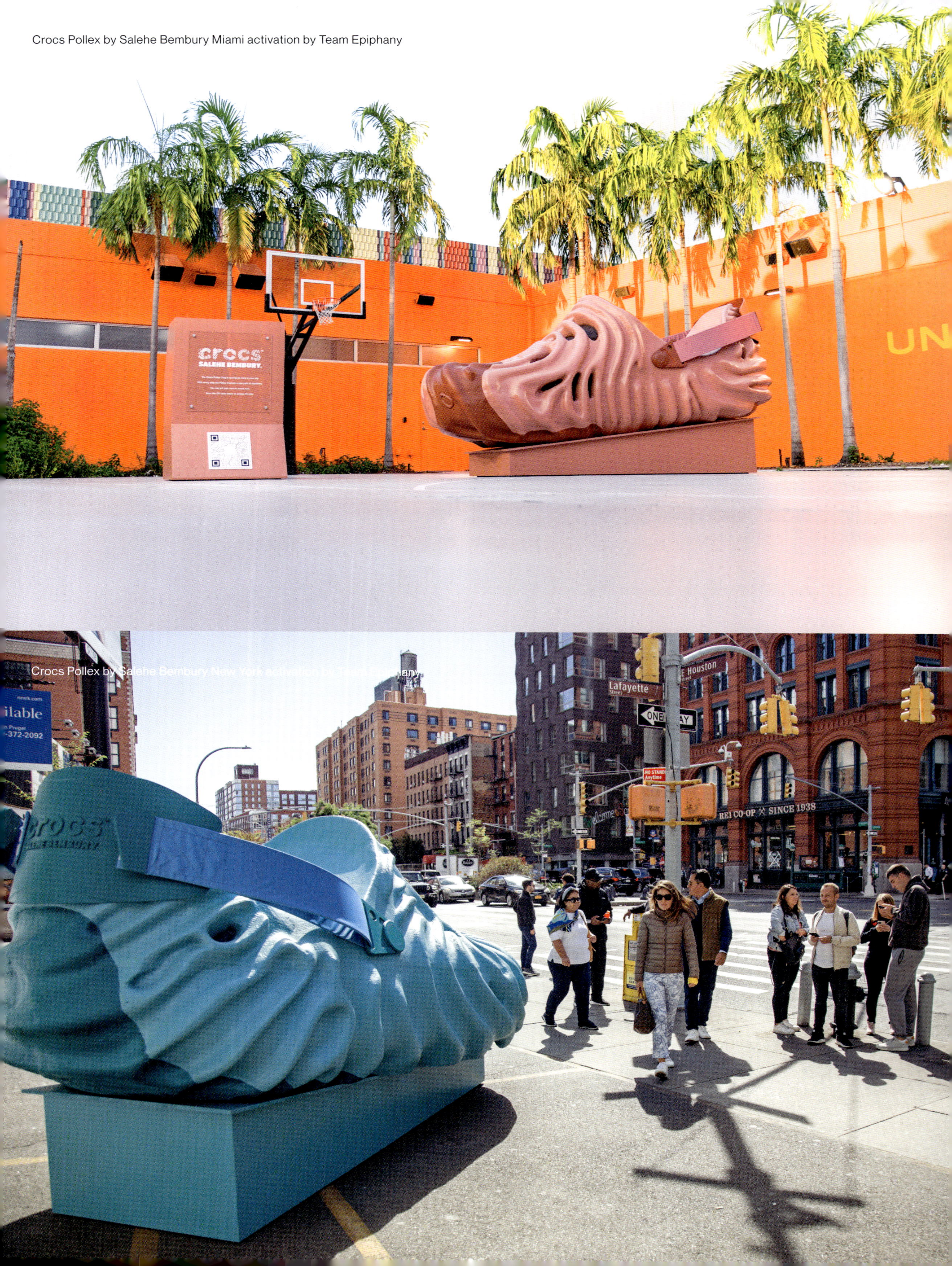

Crocs Pollex by Salehe Bembury New York activation by Team Epiphany

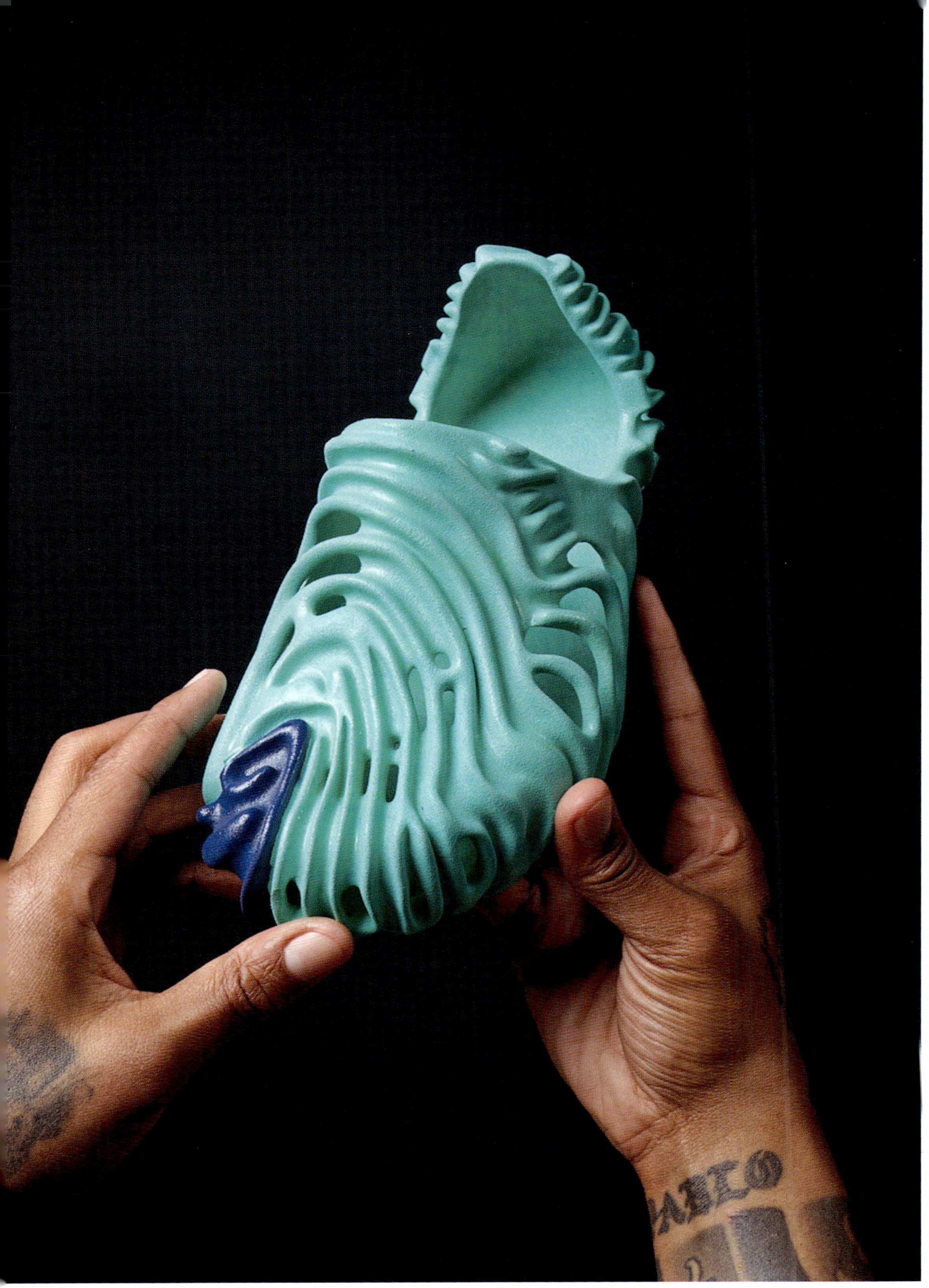

Second Crocs Pollex 3D prototype

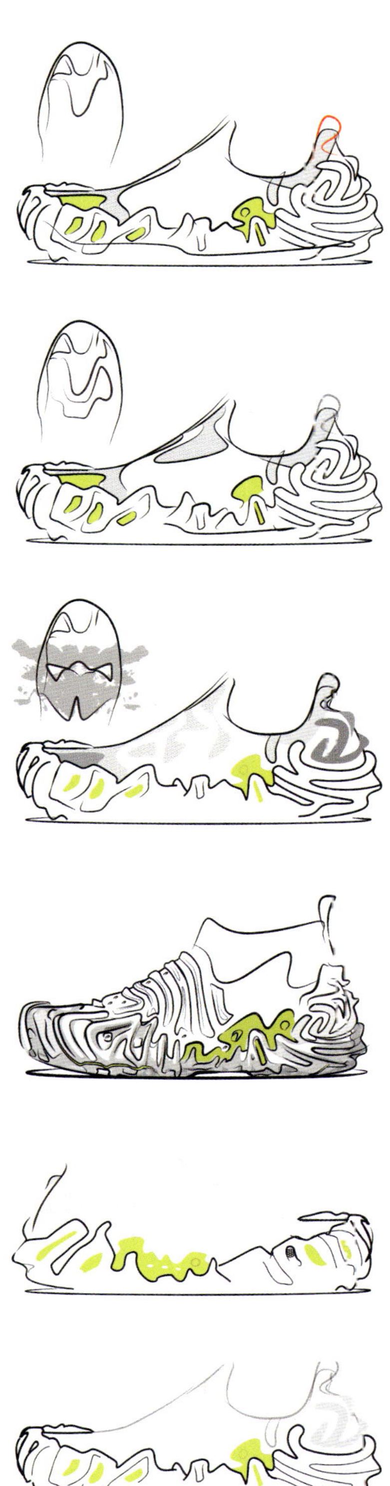

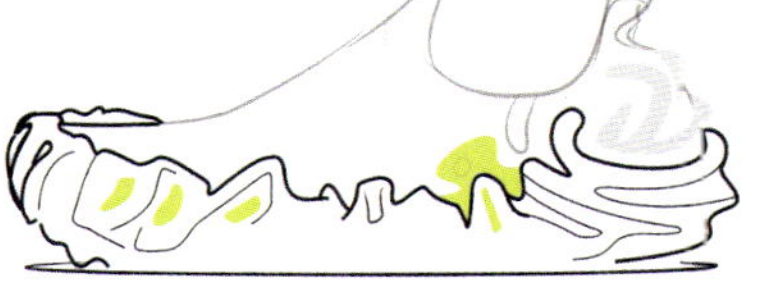

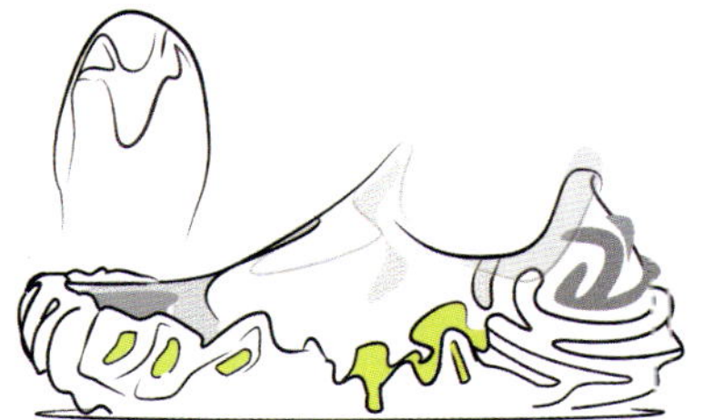

Crocs Juniper sketch

Crocs Pollex campaign featuring Cynthia Erivo and Jess Lin

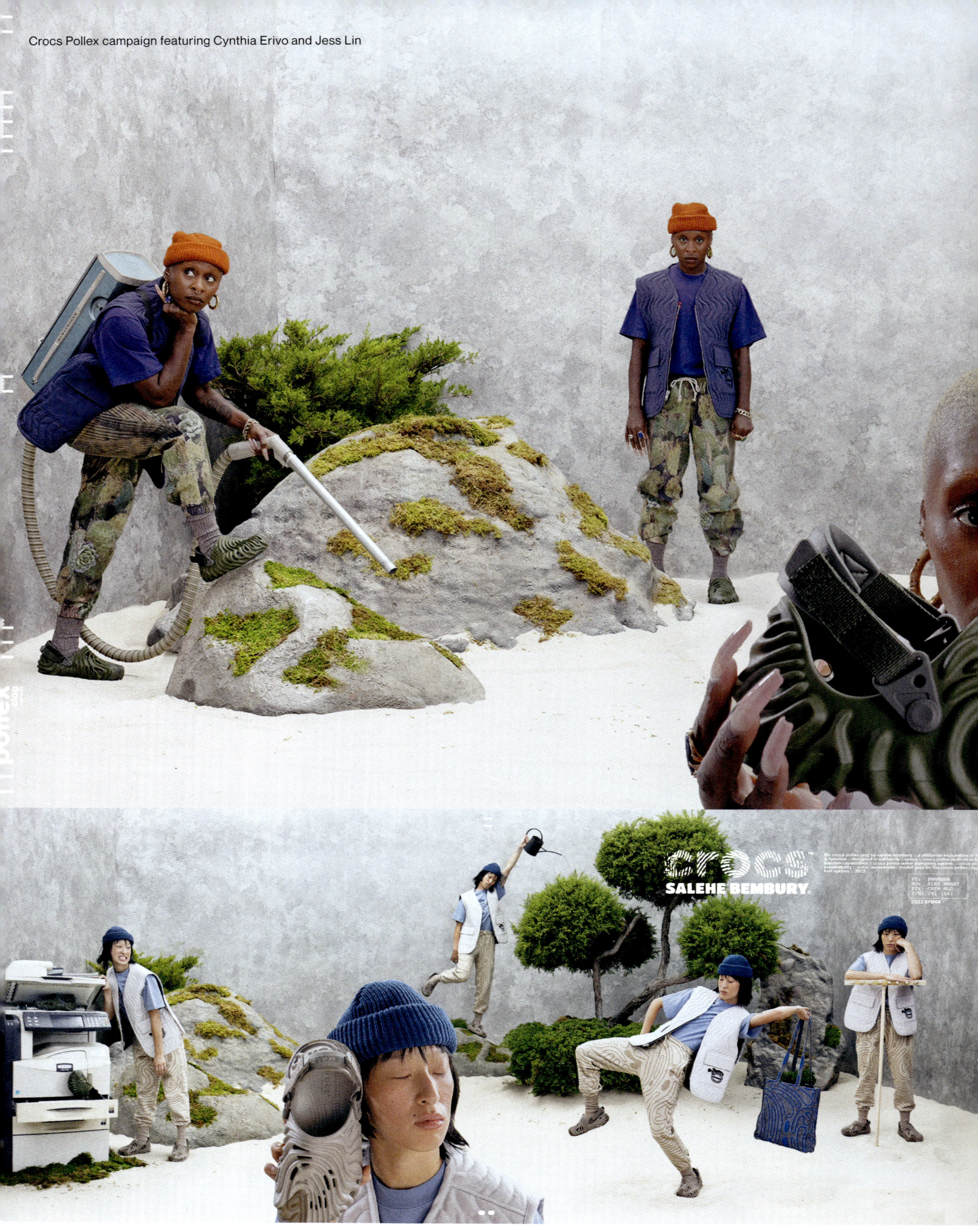

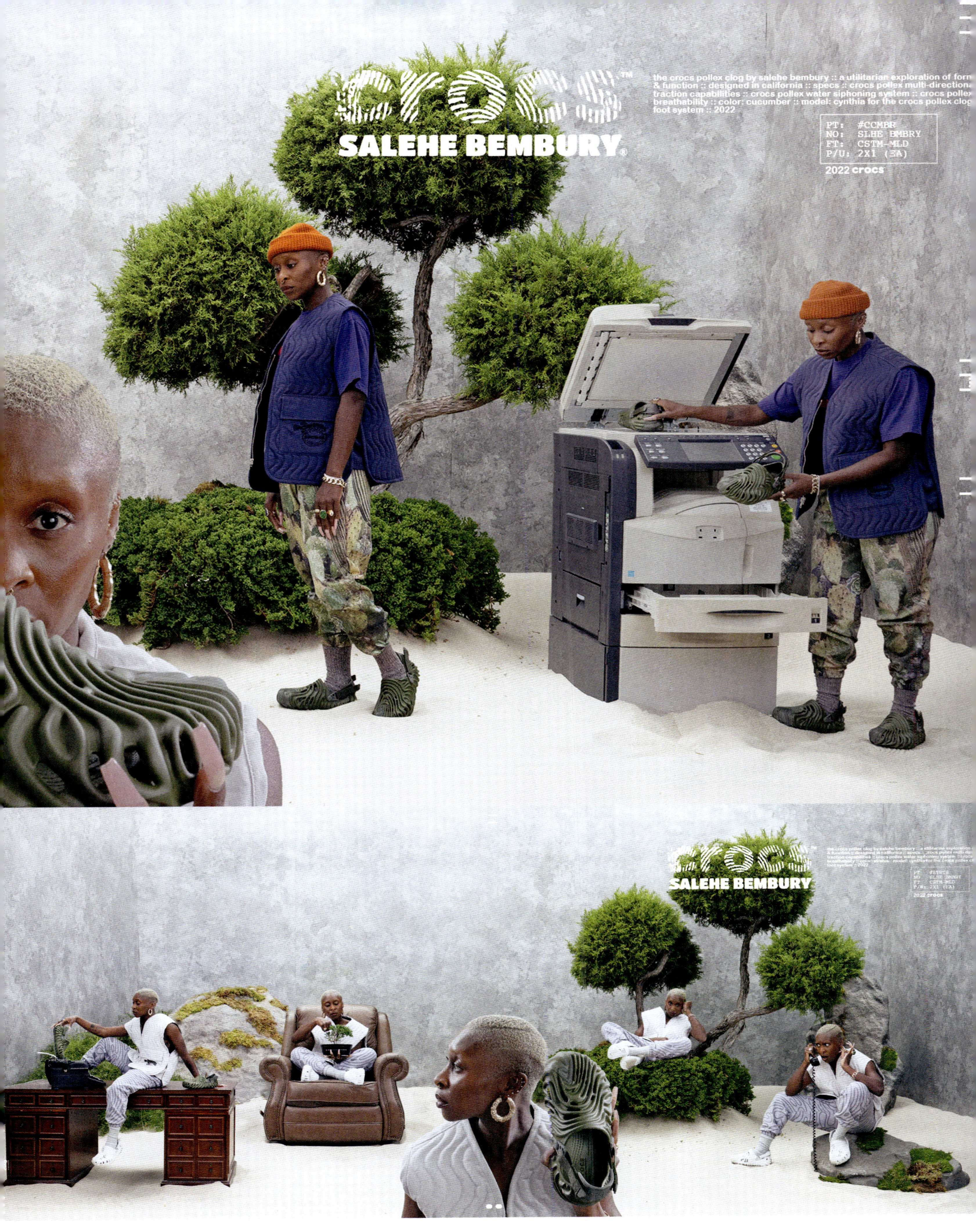
crocs
SALEHE BEMBURY
the crocs pollex clog by salehe bembury :: a utilitarian exploration of
& function :: designed in california :: specs :: crocs pollex
traction capabilities :: crocs pollex water siphoning system :: crocs
breathability :: color: cucumber :: model: cynthia for the crocs pollex
foot system :: 2022
PT: #CCMBR
NO: SLHE BMBRY
FT: CSTM-MLD
P/U: 2X1 (3A)
2022 crocs

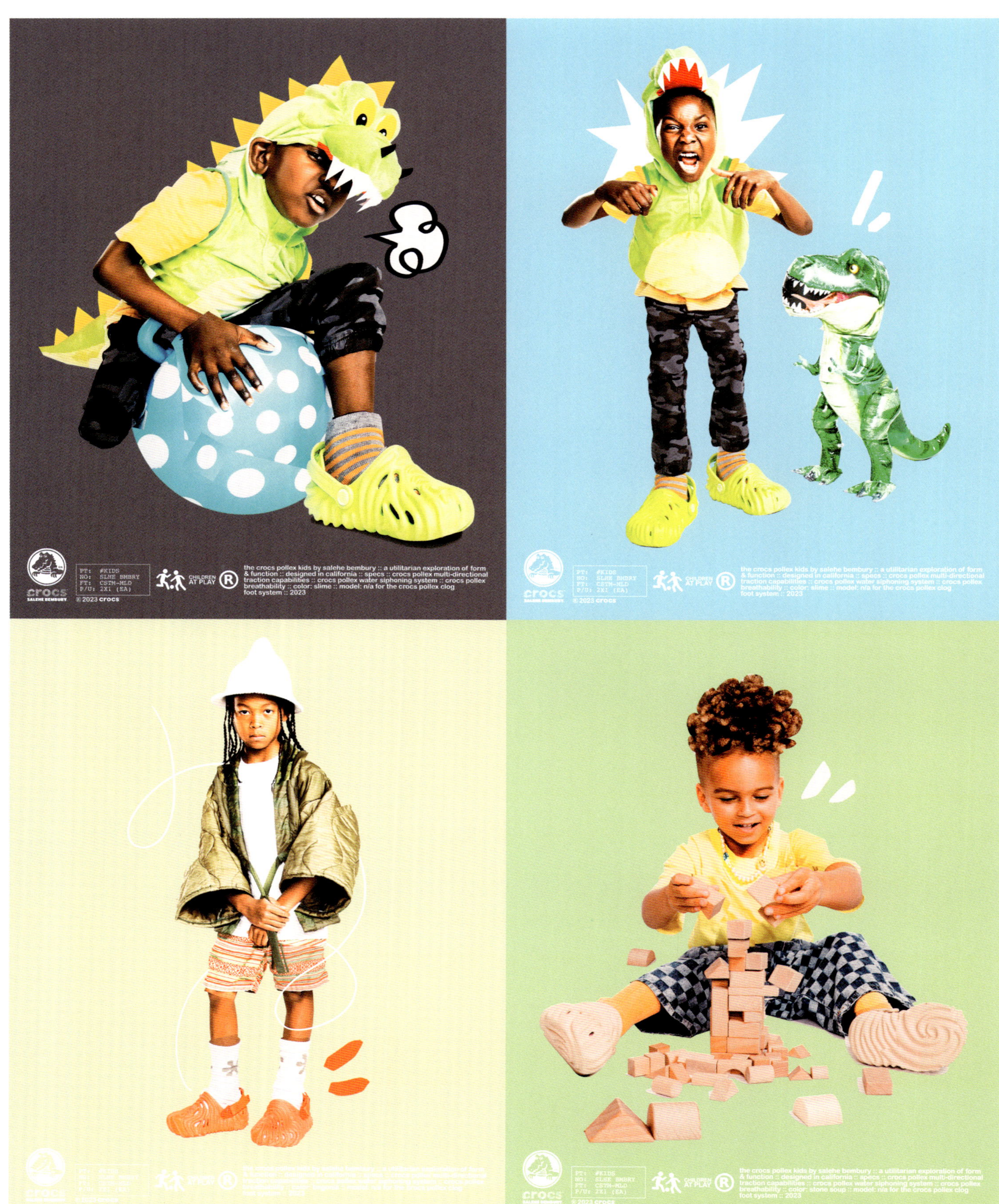

Crocs Pollex by Salehe Bembury Kids campaign

228

(2020)

CROCS

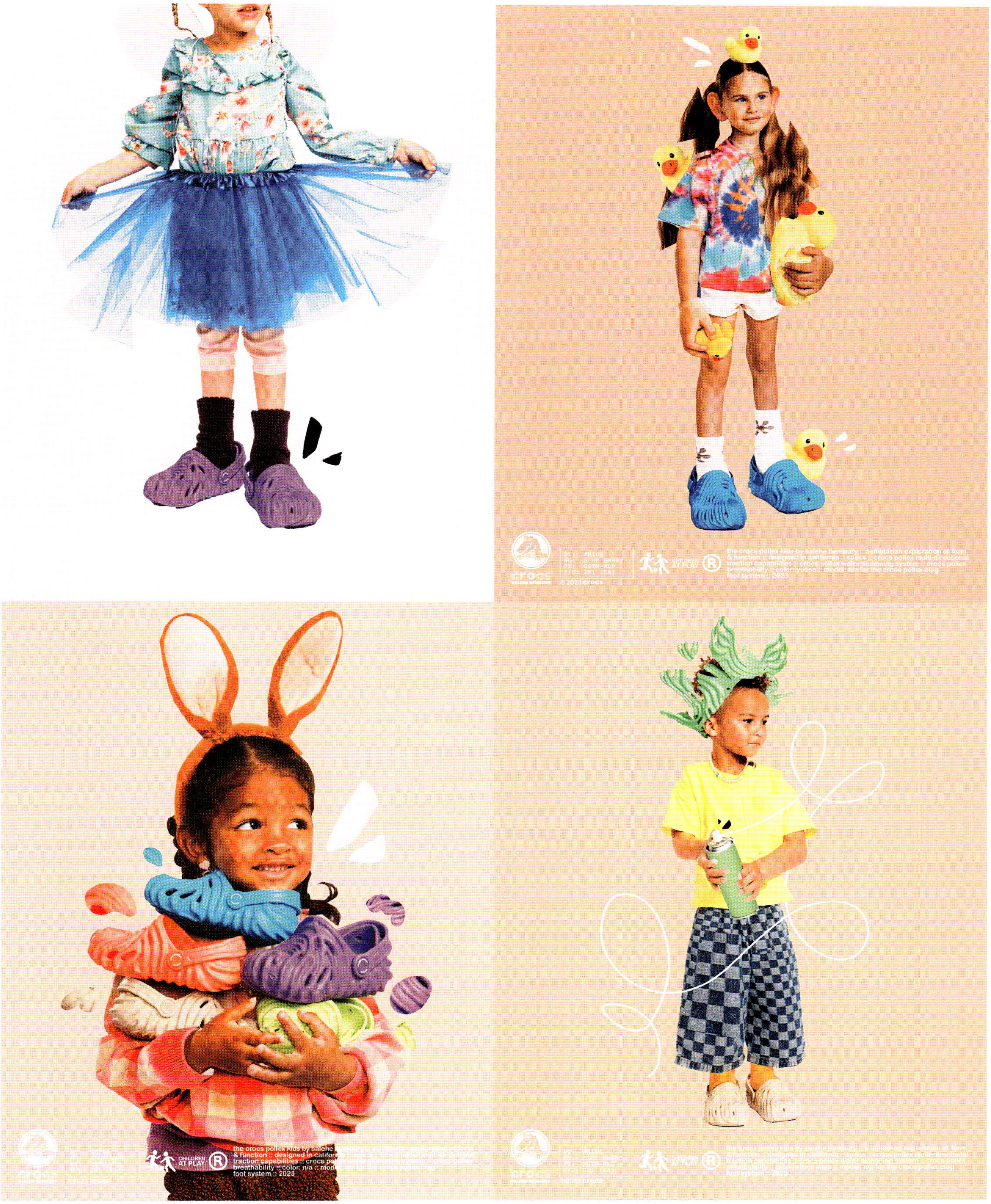

Crocs Pollex by Salehe Bembury Kids campaign

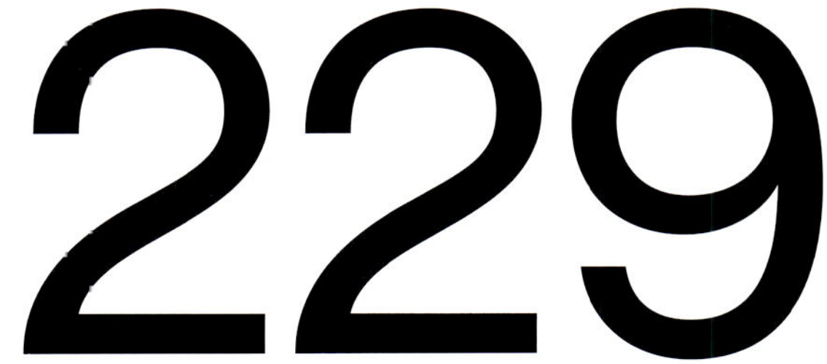

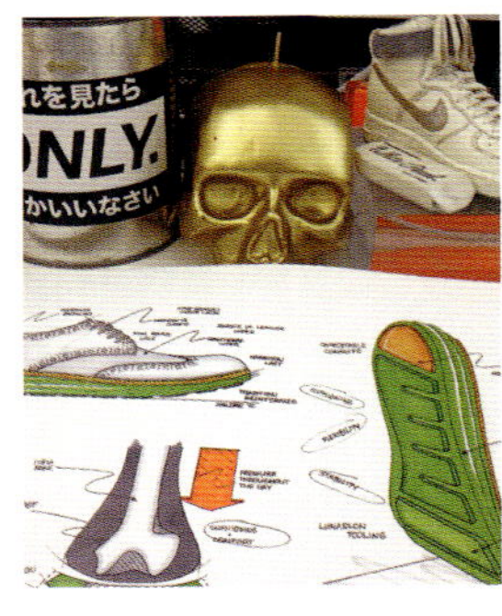
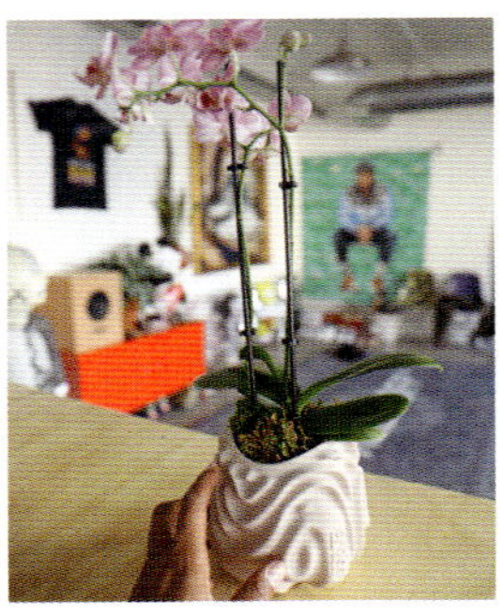
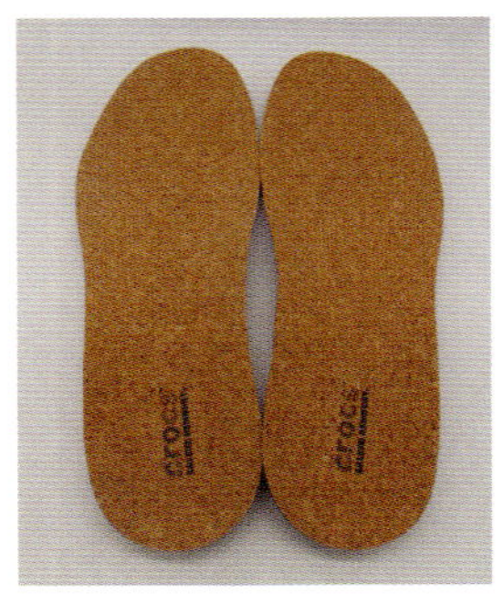
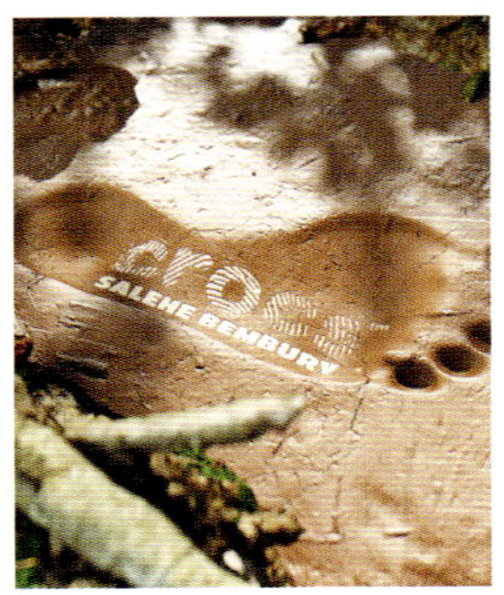

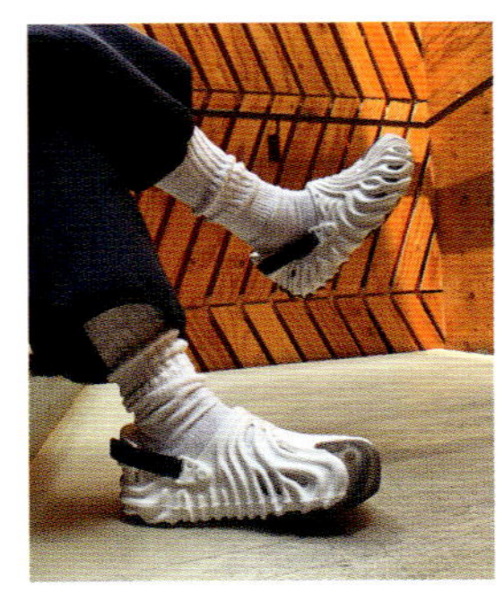
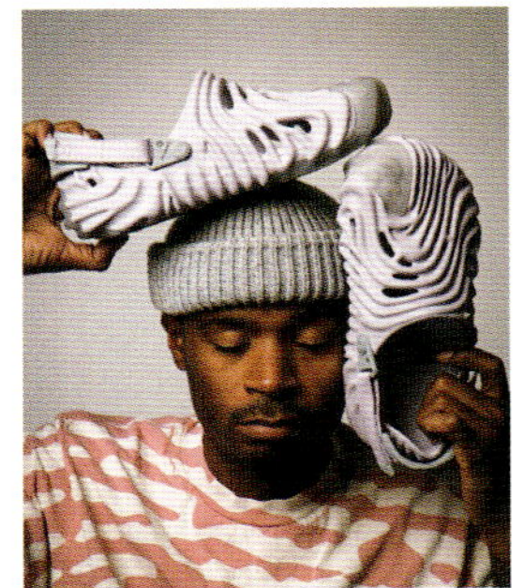
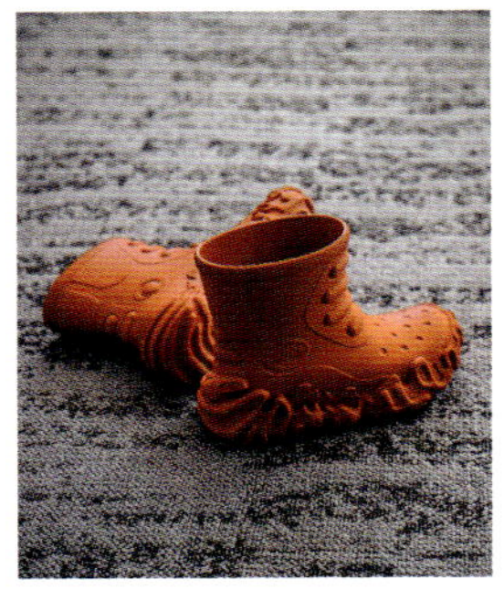
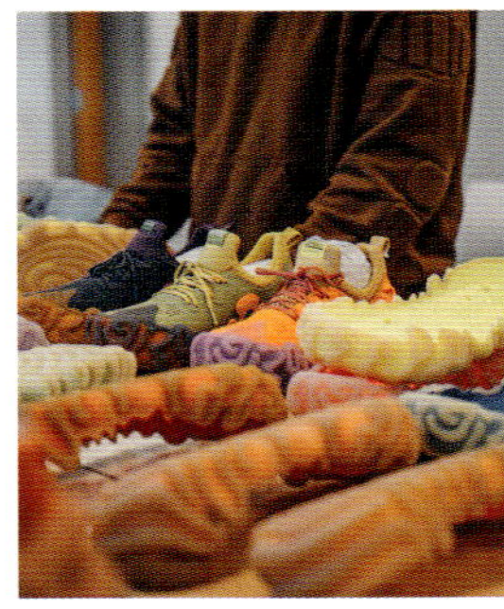
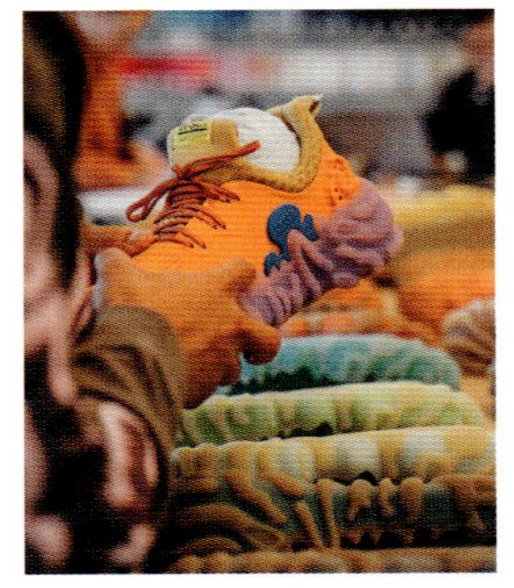
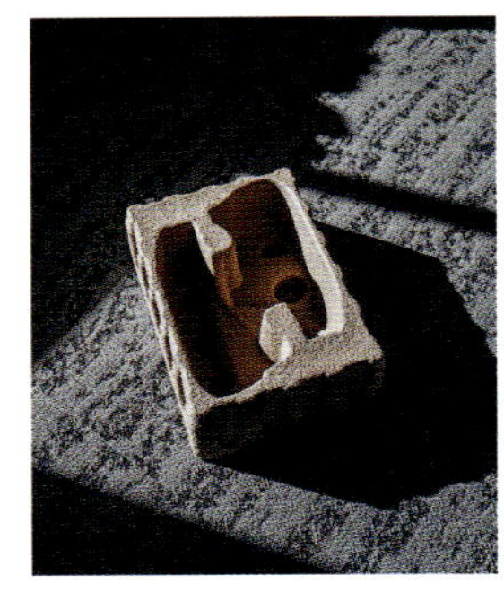
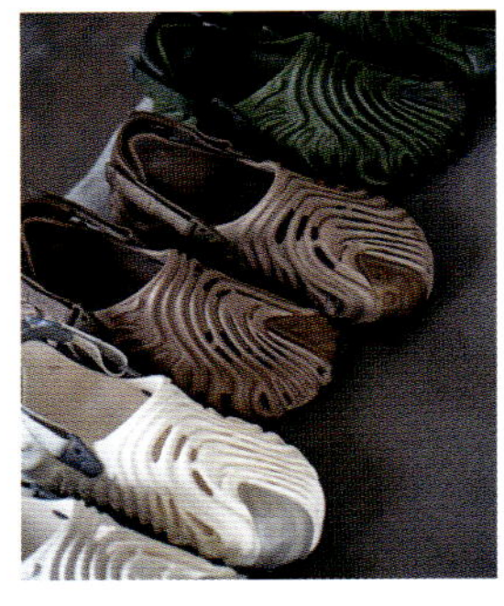
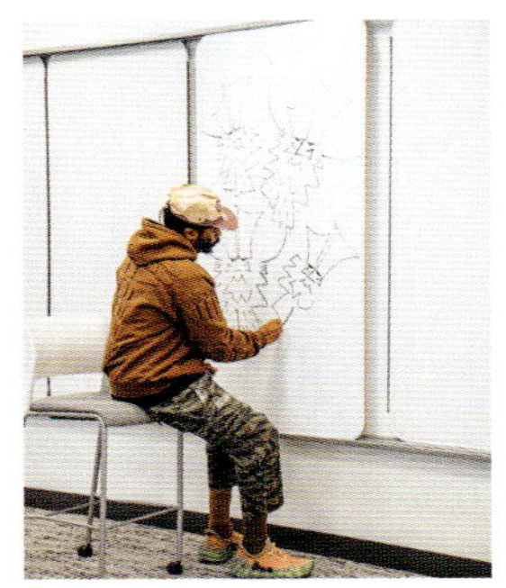
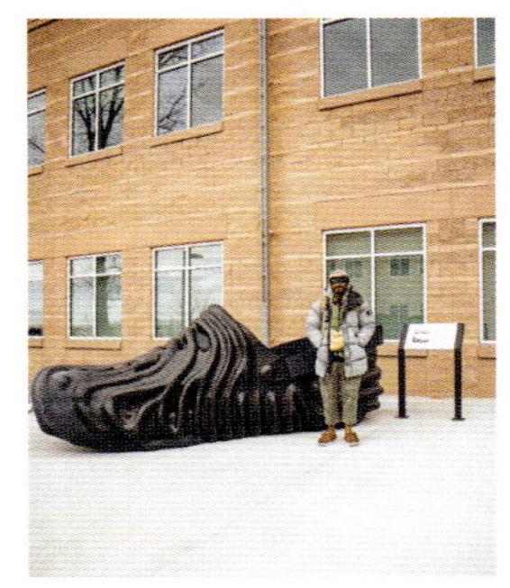
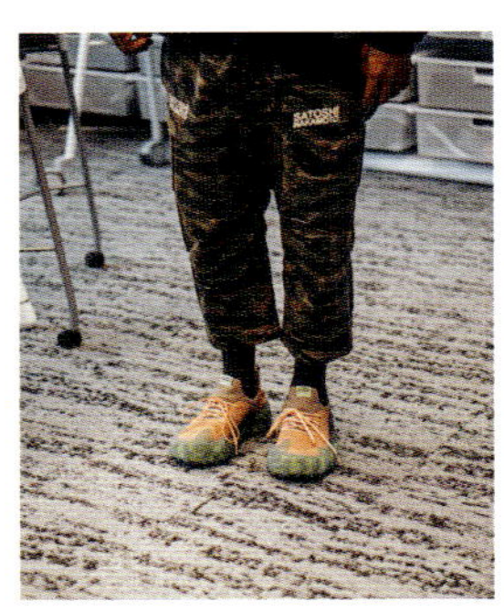
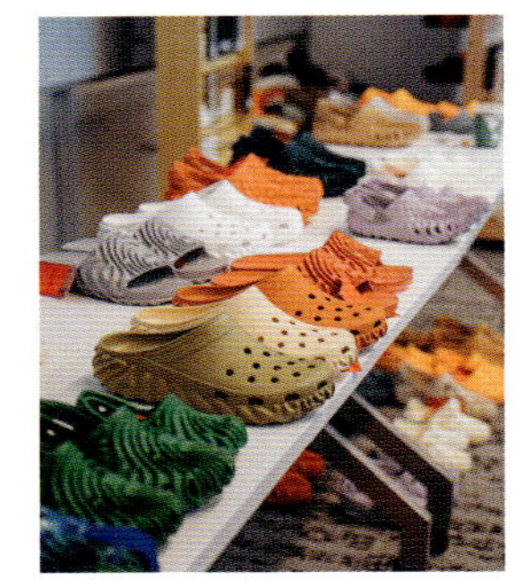
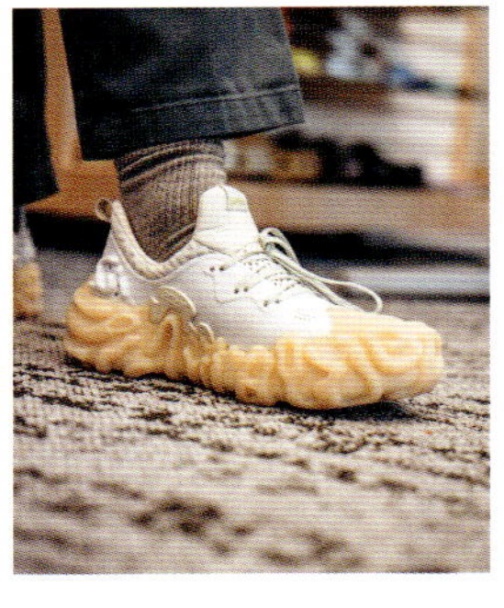
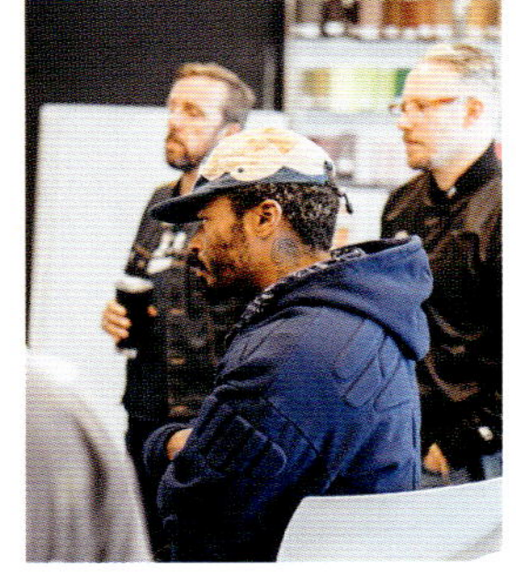
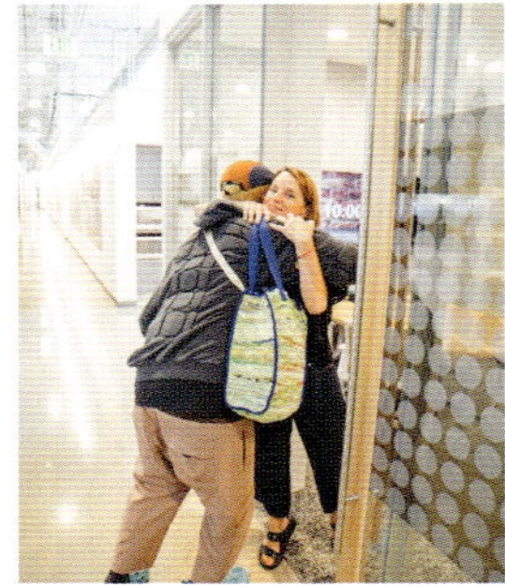
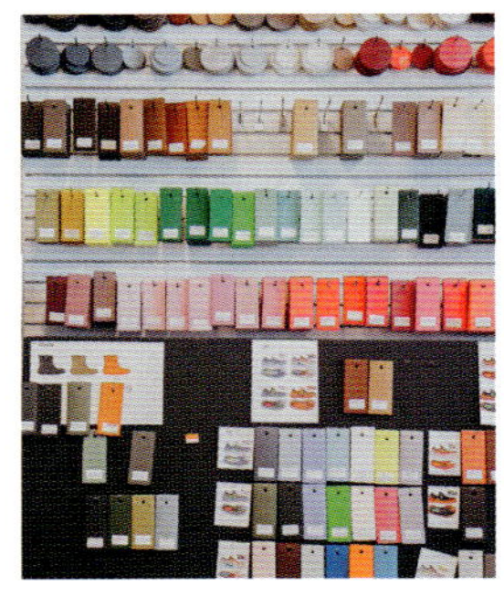
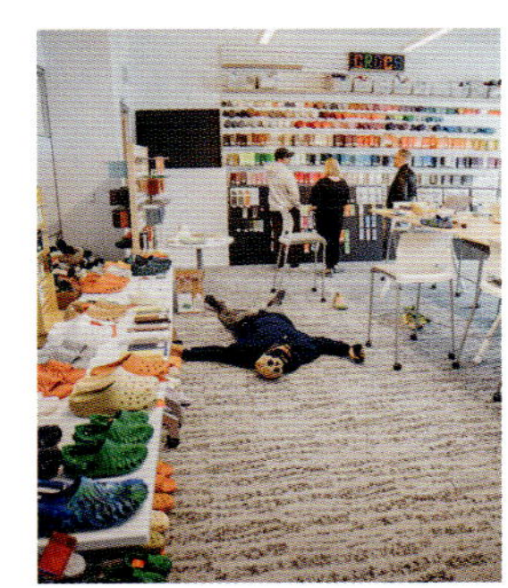
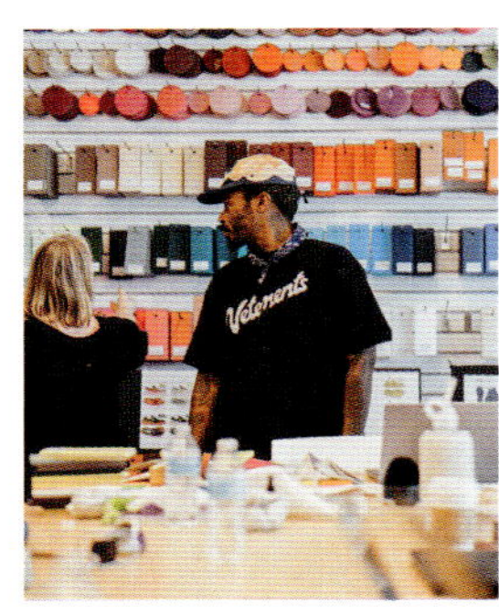

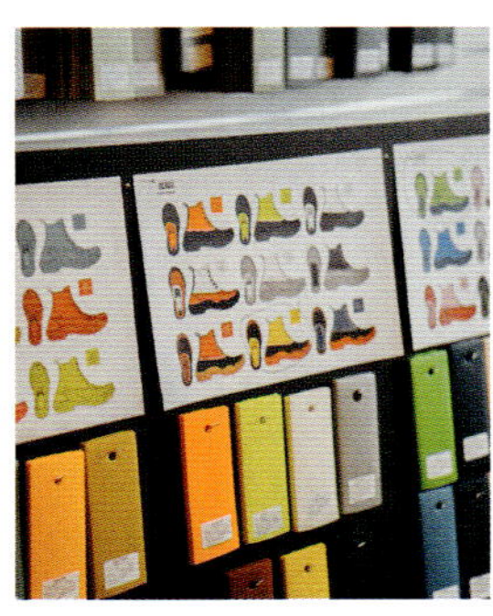
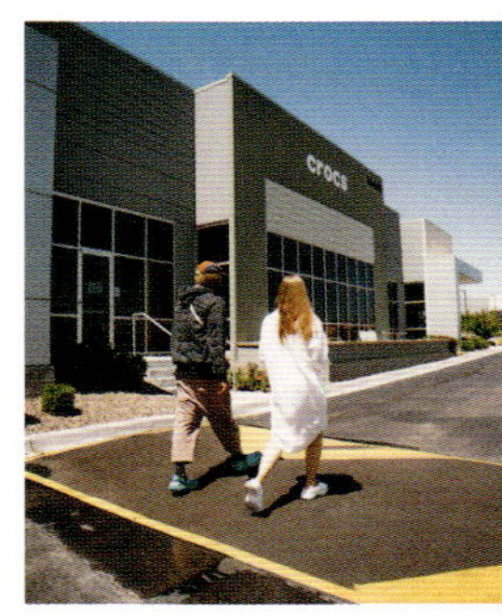

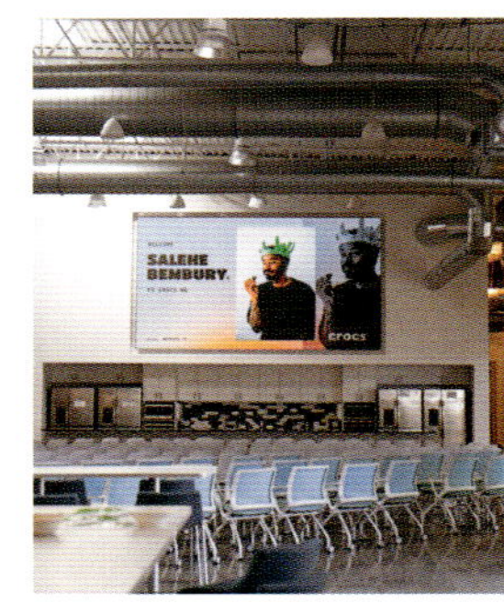

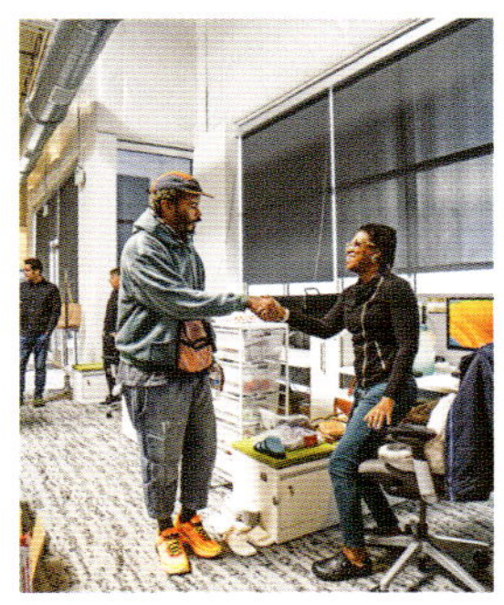

230

(2020)

CROCS

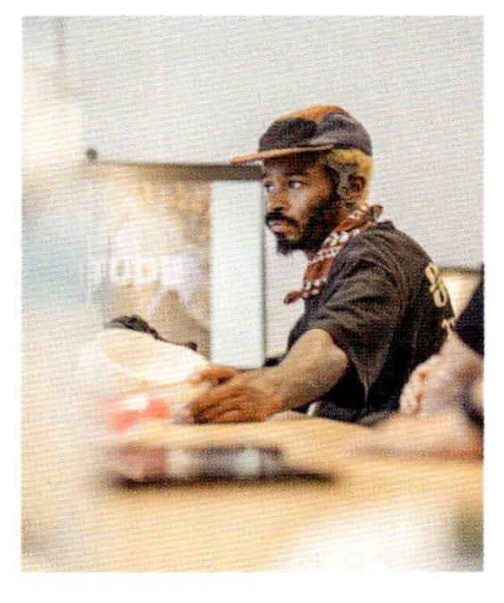
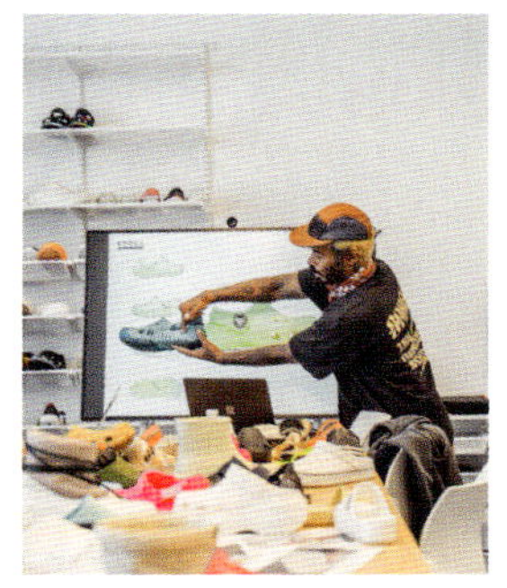
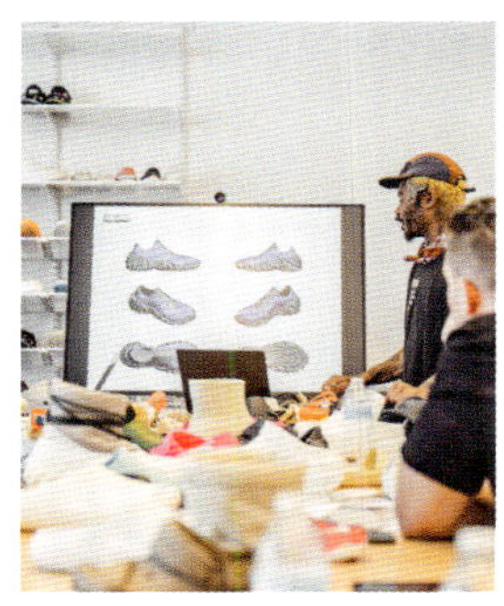
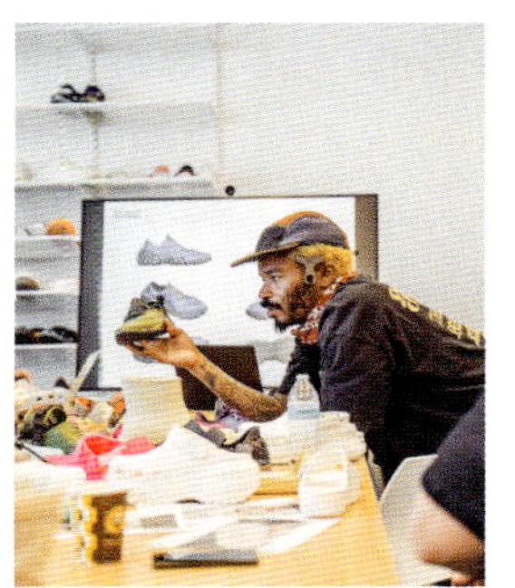
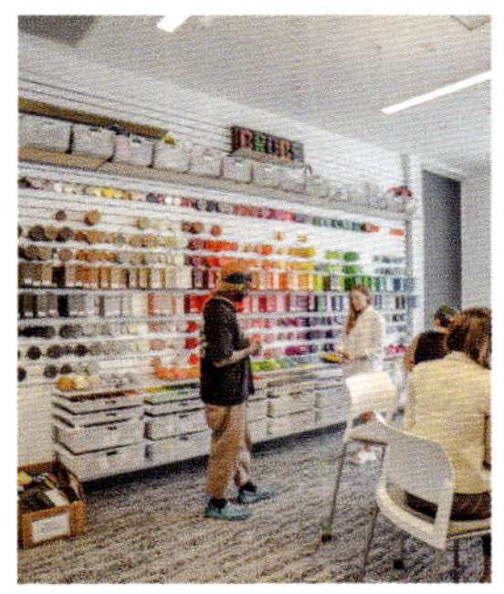
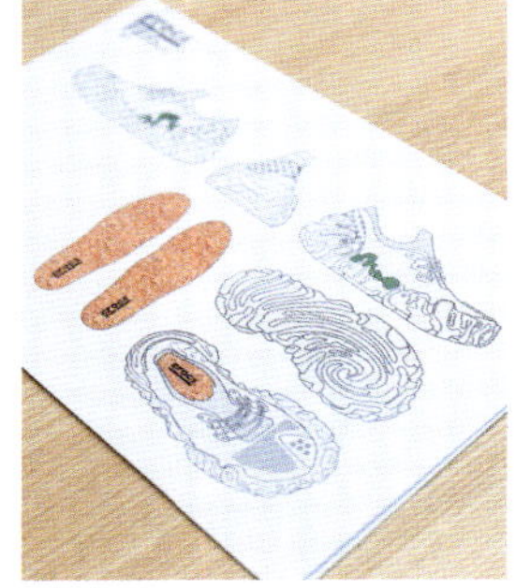
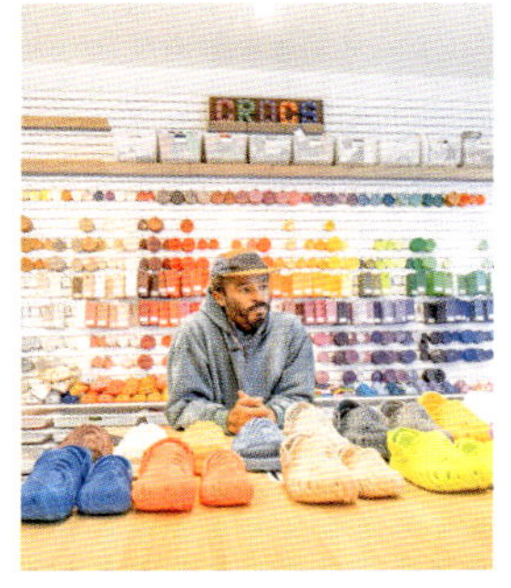
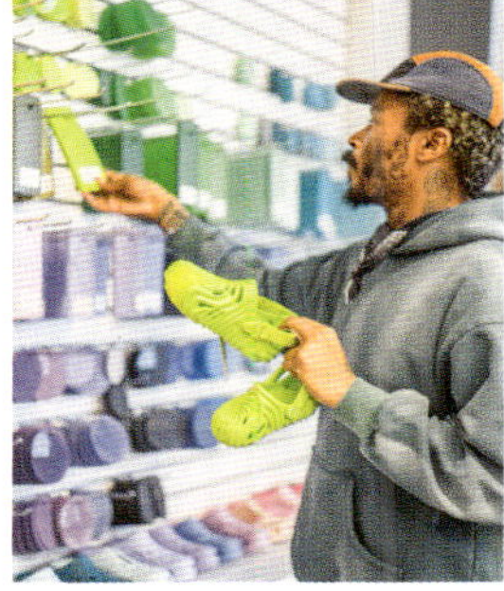
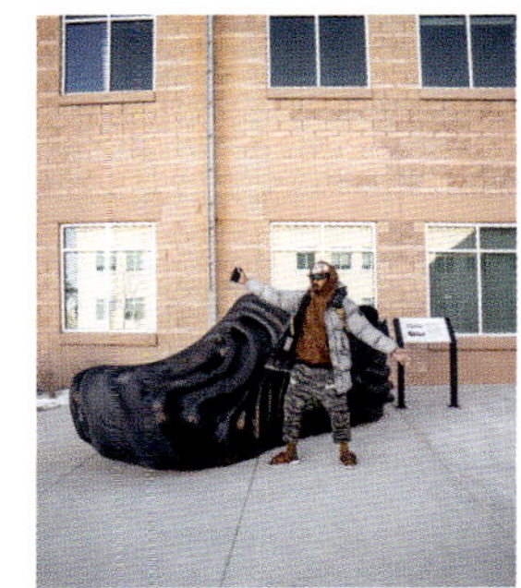
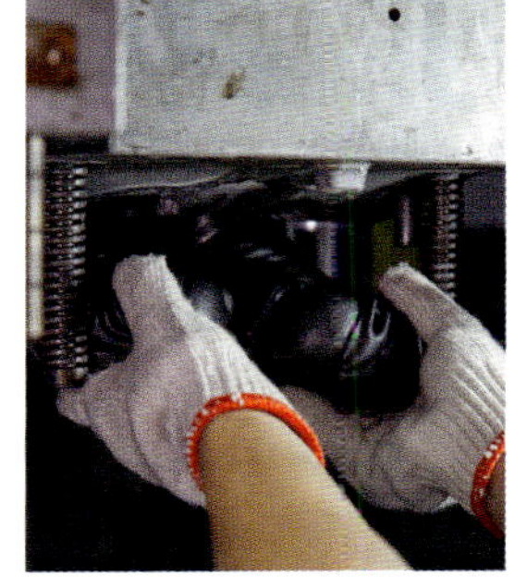
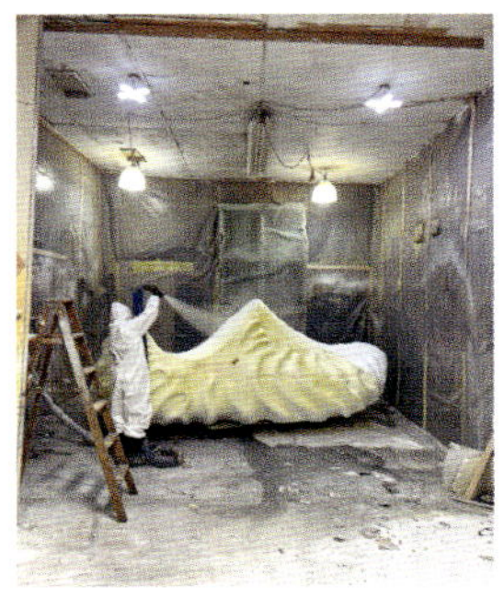
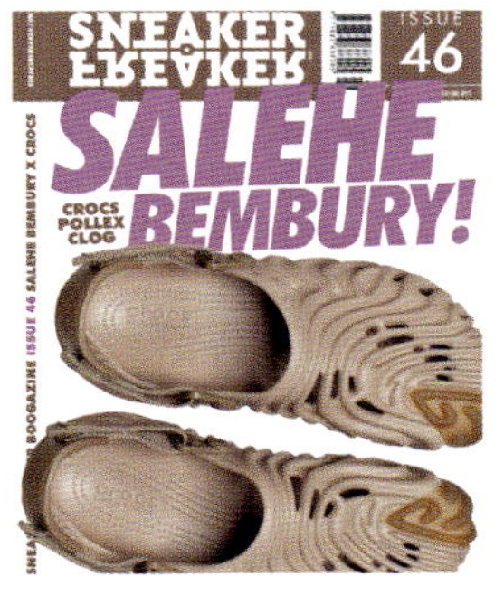
SNEAKER FREAKER
ISSUE
46
SALEHE BEMBURY!
CROCS
POLLEX
CLOG
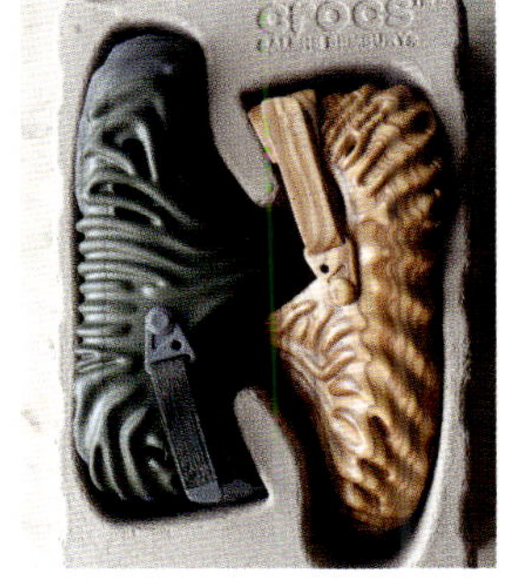
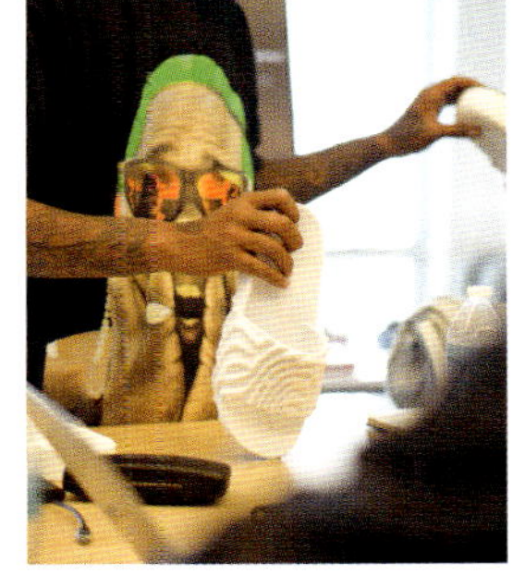
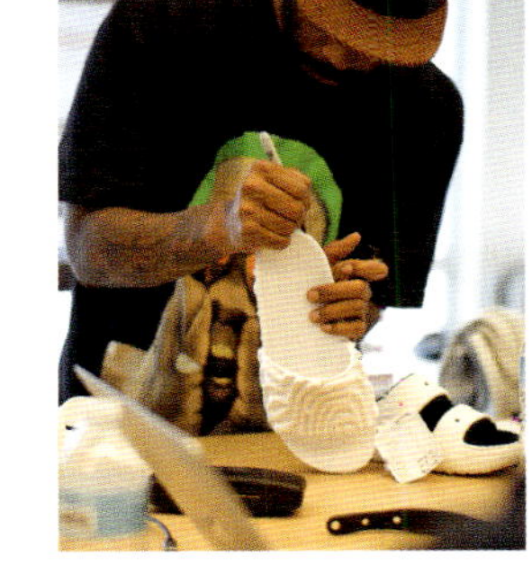
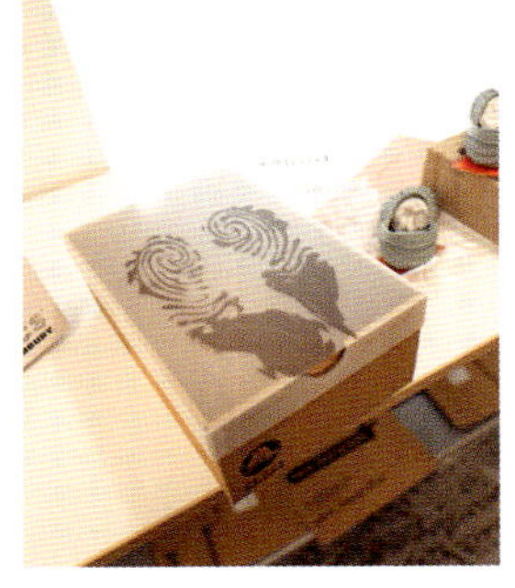
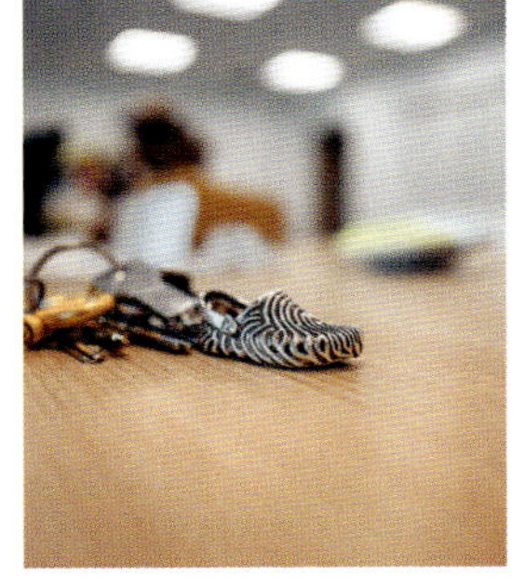
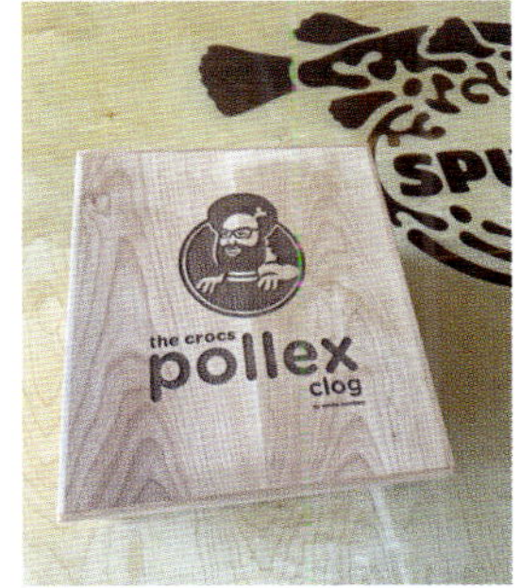
the crocs
pollex
clog
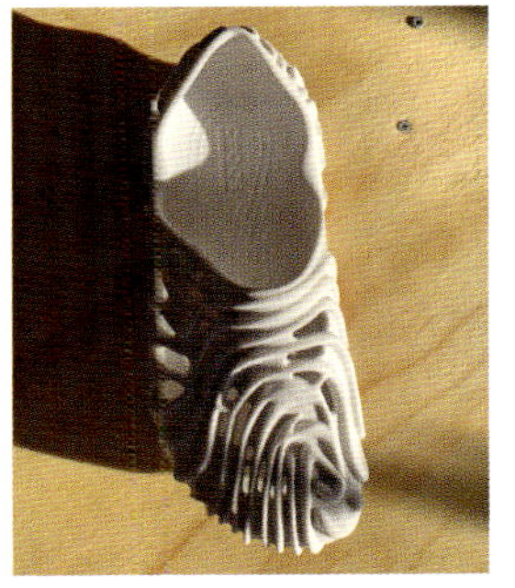
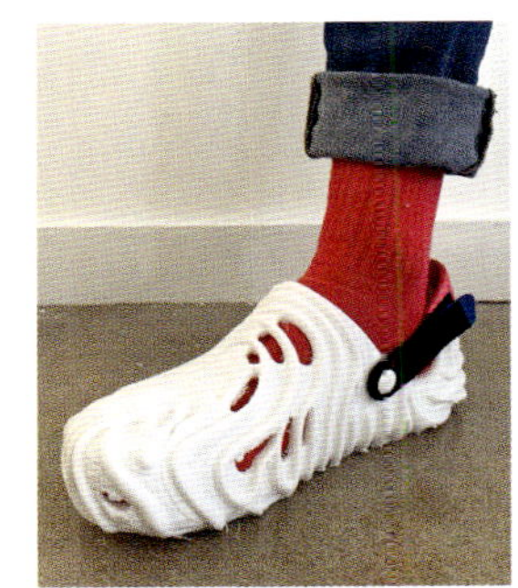
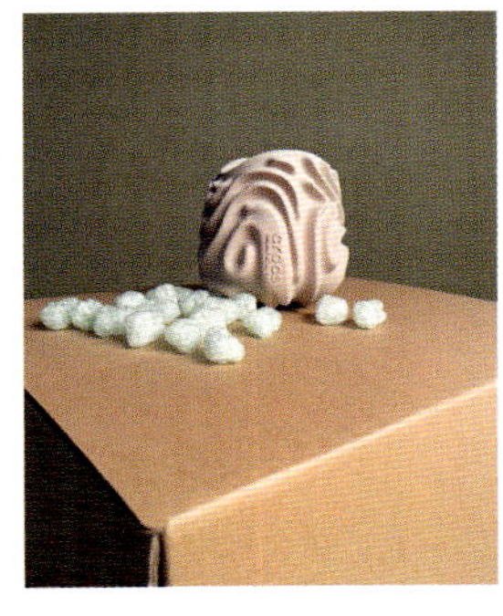
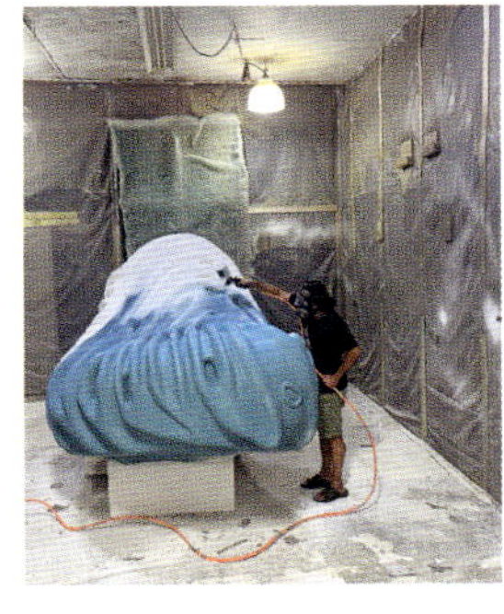
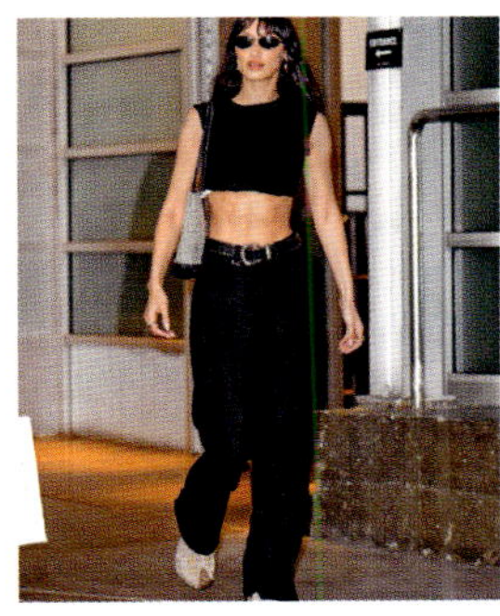
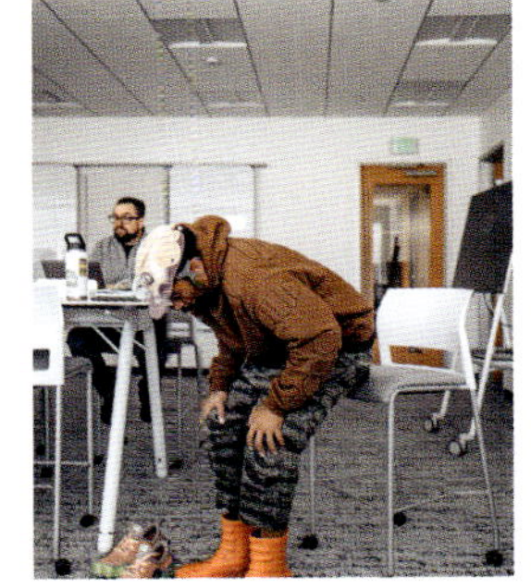
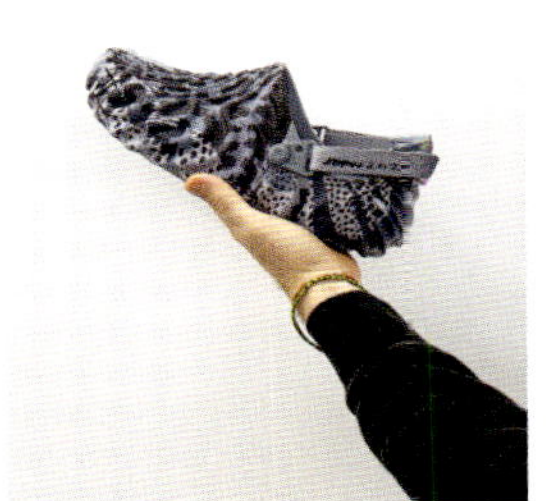

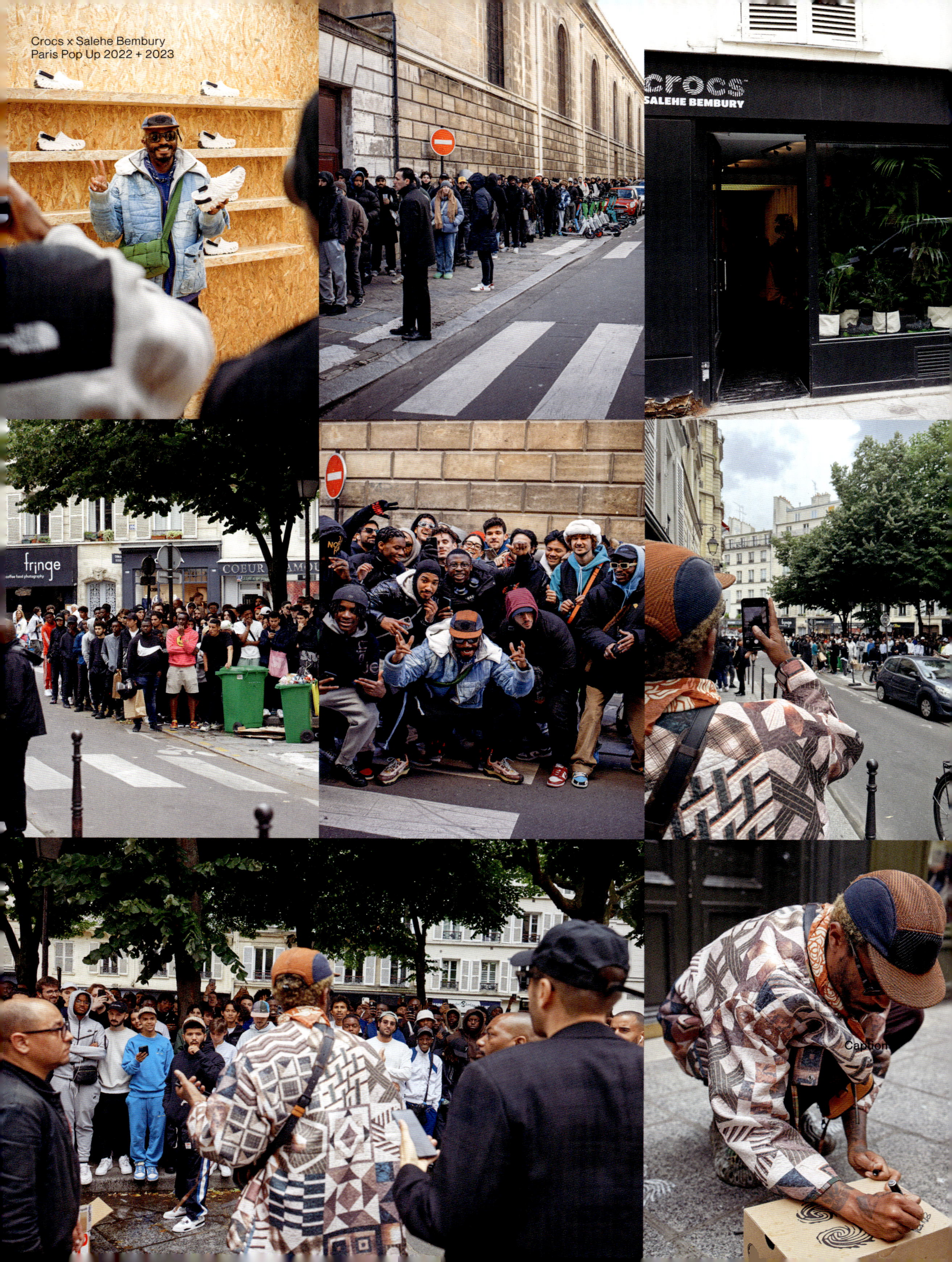

Crocs x Salehe Bembury
Paris Pop Up 2022 + 2023

Caption

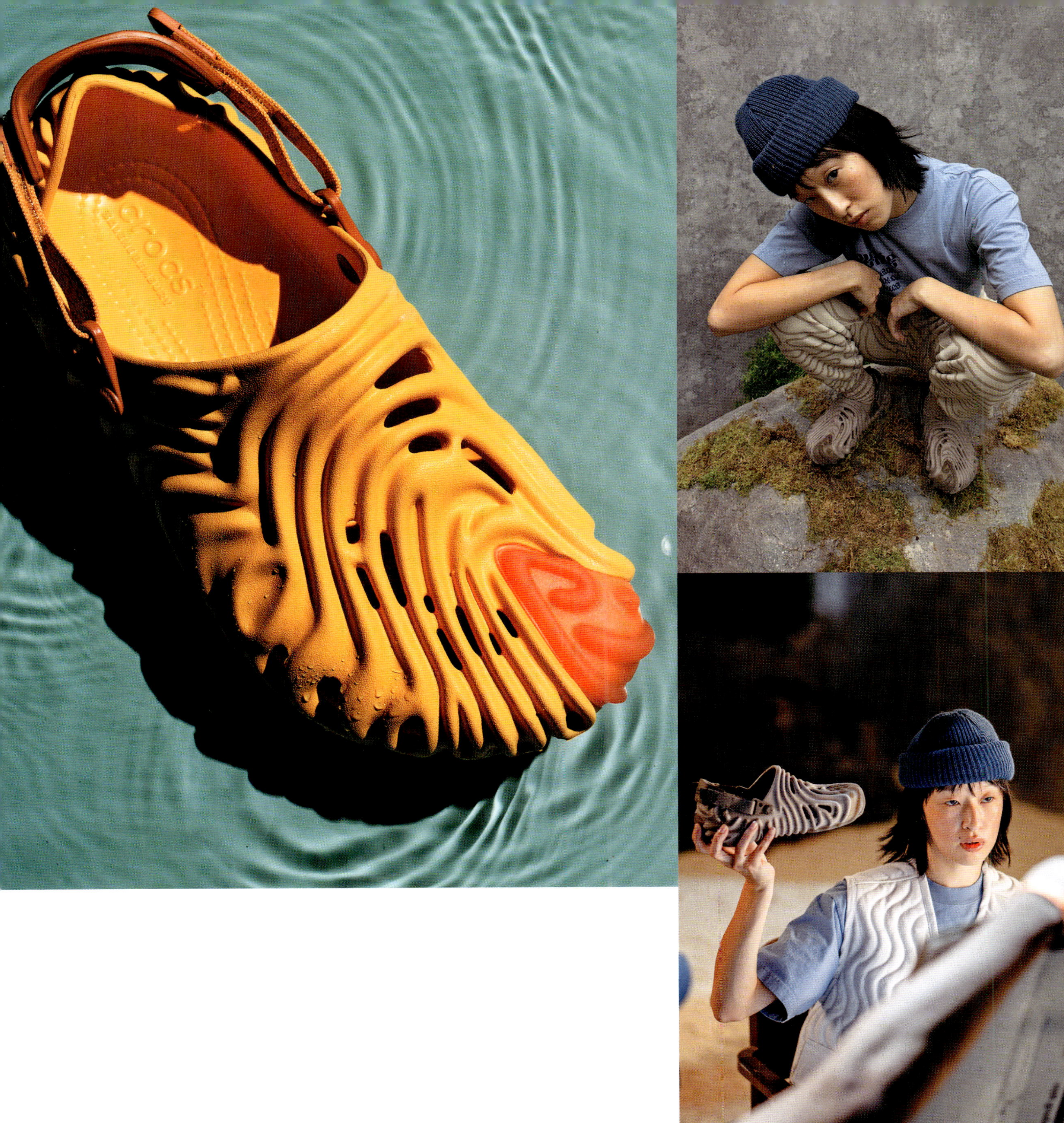

Crocs Pollex Campaign featuring Cynthia Erivo anc Jess Lin

233

CROCS

(2020)

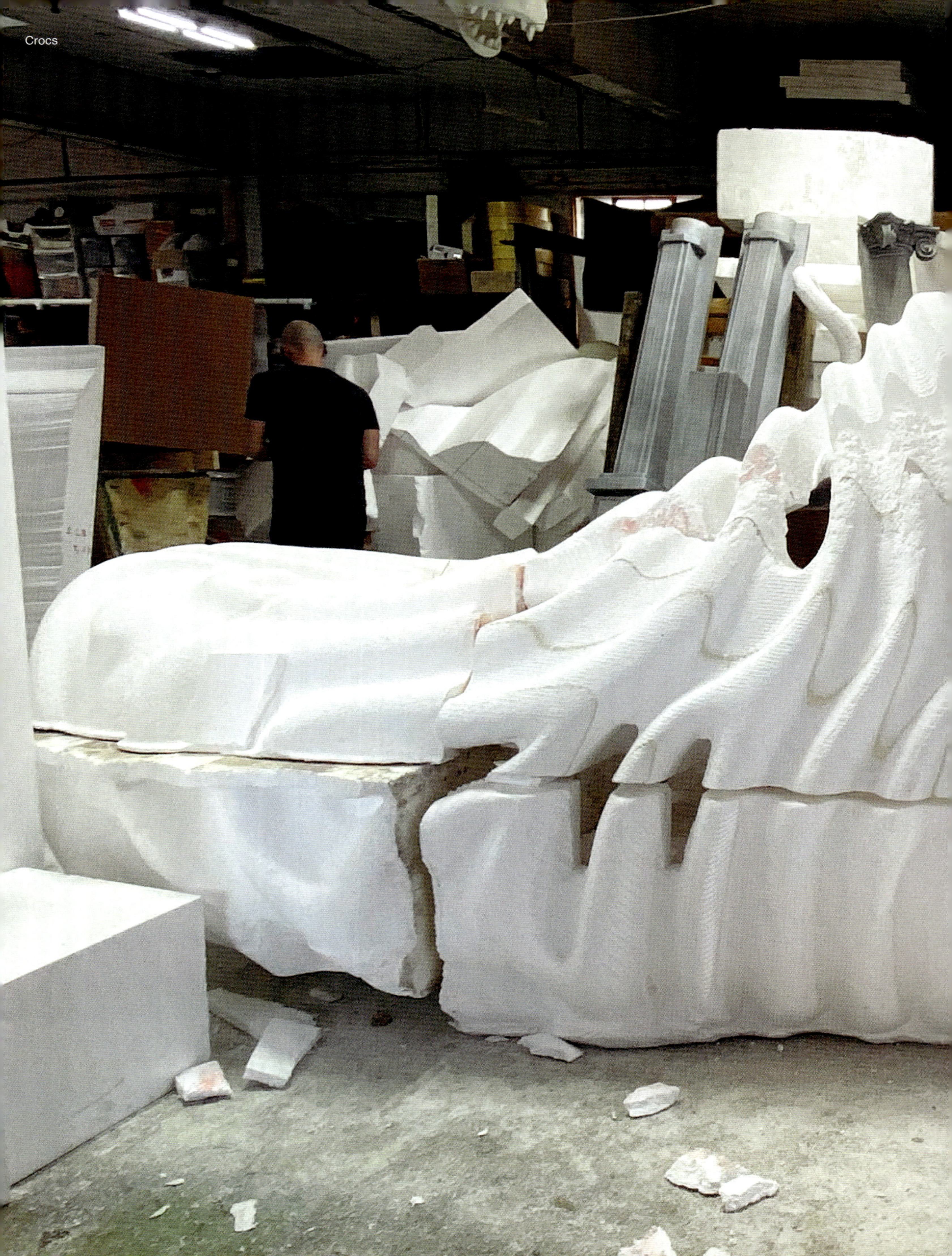

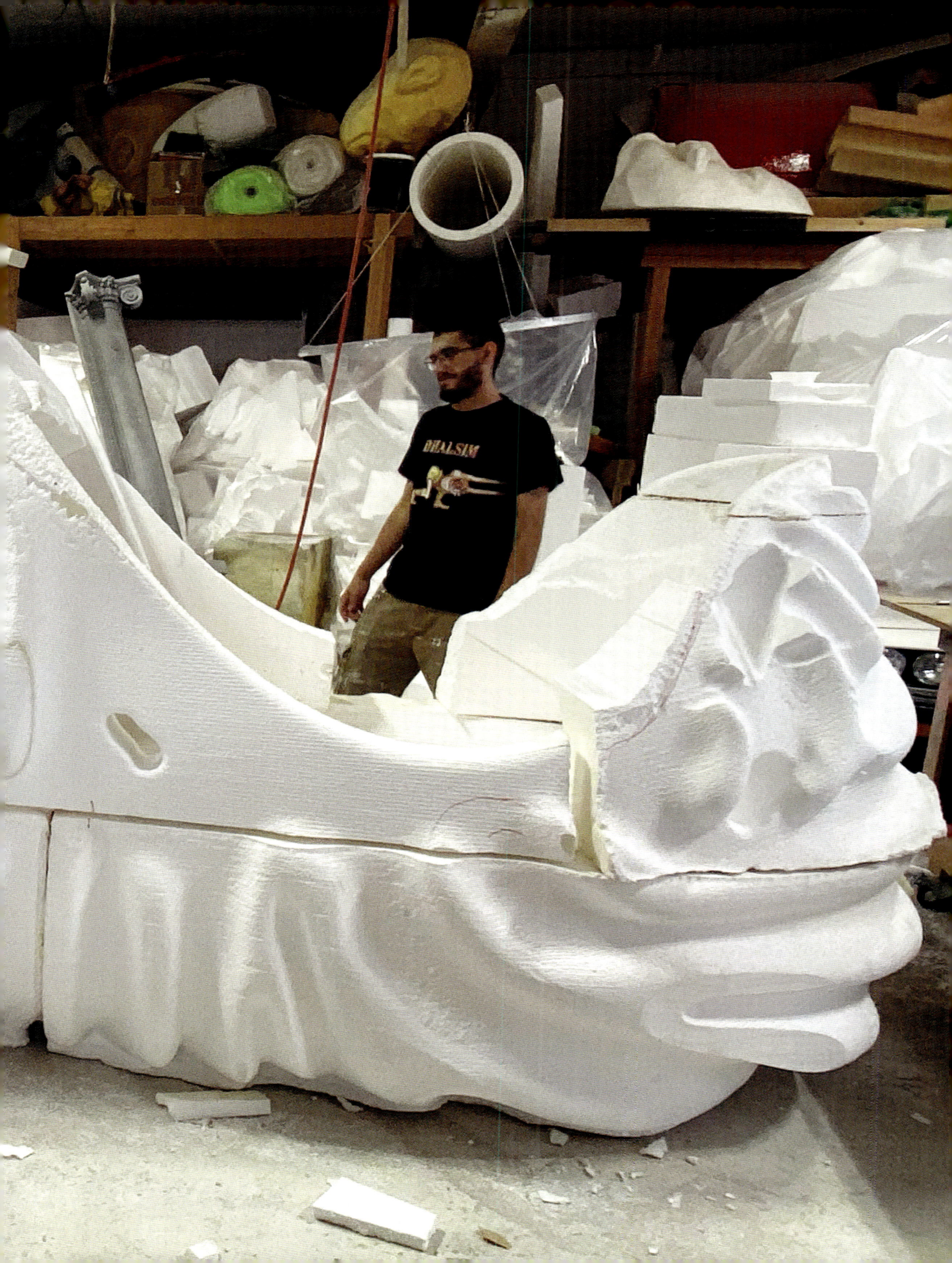
DHALSIM

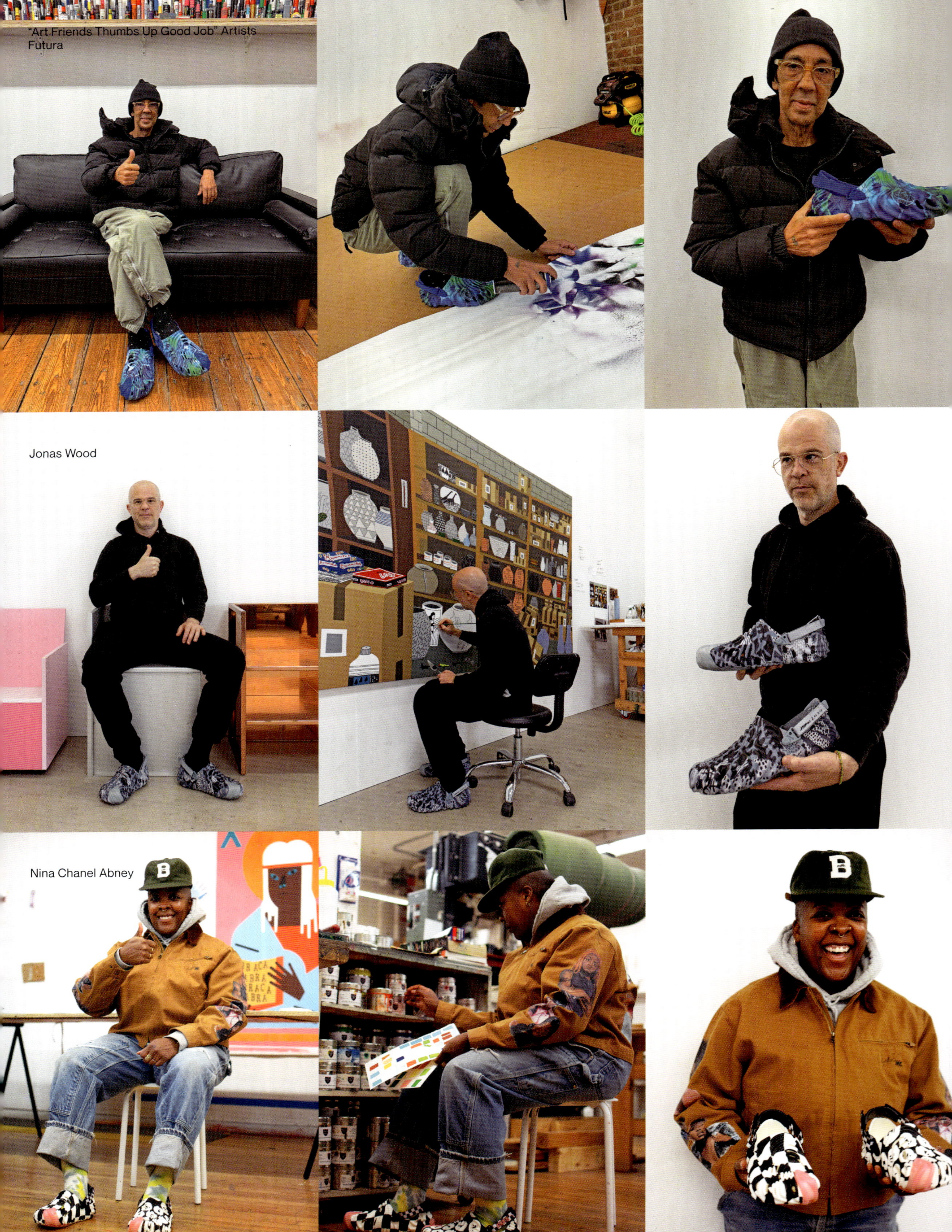

"Art Friends Thumbs Up Good Job" Artists
Futura

Jonas Wood

Nina Chanel Abney

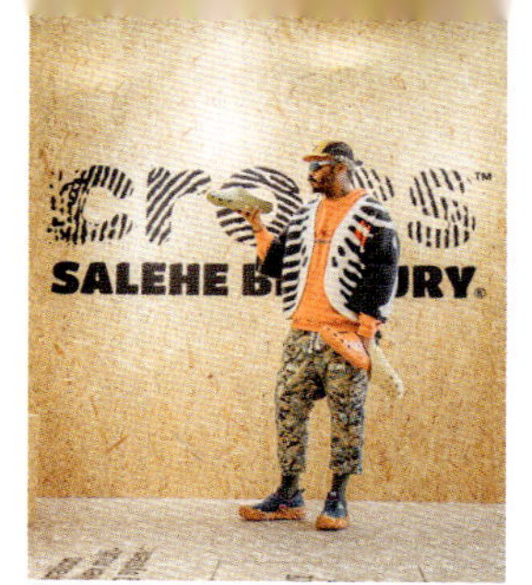
crocs
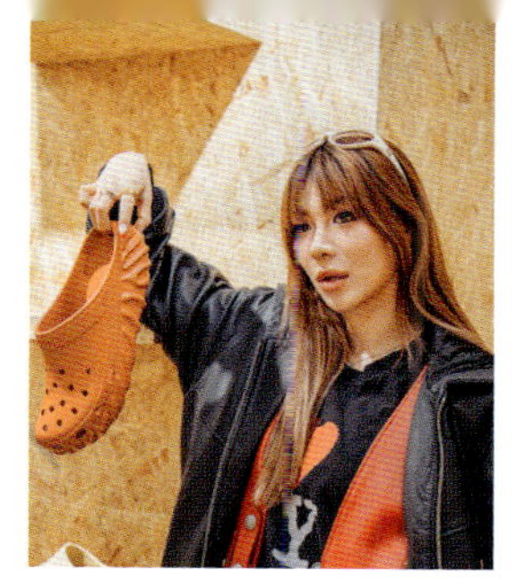
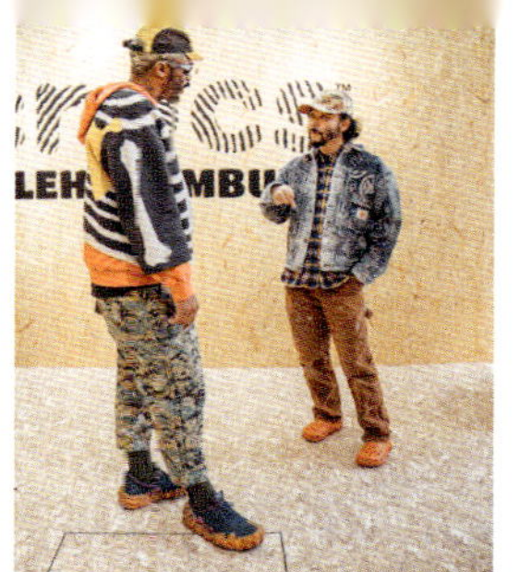
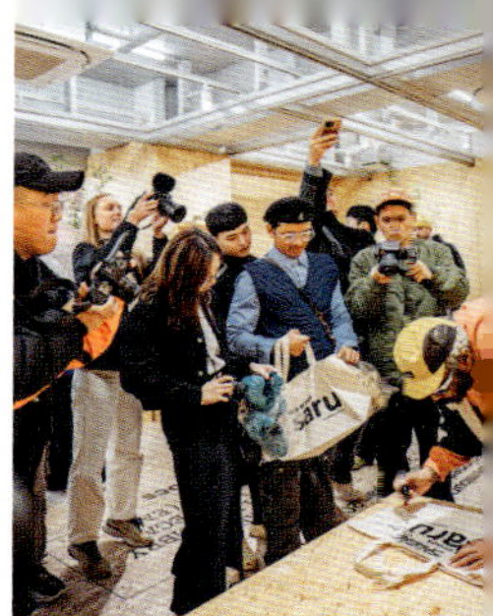
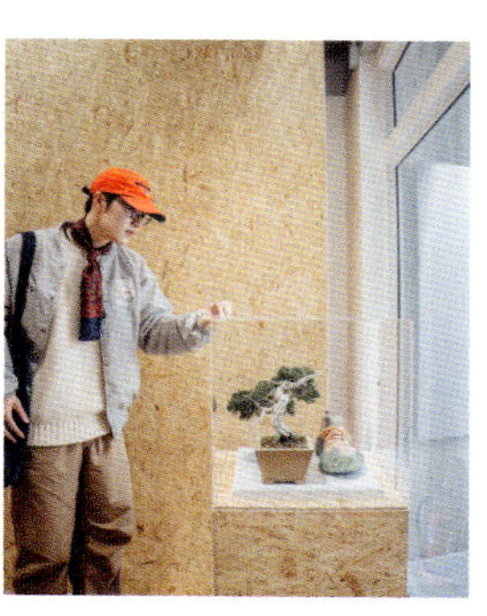
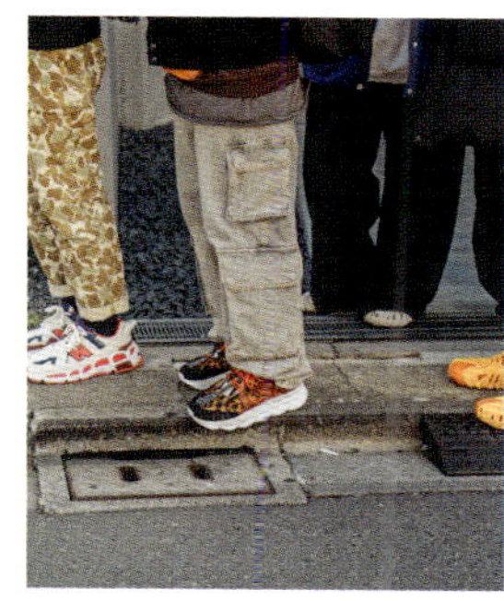
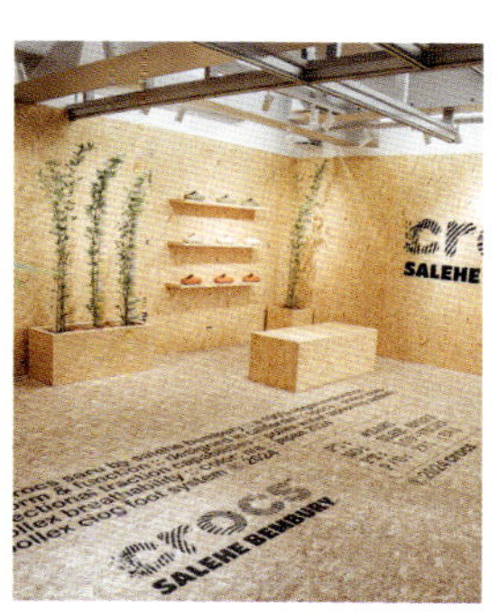
crocs
SALEHE BEMBURY
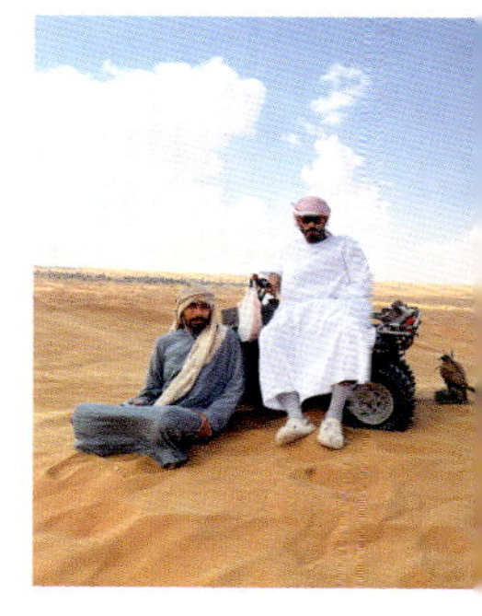
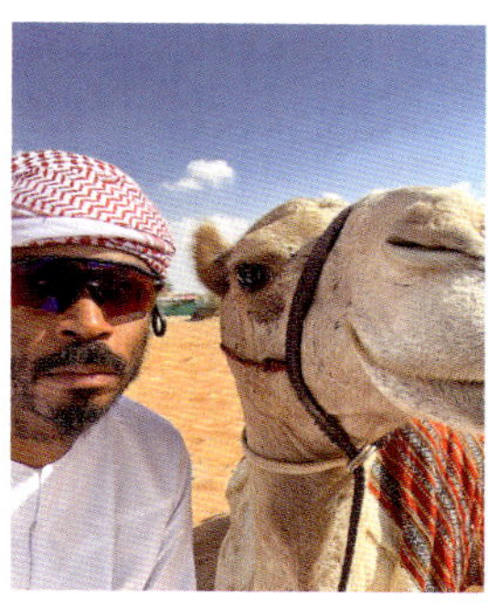
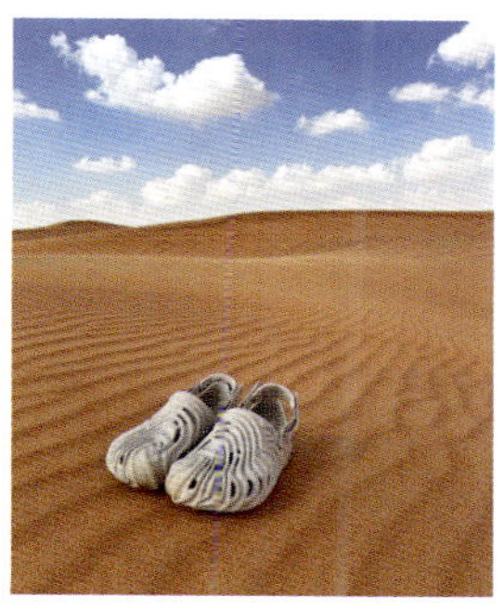
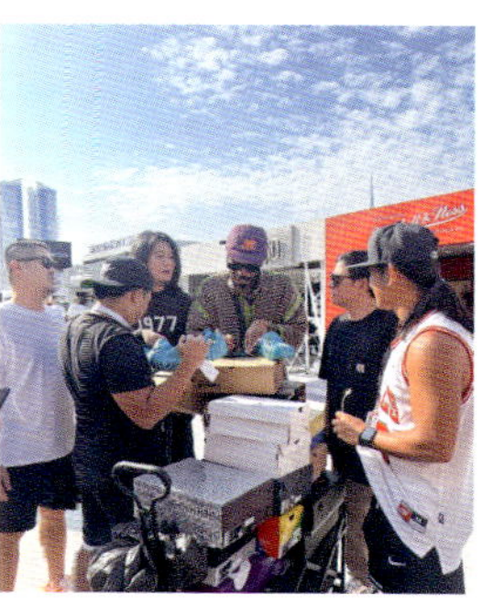
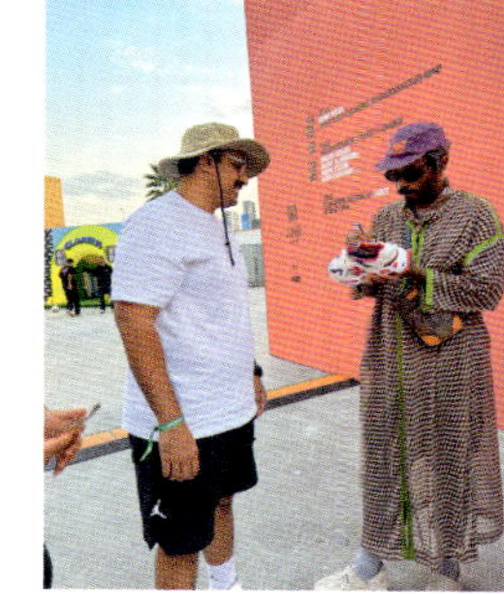
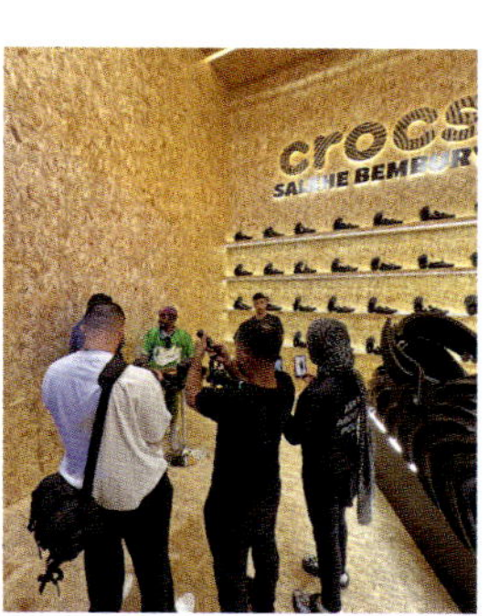
crocs
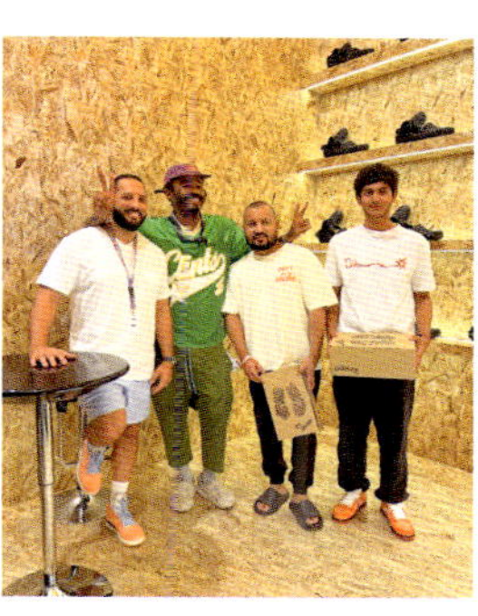
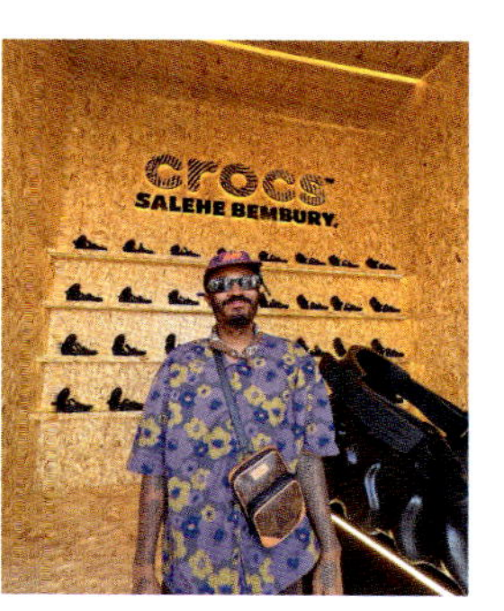
crocs
SALEHE BEMBURY
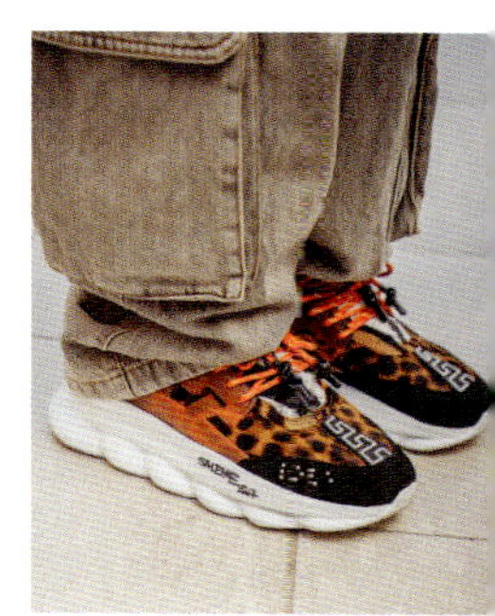

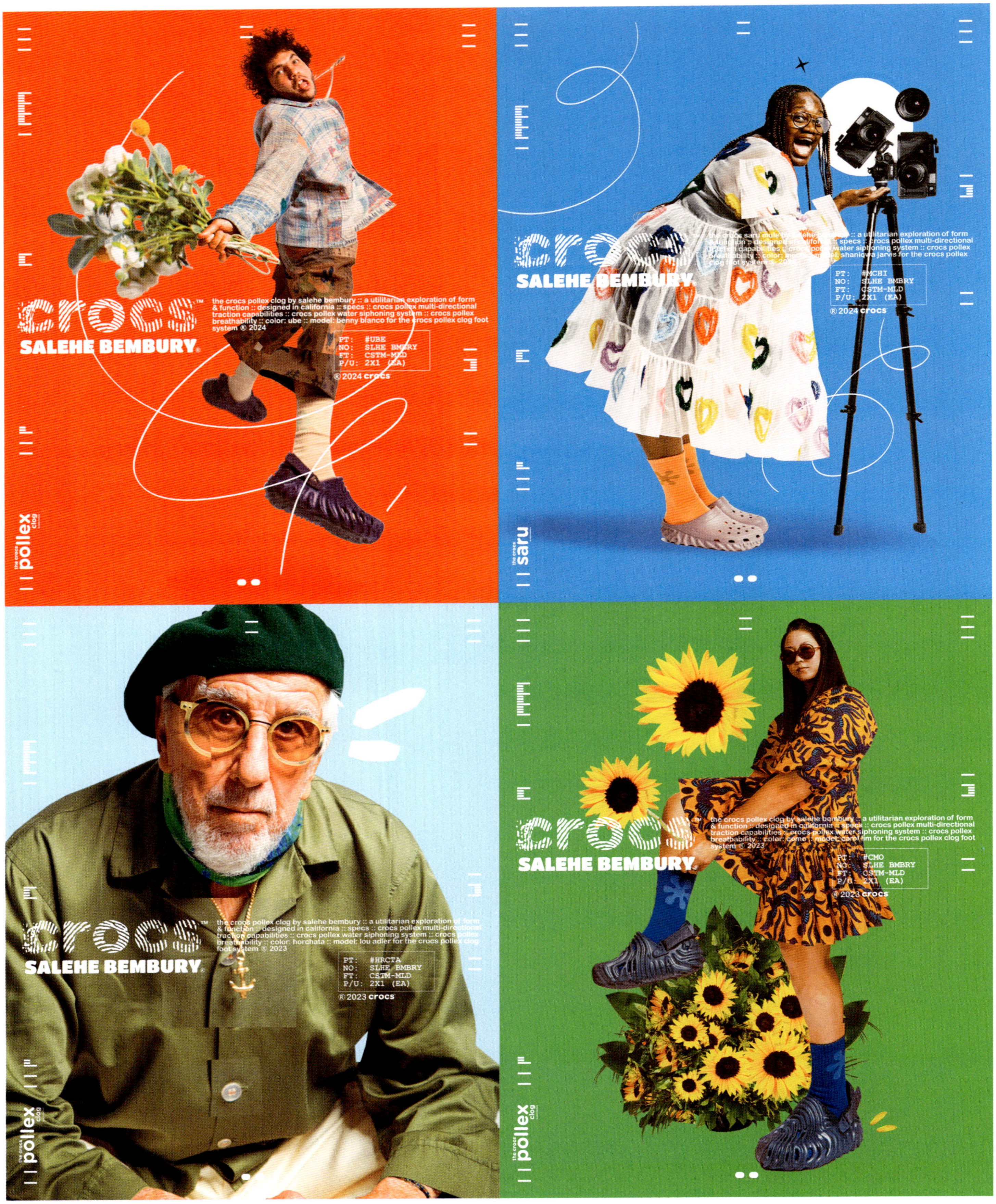

Crocs Pollex and Saru campaigns featuring: Benny Blanco, Shaniqwa Jarvis, Lou Adler, Carol Lim

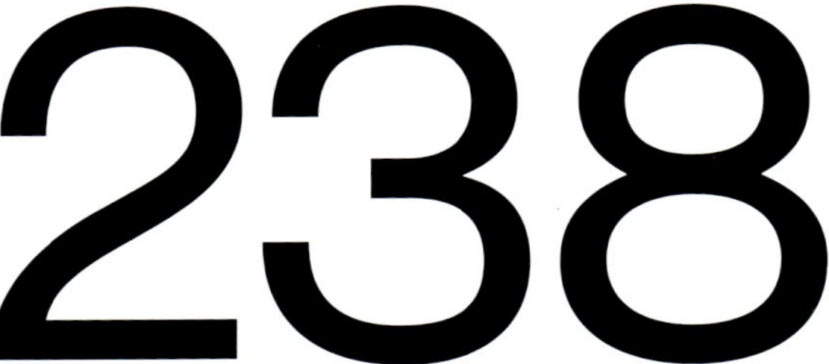

(2020)

CROCS

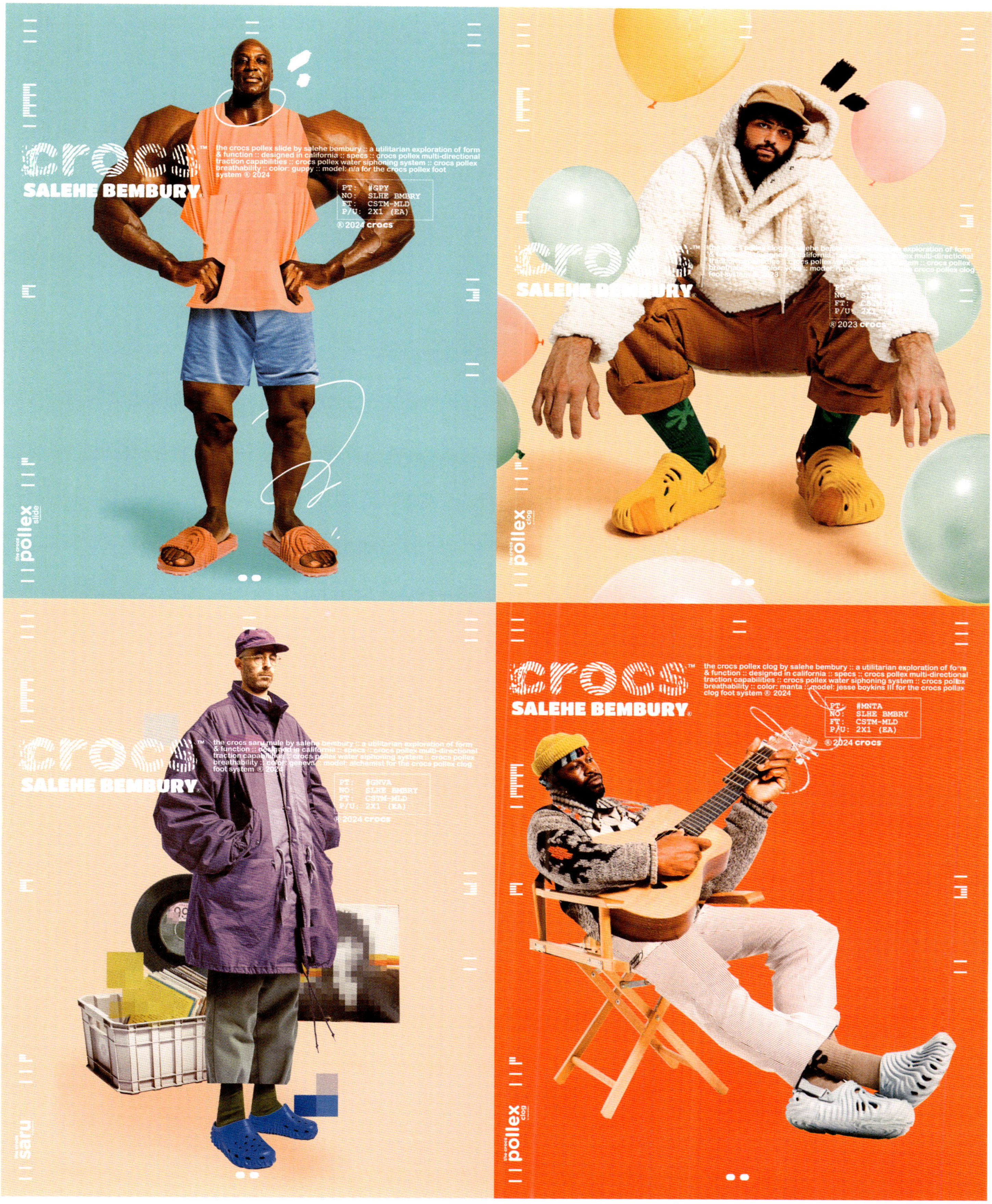

Crocs Pollex and Saru campaigns featuring: Muscles by Monty, Noah Centineo, Alchemist, Jesse Boykins

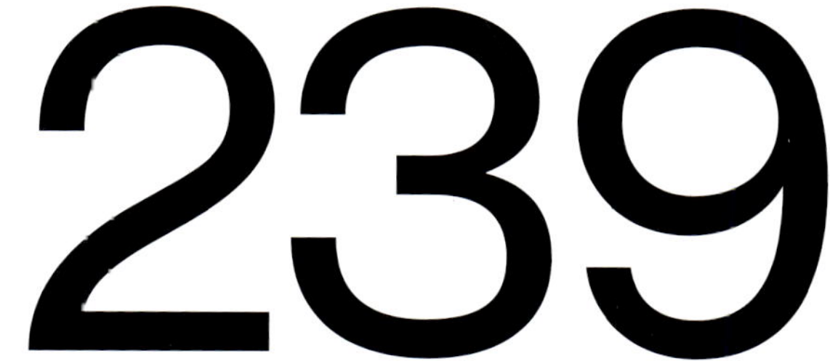

CROCS (2020)

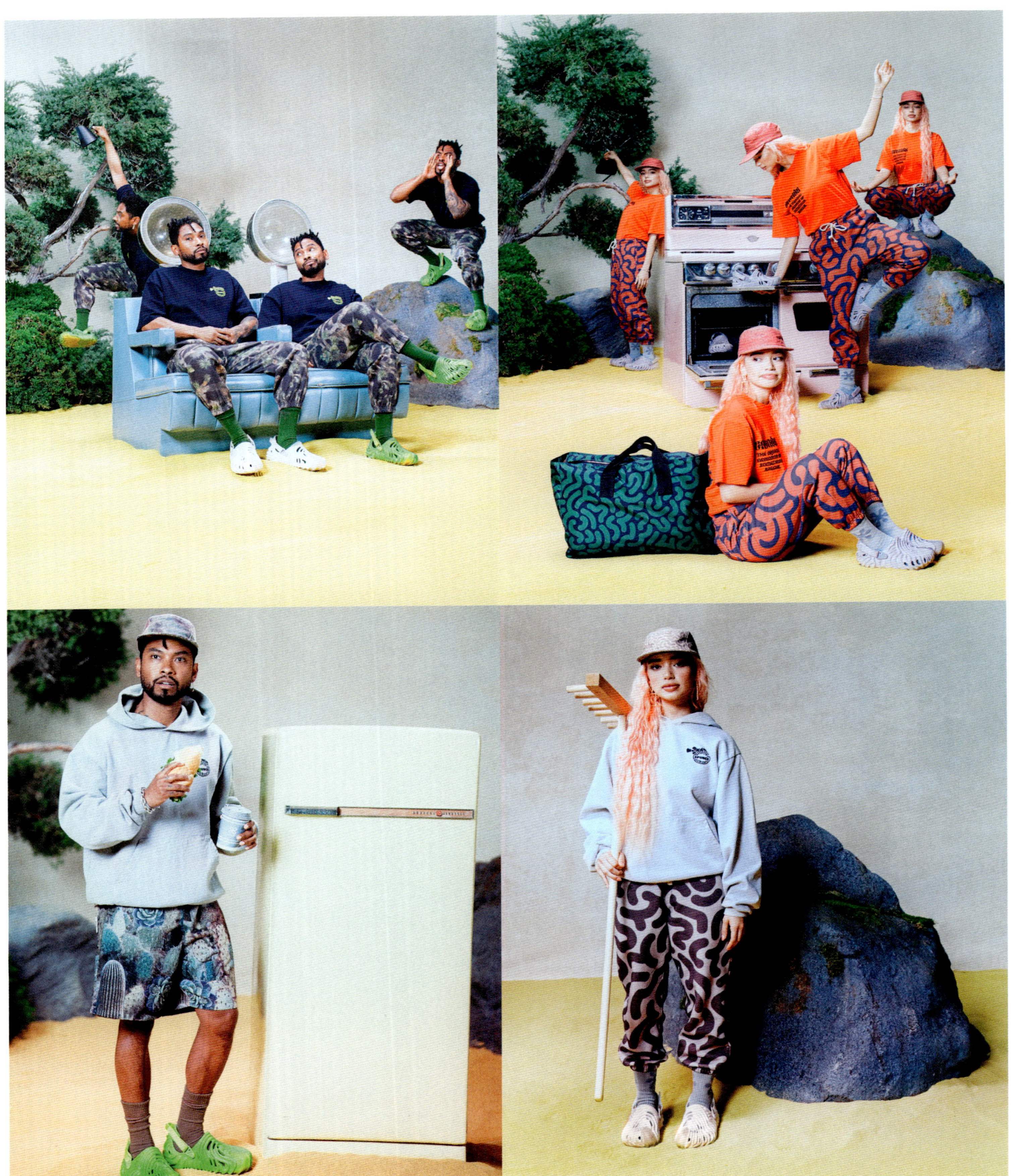

Miguel for Crocs x Salehe Bembury

Sabrina for Crocs x Salehe Bembury

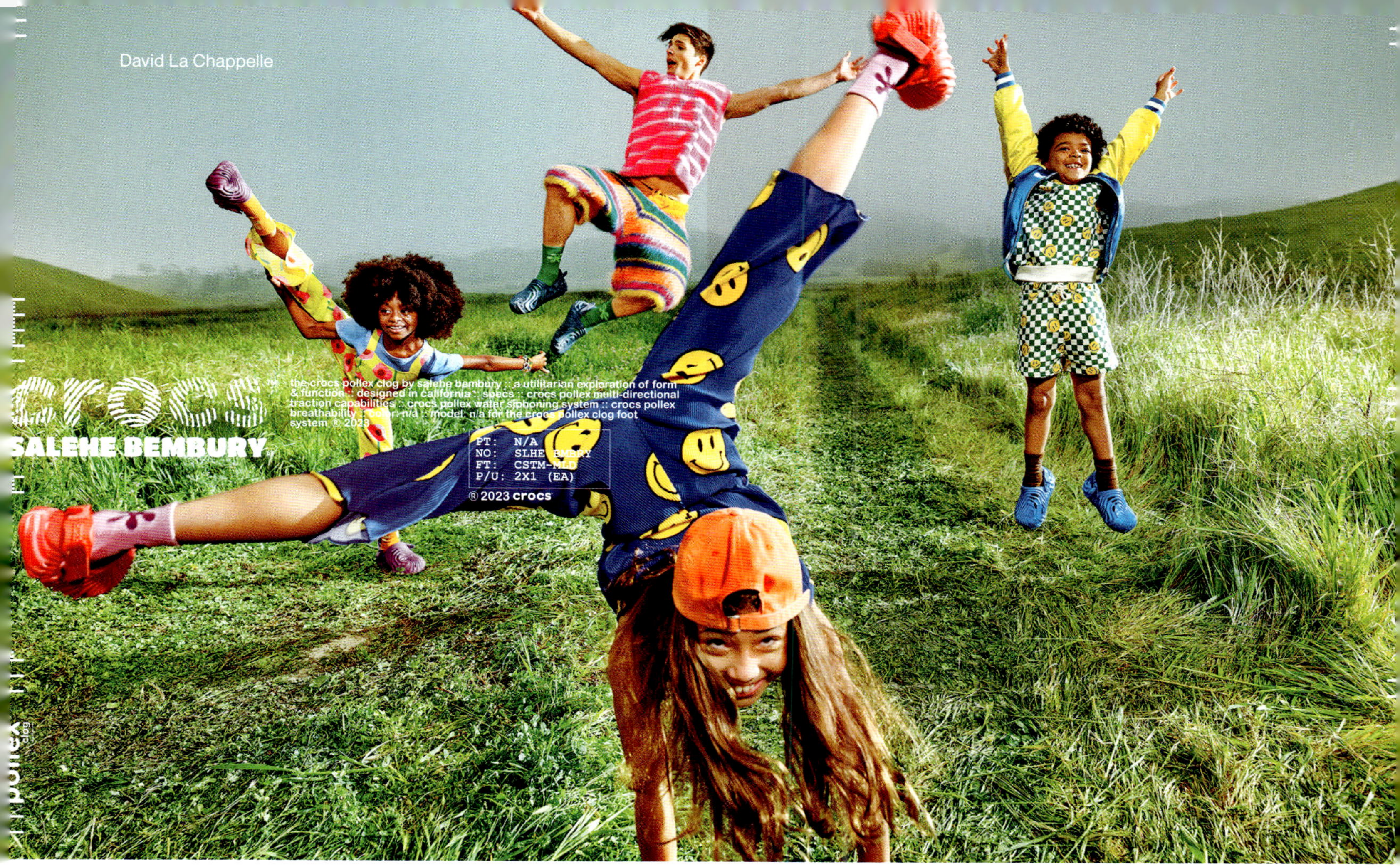

David La Chappelle

crocs™
SALEHE BEMBURY

the crocs pollex clog by salehe bembury :: a utilitarian exploration of form & function :: designed in california :: specs :: crocs pollex multi-directional traction capabilities :: crocs pollex water siphoning system :: crocs pollex breathability :: color: n/a :: model: n/a for the crocs pollex clog foot system ® 2023

PT: N/A
NO: SLHE BMBRY
FT: CSTM-MLD
P/U: 2X1 (EA)

® 2023 crocs

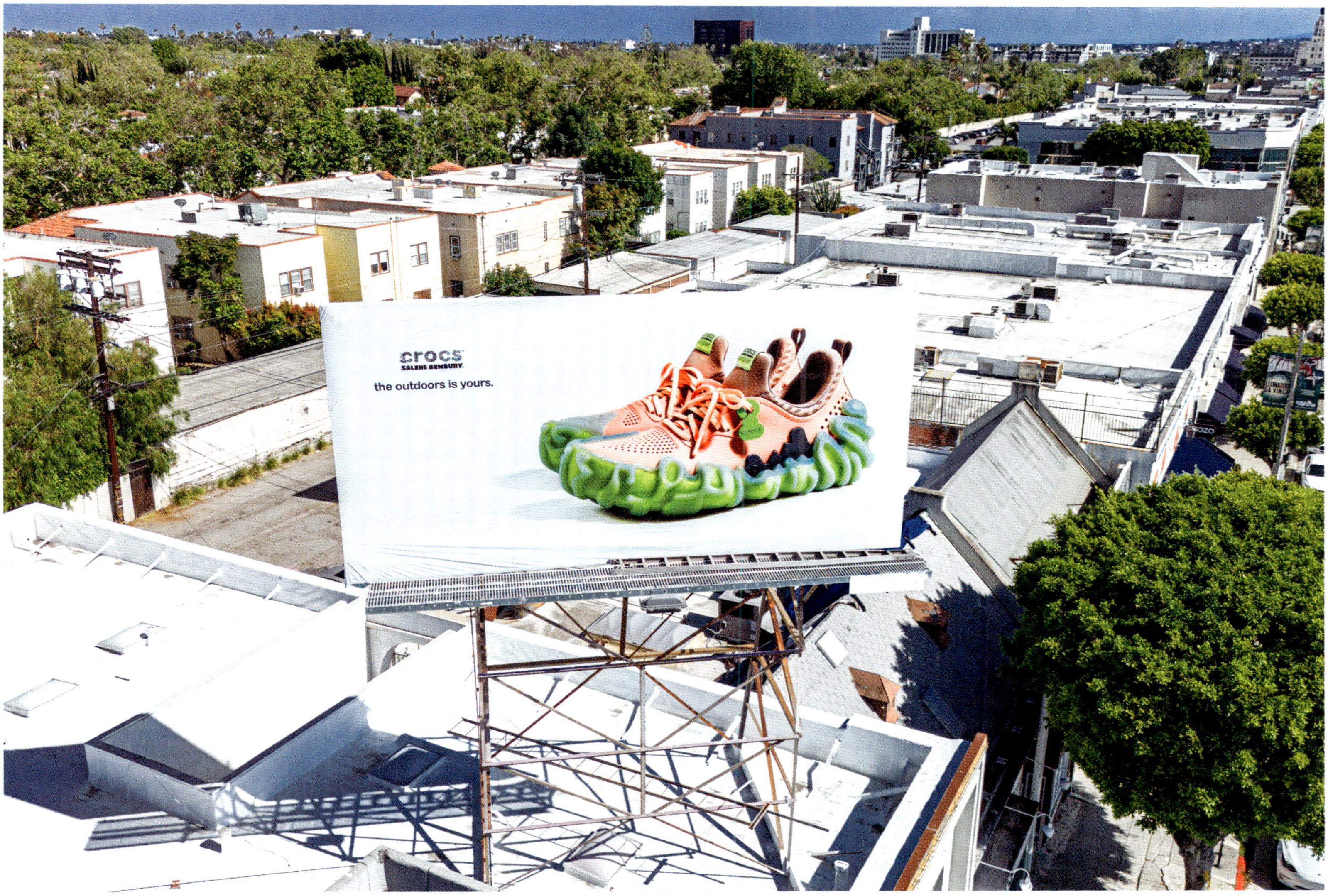

crocs
SALEHE BEMBURY
the outdoors is yours.

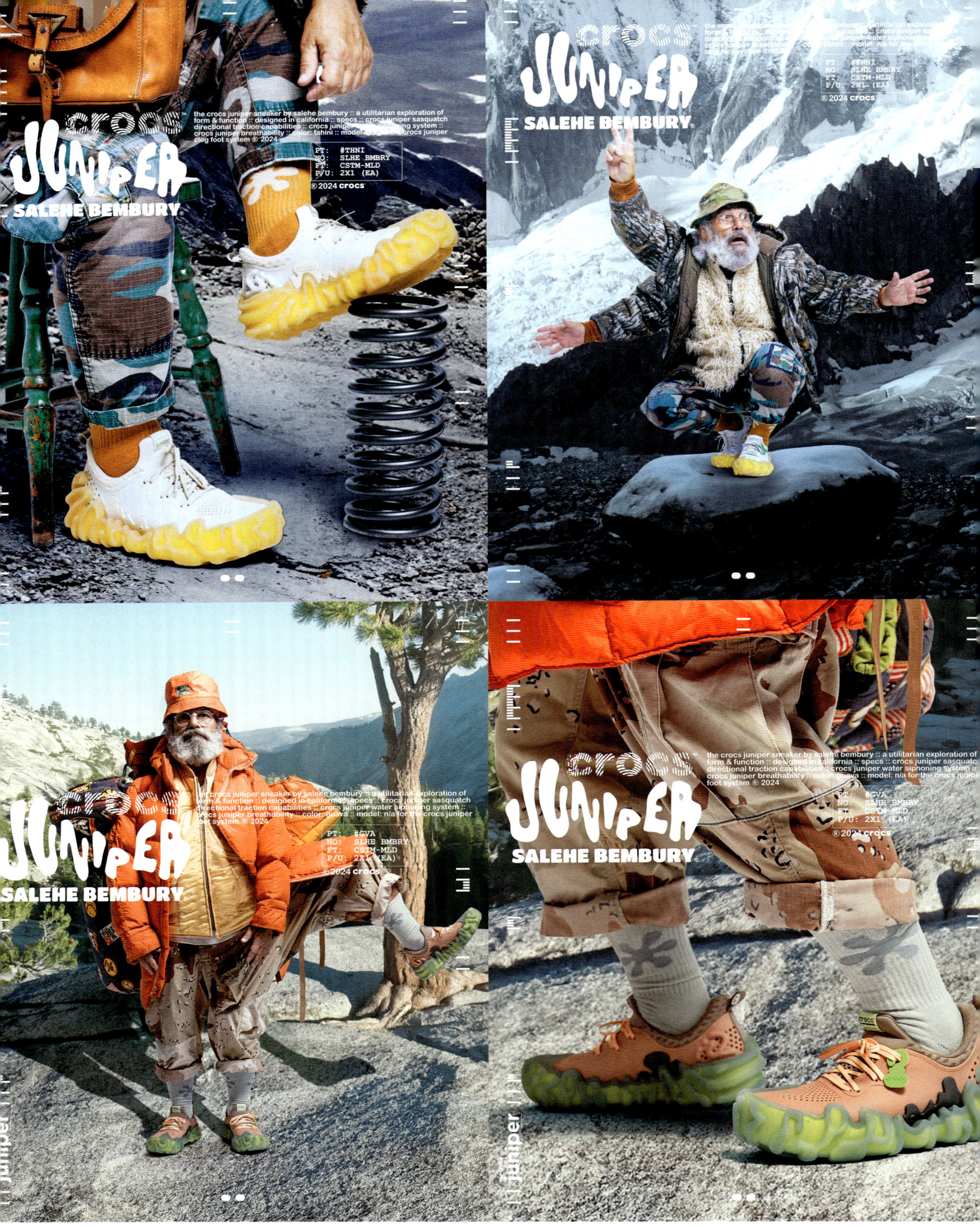
crocs
JUNIPER
SALEHE BEMBURY
the crocs juniper sneaker by salehe bembury :: a utilitarian exploration of form & function :: designed in california :: specs :: crocs juniper sasquatch directional traction capabilities :: crocs juniper
crocs juniper breathability :: color: tahini :: model
crocs juniper clog foot system ® 2024
PT: #THNI
NO: SLHE BMBRY
FT: CSTM-MLD
P/U: 2X1 (EA)
® 2024 crocs
crocs
JUNIPER
SALEHE BEMBURY
PT: #THNI
NO: SLHE BMBRY
FT: CSTM-MLD
P/U: 2X1 (EA)
® 2024 crocs
crocs
JUNIPER
SALEHE BEMBURY
the crocs juniper sneaker by salehe bembury :: a utilitarian exploration of form & function :: designed in california :: specs :: crocs juniper sasquatch directional traction capabilities :: crocs juniper water siphoning system :: crocs juniper breathability :: color: guava :: model: n/a for the crocs juniper foot system ® 2024
PT: #GVA
NO: SLHE BMBRY
FT: CSTM-MLD
P/U: 2X1 (EA)
® 2024 crocs
crocs
JUNIPER
SALEHE BEMBURY
the crocs juniper sneaker by salehe bembury :: a utilitarian exploration of form & function :: designed in california :: specs :: crocs juniper sasquatch directional traction capabilities :: crocs juniper water siphoning system :: crocs juniper breathability :: color: guava :: model: n/a for the crocs juniper foot system ® 2024
PT: #GVA
NO: SLHE BMBRY
FT: CSTM-MLD
P/U: 2X1 (EA)
® 2024 crocs
juniper

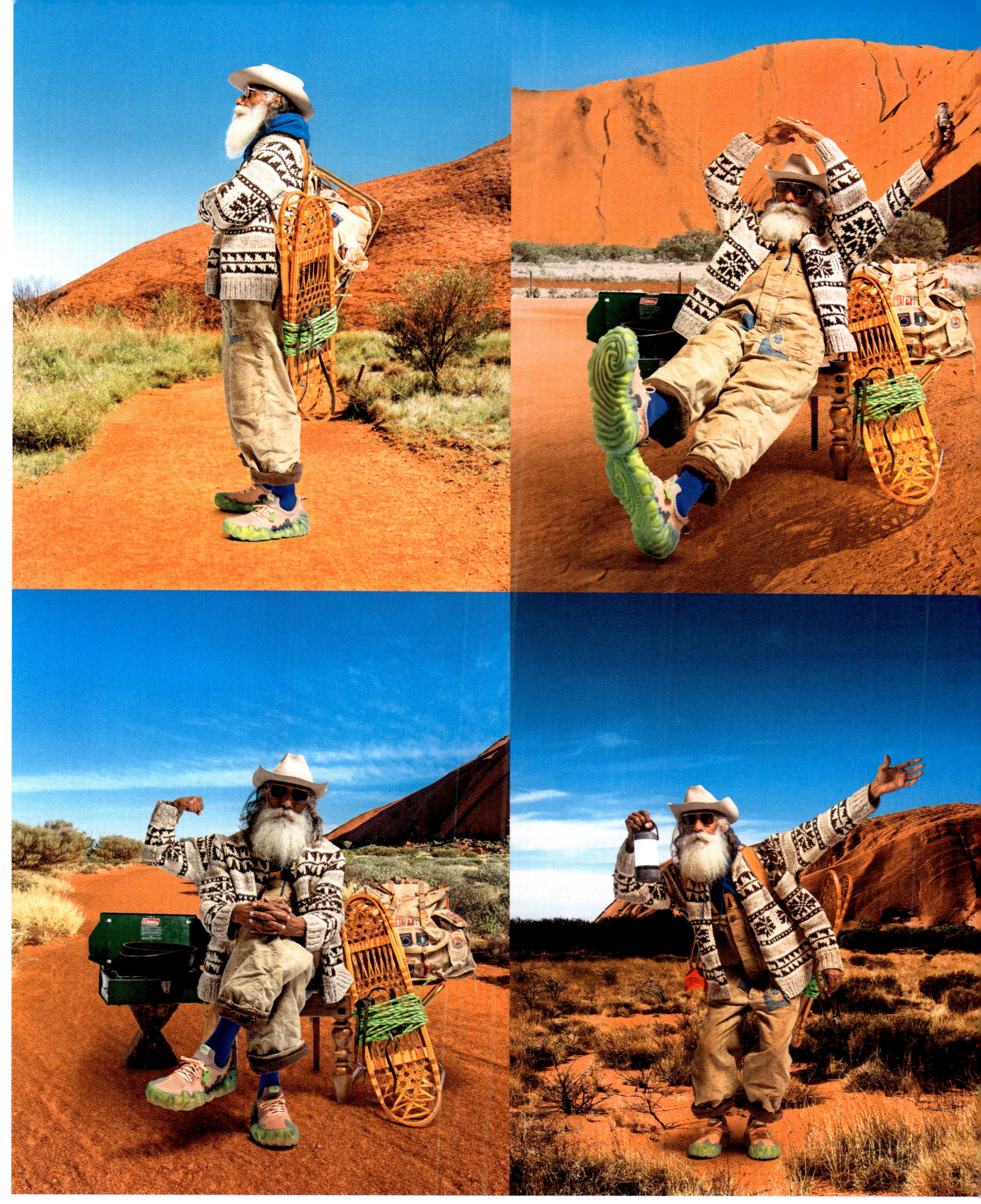

Crocs

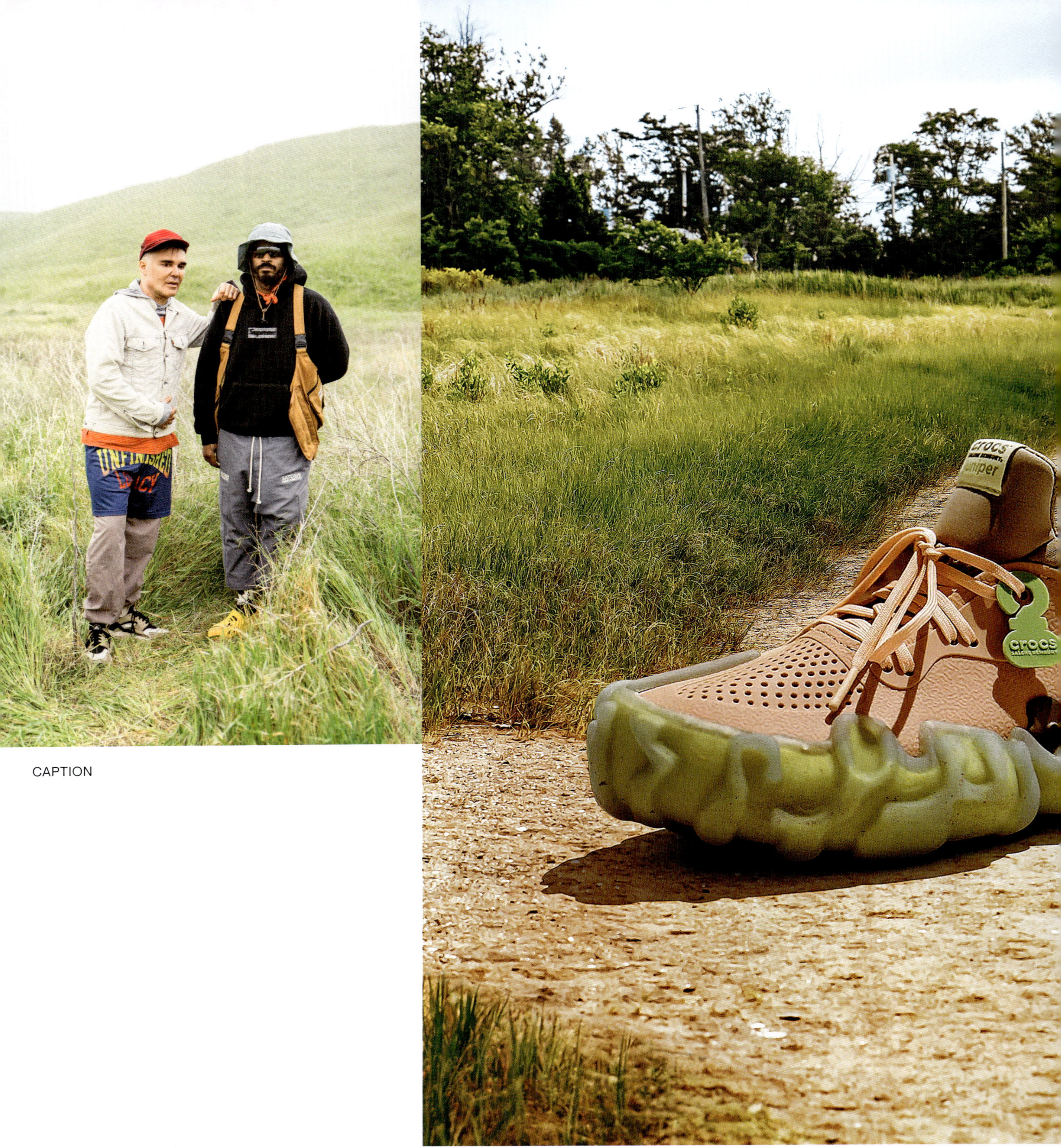

CAPTION

Carlos Jimenez Varela Crocs marketing

244

(2020)

CROCS

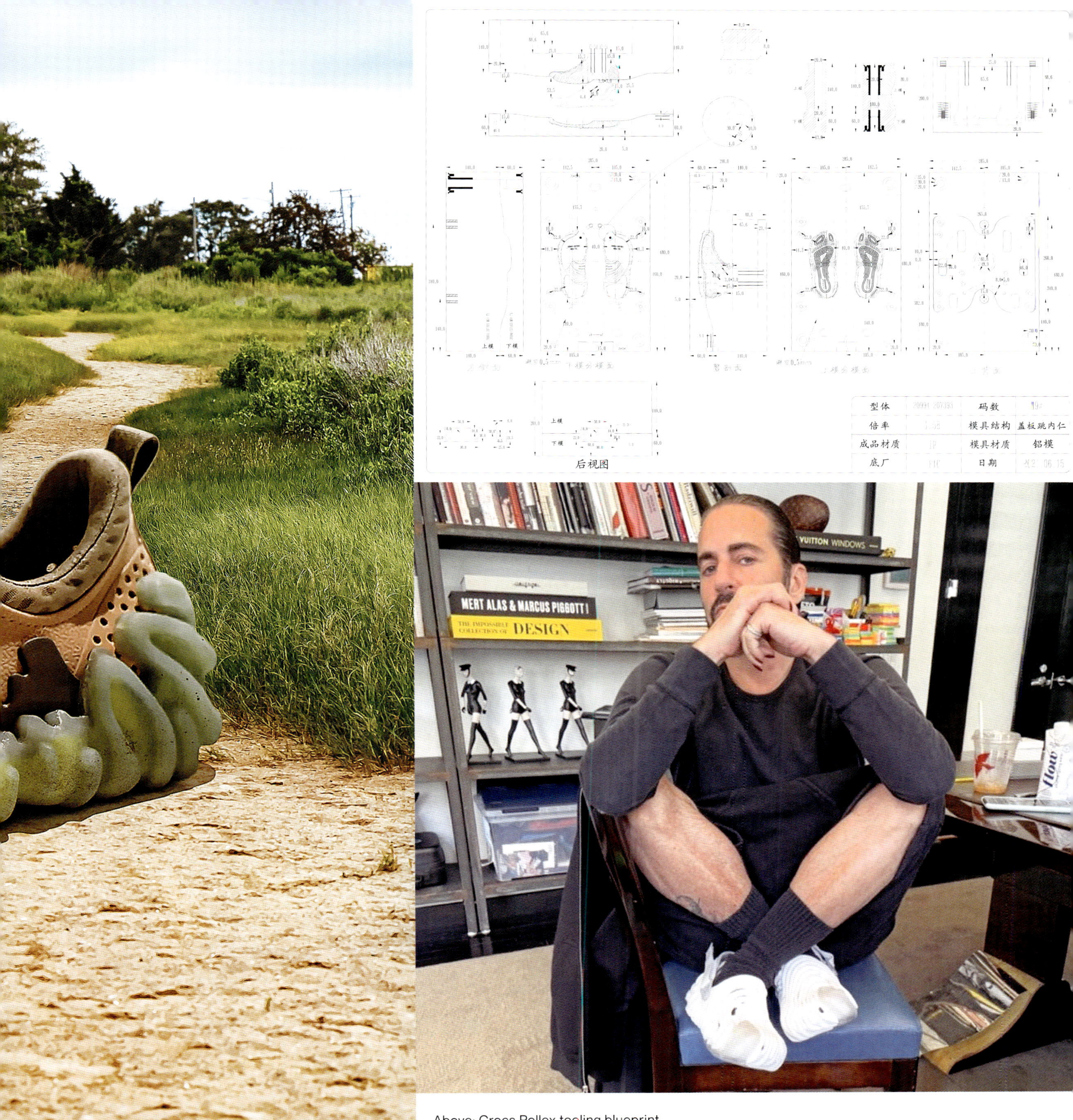

Above: Crocs Pollex tooling blueprint
Below: Marc Jacobs wearing Crocs Pollex

245

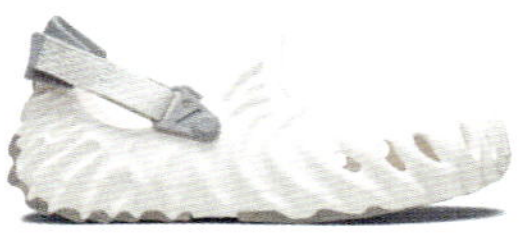
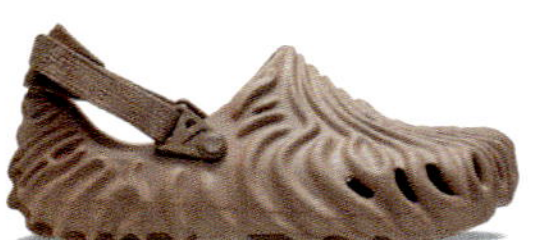
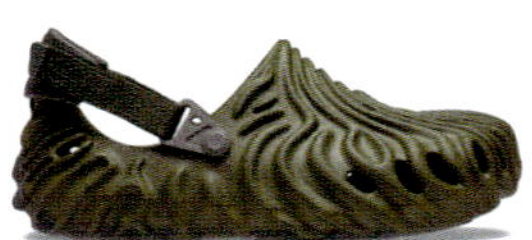
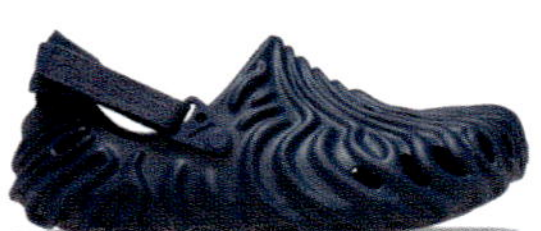
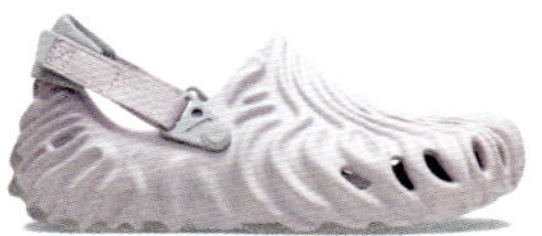
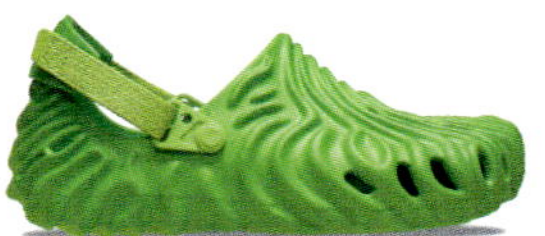
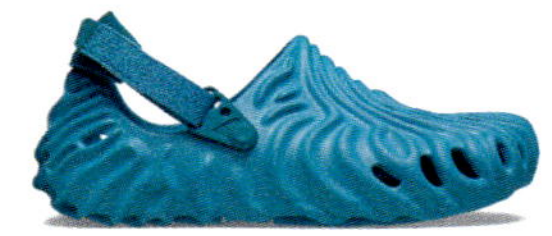
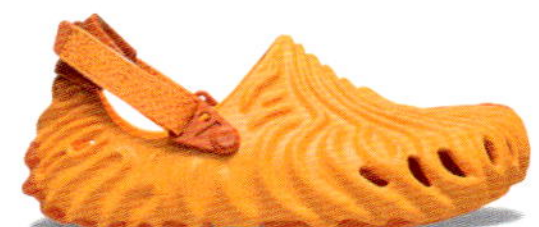
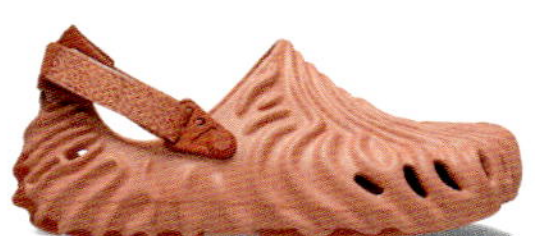
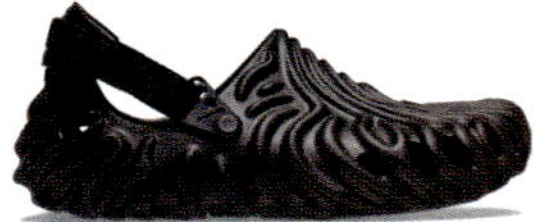
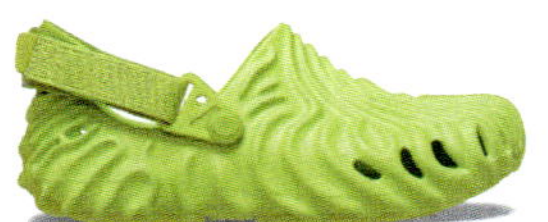
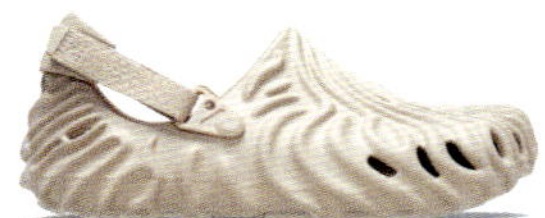
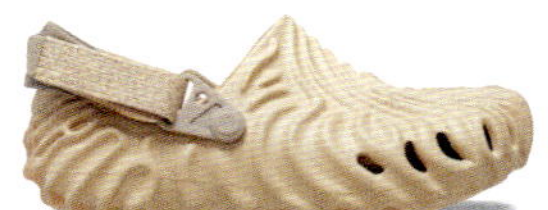
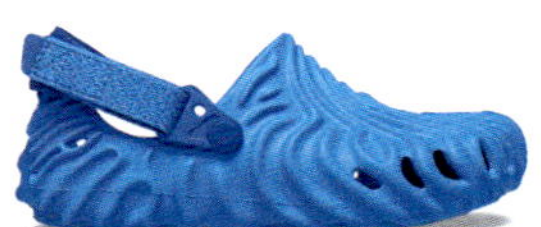
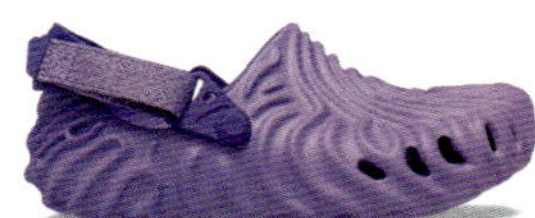
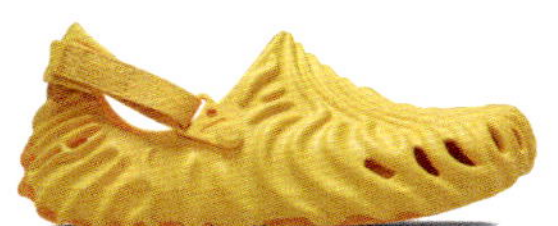
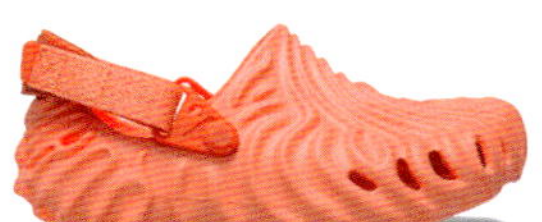
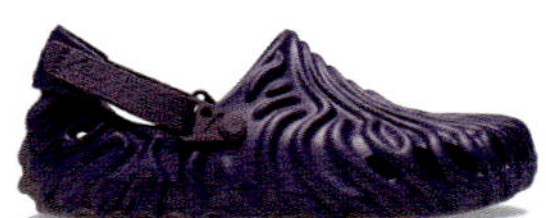
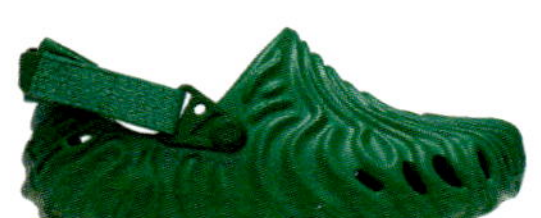

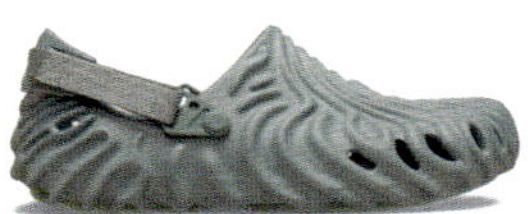
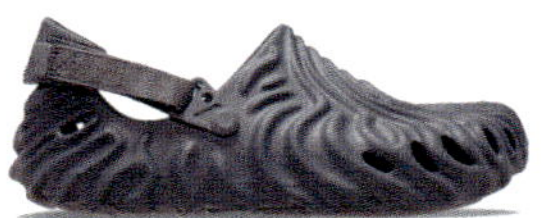

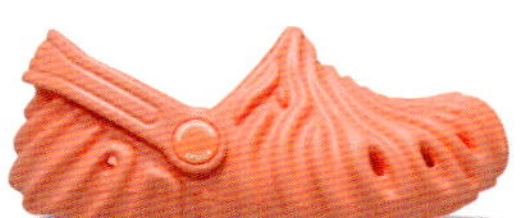
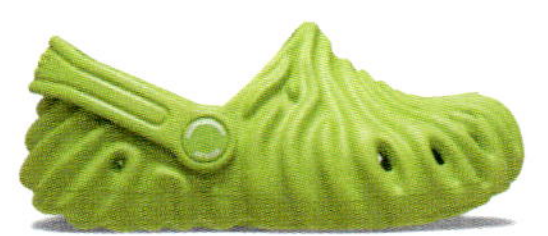
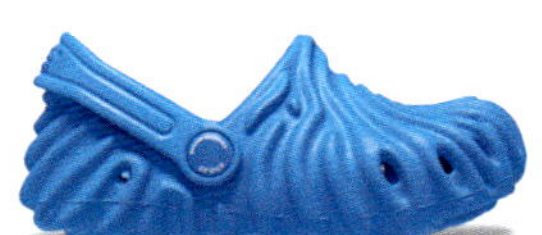
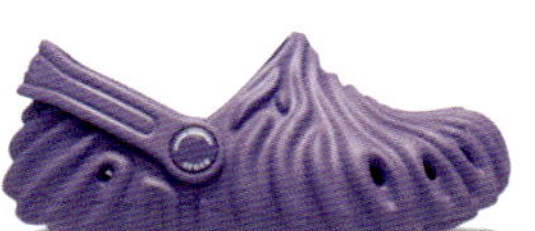
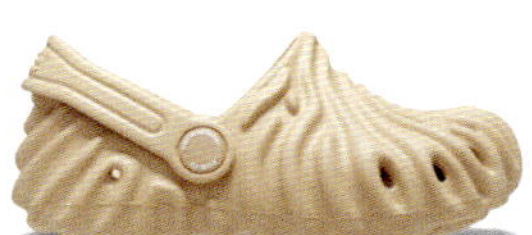
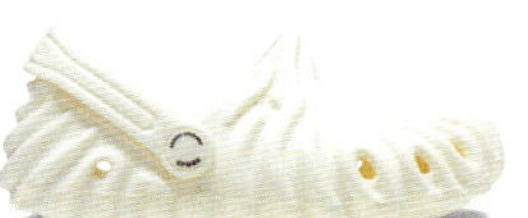
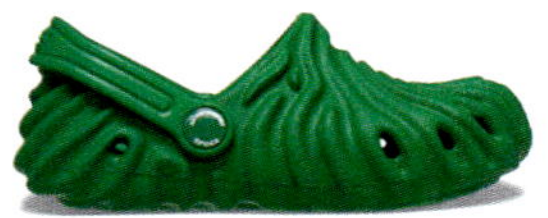
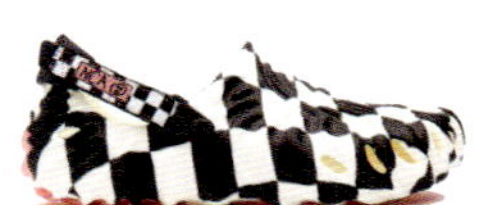
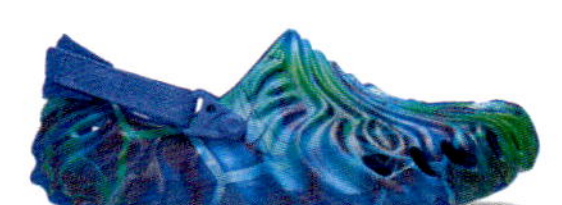
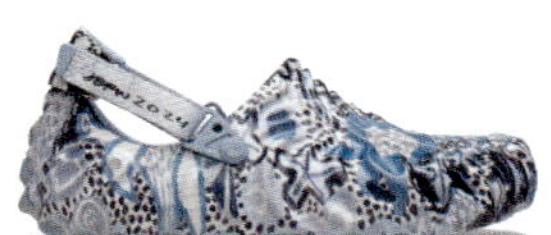
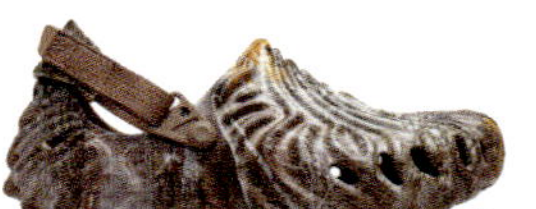

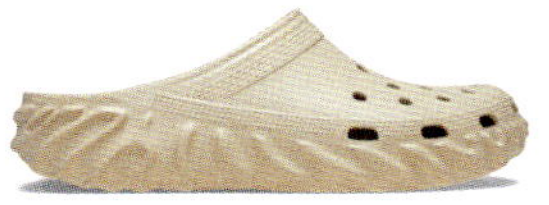
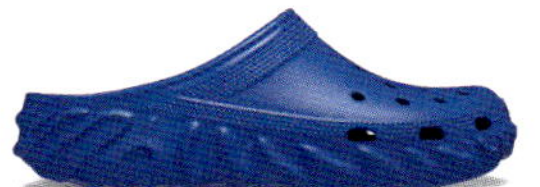
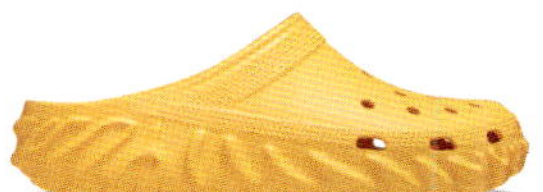
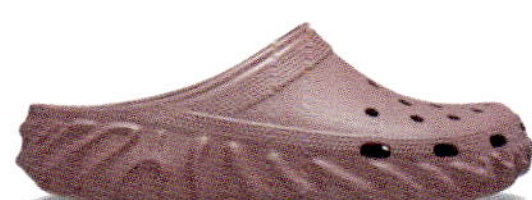
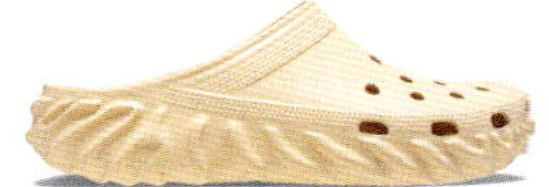
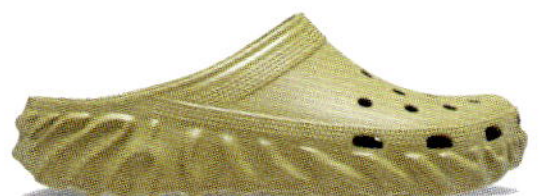
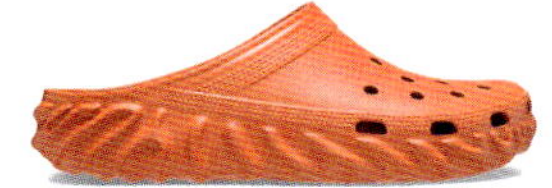
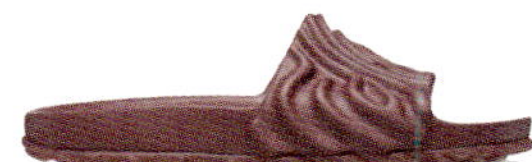

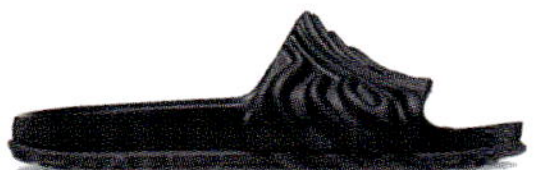

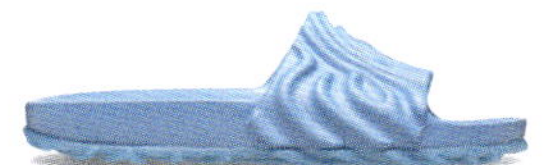
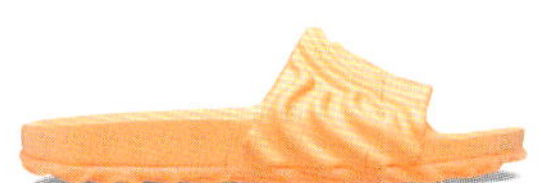
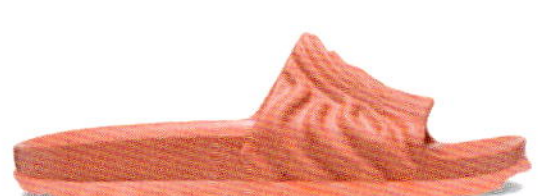
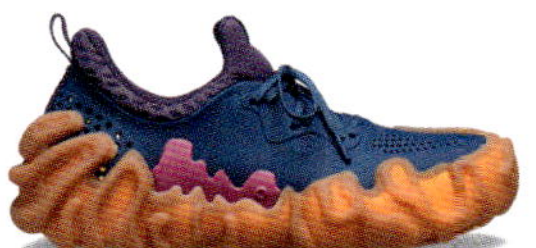
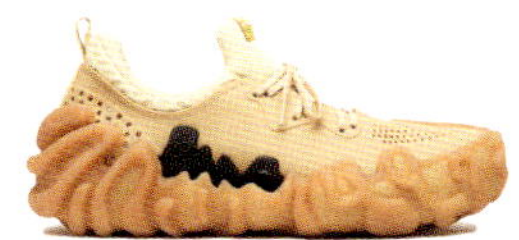
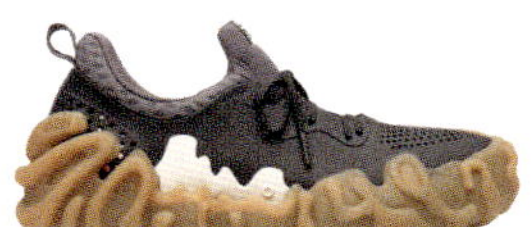
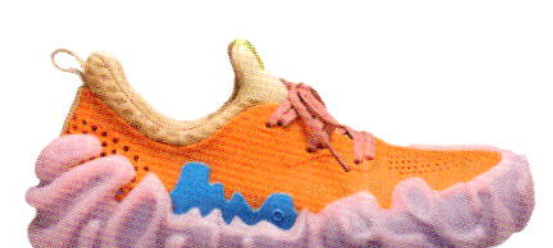
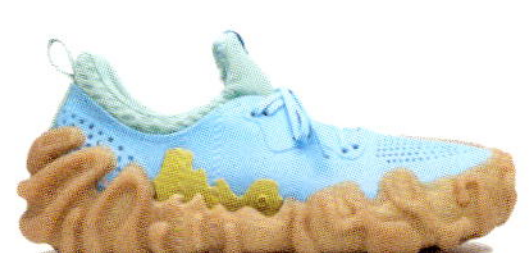
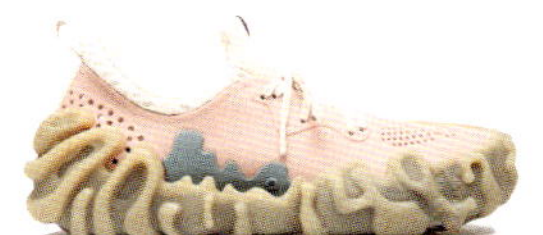
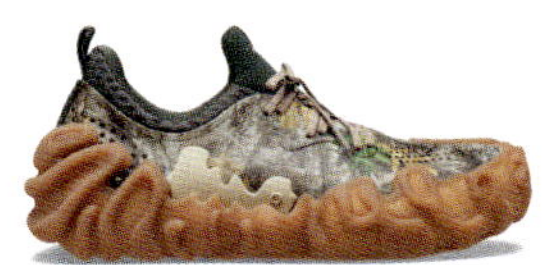
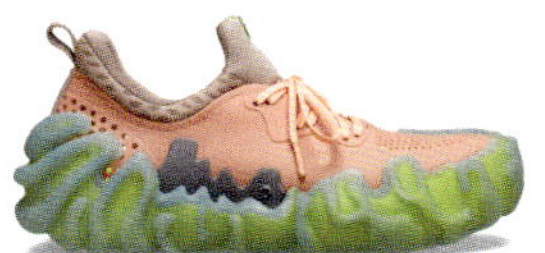
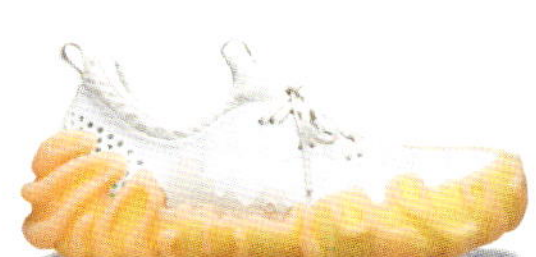
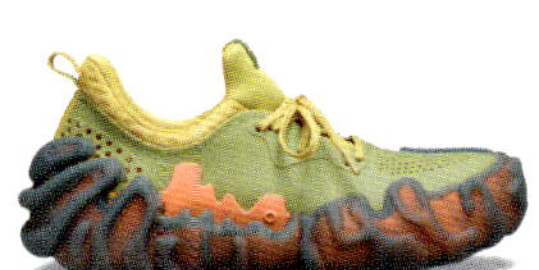
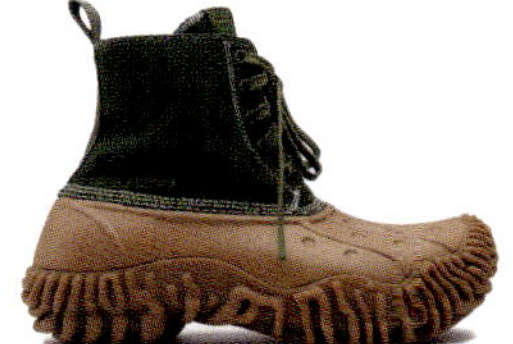
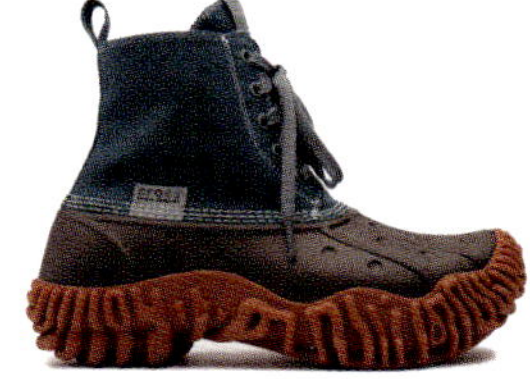
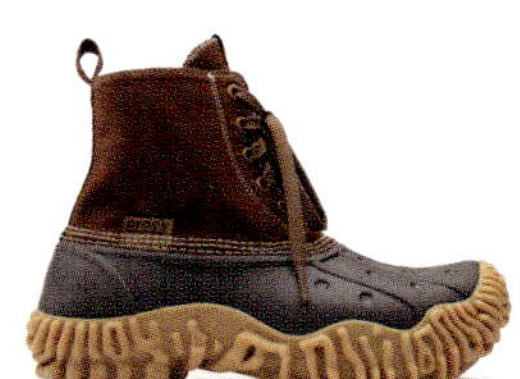
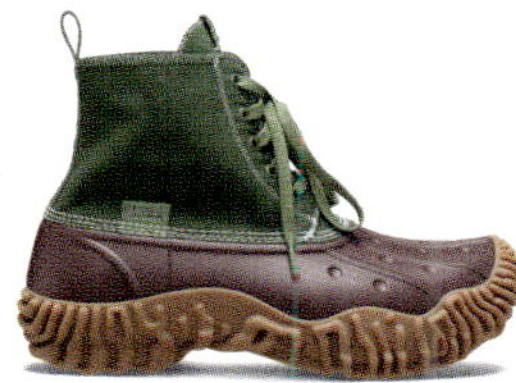
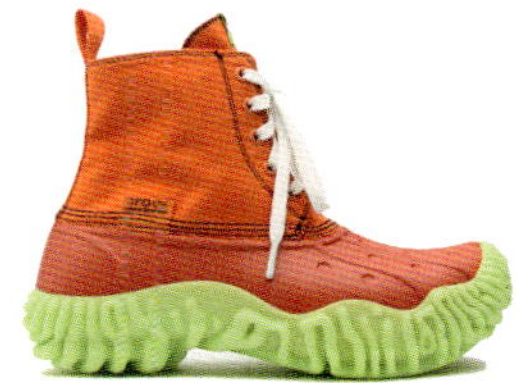
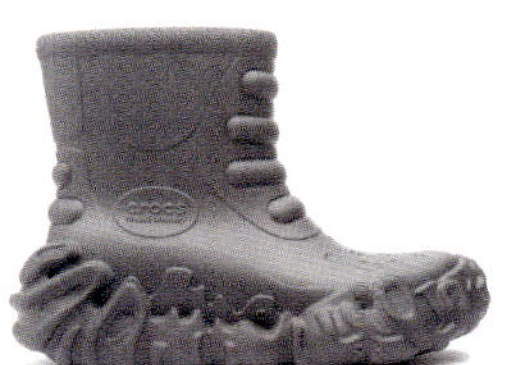
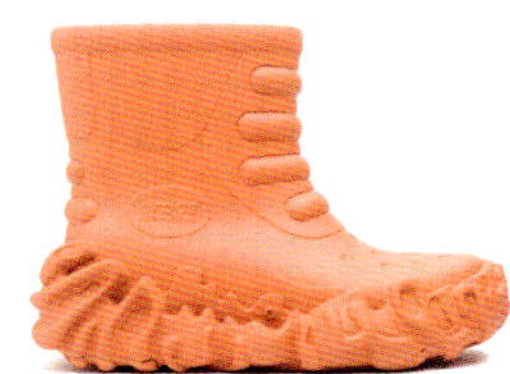
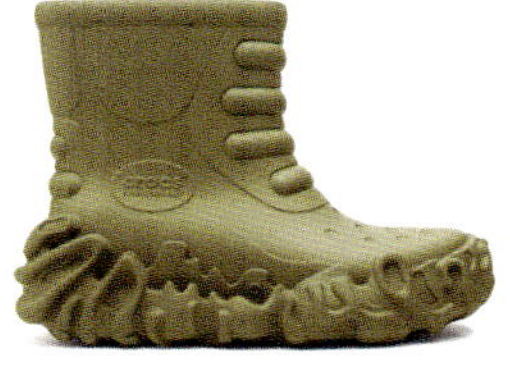

248

UNION (2021)

MAKE A MEN

WITH
TOR

UNION

MAKE WITH A MENTOR

1

1At this point in my career, Crocs was flourishing, my name was becoming better known, and I was looking for other projects to keep me motivated—things that were different from my regular footwear dealings. Simultaneously, a lot of the individuals that I used to look up to, and whose work I would obsess over, were now becoming friends and peers; now I was able to touch these people and reach out to them. Furthermore, these individuals were beginning to respect me as a peer and a player in the space. This allowed for creative alignment for collaborations, which, having been less recognizable in the past, would've been a whole lot harder.

Both Union and Chris Gibbs have been legends in the space for an extremely long time. One could argue that they are second to Supreme: James Jebbia, who started Supreme, used to work at Union, so the DNA and the lineage is significant. Union was a store I would only read about growing up—I was in New York City, they were on the West Coast, and for me the West Coast was this legend that I would read about and see pictures of, but never knew. I had met Chris a few years prior while I worked at Versace, and over the years the relationship had gradually grown. My brand was doing well and I had my own audience, so I figured, what better than to have us come together in a moment.

I proposed simply doing a t-shirt and a hoodie. The timing was perfect because it was Union's 30th anniversary and they were conceiving collaborations with a lot of other recognizable individuals in the space—brands like WTAPS, A Bathing Ape, and the kinds of brands you would expect to collaborate with Union for their 30th. So not only was I getting to collaborate with Union, but I was also being presented adjacent to many of the brands I had essentially worshipped my entire consumer life.

2

Along with the t-shirt and hoodie, I proposed doing a vinyl, which Union had never done before. Chris is a self-admittedly analog creative, and 3D is not a tool that he uses. The Union "Frontman" silhouette, which is the logo of their brand, is actually Sidney Poitier jumping in the air in the movie Raisin in the Sun, which I bet only 10% if that of the Union consumer base knows. So, given that there was this void in knowledge, and the fact that Chris does not use 3D as a design tool, I thought to myself: why don't we make the "Frontman" three-dimensional, both to educate the consumer on who they're actually wearing on their chests, and to explore a tool that's never been used in Union's history. We made the vinyl with All Rights Reserved, a prestigious vinyl and toy company based in Hong Kong that works with Kaws and many other notable artists that work with those materials.

The apparel consisted of a t-shirt and a hoodie, the fronts of which featured an illustration of Sidney Poitier, which was the educational element of the collection. The backs featured a collaborative logo lock-up with "30th Anniversary" below it, featuring my still-relatively-new fingerprint brand identity, which I used this collaboration as an opportunity to establish further. At the bottom of each was the word "organic," spelled out in the Spunge font that we created and is exclusive to us, which is a word I use to describe how a lot of my projects come to fruition. The vinyl and the apparel were released on the same day.

3

This collaboration, while it was small, was a big milestone for me because it made me realize that a lot of the people that I had looked up to were walking similar paths as myself. This comes less from a place of ego as from a place of opportunity: my design studio is filled with shoes and toys and vinyls and art, and these were all people that I had looked up to and still look up to. But this collaboration made me realize that I had entered a similar space to the one they'd been living in for a while. The ability to create a collaboration simply by texting a friend seemed like a way shorter bridge than the ones I'd had to cross before. I realized my potential; I was starting to understand what my value was; and I was becoming more comfortable with exploring my brand identity and the conversation with my consumer.

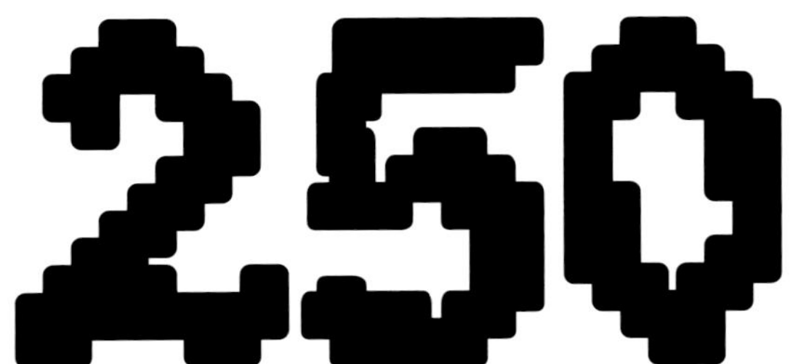

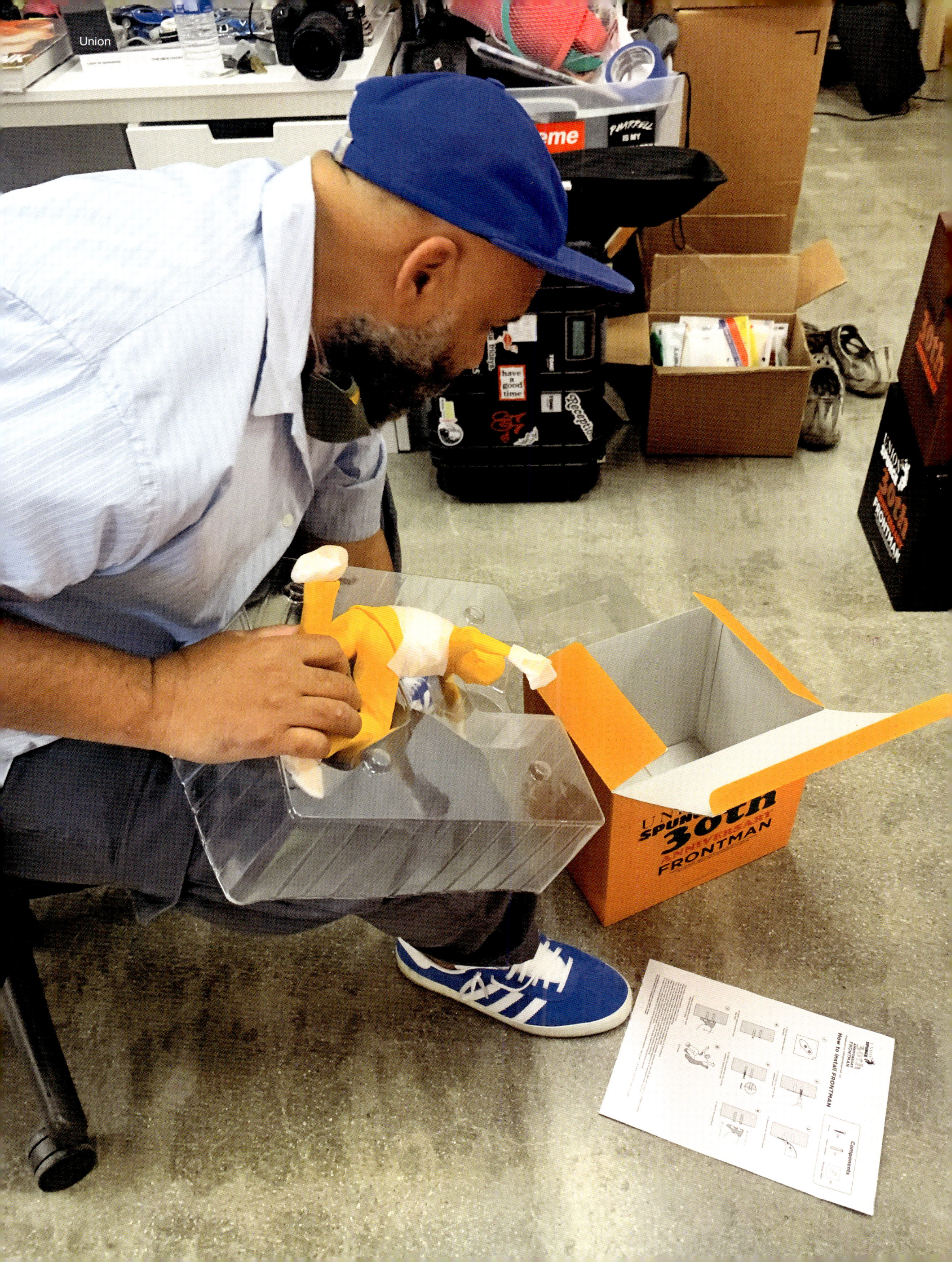

Union

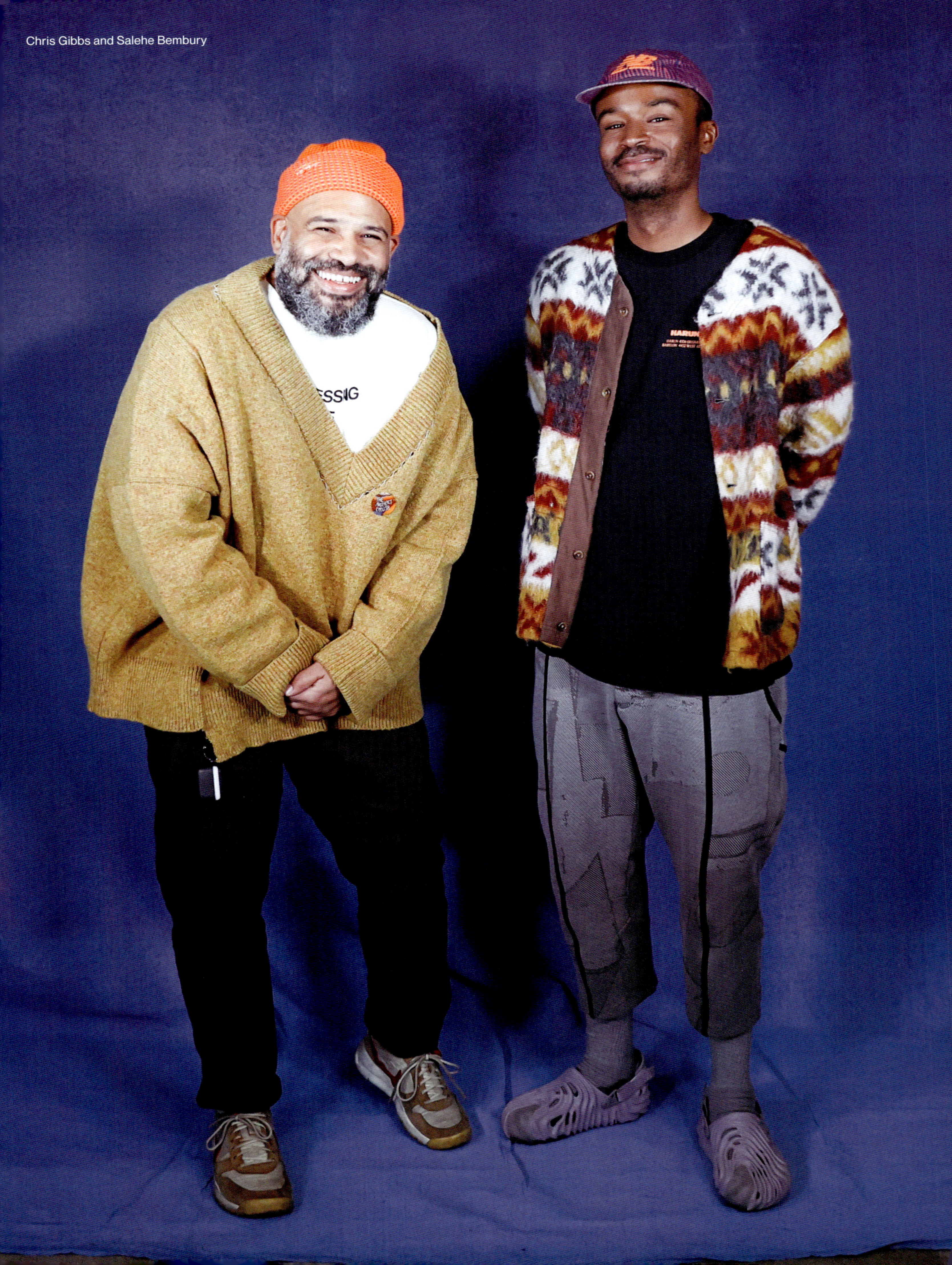
Chris Gibbs and Salehe Bembury

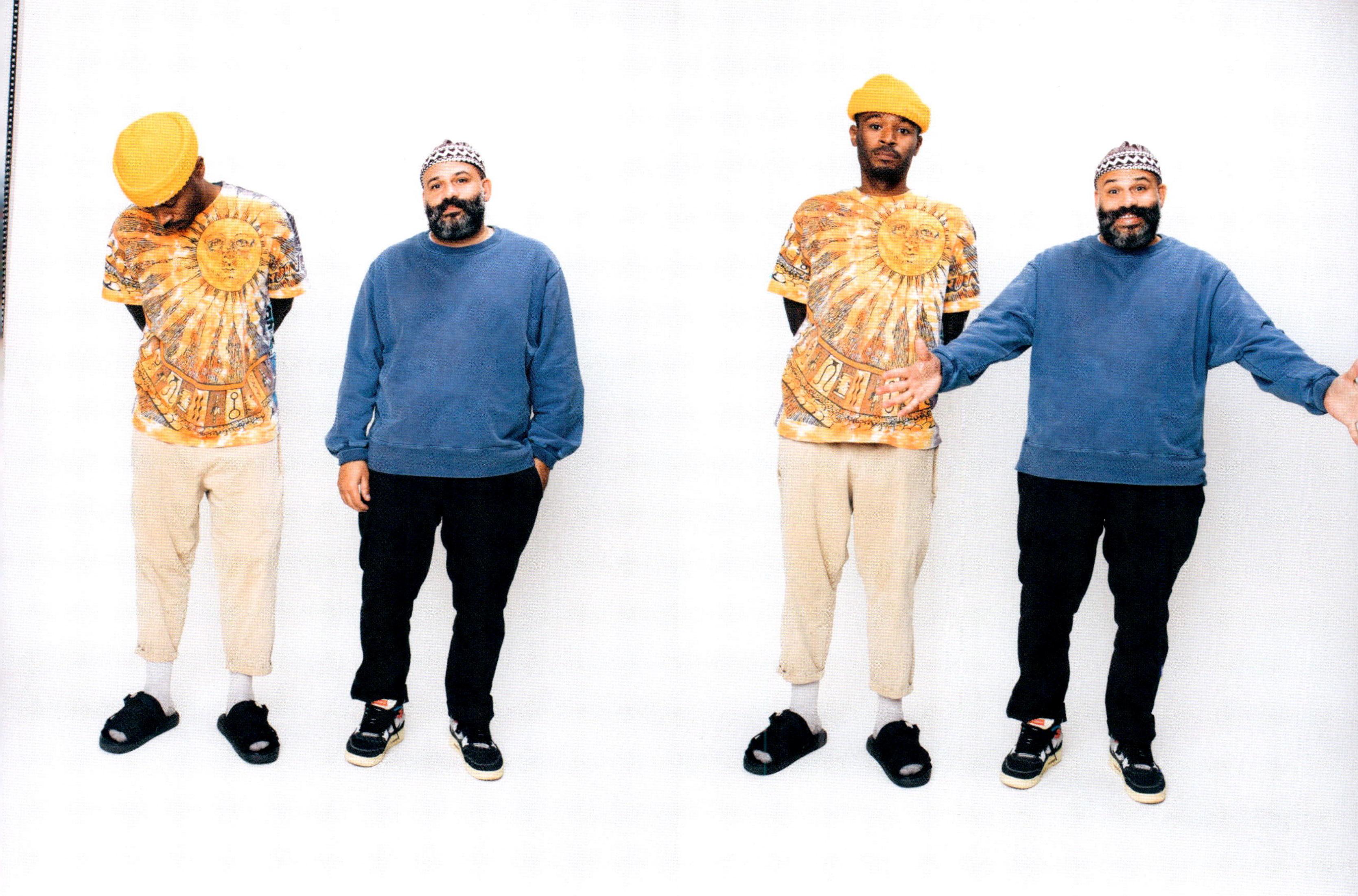

Chris Gibbs and Salehe Bembury

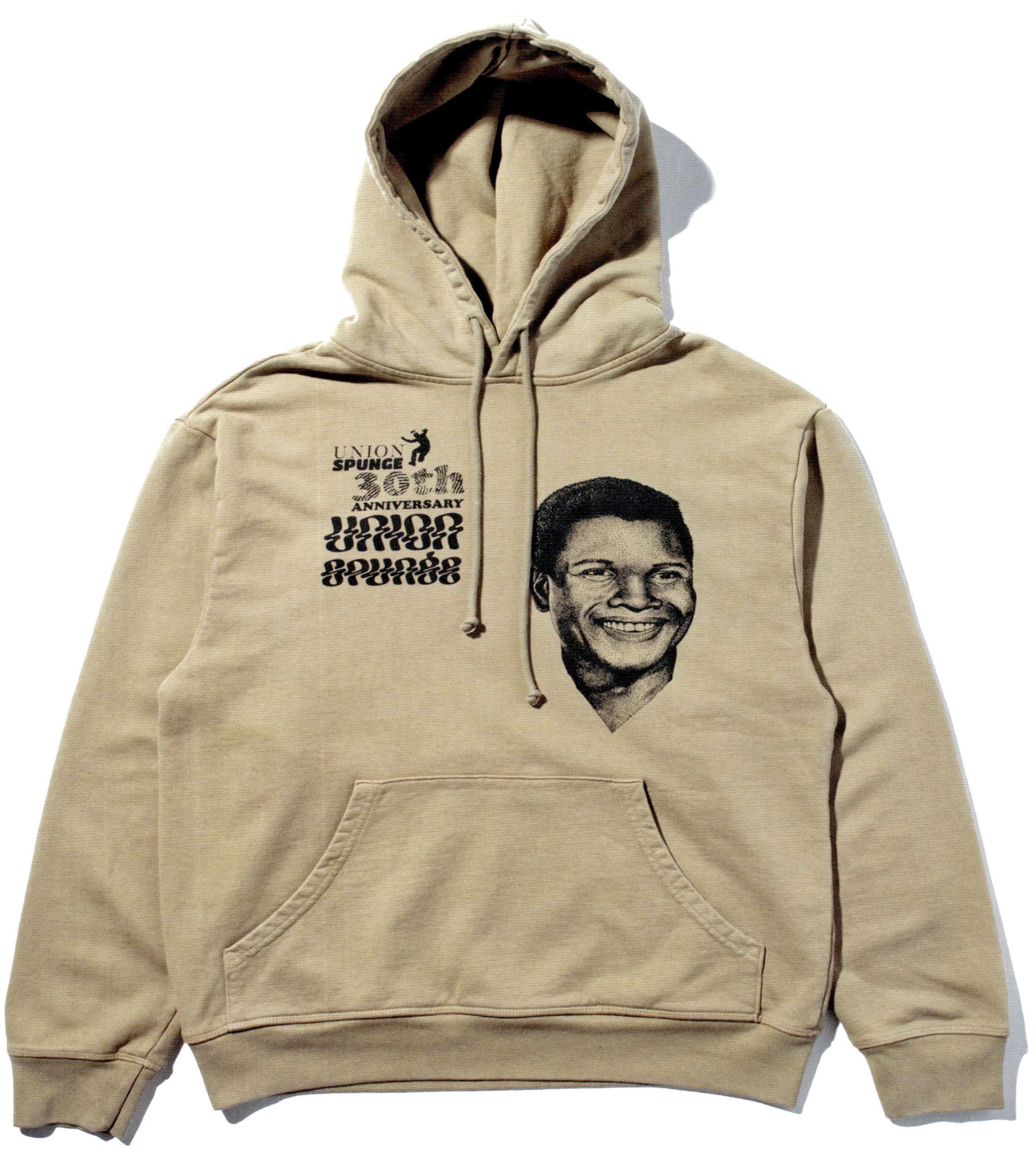

Union

254

(2021)

UNION

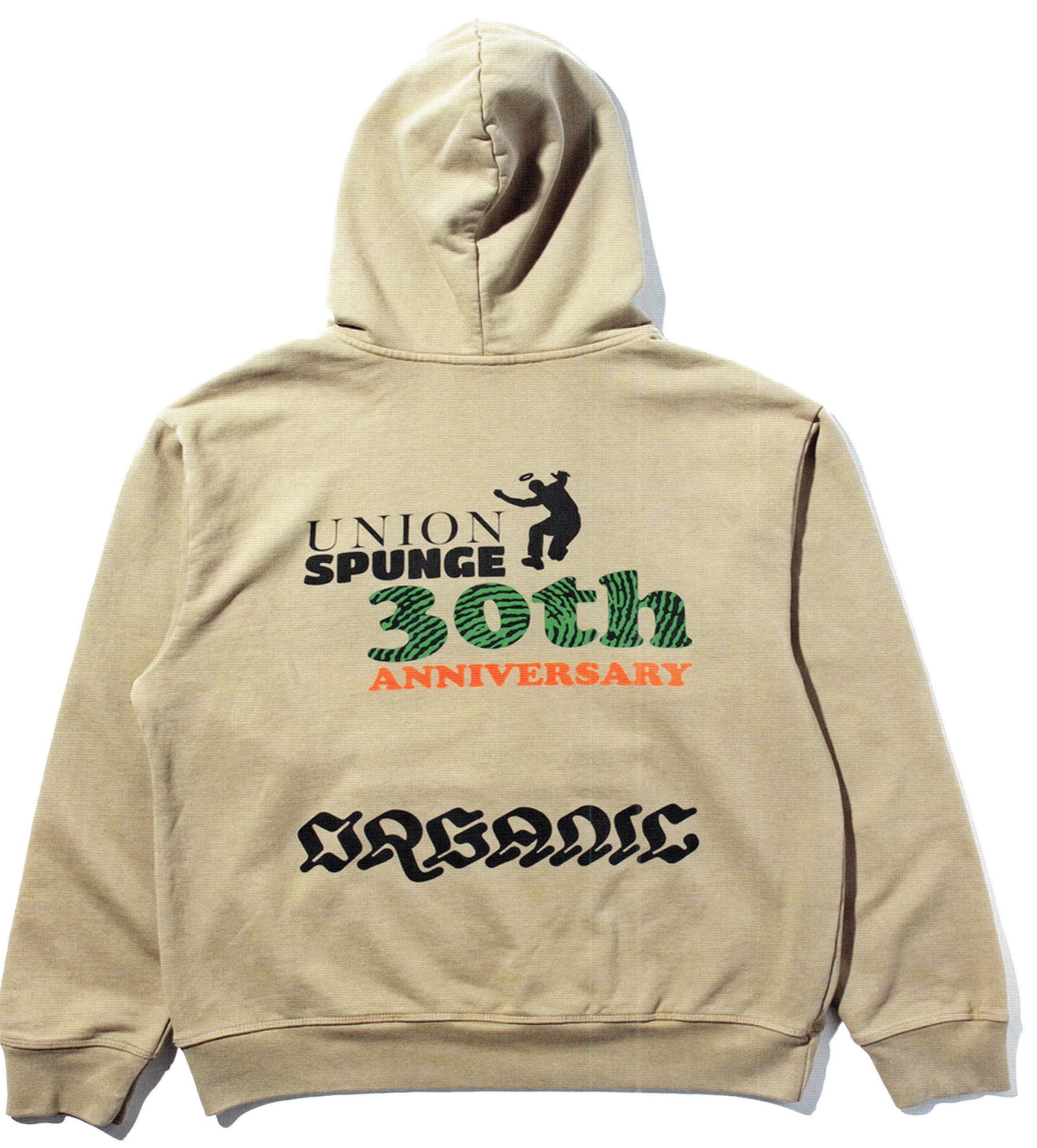

Union

256

CANADA GOOSE **(2022)**

EXPLO
NEW
SPACE

RE

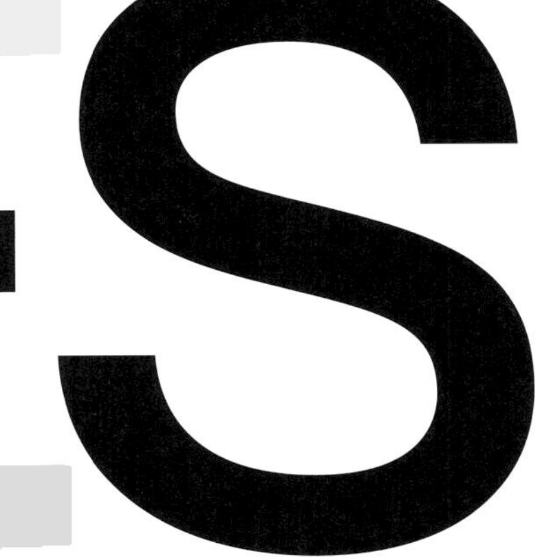

CANADA GOOSE EXPLORE NEW SPACES

1

Canada Goose was an opportunity for me to do my first proper apparel collection. I had previously made one with New Balance, but from a perspective of quality, price point, and execution, this was a first: New Balance was inexpensive and more about streetwear pieces, and the Canada Goose collection was $1,000 jackets and $800 fleeces, and just at a higher level.

It was actually a three-way collaboration between Canada Goose and the NBA. Throughout all the conversations to the final execution I tried to keep the NBA branding extremely minimal, and I kept all the logo usage on the interior of the pieces; I was really interested in elevating the partnership with Canada Goose.

2

One obstacle of the collaboration was that there wasn't much wiggle room within what I was able to do with the garments. With the New Balance apparel I essentially was allowed to do whatever I wanted, but with Canada Goose there were restrictions on materials, stitch, color, and execution. While most designers would see that as a negative, I saw it as an additional design challenge to add to the brief.

When I was given the different articles of clothing that I was allowed to work on, I asked if I could also do a jumpsuit so I could have an entire look. Initially, the collaboration was all about outerwear pieces, but I felt it wouldn't make sense if we did a campaign and the model wasn't wearing something on their legs that I'd created. So I pushed for there to be a puffy jumpsuit, so we had a full look head to toe. Unfortunately, I wasn't able to create the footwear for this collaboration, so the models are wearing shoes that I did not design.

While this was unfamiliar territory to me, I treated the project as I would a footwear project. I researched Canada Goose as a brand, I created mood boards, and then I wanted to execute similarly to how I introduce footwear, where I try to create something polarizing to get the consumer's attention. I love the idea of creating something different yet commercial, and that's how I tried to approach this project. So: I went to Home Depot. Home Depot is not necessarily my primary source of inspiration, but I sometimes go there just to be inspired, because there are so many different materials and colors–it's just an amazing place. As I walked through Home Depot, I saw a microfiber mop. Purely from a visual perspective, it was beautiful. And then I thought to myself: this could also work as a substitution for fur on a hood. The function of fur on a hood is to protect your eyes and face from harsh conditions, without you having to cover your entire face. What if I could use this as a material to serve the same exact function as fur, but it's not fur? I would be creating something the consumer has never seen; I would be using a material the consumer is familiar with but through a different lens; and at the same time I would be working sustainably by not using fur. I thought this was a triple threat of an amazing design idea.

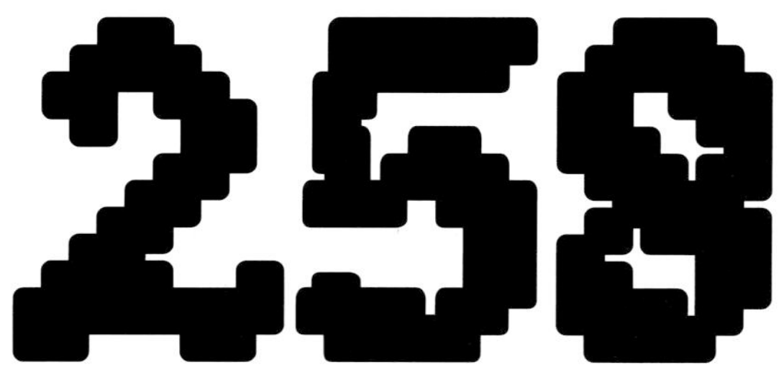

So I bought that mop and I put it on my head with a jacket Canada Goose had sent me, just to see how it would look. That was a pivotal moment, and the foundation of the collaboration: once I had figured that out, I knew everything else would fall into place, because the jacket was kind of the hero item. It felt different, but it didn't feel different to the point where it was just ridiculous. I felt like I had found the perfect balance of polarizing and commercial.

3

The finished collection consisted of a jacket, a fleece, a jumpsuit, and a vest. After the collection was created, it was time to make a campaign. I had always wanted to work with Foster Huntington. The first thing we did was go to his compound in Washington, which features two treehouses connected by a bridge, and a skate bowl. He's a kind of modern-day MacGyver wizard from the future and the past–there really are only a handful of people that inspire me on another level, and Foster is one of them. I had seen his work with Nike and Patagonia, and this was a great opportunity to do something with him. Foster did a Claymation campaign. He essentially created an armature of me that did a bunch of really cool things in nature, and it was one of my favorite and most successful campaigns.

This was a campaign of a lot of firsts–I had never even conducted a campaign on this level. A lot of them were shooting models and creating videos, but to do Claymation of myself was insane. We also created a doll of myself. We worked with a guy named Mental Ben to make this Salehe figure–a version of myself that was wearing the entire Canada Goose fit–that we then gave out promotionally. That aligned with the Claymation doll that people saw in the campaign, and it was just all very cool.

Since it was a collaboration with the NBA, the collection was launched at All-Star Weekend in February 2022. There was a whole build-out, where they put together a little cabin that mimicked the one that people saw in the campaign–you could go "digital fishing" inside, and it had the collection in there, and a TV playing NBA games. I met Evan Mobley and Clyde Drexler, and he and I had a moment. I spun the ball on my finger as a way to show him–I'm not just a fashion guy, I hoop! Given that I grew up playing basketball, and given my current explorations with Puma, it was coming from a place of authenticity. That's my childhood, and even though I hadn't had many opportunities to explore it or talk about it at the time, this felt like a nice overlap of stories.

4

With a strictly apparel collection, I was able to tell new stories, speak to new audiences, and get new opportunities. The *Source* cover with 2 Chainz is an example of that. Since I make shoes, I never really had an opportunity to have a magazine cover. if I did, it was a very small appearance, at the bottom of the magazine. But now that I was making apparel, someone could wear my work on a magazine cover, which seems like a small feat but was huge at the time. To see 2 Chainz, who is a well-known rapper and a good friend, wear my work on a magazine cover was a big deal to me. It was a very significant moment in this journey that I've been on. I even designed the chain he was wearing.

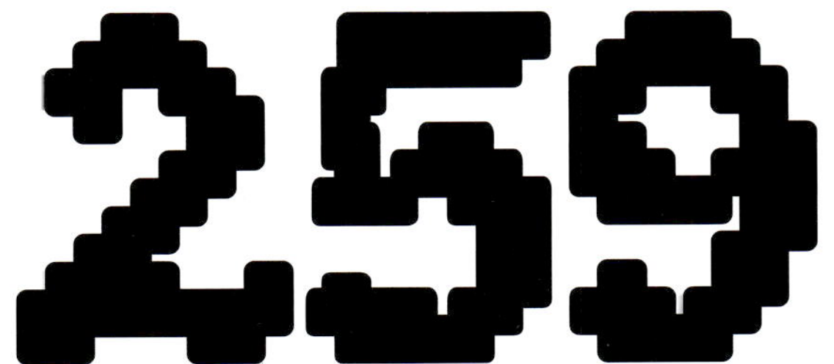

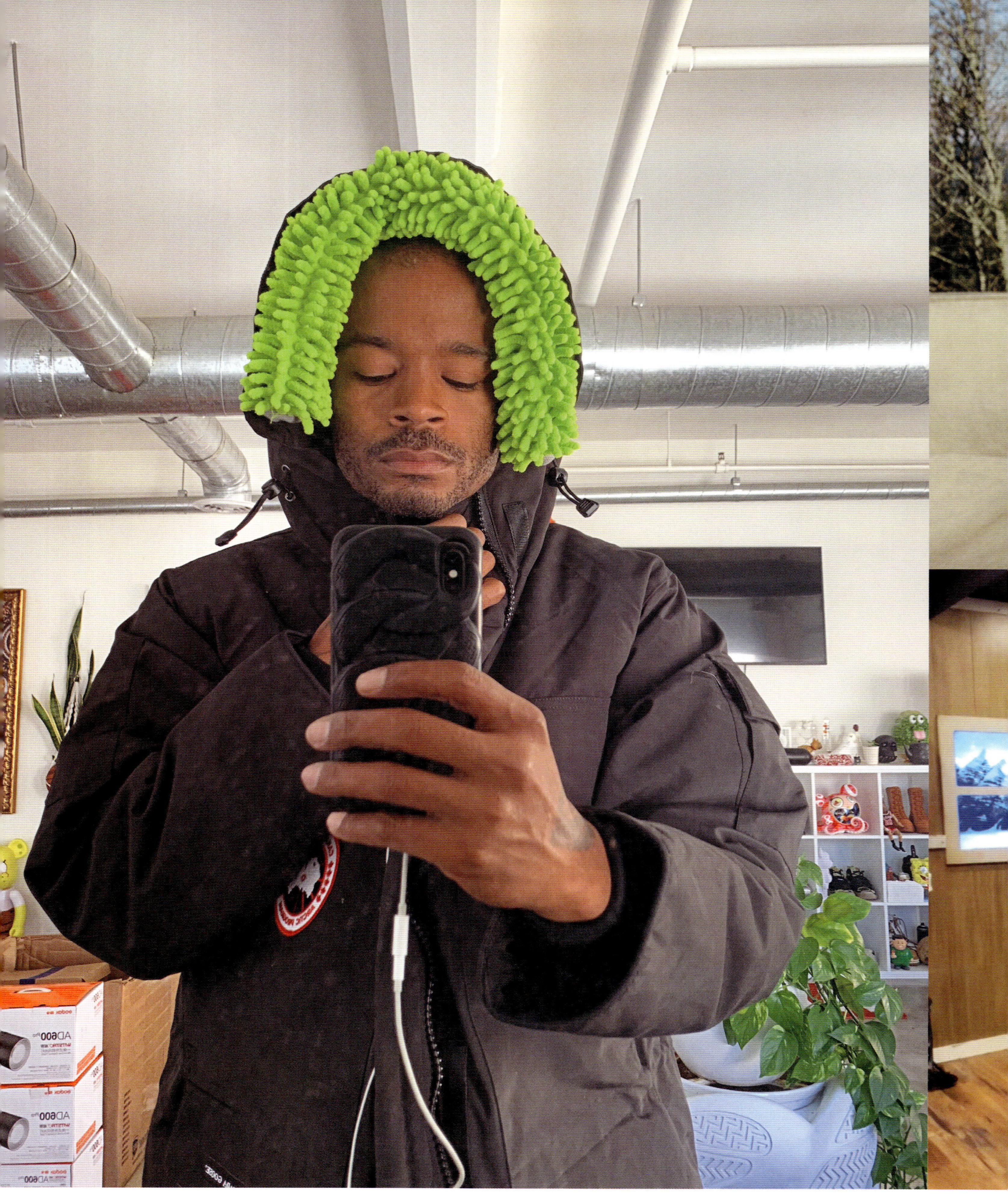

Salehe Bembury using mop for hood detail

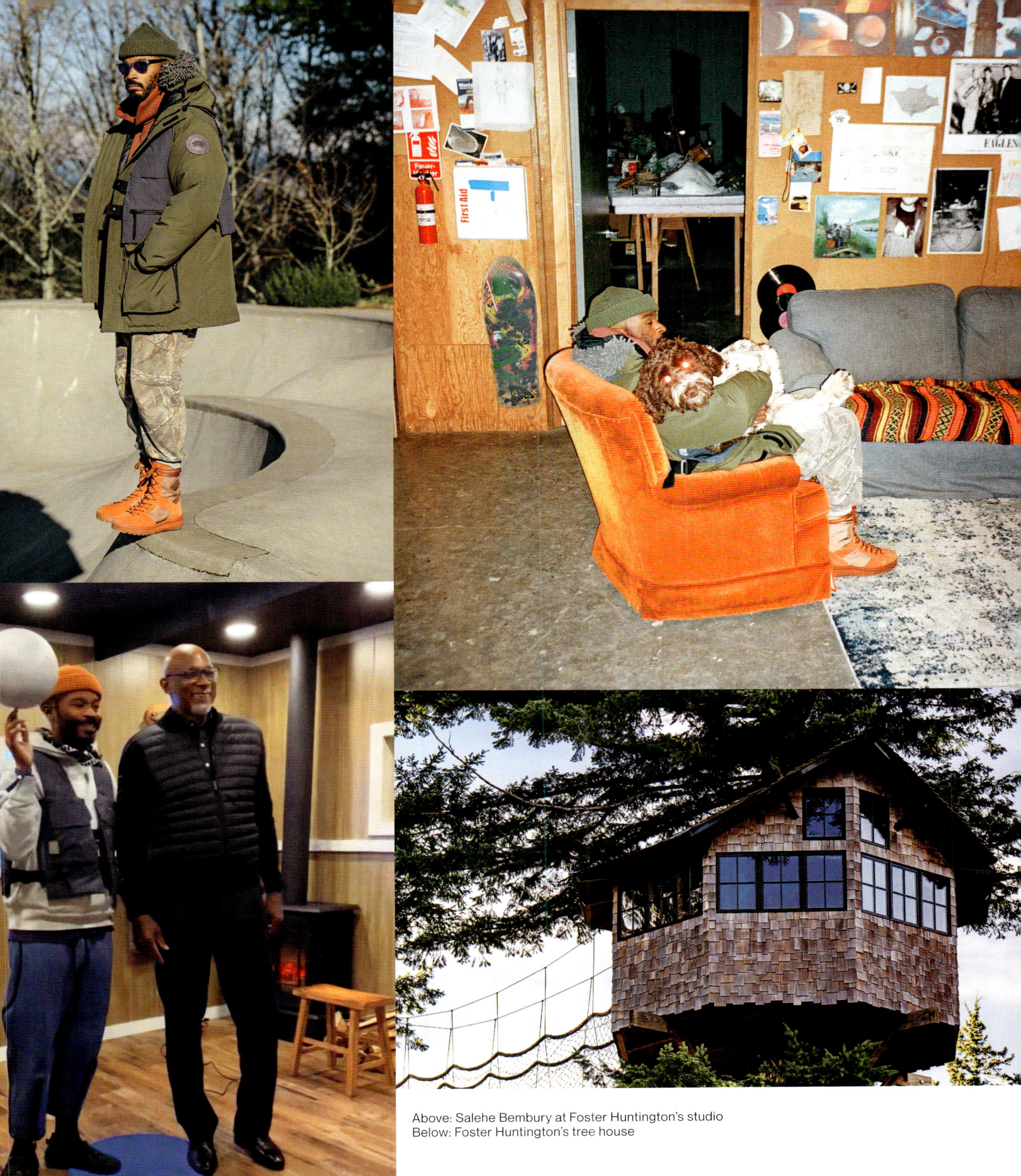

Above: Salehe Bembury at Foster Huntington's studio
Below: Salehe Bembury with Clyde Drexler

Above: Salehe Bembury at Foster Huntington's studio
Below: Foster Huntington's tree house

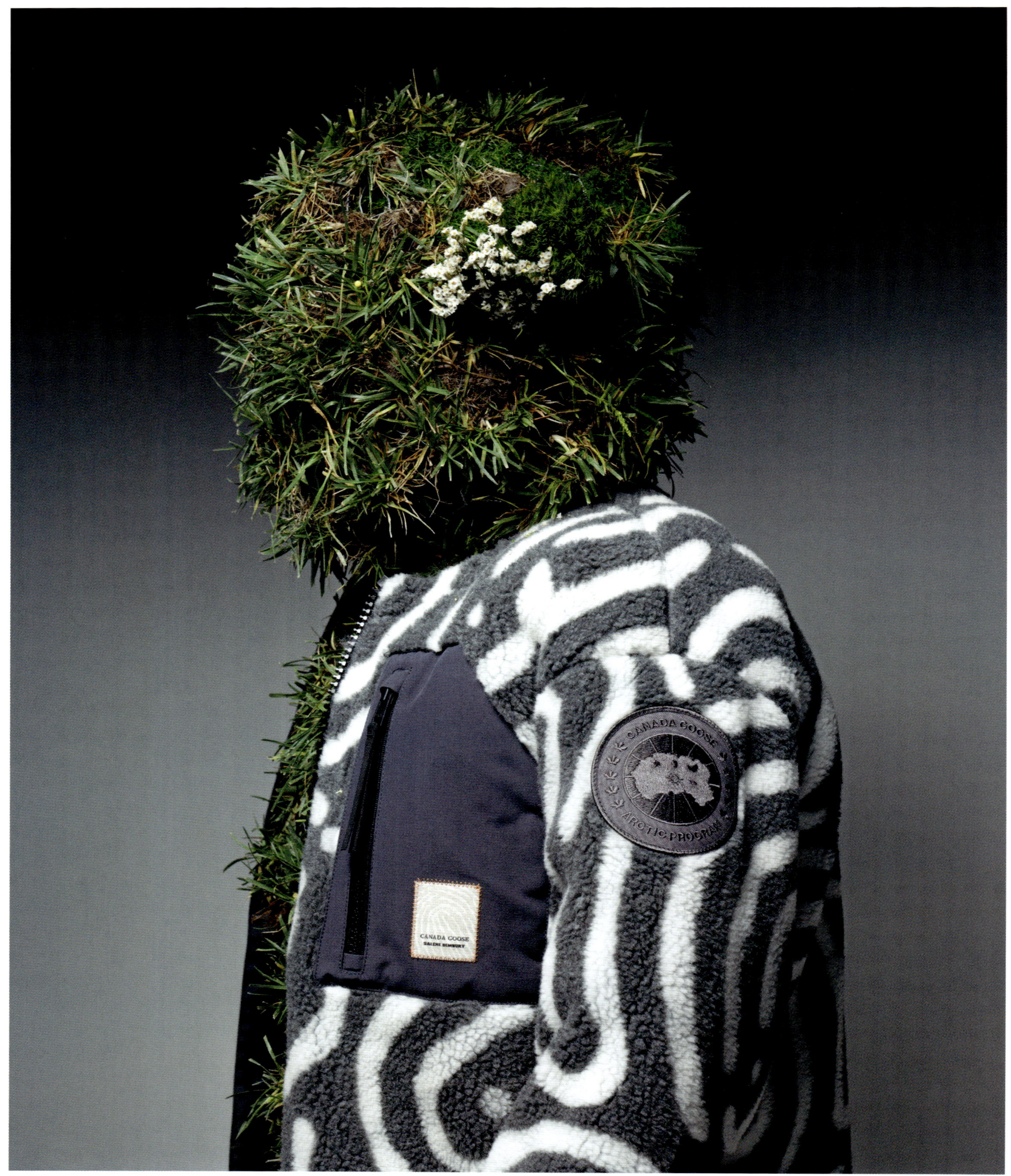

Canada Goose x Salehe Bembury Keylowna Boreal Fleece

262

(2022)

CANADA GOOSE

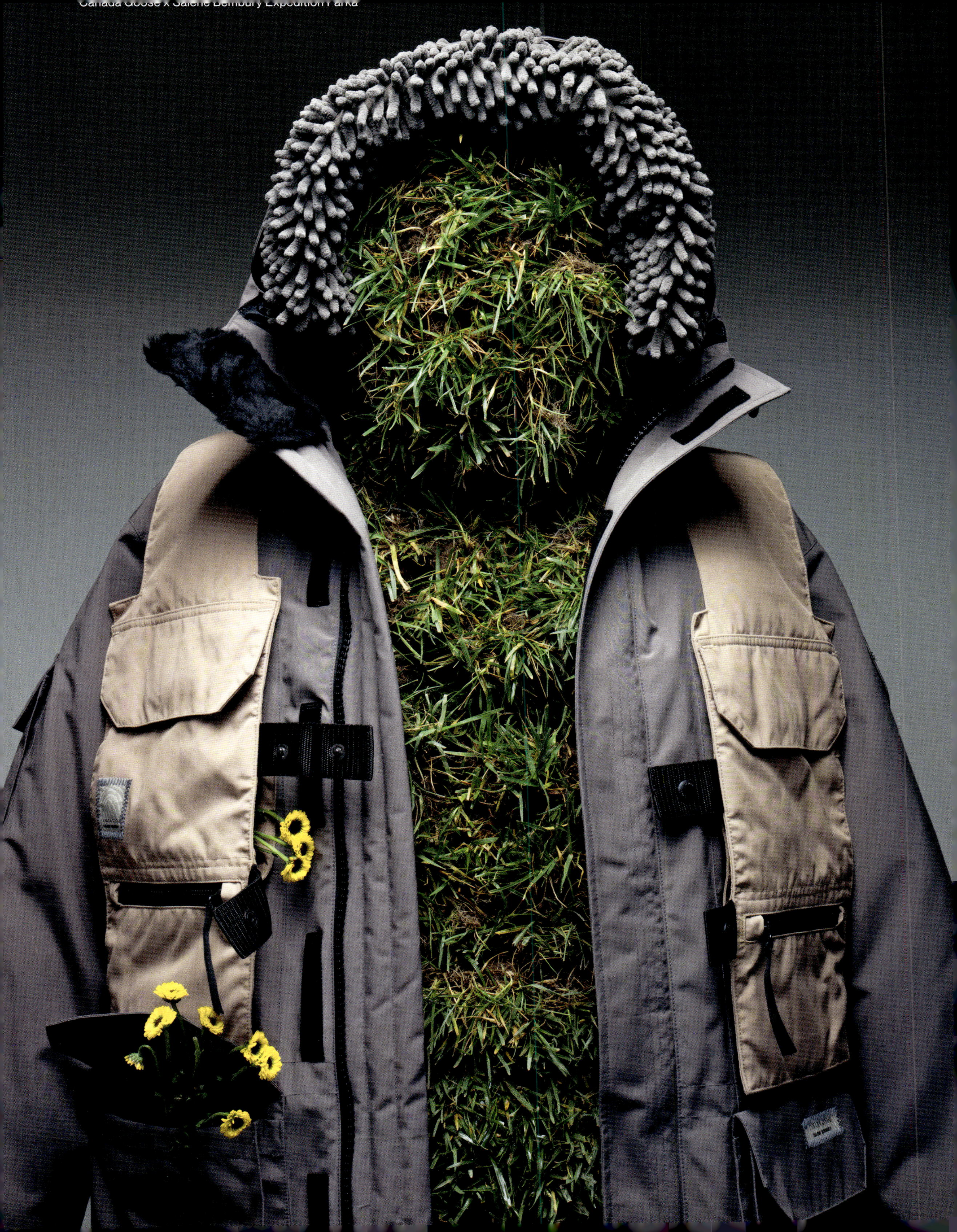

Canada Goose x Salehe Bembury Expedition Parka

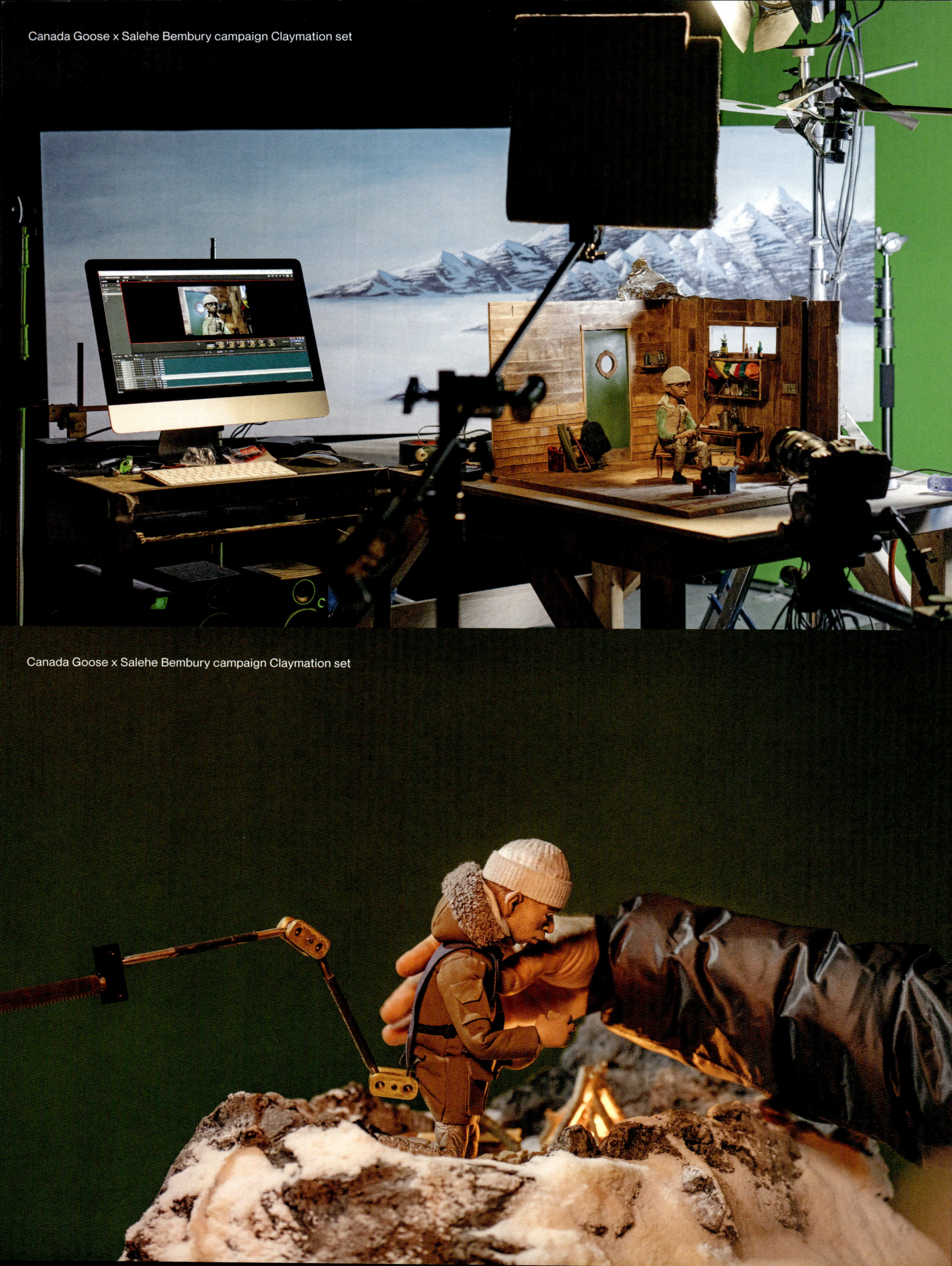

Canada Goose x Salehe Bembury campaign Claymation set

Canada Goose x Salehe Bembury campaign Claymation set

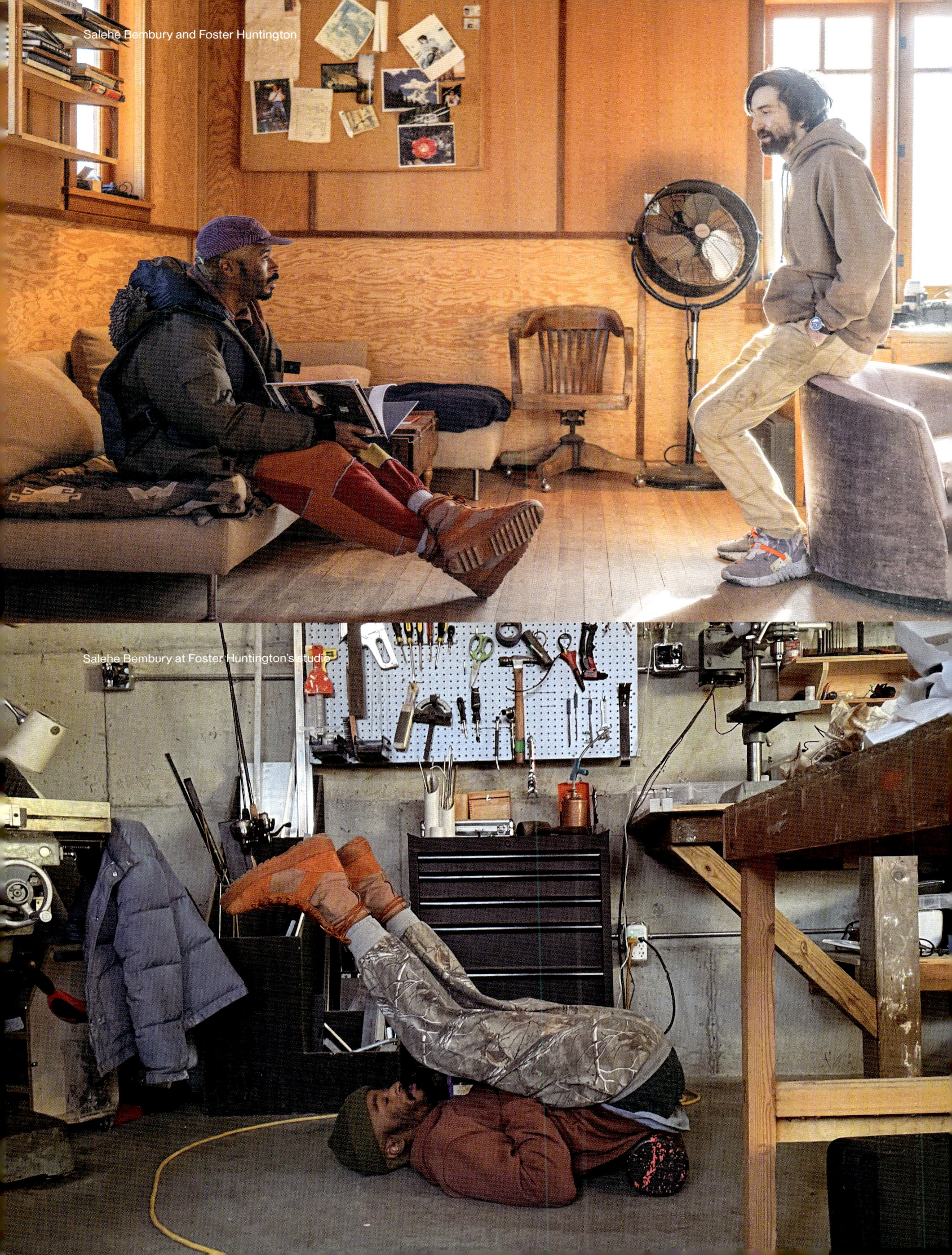

Salehe Bembury and Foster Huntington

Salehe Bembury at Foster Huntington's studio

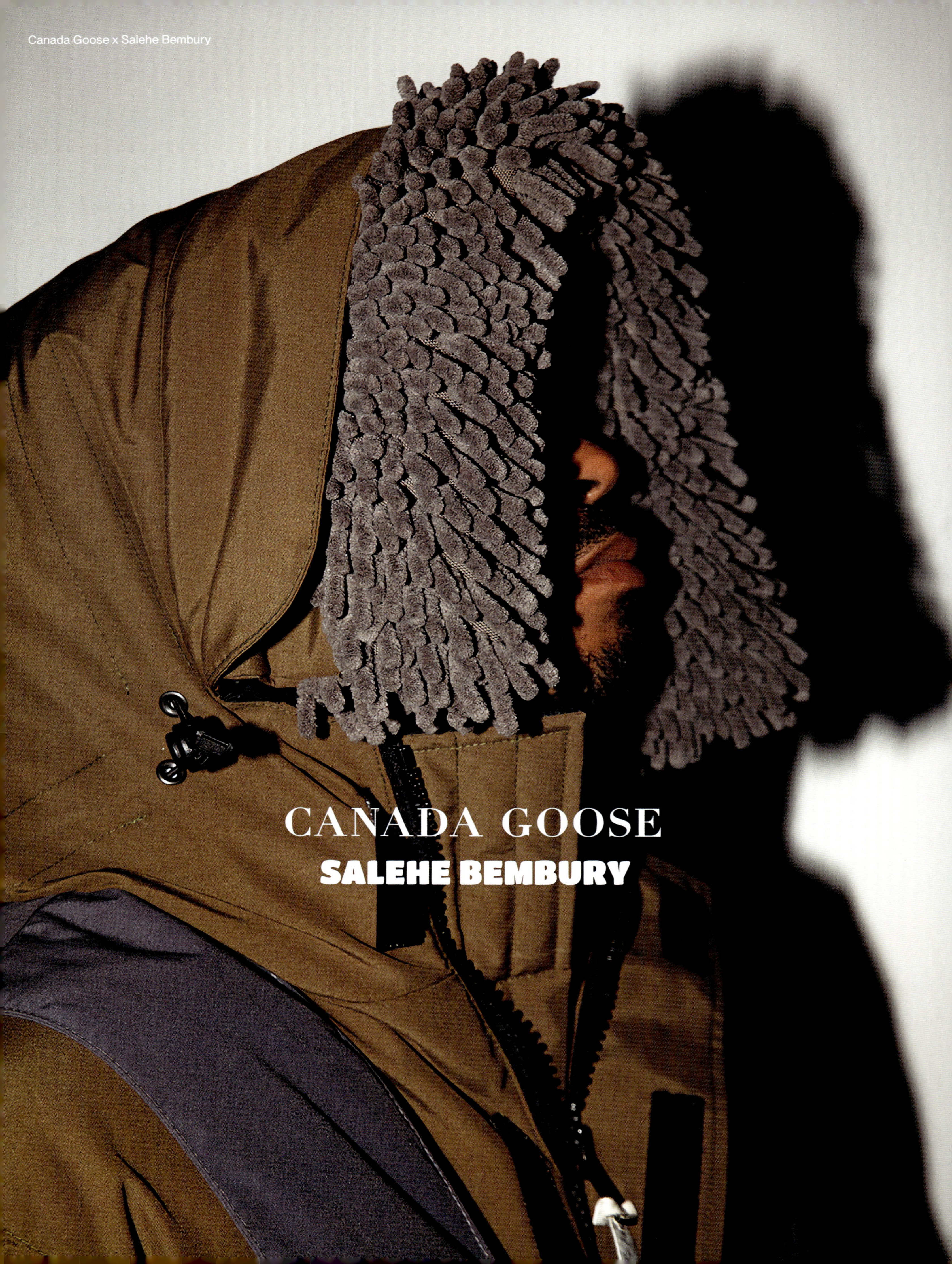
CANADA GOOSE
SALEHE BEMBURY

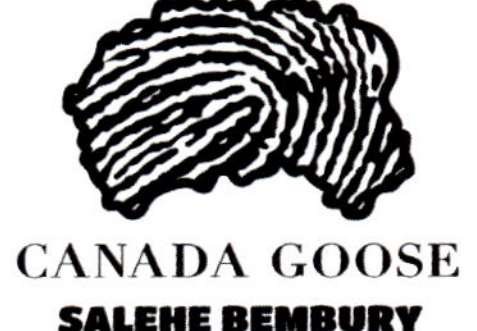

IS IT POSSIBLE TO:
1. REDUCE AMOUNT OF SPACE BETWEEN ROWS
or
2. ADD ADDITIONAL ROWS SO THERE ARE NO SPACES

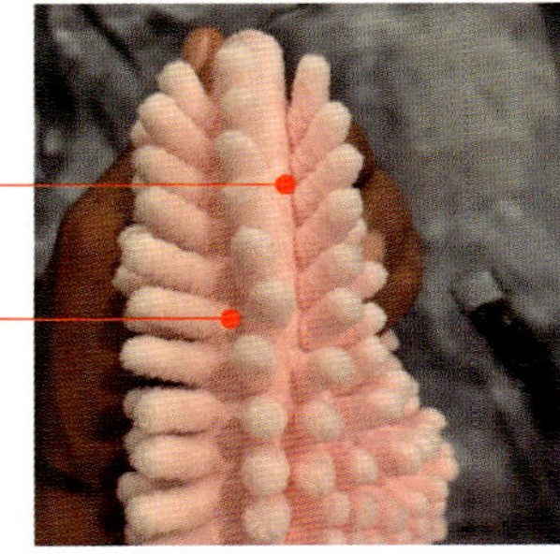

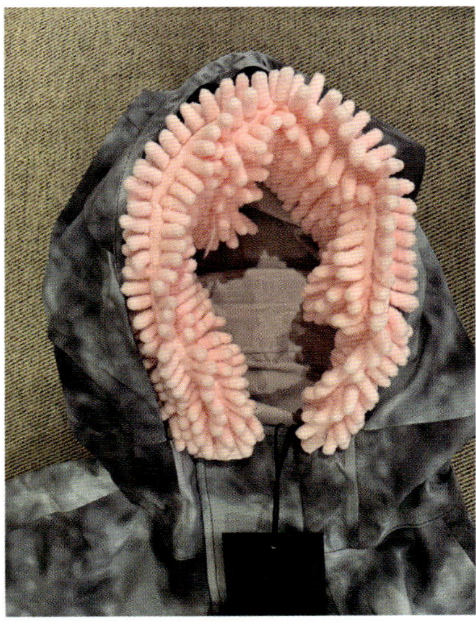

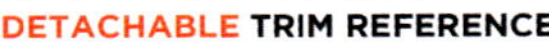

DETACHABLE TRIM REFERENCE

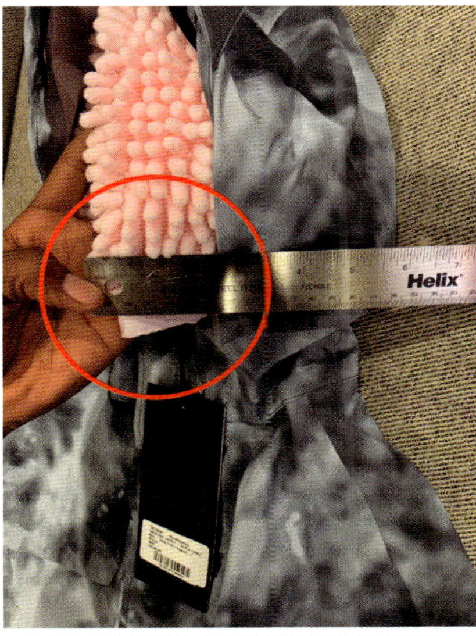

EXTEND MATERIAL 2.5 INCHES PAST HOOD

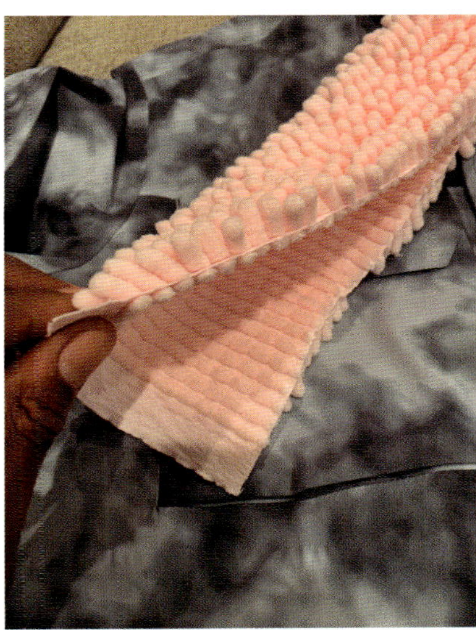

FOLD OVER MATERIAL AS REFERENCE SO THAT BOTH SIDES HAS NUBS.

Canada Goose x Salehe Bembury Expedition Parka design exploration

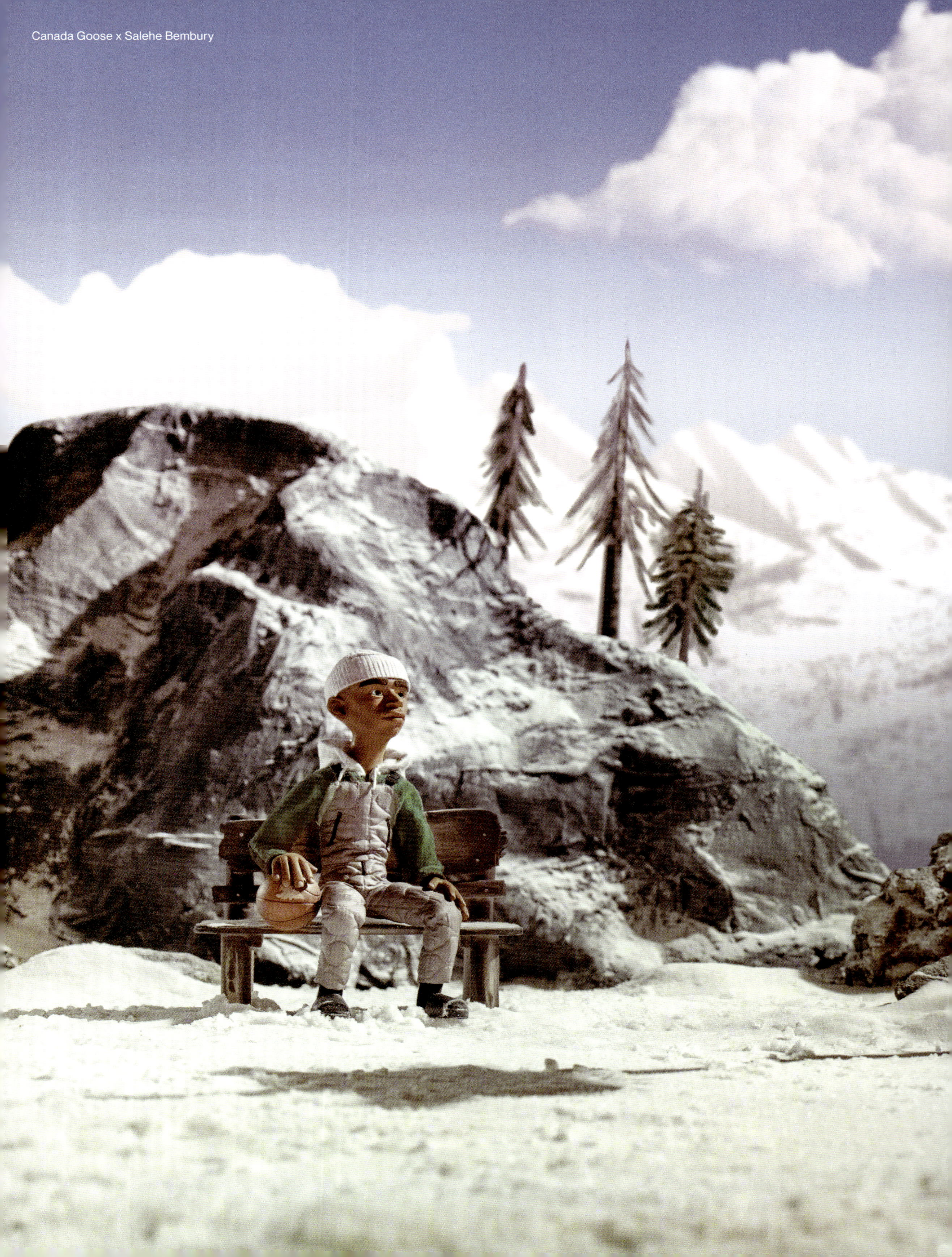

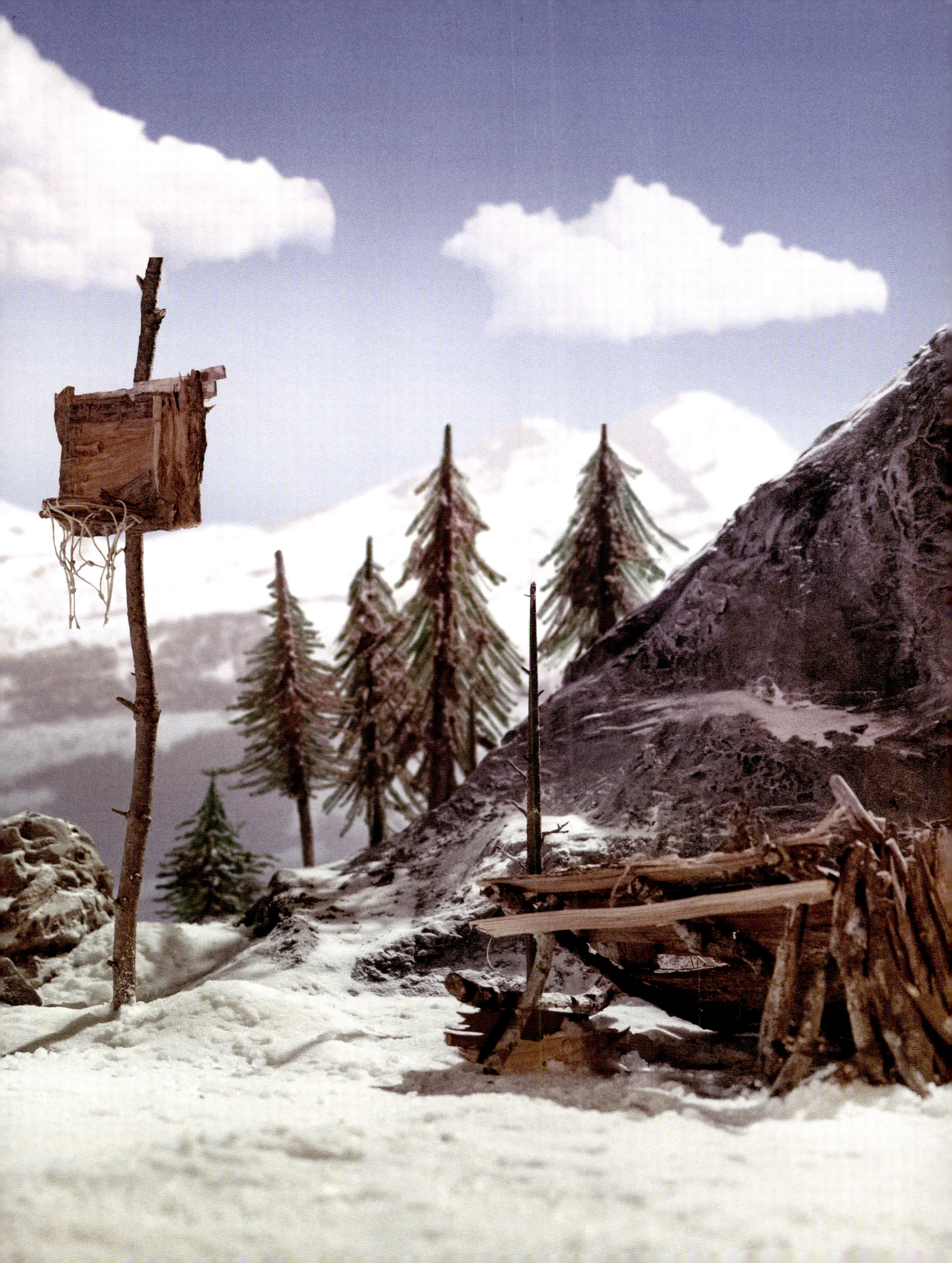

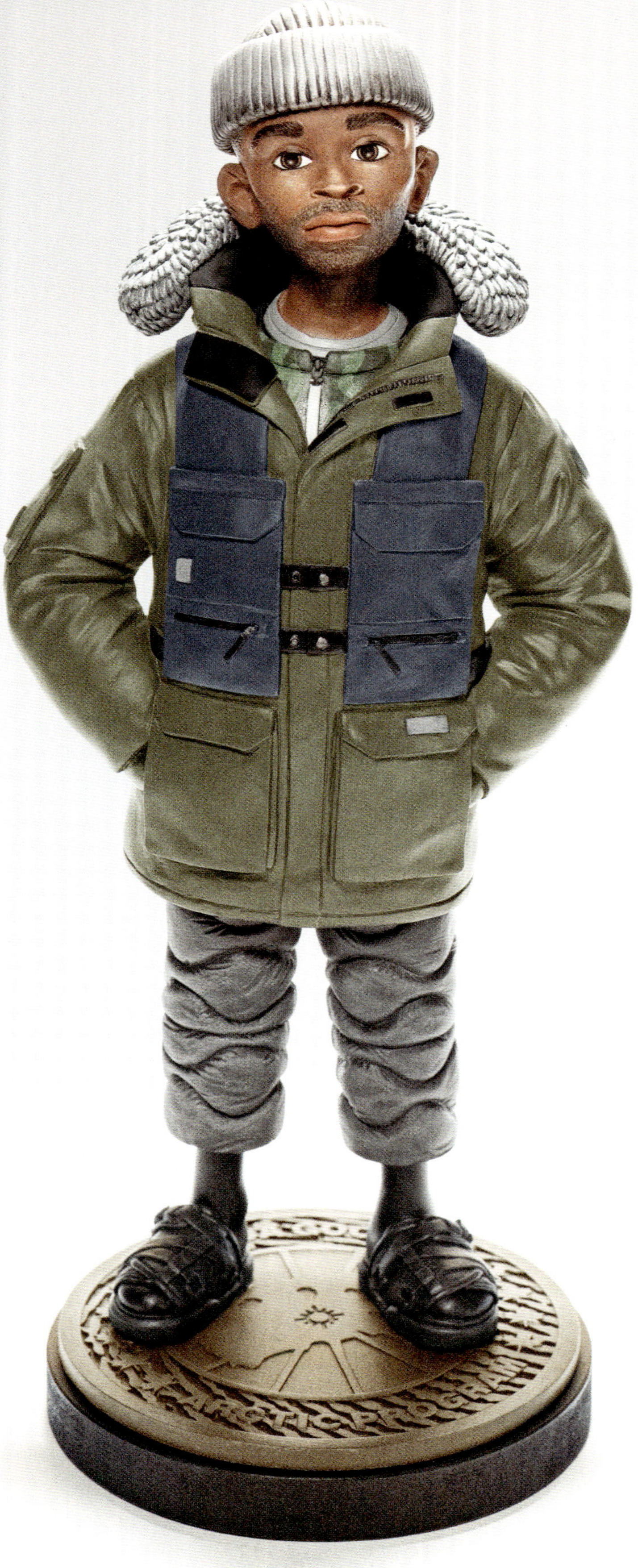

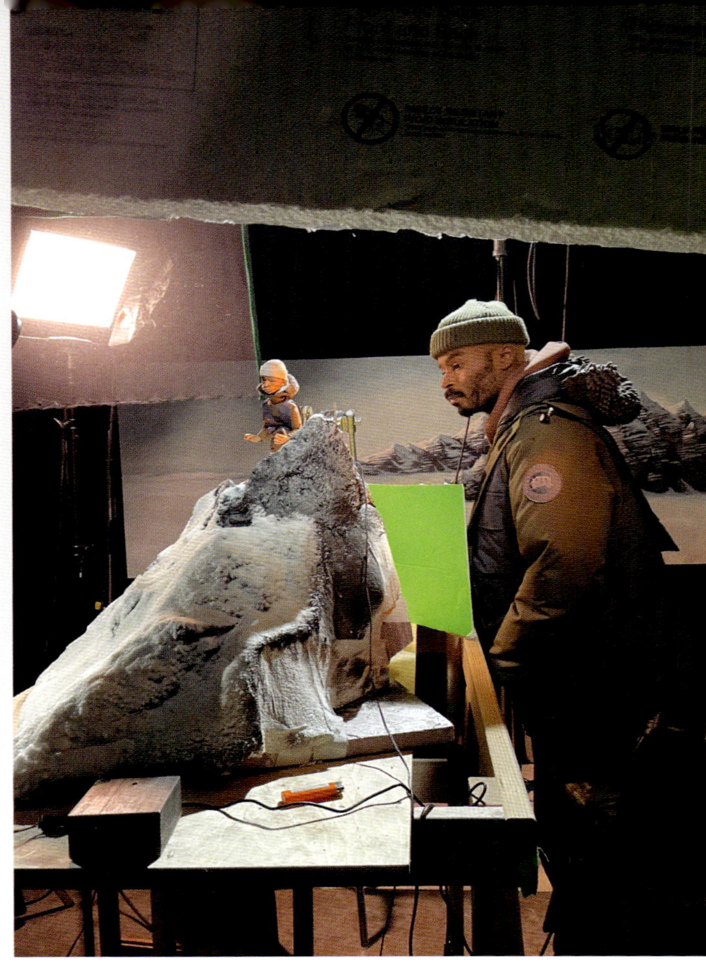

270

(2022)

CANADA GOOSE

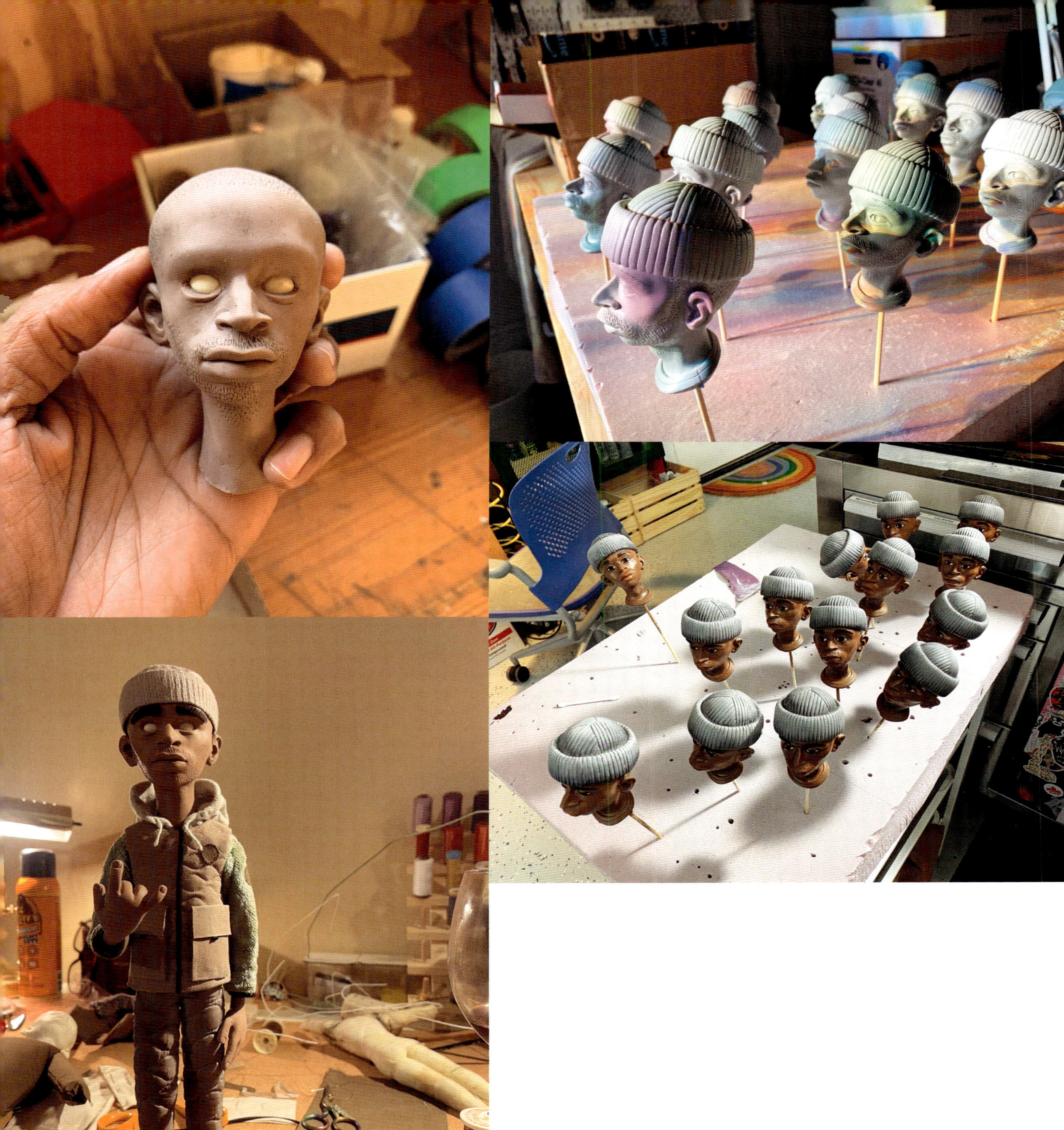

271

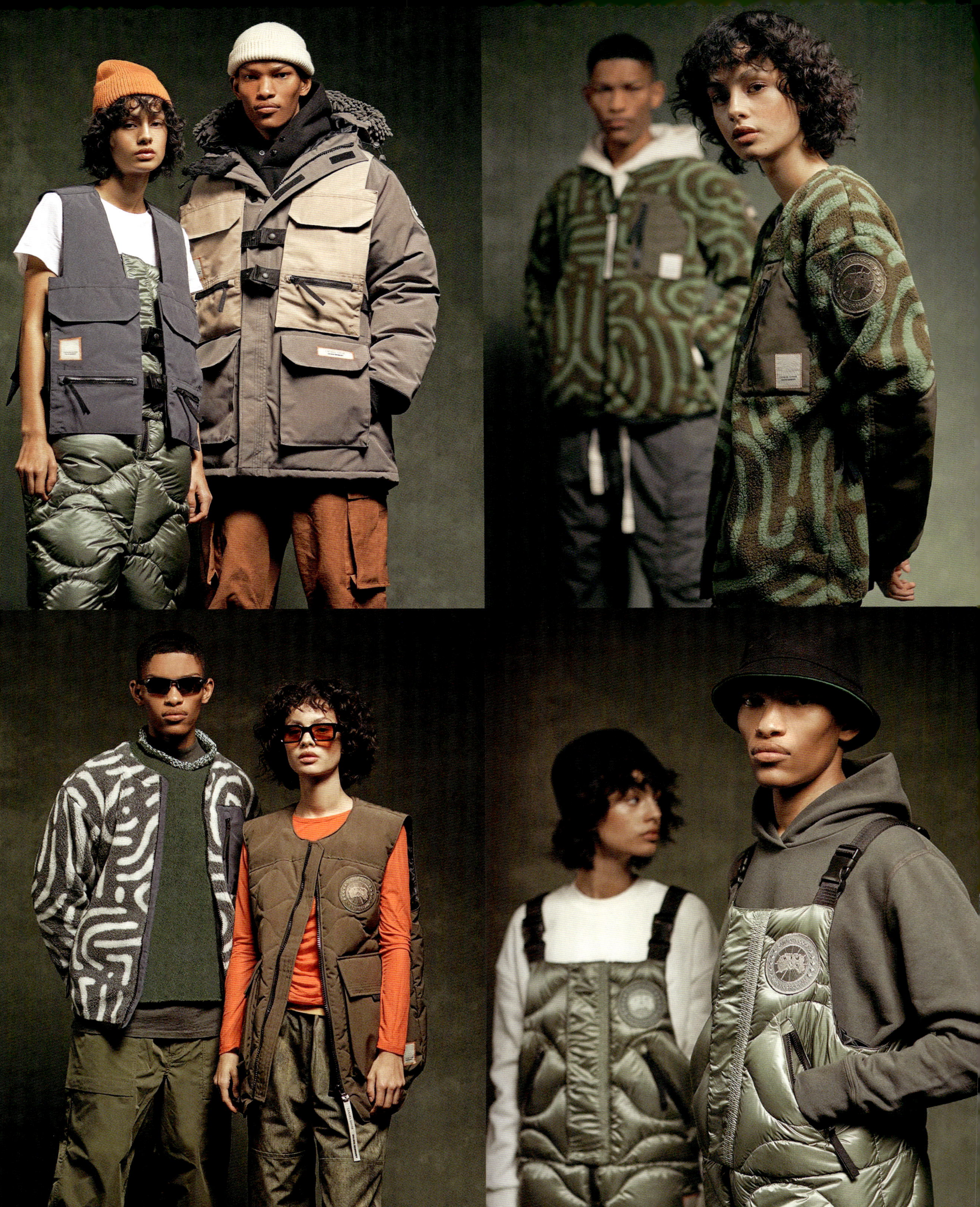

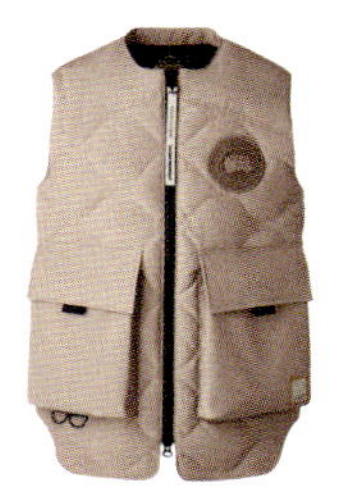
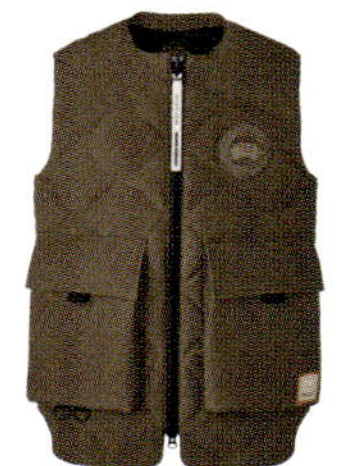
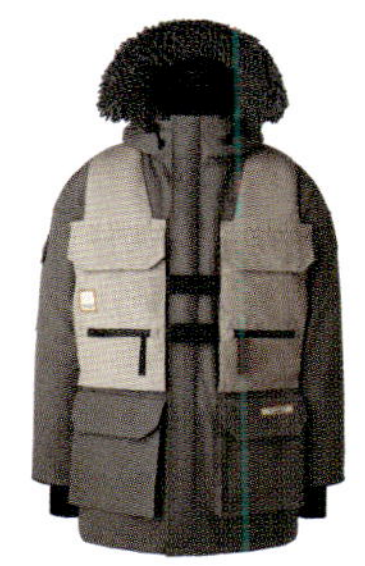
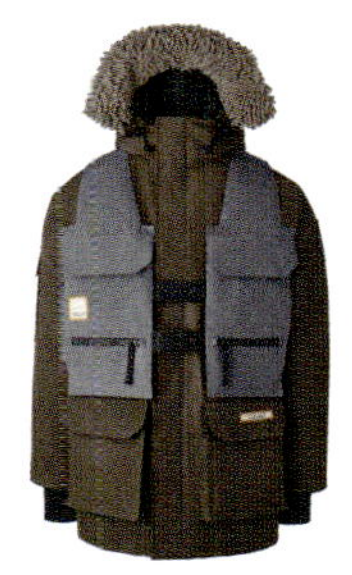
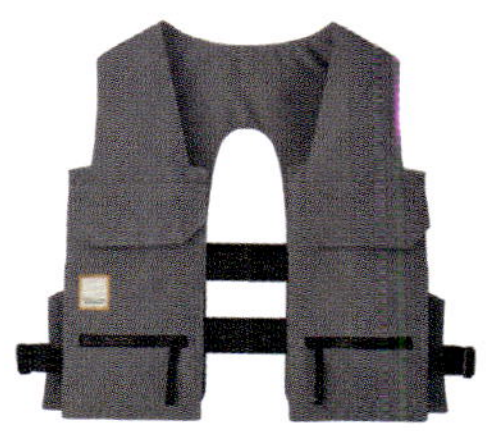
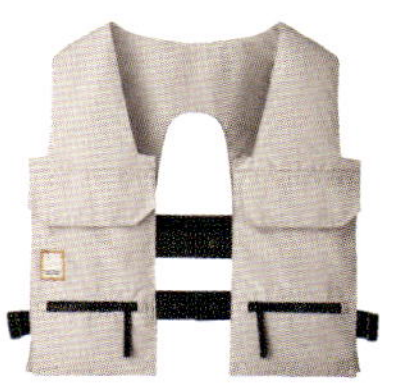
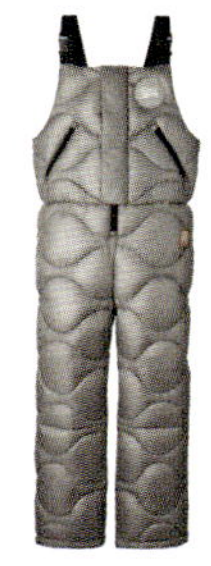
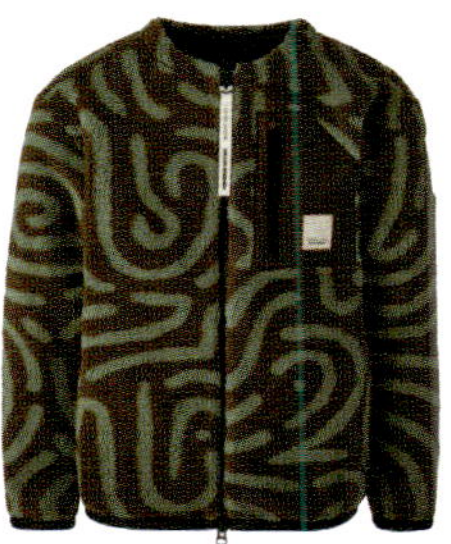
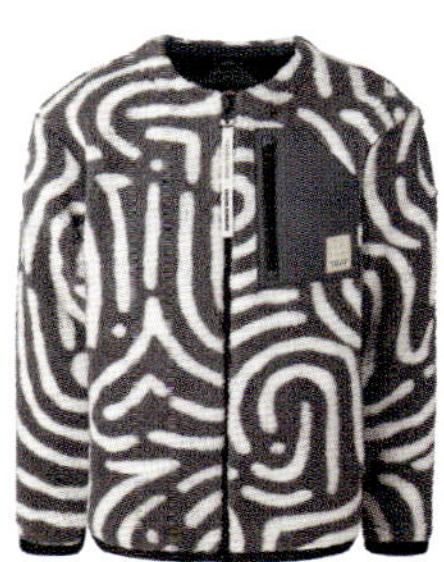

BRANDON ‘JINX’ JENKINS IN CONVERSATION WITH SALEHE BEMBURY

III

JINX: You’ve spoken about only wanting to do work that’s authentic, that aligns with you. You said something to the point of, “If someone asks me to make a golf shoe, I’m not going to make a golf shoe because I don’t currently golf.” Obviously there is a level of strategy, but it feels like a lot of times you’re responding to what’s being thrown into your world. I don’t know if that’s actually what lies underneath the surface, but it feels as if you’re more like a sail in the wind, right?

SALEHE: You’re absolutely right. I don’t know if that’s intentional, necessarily, but I think I’ve gotten to a place in my career where I can not only pursue the three Fs, but I can also pursue happiness and pursue comfort. I’ve always chased that, since I realized that that was even possible—even going back to the Versace story, of Donatella offering me that opportunity and then me being like: “But can I stay in LA?” I guess I was learning what high-level negotiation was, in real time. That taught me from that day forward: OK, my value sits at a level where I can make the situation work to my liking.

JINX: In the shift from employee to the front lines of entrepreneurship, where it’s essentially a one-man army, different skills must be asked of you.

SALEHE: I never saw it as a one-man army because we all have a job, right? We all are that one man or one woman within our job. I was blessed enough to get this entrepreneurial opportunity of putting my name on product. Then I go from having an employer to going to do that, which is now my job. It’s not like when you immediately get knighted with that opportunity, you think to yourself, “I got to hire a team.” It’s just like, now this is my new job and I guess technically my boss is me. But that’s ultimately just a shift in job, I guess.

JINX: You’d been working for different organizations, and then obviously at Versace, you were more your own boss than you ever had been. You’re the lead designer at this point. But the Takashi project is different. The Takashi thing is where you step to the side now and think: “Oh, I’m always slay, but now I’m slay front-facing to the world.”

SALEHE: Exactly right. I was familiar with Takashi, but not as closely as I got to be by being around him as long as I was. Even his illustrated poses he did, that on the surface just felt silly—I realized that he was ultimately creating moments for people.

When you look back at a lot of those photos, they seem like they were happy, positive moments. And this was at a time where if you look at the photos, I’m frowning, because I’m trying to look cool or look like what I thought a serious designer was supposed to look like. And really that wasn’t the vibe. Takashi taught me that you should spread positivity with your work. Maybe even if you’re not in that mood. I’ve seen Takashi literally be straight-faced and then meet a fan and light up. That’s inspired me because for the longest time I was taking pictures where I looked like I was depressed and trying to be cool or just throwing a peace sign.

So now—not to say that this was totally inspired by Takashi—but now I do a very performative smile with a peace sign. And now you look back on those photos and they look like really happy moments. And now my audience has come to expect that. Now when people ask me for photos, they do the exaggerated smile and peace sign, and this photo now becomes a moment of positivity and I’m acknowledging that even though I’ve met ten fans that day, this was their moment with someone that they at least made me believe they care about or respect. I’m going to respect that moment and then I’m going to get back to my day because it only takes a few seconds.

JINX: You mentioned this moment that you have with Takashi is a turning point: it goes from something you’re somewhat anxious about into understanding it’s something bigger. You’re stepping out as Salehe, the individual, but you also have this new fandom that you are experiencing in real life. What does that say about the power of design, about what’s happening in this space between you and them?

SALEHE: I think it exists on a spectrum. To some people, it’s like, damn, this motherfucker just makes me happy. And it might just be through color usage or light-hearted campaigns that are different and make you smile. Going back to that Maya Angelou quote, there are just some people that see me and they’re like, man, you make me feel good in this world of seriousness and dark images and Travis Scott looking at the floor in every picture. This guy’s playing with nostalgia and color and happiness. There are other people that are like, damn, look at this life he’s living—this motherfucker’s above the clouds one day and then the next day he’s repotting a plant with dirt all around him and then the next day he’s on a plane. Just the diversity in experience and that hunger and excitement for life, I think people see that and it’s something that they want to relate to or strive for. I think for some people, maybe just seeing my journey and my origin story and what it is now, it helps them realize that life is short and you’ve got to pursue happiness.

JINX: Did you always believe in design over everything?

SALEHE: Well, as a consumer, I didn’t realize I was a slave to storytellers. Older designers and teachers would be like, “You got to tell stories,” and that whole sentence would confuse me. I’d be like, “Wait, what? I thought I was here to design. What do you mean I got to tell stories?” It didn’t click for me for the longest time. I don’t think it clicked until I started doing collaborations, because even at Versace I would just design the shoe and then they would take it and put it into their fashion machine and you’d see models and runway or whatever. But then when it was New Balance, and even Anta, it was like: now I’m digging back into the nostalgia of Nike and thinking about different shoes I loved, and how a Jordan was inspired by a Cadillac or a jet or the Pompidou Center in Paris, and the storytelling that goes with that.

With Anta, I really thought about my whole budding outdoor brand. I went through all these photos and I found Birds Nest. And then I thought about how the foam, which was like the energy similar to the bird, lives within the bird’s nest, which is the cage and the structure. So then we created this shoe called Nest Tech, which was this foam that lived within this bird’s nest-looking cage.

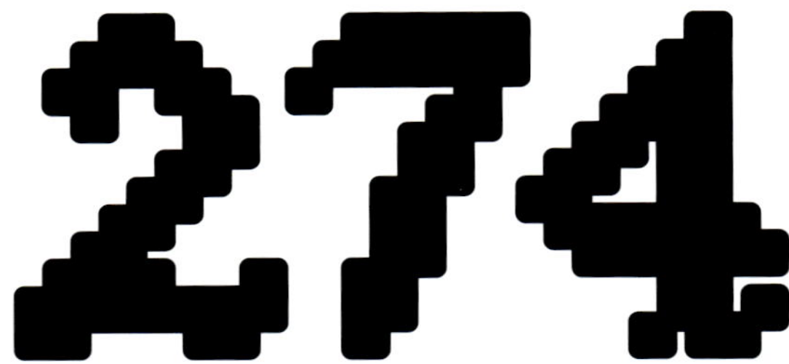

I went to China and we did this whole thing called Make and Play, where myself and four young designers cut up and reconstructed a whole bunch of shoes—very Virgil Blueprint. We took pictures of all those shoes. That was more of a story of the process and the steps that it was going to take us to get to this shoe—very much fabricated for asset purposes, but still necessary in the process. I knew that I needed to create something that made people feel like they were a part of something or made people laugh, so that when they wore the shoe it gave them a feeling—because that's what's always worked on me.

JINX: What changed for you post–New Balance?

SALEHE: Well, I guess it was the first time I was working with a brand where it was hype, because now my name was joining with this already very established brand—people automatically wanted it. So that was interesting. Even with Yeezy, Season 3 and Season 4, we were still trying to get established, still trying to find factories and stuff. A lot of the brands I worked with—including Versace, because there was no real sneaker business there, and even Cole Haan—these were all underdog stories in a sense. And then with New Balance, it was like I finally got drafted by a winning team—from a sneaker business perspective, to be very clear. I was able to approach product a little bit more honestly, slightly more comfortably, and maybe without such a specific consumer in mind. Maybe I became the consumer.

JINX: Whether we're talking about your entry point in the beginning, or working places and feeling uncomfortable because of how you were dressed and wanting to do more, to responding to outside impulse—I feel like you're in the feelings business. A lot of what you're talking about is either how you feel or how you're making other people feel. Is that what good design is about?

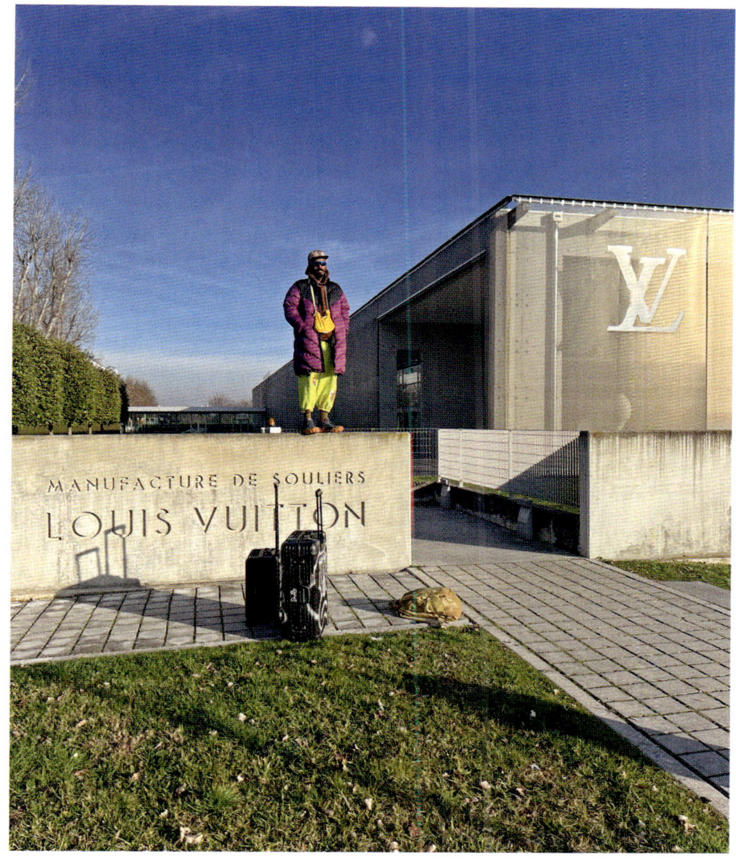

SALEHE: Good design is something that works and leaves you with a feeling, I would say. That's the problem with a lot of design these days: it doesn't work. So there's shoes that are cool for a moment on the internet, but that shit don't work as a shoe. It doesn't function. It doesn't breathe. It's not comfortable. And we can't depart from some of the very important rules to footwear or design. It has to function. If it doesn't function, it's just art. I just hold those things to be really important, and even did when I was in fashion, where those rules are valued even less. I think it has to work and it has to leave you with a feeling. And if you think about any Jordan you've loved, or any Apple computer, or anything like that, they all check those two boxes.

JINX: As you keep going further, even as you're working more as just Salehe, you're getting closer and closer to people that are close to your world. As the kid who grew up in TriBeCa liking streetwear and playing the SoHo scene, Union is pretty key and on point. And you made a point to say, it's not just that you were working with him, but that you guys were able to become contemporaries.

SALEHE: Going back to the tools that I was picking up along the way: I just think I picked up enough tools for Chris to acknowledge me and to respect me. In the beginning it was just trying to associate with whoever would associate with me. But then I got to a place where I had a portfolio or a resume that made these people respect me and made me stand out enough for them to take my call. Chris Gibbs and I were introduced through a mutual friend, but I think the reason he took that meeting is because he looked at my Instagram and was like, "Oh, okay. He's at Versace." It's very hard to come in cold. You need to have some bridges, or something that helps you shine.

JINX: But then how do you feel about that, realizing that, "Hey, I think I might be shiny, I think I might've gotten to this point." Do you acknowledge what's taking place? Do you celebrate it? Do you push it away? How do you navigate?

SALEHE: I just do a Jordan fist and get back on defense... The driving force for my entire career has been those milestone moments. It even started back in school when we were allowed to go out to lunch by ourselves. And then you're working at a job and maybe you're allowed to leave the office without telling your boss, that's a big deal. And then it's your first lookup on the Internet where your name is in it. So it's these things that I just kept trying to get. Then once I got them, they don't matter anymore, and it's on to the next one. And it could be a curse, because I don't know if it means I would never be satisfied—but it also is an amazing fuel.

JINX: Maybe never satisfied—but are you happy?

SALEHE: I'm human. I think I'm as happy as I can be. I'm literally doing what I wanted to do as a little kid. I'm driving a spaceship to work. I own a home. You know what I mean? I'm doing all the things, so how could I not be pretty satisfied? I'm Pisces, I experience emotion.

JINX: What does the design of non-apparel items open up for you? Obviously you have an education in industrial design that spans beyond footwear, but footwear is where you wanted to apply it. But now the scope is wider, in textiles and ceramics and the potential for other projects—now you're playing in a wider sandbox.

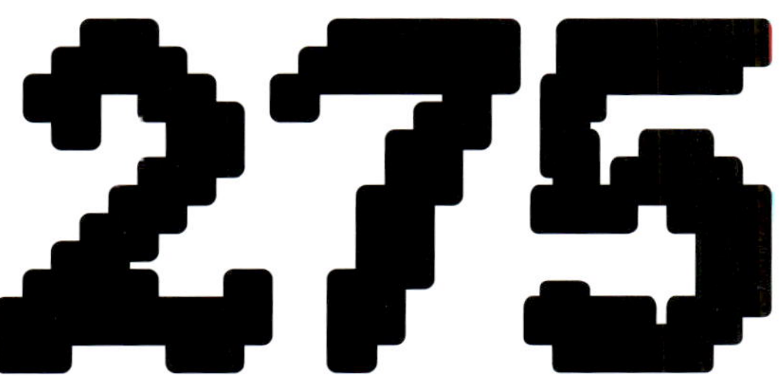

SALEHE: I remember Kanye talking about maybe *Yeezus*, and he was talking about creating as if he was three years old. And I thought that that was really cool because creating as adults, we have all of these barriers and obstacles, doubt and ego or lack thereof. When we're babies, we start as these perfect spheres of clay, and then the first time we're told "no," it's like a jab in it. And then the first time we're embarrassed, it's mangled. You know what I mean? And the first time we fail, right? So we end up as these beautiful forms of clay, but ultimately these beautiful forms of clay that are afraid to create truly. So I really try to do that, just create truly and create from the gut. There are designers that will make 50 colors and then circle three and then explore that further, blah, blah. I pick a color and I'm done. I'm like, "This works. I like it." I really think there's something to be said for designing from the heart.

I think one of the most valuable things that I have is a design language. And if you have a design language, that can really live on anything. And so on top of a design language, I have an unintentional color palette that I use as well. I get tagged in random things on Instagram often where they just have this organic design language or maybe certain colors and people are like, "Salehe vibes." And I get it now. I've kind of established this aesthetic. I can inject my sensibilities into something. So whether it's urban planning or designing a car or designing a flower pot, I can take that sensibility and apply it to that.

JINX: So much of your career has been defined by partnership. What is a good partnership?

SALEHE: I mean, on paper, a good partnership is when there's a 50/50 exchange of ideas and output and resources. Ultimately that's how it should be just because there needs to be an equal acknowledgement of both parties, so they can reach a destination that they wouldn't have been able to reach on their own. However, personally, and with the portfolio that I have in collaborator history, I think the best partnership is one where they'll just let me go. And that obviously comes from having a resume and obtaining trust, but I'm a unique collaborator in the sense that I'm also a fifteen-year veteran footwear designer. Most collaborators are musicians or influencers or people that have no background in footwear, so they need a lot of guidelines and leading and hand-holding, whereas I understand the business inside and out. And then on top of that, I also am theoretically an influencer or a talent or whatever you want to call it. So I believe that I'm in some cases the perfect collaborator, because I can kind of have all of the conversations.

These brands are bringing in the collaborators because we have the ideas. In some brands there are people with ego that believe they're just as creative and just as important as the collaborator, and they want to represent that through what they do with the brand. And that's what can make things difficult sometimes. But ultimately, you have to structure a contract before actually getting in bed with a brand, and I make sure to structure my deals in favor of my creative freedom.

JINX: What's your favorite thing you've been tagged in with "Salehe vibes?"

SALEHE: When I created the Yurt, it had the whistle on the back, and that whistle had a very purposeful function for the outdoors and more specifically, safety. But then it took on this other life on social media because you'd have people in the outdoors blowing the whistle, you'd have people just drunk in bars blowing the whistle. You'd have parents giving the shoes to their little four-year-old kids, they'd blow the whistle and laugh, so you'd see that joy. Going back to what you were saying about leaving the audience with a feeling—it was just happening nonstop for a few months because it was giving kind of new use or new meaning to a shoe, and it was community-building in the weirdest way. And that's something a shoe's never done before.

JINX: You are literally making new things as this book will be getting printed. Do you find that there are threads that you still see from your youth up until now? Can you look back at Payless Salehe, or even high-school TriBeCa Salehe, and see elements that are still present today?

SALEHE: I like to think that I haven't changed. I've grown through experience and resources, but I'd like to think I'm the same. And I really think that's worked in my favor, because there's a high level of authenticity in there, where I'm kind of just the same little kid that's doing what he loves and having fun. And when I'm on set making these commercials or campaigns, I'm always just laughing. At the end of the day, it's just shoes. And I'm very blessed to be in this position.

JINX: There's an emotional component to that, to realize how hard it is to preserve something, to preserve the good things about yourself in a world that is constantly changing. This world is different than it was four years ago. Your life is dramatically different and you're living a very singular existence. To be able to remain unchanged—not unchanged, but for pieces of you to be preserved—is actually really fucking hard.

SALEHE: I don't know if it's intentional, though. I think maybe I'm just stubborn about what I like and I know what I don't like, and I'm consistent with that. Very much so just me. I mean, the most frequent and the most rewarding critique I get of my work is when people say, "Wow, it's just so you." And I'm like, "Thanks." Because that is what I do kind of unintentionally every single time. Recently, a friend commented on something that one of my designers colored up, and she was like, "I can tell you didn't design that." And that really spoke to the fact that I actually do have this unintentional language that I speak with my audience, that sometimes I don't even realize I'm speaking.

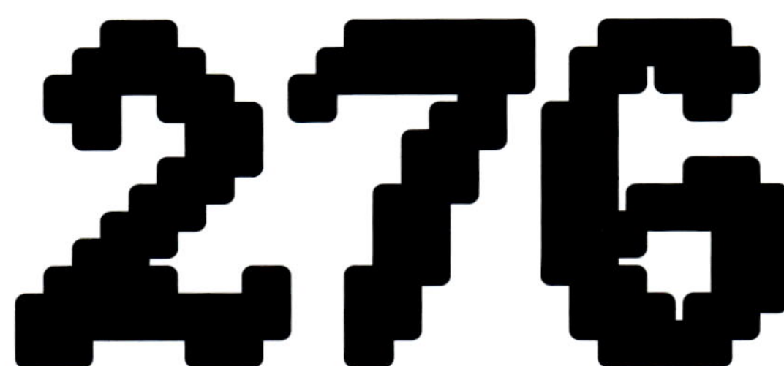

Photographed by Mark Nguyen

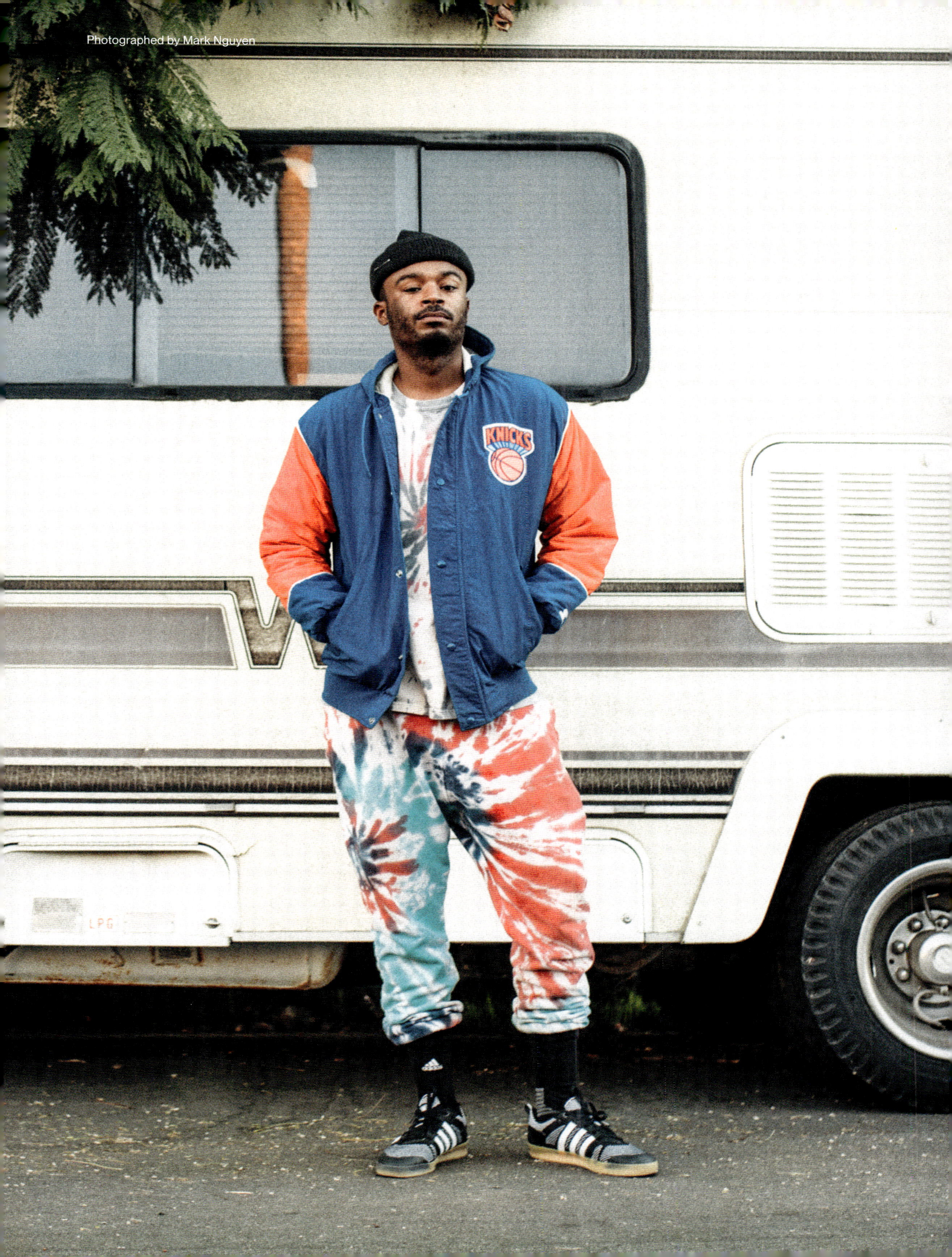

278

CLARKS (2022)

FEEL YOURS

SELF

CLARKS
FEEL YOURSELF

Being a new brand myself, with a smaller audience, I felt that aligning myself with iconic brands would immediately increase my designer value. It would increase the number of people familiar with my work, and it would allow me to tell a different story, because I wouldn't necessarily be restrained by the parameters of the brands I was already working with. Clarks wasn't a brand I grew up wearing all the time, but it was a brand that I did have from time to time, and I was interested in acknowledging the success that they were able to maintain over decades.

During this time, the stories that I was telling were focused in the outdoors, the products I was creating had a foundation in utility. But in the case of Clarks, this was essentially a lifestyle shoe. So the first task that I was met with was figuring out how to continue to tell the story that I was telling to my audience; how to incorporate the Clarks DNA and heritage into the product and how to make something that feels fresh and new both for the existing Clarks consumer and my consumer.

Clarks gave me some books–there's a great book called *Clarks in Jamaica* that I spent a lot of time reading–and I started to identify the styles and the stories that they told way before I collaborated with the company. They had a lot of amazing styles. Many companies will have silhouettes that are successful for a period of time, and then they stop making them. And for me that's the most exciting thing because the question becomes: how can we rebirth this shoe that once had success? How can we present it through a new lens, show it to a new consumer, and give it a completely new round of success?

From that research, I identified the Lugger. I didn't want to just do a color exercise–though that is something I never speak about negatively, because some of the best collaborations have been color-based. I really value the ability to add design lines to a shoe, or create something from scratch. For the Lugger, I wanted to keep the DNA of the shoe but I also wanted to add new details, both aesthetically and functionally. In this sense the project was similar to the Croc, which was something I created from scratch and something very new, but at the same time was a Croc, and something I believe any existing Crocs consumer would identify as such.

So I created a shoe, and we called it a Mud Moss Lugger. It had an asymmetrical lace going up the lateral side of the shoe, an extremely hairy suede, and featured an extremely heavy screen-printed organic shape. The front half of the shoe is essentially the Lugger, and the back half of the shoe is a new design that incorporated neoprene and an open collar. The hairy suede visual was something I had used consistently with New Balance, so this was a part of bringing my brand identity to this shoe. The organic shape had no rhyme or reason, but a lot of my designs live within organic lines and it just felt appropriate. And it also felt confident. In the past I was creating product with reservation and uncertainty, and I really was trying to make the best decisions to ultimately make something both interesting and commercial. But during this period of time I was really feeling myself, so with this Clarks shoe, I thought, fuck it, let me just put a splat on the toe. It felt very Japanese in execution. I've seen some Japanese footwear designers who will just put something crude and confident, maybe screen-printed pr painted, on top of the shoe; it'd look like traditional design principles that would scare a lot of people, but to me it screams confidence, it communicates intention. With this toe mark, and in a sense with the project as a whole, that was what I was trying to do.

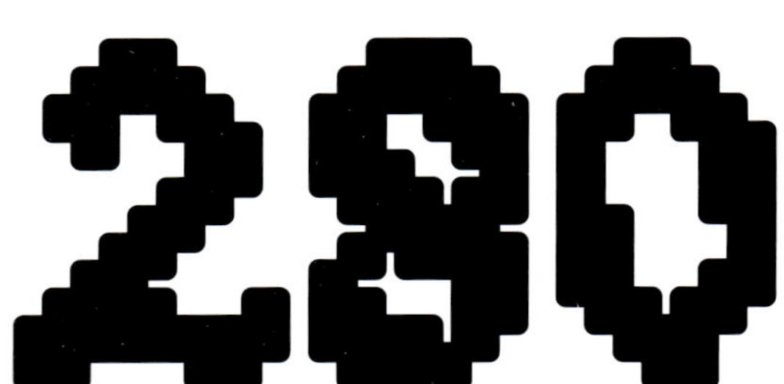

The campaign for this collaboration was done with Foster Huntington, with whom I created my Canada Goose campaign. In this space, where everyone is mimicking everyone else, he is truly a pioneer and an innovator. He created this stop-motion birds-eye view perspective of a pot, of a camper opening the pot, and all of the shoes bubbling around in a bunch of vegetables and greens. This was actually a project that had very little marketing budget. At the end of the day, no matter how great your product is, you do need the ability to market it properly, to tell stories and to reach audiences. Foster created magic with the ingredients he was given, and I was really happy with the result of the collaboration.

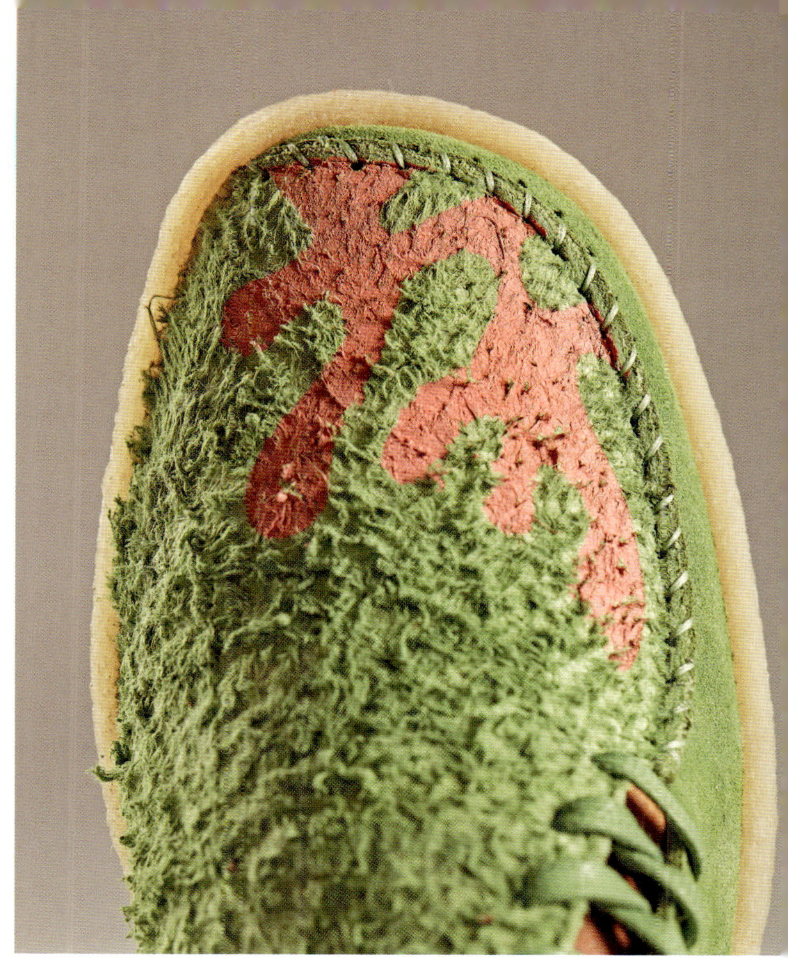

Clarks x Salehe Bembury Mudd Moss Luggger

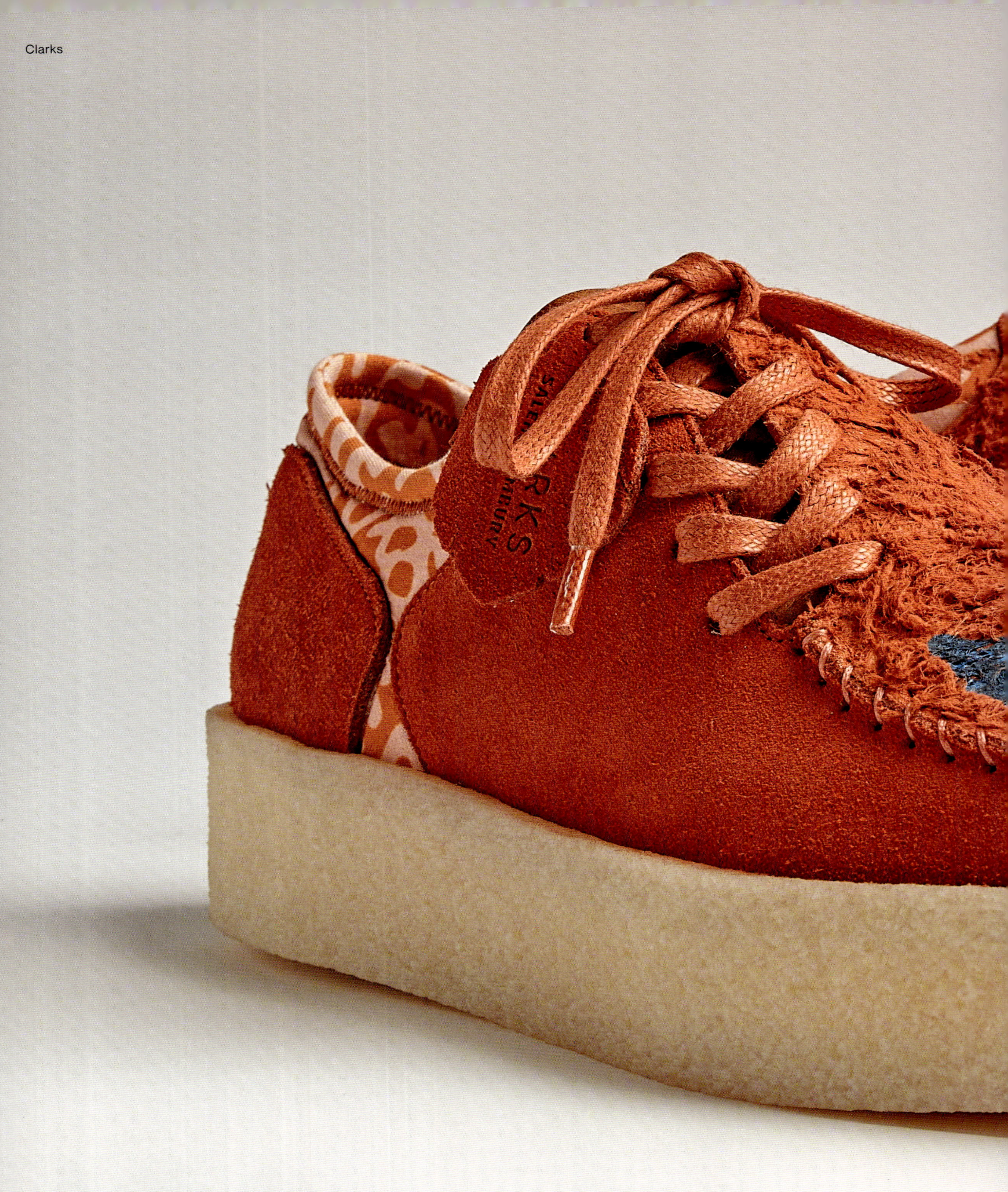

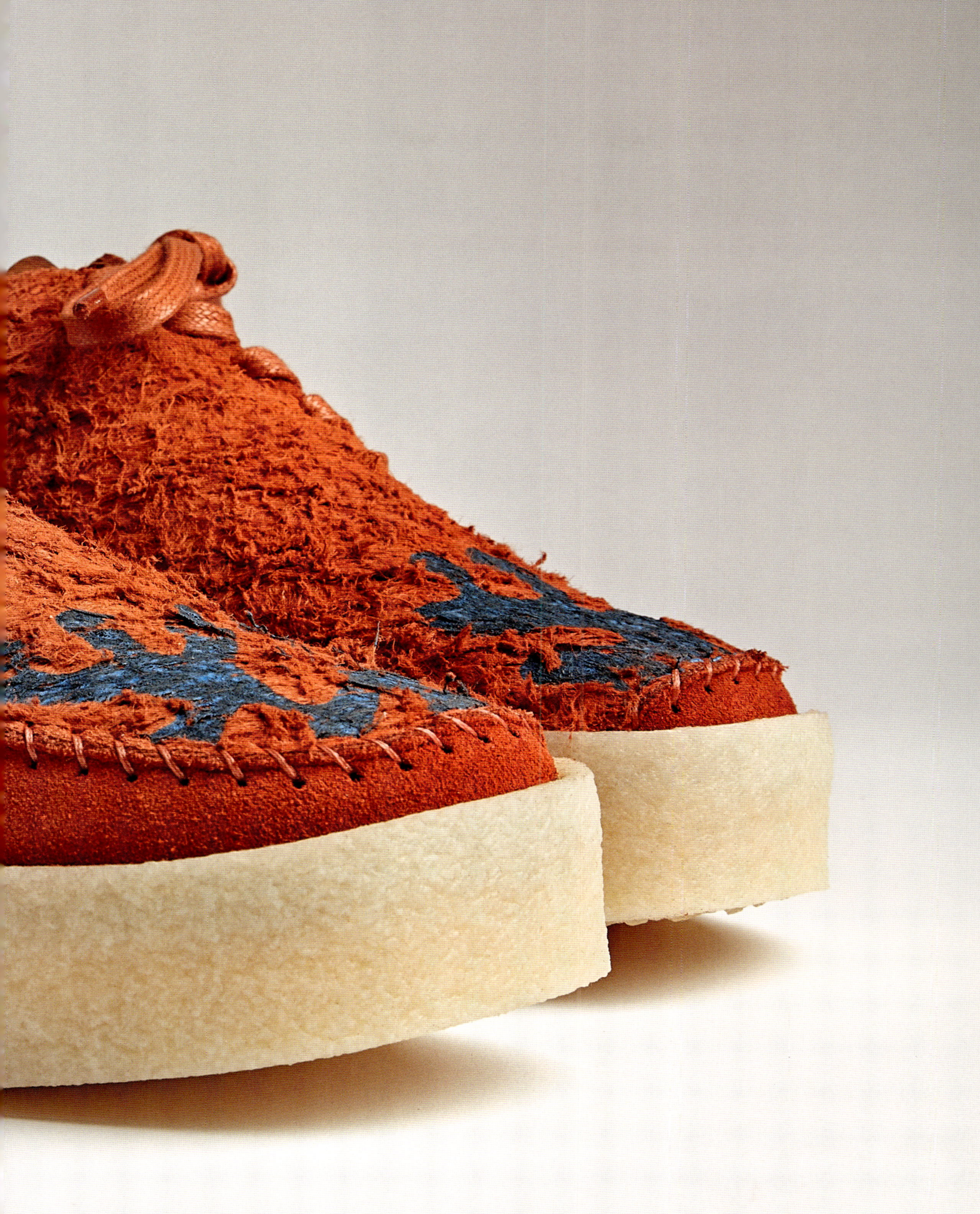

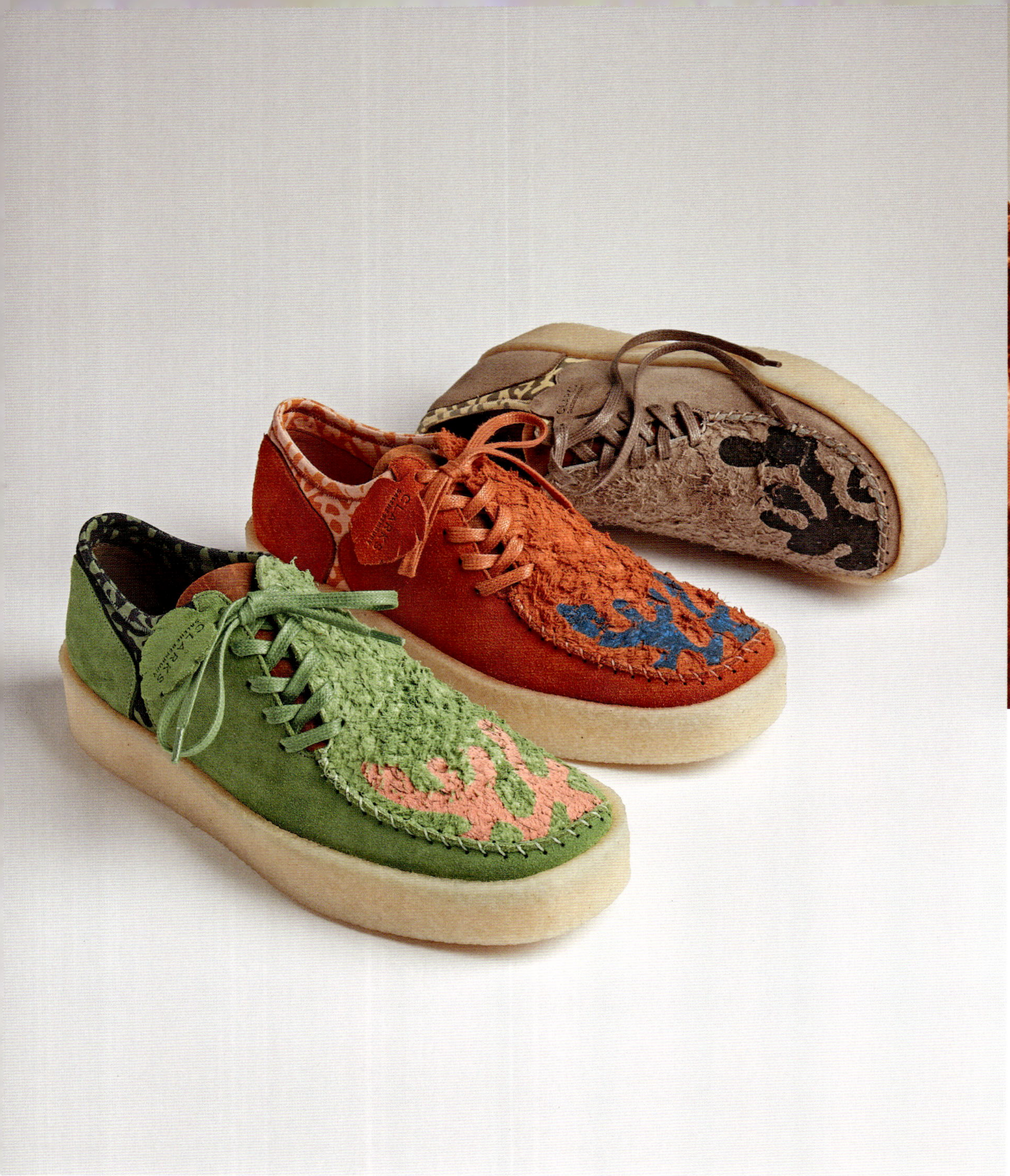

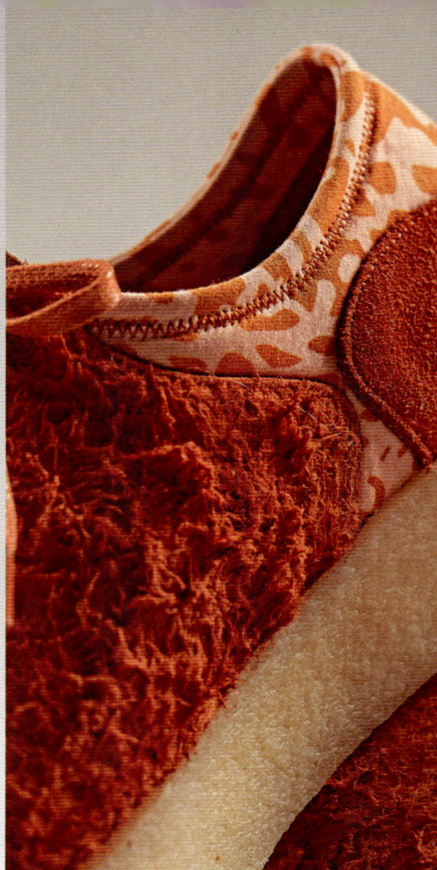

284

(2022)

CLARKS

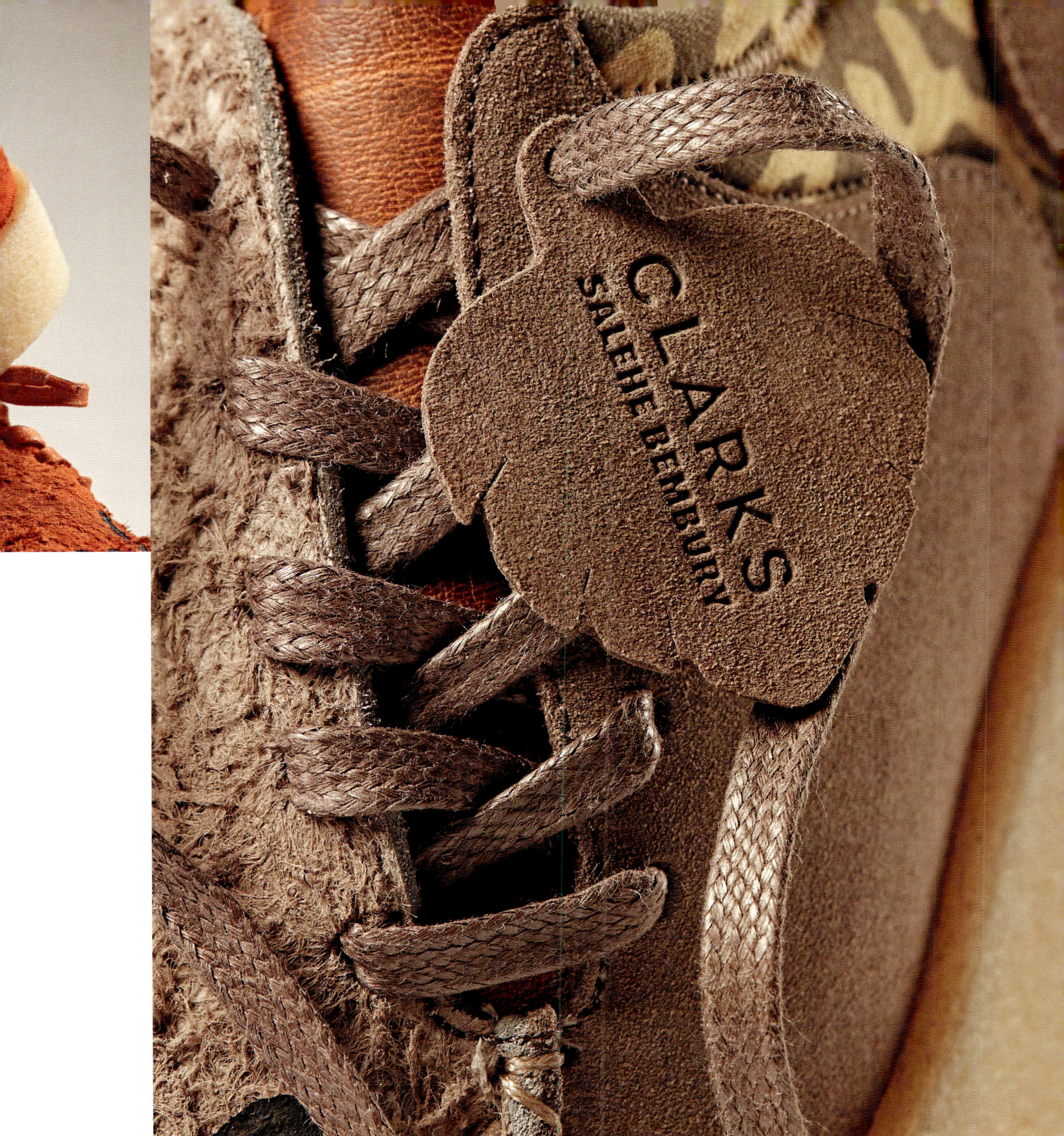

285

CLARKS

(2022)

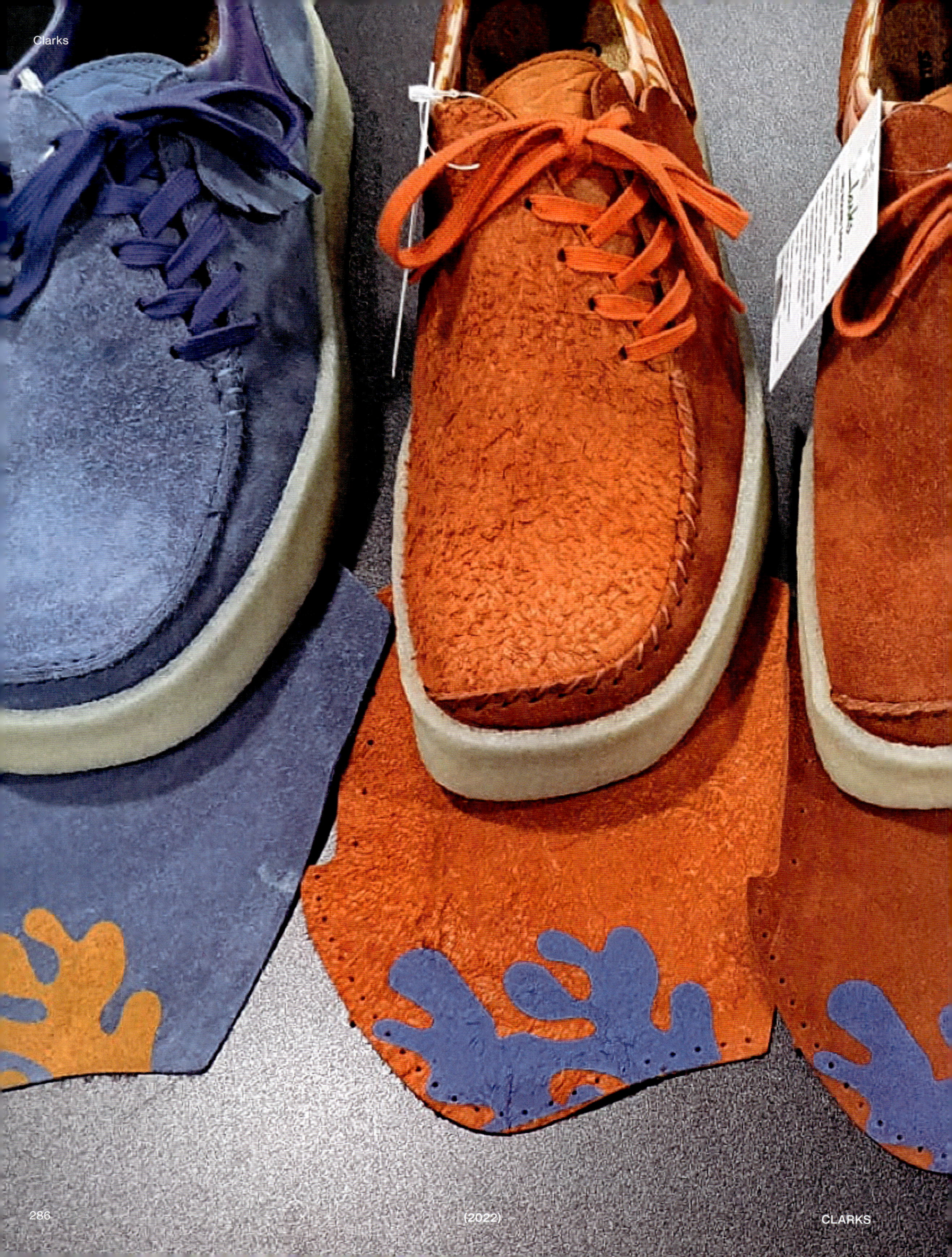

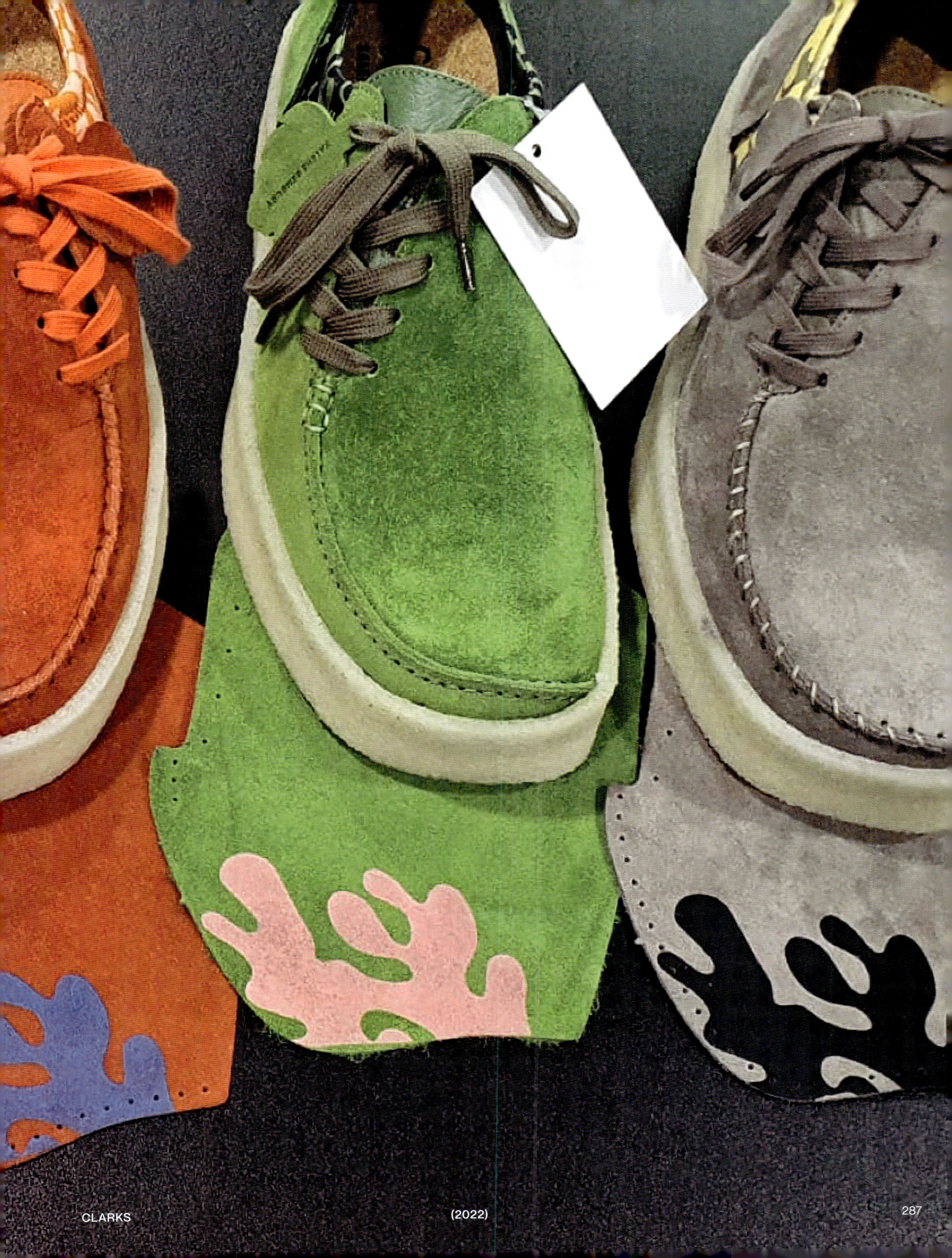

288

VANS (2021)

FOR T
F*CK C

HE
OF IT

VANS
FOR THE FUCK OF IT

With New Balance and Crocs still thriving, and the Union project behind me, I was thinking about working with iconic brands that could raise my designer status, heritage partners that could further stamp and give value to my career. It was like a video game: getting a golden mushroom, or one point up, by working with brands that the average audience member had seen and respected for decades upon decades. Being a new and independent designer, I needed to align with them to increase my momentum and my visibility.

The Vans project allowed me to tell different stories than the narratives of the outdoors and utility I had been telling to that point. Vans was a skate brand, and while I'm not a skater, I'm from Downtown New York, and a lot of my friends' interests and environments involved skate culture. I was very familiar with it, and I wanted to make sure I could tell the skate story from a place of authenticity. There have been many times when I've been offered, say, a golf deal, and I've turned it down because I do not play golf, and above all I would like everything I create to be authentic. So, while I don't skate, I did have many of the reference points, I did a lot of research, and I used my buddy Olan Prenatt, who is very well known in the skate space. Olan was in the movie *Mid90s*, directed by Jonah Hill, and since then he stayed in the industry modeling and acting. He's someone I often see in Los Angeles, he's a fellow creative, and I believe he helped me obtain that level of authenticity with the collaboration. If I had stepped on a skateboard it would not have worked.

Along with the sneakers we created, I took this as an opportunity to make clothing for Spunge. I had gained confidence and experience from the Union collaboration; we made three t-shirts that corresponded with the color palette and the fingerprint pattern used on the sneakers, and that same motif and pattern were printed on the box. This was a conscious effort to create a consistent visual langue and further establish my brand identity; I put it wherever I could, on the shoe, the packaging, and the apparel.

While I was not telling an outdoor story, this project allowed me to explore my palette and identity in a different category and still feel familiar; I believe my audience saw this sitting well next to everything I had created thus far. Without really knowing it, I was also beginning to establish a very organic way of creating my work. There wasn't an insane amount of thought being put into it, a lot of it was coming from the gut, my personal taste, and my personal experiences. Like the name says, the most valuable thing you can be is a sponge; and at this point in my career, all of those absorbed learnings were being used as tools.

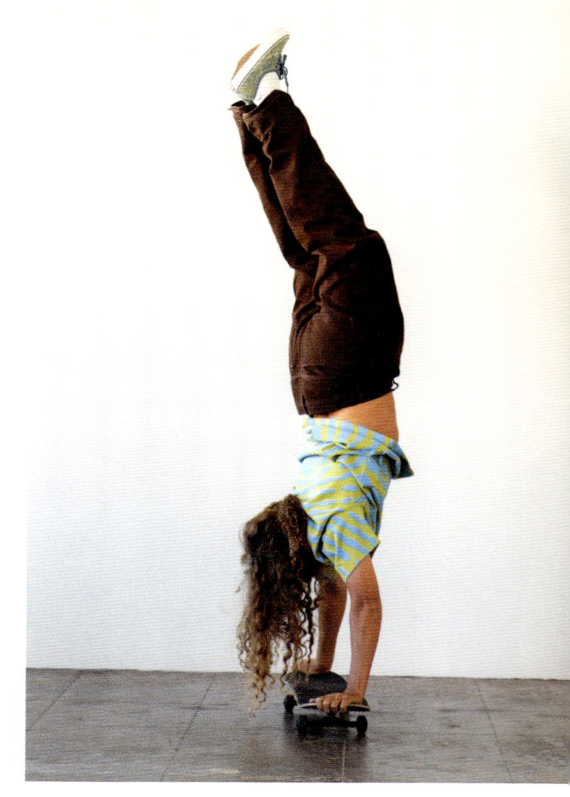

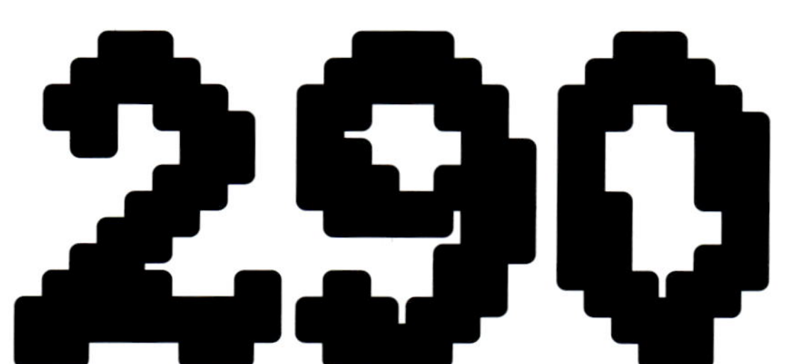

Olan Prenatt for Vans x Salehe Bembury campaign

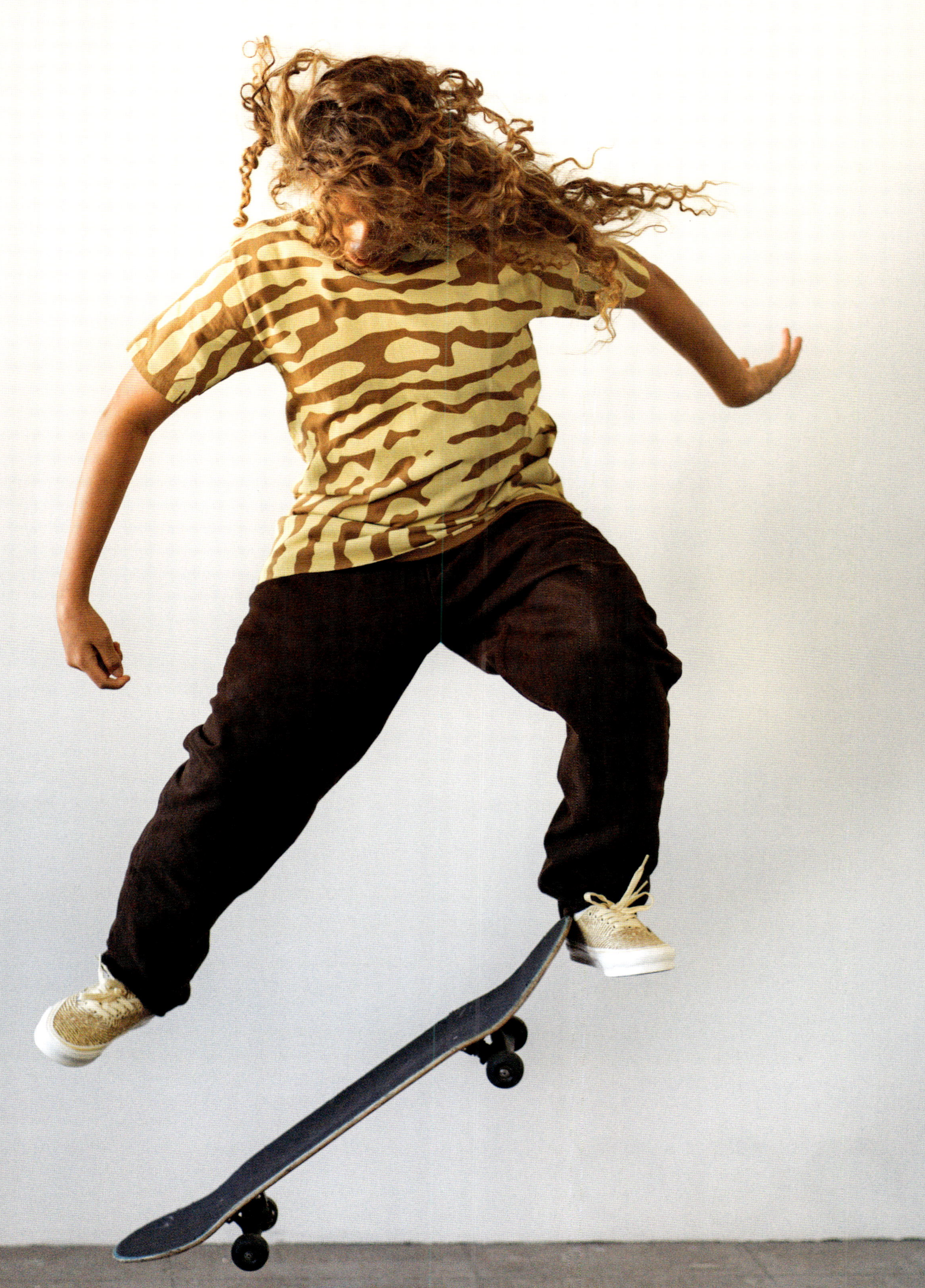

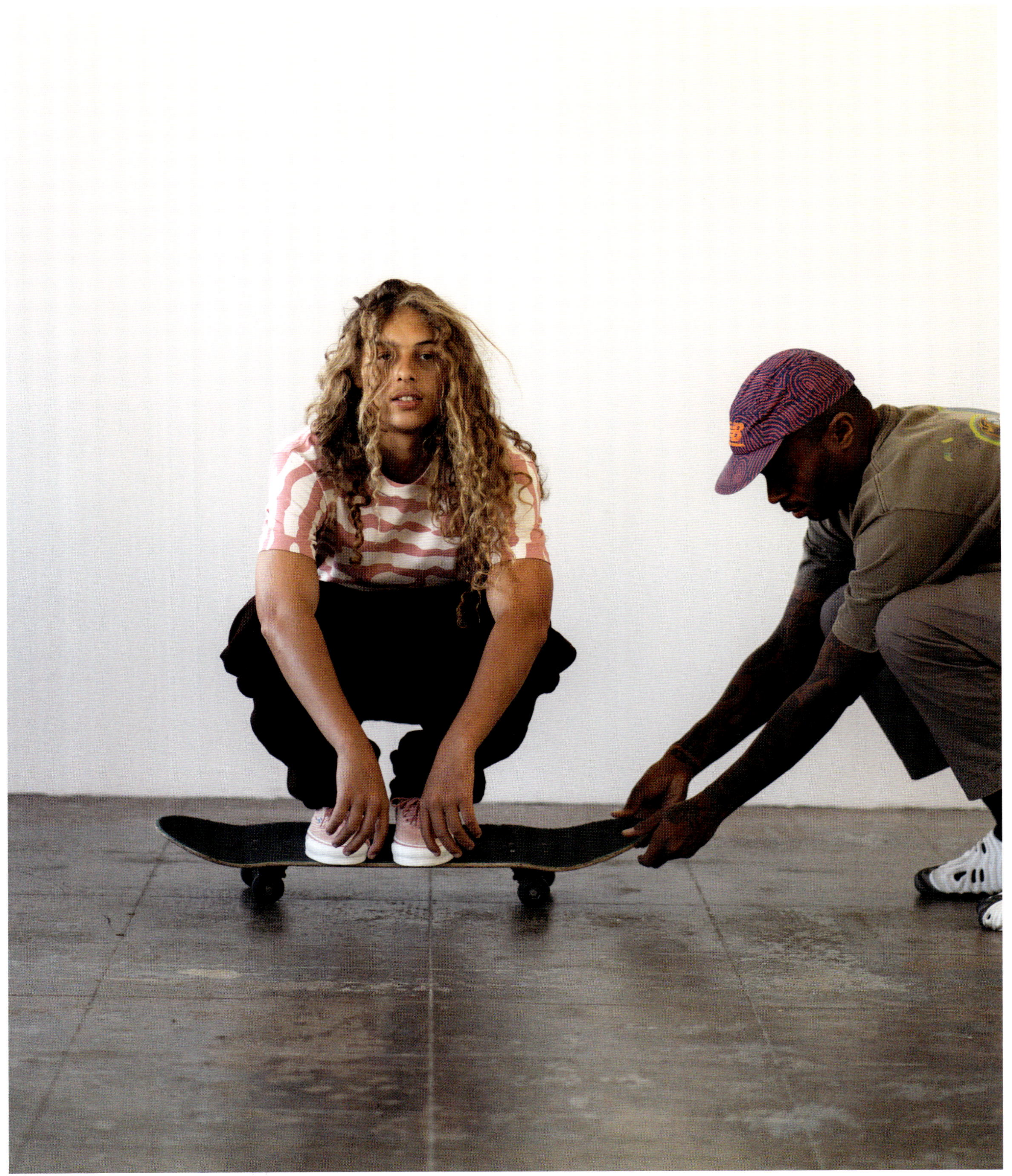

Olan Prenatt for Vans x Salehe Bembury Campaign

292

(2021)

VANS

Olan Prenatt for Vans x Salehe Bembury campaign

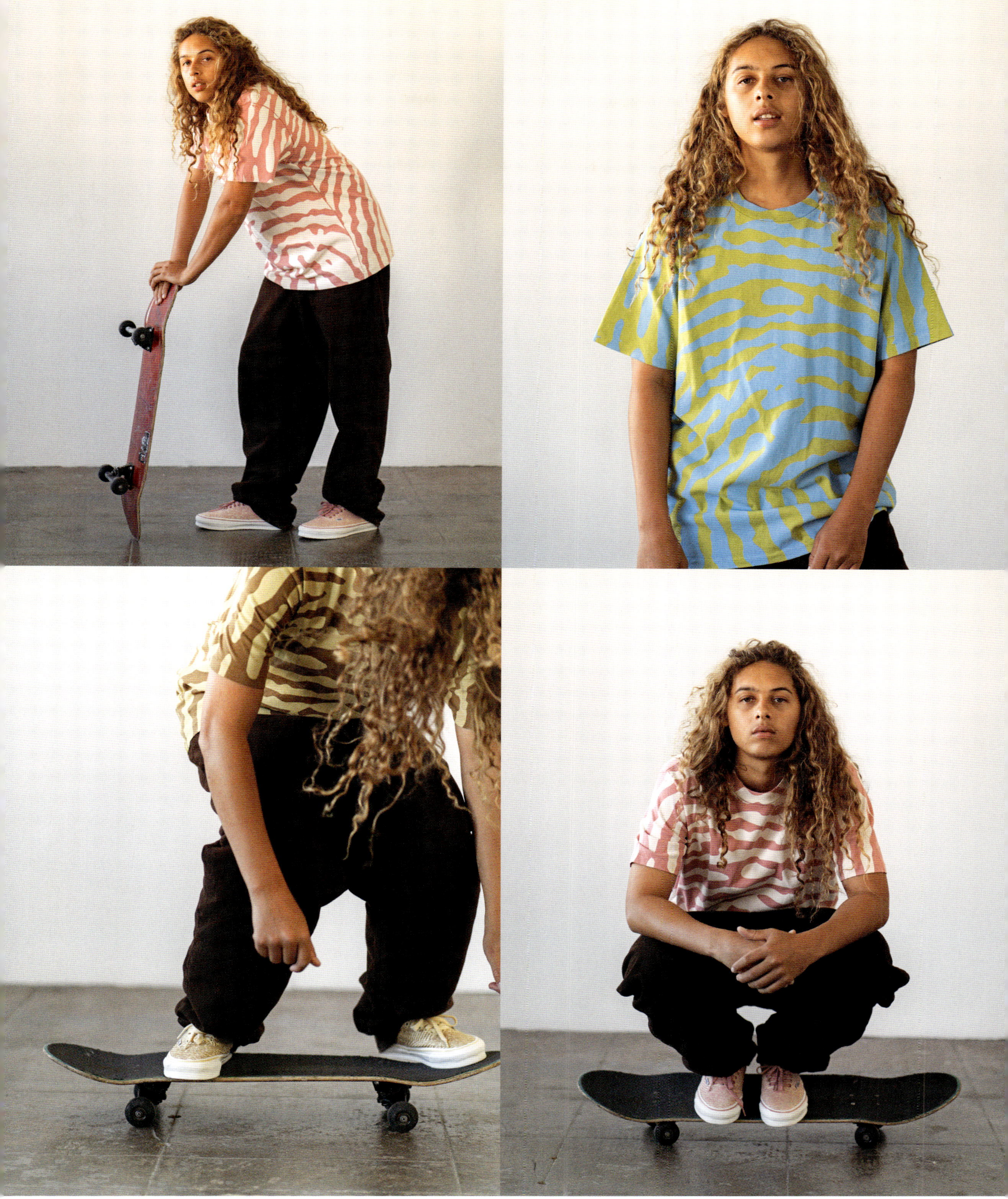

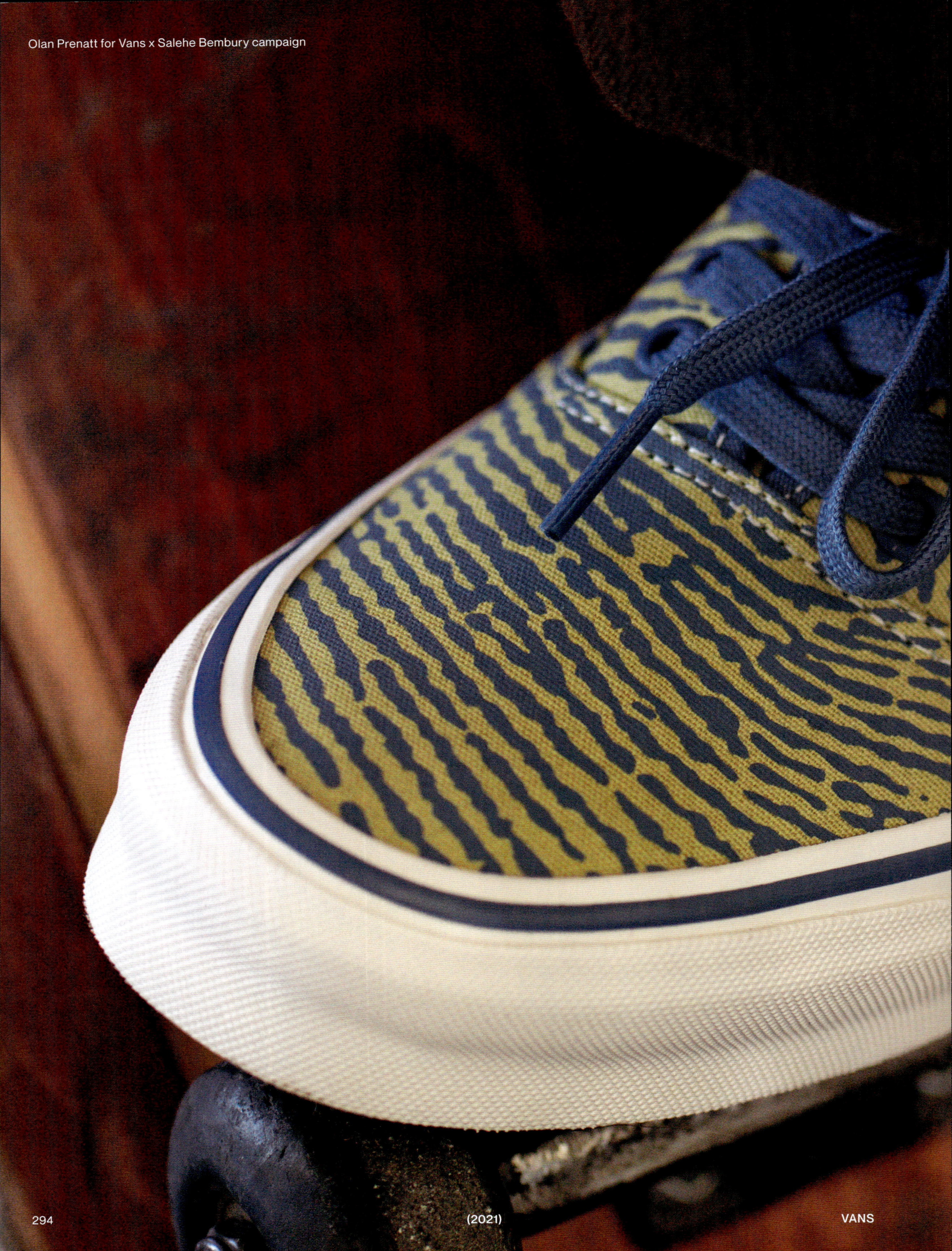
Olan Prenatt for Vans x Salehe Bembury campaign

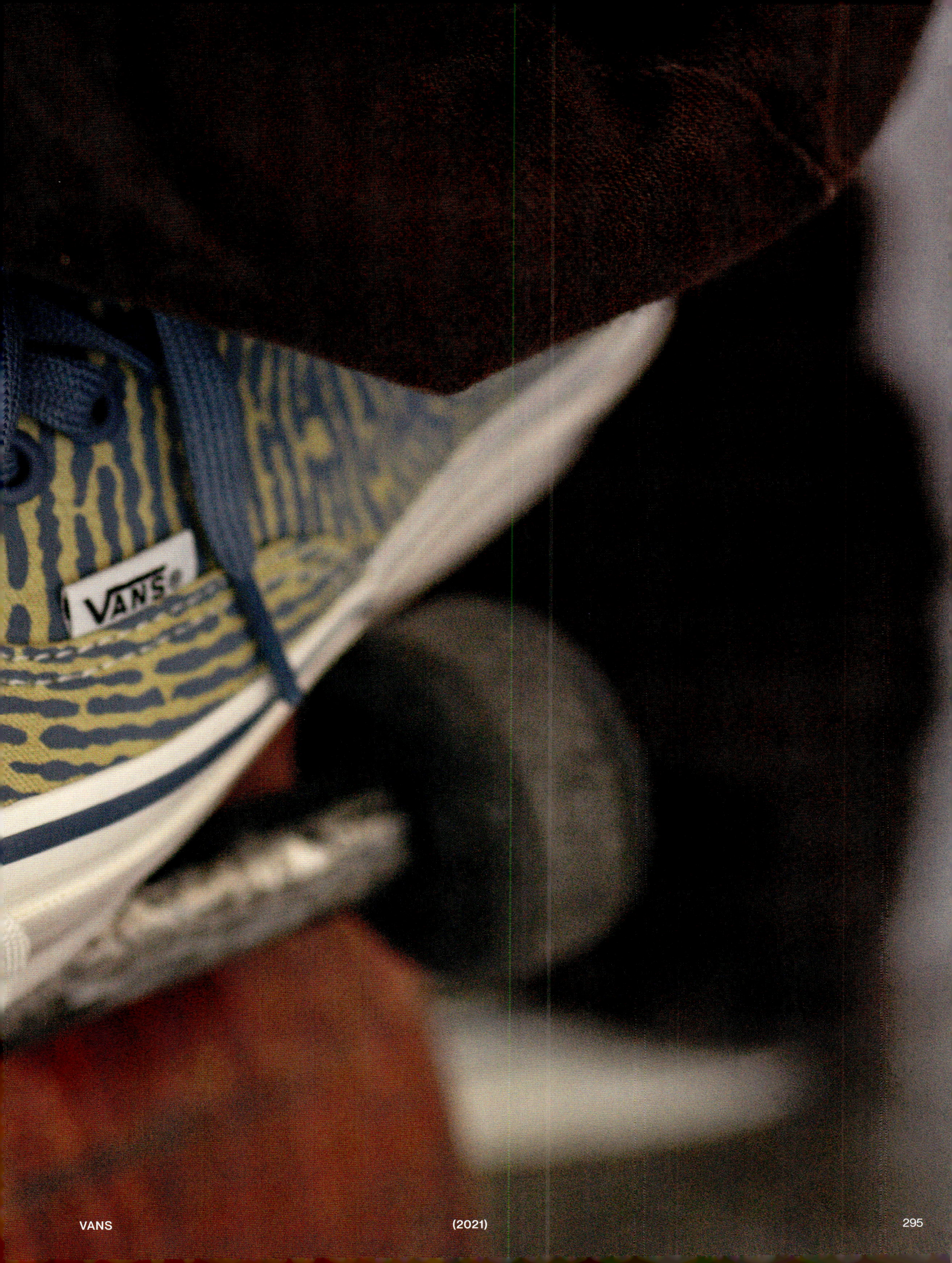
VANS

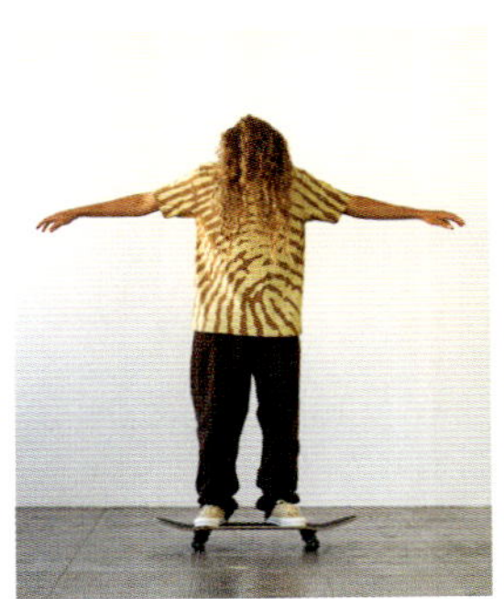
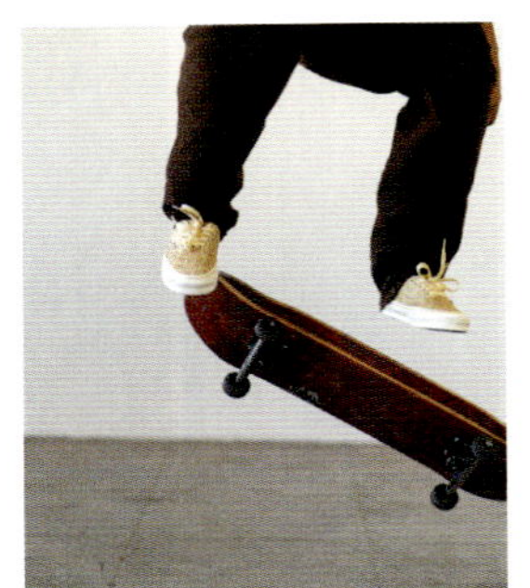
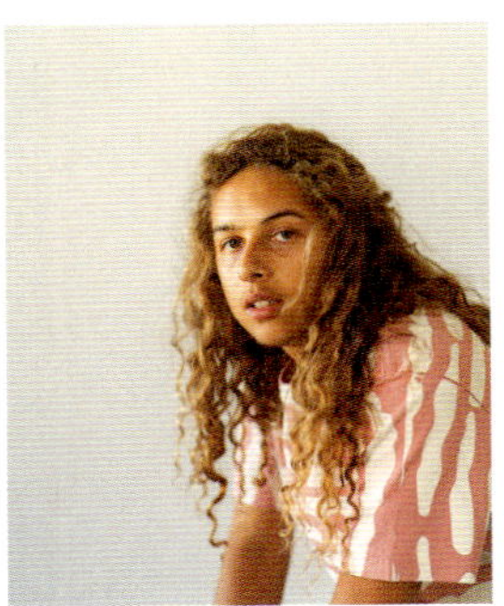
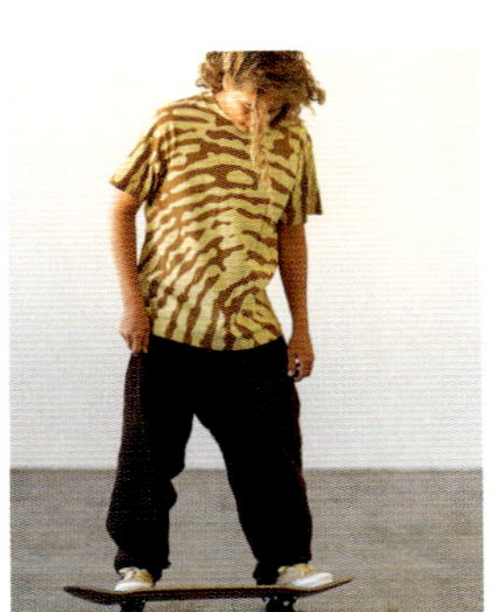
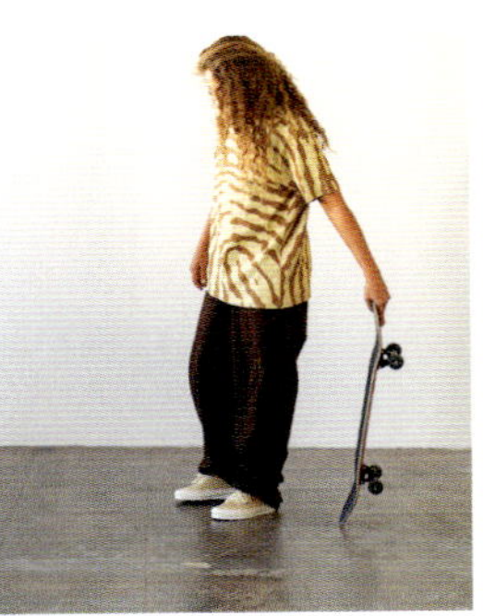
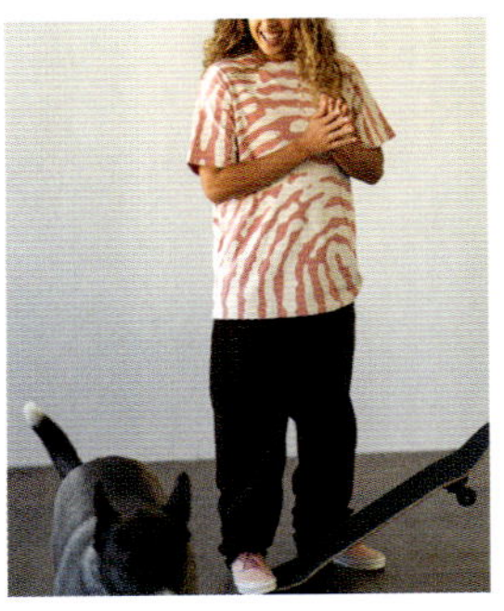
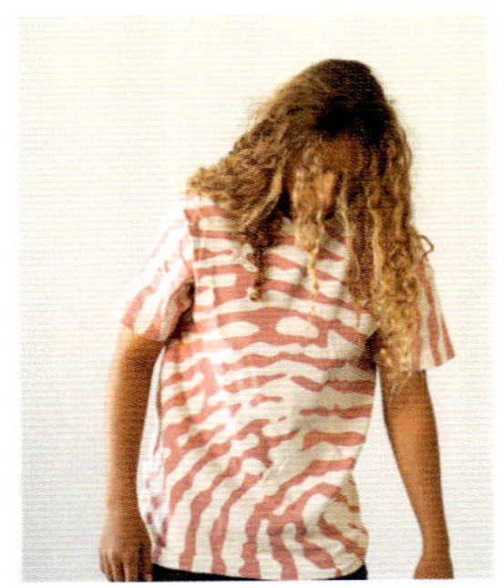
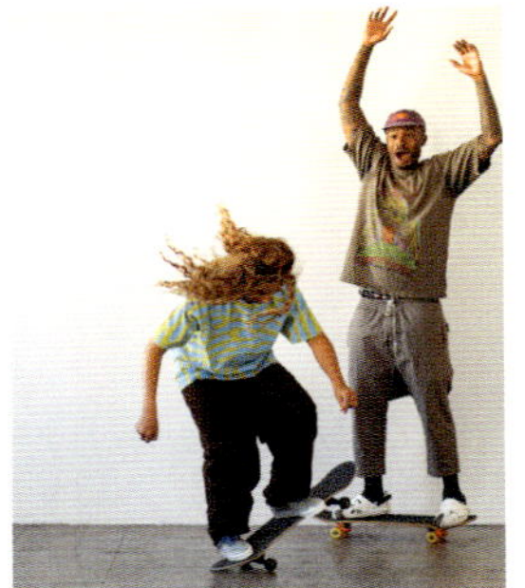
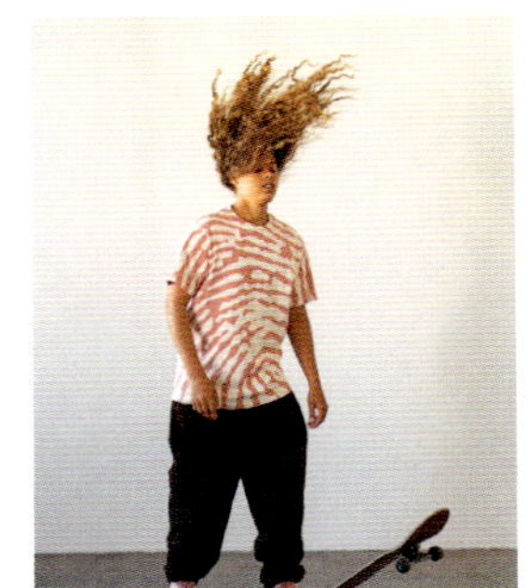
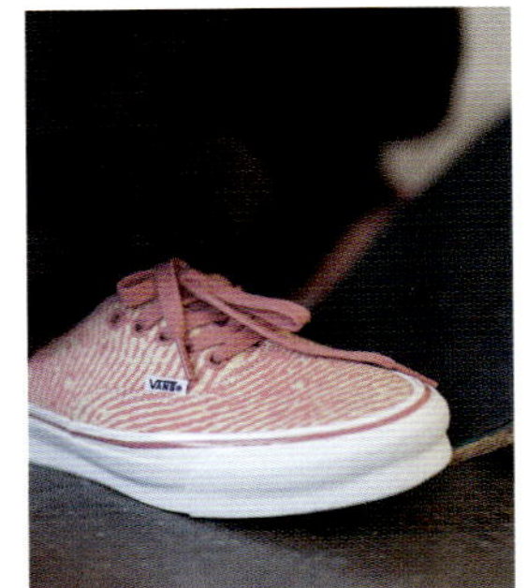
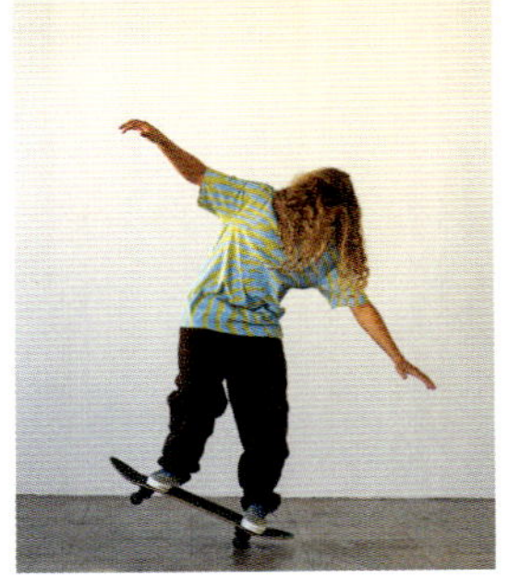
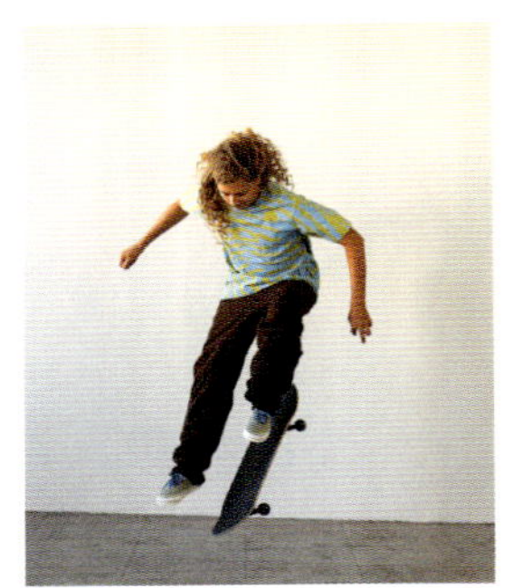
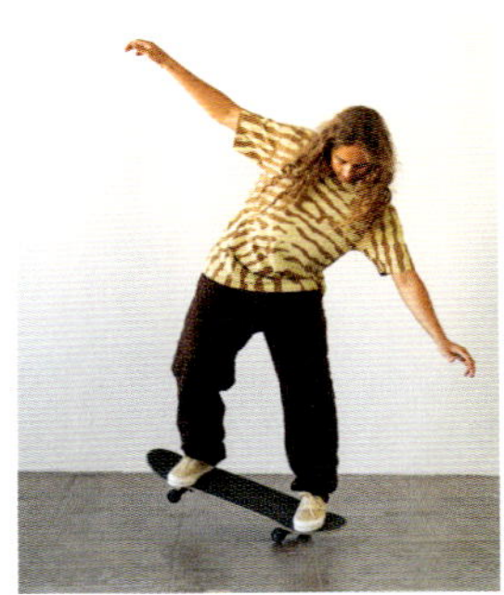
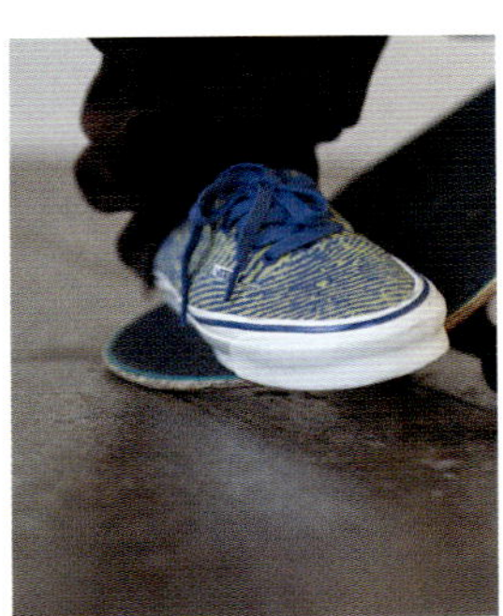
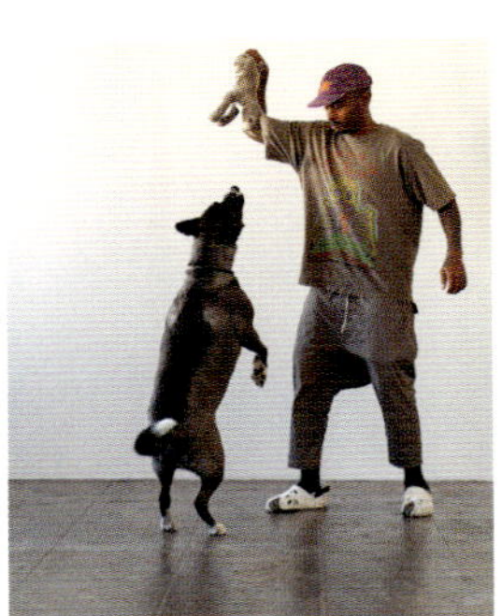

296

(2021)

VANS

Olan Prenatt for Vans x Salehe Bembury campaign

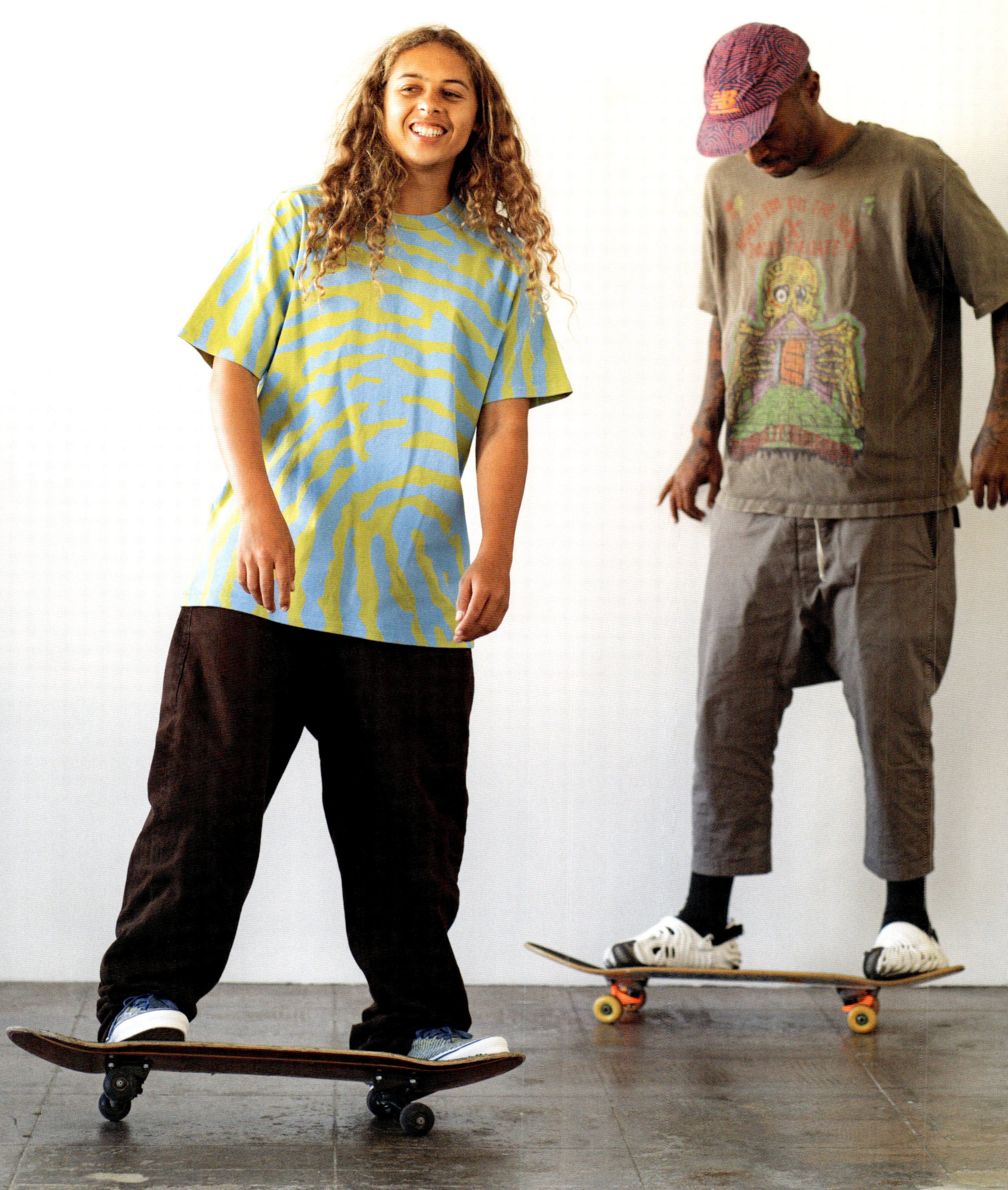

MONCLER (2023)

FAKE IT YOU M

T 'TIL
AKE IT

MONCLER

FAKE IT 'TIL YOU MAKE IT

During a design session, I was told that Moncler had been looking to collaborate with someone that would help them humanize the brand. I found that to be extremely insightful with regard to my own brand, because I'm always fascinated by how people view it externally: sometimes correctly, sometimes incorrectly, but always interesting to hear. And this project was probably my biggest example of "fake it 'til you make it," which I believe is one of the tentpoles of being a successful designer.

I was approached by Moncler to be one of the "geniuses" for their Moncler Genius program. I was somewhat familiar with the program but, given that their price points are beyond what I usually spend on my clothing, not as much of a consistent consumer. I was asked to come out to Milan to do design sessions, which I was already familiar with because I'd worked with Versace for four years and traveled to Milan every month. So this was a very familiar environment for me, in a way that it wasn't at the beginning of my time with Versace. Now I was confident within my design abilities, familiar with Milan, I had friends there, was familiar with the trip and the travel and the commuting, and I was ready to go—or so I thought.

But when I got there, it wasn't exactly what I expected. I thought the purpose of my trip would be to get the brand codes, understand the ingredients and the restrictions and the guidelines, and maybe get some inspiration and some Moncler heritage, and put it all into my figurative designer satchel and head back to LA and get to work—because the majority of my design work happens in solitude at my desk, with pen and paper and my computer and all the tools that I need to design. How it doesn't happen is surrounded by people and models, and that's exactly how I was greeted in the Moncler office. I walked in and there was a team of designers, and models waiting in the side room to try things on. They had pulled vintage clothing items and references—which they did an amazing job of, because they were all in line with my aesthetic and how I dress—and they basically just told me to design. And that was a mysterious statement to hear, because that is not how I design. I also am not a traditional fashion designer: I went to school for industrial design, a lot of my design happens with a pen and paper, or clicking on a computer. But it definitely doesn't happen by cutting up fabric, placing it on a model, stepping backwards and taking a photo and putting it on a white board. I just wasn't familiar with that process. It was one that I'd witnessed many times—with Virgil, say, in a room with some massive scissors and models standing around trying on different looks, and photographers taking photos, and it was even something I was a fly on the wall for at Versace—but had never executed myself. I tried to back out—not back out of the project, but back out of that way of working. I asked: "Can't I just learn everything I can do, take everything back to California and just work?" And that was not the case.

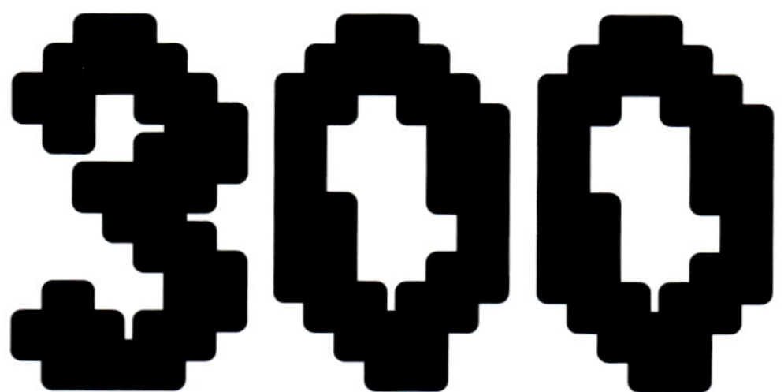

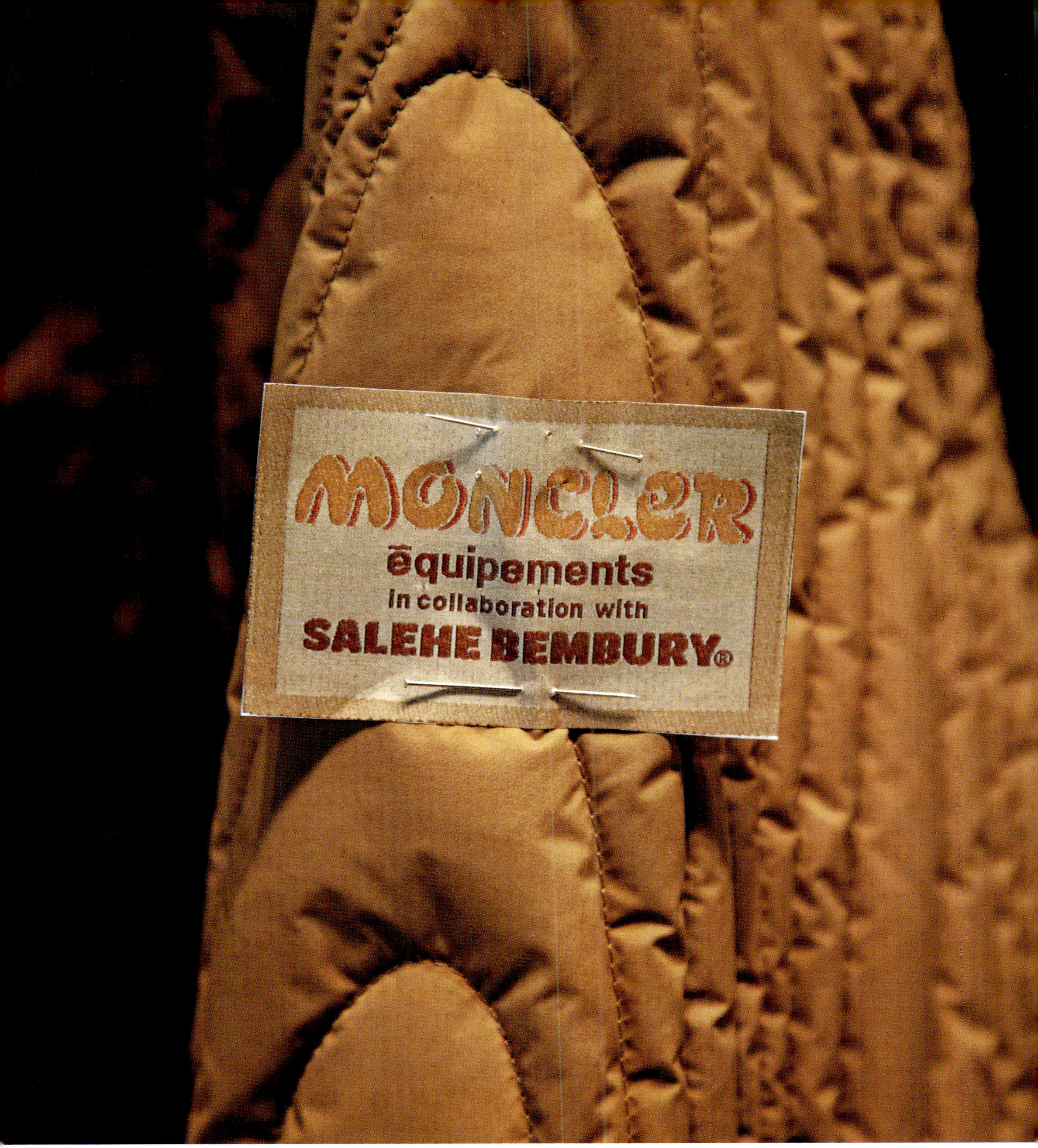

Moncler Genius fitting in Milan, Italy

So, I had to start faking it. I started taking out jackets, I brought a few samples from home. I was putting things on models, stepping back, just mimicking what I'd seen other people do in videos—I really didn't know what I was doing. At that point, I had become very comfortable with my design ability and the consistency of it and the recognizability of it. But through this method of execution, I was lost. I also knew that I was being watched, I knew that I was being photographed, I knew that I had a task to achieve. I had to make something. So I just continued. I continued playing with samples. The team was extremely helpful in realizing my vision, and after a few hours it started to feel more comfortable, more familiar, and I actually started to see my design aesthetic come through. And that started to raise my confidence in the process.

The process continued and we had about four different design meetings in Milan, and with each meeting I became more and more confident, and the collection became more and more tangible. The collection was a full ready-to-wear collection that included bags, sneakers, jackets, fleeces, vests, pants, socks, and hats. It was easily the largest collection I had ever made, and the most expensive collection I had ever made, and the stage that it was going to live on was the most significant. The stakes were high. This was a significant moment for me in my career, and a significant moment in fashion, because Moncler Genius is at the top of Moncler's product offering. The fact that they chose me to sit next to names like Rick Owens, Palm Angels, and Pharrell—a very gangster list of designers that I was honored to be next to. And even just the first launch of who they were showing was a part of Moncler Genius, that itself was surreal—Fujiwara, Jay Z, Adidas. These are names I consider to be legendary, and it was really humbling to see my name up there with them.

During the design process, I got to work with a designer that I had looked up to for years, Nate Van Hook. We co-designed the sneakers that featured in the collection, and this was really me getting an opportunity to design with one of my heroes. Nate is the super OG legend, I respect everything he's done from Yeezy to ACG, and getting to work with anyone you look up to is a treat. He has created some of the most beautiful and most detailed footwear ever, but then his sketches are the crudest, most caveman-looking things. I'm actually fascinated by that, the way he gets such beauty and poetry from his mind, but then the sketches almost look like he used a crayon. There's something so poetic about that.
So after dealing with a little bit of vulnerability with this new mode of creativity and design, I found some comfort; I worked with Nate and we created a collection that myself, Moncler, and Remo Ruffini were extremely happy with. I also was able to maintain within the work my own still-budding brand identity. There were a lot of organic shapes and fingerprints in the collection—not all literal fingerprints, the shoes had lines that felt more topographical—but from a perspective of shape, execution, and palette, it felt like it was very me. The most consistent and best critique I've ever gotten on my work is "it's so you," and I love that because I'm not intentionally doing that; I often design from the gut, and the fact that people see a consistent emotion in my work is extremely special.

The next task was to create a campaign. Since this was a high fashion brand, I stepped outside of working with my good friend and usual production partner in Nat Prinzi and Better Days, and we

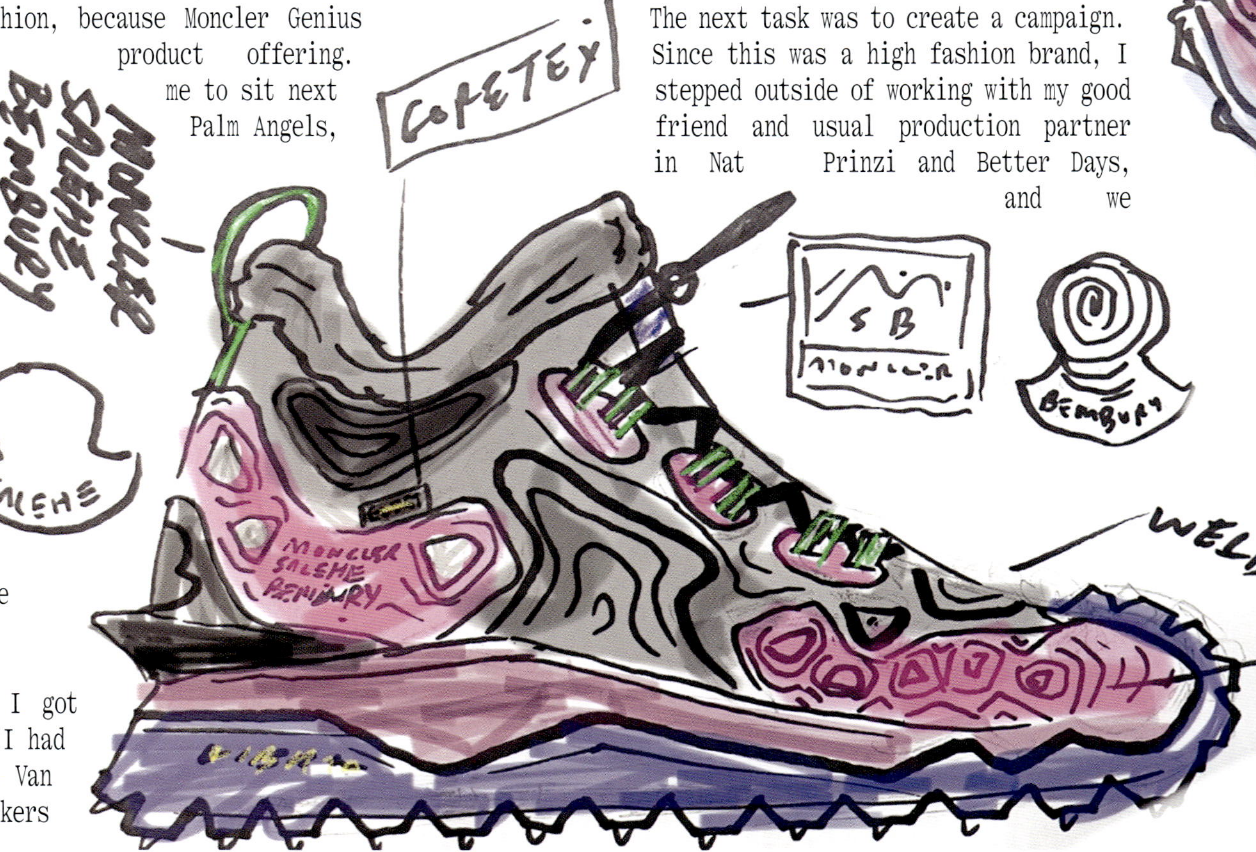

Nathan VanHook sketch of Moncler x Salehe Bembury Trail Grip Grain Sneaker

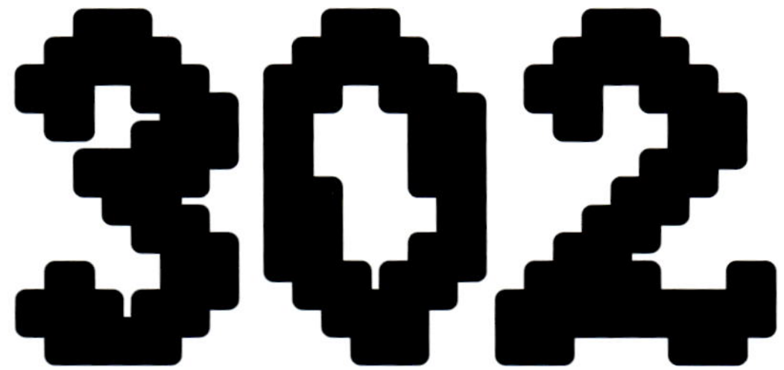

worked with new people. I don't know if this was my Kanye West moment of stepping away from Coodie and Chike to work with Hype Williams, but it was just me experimenting with a new aesthetic and new talent. It did not work out: the images and the campaign turned out to be extremely dark. With marketing, a lot of the time brands or individuals lose sight of the fact that you are ultimately trying to sell a product, and that's what happened with this campaign. The director got lost in her trying to create art, and forgot that we were trying to sell a shoe and sell a collection. The result was an extremely dark campaign where a lot of the product could not be seen. It bothered me for a long time that that campaign turned out that way, because I was a big fan of the collection and I think storytelling is a close second in terms of its significance in revealing a product to the world, so I always hoped that campaign had gone better. But at the end of the day, this is a part of the journey and the process. I don't even know if the audience noticed a difference, but I did, and it's always bothered me.

Moncler had the budget to do some billboards, and they asked where I wanted the billboards to be. I honestly didn't care too much, because I figured they had people to make those decisions the right way. But then I thought to myself: there was a building-sized billboard just inches outside of the Versace office, and that there was something poetic about the idea of putting the billboard outside of my previous fashion job. So I placed three billboards outside of the Versace office: one inches outside of it, one across the street above another road, and one around the corner. So it didn't matter which direction you were going to or coming from, you were going to see that billboard. Was it petty? Maybe. Was it intentional? Absolutely. I kind of cringed at the fact that we had all this real estate to show my work and had to end up posting all of these extremely dark images—I could've had a really cool image the size of a building, but instead I had these dark images. But this is why you have to be very particular about who you work with, so they can realize your vision.

The Moncler partnership was really positive for me just because it allowed me to tell new stories, speak to a new consumer, and helped me step outside of just being the shoe guy. I named this book "I Make Shoes" almost ironically, and this was one of the moments where I was truly stepping outside of that space and the audience was able to see me as a fashion designer. They were able to see my brand identity bleed onto other product, and I think it does so very well. Moncler Genius allowed me to create an installation which felt like a full 360-degree experience of my world: the shoes, the accessories, the clothing, the world. There always needs to be a mutual benefit for any collaboration, but in this instance there was a huge benefit for me with regard to the association, with regard to producing new product that my audience had never seen me make. It helped me prove something to the audience, it helped me prove something to myself, and it was also proof of concept that if there was an apparel brand that wanted to work with me, they have seen that play out.

My brand equity was increased significantly. Now I was selling a jacket that cost $1,500 and my name was next to a fashion house from Italy. So if we're just talking about the value of my name, where it existed five years ago and where it exists today, and the brands that helped me achieve that, this Moncler one was huge. Now I know there's a new audience looking at me, and there's an old audience that's seeing me evolve, and there are opportunities within arm's reach because of this partnership.

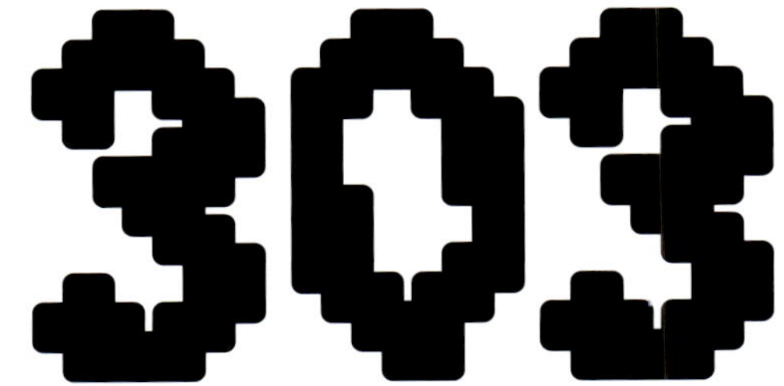

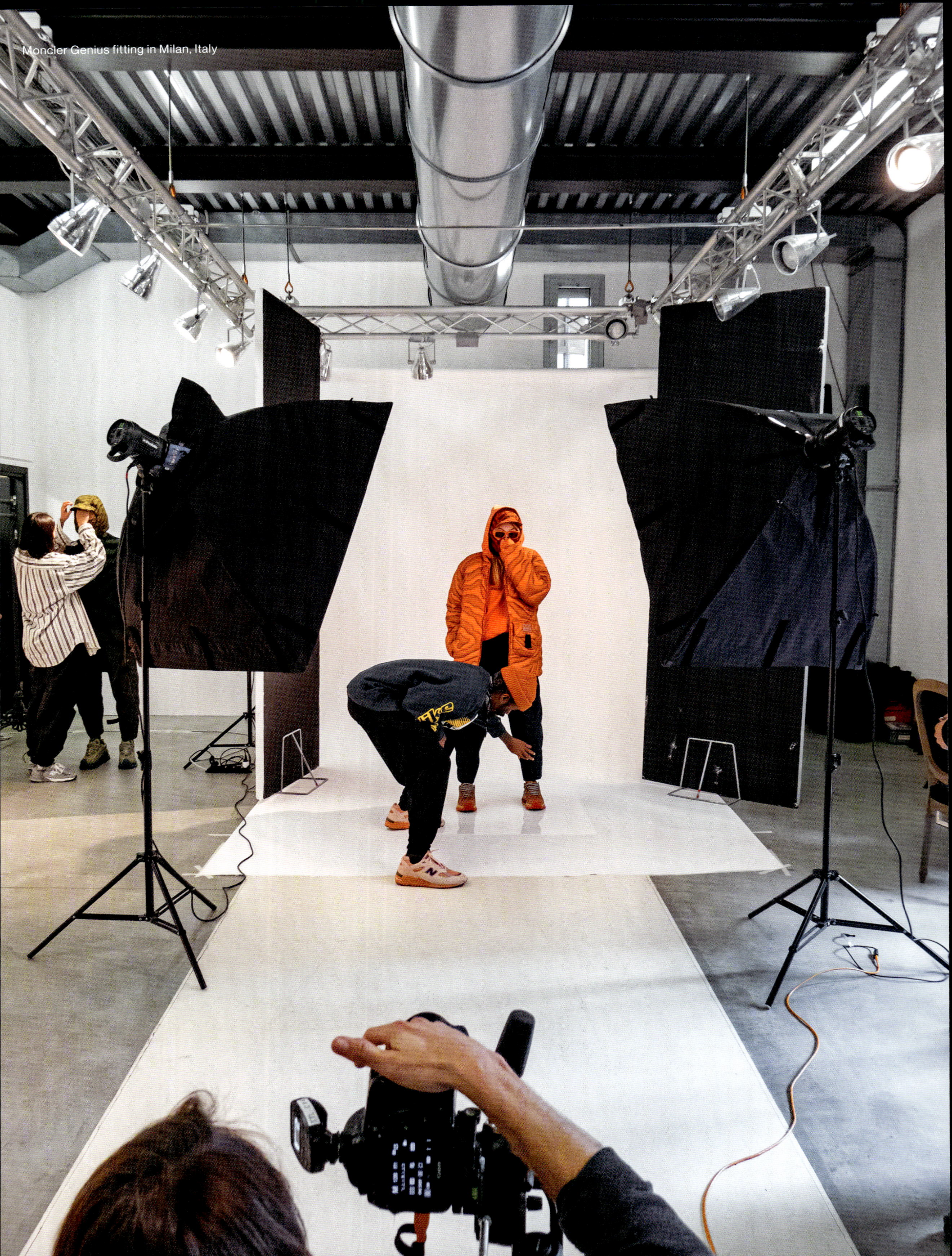
Moncler Genius fitting in Milan, Italy

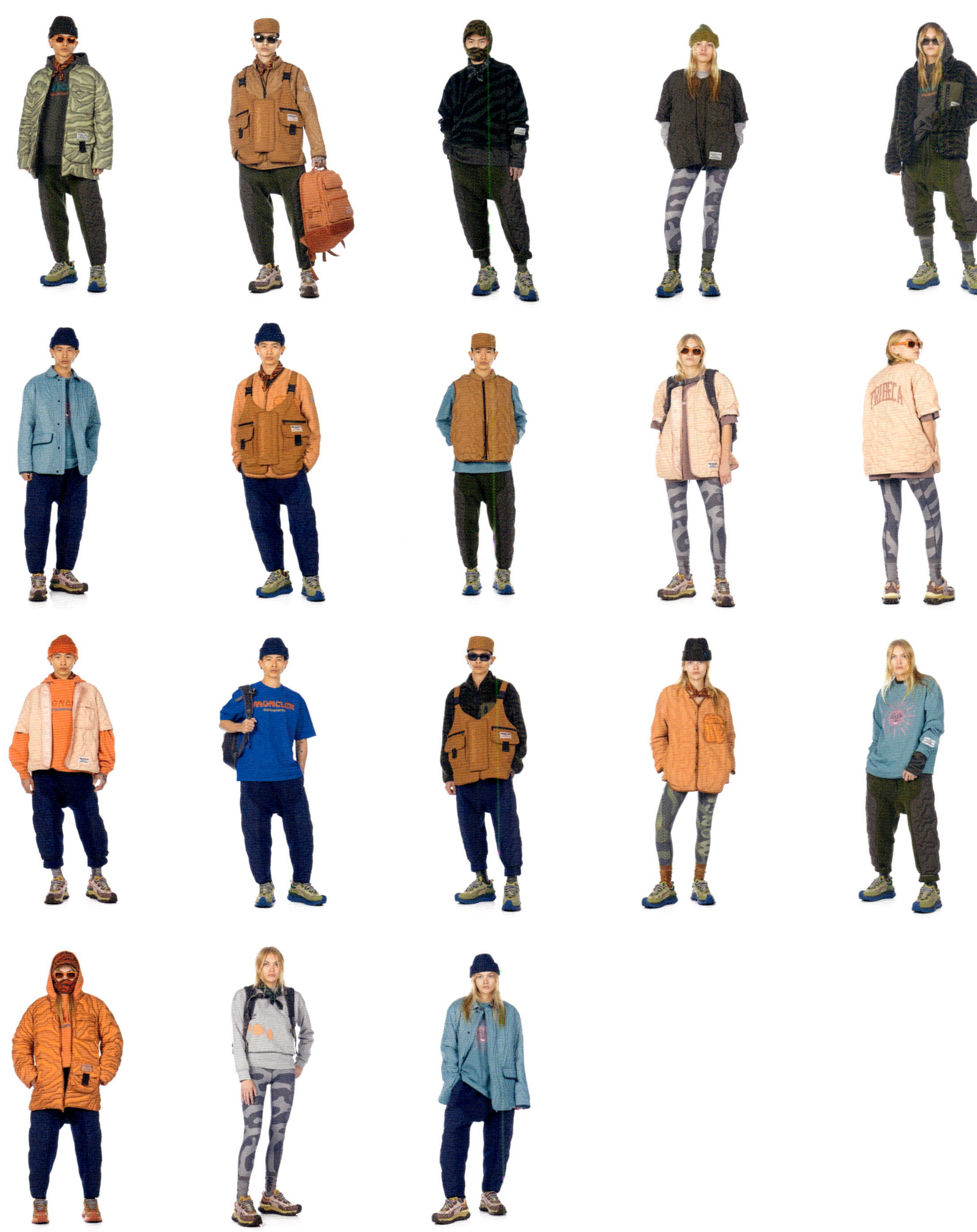

MONCLER (2023) 305

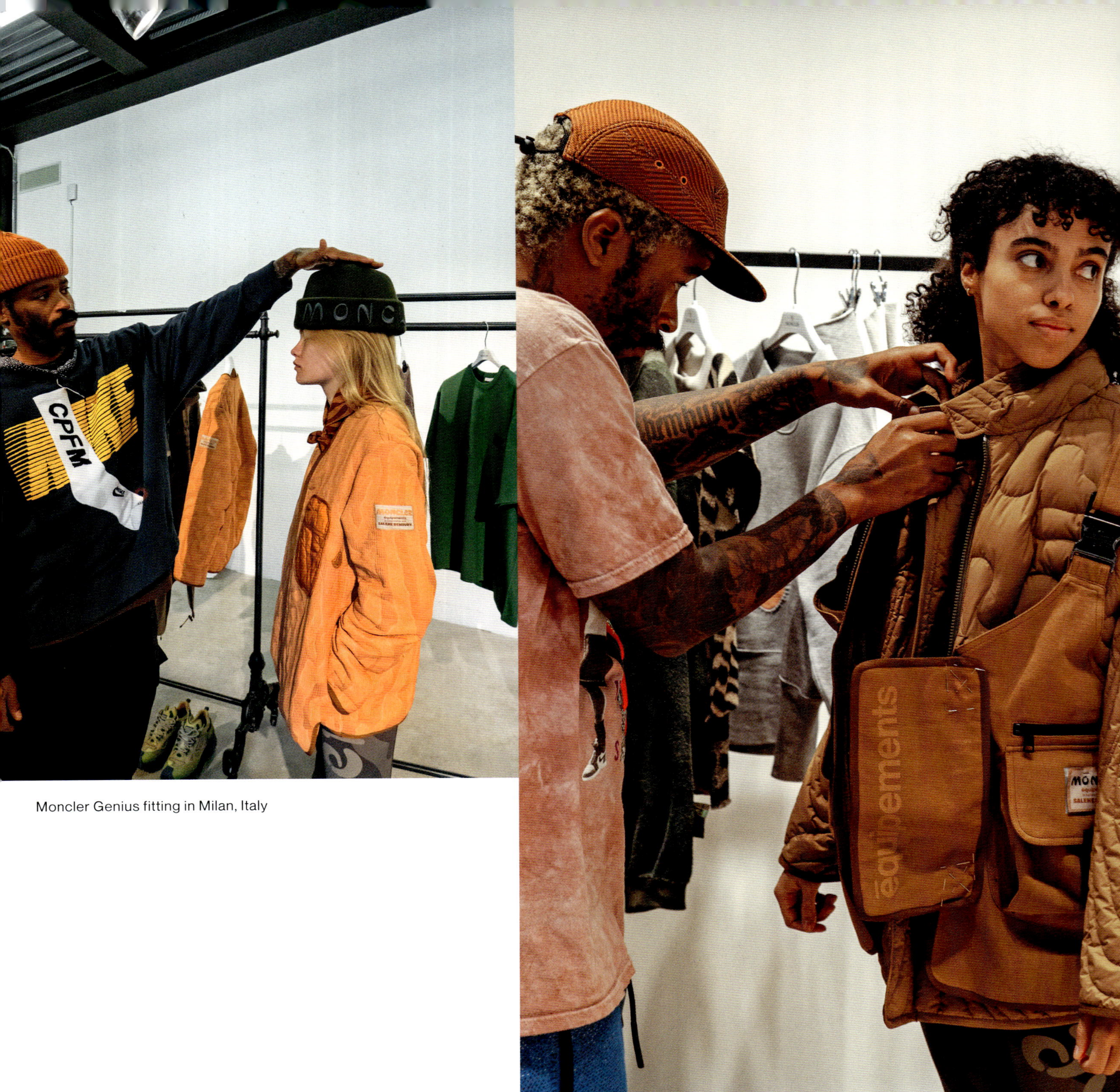

Moncler Genius fitting in Milan, Italy

Moncler Genius fitting in Milan, Italy

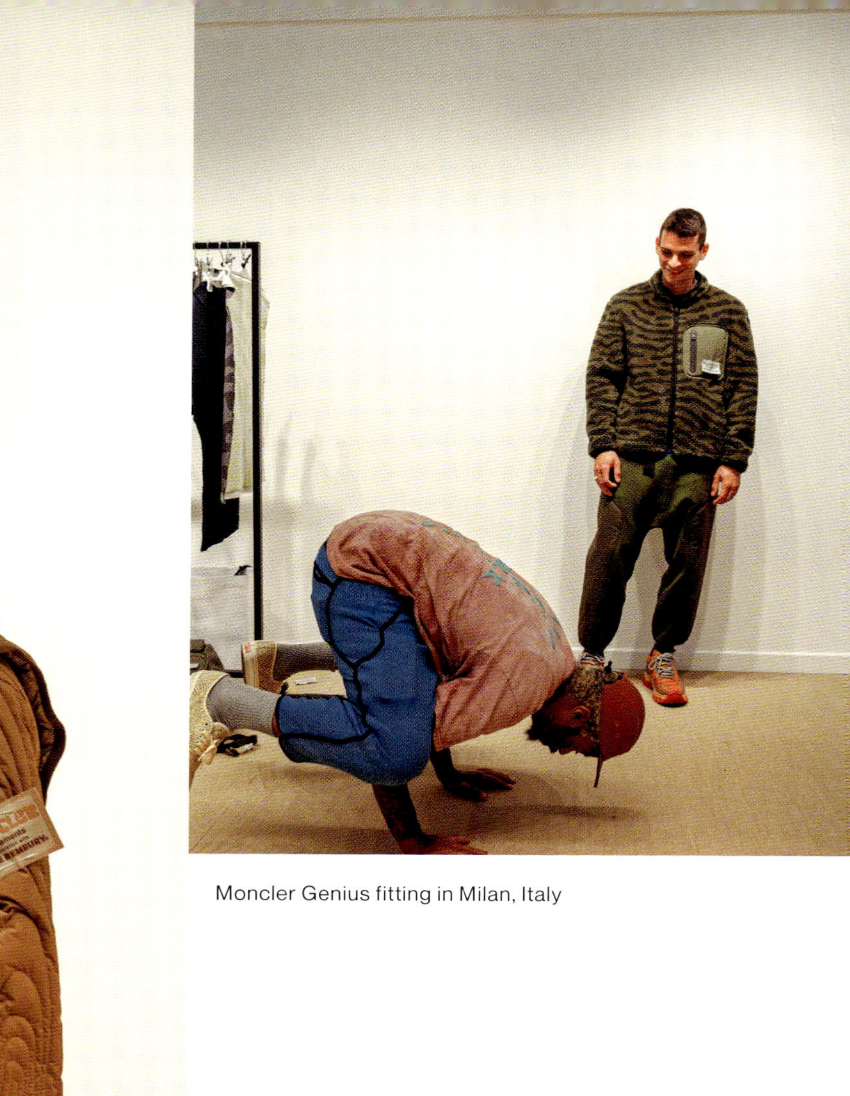

Moncler Genius fitting in Milan, Italy

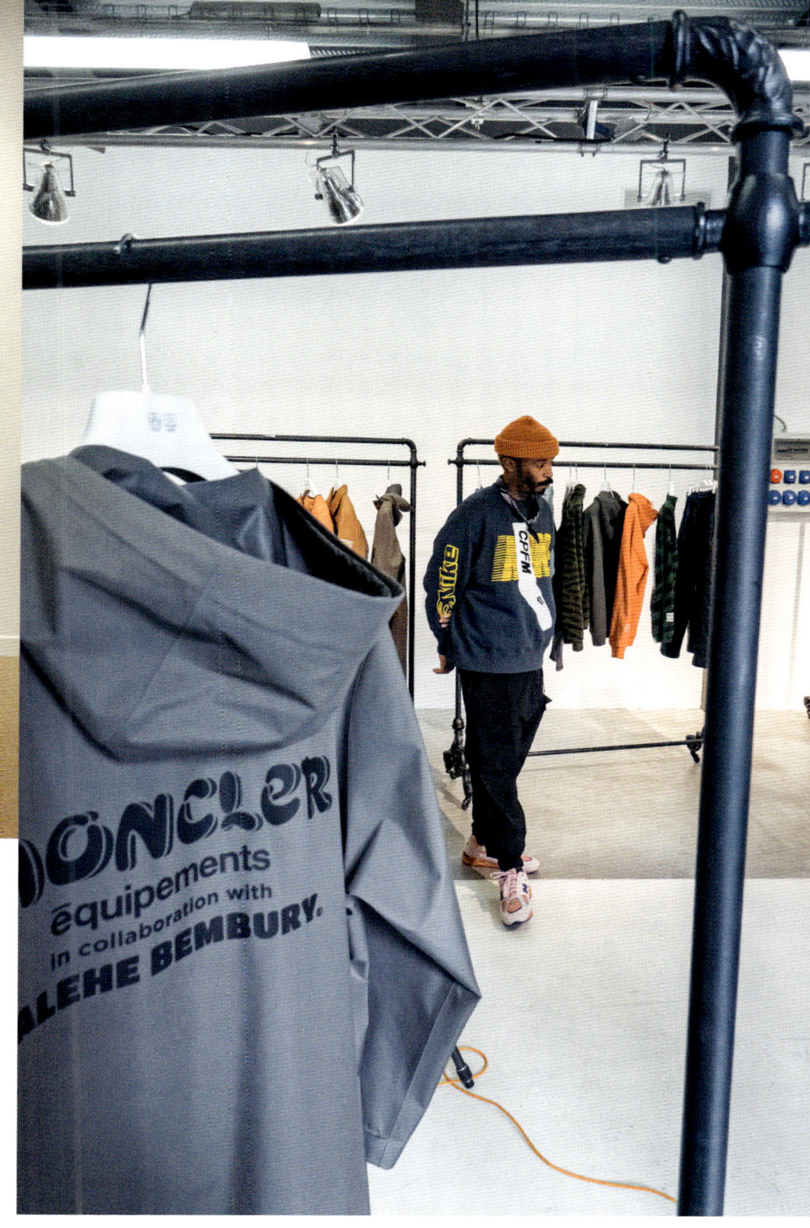

Moncler Genius fitting in Milan, Italy

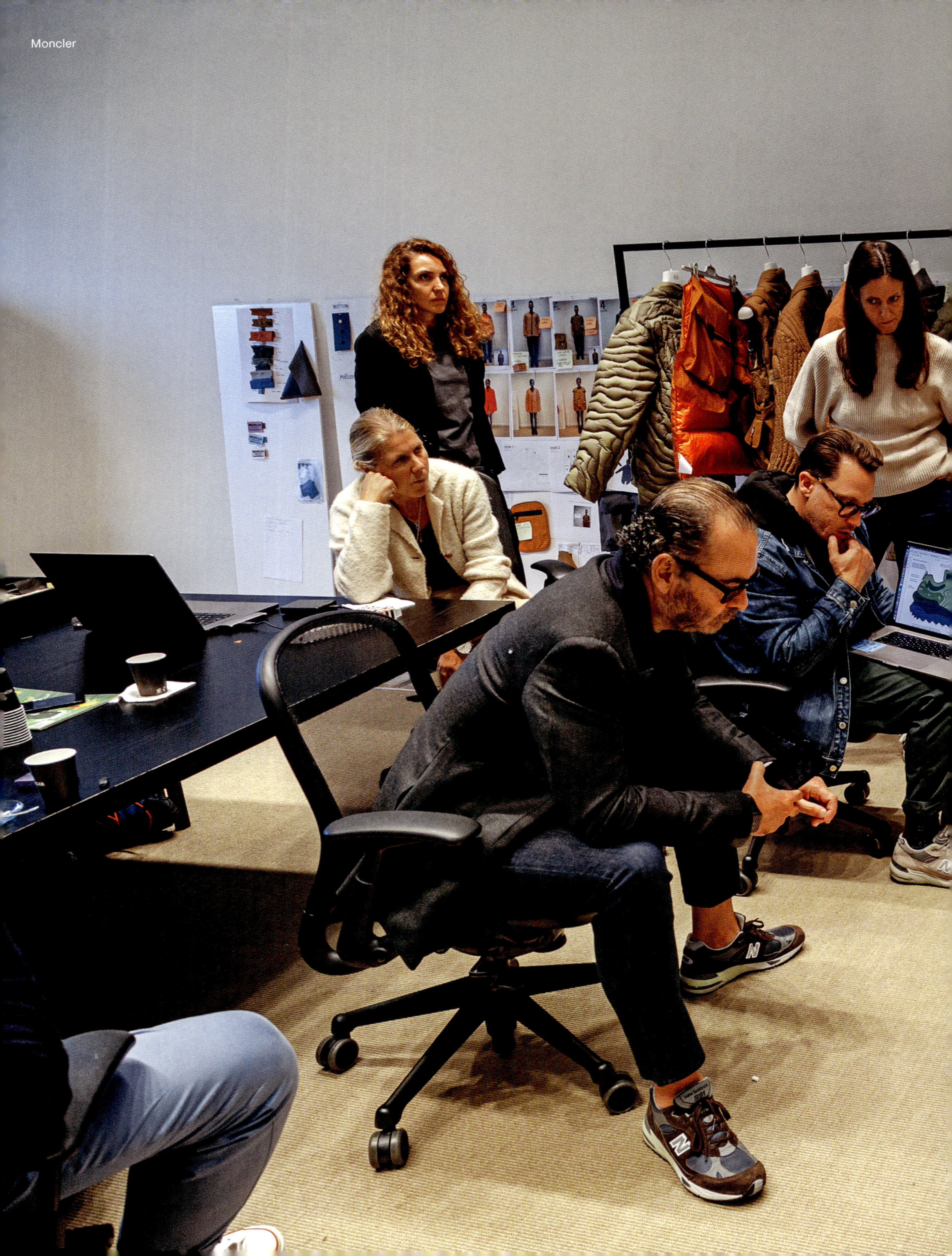

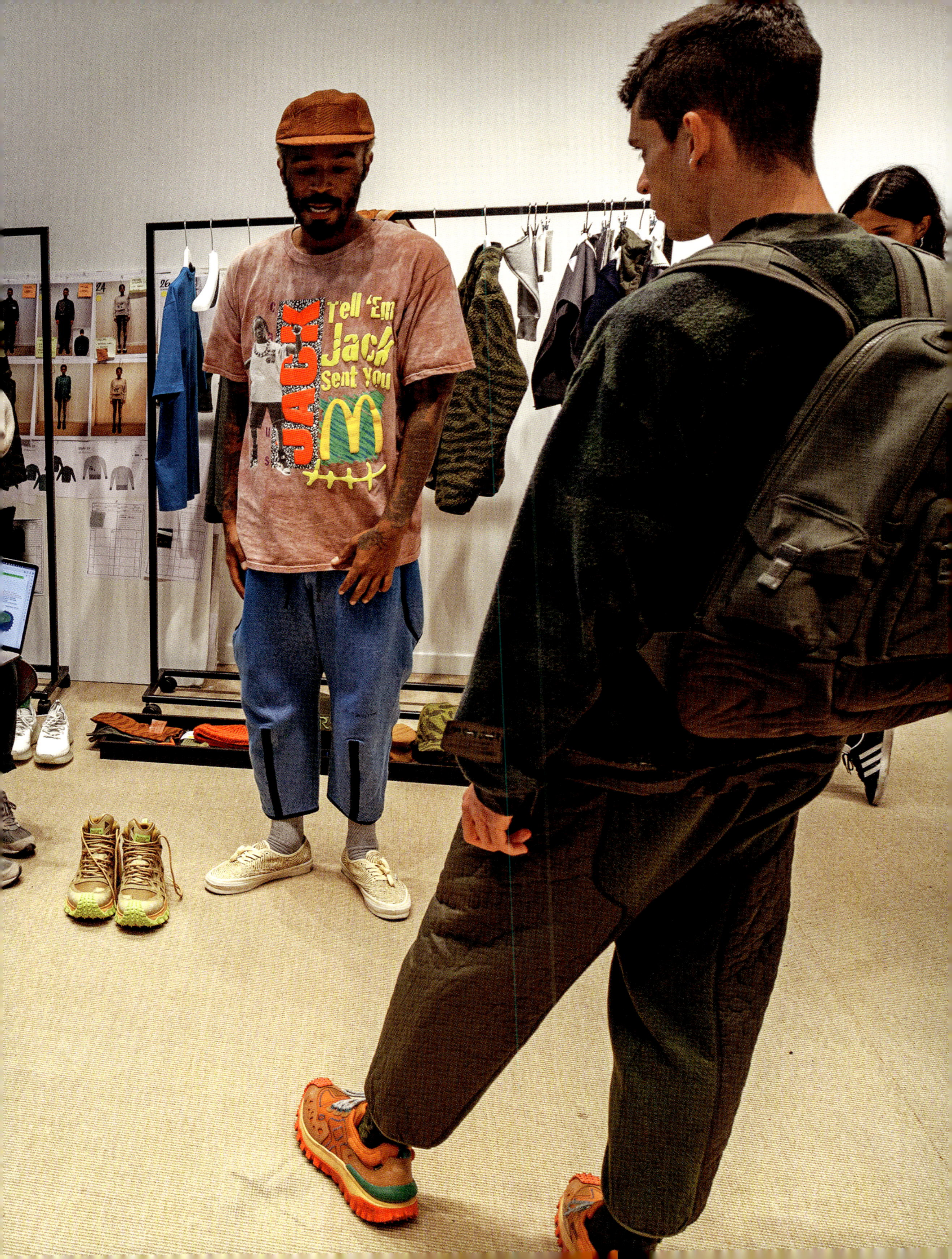
JACK
Tell 'Em
Jack
Sent You

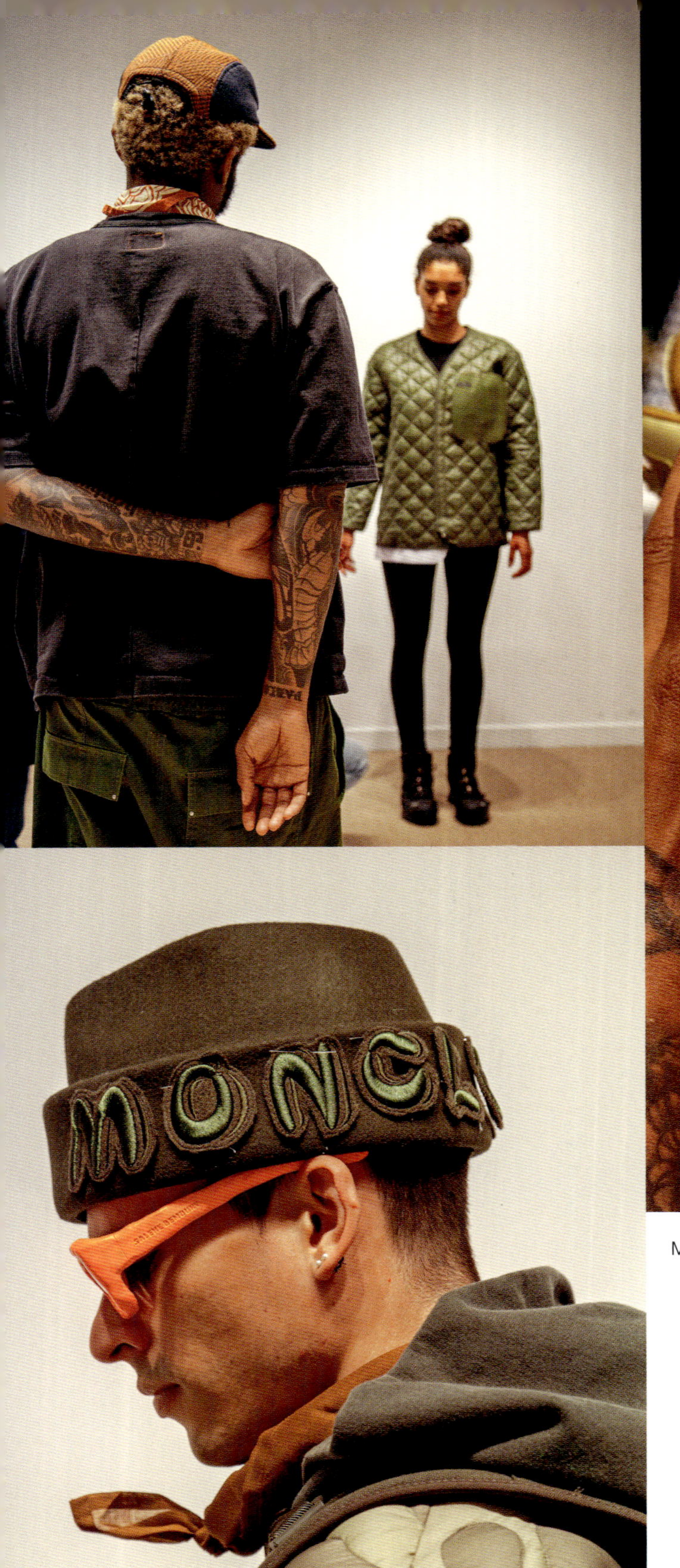

Moncler Genius fitting in Milan, Italy

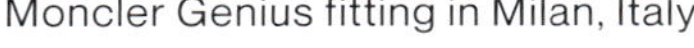

Moncler Genius fitting in Milan, Italy

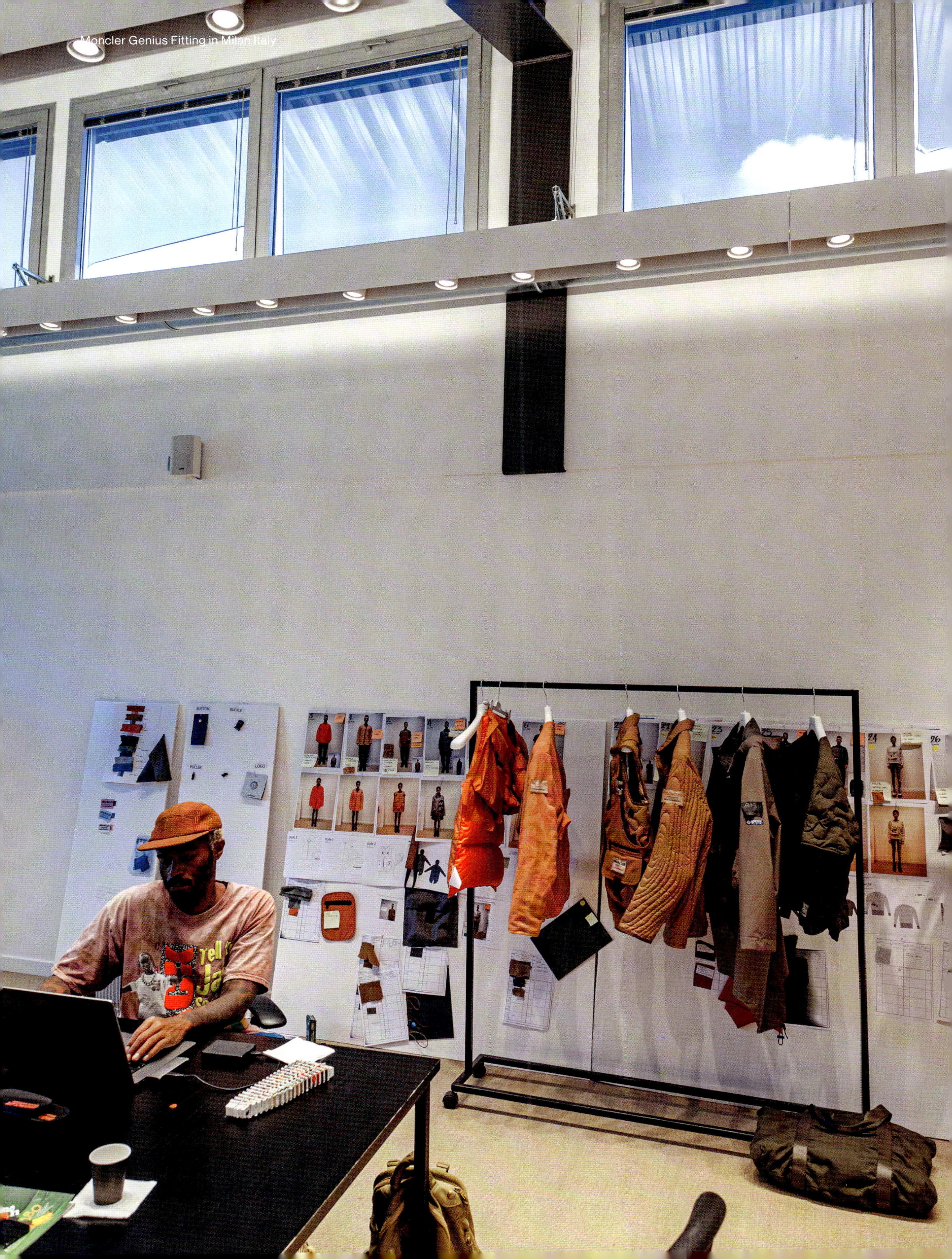

Moncler Genius Fitting in Milan Italy

Moncler Genius fitting in Milan, Italy

Moncler Genius fitting in Milan, Italy

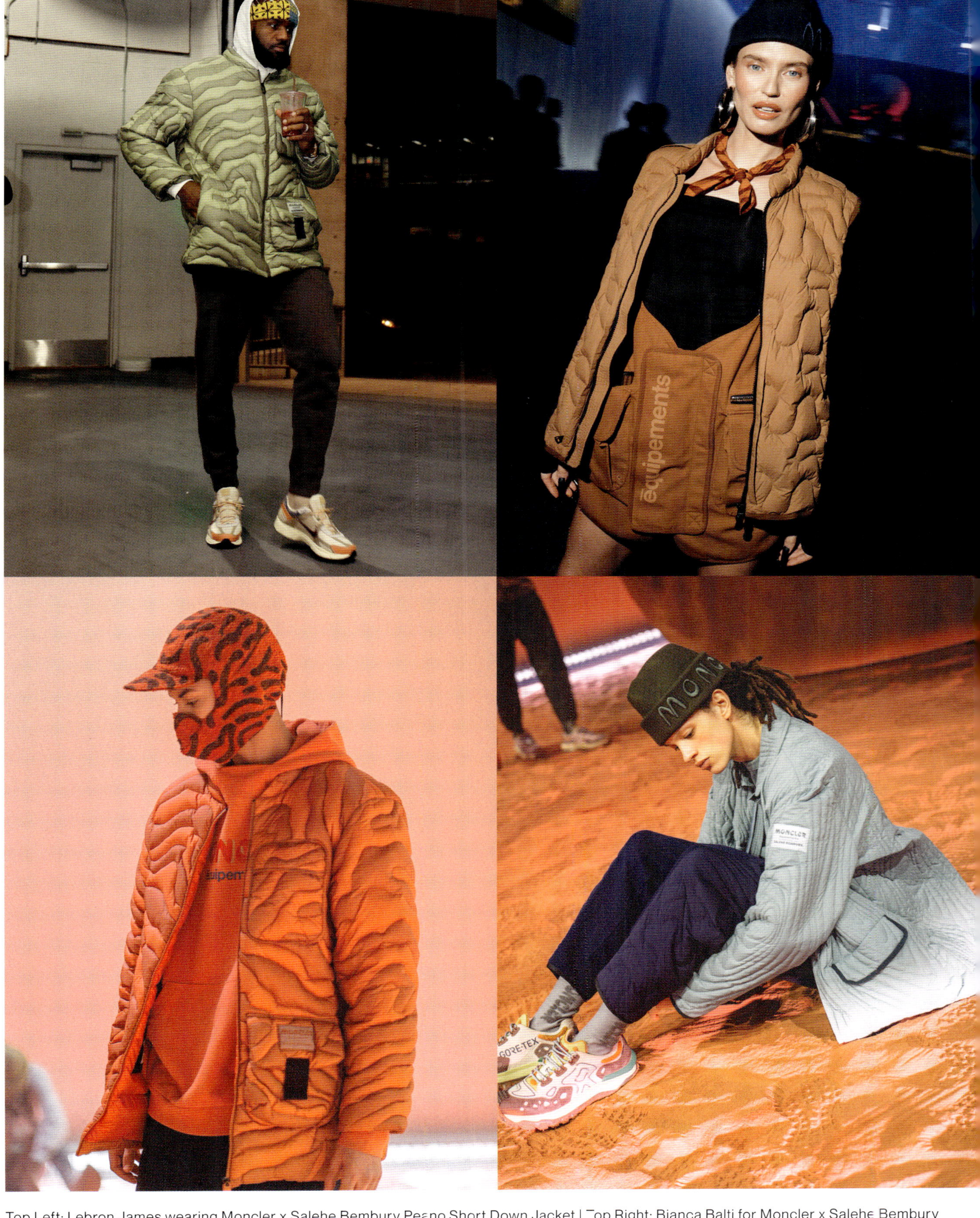

Top Left: Lebron James wearing Moncler x Salehe Bembury Peano Short Down Jacket | Top Right: Bianca Balti for Moncler x Salehe Bembury
Bottom Left: Moncler Genius 2023 | Bottom Right: Moncler Genius 2023

313

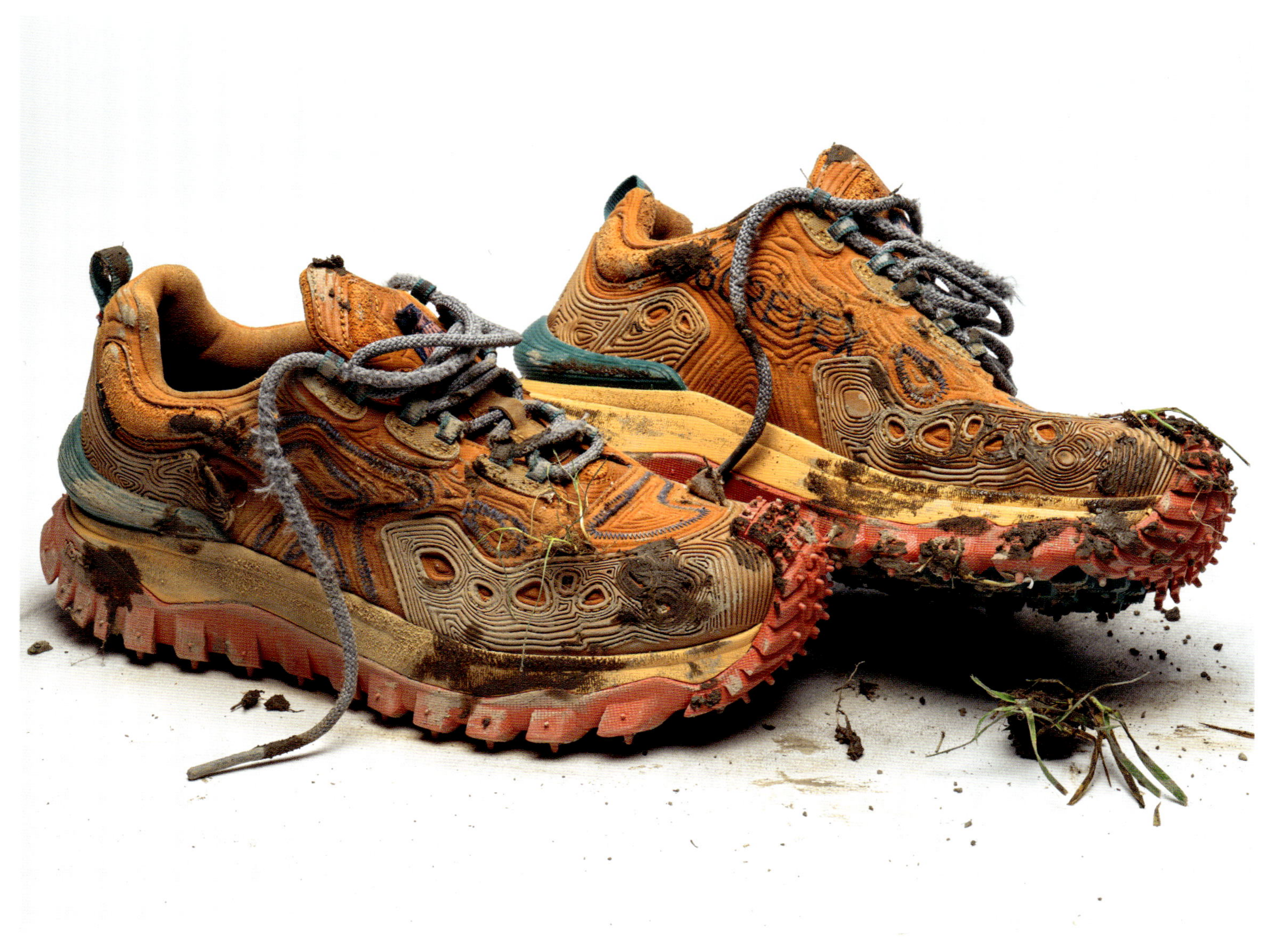

314

(2023)

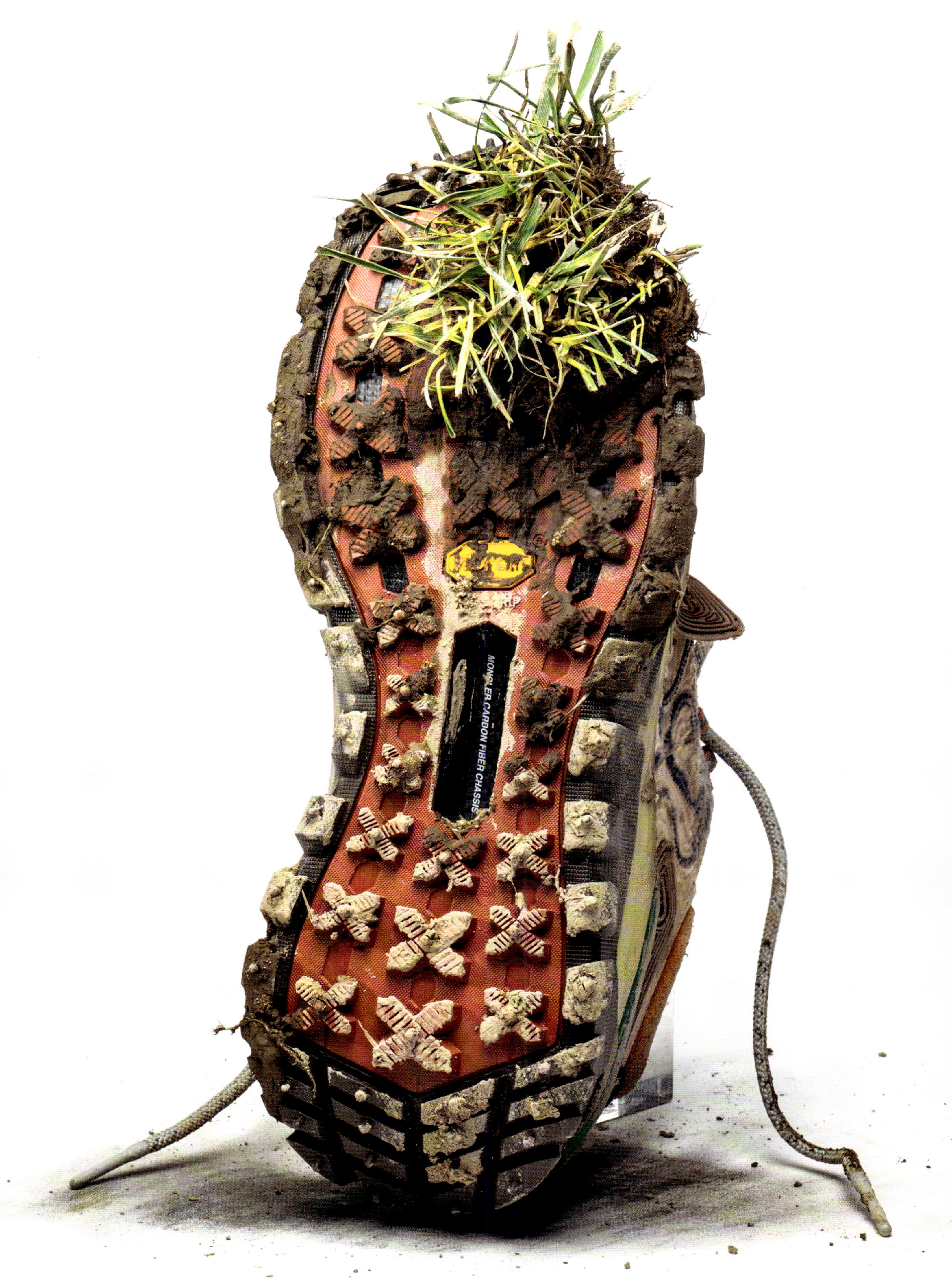
MONCLER CARBON FIBER CHASSIS

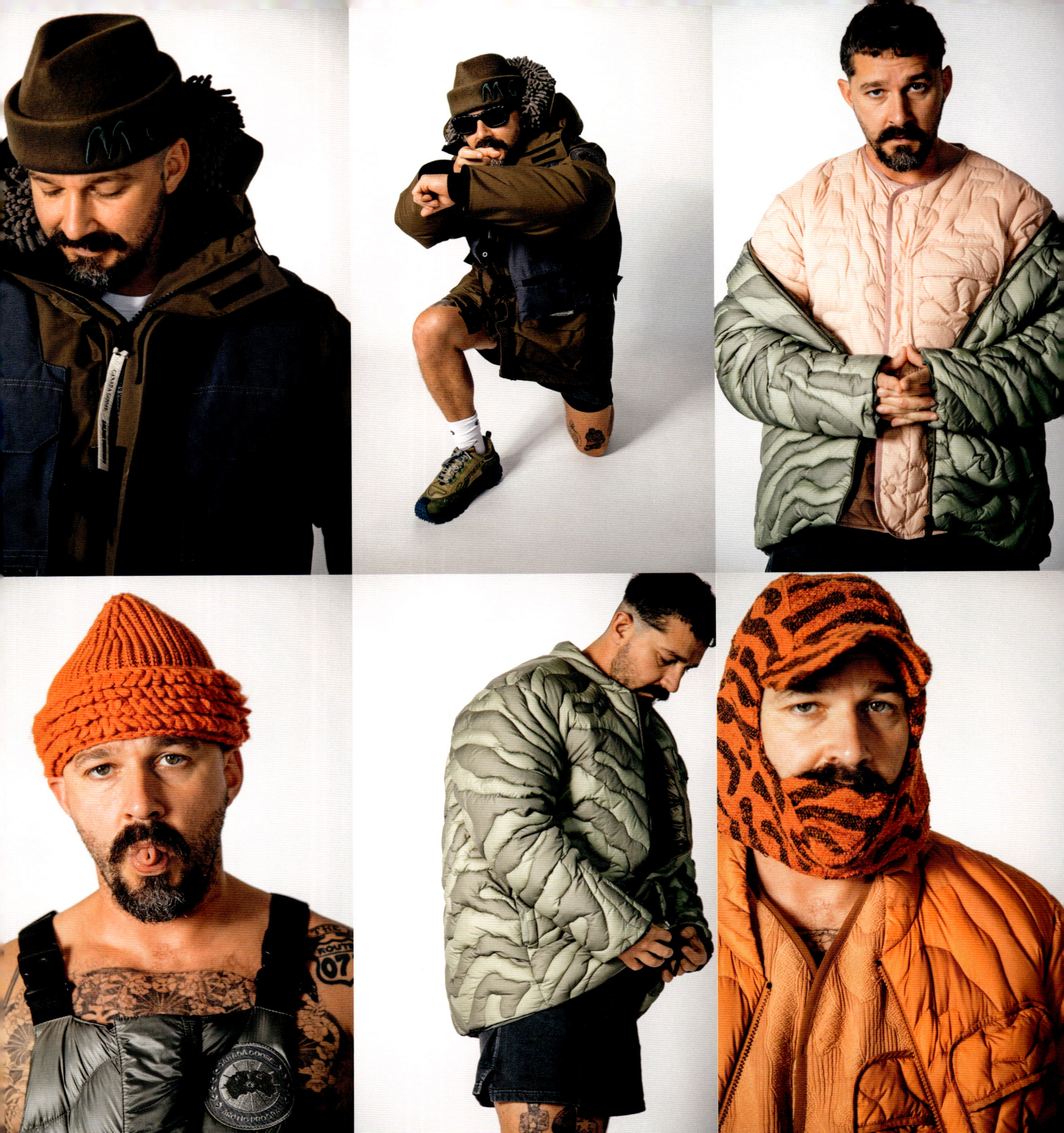

Shia Labeouf wearing various Salehe Bembury designs

Shia Labeouf wearing various Salehe Bembury designs

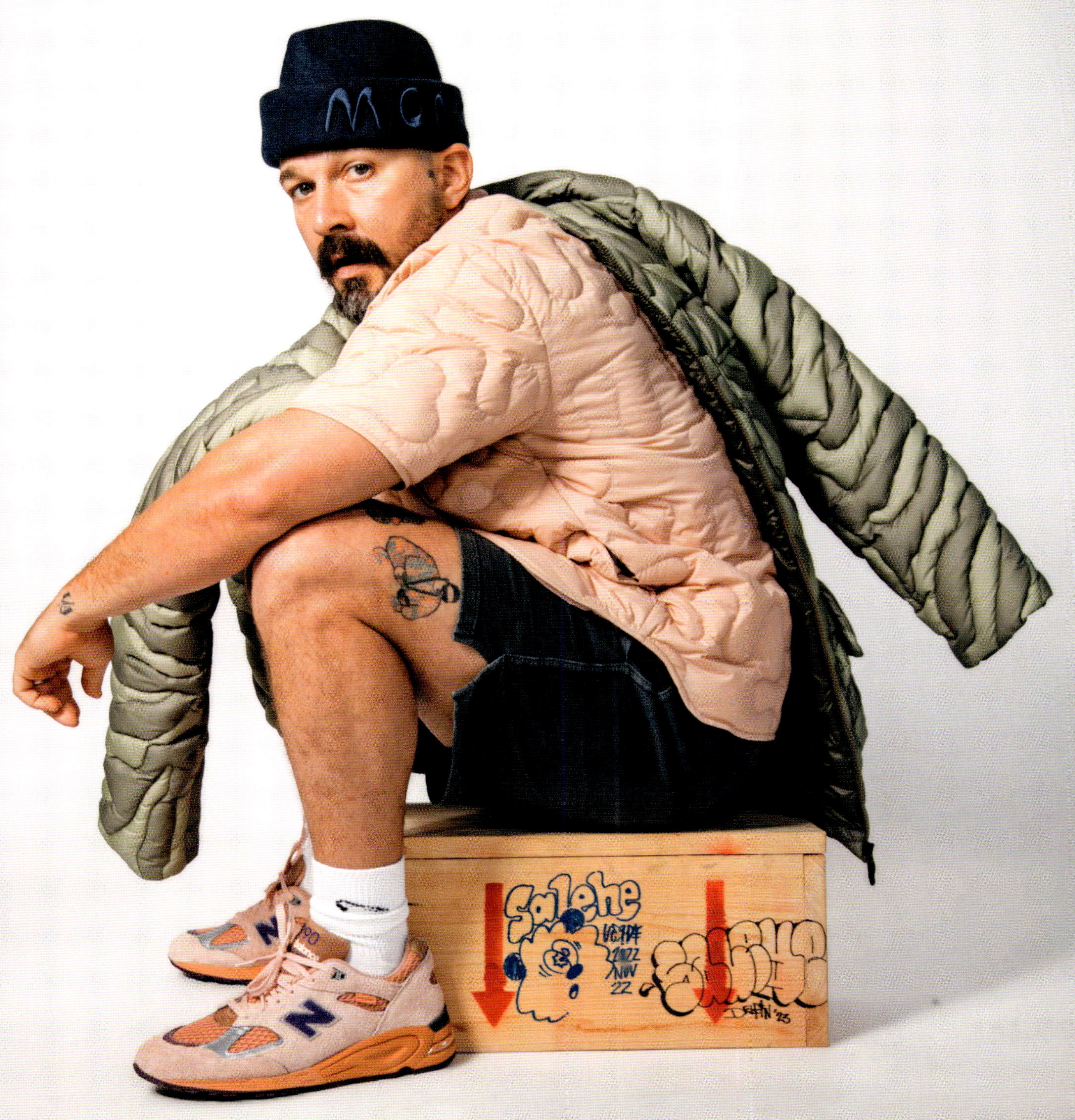

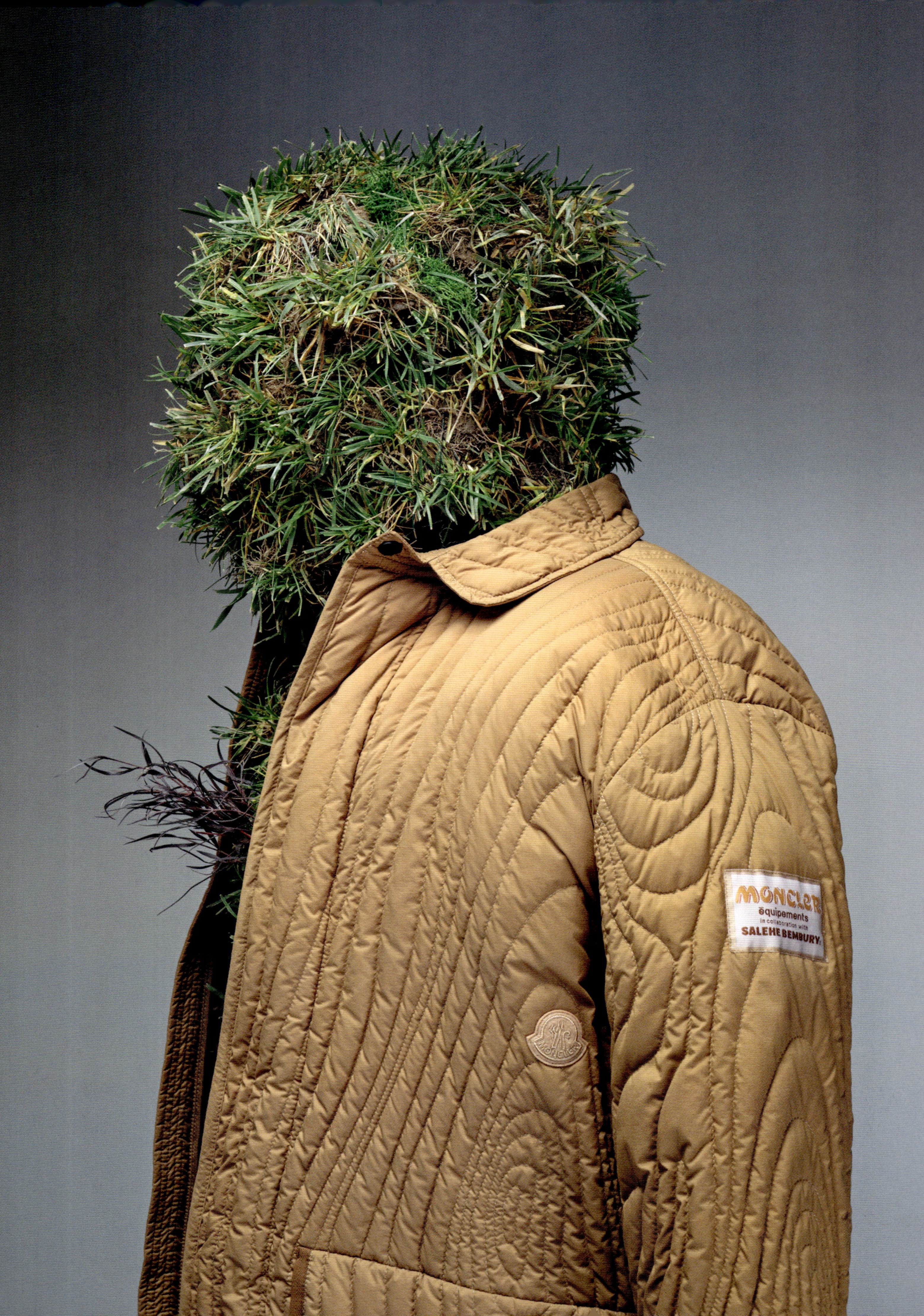
MONCLER
équipements
in collaboration with
SALEHE BEMBURY

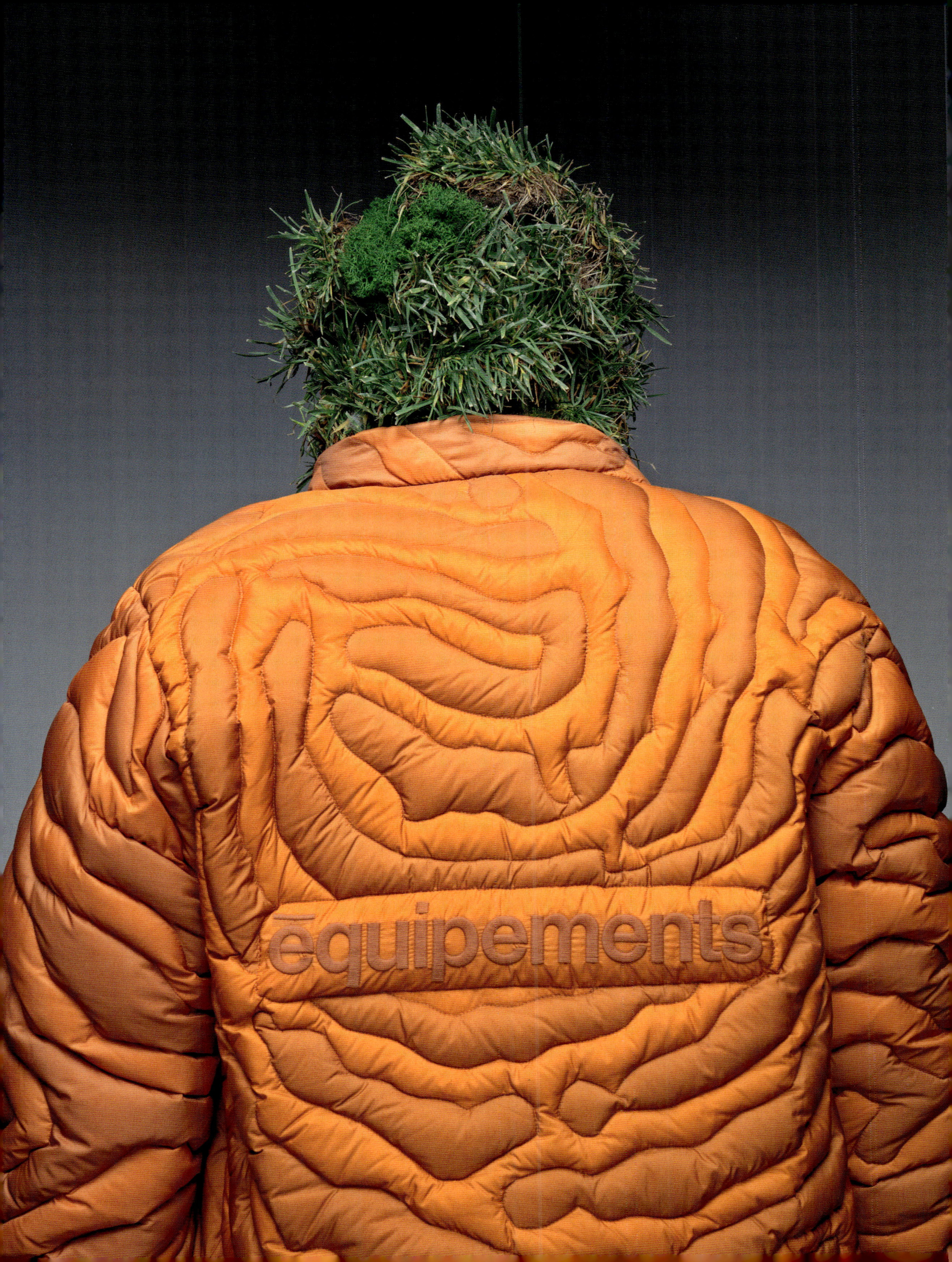
ēquipements

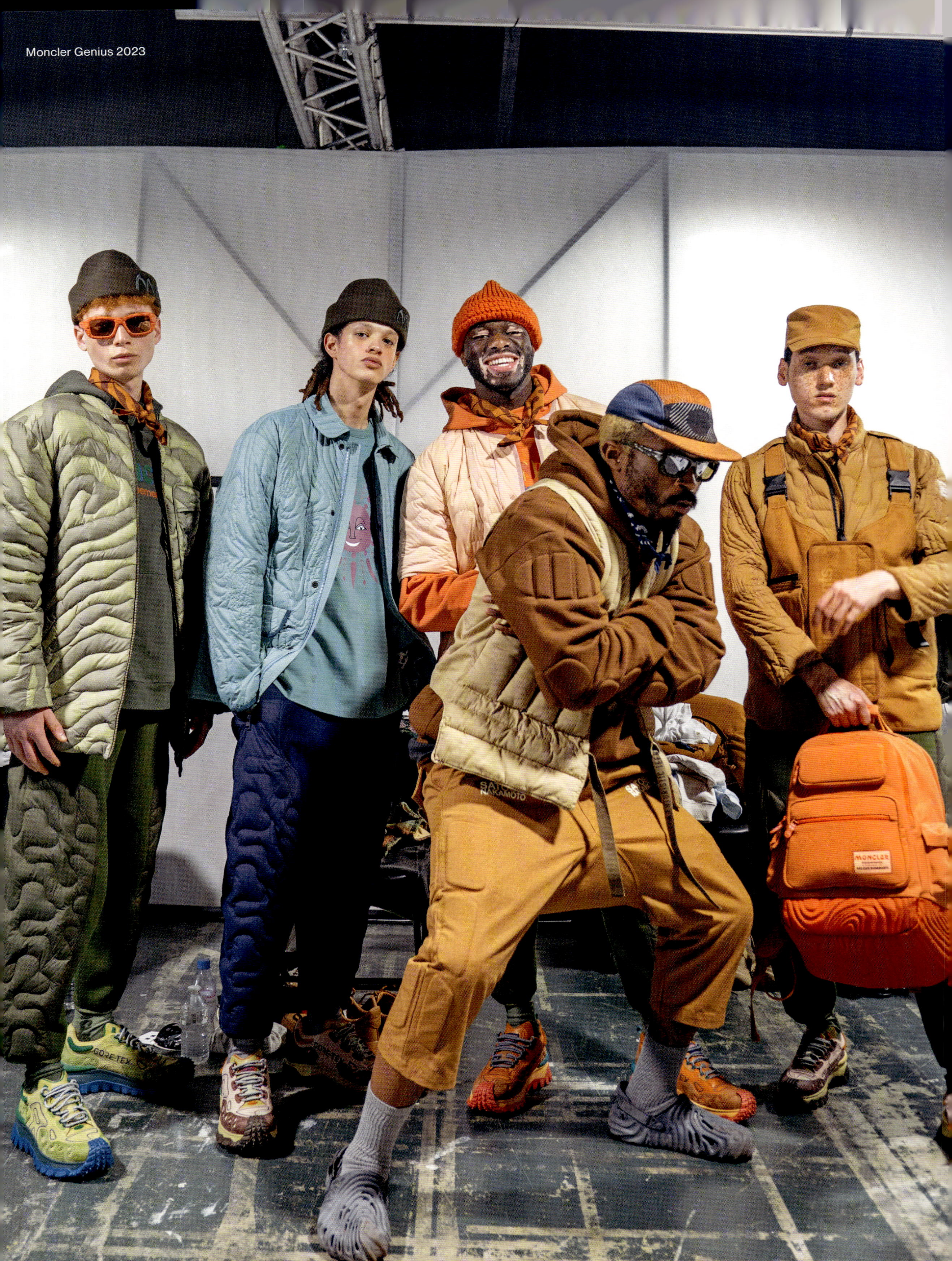
GORE-TEX
SATOSHI
NAKAMOTO
MONCLER

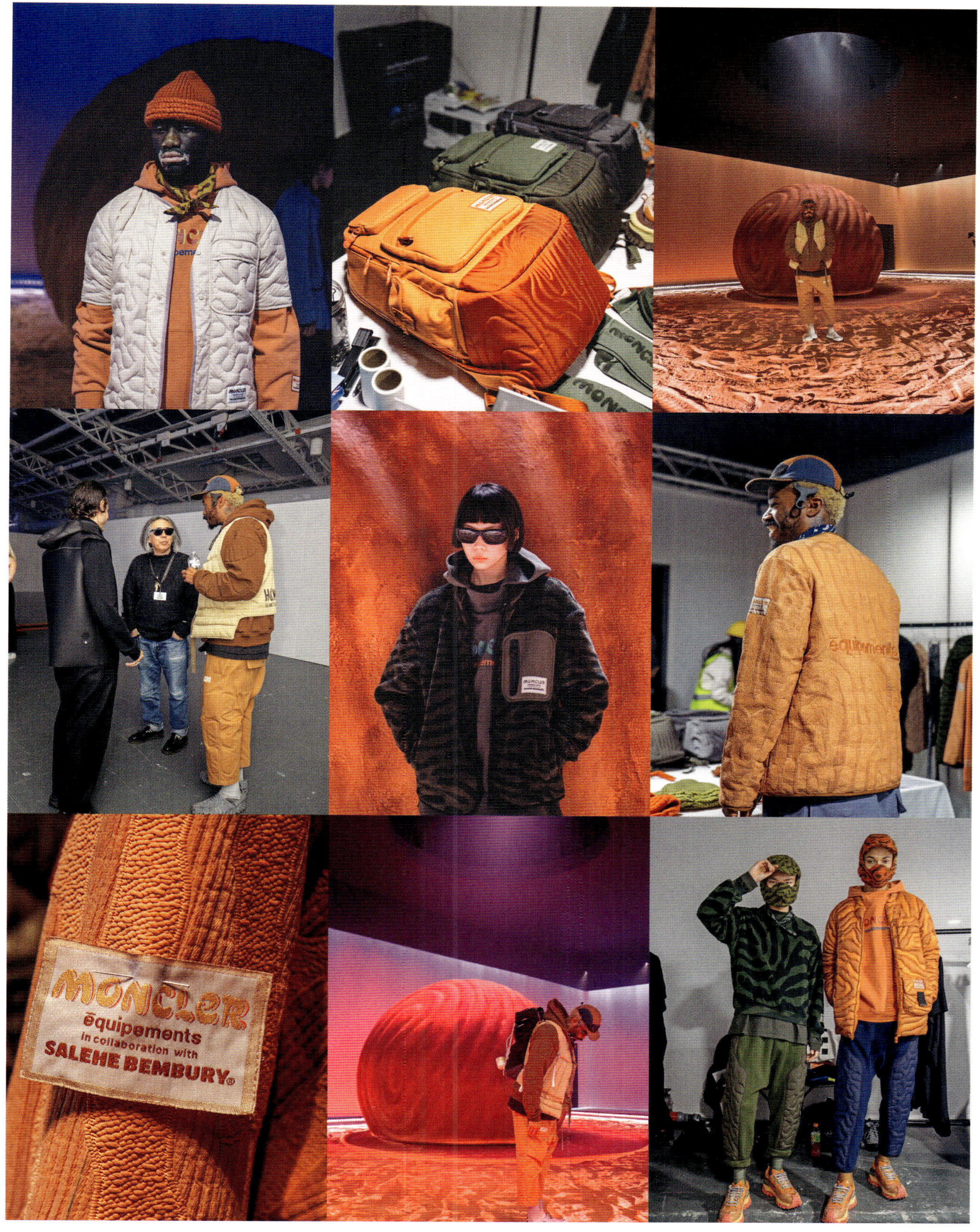

Moncler Genius 2023

321

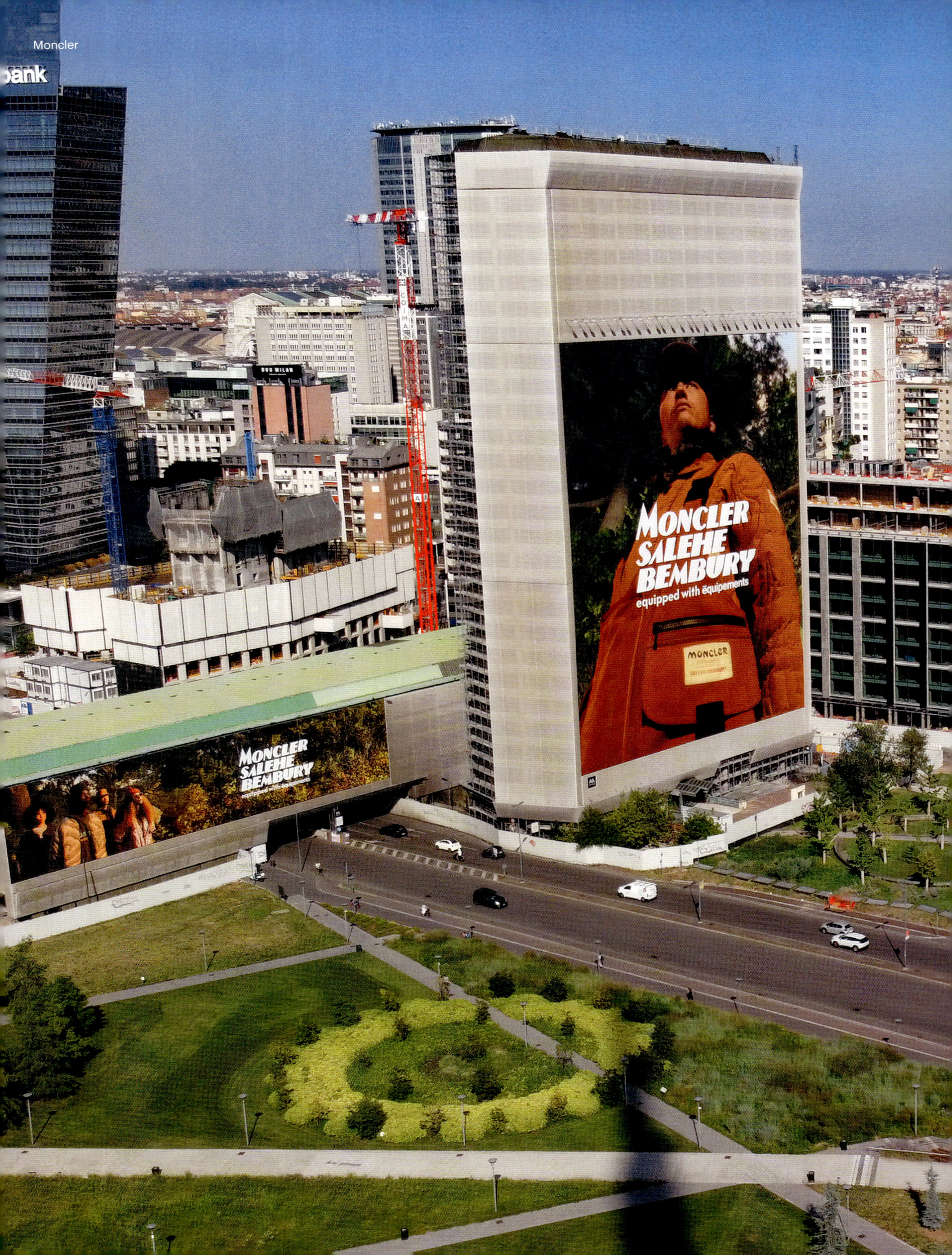

MONCLER
SALEHE
BEMBURY
equipped with ēquipements
MONCLER
MONCLER
SALEHE
BEMBURY
equipped with ēquipements

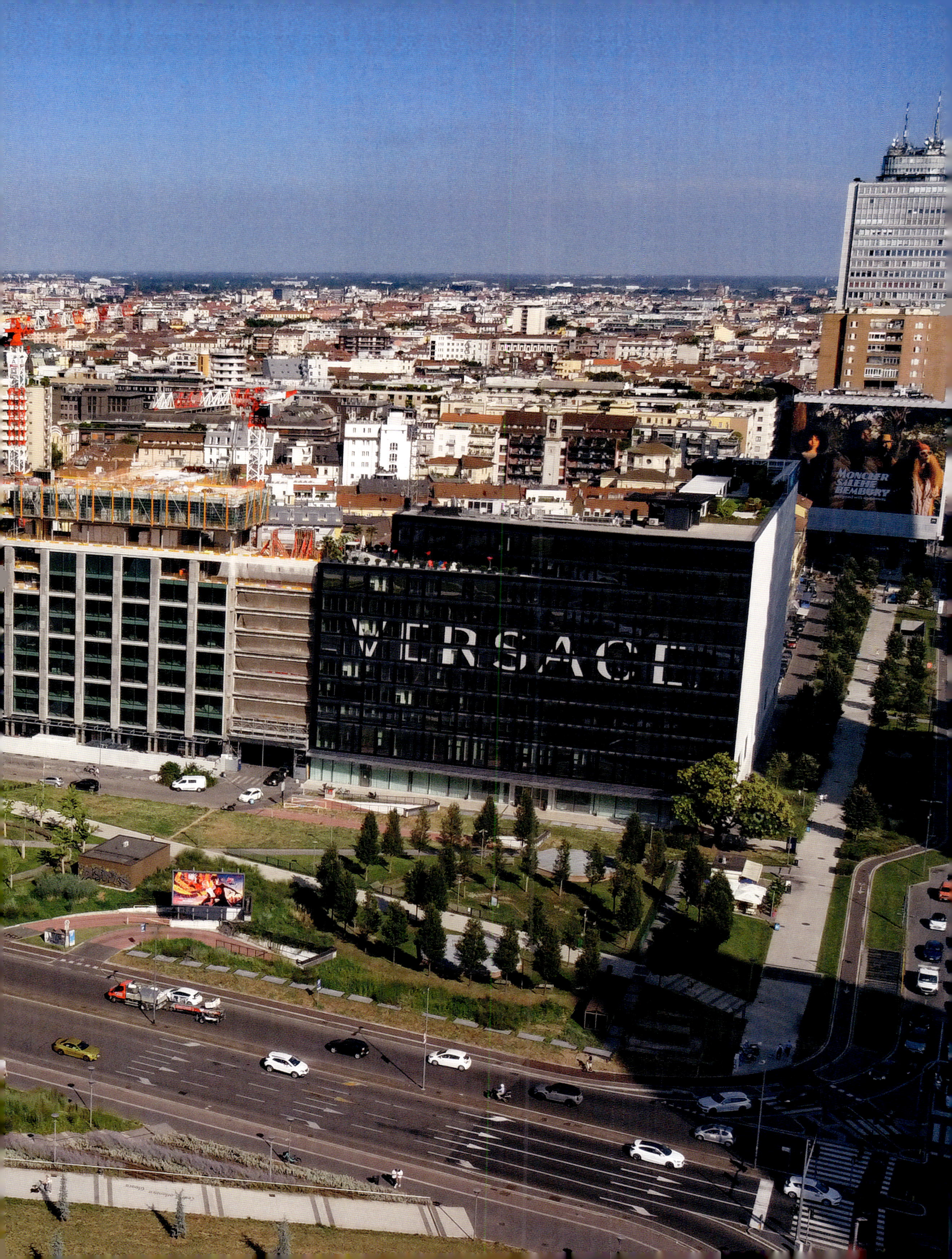
VERSACE
MONCLER
SALEHE
BEMBURY

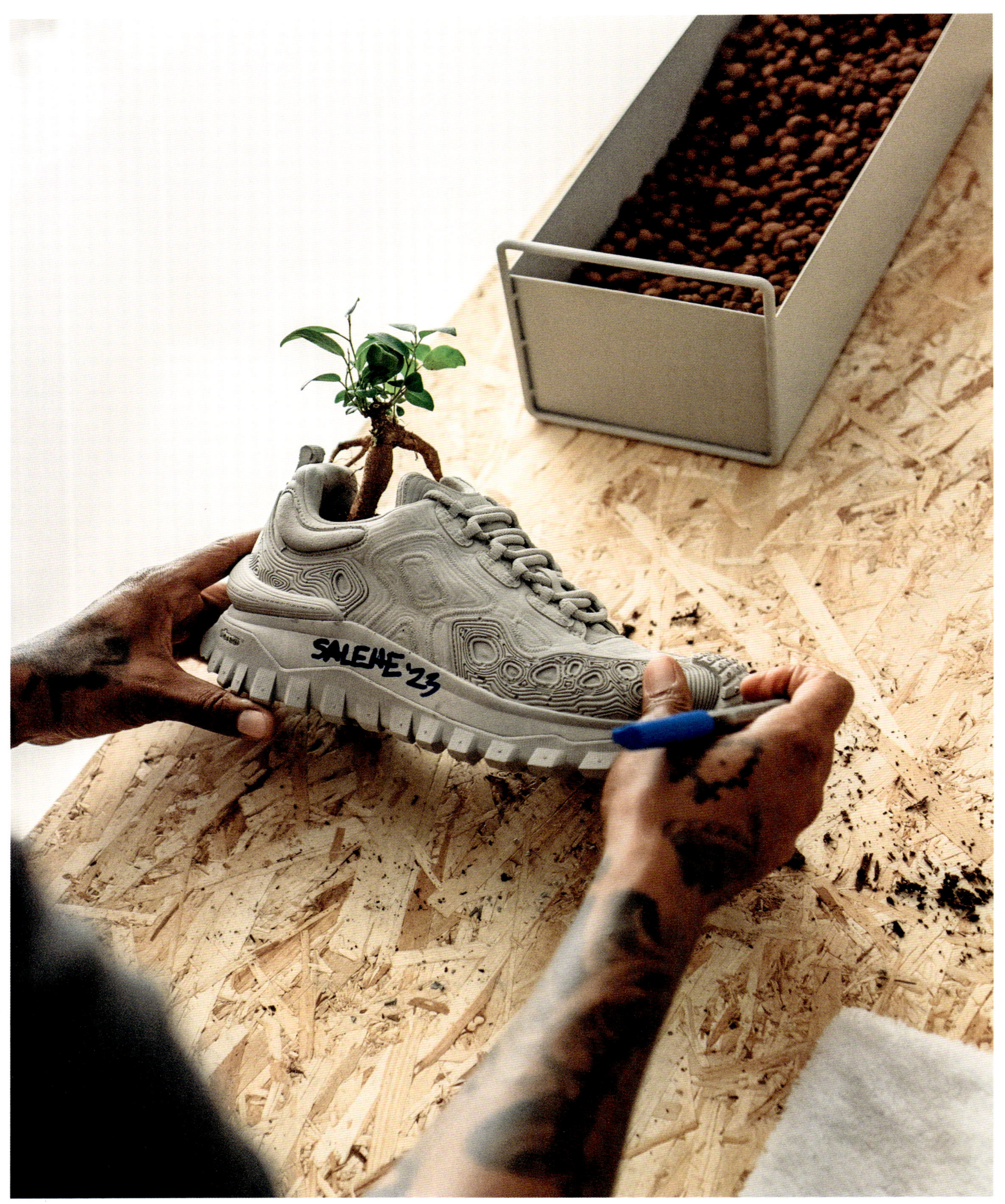

324

(2023)

MONCLER

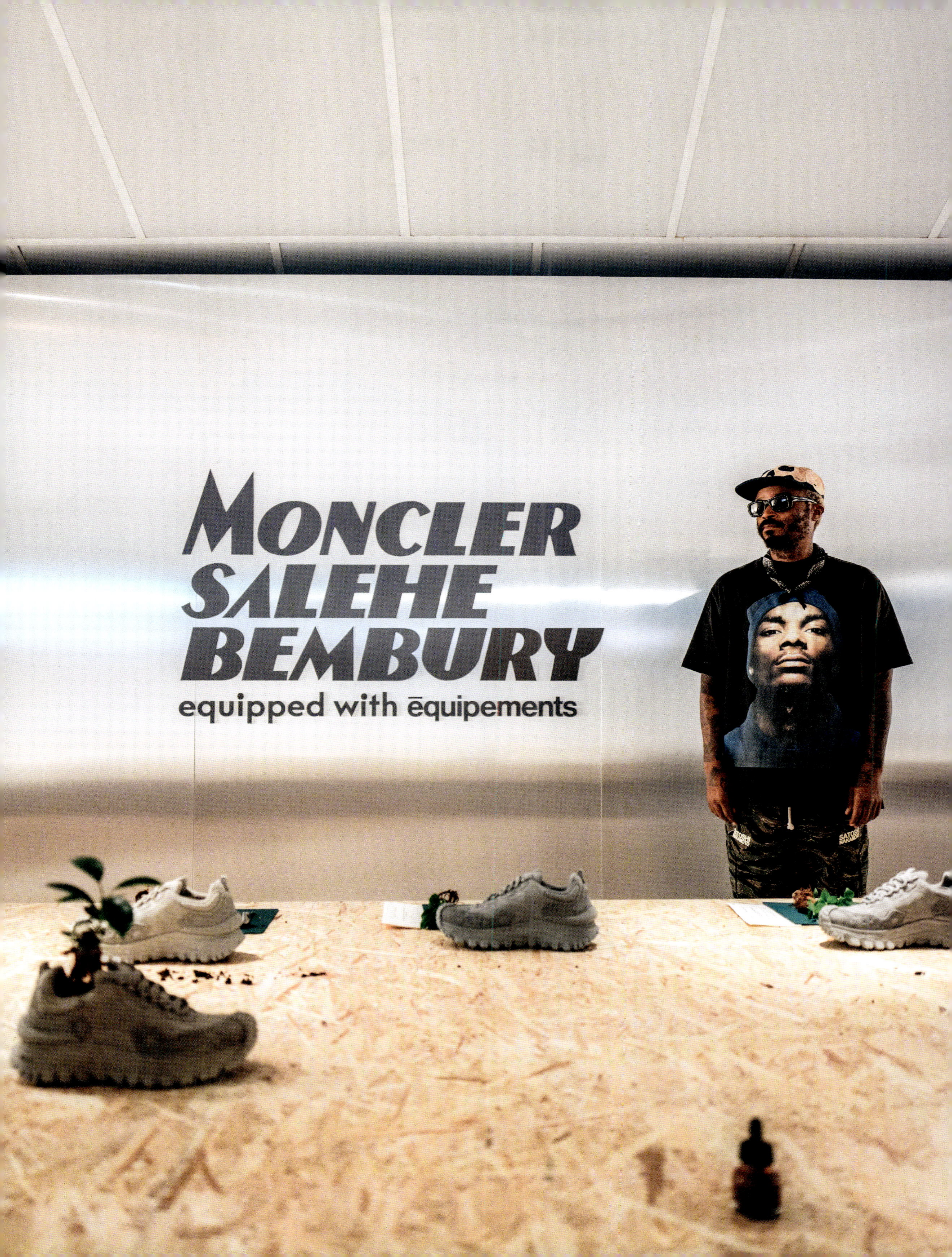
MONCLER
SALEHE
BEMBURY
equipped with ēquipements

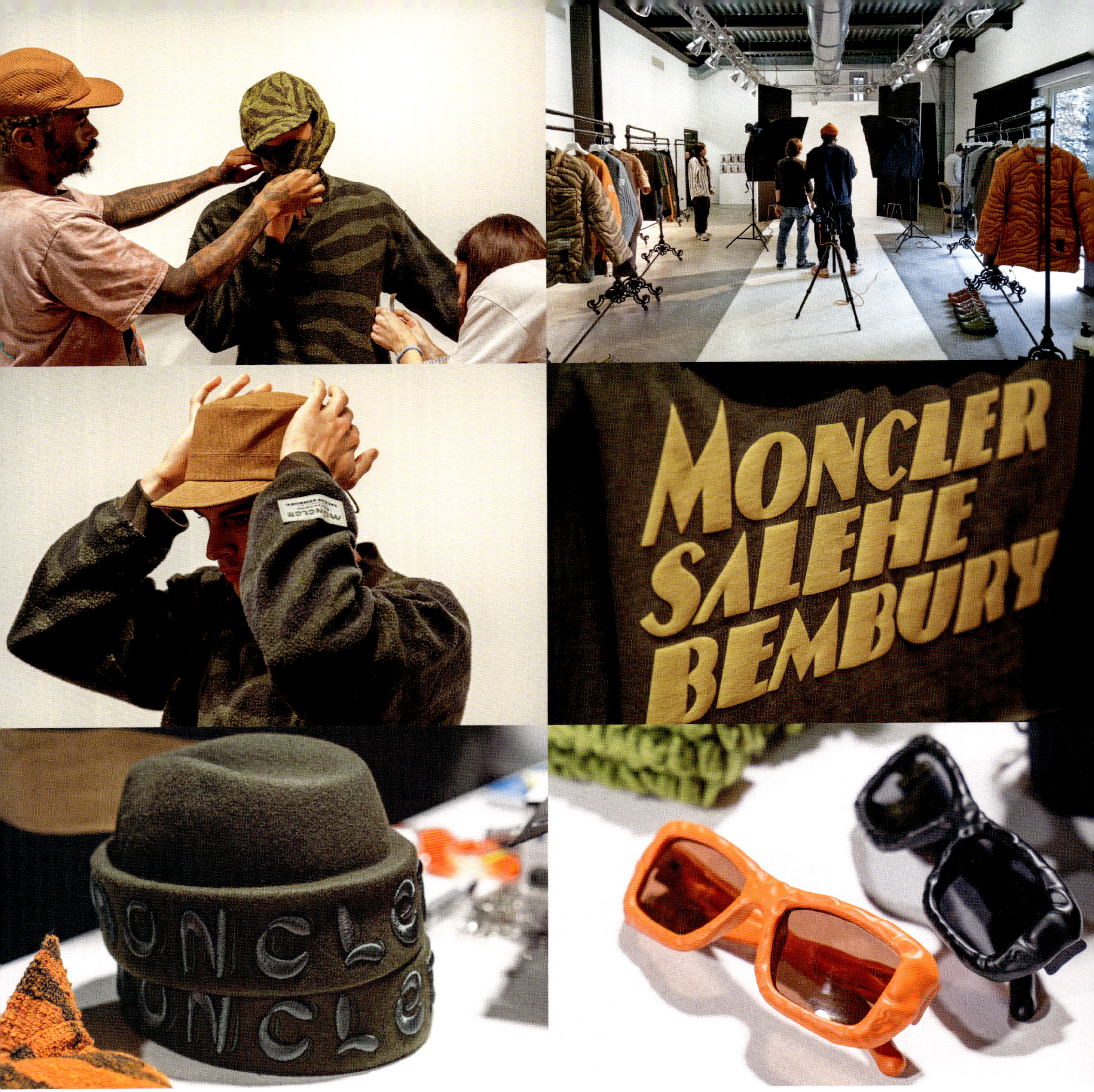

Moncler Genius fitting in Milan, Italy

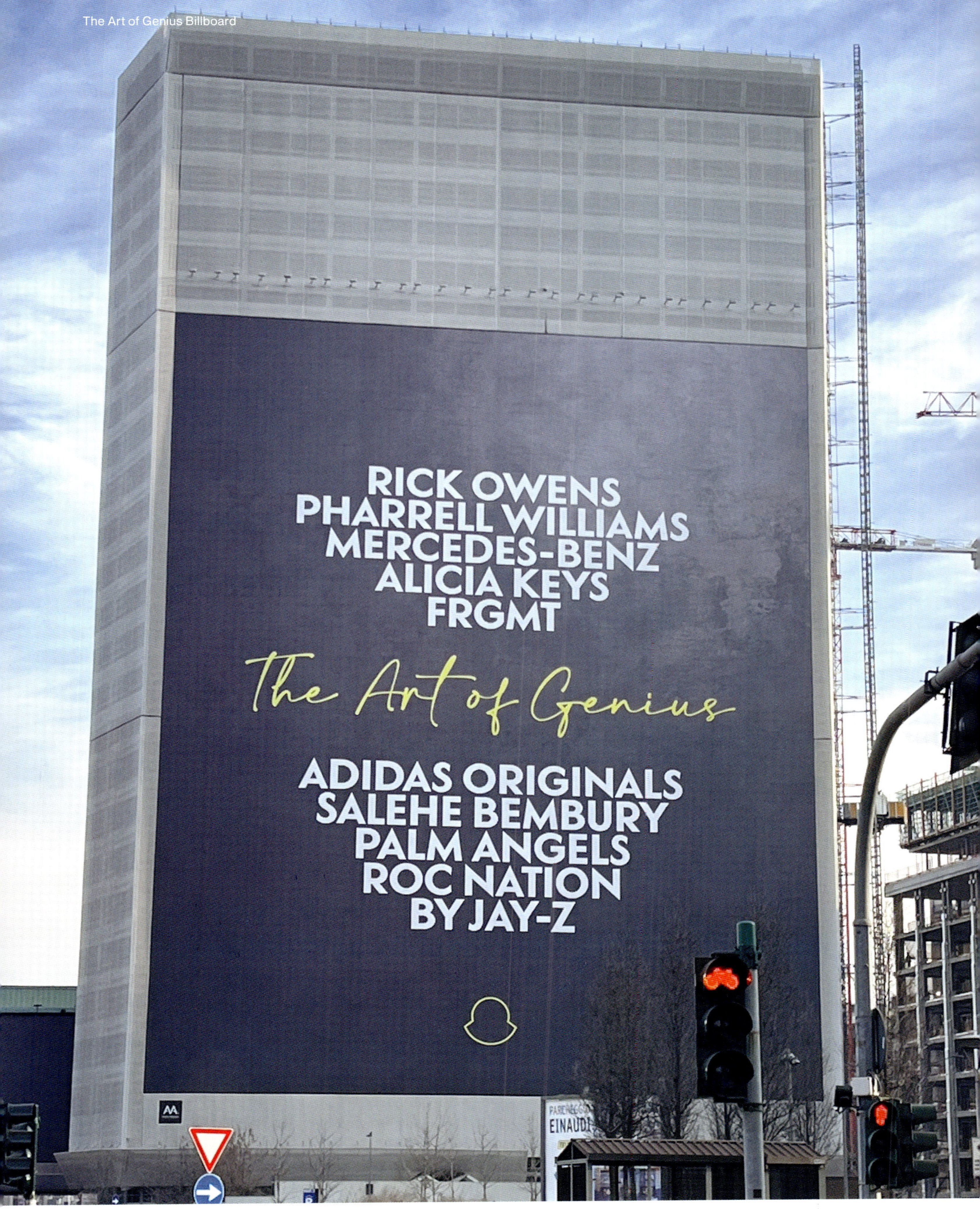
RICK OWENS
PHARRELL WILLIAMS
MERCEDES-BENZ
ALICIA KEYS
FRGMT
The Art of Genius
ADIDAS ORIGINALS
SALEHE BEMBURY
PALM ANGELS
ROC NATION
BY JAY-Z
EINAUDI

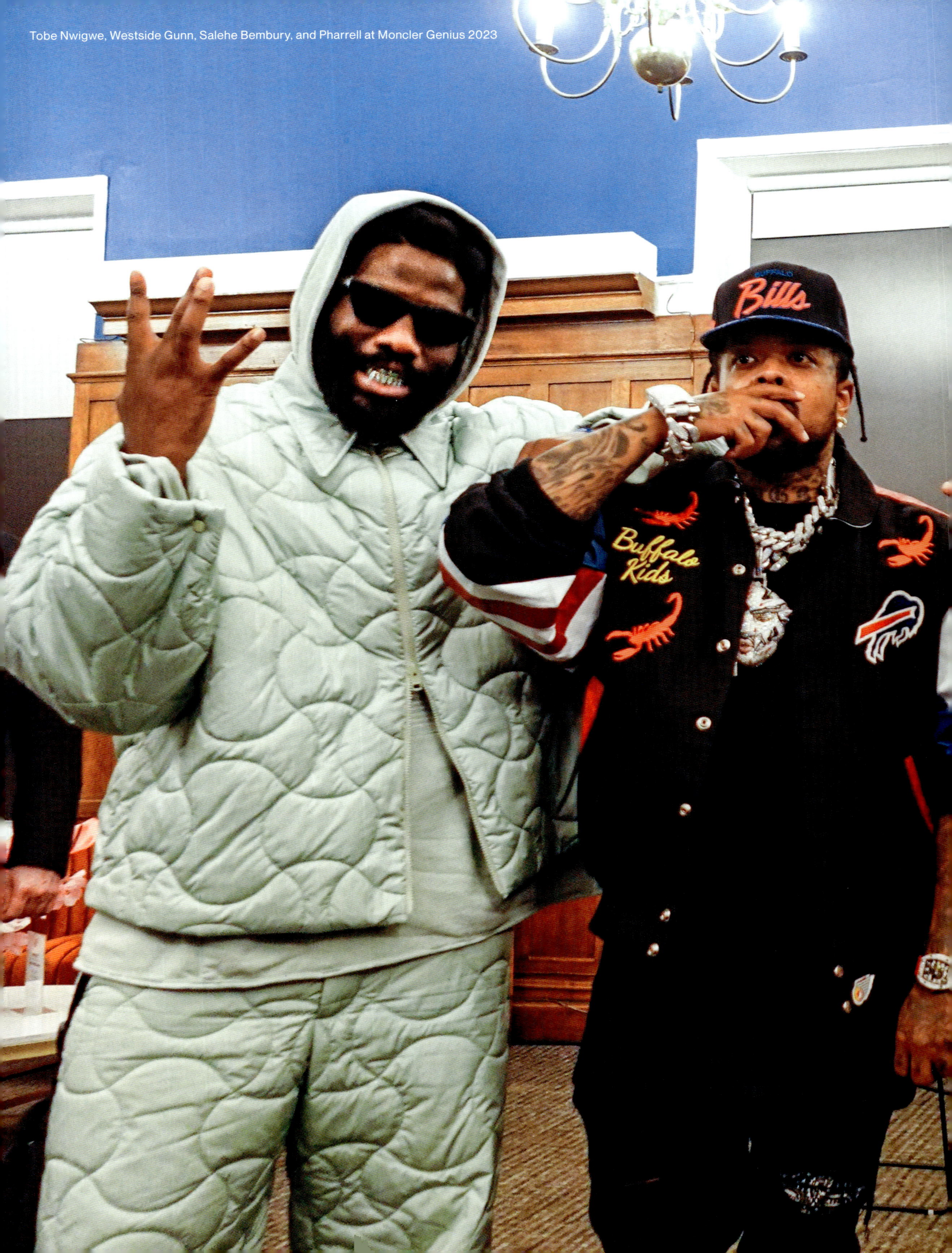

Tobe Nwigwe, Westside Gunn, Salehe Bembury, and Pharrell at Moncler Genius 2023

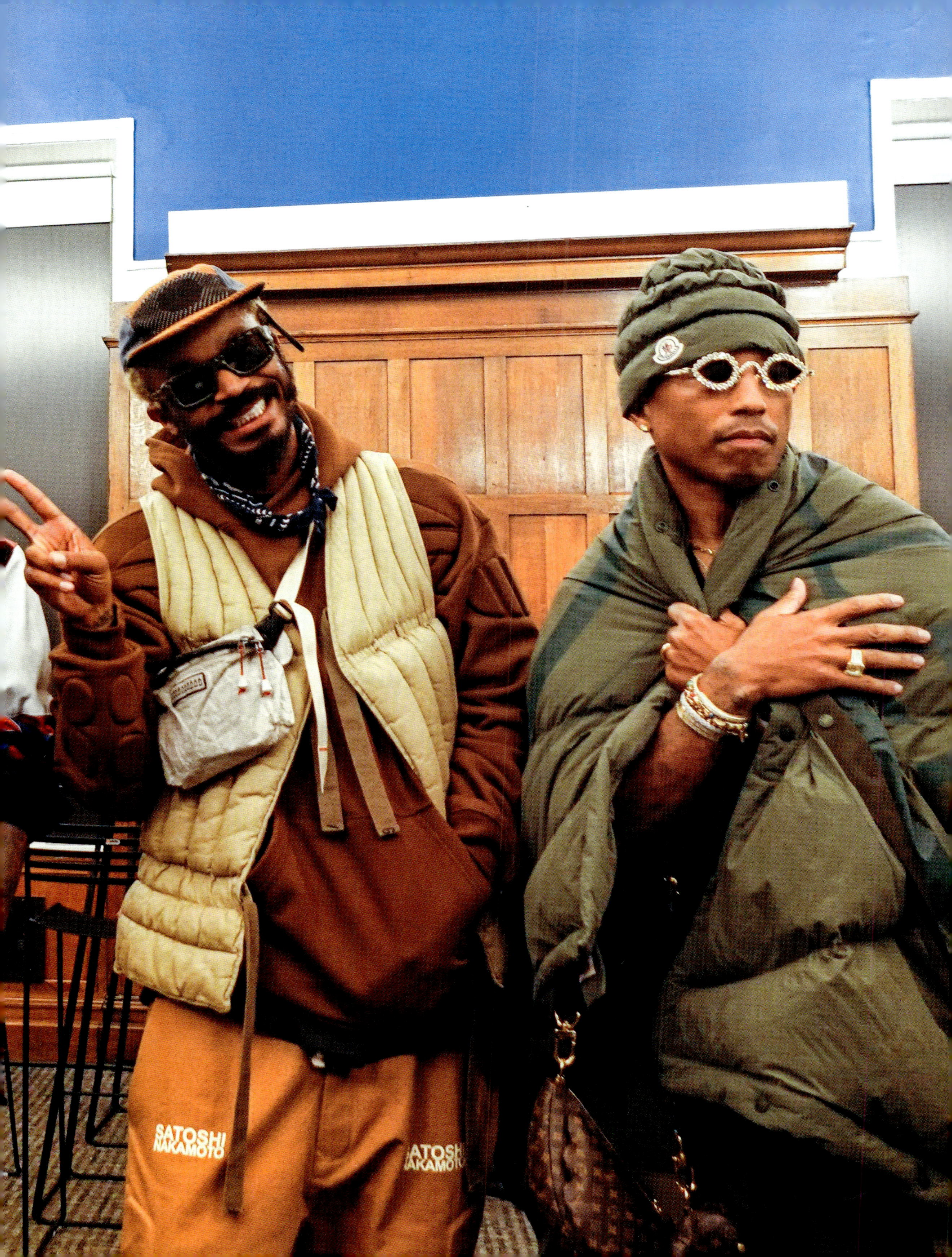
SATOSHI
NAKAMOTO

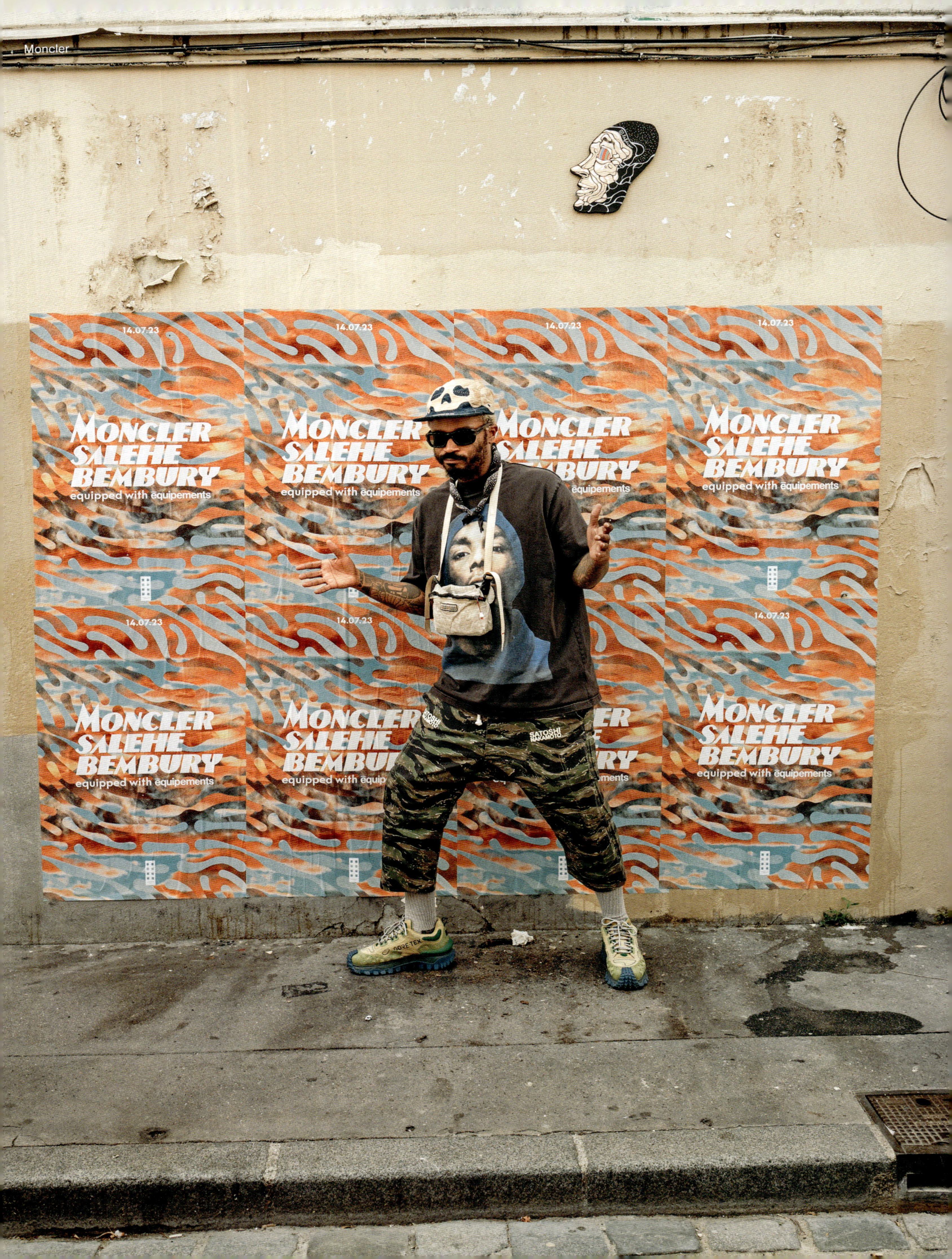
14.07.23
MONCLER
SALEHE
BEMBURY
equipped with equipements
SATOSHI NAKAMOTO

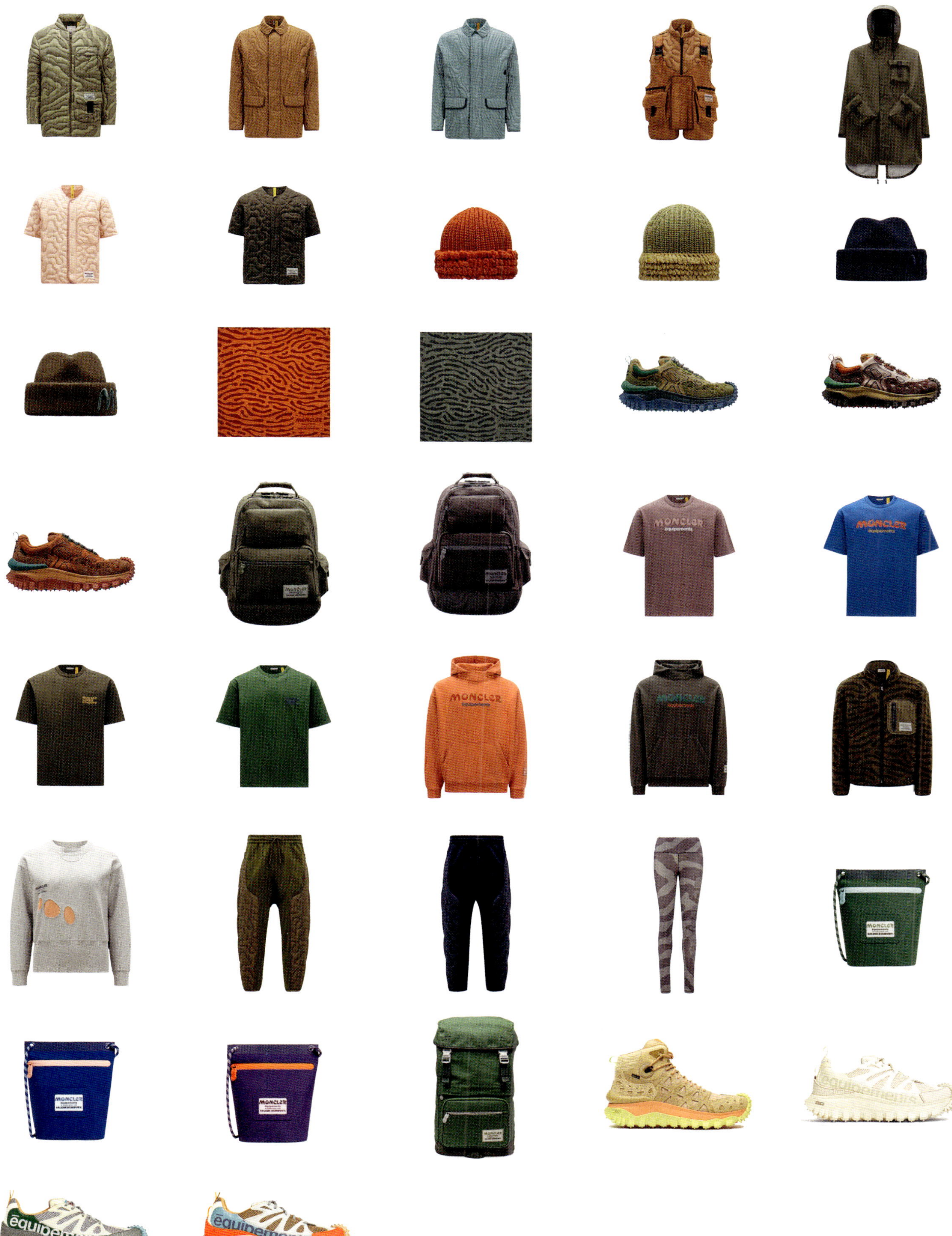
MONCLER
equipements
MONCLER
equipements
MONCLER
equipements
MONCLER
equipements
equipements
équipements
équipements

332

PUMA (2024)

CHILDH
DREAM
ADULT

HOOD
VS.
DREAM

PUMA

CHILDHOOD DREAM VS. ADULT DREAM

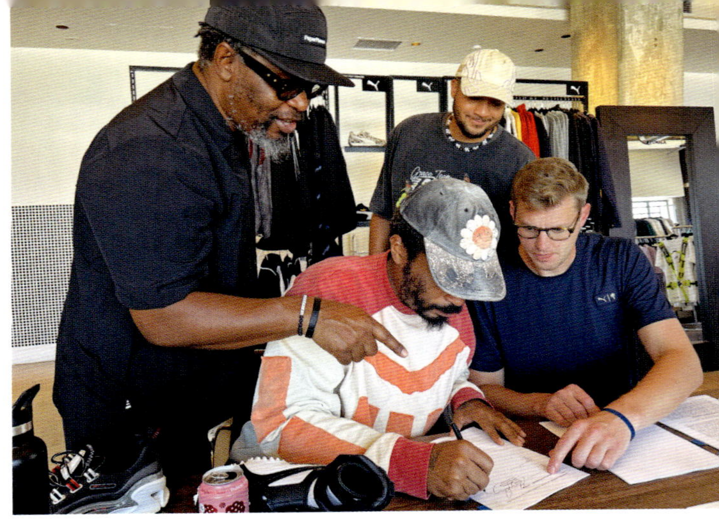

My partnership with Puma represents a shift in perspective and growth in life. I became a footwear designer because of Nike. I've told that story many times—I used to think it was unique to myself, but it is a very common story. I have never on record had the opportunity to work with Nike, but at this point in my life, I thought to myself, I would like to create more impactful product. I would like to have more moments, I would like to tell more stories. I would like to broaden what the stories are that I tell since I've lived in this outdoor space.

Jeremy Sallee from Puma DM'd me and said, "Hey, do you want to come design at Puma?" I spoke to Jeremy and said I was interested in potentially designing the Melos, but because he designs those I didn't want to step on his feet. He said he was fine with that if that was in the cards, so we had a conversation and I liked what I heard. I saw a lot of potential, I saw a lot of alignment in values and ethos, and I signed with Puma.

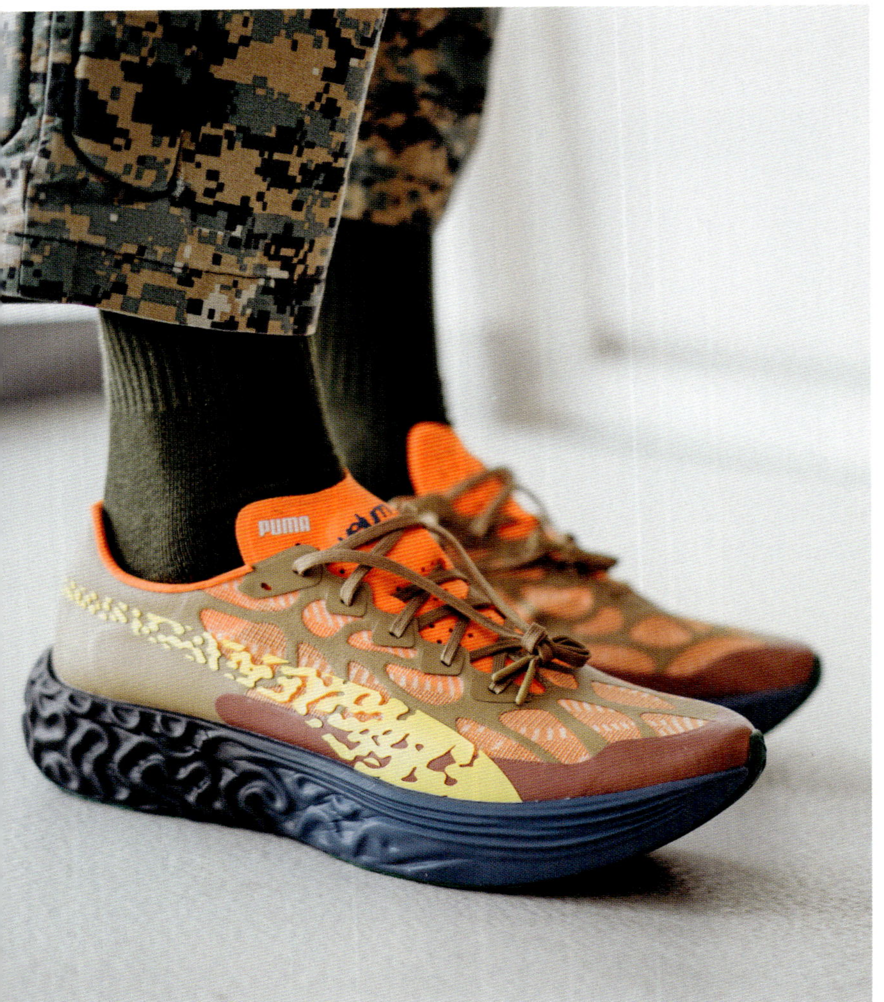

Immediately the online conversation was: Did he leave New Balance? How is he able to work with this many brands? Some were negative reactions, some positive, which really fascinated me. I think people fail to realize that some of my peers work with more brands than I do, but because they have stores they're not seen as individuals, they're seen as stores, and for some reason in peoples' minds that makes it different. But, without naming any names, some of my friends and peers have more partners than I do, but for whatever reason that's not in the narrative. I am still in partnership with New Balance and Crocs, and I'm telling drastically different stories and creating drastically different product with each of them. In my mind, and in the partners' minds, it is not a problem, and there's been much success on all sides ever since.

The Puma story thus far has included my team and I flying to Germany in the Puma private jet, which was a very new experience for me, and one which I was initially a little bit afraid of—a fear I quickly conquered. We went to Puma, got to see their archive, got to speak to their team, and really got to map out how we were going to shift the basketball narrative and introduce some extremely impactful product into the market. I've always wanted to design a basketball shoe; doing so was the foundational inspiration that motivated me to move toward footwear.

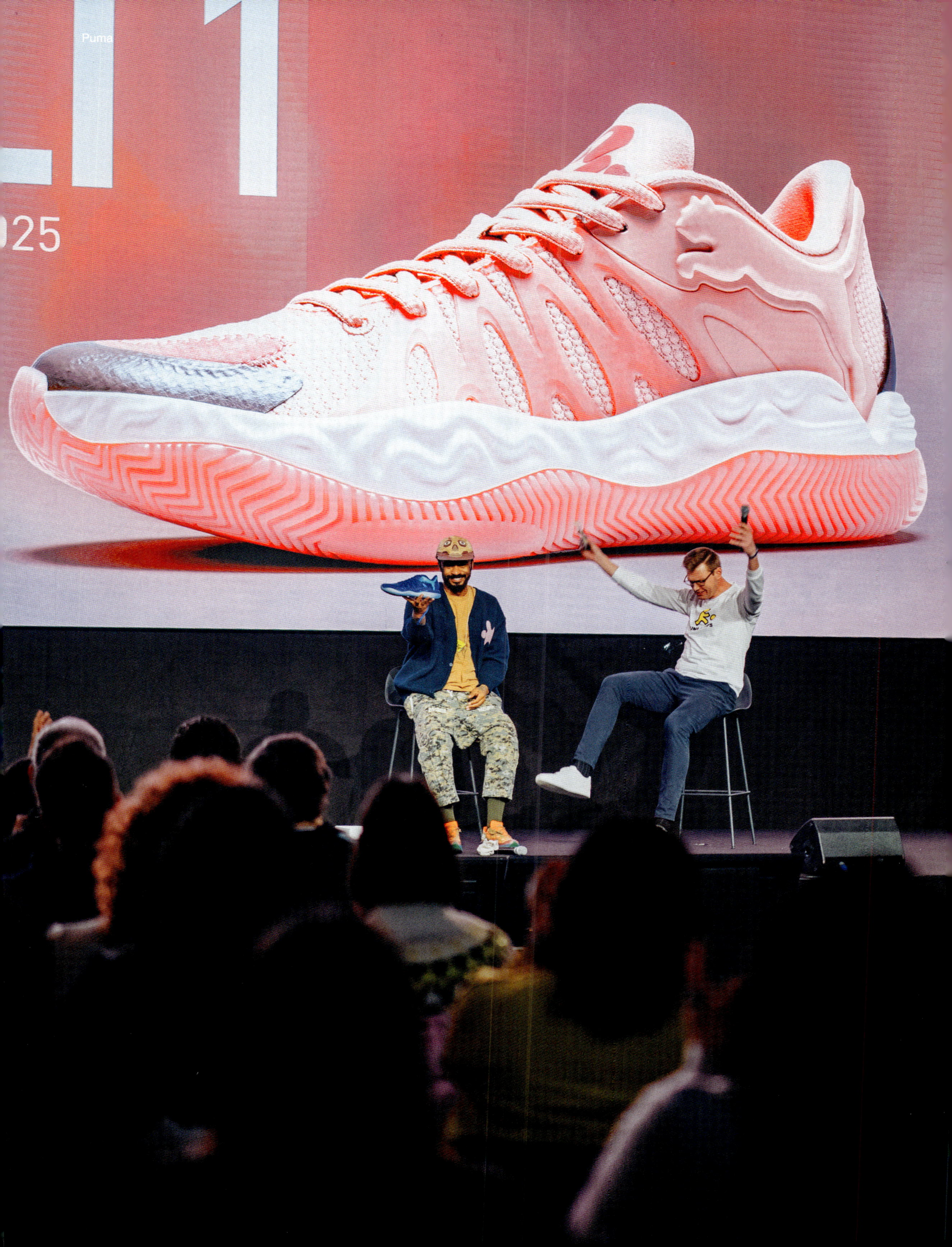

Puma

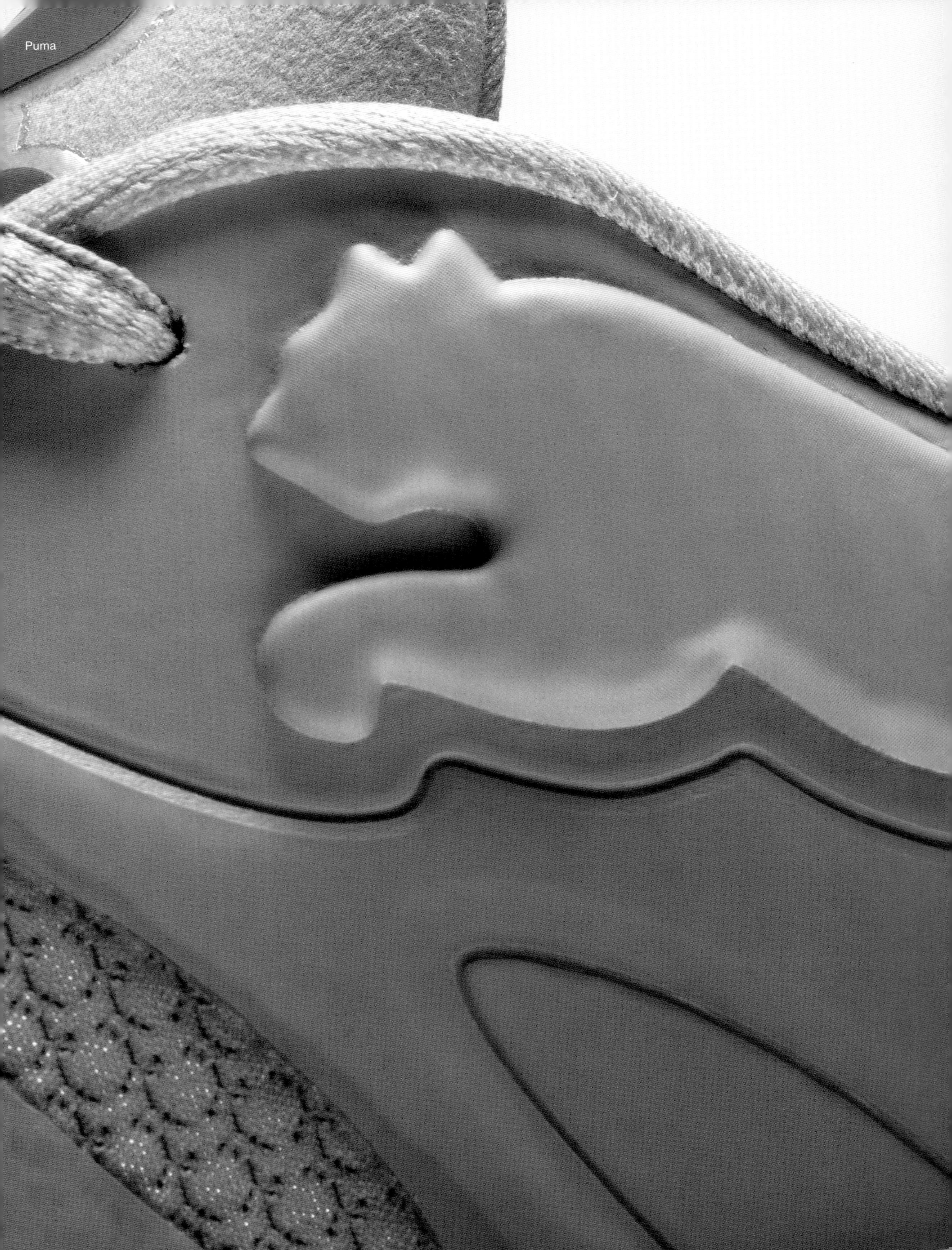

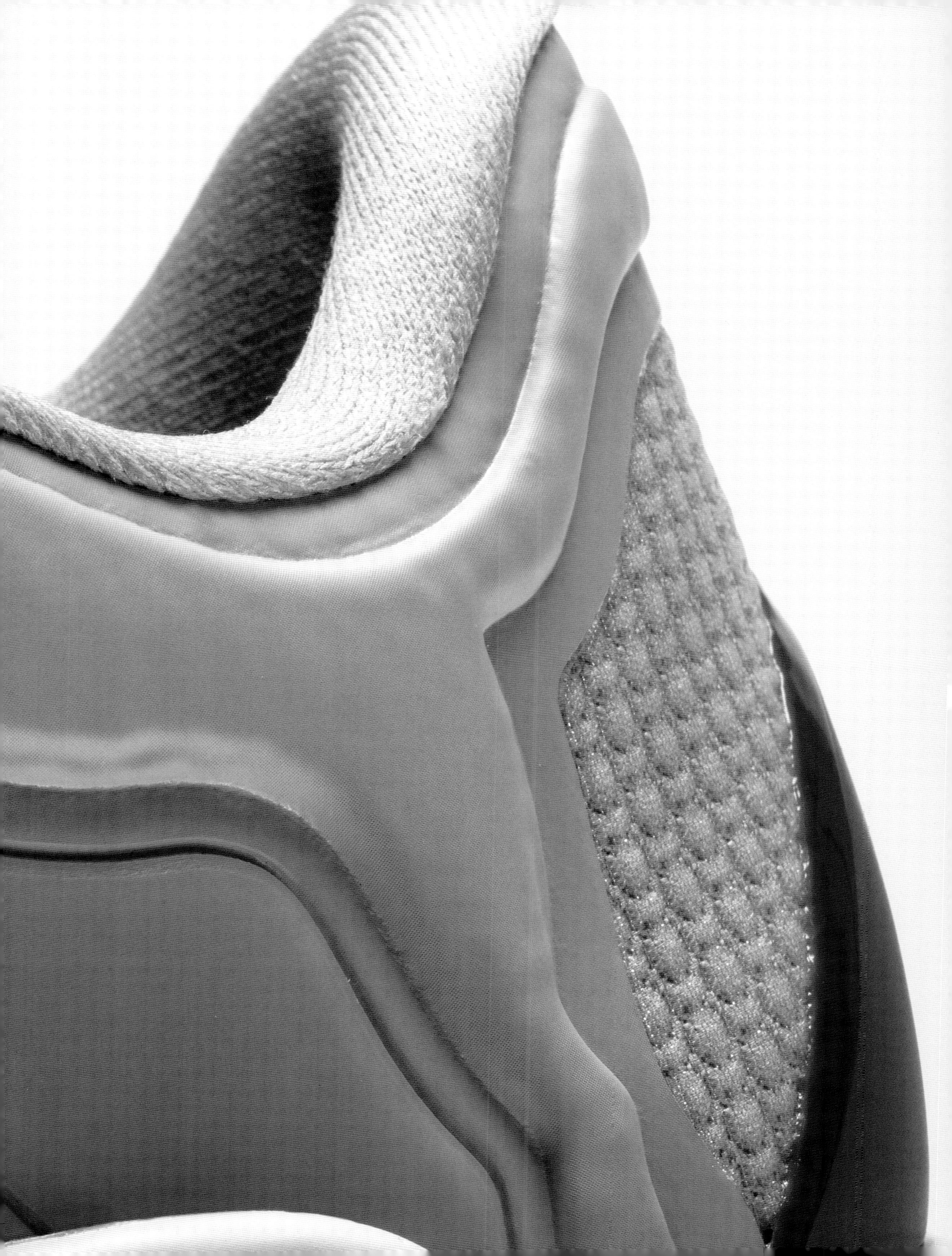

Puma Hali 1 3D print

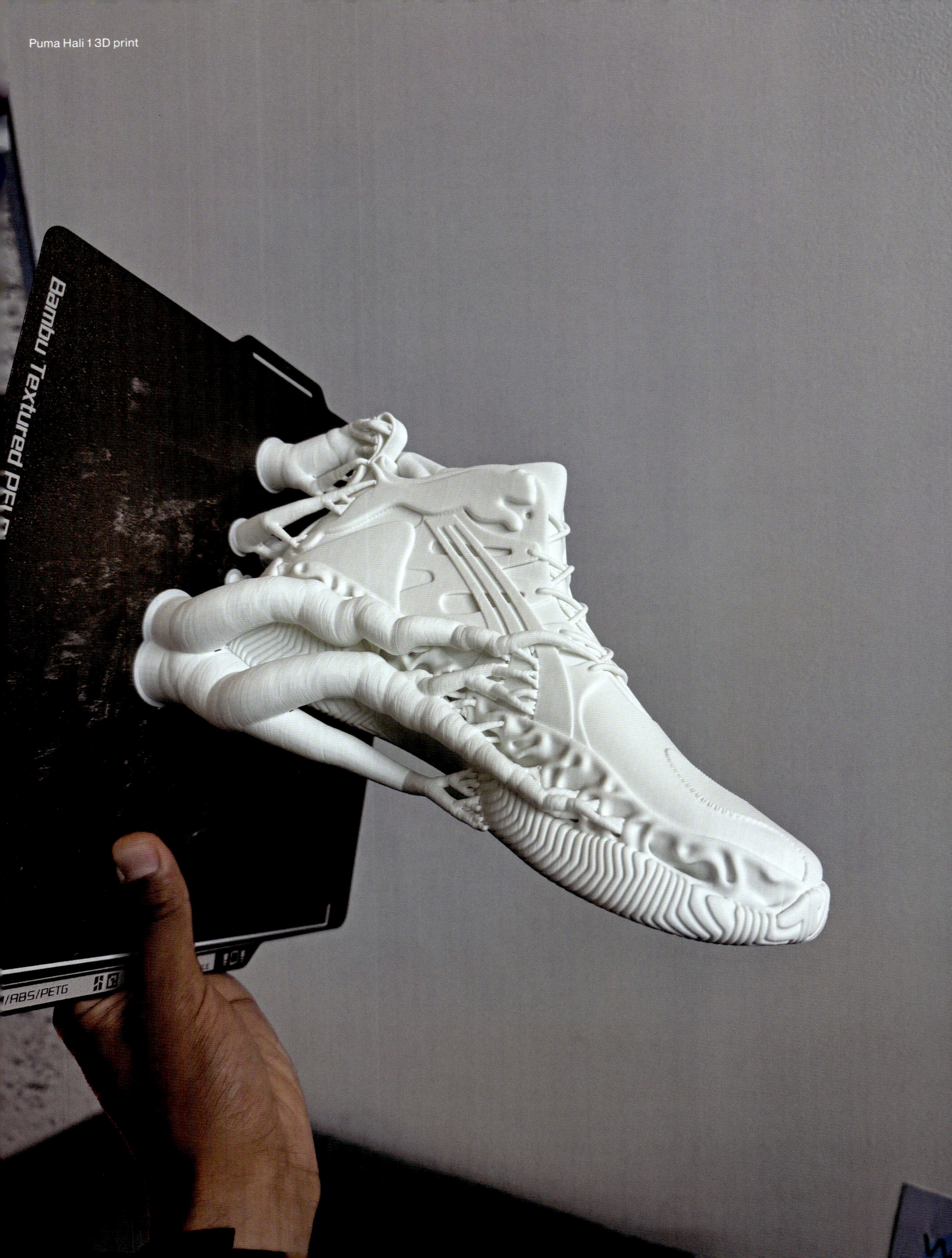

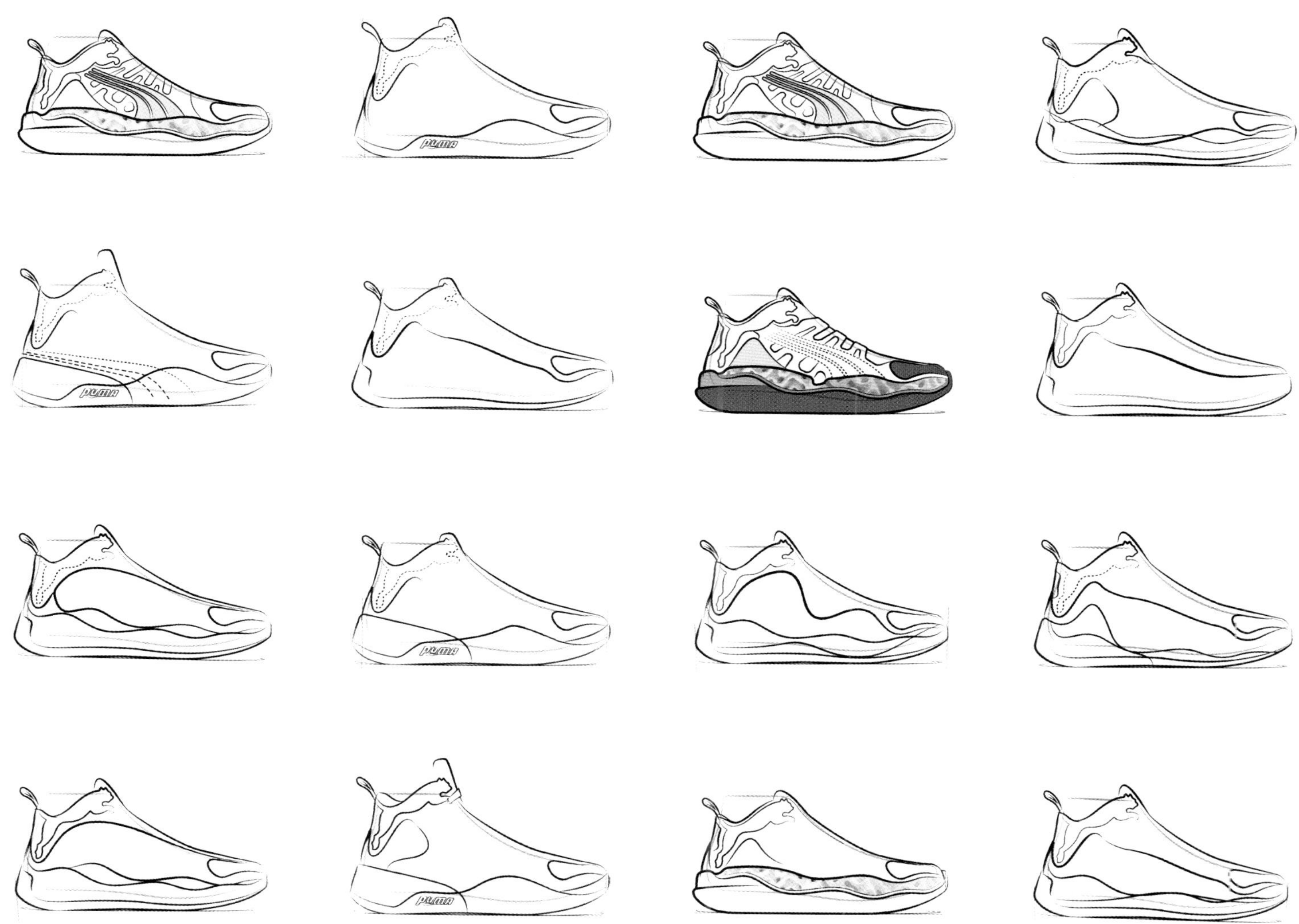

Puma Hali 1 sketches

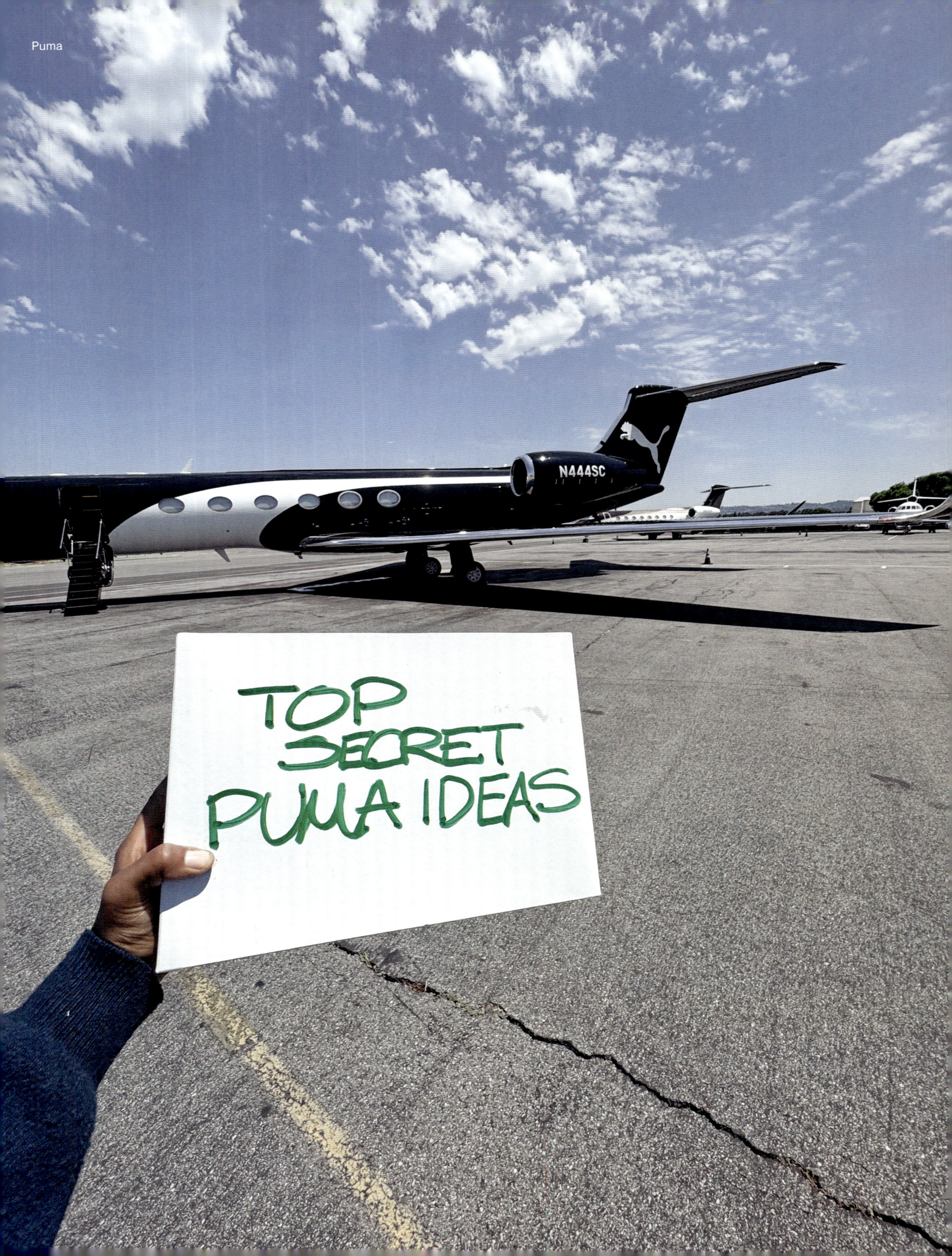
N444SC
TOP
SECRET
PUMA IDEAS

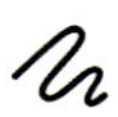

Jeremy PUMA
7/18/24, 10:34 AM

JAN 26 AT 10:36 AM

Yo you a free agent yet ?

I been one

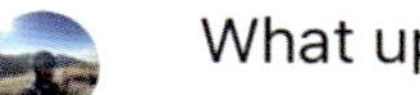

What up

You tryna do some with Us (Puma Hoops)

Somethin*

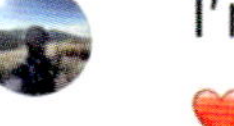

I'm open to a convo

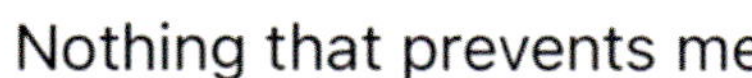

Nothing that prevents me

I told em you were the only one and they went and got the budget

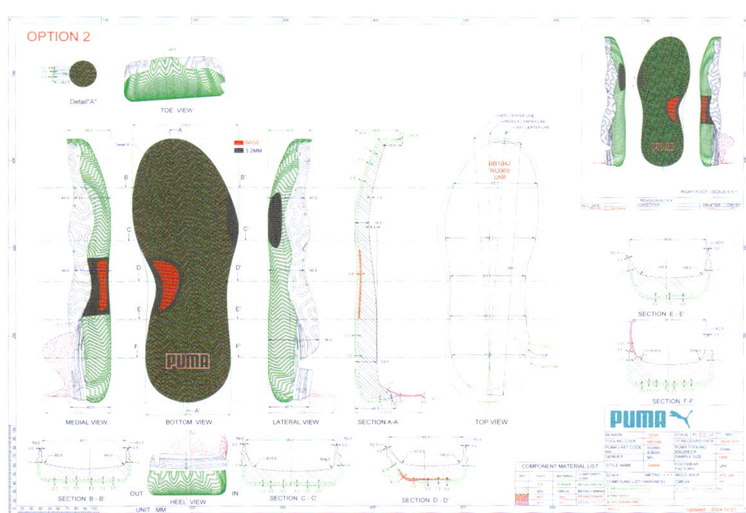

Above: Text between Jeremy Sallee and Salehe Bembury
Below: Puma CADs

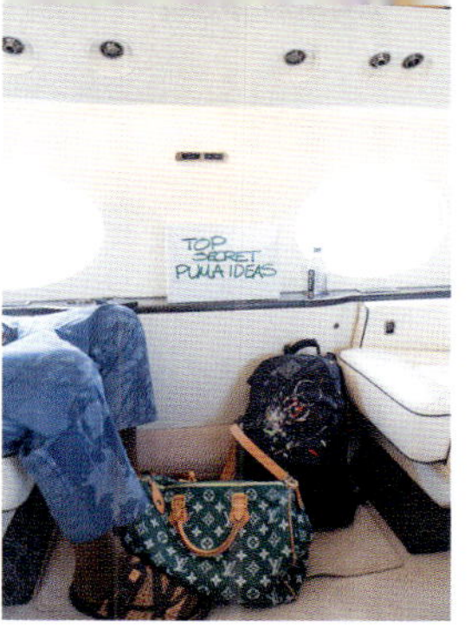

Salehe Bembury on the Puma private jet

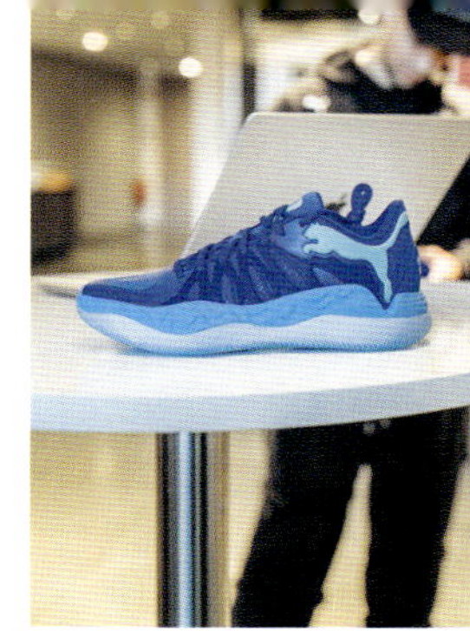
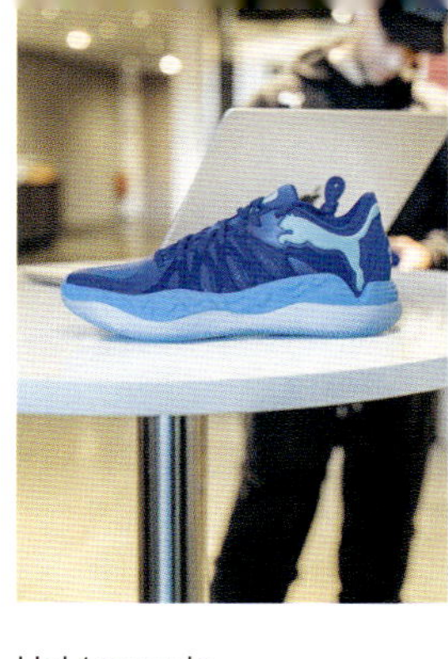

Hal 1 sample

Tyrese Haliburton Facetiming with Salehe Bembury

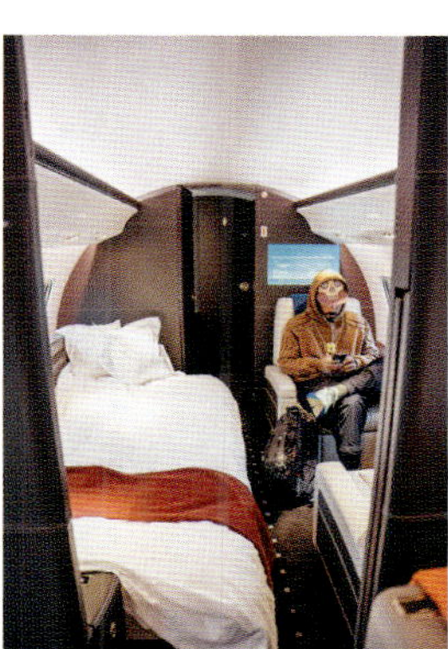

Salehe Bembury on the Puma private jet

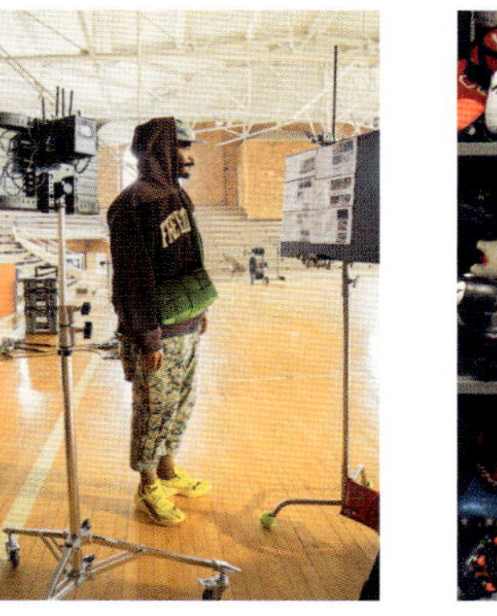
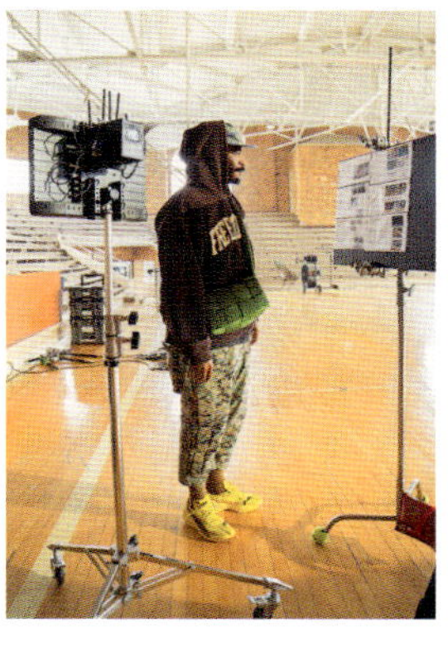

Salehe Bembury on set at Tyrese Haliburton's Puma campaign

Puma Archive

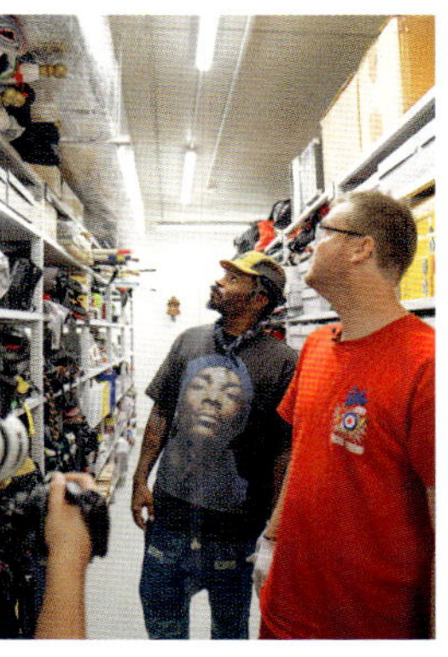

Puma Archive

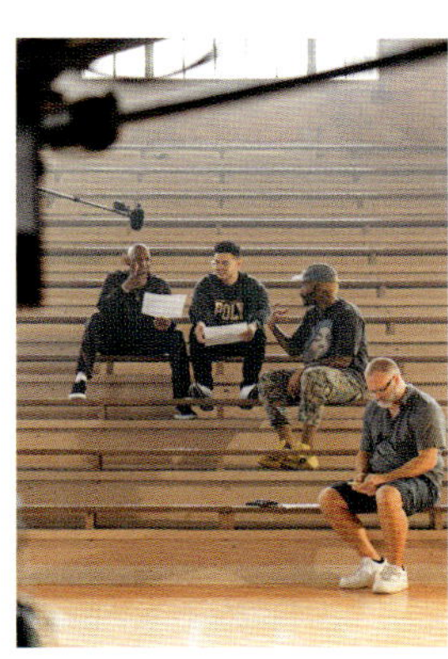

Nat Prinzi, John Haliburton, and Salehe Bembury on set at Tyrese Haliburton's Puma campaign

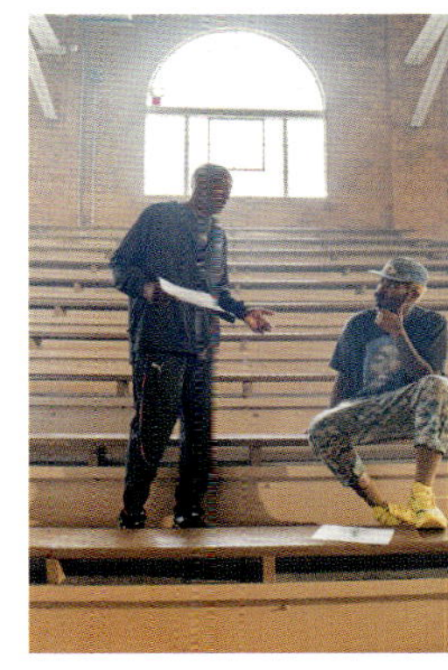

John Haliburton and Salehe Bembury on set at Tyrese Haliburton's Puma campaign

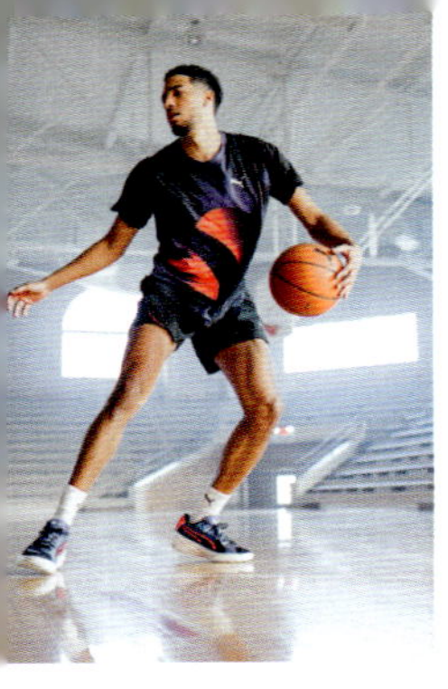

Tyrese Haliburton Puma campaign

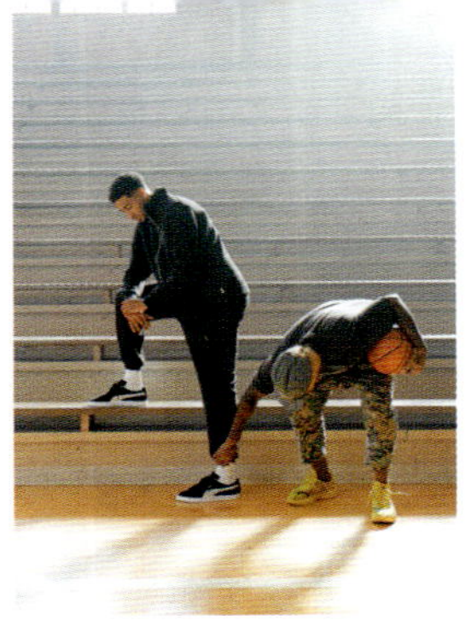

Tyrese Haliburton and Salehe Bembury on set at Tyrese Haliburton's Puma campaign

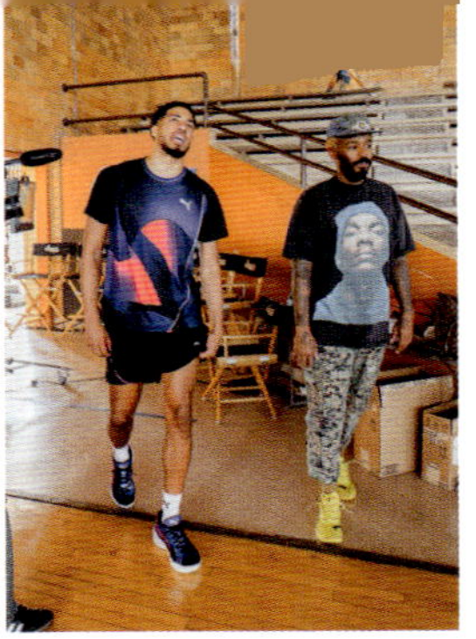

Tyrese Haliburton and Salehe Bembury on set at Tyrese Haliburton's Puma campaign

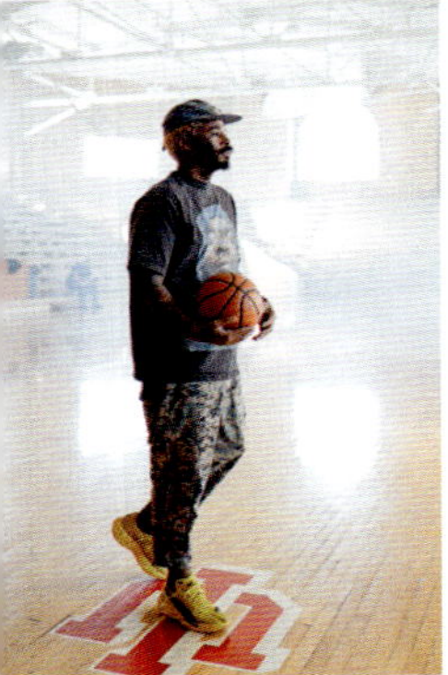

Salehe Bembury on set at Tyrese Haliburton's Puma campaign

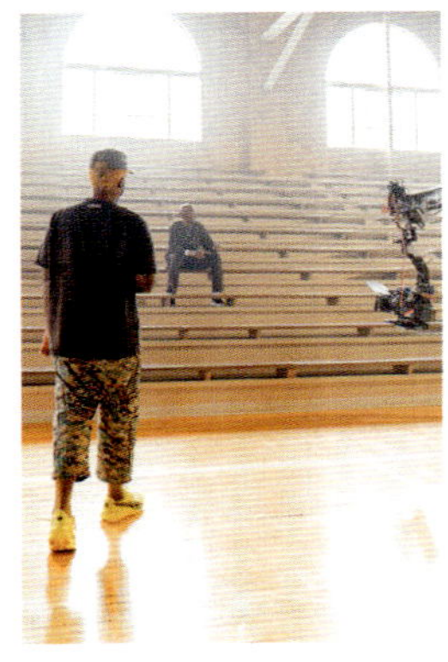

John Haliburton and Salehe Bembury on set at Tyrese Haliburton's Puma campaign

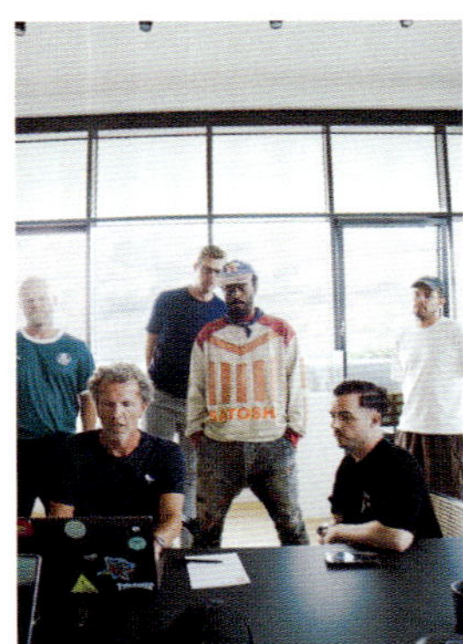

Design review in Herzogenaurach Germany

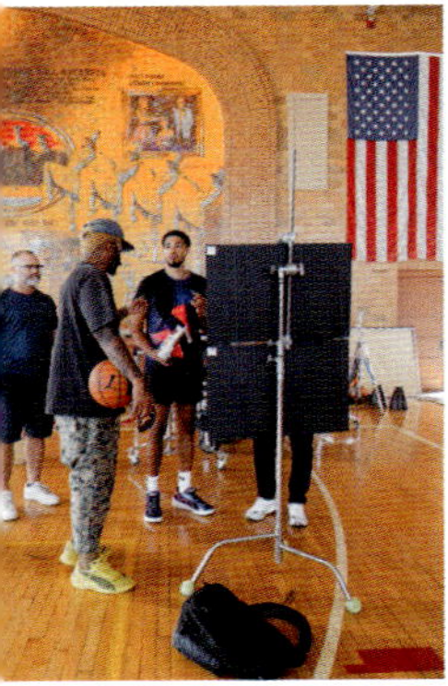

Tyrese Haliburton and Salehe Bembury on set at Tyrese Haliburton's Puma campaign

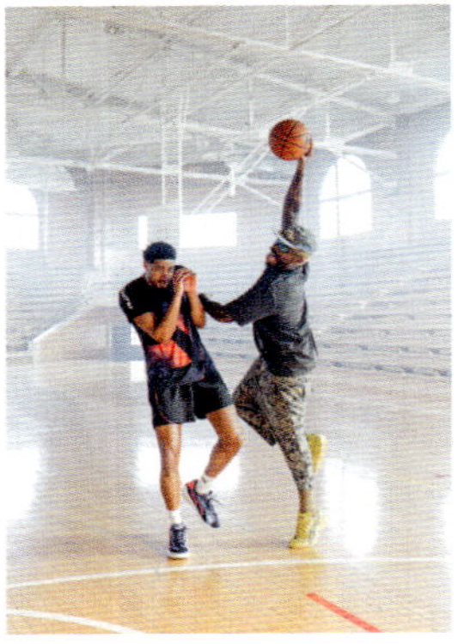

Tyrese Haliburton and Salehe Bembury on set at Tyrese Haliburton's Puma campaign

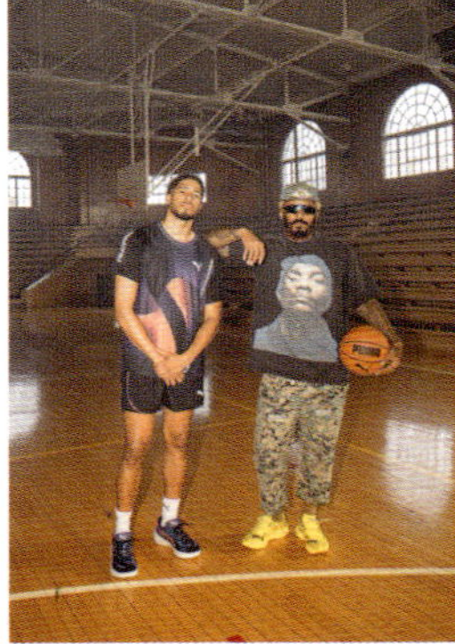

Tyrese Haliburton and Salehe Bembury on set at Tyrese Haliburton's Puma campaign

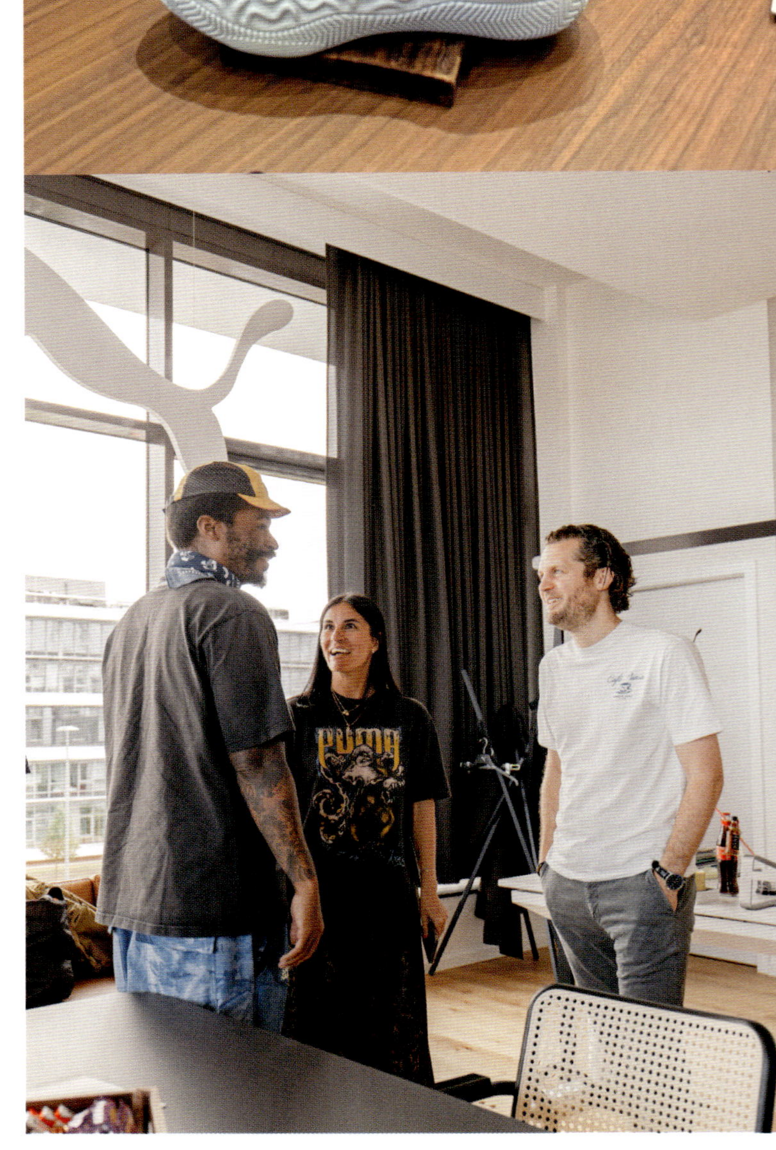

Above: Tyrese Haliburton with Hali 1 samples
Below: Salehe Bembury with Maria Valdes and Arne Freundt

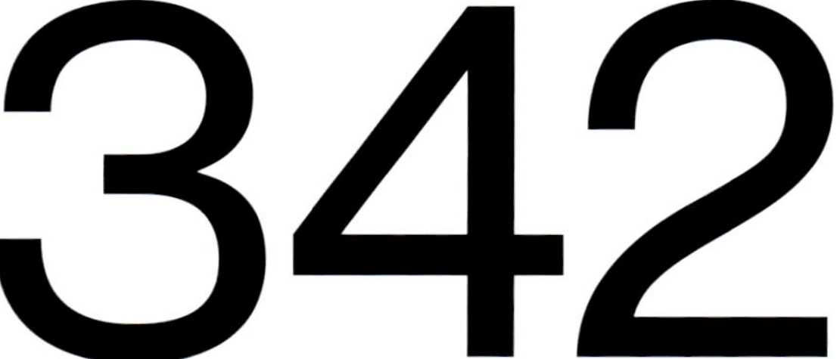

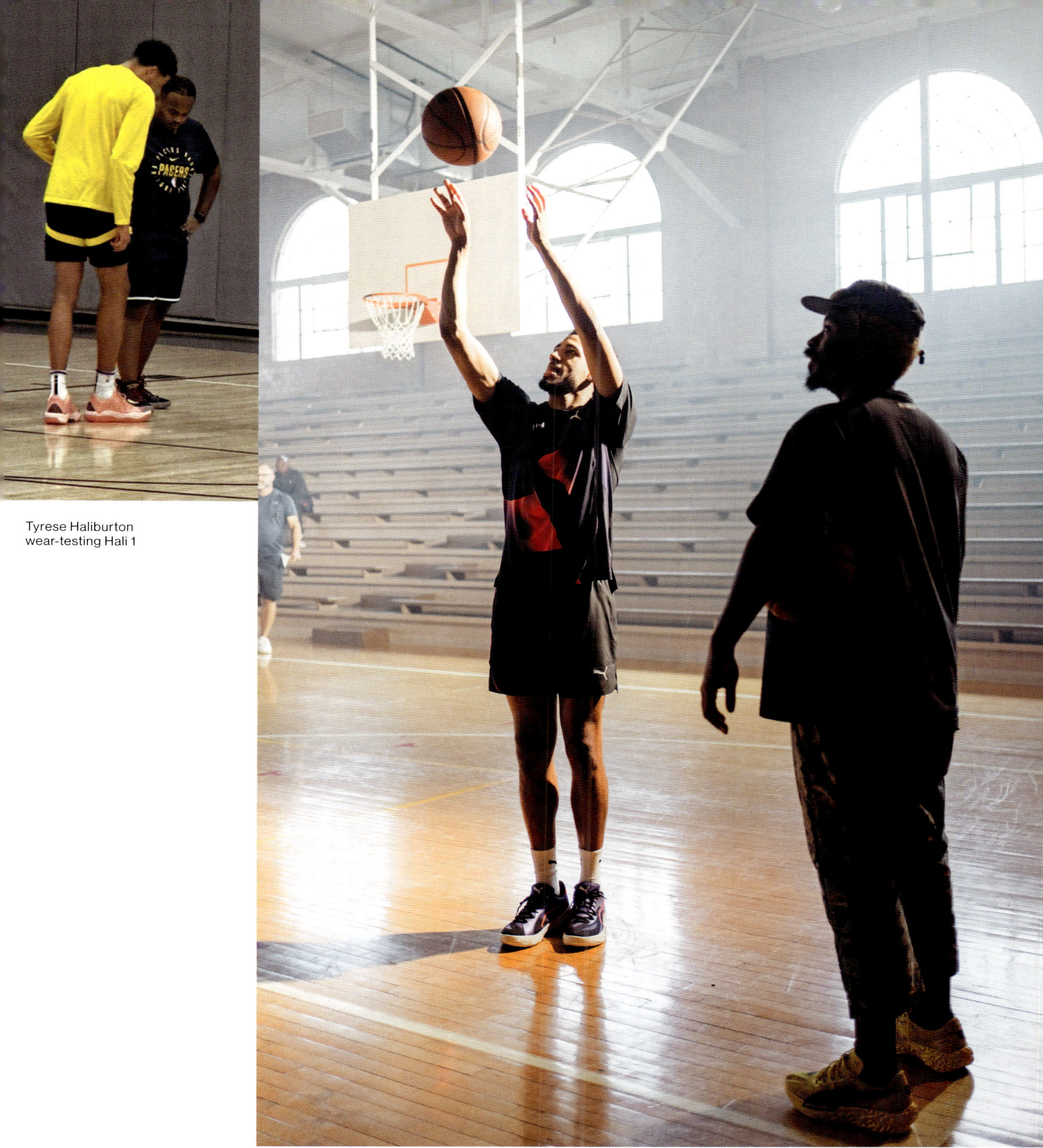

Tyrese Haliburton
wear-testing Hali 1

Salehe Bembury and Tyrese Haliburton

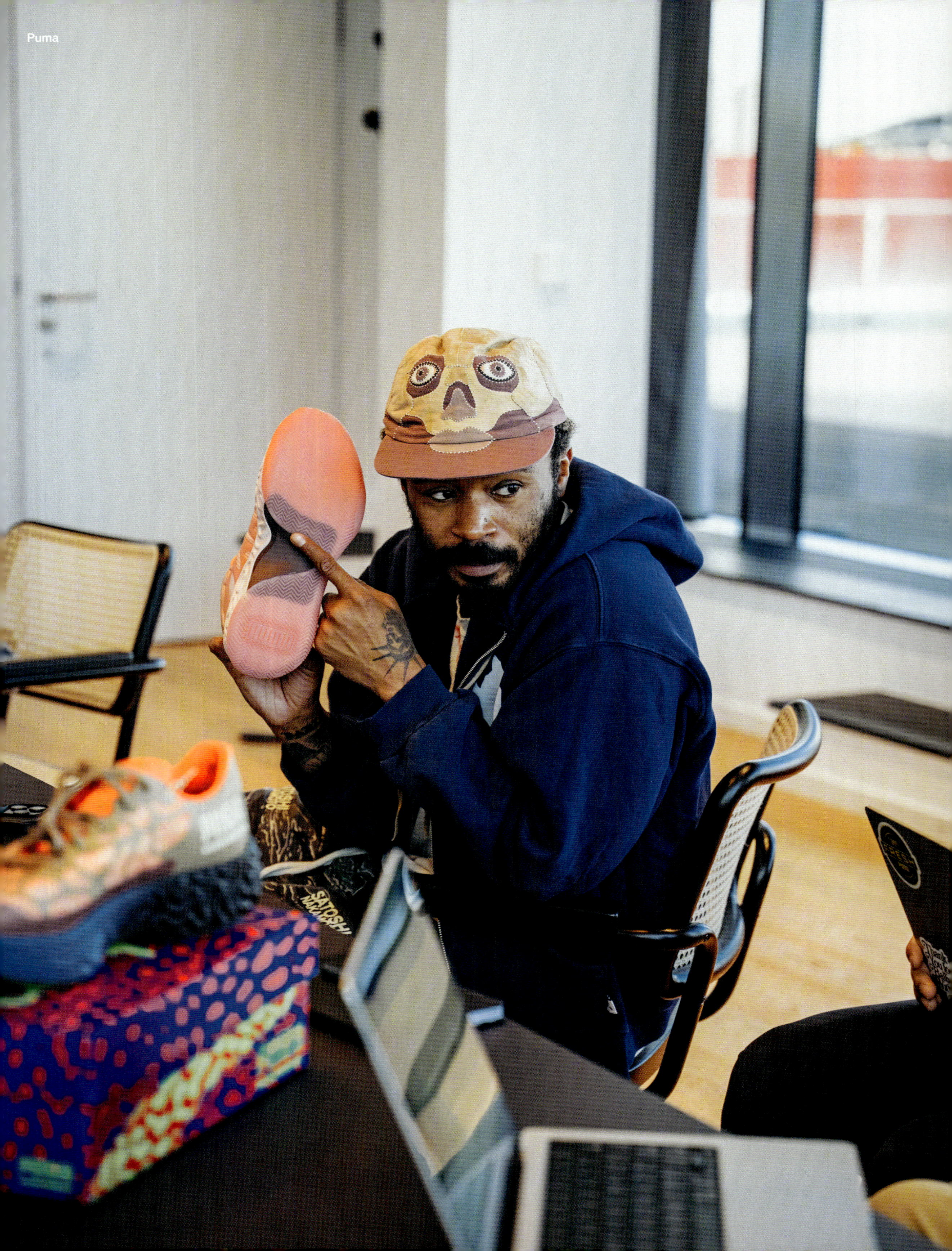

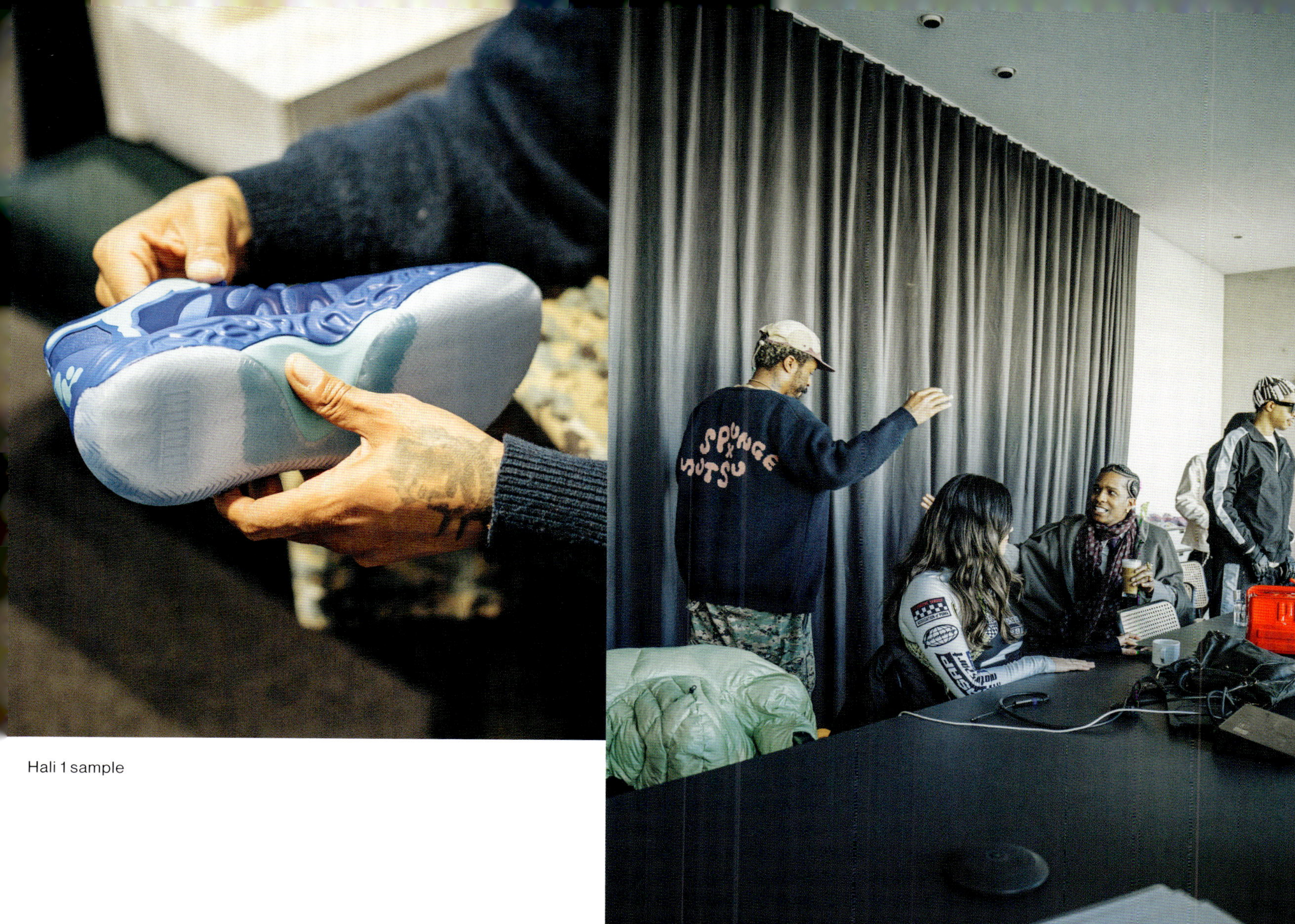

Hali 1 sample

Salehe Bembury and A$AP Rocky

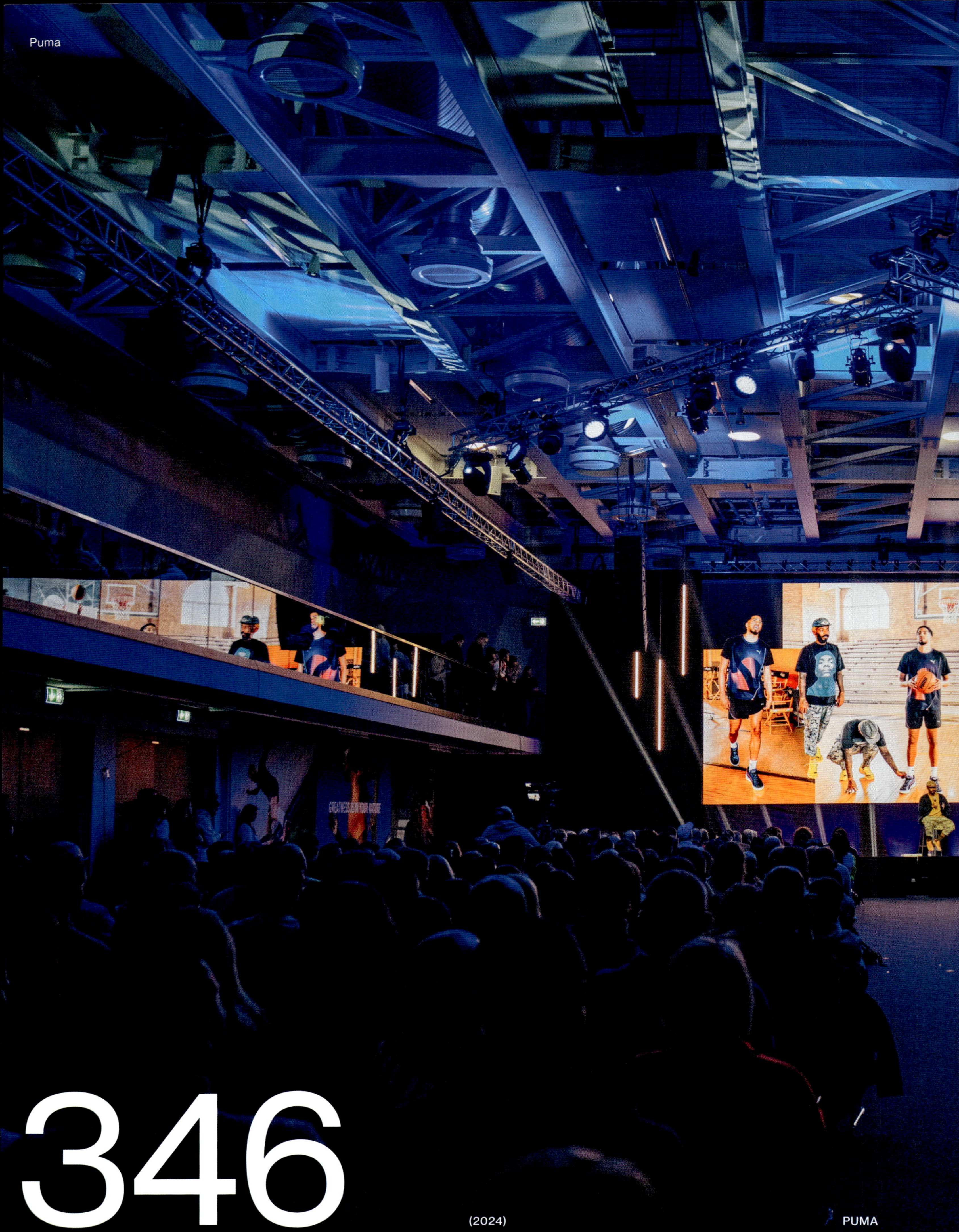

346

(2024)

PUMA

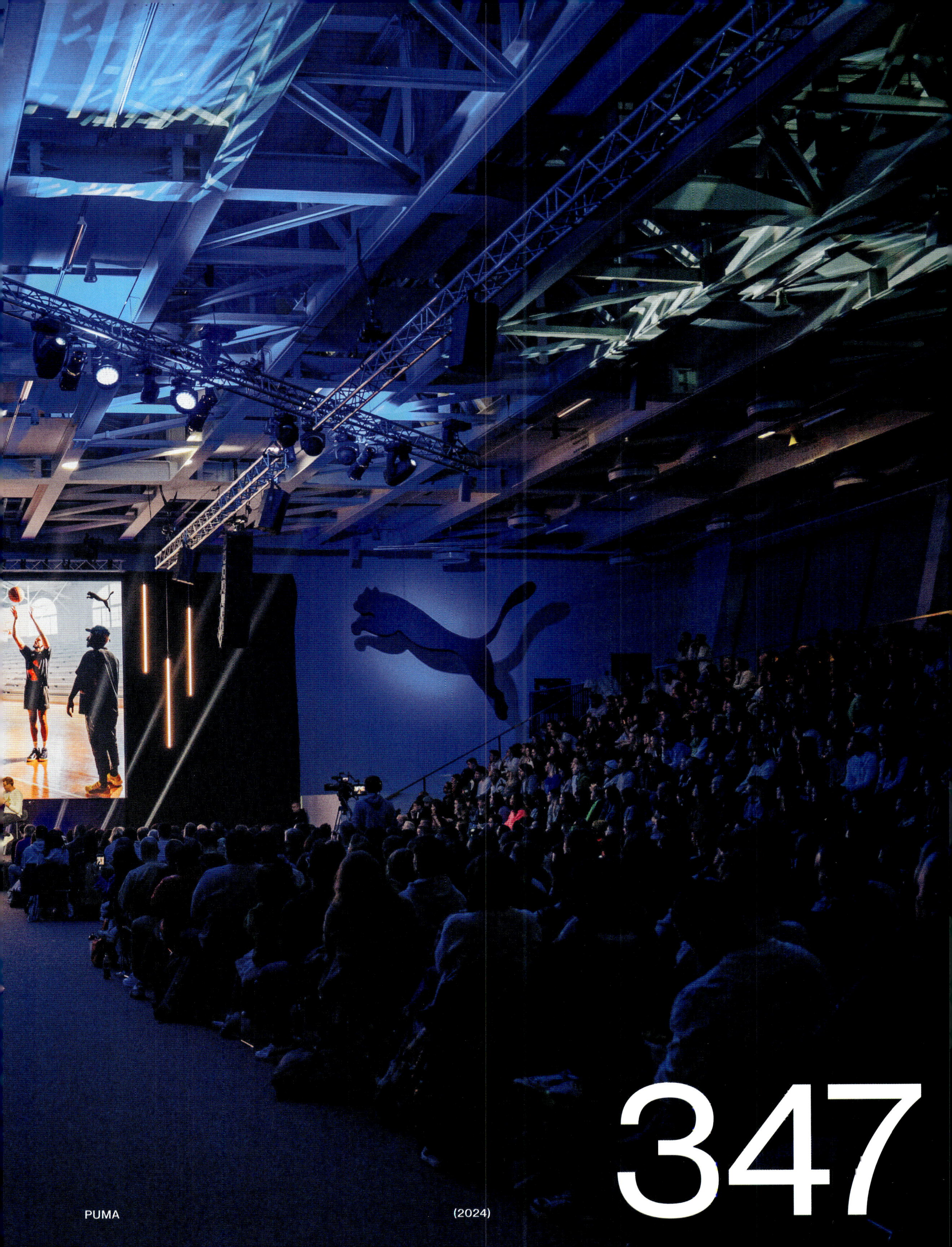

BLISS FOSTER
IN CONVERSATION WITH SALEHE BEMBURY

BLISS: How did shoes impact your childhood? What models did you grow up with?

SALEHE: Basically, sneakers were the foundation for all of the inspiration in my childhood. Growing up in the 1990s, things were not as exciting as they are now. It really felt like technology, cars, and shoes were like the only things that showed a brighter future than what a lot of the grayness and dullness of the 1990s embodied.

It's funny, I see kids now playing with all kinds of touch screens and AI and all this kind of stuff. The other day, I was having a conversation with a friend and came to the realization that we literally had a toy where it was a bunch of wires on a wooden block, and we would just move blocks and balls and different wooden shapes along these wires. And that shit was exciting for us. I just think that that's really representative of how far entertainment—not just TV shows and movies, but just entertainment in general—has come in the last twenty years.

So shoes were really more than functional items to me. They were exciting, they were whimsical, and they were attainable, which I think was the most important of the three things I listed, alongside cars and technology. I don't care for cars at all. Obviously, I love technology, but it was really shoes that embodied this futuristic aesthetic. They were attainable; they related to culture. They related to music, sitcoms, and pop culture generally. I was a big watcher of Fresh Prince of Bel Air, and sneakers were such a large part of those TV shows, of those NBA moments, of those rap music videos. Sneakers were this aspirational thing. It was this thing that I thought would give me superpowers in regard to sports. At the time, I didn't know that I was appreciating design. I was just appreciating how they made me feel and what they made me feel like I could do. In my later years, I learned that's exactly what appreciation of design is. But at the time, it was more of a feeling. Not only was it the shoes themselves, but it was the marketing and the storytelling and the journey that these brands would bring me on through the shoes. When I tied up those shoes, I immediately felt that feeling—whether it was feeling like I could fly, or feeling cool, or feeling like I could get the girl. At the time, I didn't realize that that was marketing, but now I do.

BLISS: What shoe models have influenced you?

SALEHE: Modern day Salehe wouldn't want to praise or give Nike their flowers like I'm about to do. But if I'm paying respects to what younger me was into this really is like a complete praising of Nike: of their storytelling and of the magic they would create within moments.

I think maybe one of the most stereotypical shoes to mention, but it was extremely left, was the Jordan 11. I was 10 when it was released. I remember drawing it non-stop. I actually have a small ceramic sculpture I made of it when I was 10 or 11. The Footscape, the Nike Tuned Air, all Nike Dunk SBs, I had a really close relationship with those when those were big in the early 2000s. Prestos were huge. The Nike Air Zoom Flight 95, the whole KG series, the Flightposits, the Air Maxes. It's hard to call out an individual shoe because I was more in love with Nike—and I say "was" because I've since fallen in love with many brands, and now I probably am most in love with authentic design and less necessarily where it's coming from.

I think Nike did an amazing job of balancing innovative design lines with nostalgia and familiarity. So a lot of the time, they were able to get me excited about what they were creating, but it wasn't too left that a 14-year-old kid from New York would be afraid of it. I believe now my palette has broadened in regard to what I'll wear and what interests me, but back then, it was pretty limited, and it also was defined by the logo on the side of the shoe.

Personally, and for the consumer, I believe that conditioning has dissolved. Now, people aren't as concerned with what brand their shoe is.

Bliss: How did Nike speak to young Salehe? What were the moments in the design or the storytelling that stuck with you?

SALEHE: There was a time in sneakers when a new Nike basketball sneaker would release. They'd have a page in Slam magazine that had a whole graphic for the sneaker, but it also had a phone number. To an 11- or 12-year old kid, it felt like they were giving you that player's phone number. So I would call the number, then Jason Kidd or Michael Jordan would pick up to tell you about their shoe. It would be in their voice. And this is way before AI or social media, or really any kind of technology that would make me believe that it couldn't be that player, even though it was pre-recorded.

I was 11 or 12, so I would think I was speaking to Michael Jordan, I would think I was speaking to Jason Kidd, and the magic that that would create, along with the beauty of the shoe, was unmatched. It's little things like that that I try to create within my own work that leaves the audience with a feeling. Nike did such an amazing job of doing that. So a lot of the obsession that I had with the brand came not only from design, but also simply from how they introduced the product to the market. And I like to study this within my work.

BLISS: You've established a name for yourself through collaborations and as an employee of massive companies, but there's a continuity across your whole body of work. How do you maintain the "Salehe look" through different brands with different identities?

SALEHE: During the Nike era, we saw sneakers that were inspired by animals, cars, and planes. But furthermore, those sneakers held what I believe to be a signature of the designer working on them. Whether it was Tinker Hatfield, Erica Var, or Aaron Cooper, I felt like these shoes had hand-signatures of the designers. So I went through school thinking that when I become a designer, I'm going to put my personal sauce on my design, similar to a rapper.

Once I entered the professional realm, I realized the personal signature thing usually doesn't happen, and that any good designer has to fall into line with the signature of the brand that they're working for because of price points, brand details, and brand identity generally. So I quickly realized that it really wasn't about me and it was about the customer. So in my earlier jobs working for different brands, I really tried to prioritize the brand's needs.

But one of the more rewarding and unexpected critiques of my work is that there is a common or cohesive visual language. I can absolutely see that in my collaborative work, but I've also heard that in regard to my work for brands, and I really don't have an explanation for it. I've had people tell me that they see a cohesion in the colors I use or the shapes I use, and to me, that's a surprise, because it really is not that calculated. I often design from the gut and what feels right.

Another way I maintain the "Salehe look" is by not really approaching it like a shoe; I'm approaching it like a product. I'm approaching a shoe from an angle of composition in real estate. Other designers often design a shoe in totality. But I first design

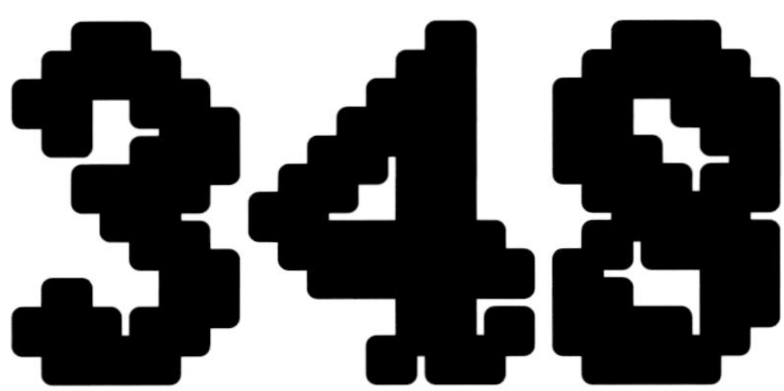

the heel, then I design the toe, then I design the stay lace row, then the outsole. All that in no particular order. I really try to honor every area of value on a shoe or on a foot, every area of function or obstacle. Consider where heat is being released, consider where utility is needed, and then consider where there's room for growth and evolution in the shoe.

I think one of the most important traits that any designer has is the ability to exercise restraint and not push the design too far. So it's really about maintaining that balance between polarizing and familiar, and ultimately having a conversation with both.

And now in my current projects there's almost this expectation that I'm going to either do something new or give something a "silly" look. So that almost works as a catalyst and a motivator for me to put new design lines down.

The first task is to foster and maintain the codes of the brand that I'm working with, and then, once those are established, once the signature details have been called out, I believe that is when I can have fun and really explore my personal brand identity.

The last thing I would like to call out is the squint test. The squint test is when you're looking at a wall of shoes or a page of designs, maybe different colors, and you ever so slightly squint your eyes so everything kind of blurs. And when you do that, it's the shoes that stand out in that blurred vision that you now have that passed the squint test.

BLISS: There was an incredible story that I know you've told about the birth of the Yeezy 350 V2, when you were working for Ye. Personally, I think of the V2 as a generation-defining shoe. You were head of men's footwear, which was an incredible opportunity for you: the highlight of your career at that time. I know that while there, you weren't there to flick up and have fun, you were on a mission. But in the end, for the V2, Ye picked up a piece of ribbon off the ground and said, "Hey Salehe, can you pin this to the side of the 350 prototype?" He liked how it looked, and that was the design. All the concepts you did and the prototypes and your rejected designs. In the end, Ye liked the trash he found on the ground best. Did that hurt?

SALEHE: No, no. It didn't hurt at all. Back then, I was Kanye's pencil. By that, I mean he would come to myself and Lucette Holland, who worked at Proenza Schouler doing women's footwear. Ye would come to us and basically describe something he dreamt about. He would send references of really low resolution images, and then it would be our jobs to bring those ideas to fruition. So really, that whole ribbon moment was, if anything, a moment of relief, because we seemingly handed him something mediocre, and then he put a ribbon, like a little stripe on it, and then it was great. And so if anything that was a moment of satisfaction. It's like in sitcoms when they have a pie and it doesn't taste good, but then someone sprinkles a little something in it, and it's delicious.

BLISS: To ask the obvious question: what was it like working at Yeezy, as compared to other huge companies that you have worked for?

SALEHE: It was unlike any company I worked for. Yeezy wasn't a startup and it wasn't a big corporation, it just sat in a completely different space. I'll say this: I've always enjoyed meeting people that have worked for Ye, because the level of ridiculousness and the stories always align. And by no means am I saying that my job or the work itself was ridiculous. I just think it's the uniqueness of "the Yeezy experience," and the fact that Ye is a one-of-one individual. So it's always fun to hear someone else's crazy story, and for that story to be just crazy enough for me to believe it happened.

I was challenged at that job a lot. Working for Yeezy opened up all of the doors that I'm experiencing right now. So I'm forever in debt to that job and to Ye for bringing me to California and bringing me into high fashion. Ultimately, that job is what made Versace look at me in a certain light. Usually, sneaker companies don't like to hire from the fashion pool of designers, and it doesn't work the other way either. I believe I was able to jump over that wall because of Ye. But yeah, it was an extremely fucking difficult job.

BLISS: Was it taxing because you were trying to keep up with the most eccentric billionaire who's ever lived?

SALEHE: Well, no. I think the taxing part came from working for someone with extremely high expectations and an endless personal output meter. Ye works incredibly hard and produces magic. He expects his team to work hard and produce magic.

BLISS: What sports do you play?

SALEHE: The sport I played my entire life is basketball. It was probably the number one thing that inspired my love for sneakers: everything from the marketing to the actual look on court. Also, back then, it really felt like every player's signature shoe aesthetic was just so drastically different. Now, for whatever reason, all basketball sneakers look the same.

I feel like there's a secret that I don't know about or something. But back in the early 2000s every sneaker looked different. Every basketball shoe had a different energy. Also, playing basketball in the shoes that I would wear with my on-court fit or my off-court fit. I guess that was the slow education of fashion that I didn't even realize was fashion. It was more just like what you wear with your sneakers. So basketball absolutely served as the inspiration.

BLISS: When I was researching, your time at Cole Haan jumped out at me. Your mentor, Jeff Henderson, gave you the liberty to take as many shoes as you wanted and cut them up. You could spray-paint them, draw on them, turn them inside out, anything. You were being treated like a serious designer for maybe the first time. Did that unlock anything for you? Did that moment register as significant?

SALEHE: I think subconsciously it did. With the brain that I had then, it was just a task, and I was kind of tripping off of being able to take scissors to a pair of shoes. I was coming off of saving up for sneakers. So now to be able to take these things that are worth $300 and cut them up for the sake of research, I was tripping off of that. My biggest motivation was the fact that I knew that Nike was kind of at the end of the tunnel; that they were going to see this stuff. And the person steering the ship was a Nike veteran, Jeff. So really, if he told me to go outside in my underwear, I probably would have asked why... but I would have done it.

BLISS: What tools do you use? Is it just your laptop and brain? What are the things that you need to work?

SALEHE: At this point in the career, it's more about identifying the most efficient tools to get the job done. In the early stages of my career, it was hand-sketching and Adobe Illustrator. But in these stages of my career, it can be anything from 3D modeling to 3D printing to even utilizing some AI. And I think I got this from studying industrial design, because they really teach us to be versatile, to be design MacGyvers with the resources around us. So now, it's a whole gambit of tools. For the Crocs and the Versace Chain Reaction, I was playing with clay and modeling forms with my hands to just start the form exploration. It's really whatever it takes

And honestly, even if I'm not capable of utilizing a tool, I may hire someone who is, because I really believe in using people with an expertise and not being a jack of all trades and a master of none.

BLISS: The number one way to waste time is to think that you somehow are the most qualified person to do literally anything, even if you've never done it.

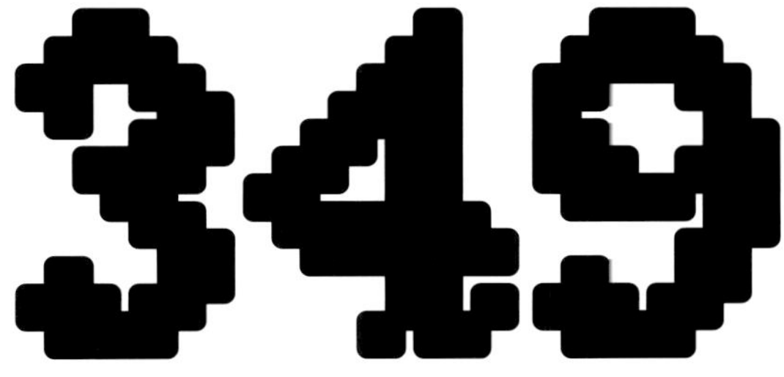

SALEHE: Exactly.

BLISS: I feel like most non-designers might think that working with clay or cutting up shoes makes for a fun story, but they might assume that no designers really do this on the daily. Could you talk a little bit about the practical function of working with weird materials and going through these eccentric design exercises?

SALEHE: Recently, on a project, I described what you're talking about as "design process theater." And this theater is something that worked on me when I was a consumer. It still works on me. We all have this idea of "what it is to be a designer" through marketing. I've absolutely participated in design process theater. But at the same time, there are different tools and different materials that can unlock parts of your brain that you can't necessarily unlock with a computer. It's no different than if you were to only use AI: then your designs wouldn't have a soul or may not have cohesion.

I don't do process theater to fit into the role of being a designer. I just do it because that's what's necessary. Coming up with a completely new outsole from scratch for Versace when they've never really made sneakers—I thought it was really necessary to get hands-on with it, you know?

BLISS: I want to hear about your media diet.

SALEHE: I never heard it called "media diet," so I love that. Mine has evolved from the days of being someone that was just on Hypebeast and Complex every day. I get a job at Versace and I have to learn how to say "Givenchy" correctly or whatever, so then it turned into me reading L'Officiel.

I would say a lot of my education came from going to fashion shows and just seeing the diversity and the juxtaposition from collection to collection. At the end of one of your videos, you were talking about young designers who want to get their start—you were like, "Fucking research!" And I really do believe that research is that important first step. A designer is only as good as their ability to research, so I try to keep my research broad.

BLISS: What's something you love that your fans would be surprised to hear from you?

SALEHE: I love Mumford and Sons. But the weird thing is I've never seen them perform. I don't research their music. I only listen to this one album that has "I Will Wait" on it. I've never heard any of their other music, except this one album. I can sing all the words bar for bar. Strangely, Pharrell used Mumford and Sons for his LV Men's show during Paris Fashion Week. I thought that was the weirdest move ever, but I was very happy to smoke a spliff and sing along word for word, unexpectedly, at my first Mumford and Sons concert.

I'm very much a chameleon and my parents did an amazing job of exposing me to many walks of life. I can sail, by the way. I'm like, an experienced sailor. So I would say many of the things that make up me would probably surprise people, just because I'm private and I give them what I would like to give them.

BLISS: I don't feel like designers get asked this enough: I want to hear about your tattoos.

SALEHE: I guess when I first started getting tattoos, I thought that they need to have some epic story so that, elbows down, they're all significant. And then, elbows up, they turn into moments of beauty. So I got a statue of liberty, for obvious reasons. This one just says "BEMBURY," but it's an ambigram so it reads both ways. A Jordan III outsole, which is just the shoe that kind of started my love for footwear. "Pablo" represents my time working with Ye. Lobster, favorite food. New York, my love. I call this one "my Versace job security tattoo"—I got it two weeks into my job. I thought "they can't fire me now," you know? Then all this stuff up here is just beauty. No significance, just flowers and pigeons and shit. Oh, I'm really proud of this one.

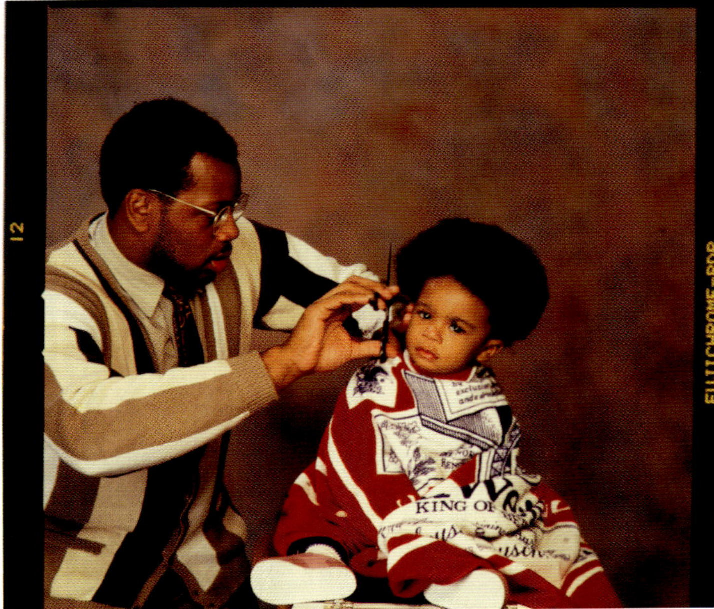

BLISS: Is that Obama with Basquiat's haircut?

SALEHE: There you go! When I was younger, I kind of felt like tattoos fit the designer uniform I was trying to achieve. In our adolescence, we all take these steps to be different, whether it's a piercing or dyeing our hair. I just saw a designer in my head that I wanted to be and he had lots of tattoos.

BLISS: I'm 34. How old are you?

SALEHE: 38.

BLISS: Okay, so we came up around the same time. As far as your online life was concerned, were you mostly a Nike Talk guy? Or were you on any other old school forums?

SALEHE: I didn't know of any other forums! What else was there?

BLISS: Style Zeitgeist was avant garde: Rick Owens and Ann Demeulemeester–type stuff. And then there was StyleForum and SuperFuture.

SALEHE: I would say the biggest difference is, back then, we had to seek this stuff out. We had to find it, you know? And now, like, you could just be scrolling in your algorithm, and it's just like, "Hey! You want to see what it looks like to be a designer?" It's just served to you automatically.

BLISS: What would you say is the most important single moment or sneaker model release or single event in the history of sneakers, specifically?

SALEHE: When it comes to shoes, if we're talking sneakers, the most valuable thing is vis-tech: visual technology. As a designer, you can use design lines to make a cool shoe and give your consumer a feeling. But if you can add something that makes them feel like there's a machine or some new technology in their shoe, it's extremely valuable. I don't know if I want to just completely give the answer to Nike, but I think Nike Air was a really important moment. And the fact that it was inspired by the Pompidou Center is beautiful: it was taking this architectural beauty and then relating that beauty to a completely different space.

BLISS: I've never heard about the Centre Pompidou inspiration. Was it just that the Pompidou has all those tubes on the outside of the building? Like the AC, the heating system, all the plumbing is on the outside so that the inside can be completely bare? And then Nike was like, "The idea of air, and it sort of looks like a tube." Is that the connection to the Pompidou?

SALEHE: That's exactly it. Tinker Hatfield designed it. He was in Paris, saw the building, and he loved how everything was visible.

BLISS: What do you feel defines our current era of sneakers? We'll say the last five years and the next five years.

SALEHE: Brands are trying to figure out the silhouette that everyone's going to be attached to; unfortunately, no one's really creating newness. It seems like a lot of these brands are just attaching themselves to ideas that have worked in the past and are just recoloring them and telling slightly different stories. Obviously, it's a risk to create something new, because there's no sales data for new ideas. But I'm kind of design-over-everything: I try to introduce new things while still maintaining that balance with a brand's heritage.

Even right now, I'm working on my first ever shoe for my own brand. When I'm working with another brand for a collaboration, I know that quantities and sales aren't the first priority. But with my own shoe, I am trying to create footwear that's commercial and can be commercial for a long time, but it's also got to be interesting and new and fresh. But also commercial.

BLISS: If it didn't sound impossible on paper, we wouldn't need designers.

SALEHE: Exactly.

BLISS: You have this design for New Balance that involves a whistle on the heel of the shoe. I like that shoe a lot. It's one of your most high-risk / high-reward designs so far. The whistle also feels very childlike, even in its placement. Like, if you asked a 6-year-old boy where the turbo boosters should go on the shoe, they would point to the back of the heel.

SALEHE: I get the child-like descriptor of my work a lot, and I don't fully see it. I often get people saying my work looks like Nickelodeon.

BLISS: I don't think your work looks child-like to me, generally. To my eyes, your work feels like it was created by an adult, but it's an adult who's recently developed a new-found relationship with their inner child. Like they had a break-through in therapy. They're still an adult, but they're going to move through life more fluidly, like they did when they were 11.

Sneaker design seems difficult because it's so political. When we were coming up, I can hear my

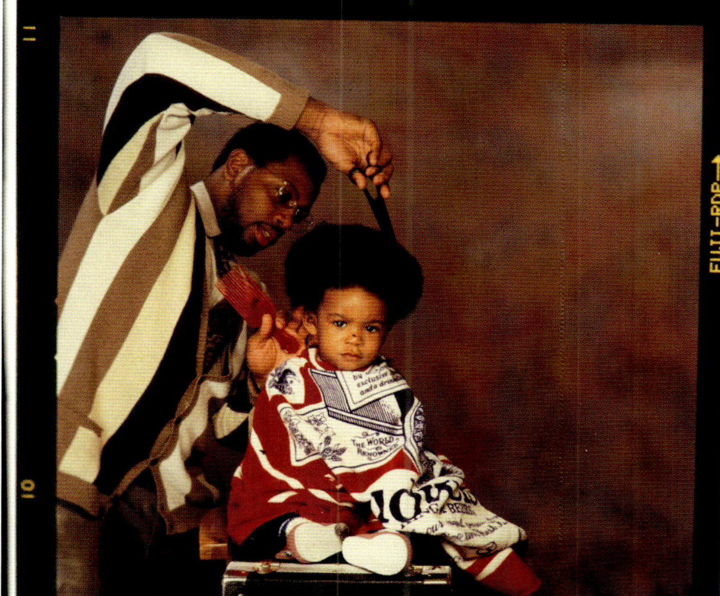

mom saying, "I know all your friends have Jordan 1s, but I'm not spending that much money on shoes. Why don't you be the trendsetter with these Payless shoes?" My mom is a smart lady, but she didn't understand that if my shoes weren't Nike, they literally couldn't be cool. With sneakers, the next king will be the son of the current king. But you have broken the fuck out of that mold. You have been able to make Crocs some-thing that a cool kid could wear to art school. How did you do this?

SALEHE: Now, I believe the consumer does not give a fuck what the logo is. People just want good design over everything. The market is fully open right now; any brand can make something cool. That means there's a lot of opportunity for brands if they have the tools to take advantage of that opportunity. Sometimes I'll go to a store and look at some shoes that a fashion house makes, and they look cool, but they clearly didn't think the design all the way through.

BLISS: For me, the coolest part of your career is when you started designing shoes that look better when they're beat up, as opposed to fresh out of the box. The Juniper Crocs, all the fuzzy New Balances, Peace Be the Journey, and even the red and blue Heat Be Hot colorway. I think all those models will only look better as they get beat up.

SALEHE: That's interesting.

BLISS: To me, that's one of the hardest things to do in sneakers. Personally, Jordan 1s are always going to be "the coolest sneaker ever." But we all know that they look best brand new, and once you put them on, it's all downhill from there. But if someone wears their Junipers on a hike, they aren't "ruining" their shoes. Based on your reaction, this wasn't a conscious decision?

SALEHE: No, and you know, so it's funny you say this. It's not exactly the answer to the question, but maybe a year ago, I saw a picture of three different shoes from three different collaborations in one photo. All the greens were cohesive. And as an audience member, you might assume that I'm sitting in my studio with color swatches everywhere ensuring that my body of work is perfectly cohesive. Nope. I design from the gut. I designed for me and for what I like.

BLISS: That specific green just vibrates with you.

SALEHE: Yeah, it's made me wonder if I need to create my specific shade. So when people see it, they know it's me. But no, the matching greens weren't intentional.

BLISS: You're not retiring are you? The book doesn't mean you're retiring, right?

SALEHE: No. I originally wanted to call this book "Chapter 1" to imply that this is the beginning. My career is like that band that's been working for a long time but just got big. I'm fifteen years in right now, so if anything, I think this book is going to do a great job of showing people all the different places I've been in my career thus far—the diversity in those places. I want it to be a creative bible and a place to share gems with young creatives. My targets are the future designers that maybe are afraid to ask for that one opportu-nity or don't necessarily know how to go about it. I'm not really a public speaker, so I think that this book can maybe accomplish some of the things that public speaking would.

Bliss: What do you want the rest of the next thirty years of your career to look like? I think it would be fun to look back at this first book and say, "Oh, damn! Salehe had no idea what was waiting for him in the future!"

Salehe: I think at this stage I would like Spunge to be me wearing myself from head to toe. To have a brand that people with taste respect and that people without taste just don't even know about.

ANDRÉ BENJAMIN

IN CONVERSATION

SALEHE BEMBURY I'm going to set the stage for how we met. I'm working on my New Balance Yurt campaign at the time. And when it comes to my marketing, I believe in tapping into humor and nostalgia—but furthermore, using someone that people like or love helps that initiative. So I'm thinking, who's someone I can use for this shoot? I had been using friends that were known, like Jesse Williams, to get over that bridge. And then I think of you. Normally, trying to get in touch with any known figure is difficult, but you, being the analog individual that you are, it's even harder. Somehow I got in touch with Eufaula and she says: "I have good news and I have bad news. The bad news is, he doesn't want to do your campaign. The good news is, he fucks with you. He wants to chill, maybe learn, maybe do a project." And I was like, what? That's fucking crazy. Awesome. Let's do it. So then you come to my studio, a very surreal experience for me. I've been around many celebrities, but this was different. You were immediately disarming because you're wearing regular shit, some Jordan threes. I don't really remember the conversation, but it was a fluid one. And throughout that conversation you tell me that you don't really use social media, especially in the period of time you've been famous. No MySpace, no Facebook, little Instagram, whatever. I noted it, but I don't think I absorbed it until later that day. You tell me you've been playing the flute, you sit down, you play the flute, and I think: I'm going to record this and put it on my IG. And I even asked you, "Can I record this?"—and this is where there was a disconnect.

ANDRÉ BENJAMIN Yeah, yeah. I didn't understand—I thought that just meant recorded personal.

S Yeah, modern day, if someone says, "Can I record this?"—it's understood, it's going online. So then you leave—good hang, potential new friend. And maybe ten minutes later I post it. Instantly viral, everywhere—Complex, which is expected. Obviously if you take a shit, people talk about it. And so your team hit me and they're like, "Hey, take that down." And then transparently—I've never said this to you before—I'm thinking to myself, everyone in the world has already posted this, so if I take this down, it doesn't change anything. But given the length of the relationship, I was like, let me just do what they say. So anyway, since that time we have brought a friendship to fruition. We hike, and during these hikes, what I found really interesting is that us as humans always deal with vulnerability, insecurity, uncertainty. But to hear someone such as yourself talk about some of those feelings, that's some core memory shit for me. Because to see someone that's a "legend" express very human perspectives about their creative output was refreshing and made me look at my work differently. A lot of that was about your music, about your return into this fucked-up world, all that. And now it's, what, six months later. So my question is: How does it feel? How's it gone? Did it take a few shows to break through?

A No, it's really just a live and direct version of what I was dealing with before. So if anxiety was a thing, if being in the public eye was a pressure for me—a lot of people don't understand. I think because we're in a celebrity culture now, people got to understand that having that much adoration from a lot of people, it's abnormal and possibly harmful. I think we'll see research on it in the future.

S Harmful to the individual, or—?

A Yes, to the individual and to the people. Because at some point now everybody wants to be famous, not understanding the results, the implications of it. So I can't remember—man, I wish I could remember this and you can probably Google it—but there's this classical composer pianist, and there was this documentary about him, and he just stopped playing. He stopped. A classical pianist, you're in front of thousands of people and it's just you and the piano and you're doing these things you've practiced. In the documentary, he's an older man now, he's like seventy, eighty. But he said, "I realize that having that much attention and adoration from a person is abnormal, is possibly shocking to the human, unless you're addicted to it." Some people like it. I see some of my celebrity friends, they're so good at it, as if they wanted that all their life. I didn't do this shit to get famous.

S What'd you do it for? Money?

A No, I mean when I started rapping, niggas wasn't making money like that. That's what people don't understand. All this money shit kind of started with Puffy, people making money off of doing it. All my heroes before me—all my heroes were Rakim. And I am sure Cube made money and NWA made a certain amount of money, but it ain't what it is now. So as a rapper, back then—

S It was the love.

A You just wanted to be fresh, have fresh gear, have a fresh ride, and have the bitches. That's what it was. From my viewpoint, you never thought, oh, I have a whole-ass empire. I've had thirty, forty employees, a hundred, even. I had an interview yesterday and the interviewer asked me, "So what do you think about the Kendrick and Drake Beef battle?" And I was like, wow. It kind of made me sad because I realized, whoa, we ain't just rapping for fun no more.

S No, no.

A Like early rap battles—we're talking shit, word play though. But now you have individuals that have a hundred people on the payroll trying to find dirt, have million-dollar deals. So is it actually worth it for you to be playing with somebody, for you to be rapping against somebody? Because you could lose that. That made me sad because you quickly realize that it's beyond that. We have empires and entities now, so it ain't just, "I'm going to say some fly shit, you going to say some fly shit, I'm going to rap better than you, blah, blah, blah." When I started rapping, it was: I just like rap music. I'm watching videos and saying, "Let's do it," because we're rapping along to the people we love. Let's try it. I didn't have big dreams of millions of dollars. So that wasn't my motivation, to my point.

S Who was big in Atlanta at the time?

A The biggest thing in Atlanta was Kriss Kross.

S I loved that.

A I loved Kriss Kross, but they were kids. So you knew the appeal of kids. I mean, at that point, they were performing for the Prince of Arabia. They were doing a pop thing, no matter what nobody say, Kriss Kross and TLC were the biggest things in Atlanta. You never thought you'd make it big talking about hood shit. I think that's when Snoop Dogg and Dogg Pound started, because they was talking some street shit and they were like, oh, okay, we're selling records too. Okay, this shit can work. We got the formula. I'm just saying, we started to see people actually making money before then. It was

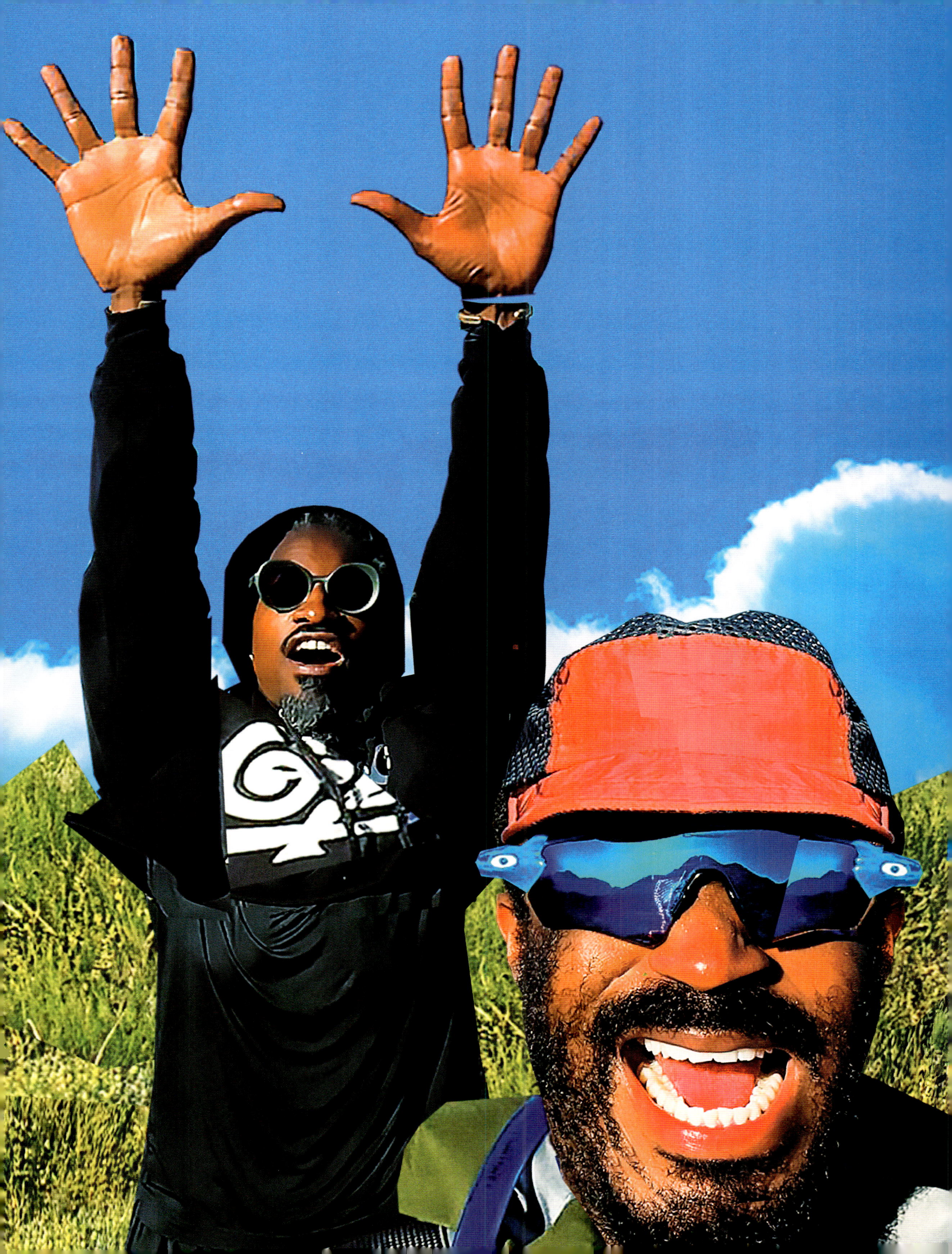

kind of like MC Hammer making the big money, you know what I mean? It was different. So that was not my motivation. It was like, I just want to test this rap shit. It was cypher, it was kind of, we in a circle, I'm going to spit my shit, you going to spit your shit. And it was just a display of what you can do.

S Was the notion of a style in the conversation yet, or was it just about rapping? You probably sounded like someone else.

A Oh yeah, for sure. I think everybody–it's kind of like, as a baby, you learn how to talk by mimicking your parents. Saying your ABCs, they sing the ABC song and you sing it just like them. Then you start to put words together. By the time you get to thirteen, fourteen, and start hanging out with your niggas in high school, you start having your own language. That's how it is. When I first started rapping, I wanted to be and sound like everybody I was listening to. I was a huge Das EFX fan. I was a huge Souls of Mischief fan, huge Tribe Called Quest fan, huge Odd Squad fan, Scarface, Ghetto Boys, UGK, Eight Ball & MJG. So all of those influences were part of everything we did. Your formative years in high school, when you start making your own decisions, listening to your own music outside of your parents, you make those decisions. And when you start skipping school and smoking and listening to Eight Ball and MJG all day, all of that influences what you do. It helps to spark or develop your style. So yeah, you start there, just rapping along with people you love and you kind of learn their style, learn their patterns.

S But I guess in the beginning it felt like you were audibly unique, but maybe not visually. I don't mean your art, but more your fashion. At what point were you like, you know what, I'm going to do this different?

A What people don't realize is the very first album–*Southernplayalisticadillacmuzik*–it says it's an Outkast album, but it was really a Dungeon Family album. And that was just our whole crew. We had the deal with the record label, so they called it an Outkast album, but some of the best work on that was like, CeeLo, "Git Up, Git Out." It was a display of all our niggas in our crew. And believe it or not, me and Big Boi were the youngest niggas in the crew. We weren't as developed or hadn't been rapping as long as everybody else–Big Gipp, Khujo, T-Mo. Even though CeeLo was my age, we went to high school together, Ceelo had been rapping way longer. I'd only been rapping two years before we got the deal. And you can hear it, you can hear it in the work. But because we were the young energy, because we were bringing something new, our influences were new. I guess we were intriguing to the record company at that point, but I was really just a team player. That first album–rest in peace, Rico Wade, a lot of that was driven by Rico's genius, by Sleepy Brown's genius. And we were just young kids playing our role, man. By the second album, I'd had enough money to buy music equipment and I started producing my own records, having my own concepts and breaking out of what was there. Not as a choice, but just naturally.

S Like that scene in *Matrix* where Neo pops out of the OS.

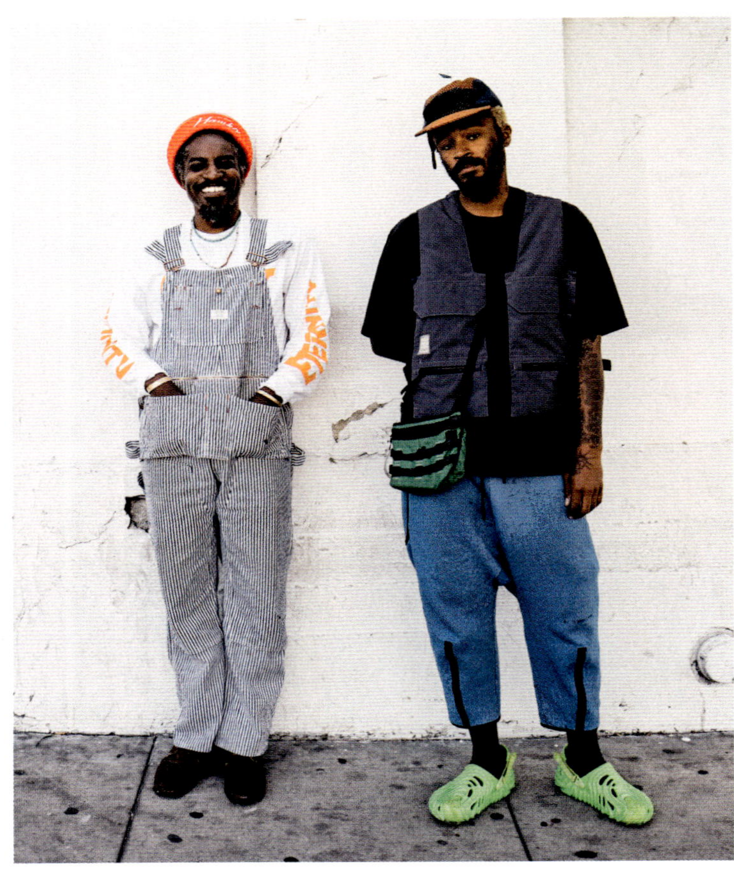

A Exactly. Just my own development. My own research and buying records, listening to records, kind of following the breadcrumbs of what players played with, what players from James Brown's crew went to play with Parliament, Funkadelic. And just kind of getting into it. I noticed that I was a fan of certain people, and you start to associate with people who are like-minded or who attract you in a way. So all the funk people, all the punk people, they felt like my clan.

S Yeah, yeah. Cloth recognized cloth.

A I felt comfortable in that space. So my decision as to what people see as this physical, stylistic change was driven by that freedom. I was like, I don't see that in rap. The only person before who was the father of it from my standpoint was Big Gipp, Goodie Mob. He understood early on the power of the visual. And then you got to think, Busta Rhymes and Missy were hot at that time too, so they were even big influences on me. To me, they were doing their version of what I felt was like funk. So one thing led to another. I draw, actually–before rapping I draw. I was always able to draw out ideas. And so I started to draw what I'm wearing, started to draw things that I would have seamstresses in Atlanta make. I was doing kind of like rag-tag designing, going to fabric stores on my own, picking fabrics, not knowing about weight or drape, horrible fabrics. But it was my first look into it. So a lot of that was just me trying out ideas and what I thought would be fresh. And in my mind, you got to think the name André 3000 came into play.

S What were you before that?

A Just André. André. In my mind, I'm talking to the future, and when you start seeing white wigs and stuff, people saw it as androgynous. But for me, in my mind, in the future everybody got white hair, certain wisdom that comes with white hair.

S Wow, I love this.

A So a lot of that imagery was just me trying out ideas, it was more about the freedom and stretching out. I felt like I carried that flag in rap. I didn't see it. Just to inject some things that I didn't see.

S So three audiences–your Atlanta inner circle, the label, and the media–were asking, what is this shit?

A Yeah, of course, of course. You start getting those questions. In my mind, I was making a play off of tunics, and it's, "Oh, he is wearing a dress." No. Young Thug was the first rapper to actually wear a dress–a dress, dress, dress. And I thought that shit was dope. For me it was just playing with the audience in a way. Don't judge physical, are you rocking to the music? And I kind of of like to just piss people off in a way, I don't know.

S Well, I've always said that to have gotten where I've gotten in my career thus far, it's not just talent, it's like ten things. It's my ability to dress, it's where I'm from, it's my name, it's my network, it's my charm, *and* it's my talent. Do you think that if you'd dressed like you dress now back then, it would have changed things?

A I don't think so. I don't think it would've gotten the same attention. But at the same time, in retrospect, because I lived it, I'm seeing now there was something bigger at play. Whatever you believe in, something was at play. I mean, it wasn't a coincidence that I was talking to Big Boi, and we'd call ourselves Outkast. That actually came because in high school we dressed different. It's funny, we actually took it back before our first album came out–we were much wilder. So we actually getting back to what we were before the Dungeon–you got to think this is 1990, I had platinum blonde hair in high school. It wasn't a style then, it was just because we knew some homegirls that were hairstylists and we thought, okay, if Kriss Kross got discovered in the mall because they looked cool, that was our plan. We're going to look fresh and we're going to walk through Greenbriar Mall. I would cut my Guess jeans back pocket patch off, dye my plain Gap jeans orange with Rit dye from the grocery store, like bright orange and then sew my Guess patch onto the Gap jeans. I'd go to school and kids would be like, "Whoa, where you get them from?"

S The best focus group there is.

A So that's kind of how me and Big Boi were in high school. I had platinum blonde hair, Big Boi had bright, sandy, like a reddish brown. And we were kind of of more to the left than we were by the time we got to *Southernplayalisticadillacmuzik*.

S What shoes were you wearing on your feet?

A Aerobic, Reebok, in different colors. It was about the colors. Cross Colours was huge at that time, so it was about the big pants. At one point we were both baldheaded. When we first met Rico, we were both baldheaded. We both went to the same high school and I got in trouble for skipping school, so they kicked me out and sent me to an alternative school. When I get to alternative school, CeeLo is there, and me and CeeLo had known each other since third grade. So by the time I get to alternative school, I'm like, whoa, let's see what you're doing. We met back up. So Big Boi is still at our high school-Big Boi is super smart, he graduated with an awesome grade point after-but he had a girl in his class that worked with Rico at a beauty supply store. And because she knew we rapped and she knew they made beats, she was like, y'all should meet. So one day we walked to catch the bus, the MARTA City Transit, to Rico's job, and he said, "I want to hear y'all rap." So we're in the parking lot and we were heavy into A Tribe Called Quest, we had a "Scenario" remix, instrumental cassette. Big Gipp had a Jeep, he pulled up, and we sat outside the truck and played the tape and just rapped for a long-ass time. And that's how we ended up meeting Rico. Rico said, "I love y'all looked different. Y'all was new, y'all was fresh." We were always pushing it in some type of way. So by the time we get around to "Hey Ya!" and all that kind of shit, in my mind-

S You were already there.

A Yeah. It's just an extension. With *ATL[iens]* you start to see it happen. Fuck. You know why podcasts work and why they're so dope? Because as humans we want to express, we want to tell our story. And so even you asking me now-I don't sit around thinking about this shit, but because you're asking me, it's making me go back and remember, "Oh shit, we were actually wild way before."

S And with the perspective you have now-

A Completely. These kinds of situations where you get to relive it and tell your story-and especially when we're in a time now where publications and people try to talk for you and make up shit-it's always good to just say it on your own.

S How would you like your story told when that day comes? A book, a movie?

A I have no idea. Well, I think all of them-all mediums-because you get something different from a book. I think if we do a movie though, in Outkast fashion, that shit ain't going to be no straight-up biopic. That shit would be boring.

S Yeah, I feel you. Was *Straight Out of Compton* boring to You?

A No, it wasn't boring because it worked in their style. They were street rappers. But if we do an Outkast movie, I might be born on another planet, you know what I mean?

S It is interesting to hear you say all mediums because I remember when we first started hiking, I was like, man, you got to make some clothing. And you were like, nah, not yet. And I'm like, okay, cool, cool. You should make a bowl. And you're like, nah, not yet. And I feel like I listed every product under the sun-not yet. And now you're saying all mediums.

A Well, when I was saying not yet, maybe what I meant is-it's not developed enough. Some of my favorite visual artists, they may have done the same image in a lot of different mediums to see which was the best way to do it. Gauguin, who is one of my favorite artists, he would do wood carvings, he would do woodcut prints, he would do paintings on canvas, sculptures of the same image. So for me it's figuring out what's the best way to say what you want to say. The most effective way. The most effective medium.

S How long was it between the flute album and your last body of work? Ten years?

A Yeah, I don't even think about it in that way.

S Well, who does think about it like that? All of your fans?

A It's strange to me. When the flute album came out people were really upset-like, nigga, we waited seventeen years or whatever, and you're going to give us the flute album? In my mind, I'm like, I never told y'all I'm about to put out a rap album. So I didn't know what y'all were waiting on.

S Well, that'd be like if you heard Will Smith coming out with a project and then it's a cookbook-you'd be like, wait a minute.

A Yeah. Recently L.L. dissed me on a show, I think he was on *The Shop*, and he was like, "yeah, not the fucking flute, B," or something. It was funny to me.

S Well, he's got to remain the forefather of hip-hop shit.

A He said, "Man, if I would've come out and played a violin album y'all would be tripping." And when he said that I was like, "That shit would probably be more interesting than your rap shit to me." So yeah, I'm all for it. The best way to say what you can say. Sometimes not saying shit and displaying something else. If you get to arguing with your girl, you can fight. But when she don't say shit-whoa.

S A buddy of mine compared that to war. He said, when you're at war, you get used to the bullets and the explosions, but then eventually the silence becomes the scariest thing because you think you don't know what's happening.

A Then you actually pay attention to every move at that point. How she put a cup down, how she walked in. Yeah. I'm not the best flute player, I know that shit. I'm not even trying to be the best. I never was trying to be the best rapper. I'm trying to connect with people in a certain way, in an interesting way. As humans, we can be whatever we want to be. If that was my goal, I would go for it. You know what I mean? But being the best rapper didn't hold value to me. I want verses that people feel in their fucking heart, not just rap. Oh, that was some slick shit that nigga said. I want people to connect the same way I did, when I grew up listening to rappers and you'd get a connection when Q-tip might say some shit. And always-I say this a lot-he may say something like "like getting stomach aches when you gotta go to work, or staring into space when you're feeling berserk. And I was like, whoa, he feels that too. It's a connection. And that's all I'm ever trying to do.

S Someone told me that if there was a celebrity that was perfectly perfect, perfect life, perfect family, and then a celebrity who's flawed and shows their traumas, the audience is going to relate way more to that person.

A Yeah, because it's human. It's a connect thing. Sometimes perfect things get boring.

S You ever do a collab with anyone that never saw the light of day, where people would be like, what the Hell?

A We worked on this song with Prince called "The Good Life," and I don't know whatever happened to it. But the chorus was "the good life, that's what we ought to be living," or something like that.

S Oh, you don't even have it? Somebody got it. You got to find that, man. Put out a search. And it was Prince singing the chorus?

A Yeah. So at one point in time, Prince had signed with Arista records for a record or two. L.A. Reid was the president.

S But you were with them too?

A Yeah, we were. They were on the top of that game. And L.A. Reid told me this story once. He said, "I told Prince, I'll give you millions of dollars if you let André and Pharrell produce your next album." And Prince said no.

S Yeah, I'm sure.

A I get it. I get it He's Prince, he doesn't need anyone. But I always think, what would Prince sound like on some new... and not even musically, because one thing I've noticed is when artists age, it's because their rhythms age, their drums age, their beats age, because the youth is always moving to a new beat. And sometimes getting people in there to be your drummer is effective. And so I always wondered, man, what would that record have sounded like with Pharrell drums? Crazy. My drums ain't that crazy, but I had a sense of song.

S Is drums what makes a song?

A Not necessarily. When you listen to records from the 1950s and 1960s, they mix the drums really, really low in the back. Drums were considered just timekeepers.

S I guess. So when Tyler says, "I just spent the weekend in Colorado working on drums," what does that mean?

A Finding good drum sounds, because hip hop put the drums forward, and rock at a certain point-a lot of black people fuck with Nirvana hard because the drums were not hidden. Even though I was recently watching an interview with Dave Grohl and he was talking about how he had gotten influenced by the Gap Band. When "Smells Like Teen Spirit" starts, that's the Gap Band. He said, "I was at a picnic and I met the Gap Band drummer, and I told him, man, I got that from you." So I love influence, man. When everybody picks up things and puts it in new genres, that's the way, man.

S You know how there's Lil Nas X? How would you feel about a "Big 3000" or something? Just someone that clearly took two other motherfuckers' names?

A I mean, of course I would feel funny about it at first, because I'm from a different generation and we didn't combine. We came from a generation where we felt like originality was king. Biting or nicking somebody just wasn't the thing But we are in an era now where it is exactly the thing. So I can't argue with what the wave is. Young people like to troll. We don't play those games.

Trolling is just another version of agitating or lying. We just don't play those games. But it's a way, and it's probably in response to something, and the youth usually respond to what was before. So I ain't mad at it. The youth always got the way.

S Have you seen how they give heart signs now? Even just something as small as that.

A I've never used an emoji in my life.

S Really? Never even to show someone you're laughing? Never?

A Well, I don't know. I don't want to use those symbols.

S Well, it's weird. I mean, you may not have been on the Internet then either, but they already had one time around with AOL. They were called emoticons. And then they kind of died and Instagram just brought 'em back like they were never here.

A Well, symbols are important, man. When you think of the Egyptians, they spoke in symbols. They wrote in symbols that meant whole sentences. So there's power in it. I guess I just detest feeling like I'm just following along.

S So, the tour. Please describe to me the emotions and the outcome of the first night, compared to maybe a show a few weeks ago.

A I get the same kind of build-up of energy, the same nervousness, the same excitement, the same journey, the same freedom, the same pureness. What I love about now is I'm able to be 49 years old and feel like I'm 17, the first time we hit the stage as Outkast.

S That's what your art grants you.

A Yeah, and we're doing it every night because the nature of what we are doing is–it's kind of like trust music. We completely trust what's happening, good or bad. And to be in that space, and for people to be watching, the reward is greater than a song they know and can sing along to. And so I say honestly, we're probably doing the most honest shit right now.

I always appreciate this walk, man. You athlete of creation, athlete of design. Most designers, scientists, they take walks, you know what I mean? You got to cultivate a space where designs pop up where you're thinking out of the box. And ideas don't necessarily come when you're at the table in the office.

S Do you have a hard drive of music? Some designers, which I'm not one of them, have a sketchbook of designs.

A I keep a sketchbook.

S No, but do you have music?

A Yeah, I have ideas. Yeah, I have.

S So if right now, I'm a record label, I'm like, "You know what André, I'm going to give you a billion dollars, but I need twelve songs right now." You got twelve songs?

A I am going to say, yeah, twelve bad ones or whatever. Yeah, just twelve sketches, ideas. But see, that's the problem too. We are in a time where humans are so entitled and feel like they have privilege and access to every piece of someone's art. Now we have the technology to analyze a Picasso painting–they have laser lights, they can go and see the layers of paint. They find that he did this painting four or five times before the one we see, changed it, worked on it. So now with entitled fans it's almost like going into Picasso's studio at night, stealing this piece while he's working on it. He didn't even have time to do his fucking craft. And people are stealing people's songs and shit. Red Hot Chili Peppers–at one point there was a dude stealing their session while they were recording. Who does that?! People should be fucking killed, knocked off for that–I think there should be art mercenaries! Y'all got to stop. This shit stole. Just like in the hood, you disrespect some shit. People should start being killed for hacking, I think. I'm just wildly talking, I don't think anybody should be killed. But you shouldn't disrespect people's work. Who are you to come in and steal people's shit and then present it?

S Just to play devil's advocate: creativity and ideas come so easy to us. So we can just be in the shower and be like, damn, that would be cool. Let me try.

A They do, but they don't. They come at a moment, but they're in us. But we work our whole lives. We worked to–

S Obtain them.

A Yes, I did. It did just come, but you had a whole life. You had to do a few things to get to that space.

S Here's the analogy. We have the seeds. A lot of motherfuckers don't even have the seeds. So even when they see a flower, they're like, fuck, I don't even have seeds. Let me take this flower. You feel me?

A Yeah.

S Where we're like, damn, they took my seed. I got a bunch of other seeds, I just watered these over.

A Nah, nah. But they don't understand how valuable the components are. Components make up a thing. Like, for instance, "Hey Ya," the song–I did that shit six years before I put it out. It wasn't completely ready. I don't think the audience were even ready for that song. What if someone stole that song? I didn't get a chance to totally finish it. That's just a fucked-up thing.

S You know how with Pablo, because it was digital music, Kanye released a first version and then a month later he released a different version of a song with all-of-a-sudden-now fucking blah-blah-blahs on it, and then he added Frank, and he added some drums. Do you wish maybe you released "Hey Ya," but then–

A No, no. Because it wasn't ready. And that's another thing, too. I think we are so rushed to put shit out, but as an artist, it's all about taste and choices. An artist knows when something is ready. They feel like it's ready to be put out once it's out. It's like once you have a child, you can't go back and change that child and say, oh no, I want this type of child. No, that child is fucking born, is out in the world. You deal with it.

S Are you familiar with Flat Earthers?

A Yeah. But we have proof now, we can actually take a Flat Earther on a fucking spaceship now and show you if you still believe it's flat. Put that to a scientist. Put that to an astronomer.

S Have you met Neil deGrasse Tyson?

A I have not, but I want to meet him. He said something the other day that was so fucking awesome. Neil said that we're in a time now that the internet has gotten so good at faking things that at a point humans will distrust the Internet, we will all turn away from it because we won't know what's real. We just won't trust it. It just won't be valuable to us. Imagine a time where I could see a video, a video of you sitting up here, but you made the whole shit up. But we believe it–it's real, he took this hike. But because we know someone can create it and it looks real, we won't believe it unless we are there. So everything will become live and direct again. If it's on the screen, we won't believe it. So there may come a time where we turn away from the Internet and we may only use it for communication, technical things like GPS, stuff to help us as actual tools. But information the way we're seeing now, that bots can make a whole country believe, can get us in trouble. No one will trust what they see. When no one trusts what they see, they turn away from it.

S Yeah, that's true. I got to go take a picture in front of these clouds real quick.

A So it's trippy what we are doing now. Musically, how we perform every night. It is something where we don't know the outcome. We can't predict it. We don't have the chorus, we don't have a beat. It's a live and direct thing where you have to be there to experience it. It is not made up. It is not predetermined. When I grew up, when people said a rapper was freestyling, he was actually freestyling. Now my kid showed me something one day and he was like, "Dad, watch this artist, this freestyle is dope." And he shows the video and I'm like, "Son, I'm sorry, he's not freestyling. He's saying a written verse. Yeah, that's just a performance, but it's not a freestyle." Freestyle is where they know they're making it up live and direct. So it's kind of–what's going to be the value?

S Some rappers freestyle.

A Some rappers freestyle, but it's an old-school thing. On the Internet they call freestyling like, "Oh, this artist came up to the radio station, he's freestyling." He's not freestyling. He's definitely saying some written shit. You can tell freestyling in its free form. You can totally tell when a nigga's saying some written shit. Proof of now is going to be the value. Proof of alive, alive and human. And that's what I want to ask you about in design. In music, I'm not scared of AI. It's a tool and I'm trying to figure out the best ways to use it. There's always new tools introduced and there's always a fear of new tools. When the drum machine came into play, drummers were like, oh fuck, what are we going to do? But that's just not the case. So I'm always trying to figure out–in design, do you use AI in some type of way as a tool to help you to do your craft?

S Do you know who Mark Ecko is?

A Yeah.

S Mark Ecko comes to my office. I've known him for a few years and I'm thinking he wants to catch up, but it turns out he's trying to pitch me on some AI company. He's either starting or investing in some shit, and I'm not really familiar and nor am I really interested. This is also at a time where everyone's fucking in my ear about NFTs and it's just like, yo, leave me the fuck alone about all this shit. But he's in my office and he's like, just try it. Just try it out. And I'm like, okay. I go, Salehe Croc, version two, made for the outdoors–and within three seconds it shows an image of a pretty good fucking shoe.

A That's what I'm saying.

S And I was like, yo, get the fuck out of my office, jokingly–but it's crazy because the Pollex, the Croc I did, it took me three weeks to make and this shit did it in three minutes. So at first it scared me, but then I started taking on this perspective, which is: every job I've worked at, the prime tools that we use are Photoshop, Illustrator, InDesign, stuff like that, right? Digital. Maybe some 3-D. But there's always this guy, let's call him Larry, that would be like sixty years old, and he always just hand-sketched. And that's because when the transition was happening, he decided, nah, I'm just going to keep sketching.

A Yeah, I'm Larry. Haaa!

S And so now he moves slower, he can't keep up with the team and is ultimately making himself obsolete. And so I thought to myself: I cannot be Larry. So I was like, this is the tool. It's no different than fighting against the Internet. Or when digital cameras first came out, I'm sure analog photographers were like, fuck this shit. You got to be in the dark room. And so I was like, you know what? I got to use this as a tool, and now I've realized that I can use it as a tool to honestly help me save time.

A It's a quicker mood-board creator.

S Exactly. Because even just if we're going back to your music for a second—and me knowing nothing about music—maybe if you wanted to just end a flute song, if you could put that into AI and then it could give you fifty versions of that just to stimulate your mind. And then one, you're like, damn, I never thought to put a low note there. And then you're like, wow, AI didn't replace any of my creativity, but it helped expand my mind because now it's like a tool. You're using it no different than a digital camera or building with 3-D or whatever. Do you credit AI on that fucking track? No, because that's still all your mind, but now you just have yet another tool to help you operate at a higher level.

A It's kind of like a drum machine. But I do see it as a tool, even in music—I'm finding now it's about how to use it. I think right now people are using it as a kind of novelty wow factor. Like, oh, we can make it sound like it's from the 1970s, but that's just AI spitting out a prompt. But at the core of AI is this superhuman brain that analyzes everything. So that's what I'm focused on. Not the actual outcome, but what the technology is and how I can use that.

S You know Terrence Howard? Did you see his Howard Stern interview?

A No, I didn't. I heard about it.

S So apparently a lot of VR technology is based off a patent that he created, which is kind of random, but also very interesting because it speaks to what you're saying about how really it's the foundational idea—the brain is what can really be the tree that all of these things branch off of.

A Well, here's my theory. I think technology is just proof of what we already are capable of. I think at a certain point, you got to know that we only use 11% to 12% of our brains. Imagine if we were at 90%, we probably could do AI shit on our own. So I think science and technology are only proof of what we already know how to do. We discovered DNA through science, but DNA had already been around. It's not a new invention, it's just a discovery of something old. So really, all of this shit is just discovering ourselves, discovering nature. Even the DNA molecule, it is a set of numbers. It's a set, it is mathematical in ways. We're still trying to figure out how the fucking Egyptians built them fucking pyramids? How did they get those big blocks? There's just no way. But what if they were just tapped into a certain technology that we lost along the way, and now we're able to find it again? When we go through dark ages—they call them dark ages—a lot of things are destroyed, and we kind of have to start over as a society. Tesla was making free energy and electricity a long, long time ago. Now we're getting back to it. So it's kind of like we rediscover lost things. So my theory is, all the shit is already out there. Nature is the inventor, and science is just the proof, or the discovery, the poking around to prove what's happening.

And now we have to be honest. Anything that's written by humans is weird because anything that's written has an editor, especially if you tell the same story through time, that'll get edited down to something else. So if we're reading a Bible that's a King James version, you better believe it's whatever the fuck King James wanted it to be. His rules, they're going to be edited in or out of the book. So I have this stupid-ass theory: what if the Bible was just a graphic novel of that time, and we've just taken it way too seriously? So this Jesus character was like a superhero. It's almost like if people discover a Batman novel two thousand years from now, or Spider-Man, this dude could do this and do this. He has to have magical powers. And now we're taking it in a way where we are praising him. Two thousand years from now, people are going to talk about some of the shit that we're doing. "Okay, this dude, he did this and he started playing this flute, and then there was this guy named Kanye"—some of that shit is going to seem magical to people two, three thousand years from now. They weren't there, so their human minds are going to create things around it, the romanticism of things. And I think we've just humanly romanticized religion where we've taken it so seriously. Yeah, there are good things and good fables, but there are good fables in niggas' raps too. When they discover somebody's raps, somebody's going to be able to learn from it and apply it to their life just like the Bible. So I have a theory that the Bible was just a great piece of literature from that time. One time they were saying that Shakespeare wrote it.

S I just don't understand why our human ability to archive hasn't been that good.

A We wouldn't even know certain languages if we wouldn't have found that one stone, the Rosetta Stone. The Rosetta Stone opened up doors for us to understand how people wrote, how they talked. It actually is a stone. It's almost like someone wrote these things in a stone and it kind of gave people pieces to find out how people wrote. Language. Without that stone, we wouldn't know what it means.

S Where was the stone?

A Oh, I don't know where they found it, but we haven't been able to document it because our materials hadn't been able to last. So imagine now if we're storing everything on a chip, and that chip goes away, or that file goes away or that server goes away—we've lost so much. So that's why I'm actually now sculpting in stone, carving in stone.

S It's a soft stone? You chisel it? Are you putting muscle into it or is it easy kind of working with?

A Well, you can do it both ways. You can use a computer to create an image and you can get a machine, or I'm going to start with my hand. I want to use both technologies to get things that I can't do by hand. So when I'm gone two thousand years from now, people will find shit. My songs may not even exist because they may just be gone, unless someone had a vinyl copy and a phonograph still exists, like a record player. Even now, if you have a cassette, but you don't have a cassette player, you're fucked. So when you say, how do we lose so much? There's just no way to store it. No way to keep it.

S Yeah, yeah. I get what you're saying. What is the eternal device?

A Well, I've heard they made new discoveries now and putting information in glass that lasts longer than a chip.

S What? Lasering patterns?

A Yeah.

S I just saw some shit on IG about how one of the biggest database companies in the world can't get hacked. Any code that a computer can write is ultimately a pattern, so a hacker could eventually figure it out. But this company can't get hacked—in the office they have a wall of lava lamps, and then they have these scanners that are scanning the lava lamps. And because lava lamps are so spontaneous and random, the codes get created from what the lava lamps are doing. So visually it looks like the most archaic thing, like why there a hundred lava lamps right there? But it's actually the most innovative thing ever.

A Yes. Sometimes using outdated technology is the way, and that's how they discovered this glass thing, putting information on glass.

S Do you want to make anything now? What are you trying?

A I'm about to make shoes. I just started with this company, making my own, but they will be manufacturing.

S I'm about to do the exact same thing. And then what kind of sneakers you making?

A I'm not sure. I have a couple ideas. I don't even know if they'll be sneakers

S Well, bro, if you need any design help, I got you.

A Of course I do.

S Do you see yourself as an icon?

A I see myself as someone that's been known for a while. "Icon" is a funny word for me. I think icons have to be careful of what made them icons.

S One hundred percent.

A I'm always on the other side looking—why would André do this? Why is he doing this? If I'm a fan, why is he doing it? Oh, oh, he designed, he helped design those. And with those opportunities, I always tell them, I want to work with you all, but if we do a collaboration, that is the only way I'm *with* that. I don't want to just be a model in a campaign. I'll wear things that I'm actually a part of.

S But so now all those people that maybe didn't know about you or didn't see you as an apparel creator are now like, holy shit, we see him in this light that we didn't see him in before. Isn't that a bridge to the exact same place as if you were just featured in a campaign for a brand?

A It's a more honest bridge. It is a thing that you can track back. Because niggas get deals all the fucking time, niggas get campaigns all the fucking time. It's really like niggas be doing it for clout. I don't want that. You know what I mean? So I just kind of value it differently. For them, it's a campaign—they got an album to promote, you know what I'm saying? "It's a good look. I'm cool."

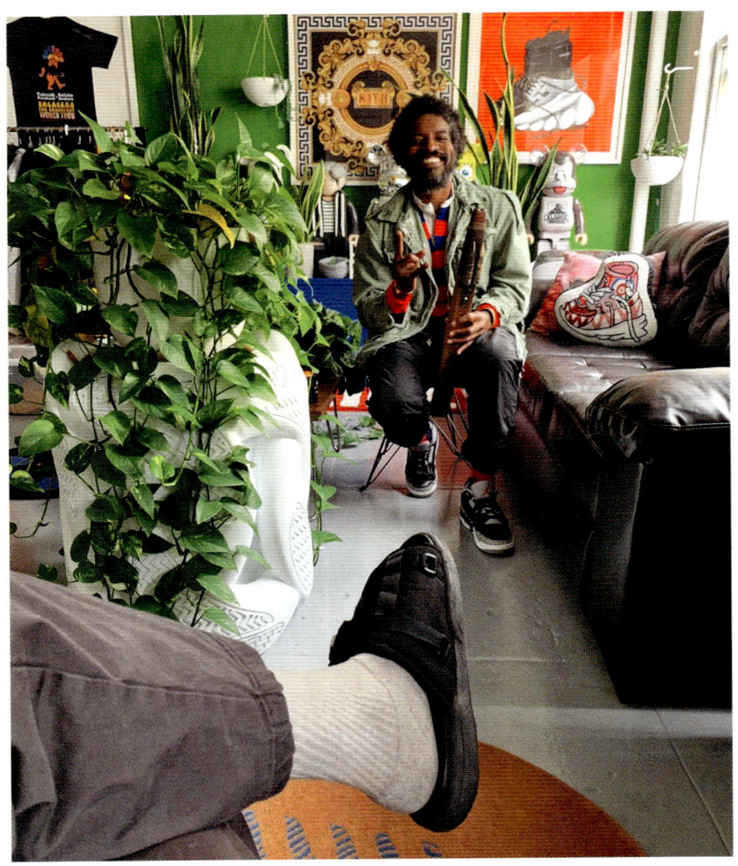

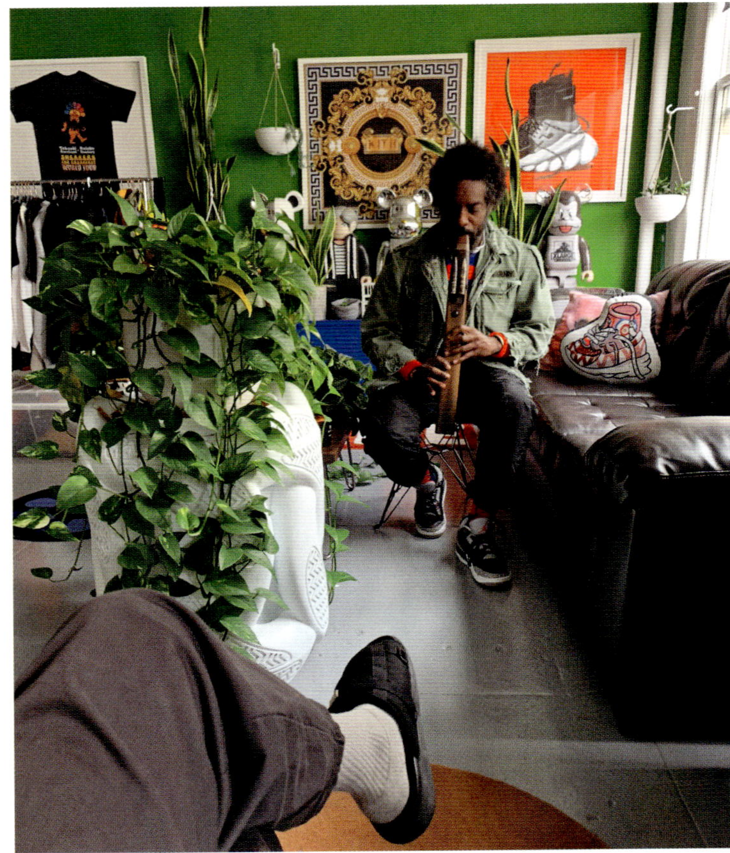

S But through your lens, it would be dope. I would imagine they're going to make overalls in the exact same cut as your favorite overalls with the pinstripe or whatever.

A That shit, yeah. But I'd rather do that with a workwear company. To me, if I can find a way to make dope instrument cases, like flute cases, and if there's a cool shirt or pants that go with it, great. But the value is where something's authentic to what I'm trying to do.

S How do you reach out to your audience as an entrepreneur, when you want to be like, okay, I'm releasing an album. Is it just like a press team, or can you just hit Instagram?

A I'm learning that because I hadn't done it in so long that I had to get help to even figure out how to release the album. Like the last flute album. I got a PR team, I got art directors, just people that I trust just to see. And so now I'm seeing the value of building a team to help get ideas–young people, old people, I don't know certain things. So I need to have people in the room to help and just to make sure that it's saying what I want it to say more than anything. A hundred percent. But I'm still trying to figure that out, man. I don't even know how to post. I've never posted anything in my life. I've never gotten a DM in my life.

S Don't. That's the plus symbol. It's so simple. You become addicted.

A That's the problem. And I'm cool, I'm cool on that. I mean, I like Pinterest, just to kind of look through things. But yeah, I'm cool on that.

S Because I know you don't care. But if you did, yeah, Instagram for you would be the most, because not only would it be you putting whatever you want out there, every fucking outlet would just pick up, "Yo, this motherfucker's eating bananas this morning."

A Yeah. But I want to actually offer something I love.

S I'm joking about the bananas, but even if you posted a sketch, or if you released a T-shirt, it's everywhere now.

A Yeah. I mean, I think the technology is dope and I will use it. I will use it to present what I'm doing.

S It kind of goes back to the AI Larry conversation.

A Yeah. I love that Cactus Plant sometimes only has just one fucking post on her shit. That shit is hard to me, man. I like Cactus's career. I just now recently know what Cactus looks like.

S Whatcha going to do with the rest of your day?

A I'm going to do actually what you're doing, man. Having somebody to hold you accountable or kind of just doing it with somebody. I can't work out on my fucking own. I hate fucking working out, but I don't mind walking. I think when you have someone, a team member, that shit just catapults everything, man.

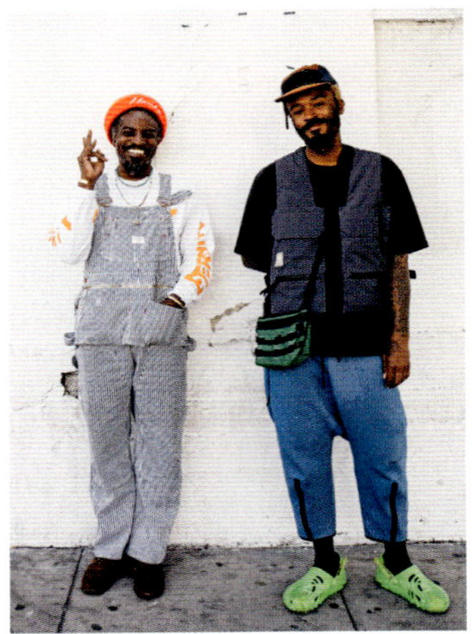

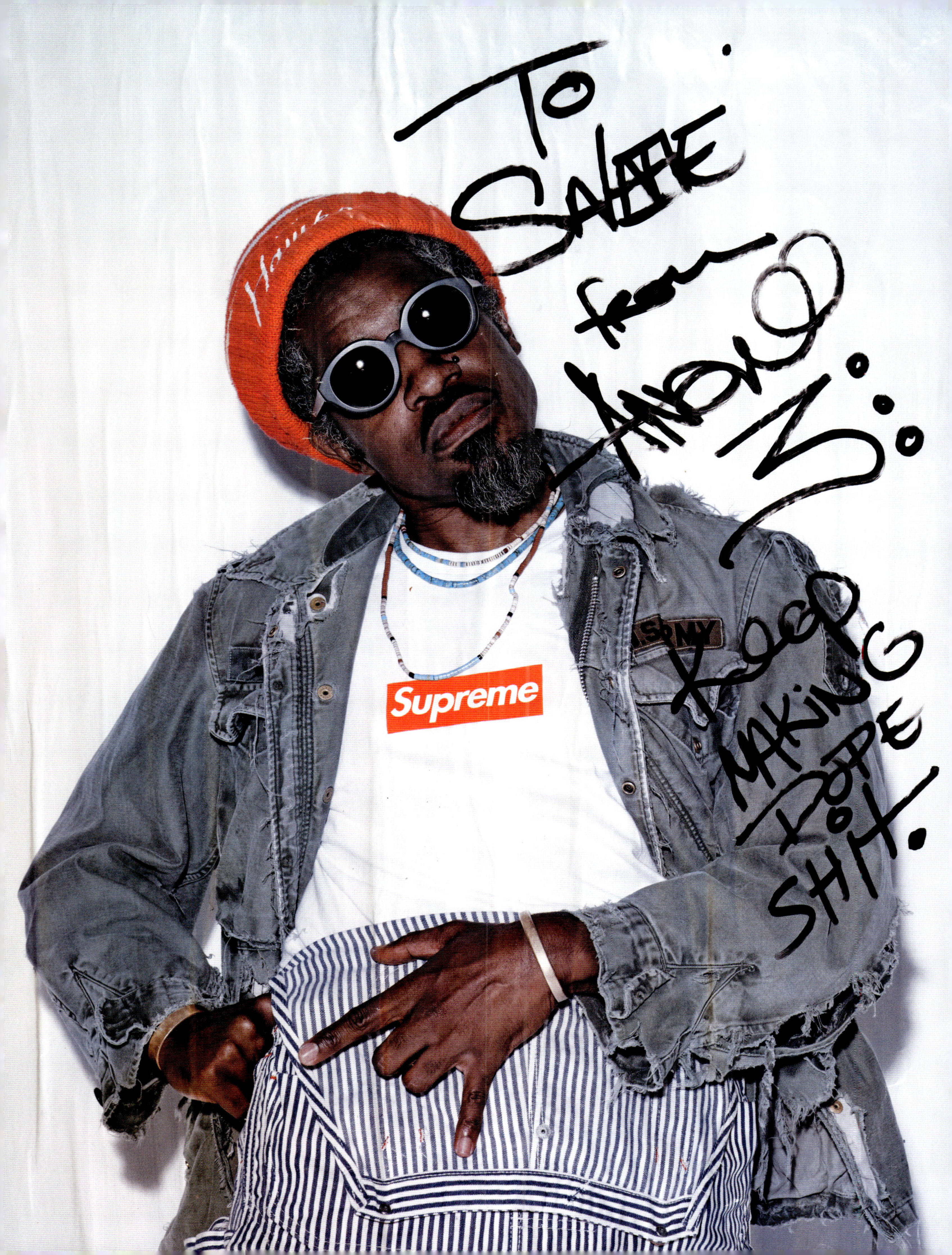
To
from
Supreme
Keep MAKING DOPE SHIT.

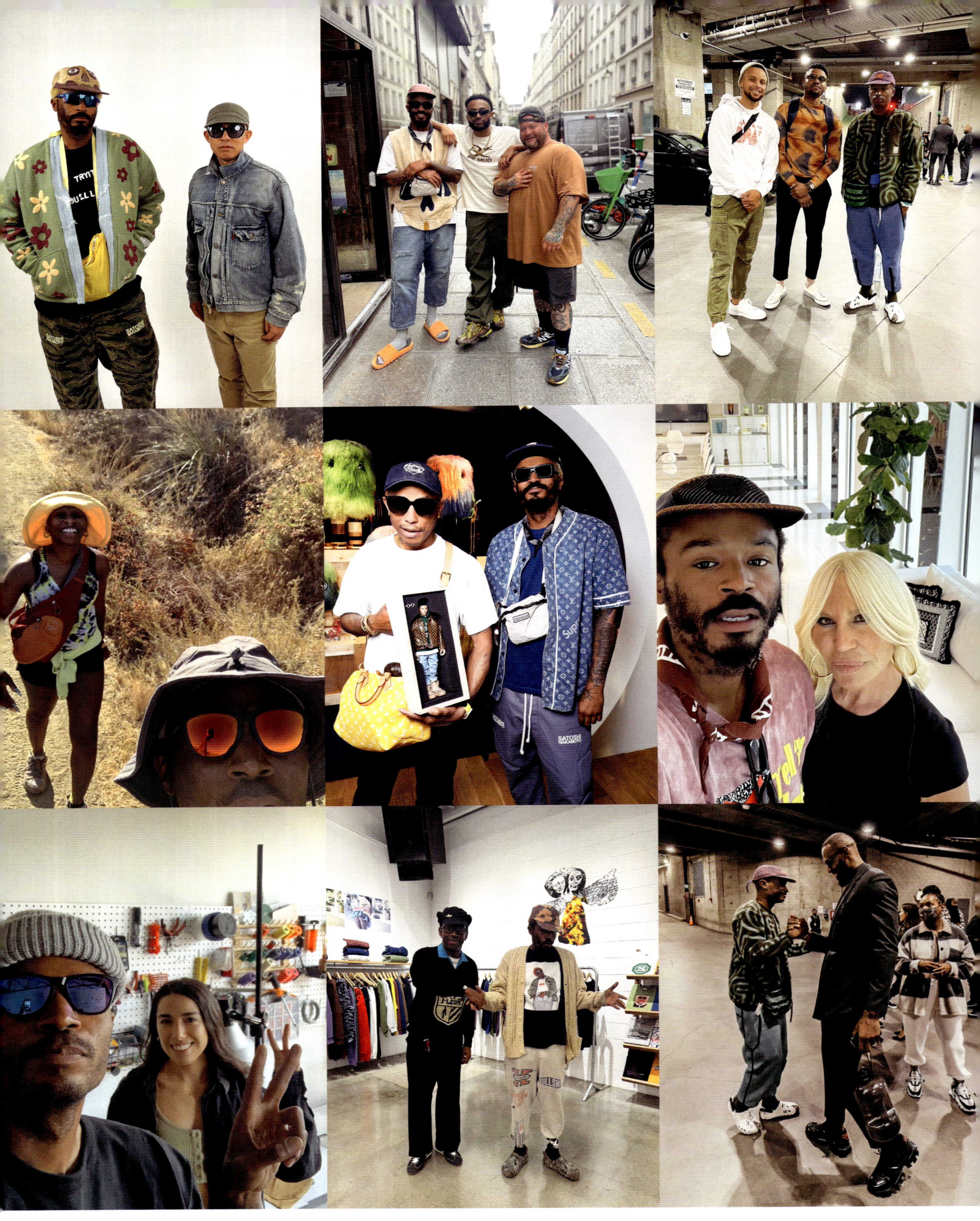

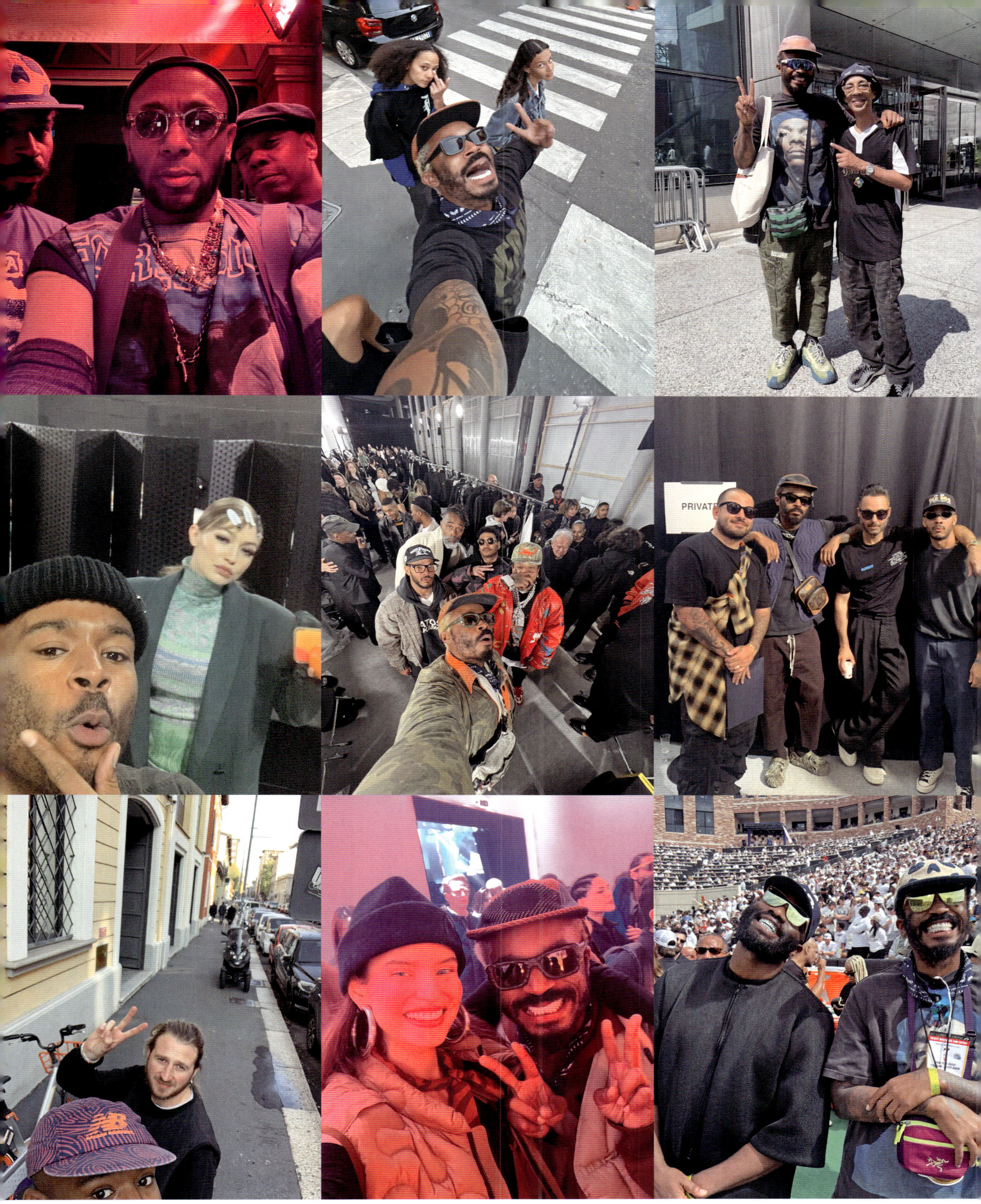

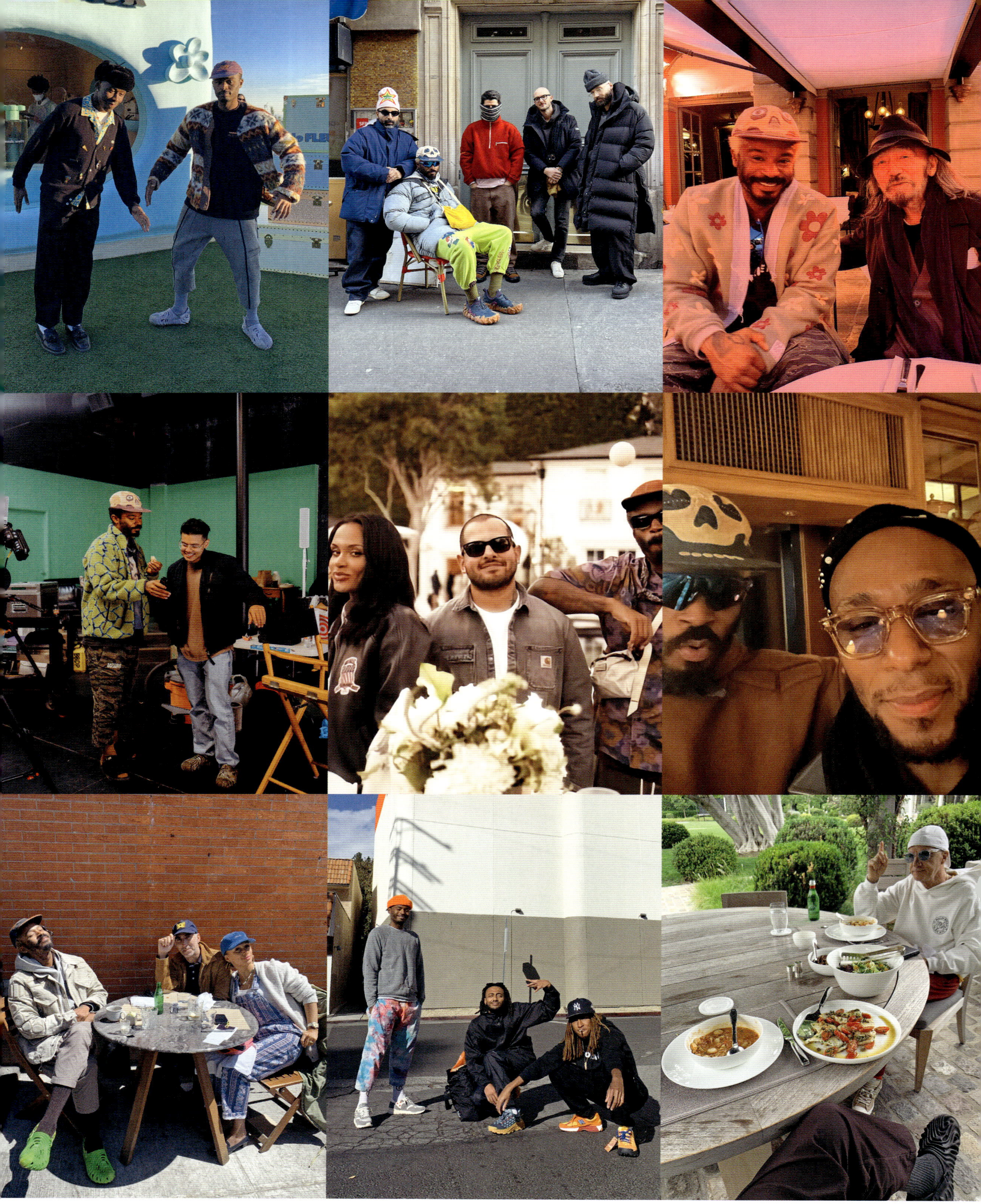

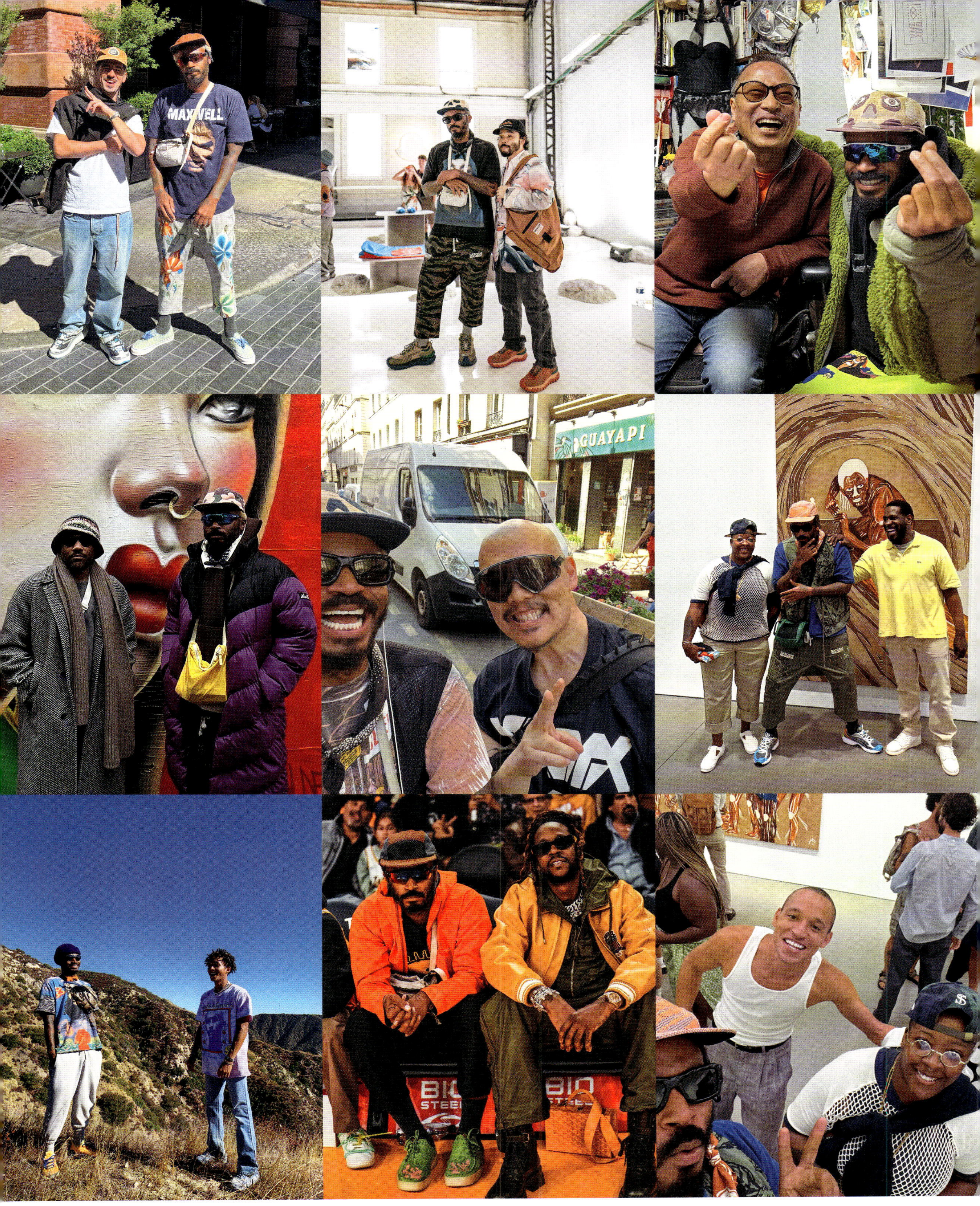
MAXWELL
GUAYAPI

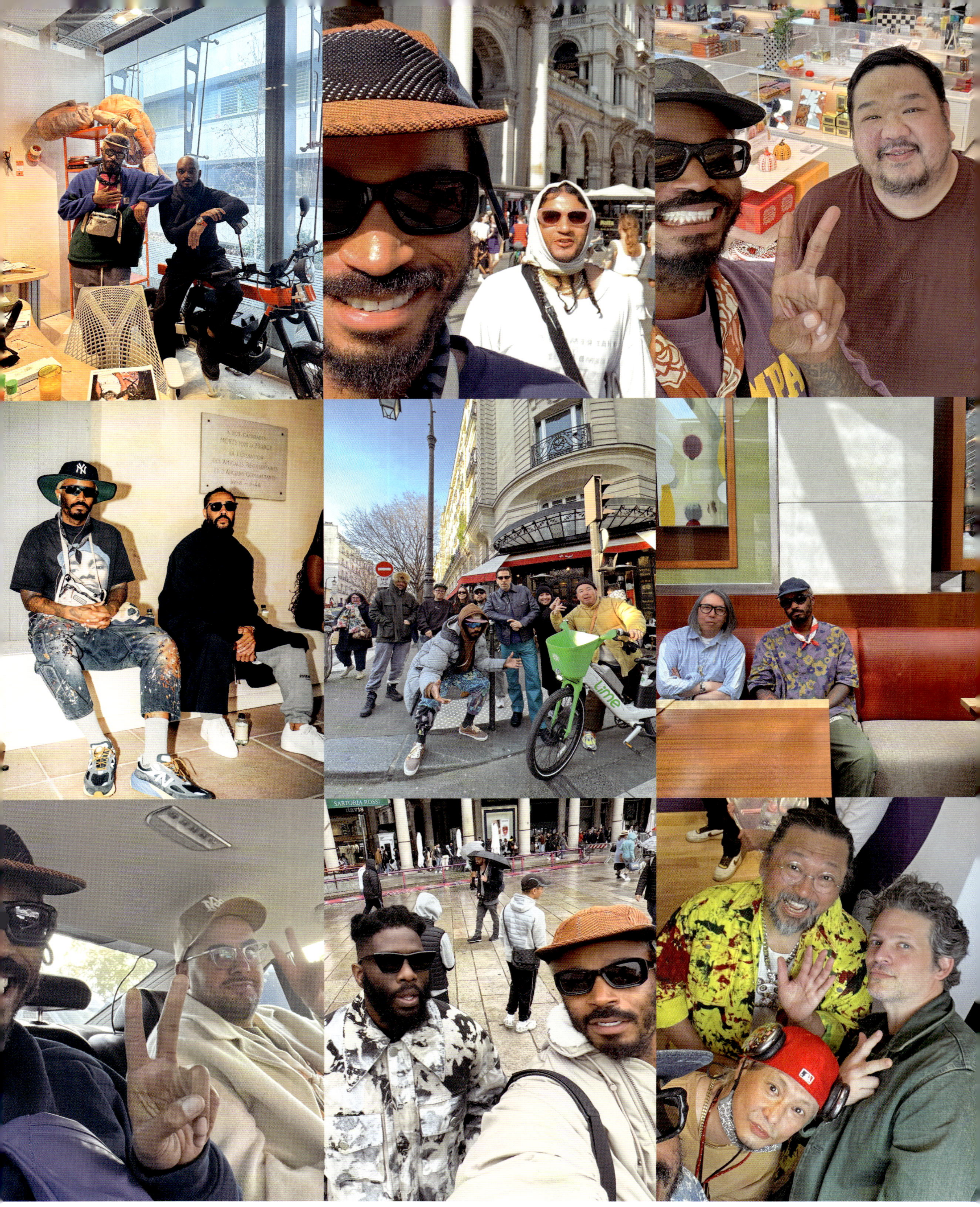
SARTORIA ROSSI
lime

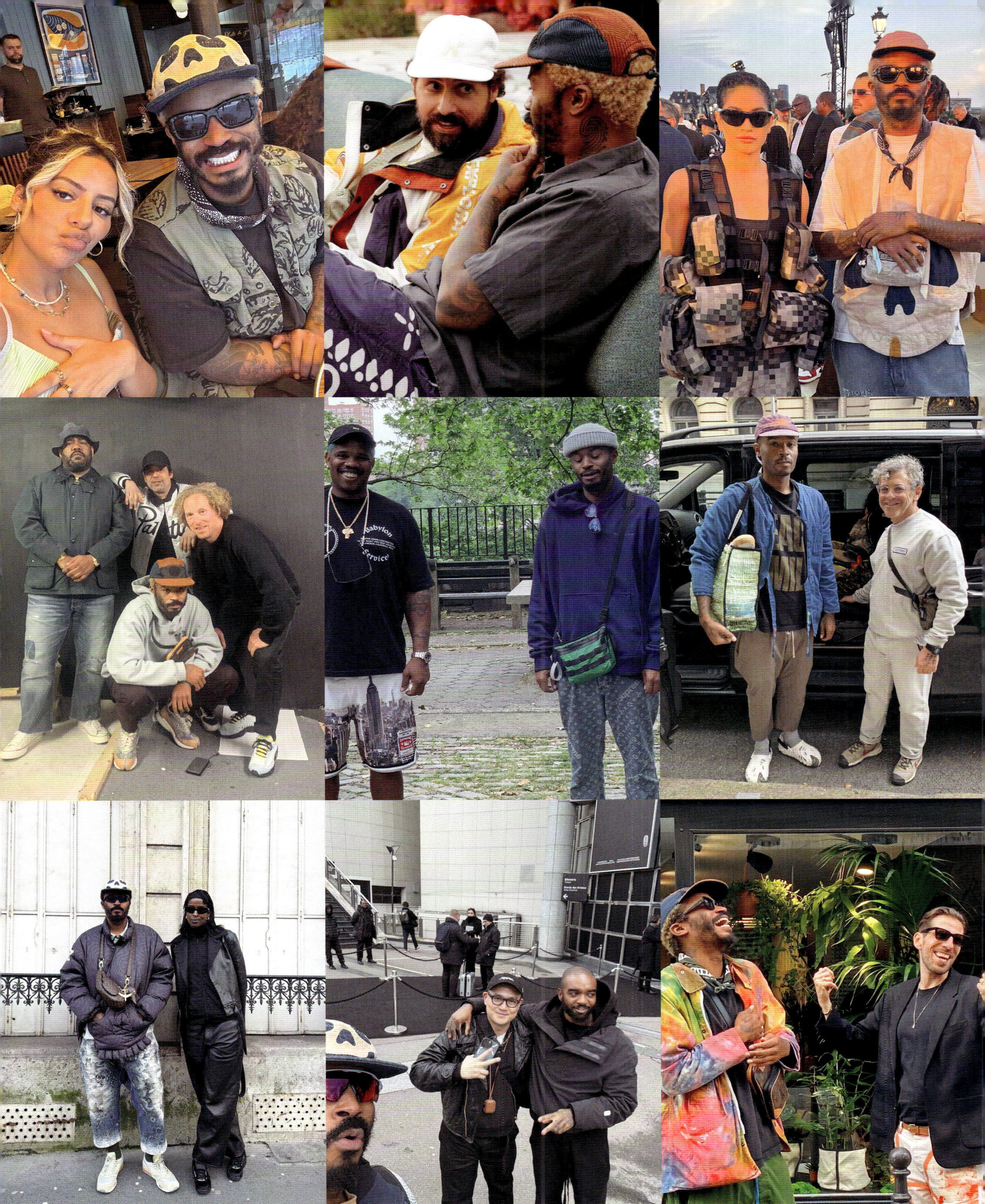

STUDIO VISITS

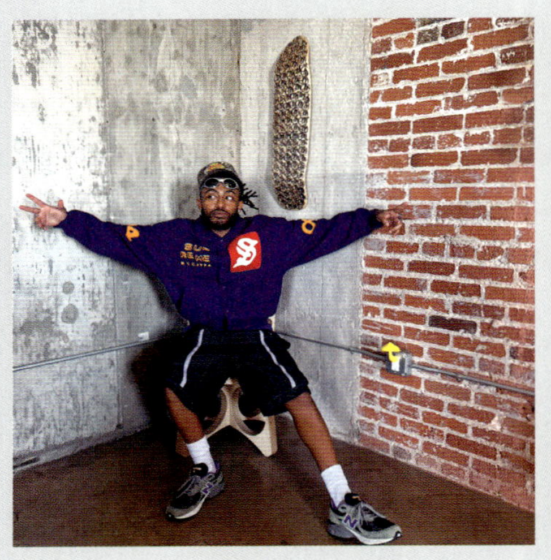

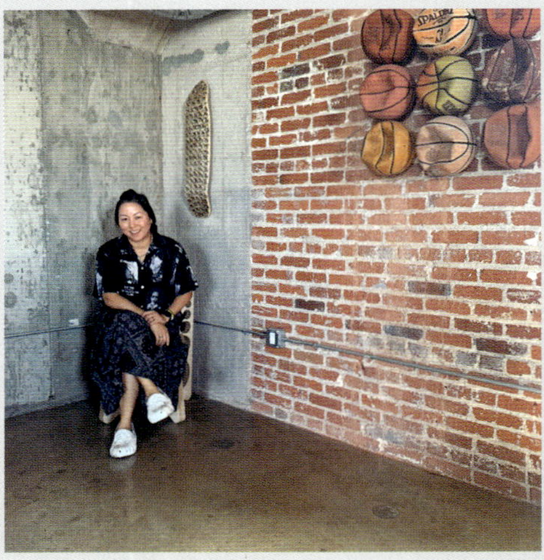

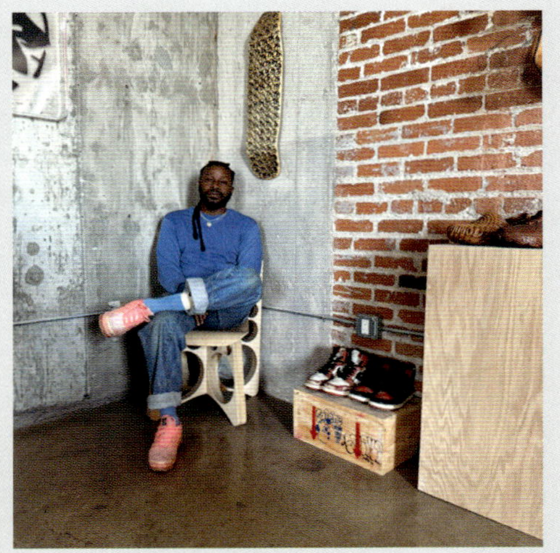

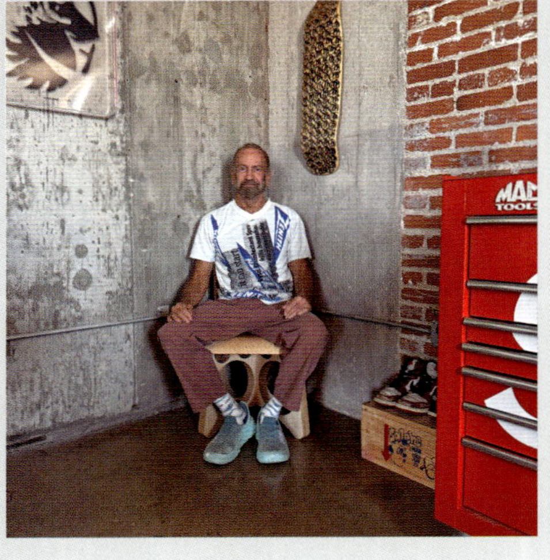

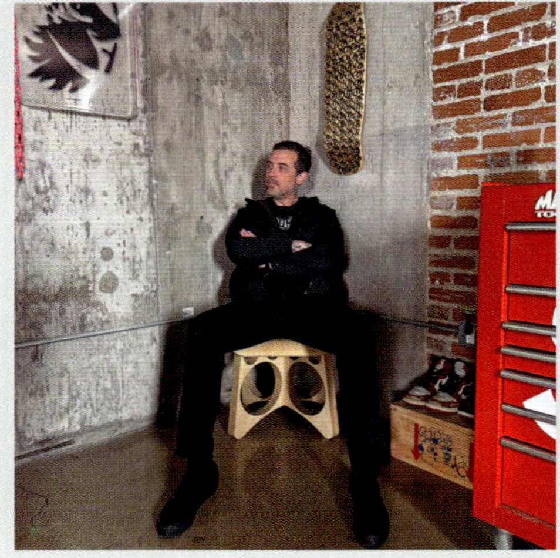

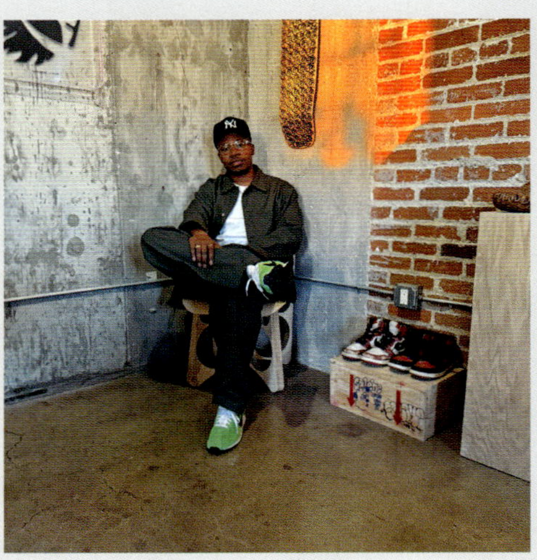

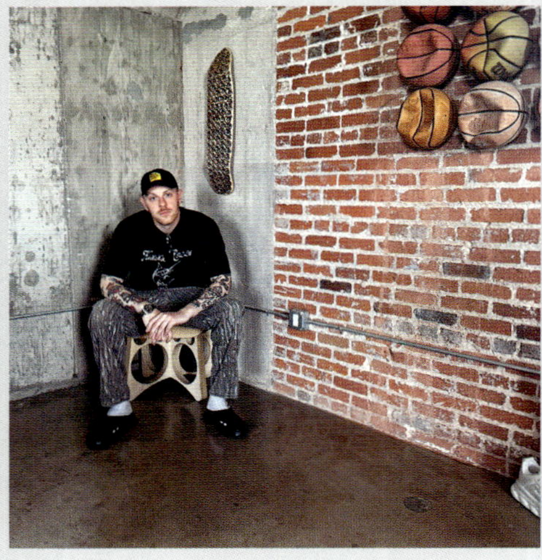

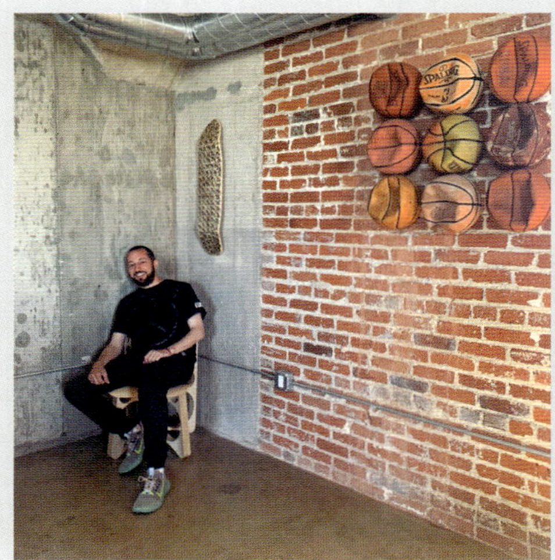

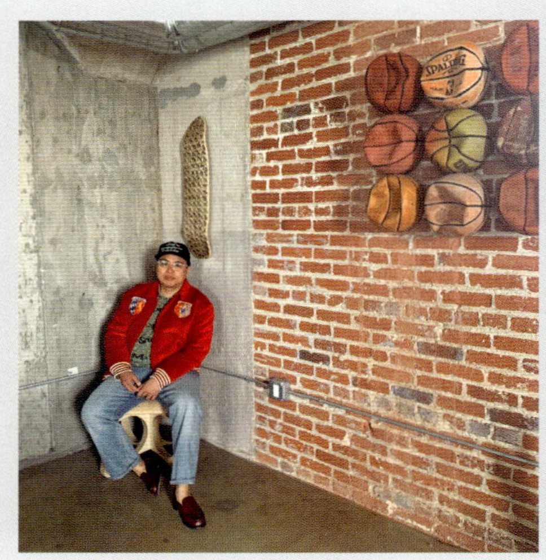

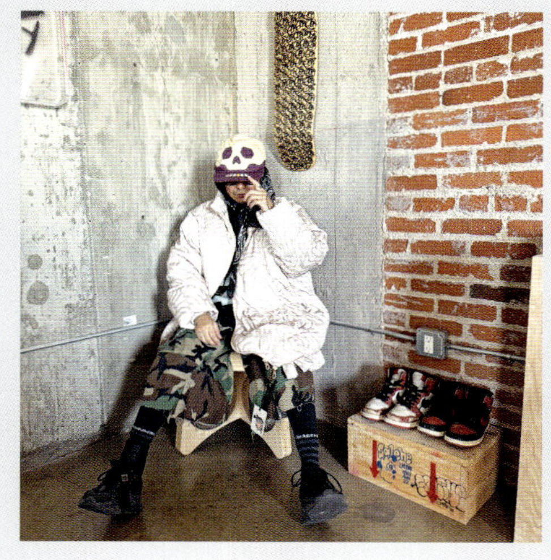
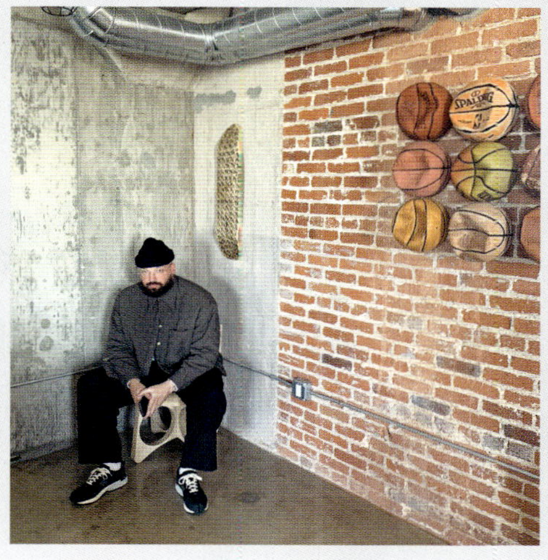
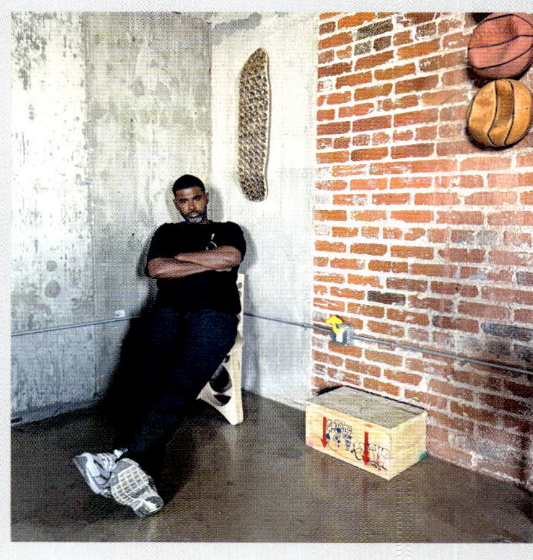
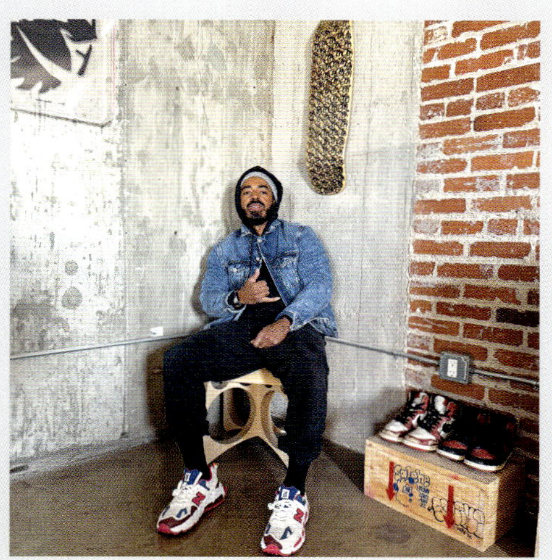
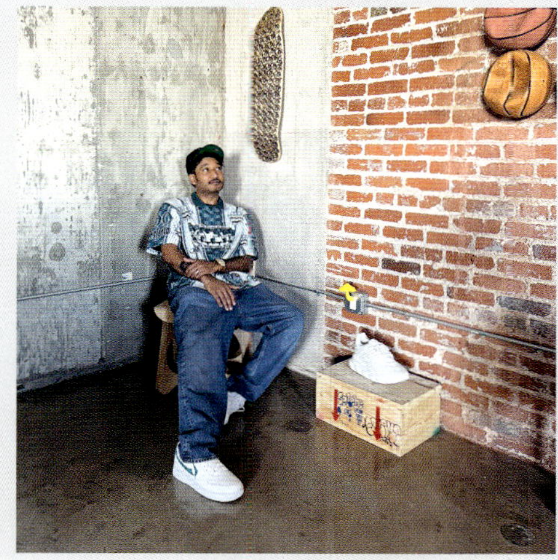
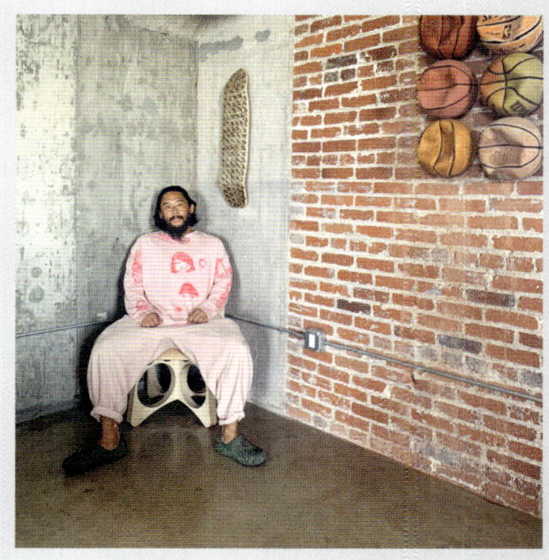
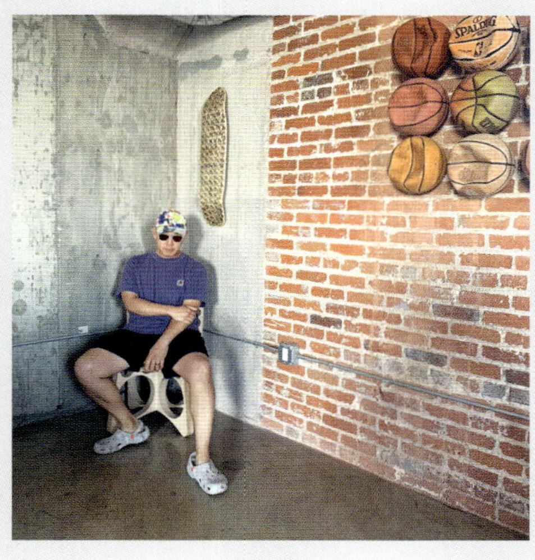
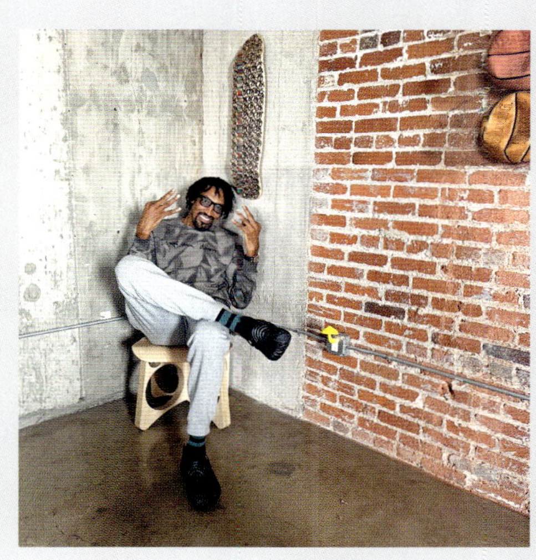
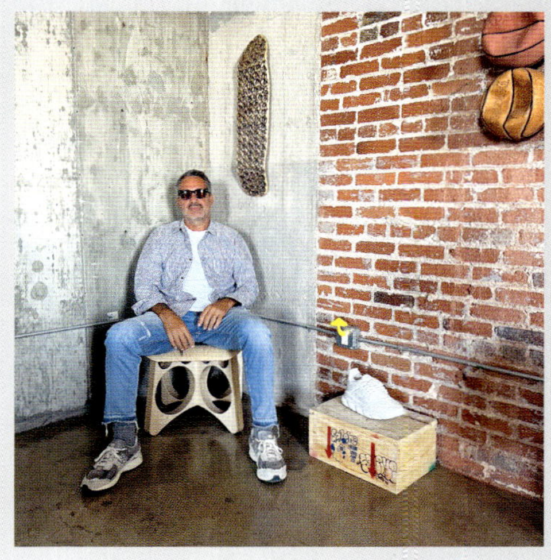
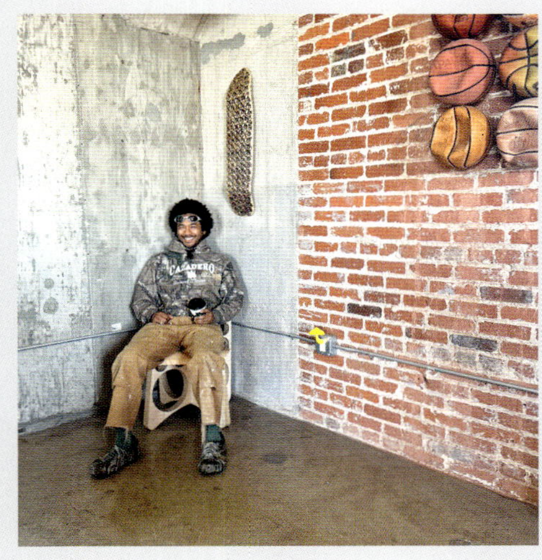
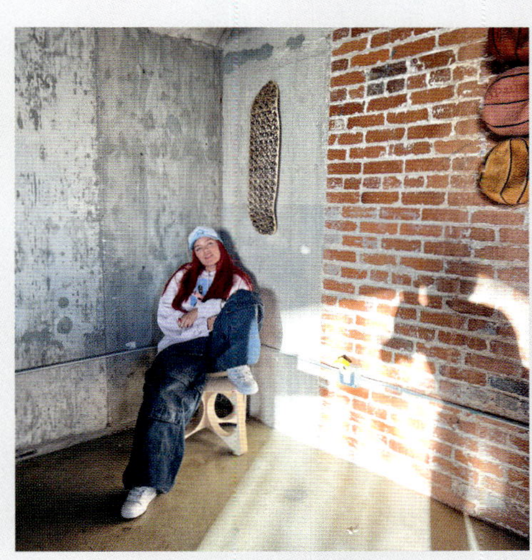
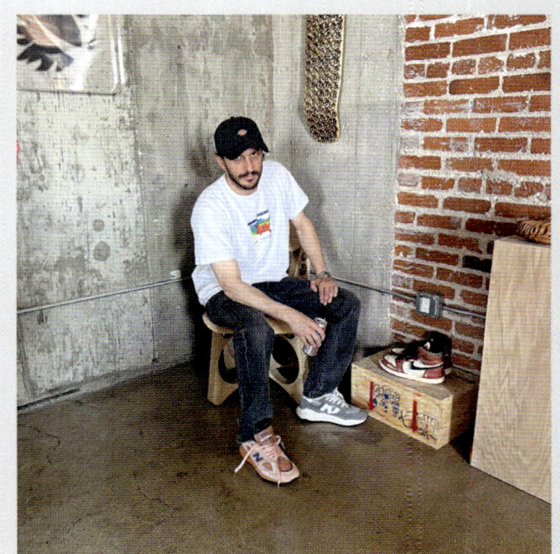

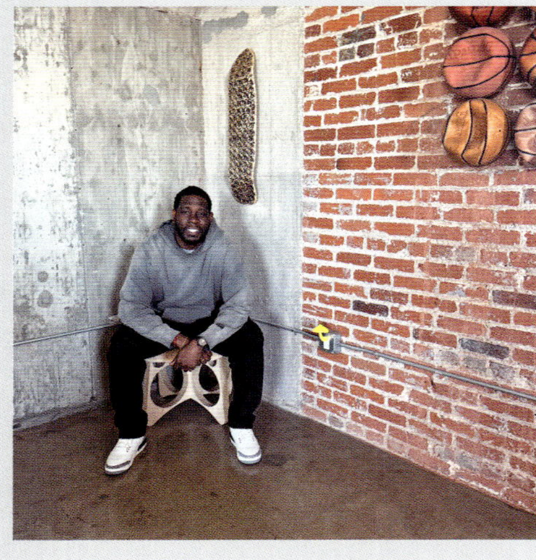
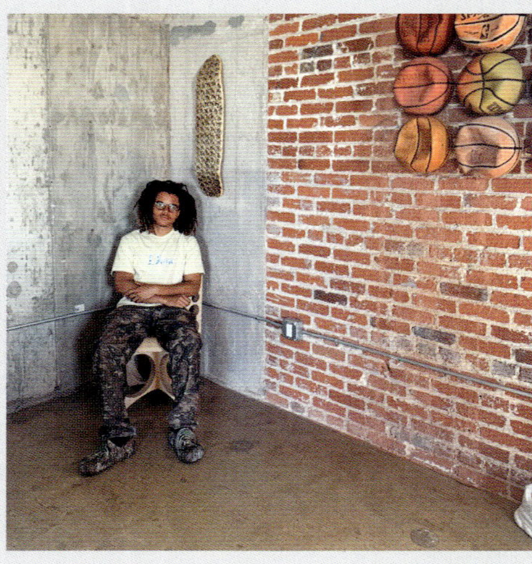
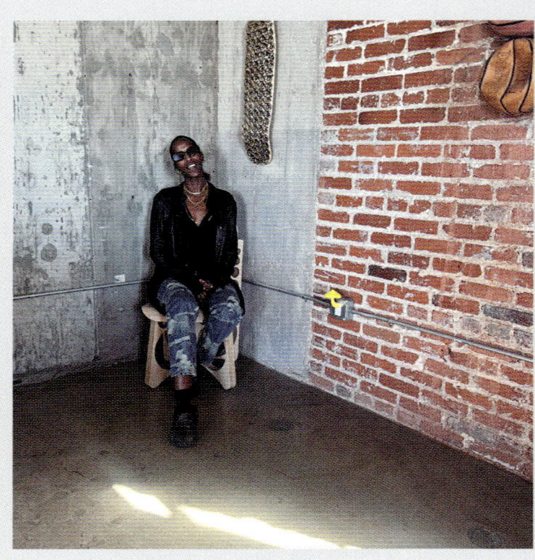
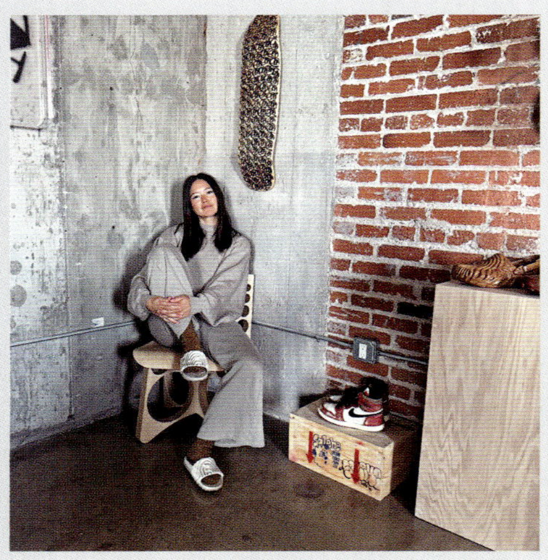
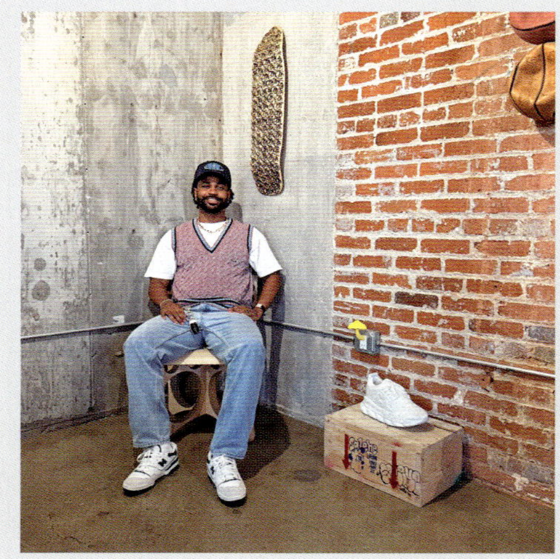
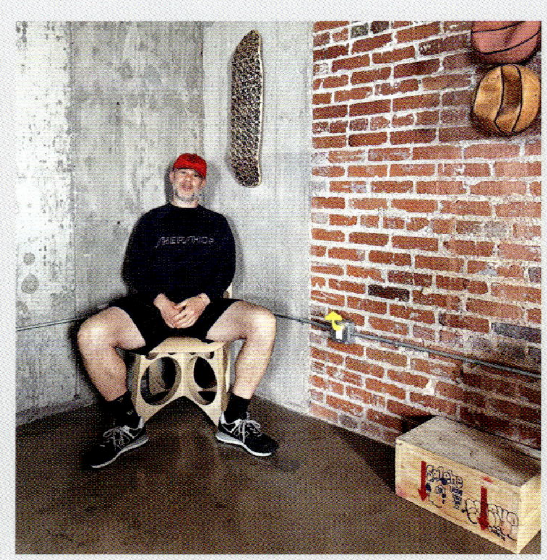
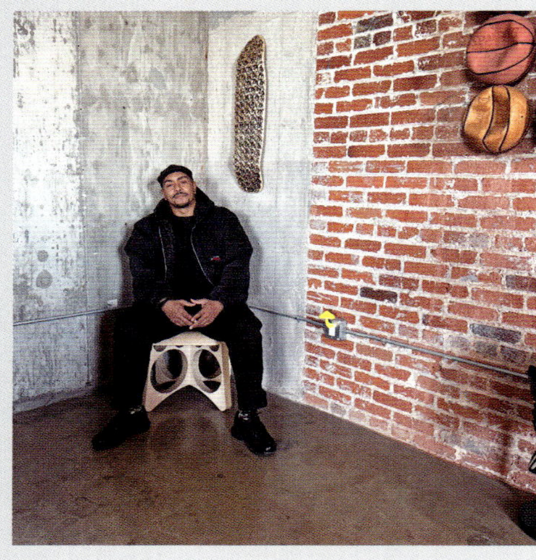
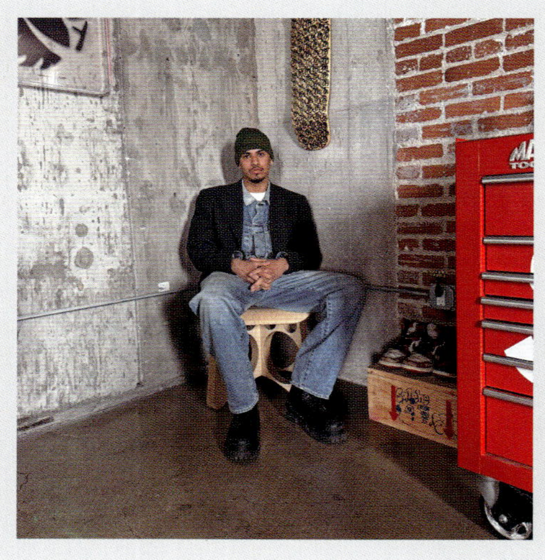
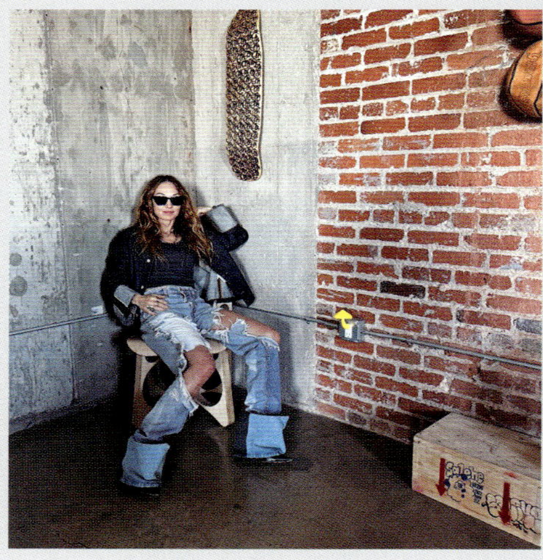
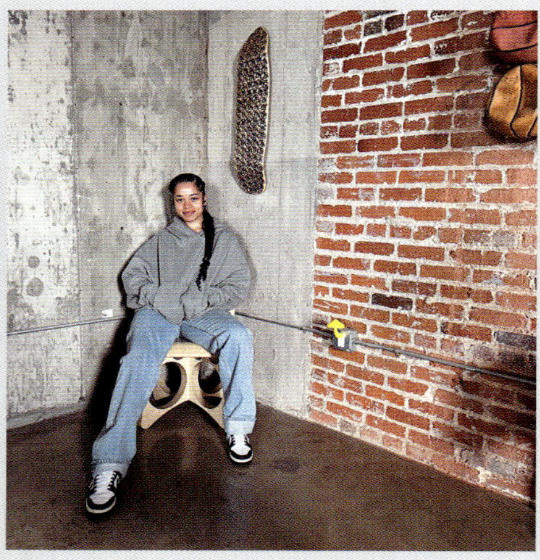
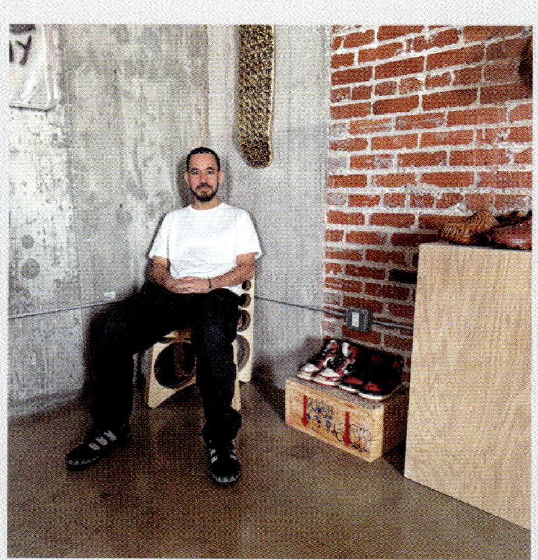
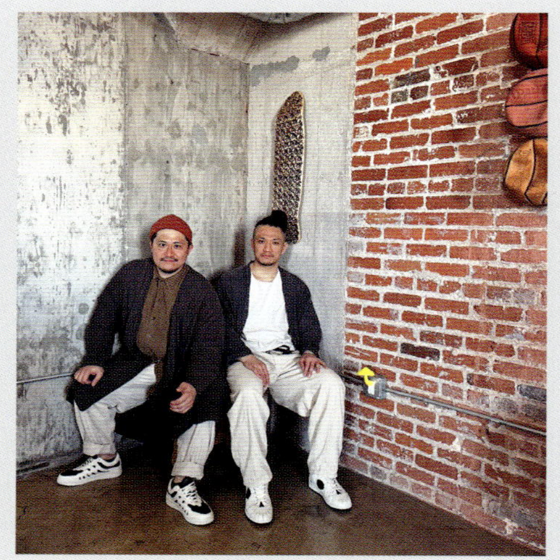

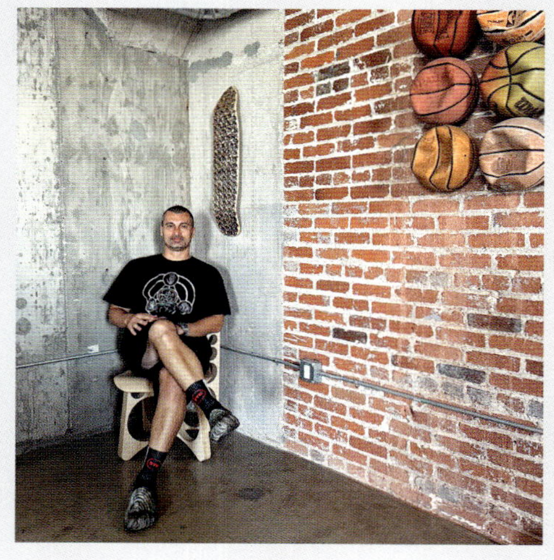
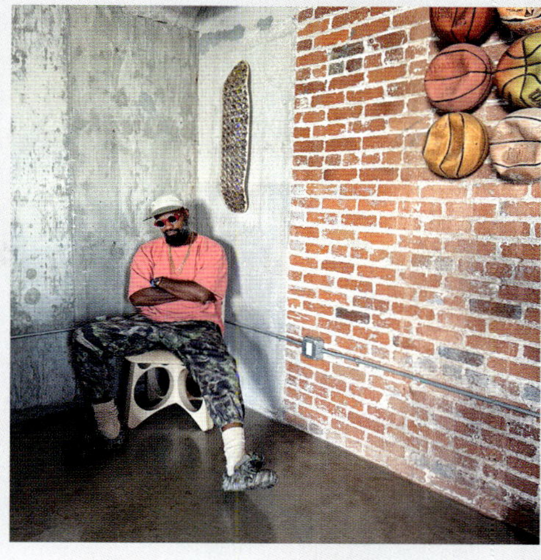
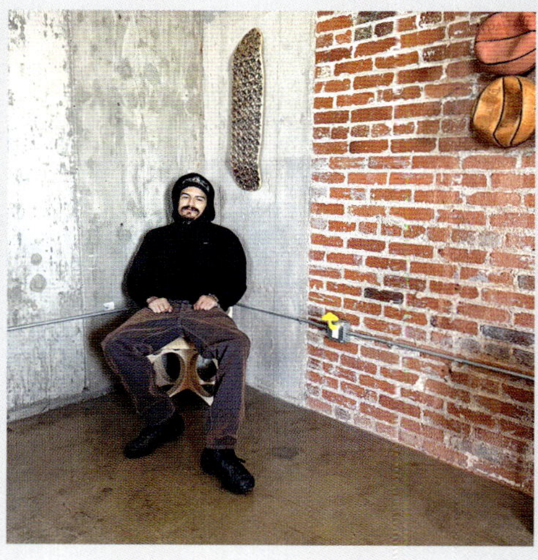
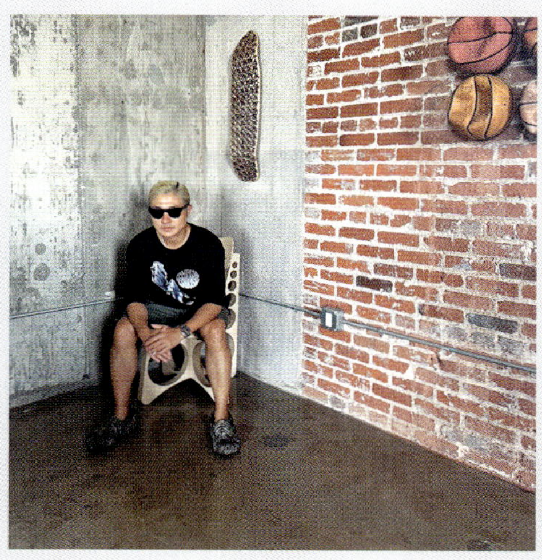
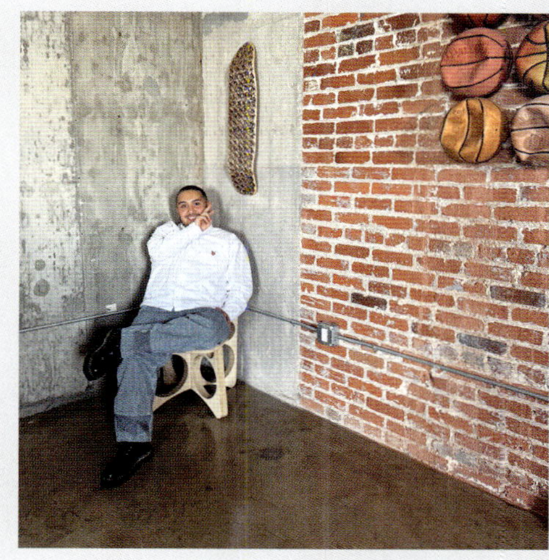
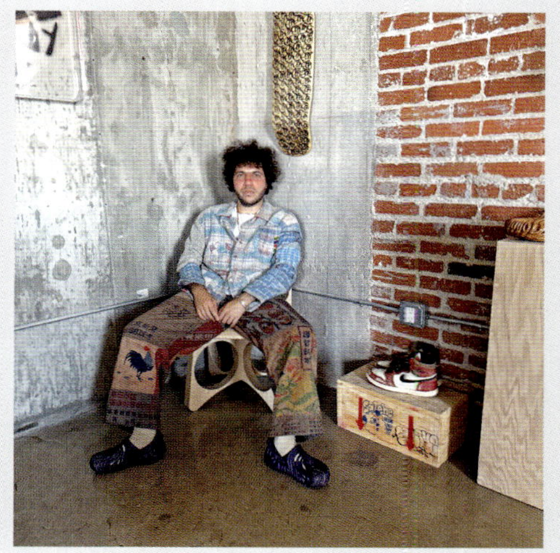
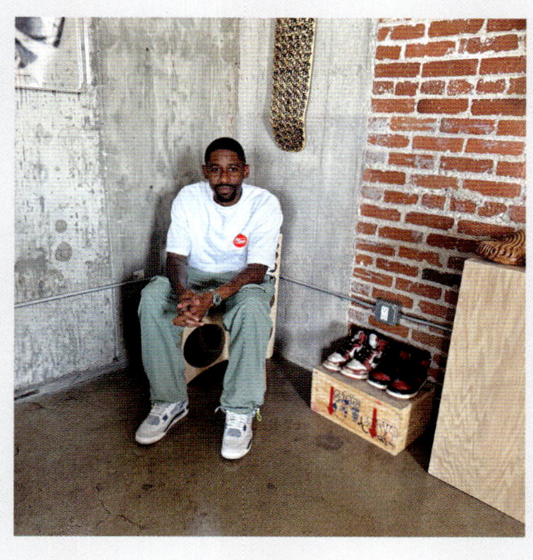
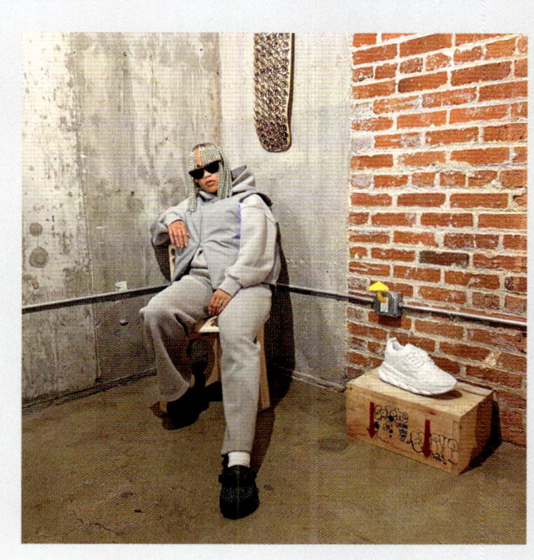
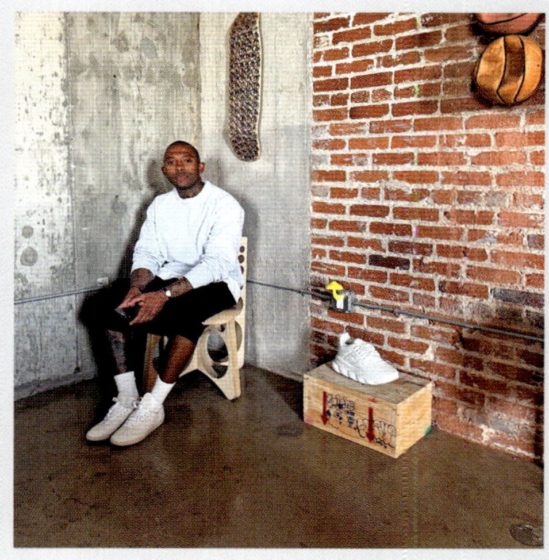
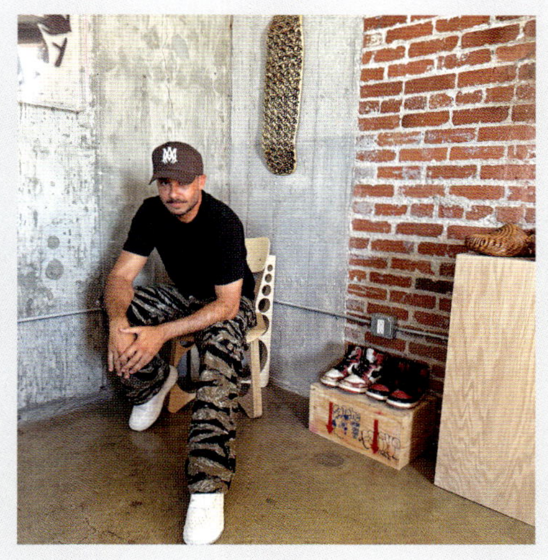
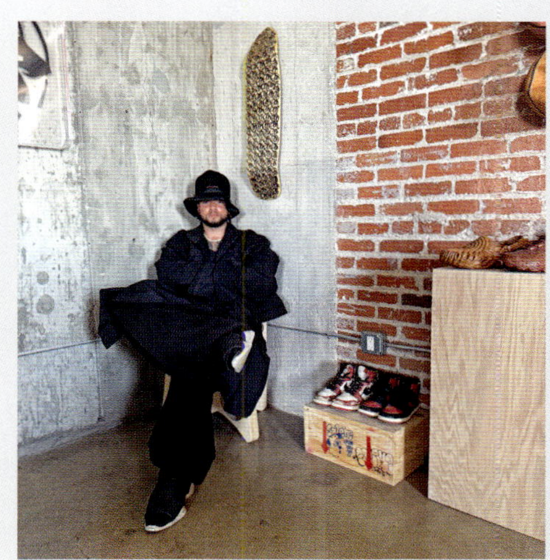
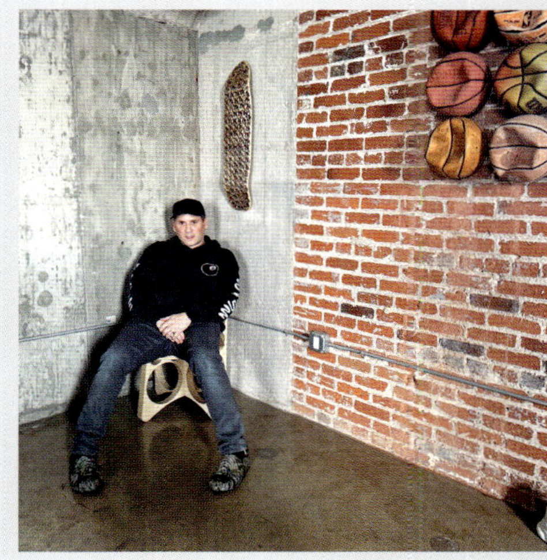

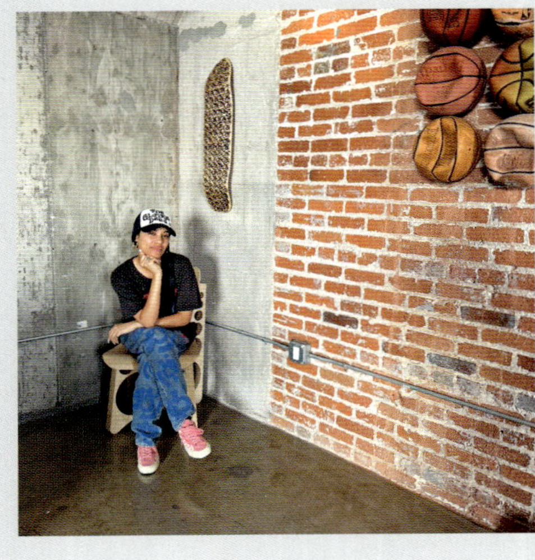
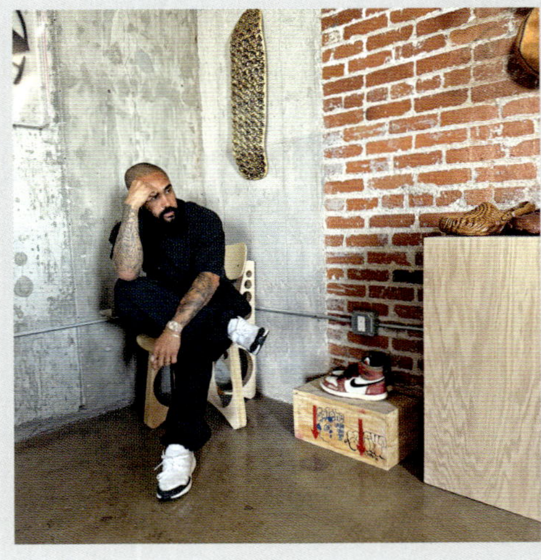
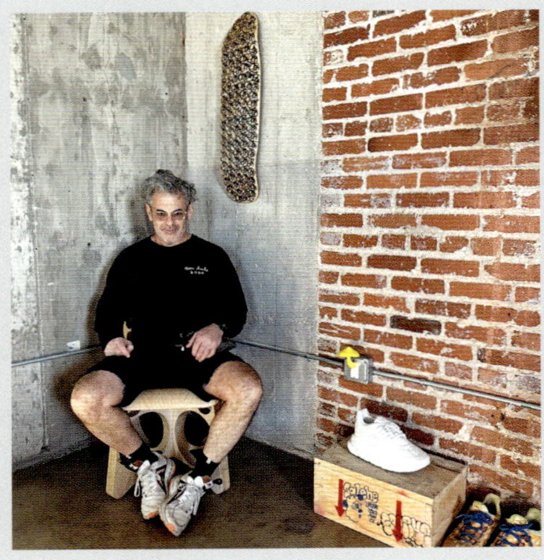
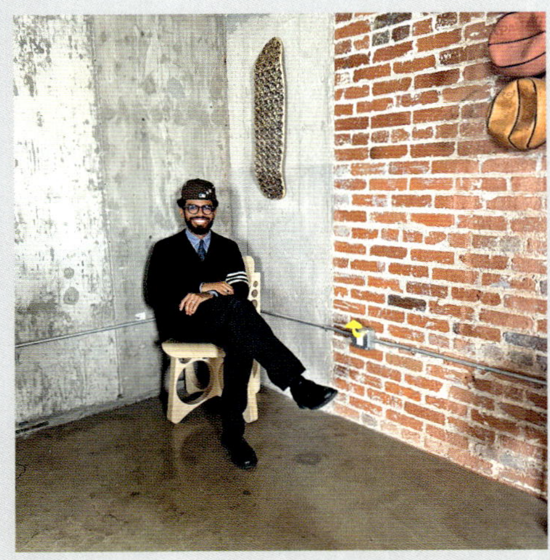
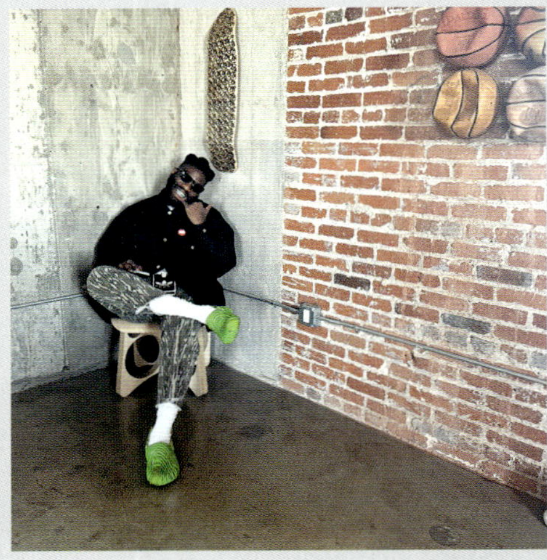
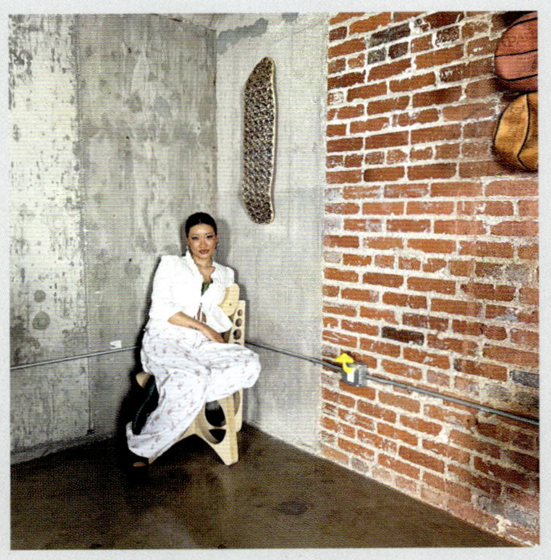
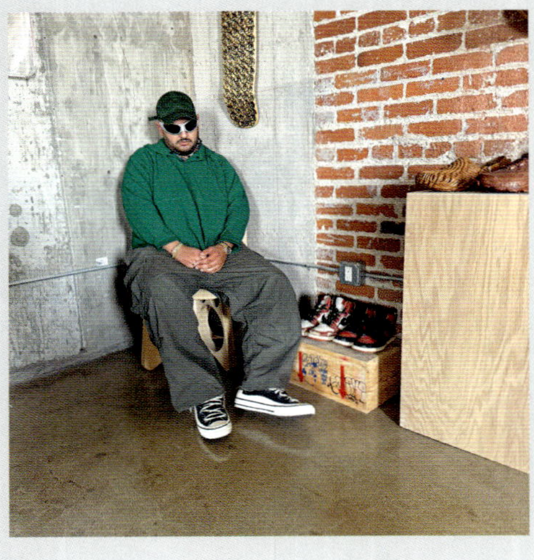
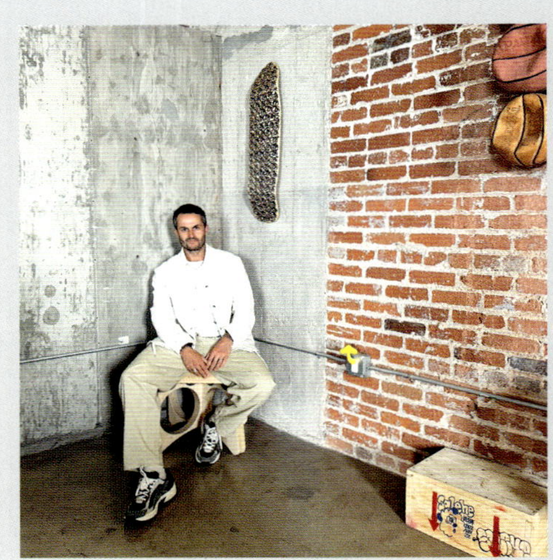
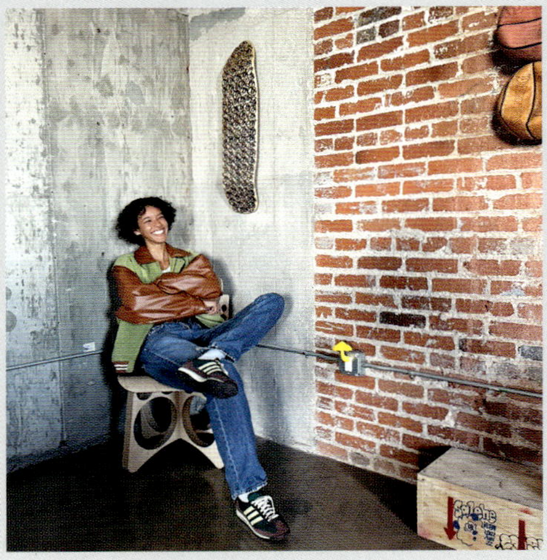
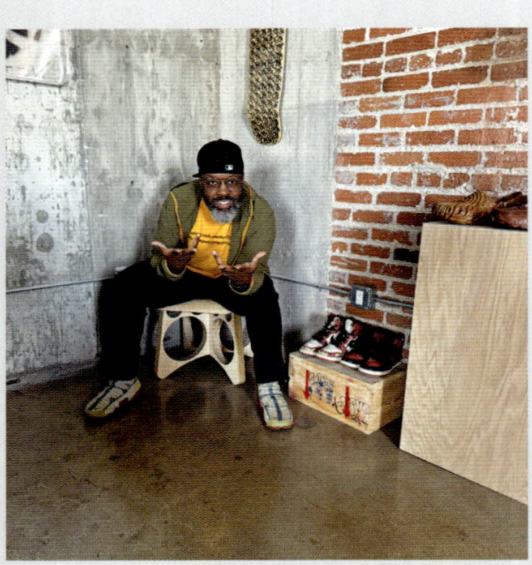
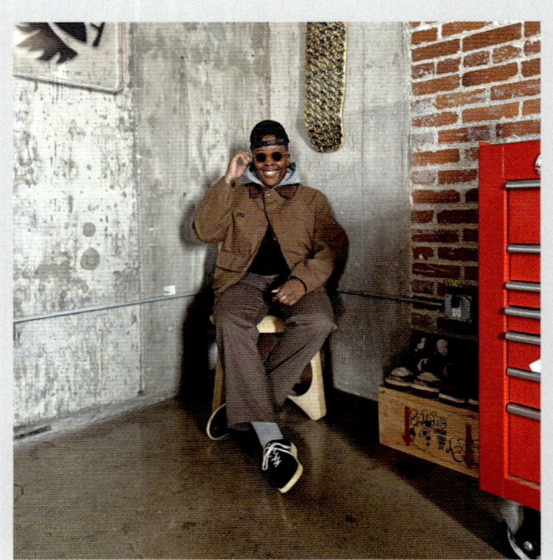
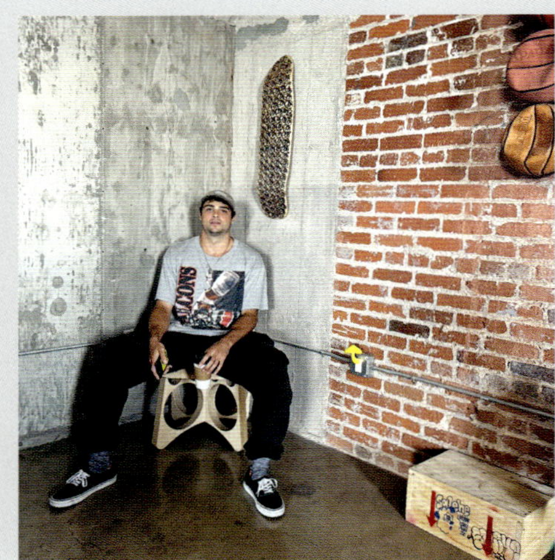

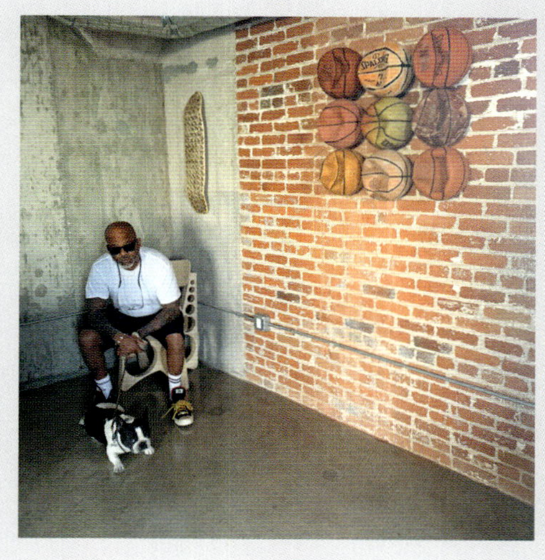
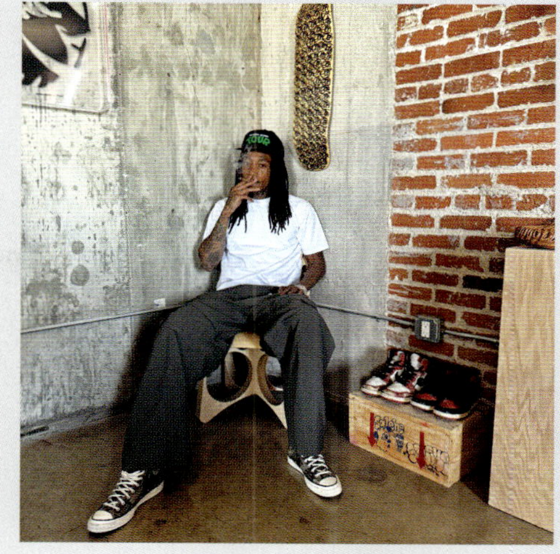
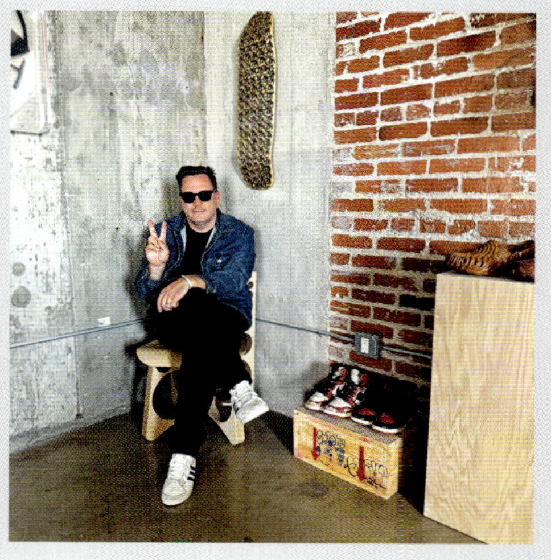
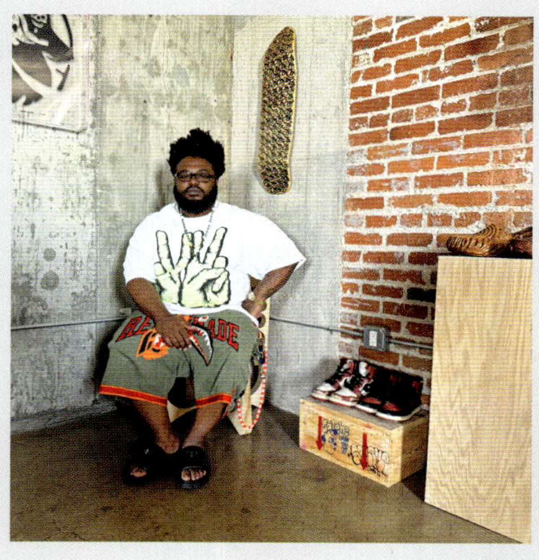
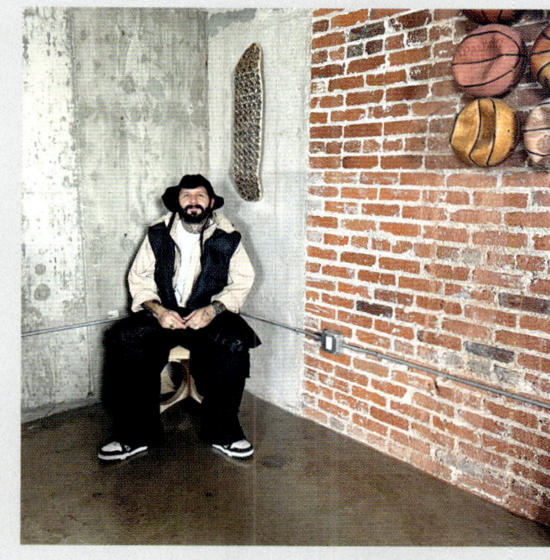
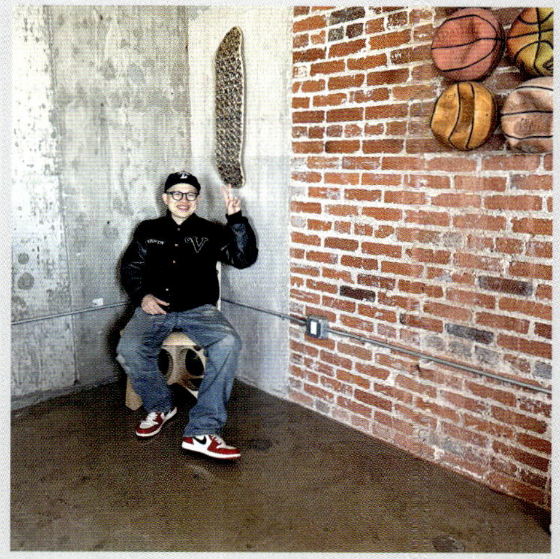
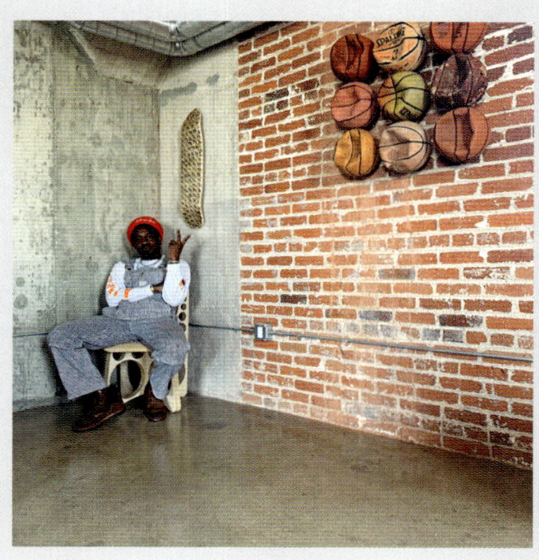
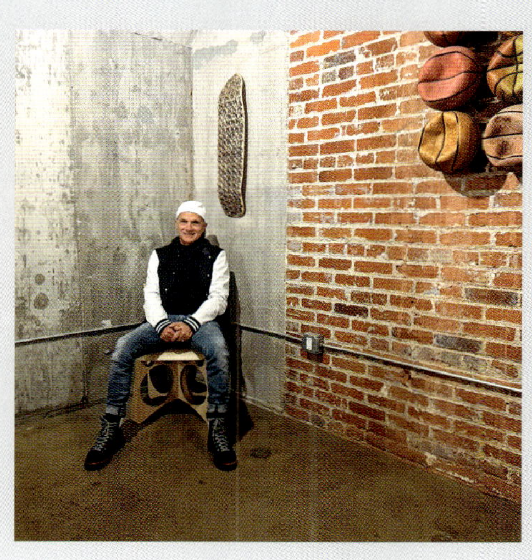
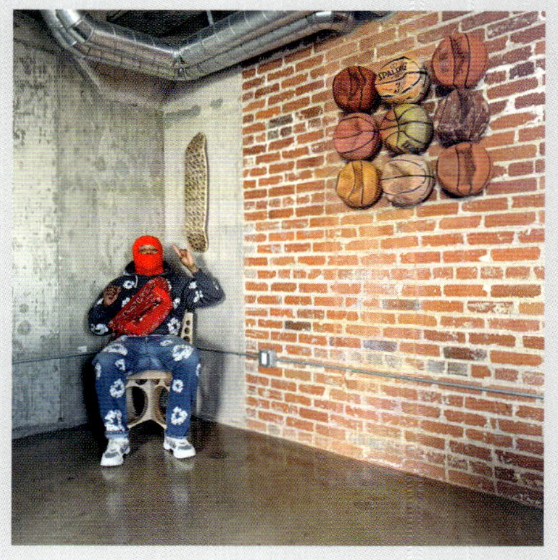
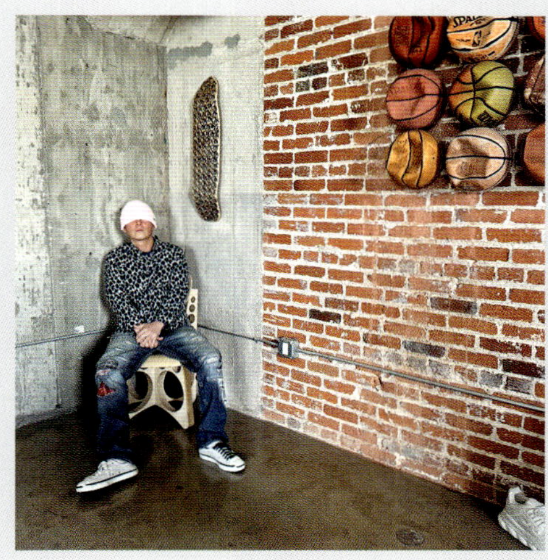
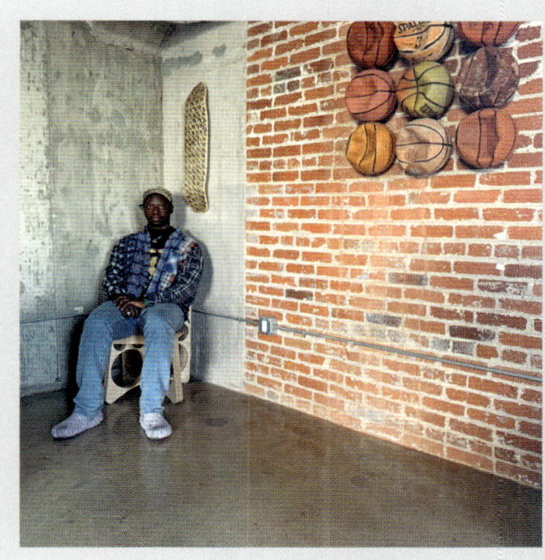
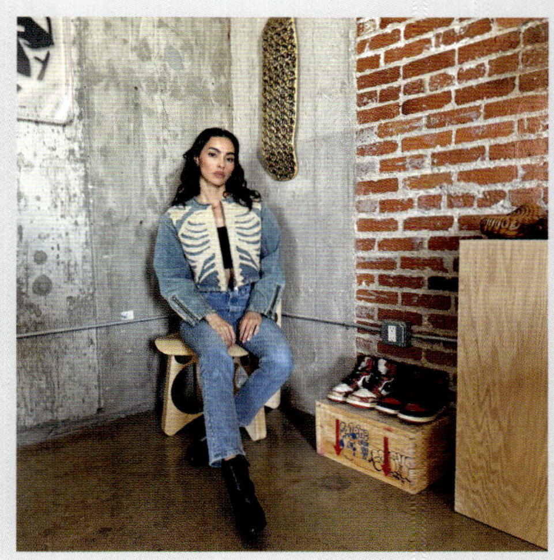

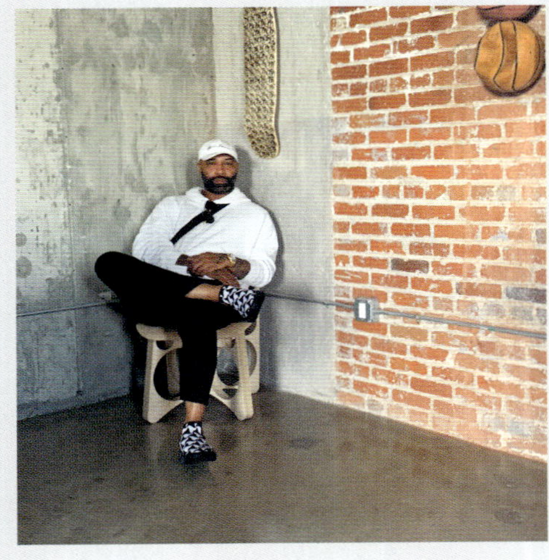
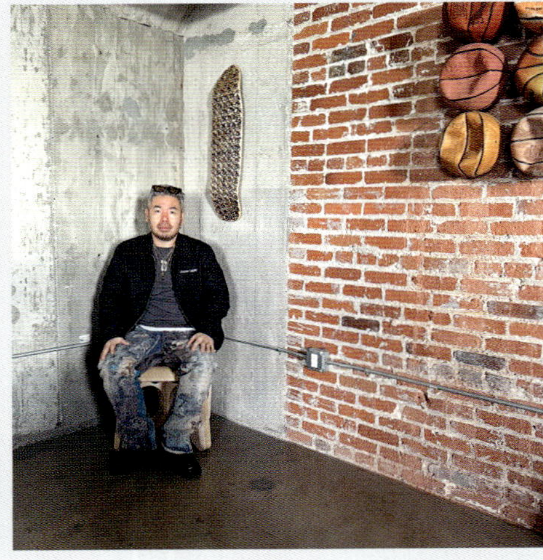
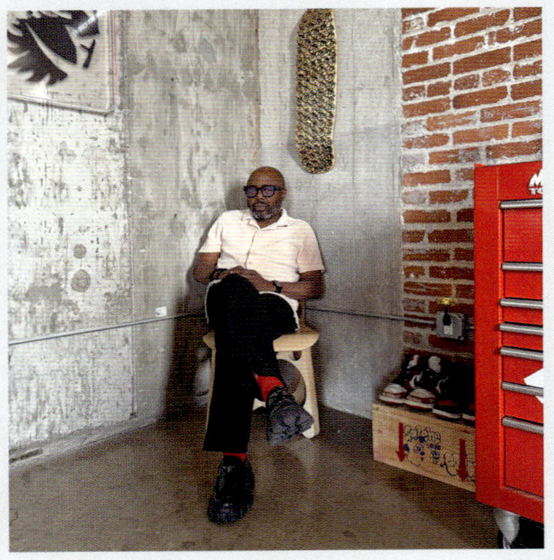
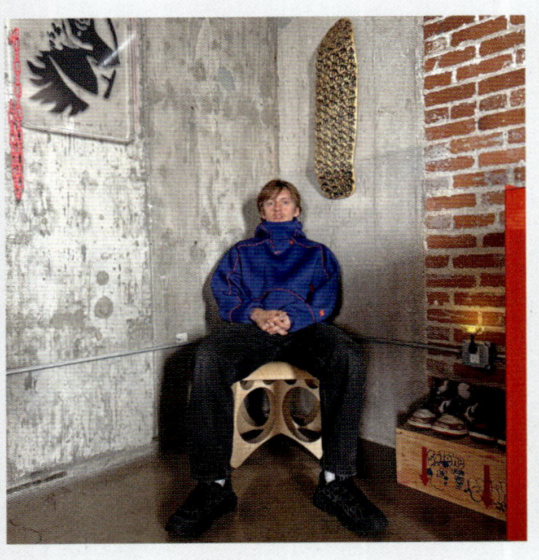
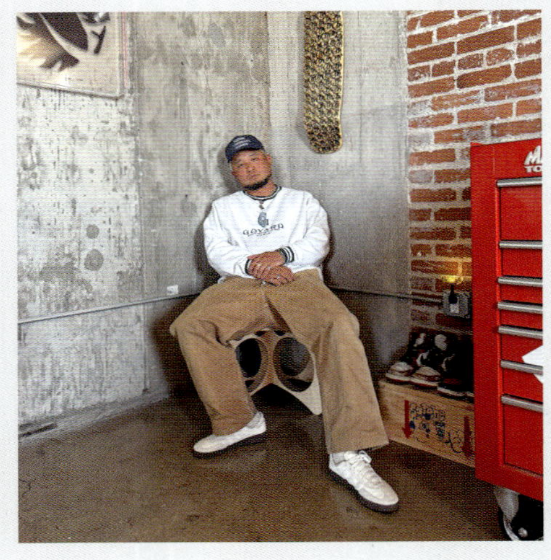
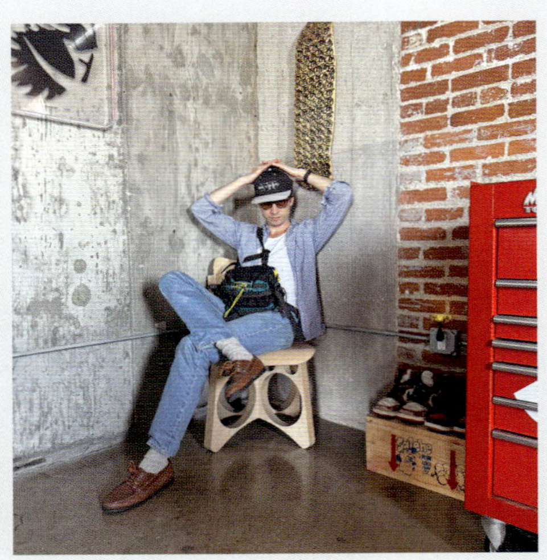
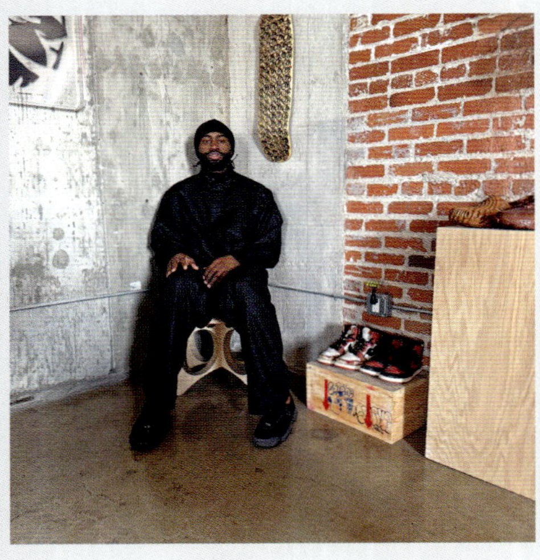
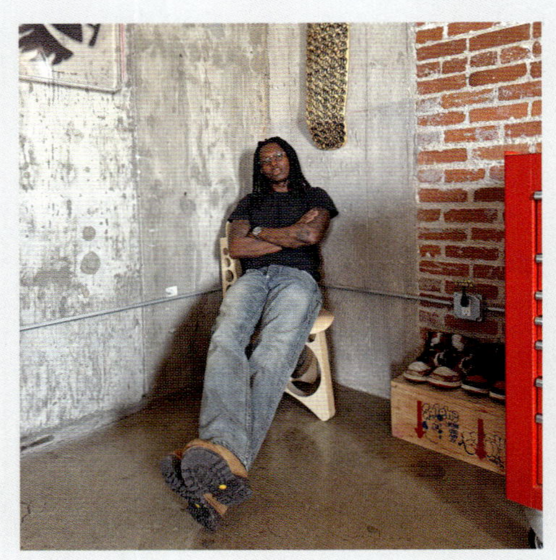
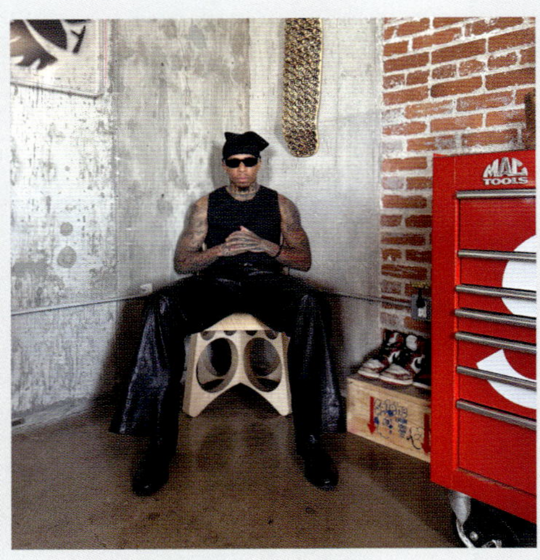
MAC TOOLS
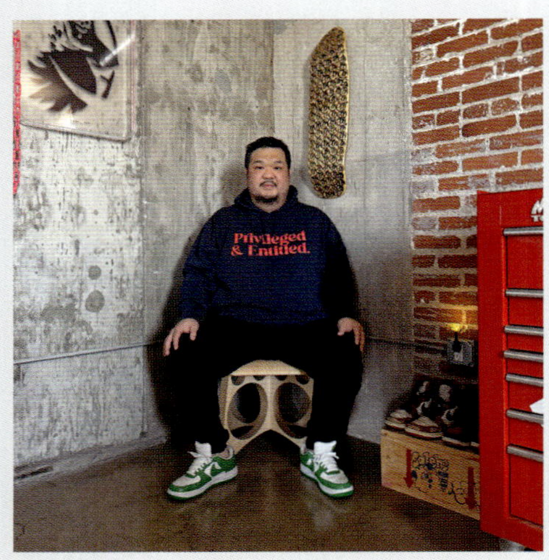
Privileged & Entitled.
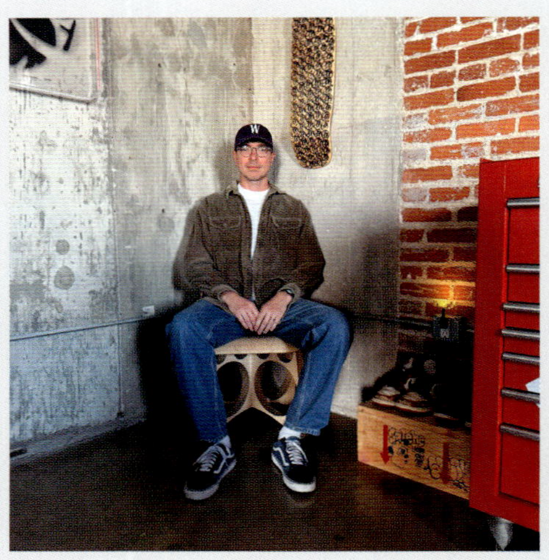
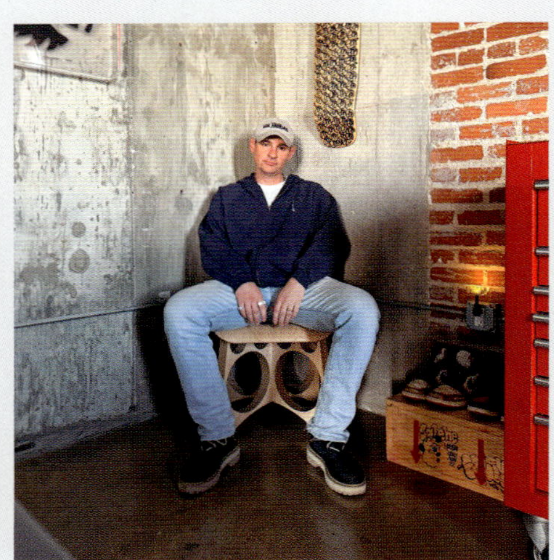

ACKNOWLEDGMENTS

"There's a frequency to gratitude, and I feel it deeply. So many beautiful souls poured light into my path — some knowingly, some without even realizing it. If you felt a moment in this book that resonated then you were part of this vibration. Thank you for the energy. Eternally."

SPECIAL THANKS

JEFF HENDERSON
DONATELLA VERSACE
KANYE WEST

2 Chainz
AC Gariel
Action Bronson
Adam Lefkoe
Adam Saleh
Adrian Fenech
Adrianne Ho
Aja Monet
Alchemist
Alec Ottevanger
Algee Smith
Alife
Alison Fullin
Allegra Versace
Amine
Amoako Boafo
André 3000
Andrea Rosen
Angelo Baque
Angie Chavez
Antoci Sculptures
Antoni Tudisco
Anwar Carrots
Archie Lee Coates
Ashleah Gonzalez
Astor Place Hair
Ava Jones
Ben Adams
Benjamin Paulin
Bianca Balti
Blake Anderson
Bliss Foster
Blossom Liu
Bobby Waltzer
Brandon 'Jinx' Jenkins
Brennan Rabb
Brian Beckwith
Brian Foresta
Brian Lynn
Bryan McGurk
Bryce Wong
Caeser Perez
Cam Stewart
Carlos Jimenez
Carnegie Mellon
Carol Lim
Carolina Stefani
Chace Infinite
Charlie Mangan
Chase Hall
Chaymin Barut
Chris Bevans
Chris Gibbs
Chris Stampd
Chris Vidal
Christopher McClean
Clea Irving
Coco Tedoro
Coltrane Curtis
Complex
Cool Rain Lee
Corey Wash
Coodie & Chike
Curtis Kulig
Cynthia Erivo
DJ Clark Kent
Damon Dash
Dan Doyle
Daniel Arsham
Daniel Bailey
Dave Chappelle
Dave Ortiz
David Blaine
David Choe
David LaChapelle
Delfin Finley
Denise Heckman
Devon Ojas
Dice The God
Digital Gravel
Dillon Kogle
Dilone
Dismas "Tek" Matheka
Don C
Don Carr
Don Sawyer
Donnell Rawlings
Eastbay
Easy Otabar
Edison Chen
Edith Bo
Emory Jones
Ernie Ramos
Errolson Hugh
Eugene Kan
Evan Funke
Fara Leff
Fardin Hazratizadeh
Fed Tan
Foster Huntington
Futura
Gabe Eng-Goetz
Gabe Gault
George Chiou
George Robertson
Gigi Hadid
Giorgia Pignetti
Go Miyazaki
Gordon Stevenson
Greg Passuntino
Heron Preston
Highsnobiety
Hiroshi Fujiwara
Hypebeast
IRAK NY
Ian Connor
J. Period
Ja Tecson
Jack Begart
Jacob Gallagher
Jacob Lehman
Jahlil Nzinga
Jaime King
Jake Mednik
James Jebbia
James King
James Law
James Lee
James Whitner
Jason Bolden
Jason Mayden
Jason Revok
Javier Hernandez
Javier Laval
Jaylen Brown
Jcro
Jeff Franklin
Jeff Henderson
Jeff Lazaro
Jeff Staple
Jeffrey Deitch
Jeremy Sallee
Jerry Lorenzo
Jess Gonsalves
Jess Lin
Jesse Boykins III
Jesse Ramos
Jesse Villanueva
Jesse Williams
Jessica Walsh
Jessie J
Jian Deleon
Jimmy Gorecki
Jimmy Iovine
Joanathan Mannion
Joe Budden
Joe Grondin
John Gray
John Mayer
Johnathan Anderson
Jonas Wood
Jonathan Mannion
Jordan Johnson
Josh Peskowitz
Josh Seidman
Josh Sperling
Josh Vides
Joshua Seidman
Jules Kim
Julian Ahye
Juliana Sagat
Justin Saunders
KB Lee
Karen Civil
Karol G
Kaws
Kelly Wearstler
Kenny Scharf
Kerby Jean Raymond
Kevin Leong
Kim Bekker
Kim Johansson
Koshin Finley
Kristen Fougere
Kunle Martins
Kyle Kivijarvi
Lauren Halsey
LeBron James
Loic Villepontoux
Lori Foglia
Lou Adler
Lucas Raynaud
Lucette Holland
Lucy Thornley
Luke Wood
Mac Martin
MadisonLST
Madsaki
Maggie Molitor
Mamoun's Falafel
Marc Ecko
Maria Valdes
Marissa Cianciulli
Martin Rose
Mary Francis
Maurizio Donadi
Maximilian Staiger
Mel D. Cole
Micah Belamarich
Michael Dupouy
Michael Ealy
Michal Kukucka
Mickey Robins
Miguel
Mike Amiri
Mike Cherman
Mike Shinoda
Miles Guidon
Molly Willhelm
Nathan Van Hook
Nathaniel Prinzi
New York Knicks
Nice Kicks
Nick Hunt
Nick Wooster
Nicole Underwood
Nigo
Nike
Niketalk
Nina Chanel
Noah Bice
Noah Centineo
Noelle Victoria
Nom De Guerre
Olan Prenatt
Pablo Vargas
Patrick Ewing Jr.
Patrick Martinez
Paul Auersperg
Paul Rivera
Paul Wachter
Pearl Paint
Pegleg NYC
Peter Verry
Pharrell Williams
Phil Russo
Phillip T. Annand
Pietro Paolo
PlayLab, Inc.
Poggy
Procell Vintage
RISD
Randi Chiemi Tagorda
Reillor Davis
Rem D. Koolhaus
Remo Ruffini
Revok
Rich Pau
Richard Brooks
Robert Lunardon
Robert Mingione
Rockers NYC
Rodrigo Corral
Ron English
Ron Holden
Ronnie Fieg
Ross Dwyer
Ruby Rose
S.K. Lam
Sabine Marcelis
Salima Nasri
Samuel Ross
Sandra Romboli
Sarah Laws
Saskia Lawaks
Sasu Kauppi
Sayre Gomez
Scott Sasso
Selena Forrest
Shae Haley
Shane Ward
Shaniqwa Jarvis
Sharifa Murdock
Shawn Ward
Shia Lebeouf
Sky Gellatly
Sneakernews
Soki Mak
Sprint Sports
Steph F. Morris
Steve Aoki
Steve Beccia
Steve Girault
Susanna D'Antonio
Syracuse University
Takashi Murakami
Take Off
Taylor Peden
Taz Arnold
Ted Junko
Teddy Santis
The Joe Budden Podcast
The Madbury Club
Thibo Denis
Thundercat
Tito Soto-Carrion
Tom Sachs
Tommy Ton
Toro y Moi
Tremaine Emory
Treis Hill
Tyler Mansour
Tyler Okonma
Tyrell Winston
Tyrese Haliburton
Ugo Mozie
VJ Kesh
Valentina Cy
Vashtie Kola
Verbal Ambush
Vhils
Vince Palacios
Virgil Abloh
Waraire Boswell
Wes Lang
Westside Gunn
Whitney Alexandra
White Trash Tyler
Wil Whitney
will.i.am
Wiz Khalifa
Yasiin Bey
Ye
Yoon Ambush
Yu-Ming Wu
Zainab Jama
Zia Ziprin
Zoe Costello

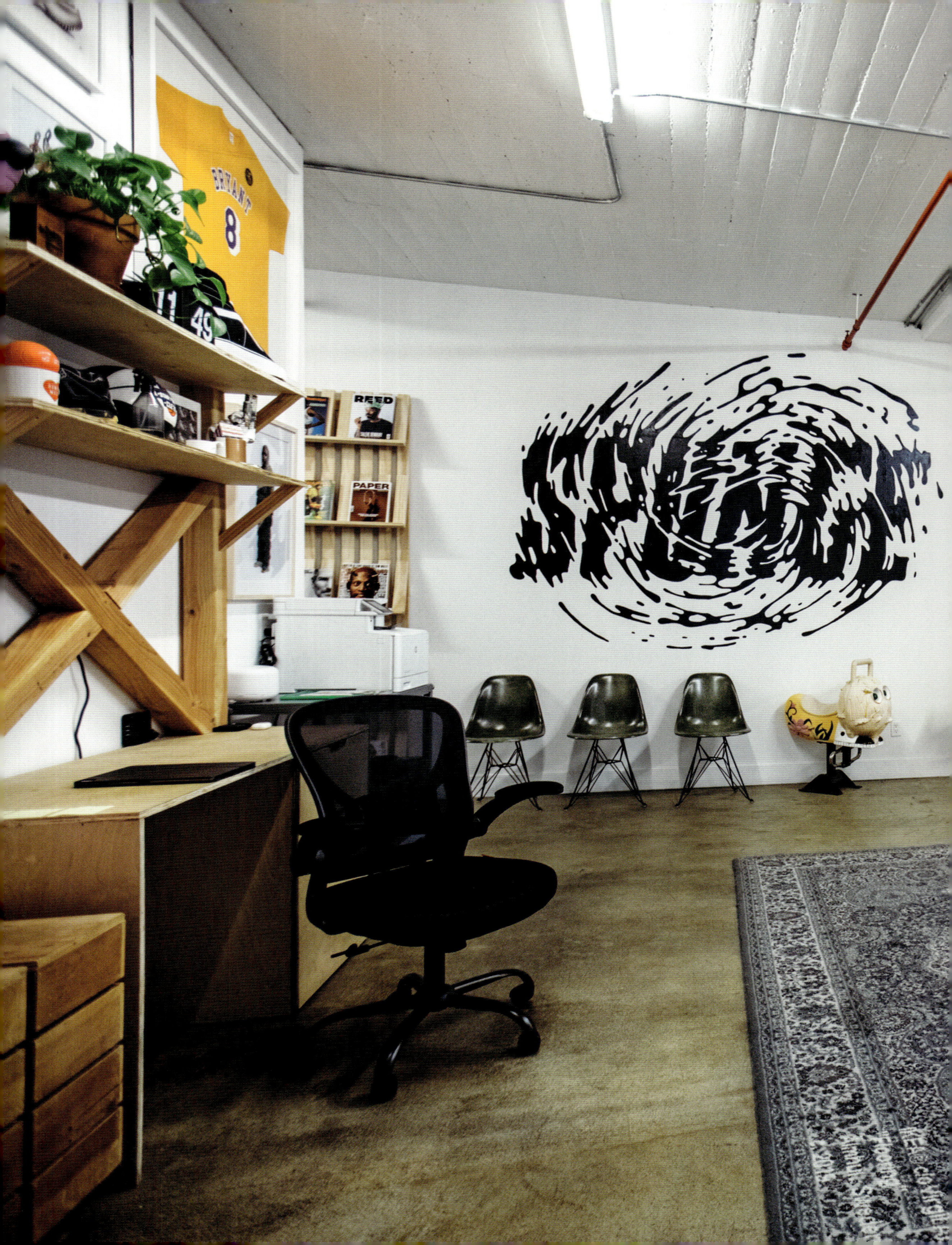
BRYANT
8
REED
PAPER

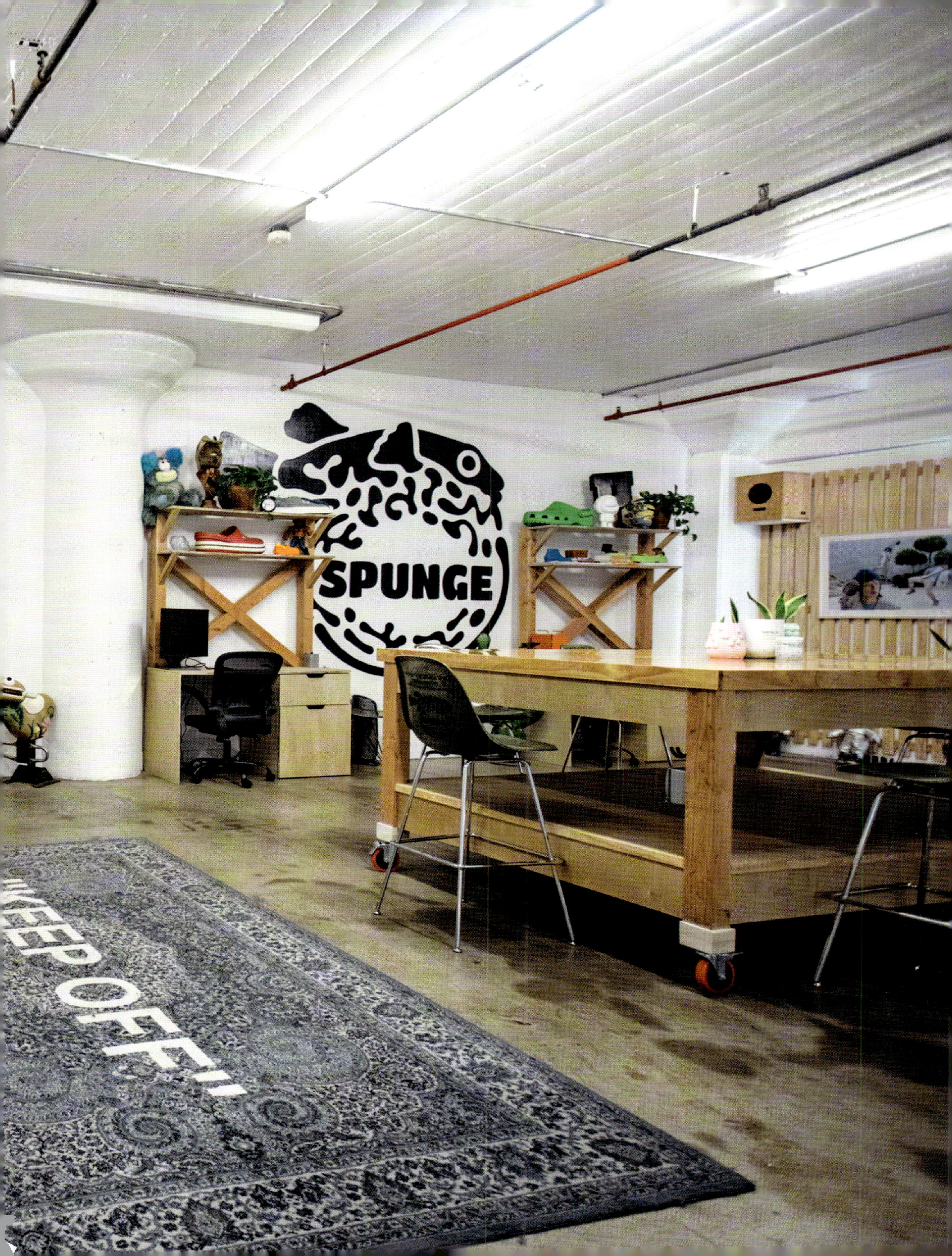
SPUNGE
KEEP OFF"

SALEHE
I MAKE SHOES

First published in the
United States of America in 2025 by
Rizzoli International Publications, Inc.
49 West 27th Street
New York, NY 10001
www.rizzoliusa.com

Design by PlayLab, Inc.

Publisher: Charles Miers
Editor: Jacob Lehman
Production Manager: Kaija Markoe
Managing Editor: Lynn Scrabis

The authorized representative in the EU for product safety and compliance is Mondadori Libri S.p.A., via Gian Battista Vico 42, Milan, Italy, 20123
www.mondadori.it

Printed in China

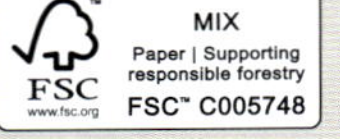

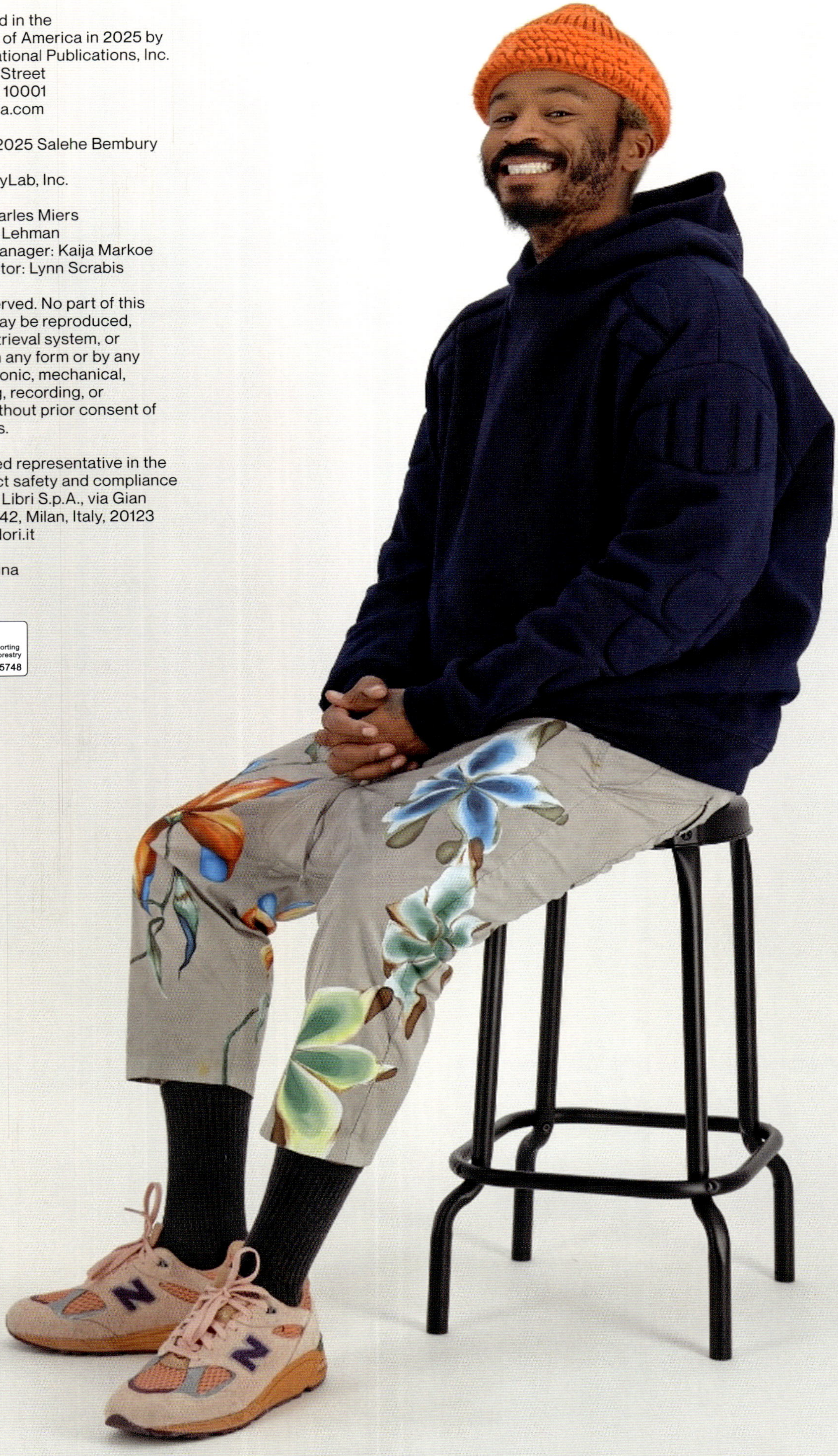

2025 2026 2027 2028 / 10 9 8 7 6 5 4 3 2 1

ISBN: 978-0-8478-4496-8

Library of Congress Control Number: 2025934809